THE OXFORD HANDBO

INTERNATIONAL LAW IN ARMED CONFLICT

THE OXFORD HANDBOOK OF

INTERNATIONAL LAW IN ARMED CONFLICT

Edited by

ANDREW CLAPHAM

and

PAOLA GAETA

Assistant Editors:

TOM HAECK

ALICE PRIDDY

The Academy, a joint centre of

OXFORD
UNIVERSITY PRESS

OXFORD
UNIVERSITY PRESS

Great Clarendon Street, Oxford, OX2 6DP,
United Kingdom

Oxford University Press is a department of the University of Oxford.
It furthers the University's objective of excellence in research, scholarship,
and education by publishing worldwide. Oxford is a registered trade mark of
Oxford University Press in the UK and in certain other countries

Published in the United States of America by Oxford University Press
198 Madison Avenue, New York, NY 10016, United States of America

British Library Cataloguing in Publication Data

Data available

Library of Congress Cataloging in Publication Data

Data available

ISBN 978-0-19-955969-5 (Hbk.)
ISBN 978-0-19-874830-4 (Pbk.)

In memoriam Antonio Cassese

PREFACE

....

This *Handbook* started life as a series of 'Academy Lectures', inaugurated in 2007 by the late Antonio Cassese, and subsequently delivered by leading scholars in their fields of expertise. A number of the original lectures can still be viewed online and they add another dimension to the edited Chapters in this *Handbook*.[1] Each lecturer was forced to fit their main points into a one-hour presentation and tackle a series of questions for an informed audience. The result is that the Chapters work as self-contained essays, which can be used along with the videos, for single seminars on multiple aspects of international law in armed conflict.

We deliberately chose to emphasize international law *in* armed conflict, rather than the humanitarian law *of* armed conflict. First, we wanted to emphasize that multiple branches of international law apply in times of armed conflict. In this *Handbook* you will find, inter alia, Chapters on human rights law, refugee law, international criminal law, and environmental law. Of course each Chapter has to explore the interaction between these branches and international humanitarian law ('IHL'), but our main message is that, today, one needs to master multiple branches of law to be able to understand the international law applicable to armed conflicts (or what might now be termed the *laws* of war). Developments, particularly at the level of the International Court of Justice ('ICJ'),[2] and in the doctrine,[3] have highlighted that, in times of armed conflict, international humanitarian law (or the law of war) is complemented by human rights law, which applies with important consequences with regard to monitoring and international adjudication. The modalities for the

---

[1] <http://www.geneva-academy.ch/the-academy/events/academy-lecture-series>.

[2] *Case Concerning Armed Activities on the Territory of the Congo (Democratic Republic of the Congo v. Uganda)*, 19 December 2005, esp §§ 178ff and Advisory Opinion on the *Legal Consequences of the Construction of a Wall in the Occupied Palestinian Territory*, 9 July 2004, § 106.

[3] Greenwood, writing before these pronouncements were made by the ICJ, highlighted the intersections between IHL and human rights law and concluded that each branch 'may have more to contribute to the other than has generally been recognized'. C. Greenwood, 'International Humanitarian Law (Laws of War)', in F. Kalshoven (ed), *The Centennial of the First International Peace Conference* (The Hague: Kluwer Law International, 2000), 161 at 190; see also Y. Dinstein, *The Conduct of Hostilities under the Law of International Armed Conflict* (Cambridge: Cambridge University Press, 2004), 20–2; for a recent set of useful essays on this topic, see R. Kolb and G. Gaggioli (eds), *Research Handbook on Human Rights and Humanitarian Law* (Cheltenham: Elgar, 2013).

applicability of the two branches of law is complex,[4] and contested in certain contexts, but what is clear is that there is significant resistance to assimilating human rights law within international humanitarian law or vice-versa.[5]

Secondly, the question of what parts of the laws of war should be included as part of *humanitarian* law, strictly speaking, remains the subject of debate.[6] Furthermore, the US Departments of Defense and State prefer the expressions 'law of war', or 'laws and customs of war', and continue to use these terms rather than international humanitarian law, even when commenting on the ICRC's *Customary International Humanitarian Law* study.[7] One might then consider a better title the 'Law of War' or 'War Law'. There are various recent books with titles that play on this rhyme,[8] but one has to consider that a new law *Handbook* with war in the title could be seen as contributing to an emphasis on the demands of war and military necessity,[9] rather than the desirability of protection through law.

Thirdly, the International Committee of the Red Cross, however, describe the development of hybrid instruments in the following way: 'While IHL and IHRL [international human rights law] have historically had a separate development, recent treaties include provisions from both bodies of law. Examples are the Convention on the Rights of the Child, its Optional Protocol on the Participation of Children in Armed Conflict, and the Rome Statute of the International Criminal

---

[4] See A. Clapham 'The Complexity of the Relationship between Human Rights Law and the 1949 Geneva Conventions', in A. Clapham, P. Gaeta, and M. Sassòli (eds), *The 1949 Geneva Conventions: A Commentary* (Oxford: Oxford University Press (forthcoming)).

[5] Dinstein, like Greenwood, is keen to keep the branches separate. Dinstein's explanation of the terminological significance is representative of many lawyers working on the law of armed conflict: 'When LOIAC [the law of international armed conflict] is referred to as "International Humanitarian Law" (IHL), it is easy to assume—wrongly—that it is "a law concerning the protection of human rights in armed conflicts". This can be a misconception. Although the expressions "human" and "humanitarian" strike a similar chord, it is essential to resist any temptation to regard them as intertwined or interchangeable. The adjective "human" in the phrase "human rights" points at the subject in whom the rights are vested: human rights are conferred on human beings as such (without the interposition of States). In contrast, the adjective "humanitarian" in the term "International Humanitarian Law" merely indicates the considerations that may have steered IHL—or LOIAC—is the law channelling conduct in international armed conflict, with a view to mitigating human suffering' (Dinstein (n 3), 20).

[6] Greenwood (n 3), 161; note Greenwood inverts the order in a later publication C. Greenwood, 'The Law of War (International Humanitarian Law)', in M. Evans (ed), *International Law* (Oxford: Oxford University Press, 2003), 789.

[7] See, most recently, letter to the ICRC of 3 November 2006, <http://www.defenselink.mil/home/pdf/Customary_International_Humanitiarian_Law.pdf>.

[8] M. Byers, *War Law: Understanding International Law and Armed Conflict* (New York: Grove Press, 2005); I. Detter, *The Law of War* (3rd edn, London: Ashgate Press, 2013); M. Sassòli, A. Bouvier, and A. Quintin, *How Does Law Protect in War? Cases, Documents and Teaching Materials on Contemporary Practice in International Humanitarian Law* (3rd edn, Geneva: ICRC, 2011); D. Kennedy, *Of War and Law* (Princeton: Princeton University Press, 2006).

[9] For a non-legal companion, see, J. Lindley-French and Y. Boyer (eds), *Oxford Handbook of War* (Oxford: Oxford University Press, 2012).

Court.'[10] By referring to international law *in* armed conflict rather than international law *of* armed conflict one can openly address the relevant human rights law without being seen as assimilating human rights law as part of the law of humanitarian law. As the quote from the ICRC implies, the relevant law now includes, not only human rights and humanitarian law, but also international criminal law. Similarly, we should add that any appreciation of the legal framework in context of armed conflicts almost inevitably should include a discussion of refugee law.

These three factors represent the primary reasons for seeking to use 'law in armed conflict' as the organizing principle. In order to illustrate the delicacy of the choice of title it may be worth entering into even more explanation. This debate goes way beyond the discussions of the interaction of different branches of international law. We can open a parenthesis here and contemplate the increasing emphasis on human rights in the doctrine being developed by humanitarian field operations and the concerns that this brings for the prospect of mixing up this work with advocacy for humanitarian intervention. The commentator David Rieff has argued against such a broadening of the traditional humanitarian role as 'silent neutrals' in armed conflict situations as he sees the embrace of human rights as inevitably linked to conditionality, militarization, and humanitarian intervention. Rieff documents the convergence of humanitarians and the human rights movement over several pages.

[T]he language of rights has proven commanding. In the minds of many aid workers, the right of victims under international humanitarian law and the Universal Declaration of Human Rights to receive assistance restored their human dignity and made them more than passive recipients of the charity of others. This shift did not take place in a vacuum. Rather, in the minds of many of its most intelligent and scrupulous practitioners, the transformation of humanitarianism was part of a broader shift in the post-Cold War era towards a rights-based universalism.[11]

Rieff's fear is of humanitarianism being co-opted by those who would support the use of force to achieve humanitarian or human rights objectives. 'For the reality is that no version of the intermingling of humanitarianism and human rights makes sense except in the context of a world order in which humanitarian military intervention, or at least its credible threat, is one standard response (it need not, however, be frequent) to a so-called humanitarian crisis.'[12]

On the other hand, Nick Stockton, formerly Executive Director of the Humanitarian Accountability Partnership based in Geneva, has argued that the 'humanitarian community has embarked upon a radical journey from being the rather selective and ad hoc conduit of charitable giving [...] towards being the champion and monitor of universal humanitarian rights and sometimes fulfiller of humanitarian claims.'[13] His

[10] International Humanitarian Law and International Human Rights Law: Similarities and differences (Advisory Service, 01/2003).

[11] D. Rieff, *A Bed for the Night: Humanitarianism in Crisis* (London: Vintage, 2002), 311.

[12] Rieff (n 11), 321.

[13] 'Performance Standards and Accountability in Realising Rights: The Humanitarian Case' Nicholas Stockton, Talk given at ODI, London, 17 March 1999 at 1, <http://www.odi.org.uk/speeches/stockton.html> and quoted by Rieff (n 11), 294.

point is not to build the case for military intervention but rather to emphasize that in providing assistance humanitarian actors take on 'a duty of care and a duty of impartiality'.[14]

There is a perceived need from the humanitarian sector for extra clarity with regard to the terms: human rights law, humanitarian law, international criminal law, and refugee law. There have been several attempts to disentangle the complex web of interacting regimes but none have moved beyond historical description and some rather obvious points of interaction. This *Handbook* takes the discussion to a more sophisticated level, and addresses some of the complex questions of law that arise when one tackles the harder questions. Which human rights violations or war crimes allegations result in exclusion from the refugee regime? What human rights protections apply to someone declared an unlawful combatant? Which human rights apply in the context of armed forces acting abroad? Are armed non-state actors bound by human rights law? When is a violation of international law an international crime in armed conflict?

The Introductory Part opens with a set of challenges thrown down by the sadly missed Antonio Cassese and continues with an introduction to the Role of the International Committee of the Red Cross by Jakob Kellenberger. From their separate perspectives of the international criminal bench and the operational humanitarian organization they take us to the heart of the problem of protecting the victims of war. We will not mention all the remaining contributors by name in this preface, suffice it to say that they all combine an ability to lecture, immense experience, a critical and scholarly approach to their writing, and perhaps most memorably from our perspective as editors, infinite patience.

The Part on Sources starts with a reflection on how judges are today shaping customary international law in new and accelerated ways. Complementing this is a Chapter on treaties which takes the reader through the multiple instruments that have been adopted over the last 150 years.

The Part on Legal Regimes covers land, air, and maritime warfare as well as the law of occupation. We chose to add specific Chapters on the law applicable to peace operations and neutrality as these topics generate particular interest in Geneva and deserve greater attention in the contemporary context.

The Part on Key Concepts tackles in quite philosophical terms a number of thorny issues relating to the law of weapons, the principle of distinction, proportionality, and non-international armed conflicts. These Chapters do not pretend to provide a comprehensive outline of all the applicable law, instead they provide a springboard for discussion and reflection on the fundamental ideas operating deep down in the DNA of the laws of war.

---

[14] 'Performance Standards and Accountability in Realising Rights' (n 13).

The Part on Key Rights emphasizes some of the themes outlined above. Rather than looking at the traditional law of targeting, we start with an essay on the right to life and the question whether those who go to war might not have to consider the lives of all those attacked from a human rights perspective. Similarly, the other Chapters in this Part dealing with torture, fair trial, the environment, cultural property, and human rights as they relate to members of the armed forces, all force the reader to see armed conflict from another angle.

The Part on Key Issues addresses topics that were not traditionally dealt with in manuals on the law of armed conflict. Aggression and self-defence are not always included due to a perceived need to keep *jus ad bellum* and *jus in bello* separate. Moreover many manuals start life as military manuals and these topics are seen as more properly the preserve of the Executive or the Legislature. But the recent inclusion of the crime of aggression in the Rome Statute of the International Criminal Court has given all leaders cause to pause for thought as the topic becomes less academic and doctrinal. The Academy lectures were delivered over the period 2008 to 2011 and issues of terrorism, unlawful combatants detained at Guantánamo, human rights, gender, and forced migration were, and sadly remain, particular preoccupations.

The last Part on Accountability presents some of the most recent developments affecting the operation of law in times of armed conflict. The Chapters on war crimes and armed groups illustrate how international law has adapted beyond a focus on states and the sole actors on the international legal stage. The obstacles to holding states themselves accountable are highlighted in the Chapter on individual claims before national courts, and the last Chapter explores some of the most pressing dilemmas in the post-conflict situation and details some of the international community's most recent initiatives.

This project was made possible due to the generosity and support of a number of institutions. First we must thank the Oak Foundation. Their generous support enabled us to mount the lecture series and develop this *Handbook*. We are extremely grateful, not only for the financial support, but also for the way in which Adrian Arena and Greg Mayne offered suggestions and help along the way. Next we should like to express our gratitude to the Graduate Institute of International and Development Studies and the Faculty of Law of the University of Geneva. All the Academy Lectures were given in one or other of these two venues and both provided generous help in arranging for filming and technical support. We should like in this context to thank particularly Jacqueline Coté, Director of Communications at the Graduate Institute, who helped ensure that we reached into the furthest crevices of International Geneva; Edgardo Amato who ensured that the technology worked perfectly; and Jean-David Curchod who expertly filmed and edited the lectures.

The Lectures, discussions, and subsequent chapters were a project of the Geneva Academy of International Humanitarian Law and Human Rights. The Academy provides post-graduate teaching, conducts academic legal research, undertakes policy studies, and organizes training courses and expert meetings. The Academy concentrates on the branches of international law applicable in times of armed conflict. We are supported, not only by the Graduate Institute and the University (as just mentioned), but also by the Swiss Federal Department of Foreign Affairs, and this project could not have been completed without their generous involvement and support.

Finally let us acknowledge the dedication and huge effort which has gone into the organization and editing of this volume from a remarkable team which started under the leadership of Aline Baumgartner, who did so much to launch this project, organize the lectures, and coordinate the editorial process, and to whom we are extremely grateful. Claire Mahon, Scott Jerbi and Katie O'Byrne took on the editing of a number of chapters and their contribution is also gratefully acknowledged. The assistant editors, Alice Priddy and Tom Haeck, have tirelessly revised and polished the texts until they shine. We owe them a huge debt of gratitude and the volume is undoubtedly immeasurably improved thanks to their careful edits. In the very last phase we were lucky to have the guiding hand of Merel Alstein on the tiller, enthusiastic help from Molly Davies from Oxford Online, Briony Ryles and Barath Rajasekaran in the final stages of proofreading and production.

The painting reproduced on the cover of this *Handbook* is by the renowned Japanese artist Yayoi Kusama. It is entitled *Lingering Dreams* and was recently featured in the retrospectives in London and New York where we came across it. This piece, painted in 1949, remains particularly poignant in the aftermath of the atomic bombing of Japan and the devastation of the War. The catalogue explains: 'In *Lingering Dreams* Kusama deftly employs the dark crimson tone laid in the foreground to suppress the entangled withered sunflowers, which conjure up the grim realities of war. The unified tone of the foreground establishes a visual shield, guiding the viewers' attention to a faint light over the horizon, alluding to an uncharted world beyond.'[15]

Our intention with this *Handbook* is simply to provide a grounding for those who would like to go further with their understanding of the law applicable in armed conflict. We do not pretend to provide all the answers, rather we should like to provide the reader with some tools to tackle the challenges of venturing into this rather bleak landscape. Our hope is that future generations will not shy away from this adventure—but rather venture on—taking with them the spirit of humanity that permeates the contributions in this book.

Andrew Clapham and Paola Gaeta
Villa Moynier, Geneva August 2013

---

[15] M. Yamamura 'Rising from Totalitarianism: Yayoi Kusama 1945–1955', in F. Morris (ed), *Yayoi Kusama* (London: Tate Publishing, 2012), 168–75 at 171.

Contents

....

PART I INTRODUCTION

PART II SOURCES

PART III LEGAL REGIMES

PART IV KEY CONCEPTS FOR HUMANITARIAN LAW

PART V KEY RIGHTS IN TIMES OF ARMED CONFLICT

PART VII ACCOUNTABILITY/LIABILITY
FOR VIOLATIONS OF THE LAW IN
ARMED CONFLICT

PART VI KEY ISSUES IN TIMES OF ARMED CONFLICT

TABLE OF CASES

....

INTERNATIONAL CASE LAW

....

Eritrea Ethiopia Claims Commission

European Court of Human Rights

European Court of Justice

Inter-American Commission on Human Rights

Inter-American Court of Human Rights

International Court of Justice

International Criminal Court

International Criminal Tribunal for Rwanda

International Criminal Tribunal for the former Yugoslavia

International Military Tribunal at Nuremberg

Permanent Court of Arbitration

Permanent Court of International Justice

Special Court for Sierra Leone

Special Tribunal for Lebanon

UN Committee Against Torture

UN Human Rights Committee

·

National Courts

Australia

Canada

Croatia

France

Germany

Greece

Israel

Italy

Netherlands

New Zealand

United Kingdom

United States

TABLE OF AGREEMENTS CONVENTIONS INSTRUMENTS, TREATIES AND NATIONAL LEGISLATION

EUROPEAN UNION

INTERNATIONAL

UN Resolutions

National

New Zealand

Pakistan

Sierra Leone

Singapore

South Africa

Switzerland

United Kingdom

United States

List of Abbreviations

AC	Appeals Chamber
ACHPR	African Court of Human and People's Rights
ACHR	American Convention on Human Rights
AFDI	Annuaire français de droit international
AFRC	Armed Forces Revolutionary Council
AJIL	American Journal of International law
AMIB	African Mission in Burundi
AMIS	African Union Mission in Sudan
AMW Manual	Manual on International Law Applicable to Air and Missile Warfare, with Commentary (2010)
AP I	Additional Protocol I to the 1949 Geneva Conventions (1977)
AP II	Additional Protocol II to the 1949 Geneva Conventions (1977)
AP III	Additional Protocol III to the 1949 Geneva Conventions (2005)
ATT	Arms Trade Treaty
AU	African Union
BELISI	Peace-Truce Monitoring Group in Bougainville
BVR	Beyond Visual Range
BYBIL	British Yearbook of International Law
CA 3	Common Article 3 to the Geneva Conventions
CanYIL	Canadian Yearbook of International Law
CAR	Central African Republic
CARICOM	Caribbean Community and Common Market
CAT	UN Convention Against Torture and Other Cruel, Inhuman and Degrading Treatment or Punishment
CCW	Convention on Conventional Weapons
CDDH	The Diplomatic Conference on the Reaffirmation and Development of International Humanitarian Law Applicable in Armed Conflicts
CSDP	Common Security and Defense Policy
CESCR	Committee on Economic Social and Cultural Rights
CETS	Council of Europe Treaty Series

CFSP	Common Foreign and Security Policy
CIA	Central Intelligence Agency
CIL	customary international law
CIS	Commonwealth of Independent States
CITES	Convention on International Trade in Endangered Species of Wild Flora and Fauna
CIVPOL	UN Civilian Police
CM	Committee of Ministers
CMS	Convention on the Conservation of Migratory Species of Wild Animals
COE	Contingent-Owned Equipment
COIN	Counterinsurgency
Commentary GC I	Commentary on the Geneva Conventions of 12 August 1949 for the Amelioration of the Condition of the Wounded and Sick in Armed Forces in the Field. Vol. I (Geneva: International Committee of the Red Cross (ICRC), 1952)
Commentary GC II	Commentary on the Geneva Conventions of 12 August 1949 for the Amelioration of the Condition of Wounded, Sick and Shipwrecked Members of Armed Forces at Sea, Vol. II ((Geneva: International Committee of the Red Cross (ICRC), 1960)
Commentary GC III	Commentary on the Geneva Conventions of 12 August 1949 Relative to the Treatment of Prisoners of War ((Geneva: International Committee of the Red Cross (ICRC), 1960)
Commentary GC IV	Commentary on the Geneva Conventions of 12 August 1949 Relative to the Protection of Civilian in Time of War ((Geneva: International Committee of the Red Cross (ICRC), 1958)
Commentary AP I and II	Commentary on the Additional Protocols of 8 June 1977 to the Geneva Conventions of 12 August 1949 (Geneva/ Dordrecht: International Committee of the Red Cross (ICRC)/Martinus Nijihoff Publishers, 1987)
CRC	Convention on the Rights of Child
CRPD	Convention on the Rights of Persons with Disabilities
CRS	Congressional Research Series
CSRT	Combatant Status Review Tribunal
D.Md	US District Court for the District of Maryland
DAM	Department of Administration and Management
DC Cir.	US Circuit Court for the District of Columbia
DCAF	Democratic Control of Armed Forces
DDC	US District Court for the District of Columbia.
DDR	disarmament, demobilization, reintegration

DFS	United Nations Department of Field Support
DHA	Department of Humanitarian Affairs
DLR	Dominion Law Reports
DOJ	(US) Department of Justice
DPA	Department of Political Affairs
DPH	direct participation in hostilities
DPKO	United Nations Department of Peacekeeping Operations
DRC	Democratic Republic of the Congo
ECCC	Extraordinary Chambers in the Courts of Cambodia
ECHR	European Convention on Human Rights
ECOMOG	Economic Community of West African States Monitoring Group
ECOWAS	Economic Community of West African States
ECtHR	European Court of Human Rights
ED VA	Eastern District of Virginia
EEZ	Exclusive Economic Zone
EHRR	European Human Rights Reports
EJIL	European Journal of International Law
ENMOD Convention	Convention on the Prohibition of Military or any other Hostile Use of Environmental Modification Techniques
EO	Executive Order
ESC	Economic and Social Council
ESCOR	Economic and Social Council Official Records
ETS	European Treaty Series
EU NAVFOR ATALANTA	European Union Naval Force Somalia – Operation Atalanta
EU	European Union
EUFOR	European Union Force
EULEX	European Union Rule of Law Mission in Kosovo
EWHC	High Court of Justice of England and Wales
FACA	Central African Republic Armed Forces
FAFN	Forces Nouvelles de Côte d'Ivoire
FAO	Food and Agriculture Organization of the United Nations
FARC	Revolutionary Armed Forces of Colombia
FARDC	Forces Armées de la République Démocratique du Congo
FF	Feuille Fédérale
FM	Field Manual
FNI	Front for National Integration
FPLC	Forces Patriotiques pour la libération du Congo
FR	Federal Register
FRPI	Forces de Résistance Patriotique d'Ituri
FSA	Free Syrian Army

FSIA	Foreign Sovereign Immunities Act of 1976
FYROM	Former Yugoslav Republic of Macedonia
GAO	Government Accountability Office
GAOR	General Assembly Official Records
GC I	Convention (I) for the Amelioration of the Condition of the Wounded and Sick in Armed Forces in the Field
GC II	Convention (II) for the Amelioration of the Condition of Wounded, Sick and Shipwrecked Members of Armed Forces at Sea
GC III	Convention (III) Relative to the Treatment of Prisoners of War
GC IV	Convention (IV) Relative to the Protection of Civilian Persons in Time of War
GCs	Geneva Conventions
GPRA	Gouvernement provisoire de la République algérienne
GPS	Global Positioning System
GWOT	Global War on Terror
GYIL	German Yearbook of International Law
HC V	Hague Convention of 1907 Respecting the Rights and Duties of Neutral Powers and Persons in Case of War on Land
HC XIII	Hague Convention of 1907 Respecting the Rights and Duties of Neutral Powers in Naval War
HCJ	Israeli High Court of Justice
HPCR	Program on Humanitarian Policy and Conflict Research at Harvard University
HRCttee	United Nations Human Rights Committee
HRL	Human Rights Law
HRW	Human Rights Watch
HuV	Humanitäres Völkerrecht
HVO	Croat Defence Council
IAC	international armed conflict
IACHR	Inter-American Commission on Human Rights
IACtHR	Inter-American Court of Human Rights
ICC	International Criminal Court
ICCPR	International Covenant on Civil and Political Rights
ICERD	International Convention on the Elimination of all forms of Racial Discrimination
ICESCR	International Covenant on Economic Social and Cultural Rights
ICHRP	International Council on Human Rights Policy
ICISS	International Commission on Intervention and State Sovereignty

ICJ	International Court of Justice
ICLQ	International and Comparative Law Quarterly
ICRC	International Committee of the Red Cross
ICSID	International Center for Settlement of Investment Disputes
ICTR	International Criminal Tribunal for Rwanda
ICTY	International Criminal Tribunal for the former Yugoslavia
IDI	Institut de droit international
IDP	internally displaced persons
IEDs	improvised explosive devices
IFOR/ SFOR	Implementation Force/Stabilization Force in Bosnia and Herzegovina
IHL	international humanitarian law
IHLRI	International Humanitarian Law Research Initiative
IHRL	international human rights law
IIHL	San Remo Institute for International Humanitarian Law
ILC	International Law Commission
ILM	International Legal Materials
ILR	International Law Reports
IMT	International Military Tribunal
IMTFE	International Military Tribunal for the Far East
INTERFET	the International Force in East Timor
IRA	Irish Republican Army
IRRC	International Review of the Red Cross
ISAF	International Security Assistance Force
IsrYBHR	Israel Yearbook on Human Rights
JAIL	Japanese Annual of International Law
JDI	Journal du Droit International
JEM	Justice and Equality Movement
JICJ	Journal of International Criminal Justice
KFOR	Kosovo Force
LJIL	Leiden Journal of International Law
LNTS	League of Nations Treaty Series
LOAC	law of armed conflict
LOC	lines of communication
LOSC	United Nations Law of the Sea Convention
LRTAP	Convention on Long-Range Transboundary Air Pollution
LTTE	Liberation Tigers of Tamil Eelam
MARPOL	International Convention for the Prevention of Pollution by Ships
MCA	Military Commissions Act (2006)
MINURCA	United Nations Mission in the Central African Republic
MINURSO	United Nations Mission for the Referendum in Western Sahara

MISAB	Mission Interafricaine de Surveillance des Accords de Bangui
MLC	Movement for the Liberation of Congo
MONUC	Mission de Organisation des Nations Unies en République Démocratique du Congo
MPEPIL	The Max Plank Encyclopedia of Public International Law
MWC	United Nations International Convention on the Protection of the Rights of All Migrant Workers and Members of Their Families
N.D. Ill.	US District Court for the Northern District of Illinois
NAM	non-aligned movement
NATO	North Atlantic Treaty Organization
NDC	Nduma Defence of Congo
NGO	non-governmental organization
NIAC	non-international armed conflict
NILR	Netherlands International Law Review
NLA	National Liberation Army
NOTAM	Notice to Airman
NOTMAR	Notice to Mariners
NUPI	Norwegian Institute of Foreign Affairs
NWP	Naval Warfare Publication
NYT	New York Times
NZAR	New Zealand Administrative Reports
OAS	Organization of American States
OASTS	Organization of American States Treaty Series
OAU (Convention)	Organization of African Unity
OCHA	UN Office for the Coordination of Humanitarian Affairs
ODI	Overseas Development Institute
ODIHR	Office of Democratic Institutions and Human Rights
OIC	Organization of Islamic Cooperation
OILPOL	International Convention for the Prevention of Pollution of the Sea by Oil
OJEC	Official Journal of the European Union
OMB	Office of Management and Budget
ONUC	Opération des Nations unies au Congo
OPCAT	Optional Protocol to the Convention Against Torture
OSCE	Organization for Security and Co-operation in Europe
OTP	Office of the Prosecutor
PCA	Permanent Court of Arbitration
PCAT	Public Committee Against Torture
PCIJ (series)	Permanent Court of International Justice
PGM	Precision Guided Munition

PIRA	Provisional Irish Republican Army
PLO	Palestine Liberation Organization
PMC	private military company
PMSC	private military and security companies
POW	prisoner of war
PSF	UN Rapid Deployment Police and Security Force
PSO	Peace Support Operation
PUSIC	Party for the Unification and Safeguarding of the Integrity of the Congo
R2P	Responsibility to Protect
RCADI	Recueil de Cours de l'Académie de Droit International de la Haye
RGDIP	Revue Générale de Droit International Public
RIAA	Reports of International Arbitral Awards
RMC	Rules for Military Commissions
ROE	Rules of Engagement
RSC	Revised Statutes of Canada
RUF	Revolutionary United Front
RUSI	Royal United Services Institute for Defence and Security Studies
SCR	Supreme Court Reports
SCSL	Special Court for Sierra Leone
SEESAC	South Eastern and Eastern Europe Clearinghouse for the Control of Small Arms and Light Weapons
SIPRI	Stockholm International Peace Research Institute
SIrUS	Superfluous Injury and Unnecessary Suffering (ICRC Project)
SOFA	Status of Forces Agreement
SSR	security sector reform
STUFTS	Ships Taken Up From Trade
SVP	Swiss People's Party
TAM	Tribunal Arbitral Mixte
TC	Trial Chamber
TCN	Third Country National
TEU	Treaty on the European Union
TS	Treaty Series
TWC	Trials of War Criminals
UCAS	Unmanned Combat Aerial Systems
UCIHL	University Center for International Humanitarian Law
UCK (KLA)	Ushtria Çlirimtare e Kosovës (Kosovo Liberation Army)
UCMJ	Uniform Code of Military Justice
UDHR	Universal Declaration of Human Rights

UKAIT	United Kingdom Asylum and Immigration Tribunal
UKHL	United Kingdom House of Lords
UN GAOR	General Assembly Official Records
UN	United Nations
UNAMID	United Nations-African Union Hybrid Mission in Darfur
UNAMIR	United Nations Assistance Mission in Rwanda
UNAVEM III	United Nations Angola Verification Mission
UNCIO	UN Conference on International Organization
UNDP	United Nations Development Programme
UNDSS	United Nations Department for Safety and Security
UNEF/UNEF II	United Nations Emergency Force/Second United Nations Emergency Force
UNEP	United Nations Environment Programme
UNFICYP	United Nations Peacekeeping Force in Cyprus
UNGA	United Nations General Assembly
UNHCHR	United Nations High Commissioner for Human Rights
UNHCR	United Nations High Commissioner for Refugees
UNICEF:	United Nations International Children's Emergency Fund
UNIFIL	United Nations Interim Force in Lebanon
UNIIIC	United Nations International Independent Investigative Commission
UNMIH	Multinational Interim Force in Haiti
UNMIK	United Nations Mission in Kosovo
UNMIS	United Nations Mission in Sudan
UNOCI	United Nations Operation in Côte d'Ivoire
UNOSOM II	United Nations Operation in Somalia II
UNPROFOR	United Nations Protection Force
UNSAS	The United Nations Standby Arrangements System
UNSC	United Nations Security Council
UNSF	United Nations Security Forces
UNTAC	United Nations Transition Authority in Cambodia
UNTEA	United Nations Temporary Executive Authority
UNTS	United Nations Treaty Series
UPC	Union of Congolese Patriots
USC	US Code
USV	Unmanned Seagoing Vessel
VCLT	Vienna Convention on the Law of Treaties
WLR	Weekly Law Reports (UK)
WMD	Weapons of Mass Destruction
YIHL	Yearbook of International Humanitarian Law
YILC	Yearbook of the International Law Commission

Notes on the Contributors

Andrea Bianchi is Professor of International Law and Head of the International Law Department at the Graduate Institute of International and Development Studies, Geneva.

Enzo Cannizzaro is a Professor of International Law and EU Law at the University of Rome La Sapienza, Italy.

Antonio Cassese† was President of the Special Tribunal for Lebanon and the International Criminal Tribunal for the former Yugoslavia, as well as Professor of International Law at the University of Florence.

Vincent Chetail is Professor of International Law at the Graduate Institute of International and Development Studies (Geneva) where he is also Director of the Programme for the Study of Global Migration.

Christine Chinkin is Professor of International Law at the London School of Economics and William W. Cook Global Law Professor, University of Michigan. She is currently a member of the Kosovo Human Rights Advisory Panel.

Andrew Clapham is Professor of Public International Law at the Graduate Institute of International and Development Studies, Geneva. He was formerly Director of the Geneva Academy of International Humanitarian Law and Human Rights.

James Cockayne is Head of the United Nations University Office in New York. He served on the Temporary Steering Committee for the International Code of Conduct for Private Security Providers.

Dana Constantin is finishing her Referendariat at the Higher Regional Court of Hamburg. In 2011, she was a Legal Attaché in the Legal Division of the International Committee of the Red Cross.

Eric David is Professor (Emeritus) of Public International Law and President of the Centre for International Law at Brussels Free University (ULB) and member of the International Humanitarian Fact-Finding Commission.

Katherine Del Mar holds a PhD in International Law from the Graduate Institute of International and Development Studies, Geneva. She is a Member of the Editorial Committee of the *Journal of International Criminal Justice*.

Giovanni Distefano is Professor of Public International Law at the University of Neuchâtel. He is also Visiting Professor at the Geneva Academy of International Humanitarian Law and Human Rights.

Knut Dörmann has served as Head of the Legal Division of the International Committee of the Red Cross (ICRC), since December 2007.

Dieter Fleck, formerly Director of International Agreements and Policy of the German Ministry of Defence, is Honorary President of the International Society for Military Law and the Law of War, Member of the Advisory Board of the Amsterdam Center for International Law, and Member of the Editorial Board of the Journal of International Peacekeeping.

Paola Gaeta is Professor in the Faculty of Law at the University of Geneva and Adjunct Professor at the Graduate Institute of International and Development Studies, Geneva. She was formerly Director of the Geneva Academy of International Humanitarian Law and Human Rights.

Tom Haeck is an international lawyer specializing in human rights and international humanitarian law.

Steven Haines is Professor of Public International Law at the University of Greenwich, London and Visiting Fellow on the University of Oxford Changing Character of War Programme.

Wolff Heintschel von Heinegg is Professor of Public Law at the Europa-Universität Viadrina in Frankfurt (Oder), Germany. He is the current Charles H. Stockton Professor of International Law at the US Naval War College in Newport, United States, a position he also held in 2003–04.

Jean-Marie Henckaerts is a Legal Adviser in the Legal Division of the International Committee of the Red Cross (ICRC). He was head of the ICRC's project on customary international humanitarian law from 2000–10 and is currently heading the ICRC's project to update the Commentaries on the 1949 Geneva Conventions and their Additional Protocols of 1977.

Derek Jinks is the Marrs McLean Professor in Law at the University of Texas School of Law, United States and he has served on the US Department of State's Advisory Committee on International Law since 2006.

Jakob Kellenberger teaches at the Swiss Federal Institute of Technology in Zurich, the University of Salamanca and is a visiting Professor at the Graduate Institute of International Studies in Geneva. He is former State Secretary for Foreign Affairs for Switzerland and President of the International Committee of the Red Cross (2000–12).

Robert Kolb is Professor of Public International Law at the University of Geneva.

Nils Melzer held the Swiss Chair of International Humanitarian Law at the Geneva Academy of International Humanitarian Law and Human Rights, Switzerland until September 2013. He is Senior Programme Advisor and Senior Fellow of the Emerging Security Challenges Programme at the Geneva Centre for Security Policy (GCSP), Switzerland.

Theodor Meron is President of the International Criminal Tribunal for the Former Yugoslavia, and President of the International Residual Mechanism for Criminal Tribunals.

Nicolas Michel is Professor of Public International Law at the Law Faculty of the University of Geneva as well as at the Geneva Graduate Institute of International and Development Studies. He is President of the Board of the Geneva Academy of International Humanitarian Law and Human Rights. He served as Under-Secretary-General for Legal Affairs, the Legal Counsel of the United Nations (2004-2008).

Yasmin Naqvi is a Legal Officer in the Appeals Chamber of the International Criminal Tribunal for the former Yugoslavia.

Manfred Nowak is Professor of International Law and Human Rights at the University of Vienna, Austria. He is also Co-Director of the Ludwig Boltzmann Institute of Human Rights in Vienna, Austria and was UN Special Rapporteur on Torture from 2004–10. He was formerly Swiss Chair of Human Rights at the Geneva Academy.

Roger O'Keefe is University Senior Lecturer in Law and Deputy Director of the Lauterpacht Centre for International Law at the University of Cambridge, and Fellow of Magdalene College, Cambridge.

Alice Priddy is a researcher at the Geneva Academy of International Humanitarian Law and Human Rights.

Eibe Riedel is Professor (Emeritus) of International, European and Comparative Public Law at the University of Manheim, Visiting Professor at the Geneva Academy of International Humanitarian Law and Human Rights, and formerly Swiss Chair of Human Rights.

Peter Rowe is Professor of Law at the University of Lancaster, England. He has been Chairman of the UK Group of the International Society for Military Law and the Laws of War.

Yves Sandoz served for 18 years as Director for International Law and Policy at the International Committee of the Red Cross. He was elected to the Assembly of the International Committee of the Red Cross in 2002.

William A. Schabas is Professor of International Law at Middlesex University, London, Professor of International Criminal Law and Human Rights at Leiden University and Professor (Emeritus) of Human Rights Law at the National University of Ireland Galway.

Michael N. Schmitt is Chairman of the International Law Department at the US Naval War Law College. He is also Honorary Professor of International Humanitarian Law at Durham University in the United Kingdom.

Paul Seger is the Ambassador and Permanent Representative of Switzerland to the United Nations in New York. Before his present assignment he served as the Legal Adviser and Head of the Directorate for International Law in the Swiss Department of Foreign Affairs.

Philip Spoerri is Director for International Law and Cooperation at the International Committee of the Red Cross

Christian Tomuschat is Professor of International and Constitutional Law at Humboldt University Berlin. He was a member of the Human Rights Committee under the International Covenant on Civil and Political Rights from 1977–86 and a member (and chairman) of the International Law Commission (1985–96).

David Weissbrodt is the Regents Professor and Fredrikson & Byron Professor of Law at the University of Minnesota, United States. He is also the Co-Director of the Human Rights Center and Human Rights Library at the University of Minnesota.

PART I

INTRODUCTION

CHAPTER 1

CURRENT CHALLENGES TO INTERNATIONAL HUMANITARIAN LAW

ANTONIO CASSESE[†]

1 HENRY DUNANT AND THE BIRTH AND DEVELOPMENT OF INTERNATIONAL HUMANITARIAN LAW

INTERNATIONAL humanitarian law (IHL) is one of the great achievements of mankind. It was born in the middle of the nineteenth century thanks to Henry Dunant, a Swiss banker.

Dunant was not known for his acumen as a banker. Perhaps our debt for the creation of the International Committe of the Red Cross (ICRC) and the elaboration of the first Geneva Conventions is owed to his professional mediocrity, besides of course his great humanitarian commitment. In 1857, Dunant launched a company for the construction of windmills in Mons-Djémila, in the north-east of Algeria (located between the towns of Sétif and Constantine): the *'Société Anonime des Moulins de Mons-Djémila'*. He hoped to produce wheat to be sold to the French army. Under the circumstances, the idea of such a project was preposterous: it required the concession of many acres of land in Algeria by the colonial power; in addition, it involved the cultivation of grain in a place where there were no roads and no rail access needed to transport the harvested wheat. As it happened, Dunant only managed to secure 19 acres, whereas he needed around 1219. He also needed a waterfall to make the windmills work and to irrigate the fields. To obtain these resources, he conceived a bold idea: to ask Napoleon III directly for the necessary land and water. He thus wrote to the Emperor and printed, at his own cost, two pocket-size books. In one of these, Dunant made the case for the establishment of a grain cultivation company in Algeria; in the other he extolled the Emperor's magnificent deeds and even asserted that he was the sole and rightful heir to the ancient Roman crown, declaring that 'one word from his [Napoleon III's] lips terrifies Europe. A line from his pen reassures Europe.'[1]

Armed with these two booklets, Dunant set out to find Napoleon III but learned that in fact the Emperor was in northern Italy leading the French army and preparing, with the support of the army of Vittorio Emanuele II, to attack the Austrian army, led by the Emperor Franz Joseph. Draped in an impeccable white suit, Dunant naively hastened to Brescia but Napoleon III had already left for the battlefront. Hurrying on to Castiglione delle Stiviere (in the province of Mantua), Dunant arrived on the evening of 24 June 1859, precisely when, in a nearby clearing in Solferino, one of the bloodiest battles since Waterloo had just been fought. In that clearing, 170,000 Austrian soldiers had clashed with a combined Franco-Italian force of 150,000. The battle had begun to rage before dawn, and it lasted until five o'clock in the afternoon with the defeat of the Austrians. Strewn about on the battlefield there remained more than 40,000 dead and thousands of wounded.

The next morning, Dunant, still in his snow-white outfit, made his way to Solferino and was horrified by the scene. In the following days the banker almost completely forgot about his Swiss-Algerian company and, working day and night, struggled to care for the wounded and the dying. Three years later, in 1862, and once again at his own expense, Dunant published a short book called *Un souvenir de Solferino* ('A Memory of Solferino'). Although only 1600 copies were printed, the book achieved an extraordinarily wide distribution. In his account, Dunant not only described the terrible suffering of the survivors at Solferino but also proposed a great idea: to promote the conclusion of an international convention that would create societies in every European state to care for the wounded in battle. In short, he launched the idea of a permanent, voluntary, and international organization that would care for victims of war.[2]

---

[1] C.Z. Rothkopf, *Jean Henri Dunant—Father of the Red Cross* (New York: Franklin Watts Inc, 1969), 39–40.

[2] The same idea had been advocated by the Italian physician Ferdinando Palasciano (1815–91), who had been a medical officer in the Bourbon army during the insurrectionist movements of the Risorgimento. Palasciano was arrested by the Bourbon troops for insubordination, and in particular for providing medical care to wounded enemies after having stated: 'The wounded, whatever army they belong to, are sacred to me and cannot be considered as enemies'. In 1861, at the International Congress

From that moment Dunant's life split in two. As a promoter of humanitarian ideas, Dunant had great success (even though he soon exited from the stage): in 1864, agreement was reached on the first Geneva Convention, concerning the Amelioration of the Condition of the Wounded and Sick in Armed Forces in the Field. This first Convention set in motion an extraordinary mechanism that led to two notable developments. First, the conclusion of other Geneva Conventions: the Convention of 1929 concerning the Treatment of Prisoners of War, the 1929 Convention on the Wounded and Sick (amending and updating the previous agreement) as well as the four Geneva Conventions of 1949 and the two Additional Protocols of 1977. Secondly, the creation of the national Red Cross societies in 1863 and of the International Committee of the Red Cross (ICRC) in 1864. As for the banking side of his life, however, Dunant was destined to fail miserably.[3]

I have lingered on the origins of the first two Geneva Conventions in order to highlight the fact that, in essence, it was the idealism and the innovative, ingenious spirit of a single man which originated the idea to create an international institution with an exclusively humanitarian character aiming to mitigate as far as possible the suffering caused by war. That exclusively humanitarian spirit—the wounded and the sick had to be cared for, regardless of whether they were friends or foes—also inspired, albeit in attenuated form, the drafting of the famous Hague Conventions, concluded in 1899 and in 1907 in The Hague, at the behest of the Russian Tsar Nicolas II. Among these was a Convention of the utmost importance containing, as an annex, the Regulation concerning the Laws and Customs of War on Land. The Hague Conventions also limit and channel the powers of belligerents and therefore are, in significant measure, of a humanitarian character: they protect individual persons. They address questions such as who may be considered a legitimate combatant and what rights are held by such a combatant when captured. In other words, these Conventions address the issue of the treatment of prisoners of war, as well as the powers and duties of an occupying state and those of the population of the occupied country. Above all, they determine the way in which hostilities may be conducted.

at the Accademia Pontaniana of Naples, he famously declared that 'all the belligerent Powers, when declaring war, should reciprocally recognize the principle of neutrality of wounded combatants during the time in which they receive care. They should furthermore recognize the principle of unlimited increase of health care personnel during the entire period of the war.'

[3] In 1867, the small private bank where Dunant worked as manager was obliged to close its doors. The bank's shareholders demanded compensation but Dunant was penniless. Regarded with contempt by the local Calvinist bankers, who had no tolerance for economic failure, and unable to live any longer in Geneva, he left and became a voluntary exile. At the age of 40 he thus began living in Paris, first doing odd jobs before gradually becoming a sort of *clochard* living on the street. In 1892 a journalist found him in the small Swiss village of Heiden, where he was living in a publicly funded shelter. At that stage Dunant was granted a new lease on life. In the end he was universally acclaimed for the actions he took to care for the sick and the wounded in war, and in 1901 he was awarded (together with Frédéric Passy, the French founder of the '*Société française pour l'arbitrage entre nations*') the first Nobel Peace Prize.

However, the states convening in The Hague were animated not only by a humanitarian spirit. They also sought to safeguard politico-military interests, agreeing a series of 'rules of the game' aimed in particular at satisfying the requirements of the Great Powers and, to some degree, also those of lesser states. In The Hague, as had previously been the case at the Conference of 1874 in Brussels,[4] the large and powerful states were pitted against the small states, each with specific interests not altogether humanitarian. The large states, assured of victory in case of war, sought to secure as far as possible the interests of belligerents, while the small states—certain to be vanquished and occupied in the case of war—sought to protect civilian populations and their territory. Even the famous 'Martens clause', that is, the clause proposed by the Russian Delegate Martens according to which, in all cases not subject to the Regulation concerning the Laws and Customs of War on Land, civilian populations 'remain under the protection and empire of the principles of international law, as they result from the uses established between civilized nations, from the laws of humanity and the requirements of the public conscience'—even this clause in reality was conceived not as a humanitarian provision but as a clever diplomatic expedient to cut short a dispute between the large and small powers.[5] In brief, at the Conferences in The Hague an effort was made to protect *persons*, but also and above all to safeguard the *interests of the states*.

The indisputable fact remains that all of these rules of the law of war (or international humanitarian law, as it is called today, conceptually merging the two components inspiring this body of law, namely the humanitarian and the politico-military components) have constituted, in the last hundred years, a formidable protective net which to some extent seeks to attenuate the devastation of war. No one can deny that the four Geneva Conventions of 1949 have shielded the 'victims of war', that is, those who do not take (or no longer take) part in hostilities, limiting the harm they suffer from the violence wrought by conflict. In short, there is no doubt that the more strictly humanitarian rules of the law of armed conflict represent significant progress for our civilization.

---

[4] The 1874 Brussels Conference was convened at the initiative of Tsar Alexander II of Russia to adopt an international agreement on the laws and customs of war. The text of the agreement was adopted, but never entered into force. However, it constituted an important step towards the codification of the laws of warfare.

[5] On the origin and meaning of the Martens clause, I take the liberty of referring to my earlier essay, 'The Martens Clause: Half a Loaf or Simply Pie in the Sky?', 11 *European Journal of International Law* (2000) 187–216.

2 The Principal Failings of Current IHL

What are the principal weaknesses of contemporary IHL, and what challenges must it face?

I will not dwell too much on certain inadequacies of the law today, such as the fact that the regime governing military occupation (*occupatio bellica*) conceived for occupations of enemy territory limited in time (a few months or a few years) is today subject to strong tensions because certain occupations persist for decades. (The Israeli occupation of Palestinian territory has lasted 40 years, and Morocco's occupation of the Western Sahara dates back 32 years.) Other acts originally had another purpose and a different temporal dimension. For example, the *armistice*, which was originally intended to be of short duration—just long enough to reach agreement on a peace treaty—has in fact been stretched out to as long as 54 years in the case of the two Koreas (whose armistice was signed in 1953). Another example is the *cease-fire agreement*, which was supposed to be followed rapidly by an armistice and then by a peace treaty, whereas in reality such an agreement may crystallize for years, as we saw, for example, when a cease-fire agreement was concluded between Israel and Syria in 1973.

These inadequacies of humanitarian law are, to some degree, physiological: it is illusory to think that the law can keep pace with evolving reality, which becomes more and more complex and tends to slip past the constraints of legal rules. Yet even if states fail to fulfil their moral obligation to ensure that the law is appropriately adapted to reality, legal rules nevertheless contain at least the general principles capable of 'taming' new phenomena, principles that it falls to judges and jurists to distil from those rules.

In my view the real weakness of humanitarian law lies elsewhere: nowadays, in the numerous wars that plague the planet, *civilians are no longer protected*. All wars, internal or international, result in massacres. Why? The reason is very simple: the segment of IHL that governs the conduct of hostilities, namely the use of the means of war (arms) and the methods of war (attacks against the enemy), is loose and flawed by lacunae. It thus fails to restrain the violence of war, which in the end always causes more harm to civilians than to the clashing forces themselves.

A. The total and asymmetric nature of modern armed conflicts

The entire body of law which we have at our disposal today—the so-called law of Geneva (aimed at protecting persons that do not, or no longer, take part in hostilities, such as civilians, sick or shipwrecked persons, or prisoners of war) and the

so-called law of The Hague (aiming above all at regulating the conduct of hostilities)—is modelled on a *Rousseauian* conception of war. According to this philoso-
pher from Geneva, war is fought between *two armies*, from which civilians must be
sheltered at all costs. War, he wrote in the *Social Contract* (1762),[6] is a relation, not
between man and man, but between state and state, and individuals are enemies
only accidentally, not as men nor even as citizens, but as soldiers.

Yet today nearly all armed conflicts are *total wars*. They belong to the category of
wars theorized by von Clausewitz in 1832 and practised by Napoleon a few decades
before: bloody conflicts not between two armies but between *entire nations in arms*.
These wars are merciless, and invariably they involve not just soldiers but the entire
civilian populations of each side, or at least of the weaker one. In the midst of these
hostilities, the distinction between military and civilian personnel, if not cancelled
altogether, becomes, *de facto*, very hazy indeed.

Moreover, with certain exceptions, such as the wars between Iran and Iraq (1980–
88) and between Eritrea and Ethiopia (1998–2000), almost all modern armed conflicts are *asymmetric*. On one side there is a state or government well supplied with
a regular army and modern armaments (jets, helicopters, tanks, missiles and so
on), while on the other side there are non-state entities (insurgents, guerrillas, or
armed terrorist groups) without any proper army, air power, or heavy weaponry.
The recent war in southern Lebanon between the Israeli army and Hezbollah, and
the wars being fought in Iraq and Afghanistan, are typical manifestations of such
modern conflicts. The likelihood that future conflicts will increasingly be *unconven-
tional* wars was recently affirmed by Robert M. Gates, then US Secretary of Defense,
in a speech of 10 October 2007. He noted that 'we expect that asymmetric warfare
will remain the mainstay of the contemporary battlefield for some time'.[7]

Given these two fundamental characteristics of modern armed conflicts, that is,
their totality and their asymmetry, how do belligerents behave?

The short answer is that, by and large, states and governments involved in armed
conflicts tend to be guided by the conception of war set forth by Rousseau. Broadly
speaking, they insist on respect for IHL, a body of law that—as mentioned above—
is itself patterned after the Rousseauian model. They therefore make an effort to
distinguish between civilians and soldiers; they respect private dwellings, schools,
places of worship, hospitals, ambulances and so on. But states and governments are
not always on their best behaviour. They frequently avail themselves of the ambiguities and the lacunae of the international rules on the conduct of hostilities, ambiguities, and lacunae whose repercussions are all the more serious when war is not just
between two armies but is total and asymmetric.

---

[6] See R.D. Masters and C. Kelly (eds), *The Collected Writings of Rousseau* (Hanover: University Press
of New England, 1994), vol 4.

[7] Robert M. Gates, Speech to the Association of the United States Army, 10 October 2007, available
at <http://www.defenselink.mil/speeches/speech.aspx?speechild=1181>, 4.

As for rebels, guerrillas, and terrorists, who do not have an extensive war-making apparatus comparable to that of a state, they normally conduct their hostilities in accordance with a different conception: that proffered by von Clausewitz. They do not wear military uniforms, they do not openly bear arms, and they do not refrain from blending in with the civilian population. Indeed, by camouflaging themselves among civilians, they may more effectively attack the enemy. Not only is this prohibited by IHL, it also confronts the adversary with a grave dilemma: attack the guerrillas and risk causing enormous civilian casualties, or abstain from attacks that could decisively contribute to defeating them? In 2007, US Rear Admiral Greg Smith, as US military spokesman in Iraq, in commenting on a US air strike on a stronghold of senior insurgent leaders in Baghdad which also killed nine children and six women, called those killings 'absolutely regrettable'. However, Smith placed the blame for them on the enemy fighters: 'We do not target civilians. But when our forces are fired upon, as they are routinely, then they have no option but to return fire'.[8]

B. Other specific deficiencies of IHL

The foregoing remarks have laid out a general context. Let us now look more closely at some *specific* gaps or deficiencies in modern IHL.

(i) *Guerrillas and terrorists are discouraged from respecting IHL*

Irregular combatants usually do not comply with the prescriptions of IHL and make no effort to distinguish themselves from civilians. On the contrary: they hide among civilians so as not to be attacked; they launch rockets or fire arms from private houses, or even from city streets (as Hezbollah did, launching rockets against Israel from trucks situated in the city centre or in a square before hastening to other locations); they camp in civilian dwellings or other civilian places, rather than in military quarters; they use civilians as human shields or hostages.

Unfortunately, IHL does not provide irregular combatants with any advantages that could induce them to respect the law of war. The only 'bonus' the current law offers such combatants is this: if they are captured by an enemy belligerent, they are not punished simply for making war, provided that 'they openly bear arms immediately prior to and during each military attack'. However, this advantage is somewhat limited by the fact that the military powers may use the means at their disposal to identify and strike a combatant that openly bears arms, even before a military encounter is initiated. For example, the great military powers have spy satellites, infrared vision equipment, deadly robot aircraft (so-called 'Predators', pilotless

---

[8] *International Herald Tribune*, 13–14 October 2007, 3 ('15 Iraqi civilians die in American airstrike').

planes capable of electronic surveillance and search for targets) and laser weaponry. With these types of modern arms and equipment, a belligerent power can easily identify and strike an irregular enemy combatant.

I would add that an irregular combatant has little incentive to abide by IHL, considering that the military powers assert that it is legitimate to strike him not only in the theatre of war but anywhere they find him, even at home or when he takes his wife and children to the cinema. Furthermore, the military powers no longer distinguish between political adversaries (who should be treated as equivalent to civilians) and men in arms.[9] For this reason, the irregular combatant, knowing that he is at a tremendous military disadvantage, may be inclined to conceal his weapons and to produce them only at the moment of attack, and may further seek to hide among the population while he prepares his next attack.

The obvious consequence of this state of affairs is that the irregular combatant puts the civilian population at great risk.

(ii) *IHL Fails to place limits on the military might of the Great Powers*

A second serious deficiency of modern IHL lies in the fact that it does not sufficiently limit the exorbitant military might of belligerent powers.

The rules of IHL prohibit attacks on civilians, but they do not specify the *precautions* that a belligerent must take when it risks striking them. As a consequence, for instance, in Kosovo the bombardment of the television station in Belgrade was not preceded by any precautionary measure. Or to cite another example, Russian armed forces, when they attack Chechen 'terrorists', consider it sufficient to warn the local population by means of loudspeakers they bring with them in helicopters.[10] And in the case of Lebanon, the Israelis considered it adequate to distribute leaflets, or to use loudspeakers or radio transmissions, or recorded messages sent via Lebanese cellular phones.[11]

Furthermore, IHL rules fail to delimit with sufficient precision the notion of *military objective*. In some of the latest conflicts, for example NATO's attack in Kosovo in 1999 and Israel's attack in Lebanon in 2006, belligerent powers substantially extend the notion of 'military objective' to the point of including, among other things, television stations. In addition, IHL rules prohibit attacks that cause so-called

---

[9] The Israeli Ambassador to the UN, Dan Gillerman, stated in 2006 that it makes no sense to distinguish between the political and military structures of Hezbollah, since '[the] Hizbollah member of parliament and the terrorist in the hills launching rockets at Israeli civilians both have the same strategy and goal. These labels cannot be allowed to give legitimacy to a gang of thugs' (UN Doc S/PV.5493, 11).

[10] See European Court of Human Rights, *Isayeva v Russia*, 57950/00, Judgment of 24 February 2005, §§ 25, 52, 72, 77, 171, 192, 193.

[11] See Human Rights Watch, *Why They Died: Civilian Casualties in Lebanon During the 2006 War* (2007), 6–7 and 66–9.

disproportionate *collateral damage* to civilians and civilian objects, ie harm that is 'disproportionate' with respect to the military advantage sought to be achieved. Yet no concrete standard is provided for the purpose of gauging the proportionality of the actions taken. Is the killing of 20 civilians in order to destroy a bridge used by the enemy 'proportionate'? Is it 'proportionate' to destroy dozens of civilian homes and the occupants inside them in order to blow up an electric power plant used exclusively for military ends?

IHL also fails clearly to provide whether certain weapons (for example, cluster bombs) capable of inflicting damage indiscriminately and thus also harming civilians are banned or whether they may be used in specific exceptional circumstances.

Nor do we find rules—in scenarios where the soldiers of a belligerent have violated on a massive scale the obligation to respect civilians—which effectively ensure that the soldiers in question will be tried in *court martial* proceedings. Even when there is a competent international tribunal, political circumstances often scuttle attempts to establish liability. For example, the 'collateral damage' caused by NATO air forces in Kosovo in 1999 demonstrates clearly how the forces of great and medium-size military powers can cause serious harm to civilians without any negative consequences for the belligerents. Not only was there never a trial, there was never even an investigation into what Belgrade characterized as war crimes. Likewise, with regard to war crimes committed in Afghanistan, the International Criminal Court would be empowered to intervene, but remains silent.

(iii) *IHL fails to control the actions of 'private contractors'*

One increasingly widespread and serious phenomenon is the so-called 'privatization of war'. Today, belligerents tend to entrust to private parties tasks that are normally discharged by military units. These tasks are various and sundry: security services, including above all bodyguard services, logistical support, construction, and maintenance of logistical apparatus such as housing or cafeteria services, the maintenance of arsenal, the management of defence and intelligence systems, prison management (including interrogation of detainees), the training of armed forces or of local police, and psychological warfare. In other words, private parties are enlisted for practically all kinds of war-related activities short of actual participation in armed combat.

May we designate such 'private contractors'—which, for example, the United States has used on a massive scale in Afghanistan and Iraq—as mercenaries, and hence criminals? No, they are not mercenaries. In the first place, these private parties are nearly always citizens of the state that employs them. Moreover, in the American case they are formally charged by the US Government with the missions they perform. And they take no direct part in armed hostilities. Why, then, have the authorities in Washington decided to rely so heavily on them? (According to several sources, the Pentagon has employed between 10,000 and 20,000 'private contractors' in Iraq alone.) And how should they be characterized? Are they equivalent to armed forces or police forces? Or are they akin to vigilantes, unrecognized by the laws of states and the international community? The question is not an academic one: the answer will determine (i) whether they may considered by the adversary as legitimate targets in warfare, as well as (ii) whether and by whom such private persons will be charged and prosecuted for the crimes they may commit against civilian populations.[12]

The 'privatization of war' confronts us with a very serious problem. For decades, if not centuries, the effort has been made to establish rules to regulate war—rules to decide who is a legitimate combatant, how hostilities are to be conducted, and how to punish those who flout the rules. But now a new trend has emerged for which these rules are ill-equipped, a trend that could produce disastrous consequences.

(iv) *IHL fails to detect violations*

A fourth deficiency of modern IHL—and hardly a minor one—is that there are not effective mechanisms for determining when a belligerent has violated that very law. The Geneva Conventions of 1949 and the First Additional Protocol of 1977 assign monitoring functions to both the Protecting Powers and the ICRC. The First Additional Protocol further establishes, in Article 90, an 'International Fact-Finding Commission', which may be charged by the belligerents with the task of ascertaining relevant facts.

Yet these organs are not functioning. The Protecting Powers must be accepted by both parties to a conflict; in addition, third states are always hesitant to become involved in conflicts, as these entail complex and politically risky actions. The ICRC, which substitutes regularly for the Protecting Powers because of their absence, is authoritative and competent, but is limited by the fact that its reports and interventions are always confidential: it therefore cannot avail itself of resort to

---

[12] The reason why the US Government relies on private parties for such operations is clear: in scenarios such as that of Afghanistan (and previously in Iraq), hundreds of thousands of persons are needed to face the vast range of military and security issues. Military personnel are often poorly trained youth, and in the last few years they include many who in their native country have committed petty crimes. Due to the harshness of war, young officers are often tempted to quit the military, and in recent times the US Government has had to grant significant financial bonuses to retain them. It is therefore preferable to turn to specialized and better prepared personnel, even if this entails high cost, as this at least spares soldiers from having to perform so many specialized and onerous tasks and allows them to concentrate on combat operations. Another 'advantage' is that the killing of private contractors causes less of a stir in public opinion than that of young soldiers or marines. Furthermore, the use of such contractors can be a way to sidestep a lot of rules. In particular, such private parties are removed from the scope of the laws of the territories in which they operate, and likewise cannot be touched by American law or international law. On the basis of agreements the US has concluded with Afghanistan and Iraq, the latter may not exercise criminal jurisdiction in cases of crimes committed by 'private contractors'; only the US may prosecute them. But since in the US the legal position of these persons is unclear, in practice they surreptitiously enjoy *de facto* immunity. It should be stressed that the use of private persons is increasingly expanding. See further Chapter 25 in this volume.

world public opinion. The International Fact-Finding Commission provided for by Article 90 has been called the 'Sleeping Beauty of the Forest',[13] considering that so far it has never been activated, partly because it is complex and cumbersome and also because substantially it is a quasi-judicial mechanism designed to intervene only on an *ex post* basis.

It is distressing to note that in the conflicts of the last 20 years, no international supervisory organ has been able to verify, on the ground, the numerous violations committed by the belligerents. Instead, it has been necessary to resort, in certain cases of massive and repeated violations, to the creation of ad hoc international criminal courts and tribunals (eg the ad hoc Tribunal for the former Yugoslavia, established in 1993, the ad hoc Tribunal for Rwanda, established in 1994, and the ad hoc Special Court for Sierra Leone, created in 2002), or to the use of inter-state tribunals, such as the Eritrea-Ethiopia Claims Commission, established in 2000, or human rights courts, such as the European Court of Human Rights, in the case of the Chechen conflict.[14] In other cases, it has been necessary to rely on independent and authoritative non-governmental organizations, such as Human Rights Watch[15] or commissions of inquiry set up by UN bodies (such as the commissions established by the Human Rights Council or by the Security Council).[16]

(v) *IHL fails to secure compensation to victims*

A further and equally important shortcoming of modern IHL is that it does not adequately protect the victims of violent conflict or their families, even after the violations have occurred, by providing an appropriate mechanism by which the offending belligerent can at least compensate the victim for damage suffered. Of course, international customary law (in accordance with Article 3 of the Fourth Hague Convention of 1907) as well as the four Geneva Conventions of 1949 (Articles 51/52/131/148) and the First Additional Protocol of 1977 (Article 91) all oblige a belligerent which has violated the rules of the law of war to indemnify the victim. Nevertheless, this obligation only has legal force between states, or at least this is the way it has thus far been interpreted. It follows that, if the party to the conflict to which the victim belongs does not demand compensation for the harm suffered (or if it obtains compensation in a lump sum to be distributed with discretion among

---

[13] F. Kalshoven, 'The International Humanitarian Fact-Finding Commission: A Sleeping Beauty?', 4 *Humanitäres Völkerrecht* (2002) 213–16, reprinted in F. Kalshoven, *Reflections on the Law of War—Collected Essays* (Leiden: Koninklijke Brill, 2007), 835–41.

[14] See *Isayeva v Russia*, 57950/00, Judgment of 24 February 2005, and *Isayeva, Yusupova and Bazayeva v Russia*, 7947/00; 57948/00; 57949/00, Judgment of 24 February 2005 (decided on the same day).

[15] See eg Human Rights Watch, *Civilians under Assault—Hezbollah's Rocket Attacks on Israel in the 2006 War* (2007), as well as *Why They Died—Civilian Casualties in Lebanon During the 2006 War*.

[16] On these commissions, see P. Alston, 'The Darfur Commission as a Model for Future Responses to Crisis Situations', 3 *Journal of International Criminal Justice* (2005) 600–7.

the victims), there is no compensation to the victim by the state or other party that committed the violation. If the victims or their families are faced with inertia on the part of the party to the conflict to which they belong, and if they endeavour to seek redress through the courts of the offending party, in most cases they are doomed to fail. Indeed, they may find that the offending party has no courts, or at any rate courts capable of granting effective remedies (as is the case with rebels or other non-state organizations, let alone terrorist organizations); or they may discover that the belligerent in question, if it is a state, enjoys a powerful defence which for centuries has protected sovereign states: the 'doctrine' of sovereign immunity, in civil actions where the state has acted in its sovereign capacity.[17]

3 How Can Armed Conflicts Be Made Less Inhumane?

Given these gaps and difficulties in the law today, what can be done to mitigate the devastation of armed conflicts?

To my mind, we must first of all exclude two options, even though in the abstract they would seem relevant. These options consist of, on the one hand, *changing international rules* to adjust them to the reality of modern conflicts; and on the other, establishing *new criminal mechanisms* for the punishment of violators.

Regarding the first option, it is unthinkable to *modernize IHL rules*. These rules have been fashioned above all by the Great Powers, and these Powers do not have an interest in tying their own hands with more precise legal standards. On the other hand, states linked politically or ideologically to guerrillas or terrorists would also oppose modifications that could end up penalizing those under their protection.

Nor is it realistic to consider *extending and strengthening the application of criminal law* to individuals that carry out attacks against civilians. Guerrillas normally do not have courts martial in which either their own combatants, or those of the enemy, may be tried for serious violations of IHL. In any case, such groups tend to flout prohibitions laid down by IHL. On the other hand, belligerent states and governments often do not prosecute captured enemy combatants but tend rather to detain them in gloomy places without giving them any rights, least of all the right to a fair and speedy trial. In addition, belligerent states and governments tend not to prosecute their own military personnel, either because their conduct often conforms to widespread practices tolerated or indeed inspired or authorized by the authorities

---

[17] See the Chapter by C. Tomuschat in this volume.

(consider the American attack in Falluja), or because any trials could damage the morale of other troops exposed to grave danger and exhausted by fighting.

In short, the world is beset by a vicious circle that is difficult to break out of: barbarity is met with barbarity, and no sanction is meted out. The exceptions are rare: soldiers are prosecuted only for egregious rapes or for 'gratuitous' killings of civilians (for example, where motivated by racial or ethnic hatred or by 'private' ends); no soldiers are tried when their crimes are in some way part of a common strategy or policy, required or tolerated by the chain of command.

A. A modest tripartite proposal

I would therefore suggest that we set aside those abstract possibilities; we need to venture out on more promising roads. As I see it, what is required is action on three levels.

(i) *The drawing up of non-binding guidelines*

On one level, authoritative 'general directives' could be worked out to delimit and specify what is permissible as regards the conduct of belligerents. When I say 'general directives' I am referring to parameters and standards that are not binding. Indeed, as I have just explained, the reluctance of the Great Powers to limit their own margin for manoeuvre makes it highly difficult if not impossible to secure the adoption of binding rules that circumscribe the enormous discretionary power states have at their disposal. Since, for that reason, international 'law-makers' keep silent, the elaboration of general parameters or directives providing greater precision, and hence limiting the power of belligerents, could indeed be a useful step forward. These standards or guidelines should be prepared by (military and legal) experts and should thereafter be approved by humanitarian bodies including Red Cross societies and the ICRC, or at least by authoritative non-governmental organizations. Such instruments would thus have no legally binding character, but they could acquire an important moral, psychological, and political force.

One may ask: 'Is it realistic to think that legal and military experts could act as a kind of international "quasi-legislator"? On the strength of what authority will they be able to agree upon directives or standards of conduct, thus acting in the stead of states?' My answer is that those legal and military experts should assign a limited task to themselves. They should follow the case-by-case method adopted by the then-President of the Supreme Court of Israel, Aharon Barak, in the Court's judgment on the legitimacy, from the standpoint of international law, of 'targeted killings'.[18] In other words, on the basis of a careful study of international practice,

---

[18] Supreme Court of Israel sitting as the High Court of Justice, *The Public Committee against Torture in Israel and Others v The Government of Israel and Others*, HCJ 769/02, Judgment of 13 December 2006.

and drawing illumination and clues from the *general principles* of IHL, these experts could elaborate a sort of *casuistry*,[19] indicating for each case the most appropriate and rational solution available under the relevant legal principles and in light of the particular circumstances of the case. In this way, belligerents could find, in that casuistry, the proper guidance for their behaviour in the course of armed conflict.

As for the subjects which should be covered by such guidelines, there are two that I think deserve priority: (i) the position of irregular combatants and 'private contractors'; and (ii) the limits that should apply to attacks by military powers carried out to target military objectives but leading to collateral damage to civilians.

On the first point, it is necessary to *incentivize irregular combatants* to spare the civilian populations in which they live and operate. In that regard, action could be taken on two fronts.

On the one hand, those combatants who treat civilians as human shields or who attack civilian dwellings or hide arms in civilian property should subsequently be 'penalized'—not with new procedural mechanisms, but with those that already exist. This 'penalization' should commence immediately where such a combatant is captured: he or she should immediately be court-martialled and, if found guilty, face serious penalties. Possible abuses on the part of the military power that has captured the irregular combatant may be avoided by recourse to certain monitoring mechanisms about which I will speak in a few moments.

On the other hand, it is also necessary to *incentivize* the civilian population to exclude, as far as possible, such combatants, or in any case to differentiate themselves from them. That could be achieved by providing, as I will explain, that where an attack against irregular combatants causes harm to civilians, compensation will only be obtained if the combatants have not 'utilized' or instrumentalized civilians in pursuit of their objectives (this, of course, within possible limits: for example, it may prove very difficult for a Palestinian living in the occupied territories to prevent an armed member of Hamas from taking refuge in his cellar or from leaving weapons there for later use).

It is furthermore necessary to propose legal regimes applying to the actions of *'private contractors'*. Such regimes would enumerate their obligations or treat them as equivalent to members of the armed forces. Provision should then be made for submitting them to the criminal jurisdiction of the state in which violations have been committed and to that of the state to which the offender belongs.

---

[19] Like the word 'sophistry', it is probable that early usage of the word 'casuistry' was derogatory: see T.F. Hoad (ed), *The Concise Oxford Dictionary of Word Origins* (Oxford and New York: Oxford University Press, 1986) 65. In this Chapter, 'a casuistry' refers to an instance of casuistic reasoning, described in the *Oxford English Dictionary* as 'that part of Ethics which resolves cases of conscience, applying the general rules of religion and morality to particular instances in which "circumstances alter cases", or in which there appears to be a conflict of duties': see *Oxford English Dictionary* (2012), 'casuistry, n.'. For similar usage and further illumination, see T. Fowler, *The Principles of Morals, Part II (being the body of the work)* (Oxford: Clarendon Press, 1887), 246–8.

Turning to the *delimitation of the power* of belligerents to take precautions when launching an attack that could claim numerous civilian lives, and to the question of how to ascertain whether 'collateral damage' to civilians is 'proportional', a detailed casuistry should be elaborated, as I mentioned earlier. To that end, the method adopted by President Barak in the judgment of the Israeli Supreme Court, to which I have already referred, should be taken as a guidepost. To begin with, two extreme cases should be identified: one in which collateral damage is clearly legitimate; and then the opposite case, in which such damage is manifestly excessive. That would leave an intermediate or 'grey' zone. It is with respect to this grey zone that a casuistry should be elaborated, with indications, for each hypothetical case, of the most reasonable and appropriate solution that may be drawn from general principles and from state practice. Furthermore, each solution should be fully reasoned. If such an approach were to yield reasonable and convincing solutions, and if these solutions were also supported by authoritative humanitarian organizations, we could offer states a set of standards by which states would hopefully comply when engaged in hostilities.

(ii) *Setting up flexible and effective monitoring mechanisms*

A second level for action could lead to proposals concerning the creation of monitoring mechanisms aimed at establishing the relevant facts in cases of grave violations of the principles and rules of IHL.

In general terms, the legal perspective—in particular the criminal law perspective—that some favour, should be abandoned. It is also time to abandon the mechanism adopted in Geneva in 1977, when Article 90 of the First Additional Protocol was approved. As I have said, this provision follows an outdated, quasi-judicial logic and lays down a quite cumbersome procedure. In contrast to this approach, what is needed are flexible bodies, not quasi-judicial ones but rather organs adapted for the minute and daily monitoring of the conduct of combatants. These supervisory mechanisms should obviously be impartial beyond any doubt and should be composed of military experts and specialists in humanitarian law who do not come from countries involved in the armed conflict in question. They should, moreover, be able to operate *right from the start* of the conflict: their intervention in the conflict should indeed be *automatic*. For example, as soon as armed conflict breaks out, the ICRC, or another authoritative humanitarian organization, could ask the belligerents to ensure that small monitoring organs can operate in their respective territories. Presumably, refusal of access to such an organ would be an embarrassment for a state. These organs would then be responsible for monitoring the conduct of the belligerents and for preparing factual reports. Initially these reports would be confidential and would be disclosed only to the parties to the conflict. However, they could be made public in cases of repeated violations of international humanitarian law. At the conclusion of the conflict all reports should automatically be published.

It could also be useful to provide for the creation of *ex post* verification mechanisms at the national level for the purpose of ascertaining whether the killing of civilians has been, under the circumstances, disproportionate.

(iii) *Compensating victims*

The third level of action, which in my view would be needed to help rectify the deficiencies of IHL, would be the adoption of mechanisms to indemnify victims of serious violations. I am thinking above all of cases of excessive 'collateral damage' and, all the more so, of cases of indiscriminate attacks. To my mind, in cases of excessive collateral damage caused by a belligerent party (not including damage resulting from civilian involvement in the activities of irregular combatants), it is necessary to compensate the *victims* or, more generally, the *community* concerned.

The idea of compensation can be an important incentive for civilians to avoid letting themselves be manipulated by guerrillas, particularly since they would realize that any excessive harm they suffer would only be indemnified if they have neither collaborated with guerrillas, nor allowed themselves to be the guerrillas' 'instruments' by permitting them to hide among the population in violation of international rules.

Whose responsibility should it be to compensate the victims of serious violations, and when is intervention necessary? In this regard, a range of solutions could be offered to belligerents, it being understood that, if they fail to accept a particular mechanism, there is the possibility that one of the mechanisms in question would be triggered automatically. As a first step a special international mechanism could be created, either within the organization of the ICRC or at least linked to it, which could be activated by victims upon the termination of the conflict. Only if this international mechanism turns into a bottleneck could victims bring their cases before the courts of the parties to the conflict. The courts would be competent to try cases following the conclusion of hostilities, but only in the capacity of 'surrogate' where international action is unavailing.

The financial resources necessary to compensate victims could be made available by the party to the conflict which has committed violations that have been verified by one of the organs that I have mentioned. But it would also be possible to set up a trust fund financed by contributions from international organizations and states, the primary function of which would be to compensate victims of violations committed by non-state organizations or rebels.

B. Who can we count on?

Now that I have proposed this tripartite action plan, let us ask ourselves who we could count on to carry such an enterprise forward.

Let us first consider whether we can rely on states or intergovernmental organizations. In my view, we cannot. Even the states that are the most sensitive to humanitarian needs, such as Switzerland, the Netherlands, or the Nordic European countries, cannot by themselves make changes to international law, let alone establish international monitoring mechanisms. In this domain more than in others in international law, it is the Great Powers that have the final word. And as I have already said, it is hardly in the Great Powers' own interest to tie their own hands.

It is therefore necessary to turn, above all, to non-governmental organizations such as the ICRC or other entities whose moral authority places them on higher ground than that of states, including for example the Holy See. There are other non-governmental organizations of high prestige as well that could be involved in the effort, such as the US-based Human Rights Watch. These organizations have already achieved great accomplishments in their quest to 'humanize' war. One of these bodies or organizations might invite a group of military and legal experts to study these themes carefully and formulate proposals along the lines I have just indicated.

I realize that it will not be easy to travel down these roads. It will take courage and imagination. But I am hopeful that some authoritative humanitarian body of great moral prestige will take affirmative steps, whether it be now or later, to drive forward or otherwise support this humanitarian enterprise.

CHAPTER 2

....

THE ROLE OF THE INTERNATIONAL COMMITTEE OF THE RED CROSS

....

JAKOB KELLENBERGER

1 INTRODUCTION

....

THE International Committee of the Red Cross (ICRC) is an impartial, neutral, and independent organization whose exclusively humanitarian mission is to protect the lives and dignity of victims of armed conflict and other situations of violence and to provide them with assistance. The ICRC also endeavours to prevent or alleviate suffering by promoting and strengthening International Humanitarian Law (IHL) and universal humanitarian principles.

The ICRC is present in some 80 countries and has around 13,000 staff members. As such, it is one of the largest international humanitarian organizations, with probably the most extensive field of action in armed conflict and other situations of violence. Field expenditure is mostly dedicated to four large assistance programmes: health services, water and habitat, economic security, and physical rehabilitation.

Of particular relevance is the extent of the access of the ICRC to persons in need of protection and assistance, the fact that the ICRC directly implements activities in the majority of its operations (from needs assessment to distribution), as well as its multidisciplinary response and its proven rapid deployment capacity. ICRC partnerships with National Red Cross and Red Crescent Societies also play an important role in a number of particularly difficult contexts such as Afghanistan, Syria, and Somalia.

2 THE ICRC's MANDATE AND ACTIVITIES

Under Article 5 of the Statutes of the International Red Cross and Red Crescent Movement[1] the ICRC is mandated to work for the faithful application of IHL, to take cognizance of any complaints based on alleged breaches of that law, to work for the understanding and dissemination of knowledge of this body of rules and to prepare any development thereof. The ICRC may also take any humanitarian initiative which comes within its role as a specifically neutral and independent institution and intermediary, and may consider any question requiring examination by such an institution.

In addition to its more 'traditional' work, the ICRC's strategic plan for 2011–14 commits the organization to further reinforcing its activities in the phase of early recovery, as well as in other situations of violence than armed conflicts. Early recovery basically refers to activities aimed at the restoration of livelihoods, basic services, and promotion of self-sustainability at different levels of the society. Early recovery activities often begin in a humanitarian (emergency) setting and are carried out in parallel with humanitarian activities. The more an organization has been involved in the emergency phase, the better its chances are of playing a useful role in the early recovery phase ('you know the place, you know the actors, you know the needs'). The term 'other situations of violence' is used primarily to describe situations of violence that cannot be classified as an armed conflict; intercommunity or urban violence for example. The ICRC will also endeavour to further strengthen its activities in the legal domain.

---

[1] The Statutes were adopted by a resolution of the 25th International Conference of the Red Cross in October 1986.

Looking back at the ICRC's history, one must take note of the fact that ICRC action often preceded the adoption of a legal basis for it. After the failed negotiations on a Convention on Prisoners of War in 1874, ICRC delegates visited prisoners of war in the winter of 1914/15, even though the first Convention on Prisoners of War was only adopted in 1929. In keeping with this legacy, one of the underlying messages of the ICRC's strategic plan for 2011–14 is that action remains the prevailing mindset of the organization.

The ICRC is widely considered to be a reference organization on IHL and does its best to live up to this reputation. As different manifestations of collective violence and their humanitarian consequences have emerged, the institution has also had to strengthen its competence in the field of other bodies of law relevant to the protection of human life and human dignity.[2]

The first question to be asked from a legal perspective is: 'What is the applicable law and how does it interact with other relevant bodies of rules, both international and domestic, in a given context?' The ICRC is increasingly faced with such a question in situations of violence where the applicable law is disputed, partly as a consequence of the blurring of lines between situations of armed conflict and other situations of organized armed violence, and partly for political or other reasons. In terms of protection provided by the law—which should never to be confused with physical protection—the effect of extensive interpretations of the applicability of IHL to situations for which it was not meant gives rise to particular concerns.

A reference organization for IHL like the ICRC can reasonably be expected to provide expertise, support, and authoritative guidance in at least three areas: better compliance with existing IHL rules; clarification of key legal concepts that may be necessary as a consequence of developments in the character of armed conflicts; the development of treaty-based IHL.

A. Compliance with IHL

For an operational international humanitarian organization, contributing to better compliance with existing rules is the most immediate and without a doubt the most demanding task. The applicability of IHL or certain of its rules is challenged in various and important contexts, a trend that could become stronger in the future.

---

[2] For example, the ICRC's dialogue with selected police forces about law applicable to the use of force in non-armed conflict situations has been strengthened in various countries.

(i) *Specific challenges related to non-international armed conflicts*

In the context of non-international armed conflicts (NIACs), this development may be attributed to the fact that some governments have an increased tendency to treat non-state armed groups as criminal organizations. Consequently, they find it difficult to accept that the ICRC's determination that the applicability of IHL depends exclusively on the degree of organization of the parties to a conflict and the conflict's intensity, the two factual criteria for establishing that a NIAC exists. Independently of the political interests involved, it is on occasion also admittedly difficult to make factually a distinction between the non-state armed groups parties to a NIAC and organized criminal groups. The lines are sometimes blurred and a group can slide from one category to the other.[3]

The applicability of Common Article 3 of the 1949 Geneva Conventions (CA 3), the bedrock provision governing NIACs, is also sometimes challenged. Non-state armed groups tend not to conform with this provision. In addition, states are prone to view acceptance of an organized non-state armed group as a party to a conflict as amounting to political promotion or legitimization of an otherwise 'criminal' group even if it is perfectly clear that the applicability of CA 3 does not confer any legal status on the non-state party to a non-international armed conflict. The 'vertical' nature of criminal law enforcement is thus preferred to the 'horizontal' nature of IHL, even though states do sometimes simultaneously resort to a selective application of IHL rules on conduct of hostilities in order to give themselves broader scope for the use of lethal force against their non-state adversaries.

Achieving better compliance with IHL by both state and non-state armed groups parties to armed conflicts remains a great challenge and is multifaceted in nature. The most obvious challenge is that states' political and psychological readiness to respect IHL rules will in practice depend to some degree on the capacity and readiness of the non-state party to likewise abide by the same rules. States might even accept that organized non-state armed groups might not be in a position to respect all the relevant norms despite a genuine willingness to do so. In practice, it is sometimes of limited practical use to remind the parties to an armed conflict that the rules have to be respected independently of the behaviour of the adversary and that there is no reciprocity requirement as a matter of law. Expectations of reciprocity serve as an important factual incentive for compliance with IHL and non-compliance is likely to increase as such expectations fade away, even if public pressure can make up for part of the lost motivation.

It is usually, for objective reasons, more difficult to enter into a structured dialogue on IHL with organized non-state armed groups involved in a NIAC than

---

[3] See eg J. McMullin, 'Organised Criminal Groups and Conflict: The Nature and Consequences of Interdependence', 11 *Civil Wars* (2009) 75–102.

with other actors.[4] It takes time to build mutual trust and understand the sensitivities of all actors involved in a conflict situation. Once a dialogue is established, the challenge may involve convincing the non-state party of its interest in respecting IHL, at least to the extent that it is able to do so in practice. Members of non-state armed groups in fact have the choice between being 'good' criminals or 'bad' criminals. The 'good' criminals could be prosecuted under domestic law for all acts of violence committed while fighting, even if their actions did not violate IHL. They will, however, become 'bad' criminals if their actions violated both bodies of law. The option of participating in an armed conflict while maintaining respect for IHL rules despite the lack of prospect for a 'reward' in terms of exemption from prosecution under domestic law, will obviously not look very attractive to members of a non-state armed group unless they are driven by strong moral convictions or are genuinely concerned with the perception of the group among the local population and at the international level. Article 6(5) of Additional Protocol II (AP II), which encourages states to refrain from imposing criminal sanctions against persons who took part in a NIAC without breaching IHL rules, does not decisively mitigate the above choice for non-state armed groups. Whether they belong to the 'good' or 'bad' criminal camp they are still deemed criminals under domestic law. Moreover, a clear majority of states appear unwilling to envisage other incentives to achieve better compliance with IHL by non-state actors.

(ii) *Mechanisms to promote or ensure compliance*

The prospects for new legal instruments that would help achieve greater compliance with IHL look uncertain even if the need for such development is widely recognized. The application of IHL is heavily dependent on political considerations due to the fact that all issues related to the use of force are closely linked to the notion of state sovereignty, which is closely guarded. One indicator of this dependence is the final result—or rather absence thereof—of actions undertaken within the framework of various existing IHL compliance mechanisms. Calls for their use invariably provoke much political debate. However, the relevant processes and final results, if any, attract much less attention and often remain unclear.

There are few treaty-based mechanisms for monitoring compliance with IHL applicable to international armed conflicts (IAC). No such mechanism exists for NIACs, putting aside the role performed by the ICRC on the basis of its right to offer its service to the parties to this kind of armed conflicts (see CA 3). The main existing monitoring mechanism, the International Fact-Finding Commission established by Article 90 of the First Additional Protocol, has never been able to exercise its function in IACs in the 20 years of its existence because of the lack of political will by

---

[4] As regards the perspective of such groups and their difficulties in applying IHL, see M. Sassòli, 'Taking Armed Groups Seriously. Ways to Improve Their Compliance with International Humanitarian Law', 1 *International Humanitarian Legal Studies* (2010) 5–51.

states involved in an armed conflict to trigger it. This, however, did not prevent the Fact-Finding Commission being granted observer status by the UN General Assembly on 23 October 2009; nor did it prevent the Security Council from calling for the possibility of its use in Resolutions, for example in paragraph 9 of Resolution 1894 adopted in 2009.

That being said, there are measures and actions that can be developed to contribute to better compliance with IHL. In this context it should be noted that one of the four areas that the ICRC identified as needing further development based on its two year study on the current state of IHL, are measures aimed at achieving better compliance with IHL (see further below). The ICRC's proposal focuses on control/monitoring mechanisms, monitoring being understood in the broadest sense as any process allowing legal assessment of a certain behaviour in order to verify its compliance with IHL.

A report of the Office of the United Nations High Commissioner for Human Rights summarizing the outcome of expert consultations on the protection of the human rights of civilians in armed conflicts[5] argues that IHL has no mechanisms similar to those available under existing UN human rights treaties in case of human rights violations. Two possible options are mentioned for addressing the issue. The first would involve the creation of a permanent commission of inquiry with a mandate to investigate violations of IHL. The second option would be to 'encourage the existing international human rights machinery to look into violations of both human rights and IHL'.[6]

However, one may wonder whether the involvement of the international human rights machinery would help ensure better compliance with IHL or instead would lead to more debate on better compliance. Taking as an example Israel and the occupied Palestinian territories, one of the more difficult compliance contexts, it is instructive to look at the results of the Fact Finding Missions established by the UN Human Rights Council that were submitted in July 2006, in November 2006 and in April 2009. These results, to the extent it is possible to speak of results, are sobering indeed. The value-added of the UN human rights machinery's inclusion of IHL as part of its mandate with the aim of ensuring better state compliance with IHL obligations does not appear to be evident in the light of these examples.

International and mixed criminal courts and tribunals can make an important contribution to the enforcement of IHL by applying criminal sanctions against persons who are responsible for serious violations of IHL amounting to war crimes. International criminal justice has a potentially preventive dimension that can hardly be overestimated, but it must also be said that such potential has yet to materialize clearly.

---

[5] Report of the Office of the High Commissioner for Human Rights: Outcome of the expert consultation on the issue of protecting human rights of civilians in armed conflict, A/HRC/11/31, 4 June 2009.

[6] Report of the Office of the High Commissioner for Human Rights, § 42.

The adoption of the Rome Statute of the International Criminal Court (ICC) on 17 July 1998 by an international community 'determined to put an end to impunity', with respect to such crimes as genocide, crimes against humanity, war crimes, and aggression, was a major step towards strengthening the notion of individual criminal responsibility for crimes under international law. The Rome Statute entered into force on 1 July 2002. The 'crime of aggression' was defined in May 2010 at the Kampala Review Conference, and may in the future fall under the jurisdiction of the Court.[7]

The ICRC, which focused primarily on the negotiations relating to war crimes, supported the idea of the establishment of an effective and independent permanent international criminal court throughout the negotiating process. Its main contribution to further negotiations after the Rome Diplomatic Conference was an extensive study of the elements of war crimes, based in particular on the case law of international and national courts.[8]

Solid field experience is indispensable in order to understand fully what better compliance with IHL means in practice. This implies dealing with myriad challenges one faces in the field, including those of a legal (and psychological) nature. Carrying out detention visits, drafting relevant reports, and discussing recommendations with responsible authorities at different levels are all vital aspects of field experience that shape awareness of how IHL is implemented. Experience of monitoring (security permitting) respect for rules on the conduct of hostilities, and of trying to convince interlocutors of one's view even when they clearly do not share it, are equally important. Needless to say, it takes much more skill and courage to make a point in the field than to make the same point in expert meetings at a safe distance from the reality at issue. To stand up for IHL rules in an armed conflict environment—with all the passions involved—is an extremely useful reality check with regard to the forces at work in the real world. No doubt, the main role and most noble purpose of the ICRC in the legal field will remain its struggle to ensure respect for IHL where it is most challenging.

B. Clarification of rules of IHL

Changes in the nature of armed conflicts and other situations of violence need not necessarily give rise to development of IHL. One of the more immediate consequences may well be the need to define more precisely certain notions of key importance in order to reflect better new forms of violence. The need for such clarification

---

[7] ICC Review Conference, Resolution RC/Res.6, 'The Crime of Aggression', Kampala, 11 June 2010, available at <http://www.icc-cpi.int/iccdocs/asp_docs/Resolutions/RC-Res.6-ENG.pdf>.

[8] K. Dörmann, *Elements of War Crimes under the Rome Statute of the International Criminal Court* (Cambridge: Cambridge University Press, 2003).

may be felt more keenly now than it was some decades ago due to increasing operational importance for the protection of persons, for example in the conduct of hostilities. In this regard, one may mention the ICRC Interpretive Guidance on the notion of 'direct participation in hostilities' under IHL, that provides greater clarity in the definition of when a civilian might be considered to participate directly in an armed conflict.[9]

The need for clarification is not limited to this example. More precise guidance is needed, for instance, on the issue of proportionality in attack, that involves determining when and to what extent military advantage can justify incidental civilian casualties and damages. Another area in need of clarification is the law of occupation, especially on the following four issues: the beginning and end of occupation; the delimitation of the rights and duties of an Occupying Power; the legal framework applicable to the international administration of territory; and the use of force in occupied territory.

ICRC guidance aimed at clarifying existing IHL rules, despite the obvious operational relevance of such efforts, should not to be confused with normative development, which is the prerogative of states. Interpretations by the ICRC, even if preceded by consultations with external experts (governmental or non-governmental) are not strictly binding on states.

C. Development of IHL

The adequacy of IHL was strongly questioned after the terrorist attacks of 11 September 2001, especially in the United States. Queries about IHL's adequacy in the face of emerging global terrorist threats were justified by the argument that the crimes committed on 11 September 2001 signalled the beginning of a new era in which previously established rules might, at least in part, no longer be adequate. There were also more down-to-earth reasons: one was the attempt to widen the scope for political action as much as possible and to narrow the restraints imposed on state action by international law. Challenges to the adequacy of IHL were, however, seriously weakened by two developments. The first were the instances of ill-treatment[10] in detention places around the world, including Guantánamo and Abu Ghraib. These situations illustrated what could happen when authorities responsible for detainees were given direct or indirect authority to disregard well-established rules

---

[9] Interpretative Guidance on the Notion of Direct Participation in Hostilities under International Humanitarian Law, adopted by the ICRC Assembly on 26 February 2009. Dr Nils Melzer is the author of the guidance published in the International Review of the Red Cross: N. Melzer, 'Interpretive Guidance on the Notion of Direct Participation in Hostilities under International Humanitarian Law', 90 *International Review of the Red Cross* (2008) 991–1047.

[10] Ill-treatment is a generic term that covers torture and other cruel, inhuman, or degrading treatment or punishment.

seen as being no longer suitable to deal with the global terrorist threat. The second development was that those who challenged certain IHL rules were not able or willing to come up with proposals for new, more 'adequate' alternatives. This left many with the impression that the main aim of claims of inadequacy was in fact to lessen rather than increase the authority of IHL and other legal protections in order to give maximum space to security-driven decisions by governments.

In the present context, the relevance of IHL hinges to a large extent on its applicability to NIACs, which are most prevalent in today's world. The advantage of the debate on IHL adequacy was that it drew attention to some of the weaknesses in the applicable body of IHL, essentially CA 3 and the relevant provisions of AP II. More specifically, these provisions lack precision on issues that have come to the centre of international attention such as internment for imperative reasons of security (see further below).[11] If, as already indicated, the need for a consolidated and up-to-date interpretation of CA 3 has been strongly felt in recent years, this has to a large extent been the result of the intense legal debate on IHL adequacy that occurred after September 11.

The more states (and non-state armed groups) can agree on a common understanding of CA 3, the better it would be for the pertinence and relevance of IHL in the years to come. We are, however, far from such a consensus. CA 3, a child of its time and of a difficult birth in addition, does not address (or at least not with the necessary precision) certain issues that have become very important since 1949. It contains only rules on the protection of persons in the power of the enemy and does not deal with the conduct of hostilities. This lack can, admittedly, be considered as partly compensated for by the results of the ICRC's Study on Customary International Humanitarian Law (see in particular rules 1–24)[12] which identifies rules on the conduct of hostilities that are applicable to any type of armed conflict. It must nevertheless be noted that a number of states tend in practice to distinguish between rules they have specifically agreed to, and rules of customary law, even though treaty and custom are considered equivalent sources of international law.

Contrary to Article 5 of AP II, CA 3 does not regulate material conditions of detention as such. As already mentioned above, it does not mention internment or define the grounds for or procedural safeguards during internment. This is a significant gap at a time when persons believed to pose an imperative threat to security

---

[11] Unfortunately, state compliance with more detailed human rights rules when undertaking administrative detention outside armed conflict is also far from adequate. See eg the briefing note of the International Commission of Jurists on Sri Lanka: International Commission of Jurists: 'Beyond Lawful Constraints: Sri Lanka's Mass Detention of LTTEE Suspects', September 2010, available at http://www.icj.org/dwn/database/BeyondLawfulConstraints-SLreport-Sept2010.pdf.

[12] J.M. Henckaerts and L. Doswald-Beck, *ICRC Study on Customary International Humanitarian Law* (Cambridge: Cambridge University Press, 2005).

are deprived of liberty without criminal charges being brought against them, has become a critical issue.

More importantly, there is disagreement between states, courts, and scholars about the scope of application of CA 3. Thus, Jean S. Pictet, in his commentary on CA 3[13] interprets 'non-international' armed conflict as 'intra-State'. The US Supreme Court determined in the 2006 *Hamdan* case that CA 3 was applicable as a matter of US treaty obligation to any armed conflict that was not of an international character, thereby recognizing that its application was not confined to the territory of a single state. For its part, the government of Israel's view is that CA 3 is only applicable to intra-state armed conflicts, therefore not to the conflict between Israel and Hamas.

The ICRC's recent project 'Strengthening Legal Protection for Victims of Armed Conflicts'—aimed at encouraging the development of treaty law—focuses consequently (but not exclusively) on strengthening IHL's applicability to NIACs. The relevance of IHL as such is at stake in today's environment of armed violence if it cannot provide clear answers to legal issues arising in this type of conflict. Out of the four topics selected from the two-year ICRC study on the current state of IHL, the one relating to detention is of immediate relevance in terms of expanding the scope of CA 3. The ICRC's proposal on detention includes developing procedural safeguards for internment, as well as elaborating on standards governing material conditions of detention and the transfer of persons. The right of ICRC visits to persons deprived of liberty in the context of NIACs is also part of the proposals related to detention.

In the present legal framework the ICRC can only offer its services to carry out detention visits, an offer that can be declined by the parties to a non-international armed conflict without violating IHL (see CA 3(2)). It is noteworthy, however, that 95 per cent of the more than 2000 detention centres visited yearly by the ICRC are located in contexts in which the parties are not legally obliged to grant the ICRC access and that such wide acceptance of the ICRC's offers makes instances of refusal of access all the more striking. The broad acceptance of ICRC visits is one more reminder of the importance of humanitarian initiatives regardless of the legal framework.

It may be said that at the present stage of the consultation process with a representative group of states from all continents, the ICRC's detention-related proposals have generated particular interest, which is not surprising in light of recent experiences in the context of the so-called 'war on terror'. The proposals with regard to detention, though crafted primarily in NIAC contexts, are also relevant for persons deprived of liberty in international armed conflicts.

---

[13] J. Pictet, *La Convention de Genève pour l'amélioration du sort des blessés et des malades dans les forces armées en campagne* (Genève: CICR, 1952), 39–65.

The other proposals arising out of the ICRC's study on the current state of IHL focus on possible normative developments in the areas of internal displacement, the protection of the natural environment (in armed conflicts) and, as already mentioned, on monitoring mechanisms, and reparations for victims of IHL violations.

Norms on reparations are more detailed in human rights law and recent experience has highlighted the need to elaborate IHL provisions in this respect. There are, under IHL, no express obligations that reparations must be afforded directly to the individuals concerned and also be provided by non-state armed groups. The protection of the natural environment has become a major political issue at the global level: whether intentionally or recklessly it is clear that the environment is often seriously damaged as a result of armed conflicts. However, IHL regulation is insufficient, with a few treaty provisions applicable in IACs, but no treaty norms provided for in NIACs.[14] While the ICRC's Customary Law study contains a few rules on protection of the natural environment,[15] some would need to be strengthened, and codified in treaty form in order to apply adequately in NIACs as well. IHL rules applicable to civilians in general also protect internally displaced persons (IDPs). Some specific IDP needs, however, are not sufficiently covered by existing treaty law, such as the right to voluntary return or the need to find long-term solutions for persons who have been displaced from their homes as a result of armed conflict.

The heated debates about the adequacy of IHL that have taken place over the past decade have almost completely overshadowed successful efforts to adapt IHL to new and unregulated situations. Indeed, one could be forgiven for having missed positive developments altogether given the focus on more controversial debates. The underlying aim of these efforts has been to help eliminate the grave humanitarian consequences caused by the use of weapons that do not permit a distinction between persons taking direct part in hostilities and others. The Conventions on the Prohibition of the Use, Stockpiling, Production and Transfer of Anti-Personnel Mines and on their Destruction, and on Cluster Munitions, are highlights in this respect. The first entered into force on 1 March 1999, the second on 1 August 2010. There were also other treaty developments, partly related to the Convention on Certain Conventional Weapons.[16]

---

[14] There is, admittedly, a specific environment-related provision in Protocol III to the Convention on Conventional Weapons (CCW) which applies in both international and non-international conflicts, that prohibits making forests or other kinds of plant cover the object of attack by means of incendiary weapons under certain circumstances. CCW Protocol III, Art 2(4).

[15] ICRC Customary Law Study (n. 12 above), Ch 14 on the natural environment, Rules 43–5.

[16] Other IHL developments since 2000, not all arms-related, should be recalled: Optional Protocol to the Convention on the Rights of the Child on the Involvement of Children in Armed Conflict, 25 May 2000; Protocol on Explosive Remnants of War (Protocol V to the 1980 Convention), 28 November 2003; Protocol Additional to the Geneva Conventions of 12 August 1949, and relating to the Adoption of an Additional Distinctive Emblem (Protocol III), 8 December 2005.

The ICRC's main value-added in the respective negotiations was its ability to credibly attest, based on its field experience, to the enormous suffering that the use of certain weapons causes to the civilian population. The ICRC's interest and involvement in weapons-related debates is not always well understood. It is a simple expression of its duty and willingness to work for the faithful application of IHL. Its role and ambition is not to get involved in disarmament negotiations, but to draw the international community's attention to the humanitarian consequences of the use of certain means of warfare. The ICRC's statement of April 2010 ('Bringing the Era of Nuclear Weapons To An End') is a typical example of this type of action. Prior to the NPT Review Conference, which took place in May 2010, the purpose of the statement was to draw attention to the humanitarian consequences of the debate on disarmament.

3 The Role of the ICRC Going Forward

The roles of the ICRC with regard to IHL as provided for in the Statutes of the International Red Cross and Red Crescent Movement, Article 5(2)(c) and (g), remain pertinent. Consequently, the ICRC will continue to work for better understanding, dissemination and faithful application of this body of rules, and it will prepare any developments thereof. The ICRC will also maintain its participation in the debate on IHL issues and proceed with its endeavours to shape this debate, based on its field experience, with a view to making these rules operational and addressing the main humanitarian issues that are not sufficiently covered by IHL (treaty law in particular). This explains the particular efforts that the ICRC has made in recent years with regard to clarification and development of IHL.

Ensuring better compliance with IHL remains a huge task and has many different facets in terms of prevention, monitoring and criminal accountability. Two related measures that are infrequently mentioned should be recalled in this context. First, according to the Geneva Conventions, the High Contracting Parties have an obligation to search for persons alleged to have committed or to have ordered the commission of grave breaches of the Conventions and to bring such persons before their own courts. However, the opening of an investigation, even if highly commendable, is just a first step. Domestic prosecutions of grave breaches and of other serious violations of IHL must be followed through if they are to have a preventive effect. Various organizations are dedicated to the monitoring of judicial proceedings for these types of crimes. Their tenacity plays an important role in efforts to prevent IHL violations.

A second measure concerns engaging non-state armed groups in a dialogue on IHL implementation. This is of increasing importance given the characteristics and structure of contemporary armed conflicts. Dialogue with non-state armed groups is particularly demanding for various reasons, which range from difficulties of access to organized non-state armed groups to psychological factors. It also demands a major effort in terms of setting priorities in the presentation of IHL rules and in terms of the need to convey IHL messages in a way that is understandable for the recipients. Much of IHL is not easily accessible to persons without the requisite expertise and not all its formulations lend themselves to easy understanding. An example can be seen in the terms 'persons in the hands of' and 'in the power of' an adversary, both of which are used in IHL treaties. It is not self-evident based on the plain language of the text that 'in the hands of' means 'under the control of' and 'in the power of' essentially means 'in the physical power of' the enemy, ie deprived of liberty. Distinctions between the rules governing the protection of persons in enemy hands and those regulating the conduct of hostilities are likewise not evident to everyone: thus, a person performing a continuous combatant function for a non-state armed group in a non-international armed conflict is not a civilian for the purposes of the principle of distinction, but is entitled to protection guaranteed to civilians upon capture. Confusion is sometimes even created by legal experts who, for example, use the notion 'combatant' in relation to both international and non-international armed conflicts even though it is a legal status inherent only to the former type of conflict.

The way in which the notion of 'unlawful combatant' has been used in recent years, namely in the context of the so-called 'war on terror', has likewise added to the confusion. It has been used, without distinction, to refer to persons detained in both international and non-international armed conflicts even though, as just noted, the notion of 'combatant' is absent in NIAC and therefore makes no legal sense in that context. It would have been helpful if the notion of 'combatant' had only been used in its proper legal meaning over the past several years. More generally it would have been helpful if a constant effort had been made to distinguish between concepts that are inherent to IACs on one side and NIACs on the other, and to use them accordingly. It would not have required a great exertion, but simply a measure of (legal) discipline.

It is submitted that IHL will remain a relevant body of international law provided that clear and convincing answers can be given to the main questions arising from today's armed conflicts not of an international character, the number of which remains significant. It should, however, be noted that the humanitarian consequences of other forms of organized armed violence are also becoming more pernicious. The number of persons who have lost their lives as a result of direct violence in some of the latter situations is higher than in some armed conflicts, even though this is, of course, a limited way of looking at the broad range of effects of different forms of organized armed violence.[17]

---

[17] The difference between the humanitarian consequences of armed conflicts and other forms of violence is not always made. For example, the Internal Displacement Monitoring Centre determined that there were some 27 million IDPs at the end of 2009, as a result of both 'conflict or violence worldwide'.

The ICRC is thus likely to be faced with an increasing number of borderline situations—those falling between armed conflict and other types of organized armed violence—and will have to rely on other bodies of international law aimed at the protection of persons, such as international human rights law (even though it does not have the ambition of becoming a reference organization for non-IHL issues). The ICRC's humanitarian interest can hardly be to militate for the applicability of IHL as *lex specialis*: this is because of its rules on targeting (with direct participation in the hostilities as the criterion in respect of persons) and its inevitable acceptance of 'incidental' loss of civilian life or damage to civilian objectives in military operations, providing the harm is not excessive in relation to the military advantage anticipated.[18]

Current trends in the development of various forms of violence make it even more important than in the past to constantly keep in mind the respective roles and interplay of IHL, international human rights law, and domestic law with a view to achieving the protective aims of these bodies of norms. Both IHL and human rights law are applicable in armed conflicts. There are situations where IHL applicability is challenged and where it may be worthwhile reflecting, from a protection perspective, if insistence on IHL applicability or insistence on full application of international human rights rules is the way to go. This, naturally, will also depend on the state of ratification of the different instruments by the relevant state. What should not be accepted is a selective use of IHL provisions.

In terms of protection, important differences between IHL and international human rights law nevertheless remain relevant. While IHL rules are adapted to the uncertainty that characterizes situations of armed conflict, human rights rules are based on the premise that a state exercises effective control over a territory or persons in peace time. In this context one may wonder whether urban violence could become an IHL challenge similar to the challenge posed by the so-called 'war on terror' over the last ten years, even if of a very different nature. On burning issues like the extraterritorial targeting of persons ('extraterritorial' in this case meaning outside a territory in which IHL is applicable), or the deprivation of liberty in the fight against terrorism, it is also useful to keep both bodies of law in mind. This is the case despite the fact that there is currently no agreement on whether a transnational armed conflict with certain terrorist groups is taking place (the ICRC believes it is not) and what the geographic . reach of such a conflict might be.

'Cyber warfare', which refers essentially to attacks on computer networks in an armed conflict is an evident example of an emerging IHL challenge. While IHL is clearly applicable, the question is whether and how certain rules established for a different context—the physical world—should be adapted for the cyber context.

---

[18] See AP I, Art 51(5)(b).

Also, what such an adjustment would mean for their application in the traditional contexts of war, on land, sea, or in the air. The ICRC is contributing to a reflection aimed at elaborating on the applicability of IHL rules to cyber warfare.

To conclude, the ICRC will not only maintain its current role as the reference organization for IHL overall, but will also continue to make the necessary efforts to fulfil this role in the areas indicated above.

PART II

SOURCES

CHAPTER 3

CUSTOMARY HUMANITARIAN LAW TODAY

FROM THE ACADEMY TO THE COURTROOM

THEODOR MERON

1 THE ROOTS OF THE REVIVAL OF CUSTOMARY INTERNATIONAL LAW

THE roots of the revival of customary humanitarian law can be traced back to the Nuremberg trials. Customary law was essential to the Nuremberg tribunals' ability to convict Nazi war criminals. The tribunals, including the International Military Tribunal, could not rely heavily on treaties because the Soviet Union had not ratified the 1929 Geneva Convention on Prisoners of War and because the application of The Hague Convention No IV was challenged on the ground that the situation of the belligerents did not conform with its *si omnes* clause, as not all the belligerents were parties. The IMT reasoned, however, that the law of war was to be found not only in treaties but also in the customs and practices of states and in the general principles of justice.[1]

For many years after Nuremberg, there were no other international criminal tribunals. Thus, customary humanitarian law lay dormant for some time, except for its invocation in inter-state disputes. In other areas of international law too, customary international law began to appear less relevant. Where international tribunals *did* rely on customary international law, as in the International Court of Justice ('ICJ')'s *Nicaragua* case in 1986,[2] they did so in a somewhat relaxed fashion. This approach relied principally on loosely defined *opinio juris* and the existence of widely ratified treaties, resolutions, and 'soft law' instruments as proof of state practice.

Only a few years ago, I would have described customary international law primarily as a theoretical matter, except for the Nuremberg case law, the ICJ's *Nicaragua* decision, and a few other exceptions. Today, however, customary international law has effectively moved from the domain of academia to the courtroom. Customary international law now comes up in almost every international court and tribunal, in almost every case, and frequently has an impact on the outcome. International courts ranging from the ICJ, the Iran–United States Claims Tribunal, and the ICSID arbitral tribunals to the regional human rights courts have pronounced on important issues of customary international law in recent years. But I believe it is in the international criminal tribunals—particularly in the International Criminal Tribunal for the former Yugoslavia ('ICTY')—that the jurisprudence on customary international law has been most rich.

2 Customary International Law in the Non-Criminal International Courts

Let us begin by looking at the application of customary international law by non-criminal international bodies, such as the ICJ.

Although several classically customary branches of international law have been codified in widely ratified conventions, other branches have so far resisted such codification. Thus, today, customary law is very much alive in institutions treating those latter branches, although it is no longer the dominant source of international law in general.

---

[1] *Goering et al,* International Military Tribunal (Nuremberg), 'Judgement and Sentences', 41 *American Journal of International Law* (1947) 172.

[2] *Military and Paramilitary Activities in and against Nicaragua (Nicaragua v United States of America)* (Merits: Judgment) [1986] ICJ Rep 14.

Likewise, where one or more parties to a dispute have not ratified the relevant international instruments, customary law governs. This is the case with the Eritrea–Ethiopia Claims Commission which, before Eritrea's ratification of the Geneva Conventions, focused on customary humanitarian law.

Even the regional human rights courts, which principally apply their own constituent instruments, occasionally invoke customary law. The Inter-American Court of Human Rights, for example, has relied on the law of state responsibility as a matter of customary international law[3] and, more recently, has ruled that amnesties for crimes against humanity violate customary international law and *jus cogens*.[4] The European Court of Human Rights has invoked the customary rules on imputability,[5] has found that the prohibition on torture is both customary and *jus cogens*,[6] and confirmed the customary law character of the prohibition of attacks against persons *hors de combat* and of the principle of *nullem crimen sine lege*.[7]

Notably absent from many of these cases, however, is a detailed discussion of the evidence that traditionally has supported the establishment of the relevant rules as customary law—the practices and legal opinions of a large number of states. The ICJ articulated the textbook methodology for identifying customary law more than 35 years ago in its seminal *Continental Shelf* cases.[8] Yet other bodies can hardly be blamed for failing to apply this approach, as the ICJ's modern cases also do not tend to follow it rigorously. Rather, where a treaty exists in a particular area of law, even where it does not bind the parties to the dispute in question, the ICJ has tended to treat the text of the treaty as a distillation of the customary rule, thus eschewing examination of primary materials establishing state practice and *opinio juris*.

For example, in the *Nicaragua* case, the Court held that Common Articles 1 and 3 of the Geneva Conventions constitute binding general principles of humanitarian law—in other words, customary law. In doing so, the Court made a major contribution to the vitality of humanitarian law. What is remarkable about the *Nicaragua* case, though, is the complete failure to inquire whether *opinio juris* and practice support the crystallization of Common Articles 1 and 3 into customary law, as pointed out in Judge Sir Robert Jennings' dissent.

---

[3] *Case of Velásquez Rodríguez v Honduras* (Judgment (Merits)) Inter-American Court of Human Rights Series C No 4 (29 July 1988).

[4] *Case of Almonacid-Arellano et al v Chile* (Judgment (Preliminary Objections, Merits, Reparations and Costs)) Inter-American Court of Human Rights Series C No 154 (26 September 2006).

[5] *Assanidze v Georgia* (App no 71503/01) (2004) 39 *EHRR* 32; *Ilaşcu and others v Moldova and Russia* (App no 48787/99) (2005) 40 *EHRR* 46.

[6] *Al-Adsani v United Kingdom* (App no 35763/97) (2002) 34 *EHRR* 11.

[7] *Korbely v Hungary* (App no 9174/02) (2010) 50 *EHRR* 48.

[8] *North Sea Continental Shelf Cases (Federal Republic of Germany v Denmark; Federal Republic of Germany v Netherlands)* (Merits: Judgment) [1969] ICJ Rep 3 ('*Continental Shelf*').

Another example of the ICJ's reliance on customary international law is the recent *Genocide* case (*Bosnia and Herzegovina v Serbia and Montenegro*, 2007).[9] While the Court was careful to confine much of its ruling to the Genocide Convention itself, it also found that the 'effective control' standard of attribution contained in the non-binding ILC Articles on State Responsibility[10] was reflective of customary international law.

In addition to a generally more relaxed approach to customary international law, the ICJ and other international courts are increasingly relying on precedent rather than repeatedly engaging in detailed analysis of the customary status of the same principles in every case. We might perhaps discern in this practice something similar to a *stare decisis* principle amongst the international tribunals. For instance, the impact of *Nicaragua* on the subsequent development of the law was such that the customary law character of Common Articles 1 and 3, and practically of the entire corpus of the Geneva Conventions, is now virtually never questioned. The same is true, under the influence of the Nuremberg tribunals, of The Hague Convention No IV of 1907. It is certainly true that, in practice, courts are giving greater weight to judicial decisions than what is suggested by the text of Article 38 of the ICJ Statute.

In calling attention to this more relaxed approach to customary international law, I do not mean to argue that these courts' holdings have been unfounded or are any less important than they would be had they followed a more traditional approach. To the contrary, at least one aspect of this more relaxed approach has been a very good development. In *Nicaragua*, the ICJ substantially strengthened customary law by downplaying the normative significance of contrary practice. State conduct inconsistent with a norm was to be treated as a breach of the rule rather than as evidence disproving the rule. And if a state defended its inconsistent conduct by appealing to exceptions and justifications contained in the rule, the significance of such a statement was to confirm the rule.

This development was essential to the effectiveness of customary law. A balance must, of course, be struck, as there is a point at which contrary practice reaches such a critical mass that the norm in question cannot be said to be customary. But without an approach acknowledging the reality of contrary practice and articulating a method of dealing with it, it might be virtually impossible to identify any norms of customary international law, for there is almost no norm that every nation consistently obeys.

It is also important to recognize that many of these judicial bodies, perhaps particularly the ICJ, would struggle to apply a more traditional approach to customary law. They lack strong fact-finding powers and their formal rules of procedure and

---

[9] *Application of the Convention on the Prevention and Punishment of the Crime of Genocide (Bosnia and Herzegovina v Serbia and Montenegro)* (Merits: Judgment) [2007] ICJ Rep 43.

[10] [2007] ICJ Rep 43, § 401.

evidence make the presentation of the large bodies of evidence required to demonstrate 'extensive and virtually uniform'[11] state practice difficult. In addition, we must remember that it is difficult to find positive, concrete state practice with respect to rules that are largely prohibitive—as the rules of humanitarian law generally are—because such rules are largely respected through abstention from violations, rather than affirmative practice.

3 The Customary Law Jurisprudence of the ICTY

International criminal tribunals, particularly the ICTY, have taken a conservative approach to the identification and application of customary international law principles. Both the centrality of customary law in ICTY doctrine and the ICTY's rigorous approach to analysing and applying it are the result of the Tribunal's obligation, as a criminal court, to respect the fundamental principle of *nullum crimen sine lege*, or the legality principle: a defendant may only be convicted on the basis of legal rules clearly established at the time of the offence.

Given that the Nuremberg tribunals rooted their convictions not only in custom, but also in treaties and general principles of criminal law, one might ask why the ICTY has relied principally on customary law. One reason is a desire to honour the statement in the Secretary-General's 1993 authoritative report to the Security Council that the Tribunal should refer to custom—although, it bears noting, the Appeals Chamber has held that this statement does not exclude reliance on treaties where there is no doubt that all the relevant states were party to them.[12] In addition, because of the generality of custom, reliance on it avoids doubts as to succession to treaties, their continuing binding character, the application of reservations, and the validity of ad hoc agreements between belligerents. And, although the Tribunal's jurisdiction is defined by its Statute, reliance on customary law ensures that the principle of legality is respected even where the alleged crimes occurred before the Statute entered into force.

The Tribunal's authority to punish is therefore circumscribed by customary law. If a criminal conviction for violating uncodified customary law is to be reconciled with the legality principle, however, it must be through clear and well-established

[11] *Continental Shelf*, § 74.
[12] *Prosecutor v Duško Tadić* (Decision on the Defence Motion for Interlocutory Appeal on Jurisdiction) ICTY-94-1-AR72 (2 October 1995).

methods for identifying customary law. The legality principle is thus a restraint on tribunals' ability to be 'progressive' in developing customary humanitarian law. Rather, tribunals must be 'conservative' in the sense of resisting fast change to the law—in particular, fast expansion of the definition of culpable conduct. This approach respects an accused's procedural right to fair notice of the law.

It might fairly be asked whether a conviction for violating uncodified customary law can ever meet this standard. After all, codification of criminal prohibitions is the modern norm in domestic systems, even in common law countries; in the United States, for example, there are no common law crimes, and in the United Kingdom there are few. Nonetheless, in my view the legality principle does not bar such a conviction.

Thus, customary law can provide a safe basis for a conviction, but only if genuine care is taken in establishing that the relevant legal principle was sufficiently firmly established as custom at the time of the offence so that the offender could have identified the rule he was expected to obey.

This, in a nutshell, has been the approach of the ICTY. In effect, the Tribunal's Chambers have superimposed on the Statute a test of whether each of the crimes within the Tribunal's jurisdiction reflects customary law. The *Galić* case, for instance, concerned a conviction for terrorization of the civilian population. The Trial Chamber based the conviction on Additional Protocol I,[13] while the Appeals Chamber grounded it in customary humanitarian law.[14] The Appeals Chamber concluded that the conduct at issue was clearly prohibited under customary law at the relevant time by examining the drafting history of the Additional Protocols, previous conventions, and soft law norms such as the Turku Declaration on Minimum Humanitarian Standards, as well as the official pronouncements and military manuals of states. As the Appeals Chamber's judgment in *Galić* makes clear,

the Judges have consistently endeavoured to satisfy themselves that the crimes charged in the indictments before them were crimes under customary international law at the time of their commission [...] This is because in most cases, treaty provisions will only provide for the prohibition of a certain conduct, not for its criminalisation, or the treaty provision itself will not sufficiently define the elements of the prohibition they criminalise and customary international law must be looked at for the definition of those elements.[15]

So, does the legality principle require a tribunal to conduct a laborious inquiry into the question whether a particular legal principle enjoyed the status of customary international law for *every* offence with which *every* accused is charged? No—such an inquiry is only required where the unlawfulness of the conduct in question at the time would not otherwise have been clear. As the ICTY Appeals Chamber stated in the *Čelebići* case, acts such as murder, torture, and rape are

[13] *Prosecutor v Stanislav Galić* (Judgment and Opinion) ICTY-98-29-T (5 December 2003).
[14] *Prosecutor v Stanislav Galić* (Judgment) ICTY-98-29-A (30 November 2006).
[15] *Prosecutor v Stanislav Galić*, § 83.

obviously unlawful and there is nothing unfair about using the international system to punish them.[16]

Many of the Tribunal's cases, however, involve conduct of less obvious criminality. In such cases, the relevant customary law must be ascertained, and it must likewise be determined whether fair notice to the accused—sufficient to satisfy the *nullum crimen* principle—was provided. This may be accomplished through either of two related approaches. The first approach might be characterized as 'methodological conservatism'—that is, the use of only firmly established, traditional methods for identifying the applicable customary norms. A second approach might be referred to as 'outcome conservatism'. Under this approach, doubts regarding the customary status of any particular legal principle are resolved in favour of the defendant, *in dubio pro reo*. This is simply another way of stating the requirement that criminal prohibitions be clear. The ICTY has blended these two approaches, and has done so in a way that, I believe, respects the fundamental principle of *nullum crimen*.

An example illustrating the Tribunal's approach is the 2003 decision in an interlocutory appeal in the *Hadžihasanović* case, which presented two issues.[17] The first was whether customary law applied the doctrine of command responsibility to internal conflicts. The five-member panel unanimously agreed that it did. The Appeals Chamber's methodology in reaching this conclusion provides an illustration of its generally meticulous approach. The Appeals Chamber specifically noted that 'to hold that a principle was part of customary international law, it has to be satisfied that State practice recognized the principle on the basis of supporting *opinio juris*'.[18]

The second issue in *Hadžihasanović* proved more contentious. At issue was whether a superior could be held responsible for punishing acts that were committed before he became the superior of the persons who committed the offences—that is, crimes that took place on his predecessor's watch. By a majority, the Appeals Chamber rejected such culpability, finding no state practice and no *opinio juris* to support the theory of liability. It also found that an expansive reading of criminal law texts, including the ICTY Statute, adequate to support such liability would violate the principle of legality.

The majority and minority decisions highlight a challenging issue raised by grounding criminal convictions in customary international law. Where a customary law principle can be shown to exist, 'it is not an objection to the application of the principle to a particular situation to say that the situation is new if it reasonably falls within the application of the principle'.[19] The difficulty lies in deciding where to

---

[16] *Prosecutor v Zejnil Delalić et al* (Judgment) ICTY-96-21-A (20 February 2001) ('*Čelebići*').

[17] *Prosecutor v Enver Hadžihasanović et al* (Decision on Interlocutory Appeal Challenging Jurisdiction in Relation to Command Responsibility) ICTY-01-47-AR72 (16 July 2003).

[18] *Prosecutor v Enver Hadžihasanović et al*, § 12.

[19] *Prosecutor v Enver Hadžihasanović et al*, § 12.

draw the line and how to determine when a new situation is so new that it cannot be said to *reasonably* fall within the principle. On this issue, reasonable judges can differ, as we did in *Hadžihasanović*. Customary international law is not a precise science.

I believe that international criminal tribunals are necessarily constrained by the principle of legality, which is widely recognized as a peremptory norm of international law. While international tribunals can clearly apply a principle of customary international law to new factual circumstances, they cannot cross the line and create new criminal prohibitions that would be applied retroactively. This is the essence of the principle of legality and it serves as a fundamental check on the ability of international *criminal* tribunals to push the progressive development of customary international law.

Still, we must distinguish between the creation of new law and the interpretation of the scope of existing law. In *Prosecutor v Aleksovski*, for example, the accused argued that a previous decision could not be used as a statement of the governing customary law, since that decision was made after the alleged commission of the crimes. The ICTY Appeals Chamber distinguished the interpretation and clarification of customary law, which is permissible, from the creation of new law, which would violate the *ex post facto* prohibition.[20] As the Appeals Chamber explained in its judgment, the *nullum crimen* principle

does not prevent a court, either at the national or international level, from determining an issue through a process of interpretation and clarification as to the elements of a particular crime; nor does it prevent a court from relying on previous decisions which reflect an interpretation as to the meaning to be ascribed to particular ingredients of a crime.[21]

The ICTY has also made important contributions to the clarification of the substantive scope of customary international law. Amongst others, the ICTY has held that torture, slavery, forcible displacement, deportation, and terrorizing the civilian population are prohibited under customary humanitarian law. Here too, I believe, the Tribunal's methodological approach to determining the substance of customary humanitarian law has been sound.

In the *Stakić* case, for instance, the Appeals Chamber had to assess the cross-border requirement of the crime of deportation.[22] In its 2006 judgment the Chamber surveyed existing international law, including the IMT judgment, the Geneva Conventions and their Additional Protocols, the ILC Draft Code of Crimes against Peace and Security of Mankind, the ICRC study on customary humanitarian law, and its own case law. It concluded that the crime of deportation requires, as a matter of customary law, a transfer across a *de jure* or a *de facto* state border and that the

---

[20] *Prosecutor v Zlatko Aleksovski* (Judgment) ICTY-95-14/1-A (24 March 2000) ('*Aleksovski* Appeal Judgment').

[21] *Aleksovski* Appeal Judgment, § 127.

[22] *Prosecutor v Milomir Stakić* (Judgment) ICTY-97-24-A (22 March 2006).

issue of whether a particular *de facto* border was sufficient must be assessed on a case-by-case basis in light of customary international law. On the facts of that particular case, the Appeals Chamber concluded that 'constantly changing frontlines' did not constitute a sufficient *de facto* border.[23]

In the *Kunarac* case—my first case—the Appeals Chamber upheld the Trial Chamber's definition of rape as reflecting customary international law, noting in particular that that there is no victim 'resistance' requirement under the customary international law definition of rape.[24] The Appeals Chamber also emphasized that the definition of rape under customary international law did not require that the victim's lack of consent result from force or threat of force; lack of consent could be inferred from coercive circumstances. Finally, the Appeals Chamber concluded that rape constituted 'a recognised war crime under customary international law, which is punishable under Article 3 of the Statute'.[25] It based this conclusion on:

The universal criminalisation of rape in domestic jurisdictions, the explicit prohibitions contained in the fourth Geneva Convention and in the Additional Protocols I and II, and the recognition of the seriousness of the offence in the jurisprudence of international bodies, including the European Commission on Human Rights and the Inter-American Commission on Human Rights. [...][26]

The ICTY has relied on customary international law not only for the basis of the underlying, substantive crimes, but also for the modes of liability. Early in its jurisprudence, the Tribunal clarified the customary doctrines of command responsibility and of joint criminal enterprise by reference to customary international law.

In addition, the ICTY has also relied on customary international law in construing procedural protections. In *Aleksovski*, the Appeals Chamber concluded that '[t]he right to a fair trial is, of course, a requirement of customary international law'.[27] In a decision in the *Perisić* case, the Trial Chamber relied on customary international law to define the right to fair trial.[28] It reasoned that 'although the right to a fair trial encompasses an equality of arms between the parties, there is no support in either customary international law, the case law of the [Human Rights Committee] or that of the [European Court of Human Rights] which supports the proposition that the principle of equality of arms affords a party a right to receive resources that are similar to his opponent'.[29] In the *Krajišnik* case, the Appeals Chamber concluded that the case law of domestic jurisdictions did not support a distinction between

---

[23] *Prosecutor v Milomir Stakić*, § 303.

[24] *Prosecutor v Dragoljub Kunarac et al* (Judgment) ICTY-96-23 and ICTY-96-23/1-A (12 June 2002), § 128.

[25] *Prosecutor v Dragoljub Kunarac et al*, § 195.   [26] *Prosecutor v Dragoljub Kunarac et al*, § 195.

[27] *Aleksovski* Appeal Judgment, § 104.

[28] *Prosecutor v Momčilo Perisić* (Decision on Motion to Appoint *Amicus Curiae* to Investigate Equality of Arms) ICTY-04-81-PT (18 June 2007).

[29] *Prosecutor v Momčilo Perisić*, § 9.

the right to self-representation during trial and on appeal.[30] Most recently, in the *Strugar* judgment, the Appeals Chamber relied on 'general principles of law recognized by all nations,'[31] as exemplified in state practice and the jurisprudence of a range of international tribunals, to conclude that the applicable standard for fitness to stand trial was 'meaningful participation which allows the accused to exercise his fair trial right to such a degree that he is able to participate effectively in his trial, and has an understanding of the essentials of the proceedings.'[32]

In some cases, of course, whether the issue is substantive or procedural, the Tribunal's assessments of the evidence supporting the relevant customary international law principles have been comparatively brief. In most of these cases, the Tribunal has relied on its own precedents instead of revisiting the same issues repetitively, an approach that can hardly be faulted. It has also relied to some extent on proxies—such as the long-standing recognition of a principle's customary status by the ICJ—in place of the comprehensive detailing of state practice.

The ICTY is not the only international institution to have approached the analysis of customary international law in such a painstaking manner. The ICRC study on customary international humanitarian law adopted a similarly traditional approach. This important study represents an unprecedented collection of state practice and opinion gathered over the course of ten years, from over 50 countries and 40 armed conflicts, and the volume of rules that the study produced represents essentially a restatement of the law. The need for this study, which was requested by states themselves, reflects the increasing importance of customary international law today. The study's two volumes on state practice that accompany the rules are perhaps even more important than the volume on rules, as they demonstrate the methodology applied and the wealth of practice considered.

In general, therefore, both the ICTY and the ICRC study have eschewed the more relaxed approach that has typically characterized modern discussions of customary international law. The two institutions share a synergy in their approach to re-establishing the centrality of customary humanitarian law which, I believe, is mutually reinforcing. Already, the ICRC study has been invoked in the ICTY's jurisprudence. For example, in the *Stakić* appeal judgment, the Appeals Chamber relied on the study as evidence of the customary international legal definition of the crime of deportation. In another interlocutory decision in the *Hadžihasanović* case, the Appeals Chamber cited the study to support the Trial Chamber's conclusions that the prohibitions of wanton destruction of cities, plunder of public or private property, and destruction of institutions dedicated to religion, and, more broadly,

---

[30] *Prosecutor v Momčilo Krajišnik* (Decision on Momčilo Krajišnik's Request to Self-Represent, on Counsel's Motions in Relation to Appointment of *Amicus Curiae,* and on the Prosecution Motion of 16 February 2007) ICTY-00-39-A (11 May 2007).

[31] *Prosecutor v Pavle Strugar* (Judgment) ICTY-01-42-A, Judgment (17 July 2008), § 44 (internal quotation marks omitted).

[32] *Prosecutor v Pavle Strugar,* § 55.

of attacks on civilian objects, were customary norms whose violation entails individual criminal responsibility.[33] In both cases, the Appeals Chamber was cautious not to rely on the study's rules alone; in the *Hadžihasanović* decision, the Chamber cited practice, rather than a black-letter rule, and in *Stakić*, the Chamber relied on Nuremberg case law, the Geneva Conventions and their Additional Protocols, the 1991 ILC Draft Code of Crimes against the Peace and Security of Mankind, and its own jurisprudence.

4 THE CUSTOMARY LAW JURISPRUDENCE OF THE OTHER INTERNATIONAL CRIMINAL COURTS

Now let me turn briefly to look at the use of customary humanitarian law by the other international criminal tribunals, particularly the International Criminal Tribunal for Rwanda ('ICTR'), the Special Court for Sierra Leone, and the International Criminal Court ('ICC').

Despite the general similarities between the law governing the ICTY and the ICTR, there is a significant difference with respect to custom and the legality principle. Since the conflict in Rwanda was non-international in character, and since Rwanda was a party to the relevant international humanitarian law treaties, it is not generally necessary to consider whether a violation of the ICTR Statute was also a violation of customary law. It is enough that the treaties with domestic force in Rwanda were violated. There has therefore been no obvious need for the ICTR, in its treatment of provisions of these treaties or its own Statute, to examine their customary law underpinnings.

Nevertheless, the ICTR has still made some contributions to the elucidation of customary humanitarian law. In the so-called *Media* case (*Prosecutor v Nahimana et al*, 2003), the Trial Chamber found that hate speech violates the customary international law prohibiting discrimination and, as a result, can constitute the crime against humanity of persecution.[34] In addition, the Chamber confirmed the distinction among hate speech in general, which is not criminalized in and of itself, speech that incites to discrimination or violence, and the crime of direct and public

[33] *Prosecutor v Enver Hadžihasanović and Amir Kubura* (Decision on Joint Defence Interlocutory Appeal of Trial Chamber Decision on Rule 98*bis* Motions for Acquittal) ICTY-01-47-AR73.3 (11 March 2005).

[34] *Prosecutor v Ferdinand Nahimana et al* (Judgment and Sentence) ICTR-99-52-T (3 December 2003).

incitement to commit genocide. The Tribunal has also frequently invoked customary law on its decisions on preliminary motions.

I turn now to the Special Court for Sierra Leone. Its Appeals Chamber has held that the *nullum crimen* principle must be applied by reference to customary law.[35] As a matter of substance, the Special Court's greatest contribution to the clarification of customary law so far is the Appeals Chamber's finding that the prohibition on child recruitment in internal and international armed conflicts had crystallized into customary international law prior to November 1996, which is the starting point of the Court's temporal jurisdiction. Based on that reasoning, the Trial Chambers convicted four accused, in two separate cases, of recruiting, enlisting, and using children to participate in hostilities. All but one of these convictions were upheld on appeal.

The Special Court's recognition that the recruitment of child soldiers violated a customary international law prohibition has been cited with approval by the ICC in the Pre-Trial Chamber's decision on the confirmation of charges in the *Lubanga* case.[36] There, the Pre-Trial Chamber rejected the accused's argument that the indictment violated the principle of legality because the charge of child recruitment was not prohibited under customary international law at the time of the offence. The Pre-Trial Chamber agreed with the Special Court's conclusion that, as far back as 1996, child recruitment was an offence under customary law.

Primarily, however, the Pre-Trial Chamber based its decision on the fact that the offence of child recruitment is clearly proscribed in the Rome Statute, which was in force in the Democratic Republic of Congo at the time the alleged offence was committed. This approach illustrates a fundamental difference between the ICC and the ad hoc tribunals. The ICC Statute more closely resembles a civil law code. Unlike pleadings in the ICTY, therefore, the gravamen of future pleadings in the ICC will be the interpretation of the Statute, not its customary law underpinnings.

Nevertheless, Article 21 of the Rome Statute, which concerns applicable law, opens the door wide to additional sources of international law, including custom as well as 'general principles'. If the ICC chooses to take advantage of this Article in defining the scope of criminal liability, it should be guided by the legality principle and should, in my view, adopt a cautious approach to the interpretation of custom. The principle of legality is recognized in Article 11 of the Statute, which provides that the ICC's jurisdiction does not extend to crimes committed before the Statute's entry into force for the ICC or for the state concerned, if it became a party to the Statute at a later date.

---

[35] *Prosecutor v Sam Hinga Norman* (Decision on Preliminary Motion Based on Lack of Jurisdiction (Child Recruitment)) SCSL-2004-14-AR72(E) (31 May 2004).

[36] *Prosecutor v Thomas Lubanga Dyilo* (Decision on the Confirmation of Charges (Public Redacted Version)) ICC-01/04-01/06 (29 January 2007).

Moreover, in the case of a referral of a situation to the ICC by the Security Council acting under Chapter VII of the UN Charter and in accordance with Article 13(b) of the Statute—as, for instance, with the Darfur atrocities—or when the ICC's jurisdiction is based on a special acceptance by the state concerned, a defendant might argue that he or she is subjected to *ex post facto* legislation. The success of such an argument would turn on whether the act constituted an offence at the time of its commission. In such a case, the ICC will have a rare opportunity to clarify the customary law status of the Statute's provisions.

5 CONCLUSION

This Chapter has demonstrated that, contrary to what some may assume, customary international law is undergoing a remarkable revival. It has effectively moved from the academy to the courtroom. Nowhere is this more apparent than in the jurisprudence of the international criminal tribunals.

I do not foresee any end to the importance of customary humanitarian law. Sadly, there continues to be a shortage of treaty law regulating non-international armed conflicts—yet almost every conflict in the world today is non-international. It is in these internal conflicts, frequently so brutal, that the great majority of violations of humanitarian law and fundamental human rights occur. International courts will therefore necessarily have to rely on custom to fill the gaps and provide the necessary detail so as to be able to punish those who have committed these offences.

Clearly, those who predicted the demise of customary law in the era of codification and treaty regimes have been proven wrong, at least with respect to international humanitarian law. As for those who believe that codification is always the best solution, I would point to the danger that diplomatic conferences would drift to the minimum common denominator.

Finally, as the ICJ made clear in the *Nicaragua* case, violations of customary law cannot be allowed to undermine or modify the law. In an age where many states are keen to rely on fears of terrorism and other threats to question fundamental principles of international law, such as the absolute prohibition on torture, international courts must stand firm: violations of the law cannot be allowed to 'dictate the law'.[37]

---

[37] International Committee of the Red Cross, Response of Jean-Marie Henckaerts to the Bellinger/ Haynes Comments on Customary International Law Study, 46 *ILM* (2007) 959, 961.

CHAPTER 4

TREATIES FOR ARMED CONFLICT[1]

ROBERT KOLB AND KATHERINE DEL MAR

1 IMPORTANCE OF TREATIES IN THE LAW OF ARMED CONFLICT

WRITTEN law, and within that category, treaty law,[2] has traditionally been, and remains today, a particularly important source of the law of armed conflict

---

[1] This Chapter will not analyse the question of the effect of war or armed conflict on treaties, namely their suspension or termination because of the outbreak of hostilities. This topic has been considered by the International Law Commission. Moreover, that question concerns treaties concluded in peacetime and for the purposes of peacetime, whereas the focus of this Chapter is on treaties designed to apply specifically during armed conflicts, ie those treaties that essentially apply, *ratione matariae*, from the very moment an armed conflict breaks out.

[2] A treaty is defined as follows in the Vienna Convention on the Law of Treaties of 1969, 23 May 1969, entered into force on 27 January 1980, UNTS, vol 1155, 331 (VCLT): '"Treaty" means an international agreement concluded between States in written form and governed by international law [...] whatever its particular designation'. The VCLT only covers agreements between states and in written form. However, under customary international law or under other conventions (such as the VCLT of 1986 concerning treaties concluded by international organizations), the definitions of treaties may differ. Thus, under customary international law, the four essential and cumulative criteria for determining the existing of a binding agreement under international law are the following: (i) a meeting of minds

or international humanitarian law (IHL).[3] There are several reasons for this preeminence.

First, questions of warfare are relatively detailed and technical matters. Apart from a body of broad principles and flexible general rules adaptable to the ever-changing circumstances of armed conflict, this area of the law is prescribed in a set of detailed rules of an 'administrative' rather than 'constitutional' legal character. The law of armed conflict is an area of international law most intimately character-ized by the complex interplay of some general principles (necessity, proportionality, unnecessary suffering, distinctions, humanity, etc.) over which lies a web of detailed rules containing specific prescriptions of a procedural or substantive nature. Such specific rules can only reasonably be set out in a written form. The medium of trea-ties is their most natural form of expression.

Secondly, one has to bear in mind that IHL principally addresses itself to non-lawyers. IHL has to be applied mainly by soldiers and higher military officials; sometimes even by ordinary citizens in international armed conflicts,[4] and more frequently in non-international armed conflicts.[5] These individuals invariably have no formal legal training. They cannot be asked to undertake complex and nuanced tasks of interpretation. The law must tell them clearly and in detail what conduct is expected from them in a whole set of situations. Only treaty law allows for such detailed legal regulation. Alberico Gentili, one of the founding fathers of classical international law, wrote with some derision: 'In fact, a soldier ought to know arms and not the law, and it is proper that military men should be ignorant of the law. It is military custom to regard as ridiculous and silly the subtleties of the courts'.[6] Moreover, since the creation of the International Committee of the Red Cross (ICRC), following the battle of Solferino in 1859, IHL advocates have been heav-ily involved in the dissemination of IHL rules to the general public. This in turn imperatively requires a set of precise and written norms.

Thirdly, the law of armed conflict is designed to apply in situations of great social and psychological stress, namely during warfare. In such situations, there is usually no time and no possibility to consult legal writings or to have complex discussions

on some object; (ii) the international legal personality of the subjects agreeing (*jus tractatus*), except for the individual who possesses no power of concluding treaties; (iii) the legal effect of the compact (if an agreement is not designed to have legal effects but is confined to be a political agreement or a gentlemen's agreement, it will not be a treaty); (iv) the fact of being governed by international law (states or other international subjects may conclude commercial and other contracts, which are not treaties).

[3] On these terminological questions, see R. Kolb and R. Hyde, *An Introduction to the International Law of Armed Conflicts* (Oxford: Hart Publishing, 2008), 16–17.

[4] For example, industrialists in whose factories prisoners of war may work: see for instance the *I.G. Farben* or *Krupp* cases, in: United Nations War Crimes Commission, *Law Reports of Trials of War Criminals*, vol X, London, 1949, 1ff, 69ff.

[5] In non-international armed conflicts, a government may fight against armed factions comprised of its own citizens.

[6] A. Gentili, *De iure belli, libri tres* (1598, reprinted: Oxford: Carnegie Classics, 1933), 204.

about how to balance general principles in order to shape a contextual rule. Of course, there is a place for such a process in armed conflicts. For instance, higher officials will undertake such an exercise in the targeting phase of a planned armed attack. But for most military and administrative operations of warfare, there must be ready-made and concrete rules at hand. These can, once again, only be provided in the written form of a treaty.

Fourthly, the law of armed conflict regulates not only the conduct of hostilities, but also situations where individuals are detained or are under the control of a party to the armed conflict. In such situations, there is a particularly high risk of such individuals being subjected to harsh and abusive treatment. Customary norms are not in these instances the most suitable rules to regulate such situations, as they are less easily discernible, less precise, and often more controversial. The written treaty law here has a fundamental role to perform: to set clear and detailed rules to constrain effectively the conduct of the military personnel with regard to the treatment of those detained or under its control.

Fifthly, treaties are also important devices for unifying the law. National legislation and military manuals could certainly satisfy all the requirements set out above, thereby providing soldiers with the detailed technical rules of the law of armed conflict that they must apply. But the law would inevitably differ considerably from one state to another. These differences would be highly problematic in the light of the paramount principle of reciprocity, or of equality of belligerents.[7] To a large extent, the law of armed conflict can only practically function if it is premised on the equality and non-discrimination of the belligerents. A party to an armed conflict is unlikely to agree to be bound by rules to which its adversary will not pay heed. Such adverse discrimination would put it at a comparative military disadvantage. This is particularly true in international armed conflicts, where IHL applies equally to the sovereigns in question, regardless of their respective *jus ad bellum* motives. Treaties ratified by a large number of states (or indeed by all states) create a unique legal space by establishing uniformity in the applicable rules and consequently extending the scope of reciprocity and equality of belligerents. This function obviously could also be performed by customary international law, but its evolution would be longer, more burdensome, haphazard, and riddled with more uncertainties.

Sixthly, treaties allow for a more efficient and more rational modification of the law when some change is needed. This is frequently the case in IHL, which has to keep a pace with a highly complex and evolving field of human experience, namely warfare. It is a truism to affirm that the law of armed conflict always tends to be one war behind. Through the creation of a new protocol, or the modification of some treaty rules, change can sometimes be achieved relatively quickly through the conventional process. The same is true for minor or technical amendments, which may

---

[7] On the importance of this principle, cf. H. Meyrowitz, *Le principe de l'égalité des belligérants devant le droit de la guerre* (Paris: A. Pedone, 1970).

be considered particularly pressing. For example, it was only through the creation of a new treaty, Additional Protocol III of 2005 to the four Geneva Conventions,[8] that the new emblem of the red crystal could reasonably be adopted and the rules concerning its use clearly articulated.

All these reasons explain why the law of armed conflict is one of the branches of public international law that has been the most intensely codified through treaties.

2 TREATIES AND CUSTOMARY INTERNATIONAL LAW

This is not the place to dwell on the multiple issues that arise out of consideration of the relationship between treaty-based IHL rules and customary law.[9] Only some aspects will be analysed here: first, the specific utility and functions of customary international law (CIL) in IHL alongside the many conventional sources; secondly, the extent to which the various conventional sources reflect CIL; thirdly, the seminal role of customary practice in some recent efforts to codify specific branches of IHL.

(a) If IHL is essentially governed by treaties, what is the role performed by CIL in this area of the law? What are the distinctive or comparative advantages of IHL rules that form part of CIL compared with those contained in IHL treaties? In particular, what can only be achieved by CIL and not by treaty law?

First, CIL provides for a minimum standard of universally applicable IHL rules, independent of the current state of ratifications or accessions to an IHL treaty. Treaty law is relative law: it applies only to states (or other subjects of international law) that have formally consented to be bound by the treaty obligations, ie through ratification or accession to a treaty. *Pacta tertiis nec nocent nec prosunt*. Some IHL treaties of primary importance are far from being universally ratified or acceded to.[10] The most famous examples are the Additional Protocols I and II (1977) to the four Geneva Conventions of 1949. These treaties contain some rules of paramount importance, such as those concerning the protection of civilian populations from attack.[11]

---

[8] Protocol additional to the Geneva Conventions of 12 August 1949, and relating to the Adoption of an Additional Distinctive Emblem (Protocol III), 8 December 2005, entered into force 14 January 2007.

[9] See on this point the recent contribution of Y. Dinstein, 'The Interaction Between Customary International Law and Treaties', 322 *Recueil des cours de l'Académie de droit international de La Haye (RCADI)* (2006) 243–427; Paul Tavernier and Jean-Marie Henckaerts (eds), *Droit international humanitaire coutumier: enjeux et défis contemporains* (Brussels: Bruylant, 2008).

[10] See (C) below.

[11] Articles 48ff of Additional Protocol I (AP I) (1977), and the weaker rules of Arts 13ff of Additional Protocol II (AP II), (1977).

To the extent that some of the rules contained in these multilaterally—but not universally—ratified conventions reflect customary law, evinced by general state practice and *opinio juris*,[12] they will be applicable to all the states in the world. General international law on treaties can thus be transformed into universal international law by CIL. This is an important function in a world composed of a growing number of states; in a world where new states emerge, which for a transient time will not be bound by the conventions; and in a world where armed conflicts are endemic. In other words, CIL ensures a common standard of rules applicable in all situations of armed conflict everywhere in the world independent of the acceptance of treaties by the states concerned. If one reflects upon the fact that the non-ratification of a treaty by one party to a conflict does not simply entail the non-application of that treaty to that state alone, but rather its non-application to all the relations between that state and other belligerent parties, then the importance of this residual unifying function of CIL is very apparent. Since the Korean war of 1950,[13] where the Geneva Conventions were still widely non-ratified, through to the Ethiopia/Eritrea war of 1998–2000, where Eritrea had not acceded to the Geneva Conventions until August 2000, there has been a considerable need to apply CIL because of formally inapplicable treaty norms.

Secondly, CIL remains the paramount vehicle for binding different non-state subjects and entities to IHL. IHL treaties are open to accession only by states[14] (or 'Powers',[15] where this term is customarily interpreted as meaning states). Thus, if armed forces under the command of an international organization participate in hostilities—as occurred with UN blue helmets, dragged into an armed conflict in the Congo in 1960–63—CIL of the law of armed conflict applies to these individuals since the UN is not party (and under the current interpretation could not become a party) to the relevant IHL treaties.[16] The same may also be the case for insurgents or other similar entities in the context of a non-international armed conflict. In such a case, treaty law is ordinarily held to be applicable because the conflict takes place on the territory of a state that has ratified the treaty. The idea is that the ratification or accession to a treaty and its incorporation into the municipal law of a state has as a corollary effect that all individuals on the territory will be bound by these rules,

---

[12] Statute of the International Court of Justice, annexed to the Charter of the United Nations, Art 38(1)(b); *North Sea Continental Shelf, Judgment* [1969], § 77.

[13] Cf. D.W. Bowett, *United Nations Forces. A Legal Study of United Nations Practice* (London: Stevens & Sons, 1964), 53ff.

[14] See eg Art 4 of the Convention on Prohibitions or Restrictions on the Use of Certain Conventional Weapons Which May be Deemed to be Excessively Injurious or to Have Indiscriminate Effects, 10 October 1980, entered into force 2 December 1983, UNTS, vol 1342, 137.

[15] See eg Art 6 of the Hague Convention IV Respecting the Laws and Customs of War on Land (The Hague Convention IV) (1907), Arts 60, 59, 139, and 155 respectively of Geneva Conventions I–IV.

[16] On this question, see R. Kolb, *Droit humanitaire et opérations de paix internationales* (2nd edn, Geneva/Basel/Munich/Brussels: Helbing & Lichtenhahn, 2006), esp 21ff.

especially if they take up arms during an insurrection.[17] In addition to this indirect reach of treaty law, CIL also applies to non-state actors, albeit only that branch of customary IHL applicable during non-international armed conflicts. This general reach of CIL *ratione personarum* was stressed by the Institute of International Law in its Resolution on 'The Application of International Humanitarian Law and Fundamental Human Rights in Armed Conflicts in Which Non-State Entities are Parties' (1999), in Articles II and IV.[18]

Thirdly, CIL can be seen as a subsidiary source of the law of armed conflict. It may in some circumstances fill gaps and/or remove uncertainties lurking in the interstices of treaty law. Such gaps are particularly numerous in lesser developed areas of IHL and in rapidly evolving areas. The best example is the branch of IHL applicable to non-international armed conflicts. To a tiny set of treaty rules, namely Common Article 3 to the four 1949 Geneva Conventions and Additional Protocol II of 1977, there is today the complement of a whole series of CIL rules that have progressively emerged through case law, as well as through institutional and state practice.[19]

In a similar vein, specific treaty-based norms may benefit from some clarification found in unwritten practice. CIL can thus also develop conventional rules by adding precision to them. In this process, customary practice may derogate from

---

[17] On this construction, see Commentary AP I and II, 1345: 'The question is often raised how the insurgent party can be bound by a treaty to which it is not a High Contracting Party. It may therefore be appropriate to recall here the explanation given in 1949: the commitment made by a State not only applies to the government but also to any established authorities and private individuals within the national territory of that State and certain obligations are therefore imposed upon them. The extent of rights and duties of private individuals is therefore the same as that of the rights and duties of the State. Although this argument has occasionally been questioned in legal literature, the validity of the obligation imposed upon insurgents has never been contested'. See also J. Pictet, *Le droit humanitaire et la protection des victimes de la guerre* (Leiden: Brill, 1973), 58: 'On a d'ailleurs fait remarquer que lorsqu'un Etat ratifie les Conventions, il le fait au nom de tous ses ressortissants, y compris ceux qui s'insurgent contre l'ordre établi, bien que ces derniers aient tendance, par définition, à répudier tous les actes de l'Etat'; J. Pictet (ed), *Geneva Convention II, Commentary* (Geneva: ICRC, 1960), 34: 'On the other hand, what justification is there for the obligation on the adverse Party in revolt against the established authority? Some doubt has been expressed as to whether insurgents can be legally bound by a Convention which they have not themselves signed. The answer is provided in most national legislations; by the fact of ratification, an international Convention becomes part of law and is therefore binding upon all the individuals of that country'; D. Fleck (ed), *The Handbook of International Humanitarian Law* (2nd edn, Oxford: Oxford University Press, 2008), 620. For other authors, it is precisely the customary nature of the minimum rules contained in Common Article 3 (or in AP II) that command their application by any government and rebels, independently from any state of ratifications: see F. Bugnion, *Le Comité international de la Croix-Rouge et la protection des victimes de la guerre* (Geneva: ICRC, 1994), 381–4.

[18] The text of this resolution is available on the website of the Institute of International Law at <http://www.idi-iil.org/idiE/resolutionsE/1999_ber_03_en.PDF>. See also D. Schindler and J. Toman, *The Law of Armed Conflicts* (Leiden/Boston: Hotei Publishing, 2004), 1206–7.

[19] See T. Meron, 'International Law in the Age of Human Rights', 301 *RCADI* (2003) 24ff. See also the ICRC study on CIL, J.M. Henckaerts and L. Doswald-Beck, *Customary International Humanitarian Law*, vols I–III (Cambridge: Cambridge University Press, 2005).

a written norm, which in turn it complements. An example of the former is the application of Article 118, paragraph 1, of Geneva Convention III requiring that prisoners of war (POWs) shall be released and repatriated without delay after the cessation of active hostilities. This Article has today to be interpreted in light of the customary practice according to which repatriation (ie return to the country of origin) shall not be undertaken against the express wish of the POW. The concern of Geneva Convention III was to impede delay and excuses for the non-repatriation of POWs as witnessed after World War I, and also, specifically, to stop persons being unwillingly sent to a place other than their country of origin. It thus provided for mandatory return to the country of origin of the prisoner. However, since the Korean War of 1950, the concern has shifted to the case of POWs who do not wish to be sent back by force to their country of origin, because of well-founded fears of being persecuted upon return.[20] The relevant state practice—not then reflected in the text of Geneva Convention III—eventually changed under the pressure of refugee and human rights law. Consequently, the ICRC now conducts individual interviews with POWs to determine if a POW wishes to return to his or her country of origin, in order to avoid unwelcome pressure to return home being placed on these individuals by the detaining power. If the POW does not wish to return to his or her country of origin, another destination for return that corresponds with the wishes of the POW is sought. The Permanent Court of Arbitration in 2003 implicitly ruled that this practice amounted to a customary rule.[21] Thus, CIL has modified a treaty rule contained in Geneva Convention III or filled a justice gap within that rule (*rechtspolitische Lücke*). This is also an example of the influence of human rights law on IHL. Another example demonstrates how CIL can complement a treaty norm by providing it with more contextual precision. Article 30 of Geneva Convention I stipulates that medical and religious personnel, whose retention is not indispensable for the care of POWs of their country, shall be returned to the party to the conflict to whom they belong as soon as military requirements permit. In the practice of states, and initiated by the ICRC, these release operations are usually linked with the repatriation of seriously wounded and sick POWs, who must be sent back to their state of origin as quickly as circumstances allow according to Article 109 of Geneva Convention III. This solution avoids multiple repatriation flights or convoys and also ensures the care of seriously injured POWs during transit. The interrelationship between these two provisions can only be understood in the light of customary practice.[22]

---

[20] Cf C. Shields Delessert, *Release and Repatriation of Prisoners of War at the End of Active Hostilities* (Zurich: Schulthess Polygraphischer Verlag, 1977).

[21] Arbitral Award of 1 July 2003, *Prisoners of War*, Eritrea's Claim 17, § 147: '[T]here must be adequate procedures to ensure that individuals are not repatriated against their will'.

[22] Cf F. Bugnion, *Le Comité international de la Croix-Rouge et la protection des victimes de la guerre* (Geneva: ICRC, 1994), 790.

CIL shaped by military practice can moreover sometimes be used fruitfully in order to interpret general principles contained in treaties, which need to be concretized. Thus, for example, in the context of 'military necessity', it is indispensable for an IHL lawyer to have some intimate knowledge of field practice in order to assess, for example, when the destruction of an enemy's property is normally considered to be 'imperatively demanded' (Article 23(d), of The Hague Regulations, 1907).[23]

In sum, CIL presents the advantage of offering a minimum standard of rules applicable in all circumstances of armed conflicts to all actors effectively participating therein. CIL is free of the loopholes and inequalities flowing from the different status of ratifications of treaties, which exclude non-state entities from becoming parties, or which suffer from other limitations (denunciations, reservations, etc). CIL thus provides a minimum yardstick of IHL rules that apply to international peace operations of the UN where, quite apart from the applicable military Rules of Engagement (ROE), the treaty law applicable to the different national contingents may greatly differ because of unequal ratification/accession to treaties by the respective states. In Somalia, during the phase of UNOSOM II in 1992, there were 23 national contingents participating in the operation, with *prima facie* different IHL rules applying to each contingent.

(b) Which rules of conventional IHL reflect CIL? Which rules of treaty-based IHL have shaped new CIL? These two questions relate to the codification of preexisting CIL and to the progressive development of CIL. A great deal of rules in IHL treaties codify preexisting CIL. After all, treaty-based IHL seeks to reflect military and humanitarian practice. Thus, the provisions on the right of humanitarian initiative by the ICRC (Common Article 3 and Articles 9, 9, 9, and 10, respectively of Geneva Conventions I–IV) codify an ancient practice dating to the formative stage of the 1860s. Conversely, Article 54 of Additional Protocol I on the protection of objects indispensable to the survival of the civilian population during the hostilities phase was not reflective of CIL in 1977. However, the PCA in the Eritrea/Ethiopia *Western Front, Aerial Bombardment and Related Claims* case (Eritrea's Claims 1, 3, 5, 9–13, 14, 21, 25, and 26, Award of 19 December 2005), found that the provision had since crystallized into CIL, even without any compelling state practice to that effect.[24]

Overall, what rules of conventional IHL are to be considered CIL? The rule of thumb today is that the substantive rules (as opposed to procedural provisions) contained in the many multilateral treaties on IHL represent CIL. This tendency to harmonize and to equalize these two sources of international law stems from the fact that military and state practice can only be one and the same; practice cannot be split according to the sources. If the treaties are expressive of, and seek to

---

[23] Regulations Respecting the Laws and Customs of War on Land, annexed to the Convention Respecting the Laws and Customs of War on Land (The Hague Convention IV), 18 October 1907, entered into force 26 January 1910.

[24] At § 96ff.

influence, the actual practice of warfare, they perforce must reflect what states and other international actors consider to be the law during armed conflict. But that is also roughly the test for CIL. If the two sources contained significant differences, a legal schizophrenia would result: international subjects would be bound by CIL, reflective of their practice and *opinio juris*, whereas the treaty-based law would largely be irrelevant or modified by subsequent practice.[25] Thus, as in the *Nicaragua* (1986) case,[26] we are confronted with two sets of largely (albeit not completely) identical rules of behaviour in conventional international law and CIL.

However, clear evidence of actual military practice is exceedingly difficult to obtain, especially if it is based not only on the activities of some selected states, but on a universal approach confronting the practice of all states in the world. Consequenlty, there is a strong temptation to find a proper expression of *opinio juris* (which in turn is supposed to underlie the true practice) in norms contained in IHL treaties. This presumptive approach has a long standing. The International Military Tribunal of Nuremberg stated that the Hague Regulations of 1907 (Convention IV) completely reflected CIL.[27] The ICJ has affirmed in a more general way that the great majority of substantive rules of conventional IHL reflect CIL. In the *Legality of the Threat or Use of Nuclear Weapons* Advisory Opinion (1996), the Court stated as follows:

The extensive codification of humanitarian law and the extent of the accession to the resultant treaties, as well as the fact that the denunciation clauses that existed in the codification instruments have never been used, have provided the international community with a corpus of treaty rules the great majority of which had already become customary and which reflected the most universally recognized humanitarian principles. These rules indicate the normal conduct and behaviour expected of States.[28]

The ICTY in the *Tadić* case (1995) affirmed that many rules contained in Additional Protocol II and concerning non-international armed conflicts are reflective of CIL.[29] More recently, and in the same vein, the PCA in its *Eritrea/Ethiopia* cases, affirmed in a more balanced way that the great majority (but not all) of the rules contained in the four Geneva Conventions and Additional Protocol I reflected CIL.[30] Whereas

[25] If the conventional law was held to prevail by virtue of the *lex specialis* rule, there would be an enormous number of violations of the law, which is an impractical solution.

[26] In this case, the rules at stake were those on the use of force under the Charter and under CIL (*jus ad bellum*): ICJ Rep 1986, 92ff.

[27] *Nuremberg Judgment of the IMT*, 1947: 41 *American Journal of International Law*, (1947) 248–9. For the customary nature of Art 42 of the Regulations, see also the *Armed Activities* case (*DRC v Uganda*), ICJ Rep 2005, § 172.

[28] ICJ Rep 1996-I, 258, § 82.   [29] At § 117. The judgment is published in 35 *ILM* (1996) 32ff.

[30] See *Central Front*, Ethiopia's Claim 2, decision of 28 April 2004, §§ 13ss; *Central Front*, Eritrea's Claims 2, 4, 6, 7, 8, 22, decision of 28 April 2004, §§ 21ss; *Prisoners of War*, Ethiopia's Claim 4, decision of 1 July 2003, §§ 22ss; *Prisoners of War*, Eritrea's Claim 17, decision of 1 July 2003, §§ 31ss; *Civilians Claims*, Ethiopia's Claim 5, decision of 17 December 2004, §§ 22ss; *Civilians Claims*, Eritrea's Claims 15, 16, 23, and 27–32, decision of 17 December 2004, §§ 26ss; *Western and Eastern Fronts*, Ethiopia's Claims

the Geneva Conventions have consistently been considered to reflect CIL, the PCA underscored that most of the provisions in Additional Protocol I reflect CIL, but not all of them, some consisting rather in progressive development of the law. According to the PCA, the provisions concerning the conduct of hostilities and correlative protection of the civilian population (Articles 48ff) nowadays reflect CIL without exception. In relation to Protocol II to the Conventional Arms Treaty of 1980, on mines, booby-traps, and other devices, the PCA held that the conclusion of this treaty was too recent,[31] and state practice still too uncertain to affirm the customary nature of its provisions. The Court, however, adds that some of these provisions represent accepted general principles of IHL and thus reflect CIL, eg the provisions on the registration of mines and the localities where they are placed, and the prohibition of their indiscriminate use. Finally, the PCA asserts the presumption whereby the substantive provisions of treaty-based IHL in the *codification treaties* reflect CIL. There is thus a shift in the burden of proof: the party contesting the customary status of IHL rules bears the onus in demonstrating otherwise.

Thus, according to the recent case law, there is a considerable tendency to merge treaty-based IHL and customary IHL. The equation seems roughly to be: written (codified) IHL = customary IHL. This same conclusion was reached by the above-mentioned ICRC study on the subject matter.[32] This view, based on a large harmonization of the treaty-based and customary sources, is today challenged only by states not having ratified or acceded to some important treaties, as is the case of the United States, Israel, or India, which are not parties to Additional Protocol I. These states thereby seek to cling to what they may consider an 'advantage' of not being bound by this Protocol and other instruments, in order consequently also not to be bound by CIL creeping through the backdoor of these treaties.

(c) In some areas of IHL, there is still no codification of the relevant rules; CIL governs alone. To the extent efforts of codification are undertaken, CIL will guide the work of the drafters of relevant future treaties. This is the case, for example, in the context of aerial warfare, especially with regard to air-to-air combat.[33] An effort of 'codification' is taking place in this area with the drafting of a 'Third Draft Manual

1 and 3, decision of 19 December 2005, §§ 14ss; *Western Front, Aerial Bombardement and Related Claims, Eritrea's Claims* 1, 3, 5, 9–13, 14, 21, 25, and 26, decision of 19 December 2005, §§ 10ss. The arbitral awards are available online at the website of the PCA <http://www.pca-cpa.org>.

[31] This Protocol was adopted in 1980, with amendments in 1996.

[32] Cf J.M. Henckaerts and L. Doswald-Beck, *Customary International Humanitarian Law*, vols I–III (Cambridge: ICRC, 2005). For the somewhat reserved reaction by the United States to that study, see 46 *ILM* (2007) 511ff. The study is concentrated on the two Additional Protocols of 1977, which are more controversial, whereas the rules of the Geneva Conventions are recognized today to reflect CIL. On this ICRC study, see also M. Bothe, 'Customary IHL: Some Reflections on the ICRC Study', 8 *Yearbook on International Humanitarian Law* (2005) 143ff.

[33] On air warfare, see A. Bouvier and M. Sassoli, *How Does Law Protect in War?*, vol I (2nd edn, Geneva: ICRC, 2006), 241ff. The air-to-land combat is covered in other treaties, such as Additional Protocol I.

on Air and Missile Warfare' for the use of professional armies.[34] On such topics, a rather particular relationship exists between CIL and treaty-based law: the former makes an original and unilateral contribution to the latter; and the latter grows in a legislative way in the shadow of the former.

3 MAIN TREATIES

There are today a great number of treaties dealing with armed conflict or related matters, such as human rights treaties which apply in times of peace, internal disturbance and in times of armed conflict.[35] This is not the place to give an exhaustive list of all the treaties relevant to armed conflict.[36] The main treaties codifying general rules of the law of armed conflict are the following:

- *St Petersburg Declaration Renouncing the Use, in Time of War, of Explosive Projectiles under 400 Grammes Weight* (1868) (Declaration of St Petersburg).[37] This text remains important today with respect to the general principles stated in its Preamble and those parts that deal with the legitimate aims of war and the principle of the limitation of means.
- *The Hague Conventions I–XIV of 1907,*[38] in particular Convention IV respecting the Laws and Customs of War on Land with its annexed Regulations on

---

[34] Program on Humanitarian Policy and Conflict Research, Harvard University, Manual on International Humanitarian Law Applicable to Air and Missile Warfare, including Commentary, 15 May 2009.

[35] On this aspect, see R. Kolb, 'Relationship between International Humanitarian Law and Human Rights Law', in *Encyclopaedia of Public International Law*, <http://www.mpepil.com>.

[36] A complete overview is available on the website of the ICRC: <http://www.icrc.org/ihl.nsf/INTRO?OpenView>. See also D. Schindler and J. Toman, *The Law of Armed Conflicts* (Leiden/Boston: Martinus Nijhoff Publishers, 2004). For an overview of the main instruments and some commentaries to them, see C. Greenwood, 'Legal Sources', in D. Fleck (ed), *The Handbook of International Humanitarian Law* (Oxford: Oxford University Press, 2008), 27ff.

[37] 29 November and 11 December 1868, entered into force 11 December 1868, currently (as of May 2012) 20 states parties.

[38] Convention for the Pacific Settlement of International Disputes (The Hague Convention I), 18 October 1907; Convention Respecting the Limitation of the Employment of Force for the Recovery of Contract Debts (The Hague Convention II), 18 October 1907, entered into force 26 January 1910; Convention Relative to the Opening of Hostilities (The Hague Convention III), 18 October 1907, entered into force 26 January 1910, currently (as of May 2012) 34 states parties; for The Hague Convention IV and its annexed Regulations, see n 23 above, currently 35 states parties; Convention Respecting the Rights and Duties of Neutral Powers and Persons in Case of War on Land (The Hague Convention V), 18 October 1907, entered into force 26 January 1910, currently 32 states parties; Convention Relating to the Status of Enemy Merchant Ships at the Outbreak of Hostilities (The Hague Convention VI),

Land Warfare, and Convention V respecting the Rights and Duties of Neutral Powers and Persons in Case of War on Land. The Hague Convention IV with its Regulations remains very relevant today in a great array of situations, namely with respect to prohibited means and methods of warfare (see especially Article 23 of the Regulations) and in the context of occupied territories (see Articles 42ff of the Regulations). Those rules of The Hague Convention V concerning rules on the law of neutrality in land warfare, are also still important.

- *The Geneva Conventions I–IV of 1949.*[39] These treaties are currently the major IHL conventions. They are universal in scope, having been ratified by all existing states. They reflect an ideological shift with respect to Hague Law of 1907 in three respects. First, Hague Law is essentially based on a military and administrative approach to warfare: it contains primarily rules for the military branch, spelling out their rights during warfare and their powers in certain situations such as occupied territories. In contrast, Geneva Law is based on the protection of individuals, namely the so-called victims of war or persons in need of protection since they are *hors de combat*. A military approach has thus given way to a humanitarian one. Secondly, Hague Law is formulated in a series of short provisions containing general rules, with an important number of gaps or uncertainties lurking under the surface. States in 1899 and 1907 were not ready to limit significantly their sovereignty in wartime. After the appalling experiences of World War II, the Geneva Conventions mark a shift towards a much more detailed and complete codification of the applicable rules. The norms of Geneva Law are much more numerous, much more detailed, and much more comprehensive. Thirdly, Hague Law does not make clear to what extent it can be derogated from by way of special agreements. Geneva Law, on the contrary, contains specific rules ensuring that its provisions will not be displaced by all sorts of ingenious devices invented by the state parties: Articles 6/6/6/7, 7/7/7/8 respectively of Geneva Conventions I–IV,

---

18 October 1907, entered into force 26 January 1910, currently 29 states parties; Convention Relating to the Conversion of Merchant Ships into War-Ships (The Hague Convention VII), 18 October 1907, entered into force 26 January 1910, currently 32 states parties; Convention Relative to the Laying of Automatic Submarine Contact Mines (The Hague Convention VIII), 18 October 1907, entered into force 26 January 1910, currently 27 states parties; Convention Concerning Bombardment by Naval Forces in Time of War (The Hague Convention IX), 18 October 1907, entered into force 26 January 1910, currently 35 states parties; Convention for the Adaptation to Maritime War of the Principles of the Geneva Convention (The Hague Convention X), 18 October 1907, entered into force 26 January 1910, currently 33 states parties; Convention Relative to Certain Restrictions with Regard to the Exercise of the Right of Capture in Naval War (The Hague Convention XI), 18 October 1907, entered into force 26 January 1910, currently 31 states parties; Convention relative to the Creation of an International Prize Court (The Hague Convention XII), 18 October 1907, has not entered into force, currently 1 state party; Convention Concerning the Rights and Duties of Neutral Powers in Naval War (The Hague Convention XIII), 18 October 1907, entered into force 26 January 1910, currently 28 states parties; Declaration Prohibiting the Discharge of Projectiles and Explosives from Balloons (The Hague Convention XIV), 18 October 1907, entered into force 27 November 1909, currently 20 states parties.

[39] See n 15 above.

and Article 47 of Geneva Convention IV. Thus, Geneva Law is a public order or public policy law, not to be derogated from under any circumstances.

- *The Convention for the Protection of Cultural Property in the Event of Armed Conflict* (Hague Convention on Cultural Property in Case of Armed Conflict 1954), with its two Additional Protocols of 1954 and of 1999.[40] This Convention deals with the protection of monuments and works of art, ie buildings, libraries as well as other objects of cultural interest or deposits of protected objects. A definition of protected cultural property can by found in Article 1 of the Convention. States parties drew up lists of these objects and communicated them to the other parties. The lists of world cultural heritage of the UNESCO contribute to the definition of such sites and objects. Finally, there is a distinctive emblem with which the protected objects are marked during armed conflicts.[41]

- *Additional Protocols I, II and III to the Geneva Conventions of 1949* (1977 and 2005). Additional Protocol I (1977) is an important update to the Geneva Conventions, developing the rules of the Geneva Conventions on the protection of persons, but also inserting new rules on means and methods of warfare, such as those governing attacks against military objectives and the correlative immunity of civilian objects and persons from attacks (Articles 48ff). Additional Protocol II (1977) is the first treaty relating to the law of armed conflict dedicated exclusively to non-international armed conflicts (roughly speaking to 'civil wars'). In 2005 Additional Protocol III was adopted adding a further protective emblem (the red crystal) to the former ones. Additional Protocol I was first applied in the Kosovo War of 1999, between the Federal Republic of Yugoslavia and those NATO states that were at that time parties to the Protocol. Additional Protocol II was first applied, by special agreement, to the civil war in El Salvador during the 1980s.

- *Rome Statute of the International Criminal Court*, adopted at Rome (1998).[42] This treaty does not deal directly with the law of armed conflict; it rather deals with international criminal law in the specific institutional context of the International Criminal Court (ICC). However, as the violation of the law of armed conflict may entail individual criminal responsibility, the Statute is interesting for the scholar specialized in IHL. Although it is not a codification of international criminal law, the provisions that address the *ratione materiae* of the ICC, and in particular the

[40] 14 May 1954, entered into force on 7 August 1956, currently (as of May 2012) 123 states parties; Protocol for the Protection of Cultural Property in the Event of Armed Conflict, 14 May 1954, entered into force 7 August 1956, currently (as of May 2012) 100 states parties; Second Protocol to the Hague Convention of 1954 for the Protection of Cultural Property in the Event of Armed Conflict, 26 March 1999, entered into force 9 March 2004, currently 53 states parties.

[41] According to Art 16 of the Convention the emblem takes the form of 'a shield, pointed below, per saltire blue and white (a shield consisting of a royal-blue square, one of the angles of which forms the point of the shield, and of a royal-blue triangle above the square, the space on either side being taken up by a white triangle)'.

[42] 17 July 1998, entered into force 1 July 2002, UN Doc A/CONF.183/9.

long enumerated list of war crimes under Article 8, indirectly touch upon and develop the law of armed conflict.

Furthermore, there are a series of treaties limiting the production or use of particular weapons. Again, only some prominent examples will be given:

- *Protocol for the Prohibition of the Use in War of Asphyxiating, Poisonous or Other Gases, and of Bacteriological Methods of Warfare* (Geneva, 1925).[43] This Gas Protocol is widely ratified and remains important. The Protocol places a ban only on the use, not the production or possession of such arms. This was due to the fact that many states in 1925 insisted—through relevant reservations—that they remained free to use prohibited gases to the extent that such weapons were first used against them or their allies (reprisals). Thus, it remained necessary to adopt further instruments limiting the production and possession of biological and chemical weapons. The Protocol of 1925 covers both chemical weapons and biological (bacteriological) ones, ie weapons based on non-organic poisonous substances or on organic (living) poisonous substances.[44]
- *Convention on the Prohibition of Development, Production and Stockpiling of Bacteriological (Biological) and Toxin Weapons and on their Destruction* (London, Moscow, Washington, 1972).[45] This agreement was limited to biological weapons as no agreement on the international supervision of a prohibition on chemical weapons could be agreed upon (the Vietnam War was still fresh in people's minds). With regard to biological weapons, the problem of supervision was thought to be dispensable since the use of such weapons no longer presented, by that time, any direct military advantage. Article 1 of the Convention defines the type of substances covered by the treaty.
- *Convention on the Prohibition of Military or Other Hostile Use of Environmental Modification Techniques* (New York, 1976).[46] This Convention does not protect the environment in general terms but merely seeks to prohibit the deliberate and large-scale misuse of the environment for military purposes.
- *Convention on Prohibitions or Restrictions on the Use of Certain Conventional Weapons Which may be Deemed to be Excessively Injurious or to Have Indiscriminate Effects* (Geneva, 1980), with its Protocols I–V: on non-detectable fragments (Protocol I);[47] on mines, booby-traps and other devices (Protocol II);[48]

---

[43] 17 June 1925, entered into force 8 February 1928, currently (as of May 2012) 133 states parties.

[44] See § 1 of the Preamble and § 1 of the text. The latter reads: '[The High Contracting Parties accept such prohibition, i.e. that on chemical weapons and] agree to extend this prohibition to the use of bacteriological methods of warfare....'.

[45] 10 April 1972, entered into force 26 March 1975, currently (as of May 2012) 164 states parties.

[46] 10 December 1976, entered into force on 5 October 1976, currently (as of May 2012) 73 states parties.

[47] 10 October 1980, entered into force 2 December 1983, currently (as of May 2012) 107 states parties.

[48] 10 October 1980, entered into force 2 December 1983, currently (as of May 2012) 92 states parties.

on incendiary weapons (Protocol III);[49] on blinding laser weapons (Protocol IV);[50] and on explosive remnants of war (Protocol V).[51] This is the most important modern treaty that restricts the use of conventional weapons. It is an umbrella treaty, which is concretized through successive Protocols on the prohibition of specific weapons. It was drafted as a by-product of the negotiations leading to the creation in 1977 of Additional Protocols I and II. There, glaring opposition to weapons of mass destruction had overshadowed the whole quest for the prohibition of weapons more generally. The ICRC was finally able to make some progress after the Conference of 1977, once the controversial problem of the weapons of mass destruction had been eliminated from the discussions. Focus was placed on conventional weapons and the result was the 1980 Convention.

- *Convention on the Prohibition of the Development, Production, Stockpiling and Use of Chemical Weapons and on Their Destruction* (Paris, 1993).[52] The 1972 Convention on biological weapons had left open the possibility of lawfully using chemical weapons. The question of prohibiting chemical weapons came to the fore during the Iraq–Iran War in the 1980s. There was now readiness, following the end of the Cold War, to eliminate completely chemical weapons. The Convention was finally adopted through the channeling efforts of the UN General Assembly. Article 2 of the Convention contains a definition of the prohibited substances and devices. A detailed mechanism of control was agreed upon.
- *Convention on the Prohibition of the Use, Stockpiling, Production and Transfer of Anti-Personnel Mines and on Their Destruction* (Oslo, 1997).[53] The amended Protocol II on prohibitions and restrictions on the use of mines, booby-traps and other devices (1996) annexed to the 1980 Weapons Convention did not satisfy all those in the international community, in particular NGOs that wanted to place a general ban on anti-personnel mines. It is estimated that more than 100 million such mines are scattered throughout the world. These mines kill and injure thousands of people every month. This Convention seeks to fill the gap by imposing a total ban. However, it has not been ratified by some important mine-producing states.

[49] 10 October 1980, entered into force 2 December 1983, currently (as of May 2012) 103 states parties.
[50] 13 October 1995, entered into force 30 July 1998, currently (as of May 2012) 94 states parties.
[51] 28 November 2003, entered into force 12 November 2006, currently (as of May 2012) 59 states parties.
[52] 13 January 1993, entered into force 29 April 1997, currently (as of May 2012) 188 states parties.
[53] 18 September 1997, entered into force 1 March 1999, currently 156 states parties.

4 PROBLEMS OF RATIFICATION OF IHL TREATIES

Treaties on IHL have, until now, only been open for ratification or accession by states. The term 'Powers' contained in the accession clauses of the Geneva Conventions and of other IHL instruments have consistently been interpreted as allowing only states to become parties to these instruments.[54] This position was implicitly reaffirmed with regard to Palestine in 1989. Having received a letter declaring that the Palestine Liberation Organization (PLO) wanted to accede to the four Geneva Conventions, the depositary Switzerland sent a notification to the states parties noting that 'due to uncertainty within the international community as to existence or non-existence of a State of Palestine' it was not in a position to decide whether the communication of the PLO could be treated as an instrument of accession.[55] In 1960, the 'Gouvernement provisoire de la République algérienne' (GPRA) decided to accede to the Geneva Conventions. This was done in the name of Algeria. Thus, the accession became effective at the moment of independence. When the Geneva Conventions were drafted, it was believed that only states possessed armies and made war. Thus only states should be able to become parties to these Conventions, since only they could fulfil all the obligations contained in them. That is also one of the reasons why international organizations, such as the UN, never acceded to any IHL Conventions. This conception has not changed. Consequently, as far as IHL Conventions are concerned, there is still a 'states-only' rule on ratification or accession.

However, this does not mean that entities other than states cannot be subjected to IHL treaty law, as distinct from customary IHL. Thus, states not parties to specific treaties, rebels within a territory torn by insurrection, provisional governments in exile, and a series of other non-state entities, can by unilateral declaration subject themselves to one or more IHL treaties, either in totality or in part. There are three legal devices by which this can be achieved:

- *Article 2, paragraph 3, GC I–IV, for international armed conflicts.* If some belligerent states in an armed conflict are parties to the Geneva Conventions but others are not, the Conventions—even where they formally apply—would be jeopardized. Indeed, reciprocity remains an essential element of the practical working of the law of armed conflict; and it is precisely this reciprocity that would be undermined by the gaps in application generated by the involvement of states

---

[54] See eg J. Pictet, *Geneva Convention I, Commentary* (Geneva: ICRC, 1952), 408: 'The invitation [to accede to the convention] is addressed to all States…'.

[55] D. Schindler and J. Toman, *The Law of Armed Conflicts* (Leiden/Boston: Martinus Nijhoff Publishers, 2004), 649.

which are non-parties. For this reason Article 2, paragraph 3, common to the Geneva Conventions, tries to extend as much as possible the reach of these treaties. It provides, '[the Contracting states] be bound by the Convention in relation to the said Power [not being a party to the Convention], if the latter accepts and applies the provisions thereof'. This acceptance can be express or tacit, made by way of declaration or by way of effective application. An example of a comprehensive acceptance of the Geneva Conventions is found in the declarations of the United Kingdom during the Suez war of 1956. An example of a partial acceptance of the Geneva Conventions can be found in the Korean War of 1950.[56] There, South Korea declared that it would apply Common Article 3; North Korea said it would apply Geneva Convention III on prisoners of war; the United States said that it would apply the 'humanitarian principles' of the Conventions; the UN said that it would respect these 'humanitarian principles' and Geneva Convention III.[57] With the universal acceptance of the Geneva Conventions today, this provision, albeit not obsolete, is rarely applicable. In some rare cases, a treaty not yet in force may be applied in advance by special agreement. Thus, during the 1973 Middle East War, there was an agreement to apply the draft provisions on the protection of the civilian population of Additional Protocol I.[58]

- *Article 3, paragraph 3, GC I–IV, for non-international armed conflicts (or beyond).* It was felt by the drafters of the Geneva Conventions in 1949 that the law on non-international armed conflicts remained underdeveloped, and that the parties to such conflicts should accept to apply more IHL rules than those strictly applicable to non-international armed conflicts, possibly even the entirety of the Geneva Conventions, by way of a special agreement. This ad hoc means of rendering applicable IHL conventions has been extensively relied upon. Thus, for example, the Geneva Conventions have, by agreement between the warring parties, been integrally applied in Yemen (1964) and in Nigeria (1969). Further, one may recall the important special agreement concluded on 22 May 1992 by the belligerents in the former Yugoslavia.[59] In that agreement, they recognized the applicability to their conflict of a series of sources of the law of armed conflict.[60]

---

[56] The Geneva Conventions were not at that time in force for the belligerents. Thus, Art 2, § 3, was at best applied by analogy.

[57] See F. Seyersted, *United Nations Forces in the Law of Peace and War* (Leyden: A.W. Sijthoff, 1966), 182ff.

[58] See F. Bugnion, *Le Comité international de la Croix-Rouge et la protection des victimes de la guerre* (Geneva: ICRC, 1994), 472.

[59] Agreement concluded under the auspices of the ICRC by the representatives of the Republic of Bosnia-Herzegovina, the Serbian Democratic Party, and the Croatian Democratic Community, signed in Geneva on 22 May 1992.

[60] For example, under para 2.3. of the Agreement, the Parties agreed to apply Arts 13 to 34 of the Fourth Geneva Convention.

This agreement became one of the bases for the prosecution for war crimes by the ICTY.[61]

- *Unilateral Declarations of Application*. For entities that are not states, or in relation to IHL treaties that do not contain clauses such as the aforementioned provisions of the Geneva Conventions, the possibility remains for a non-state actor to accept unilaterally to be bound by all or some of the rules contained in an IHL treaty by making a declaration to this effect. This will often be done in the hope that the opposing belligerent will find good reasons, particularly on the basis of reciprocity or humanity, to apply treaty-based IHL rules. Thus, the UN declared in the Korean War of 1950 that it would respect Geneva Convention III. Moreover, the Palestinian Liberation Organization unilaterally accepted, in a declaration made in 1982, to respect the provisions of the four 1949 Geneva Conventions and of Additional Protocol I of 1977. Whilst refusing to recognize a particular entity as a state, some states have nevertheless expressly acknowledged the willingness of non-state actors to apply the rules contained in an IHL treaty.

The common aim of all these devices is to extend the reach of IHL to situations where it would not formally apply. By filling such gaps in the scope of IHL rules though the use of liberally construed ad hoc devices, it is thought that the belligerents will find a common framework of rules for fighting a limited war. Such limitations will be more beneficial to them than a progressive escalation into a total war. There is, moreover, a chance that humanitarian concerns will be properly respected.

5 RESERVATIONS TO IHL TREATIES

Much ink has been spilt on examining reservations to treaties in general and human rights treaties in particular. Less attention has been paid to reservations to IHL treaties, which have a special humanitarian character, yet must be distinguished

[61] In the case of *Prosecutor v Stanislav Galić*, the ICTY Trial Chamber held that 'by virtue of the 22 May 1992 Agreement the parties to the conflict clearly agreed to abide by the relevant provisions of Additional Protocol I protecting civilians from hostilities. Therefore, Article 51, along with Articles 35 to 42 and 48 to 48 of Additional Protocol I, undoubtedly applied as conventional law between the parties to the conflict'. ICTY (Trial Chamber I), *Prosecutor v Stanislav Galić*, Case No IT-98-29-T, Judgment and Opinion, 5 December 2003, § 25. On appeal, the Appeals Chamber did not consider it necessary to address the argument that the Agreement of 22 May 1992 was not binding on the parties and did not give rise to individual criminal responsibility, because it was satisfied that the prohibition of terror against the civilian population, set out in Art 51(2) of Additional Protocol I, was part of customary international law at the relevant time: ICTY (Appeals Chamber), *Prosecutor v Stanislav Galić*, Case No IT-98-29-A, Judgment, 30 November 2006, § 86.

from human rights treaties because they comprise inter-state obligations applicable among states. This section will briefly address the following aspects of this complex and evolving topic of reservations, currently under examination by the International Law Commission: first, the permissibility of reservations to IHL treaties; secondly, the formulation of such reservations; thirdly, the compatibility of these reservations with the IHL treaties to which they are attached; fourthly, the legal effects of the said reservations; and fifthly, the withdrawal of reservations to IHL treaties.

Permissibility of Reservations to IHL treaties. A reservation to a treaty is 'a unilateral statement, however phrased, made by a state, when signing, ratifying, accepting, approving or acceding to a treaty, whereby it purports to exclude or to modify the legal effect of certain provisions of the treaty in their application to that State'.[62] In the absence of an express prohibition of reservations to an IHL treaty, states may make reservations purporting to modify the legal effect of certain IHL treaty provisions.[63] Not all IHL treaties allow for reservations. For example, the Rome Statute of the ICC (if we consider it an IHL treaty for present purposes) must be accepted as a whole by states parties;[64] states cannot pick and choose the rules in the Rome Statute that best suit them, and make reservations concerning rules that they find less attractive.[65] Indeed, as the Rome Statute is a treaty containing rules both governing the functioning of a judicial institution and setting out the law that this institution must apply, it is difficult to see how reservations could work in practice. In contrast, most IHL treaties allow for reservations. The logic behind allowing for reservations is to encourage as many states as possible to become parties to these important instruments. States that may not wish to be bound by one or a number of provisions in an IHL treaty are not therefore discouraged from becoming parties and therefore from being bound by the bulk of the important rules contained therein, as they can attach reservations to the specific provisions to which they do not wish to be bound.

This wide degree of participation by states in IHL treaties is particularly important for IHL where the rationale of reciprocity between warring parties is omnipresent. It is highly desirable that IHL rules that do not form part of CIL apply equally among parties to an armed conflict, and that human suffering during armed conflicts is consequently mitigated as much as possible under international law. If this were not the case, a party to a conflict may not wish to adhere to IHL rules to which the other party was not legally bound, even if such rules mitigate suffering during war, as these additional obligations may place the adhering party at a comparative military disadvantage. It is thus desirable to encourage states to take on additional IHL treaty obligations and to become parties to these treaties by allowing them to make reservations to certain provisions they may not agree with. In addition to

---

[62] Article 2, § 1(d) of the VCLT, n 2 above.   [63] See Art 19 of the VCLT.
[64] Article 120 of the Rome Statute of the ICC provides '[n]o reservations may be made to this Statute'.
[65] Although one should note the effect of Art 124.

enlarging the scope of application of IHL treaties, a high degree of participation in IHL treaties is also important because it strengthens 'the authority of the moral and humanitarian principles which are [their] basis'.[66]

Although reservations to some IHL treaties are permissible, no reservations have ever been made to a number of them. This is the case with the Declaration of St Petersburg, and The Hague Conventions III, V, VII, XI, XII (indeed, this last treaty has only one ratification), and XIV, and arguably the 1976 Convention on the Prohibition of Military or any Hostile Use of Environmental Modification Techniques to which only one state (Turkey) has attached an interpretative declaration, rather than a reservation. A whole series of examples may, however, be furnished concerning reservations made with respect to other IHL treaties. Small numbers of states made reservations to Hague Conventions IV, VI, VIII, IX, X, and XIII. For example, four states made reservations to Article 44 of Hague Convention IV, which prohibits a belligerent from forcing the inhabitants of an occupied territory to furnish information about the army of the other belligerent or its means of defence. A large number of states have made various reservations to the universally ratified Geneva Conventions, and to the widely ratified Additional Protocols I and II. Unlike earlier IHL treaties, reservations made by some states to Articles in these treaties met with objections from other states. We deal with an example below.

Formulation of Reservations to IHL Treaties. Reservations must be made by a state when signing, ratifying, accepting, approving, or acceding to a treaty. Not all unilateral statements made by states when consenting to be bound by a treaty are reservations. Some statements do not purport to modify the legal effect of provisions of the IHL treaty to which they attach; they are simply statements concerning a state's understanding of the treaty, or certain provisions contained therein, and are called 'interpretative declarations'. Indeed, some unilateral statements do not even purport to interpret part of the IHL treaty to which they are attached. An example is the declaration made by the United Kingdom to Hague Convention VIII, which provides that '[b]y signing this Convention the British Plenipotentiaries declare that the only fact that said Convention does not prohibit such a deed or such a proceeding must not be considered as depriving the Government of His Majesty of the right to contest the legality of said deed or proceeding'.[67]

It is not important whether a statement is called a reservation or an interpretative declaration in order to determine whether it constitutes the former or the latter. The United Kingdom made a 'reservation' upon ratification of Additional Protocol I, which provided that under Article 44, § 3, the term 'deployment' in the sentence 'while he is engaged in a military deployment preceding the launching of an attack' includes 'any movement towards a place from which an armed attack is to

---

[66] *Reservations to the Convention on Genocide, Advisory Opinion*, ICJ Rep 1951, 15 at 24.

[67] Statement by the United Kingdom made at signature at maintained at ratification of The Hague Convention (VIII), reproduced in the IHL treaty database available on the website of the ICRC.

be launched'. According to Professor Shearer, '[i]t is arguable that this is not really a reservation, but an interpretative statement, and that the word deployment is capable of this wider meaning'.[68] It is often difficult to distinguish interpretative declarations from reservations. This is particularly the case where some statements purport to 'interpret' certain provisions, but in so doing attach a wider or narrower meaning to a provision than otherwise exists on its plain reading. Roughly speaking, when a unilateral statement made by a state provides an interpretation of a provision or a term included in an IHL treaty that may be later proven incorrect, it is more likely that the statement will be considered an interpretative declaration rather than a reservation. In contrast, a statement containing an 'interpretation' which cannot be proven incorrect, meaning that the state making the interpretation is in effect asking other states parties to accept it, will more likely be a reservation. However, if states wish to go beyond the scope of a treaty provision, and undertake more onerous obligations to, for example, extend the protection afforded to some individuals under IHL to others not otherwise covered, then this 'humanitarian' extension will not constitute a reservation as the legal effect of the treaty provisions are not being excluded or modified, only extended.

Compatibility of Reservations with IHL Treaties. Even though reservations are permissible for some IHL treaties, states are not at liberty to make reservations to just any rule contained in the respective treaty. An IHL treaty may of course specify to which articles states may attach reservations.[69] However, in the absence of such a provision, the freedom of states to make reservations is limited under customary international law. The rationale behind this limitation is that although states wish to encourage a very high level of participation in some treaties, and thus allow states to make reservations, this participation does not come at the cost of undermining the most fundamental provisions of the treaty in question. The most important parts of IHL treaties are thus protected from reservations, and any attempts to modify the legal effect of these parts of the treaty will be invalid. The difficulty is of course identifying these parts, and consequently the invalid reservations that are attached. The test articulated by the International Court of Justice in 1950,[70] now customary in nature and codified in Article 19(c) of the 1969 Vienna Convention on the Law of Treaties (VCLT),[71] is the 'object and purpose' test.[72] If a reservation is incompatible with the object and purpose of the treaty, it will be invalid.

---

[68] I.A. Shearer, 'Commentary on Paper Presented by K J Keith', 9 *Australian Year Book of International Law* (1980) 41–5 at 44.

[69] Article 19(b) of the VCLT, n 2 above.

[70] *Reservations to the Convention on Genocide, Advisory Opinion,* ICJ Rep 1951, 15 at 24.

[71] Article 19 of the VCLT, n 2 above, provides '[a] State may, when signing, ratifying, accepting, approving or acceding to a treaty, formulate a reservation unless [...] (c) [...] the reservation is incompatible with the object and purpose of the treaty'.

[72] For a discussion concerning the object and purpose of a treaty, see Alain Pellet, 'Article 19— Convention de Vienne de 1969', in Olivier Corten and Pierre Klein (eds), *Les Conventions de Vienne sur le Droit des Traités. Commentaire article par article,* vol I (Brussels: Bruylant, 2006), 641–796.

It is up to each state party to an IHL treaty individually to determine if a reservation made by another state party to the treaty is invalid. In appraising a reservation each state is 'to be guided in their judgment by the compatibility or incompatibility of the reservation with the object and purpose of the [IHL treaty]', and in undertaking this appraisal states must exercise good faith for '[i]t must clearly be assumed that the contracting states are desirous of preserving intact at least what is essential to the object of the [IHL treaty]'.[73] Following its individual evaluation of a reservation, a state party may thus accept or object to another state's reservation. For example, Germany objected to reservations made by Guinea-Bissau to Geneva Conventions I, II, and III. It stated that the reservations 'exceed, in the opinion of the Government of the Federal Republic of Germany, the purpose and intent of these Conventions and are therefore unacceptable to it. This declaration shall not otherwise affect the validity of the said Geneva Conventions under international law as between the Federal Republic of Germany and the Republic of Guinea-Bissau'.[74] There may of course be divergent views concerning the validity of some reservations, and this will alter the legal effect of these reservations on a bilateral basis, discussed below. However, these divergent views will not affect the ability of the state making the reservation to become a party to the IHL treaty.

It is important at this juncture to make a distinction between reservations to IHL treaties, and reservations to human rights treaties in relation to two aspects: the 'object and purpose' test, and the role of objections to reservations. It has been argued in the context of human rights treaties, that the object and purpose of these treaties is extremely broad and covers all the provisions contained in a treaty. Consequently, it is argued, because a reservation purports to change the legal effect of conventional human rights obligations, and that each right secures the objectives of the human rights treaty, most reservations are not permissible. The treaty body to the International Covenant on Civil and Political Rights (ICCPR), the Human Rights Committee, thus stipulated in its General Comment No 24 that '[i]n an instrument which articulates very many civil and political rights, each of the many articles, and indeed their interplay, secures the objectives of the [ICCPR]'.[75] The same is not the case for IHL treaties. Although a certain number of important provisions interrelate, and reservations to these provisions would be *prima facie* impermissible, there are other stand-alone provisions, reservations to which would not be contrary to the object and purpose of the respective IHL treaty. An example is Article 28 of Geneva Convention III, which provides, inter alia, that prisoners of war shall be able to procure tobacco for daily use. Rather than being contrary to the object and

---

[73] *Reservations to the Convention on Genocide, Advisory Opinion*, ICJ Rep 1951, 15 at 26–7.

[74] UNTS, vol 970, 1975, 367, also reproduced in the IHL treaty database available on the website of the ICRC.

[75] Human Rights Committee, 'General Comment No. 24: Issues relating to reservations made upon ratification or accession to the Covenant or the Opinion Protocols thereto, or in relation to declarations under article 41 of the Covenant', 4 November 1994, CCPR/C/21/Rev.1/Add.6, 7.

purpose of Geneva Convention III, a reservation to this outdated rule would be in keeping with current international health standards.

In the context of human rights treaties, it has also been argued that objections by states parties to a human rights treaty simply do not fit within the normative framework of these treaties. The Human Rights Committee stated that '[human rights treaties] are not a web of inter-State exchanges of mutual obligations. They concern the endowment of individuals with rights. The principle of inter-State reciprocity has no place'.[76] In the view of the Committee, it alone was the appropriate entity to evaluate reservations to the ICCPR, and objections by states to reservations only served to 'provide some guidance to the Committee'.[77] The position is different for IHL treaties, which create inter-state obligations. Unlike human rights treaties, IHL treaties continue to be based on the notion of reciprocity. Objections by states parties to an IHL treaty thus remain the means by which the legal effects of reservations to IHL treaties are determined. Furthermore, IHL treaties have no treaty body attached to them, like some human rights treaties. There is thus no possibility for a third party to be the sole evaluator of reservations to IHL treaties. This role continues to be played by states.

Legal Effects of Reservations. There are two schools of thought for determining the legal effects of reservations: the 'permissibility school' and the 'opposability school'. According to the former approach, a reservation must be objectively considered compatible with the object and purpose of the treaty, and only those reservations which are objectively compatible may be either accepted or objected to by other states parties. In contrast, according to the 'opposability school', the validity of a reservation turns on whether it is either accepted or objected to by other states parties, which may be guided in making such an assessment by the object and purpose test. Once a state party accepts or objects to a reservation made by another, then the legal effects must be understood in terms of the bilateral relationship between these two states. If a reservation made by state A is expressly or implicitly accepted by state B,[78] then the IHL treaty enters into force between these two states, with the exception of the provision(s) or parts thereof excluded from applying as a result of state A's reservation.[79] Thus, even though state B has not made the same reservations as state A (or even any reservations), state B may nevertheless avail itself of state A's reservations on the basis of reciprocity. Consequently, those parts of the treaty to which the reservations of state A attach, will not apply between state A and state B.

---

[76] Human Rights Committee, 'General Comment No. 24', 17.

[77] Human Rights Committee, 'General Comment No. 24', 17.

[78] A state is considered to have 'implicitly' accepted another state's reservation if its conduct evinces acceptance (Art 45 1969 VCLT, n 2 above), and in any event if after a 12-month period it has not objected to the reservation (Art 20(5) 1969 VCLT).

[79] Article 21(1) 1969 VCLT, n 2.

That reservations operate in this reciprocal manner even when they are accepted by other states may itself provide an incentive for states not to make reservations to IHL treaties. As Mr Duffy, the Attorney-General of Australia, noted with respect to the prospect of Australia making a reservation on the prohibition of reprisals in Additional Protocol I, '[a] reservation would operate reciprocally between Australia and a future enemy also party to the protocol. If we [made a reservation on the prohibition on reprisals], it would reduce the level of protection afforded by the protocol to Australian civilians and civilian objects'.[80] However, reciprocity in relation to some reservations made by states to IHL treaties is not always tenable. This was the case, for example, when Israel made a reservation to three of the four 1949 Geneva Conventions stating that 'while respecting the inviolability of the distinctive signs and emblems of the Convention, Israel will use the Red Shield of David as the emblem and distinctive sign'.[81] Even the acceptance of this reservation by other states parties to the Geneva Conventions would not have entitled them to depart from the requirements set out in the Geneva Conventions concerning their use of distinctive signs and emblems.[82] To do so they would have to make their own respective reservations. The situation regarding Israel's use of the emblem has now changed following its ratification of Additional Protocol III on 22 November 2007.

A state may wish to object to a reservation and in such a case the legal effects will depend on the wording of its objection. A 'simple objection' to an IHL treaty, where a state party objects to the reservation, but does not oppose the entry into force of the treaty between itself and the reserving state, will result in the IHL treaty applying between the reserving state and the objecting state. However, if the reservation excluded a treaty provision, or the reservation purported to modify a treaty provision, then the excluded or the modified parts of a treaty will not apply between the reserving state and the objecting state. The legal effect of a 'simple objection' in such a case is thus much the same as the legal effect of an acceptance of a reservation. A straightforward example of a 'simple objection' is the statement made by Germany, quoted above.[83]

Even though a state may reject a reservation made by another state, the reserving state may nevertheless purport to apply its legally invalid reservation in practice, creating a situation with serious humanitarian consequences. An example is the reservation to Article 85 of Geneva Convention III made by the Democratic Republic of Vietnam (North Vietnam). This reservation provided that '[t]he

[80] Comment made on 22 August 1990, reprinted in 13 *Australian Year Book of International Law* (1990–91) 421 at 445.

[81] Final Record of the Diplomatic Conference of Geneva of 1949, vol I, Federal Political Department, Bern, 348, reproduced in the IHL treaty database available on the website of the ICRC.

[82] This point is made by D.W. Greig, 'Reservations: Equity as a Balancing Factor?', 16 *Australian Year Book of International Law* (1995) 21 at 140.

[83] See p 71 above.

Democratic Republic of Vietnam declares that prisoners of war tried and convicted of war crimes or crimes against humanity, in accordance with the principles laid down by the Nuremberg Judicial Tribunal, shall not benefit from the provisions of the present Convention as is specified in Article 85'.[84] It is uncontroversial that this reservation is contrary to the object and purpose of the Geneva Conventions which are to promote IHL and to extend its protection to all those falling into the hands of an adverse party. The United States, among other states, objected to this reservation, stipulating that it was '[r]ejecting the reservations which States have made with respect to the Geneva Convention relative to the treatment of prisoners of war, the United States accepts treaty relations with all parties to that Convention, except as to the changes proposed by such reservations'.[85] However, during the international armed conflict in Vietnam, North Vietnam unlawfully applied its reservation and refused to grant prisoner of war status to captured pilots of the US armed forces on the basis that all were categorically 'war criminals' who were not entitled to the protection afforded under Geneva Convention III. The disastrous result was that US armed servicemen were mistreated whilst being detained by North Vietnam. As the Deputy Legal Advisor of the US Department of State, George Aldrich, remarked at the time, '[a]lthough [the North Vietnamese] excuse was untenable, neither the convention nor general international law has provided any effective remedy for this flagrant disregard of international obligations, and our persistent efforts to bring about some type of impartial inspection of detention conditions continued to be rebuffed'.[86] The importance of the work of the ICRC cannot be underestimated in this context, as with many situations involving violations of IHL.

If a state makes a 'radical objection' to a reservation, and opposes the entry into force of the IHL treaty between itself and the reserving state, then the treaty will not enter into force between the reserving state and the objecting state. Regardless of the problematic content of a reservation, to radically object to it would entail very serious consequences for both the reserving state and the objecting state, as none of the conventional obligations contained in the IHL treaty would apply between these two states if ever they were both parties to the same international armed conflict. This situation would not affect treaty relations with other states parties to the IHL treaty if these states have either accepted the reservation, or only made a simple objection to it. It must also be stressed that the rules of IHL that form part of customary international law would continue to apply between the reserving state and the radically objecting state.

---

[84] Notification by the depositary addressed to the ICRC on 23 July 1957, reproduced in the IHL treaty database on the website of the ICRC.

[85] Text of the United States of America reservations/declarations to the Geneva Conventions is contained in UNTS, vol 213, 1955, 379–84, reproduced in the IHL treaty database on the website of the ICRC.

[86] 67 *American Society of International Law Proceedings* (1973) 143.

Withdrawal of Reservations to IHL Treaties. States' attitudes towards IHL rules change over time. For example, a state may wish to withdraw a reservation that it once made allowing it to behave in a certain way that it now considers unacceptable. In addition, it may not want to leave open the possibility for it to behave in a certain way any more than it may want other states to be allowed to behave in this way. Under customary international law, codified under Article 22(2) of the VCLT, a state may withdraw a reservation at any time, unless the treaty in question provides otherwise. For example, following Iraq's use of chemical weapons in the Gulf War, Australia made clear that 'the Australian Government did not consider the use of chemical weapons justified under any circumstances'.[87] Australia subsequently withdrew its reservation to the 1925 Protocol for the Prohibition of the Use in War of Asphyxiating, Poisonous or Other Gases, and of Bacteriological Methods of Warfare, which had left open the possibility for Australia to use chemical weapons in certain circumstances. A withdrawal of a reservation will only take effect once the other states parties to the IHL treaty have been duly notified, in accordance with Article 22 3(a) of the VCLT. Notification is a requirement that derives from the principle of legal security.[88] It is thus not sufficient that a state merely withdraws its reservation to a multilateral treaty in domestic law; it must also be accompanied by a notification at the international level in order for such a withdrawal to take effect.[89]

6 LEGAL RELATIONSHIPS BETWEEN IHL TREATIES

Succession of treaties which contain rules on the same or similar subject matters raises the problem of the relationship between these different IHL (or related) instruments. Broadly speaking, three types of relations may be distinguished:

- *Lex posterior 'derogat' vel 'abrogat' legi priori*. Sometimes, a posterior IHL treaty is concluded on the same subject matter and is intended by the states adopting it to replace, ie to supersede completely, an older IHL treaty on the same object. Thus,

[87] Comment made by Mr Hayden on behalf of the Government of Australia, reprinted in 11 *Australian Year Book of International Law* (1984–87) 577 at 623.

[88] *Armed Activities on the Territory on the Congo (New Application: 2002) (Democratic Republic of the Congo v Rwanda)*, Jurisdiction of the Court, Judgment, ICJ Rep 2006, 6, 25, § 41.

[89] ICJ Rep 2006, 6, 26, § 42.

for example, in the context of the amelioration of the condition of the wounded and sick members of armies during warfare, there have been a series of conventions, each one improving on previously concluded treaties and which were designed to take their place. Hence, the Convention of 1864 for the Amelioration of the Condition of the Wounded in Armies in the Field[90] was replaced by the 1906 Convention for the Amelioration of the Condition of the Wounded and Sick in the Armies in Field.[91] Article 31 of the latter reads: '[t]he present convention, when duly ratified, shall supersede the Convention of August 22, 1864, in the relations between the contracting states'. The same derogatory relations exist between the aforementioned Convention of 1906 and the 1929 Convention for the Amelioration of the Condition of the Wounded and Sick in Armies in the Field;[92] and later between the aforementioned 1929 Convention and the Geneva Convention I of 1949 on the Amelioration of the Condition of the Wounded and Sick in Armed Forces in the Field.[93] If all the parties to the earlier treaty become parties to the later one, the former treaty is extinguished (abrogated) *erga omnes*; if some but not all of the parties to the older treaty also become parties to the new treaty, then this new treaty will apply between parties to it (and will derogate in their relationships the older one), whereas the older treaty will continue to apply between states only parties to the old convention, or between these states and states also parties to the new treaty. Even in cases of extinction of an older treaty by a wholesale replacement through a new treaty, this will not mean that the older text is deprived of any legal meaning whatsoever under the new regime. It can still be used for the interpretation of provisions contained in the new treaty. This may happen where the older provision was clearer or in relation to which some practice had developed, which may be relevant for the application of the new rule.

- *Lex posterior 'amplificat' legi priori*. It is frequently the case that a newly concluded IHL treaty does not replace an older IHL convention but rather builds upon it. That may mean, on the one hand, that the new convention includes new rules not contained in the older one. Both treaties then remain applicable in their respective material and other scopes of application. It may also mean, on the other hand, that the new convention in part derogates from the older one and in part develops the law of armed conflict. This latter case, where the elements of amendment

---

[90] D. Schindler and J. Toman, *The Law of Armed Conflicts* (Leiden/Boston: Martinus Nijhoff Publishers, 2004), 365ff.

[91] Schindler and Toman, *The Law of Armed Conflicts*, 385ff.

[92] Schindler and Toman, *The Law of Armed Conflicts*, 409ff. See Art 34 of the 1929 Convention: 'The present Convention shall replace the Conventions [of 1864 and 1906] between the High Contracting Parties'.

[93] Schindler and Toman, *The Law of Armed Conflicts*, 459ff. See Art 59 of Geneva Convention I: 'The present Convention replaces the Conventions of [1864, 1906, and 1929] in relations between the High Contracting Parties'.

and addition are inextricably interwoven, is most frequent. Three examples may briefly be mentioned.

- In relation to a *simple addition* to an older convention, one may invoke the case of the Gas Protocol of 1925, which prohibits only the *use* of certain chemical and biological agents, and the Biological (1972) and Chemical (1993) Weapons Conventions,[94] which concern only the *production* and *possession* of such weapons. The latter texts do not deal at all with the use of such arms (that aspect being covered already by the Gas Protocol), but only with the development, production and stockpiling of them.[95]

- With respect to a *partial amendment and partial development* of the law, one can mention the Regulations of Hague Convention IV (1907) with respect to Geneva Conventions III and IV. Thus, Article 154 of Geneva Convention IV[96] reads as follows: '[i]n the relations between the Powers who are bound by the Hague Conventions [...] and who are parties to the present Convention, this last Convention shall be supplementary to [the] above-mentioned Convention of the Hague'. Thus, for example, Geneva Convention IV builds on the law of occupation of the Hague Regulations of 1907, the two texts must therefore be read in conjunction with one another.[97] As far as the establishment and definition of occupation is concerned, the matter remains regulated by Article 42 of the Hague Regulations. Geneva Convention IV is silent on that point because it implicitly operates a *renvoi* to the older text. As far as respect for the local legislation and institutions is concerned, Article 43 of the Hague Regulations is supplemented by some more details provided in Article 64 of Geneva Convention IV. This is evident insofar as it permits (or even mandates) suspension or abrogation of local legislation if that legislation is oppressive, ie if it contravenes the humanitarian standards guaranteed in Geneva Convention IV itself. A further example of such an interaction between the old and the new norms can be found in Article 4 of Geneva Convention III and in Articles 43–44 of Additional Protocol I. These treaties deal with the definition of a combatant, ie those individuals entitled to fight and to attain POW status upon capture.

---

[94] See (C) above.

[95] Thus, Art VIII of the 1972 Biological Weapons Convention reads: 'Nothing in this Convention shall be interpreted as in any way limiting or detracting from the obligations assumed by any State under the Protocol for the Prohibition of the Use in War of Asphyxiating, Poisonous or Other Gases, and of Bacteriological Methods of Warfare...'. See also Art XIII of the 1993 Chemical Weapons Convention.

[96] There are no analogous provisions in the first two Conventions: Geneva Conventions I and II supersede older Conventions. Geneva Convention III contains an analogous 'complemetation' clause in Art 135.

[97] For more details on this quite complex relationship, see R. Kolb and S. Vité, *La protection des populations civiles soumises au pouvoir d'une armée étrangère—La complémentarité du droit de l'occupation militaire et des droits de l'homme à la lumière des interventions en Afghanistan et en Irak* (Brussels: Bruylant, 2008).

- *Lex posterior 'compleat' legi priori.* Finally, a newer body of law can complement the older one without being formally an addition or a revision of it. We may here consider some relationships going beyond purely IHL–IHL relations and of purposed revision of older conventions. Thus, human rights law (HRL) today complements IHL in many ways without being itself a body of IHL subject to the same conditions of applicability or destined to revise older IHL laws.[98] Hence, for example, HRL may serve as a yardstick of interpretation of IHL, for example in such areas as detention of persons or rules governing the fair trial of protected persons. HRL here provides not only more detailed textual rules,[99] but also offers a rich network of adjudicatory organs, which have given flesh to most of these norms by a further detailed body of jurisprudence. Thus, for example, when IHL provides for the detention of persons,[100] HRL may assist concretizing the rights and duties involved by offering its own rich experience. In some cases, the interplay of both sources is even more apparent: in the case of belligerent occupation of territories, the fundamental guarantees of civilians are a mix of IHL and HRL. In some areas, HRL may even provide a sort of derogatory *lex specialis* to IHL. This is the case, for example, in the context of Article 43 of Geneva Convention IV. That provision reads as follows: '[a]ny protected person who has been interned or placed in assigned residence shall be entitled to have such action reconsidered as soon as possible by an appropriate court or administrative board designated by the detaining power [...]'. The Geneva Conventions consequently allow for a review by an executive body. However, if HRL is applicable to such internment of enemy civilians (as it is), its own rules on fair trial conclusively require adjudication of the matter by an independent and impartial court.[101] The two obligations under IHL and HRL are here partly incompatible. To the extent both bodies of the law apply, the stronger obligations under HRL will have to prevail over the weaker ones in IHL. A state must respect *all* its obligations under international law. If it sets up an administrative board for adjudicating on our question, it would respect its obligations under IHL but violate those rules under HRL. The consequence is that it must respect the stricter obligation under HRL in order not to violate that applicable body of law. All these aspects can be analysed as relationships between different conventions and between treaties and CIL.

[98] For details, see R. Kolb, 'Relationship between International Humanitarian Law and Human Rights Law', in *Encyclopaedia of Public International Law*, <http://www.mpepil.com>.

[99] For example, Art 6 of the European Convention on Human Rights or Art 14 of the ICCPR in fair trial matters.

[100] See Geneva Convention III, Arts 21ff; and Geneva Convention IV, Arts 76, 78, 79ff.

[101] Except if use has been made of a suspension or derogation clause in times of national emergency, and to the extent that this use is allowed.

7 INTERPRETATION OF IHL TREATIES

The interpretation of IHL treaties is to be performed within the general framework of rules on treaty interpretation as they exist in CIL and are codified in Articles 31–33 of VCLT.[102] Is there some specificity for IHL treaties? Roughly, it can be said that there were two historical phases eliciting quite different approaches to the question of interpretation:

- *First phase (1899–1949): narrow interpretation, residual rule of state freedom.* In the Hague phase of the law of armed conflict (1899–1949), the tendency was to interpret norms of that branch of the law restrictively. War consisted in a struggle for survival or in the pursuit of vital interests of sovereign states. Limitations on state freedom in such a crucial matter could not be easily presumed or imposed. The maxim '*Kriegsräson geht vor Kriegsmanier*' was refuted as a general rule, since 'laws' of war are binding and cannot be compared to 'usages' of war.[103] But it was also understood that limitations on a state's freedom to pursue its vital interests through belligerency could only be construed in a restrictive way. The polar star of interpretation in this '*Lotus*' or state-centred phase of international law[104] was the so-called *Lotus* principle: 'What is not prohibited is permitted in the law'.[105] This expressed not only a substantive rule for the handling of gaps; it informed also the interpretation of the texts, enjoining the interpreter to look for a narrow construction of state duties. In other words, the Martens Clause[106] contained in the preamble of the 1899 and 1907 Hague Convention IV was not yet taken seriously as a binding norm of IHL.

[102] On these rules, see A. Aust, *Modern Treaty Law and Practice* (2nd edn, Cambridge: Cambridge University Press, 2007), 230ff. For more details, see O. Corten and P. Klein (eds), *Les Conventions de Vienne sur le droit des traités, Commentaire article par article*, vol II (Brussels: Bruylant, 2006), 1289ff; and R. Kolb, *Interprétation et création du droit international* (Brussels: Bruylant, 2006).

[103] See R.F. Roxburgh (ed), L. Oppenheim, *International Law*, vol II (3rd edn, London: Longmans, Green & Co, 1921), 91–2.

[104] On this phase of international law more generally, see the illuminating passages in P.M. Dupuy, 'L'unité de l'ordre juridique international, Cours général de droit international public', 297 *RCADI* (2002) 93ff.

[105] See the references in P.A. Pillitu, *Lo stato di necessità nel diritto internazionale*, (Perugia: Pubblicazioni della Facoltà di giurisprudenza, Università di Perugia. Facoltà di giurisprudenza, 1981), 359.

[106] On this clause, see R. Kolb and R. Hyde, *An Introduction to the International Law of Armed Conflicts* (Oxford: Hart Publishing, 2008), 61ff; H. Strebel, 'Martens Clause', in R. Bernhardt (ed), *Encyclopaedia of Public International Law*, vol 3, 252–3. F. Münch, 'Die Martens'sche Klausel und die Grundlagen des Völkerrechts', 36 *ZaöRV* (1976) 347ff; S. Miyazaki, 'The Martens Clause and International Humanitarian Law', *Essays in Honour of J. Pictet* (Geneva: ICRC, 1984), 433ff; V.V. Pustogarov, 'The Martens Clause in International Law', 1 *Journal of the History of International Law* (1999) 125ff; A. Cassese, 'The Martens Clause: Half a Loaf or Simply Pie in the Sky?', 11 *EJIL* (2000) 187ff; T. Meron, 'The Martens Clause, Principles of Humanity, and Dictates of Public Conscience', 94 *AJIL* (2000) 78ff; R. Ticehurst, 'The

- *Second phase (1949 onwards): broad interpretation, active rule of humanity.* In the Geneva phase of IHL (1949–today, and especially since 1993), the law of armed conflict centred on military concerns progressively became also a 'humanitarian law', ie a body of law furthering humanitarian concerns. The old principle of limitations of means and methods of warfare informing the Hague Law was now amplified by the new principle of humanity informing the Geneva Law. Thus, the interpretation of IHL provisions progressively became more liberal and more expansive. HRL equally pushed in that direction. The polar star of the new layer of the law was the humanitarian protection of war victims, and a broad and not a literal construction was felt to be necessary in order to better serve that fundamental civilizing purpose. Moreover, if it is held that IHL contains a great number of public order, public policy or *jus cogens* norms,[107] it seems quite understandable that the interpretation of such texts has to be expansive rather than narrow. This new orientation represents a shift from a 'state-centred' view of the law of armed conflict to a 'human-centred' view of IHL. It has sometimes been called the 'humanization' of IHL. The recent state and especially judicial practice is replete with examples of such broad interpretations.[108]

A particularly bold (and not unproblematic) example of such a line of reasoning can be found in the context of armed reprisals during warfare. The ICTY, in the *Kupreškić* case (2000),[109] considered that under CIL all civilians are protected against belligerent reprisals in all circumstances. The ICTY Trial Chamber relied on a series of arguments to conclude that there is such a general prohibition. The Chamber invoked the principle of humanity and the Martens Clause; the *jus cogens* character of the protective rules and the Kantian imperative; the absence of reciprocity in the fundamental protections of IHL, which must be respected in all circumstances independently from performance by the other parties; the underlying logic of Common Article 3 to the GC, which must be applicable *a fortiori* in an international armed conflict; the modern tendencies of state practice, that many states abstain from claiming such reprisals; and the negative reactions of the UN General Assembly to cases of such reprisals. These statements go somewhat beyond the actual state of the law,[110] but they provide a good example of the type of argument often underlying modern interpretations of IHL norms. The point is obviously to find an interpretation which takes into account military and humanitarian needs in a balanced way.

Martens Clause and the Laws of Armed Conflict', in N. Sanajaoba (ed), *A Manual of International Humanitarian Laws* (New Dehli: Regency Publications, 2004), 312ff.

[107] Cf E. David, *Principes du droit des conflits armés* (4th edn, Brussels: Bruylant, 2008), 106–14.

[108] See T. Meron, 'International Law in the Age of Human Rights', 301 *RCAD* (2003) 24ff.

[109] At §§ 515ff, 527ff of the judgment of 14 January 2000.

[110] See J.M. Henckaerts and L. Doswald-Beck, *Customary International Humanitarian Law*, vol I (Cambridge: ICRC, 2005), 513ff.

8 SPECIAL AGREEMENTS

There are a series of cases, where the applicability of IHL may be in doubt. There are moreover situations where only a limited number of rules would normally apply. In both cases there may be a need for additional protective rules.

Thus, for example, certain conventional rules may be applicable due to the fact that a state participating in a conflict is not a party to a specific IHL convention. This was the case, for example, of the 1929 Geneva Convention on prisoners of war, not ratified by the Soviet Union, during World War II. Moreover, there may be gaps in the law of armed conflict. For a long time, codification was rather piecemeal: first it covered only wounded and sick combatants in land warfare; then these protections were extended to the sea; then protection was extended to combatants in captivity (prisoners of war); then the law started to contain rules on the protection of civilians, in the beginning in a rather limited way, then the law was extended to non-international armed conflicts. In all these phases, there remained gaps in protection. For example, in the case of a non-international armed conflict, the applicable rules are less numerous. During the Spanish Civil War (1936–39), the two belligerents, the Madrid Government and the Burgos Junta, agreed to treat certain prisoners as having POW status by way of analogy. Further, it might sometimes be wise to apply at least some rules from the law of armed conflict by analogy to a situation of internal disturbance not as such being an armed conflict.

Furthermore, there may be situations where there is a gap due to the particular circumstances. Thus, for example, certain weapons are not clearly prohibited. One may mention the discussions with regard to weapons containing uranium. If customary international law applies, its precise content may be doubtful. To all these cases, one must add that often a state may deny the existence of an international or non-international armed conflict, or a situation of occupation as defined by the Geneva Conventions. The Israeli occupied territories or the Western Sahara under Moroccan rule spring to mind. Finally, an armed conflict may be of a mixed international and non-international character. In cases of a mixed conflict, it may be difficult to establish exactly what law applies to what precise situation, since there may be a highly complex merging of belligerent activities.

All the situations described above—to which others could be added—have one point in common: the application of the law is rendered difficult or stymied by a controversy over its applicability or by an insufficient reach of the rules. In such cases, a simple device may overcome the above-mentioned difficulties. If the parties agree, they may conclude one or more 'special agreements' in which they explicitly recognize that certain rules apply in a given situation, even if these rules might otherwise not be applicable. These special agreements may be concluded in written form, but they may also be concluded informally, orally, or by actual conduct.

The Geneva Conventions of 1949, in Article 3, paragraph 3 and Articles 6/6/6/7, respectively, encourage the conclusion of such 'special agreements'. However, the parties ultimately remain free to accept such agreements or not. If such a special agreement is concluded, the reach of the law of armed conflict is increased. Apart from the rules of IHL that non-controversially apply by virtue of either treaty law or CIL, there will be an additional layer of the rules contained in the special agreement. Such special agreements are practically speaking very important. They help to solve many doubts and quarrels on the applicability or application of rules of IHL. Hundreds of such special agreements have been concluded between belligerents: some are of minor importance, simply organizing the execution of conventional and undisputed duties; others are of great importance, putting beyond doubt, and giving precision to, the rules applicable in a particular armed conflict.

The belligerents themselves are often on such hostile terms with one another that they are unable to take the initiative of proposing such an agreement, or negotiating its conclusion. There is normally the need for the mediation of a third party. In practice, the ICRC most frequently takes such initiatives. Some examples of categories or of particular agreements can be given here:

(1) Article 3, paragraph 3, deals formally with non-international armed conflicts, but the special agreements it provides for have been concluded also outside this narrow compass. The drafters of the Geneva Conventions were aware that only very few rules applied to non-international armed conflicts. Thus, they inserted a provision encouraging the parties to accept further obligations. In practice, this provision has been very important.

(2) Articles 6/6/6/7, respectively, of Geneva Conventions I–IV deal with open-ended special agreements. Article 6 of Geneva Convention I reads as follows: 'In addition to the agreements expressly provided for in Articles 10, 15, 23, 28, 31, 36, 37 and 52, the High Contracting Parties may conclude other special agreements for all matters concerning which they may deem it suitable to make separate provision. No special agreement shall adversely affect the situation of the wounded and sick, of members of the medical personnel or of chaplains, as defined by the present Convention, nor restrict the rights which it confers upon them'. Many such special agreements have been concluded, be it under Article 6, or, for parties not yet bound by the Geneva Conventions, under CIL. Hence, for example, in the civil war of Yemen (1962), the belligerents undertook the obligation to respect the essential provisions of the Geneva Conventions, including Common Article 3, where Yemen had not yet ratified the Geneva Conventions.

What can be said on the legal status of such agreements?

- First, it must be noted that they will *apply only circumstantially*: to the parties concluding them; for the conflict at stake; and under the conditions stipulated in the agreements. Hence, such special agreements do not add objective rules to the corpus of the law of armed conflict. They simply allow gaps and weaknesses in the law to be filled in the context of a specific conflict or situation by way of specific obligations. The special agreements terminate at the end of the armed conflict at issue.

- Secondly, such special agreements may have *two different aims*. Some special agreements are purely executory. They will not add new obligations nor will they clarify the law applicable. Rather, their aim is to execute the obligations contained in IHL treaties in a particular context. Thus, for example, Articles 109ff of Geneva Convention III stipulate that POWs who are seriously wounded or seriously sick shall be repatriated as soon as possible, without having to wait until there is a cessation of hostilities. In order to put into effect this provision, there must be a handing over of these prisoners to the adverse belligerent. To that effect, an agreement on the conditions of this transfer will be necessary. Other special agreements may be comprised of fresh obligations. Thus, for example, they may undertake to respect a treaty which is not formally applicable.

- Thirdly, it must be stressed that the *law limits the content* of such special agreements. These must be either agreements in order to execute obligations or rights contained in the law of armed conflict (and hence by definition compatible with it) or agreements which will give additional protections and do not, in the context of the Convention I, 'adversely affect the situation of the wounded and sick, of members of the medical personnel or of chaplains, as defined by the present Convention, nor restrict the rights which it confers upon them'.[111] The Geneva Conventions thus allow for an increase in the protection already enjoyed by protected persons through special agreements; they conversely do not allow special agreements to restrict or deny the enjoyment of any of the conventional rules protecting such persons. As to this last aspect, an example from World War II may be recalled. By agreements between the Vichy Government and Germany, the position of French POWs in Germany had been jeopardized, with the POWs losing their POW status. They in fact became civil workers in the German industry. By this device, they no longer enjoyed the protection afforded them by the Geneva Convention on POWs of 1929. Such an agreement would not be in conformity with the Geneva Conventions of 1949 as it would restrict the rights of protected persons.

---

[111] Geneva Convention I, Art 6.

9 DENUNCIATION OF IHL TREATIES

Most IHL treaties contain denunciation clauses.[112] Geneva Conventions I–IV contain a typical denunciation clause. It is a reproduction of the denunciation clauses found in older treaties, especially the Hague Conventions. It is contained in Articles 63/62/142/158 of Geneva Conventions I–IV, and reads as follows:

Each of the High Contracting Parties shall be at liberty to denounce the present Convention.

The denunciation shall be notified in writing to the Swiss Federal Council, which shall transmit it to the Governments of all the High Contracting Parties.

The denunciation shall take effect one year after the notification thereof has been made to the Swiss Federal Council. However, a denunciation of which notification has been made at a time when the denouncing Power is involved in a conflict shall not take effect until peace has been concluded, and until after operations connected with the release, repatriation and re-establishment of the persons protected by the present Convention have been terminated.

The denunciation shall have effect only in respect of the denouncing Power. It shall in no way impair the obligations which the Parties to the conflict shall remain bound to fulfil by virtue of the principles of the law of nations, as they result from the usages established among civilized peoples, from the laws of humanity and the dictates of the public conscience.

This typical clause shows that if denunciation is not prohibited, it is subjected to severe limitations. First, it takes effect only one year after its notification to the depositary. Secondly, in any event, a denunciation produces no effects for an armed conflict already underway at the time of denunciation. Even one year after notification, it would be inappropriate to allow a party to take a military advantage in war by denouncing the treaty after hostilities have commenced. The humanitarian purpose of IHL treaties could then easily be thwarted. Hence, a denunciation during an armed conflict can only take effect after the end of the armed conflict for all relevant purposes (ie end of active hostilities for the law on means and methods of warfare; and release of all the protected persons for the law on humanitarian protection of war victims). Thirdly, the clause underscores that a denunciation will not liberate the non-denouncing parties in their dealings among themselves: these other treaty parties remain bound by the convention *inter se*. They will be freed from its application only towards the denouncing party. This rule mirrors the rejection of the *si omnes* clause in Article 2, paragraph 1, of the 1949 Geneva Conventions. Fourthly, the provision recalls that CIL and the Martens Clause remain applicable to the denouncing state. To the extent that today most of the substantive obligations of IHL are considered to be of a customary nature, there is little to be gained legally, but much to be lost politically, by a denunciation

---

[112] The *jus cogens* character of many of their norms must not induce one to think dogmatically that such denunciation is impossible. In any event, in the case of such denunciation, the applicability of the norms of *jus cogens* would remain unaffected because and to the extent they reflect CIL.

of an IHL treaty. It is therefore not surprising that since 1945 no state has attempted to denounce an IHL convention.

If an IHL convention does not contain a denunciation clause, Article 56 of the Vienna Convention on the Law of Treaties applies as a reflection of CIL. This provision reads as follows:

A treaty which contains no provision regarding its termination and which does not provide for denunciation or withdrawal is not subject to denunciation or withdrawal unless: (a) it is established that the parties intended to admit the possibility of denunciation or withdrawal; or (b) a right of denunciation or withdrawal may be implied by the nature of the treaty.[113]

The general rule is thus that a treaty cannot be denounced. Otherwise, it would be too easy to escape unwelcome treaty obligations at will. As for (a), if an intention of the drafters to allow denunciation can be shown, possibly through the *travaux préparatoires*, then denunciation must be admitted (such was the case, for example, for the UN Charter). As for (b), it could be argued that IHL treaties can be denounced by their 'nature': the argument would be buttressed by the many denunciation clauses in most IHL treaties by way of analogy. However, on the other hand, it could be held that the drafters must have intended to protect their particular treaty from denunciation if they did not insert a denunciation clause. The rich conventional IHL practice, which they invariably take advantage of in the process of drafting a new treaty, clearly puts them on notice of the possibility of inserting such a clause. If they have chosen not to insert such a clause, this must be considered a 'qualified silence' which *a contrario* excludes any denunciation.

In regard to the absence of any denunciation practice, this point remains somewhat theoretical. In view of the essential civilizing and public order character ascribed today to IHL treaties (as to the ICCPR), the better position is probably that they should not be denounceable unless they specifically provide otherwise. Moreover, the general presumption of Article 56 against denunciation, as well as the protective object and purpose of these treaties, also militates in favour of excluding denunciation in the absence of particular clauses allowing otherwise.

A last question could be asked: if the denunciation clauses have never been invoked in the last 50 years, has subsequent practice not rendered them obsolete? The answer to this question is that such desuetude can obviously intervene. However, the simple non-use of a provision does not entail its obsolescence. There must moreover be a general *opinio juris* that the provision at stake shall be regarded as no longer applicable in the future.[114] In our context, such an *opinio juris* cannot

---

[113] See A. Aust, *Modern Treaty Law and Practice* (2nd edn, Cambridge: Cambridge University Press, 2007), 289ff. For more details, see O. Corten and P. Klein (eds), *Les Conventions de Vienne sur le droit des traités, Commentaire article par article*, vol III (Brussels: Bruylant, 2006), 1951ff.

[114] M. Kohen, 'Article 42', in O. Corten and P. Klein (eds), *Les Conventions de Vienne sur le droit des traites. Commentaire article par article* (Brussels: Bruylant, 2006), 1593–1614 at 1606: '[U]n Etat peut, pour des raisons politiques ou autres, décider de ne pas se prévaloir d'un traité, sans que cela

be shown. The states parties have not given up in an unambiguous or indeed in any way their exceptional right to denounce; they just considered that no circumstances arose making the use of such a right necessary. Thus, no desuetude can be implied.

10 LEGAL EFFECTS OF A BREACH OF AN IHL TREATY

If the provisions of an IHL treaty are breached, remedies for the aggrieved state may flow from the rules of IHL itself (such as rules concerning Protecting Powers, the ICRC in its role as a substitute or acting in its own right, or from the commissions of inquiry), and from general international law (for example, the law of state responsibility). Can a state aggrieved by a material breach by another state party avail itself of the possibility of suspending or terminating the breached treaty according to the Vienna VCLT? Article 60(5), VCLT responds in the negative: 'Paragraphs 1 to 3 [on termination and suspension] do not apply to provisions relating to the protection of the human person contained in treaties of a humanitarian character, in particular to provisions prohibiting any form of reprisals against persons protected by such treaties'.[115]

Article 60(5), was inserted at the Vienna Conference on the suggestion of the Swiss Government, which is the depositary of the Geneva Conventions. The point is precisely to rule out a termination or suspension of certain treaties containing 'absolute' or 'public order' provisions for the protection of individuals. Such treaties are not subjected to the ordinary reciprocity (*do ut des*) of inter-state treaties: 'you violate, I suspend or terminate'. They are to some extent stipulations in favour of a third beneficiary, the protected human being, and have moreover a fundamentally civilizing nature. Therefore such treaties have to be respected even if breached by the other party. The wounded and sick; POWs; the civilians, from the other side always have the right to be humanely treated, regardless of the extent to which IHL

---

signifie qu'il y renonce à l'avenir. Enfin, le simple fait de ne pas appliquer un traité peut témoigner d'une volonté de le suspendre durant un certain temps et non nécessairement d'y mettre fin'. See also the European Communities case (*Commission v France*), no 7/71, 1971, in: 48 *ILR* 223. On the concept, see also R. Kolb, 'La désuétude en droit international public', 111 *RGDIP* (2007) 577ff; G. Le Floch, 'La désuétude en droit international public', 111 *RGDIP* (2007) 609ff.

[115] For a detailed commentary of this provision, see B. Simma and C. Tams, 'Article 60', in O. Corten and P. Klein (eds), *Les Conventions de Vienne sur le droit des traites. Commentaire article par article* (Brussels: Bruylant, 2006), 2129–79 at 2157ff.

rules are respected by other belligerents in an armed conflict. The rationale behind this is that even if violations do occur, they should not spread to further violations due to the suspension or termination of treaty commitments. A distinction must be made with reprisals, which form part of customary IHL, the effects of which do not amount to treaty suspension or termination. In modern IHL, the rule is that reprisals are prohibited against protected persons and some protected objects.[116] Both branches of the law, treaty law and general IHL on reprisals, thus reflect the same basic concern for maintaining a minimum standard of civilization and of humanity.

[116] Belligerent (armed) reprisals are prohibited against the following persons and objects:
- against the wounded, sick or shipwrecked combatants, and all other persons covered under Geneva Conventions I and II: Art 46 GC I, Art 47 GC II;
- against prisoners of war under Geneva Convention III, Art 13, paragraph 3;
- against civilians who find themselves in the hands of a party to the conflict of which they are not nationals, ie protected civilians outside warfare situations: Geneva Convention IV, Art 33, paragraph 3;
- against the wounded, sick, or shipwrecked military persons or civilians covered by Part II of Additional Protocol I of 1977, Art 20;
- against civilians during hostilities, ie in the context of targeting: Protocol I, Art 51(6). This is a most important limitation: it means that all the limitations on targeting flowing from the principle of distinction are not any more subject to the exception of reprisals;
- against civilian objects during hostilities, ie in the context of targeting: Protocol I, Art 52(1);
- against historic monuments, works of art, or places of worship which constitute the cultural or spiritual heritage of peoples: Protocol I, Art 53(c);
- against objects indispensable to the survival of the civilian population: Protocol I, Art 54(4);
- against the natural environment: Protocol I, Art 55(2);
- against works and installations containing dangerous forces: Protocol I, Art 56(4).

PART III

LEGAL REGIMES

CHAPTER 5

LAND WARFARE

YVES SANDOZ

1 INTRODUCTION

In recent years, multiple questions have arisen with regard to the status and permissibility in international humanitarian law (IHL) of aerial bombing and the use of nuclear weapons. Nonetheless, the fact cannot be ignored that most contemporary armed conflicts are conducted on land. Therefore, questions about land warfare remain as topical as ever.

Land warfare, aerial warfare, and maritime warfare each have their own specific features. Advanced technology, in particular the possibility to project destructive devices over very great distances, combined with the increasing dependence of states on computer systems in the conduct of military operations have given rise to considerable debate in relation to aerial warfare. It is especially in such contexts that the meaning or interpretation of certain principles of IHL, including those of precaution and proportionality, are under scrutiny. It is nonetheless worth recalling that these principles apply in all circumstances and, hence, it is also appropriate to consider their significance in land warfare.

This Chapter will review the principles and rules of IHL that apply to land warfare. Those rules that have retained their full relevance—which is the case for most of them—will be highlighted. Equally important, those few rules that deserve to be clarified or rendered more precise or that, in some cases, could justifiably be considered afresh will also be discussed.

This review will proceed first by presenting IHL from the perspective of the foot soldier, outlining in detail his or her rights and duties. This emphasizes the fact that compliance with IHL depends first on the conduct of each individual soldier. Of course, in focusing on the individual soldier, it would be wrong to ignore the responsibility of the chain of command. Decisions made by commanders and the high command contrary to the principles of IHL, including the use of prohibited weapons, giving orders that breach humanitarian rules, failure to prevent violations and failing to fulfil duties to train their subordinates, will all be examined in less detail towards the end of the Chapter.

It should be noted that questions relating to the use of artillery will not be considered in this contribution. Under IHL, shelling and the use of land-to-air missiles are subject to the same constraints as aerial bombing. That aspect of land warfare will be dealt with in the Chapter on air warfare.[1]

2 Principles and Rules of IHL to be Observed by Foot Soldiers

A. General observations

War should not be an excuse for someone who has joined the army to turn into a brigand. A soldier is not a bandit and must not behave like one. That is the first and simplest of the rules of land warfare and it can never be recalled often enough. In contemporary conflicts, however, non-compliance with that rule has consistently led—and still does—to the greatest human suffering, particularly in non-international armed conflicts.

We are all too aware how great the temptation is for all those who have power to abuse it. Clearly, a gun does not confer governing powers but it does give power and the temptation to abuse it. A soldier's education and training in IHL are therefore of vital importance. This point will be discussed further below.

A soldier's first duty is to 'respect and protect' civilians and civilian property. Secondly, the individual soldier is also under a similar obligation towards all those *hors de combat*—that is, soldiers who are wounded or sick and therefore no longer able to take part in the hostilities—as well as towards those who decide to surrender and clearly signal their intention to do so. Thirdly, soldiers are subject to certain restrictions with regard to enemy combatants.

---

[1] See Ch 6.

B. Respect for and protection of civilians and civilian property

(i) *The humanitarian face of the principle of military necessity*

In the Code that he drafted during the American Civil War[2] at the request of President Abraham Lincoln, Francis Lieber placed particularly strong emphasis on the principle of military necessity. This principle may appear at first sight to be non-humanitarian since it seems to allow everything that is necessary to win wars. The humanitarian counterpart of this principle is, however, that nothing is allowed that is not *justified* by military necessity. In other words, gratuitous violence and subjecting civilians to abuse are strictly prohibited. War is no justification for rape or other kinds of sexual abuse, violations of the physical or moral integrity of people held at gunpoint, pillaging, theft, harassment, constraints, or threats.

It must be pointed out that such acts, which are crimes in peacetime, are crimes in wartime as well. Lieber went as far as advocating the death penalty for some of these crimes.[3] Concern not to let such crimes go unpunished led to the introduction of the notion of war crimes for serious breaches of IHL, along with an obligation to punish those crimes at the national level. The principle of universal jurisdiction together with creation of the ad hoc international courts and the International Criminal Court are designed to ensure individual accountability for war crimes. It should be noted, however, that none of the international mechanisms replace the role of national courts. Instead these mechanisms complement national courts by coming into operation where national authorities are unwilling or unable to prosecute those accused of war crimes.[4] It should also be stressed that the death penalty is not a permissible sentence in any of the international courts.

(ii) *The principle of humanity and the obligation to 'protect' civilians*

IHL standards not only prohibit all hostile acts deliberately directed against civilians, they also apply to the indirect effects of hostilities on civilians. For example, where there is a military necessity for troops to occupy villages or densely populated territories, the basic necessities of the civilian population such as access to drinking water and to all other commodities essential to survival must be properly assessed and taken into account by combatants.[5] This obligation may rule out the

---

[2] *Instructions for Government of Armies in the United States in the Field*, prepared by Francis Lieber, promulgated as General Orders No 100 by President Lincoln, 24 April 1863 ('the Lieber Code').

[3] See in particular Lieber Code, Arts 44, 47.

[4] On war crimes, see the Chapter by Theodor Meron in this volume, 'Customary Humanitarian Law Today: From the Academy to the Court Room'. For an introduction to the work of the ICC see W. Schabas, *An Introduction to the International Criminal Court* (4th edn, Cambridge: Cambridge University Press, 2011).

[5] Geneva Convention IV, Art 55(1); Additional Protocol I, Art 69(1).

use of certain weapons such as anti-personnel mines for those states that have not accepted their total ban.

A further obligation demands that soldiers demonstrate respect and facilitate relief actions for populations or groups of people that need them.[6] No attacks are permitted on such actions, and no goods may be taken from them. Respect must be shown for the personnel accompanying relief efforts. Those involved in combat are also required to facilitate full access to relief for the vulnerable people for whom it is intended.

IHL prohibits forced displacement,[7] and every possible effort should be made to avoid creating conditions that render displacement unavoidable. In some extreme cases, if civilians are caught in the midst of fighting and military necessity urgently requires it, the population will move out of the area of its own accord or orders may be given for people to be displaced.[8] In both cases, the population being displaced must be given as much protection and support as possible.[9]

Of course, such behaviour requires thorough training and remains an ideal that is not easily attainable, especially if soldiers face a hostile environment or if enemy combatants have mingled with the population and soldiers are in constant fear of direct attack. In the latter case and in situations where civilians occasionally take part in hostilities, the immunity of their hiding places is no longer absolute. The following section will provide more detail on what attitude should be adopted by combatants facing such situations.[10] At this point, however, it should be noted that soldiers in situations of stress, however well trained, require sound and ongoing supervision.

(iii) *The principle of distinction*

Sparing civilians and civilian property requires the ability to recognize and distinguish them from military objectives. The principle of distinction is thus at the very heart of IHL, not as an ultimate aim but as a vital means of sparing civilians. As far as soldiers are concerned, this means they must recognize the distinction between combatants and civilians and grant civilians the protection required by IHL.

Even when IHL only addressed armed conflict between states, the question arose as to whether the rules should apply to armed elements not directly connected with a state's armed forces. There was a risk that this would make the system less rigorous; at the same time, not including such elements would result in a lack of legal

---

[6] Geneva Convention IV, Art 23; Additional Protocol I, Art 70.

[7] Geneva Convention IV, Art 49; Additional Protocol II, Art 17. See also J.-M. Henckaerts and L. Doswald-Beck, *Customary International Humanitarian Law*, vol 1 (Cambridge: Cambridge University Press, 2005) ('Customary Law Study'), Rule 129.

[8] Customary Law Study, Rule 129.   [9] Customary Law Study, Rules 131, 132, 133.

[10] See 2(B)(viii) below. See also the Chapter by Nils Melzer in this volume, 'The Principle of Distinction between Civilians and Combatants'.

control. In the end, states deemed it preferable to integrate armed elements not directly associated with a state's armed forces into the system, while at the same time establishing strict conditions for their integration.

First, those armed elements must be in a relation of dependence with the government. Additionally, they must bear a distinctive sign, carry their weapons openly when fighting, be organized in a hierarchical structure, and comply with IHL.[11] At this juncture, the precise meaning of these conditions will not be elaborated.[12] However, it should be stressed that the importance of preserving the principle of distinction by including the obligations to bear a distinctive sign and to carry weapons openly in combat remains of crucial importance.

The same principle of distinction was at the heart of the arduous negotiations surrounding the drafting of the Additional Protocols of 1977 to the Geneva Conventions. Newly independent states or those still fighting for their independence were convinced that they would have no chance of defeating colonial or ex-colonial powers if they complied consistently with the principle of distinction by permanently identifying themselves as combatants by wearing a uniform or bearing distinctive signs.[13] When faced with organized armies with far superior equipment, those new states considered that they had no choice other than to resort to the guerrilla technique of mingling with the population 'like fish in water', to use the expression attributed to Mao-Tse Tung.[14]

The universal vocation of IHL had to be safeguarded without emptying the law of its substance. As it happened, these goals were contradictory and virtually impossible to implement. To turn down the insistent request of most states allowing for guerilla techniques would be tantamount to making IHL a parlour game for the exclusive club of Western states. On the other hand, to accept it amounted to doing away with the principle of distinction. The compromise that was finally reached with considerable effort[15] ensured that reluctant states were kept 'on board' by accepting the principle of guerrilla warfare, that is, the right to merge into the civilian population between combat phases. But the essential features of the principle of distinction were nonetheless retained by requiring combatants to carry their weapons openly when engaging directly in hostilities.[16]

What does this actually mean for foot soldiers? Ruse and camouflage, which are among the most accepted and widely used methods of warfare, are not outlawed.

[11] Geneva Convention III, Art 4; Additional Protocol I, Art 44(3); Customary Law Study, Rule 106.

[12] See Ch 12.

[13] See eg Customary Law Study, Practice Relating to Rule 106. Conditions for Prisoner of War Status.

[14] Mao Tse-Tung, 'The Political Problems of Guerrilla Warfare', in *On Guerrilla Warfare*, first published 1937, trans Samuel B. Griffith II (Champaign: First Illinois Paperback, 2000).

[15] See Commentary AP I and II, paras 1684ff; M. Bothe, K.J. Partsch, and W.A. Solf, *New Rules for Victims of Armed Conflicts* (The Hague: Nijhoff, 1982), 241ff.

[16] See Additional Protocol I, Art 44(3).

However, what is prohibited is the act of pretending, when in sight of the enemy, to have protected status in order to commit an act of hostility. Such behaviour would render protection of civilians (or those who are *hors de combat*) impossible to achieve. How could a soldier be asked to show the full respect due to a wounded person or an enemy combatant who surrenders or, indeed, a civilian if there is every reason to doubt that their apparent status is bona fide? This principle of distinction is elaborated in specific provisions of IHL discussed later in this Chapter.[17]

(iv) *Prohibition of denial of quarter or threats to deny quarter*

The prohibition on denial of quarter is set out in Additional Protocol I, and can also be included in the general framework of the principle of distinction. Article 40 of Additional Protocol I provides that '[i]t is prohibited to order that there shall be no survivors, to threaten an adversary therewith or to conduct hostilities on this basis'. Such actions would amount to killing the wounded and those who surrender or, in the case of a town or another place under siege, not sparing captured civilians. These or similar actions would also be contrary to other rules of IHL and would be the very negation of the principle of distinction.

In fact, Article 40 includes a prohibition to 'threaten' such behaviour as a means of putting pressure on the adversary, even when there is no intention to follow through in a concrete manner. Threatening to behave contrary to IHL is not included in the category of acceptable war ruses. Moreover, it should be noted that offering to give fair treatment to enemy combatants who might surrender (rather than threatening to execute them) improves the chances of obtaining their acceptance of defeat. A link can also be established to the prohibition of 'threats of violence the principal purpose of which is to spread terror among the civilian population'.[18]

(v) *Evacuation of besieged areas*

The rules on siege have changed radically over time. The Lieber Code reflected the notion that the population of the belligerent state has a degree of 'guilt'. The Code stated that it is 'lawful to starve the hostile belligerent, armed or unarmed, so that it leads to the speedier subjection of the enemy'.[19] It might therefore be thought that the Code distinguishes between civilians and soldiers and only includes the latter in the category of 'belligerent'. The Code also noted that 'the principle has been more and more acknowledged that the unarmed citizen is to be spared in person, property, and honor', but added 'as much as the exigencies of war will admit'.[20] As far as blockades were concerned, Lieber considered that those 'exigencies' prevent the provision of supplies to civilians. He went even further, saying: 'When a commander of a besieged place expels the non-combatants, in order to lessen the number of

---

[17] See 2(B)(iv)–(vii) below.   [18] See Additional Protocol I, Art 51(2).
[19] Lieber Code, Art 17.   [20] Lieber Code, Art 22.

those who consume his stock of provisions, it is lawful, though an extreme measure, to drive them back, so as to hasten on the surrender'.[21]

The Fourth Geneva Convention now takes the opposite position, but without totally contradicting the Lieber Code. GCIV requires the parties to the conflict to 'endeavour to conclude local agreements for the removal from besieged or encircled areas of wounded, sick, infirm, and aged persons, children and maternity cases'.[22] '[E]ndeavour to conclude' is not a particularly demanding requirement. It may nonetheless be suggested that the normative changes observed with regard to relief actions carried out for the civilian population, and the modifications applied to blockades, indicate an evolution in thinking.

Lieber's argument, namely that civilians, by drawing on the stocks of food, speed up shortages and hence compromise the forces who must provide for them, was not reflected in the Protocol with regard to relief actions and should therefore no longer be considered as valid. Similarly, with regard to evacuation, the conclusion can be drawn that the wounded and civilians must be removed from a besieged area as far as possible. The language 'endeavour to' from the Protocol must be interpreted as meaning, on the one hand, that the parties to the conflict must take initiatives and, on the other hand, that they must in principle accept proposals that are made to them in good faith. A humanitarian organization may also take the initiative of making such proposals, given that its role in carrying out an evacuation is often useful, if not indispensable. In practice, the ICRC has taken such initiatives and has carried out evacuations, with the agreement of all interested parties.

(vi) *Prohibition on using human shields*

In no case may soldiers attempt to protect themselves or to protect property by using civilians as human shields.[23] This term describes any situation in which civilians are deliberately placed around a military target to ward off attack by the enemy and sometimes to reduce military casualties, for example by tying civilians to armoured vehicles or by detaining groups of civilians near or within the target area. The prohibition on the use of human shields is thus also covered by the principle of distinction. The appropriate military response to such abuse is a delicate matter, which we will examine below.[24]

(vii) *Prohibition of perfidy*

'Acts inviting the confidence of an adversary to lead him to believe that he is entitled to, or is obliged to accord, protection under the rules of international law

---

[21] Lieber Code, Art 18.   [22] Geneva Convention IV, Art 17.
[23] Customary Law Study, Rule 97.   [24] See 2(B)(ix) below.

applicable in armed conflict, with intent to betray that confidence, shall constitute perfidy'.[25] That definition, from Additional Protocol I, gives rise to a certain ambiguity because of the way in which the relevant Article is constructed. Before giving this definition, the Article states that it is 'prohibited to kill, injure or capture an adversary by resort to perfidy'. The ICRC Commentary makes clear that, while Article 37 is concerned only with a particular category of acts of perfidy, it does not implicitly authorize acts of perfidy in other circumstances.[26] The Article's final paragraph gives further content to the notion of perfidy by pointing out that ordinary 'ruses of war are not prohibited [...] because they do not invite the confidence of an adversary with respect to protection' under international law, and therefore do not violate that law.

Article 37 of Additional Protocol I is often linked with the Article condemning the abusive use of protective emblems.[27] It must nonetheless be pointed out at this juncture that the most frequent form of deceit is simply that of feigning to be a civilian by violating the rule of 'carrying arms openly'.[28] That takes us straight to the domain of terrorism, most notably, suicide attacks. Another possible violation of Article 37 would be to feign surrender or being wounded in order to use this deception to then injure or capture those accepting the surrender or against those providing relief for the wounded.

In fact, given the heading of the Article and its content, acts carried out with the intention of killing, wounding, or capturing an adversary have fairly generally been assimilated with the elements constituting perfidy.[29] What must be borne in mind is that the drafters have clearly demonstrated that perfidy that is committed with the aim of killing, wounding, or capturing is classified as a war crime.[30]

As Article 37 of Additional Protocol I makes clear, a distinction must nonetheless be made between perfidy and ruses of war. Camouflage, the dissemination of misinformation, the use of decoys, and other similar practices are not prohibited since they do not fall within the definition of perfidy. The perpetrators of such ruses, if they are captured, may therefore not be punished in respect of those acts.

---

[25] Additional Protocol I, Art 37 gives the following examples of perfidy: (a) the feigning of an intent to negotiate under a flag of truce or of a surrender; (b) the feigning of an incapacitation by wounds or sickness; (c) the feigning of civilian, non-combatant status; and (d) the feigning of protected status by the use of signs, emblems, or uniforms of the United Nations or of neutral or other states not parties to the conflict.

[26] Commentary GC IV on Art 37, [1490]–[1492].

[27] See 2(C)(iii), (iv), (v) below.   [28] See 2(B)(iii) above.

[29] Commentary GC IV on Art 37, [1493].

[30] See further, Customary Law Study, Rule 65; *Rome Statute of the International Criminal Court* ('Rome Statute'), Art 8(2)(b)(ix) which contains the phrase 'killing or wounding treacherously'.

(viii) *The principles of precaution and proportionality*

The principle of distinction inherently requires respect for two further principles: those of precaution and proportionality.[31] These principles must first and foremost be respected at the level of the military command, in the choice of military objectives and the means to be used to achieve them.[32] But they must also be borne constantly in mind by soldiers engaged in an operation in accordance with the general obligation to endeavour to ensure respect for and protection of the civilian population.

As far as proportionality is concerned, some states have considered that respect for this principle was to be gauged in relation to the attack as a whole.[33] Nonetheless, such a conclusion does not permit soldiers to dispense with evaluating different stages of an operation from the perspective of proportionality. The death of a hundred children in an attack on a school where two enemy soldiers were said to have taken refuge cannot be 'excused' by weighing those deaths against the overall outcome of a large-scale attack. The execution of orders given in a particular situation must, moreover, be aligned with the development of that situation. For example, if orders were given to destroy a building when it was presumed to be empty and civilians or wounded soldiers in the meantime have taken refuge there, the soldier who has been given the order to destroy must adapt his or her behaviour to the new situation.

Respect for the principles of precaution and proportionality also present particularly thorny problems in particular circumstances, discussed in the following two sections.

(ix) *Searching for guerrilla fighters and civilians who have taken part in the hostilities*

As we saw above, the issue of guerrilla warfare has been divisive. As soon as guerrilla tactics are accepted as a means of warfare, the search for guerrilla fighters in civilian areas cannot be ruled out. However, as actions intended to locate guerrilla fighters can create considerable tension between those subjected to such searches and those who carry them out, they must be conducted in full compliance with the principle of precaution. In other words, everything possible must be done to spare civilians. The integrity, dignity, and property of civilians must be respected in all circumstances. It is also vital in such circumstances to bear in mind the prohibition of collective punishment.

---

[31] See Customary Law Study, Rules 14–21. See also Ch 11.
[32] See 2(C) and 3(E) below.
[33] See Commentary AP I and II, paras 2204ff, in particular para 2217, note 15.

A similar situation arises when there is a search for civilians who have participated directly in the hostilities. Such individuals lose their immunity only during such direct participation, provided that it is occasional. This particularly contentious matter is dealt with in other Chapters.[34] However, what we wish to focus on here is the problem posed by the actual search for those civilians who have participated directly in the hostilities. Direct participation in hostilities by civilians is a crime and those who have committed such offences must be apprehended. As they are not combatants, the means to be used in this respect stem from 'law enforcement' rules, which present more rigorous restrictions than those found in IHL, particularly as concerns the right to shoot without warning and the admissibility of collateral damage.

It would be worth reviewing questions related to the use of force during searches for combatants and criminals. This issue is particularly complex in situations involving serious organized crime or where acts connected with organized crime are committed alongside the conflict. The difference in approach between law enforcement and the law of armed conflict is extremely difficult to put into practice in the rules of engagement of military units.

(x) *Response to the use of human shields*

Previous sections have clarified that civilians may not be used as human shields. Clearly, acts committed by guerrilla fighters from a location where civilians are sheltering would violate humanitarian norms, as would any use of civilians for protection or to discourage the adversary from attacking property constituting a military target. Nonetheless, the crime of using human shields is not an excuse for committing other crimes. Given the circumstances, the obligation of doing everything possible to spare civilians and to avoid collateral damage prevails. That requirement concurs with the prohibition on making civilians the target of reprisals.

C. Respect for and protection of other non-combatants

As far as individuals are concerned, the demarcation line that must be clearly drawn for combatants separates those fighting from everyone else. The underlying philosophy is still that formulated by Jean-Jacques Rousseau in a frequently quoted passage: 'War is a relation, not between man and man, but between State and State, in which individuals are enemies only accidentally, not as men, nor even as citizens, but as soldiers'. As soon as they lay down their arms, they 'become once more merely men, whose life no one has any right to take'.[35] This is the basis on which IHL was founded, its initial objective being to protect wounded soldiers.[36]

---

[34] See Chs 12, 23, and 24.

[35] Jean-Jacques Rousseau, *The Social Contract*, first published 1762, trans G.D.H. Cole (New York: Cosimo Classics, 2008), Book I, Ch IV, 19–20.

[36] See H. Dunant, *A Memory of Solferino*, first published 1862 (ICRC, 1986).

(i) *Respect for and protection of the wounded and sick*

Wounded soldiers on the battlefield were the first victims addressed by IHL. The definition given today in Additional Protocol I of 1977 is broader.[37] It deals not merely with wounded soldiers but with all wounded persons—which is important because conflicts no longer take place between two armies on a well-defined battlefield—and not merely with the wounded or sick *stricto sensu* but with all those who are particularly vulnerable and who need immediate care, such as the infirm and maternity cases.

However, a constitutive element is added to the definition, which requires that wounded and sick people only be considered and treated as such if they refrain from all acts of hostility. A wounded soldier who continued using his weapon would therefore not be included and would not enjoy the immunity granted to those in that category. This distinction has been implicit since the beginnings of IHL although it is now mentioned explicitly. Moreover, anyone who pretends to be wounded or sick so that he or she can commit a hostile act against persons providing relief commits an act of perfidy.[38]

The foot soldier's obligation towards the wounded or sick, as defined, is first to show respect for such persons, which means not causing them harm. Soldiers may obviously take up weapons but may not commit harmful acts against wounded or sick persons. In the heat of battle, this obligation of abstention must be stressed. As soon as possible, however, more must be done, which is why IHL also refers to protection and humane treatment. Wounded people must be taken into care to avoid others abusing them (the concept of protection); they must be given first aid and passed on to the medical services. The wounded or sick are thus dealt with humanely and without discrimination of any kind.[39] That means that the wounded must be dealt with and their evacuation must be organized solely on the basis of medical criteria, regardless of whether they are members of the same army or of the enemy army.

It is not always easy to comply with these requirements, particularly in situations of intense fighting, when soldiers risk their lives, have seen some of their comrades being killed or wounded, and are under tremendous pressure. But these obligations are clearly stipulated and it is therefore vital for soldiers to receive clear instructions and for commanders to issue orders consistent with IHL in relation to these matters.[40]

(ii) *Respect for and protection of medical personnel, vehicles, and units*

For the obligation to respect and protect the wounded and sick to play an effective role, it is important for the wounded and sick to be taken care of swiftly by medical

---

[37] Additional Protocol I, Art 8(a).   [38] See 2(B)(vii) above.
[39] Additional Protocol I, Art 9(1).   [40] See further Customary Law Study, Ch 34.

personnel, transported by ambulance or other medical vehicles (including transport by water or air if necessary) and given hospital treatment. This explains the immunity granted to medical personnel, vehicles and units, naturally subject to the condition that such individuals in no way take part in the hostilities. However, for medical personnel and property to be protected effectively, they must be easy to identify.

(iii) *The choice and meaning of the distinctive emblem*

The initial emblem chosen under IHL to identify protected people and goods was a red cross on a white background. It is the reverse image of the Swiss flag and was chosen as a compliment to Switzerland, the host state of the diplomatic Conferences which elaborated, adopted and revised the Geneva Conventions. The choice of this emblem was not very fortunate in that some considered the cross as a Christian symbol. This did not reflect the thinking behind an emblem that would be widely viewed as being neutral and universal. Other emblems were subsequently introduced to resolve that misunderstanding but the aim remained to avoid confusion and prevent any action that may weaken the protection given to the wounded and sick.

This Chapter will not discuss this matter in further detail although it should be noted that the subject has been highly emotive and political and led to a number of controversies.[41] The current solution is to recognize three emblems that states may adopt as they choose: the red cross, the red crescent, and the red crystal, each on a white background.[42] Medical personnel and medical vehicles and units entitled to protection may display the emblem chosen by their state—there may only be one emblem per state—as a means of identifying protected persons or property. For the sake of completeness, we should add that because visual means of identification may in some cases be insufficient, the possibility of using other visual, acoustic, or electronic signals, particularly in order to identify medical aircraft or ships, was introduced in a technical annex when the Additional Protocols of 1977 were adopted. However, this is of particular concern for anti-aircraft defence and maritime warfare and is therefore of little relevance to land forces.

Soldiers are required to show respect for persons and property bearing one of the above-mentioned emblems.[43] This includes not targeting them and ensuring as far

---

[41] For an updated history of the question, see F. Bugnion, *Red Cross, Red Crescent and Red Crystal* (Geneva: ICRC, 2007).

[42] It is worth noting the customary evolution that occurred on this subject. The red crescent and the red lion-and-sun (formerly used only by Iran, which renounced it in favour of the red crescent) are only tolerated under Geneva Convention I, Art 38, for countries which already use them. This customary evolution was then recognized by states in 2005 when they introduced the possibility of using the red crystal, for states refusing either the cross or the crescent, in a new Protocol (Additional Protocol III to the Geneva Conventions).

[43] Customary Law Study, Rule 30.

as possible that such persons and property are able to fulfil their medical function. It should be pointed out, however, that while the emblem makes it easier to identify a protected person or property, this person or property is protected independently of the emblem. For example, a hospital may not be attacked under the pretext that it was not marked by a red cross. Conversely, a red cross wrongly placed on a military target does not confer immunity on it.

Furthermore, protection granted to people and property entitled, from the out-set, to be identified by a protective emblem is not unconditional and may be questioned if the person or the property no longer meets the initial conditions. That would be the case, for example, if a hospital had been converted into barracks or a munitions store, or if a medical officer used his protection to commit acts of sabotage or to spy.

The party associated with the goods and persons that are protected and identified by one of the recognized emblems is thus responsible, first, for complying strictly with the rule and, secondly, for immediately putting a stop to any abuse committed unwittingly by soldiers or any other persons connected with that party. This is essential because the entire system is based on good faith. If abuse is committed on a large scale or is repeated regularly, all property and persons entitled to protection suffer. A soldier will clearly be reluctant to spare ambulances if they are used regularly to launch surprise attacks.

The priority is therefore to prohibit and to condemn manifest and deliberate abuse. It is, however, not always easy to establish whether abuse has been committed and even when proof of it has been provided, the reaction must be proportionate.

(iv) *Identifying, reacting to, and combating abuses of the distinctive emblem*

As IHL authorizes medical personnel to carry weapons, the use of those weapons may lead to confusion. The principal reason why those who drafted the Geneva Conventions authorized medical personnel to carry weapons was to help ensure that wounded persons were protected against abuse that might be committed against them, for example, as they were being transported to a hospital for medical care. Armed conflicts are frequently accompanied by disturbances and inadequate law-enforcement, making banditry and pillaging more likely. The weapons carried by medical personnel are not intended to be used to stop the advance of enemy troops. In particular, they are not to be used to prevent enemy troops from occupying a hospital. Nonetheless, such situations are not without ambiguity, especially if the first soldiers to enter a hospital vent their anger against the wounded and their property. In such cases, the use of weapons by medical personnel would be legitimate.

Even in the case of abuse, the reaction must be proportionate. Obviously, if a medical soldier deliberately shoots at a soldier from the opposing party, the latter cannot be expected not to retaliate, with the risk of killing the person at fault. The solution must be more refined, however, if shots are fired from a hospital or from a medical convoy or if the medical areas are not free, as they should be, from activities intended to support the war effort. A medical facility being used in this way loses its absolute protection, but the approach in those cases is not all or nothing. The principles of precaution and proportionality then assume their full meaning and an attempt must be made to find a solution which safeguards the integrity of the protected persons as far as possible, particularly if they have absolutely nothing to do with the abusive use of the protected property. It is important for abuse to be stopped without delay and for those who have committed it to be punished. To that end, IHL provides for a scale of measures to combat such abuse.

The use of the red cross (red crescent or red crystal) is regulated even during peacetime. The idea behind this is that the emblem must be safeguarded and that obvious misuse would tarnish its image and jeopardize respect for it in wartime. As the emblem is one of the best known in the world, the temptation to misuse it is great and there are countless examples of misuse, some of limited consequence, such as a doctor using the emblem to identify his surgery or a pharmacist using it to identify his chemist's shop, while others are far more serious. The Geneva Conventions require states to put a stop to such uses.[44] Many have adopted national laws, even if cases of abuse are generally settled amicably, with those perpetrating the violation agreeing to abandon a practice they did not know was unlawful.

Misuse of the emblem in wartime is obviously more serious because, as has already been pointed out, it weakens the entire system of protection, which is based on trust. However, IHL makes another distinction between misuse for the purpose of committing an act of active hostility, implying the use of force, and other misuses. Evidently, both kinds of misuse must be stopped, but states insisted on emphasizing the particular seriousness of the former misuses, which constitute cases of perfidy[45] and are qualified as war crimes. With regard to the latter misuses, an appeal was simply made to the parties to stop such misuse. Specific measures—penal, disciplinary, or administrative—must be taken at the national level in order to deal with perpetrators of abuse.

The seriousness of all misuse should be emphasized, even if it does not go hand in hand with acts of hostility or is justified by a good cause. One famous example of this type of misuse was the 2008 mission to rescue Ingrid Betancourt and other hostages, in which a red cross symbol was misused to deceive their captors.[46] Even when dealing with belligerents who commit war crimes such as taking hostages, practices that involve the misuse of the emblem cannot be tolerated because they jeopardize all humanitarian activity carried out under the banner of a protective

---

[44] Customary Law Study, Rule 59.   [45] See 2(B)(vii) above.

[46] 'Betancourt rescuers "misused Red Cross and broke Geneva Convention"', *The Telegraph* (17 July 2008).

emblem. The ICRC immediately complained about this misuse of the emblem and the Colombian Government finally apologized.

Medical personnel and goods are not immune from being seized. If a hospital is in a territory over which an enemy army gains control, the medical personnel at the hospital must be treated with respect, as must the wounded and sick in the hospital. It is vital for foot soldiers to be aware of this rule in both international and non-international armed conflicts. Medical personnel must therefore initially be authorized to continue their work and be given the means of doing so, as the logical consequence of respecting and protecting the wounded and sick who are dependent on these individuals and of treating them humanely.

After such a seizure of a hospital, top-level military authorities must decide what course of action to take. In international armed conflicts, permanent medical personnel—that is, those individuals appointed to a medical mission for the entire duration of the conflict—must be repatriated as a matter of principle, except for a temporary period if the medical services are overburdened and their support is indispensable to deal with the increased number of wounded and sick people.[47] Temporary medical personnel who may be assigned to military tasks during the armed conflict become prisoners of war and their medical skills may be used during their captivity.[48] During non-international armed conflicts, such distinctions are not made and there is no obligation to repatriate captive medical personnel. Nonetheless, captive medical personnel cannot be punished simply for having carried out medical activities for the enemy.[49]

This section has explained that where a hospital comes under the control of the enemy, the new controlling party bears responsibility for patients in the hospital. Medical vehicles may also be intercepted and requisitioned but on the explicit condition that this is not detrimental to the wounded or sick in them.[50]

(v) *Respect for persons and property protected by other emblems*

IHL recognizes certain other people and property as being worthy of benefiting from special protection, either because of their intrinsic value or because of their function. In order to avoid confusion and to clearly retain the 'medical' identity of those already protected, it was not considered desirable to extend the protection afforded by the red cross, red crescent, and red crystal. Other emblems were therefore designed and incorporated into IHL treaties. These emblems are intended to be used to mark areas under special protection, cultural property, civil protection organizations, and dangerous installations (dams, dykes, or nuclear power stations).[51]

---

[47] See Geneva Convention I, Art 28.   [48] See Geneva Convention I, Art 29.
[49] See Additional Protocol II, Art 10.   [50] See Geneva Convention I, Art 35.
[51] The distinctive emblem for the protection of cultural property is described in Art 16 of the Hague Convention for the Protection of Cultural Property in the Event of Armed Conflict (1954) and the other emblems mentioned above are described in Additional Protocol I, Annex I.

These additional emblems make it possible to identify people and property that are entitled to special protection and that, first and foremost, must be spared in case of attack. It is therefore important for soldiers to be familiar with these emblems as well. IHL goes further by also referring to the flag of truce and by prohibiting misuse during armed conflict of all 'internationally recognized protective emblems, signs or signals',[52] although an exhaustive list of such emblems is not given.

Like medical personnel, people involved in civil defence tasks may also be armed due to the nature of some of the tasks required of them, such as 'emergency assistance in the restoration and maintenance of order in distressed areas' and 'assistance in the preservation of objects essential for survival'.[53] The personnel concerned are not, however, to use their weapons to resist an enemy advance. Again, this may create ambiguity in some circumstances. It is the duty of soldiers, and particularly unit commanders, properly and calmly to assess the situation in such cases.

D. The attitude of combatants towards enemy combatants

The protection of non-combatants is the main aim of IHL. Soldiers enter into the category of non-combatant as soon as they are wounded or taken prisoner. However, some humanitarian norms are of direct relevance to able-bodied soldiers as well.

(i) *Restriction on the use of certain weapons or projectiles*

IHL prohibits the use of means and methods of warfare that are of a nature to cause superfluous injury or unnecessary suffering.[54] 'Unnecessary suffering' has been defined by the International Court of Justice as 'harm greater than that unavoidable to achieve legitimate military objectives'.[55] While responsibility for the choice and distribution of weaponry lies with the high command,[56] at this juncture it is sufficient to note that soldiers are immediately implicated if they modify a projectile in violation of the principle. For example, the use of dum-dum bullets, which are designed to expand on impact, will invariably cause injury and suffering greater than that required to achieve the legitimate military objective of placing enemy combatants *hors de combat*.

---

[52] Additional Protocol I, Art 38.   [53] Additional Protocol I, Art 61(a)(xi), (xiv).

[54] Customary Law Study, Rule 70.

[55] *Legality of the Threat or Use of Nuclear Weapons*, Advisory Opinion [1996] ICJ Rep 226, 257. An attempt to give objective criteria to what should be considered weapons causing superfluous injury or unnecessary suffering has been undertaken by a group of medical and legal experts. The result was published by the ICRC: R.B. Coupland (ed), *The SIrUS Project* (Geneva: ICRC, 1997). Although the proposed criteria give useful indications, they remain contested and their validity has not been formally recognized by states. For further discussion of this issue, see the Chapter by Steven Haines in this volume.

[56] See 4(C) below.

(ii) *Is there a 'right to kill'?*

It has often been asked whether soldiers have a 'right to kill'. The answer varies. The law of war clearly does not set restrictions on the use of force that are as severe as those imposed on a police officer in an operation against criminals. A soldier who shoots an enemy from a distance will not be accused of having killed rather than wounded the adversary. However, the prohibition of the use of poison is a clear indication that people should not be killed at all costs during armed conflict. Moreover, IHL does not permit a soldier to kill an enemy who is at his mercy if the enemy can instead be taken captive without risk. An example of such a case would be a situation where an armed group found itself in the presence of an enemy soldier who was asleep and could therefore be apprehended with minimal risk.

Soldiers are also under an obligation to spare an enemy who shows an intention to surrender.[57] Similar to a situation involving the wounded, soldiers must take those captured to a place of safety to the rear of the fighting.[58]

Restrictions regarding the use of force and the repulsion retained in IHL for what would amount to cold-blooded murder is clearly apparent in Article 41 of Additional Protocol I.[59] That provision envisages an advance commando who captures an enemy soldier but is unable to take him or her to a safe place or to keep the individual under control. In such a case, the temptation to resort to summary execution may be significant, but IHL is unequivocal in the obligation to release the soldiers and even to provide feasible precautions for their safety.

(iii) *Attitude to child soldiers*

As we shall see, the recruitment of child soldiers is forbidden.[60] A question that might be raised is whether soldiers must adopt a particular approach if they find themselves face to face with child soldiers. IHL does not distinguish between adult and child soldiers when it comes to retaliation in the face of a direct threat. As is the case for all protected persons, protection ceases as soon as the person commits a direct act of hostility. Conversely, as soon as a child is disarmed and taken captive, he or she must be treated as a child.

(iv) *The excuse of 'superior orders'*

Being ordered by a superior officer to violate IHL does not absolve the person who commits the violation of responsibility for the action. Nonetheless, an assessment must be made, from the penal point of view, of the ability of the person to understand that the action taken was a violation, the seriousness of the act, and the degree of pressure to which he or she was subjected. Account should be duly taken of all such factors in cases, for example, involving very young or uneducated

---

[57] Customary Law Study, Rule 46.　　[58] Geneva Convention III, Art 7.
[59] See Commentary AP I and II, paras 1625ff.　　[60] See 3(F) below.

soldiers who were compelled under threat of death to kill a civilian or an enemy soldier.[61]

3 Principles and Rules of IHL that Apply to Commanders

A. Responsibility of the commander for violations committed by subordinates

Military commanders have varying degrees of responsibility for acts committed by soldiers under their command. Commanders naturally have a major responsibility not only for actions they themselves take which amount to violations of humanitarian standards but also if they issue orders to others to commit such acts. A commander could also be sentenced as an accomplice if he or she encouraged such violations or knowingly allowed them to be committed or might reasonably have known they were going on. Lastly, even if breach is not a criminal offence, the commander also has some responsibility to train subordinates in their obligations under IHL.[62]

B. Responsibility for planning and carrying out an attack

Commanders are directly responsible for complying with humanitarian law standards when planning and preparing attacks. In particular, they are required to comply strictly with the restriction under those provisions regarding military objectives as well as with the principles of precaution and proportionality.

(i) *The principle of precaution*

Before launching an attack, operations must be assessed thoroughly so as to spare civilians as far as possible. First and foremost, a commander must make sure that a chosen target is actually a military target. If this is determined to be the case, commanders must then assess the risks to the civilian population and civilian property

---

[61] See eg L. Green, *Superior Orders in National and International Law* (Leiden: Sijthoff, 1976) and 'Superior Orders and Command Responsibility', 175 *Military Law Review* (2005) 309–84.
[62] See Additional Protocol I, Arts 86(2), 87.

caused by the attack, with special attention to people and property entitled under IHL to enhanced protection. Such risks must be reduced as far as possible by the choice of means, most notably by using weapons that are as accurate as possible, as well as the time chosen for the attack. For example, a bridge or a railway station which fulfil the criteria for military objectives are preferably attacked at a time when no or few civilians are present. When other military objectives achieve an equivalent benefit but cause less damage to civilians, these are to be given preference. This would be the case, for example, where military rail traffic could be brought to a standstill by destroying a rail track rather than by destroying a railway station.[63] As far as possible, the civilian population must also be warned so that they can take shelter.[64]

(ii) *The principle of proportionality*

If the risk of incidental damage to civilians caused by an attack is out of proportion with the direct and tangible military advantage to be achieved, such an attack is not to be carried out.[65] The assessment of the proportionality between these very different elements is undoubtedly complex but that should not be a pretext for avoiding a serious assessment, particularly as the disproportion is sometimes blatant.

C. Responsibility for the methods of warfare and choice of weapons

The commander bears chief responsibility if orders are given to use methods (such as systematically blocking the delivery of relief supplies so as to starve the civilian population or the decision to deny quarter) or means (particularly the use of arms contrary to the prohibitions or restrictions governing them) that are prohibited by IHL.

D. Prohibition of reprisals

Humanitarian norms strictly forbid reprisals against protected persons and objects.[66] The desire for vengeance which may be felt in respect of members of enemy forces who have committed atrocities is no excuse for subjecting protected persons to violence. This is true in all armed conflicts, even if the expression 'reprisals' is not used in non-international armed conflicts. The aim of the law is to avoid the onset of a

---

[63] See Additional Protocol I, Art 57(3); Customary Law Study, Rule 21.
[64] See Additional Protocol I, Art 57(2); Customary Law Study, Rule 20.
[65] See Additional Protocol I, Arts 51(5)(b), 57(2)(a)(iii); Customary Law Study, Rule 14.
[66] See Geneva Convention I, Art 46; Geneva Convention II, Art 47; Geneva Convention III, Art 13; Geneva Convention IV, Art 33; Additional Protocol I, Arts 53, 54(4), 55(2), 56(4).

spiral of intensifying hatred and violence such as has unfortunately been seen all too often. Commanding officers have particularly great responsibility in this respect, not only in terms of avoiding becoming involved in such practices themselves but also in terms of maintaining control over their troops.

E. Prohibition of taking hostages and of collective punishments

The practice of taking civilians hostage and sometimes making them pay for the acts of hostility committed by enemy troops or rebels has been widespread in various circumstances and was particularly rife during World War II.[67] Such acts are strictly prohibited by IHL in all categories of armed conflict.[68] Collective punishments are also prohibited at all times and in all places, including for detainees, who should not be made to pay for unlawful acts committed by their fellow detainees. Lastly, escape does not constitute a criminal offence. It may certainly be prevented by the use of force if necessary but an abortive attempt, even if it is collective, may give rise only to disciplinary sanctions and only for those who were directly involved.

F. Responsibilities for acts committed against subordinates and other persons under the commander's responsibility

Generally, IHL tends to establish rights and duties with regard to the other party to the conflict. The relationship between those involved directly in the conflict and their own people and army is not at the heart of humanitarian law. This fact distinguishes it from human rights law, which is primarily concerned with the relationship between a government and its own people. A degree of evolution has nonetheless been observed in this respect.

It is first of all internal law and military laws and regulations that will govern the responsibility of a commander towards subordinates. Such regulations do not directly concern IHL *a priori*. Clearly, IHL requires all wounded, including the party's own, to be treated humanely and impartially, but most of all the intention is to protect the enemy wounded, who obviously run a greater risk of being subjected to discrimination or ill-treatment.

---

[67] On this, see G. Best, *Humanity in Warfare* (London: Weidenfeld and Nicolson, 1980), 294ff.

[68] See Geneva Convention IV, Art 34; Common Art 3(1)(b).

The way in which a commander treats able-bodied subordinates is no longer totally alien to IHL. Additional Protocol I introduced minimum standards to be observed with regard to people 'affected by a situation' of international armed conflict 'who are in the power of a Party to the conflict and who do not benefit from more favourable treatment'[69] under the Geneva Conventions or under Additional Protocol I. Soldiers are therefore covered by this provision with regard to their superior officers and benefit from minimum treatment guarantees and judicial guarantees. This applies as well to traitors and deserters if they are taken captive by their own army. This Chapter will not discuss the details of these fundamental guarantees, which are taken from human rights law.

The philosophy of IHL is that the civilian population must foremost be protected against enemy abuse. This leads, first, to very detailed regulations governing occupation; and, secondly, to matters relating to blockades, particularly the obligation to give right of passage to certain relief, including *a priori* relief intended for the adverse party. However, in this respect the Additional Protocols of 1977 shifted IHL in the direction of human rights law by also taking an interest in the way in which a party to the conflict treats its own people. Relief actions must be carried out on behalf of all populations lacking essential goods and must therefore in principle also be accepted by a government for its own people. Clearly, when starvation of civilians is forbidden as a method of warfare, it is the civilians of the adverse party who are targeted. However, arbitrary refusal of a relief action on behalf of one's own people would also violate IHL as set forth in the Additional Protocols of 1977. Such actions, if they are necessary and respect the principles of impartiality and neutrality that apply to them, must be facilitated. Commanders are duty bound to avoid abuses by soldiers under their command. The behaviour of soldiers must also be controlled at all times with regard to the population, including the people whom they are defending.

4   Responsibility of the High Command

The cascade of responsibilities obviously does not stop with military commanders in the field but extends to the highest level, which may even be the head of state if he or she is also the commander-in-chief of that state's armed forces. That responsibility can be gauged from the level and extent of the decisions taken.

---

[69] Additional Protocol I, Art 75(1).

A. Humanitarian assistance

As noted above,[70] pursuant to the principle of humane treatment and the prohibition on starvation as a method of warfare,[71] there is an obligation under IHL to provide assistance to those who need it in times of armed conflict.[72] A decision to carry out a large-scale blockade—that is, cutting a territory off from its supplies—invariably stems from the high command. The obligation to provide, or accept offers of,[73] humanitarian assistance falls on the party in control of the relevant territory, including occupied territories.

The Fourth Geneva Convention preserves a very strict definition of a blockade. Only the passage of medical and religious items for the whole civilian population on belligerent territories are permitted, the free passage of foodstuffs and clothing being limited to children under 15, expectant mothers, and maternity cases, under very strict conditions. These very strict conditions do not apply to occupied territories: on the contrary, the Occupying Power has the duty to accept relief if it is unable to provide essential goods to the population on these territories.[74] The concern shown by the ICRC during World War II to take supplies to starving populations met with strong resistance from both Allied and Axis powers.[75] It was not until the televised atrocities of the Nigeria–Biafra conflict in the 1960s that the attitude of states changed radically. Under pressure from public opinion (that famous 'public conscience' dear to de Martens[76]), the concept of humanitarian assistance was overhauled in the 1977 Additional Protocols.

The revisions meant that all goods essential for the survival of the population—primarily foodstuffs and medicines, of course, but also clothing, shelter, or any indispensable item under the circumstances—must be dispatched when the population is without such relief, for use by all the people.[77] Additionally, it is prohibited

---

[70] See 2(B)(ii) above.   [71] See Additional Protocol I, Art 54; Additional Protocol II, Art 14.

[72] Geneva Convention IV, Art 27; Common Art 3. See further, H.-P. Gasser, 'Protection of the Civilian Population', in D. Fleck (ed), *The Handbook of International Humanitarian Law* (Oxford: Oxford University Press, 2008), §§ 524–5.

[73] In practice, offers to deliver and supervise delivery of assistance often come from the ICRC. Under the Geneva Conventions and Additional Protocol I, the ICRC can act as a substitute for a Protecting Power: see Geneva Conventions, Common Art 3; Additional Protocol I, Art 5. In practice, the ICRC is constantly engaged in fulfilling this substitute role in various capacities.

[74] Geneva Convention IV, Arts 23 and 59.

[75] See *Reports of the ICRC on its activities during the Second World War, Vol III (Relief activities)*, (ICRC: Geneva, 1948); F. Bugnion, *The ICRC and the Protection of War Victims* (ICRC: Geneva, 2003), 167–243.

[76] See the 'Martens Clause' in The Hague Convention with Respect to the Laws and Customs of War on Land (1899), Preamble: 'populations and belligerents remain under the protection and empire of the principles of international law, as they result from the usages established between civilized nations, from the laws of humanity, and the requirements of the public conscience'.

[77] See Additional Protocol I, Art 70; Additional Protocol II, Art 18. For discussion of the debate on the 'right to assistance', see eg M. Bettati, 'The Right of Humanitarian Intervention or the Right of Free

to 'attack, destroy, remove or render useless [...] agricultural areas for the production of food-stuffs, crops, livestock, drinking water installations and supplies and
irrigation works', unless these are being used in direct support of military action[78] —
though it must be said that a provision contemplating the deliberate destruction
of fertile fields in any circumstances seems unbearable from a humanitarian and
planetary perspective. These obligations apply also in non-international armed
conflicts, but according to Article 18(2) of AP II the consent of the state is necessary
also for relief sent to the civilian population in the territory under the control of the
opposing non-state armed forces. This consent is nevertheless not required by CA 3
of the Geneva Conventions and may anyway not be refused without good reasons.
An arbitrary refusal could be considered a violation of the prohibition to starve the
civilian population.[79]

Continuing review of the principles of blockades is desirable, despite the amendments that have been introduced. This is particularly so in the light of recent experiences in Iraq and the former Yugoslavia, both sets of sanctions being of dubious
efficacy and very painful for the people affected, despite the authorization given for
the passage of some relief.

B. Prevention of forcible displacement

Forcible displacement of the civilian population without reasons of imperative military necessity or civilian security is prohibited under IHL in both international and
non-international armed conflicts.[80] The prohibition of the transfer of civilians by
force was first articulated in the Lieber Code, which provides that 'private citizens
are no longer [...] carried off to distant parts'.[81] Forcible displacement is now a war
crime under the Statute of the International Criminal Court.[82] Movement of groups
of civilians by force is often ordered for unlawful reasons[83] such as 'ethnic cleansing',
which aims deliberately to change the demographic composition of a certain territory. In such cases, the main responsibility for what is a clear violation of IHL in all
types of conflict resides at the highest level.

Access to Victims?' and Y. Sandoz, ' " Droit" or "Devoir d'ingérence" and the Right to Assistance: the
Issues Involved', 49 *Review of the International Commission of Jurists* (1993) 1–11 and 12–22.

[78] Additional Protocol I, Art 54.   [79] Additional Protocol II, Art 14.

[80] Geneva Convention IV, Art 49; Additional Protocol I, Art 85(4)(a); see also Customary Law
Study, Rule 129.

[81] Lieber Code, Art 23.   [82] ICC Statute, Art 8(2)(b)(viii), Art 8(2)(e)(viii).

[83] For a detailed overview of the legal regulation of forced displacement, see G. Dawson and S. Farber,
*Forcible Displacement Throughout the Ages: Towards an International Convention for the Prevention and
Punishment of the Crime of Forcible Displacement* (The Hague: Martinus Nijhoff, 2012).

C. Equipping armies with authorized weapons

The 1868 Declaration of Saint Petersburg introduced the principle prohibiting weapons causing 'superfluous injury', that is, more serious harm than needed to achieve legitimate military objectives.[84] This principle has since been affirmed in numerous treaties.[85] This principle covers, inter alia, weapons such as poison, which inevitably lead to death as well as weapons designed to cause permanent infirmity. Determining which weapons are prohibited by this principle remains a question that must be settled by states and anchored in conventions. It is the responsibility of superior authorities to refrain from equipping their troops with prohibited weapons or projectiles and to give clear instructions with respect to the use of restricted weapons.

D. No recruitment of child soldiers

Children are accorded a special protected status under IHL, which requires that they be treated with respect and provided with the aid and care that they need.[86] A particularly heinous breach of this principle is the recruitment of child soldiers. Recruiting child soldiers will entail the responsibility of the highest level of command if it forms part of a deliberate policy, and there will be shared responsibility if a complacent attitude to such practices has been adopted.

The explicit ban on the recruitment of child soldiers under Article 77(2) of Additional Protocol I applies in particular to 'children who have not attained the age of fifteen years'.[87] It is, therefore, only a war crime if the children recruited are under 15 years of age—a limit considered by many to be insufficient and which is nevertheless frequently ignored. Nonetheless, it is the authorities' duty to avoid, as far as possible, sending children aged between 15 and 18 into battle.[88]

---

[84] See 2(D)(i) above.

[85] Additional Protocol I, Art 35(2); Convention on Prohibitions or Restrictions on the Use of Certain Conventional Weapons which may be deemed to be Excessively Injurious or to have Indiscriminate Effects, concluded at Geneva (10 October 1980), entry into force 2 December 1983, 1342 UNTS 137 ('Convention on Certain Conventional Weapons'), Preamble; Protocol II to the Convention on Certain Conventional Weapons, Art 6(2); Amended Protocol II to the Convention on Certain Conventional Weapons, Art 3(3); Convention on the Prohibition of the Use, Stockpiling, Production and Transfer of Anti-Personnel Mines and on their Destruction, concluded at Oslo (18 September 1997) entry into force 1 March 1999, 2056 UNTS 211, Preamble; Rome Statute, Art 8(2)(b)(xx). See Ch 11 in this volume.

[86] Geneva Convention IV, Art 24; Additional Protocol I, Art 77(1); see further H.-P. Gasser, 'Protection of the Civilian Population', in D. Fleck (ed), *The Handbook of International Humanitarian Law* (Oxford: Oxford University Press, 2008), § 505; B.F. Klappe, 'International Peace Operations', in Fleck (ed), *The Handbook of International Humanitarian Law*, §§ 1373–4.

[87] See also Convention on the Rights of the Child (1989) 1577 UNTS 3, General Assembly Resolution 44/25 (20 November 1989), entry into force 2 September 1990 ('Convention on the Rights of the Child'), Art 38, which essentially repeats the rules in Additional Protocol I, Art 77.

[88] On this issue, see G. Goodwin-Gill, 'The Challenge of the Child Soldier', in H. Strachan and S. Scheipers (eds), *The Changing Character of War* (Oxford: Oxford University Press, 2011), 410–28.

In a positive development, the Optional Protocol of 2000 to the Convention on the Rights of the Child on the involvement of children in armed conflict[89] raises the age limit to 18 years for both direct participation in conflict and compulsory recruitment into armed forces. In addition, UNICEF's Paris Principles on Children Associated with Armed Conflict of 2007 lay out further detailed guidelines for protecting children under 18 years old from recruitment and providing assistance to those already involved with armed groups or forces. Principle 2.1 defines 'a child associated with an armed force or armed group' as 'any person below 18 years of age who is or who has been recruited or used by an armed force or armed group in any capacity, including but not limited to children, boys, and girls used as fighters, cooks, porters, messengers, spies or for sexual purposes'. The Principles were developed by states, international organizations, and non-governmental organizations with the purpose of influencing law and practice to better protect children from exploitation and violence.

E. Training soldiers in IHL

The duty of commanders to provide information and training on the rules of IHL is part of the overall responsibility of the highest authorities to set in place a serious training policy,[90] although there are unfortunately no real sanctions for violations of this obligation. To be effective, training in IHL must form part of general military education.

The complicated nature of IHL training must be acknowledged, as must the maturity required of the soldier to assimilate both the commitment required in battle and the clear thinking that allows soldiers to demonstrate restraint at all times with regard to people and property that are not participating in the fighting. This is another reason to contest the very young age at which international law tolerates the inclusion of combatants in the armed forces.

F. Responsibility to stop all violations of IHL and
to punish serious violations

The obligation to stop all violations and to punish serious violations of humanitarian norms[91] implies consistent organization of the army and the legal authorities. The latter must preserve their independence. The effectiveness of sanctions

---

[89] Optional Protocol to the Convention on the Rights of the Child on the involvement of children in armed conflict, UN Doc A/RES/54/263 (25 May 2000), entry into force 12 February 2002.

[90] Customary Law Study, Rule 124.   [91] Customary Law Study, Rule 153.

deserves, moreover, to be reviewed thoroughly, the aim being to achieve an objective that is not merely repressive but also educational and preventive.[92]

5 THE PROBLEM OF NON-INTERNATIONAL ARMED CONFLICTS

The remarks in this Chapter apply strictly to international armed conflicts and mostly in the context of non-international armed conflicts as well, apart from some particular points that have been mentioned. A recent study of customary IHL carried out under the aegis of the ICRC confirmed a tendency for the rules applicable in both types of armed conflict to come closer together.[93] This is in any case true for the rules of behaviour for foot soldiers and also of the rules prohibiting or restricting the use of certain weapons.

Things are a little less clear at the higher levels of command. For example, there are differences in the way captive soldiers are treated. The status of prisoner of war does not apply in non-international armed conflicts; a soldier who is a member of the rebel forces may be tried simply for having taken up arms, even if he has not violated IHL. Clearly, fundamental legal guarantees and those governing treatment must nonetheless be upheld in this respect. This is true for both parties to the conflict. IHL does not, however, clarify the obligations of the rebel authorities towards the individuals detained by them, especially when they do not have an infrastructure similar to governments, which would allow the obligations to be clearly fulfilled.

The obligation to send back medical personnel is also not expressed clearly with regard to non-international armed conflicts, although medical personnel have no cause to be concerned simply because they have carried out their medical mission, regardless of which side they were on.[94]

The conditions of detention must in all cases comply with the minimum requirements for all detainees but IHL applicable in non-international armed conflicts does not impose respect for all the detailed rules provided for prisoners of war or civilian internees during international armed conflicts, and thus the law of

---

[92] For an in-depth reflection on the role of the sanction, see in particular the special issue of the *International Review of the Red Cross* on the subject, No 870 (June 2008).

[93] See generally Customary Law Study.

[94] There is a general protection of medical duties in non-international as well as in international armed conflicts: Additional Protocol I, Art 16; Additional Protocol II, Art 10; Customary Law Study, Rule 26.

non-international armed conflict remains less clear on the content of those minimum requirements. More precise information about the content of these obligations must be sought elsewhere, particularly in human rights law.

The responsibility of the rebel authorities towards the population in a territory under their control is also unclear. The notion of occupation cannot be transposed to non-international conflicts and human rights law primarily defines the responsibilities of the legitimate government, although a slight shift towards the responsibility of non-state actors can be observed.[95]

As far as relief is concerned, the principle governing action on behalf of the population lacking basic goods also applies to non-international conflicts, but in general the government needs to accept the action, including for action in territory controlled by rebel forces. The government, however, cannot arbitrarily refuse such action.[96]

6 CONCLUDING REMARKS

If, as we have seen, most of the rules of IHL today remain fully relevant in land warfare, some deserve clarification or even expansion. Making needed changes, however, requires further study, as any such attempts risk weakening current standards. Moreover, the underlying cause of many problems frequently lies in weaknesses in implementation more than in the substance of the rules.

Any future reflection should also take account of two essential elements. First, the rules of IHL are only respected in practice if they are useful for all those involved in armed conflicts. Rules that would give a definite advantage to one of the parties to the conflict would have little chance of being upheld. Secondly, IHL must remain straightforward and easily comprehensible for those who must apply it, particularly for foot soldiers.

---

[95] See eg E. Zegveld, *The Accountability of Opposition Groups in International Law* (Cambridge: Cambridge University Press, 2002); and A. Clapham, *Human Rights Obligations of Non-State Actors* (Oxford: Oxford University Press, 2006).

[96] As with international armed conflicts, starvation of civilians is prohibited under Additional Protocol II, Art 14, and such an arbitrary refusal would constitute a violation of this provision.

CHAPTER 6

....

AIR WARFARE

....

MICHAEL N. SCHMITT[1]

1 INTRODUCTION

....

By World War II, airpower had become a defining element of warfare. In that conflict, the Battle of Britain saved the United Kingdom from invasion, General Doolittle's daring raid made possible the first blow against the Japanese mainland, and the retaking of territory conquered by Germany and Japan would not have been possible but for Allied air superiority. Yet airpower also subjected civilian populations on both sides of the conflict to horrendous suffering in such operations as the 'Blitz', the fire-bombing of Dresden, and the dropping of atomic bombs on Hiroshima and Nagasaki. In Vietnam, Operations Rolling Thunder and Linebacker and the bombing of Viet Cong sanctuaries in Laos and Cambodia not only captured international attention, but also influenced the length and eventual conclusion of these conflicts. By the 1990s, airpower had become a (perhaps 'the') central element of operational strategy. Its potential was vividly illustrated by the 100-day Coalition air campaign during Operation Desert Storm in 1991 that enabled the defeat of Iraqi ground forces in 100 hours of follow-on land operations. Similarly, Operation Allied Force, the 78-day air assault against the Federal Republic of Yugoslavia in 1999, stopped the slaughter of Kosovar Albanians by

[1] The views expressed in this Chapter are those of the author in his personal capacity and do not necessarily represent those of the US Government.

Slobodan Milošević's security forces. And in the decade before the Second Gulf War of 2003, no-fly zones in the north and south of Iraq protected civilians from Saddam Hussein's security forces.

Airpower continues to dominate the twenty-first-century battlespace. Combined with Special Forces, it allowed Afghan indigenous forces to overthrow the Taliban almost effortlessly in 2001. Airpower remains the primary means by which insurgents are targeted in that on-going conflict. In 2003, decapitation airstrikes against Saddam Hussein kicked off Operation Iraqi Freedom. The air supremacy that was established in a matter of days enabled the rapid defeat of Iraqi conventional forces. Both conflicts, however, illustrated the limitations of airpower in combatting an insurgency. During Operation Unified Protector in 2011, NATO aircraft protected a rebellious civilian population from Libyan security forces and made possible the overthrow of long-time dictator Muammar Gaddafi. Perhaps most controversially, airpower is today the primary means by which the United States is carrying out its campaign against transnational terrorism.

Despite its decisive role in modern warfare, the air paradoxically remains the operational domain that is least regulated by treaty law.[2] While treaties addressing land and maritime warfare stretch back well over a century,[3] and military activities in space have been regulated by international law for a decade,[4] states have never adopted any international humanitarian law instrument devoted exclusively to air warfare. This does not mean that hostilities in the air are ungoverned. A number of the general international humanitarian law treaties contain provisions that constrain air operations. Moreover, state practice and *opinio juris* have combined to create a rich, albeit somewhat abstruse, body of applicable customary international law.

This Chapter is structured in two parts. It lays the groundwork for discussion with a survey of the historical *lex scripta* directly applicable to air operations, including efforts to craft restatements of the law of air warfare. However, most discussion is reserved for the second part, which considers the extant law of air operations from the perspective of airmen. It does so by examining the law governing the four questions that are central to their operations—where can they fly, at what can they shoot, how must they conduct air operations, and what weapons may they use.[5]

---

[2] Cyberspace, which is increasingly characterized as an operational domain by some states, is even less regulated. The United States recently recognized it as a domain of warfare in Department of Defense, *Strategy for Operating in Cyberspace* (2011), available at <http://www.defense.gov/news/d20110714cyber.pdf>.

[3] See eg Hague Conventions VI, VII, VIII, IX, XI, and XII, 18 October 1907.

[4] See eg Treaty on Principles Governing the Activities of States in the Exploration and Use of Outer Space, Including the Moon and Other Celestial Bodies, Art V, 27 January 1967.

[5] The Chapter generally addresses the law of air warfare in the context of an international armed conflict. However, most of the law discussed, especially that dealing with targeting, applies equally in non-international armed conflicts. Greater precision on this issue can be drawn from the Harvard Program on Humanitarian Policy and Conflict Research, *Manual on International Law Applicable to Air and Missile Warfare, with Commentary* (2010) (hereinafter AMW Manual).

2 CODIFICATION OF THE LAW
OF AIR WARFARE

Air warfare began in the eighteenth century when French forces at the Battle of Fleurus in 1794 famously used the balloon *Entreprenant* to monitor Austrian movements. Extension of hostilities into this new domain of warfare continued apace in the following century. For example, Austrian forces launched unmanned bomb-carrying balloons against Venice in 1849, observation balloons were used during the American Civil War (the North formed an aerial unit, the Union Army Balloon Corps), and technologically advanced states began to build dirigible airships.

By the end of the century, air warfare had captured the attention of the international legal community. In response, delegates to the First Hague Peace Conference in 1899 adopted Declaration 1, in which Parties agreed 'to prohibit, for a term of five years, the launching of projectiles and explosives from balloons, or by other new methods of a similar nature'.[6] The five-year limitation reflected the uncertainty of states as to how to treat this new technology. On the one hand, the ban answered their humanitarian (and operational) concerns. On the other, the five-year time-frame indicated an unwillingness to shoulder permanent prohibitions, at least not until the states had a better sense of the opportunities aerial platforms might offer. Their dilemma was that while aircraft could theoretically cause untold suffering, they might also contribute measurably to military victory. This tension between humanity and the need for military effectiveness infuses efforts to regulate new means and methods of warfare to this day.[7]

In 1903, the Wright brothers conducted the first sustained flight of a 'heavier than air vehicle', thereby launching the age of the aircraft. Hague Declaration 1 expired two years later. At the Second Hague Peace Conference in 1907, states were hesitant to permanently ban these new aerial machines, for they had begun to glimpse their battlefield utility. Instead, the conference adopted Hague Declaration XIV, which restated the prohibition in its 1899 counterpart, but again limited it temporally.[8] Declaration XIV was only to remain in effect until the Third Peace Conference. As that conference was never held, the treaty technically remains in effect for states parties. Its impact on the conflicts to come proved negligible, as Austria-Hungary, France, Germany, Italy, Japan, and Russia never became parties, and the United

---

[6] Declaration (IV, 1) to Prohibit for the Term of Five Years the Launching of Projectiles and Explosives from Balloons, and Other New Methods of a Similar Nature, 29 July 1899.

[7] On the balancing of these two interests, see M. Schmitt, 'Military Necessity and Humanity in International Humanitarian Law: Preserving the Delicate Balance', 50 *Virginia Journal of International Law* (2010) 795.

[8] Declaration (XIV) Prohibiting the Discharge of Projectiles and Explosives from Balloons, 18 October 1907.

States announced in 1942 that it would no longer abide by its terms. Moreover, like Declaration 1, the treaty contained an 'all participation' clause by which the instrument only applied during conflicts in which all the belligerents were party to it. In effect, Hague Declaration 1 is meaningless today.

The only other treaty affecting air operations during the early years of the twentieth century was the 1907 Hague Convention IV, with its Annexed Regulations.[9] Although principally addressed to land warfare, Article 25 of the Convention prohibited the 'attack or bombardment, by whatever means, of towns, villages, dwellings, or buildings which are undefended'. The 'whatever means' verbiage was intended to include air attack.[10] Arguably, Article 26's obligation to warn prior to attack or bombardment and Article 27's admonition to spare certain enumerated protected places (both precursors to the contemporary requirement to take precautions in attack) also extended to air attack.

These two instruments exerted little influence on the development of air warfare. Five years after their adoption, the tactic of modern bombardment was born when Italian aircraft bombed a Turkish camp in Libya. Aircraft were also used in the Balkan War of 1912 and by the United States against Pancho Villa in 1916.

The sole attempt to directly address the law applicable to air warfare before the outbreak of World War I came in 1911. In that year, the *Institut de droit international* adopted a resolution stating that air warfare was lawful only on the condition that it placed civilians and civilian property at no greater risk than land or maritime warfare.[11] The bombing of cities and the destruction of civilian property from the air during World War I demonstrated the ineffectiveness of this non-binding declaration by a group of eminent jurists.

World War I was the first conflict where air operations played a critical role. Aircraft were widely used by both sides for observation, bombing, and dog fighting. In the aftermath of the war, the 1921–22 Washington Conference on the Limitation of Armament considered whether and how to address this relatively new method of warfare. By then, a number of states were actively building air forces, the prime example being the establishment of the Royal Air Force in 1918. The conference could reach no agreement on limiting aircraft, but did appoint a Commission of Jurists to examine legal issues associated with air operations.[12] In 1923, the Commission

---

[9] Convention (IV) Respecting the Laws and Customs of War on Land and its annex: Regulations concerning the Laws and Customs of War on Land, 18 October 1907.

[10] Article 29 provided that personnel in balloons were not to be treated as spies, while Art 53 addressed the seizure of air 'appliances' by an occupation force.

[11] 'La guerre aérienne est permise, mais à la condition de ne pas présenter pour les personnes ou les propriétés de la population pacifique de plus grands dangers que la guerre terrestre ou maritime.' Institut de Droit International, Le régime juridique des aerostats, Section II, (Madrid, 21/22 April 1911), available at <http://www.idi-iil.org/idiF/resolutionsF/1911_mad_02_fr.pdf>.

[12] Including members from Great Britain, United States, France, Italy, Japan, and the Netherlands.

issued its general Report on the Revision of the Rules of Warfare, which included 'Rules of Air Warfare'.[13]

The Hague Rules of Air Warfare were generally recognized as an authoritative soft law pronouncement, much of which undoubtedly became customary law over the ensuing decades. Of particular note are Chapter III on 'Belligerents', which set forth the principle that only military aircraft may conduct combat operations, and Chapter IV, which dealt with the conduct of hostilities. Two of the instrument's Articles were especially relevant to the air operations that took place in the next World War. Article 22, an early version of the principle of distinction, provided that '[a]ny air bombardment for the purpose of terrorizing the civil population or destroying or damaging private property without military character or injuring non-combatants, is forbidden'. Article 24 built on that principle by offering human-itarian law's first definition of 'military objectives': 'air bombardment is legitimate only when it is directed against a military objective, ie an objective whereof the total or partial destruction would constitute an obvious military advantage for the belligerent'.[14] Today, these two articles, which undoubtedly reflect customary law, are codified in Articles 51 and 52 of the 1977 Additional Protocol I to the 1949 Geneva Conventions.[15]

The Rules also contained a listing of military objectives: 'military forces, military works, military establishments or depots, manufacturing plants constituting important and well-known centres for the production of arms, ammunition or characterized mili-tary supplies, lines of communication or of transport which are used for military purposes'.[16] The notion of an exhaustive list has since been rejected as under-inclusive, in particular because it would inevitably fail to account for civilian objects that become military objectives through use (or future use) by the enemy for military purposes.[17]

Beyond the 1925 Gas Protocol, which extends to delivery by air, no other major international effort to address air warfare was undertaken before World War II. Nevertheless, it became clear during that period that air warfare could not only sig-nificantly influence the course of battle, but also tragically affect the civilian popu-lation. The paradigmatic example was the infamous bombing of Guernica during the Spanish Civil War. Such events sometimes led states to assert that despite the

---

[13] Rules Concerning the Control of Wireless Telegraphy in Time of War and Air Warfare (Drafted by a Commission of Jurists, The Hague, December 1922–February 1923) (hereinafter Hague Rules of Air Warfare).

[14] Other aspects of Art 24 address the bombardment of populated areas, including an early version of the rule of proportionality allowing for the bombardment of such areas when 'there is a reasonable presumption that the military concentration is important enough to justify the bombardment, taking into account the danger to which the civil population will thus be exposed', Art 24(4).

[15] Protocol Additional to the Geneva Conventions of 12 August 1949, and Relating to the Protection of Victims of International Armed Conflicts, 8 June 1977 (hereinafter Additional Protocol I).

[16] Hague Rules of Air Warfare, Art 24(2).   [17] Additional Protocol I, Art 52.2.

dearth of treaty law on point, a customary body of norms had emerged to govern air warfare. For instance, in 1938, Neville Chamberlain famously articulated three fundamental rules of air warfare in the House of Commons: the civilian population may not be attacked; targets must be military objectives; and care must be taken in attack to avoid harm to civilians.[18] Moreover, irrespective of the direct bombing of civilian populations during World War II by both sides, the parties to the conflict characterized the 1923 Hague Rules as reflective of customary law and accused their opponents of violations.

Some progress has been made since World War II in codifying the law of air warfare. Each of the four 1949 Geneva Conventions mentioned aircraft, albeit primarily with respect to their medical functions, not their use in the conduct of hostilities.[19] Certain instruments that are not specific to warfare also contain rules restricting air operations. Examples include the 1956 Hague Cultural Property Convention, various aspects of the Protocols to the 1980 Convention on Conventional Weapons, and the Cluster Munitions Convention.[20] However, the 1977 Protocol Additional I to the 1949 Geneva Conventions, the first comprehensive attempt to regulate conduct of hostilities norms since the 1907 Hague Regulations, represents the high water mark with respect to regulating air warfare.

While Additional Protocol I, building upon the provisions found in the 1949 Geneva Conventions, addresses medical aircraft in some depth,[21] the most significant aspects of the instrument are found in Section I of Part IV. That section sets forth the general protection of the civilian population against the effects of hostilities by codifying such customary norms as the principle of distinction, the prohibition on indiscriminate weapons and attacks, the rule of proportionality, and the requirement to take precautions in attack.[22] It also extends protection from, or delineates restrictions on, attacks against specified objects that range from nuclear electrical generating stations to the environment.[23]

[18] A. Roberts and R. Guelff (eds), *Documents on the Laws of War* (3rd edn, Oxford: Oxford University Press, 2000), 140.

[19] Convention (I) for the Amelioration of the Condition of the Wounded and Sick in Armed Forces in the Field, 12 August 1949 (hereinafter Geneva Convention I), Arts 13, 36, 37; Convention (II) for the Amelioration of the Condition of Wounded, Sick and Shipwrecked Members of Armed Forces at Sea, 12 August 1949 (hereinafter Geneva Convention II), Arts 12, 13, 15, 39, 40; Convention (III) Relative to the Treatment of Prisoners of War, 12 August 1949 (hereinafter Geneva Convention III), Arts 4, 75; Convention (IV) Relative to the Protection of Civilian Persons in Time of War, 12 August 1949 (hereinafter Geneva Convention IV), Arts 22, 111.

[20] Hague Convention for the Protection of Cultural Property in the Event of Armed Conflict with Regulations for the Execution of the Convention, 14 May 1954; Convention on Prohibitions or Restrictions on the Use of Certain Conventional Weapons Which May be Deemed to be Excessively Injurious or to Have Indiscriminate Effects, 10 April 1981 (hereinafter Conventional Weapons Convention); Convention on Cluster Munitions, 3 December 2008.

[21] Additional Protocol I, Arts 24–31.   [22] Additional Protocol I, Arts 48, 51, 52, 57.

[23] Additional Protocol I, Arts 53–6.

Article 49(3) contains an important limiting clause on the scope of the Protocol: 'the provisions of this Section apply to any land, air or sea warfare which may affect the civilian population, individual civilians or civilian objects on land. They further apply to all attacks from the sea or from the air against objectives on land but do not otherwise affect the rules of international law applicable in armed conflict at sea or in the air'. Therefore, the treaty cannot be characterized as a thorough restatement of the legal architecture governing air warfare since it does not address air-to-sea, sea-to-air, ground-to-air, or air-to-air combat except as they have incidental effects on civilians or civilian objects on the ground.

Given the extensive air-to-air, air defence, and sea-based air warfare that had occurred during and since World War II, this approach seems curious. The Commentary to the Additional Protocols published by the International Committee of the Red Cross (ICRC) is revealing. It notes that '[a]s regards air warfare, there is no precise written law on this subject, apart from some unclear customary law (for example: external marks indicating the nationality of aircraft)'.[24] It continues:

Admittedly both sea and air warfare are subject to restrictions imposed by treaties of general application, such as, for example, the Hague Convention of 1954 for the Protection of Cultural Property and the Geneva Protocol of 1925 for the Prohibition of the Use in War of Asphyxiating, Poisonous or other Gases, and of Bacteriological Methods of Warfare, but there are hardly any specific rules relating to sea or air warfare, and insofar as they do exist, they are controversial or have fallen into disuse.[25]

An unofficial commentary prepared by three eminent scholar-practitioners who participated in the Diplomatic Conference leading to adoption of Additional Protocol I explains that the ICRC had done little preparatory work with regard to air warfare. That being so, concern was expressed that trying to address air (or naval) warfare might have the effect of scuttling the entire effort.[26] The omission of air warfare was, however, controversial. For instance, a number of Arab states tried to draw attention to the issue by citing the shooting down of a Libyan airliner by Israeli aircraft.[27] Despite these efforts, the original draft provision survived as set forth above because of the desire to complete the rest of the instrument in the time allotted for the Conference and because its participants 'recognized that care should be taken to avoid changing [the law or air and naval warfare] inadvertently'.[28]

Additional Protocol I has nevertheless exerted significant influence on the conduct of air warfare. Most air warfare today consists of ground-to-air operations in the form

[24] Y. Sandoz et al (eds), *Commentary on the Additional Protocols of 8 June 1977 to the Geneva Conventions of 12 August 1949* (International Committee of the Red Cross, 1987) (hereinafter Additional Protocols Commentary), § 1896.

[25] Additional Protocols Commentary, § 1897.

[26] M. Bothe et al, *New Rules for Victims of Armed Conflicts: Commentary on the Two 1977 Protocols Additional to the Geneva Conventions of 1949* (The Hague: Martinus Nijhoff Publishers, 1982) (hereinafter Bothe et al), 290.

[27] Bothe et al, 290.   [28] Bothe et al, 290-1.

of close air support and deliberate targeting and is therefore regulated by the instrument for parties thereto. It is significant that 172 states, with the notable exceptions of Israel, Turkey, and the United States, are party to Additional Protocol I. Even non-party states acknowledge, publicly or in practice, that its provisions relevant to air-to-ground operations in great part reflect current customary international law. And despite its limitation to air-to-ground operations, most states treat the general norms it enunciates regarding such issues as proportionality and precautions in attacks as reflective of customary international law applicable in all air operations.

In 2003, Harvard University's Program on Humanitarian Policy and Conflict Research launched a major project under the direction of the eminent scholar, Yoram Dinstein to thoroughly examine the contemporary law of air warfare. Many of the world's top academics and practitioners participated in the effort. Six years later, the group produced the *Manual on International Law Applicable to Air and Missile Warfare* (AMW Manual), which represents the most authoritative and comprehensive treatment of air warfare to date. Although non-binding, it serves states and scholars as a reliable catalogue of those customary international law rules that govern twenty-first-century air warfare. In this Chapter, heavy reliance is therefore placed on this Manual, for which the author served as a member of the core drafting team.

3 THE LAW OF AIR WARFARE

Air warfare is complex, as is the law that governs it. The AMW Manual, for instance, consists of 175 Rules with extensive accompanying commentary. However, reduced to essentials, the key provisions of the law of air warfare address one of four issues on which airmen focus: (1) Where may air operations be conducted? (2) Who and what may be attacked? (3) How must air operations be conducted? (4) What weapons may be used? Each of these questions will be addressed in turn.

A. Where may air operations be conducted?

During an international armed conflict, air operations may be conducted over the territory of any of the belligerent states. They may also be conducted in international airspace, that is, all airspace over international waters. International waters begin at the outer limit of a coastal state's territorial sea.[29]

---

[29] US Navy/US Marine Corps/US Coast Guard, *The Commander's Handbook on the Law of Naval Operations*, NWP 1-14M/MCWP 5-12.1/COMDTPUB P5800.7A (2007), § 1.9 (hereinafter US Commander's Handbook).

Belligerent military activities in neutral territory, including in neutral airspace, have long been prohibited. The general principle that neutral territory is inviolate appears in Article 1 of both the 1907 Hague Conventions V and XIII.[30] The Hague Rules of Air Warfare and the AMW Manual apply the general principle to neutral airspace.[31] It is unquestionable that the prohibition on conducting belligerent military operations in neutral airspace is customary in nature.[32] The prohibition includes both flying through neutral airspace and conducting air operations from belligerent airspace into neutral airspace, as with launching a missile into the area. It also extends to combat search and rescue operations.[33]

Neutral national airspace includes all airspace over a neutral's land and territorial sea. Note, in this regard, that there is no right of innocent passage for aircraft, as there is for warships sailing through territorial waters.[34] However, the rights of transit passage through an international strait and archipelagic sea lanes passage do apply to aircraft.[35] Neutrals enjoy certain rights in maritime zones beyond the territorial sea, such as the exclusive economic zone, but do not posses analogous rights in the airspace lying above them.

Although the principle of sovereignty generally allows states to consent to activities on their territory, a neutral state may not agree to the presence of belligerent aircraft in its airspace during an armed conflict. Allowing belligerent aircraft to use the airspace would breach its obligations under the law of neutrality. Indeed, in the event of a violation of neutral airspace, the neutral state is obliged to take whatever measures are necessary to expel the violating aircraft or otherwise terminate the breach of their neutrality.[36] Action by the neutral may include attacking the belligerent aircraft if required in the circumstances.[37]

If the neutral state fails to comply with its duty to exclude belligerent activities from its airspace, either because it cannot or simply because it elects not to do so, opposing belligerents are entitled to take measures, including the use of force, to put an end to its enemy's use of the airspace. They must first warn the neutral state to enforce its neutrality and give it an opportunity to do so unless doing so is not

---

[30] Convention (V) Respecting the Rights and Duties of Neutral Powers and Persons in Case of War on Land, 18 October 1907 (hereinafter Hague Convention V); Convention (XIII) Concerning the Rights and Duties of Neutral Powers in Naval War, 18 October 1907 (hereinafter Hague Convention XIII).

[31] Hague Rules of Air Warfare, Art 40; AMW Manual, Rule 170(a).

[32] Hague Convention V, Arts 2, 3; Hague Convention XIII, Art 2; US Commander's Handbook, § 7.3; UK Ministry of Defence, *The Joint Service Manual of the Law of Armed Conflict*, JSP 383 (2004) (hereinafter UK Manual), § 1.43; AMW Manual, Rule 166.

[33] AMW Manual, Rule 171(d).   [34] US Commander's Handbook, § 2.5.2.1.

[35] US Commander's Handbook, §§ 2.7.1.1, 2.7.1.2; AMW Manual, Rule 172(a)(ii).

[36] Hague Convention V, Art 5; Hague Air Rules, Arts 42, 47; US Commander's Handbook, § 7.3; UK Manual, § 1.43; AMW Manual, Rules 168(a), 170(c).

[37] AMW Manual, Rule 172(b).

feasible in light of the nature of the violation (eg an attack is underway from neutral airspace).[38]

It is sometimes asserted that belligerents may exclude civil (and neutral military) aircraft from particular airspace by establishing exclusion or no-fly zones. The former are set up outside the territory of the belligerents, whereas the latter are located in belligerent airspace. Such zones are legal fictions in that they do not absolve a belligerent of its responsibilities under international humanitarian law. In particular, they do not create a so-called 'free fire zone', since aircraft within an exclusion or no-fly zone may only be attacked if they fully qualify as military objectives.[39] Of course, belligerents may take measures to control the activities of civil aircraft in the immediate area of operations and to ensure force protection.[40] In particular, they may do so in the 'contact zone' (the area where opposing forces are facing each other), a principle recognized as early as the Hague Rules of Air Warfare.[41]

The extent, location, and duration of an exclusion zone must be limited to that which is necessary in the circumstances; anyone who may encounter the zone must be notified of its existence; and the zone may not bar access to the airspace of neutrals.[42] Because zones may not be enforced against aircraft that do not qualify as military objectives, they are, in effect, merely areas of heightened risk. Although they do not alter the applicable legal regime, the fact that an aircraft has penetrated an exclusion zone may, depending on the circumstances, contribute to verification of that aircraft as an enemy military aircraft that may be attacked.

No-fly zones are on a slightly firmer normative foundation in that they exist either in airspace over which the belligerent enjoys sovereignty or over the enemy's territory, an area where the prerogatives of sovereignty are diminished by virtue of the armed conflict. Therefore, the state declaring the zone has the right under international law to exclude aircraft that have not been granted its consent to fly in the area, at least over its territory or territory that it has occupied. Nevertheless, the state's right to engage civil aircraft in such areas is no greater than that which it would enjoy during peacetime (a controversial subject) or pursuant to international humanitarian law, as when a civilian aircraft is used for military purposes.

Blockade, by contrast, is a distinct legal regime that has rested on legal *terra firma* for over a century. The method of warfare consists of belligerent operations to prevent all vessels from entering or exiting specified ports or coastal areas belonging to, or under the control of, the enemy.[43] There are strict and complicated requirements for the establishment and maintenance of a naval blockade, the discussion of which

---

[38] US Commander's Handbook, § 7.3; UK Manual, § 1.43; AMW Manual, Rule 168(b); L. Doswald-Beck (ed), *San Remo Manual on International Law Applicable to Armed Conflicts at Sea* (Cambridge: Cambridge University Press, 1995), § 22 (hereinafter San Remo Manual).

[39] AMW Manual, Rule 105(a) and (b).   [40] AMW Manual, Rule 106.

[41] Hague Air Rules, Art 30.   [42] AMW Manual, Rule 107.

[43] US Commander's Handbook, § 7.7.1.

lies beyond the scope of this Chapter.[44] However, what is significant in respect of air warfare is that aircraft may be used to enforce a naval blockade.[45] In particular, because a vessel which resists capture while attempting to breach a naval blockade qualifies as a military objective, force, including an attack from the air, may be used against it.[46]

Although aerial blockades are of more recent vintage, they are increasingly viewed as lawful.[47] Such blockades are intended to prevent aircraft from entering or exiting specified airfields or coastal airspace that the enemy controls. They must conform to all the requirements (eg, effectiveness) and limitations (eg, does not bar access to neutral territory) of a naval blockade and are generally announced through a Notice to Airman (NOTAM). In addition to aircraft, naval and ground forces may be employed to render the blockade effective.

Lines of naval blockade are usually established in international waters and enforcement is permitted once it becomes clear that a vessel will try to breach the blockade. Due to the speed of modern aircraft, a line of aerial blockade would have to be placed at a significant distance from the coast to be effective. However, this fact does not preclude such a blockade from being established as a matter of law.

B. Who and what can be attacked?

The principle of distinction applies in air warfare precisely as it does in land or sea warfare.[48] Article 48 of Additional Protocol I reflects the customary norm: 'the Parties to the conflict shall at all times distinguish between the civilian population and combatants and between civilian objects and military objectives and accordingly shall direct their operations only against military objectives'.[49] This broad principle is operationalized in a number of international humanitarian law rules, the most important of which are found in Articles 51 and 52 of Additional Protocol I. Like Article 48, the two Articles are universally regarded as customary in nature.[50]

---

[44] US Commander's Handbook, § 7.7.2; UK Manual, §§ 13.65–13.76; San Remo Manual, Rules 93–104.

[45] US Commander's Handbook, § 7.7.2.3; UK Manual, § 13.69.

[46] US Commander's Handbook, §§ 7–10; San Remo Manual, Rule 98.

[47] US Commander's Handbook, § 7.7.1; AMW Manual, Rule 147; San Remo Manual, 177.

[48] The International Court of Justice has recognized the principle as one of two 'cardinal principles' of international humanitarian law, the other being unnecessary suffering. ICJ, *Legality of the Threat or Use of Nuclear Weapons*, Advisory Opinion, 8 July 1996, § 78.

[49] See eg US Commander's Handbook, § 5.3.2; J.M. Henckaerts and L. Doswald-Beck (eds), *Customary International Humanitarian Law* (Cambridge: Cambridge University Press, 2005) (hereinafter Customary International Humanitarian Law Study), Rules 1, 7; AMW Manual, Rule 10(a); San Remo Manual, Rule 39.

[50] US Commander's Handbook, § 8.3; AMW Manual, Rule 11; Customary International Humanitarian Law Study, Rules 7, 9, 10; Statute of the International Criminal Court, 17 July 1998 (hereinafter Rome Statute), Arts 8(2)(b)(i) and (ii), 8(2)(e)(i), (ii), (iii), (xii).

Article 51(2) of Additional Protocol I provides that 'the civilian population as such, as well as individual civilians, shall not be the object of attack'. Persons who are not civilians (ie, those who are members of the armed forces) are subject to attack, with the exception of those who are *hors de combat* or specially protected, such as medical or religious personnel.[51]

Between 2003 and 2008, the ICRC convened an international group of experts to consider the legal issues surrounding the targeting of civilians who directly participate in hostilities. The result of this effort was the ICRC publication of *The Interpretive Guidance on the Notion of Direct Participation in Hostilities Under International Humanitarian Law*.[52] During the project, the group achieved consensus that members of an organized armed group are to be treated as members of the armed forces with regard to how and when they may be targeted.[53] Accordingly, such individuals are liable to being targeted from the air based solely on their status as members of the group; they may be attacked at any time so long as other requirements of international humanitarian law, such as the rule of proportionality and the requirement to take precautions in attack, are met.

The ICRC took the further position that this characterization applies only to members of the group who have a 'continuous combat function'.[54] Certain of the experts, including this author, rejected the approach, arguing that it is unfounded in law and perversely produces a disparity in treatment between members of the regular armed forces without a combat role, on the one hand, and members of an organized armed group who do not have a continuous combat function, on the other.[55] The former are targetable at all times, whereas the latter may only be attacked if and while they directly participate in hostilities. Such incongruence appears inconsistent with the underlying object and purpose of the relevant international humanitarian law norms.

Pursuant to Article 51(3) of Additional Protocol I (international armed conflict) and Article 13(3) of Additional Protocol II (non-international armed conflict),[56] civilians who are not members of an organized armed group lose their protection from attack and need not be considered in proportionality or precautions in attack

---

[51] Geneva Convention I, Arts 24, 25; Additional Protocol I, Art 41; US Commander's Handbook, §§ 8.2.3, 8.2.4.1, 8.2.4.2; UK Manual, § 5.6; AMW Manual, Rules 15(b), 71; Customary International Humanitarian Law Study, Rules 25, 87.

[52] N. Melzer (ed), *Interpretive Guidance on the Notion of Direct Participation in Hostilities under International Humanitarian Law* (Geneva: ICRC, 2009) (hereinafter Interpretive Guidance).

[53] Interpretive Guidance, 21.   [54] Interpretive Guidance, 70.

[55] See the various articles set forth in 'Forum: The ICRC Interpretive Guidance on the Notion of Direct Participation in Hostilities Under International Humanitarian Law', 42 *New York University Journal of International Law and Politics* (2010).

[56] Additional Protocol I, Art 51(3); Protocol Additional to the Geneva Conventions of 12 August 1949, and Relating to the Protection of Victims of Non-international Armed Conflicts, Art 13(3), 8 June 1977 (hereinafter 'Additional Protocol II').

calculations (see below) for such time as they directly participate in hostilities.[57] The experts involved in the direct participation project agreed that the two articles reflect customary international law.

In one of the project's notable achievements, consensus was achieved among the majority of experts on three 'constitutive elements' that comprise acts of direct participation. First, '[t]he act must be likely to adversely affect the military operations or military capacity of a party to an armed conflict or, alternatively, to inflict death, injury, or destruction on persons or objects protected against direct attack (threshold of harm)'. Secondly, there must be a direct causal link between the act and the harm likely to result either from that act, or from a coordinated military operation of which that act constitutes an integral part (direct causation). Finally, for the act to amount to direct participation, it 'must be specifically designed to directly cause the required threshold of harm in support of a party to the conflict and to the detriment of another (belligerent nexus)'.[58]

Of the constitutive elements, only that requiring direct causation proved contentious. Although all the experts agreed that direct causation is required for an act to qualify as direct participation, controversy was sparked when the Interpretive Guidance characterized the assembly and storage of improvised explosive devices (IEDs) as indirect, rather than direct, participation.[59] In that, until recently, IEDs caused the greatest number of casualties among coalition troops in Afghanistan and Iraq, many militaries took the position that such activities were direct and that those involved in them could be targeted. The very existence of the debate has nevertheless complicated, and will continue to complicate, the development of multinational rules of engagement. The same is true with respect to the ICRC's controversial, and in this author's estimation unsupportable, assertion that individuals who voluntarily shield military objectives are not direct participants.[60]

Once these three criteria have been met, the individual engaging in the qualifying activity may be attacked 'for such time' as he or she is so engaged. The 'for such time' verbiage had long been the source of controversy.[61] Unfortunately, the direct participation project proved unable to resolve the dispute. At the risk of oversimplification, the ICRC argues that the period of direct participation, and therefore susceptibility to attack, encompasses 'preparatory measures [...] as well as the deployment to and the return from the location of its execution'.[62] An alternative view held by a

---

[57] Article 51(3) of Additional Protocol I reads: 'Civilians shall enjoy the protection afforded by this Section, unless and for such time as they take a direct part in hostilities'. Article 13(3) of Additional Protocol II is identical except for replacement of the word 'section' with 'part'.

[58] Interpretive Guidance, 16.   [59] Interpretive Guidance, 54.

[60] Interpretive Guidance, 56–7.

[61] For instance, the Israeli Supreme Court found the provision to constitute customary international law over arguments to the contrary presented by the government in the 'Targeted Killings' case. HCJ 769/02, *The Public Committee against Torture in Israel v The Government of Israel*, § 30 [2006] (Isr).

[62] Interpretive Guidance, 65.

significant number of the experts is that the period of participation extends as far 'upstream' and 'downstream' as a causal connection exists.[63] Moreover, the ICRC was of the view that the loss of the protection only occurs during each separate act, such that there are intervals of protection and susceptibility to attack.[64] Those on the other side of the issue, including this author, take the position that such an interpretation creates an unacceptable 'revolving door' of targetability that makes little sense operationally. The latter group translates the 'for such time' phraseology more broadly as comprising the entire period during which the individual is engaged in sequential acts of direct participation.

Direct participation has become a prominent issue during air operations because the targeting of individuals is, for operational reasons, often likely to be carried out from the air.[65] There was, for instance, a public controversy as to whether NATO could lawfully target those involved in the Afghan drug trade on the basis that the Taliban relied on funds it generated.[66] Ultimately, it was determined (correctly) that the majority of the individuals in question were not direct participants in hostilities as a matter of law.

The continuous combat function debate has likewise complicated targeting from aircraft. In great part, this is because it is often difficult to determine from the air whether members of an organized armed group who are being considered for attack have such a continuous combat function. In a coalition like the International Security Assistance Force (ISAF), with members on both sides of the debate, achieving agreement as to the lawfulness of a particular strike can accordingly prove challenging.

Article 52(1) of Additional Protocol I is Article 51's counterpart for civilian objects. It provides that '[c]ivilian objects shall not be the object of attack or of reprisals. Civilian objects are all objects which are not military objectives [...]'. Since civilian objects are defined in the negative, the Article goes on to set forth the definition of military objectives: 'Military objectives are limited to those objects which by their nature, location, purpose or use make an effective contribution to military action and whose total or partial destruction, capture or neutralization, in the circumstances ruling at the time, offers a definite military of advantage'.[67] It is incontestable that the prohibition applies in air operations.

This definition of military objectives, and derivatively civilian objects, is universally accepted as an accurate expression of customary international law. It appears

---

[63] Y. Dinstein, *The Conduct of Hostilities under the Law of International Armed Conflict* (2d edn, Cambridge: Cambridge University Press, 2010), 148.

[64] Interpretive Guidance, 70.

[65] The complexity of the issues was aptly illustrated in the Israeli Supreme Court's decision in the Targeted Killings case, which predated issuance of the Interpretive Guidance.

[66] On the subject, see M. Schmitt, 'Targeting Narcoinsurgents in Afghanistan: The Limits of International Humanitarian Law', 12 *Yearbook of International Humanitarian Law* (2009) 301.

[67] Additional Protocol I, Art 52(2).

in other treaties, most military manuals, and restatements produced by international law experts.[68] However, two issues have proven contentious. Both are especially acute in the context of air warfare because aircraft permit strikes deep into enemy territory against targets that would normally not be reachable by land-based weaponry.

The first deals with objects that qualify as military objectives by nature. As noted in the ICRC's commentary on Article 52 of Additional Protocol I, 'this category comprises all objects directly used by the armed forces'.[69] For example, all military bases, aircraft, equipment, and warships satisfy the nature criterion. The controversy arises over the additional requirements set forth in the text of the Article—that the object makes an effective contribution to military action and that attacking it offers a definite military advantage. As a rule, the closer equipment is to the battlefront, the more likely it is that it contributes, or will contribute, to the enemy's military action. Similarly, the closer equipment is to the battlefront, the more likely it is that putting it out of action will yield the attacker a military advantage. However, the reach of air operations brings objects into range that, although military in nature, do not self-evidently contribute to the enemy's immediate military action such that their destruction or damage will give the attacker a military advantage.

Most commentators agree that objects that qualify by nature always make an effective contribution to military action because the condition is not context specific. It is the second requirement that is problematic. One school of thought holds that damaging, destroying, or neutralizing an object that makes an effective contribution to the enemy's military action ineludibly offers an attacker a definite military advantage. In other words, so long as a potential target is military in nature, it is a military objective. By this approach, every military installation or piece of equipment is legally subject to air attack regardless of whether it is being used, or going to be used, during the conflict (so long as other rules such as proportionality and precautions in attack are respected). Consequently, an air campaign may be conducted wherever the enemy and its equipment and facilities are located. As an example, naval vessels are legitimate targets even during a distant low-intensity land conflict in which they play no part.

A competing school of thought suggests that the inclusion of the reference to definite military advantage in Article 52 of Additional Protocol I was intended to impose a further requirement beyond qualification as a military objective based solely on an object's nature. For instance, in the example above the naval vessels would not be subject to air attack despite being objects that are military because

---

[68] Protocol (to the Conventional Weapons Convention) on Prohibitions or Restrictions on the Use of Mines, Booby-Traps and Other Devices, 10 October 1980 (hereinafter Mines Protocol), Art 2(4); Protocol on Prohibitions and Restrictions on the Use of Incendiary Weapons, 10 October 1980, Art 1(3); US Commander's Handbook, § 8.2; UK Manual, § 5.4.1; AMW Manual, Rule 1(y); Customary International Humanitarian Law Study, Rule 8.

[69] Additional Protocols Commentary, § 2020.

sinking them would offer an attacker no definite military advantage in that particular situation.

The second contentious issue surrounds interpretation of the term 'military objectives'. There is widespread agreement that it encompasses any objects that are either 'war-fighting' or 'war-supporting'. War-fighting objects are those actually used to conduct hostilities or otherwise directly employed in military operations, while war-supporting objects are those in which the nexus between military operations and the object is relatively clear and direct. Military aircraft or airfields exemplify the former; the paradigmatic illustration of the latter is a factory that produces munitions.

The United States has adopted a broader approach. In its *Commander's Handbook on the Law of Naval Operations*, the term 'military action' found in the Additional Protocol I definition of military objectives is replaced with 'war-fighting or war-sustaining capability'.[70] In explanation, the Handbook notes 'economic objects of the enemy that indirectly but effectively support and sustain the enemy's war-fighting capability may also be attacked'.[71] Restated, a war-sustaining object is one without a direct nexus to military operations, but that ultimately makes such operations possible. Oil export infrastructure in a country that is reliant on export income to fund its war effort is the classic example. The differing approaches are especially relevant in the air context because the precision and range of aircraft and their associated weaponry render them uniquely suitable for conducting strikes against those categories of targets that sustain an enemy's ability to prosecute the war. For instance, the most efficient and effective manner of collapsing the enemy's oil export system would usually be through air attack (although the development of cyber operations offer an attractive option to air operations).

With regard to air-to-air operations, all military aircraft constitute military objectives unless they enjoy protected status under the law of armed conflict.[72] Through application of the use or purpose criteria in the definition of military objectives, other aircraft may qualify as military objectives by virtue of the activities in which they engage. It is important to emphasize that the aircraft need not conduct attacks to lose their protection as civilian objects. So long as the acts in question make an effective contribution to the enemy's military action and attacking the aircraft would provide a definite military advantage, they are military objectives. The AMW Manual offers the following examples of qualifying activities:

Engaging in hostile action in support of the enemy, e.g., intercepting or attacking other aircraft; attacking persons or objects on land or sea; being used as a means of attack; engaging in electronic warfare; or providing targeting information to enemy forces.

Facilitating the military actions of the enemy's armed forces, e.g., transporting troops, carrying military materials, or refuelling military aircraft.

[70] US Commander's Handbook, § 8.2.   [71] US Commander's Handbook, § 8.2.5.
[72] AMW Manual, Rule 26.

Being incorporated into the enemy's intelligence gathering system, e.g., engaging in reconnaissance, early warning, surveillance or command, control and communications missions.

Refusing to comply with the orders of military authorities, including instructions for landing, inspection and possible capture, or clearly resisting interception.[73]

Certain aircraft are entitled to special protection under international humanitarian law. For instance, Article 18 of the 1929 Geneva Convention for the Amelioration of the Condition of the Wounded and Sick in Armies in the Field provided that '[a]ircraft used as means of medical transport shall enjoy the protection of the Convention during the period in which they are reserved exclusively for the evacuation of wounded and sick and the transport of medical personnel and material'.[74] The protection only attached while the aircraft, which had to be marked, was over territory in the control of its own forces.

The 1949 Geneva Convention (I) for the Amelioration of the Condition of the Wounded and Sick in Armed Forces in the Field also deals with medical aircraft.[75] Article 36 grants protection to medical aircraft, although only when 'flying at heights, times and on routes specifically agreed upon between the belligerents concerned'. Flights over enemy territory are expressly prohibited in the absence of an agreement thereto between the parties to the conflict. Article 37 of Geneva Convention I allows medical aircraft to 'fly over the territory of neutral Powers, land on it in case of necessity, or use it as a port of call'. Prior notice is required and the aircraft in question are 'immune from attack only when flying on routes, at heights and at times specifically agreed upon between the Parties to the conflict and the neutral Power concerned'.

Additional Protocol I updates the 1949 protections for parties to the Protocol with a number of provisions regarding medical aircraft. Article 24 sets forth the basic scheme. As with the 1929 Convention, protection is automatic over areas not in enemy control so long as the medical aircraft performs only medical functions; there is no requirement for a pre-flight agreement with the enemy.[76] In airspace over zones where belligerent forces are in contact, an agreement is essential to ensure protection, although medical aircraft do not lose protection simply by being in the area.[77] Over areas controlled by the enemy, consent is required for flights.[78] As with civilian aircraft, 'the Parties to the conflict are prohibited from using their medical aircraft to attempt to acquire any military advantage over an adverse Party' wherever they fly.[79]

Given these treaty law standards and the substantial state practice involving medical aircraft, the experts participating in the AMW Manual project concluded that

[73] AMW Manual, Rule 26 (a)–(d).

[74] Geneva Convention for the Amelioration of the Condition of the Wounded and Sick of Armies in the Field, Art 18, 27 July 1929.

[75] Geneva Convention I.   [76] Additional Protocol I, Art 25.

[77] Additional Protocol I, Art 26.   [78] Additional Protocol I, Art 27.

[79] Additional Protocol I, Art 28.

customary law requires no consent from the opposing party when medical aircraft fly over areas controlled by friendly forces.[80] However, '[i]n and over areas physically controlled by the enemy, as well as in and over these parts of the contact zone which are physically controlled by friendly forces or the physical control of which is not clearly established, the protection of medical aircraft can be fully effective only by virtue of prior consent obtained from the enemy'.[81] Note the careful wording, as the experts did not conclude that protection only attaches once consent has been granted.

In contrast to medical aircraft, search and rescue aircraft and helicopters enjoy no protection under international humanitarian law. In fact, searching for downed aircrew or other military personnel is considered a military activity. As a result, civilian aircraft that engage in search and rescue operations lose their protection from attack for such time as they are doing so.[82]

United Nations (UN) aircraft are protected from attack so long as the UN forces they support are entitled to protection as civilians. Those forces lose protection if they become a party to the conflict. Of course, individual UN aircraft may become legitimate targets should they qualify as military objectives (see above).[83] While humanitarian relief aircraft benefit from no special protective regime, the activities they engage in are entitled to 'respect and protection', as are the individuals engaging in them.[84]

International humanitarian law contains no express rule regarding civilian airliners, although it is generally agreed that particular care must be taken in situations involving them.[85] This consensus is in part a reflection of international outrage over a number of instances in which civilian airliners have been downed, such as the shooting down of KAL 007 by Soviet aircraft in 1983. As to the application of international humanitarian norms vis-à-vis civilian airliners, there is no doubt that they may become military objectives through use or purpose, as when they are used to observe and report on military operations or fitted out to carry troops and military equipment. Of course, the resulting incidental injury and death from the shooting down of a civilian airliner would usually be excessive relative to the military advantage likely to be achieved, thereby breaching the rule of proportionality (discussed below).

Finally, even in the absence of explicit protection, international humanitarian law recognizes that aircraft may be granted protection by special agreement between the parties to a conflict.[86] Such 'cartel aircraft', which may include military aircraft,

---

[80] AMW Manual, Rule 77.   [81] AMW Manual, Rule 78(a).

[82] Additional Protocol I, Art 28(4).

[83] Convention on the Safety of United Nations and Associated Personnel, 9 Decenber 1994, Art 7(1); AMW Manual, Rule 98.

[84] Additional Protocol I, Arts 70, 71; AMW Manual, Rules 100–104.

[85] US Commander's Handbook, § 8.6.3; UK Manual, § 12.28; AMW Manual, Rule 58; San Remo Manual, § 53.

[86] US Commander's Handbook, § 8.6.3; UK Manual, § 12.28; AMW Manual, Rule 64; San Remo Manual, § 53(b).

are used for purposes like transporting prisoners of war or *parlementaires* (individuals engaged in negotiations). The agreements affording them protection typically delineate conditions for particular flights, such as speed, course, and altitude. Deviation from these conditions can result in a loss of protection.

In certain circumstances, protected persons and objects may be attacked in reprisal. Reprisals are actions that would otherwise be unlawful under international humanitarian law, but which are allowed in order to force the enemy to desist from its own unlawful conduct.[87] The classic example is an attack against enemy civilians in order to compel the enemy to stop attacking civilians. Reprisals are particularly likely to be taken through air operations because the range of aircraft makes it possible to strike many potential reprisal targets that would not otherwise be vulnerable to attack.

Consensus is lacking as to the legality of various types of reprisals. However, it is agreed that reprisals are unlawful as a matter of customary international law when directed against prisoners of war; interned civilians; civilians in occupied territory and their property; those who are *hors de combat*; and medical personnel, facilities, vehicles, and equipment.[88] As a general matter, these are not the sort of reprisal targets prone to air attack.

Additional Protocol I prohibits numerous forms of reprisals regarding which consensus as to their customary character is lacking. These include reprisals against the civilian population and individual civilians; civilian objects; cultural objects; places of worship; objects indispensible to the civilian population; the natural environment; and dams, dykes, and nuclear electrical generating stations.[89] Such individuals and objects are all highly vulnerable to air attack. A number of states that are party to the treaty have issued understandings with respect to reprisals directed against civilians. The understandings effectively make the prohibition conditional on compliance with international humanitarian law by the adverse party.[90]

---

[87] Responsibility of Germany for Damage Caused in the Portuguese Colonies in the South of Africa (Naulilaa Arbitration) (*Portugal v Germany*) (1928) 2 RIAA 1011 at 1025; US Commander's Handbook, § 6.2.4; F. Kalshoven, *Belligerent Reprisals* (2nd edn, Leiden: Brill Academic, 2005), 33.

[88] Geneva Convention I, Art 46; Geneva Convention II, Art 47; Geneva Convention III, Art 13; Geneva Convention IV, Art 33; Mines Protocol, Art 3 (prohibiting the use of booby traps as a means of reprisal against the civilian population); US Commander's Handbook, § 6.2.4.2; UK Manual, §§ 16, 18; Customary International Humanitarian Law Study, Rule 146.

[89] Additional Protocol I, Arts 20, 51(6), 52(1), 53(c), 54(4), 55(2), 56(4).

[90] For instance, the United Kingdom noted that:

The obligations of Articles 51 and 55 are accepted on the basis that any adverse party against which the UK might be engaged will itself scrupulously observe those obligations. If an adverse party makes serious and deliberate attacks, in violation of Article 51 or Article 52 against the civilian population or civilians or against civilian objects, or, in violation of Articles 53, 54 and 55, on objects or items protected by those Articles, the UK will regard itself as entitled to take measures otherwise prohibited by the Articles in question to the extent that it considers such measures necessary for the sole purpose of compelling the adverse party to cease committing

C. How must air operations be conducted?

Compliance with three international humanitarian law rules is required before an attack on a member of the armed forces, a civilian direct participant in hostilities, or a military objective may be lawfully attacked: the prohibition on indiscriminate attacks; the rule of proportionality; and the requirement to take precautions in attack. Although not unique to air warfare, the application of each in the context of air warfare raises particular issues.

Indiscriminate attacks are those 'of a nature to strike military objectives and civilians or civilian objects without distinction'.[91] They are unlawful both as a matter of treaty and of customary international law.[92] Such attacks must be distinguished from direct attacks on protected persons or objects. In an indiscriminate attack, the attacker conducts the operation without regard for any effect the attack may have on them.

Two forms of indiscriminate attack are particularly pertinent to air warfare. The first is an attack that is simply not directed at a military objective.[93] In the air environment, a violation of this norm might, for example, involve releasing weapons without aiming at a specific target, as in jettisoning live bombs that were not dropped during an attack without regard for what they are likely to hit. This might be done because of a desire not to 'waste' the weapon or because of the risks associated with landing with live ordnance. Whatever the reason, the violation occurs when the bombs are released unaimed.

The second form of indiscriminate air attack involves treating 'as a single military objective a number of clearly separated and distinct military objectives located in a city, town, village or other area containing a similar concentration of civilians or civilian objects'.[94] For instance, an enemy city may contain a district with a number of important military objectives, such as a headquarters, barracks for troops stationed there, and communications and transportation support facilities. It would be unlawful to conduct an airstrike blanketing the entire area if each of the military objectives can be targeted separately.

---

violations under those Articles, but only after formal warning to the adverse party requiring cessation of the violations has been disregarded and then only after a decision taken at the highest level of government.

UK Additional Protocol Ratification Statement, § (m). Interestingly, France did not reserve as to Art 51(6), but did make a statement regarding Art 51(8) that seems to leave open the possibility of reprisals against civilians. French Additional Protocol Ratification Statement, § 11, available at <http://www.icrc.org/ihl.nsf/NORM/D8041036B40EBC44C1256A34004897B2?OpenDocument>.

[91] Additional Protocol I, Art 51(4).

[92] Additional Protocol I, Art 51(4); Rome Statute, Art 8(2)(b)(xx); US Commander's Handbook, § 9.1.2; UK Manual, § 6.4; AMW Manual, Rule 13; Customary International Humanitarian Law Study, Rules 12, 71.

[93] Additional Protocol I, Art 51(4)(a).   [94] Additional Protocol I, Art 51(5)(a).

It must be cautioned that the test for compliance is one of feasibility; the prohibition is not a blanket ban on carpet-bombing, saturation bombing, or other means of target area bombing. Such methods of air warfare are lawful if there is operationally or technically no way to strike the military objectives individually (and the operation will comply with the rule of proportionality and the requirement to take precautions in attack). Factors that might affect the operational or technical feasibility of an operation include unavailability of precision (or sufficiently accurate) weapons, enemy air defences, a lack of targeting data sufficiently detailed to individually target, or the need to preserve guided weapons for operations requiring greater precision, such as those against high priority targets in densely populated areas.

Even if a lawful target is to be attacked by a discriminate method of air warfare, the operation must comply with the rule of proportionality. Codified in Articles 51(5)(b) and 57(2)(iii) of Additional Protocol I, this customary international law rule prohibits 'an attack which may be expected to cause incidental loss of civilian life, injury to civilians, damage to civilian objects, or a combination thereof, which would be excessive in relation to the concrete and direct military advantage anticipated'. It is an express acknowledgement that collateral damage (injury to civilians and damage of civilian objects) is often unavoidable during attacks. When this is the case, the rule permits the attack to proceed so long as the collateral damage expected is not excessive relative to the military advantage the attacker reasonably expects to attain. The rule of proportionality is especially important in the context of air warfare because air weapons may lack the precision of their land counterparts, often have greater blast and radius of effects, and are sometimes launched when the situation on the ground lacks clarity.

Assessment of whether an air attack has complied with the rule must be based on the reasonableness of the attacker's conclusions at the time. This is apparent from the terms 'expected' and 'anticipated' in the rule. As a matter of law, therefore, it is improper to characterize an attack as a proportionality violation solely based on the actual civilian casualties or damage to civilian objects that resulted; the *ex ante* expectation of collateral damage is the determinative factor. The same is true with regard to military advantage. For instance, consider the 50 unsuccessful decapitation strikes conducted by US air forces during Operation Iraqi Freedom. Their lawfulness depends on the military advantage that would have resulted had those attacks been successful and the degree of collateral damage that the mission planners expected. Of course, actual collateral damage caused and military advantage achieved may bear on the reasonableness of an attacker's expectations.

Air attacks are frequently employed to strike 'dual-use' targets. A dual-use target is one that serves both military and civilian purposes. 'Lines of communication' (LOC) such as major highways, airports, and rail lines exemplify the concept. Since they are fixed and lie behind enemy lines, LOCs are typically targeted from the air. The fact that these and other dual use targets continue to be used by civilians does not shield them from attack. On the contrary, any use by the military, even if such use is slight relative to civilian usage, renders an object a military objective subject to attack. Aspects of the target system that can be distinguished as purely civilian factor into the proportionality calculation. For example, on a dual-use airfield, the runway and taxiways are military objectives as such. However, certain of the hangers might only be used for civilian purposes. Should this be the case, expected damage to them would be included in the proportionality assessment. Civilians working at the airfield (other than those who qualify as direct participants in hostilities) expected to be injured or killed during the attack also qualify as collateral damage.

All direct effects, like blast damage or deaths caused by the collapse of a targeted building, are factored into the proportionality calculation.[95] Application of the rule is less clear with respect to indirect effects, also known as reverberating or knock-on effects.[96] The majority view today is that any reasonably foreseeable collateral damage must be considered when performing proportionality calculations. As an example, an attack on a dual-use electrical generating system may deprive many civilian users of electricity. The mere loss of electricity is not collateral damage since it does not involve loss of life, injury, or physical damage. However, if the absence of electricity would, for example, foreseeably cause damage at a manufacturing facility, this indirect effect of the attack would have to be considered when determining whether a proposed strike will comply with the rule of proportionality.

Even when the target is a lawful military objective or an individual subject to attack, and the planned attack would comply with the proportionality rule, international humanitarian law still requires the taking of precautions in attack. Set forth in Article 57 of Additional Protocol I, and considered generally reflective of customary international law, the norm requires that 'constant care shall be taken to spare the civilian population, civilians and civilian objects'.[97] The fact that most informed criticism of contemporary air attacks alleges that the attacker failed to take sufficient precautions to avoid collateral damage attests to the rule's centrality in air operations.[98]

By the requirement, those who plan or decide on attacks must do 'everything feasible' to verify that that target is a lawful one.[99] The critical aspect of this rule is the

[95] Direct effects are the immediate effects generated by the weapon, whereas indirect effects are those which are more remote in the causal sense. For instance, in an attack on an electrical generating facility, direct effects include the physical damage caused by the explosion. Indirect effects are those resulting from the loss of electricity.

[96] AMW Manual, commentary accompanying Rule 14.

[97] Additional Protocol I, Art 57(1); AMW Manual, Rule 30.

[98] For instance, see the criticism of leadership strikes during Operation Iraqi Freedom. Human Rights Watch, *Off Target: The Conduct of the War and Civilian Casualties in Iraq* (HRW, New York, 2003), 21–41. The assessment is analysed at M. Schmitt, 'The Conduct of Hostilities During Operation Iraqi Freedom: An International Humanitarian Law Assessment', 6 *Yearbook of International Humanitarian Law* (2003) 90–2.

[99] Additional Protocol I, Art 57(2)(a)(i); AMW Manual, Rule 32(a).

reference to feasibility. Feasible has been widely interpreted as meaning that which is 'practicable or practically possible, taking into account all circumstances ruling at the time, including humanitarian and military considerations'.[100] In practice, it relieves commanders from taking measures to verify a target that do not make sense militarily. For instance, an unmanned aerial system need not necessarily be used to monitor the target area during an attack if it is needed elsewhere for use in a higher priority strike or for other more important purposes. Of course, the attacker must have a reasonable basis for belief that the target is what he believes it to be before attacking; mere speculation does not suffice.

Precautions in attack also include selecting from among the available methods or means of warfare (tactics or weapons) those that are likely to result in the least collateral damage.[101] As with verification, a feasibility caveat lies at the core of application. To illustrate, precision weapons do not have to be used in an attack if they need to be conserved for higher priority targets or to avoid greater collateral damage in future strikes; this is so even when their employment might reduce the likelihood of collateral damage. Similarly, although flying at lower altitudes might allow aircrew to visually confirm a target, doing so within the threat envelope of enemy air defences is seldom operationally feasible.

A comparable requirement attends target selection. When multiple targets can be struck to achieve the same objective, an attacker must select the one likely to result in the least collateral damage.[102] For example, an attacker may seek to deprive an enemy military facility of power received through the civilian electrical grid. An attack on the grid's substations would place adjacent residences at high risk. If it is feasible to use a carbon filament bomb to attack the power lines running into the facility while avoiding civilian harm, such an attack is required. This rule applies only when a similar military advantage can be attained. There is no requirement that an attacker forfeit any degree of military advantage to avoid collateral damage (so long as the collateral damage in question is not excessive in violation of the proportionality rule). Moreover, the alternative course of action must be technically and operationally feasible.

Finally, the international humanitarian law requirement to take precautions in attack mandates the issuance of warnings when an attack can be expected to affect the civilian population.[103] This requirement is subject to the caveat 'unless

[100] Protocol (to the Convention on Prohibitions or Restrictions on the Use of Certain Conventional Weapons Which May be Deemed to Be Excessively Injurious or to Have Indiscriminate Effects) on Prohibitions or Restrictions on the Use of Mines, Booby-Traps and Other Devices as amended on 3 May 1996 (hereinafter Amended Mines Protocol), Art 3(10); UK Additional Protocols Ratification Statement, § (b). See also US Commander's Handbook, § 8.3.1; UK Manual, § 5.32 (as amended); AMW Manual, Rule 1(q); Customary International Humanitarian Law Study, Rule 15.
[101] Additional Protocol I, Art 57(2)(a)(ii); AMW Manual, Rule 32(b).
[102] Additional Protocol I, Art 57(3); AMW Manual, Rule 33.
[103] Additional Protocol I, Art 57(2)(c); AMW Manual Rule 37. Attacks on certain objects are subject to a specific warning regime. AMW Manual Rule 38.

circumstances do not permit'.[104] In air attacks, it will seldom be feasible to provide warnings because doing so would typically endanger attacking aircraft by allowing the enemy an opportunity to move air defences into the target area. Warnings could deprive the attacker of an element of surprise necessary for mission success. As an example, many airstrikes currently being conducted in and near Afghanistan target senior insurgent leaders. Warning the civilian population of an imminent attack would cause the insurgent targets to move, thereby guaranteeing mission failure.

It is sometimes reasonable to issue warnings of a general nature as to impending airstrikes. Doing so allows civilians to leave the threatened area or take measures to shelter themselves during an air attack. Yet, even general warning might sacrifice the element of surprise or heighten risk to attackers. The feasibility of warnings must, therefore, be assessed on a case-by-case basis.

D. What weapons may be used?

International humanitarian law prohibits the use of weapons that cannot be directed at a specific target or which have uncontrollable effects.[105] It also prohibits the use of weapons that cause unnecessary suffering or superfluous injury to combatants.[106] These prohibitions are unlikely to have much impact on modern air warfare both because of advancing weapons technology (even among the less technologically advanced air forces) and because of the requirement to perform a weapons review before fielding new weapons.[107]

The prohibitions and restrictions on weaponry most likely to affect air operations are treaty-based norms governing three common air-delivered weapons. The first is the prohibition on using air-delivered land mines in the 1997 Ottawa Convention.[108] For states not party to that treaty, the 1996 Amended Protocol II to the Convention on Conventional Weapons imposes special requirements regarding self-destruction and self-deactivation for parties thereto.[109] The trend towards state acceptance of a ban on anti-personnel land mines can be expected to mature into customary international law over time.

---

[104] Additional Protocol I, Art 57(2)(c); AMW Manual Rule 37.

[105] Additional Protocol I, Art 51(4)(b)(c); Rome Statute, Art 8(2)(b)(xx); Amended Mines Protocol, Art 3(8)(b); US Commander's Handbook, § 9.1.2; UK Manual, § 6.4; AMW Manual, Rule 5(a); Customary International Humanitarian Law Study, Rules 12, 71.

[106] Declaration Renouncing the Use, in Time of War, of Explosive Projectiles Under 400 Grammes Weight, Preamble, 29 November/11 December 1868; Rome Statute, Art 8(2)(b)(xx); Conventional Weapons Convention, Preamble; Convention on the Prohibition on the Use, Stockpiling, Production and Transfer of Anti-Personnel Mines and on Their Destruction, Preamble, 3 December 1997 (hereinafter Ottawa Convention); US Commander's Handbook, § 9.1.1; UK Manual, § 6.1; AMW Manual, Rule 5(b); Customary International Humanitarian Law Study, Rule 70.

[107] Additional Protocol I, Art 36; AMW Manual, Rule 9.   [108] Ottawa Convention, Art 1(1).

[109] Amended Mines Protocol, Art 6.

Cluster munitions are, contrary to occasional mischaracterization, not prohibited by customary international law. Instead, the 2008 Dublin Convention on Cluster Munitions governs their use by parties to that instrument. The Convention is rather limited in scope. By Article 2(2), it only applies to munitions containing submunitions that weigh less than 20 kilograms, and not to:

(a) a munition or submunition designed to dispense flares, smoke, pyrotechnics or chaff; or a munition designed exclusively for an air defence role;
(b) a munition or submunition designed to produce electrical or electronic effects;
(c) a munition that, in order to avoid indiscriminate area effects and the risks posed by unexploded submunitions, has all of the following characteristics:
   (i) each munition contains fewer than ten explosive submunitions;
   (ii) each explosive submunition weighs more than four kilograms;
   (iii) each explosive submunition is designed to detect and engage a single target object;
   (iv) each explosive submunition is equipped with an electronic self-destruction mechanism;
   (v) each explosive submunition is equipped with an electronic self-deactivating feature.

Treaty law also restricts the use of air-delivered incendiary weapons. Article 2(2) of Protocol III to the Conventional Weapons Convention prohibits their employment against military objectives located in a concentration of civilians. This provision is the subject to reservations issued by a number of states. For instance, the United States 'reserves the right to use incendiary weapons against military objectives located in concentrations of civilians where it is judged that such use would cause fewer casualties and/or less collateral damage than alternative weapons, but in so doing will take all feasible precautions with a view to limiting the incendiary effects to the military objective and to avoiding, and in any event to minimizing, incidental loss of civilian life, injury to civilians and damage to civilian objects'.[110] The reservation was deemed necessary because incendiaries are the weapon of choice when targeting facilities containing chemical or biological weapons; the resulting fire consumes chemicals and biological contagions, thereby preventing their spread.

Unmanned combat aerial systems (UCASs), or drones, have become a contentious weapons system over the past decade. Modern militaries increasingly turn to them to conduct attacks since they avoid risk to aircrew, loiter in the target area for extended periods, have impressive 'ISR' (intelligence, surveillance, and reconnaissance) capabilities, and offer an on-the-spot ability to track and kill a target. UCASs are the primary means used to attack individuals in counter-terrorist strikes globally and have played a central role in conventional combat operations in Afghanistan,

[110] Convention on Cluster Munitions, 3 December 2008.

Iraq, Libya, and elsewhere. All advanced air forces are increasingly relying on drone technology.

The sole issue of legal significance regarding the employment of drones involves their use in cross-border operations. This author takes the position that they may be so used in limited self-defence situations,[111] such as when the territory of a third state is being used as a base of operations and that state is unable or unwilling to police its territory.[112] As noted above, they may also sometimes be employed in cross-border operations during an armed conflict, for example, when a belligerent breaches neutrality by operating from neutral territory and the neutral state is unable or unwilling to address the breach. The law governing such operations is no different than that which governs any cross-border operation, such as a ground incursion by Special Forces or artillery fire across a border.

Unmanned systems are subject to the same international humanitarian law norms as other weapons systems. Application of those norms is most affected by fielding of the UCAS in the context of the requirement to take precautions in attack. In particular, recall the obligation to select that method or means of warfare that will minimize collateral damage. The ability of the UCAS to employ a multifaceted sensor suite to identify the target with greater reliability than might be possible using other systems, and of the system to loiter over a target and delay an attack until the point when collateral damage avoidance is maximized, means that as a matter of law its use will sometimes be compulsory. This point must be tempered by the caveat that any such requirement is shaped by the feasibility of doing so in the circumstances.

UCASs are sometimes criticized on the grounds that drone strikes cause civilian casualties and that the systems are employed without risk to the operator. Such criticisms are counter-normative and counter-factual. Operationally, drone strikes are less likely to cause collateral damage than many other systems. Some critics point to the fact that they can be used in high threat environments because they are unmanned and therefore make possible strikes, and resulting collateral damage, that might otherwise not be feasible. In fact, the situations in which this is the case are very rare. More to the point, international humanitarian law does not prohibit collateral damage; it prohibits attacks that are expected to result in excessive collateral damage. The criticism that the systems make possible attack without risk is a moral argument, not a legal one. The law of targeting is about balancing military necessity and humanitarian considerations, not ensuring a 'fair fight'.

---

[111] Pursuant to Art 51 of the UN Charter and its customary international law counterpart.

[112] M. Schmitt, 'Responding to Transnational Terrorism under the Jus ad Bellum: A Normative Framework', in M. Schmitt and J. Pejic (eds), *International Law and Armed Conflict: Exploring the Faultlines* (Leiden: Martinus Nijhoff Publishers, 2007), 157–96.

4 Concluding Thought

Of the recognized domains of warfare, the air is the least regulated by international humanitarian treaty law. This lacuna is best explained by the hesitancy of states to negotiate limitations on weapons systems and methods of warfare that are exceptionally useful militarily. In other words, it reflects the inherent tension that states feel between the concerns of military necessity and humanitarian considerations that pervade all of international humanitarian law. Customary international humanitarian law, developed through state practice, has nevertheless filled much of the vacuum.

CHAPTER 7

....

MARITIME WARFARE

....

WOLFF HEINTSCHEL VON HEINEGG

1 INTRODUCTION

....

THIS contribution deals with the principles and rules of international law applicable to international armed conflicts at sea, ie with the law of naval warfare and the law of maritime neutrality.[1] Although naval engagements during non-international armed conflicts occurred in the past,[2] the law governing such conflicts is not addressed here.

[1] Note that, although the subject matter of that law is armed conflict, it would be imprecise to use the term 'international humanitarian law'. The law of neutrality in most parts is not humanitarian in character, nor is it correct to say there is a humanitarian character in the law of the sea that has a considerable impact on the exercise of belligerent rights at sea.

[2] For an analysis of the applicability of the law of naval warfare to non-international armed conflicts, see W. Heintschel von Heinegg, 'Methods and Means of Naval Warfare in Non-International Armed Conflicts', 42 *IsrYBHR* (2012) 55–81.

The legal framework governing armed hostilities at sea is mostly covered by the Hague Conventions of 1907.[3] Other treaties date back to 1856,[4] 1936,[5] and, as regards the strictly humanitarian aspects, to 1949.[6] In view of the considerable age of the Hague Conventions it is obvious that they do not any longer meet the realities of modern weaponry and of contemporary methods and means of naval warfare. However, their basic principles as well as those of the other treaties mentioned are still generally recognized as customary in character. Moreover, there are two private drafts;[7] one by the San Remo Institute—the San Remo Manual[8]—and the other by the International Law Association—the Helsinki Principles[9]—that are widely accepted as being declaratory of the present law of naval warfare and maritime neutrality.[10] Hence, despite the fact that many states are reluctant to engage in

[3] Hague Conventions of 18 October 1907: No VI Relating to the Status of Enemy Merchant Ships at the Outbreak of Hostilities; No VII Relating to the Conversion of Merchant Ships into War-Ships; No VIII Relative to the Laying of Automatic Submarine Contact Mines; No IX Concerning Bombardment by Naval Forces in Time of War; No XI Relative to Certain Restrictions with Regard to the Exercise of the Right of Capture in Naval War; No XIII Concerning the Rights and Duties of Neutral Powers in Naval War.
  Mention must also be made of the Declaration of London Concerning the Laws of Naval War, signed on 26 February 1909 which did not, however, enter into force because it was not ratified by any signatory. See also *The Laws of Naval War Governing the Relations between Belligerents*, Manual adopted by the Institute of International Law, Oxford, 6 November 1913. These treaties and documents as well as the others referred to above and below are reprinted in A. Roberts and R. Guelff, *Documents on the Laws of War* (3rd edn, Oxford: Oxford University Press, 2001). See also the compilation of treaties at <http://www.vilp.de>.
  [4] Declaration Respecting Maritime Law, Paris, 16 April 1856.
  [5] Procés-verbal relating to the Rules of Submarine Warfare Set Forth in Part IV of the Treaty of London of 22 April 1930, London, 6 November 1936. For a short analysis see E.I. Nwogugu, 'Submarine Warfare—Commentary', in N. Ronzitti (ed), *The Law of Naval Warfare* (Dordrecht: Martinus Nijhoff, 1988), 353–65.
  [6] Geneva Convention for the Amelioration of the Conditions of Wounded, Sick and Shipwrecked Members of Armed Forces at Sea, 12 August 1949 (hereinafter: GC II). See also Protocol Additional to the Geneva Conventions of 12 August 1949, and Relating to the Protection of Victims of International Armed Conflict (Protocol I), 8 June 1977 (hereinafter: AP I).
  [7] See, however, also: Program on Humanitarian Policy and Conflict Research at Harvard University (HPCR), *Manual on International Law Applicable to Air and Missile Warfare* (Bern, 15 May 2009) (HPCR Manual).
  [8] International Institute of International Humanitarian Law, *San Remo Manual on International Law Applicable to Armed Conflicts at Sea*. See also the Explanations to the Manual in: *San Remo Manual on International Law Applicable to Armed Conflicts at Sea* (L. Doswald-Beck (ed), Cambridge, 1995) (San Remo Manual).
  [9] Helsinki Principles on the Law of Maritime Neutrality, *Final Report of the Committee on Maritime Neutrality*, International Law Association, Report of the 68th Conference, 496ff (Taipei, 1998).
  [10] The drafts are regularly referred to in manuals on the law of naval operations. See Office of the Chief of Naval Operations, US Dept of the Navy, *The Commander's Handbook on the Law of Naval Operations* (July 2007 edn, Naval Warfare Pub No NWP 1-14M); UK Ministry of Defence, *The Manual of the Law of Armed Conflict*, Ch 13 (Oxford, 2004) (UK Manual); German Navy, *Commander's Handbook—Kommandanten-Handbuch* (Bonn, 2002) (German Handbook).

a reaffirmation and codification of that law, there exists a generally accepted and operable set of customary rules and principles.[11]

It needs to be emphasized that—despite the considerable impact the 1982 UN Law of the Sea Convention (LOSC)[12] has had on the law governing armed hostilities at sea—the law of the sea has not led to an absolute demilitarization of the world's oceans and, thus, not to a prohibition on the exercise of belligerent rights at sea. Efforts aimed at demilitarization met with strong opposition from the predominantly Western sea powers.[13] Hence, for the time being, military operations at sea—whether in times of peace or in times of international armed conflict—are not prohibited. It may, moreover, not be left out of consideration that already the wording of the third sentence of Article 87 paragraph 1 of LOSC ('inter alia') reveals that the list of high seas freedoms in list (a)–(f) is far from being exhaustive. Accordingly, the freedom of the high seas also comprises other uses. Moreover, it is emphasized in the second sentence that the freedom of the high seas is to be exercised not only 'under the conditions laid down by this Convention' but also 'by other rules of international law'. Hence, the admissibility of, for example, nuclear tests is to be judged in the light of the Seabed Treaty of 11 February 1971.[14] The legality and admissibility of other military uses follow from either the law of naval warfare and neutrality at sea,[15] or from other rules and principles of customary international law.

[11] It is important to mention older publications that are of continuing interest and value, such as R.W. Tucker, *The Law of War and Neutrality at Sea* (Washington, DC: Naval War College, 1957); C.J. Colombos, *The International Law of the Sea* (6th edn, London: Longmans, 1967), 477ff; E. Castrén, *The Present Law of War and Neutrality* (Helsinki: Suomalaisen Kirjallisuuden Sueran Kirjapainor Oy, 241ff, 492ff); L. Oppenheim, *International Law* vol II. (7th edn, London: H. Lauterpacht, 1952), 457ff, 768ff; Ch. Rousseau, *Le Droit des Conflits Armés* (Paris: Pedone, 1983), 213ff, 409ff; D.P. O'Connell, *The International Law of the Sea*, vol II (ed I.A. Shearer) (Oxford: Clarendon Press, 1984), 1094ff.

[12] United Nations Convention on the Law of the Sea of 10 December 1982; entry into force on 16 November 1994. See also the Agreement relating to the Implementation of Part XI of the Convention, entered into force on 28 July 1994.

[13] For further details, see R.R. Churchill and A.V. Lowe, *The Law of the Sea* (3rd edn, Manchester: Juris Publishing, 1999), 426; R. Wolfrum, 'Restricting the Use of the Sea to Peaceful Purposes, Demilitarization in Being?', 24 *GYIL* (1981) 200–41; T. Treves, 'La notion d'utilisation des espaces marines à fins exclusivement pacifiques dans le nouveau droit de la mer', 26 *AFDI* (1980) 687–99.

[14] Wolfrum (n 13), 220–4; H.S. Levie, *Mine Warfare at Sea* (Dordrecht et al: Martinus Nijhoff, 1992), 138.

[15] See the references in n 11. For more recent analyses of the law of naval warfare and maritime neutrality, see G.P. Politakis, *Modern Aspects of the Laws of Naval Warfare and Maritime Neutrality* (London: Kegan Paul, 1998); W. Heintschel von Heinegg, *Seekriegsrecht und Neutralität im Seekrieg* (Berlin: Duncker and Humblot, 1995).

2 ENTITLEMENT TO EXERCISE BELLIGERENT RIGHTS AT SEA

In land warfare there is no prohibition on entrusting those who are not combatants proper with the exercise of belligerent rights.[16] However, in the law of naval warfare, as in the law of air warfare,[17] the exercise of belligerent rights is reserved to warships.

According to Article 29 of LOSC, which is widely considered as reflecting customary international law,[18] a 'warship' is defined as a ship

- belonging to the armed forces;
- bearing the external marks distinguishing such ships of its nationality;
- under the command of an officer duly commissioned by the government of the state and whose name appears in the appropriate service list or its equivalent; and
- manned by a crew which is under regular armed forces discipline.

Only state ships that meet the conditions of this definition are entitled to take belligerent measures. It is important to stress that 'belligerent measures' are not restricted to the use of armed force against enemy military objectives, they also comprise so called prize measures, ie visit, search, diversion, capture, and seizure of (enemy and neutral) merchant vessels, civil aircraft and/or their cargoes.[19] In view of the rights of belligerents *vis-à-vis* neutral navigation (and aviation) it is, for reasons of transparency, important that only those state ships that fulfil the requirements of the definition interfere with neutral vessels and neutral civilian aircraft. That approach is confirmed by the prohibition of privateering that dates back to the 1856 Declaration of Paris.[20]

The definition of warships covers all seagoing vehicles—surface or subsurface—irrespective of their design, construction, or equipment. Hence, not only traditional warships, like frigates, destroyers, or submarines, qualify as warships, but so too do small speed boats, like those in use by the Iranian *Pasdaran*, or transport ships and tankers, because there is no necessity for a warship to be armed.[21] Vessels other than warships which belong to, or are operated by, the state for exclusively non-commercial purposes and used for the performance of supporting tasks for the (naval)

---

[16]   However, if and for such time civilians directly participate in the hostilities, they lose their protection against attack.

[17]   HPCR Manual, Rule 17. See also Art 13 of the Rules of Aerial Warfare, The Hague, 17 *AJIL* (1923) Suppl. 245: 'Military aircraft are alone entitled to exercise belligerent rights'.

[18]   See, inter alia, San Remo Manual, para 13(g).

[19]   San Remo Manual, paras 112ff; W. Heintschel von Heinegg, 'Visit, Search, Diversion and Capture in Naval Warfare—Conditions of Applicability: Part II, Developments since 1945', 30 *CanYIL* (1992) 89–136.

[20]   See n 4.   [21]   O'Connell (n 11), 1106.

forces, but which have civilian crews, are auxiliaries. Other vessels performing governmental tasks such as police vessels, customs vessels and state-owned yachts are
state ships but not warships.

There are, however, some unresolved issues. The first relates to the question
whether the exercise of belligerent rights is indeed limited to state ships that meet all
the requirements of the definition of a warship. Indeed, as regards the relationship
between the belligerents' naval forces, it may seem rather odd if a lawful target,
such as an enemy warship, could only be attacked by a warship and not by another
state ship. Therefore, it could be argued that, in view of the object and purpose of
the rule—ie transparency *vis-à-vis* neutral navigation through the prohibition of
privateering—the scope of applicability of the rule is limited to the exercise of belligerent rights against neutral vessels and aircraft. Then, hostile acts against enemy
naval forces could be taken by any state ship. However, it is far from settled whether
the formal approach underlying the traditional law of naval warfare has been abandoned by states.[22]

The second unresolved issue concerns unmanned seagoing vehicles (USVs). At
first glance, such systems do not qualify as warships simply because they are not
manned by a crew. We should bear in mind, however, that very often USVs are
either integral components of a warship's weapons systems, or otherwise controlled
from a military platform. If that military platform is a warship or a military aircraft
the USV could be considered as sharing the legal status of the respective platform.
If, however, USVs are not part of, or controlled by, a warship, especially if they
operate autonomously on a pre-programmed course, it is impossible to follow that
approach. Of course, if operated by the armed forces or by another governmental
institution, they constitute state craft enjoying sovereign immunity.[23] That, however,
does not mean that they are 'warships' within the definition and thus entitled to the
exercise of the entire spectrum of belligerent rights. Some of the problems could be
solved if the scope of applicability of the rule on the exercise of belligerent rights
could be limited to prize measures taken against neutral merchant vessels and civil
aircraft. Another solution could be to interpret the definition of 'warship' in a more
liberal way as in the case of the definition of 'military aircraft'.[24] At present, however,
there is no sufficient state practice that would justify either approach.

The third issue relates to civilian mariners on board warships. The use of civilians
on board warships, especially of service personnel, is common practice. In most
cases they are not 'under regular armed forces discipline' although they are part of
the crew. The definition of warships, however, does not imply that the entire crew is
subjected to military discipline. It suffices if the warship is manned by *a* crew that
fulfils that requirement. The use of the indefinite article is of importance in view of

---

[22] For example, the *German Navy's Handbook* (n 10), para 83, still contains the traditional rule
reserving the exercise of belligerent rights to 'warships'.
[23] See NWP 1-14M (n 10), para 2.3.6.   [24] HPCR Manual, Rule 1(x).

the different wording of Article 4 of the 1907 Hague Convention No VII,[25] which provides that *the* crew of a converted merchant vessel 'must be subject to military discipline'. The use here of the definite article makes sense in view of the fact that the ship concerned used to be a merchant vessel and is now to be used as a warship. No such necessity exists in cases of ships that were from the outset designed and constructed as warships. Of course, there is no final answer to the question about the exact percentage of crew members who need to be under military discipline. In any event, the use of civilian mariners on board a warship does not alter that ship's status under international law, and it continues to be entitled to conduct all military operations, including prize measures, during an international armed conflict. It should not be forgotten, however, that despite the fact that there is no prohibition under the law of international armed conflict to use civilians for military purposes, they, after capture by the enemy, run the risk of being prosecuted for having directly participated in the hostilities.

3 The Legal Framework Applicable to the Conduct of Hostilities at Sea

A. Basic principles applicable to naval warfare

Although the law of naval warfare has its roots in older treaties, there is general agreement that the basic principles underlying contemporary international humanitarian law are equally applicable. This, especially, holds true for the principle of distinction, the principle of humanity, and for the prohibition of unnecessary suffering and superfluous injury.[26]

However, the obligations of belligerents engaged in naval warfare with regard to the protection of the natural environment are still largely unsettled. In this context, the Convention on the Prohibition of Military or any other Hostile Use of Environmental Modification Techniques (ENMOD Convention) hardly involves any problems. In accordance with this Convention, a modification of the natural environment is prohibited if the environment so modified is to be used with hostile intent to the detriment of another state, ie as a weapon. Disregarding nuclear weapons whose employment could, for example, cause huge tidal waves (tsunamis), no conventional weapons or techniques are now known whose employment could produce the above-mentioned effects. Likewise, there are no problems with

---

[25] See n 3.   [26] San Remo Manual, paras 38ff.

regard to naval forces attacking targets on land. In this case, Article 55 and the basic rule laid down in Article 35, paragraph 3 of the 1977 Additional Protocol I of 1977 will apply.

Things are different, however, with regard to the employment of means and methods of naval warfare that are not directed against land targets, or that do not affect civilians or civilian objects on land. Although Article 35, paragraph 3 of AP I will apply in this case, currently no conventional weapons are known whose employment could cause the qualified damage to the natural environment. In this context, however, account should be taken of the fact that today the natural environment ranks among the objects meriting protection in accordance with international humanitarian law. Therefore, any damage to or destruction of the natural environment that does not imply a military advantage and is carried out arbitrarily is prohibited. With regard to the employment of methods and means of warfare, the parties to an international armed conflict at sea are furthermore obliged to pay due regard to the natural environment and the provisions of international law established for its protection. This applies especially to rare or fragile ecosystems and the habitat of species that are endangered, threatened or in danger of extinction and of other forms of marine life.[27]

B. Geographical area

The area of naval warfare is the three-dimensional space in which acts of naval warfare may be carried out.[28]

First, the territory, internal waters, archipelagic waters and territorial sea areas of neutral states are inviolable. Subject to special rules on maritime neutrality, belligerent rights may not be exercised within those areas because that would constitute a violation of the neutral states' sovereignty. However, the sovereignty of neutral states does not extend to the contiguous zone, the continental shelf, the fishery zone and the exclusive economic zone. Hence, all acts of naval warfare may be carried out in these sea areas of a neutral state if the principle of due regard is adequately observed.[29]

Areas in which military activities are prohibited due to international agreements are not part of the area of naval warfare. In addition to those areas which have been permanently neutralized by international agreements (eg the Aåland Islands) this also applies to areas for which the parties to the conflict have agreed that they shall only be excluded from hostilities for the duration of the conflict or a particular period (eg undefended cities, demilitarized zones, and zones devoted to humanitarian purposes into which wounded and sick persons will be taken for medical care).

[27] San Remo Manual, paras 11, 35, 44.   [28] San Remo Manual, paras 10ff.
[29] San Remo Manual, paras 12, 34, 35; NWP 1-14M (n 10), para 7.3.8.

Consequently, the area of maritime warfare comprises:[30]

- the land territory of the parties to the conflict;
- their internal waters;
- where applicable, their archipelagic waters;
- their territorial seas;
- neutral contiguous zones, fishery zones, continental shelf areas, and exclusive economic zones;
- the high seas; and
- the airspace above those areas.

If the territorial seas of the parties to the conflict form part of an international strait the right of transit passage of neutral navigation and aviation may not be impaired or suspended.[31] The same holds true for the right of archipelagic sea lanes passage.[32] In the event of armed hostilities on the high seas, the parties to the conflict are obliged to pay due regard to the legitimate interests of other states.[33]

C. Military objectives

According to the principle of distinction, attacks, including those at sea, must be confined to military objectives. On the one hand, international law permits the employment of that kind of force that is required for the destruction of such objects, but on the other, any collateral damage that is excessive, and therefore no longer justified by considerations of military necessity, must be avoided, as must superfluous injury and unnecessary suffering. Moreover, the parties to the conflict must take all feasible precautions in order to ensure that civilians and civilian objects remain as unaffected as possible by the hostilities.[34]

The definition of military objectives in Article 52, paragraph 2 of AP I has been recognized as customary in character and it therefore applies not only to naval attacks on land targets, but also to any other use of weapons at sea.[35] Accordingly, military objectives are:

objects which by their nature, location, purpose or use make an effective contribution to military action and whose total or partial destruction, capture or neutralization, in the circumstances ruling at the time, offers a definite military advantage.

---

[30] San Remo Manual, para 10.   [31] San Remo Manual, para 27.
[32] San Remo Manual, para 27.   [33] San Remo Manual, paras 12, 36, 37.
[34] NWP 1-14M (n 10), para 7.3; German Handbook, paras 308ff; UK Manual, paras 13.24ff; San Remo Manual, paras 38ff.
[35] H.B. Robertson, 'The Principle of Military Objective in the Law of Armed Conflict', in M.N. Schmitt (ed), *The Law of Military Operations: Liber Amicorum Professor Jack Grunawalt*, vol 72 (Newport, Rhode Island: US Naval War College International Law Studies, 1998); San Remo Manual, para 40; UK Manual, para 13.26; NWP 1-14M (n 10) para 8.2.

It must be stressed that this definition contains two main elements, both of which must be fulfilled:

- effective contribution to military action; and
- definite military advantage by neutralization.

In this context it must be noted that 'capture' is merely an alternative to attack. As such it must be strictly distinguished from capture based on the law of prize. Hence, there is no need for a judgment delivered by a prize court. Upon seizure, ownership of lawful enemy military objectives automatically passes to the capturing state.

(i) *Enemy warships, auxiliaries, and military aircraft*

It follows from the definition of military objectives that enemy warships and military aircraft may always be attacked and captured without prior warning because they contribute to the enemy's military action by nature and, obviously, their destruction or neutralization will always constitute a definite military advantage. The same applies to enemy auxiliary vessels. The fact that these vessels do not qualify as warships only means that they are forbidden to carry out acts of naval warfare. Still, they are effectively contributing to the enemy's military activities and their neutralization will constitute a definite military advantage.

These principles were illustrated during the Falklands/Malvinas Conflict (1982). After the sinking of the Argentine warship *General Belgrano* some claimed that the British submarine's attack had been illegal because it had taken place outside the British exclusion zone and the *General Belgrano* had been moving away from that zone.[36] This claim would only be correct if the United Kingdom had, in a legally binding manner, confined attacks on military objectives to the area inside the zone. Since no such undertaking had been given, and there was no doubt that the *General Belgrano* was an enemy warship, its sinking was lawful. The sinking would have been permissible even if it had taken place, for example, in the Indian Ocean. The 'ships taken up from trade' (STUFTS) which were used by the United Kingdom were also lawful military objectives, because they were auxiliary vessels. The fact that they were not attacked by Argentine naval and air forces, was no indication of any legal opinion on the part of Argentina to the effect that those ships were protected from attacks by international law, but merely the result of a lack of appropriate air and naval capabilities.

Of course, ships and aircraft qualifying as lawful military objectives may not be attacked if they have clearly expressed their intention to surrender. A ship can do this by hoisting its flag. That presupposes visual contact. Today, however, targets are

---

[36] For the historical facts, see D. Rice and A. Gavshon, *The Sinking of the Belgrano* (London: Martin Secker & Warburg Ltd, 1984).

attacked 'beyond visual range' (BVR) and it is unsettled whether a given conduct (eg electronic signals) is to be considered a clear expression of surrender.[37]

The crews of captured or destroyed enemy warships, auxiliary vessels, and military aircraft are entitled to prisoner of war status. Moreover, after each engagement, the parties to the conflict shall, without delay, take all possible measures to search for and collect the shipwrecked, wounded and sick, to protect them against pillage and ill-treatment and to ensure their adequate care, and to search for the dead and prevent their being despoiled.[38] As the wording 'after each engagement' suggests, this obligation does not apply at all times, but only when it does not conflict with military considerations. It does not apply as long as search and collection would imply disproportionately high risks to one's own security.[39]

(ii) *Enemy merchant vessels and civil aircraft*

Merchant vessels and civil aircraft are enemy in character if they either fly the flag or bear the markings of the opposing party to the conflict, or if their enemy character may be presumed because of, eg, ownership, charter or control. Information to this effect will, as a rule, be provided by the intelligence services.

Within the geographical area of naval warfare, enemy merchant vessels and civil aircraft may be intercepted, visited, searched, and captured under the law of prize. Unless they enjoy special protection, they will always constitute 'good prizes'.[40] However, in principle, attacks on these vehicles are inadmissible, because they do not qualify as lawful military objectives by the mere fact of their enemy character/nature. In this context, it is important to note that, according to the 1936 London Protocol, an attack on an enemy merchant vessel is admissible in the cases of 'persistent refusal to stop on being duly summoned, or of active resistance to visit or search'. If an enemy merchant vessel is armed or sailing under convoy of enemy warships, this is a clear indication that it intends to actively resist visit and search. Therefore, it may be attacked in these cases. Moreover, it was clarified in the report by the committee of legal experts concerning the London Naval Treaty of 1930 that:

the expression 'merchant vessel', where it is employed in the declaration, is not to be understood as including a merchant vessel which is at the moment participating in hostilities in such a manner as to cause her to lose her right to the immunities of a merchant vessel.

Today there is agreement that the prohibition of attacks on enemy merchant vessels (and enemy civil aircraft) does not apply if they are effectively contributing to the

---

[37] If the commander of a warship wishes to surrender she/he should take all feasible measures to inform the enemy of her/his intention and comply with all orders.

[38] Article 18 GC II.

[39] For a discussion, see Commentary GC II, 130ff.

[40] NWP 1-14M (n 10), para 8.6.2.1; German Handbook, para 372; UK Manual, para 13.99; San Remo Manual, para 135.

enemy's military action and if their destruction or neutralization offers a definite military advantage in the circumstances ruling at the time.

Hence, enemy merchant vessels may be attacked, as lawful military objectives, if they:[41]

- engage in belligerent acts on behalf of the enemy, eg by minelaying or mine clearance or by taking prize measures against other merchant vessels;
- act as auxiliary vessels to the enemy's armed forces, eg by transporting troops or replenishing warships;
- are incorporated into or assisting the enemy's intelligence and communication system, eg by engaging in reconnaissance, early warning, surveillance or other command, control, communications, and information missions;
- are sailing under convoy of enemy warships or enemy military aircraft;
- carry arms enabling them to inflict considerable damage on warships (this does not include light weapons used for the crew's self-defence, for instance, against pirates, and purely defensive systems such as chaff); or
- otherwise make an effective contribution to the enemy's military action, eg by carrying military cargo.

These rules also apply to enemy civil aircraft. They must, however, be adapted to the special features of aviation.[42]

It goes without saying that even when, on the conditions mentioned, enemy merchant vessels and civil aircraft constitute lawful military objectives and may thus be attacked, the principles applicable to naval warfare and the rules concerning precautions in attack will apply.

(iii) *Land targets*

Naval attacks against land targets are regulated in the 1907 Hague Convention Concerning Bombardment by Naval Forces in Time of War (Hague IX). For many states, however, this Convention is no longer applicable because it has been superseded by the 1977 Additional Protocol I. Therefore, in addition to the principles and rules already mentioned (principle of distinction, precautions in attack), attacks on land targets, whether conducted by naval guns or missiles or by naval aviation, are, in particular, subject to the provisions of Articles 50–60 of AP I.

---

[41] San Remo Manual, paras 67, 70; NWP 1-14M (n 10), para 8.6.2.2; UK Manual, para 13.47; German Handbook, para 333.

[42] San Remo Manual, para 63; UK Manual, para 12.43ff.

D. Enemy vessels and aircraft enjoying (special) protection

Enemy vessels and aircraft serving humanitarian or other protected tasks may be neither attacked nor captured as long as their use is confined to the fulfilment of these tasks. While, due to the diversity of their functions, the protected status of these vehicles is designed in different ways, they must neither take part in hostilities nor wilfully interfere with the movements of armed forces. Besides, they are obliged to identify themselves and submit to inspections by enemy forces as well as comply with directions ordering them to leave a particular sea area.

(i) *Hospital ships*

Hospital ships are 'ships built or equipped [...] specially and solely with a view to assisting the wounded, sick and shipwrecked, to treating them and to transporting them'.[43] It makes no difference whether they are transporting wounded, sick, and shipwrecked members of the armed forces or wounded, sick, and shipwrecked civilians. All that matters is that they are not performing any other tasks, especially none of a military nature.[44]

In principle, the tonnage and the location of employment are of no significance. Nevertheless, to ensure maximum security, only hospital ships of over 2,000 tons gross should be utilized.[45]

Hospital ships may be utilized by the naval forces of a party to the conflict (military hospital ships) or by officially recognized relief societies and private persons. In the latter case, they must be given an official commission by the party concerned.[46] Hospital ships utilized by neutral relief organizations or neutral private persons require the consent of their respective governments and an authorization granted by a party to the conflict whose directions they must accept.[47]

Hospital ships may in no circumstances be attacked or captured, but shall at all times be respected and protected.[48] Of course, during and after an engagement they will act at their own risk.[49] This means that no violation of international law will be committed if they are located in the area of operations and affected by hostilities. Their lifeboats are protected as well. This protection is granted on condition that ten days before their employment their names and descriptions are notified to the parties to the conflict. The characteristics which must appear in this notification shall

---

[43] Article 22, para 1 of GC II.

[44] For instance, the so-called 'fighting hospital ships' employed during the second Gulf War did not qualify as a protected hospital ships because their use was not confined to taking care of casualties but also extended to the transport of armed forces and weapons. Neither will a Naval Rescue Coordination Centre embarked on a combat support ship confer on this vessel the status of a hospital ship.

[45] Article 26 of GC II.   [46] Article 24, para 1 of GC II.   [47] Article 25 of GC II.

[48] Article 22, para 1 of GC II.   [49] Article 30, para 4 of GC II.

include registered gross tonnage, the length from stem to stern, and the number of masts and funnels.[50]

The religious, medical, and hospital personnel of hospital ships and their crews shall also be respected and protected. They may not be captured during the time they are in the service of the hospital ship, whether or not there are wounded and sick on board.[51] This extensive protection of the personnel is to be explained by the consideration that hospital ships can only effectively perform their humanitarian functions if they can constantly rely on their trained and skilled personnel.

Hospital ships shall be distinctively marked in accordance with Article 43 of GC II and, because of the diminishing relevance of visual means of identification, they should also use such acoustic, optical, and electronic means of identification as agreed upon by the parties to the conflict.[52] The markings and other means of identification are not constitutive for protected status but shall only facilitate identification of these vehicles. In view of the problems involved in clear identification even today, the parties to the conflict should follow the example of the Falklands/Malvinas Conflict and, whenever practically possible, conclude agreements to define certain sea areas as so-called red cross boxes in which hospital ships of either side are safe to operate.[53]

The protection of hospital ships may not cease as long as they perform their protected function and they do not perform acts harmful to the enemy.[54] It is unsettled whether the prohibition, in Article 34, paragraph 2 of GC II, prohibiting the possession or use of 'a secret code for their wireless or other means of communication' is of continuing validity. This provision appears to imply a prohibition on possession and use of secure communication equipment for both sending and receiving encrypted communications. However, the English version is not the only authoritative text of the Convention. The equally authoritative French (and Spanish) text provides that 'les navires-hôpitaux ne pourront posséder ni utiliser de code secret pour leurs émissions par T.S.F. ou par tout autre moyen de communication'. According to Article 33, paragraph 3 of the Vienna Convention on the Law of Treaties 'the terms of the treaty are presumed to have the same meaning in each authentic text'.[55] Therefore, the conclusion is justified that only the possession or use of secure communications equipment for transmitting, not for receiving, messages in secret code is prohibited. While some states, like the United Kingdom during

[50] Article 22, para 2 of GC II.   [51] Article 36 of GC II.   [52] San Remo Manual, para 169.

[53] *S.S. Junod, La protection des victims du conflit armé des îles Falkland—Malvinas (1982): Droit international humanitaire et action humanitaire* (2nd edn, Geneva: ICRC, 1985).

[54] Article 34, para 1 of GC II. Note that the conditions enumerated in Art 35 of GC II shall not be considered as depriving hospital ships of their protection.

[55] For an equal consideration of the other authentic texts, see J. Ashley Roach, 'The Law of Naval Warfare at the Turn of Two Centuries', 94 *AJIL* (2000) 64 at 75; Commentary AP I and II, 1262–3.

the Falklands/Malvinas conflict,[56] hesitate to share this interpretation others, like the United States[57] and Germany,[58] obviously are prepared to provide hospital ships with equipment that would enable them to receive messages in secret code. Indeed, that would not only be in accordance with the generally accepted rules on the interpretation of multilingual treaties. It would also guarantee the effective performance of the genuinely humanitarian function of hospital ships. If hospital ships were not allowed to receive encrypted messages the respective enemy would be in a position to intercept messages sent to them and to deduce from that message the location of a future military operation.[59] If a 'Red Cross Box' is not a feasible alternative the hospital ship would be prevented from performing its humanitarian function because the respective flag state would be forced to, at least, delay the message in order not to jeopardize the military operation in question.[60] In view of the overall importance of the protection of the wounded, sick, and shipwrecked an interpretation leading to such a result would be manifestly absurd or unreasonable. Hence, it is no surprise that the San Remo Manual provides:

In order to fulfill most effectively their humanitarian mission, hospital ships should be permitted to use cryptographic equipment. The equipment shall not be used in any circumstances to transmit intelligence data nor in any other way to acquire any military advantage.[61]

This statement implies that hospital ships should be permitted to also use cryptographic equipment for the sending of messages. Indeed, in the explanations to the San Remo Manual,[62] the commentators state:

The participants were of the opinion that as the inability to receive encrypted information jeopardises the ability of hospital ships to operate effectively, the rule ought to concentrate on the sending of military intelligence. Therefore, in order to fulfil their humanitarian mission effectively, hospital ships should be permitted to use cryptographic equipment (modern terminology for a secret code) which in modern technology is an integral part of most communications systems. This cryptographic equipment may not be used for any purpose other than the humanitarian tasks of the vessel, obviously not to transmit intelligence data, nor for any other incompatible purpose.

---

[56] The British did not want to send messages in the clear because they did not want the Argentine forces to get in advance information about the possible movements of their forces. Instead, they created so-called 'Red Cross Boxes' where the hospital ships were deployed and where they waited to receive wounded soldiers.

[57] NWP 1-14 (n 10), para 8.6.3: 'As a practical matter, modern navigational technology requires that the traditional rule prohibiting 'secret codes' be understood to not include modern encryption communications systems.'

[58] German Handbook, para 357: 'Devices designed for the reception of encrypted messages should also be permitted when they are employed solely for the effective performance of humanitarian tasks.'

[59] Already in 1970 the late Professor O'Connell noted that dilemma. See D.P. O'Connell, 'International Law and Contemporary Naval Operations', 64 *BYBIL* (1970) 19–85 at 59ff.

[60] During the Falklands/Malvinas conflict the 'Red Cross Box' created considerable problems because the hospital ships were not informed prior to the arrival of the wounded and were, thus, not well prepared to treat them efficiently. See Junod (n 53), 26.

[61] San Remo Manual, para 171.   [62] Explanations to the San Remo Manual, para 171.4.

Seemingly, according to the San Remo Manual, hospital ships would not be prohibited to send encrypted messages as long as they are strictly related to the humanitarian function of the hospital ship and not used for any militarily useful purposes. In view of the importance of the humanitarian function and in view of modern communications technology it would indeed make sense if Article 34, paragraph 2 of GC II could be interpreted in that way. In this context it needs to be borne in mind that the prohibition of a 'secret code' is solely designed to reinforce the prohibition of committing acts harmful to the enemy in Article 34, paragraph 1 of GC II. Moreover, according to Article 35(1) of GC II a hospital ship may have on board an 'apparatus exclusively intended to facilitate navigation or communi-cation'. Today, modern means of communication necessitate the use of equipment that could be considered as violating the 'secret code' prohibition of Article 34 of GC II. The same holds true for navigation equipment, eg if using military GPS. The rules on medical aircraft in Article 28(2) of the 1977 Additional Protocol I take that development into account. While medical aircraft are prohibited from being 'used to collect or transmit intelligence data' this implies that they are allowed to receive and transmit messages in a secret code as long as the respective data are not of a military nature.

Hence, an extensive interpretation would certainly be in accordance with the object and purpose of Article 34, paragraph 2 of GC II. However, every inter-pretation finds its limits in the 'ordinary meaning to be given to the terms of the treaty'. These terms merely justify an interpretation allowing hospital ships the use of equipment for the receiving, not for the sending, of encrypted messages. The San Remo Manual together with the explanations does not serve as evidence for a view to the contrary. In the explanations it is made clear that paragraph 171 does not reflect the law as it stands. Rather, the majority view was that 'the present law still prohibits the use of such equipment and that this law has not fallen into desuetude. [Therefore the majority was] of the opinion that the text needed to reflect this fact and that the participants were encouraging a change in the law'.[63]

Since the sending of encrypted messages by hospital ships cannot be based upon the *lex lata*, states whose interests are specially affected should endeavour to con-tribute to a modification of the law. While a codification conference is not a realistic option, those states should rather convince other states to recognize a deviating practice as reasonable in order to safeguard the specially protected humanitarian function of such ships *de lege ferenda*. Numerous statements to that effect would certainly contribute to a modification of the law as it now stands.

---

[63] Explanations to the San Remo Manual, 171.5. Therefore, the participants could not agree on the formulation 'may' but merely on the formulation 'should be allowed to'.

An attack or other enforcement action is permissible only if a hospital ship has ignored a previous warning setting a reasonable time limit for abandoning the action or reversing the refusal in question. Even then, it may only be attacked if:[64]

- temporary arrest, diversion or capture are practically impossible;
- no other means of military control are available;
- non-compliance with the requirements for protection is serious enough to justify the assumption that the hospital ship may qualify as an admissible military objective; and
- the loss of life and collateral damage are not out of all proportion to the concrete and direct military advantage anticipated.

(ii) *Coastal rescue craft and other medical transports*

To the extent permitted by the requirements of combat operations, small coastal rescue craft employed by states or by officially recognized relief organizations, including their lifeboats, are protected as well.[65] This shall also apply if no prior notification to that effect has been provided. Nevertheless, any details concerning these small craft which will facilitate their identification and recognition should be submitted beforehand.

Other medical transports shall be respected and protected as well. If they are transporting equipment exclusively intended for the treatment of wounded, sick, and shipwrecked members of armed forces or for the prevention of disease, and if the particulars of their voyage have been notified to the enemy and approved by the latter, they may be intercepted and searched but not captured and attacked. The equipment on board must not be seized. Other medical transports shall be protected as well, in particular they must not be withdrawn from their medical mission. They will continue, however, to be subject to the law of war. They may be ordered to stop, divert, or keep a particular course. Such orders must be complied with. As soon as they are no longer carrying any wounded, sick, and shipwrecked, the transports concerned may be captured and seized.

These craft shall be marked. Their protected status will exist as long as they are employed for the performance of their usual tasks, identify themselves, and comply with an order to stop, submit to visit and search, or keep a particular course, and do not wilfully interfere with the movements of armed forces. They may, however, only be attacked if diversion or capture are practically impossible, no other means of military control are available, non-compliance with the requirements for protection is serious enough to justify the assumption that they may

---

[64] San Remo Manual, paras 49ff; UK Manual, paras 13.35ff.

[65] Article 27 of GC II; San Remo Manual, para 47(b); UK Manual, para 13.33; NWP 1-14M (n 10), para 8.6.3.

qualify as lawful military objectives, and the loss of life and collateral damage are not excessive in relation to the concrete and direct military advantage anticipated.

(iii) *Cartel vessels and aircraft as well as other vehicles granted safe conduct*

As a rule, cartel vessels and aircraft are used for the transport of prisoners of war or of *parlementaires*. Just like other vehicles given safe conduct, they shall only enjoy protection if this has been agreed between the parties to the conflict and as long as they observe the conditions laid down in the respective agreement.[66]

(iv) *Ships engaged in local trade and coastal fishery*

Vessels utilized solely for coastal fishery (not deep ocean fishery!) or for small-scale local trade as well as their fishing equipment, their rigging, their shipboard equipment and their cargo may not be captured, seized, or attacked because they are intended for no other purpose than to satisfy the basic needs of the civilian population.[67] These craft too will only be protected if they are performing their usual tasks and do not interfere with the movements of naval forces or otherwise take part in the hostilities.

(v) *Other protected vessels*

Finally, the following vessels are also exempt from capture or seizure and attack:[68]

- ships performing humanitarian tasks, especially those carrying relief shipments for the civilian population;
- ships enjoying special protection in accordance with the Hague Convention of 1954 because they are carrying cultural property;
- ships that have been assigned religious (eg pilgrim ships), scientific, or humane tasks; research ships which, for instance, are also collecting data that can be used in a military context are not protected;
- ships built and employed for the sole purpose of fighting marine pollution; and
- their lifeboats and life rafts.

E. Means and methods of naval warfare

It follows from the applicability of the basic principles of international humanitarian law to naval warfare that the belligerents are prohibited from engaging in indiscriminate

---

[66] San Remo Manual, para 47(c); UK Manual, para 13.33(c).

[67] Article 3 of the 1907 Hague Convention XI; NWP 1-14M (n 10), para 8.6.3; UK Manual, para 13.33(b); German Handbook, para 370; San Remo Manual, para 47(g).

[68] German Handbook, para 371; San Remo Manual, para 47; UK Manual, para 13.33; NWP 1-14M (n 10), para 8.6.3.

attacks or to use methods and means of naval warfare that cause, or are expected to cause, unnecessary suffering or superfluous injury. Moreover, they are, of course, under an obligation to comply with general or specific prohibitions on certain weapons, such as chemical or biological weapons.

The law of naval warfare provides such specific rules on means and methods whose employment is to be considered a special feature of naval combat operations.

(i) Naval mines and torpedoes

Naval mines are lawful means of naval warfare. This holds true for the old submarine contact mines as for modern naval mines. It does make a difference whether the mines concerned are anchored or unanchored naval mines.[69] The same applies with regard to torpedoes, which means that it does not matter whether they are wire-guided, actively homing in on their targets, or operated by a combination of different technologies.[70]

However, the use of naval mines and torpedoes involves the risk of damaging vessels and objects not qualifying as lawful military objectives, especially neutral and protected vessels. Therefore, certain principles aiming at protecting, as far as possible, innocent navigation from these hazards were agreed upon in the 1907 Hague Convention VIII. According to the Convention, naval mines must be so constructed as to become harmless as soon as they have broken loose from their moorings or when they can no longer be adequately controlled for other reasons. Torpedoes must become harmless when they have missed their mark. Although the provisions of Hague Convention VIII are formally applicable only to automatic submarine contact mines, today they are regarded as customary law that also applies to modern (and highly sophisticated) naval mines and torpedoes.

Taking into account that modern naval mines and torpedoes are highly discriminating weapons, the established rules regarding the use of these means of naval warfare can be summarized as follows:[71]

- Torpedoes must not be employed unless they sink or become harmless in some other way after having terminated their run.
- Naval mines may be used only for legitimate purposes; this also includes the denial of sea areas to the enemy.
- Subject to the rules concerning floating naval mines, the use of naval mines is restricted to those types that can be neutralized once they have broken loose from

---

[69] For an in-depth analysis, see H.S. Levie, *Mine Warfare at Sea* (Dordrecht et al: Martinus Nijoff, 1992), 23ff; W. Heintschel von Heinegg, 'The International Law of Mine Warfare at Sea', 23 *IsrYBHR* (1993) 53–76.

[70] San Remo Manual, para 79; NWP 1-14M (n 10), para 9.4; UK Manual, para 13.51.

[71] Articles 1–5 of the 1907 Hague Convention VIII; San Remo Manual, paras 80–92; NWP 1-14M (n 10), para 9.2; UK Manual, paras 13.52ff; German Handbook, paras 377ff.

their moorings or their control can no longer be adequately ensured for other reasons.

- The employment of free floating naval mines is prohibited unless they are employed against a military objective and they become harmless within one hour after ceasing to be under control.
- The laying of naval mines or the arming of naval mines and minefields that have already been laid must be notified unless they can only hit ships that are lawful military objectives.
- The parties to the conflict are obligated to map the location of the naval mines they have laid.
- If naval mines are laid in the internal waters, territorial seas, or archipelagic waters of the parties to the conflict, shipping of neutral states should be provided an opportunity to leave these sea areas beforehand.
- The laying of naval mines is prohibited in neutral internal waters, neutral archipelagic waters, and neutral territorial seas.
- The laying of naval mines must not have the effect of barring neutral territory or neutral waters.
- The party to the conflict laying naval mines must pay due regard to the legitimate interests in freedom of navigation on the high seas, eg by keeping open safe alternative routes for neutral shipping.
- The rights of transit passage and archipelagic sea lanes passage must not be impaired or suspended unless safe and equally convenient alternative routes are open to sea and air traffic.
- After termination of hostilities, each party to the conflict undertakes to do its utmost to render harmless the naval mines it has laid. With regard to the mines laid in the enemy's territorial sea, the enemy's internal waters or the enemy's archipelagic waters, the party to the conflict which laid them shall notify the former opponent of their position.

(ii) *Missiles*

Missiles and other projectiles using over-the-horizon or beyond-visual-range technologies are admissible means of naval warfare. This requires, however, that they are either equipped with sensors or receive enough data from external sources to adequately ensure that they can only be directed against lawful military objectives.[72]

(iii) *Submarines*

Submarines are warships proper, ie as long as they meet the requirements of the definition laid down in Article 29 of LOSC and in the corresponding customary

---

[72] San Remo Manual, para 78; UK Manual, para 13.50; German Handbook, para 380.

rule, they are lawful means of warfare and thus entitled to actively take part in hostilities at sea.[73] This includes combat activities against enemy military objectives as well as prize measures against enemy and neutral merchant vessels. It needs to be emphasized that submarines are subject to the same rules and principles of international law applicable to surface warships.[74] Since there is agreement on the fact that, for instance, enemy and neutral merchant vessels can, on the conditions mentioned, also be lawful military objectives,[75] today the relevance of this principle is confined to measures based on the law of prize. If crew, passengers, and papers of a merchant vessel subject to capture cannot be taken to a place of safety, destruction based on the law of prize must be avoided.

(iv) Naval blockade

A naval blockade is a method of warfare.[76] A blockade is used to prevent naval vessels and aircraft from entering or exiting enemy coastal areas or ports. It is aimed at preventing imports and exports from the enemy area concerned as well as maritime and air transport from and to that area. In contrast to the law of prize, which only allows action against certain vehicles and goods that furthermore must be intended for the enemy's armed forces, a blockade may be used to comprehensively prevent enemy commerce, ie imports and exports. The practical consequences of these findings are quite extensive. Thus, the practice in the Iran–Iraq conflict (1980–88) of preventing the export of petroleum exclusively by attacking tankers was illegal. Even though revenues from sales will enable the enemy to sustain or intensify the war effort, export goods will never constitute contraband. The only admissible way of preventing exports is by establishing and enforcing a blockade.

Although a naval blockade is directed exclusively against enemy territory, it also affects neutral vessels and aircraft. Therefore the issue of naval blockade is sometimes dealt with in the context of maritime neutrality.[77]

[73] NWP 1-14M (n 10), para 8.7, 7.10; German Handbook, para 381; Helsinki Principles (n 9), para 5.2.10. See also W. Heintschel von Heinegg, 'The International Legal Framework of Submarine Operations', 39 *IsrYBHR* (2009) 331–56.

[74] San Remo Manual, para 45.

[75] See text accompanying nn 41 and 42. Further, San Remo Manual, para 67; Helsinki Principles (n 9), para 5.1.2.

[76] See W. Heintschel von Heinegg, 'Blockade', in *Encyclopedia of Public International Law* (ed R. Wolfrum), available at <http://www.mpepil.com>.

[77] See the references in n 10. See further NWP 1-14M (n 10), para 7.7; German Handbook, paras 291ff.

(a) *Establishment and maintenance of a blockade*

A blockade must be declared and notified by the government of the party to the conflict or by a commander authorized by his government.[78] The declaration must include:

- the exact date on which the blockade is to begin;
- the exact coordinates of the blockade line; and
- the period of grace granted neutral vessels and aircraft to leave the blockaded area.

Likewise, the blockading power is obliged to declare and notify:

- any expansion or prolongation,
- reestablishment; and
- any temporary or final lifting of the blockade.[79]

The enemy as well as all neutral states must be notified of the declaration of a blockade. This may usually be achieved by a Notice to Mariners (NOTMAR).

(b) *Effectiveness*

In order to be legally binding, a naval blockade must be effective.[80] Effectiveness is a question of fact, ie it depends on the circumstances of each individual case. In general, however, a blockade is effective if, due to the presence of naval and air forces or other assets for maintaining and enforcing the blockade, there is a high probability that leaving or heading for the blockaded area will be detected and prevented or if, for other reasons, such movements will involve considerable hazards. Therefore, even a so-called long-distance blockade is not inadmissible in any case.[81] The fact that the blockading force is temporarily absent due to stress of weather or for the purpose of pursuing a blockade runner will not jeopardize the effectiveness of a blockade.[82] Neither is there any need to close every avenue of approach or exit so that, for instance, air transports do not have to be prevented.[83]

If a blockade no longer meets these requirements it will become legally void. An expulsion or destruction of the blockading force by the enemy will terminate effectiveness, even if new forces are entrusted with maintaining and enforcing the blockade straightaway. Such cases require a renewed declaration and notification of the blockade.

---

[78] San Remo Manual, para 93.   [79] San Remo Manual, para 94.

[80] See the 1856 Paris Declaration (n 4), para 4; San Remo Manual, para 95; UK Manual, para 13.67; German Handbook, paras 293ff.

[81] San Remo Manual, para 96: 'The force maintaining the blockade may be stationed at a distance determined by military requirements'.

[82] German Handbook, para 293.   [83] German Handbook, para 293.

(c) Further conditions of admissibility

Maintenance and enforcement of a blockade do not always require the employment of surface forces. It is also admissible to use a combination of means and methods of warfare that are consistent with international humanitarian law.[84] Thus it may be sufficient, for instance, to blockade an enemy port by the employment of naval mines.[85] It must be ensured, however, that vessels enjoying special rights of access (eg distressed vessels) can be given a timely warning and directed into a port without any damage.

As a method of warfare solely directed against enemy, or enemy controlled, territory, a naval blockade must not bar access to neutral ports and coasts.[86]

A blockade must be implemented impartially.[87] This means that it must be enforced against vessels and aircraft of all states. Preferential treatment of the vehicles of a particular nationality, including those of one's own nation, renders the blockade legally invalid.

A blockade must never be devoted to the sole objective of starving the civilian population or depriving it of vital items (prohibition of the so-called hunger blockade). A blockade is also inadmissible, if it is certain or to be anticipated that the negative effect on the civilian population is excessive in relation to the concrete and direct military advantage anticipated.[88]

(d) Special entry and exit regulations

Although neutral warships and neutral military aircraft enjoy no right of access to the blockaded area, their entry or exit may be authorized. Such special authorization may be made subject to conditions the blockading power considers appropriate.[89]

Neutral vessels and aircraft in evident distress should be authorized entry into as well as subsequent exit from the area. Of course, this authorization may also be subject to special conditions.

If there is a shortage of foodstuffs and pharmaceuticals or other essential items for the civilian population in the blockaded area, the blockading power is obligated to authorize the passage of relief consignments.[90] This also applies to pharmaceuticals intended for the wounded and sick members of the armed forces.[91] The blockading power will continue to be entitled, however, to determine the technical details for a passage of this kind, including visit and search. Moreover, it can

---

[84] San Remo Manual, para 97: 'A blockade may be enforced and maintained by a combination of legitimate methods and means of warfare provided this combination does not result in acts inconsistent with the rules set out in this document.' See also UK Manual, para 13.69.

[85] As in the case of Haiphong.

[86] San Remo Manual, para 99; UK Manual, para 13.71.

[87] NWP 1-14M (n 10), para 7.7.2.4; San Remo Manual, para 100.

[88] San Remo Manual, para 102.   [89] NWP 1-14M (n 10), para 7.7.3.

[90] San Remo Manual, para 103; UK Manual, para 13.75; German Handbook, para 300.

[91] San Remo Manual, para 104.

make the authorization conditional upon the fact that local distribution of relief supplies is monitored by a protecting power or a humanitarian relief organization (eg International Committee of the Red Cross) ensuring impartiality. Use of the relief consignments is to be confined to their original purpose.[92]

(e) *Breach of blockade*

A vessel or aircraft which has attempted to leave or enter the blockaded area while being aware of the blockade is subject to capture as long as it is being pursued by a warship or military aircraft. If pursuit is abandoned, for instance, because the vessel has reached a neutral territorial sea, it may no longer be captured even if it is subsequently encountered on the high seas again. A vehicle that has been captured because of a breach of blockade is subject to confiscation. If it actively resists capture despite prior warning, it may be attacked.[93]

An attempt of breach of blockade occurs if a vessel leaves a blockaded port or if an aircraft takes off from an airport in the blockaded area or if they are on a course destined to such port or airport. According to the US Manual, it 'is immaterial that the vessel or aircraft is at the time of interception bound for neutral territory, if its ultimate destination is the blockaded area'.[94] This implies that the doctrine of continuous voyage may be applied to naval blockades. There are, however, good reasons to maintain that the doctrine of continuous voyage may not be applied to blockades.[95] Moreover, Article 19 of the 1909 London Declaration provides: 'Whatever may be the ulterior destination of a vessel or of her cargo, she cannot be captured for breach of blockade, if, at the moment, she is on her way to a non-blockaded port.'

(f) *Zones*

Under the conditions of modern naval warfare it is indispensable to monitor and control as far as possible the area of operations and the objects within the respective sea area. The law of naval warfare recognizes this by, inter alia, accepting interference with neutral navigation (and aviation) for force protection or other legitimate purposes. As long as the principle of proportionality is observed, the respective control measures may be extended beyond the actual area of operations.

(g) *Control of the immediate vicinity of operations and warning zones*

The immediate area or vicinity of operations is that area within which hostilities are taking place or belligerent forces are actually operating.[96] Within that area belligerents are entitled to establish special restrictions for neutral maritime and air transport. They may, for instance, require vessels and aircraft to clearly identify

---

[92] San Remo Manual, para 103.   [93] San Remo Manual, paras 60(e), 67(a).
[94] NWP 1-14M (n 10), para 7.7.4.   [95] See Heintschel von Heinegg, 'Blockade' (n 76), para 41.
[96] NWP 1-14M (n 10), para 7.8. See also San Remo Manual, para 131.

themselves or refrain from certain activities when approaching a force (so-called defence bubbles which are also admissible in peacetime). If this is absolutely necessary for the safety of the units or the success of the respective mission, the access of neutral vehicles to the area of operations may be barred completely. Such measures, however, are only admissible in the area within which combat activities are taking place or units of the naval or air forces are actually operating, or in the adjoining environment. Access to neutral ports or coasts or passage through international straits in which the right of transit passage applies must not be impeded under any circumstances, unless another route of similar convenience with respect to navigational and hydrographical characteristics is available. The recognition of special belligerent rights in the immediate vicinity of operations is due to the fact that the presence of vessels and aircraft in that area will legitimately be considered a high threat, both for the vehicles concerned and for the belligerent units operating in the area.

Warning zones are designed to warn others of certain dangers caused by either the lawful uses of the seas or international air space (eg weapons exercises), measures of force protection ('defensive bubbles'), or activities taken in order to accomplish a particular mission. Their legality is generally recognized both in times of peace and in times of war.[97]

(h) *Exclusion zones*

In view of the illegality of the war zones established especially by the Nuremberg Tribunal[98] and the doubts raised as to the legality of the zones established by the belligerents of the Falklands/Malvinas conflict (1982)[99] and of the Iran–Iraq War (1980–88),[100] it is not absolutely clear whether and to what extent so-called exclusion zones are in accordance with the law of naval warfare. Still, because of their recognition in national military manuals,[101] the San Remo Manual,[102] and the Helsinki Principles[103] some general conclusions are possible.

---

[97] NWP 1-14M (n 10), para 7.8, para 4.4.7. See also HPCR Manual, Rule 106.

[98] The IMT, in its judgment against Admiral Dönitz, held that 'the proclamation of operational zones and the sinking of neutral merchant vessels which enter those zones presents a different question. This practice was employed in the War of 1914–18 by Germany and adopted in retaliation by Great Britain. The Washington conference of 1922, the London Naval Agreement of 1930, and the Protocol of 1936, were entered into with full knowledge that such zones had been employed in World War I. Yet the Protocol made no exception for operational zones. The order of Doenitz to sink neutral ships without warning when found within these zones was, therefore, in the opinion of the Tribunal, a violation of the Protocol', 22 *IMT* 635ff.

[99] See R.P. Barston and P. Birnie, 'The Falkland Islands/Islas Malvinas Conflict—A Question of Zones', 7 *Marine Policy* (1983) 14–24.

[100] See W.J. Fenrick, 'The Exclusion Zone Device in the Law of Naval Warfare', 24 *CanYIL* (1986) 91–126.

[101] NWP 1-14M (n 10), para 7.9; UK Manual, paras 13.77ff; German Handbook, paras 304ff.

[102] San Remo Manual, paras 105ff.   [103] Helsinki Principles, para 3.3.

An exclusion zone is the three-dimensional space in which a party to the conflict claims comprehensive control rights or denies access to vessels and aircraft in order to protect them from the effects of armed conflicts. Due to their extensive effects on neutral maritime and air transport, such exclusion zones are admissible only in exceptional cases and are subject to stringent requirements. They must not be devoted to the purpose of evading the requirements of the law of blockade or of absolving the parties to the conflict of the obligation to positively identify lawful military targets. A vehicle that may not be attacked, ie especially neutral merchant vessels and civil aircraft, will never lose this protection for the sole reason that they have entered an exclusion zone without authorization.

If a party to the conflict thus feels compelled in specific exceptional circumstances to establish (and enforce) an exclusion zone, the following restrictions apply:[104]

- Inside the exclusion zone the same rules and principles of international law applicable in international armed conflict will apply as outside.
- Location and size of the zone and the duration of its existence as well as the measures to be taken in it must not be disproportionate to the absolutely necessary and legitimate needs of security and defence.
- Due regard must be paid to the rights of the neutral states regarding the use of the seas.
- Safe passages for sea and air traffic must be kept open if, due to its spatial dimensions, the zone considerably restricts free and safe access to neutral ports and coasts or if routes normally used by international sea and air traffic are affected.
- The beginning and duration of the zone's existence and its location and size as well as the restrictions imposed on neutral vehicles in this area must be publicized, including the notification of all other states.

If a neutral vessel or aircraft observes the restrictions imposed on it in an exclusion zone by one of the parties to the conflict, the opposing party to the conflict may not consider such compliance as a form of contributing to the enemy's military action.

---

[104] See the preceding references in nn 101–103.

4 Capture and Destruction of Enemy Merchant Vessels and Civil Aircraft under Prize Law

A. Enemy merchant vessels and their cargoes

Unless performing special tasks, especially of a humanitarian character, enemy merchant vessels and civil aircraft may be subjected to all measures based on the law of prize. Hence, they may be captured at any time within the region of naval warfare.[105] Capture does not require prior interception followed by visit and search. Capture only means the assumption of command. Ownership of these vehicles will pass to the capturing state only as a result of a judgment delivered by a prize court.[106]

In exceptional situations, captured enemy merchant vessels and civil aircraft may be destroyed as prizes if, owing to the circumstances, there is no chance of taking them into an own or allied port.[107] Such destruction under the law of prize must be strictly distinguished from cases in which an enemy merchant vessel qualifies as a lawful military objective. It is only admissible if, prior to destruction:

- passengers and crew have been placed in a place of safety; for this purpose the ship's boats are not regarded as a place of safety unless the safety of the passengers and crew is assured, in the existing sea and weather conditions, by the proximity of land, or the presence of another vessel which is in a position to take them on board;
- the ship's papers have been safeguarded; and
- if feasible, the personal effects of passengers and crew have also been taken to a safe place.[108]

The cargo of enemy vehicles is subject to seizure and confiscation if it can be established that it consists of enemy goods or contraband. Goods owned by neutrals and not constituting contraband must be returned to the owners. If this is not possible, the owners must be indemnified.

---

[105] San Remo Manual, paras 135, 141. See also HPCR Manual, Rule 134.

[106] See P. Reuter, 'Étude de la règle: "Toute prise doit être jugée"' (Paris: Les éditions internationales, 1933).

[107] San Remo Manual, para 139; HPCR Manual, Rule 135.

[108] San Remo Manual, para 139; HPCR Manual, Rule 135.

B. Crews and passengers of captured enemy merchant vessels and civil aircraft

The officers and crew members of captured enemy merchant vessels and civil aircraft are entitled to prisoner of war status.[109] However, they may also be released. The passengers are subject to the discipline of the captor. Passengers who are nationals of a neutral state will be released unless they have directly taken part in the hostilities, actively resisted capture, or if they had been employed in the service of the enemy. In such cases they will also become prisoners of war.

5 MARITIME NEUTRALITY

A. Preliminary remarks

At present the continuing validity and binding force of the law of neutrality is far from generally accepted. In view of the political implications and economic interests, but also due to the comparatively long time for which the international agreements have been in force, there is no full consensus among states about the scope of the law of neutrality. Even today, some states take the view that the applicability of the law of neutrality is limited to a state of war *strictu sensu*. However, there are considerably different conceptions about the features distinguishing 'war' from 'international armed conflict'. While some states continue to regard a declaration of war as a precondition, others base their assessment on the extent and intensity of the armed conflict.[110]

Irrespective of these uncertainties, however, there is general agreement on the fact that in each international armed conflict at sea there is a need to protect states that are not involved in the conflict, their nationals and the aircraft and vessels operated under their flag. The law of maritime neutrality, however, not only comprises protective regulations, but also obligations to be fulfilled by neutral states and their nationals because the law of maritime neutrality also has an aim to prevent the escalation of an international armed conflict.[111]

---

[109] Article 4A, para 5 of GC III.

[110] See W. Heintschel von Heinegg, '"Benevolent" Third States During International Armed Conflicts: The Myth of the Irrelevance of the Law of Neutrality', in M.N. Schmitt and J. Pejic (eds), *International Law and Armed Conflict: Exploring the Faultlines. Essays in Honour of Yoram Dinstein* (Leiden: Martinus Nijhoff, 2007), 543–68.

[111] Heintschel von Heinegg (n 110), 543–68.

B. Fundamental features of maritime neutrality

(i) *Neutral status*

As long as states explicitly proclaim their neutrality once an international armed conflict has come into existence, their neutral status is beyond doubt. In present-day armed conflicts, however, it has become very rare to issue such declarations of neutrality. This is the result, among other things, of the fact that, according to traditional law, neutral states are especially committed to the strict observance of impartiality and abstention so that, for instance, the export of goods to one of the parties to the conflict could be considered by the other party to the conflict as a violation of the state's neutral duties.

It is true that the law of maritime neutrality also involves obligations of absten-tion and impartiality, but these are far less stringent than the ones laid down in the traditional law of neutrality. Regarding the law of maritime neutrality, it is therefore generally agreed that every state that is not a party to the conflict is a neutral state.

The terms 'neutral vessels' and 'neutral aircraft' refer to all vessels and aircraft either flying the flag or bearing the markings of a neutral state. In this context it must be emphasized that the flag and the marks only provide *prima facie* evidence. Consequently, vessels and aircraft, although flying a neutral flag, or bearing neutral marks, may be treated as enemy in character, if, for example, a vessel is found to be registered in the enemy state or if there is other evidence justifying doubt as to its entitlement to fly the neutral flag.[112]

(ii) *Neutrality and the Charter of the United Nations*

According to the Charter of the United Nations, states are obliged to settle their disputes by peaceful means. In particular, it is prohibited to resort to the threat or use of military force. If the UN Security Council determines a threat to or a breach of the peace, or the existence of an act of aggression according to Chapter VII of the Charter, it can decide upon non-military or military enforcement measures designed to maintain or restore international peace and security. When called upon by the Security Council, the members of the United Nations are obliged to support the United Nations or the states authorized by the Security Council to execute the enforcement measures. In particular, they are forbidden to render any kind of assis-tance to the state against which enforcement action is taken. At best, an exception will be made in the case of humanitarian relief shipments that, as a rule, require the consent of the Security Council.

These obligations laid down in the Charter of the United Nations will take prec-edence over the obligations arising from the law of maritime neutrality.[113] If the

---

[112] San Remo Manual, paras 7–9.
[113] San Remo Manual, paras 7–9. See also Helsinki Principles (n 9), para 1.2; HPCR Manual, Rule 165.

Security Council has made use of its powers under Chapter VII of the Charter, no state will be allowed to escape the resulting duties by invoking the law of (maritime) neutrality. Of course, this precedence is of practical significance only in those cases in which the Security Council decides on enforcement measures or at least names the lawbreaker. Without an authoritative decision of the Security Council there is at best only the theoretical possibility of declaring a breach of the law because, in practice, not infrequently both or all parties to the conflict will plead that they are only making use of their right of self-defence. Consequently, in the absence of a Security Council decision the states not involved in the conflict remain free to claim neutral status.

C. Neutral sea areas

The outbreak of armed hostilities at an international level does not alter the continued validity of the international law of peace with regard to the relationship between the parties to the conflict and neutral states. The international law of peace, however, is modified by the law of maritime neutrality to the extent that this is required for the purpose of preventing an escalation of the armed conflict. On the one hand, the parties to the conflict are obliged to respect the inviolability of neutral territory, neutral internal waters, neutral territorial seas, and the neutral airspace above these areas.[114] Within and above these areas all hostilities, that is the use of armed force and of other measures of maritime war (including measures based on the law of prize) are prohibited.[115] There is one exception to this principle which applies to measures of self-defence, in the event that one of the parties to the conflict is under (imminent) attack in these areas. On the other hand, a neutral state is obliged to prevent the parties to the conflict from abusing these areas as a sanctuary or base of operations. If the neutral state is unwilling or unable to do so, the aggrieved belligerent is entitled to take all measures necessary to terminate the violation of neutral territory or neutral waters.[116]

(i) *Belligerent warships in neutral ports and roadsteads*

A neutral state is entitled to close all or some of its ports and roadsteads to warships of the parties to the conflict. In doing so it must not discriminate against any of these parties. If, at the outbreak of hostilities, a warship of a party to the conflict is in a neutral port or roadstead, and if the neutral state decides to close its ports and roadsteads, the warship must be afforded a 24-hour period of grace in which to

---

[114] San Remo Manual, paras 14–17; Helsinki Principles (n 9), paras 1.4, 2.1.
[115] San Remo Manual, paras 14–17; Helsinki Principles (n 9), paras 1.4, 2.1. See also UK Manual, paras 13.7ff; NWP 1-14M (n 10), para 7.3; German Handbook, paras 236ff.
[116] San Remo Manual, para 22; HPCR Manual, Rule 168(b).

depart. Except for cases of distress, belligerent warships are only allowed to call at those ports and roadsteads that have been kept open. The neutral state is obliged to take all measures required to enforce the closure.

Unless the neutral state has adopted regulations to the contrary, the period for which a warship of the parties to the conflict stays in its ports and roadsteads must not exceed 24 hours.[117] A warship's stay exceeding 24 hours is admissible only on the occasion of damage or due to the existing sea conditions. As soon as the cause of the delay has been removed, the warship must immediately leave. If it does not, or is unable to comply with an appropriate request, the warship shall be arrested and its crew shall be interned.

Unless otherwise provided for by the laws and regulations of the neutral state, not more than three warships of one party to the conflict may be in one of the neutral state's ports or roadsteads at the same time. When warships of both parties to the conflict are present in a neutral port or roadstead at the same, not less than 24 hours must elapse between the departure of the vessels of the respective parties.[118] The order of departure is determined by the order of arrival, unless an extension of stay has been granted to the ship that was the first to arrive. A warship of a party to the conflict may not leave a neutral port or roadstead less than 24 hours after the departure of a merchant ship flying the flag of its adversary.[119]

Belligerent warships are prohibited to make use of neutral ports or roadsteads to replenish or increase their military supplies or their armaments.[120] Augmentation of the crews is forbidden too. These rules are to be explained by the fact that it is prohibited to misuse neutral territory and neutral waters as bases for acts of naval warfare. In neutral ports or roadsteads, the warships of the parties to the conflict are therefore also forbidden to erect or employ any apparatus for communicating with friendly or allied forces. Naturally, there will still be a chance of contacting the embassy or other diplomatic missions by other means. However, belligerent warships may replenish *food and fuel*. Article 19, paragraph 1 of the 1907 Hague Convention XIII restricts the quantity of food to the 'peace standard'. The quantity of fuel shall be limited to that what is required for reaching the 'nearest port in their own country' (Article 19, paragraph 2). In practice, it is up to the neutral states to determine the conditions for the replenishment with food and fuel. In doing so, they must observe the principle of impartiality and the prohibition of the abuse of neutral areas as bases for acts of naval warfare.

Prizes are enemy or neutral merchant ships that have been captured and seized. A prize may only be brought into a neutral port because of unseaworthiness, adverse sea conditions, or want of fuel or provisions.[121] It must leave as soon as the

---

[117]   San Remo Manual, para 21; Helsinki Principles (n 9), para 2.2.
[118]   San Remo Manual, para 21; Helsinki Principles (n 9), para 2.2.
[119]   San Remo Manual, para 21; Helsinki Principles (n 9), para 2.2. NWP 1-14M (n 10), para 7.3.2.1.
[120]   San Remo Manual, para 20.   [121]   NWP 1-14M (n 10), para 7.3.2.3.

circumstances allowing entry into the neutral port have ceased to exist. If it fails to comply with an appropriate request, the neutral port state is obliged to use all means available to effect the release of the prize together with its officers and crew and to intern the members of the prize crew (the officers from the belligerent warship that captured the prize).

(ii) *Neutral territorial seas and the right of innocent passage*

The sovereignty of a coastal state extends to its territorial sea, the breadth of which must not exceed 12 nautical miles measured from the baselines drawn in accordance with the international law of the sea. The parties to the conflict are obliged to respect the inviolability of a neutral state's territorial sea and the airspace above. All hostilities and every exercise of belligerent rights within the boundaries of the neutral territorial sea constitute a violation of the neutral state and are strictly forbidden. The principle of inviolability and the resulting duties, however, apply only in those territorial sea areas that are in compliance with the international law of the sea. As in peacetime, excessive claims are invalid in times of international armed conflict.

As a general rule, within the territorial sea the right of innocent passage is applicable to the ships of all states, including those of the belligerents. There is no corresponding right of overflight. However, neutral coastal states are entitled to suspend temporarily, without discriminating in form or fact among foreign ships, the innocent passage of foreign ships in specified areas of its territorial sea if such suspension is essential to the protection of its security. If such suspension is duly published it shall apply not only to warships of the parties to the conflict but to the ships of all states.[122] These rules of the international law of the sea are modified by the law of maritime neutrality to the effect that a neutral coastal state may completely or partially close its territorial sea only to the warships, auxiliaries, and prizes of the parties to the conflict.[123] It is also admissible to prohibit only the passage of certain warships, such as submarines. International straits and archipelagic waters, however, in which special rights of transit apply must be exempted from such prohibitions.[124] If a neutral state decides to close its territorial sea to warships and prizes of the parties to the conflict, it must not discriminate against any of these parties. If the closure is duly published, the right of innocent passage of the ships concerned will be suspended until the end of the armed conflict. The only exceptions will be made in cases of distress or, following an appropriate approval by the authorities of the neutral state, for medical transports. The neutral state is obliged to use all means available to enforce the closure of its territorial sea.

---

[122] Article 25, para 3 of LOSC (n 12).   [123] Helsinki Principles (n 9), para 2.3.
[124] San Remo Manual, paras 27–30.

A neutral coastal state, however, is not obliged to suspend the right of innocent passage but may keep its territorial sea open for the warships, auxiliaries, and prizes of the parties to the conflict. If these vessels make use of the right of innocent passage, they will be subject to the general rules of the international law of the sea. In neutral territorial seas, submarines and other underwater vehicles are therefore required to navigate on the surface and to show their flag. In addition, the activities enumerated in Article 19 of LOSC continue to be prohibited.[125]

It must be emphasized that in and over international straits all surface and subsurface vessels as well as aircraft of the parties to the conflict and neutral states enjoy the right of transit passage. Submarines may transit international straits while submerged. Only the Bosporus and the Dardanelles are clearly exempt from this rule.[126] Neutral states are not permitted to hamper or suspend transit passage.[127]

The parties to the conflict must also respect the inviolability of archipelagic waters provided they are in conformity with the provisions of the international law of the sea. No acts of naval warfare may be executed in neutral archipelagic waters. Moreover, it is prohibited to misuse these waters as bases or places of sanctuary. If only the right of innocent passage is applicable in archipelagic waters, the neutral archipelagic state is entitled but not obliged to close them to the warships and prizes of the parties to the conflict. In and above those parts of archipelagic waters which are usually used for international navigation or for which the archipelagic state has designated specific sea lanes and air routes all vessels and aircraft of the belligerents enjoy the right of archipelagic sea lanes passage. The neutral archipelagic state may neither interfere with nor suspend this right.[128]

---

[125] Article 19 contains the following activites: any threat or use of force against the sovereignty, territorial integrity, or political independence of the coastal state, or in any other manner in violation of the principles of international law embodied in the Charter of the United Nations; any exercise or practice with weapons of any kind; any act aimed at collecting information to the prejudice of the defence or security of the coastal state; any act of propaganda aimed at affecting the defence or security of the coastal state; the launching, landing, or taking on board of any aircraft; the launching, landing, or taking on board of any military device; the loading or unloading of any commodity, currency, or person contrary to the customs, fiscal, immigration, or sanitary laws and regulations of the coastal state; any act of wilful and serious pollution contrary to this Convention; any fishing activities; the carrying out of research or survey activities; any act aimed at interfering with any systems of communication or any other facilities or installations of the coastal state; any other activity not having a direct bearing on passage.

[126] Passage through the Turkish Straits is regulated by the 1934 Montreux Convention. Therefore, according to Art 35 lit(c) of LOSC (n 12), the right of transit passage does not apply. It is unsettled whether the Strait of Magellan and the Danish Straits are likewise exempted from the transit passage regime.

[127] San Remo Manual, para 29.   [128] San Remo Manual, para 29.

D. Neutral trade

The outbreak of an international armed conflict basically has no effect whatsoever on the right of neutral states and their nationals to engage in trade. This applies not only to the exchange of goods between neutral states but also to the exchange between neutral states and the parties to the conflict. Trade relations between a neutral state and a party to the conflict, however, involve considerable risks for the opposing party to the conflict since it may comprise war material. Hence, Article 6 of the 1907 Hague Convention XIII prohibits the supply of war material and Article 8 prohibits the fitting out of ships for use in war.

According to Article 7 of the 1907 Hague Convention XIII, however, a neutral state is not bound to prevent the export or transit, carried out for the account of either party to the conflict, of arms, ammunition or, in general, anything which could be of use to belligerent armed forces. Today, this rule may be modified so that the approval of such shipments constitutes a violation of the law of neutrality insofar as exports of war materials are government-controlled. This, however, is far from settled.

In the context of neutral trade, there is no need to go into this issue in greater detail since it only concerns intergovernmental relations. What matters here are the measures taken by the belligerents against merchant vessels and civil aircraft of neutral states. Insofar, it is generally agreed that the parties to an international armed conflict are entitled to control neutral merchant vessels and neutral civil aircraft and especially to prevent the transport of contraband. The pertinent rules and principles are summarized under the term 'law of prize'.[129] It must be emphasized that neutral merchant vessels and civil aircraft may be liable to attack if they are engaged in activities rendering them lawful military objectives.[130]

(i) *Contraband*

The term contraband refers to goods that are directly or indirectly destined for an area controlled by the opposing party to the conflict and that are susceptible for use in armed conflict. It covers only imports, export articles do not constitute contraband.[131]

The traditional differentiation between absolute and conditional contraband,[132] which is behind the provisions of the 1909 London Declaration concerning the Laws of Naval War, is no longer relevant today. This is due to the fact that the two

---

[129] San Remo Manual (Part V, paras 112ff) uses the term 'measures short of attack'.

[130] San Remo Manual, paras 67 and 70; Helsinki Principles (n 9), para 5.1.2(4); HPCR Manual, Rule 174.

[131] San Remo Manual, paras 146ff; Helsinki Principles (n 9), paras 5.2.2ff; NWP 1-14M (n 10), para 7.4.1.

[132] For the traditional distinction between absolute and conditional contraband, see Colombos (n 11), 675ff.

prerequisites of this definition cannot be specified in a way to make them generally applicable. In any case, however, there must be sufficient proof that the goods concerned are ultimately intended for the enemy armed forces. Moreover, there is now agreement on the necessity of a prior publication of lists specifying either the contraband goods or the so-called free goods.[133]

Contraband is subject to seizure and confiscation.[134] It makes no difference whether it is found on board of a neutral merchant vessel or on board of a neutral civil aircraft. The ownership rights under civil law and other legal relationships do not matter either. Goods and items not included in a list of contraband are free goods that may not be condemned or confiscated. Certain items enjoy special protection under international humanitarian law which necessarily makes them free goods.[135]

(ii) *Navicerts and aircerts*

In order to facilitate the monitoring of neutral commerce, the parties to the conflict may issue certificates, which indicate that a neutral merchant vessel (so-called navicert) or a neutral aircraft (so-called aircert) has been examined and does not carry any contraband.[136] Subject to the consent of the port state, the examination can also be carried out in neutral ports. A navicert or aircert reduces interference with neutral commerce, because it can render interception and the ensuing visit and search unnecessary. The certificates will not, however, guarantee an unimpeded voyage. Therefore, the issuing party to the conflict is particularly entitled to interception, visit and search and capture when new facts have come to light after the issuance of the certificate. On the other hand, absence of a certificate is not, in itself, a sufficient ground for capture of a neutral merchant vessel or civil aircraft. A party to the conflict must not take the fact that a vessel or aircraft is carrying a certificate issued by the opponent as a basis for discriminating against said vessel or aircraft.[137]

(iii) *Neutral merchant vessels and civil aircraft*

The international law of peace is modified by the law of maritime neutrality to the effect that neutral merchant vessels and neutral civil aircraft are obliged to tolerate the following measures based on the law of prize taken by the parties to the conflict:

- interception and visit and search;
- diversion; and
- under certain conditions, capture and destruction.

---

[133] San Remo Manual, paras 149 and 150.
[134] San Remo Manual, para 147. See also NWP 1-14M (n 10), para 7.4.
[135] San Remo Manual, para 150.
[136] NWP 1-14M (n 10), para 4.4.2; San Remo Manual, para 22; Helsinki Principles (n 9), para 5.2.6.
[137] San Remo Manual, para 123.

The obligation to tolerate those measures does not apply if a neutral merchant vessel is sailing under convoy of neutral warships and if the following prerequisites are met:

- the vessel is bound for a neutral port;
- it is sailing under convoy of a neutral warship under the same flag or of another neutral warship belonging to a state with which the merchant vessel's flag state has concluded an agreement providing for such escort services;
- the flag state of the neutral warship warrants that the neutral merchant vessel is not carrying any contraband or otherwise engaged in activities inconsistent with its neutral status; and
- the commander of the neutral warship provides, if requested by the commander of the warship or military aircraft of the party to the conflict, all information as to the character of the merchant vessel and its cargo which otherwise could only be obtained by interception and visit and search.

In the case of neutral civil aircraft a similar rule applies.[138]

Interception and visit and search are the measures based on the law of prize which a belligerent may take in order to verify the enemy or neutral character of a merchant vessel or civil aircraft, the nature of its cargo (contraband) or its actual function. In and over neutral internal waters, neutral territorial seas, and neutral archipelagic waters measures based on the law of prize are prohibited.[139] Neutral merchant vessels and civil aircraft are obliged to comply with all orders.

If visit and search at sea is impossible or too dangerous, the commander of the intercepting warship may order the neutral merchant vessel by way of diversion to proceed to a particular sea area or port for the purpose of visit and search.[140]

Capture denotes the assumption of command over a vessel or aircraft. It must be distinguished from confiscation that is effected by a judgment delivered by a prize court.

Neutral merchant vessels and neutral civil aircraft are subject to capture and confiscation if they:

- are carrying contraband;
- are on a voyage undertaken solely for the purpose of transporting members of the enemy's armed forces;
- are under direct control of or have been chartered by the enemy;
- present irregular or fraudulent papers or do not carry the required documents or if the papers are destroyed or concealed;

---

[138] HPCR Manual, Rule 140; San Remo Manual, para 153.

[139] The exercise of prize measures is an exercise of belligerent rights that is prohibited in areas where neutral states enjoy territorial sovereignty. See the text accompanying nn 28 and 29.

[140] San Remo Manual, para 121. It must be noted that diversion is also lawful as an alternative to visit and search. See San Remo Manual, para 126.

- disregard legitimate orders; or
- are breaching, or attempting to breach, a blockade.[141]

Usually, capture is effected by sending a prize crew on board of the vehicle in order to assume command. Possible resistance on the part of the crew can be overcome by reasonable and proportionate enforcement action. All documents relating to the vessel and its cargo must be preserved as they are evidence to be presented to the competent prize court. In exceptional cases captured neutral merchant vessels may be destroyed if the crew, passengers, and documents can be taken to a safe place.[142] Each destruction based on the law of prize must be confirmed by a judgment delivered by a prize court.[143]

The crews of captured neutral vessels and aircraft, who are nationals of a neutral state, must be released and repatriated as soon as possible. If, however, the vessel qualifies as a lawful target, the neutral crew will be made prisoners of war. The passengers must also be released, unless they are members of the enemy's armed forces; en route to serve in the enemy's armed forces; or officially employed in the service of the enemy.

6 CONCLUDING REMARKS

The law of naval warfare and maritime neutrality might be considered a remnant from a distant past. Especially the rules on visit, search, and capture do not seem to be of any significant relevance any longer. Why should belligerents be entitled to apply prize measures in sea areas remote from the actual armed hostilities? Why should they be entitled to interfere with neutral merchant vessels and civil aircraft if any such interference would imply considerable financial losses and, probably, also the use of force against the vessels and aircraft? Indeed, some governments have decided that apart from those rules pertaining to armed hostilities at sea many of the traditional rules of prize law and of maritime neutrality have become obsolete. However, that position is certainly not shared by other governments. For instance, the United States and Germany continue to recognize the continuing validity of all the rules and principles dealt with in the present contribution. Of course, at present, it is hardly imaginable that the US Navy or the German Navy will apply prize measures directed against neutral navigation and aviation if they are engaged

---

[141] San Remo Manual, paras 146 and 153; HPCR Manual, Rule 140.
[142] San Remo Manual, para 151.
[143] San Remo Manual, para 151(2): 'Destruction shall be subject to adjudication'.

in an international armed conflict. The fact that such conduct is not likely to occur, however, does not mean that the respective rules and principles have become obsolete by desuetude. It may be recalled that similar statements were made with regard to occupation law and blockade. Many believed that belligerents would no longer occupy enemy territory or establish and enforce a naval blockade. Recent events have shown that the allegations of the irrelevance of occupation law and of blockade law were premature. It may not be forgotten that the law of naval warfare and maritime neutrality offers options belligerents may choose to make use of or not. If they decide to make use of those instruments it is far better that international law provides accepted rules the belligerents and the neutrals are obliged to comply with rather than claiming a legal vacuum and desperately hoping for the UN Security Council to take action.

CHAPTER 8

....

THE LAW OF OCCUPATION

....

PHILIP SPOERRI[*]

1 INTRODUCTION

....

FOR many years, occupation and the legal questions that it raised concerned a limited number of contexts such as the Palestinian territories, Northern Cyprus, or the brief occupation of Kuwait by Iraq. Most legal issues had been comprehensively discussed, if not necessarily agreed upon. In terms of legal topics to be explored, occupation appeared to be a topic of the past or at least a topic followed by a very small number of experts.

Undeniably, the occupation of Iraq in 2003–04 brought the topic back into the focus of attention and raised a number of new questions. Apart from this specific event, however, recent years have been characterized by a multiplication of extraterritorial military interventions. Some of these interventions have given rise to new forms of foreign military presence in the territory of a state, sometimes consensual but very often imposed. These new forms of military presence have thus renewed interest in the law of occupation. In this respect, the topic has attracted considerable comment, in particular in the legal doctrine. Some commentators challenge the

* The author would like to thank Tristan Ferraro for his contribution to this article. Mr Ferraro has been in charge of an exploratory process undertaken by the ICRC on 'Occupation and Other Forms of Administration of Foreign Territory' with the purpose to analyse whether and to what extent the rules of occupation law are adequate to deal with the humanitarian and legal challenges arising in contemporary occupations. A report of the process was published by the ICRC in June 2012.

relevance of the law of occupation head-on while others emphasize that this body of law still serves useful purposes.

Another observation is that the phenomenon of occupation is most often only observed through the lens of contexts such as the occupation of Iraq in 2003–04 and even more so the long-lasting Israeli occupation of Palestinian territories. Looking at the law of occupation on the basis of these two cases alone can be problematic, however, as they are actually cases with a number of specific or atypical features, hence not necessarily lending themselves to general conclusions on the state of the law of occupation. Indeed, it would be a mistake to believe that the contemporary phenomenon of occupation is limited to these two situations. Former Yugoslavia, the Democratic Republic of Congo, Eritrea/Ethiopia, Nagorno-Karabakh and other volatile situations have recently shown that occupation is by no means a side issue in the present landscape of belligerency.

In many of the above-mentioned situations, the law of occupation has been responsive to the challenges at hand, in particular those relating to humanitarian emergencies, arising from the effective control of a territory—or part thereof—by foreign forces. Yet, the applicability and application of the law of occupation to such contexts also raises a number of legal issues. In this respect, several important questions are of concern including the beginning and end of occupation, the delimitation of the rights and duties of the Occupying Power (including the highly debated issue of transformative occupation and the sensitive topic of prolonged occupation), as well as the interaction between the law of occupation and human rights law or the legal framework governing the use of force in occupied territory.

The limited scope of this contribution does not allow for a comprehensive analysis of all questions raised by contemporary occupation. Rather, after having described the general features and principles of the law of occupation, this Chapter will address a few selected issues which, from the author's perspective, have had particularly important operational implications on the ground insofar as their legal dimension may have a direct impact on the population living in a territory subject to the effective control of a foreign army.

2 THE GENERAL LEGAL FRAMEWORK GOVERNING OCCUPATION

For a significant period of time, occupation was seen and perceived only as a matter of inter-state relationships. Based on the premise that occupation constitutes only a temporary situation neither causing nor implying any devolution of sovereignty, the law of occupation, as reflected in The Hague Regulations of 1907 (Hague Regulations), was mainly geared towards the maintenance of the sovereign rights of the ousted government until belligerents agreed upon the conditions for its return.

However, this nineteenth-century reality on which the law of occupation was premised has radically changed. A turning point was undeniably the response in perception, and then in specific legal development, following the horrors committed by the Nazi regime in occupied territories during World War II. Situations of contemporary occupation are more and more characterized by the tension existing between the Occupying Power and the local population (or at least some components thereof) as well as by an incremental role played by the Occupying Power in the administration of the occupied territory.

These facts and the lessons learnt from the World War II experience prompted important legal changes and compelled international humanitarian law (IHL) drafters to focus more on the welfare of the population living under occupation. The need for enhanced protection of the occupied population thus became a crucial part of the Geneva Conventions of 1949, particularly the Fourth Geneva Convention relative to the protection of civilian persons in time of war (GC IV), filling in the gaps existing in the law at the time, notably by ensuring that their basic needs were met.

Despite this important legal evolution, recent occupations have shown that the law of occupation still faces difficult challenges. The applicability of the law of occupation to situations of effective foreign control over a territory has been recurrently contested by invading states, which clearly illustrates the reluctance of those states to be considered as Occupying Powers.[1] This trend of denying the applicability of the law of occupation can be partly explained by the fact that the concept of occupation suffers a pejorative connotation and has been frequently referred to as an 'unlawful' situation running contrary to the overall objective of international peace and security foreseen by the United Nations Charter. Consequently, the reference to 'unlawful occupation' can be misleading as it confuses the question of the lawfulness of the resort to the use of force with that of the rules of conduct to be applied once armed force has been used and, as such, affects the separation between *jus ad bellum* and *jus in bello*. From a purely IHL perspective, the law of occupation applies equally to all occupations, be they the result of a lawful or unlawful use of force within the *jus ad bellum*.[2] Another important reason for contesting a situation of occupation regularly

---

[1] See for a short overview on this phenomenon of reluctance and the particular 'odium' attached to the word occupation over the last decades, see Y. Dinstein, *The International Law of Belligerent Occupation* (Cambridge: Cambridge University Press, 2009), 9–12.

[2] As stated by the US Military Tribunal in the famous *Hostages* case, 'international law makes no distinction between a lawful and an unlawful occupant in dealing with the respective duties of occupant and population in occupied territory [...] Whether the invasion was lawful or criminal is not an important factor in the consideration of this subject', US Military Tribunals at Nuremberg, *USA v Wilhem List et al (The Hostages Trial)*, Trials of War Criminals before the Nuremberg Military Tribunals, vol.11 (1950), 1247.

arises in situations where a country, having taken control of a territory, disputes the sovereign claim to this territory by the other side. A long list of past and present situations of this kind can be drawn up with the invariable finding that one side will invoke the law of occupation and the other side will vehemently and irrevocably deny it.

As a preliminary remark, it is worth mentioning that the law of occupation only applies in international armed conflict. Despite some proposals to expand the applicability of this body of law to non-international armed conflicts,[3] the majority view maintains that the retaking by government armed forces of national territory previously held by insurgents is not occupation, nor can insurgents occupy part of the national territory within the law of occupation's meaning.[4] This, however, does not mean that no IHL rules apply for the insurgent side since they must—when exercising control over parts of the national territory—always abide by the provisions of Common Article 3 of the Geneva Conventions of 1949 and by Additional Protocol II when applicable.

Turning now to the substance and content of the law of occupation, it must be pointed out that this area of law is made up of a significant web of well-recognized customary and treaty rules mainly drawn from the Hague Regulations and GC IV. Even if scattered across various IHL instruments and sources, occupation law norms generally share a common rationale, which revolves around four general principles.[5]

First, the Occupying Power does not acquire any sovereignty over the territory it occupies. In this respect, it is not entitled to bring about changes in the status and intrinsic characteristics of the occupied territory.

Secondly, the rights exerted by the Occupying Power are merely transitory and are accompanied by the obligation to respect (unless absolutely prevented) the laws in force in the occupied territory, as well as to maintain as normal a life as possible in occupied territory. The law of occupation also requires the Occupying Power to administer the occupied territory for the benefit of the local population while preserving its own security needs. Overall, the main purpose of the limits imposed by IHL upon the Occupying Power primarily aims at providing a minimum of humanitarian protection to the occupied civilian population.

Thirdly, in the exercise of its powers, the Occupying Power must always take into account two fundamental parameters: the fulfilment of its military needs and the respect for the interest of the occupied population. IHL strikes a careful balance

---

[3] M.J. Kelly, *Restoring and Maintaining Order in Complex Peace Operations: The Search for a Legal Framework* (The Hague: Kluwer Law International/Martinus Nijhoff Publishers, 1999), 111ff.

[4] Dinstein (n 1), 33ff.

[5] C. Greenwood, 'The Administration of Occupied Territory in International Law', in E. Playfair (ed), *International Law and the Administration of Occupied Territories* (Oxford: Clarendon Press, 1992), 241–66; E. Benvenisti, *The International Law of Occupation* (Princeton: Princeton University Press, 1992), 7–31.

between these two. While military necessities in some instances may gain the upper hand, they should nonetheless never result in a total disregard for the needs of the local population. This principle shall apply to all the decisions and policies under-taken by the occupier in the occupied territory.

Fourthly, the Occupying Power must not exercise its authority in order to further its own interests (other than military), or use the inhabitants, the resources, or other assets of the territory it occupies for the benefit of its own territory or population.

When considering issues arising from occupation, these general principles gov-erning occupation ought always to be borne in mind. These principles underpin the main provisions of the law of occupation as reflected in the Hague Regulations and GC IV.

Moving from general principles to specifics: one important feature of occupation law to bear in mind is that it was/is designed to allow the Occupying Power to exer-cise a temporary power of administration and, while doing so, to take into account its own security needs.[6] Large parts of the rules on occupation are dedicated to restrictions and limitations in the exercise of that power, as well as to responsi-bilities for the welfare of the population in occupied territory incumbent upon the Occupying Power. Responsibilities include matters such as: humane treatment, satisfaction of the occupied population's needs, respect for private property, man-agement of public property, functioning of educational establishments, ensuring the existence and function of medical services, allowing relief operations to take place as well as allowing impartial humanitarian organizations such as the ICRC to carry out their activities. In turn, and in order to fulfil those important responsi-bilities while ensuring its own security, the Occupying Power is granted important rights and powers, which may also take the form of measures of constraint over the local population when necessity so requires. These prerogatives, however, do not alter or detract the foreign forces from their core responsibility according to which the Occupying Power shall ensure that the basic needs of the occupied population are effectively met.

Consequently, the law of occupation is both permissive (accepting that an occupier exercises certain powers) and prohibitive (putting limits on the occu-pier's actions). Despite some critical opinions on whether the existing rules are sufficient to provide answers to all issues arising in specific cases of contemporary occupations, it is submitted here that the rules of the law of occupation are flex-ible enough to take these specific issues into account, capable of standing the test of time. When working on specific issues of occupation law as a practitioner, the pertinence and detail of responses under the law of occupation to contemporary issues is remarkable. Stated in a general manner, this body of law must still be regarded as a very relevant and useful tool that is, on the whole, adequate to meet

---

[6] Benvenisti (n 5), 7–31; H.P. Gasser, 'Belligerent Occupation', in D. Fleck (ed), *The Handbook of International Humanitarian Law* (2nd edn, Oxford: Oxford University Press, 2008), 270–311.

the challenges of today's occupations. The extent of the fault line between law of occupation and the policies carried out in recent occupations should therefore not be overemphasized.

Nevertheless, this assessment does not mean that the provisions regulating situations of occupation law are static and hermetic to any evolving interpretation in line with the aim and purpose of this body of law. In this respect, the ICRC considers that certain practical issues linked to occupation still raise legal questions which deserve to be thoroughly examined. In order to illustrate this, legal issues relating to the beginning and end of occupation, to the relationship between IHL and human rights law through the lens of use of force in occupied territory and eventually to transformative occupation, will be discussed below. This selection of themes is not meant to be an exhaustive list of legal challenges for the law of occupation, but allows for consideration of how this body of law responds to challenges raised by contemporary occupations.

3 The Beginning and End of Occupation

When referring to fresh interest in the law of occupation over the past decade, the attention of the legal community has focused primarily on a number of substantive rules rather than addressing issues raised by the conditions of the establishment and termination of occupation. Surprisingly, relatively little interest has been paid to the standards used to determine when a case of occupation begins and when it comes to an end.[7] This is regrettable since the question as to whether an occupation is established or not is central for the application of occupation law and must be answered before any substantive questions can be addressed. Hence, this question is of fundamental importance.

Past practice demonstrates that most Occupying Powers have devised claims for the inapplicability of occupation law while maintaining effective control over a foreign territory or part thereof. States are reluctant to be perceived as Occupying Powers. This situation is all the more aggravated by the fact that IHL instruments do not provide clear standards for determining when an occupation starts and terminates. Not only is the definition of occupation vague under IHL, but other factual elements—such as the continuation of hostilities and/or the continued exercise of

---

[7] However, a detailed analysis of the issue has been published recently, T. Ferraro, 'Determining the Beginning and End of an Occupation under International Humanitarian Law', 94(885) *International Review of the Red Cross* (2012) 133–63.

some degree of authority by local authorities or by the foreign forces during and after their phasing out—may render the legal classification of a situation very complex. This exemplifies the need for more precise guidance regarding when and how the law of occupation applies.

If the contours of the occupation concept have been sketched in Article 42 of the Hague Regulations, the absence of any clear-cut criteria in treaty law requires a careful examination of the interpretation given to this provision over time.

Despite its vagueness, Article 42 of the Hague Regulations continues to be the cornerstone against which any determination as to whether a situation amounts to an occupation has to be made. The pivotal role of this specific provision of the Hague Regulations has been recognized and reconfirmed in recent international jurisprudence of the International Criminal Tribunal for the former Yugoslavia (ICTY) and the International Court of Justice (ICJ).[8] This confirms that this norm still provides the core elements of the notion of effective control, a notion which lies at the core of the determination as to whether a territory can be considered as occupied for the purposes of IHL. Indeed, the notion of effective control, while not found in treaty law, has been associated very early on with the concept of occupation and has been developed in the legal discourse pertaining to occupation in order to describe the circumstances and conditions under which the existence of a state of occupation could be determined.[9]

The test of effective control—which has been developed and articulated by international jurisprudence,[10] some army manuals,[11] and in doctrine[12]—has established the fundamental importance of the exercise of authority by foreign forces in lieu of the territorial sovereign through their non-consensual and continued presence in the concerned territory as the key elements to take into account for the determination as to whether a situation amounts to an occupation for the purposes of IHL or not. These three elements (ie (1) foreign military presence, (2) the ability of the foreign forces to exert authority in the concerned territory in lieu of the local government, and (3) its non-consensual nature) are directly derived from the terms of Article 42 of the Hague Regulations. Cumulatively taken, these elements also reflect the tension of interests between the local government, the Occupying Power, and the

[8] ICTY, *Prosecutor v M. Naletilić and V. Martinović*, Judgment, Case no IT-98-34-T, Trial Chamber, 31 March 2003, §§ 215–16; ICJ, *Advisory Opinion on the Legal Consequences of the Construction of a Wall in the Occupied Palestinian Territory*, 9 July 2004, § 78; ICJ, *Armed Activities on the Territory of the Congo (DRC v Uganda)*, decision of 19 December 2005, §§ 172–7.

[9] Dinstein (n 1), 43–4.   [10] See n 7.

[11] See notably, United Kingdom, UK Ministry of Defence, *The Manual of the Law of Armed Conflict* (Oxford: Oxford University Press, 2004), point 11.3 at 275; United States of America, *US Field Manual 27-10 'The Law of Land Warfare'*, 1956, § 355.

[12] Y. Shany, 'Faraway So Close: The Legal Status of Gaza after Israel's disengagement', 8 *Yearbook of International Humanitarian Law* (2005) 369–83 at 374ff; E. Benvenisti, 'The Law on the Unilateral Termination of Occupation', in T. Giegerich (ed), *A Wiser Century?: Judicial Dispute Settlement, Disarmament and the Laws of War 100 Years After the Second Hague Peace Conference* (Berlin: Duncker & Humblot, 2009), 371–82 at 371–5.

local population, which always characterizes a situation of belligerent occupation.[13] In light of the consensus surrounding the three elements, the latter should be established as prerequisites for the effective control test—or put in other words: they should be considered as the constitutive and cumulative conditions of the concept of occupation for the purposes of IHL.

When pointing out that these cumulative conditions are indispensable for establishing a situation of occupation, the crux remains that these conditions still need further clarification and interpretation in order to define as tightly as possible a determination of the existence of an occupation.

A. The necessary presence of foreign forces

This criterion is generally seen as the only way to establish and exert firm control over a foreign territory. It is for this reason that the presence of foreign forces is viewed as a prerequisite for the establishment of an occupation since it makes the link between the notion of effective control and the ability to fulfil the obligations incumbent upon the Occupying Power.[14] It is also widely recognized that an occupation cannot be established or maintained solely through the exercise of power from outside the boundaries of the occupied territory. Rather, it calls for at least some foreign 'boots' on the ground. Therefore, only effective control on land would characterize military occupation within the meaning of IHL. However, the prerequisite of foreign troops on the ground does not mean that effective control requires their presence on each square metre of the occupied territory. On the contrary, the size of the foreign forces cannot be pre-determined and could vary according to the circumstances. Particularly relevant circumstances are the geographical characteristics of the territory, the density of the population or the degree of resistance encountered on the ground. In this respect, effective control can perfectly well be enforced by positioning foreign troops in strategic places within the occupied territory rendering the Occupying Power capable of sending troops within reasonable time in order to make its authority felt in the concerned area.

[13] M. Bothe, '"Effective control"—a situation triggering the application of the law of belligerent occupation', background document, ICRC Project on occupation and other forms of administration of foreign territory, 1st Expert Meeting, ICRC Report on occupation and other Forms of Administration of Foreign Territory, Report prepared and edited by T. Ferraro, ICRC Geneva, April 2012, 3. See also M. Zwanenburg, 'The Law of Occupation Revisited: The Beginning of an Occupation', 10 *Yearbook of International Humanitarian Law* (2007) 99–130 at 109–10.

[14] See the ICRC, Report on Occupation and Other Forms of Administration of Foreign Territory (11 June 2012).

B. The exercise of authority over the occupied territory

There is broad agreement that once enemy foreign forces have established a presence in a territory, what counts for the purposes of determining the applicability of occupation law, is the ability of the foreign forces to exert authority in the foreign territory and not the actual and concrete exercise of such authority as recently upheld by the ICJ in December 2006 in the *Democratic Republic of Congo (DRC) v Uganda* case.[15] In this respect, reliance on a test based on the ability of the Occupying Power to exert authority is justified by the fact that this prevents any attempt by the occupier to evade its duties under the law of occupation through the voluntary non-exercise of authority or through the installation of a puppet government. It is also important to specify that occupation law does not require an exclusive exercise of authority by the Occupying Power. It allows for authority to be shared by the Occupying Power and the occupied government, provided the former continues, to bear the ultimate and overall responsibility for the occupied territory. In other words, the continued exercise of power by the local authorities does not mean that occupation has not been established and maintained, provided the ongoing local government's activities derive from an authorization of the Occupying Power.

C. The non-consensual nature of belligerent occupation

The absence of consent from the state whose territory is subject to the foreign forces' presence has been identified as a precondition for the existence of a state of belligerent occupation. Without this condition, the situation would amount to a 'pacific occupation' not subject to the law of occupation. In this respect, it should be noted that, according to Article 2, paragraph 2 of GC IV, the absence of armed resistance from the territorial sovereign shall not be interpreted as a form of consent barring the application of the law of occupation. As to the characteristics of consent for the purposes of occupation law, it should be genuine, valid and explicit to entail the inapplicability of occupation law. It should be recognized here that the evaluation of those elements is very difficult, particularly in cases of 'engineered consent', which can be defined as a process by which states intervening in a foreign territory would ensure by any means or legal constructions that the presence of their armed forces would appear as being consented to by the host state. Nonetheless, the complexity inherent in the interpretation of the notion of consent would not detract from its overall importance for the purposes of determining occupation law applicability.

It is important to stress that the analysis performed here relating to the criteria permitting a determination of the existence of a state of occupation is based on a

---

[15] ICJ, *DRC v Uganda*, § 173.

concept of a 'classical' case of occupation. For these cases, the establishment of the criteria or the absence of them, would equally apply to the beginning or ending of an occupation. This analysis does not exclude the possibility that the *sui generis* character of some situations may impact on the criteria previously identified by the experts, in particular in terms of the means to exercise effective control.[16]

In addition, recent military operations have underlined the necessity to define more precisely the legal criteria determining a state of occupation when such a situation involves multinational forces. Are the criteria for beginning and end of occupation the same in this very case? Who are the Occupying Power(s) among a coalition?

In this respect, it is meanwhile well accepted that occupation law could be applicable *de jure* to multinational operations,[17] including those under UN command and control, provided of course that the conditions for its applicability were met. Therefore, the criteria for assessing a state of occupation involving UN forces ought not to differ from those concerning more classical forms of occupation. As to the criteria for identifying which countries participating in a coalition would be considered Occupying Powers for the purposes of IHL, a functional approach would appear to be the appropriate tool for making these determinations. Concretely this means that those coalition members should be considered as Occupying Powers in cases where national contingents have been assigned with responsibility for and/or would exert effective control over parts of the concerned territory. In other words, it would be the actions performed by the foreign forces and the functions they have been specifically tasked to carry out that render the states to which they belong as Occupying Powers. Those states within a wider coalition performing tasks typical and normally carried out by an Occupying Power within the framework of IHL should be labelled as such and be bound by the rules contained in the relevant occupation law instruments.

Finally, linked to the applicability of the law of occupation is the question of how to determine the legal framework applicable to the invasion and withdrawal phases. On this issue, we simply refer to the ICRC practice, namely a broad interpretation

---

[16] According to a rule of thumb proposed by Adam Roberts, foreign forces have foreign territory under control when they see the occupied population eye to eye. See A. Roberts, 'What is a Military Occupation?', 55 *British Year Book of International Law* (1984) 249–305 at 250. In line with this viewpoint one could, for example, argue in some situations that the small size of a territory and with the technology at hand such control can be established from some distance. See P. Spoerri, *Die Fortgeltung Völkerrechtlichen Besatzungsrechts während der Interimsphase palästinesischer Selbstverwaltung in der West bank un Gaza* (Frankfurt am Main: Europäische Hochschulschriften, 2001), 237. See also Ferraro (n 13), 157–8.

[17] T. Ferraro, 'The Application of the Law of Occupation to Peace Forces', in Dr G.L. Beruto (ed), *International Humanitarian Law, Human Rights Law and Peace Operations, 31st Round Table on Current Problems of IHL*, San Remo, 4–6 September 2008, International Institute of Humanitarian Law, 120–39.

favouring the applicability of GC IV with the aim of maximizing the legal protection conferred to the civilian population.[18]

4 Delimiting the Rights and Duties of the Occupying Power: The Question of 'Transformative Occupation'

When observing the application of the law of occupation over the years and decades, one must conclude that states frequently transgress and interpret occupation law's prescriptions in a self-serving manner in order to reduce constraints on their discretionary powers. This observation may certainly be made more generally with regard to the application of IHL, however it deserves particular mention in the present context. The reasons for this phenomenon may be linked to the particular *rapport de force* in such situations, but it may also be indicative of a pervading scepticism regarding the relevance of the law of occupation to contemporary circumstances.

Occupation law is regularly challenged on the basis that it is ill-suited for contemporary situations. The claim is that states find themselves today in roles which differ considerably from those of classical belligerent occupation and that the law of occupation is not sufficiently equipped to cope with the specificities of these situations.[19]

Occupation law does not authorize a foreign power to introduce wholesale changes in the legal, political, institutional, and economic structures of the territory under effective control and this has been invoked as one argument to bolster the claim that the law of occupation is ill-suited to today's situations. Indeed, it has been contended that occupation law places an undue emphasis on preserving the continuity of the socio-political situation of the occupied territory. Further, it has been argued that the transformation of an oppressive governmental system or the rebuilding of a society in complete collapse by means of occupation could be in the interest of the international community and be authorized under *lex lata*.[20]

---

[18] On this specific issue, see the debate between M. Zwanenburg, M. Bothe, and M. Sassòli, 'Is the Law of Occupation Applicable in the Invasion Phase?', 94(885) *International Review of the Red Cross* (2012) 29–50.

[19] D.J. Scheffer, 'Beyond Occupation Law', 97 *American Journal of International Law* (2003) 842–60; G.T. Harris, 'The Era of Multilateral Occupation', 24 *Berkeley Journal of International Law* (2006) 1–78; D.P. Goodman, 'The Need of Fundamental Change in the Law of Occupation', 37 *Stanford Law Review* (1985) 1573–1608.

[20] M. Patterson, 'Who's Got the Title? Or, the Remnants of Debellatio in Post-Invasion Iraq', 47 *Harvard International Law Journal* (2006) 467–88.

Examples of far-reaching political and institutional changes undertaken in recent occupations have brought to light the tension between occupation law's requirement to respect the laws and institutions in place, and the perceived need to fundamentally alter the institutional, social, or economic fabric of the occupied territory. To defuse this tension, some commentators contend that IHL should permit certain transformative processes and recognize the occupier's role in this respect. Such a position raises the question of the limitations posited by IHL with regard to the occupier's rights and duties set forth most notably in Article 43 of the Hague Regulations and Article 64 of GC IV. If occupation law does not give a 'carte blanche' to the Occupying Power, some contemporary interpretations of the rights and duties tend to grant increasing leeway in the administration of the occupied territory. One conclusion from this observation is that it is necessary to identify more clearly how much or how little room for manoeuvre an occupier actually has in such matters. The answer requires taking a deeper look into the two above-mentioned provisions which constitute the cornerstone of the occupier's powers under the law of occupation.

A. The scope of authority of the Occupying Power

Without engaging in an exhaustive analysis,[21] it is generally accepted that Article 43 of the Hague Regulations combined with Article 64 of GC IV grants the Occupying Power broad authority over foreign territory under its effective control. If, in the past, the role played by Occupying Powers implied minimal interference in life in the occupied territory, current IHL obligations and recent practice suggest that occupiers have adopted a much more interventionist approach and are generally involved in almost all aspects of life in the occupied territory. In this respect, Articles 43 of the Hague Regulations and 64 of GC IV should be interpreted broadly to allow the Occupying Power to fulfil its duties under occupation law, in particular the administration of the occupied territory for the benefit of the local population while ensuring the security of its own armed forces.

While Article 43 appears to contain two interrelated parts (the obligation to restore and maintain public order and security, and the duty to respect the laws in force in occupied territory), the *travaux préparatoires* of this instrument and subsequent state practice indicate that this provision comprises in reality two separate obligations, which delimit generally the occupier's scope of authority under IHL. On the one hand, it is considered that the positive obligation to restore and

---

[21] M. Sassòli, 'Legislation and Maintenance of Public Order and Civil Life by Occupying Powers', 16 *European Journal of International Law* (2005) 661–94; C. McCarthy, 'The Paradox of the International Law of Military Occupation: Sovereignty and the Reformation of Iraq', 10 *Journal of Conflict and Security Law* (2005) 43–74.

maintain public order and safety is essentially aimed at protecting the local population from the breakdown of orderly civil life in occupied territory and entails—as a
minimum—an obligation to take necessary measures to stop or prevent a collapse
in civil life. On the other hand, the second part of Article 43 constitutes a general
rule about the legislative powers of the occupier. It must, however, be mentioned
that an argument can be made that these two obligations are not in fact so hermeti-
cally disconnected insofar as the first part of Article 43 of the Hague Regulations
helps identify the subject matters on which the Occupying Power could legislate
under the provision's second part.

As to the interpretation of the clause on the obligation to 'restore and ensure
public order and safety' contained in the first part of Article 43, it must be noted that
the English version differs substantially from the authoritative French text, which
refers to the restoration and maintenance of *'l'ordre et la vie publics'*. It is therefore
submitted that Article 43 of the Hague Regulations, as reflected in the French version, imposes on the Occupying Power an obligation 'to restore public order and
civil life' (emphasis added), whose meaning is much broader than the term 'public
safety' used in the English version.

Whereas 'public order' means security or general safety, the meaning of 'civil
life' has been described in the International Declaration concerning the Laws and
Customs of War (Brussels, 27 August 1874) as including the social functions and
ordinary transactions that constitute daily life in the occupied territory. In this
respect, this broad interpretation of the concept of 'civil life' is still relevant and
in fact represents the only interpretation corresponding to the evolution of the
Occupying Power's role over time. Consequently, the role of an Occupying Power
can no longer be regarded as a disinterested invader but rather as a fully-fledged
administrator. In addition, the ever-increasing role of the Occupying Power in
occupied territory has been expressly recognized by Article 64 of GC IV, which
has replaced the negative test proposed in Article 43 of the Hague Regulations[22]
with a positive authorization, whereby the occupier could subject the population
of the occupied territory to provisions which are essential to enable it to exert its
functions under occupation law.

As to the clarification of the terms 'unless absolutely prevented' contained in
the second part of Article 43 of the Hague Regulations, which is generally interpreted as delimiting the scope of the occupier's legislative powers, it can be asserted
that the expression is referring to the exception of necessity. This means that the
clause should not be restricted to military necessity but be interpreted as referring
to 'necessity' broadly defined, which would justify an expansion of the grounds

---

[22] Article 43 of the Hague Regulations: 'the authority of the legitimate power having in fact passed
into the hands of the occupant, the latter shall take all the measures in his power to restore and ensure,
as far as possible, public order and safety, *while respecting, unless absolutely prevented, the laws in force
in the country*' (emphasis added).

permitting changes to local laws. In this regard, it is submitted here that the concept of necessity comprises three strands: military, legal, and material necessity allowing the Occupying Power to legislate on almost all aspects of life in the occupied territory.

The clause 'unless absolutely prevented' contained in Article 43 of the Hague Regulations should nonetheless not be interpreted as conferring upon the Occupying Power a blank cheque in the field of legislation. Therefore, the notion of necessity for the purposes of Article 43 requires further elaboration. To that end, it is Article 64 of GC IV that helps in delineating more precisely the meaning and scope of the terms 'unless absolutely prevented'. Following the terms of Article 64, paragraph 2 of GC IV, the concept of necessity for the purposes of Article 43 of the Hague Regulations would encompass the duty of the Occupying Power to fulfil its obligations under GC IV,[23] namely to maintain orderly government in occupied territory as well as its ability to ensure its own security. In those three areas, the Occupying Powers could change the pre-existing legal system in occupied territory and issue its own legislation. In others words, Article 64, paragraph 2 of GC IV posits some clear limits to the general rule on the occupier's legislative powers set forth in Article 43 of the Hague Regulations.

After having provided clarification on some elements of Articles 43 of the Hague Regulations and 64 of GC IV, it is still necessary to attempt to circumscribe more precisely the scope of the occupier's legislative powers. What appears not to be an issue of disagreement is the Occupying Power's entitlement to legislate in order to fulfil its obligations under GC IV or to enhance civil life in occupied territory. A more controversial issue is whether an Occupying Power could legislate with the aim of implementing human rights law in the area under its effective control.

On this issue, it should be recalled that a proposal aimed at giving the Occupying Power the right to repeal local legislation contrary to international human rights law was defeated during the negotiations of GC IV. The rejection of this Mexican proposal was mainly due to the embryonic character of human rights law at the time of the negotiations. Considering the development and importance of human rights law today and the recognition of its applicability in situations of occupation,[24] there is a strong trend in the literature to argue that the Occupying Power does not have to and should not respect local legislation that is contrary to human rights law.[25] Furthermore, it might also be contended that the implementation of human

[23] The reference made to the fulfilment of the Occupying Power's obligations under GC IV should be interpreted more broadly so that it not only comprised all IHL obligations but also the Occupying Power's obligations under public international law at large.

[24] See, for instance, the ICJ jurisprudence, notably the *Advisory Opinion on the Legal Consequences of the Construction of a Wall in the Occupied Palestinian Territory* (n 8), and *DRC v Uganda*, (n 8).

[25] Sassòli (n 22), 676–8; A. Roberts, 'Transformative Military Occupation: Applying the Laws of War and Human Rights', 100 *American Journal of International Law* (2006) 580–622 at 588–9; Y. Dinstein, 'Legislation under Article 43 of the Hague Regulations: Belligerent Occupation and Peacebuilding', in

rights law in occupied territory is not only legitimate but also very relevant where occupation law is silent, for instance, on questions such as freedom of opinion and freedom of the press, or where occupation law is rather vague, such as on the right to education or the right to health.

With regard to human rights law, one must distinguish between the recognized fact that human rights law sets forth obligations that Occupying Powers are bound to respect *vis-à-vis* the local population and the occupier's role in legislating in the field of human rights. The ability of the Occupying Power to legislate needs to be carefully delimited insofar as the implementation of human rights in occupied territory might amount to an agenda for societal reforms, which could be at odds with the conservationist principle underlying the law of occupation and could go beyond what the Occupying Power is permitted to do under occupation law. A means of delimiting such legislative ambitions would be that the resulting changes must pass the test that they are absolutely necessary under the Occupying Power's human rights obligations and must stay as close as possible to local standards as well as to local cultural, legal, institutional, and economic traditions.

The necessity to delimit with more precision the scope of the powers assigned by IHL to the Occupying Power takes on its full importance when it comes to addressing the issue of so-called 'transformative occupation'. This notion, which was at the core of the discussions surrounding the recent occupation of Iraq, can be described as an operation with the main objective of overhauling the institutional and political structures of the occupied territory.

B. The case of 'transformative occupation'

The notion of transformative occupation has been promoted by a number of authors as a progressive interpretation of the law of occupation or as necessary evolution requiring an update of this *corpus juris*.[26] It is suggested here that one needs to take a very cautious approach *vis-à-vis* a concept that entails important risks and is contrary to occupation law's basic premises. Transformative occupation as defined above has no legal basis and does not find any justification under current IHL. The underlying rationale for this assertion is that the Occupying Power does not acquire any sovereign rights over the occupied territory and is therefore not entitled to bring about changes in the occupied territory or to undertake reforms

Humanitarian Policy and Conflict Research, Occasional Paper Series, Fall 2004, Harvard University, 6; C. McCarthy, 'Legal Reasoning and the Applicability of International Human Rights Standards During Military Occupation', in R. Arnold and N. Quénivet (eds), *International Humanitarian Law and Human Rights Law: Towards a New Merger in International Law* (The Hague: Martinus Nijhoff Publishers, 2008), 101–20.

[26] J. Yoo, 'Iraqi Reconstruction and the Law of Occupation', 7 *University of California Davis Journal of International Law and Policy* (2004–05) 7–22.

that could not be reversed by the legitimate government once the occupation is over. In the same vein, the transitory character of the rights and duties incumbent upon the foreign administrator preclude bringing definitive and large-scale changes into the institutional structures of the occupied territory.[27]

Indeed, the idea behind occupation law is to prevent the Occupying Power from modelling the governmental structure of the occupied territory according to its own needs or perceptions, thus disregarding the intrinsic characteristics of the occupied society. Irrespective of the legitimacy or legality of the operations that led to the occupation, it can be stressed that the Occupying Power cannot be considered a neutral entity acting only in the interest of the occupied territory and therefore should not engage in institutional reforms. In this respect, the importance of the conservationist principle lying at the heart of occupation law needs to be under-lined and promoted. This principle reflects the dictates of prudence and the basic legal premises on which the international community is built, according to which fundamental decisions about a territory's institutional structures should be made by the legitimate sovereign institutions and not by outsiders such as Occupying Powers.[28]

All this said, the position held which holds 'transformative occupation' is unlaw-ful under IHL is without prejudice to the possibility that the Security Council, by application of Articles 25 and 103 of the UN Charter, decides to override IHL stric-tures, in particular those flowing directly from the conservationist principle, and to mandate—through an explicit resolution—an Occupying Power to overhaul the institutions of an occupied territory.

It is furthermore important to emphasize that it is necessary to differentiate between fully-fledged transformative projects entailing disruptions of sovereignty, and smoother changes that aim, for example, to ensure that the basic infrastructure of the occupied society operates in accordance with the relevant occupation law norms. Illegality of the transformative occupation concept under IHL should not be confused with a general prohibition against carrying out changes in the occupied territory.

Respect for the conservationist principle does not mean that the situation in an occupied territory should be completely frozen for the period of the occupation. On the contrary, compliance with the obligation to restore and maintain public order and civil life could even call for some transformations/changes and oblige the occupier to engage in important reforms. Circumstances warranting such changes would include cases where local laws in force are contrary to IHL provisions or

[27] G. Fox, 'The Occupation of Iraq', 36 *Georgetown Journal of International Law* (2005) 195–297; V. Koutroulis, 'Mythes et réalités de l'application du droit international humanitaire aux occupations dites "transformatives"', 40 *Revue Belge de Droit International* (2007) 365–400; G. Fox, 'Transformative Occupation and the Unilateralist Impulse', 94(885) *International Review of the Red Cross* (2012) 237–66.
[28] Roberts (n 25), 580–622.

prevent the Occupying Power from fulfilling its duties under occupation law. In this respect, some arguments could be put forward as possible justifications for *some* transformations during occupation: respect for IHL and human rights law; consent of the local population; the particular characteristics of prolonged occupation; and the case of occupied failed states.

5 The Relationship Between the Law of Occupation and Human Rights Law in Light of the Issue of the Use of Force in Occupied Territory

Human rights law can play an important role in delimiting the Occupying Power's rights and duties, particularly in relation to the population in the occupied territory. Indeed, the creation of a robust human rights law regime has significantly altered international expectations with regard to the treatment of inhabitants of occupied territory in particular since this body of law has been, over time, widely recognized as applicable in situations of occupation.[29] Therefore, human rights law may arguably impose formal obligations on the occupier in the course of its administration of the occupied territory.[30]

Recently, the ICJ underlined the relevance of human rights law in times of occupation and the occupier's legal obligation to take human rights law into account with regard to both its actions and policies in the occupied territory.[31] Consequently, the argument was made that human rights law could serve as a basis for changing

---

[29] However, divergent views still exist and continue to support the position that human rights law is not applicable in occupied territory. See, for instance, M.J. Dennis, 'Application of Human Rights Treaties Extraterritorially in Times of Armed Conflict and Military Occupation', 99 *American Journal of International Law* (2005) 119–41. The state of Israel still considers that human rights law has no extraterritorial application and therefore is not binding upon an Occupying Power, see O. Ben Naftali and Y. Shany, 'Living in Denial: The Application of Human Rights in Occupied Territories', 37 *Israel Law Review* (2003–04) 25–40.

[30] One should notice that a proposal aimed at giving the occupier the right to repeal local legislation contrary to human rights law was rejected during the negotiation of GC IV. The rejection of this Mexican proposal was mainly due to the embryonic character of human rights law at the time of the negotiations.

[31] ICJ, *Advisory Opinion on the Legal Consequences of the Construction of a Wall in the Occupied Palestinian Territory* (n 8), §§ 102ff; ICJ, *DRC v Uganda* (n 8), § 178.

For the relationship between international human rights law and international humanitarian law, see the Chapter by D. Jinks in this volume.

existing local laws[32] or even be used to justify transformative objectives.[33] This illustrates that contemporary occupation contexts cannot be considered without addressing the issue of human rights law. Undoubtedly, actions of the occupier must be examined not only through the lens of IHL but also through that of human rights law. Consequently, the question at stake is no longer whether human rights law applies or not in occupied territory but rather to identify how, and to what extent, this body of law applies in such circumstances.[34]

The key word for the purposes of examining the relationship between occupation law and human rights law is *complementarity*. Cordula Droege has pointed out that:

complementarity means that human rights law and humanitarian law do not contradict each other but, being based on the same principles and values, can influence and reinforce each other mutually. In this sense, complementarity reflects a method of interpretation enshrined in Article 31(3)(c) of the Vienna Convention on the Law of Treaties, which stipulates that, in interpreting a norm, *any relevant rules of international law applicable in the relations between the parties* shall be taken into account. This principle, in a sense, enshrines the idea of international law understood as a coherent system. It sees international law as a regime in which different sets of rules cohabit in harmony. Thus human rights can be interpreted in the light of international humanitarian law and vice versa.[35]

Complementarity in this understanding also means that human rights law and IHL, in particular the law of occupation, are mutually influencing. The proposed approach for the interaction between IHL and human rights law is therefore based on both complementarity and cross-interpretation, the latter meaning that the two bodies of law have to be interpreted *vice versa*. The interpretation would therefore mean that not only could human rights law be interpreted in light of IHL, as highlighted in the ICJ jurisprudence, but IHL could also be interpreted in light of human rights law. In this regard, the *lex specialis derogat legi generali* principle would be turned into a *lex specialis compleat legi generali* principle.[36] In light of the latter position, the *lex specialis derogat legi generali* principle would not disappear entirely but would only intervene when a clear conflict between two norms of occupation law and human rights law arises.

---

[32] Sassòli (n 22), 673–5.   [33] Roberts (n 25), 580–622.

[34] The present author holds the view that human rights law obligations apply in territory or parts thereof over which foreign forces have effective control as understood by IHL. In this respect, it is submitted here that effective control under IHL is of a higher threshold than effective control for the purposes of human rights law. Therefore, when foreign forces enforce effective control over foreign territory, this state of fact suffices to trigger human rights law obligations incumbent upon the Occupying Power.

[35] C. Droege, 'Parallel Application of IHL and International Human Rights Law: An Examination of the Debate', 40(2) *Israel Law Review* (2007) 468–660 at 521–2.

[36] N. Lubell, 'Elective Affinities? Human Rights and Humanitarian Law', 90(871) *IRRC* (2008) 501–48, 655; see also R. Kolb and G. Gaggioli, 'A Right to Life in Armed Conflicts? The Contribution of the European Court of Human Rights', 37 *Israel Yearbook on Human Rights* (2007) 115–63, 118ff.

In order to illustrate the relationship described, the following example of the use of force in occupied territory may render this particular issue more concrete.

One of the most important challenges in contemporary occupations is to determine how and when law enforcement rules as well as conduct of hostilities rules apply in relation to the use of force by the Occupying Power.[37] Under Article 43 of the Hague Regulations, the Occupying Power has an obligation to provide—as far as possible—security in occupied territory through maintenance of public order. The latter task can range from managing riots and disturbances to enforcing the law against criminal acts. In other words, the Occupying Power not only exercises its military authority over enemy forces, but actually must fulfil the duty to exercise a policing function in the territory under its effective control.[38]

What we have observed in recent occupations is that the regulation of the use of force *vis-à-vis* civil unrest and ongoing armed opposition is not a clear-cut matter.[39] Although the occupier is supposed to ensure security by means of law enforcement, uncertainty persists with regard to the applicable legal regimes, in particular in relation to situations where it is difficult to distinguish hostilities from civil unrest, or where the Occupying Power is confronted by both at the same time in the entire, or parts of, the occupied territory.[40]

As it stands, the law of occupation leaves a significant degree of uncertainty when it comes to determining whether a specific action is guided by law enforcement rules and standards or whether one is clearly in a situation governed by the IHL rules applicable to the conduct of hostilities. This situation inevitably opens the door for different interpretations on how the use of force may be exercised in occupied territory, in what circumstances, and according to which body of law. We are therefore once again back to the question of the application of human rights law in relation to the use of force in occupied territory.

In light of past practice, it appears that the use of force by the Occupying Power can be based on two alternative models. The first relates to law enforcement activities carried out within the framework of Article 43 of the Hague Regulations. This law enforcement paradigm presupposes a relatively secure grip by the foreign authority over the occupied territory. The second model, which applies exclusively to the conduct of hostilities, is based on the premise that violent actions carried out by organized armed groups or by the remaining occupied forces still endure or have resumed.

---

[37] R. Kolb and S. Vité, *Le droit de l'occupation militaire, perspectives historiques et enjeux juridiques actuels* (Brussels: Bruylant, 2009), 347ff.

[38] Y. Dinstein, 'The Israel Supreme Court and the Law of Occupation: Article 43 of the Hague Regulations', 25 *Israel Yearbook on Human Rights* (1995) 1–20.

[39] Dinstein, *The International Law of Belligerent Occupation* (n 1), 94–105.

[40] K. Watkin, 'Controlling the Use of Force: A Role for Human Rights Norms in Contemporary Armed Conflict', 98 *American Journal of International Law* (2004) 1–34. See also, K. Watkin, 'Use of Force During Occupation: Law Enforcement and Conduct of Hostilities', 94(885) *International Review of the Red Cross* (2012) 267–316.

Based on the fundamental distinction between these two models, it could be argued that their correlative rules and standards governing the use of force are also inherently distinct. Within the framework of the law enforcement paradigm, stricter standards apply as a consequence of the prohibition for the Occupying Power to arbitrarily deprive individuals of their right to life. This means that the use of lethal force by the Occupying Power while assuming its policing functions is only authorized under very strict circumstances. Concretely, the Occupying Power would only be able to use lethal force when strictly unavoidable in order to protect life and when less extreme means are insufficient to achieve that objective.[41]

The second paradigm—which relates to the conduct of hostilities—provides more leeway to the Occupying Power when engaged in the use of force. In the case of hostilities, the occupying forces are normally authorized to attack enemy combatants as well as civilians participating directly in hostilities. The law of armed conflict also allows—albeit under strictly pre-established conditions—a certain level of civilian losses, often referred to in a generic way as 'collateral damage'.[42] As such, this second model constitutes the realm of IHL as the *lex specialis*.

The real challenge in situations of occupation lies in the fact that there is no or little further guidance in order to determine when a factual situation falls into one or the other of these paradigms—law enforcement or conduct of hostilities—nor does it explain how to switch from one paradigm to the other.[43] This uncertainty has very serious implications, since such a determination is essential when it comes to the use of force in occupied territory because the two paradigms may apply concurrently or simultaneously. Depending on the choice made, the consequence can be very different.[44]

Indeed, the Occupying Power may well be engaged in the conduct of hostilities (for instance against remaining enemy armed forces or other organized armed groups), but may also carry out, at the same time, law enforcement tasks as required by the law of occupation (such as quelling spontaneous demonstrations by the civilian population). In such circumstances, the challenge ahead will be to identify when

[41] See Droege (n 35), 537–9.

[42] See, for instance, Art 57(2)(b) of Additional Protocol I: 'an attack shall be cancelled or suspended if it becomes apparent that the objective is not a military one or is subject to special protection or *that the attack may be expected to cause incidental loss of civilian life, injury to civilian objects, or a combination thereof, which would be excessive in relation to the concrete and direct military advantage anticipated*' (emphasis added).

[43] The limited character of this contribution does not allow for an analysis on the interaction between the two paradigms and the identification of criteria which would allow a determination of when and how to swap between the law enforcement model and the conduct of hostilities paradigm. This question is examined in detail in the ICRC Report on Occupation and Other Forms of Administration of Foreign Territory (n 13).

[44] University Centre for International Humanitarian Law, *Expert Meeting on the Right to Life in Armed Conflict and Situations of Occupation*, Report, 2005, 20–9, available at <http://www.adh-geneve.ch/docs/expert-meetings/2005/3rapport_droit_vie.pdf>.

each model applies and when it becomes necessary to switch from one to the other in light of the situation prevailing in the occupied territory.

An additional challenge posed by the issue at stake arises from the necessity to identify the exact content of the rules governing law enforcement in a situation of occupation. In this respect, one would have to determine whether the rules and standards governing the use of force in law enforcement operations derive from human rights law as applicable in peacetime, IHL or from a complementary combination of these two bodies of law.

One position advocates that that the human rights law regime would be the relevant or even prevalent one bearing in mind its ability to govern the use of force in all circumstances. The starting point for this position lies in the fact that while IHL and human rights law apply simultaneously in occupied territory, the former should not necessarily be considered as the *lex specialis* derogating from the latter in its entirety. On the contrary, it has been contended that IHL should only be considered as a complementary body of law since human rights law would generally provide adequate and sometimes more precise answers to issues linked with the use of force in occupied territory.[45]

The supporters of this theory stress that a comparison between IHL and human rights law would demonstrate that the difference in tools and reasoning would not result in substantially different outcomes. Although the human rights law regime would generally go a bit further in terms of protection—as it is based on a peacetime paradigm—the variations between the two legal regimes would only be a matter of degree. Furthermore, these slight differences would even tend to disappear progressively under the decisions of the human rights bodies, in particular the ECtHR. Such prevalence has in fact developed a set of human rights provisions applicable in situations of armed conflict, adjusted to the specificities of such a situation. The supporters of this theory therefore believe that the human rights law regime would apply also to belligerent relationships.

Those who believe that human rights law prevails in occupation situations find the argument compelling that this legal regime governs simultaneously the activities of law enforcement and military operations, both being generally conducted by the Occupying Power while enforcing its effective control of the foreign territory. According to the supporters of human rights law's prevalence in situations of occupation, the latter is mainly due to the flexibility of human rights law, meaning that the rules and standards could be easily adjusted to the large variety of situations faced by the Occupying Power.[46] This flexibility is notably characterized by the

---

[45]   ICRC, Report on Occupation and Other Forms of Administration of Foreign Territory, (n 13).

[46]   The flexibility of the human rights law rules pertaining to the use of force would permit their application in almost all factual situations faced by the Occupying Power, ranging from the enforcement of the law against criminal acts such as robbery or drug trafficking, to open hostilities pitting the occupying forces against insurgent armed groups. This benefit would in itself justify considering

fact that the resort to force under human rights law is assessed in light of the level of control exerted by the occupying forces over a specific situation and the level of threat faced. Resort to human rights law would thus prove particularly useful when the occupying forces were not in a position to establish with certainty whether a hostile act or intent threatening them did or did not have a nexus with the armed conflict.

Despite the efforts made by some in promoting the central role of human rights law in situations of occupation, the arguments put forward in relation to the use of force are, however, not convincing.

The emphasis placed on the similarities between human rights and IHL regimes by the promoters of the theory of the prevalence of human rights law in relation to the use of force, not only in terms of governing principles, but also in terms of practical results, is a false premise. It is not difficult to point out that IHL and human rights law contain important differences, be they at the level of their general rationale or at the level of their core rules. In particular, the point made here is that the logic governing the use of force under a human rights law-based law enforcement paradigm cannot be compared with the conduct of hostilities paradigm since they differ significantly due to the different realities the respective norms were intended to address: armed conflicts for IHL and peacetime for human rights law. The two regimes also vary significantly in how they address the issue of the use of force. While human rights law considers the use of force from an individualized perspective, IHL's logic is based on a broader and collective approach for the use of force— the reason being that it has in mind the juxtaposition of two or more parties.

Furthermore, some important differences still exist between the rules and standards governing the two paradigms and legal regimes. The use of force paradigm appears to be more limited in its application by placing an important emphasis on limiting the use of force to situations of absolute necessity. As a result, under this paradigm the use of force could never be regarded as necessary unless it was clear that there is no feasible possibility of protecting the prospective victim by apprehending the suspected perpetrator. Looking at this matter from an IHL angle, the use of lethal force is inherent to waging war and aims to avoid or limit death, particularly of persons protected against direct attack.

For example, the issue of proportionality illustrates the differences between the two paradigms. The aim of the IHL principle of proportionality is to limit incidental damage to protected persons and objects, while nevertheless recognizing that an operation could be carried out even if such casualties were likely, provided of course that it would not be excessive in relation to the concrete and direct military advantage anticipated. In contrast, the aim of the principle of proportionality under human rights law is to prevent harm from happening to anyone but the person against whom force is being used and under human rights law, even such a person would have to be spared lethal force if there was another, non-lethal way of achieving the aim of the law enforcement operation.

In light of the above, the thesis according to which the law enforcement regime would provide adequate rules and standards in order to quell threats stemming from insurgent groups in occupied territory is not convincing. It is also submitted that the legal test such as proposed in the *McCann* or *Issayeva* jurisprudence of the ECtHR would not prove sufficient to allow the occupier to undertake efficient military operations.[47] It is hard to imagine or unlikely that states exerting effective control over a foreign territory would consider embarking on military operations against the enemy in occupied territory under the law enforcement regime. The latter would always be more constraining in terms of preparation, execution, and *ex post facto* assessment than IHL in relation to the targeting of individuals. The human rights law regime would certainly not provide all the answers on the issue of the use of force in an occupied territory.

In contrast to the human rights are prevalent theory, it is argued here that human rights law would only be a good fit with respect to the activities falling strictly under the occupier's duty to ensure public order and safety in the occupied territory (policing activities).

The position according to which human rights law is the only referral body of law for law enforcement operations carried out within the framework of the Occupying Power's obligation to restore and maintain public order and safety, as reflected in Article 43 of the Hague Regulations, is not justified. This position simply disregards the provisions contained in IHL. It is important in this context to correct the misconception that occupation law per se could not provide a valuable legal framework regulating the use of force in law enforcement operations. In fact, the law enforcement paradigm can actually be applied in occupied territory not as a matter of human rights law, but as a matter of the law of occupation as set forth in key provisions of the Hague Regulations and GC IV.

The opinion of the present author is that the combination of Article 43 of the Hague Regulations, and Articles 27 and 64 of GC IV therefore form the backbone of the law enforcement role of the occupier. These provisions provide the essential elements of a legal framework permitting the regulation of the use of force in an occupied territory. However, while insisting that standards governing the use of force in law enforcement are based on the law of occupation, they could effectively be supplemented by standards stemming from human rights law. IHL, and occupation law in particular, would thus provide the principal legal basis, while human rights law would operate as a complement with additional standards such as precaution and proportionality. Such an approach to law enforcement in

---

the human rights law regime as the central piece of the legal framework governing the use of force in occupied territory.

[47] ECtHR, *McCann v UK*, Judgment of 27 September 1995, No 18984/91; ECtHR, *Issayeva, Yusupova, and Bazayeva v Russia*, Judgment of 24 February 2005, Nos 57947/00, 57948/00, and 57949/00.

occupied territory is very likely a concept more acceptable to many states, because rooting law enforcement rules in IHL takes more fully into account the particular realities of occupation situations, and offers a way around the difficulties of one particularly contentious issue, the extraterritorial application of human rights law.[48]

---

[48] ICRC, Report on Occupation and Other Forms of Administration of Foreign Territory (n 13).

CHAPTER 9

THE LAW APPLICABLE TO PEACE OPERATIONS

DIETER FLECK[*]

1 INTRODUCTION

PEACE operations comprise all military (peacekeeping and peace enforcement) operations performed in support of diplomatic efforts to establish and maintain peace.[1] Such operations generally do not take place during armed conflicts. Their aim is rather to prevent active hostilities and secure post-conflict peace-building. It is only in exceptional situations that peacekeepers, as noted in the 1994 UN Safety Convention[2]

[*] The author would like to express his gratitude to Professor Terry D. Gill for critical comments on a draft of this contribution. All views and opinions are personal. The author can be reached at DieterFleck@t-online.de.

[1] Cf D. Fleck (ed), *The Handbook of International Humanitarian Law* (3rd edn, Oxford: Oxford University Press, 2013), Section 1301.

[2] Article 2(2) of the Convention on the Safety of United Nations and Associated Personnel of 9 December 1994; see also Preamble, para 3, of the Optional Protocol of 8 December 2005. As stated by M.H. Arsanjani in the United Nations Audiovisual Library of International Law, <http://untreaty.un.org/cod/avl/pdf/ha/csunap/csunap_e.pdf>, the purport of Art 2(2) is not entirely clear and is open to interpretations which may not have been anticipated at the time of the negotiation of the Convention, see also M.H. Arsanjani, 'Defending the Blue Helmets: Protection of United Nations Personnel', in L. Condorelli, A.-M. La Rosa, and S. Scherrer (eds), *Les Nations Unies et le droit international humanitaire/The United Nations and International Humanitarian Law*, Proceedings of the international symposium held on the occasion of the 50th anniversary of the United Nations, Geneva,

and in the 1999 Secretary-General's Bulletin,[3] may be engaged in enforcement action 'as combatants', in which case the relevant body of international humanitarian law applies also to a United Nations force and consequently also to a force authorized by the United Nations, and irrespective of the specific classification of the mission.[4] Hence most of the law of peace operations is derived from other branches of international law.

The relevant rules and provisions are difficult to trace in areas between peace and armed conflict. Important legal and policy rules had and still have to be 'invented through trial and error under the stress of urgent circumstances',[5] and in contrast to the law of armed conflict there is no systematic codification and almost no established custom governing peace operations in a comprehensive manner. While the idea of peacekeeping as such and its basic elements of consent, impartiality and limited use of force (in self-defence and defence against armed attempts to frustrate the execution of the mandate) may now be considered as customary international law,[6] there are still many grey areas and overlaps between various types of missions, both conceptually and in practice, which pose legal questions and can have important policy implications.

The term 'peace operation' is of comparable recent coinage.[7] It entails 'three principal activities: conflict prevention and peacemaking; peacekeeping; and peacebuilding'.[8] A variety of professionals, military and civilian, are directly or indirectly involved. A complex legal regime comprising peacetime rules of international law, international humanitarian law (ie the law of armed conflict), and national law must be adhered to and properly implemented by the peace forces, their commanders,

19, 20, and 21 October 1995 (Paris: Éditions Pedone, 1996), 115, 132–45. C. Greenwood in D. Fleck (ed), *The Handbook of International Humanitarian Law* (2nd edn, Oxford: Oxford University Press, 2008), Section 208, para 4, convincingly explains that while the effect of this provision is that the threshold for the application of international humanitarian law is also the ceiling for the application of the Convention, it seems highly unlikely that those who drafted this Convention intended it to cease application as soon as there was any fighting, however low-level, between members of a UN force and members of other organized armed forces as this would reduce the scope of application of the Convention to almost nothing.

[3] Section 1(1) of the Secretary-General's Bulletin *Observance by United Nations forces of international humanitarian law*, UN Doc ST/SGB/1999/13 of 6 August 1999.

[4] C. Greenwood, 'International Humanitarian Law and United Nations Military Operations', 1 *Yearbook of International Humanitarian Law* (1998) 3–34 at 11, 33.

[5] M.J. Matheson, *Council Unbound: The Growth of UN Decision Making on Conflict and Post-conflict Issues after the Cold War* (Washington, DC: United States Institute of Peace Press, 2006), 99.

[6] This is confirmed by the ICJ, *Certain Expenses of the United Nations (Article 17, paragraph 2, of the Charter)*, Advisory Opinion of 20 July 1962, [1962] ICJ Rep 151, (see below, n 31, and accompanying text), by the Secretary-General's reports on the issue, and the reactions of member states in over 50 years of practice.

[7] See N. White, 'Peace Operations', in V. Chetail (ed), *Post Conflict Peacebuilding. A Lexicon* (Oxford: Oxford University Press, 2009), 213–27.

[8] Report of the Panel on United Nations Peace Operations (*Brahimi Report*), UN Doc A/55/305, S/2000/809 (21 August 2000), § 10; see *Glossary of UN Peacekeeping Terms*.

international organizations, and participating states;[9] yet the scope and exact meaning of relevant rules is often uncertain and disputed.

A wealth of literature has developed over time.[10] Clear legal distinctions continue to apply between operations based on and executed with full consent of the host state and enforcement operations involving the use of force even against the latter's authorities. A handbook providing a comprehensive overview and in-depth discussion of the applicable law in the form of black-letter rules and critical commentaries is now available.[11] Differentiating between enforcement operations, peace enforcement operations, and peace (support) operations and also dealing with the legal issues of self-defence, humanitarian intervention, and intervention on invitation, it is designed to provide transparent information and support a progressive discourse between practice and academic research.

This Chapter looks into some salient issues within the wider field of peace operations, focusing on existing gaps and policy problems of legal regulation. It starts with certain frictions that have evolved during the genesis of these operations and their current legal challenges (2). The following sections suggest a critical look at the existing legal basis and political control of these operations (3), comment on the status of peacekeepers in the host country and in transit states (4), and examine select issues of applicable law and policy for the conduct of peace operations. These include security and safety; command and control; freedom of movement, communications, and logistic support; and relevant operational law issues including compliance by peacekeepers with human rights obligations, protection of civilians, force protection, and operational detentions (5). Problems concerning the accountability of sending states, international organizations, and individual wrongdoers are discussed in context with fact-finding, judicial control, and the desirability of their improvement (6). Finally, some conclusions are drawn, focusing on implementation gaps and desirable legal developments (7).

---

[9] See Fleck (n 1), Sections 1305–9.

[10] For a prominent look into legal issues which has already become historic, see A. Cassese (ed), *United Nations Peace-keeping: Legal Essays* (Alphen aan den Rijn, Netherlands: Sijthoff & Noordhoff, 1978); for more information, see United Nations Dag Hammarskjöld Library, *Peace-keeping Operations. A Bibliography.*

[11] T.D. Gill and D. Fleck (eds), *The Handbook of the International Law of Military Operations* (Oxford: Oxford University Press, 2010).

2 Past and Current Legal Challenges

While the creation of legal bases for peace operations had been envisaged both after World War I[12] and World War II,[13] practice did not develop according to existing rules. Peacekeeping operations in the stricter sense are essentially based on the principles of consent of the parties, impartiality, and non-use of force except in self-defence and defence of the mandate.[14] For other peace operations, especially those with enforcement mandates, this set of core principles is not automatically applicable and may not be fully appropriate. But—as will be shown below—essential elements of the aforementioned three principles may prevail even in such cases. All peace operations are executed within the framework of the UN Charter (Chapters VI, VII, and VIII). Even those operations in which the element of coercion can be neglected differ considerably in mandate, size, and duration.[15] It should also be considered that peacekeeping and peace enforcement tasks may be present in one and the same operation.

In the Korean War the Security Council did take coercive action even though not all Council members supported the decision. Soon after the General Assembly established the United Nations Temporary Commission on Korea[16] and recognized the Government of the Republic of Korea as having 'effective control and jurisdiction over that part of Korea where the United Nations was able to observe and consult and in which the great majority of the people of Korea reside',[17] the Security Council determined the existence of a breach of the peace due to an 'armed attack on the Republic of Korea by forces from North Korea' and called upon 'the authorities in North Korea to withdraw forthwith their armed forces to the 38th parallel'.[18]

---

[12] See Art 16 of the League of Nations Covenant of 28 June 1919. Plans for an international force to secure a plebiscite in Vilna during the Polish-Lithuanian conflict in 1920–21 could not be implemented. Based on an agreement between Colombia and Peru, a League of Nations Commission with 50 Colombian soldiers placed under its control was established to administer the border city of Leticia from 1933–34. To secure the 1935 plebiscite which ended the 15 years' administration of the Saar territory by the League of Nations under Art 49 of the Versailles Treaty, a multinational force was used to maintain order during the elections.

[13] See Art 42 of the UN Charter of 26 June 1945.

[14] United Nations, Department of Peacekeeping Operations (DPKO) and Department of Field Support (DFS), *United Nations Peacekeeping Operations: Principles and Guidelines* (New York: DPKO, 2008), available at <http://pbpu.unlb.org/pbps/Library/capstone_doctrine_eng.pdf> (cited as 'Capstone Doctrine'), Chs 1 and 3.

[15] See for general information, <http://www.un.org/Depts/dpko/dpko/intro/>. A historical overview and legal assessment of the practice of peace-keping operations is provided by M. Bothe, 'Peacekeeping', margin numbers 1–71, before Ch VII, in B. Simma (ed), *The Charter of the United Nations* (3rd edn, Oxford: Oxford University Press, 2012).

[16] UNGA Res 112 (III) of 14 November 1947.

[17] UNGA Res 195 (III) of 12 December 1948; UNGA Res 293 (IV) of 21 October 1949.

[18] UNSC Res 82 (1950), adopted by 9 votes to 0, with 1 abstention (Yugoslavia) and one member absent (USSR).

Two days later the Council, responding to an appeal from the Republic of Korea, recommended 'that the Members of the United Nations furnish such assistance to the Republic of Korea as may be necessary to repel the armed attack and restore international peace and security in the area'.[19]

In the absence of any armed forces directly available to the Security Council under Article 43 of the UN Charter, action by states was recommended, and states providing military forces and other assistance were invited to put these under a United States led unified command which was authorized 'at its discretion to use the United Nations flag in the course of operations against North Korean forces concurrently with the flags of the various nations participating'.[20] The Council clearly acted under Chapter VII of the Charter, even if there was no practice at the time to explicitly say so in the text of the Resolutions. Authorization of military action by a group of states willing to act was in accordance with Article 48(1) of the Charter. It may be noted that action was taken in support of a non-member of the United Nations[21] and against an entity that was not recognized as a state by the acting Council members.[22]

The absence of the USSR (in protest against the representation of China in the United Nations by the Taiwan Government) had enabled the Security Council to act, although 'concurrent votes of the permanent members' are required under Article 27(3) of the Charter and none of the members could have presumed that the USSR, if present, would have voted in favour of these Resolutions. Considering that the object and purpose of this Charter provision is to prevent decisions from being taken against the declared will of a permanent member, it had been suggested to read the phrase 'present and voting' into its text.[23] Member states have accepted this reading, interpreting the Charter in accordance with a principle that was later codified in Article 31(3)(b) of the Vienna Convention on the Law of Treaties.[24] Yet the Council, which had requested the United States to report as appropriate on the course of action taken, was unable to act on these reports on the return of the USSR to its sessions.

It was in this situation that the General Assembly, which may not make recommendations with regard to issues on which the Security Council is 'exercising

[19] UNSC Res 83 (1950), adopted by 7 votes to 1 (Yugoslavia), with 2 members (Egypt and India) not participating in the voting, and one member (USSR) absent.

[20] UNSC Res. 84 (1950), adopted by 7 votes to 3 (Egypt, India, and Yugoslavia), with one member absent (USSR).

[21] The Republic of Korea and the Democratic People's Republic of Korea were admitted to membership not before 17 September 1991 (UNGA Res 46/1).

[22] The Democratic People's Republic of Korea was not considered under UNGA Res 195 (III) as being 'based on elections which were a valid expression of the free will of the electorate'.

[23] H. Kelsen, 'Organization and Procedure of the Security Council', 59 *Harvard Law Review* (1946) 1087–1121.

[24] B. Simma, S. Brunner, and H.-P. Kaul in Simma (ed) (n 15), margin numbers 46–51 at 47, 51.

[...] the functions assigned to it',[25] had adopted its *Uniting for Peace Resolution*,[26] deciding that

if the Council, because of lack of unanimity of its permanent members fails to exercise its primary responsibility for the maintenance of international peace and security in any case where there appears to be a threat to the peace, breach of the peace or act of aggression, the General Assembly shall consider the matter immediately with a view to making appropriate recommendations to Members for collective measures, including in the case of a breach of the peace or act of aggression the use of armed force when necessary, to maintain and restore international peace and security. If not in session at the time the General Assembly may meet in emergency special session within twenty-four hours of the request therefor. Such emergency special session shall be called if requested by the Security Council on the vote of any seven members or by a majority of the Members of the United Nations.

Most peace operations were based on the consent, or at least acceptance, of the states affected and participating, thus leaving *Uniting for Peace* procedures widely uninvoked. Yet military forces were sent to operate on foreign territory without explicit legal basis in the Charter, without special agreement in accordance with its Article 43, and without involving the Military Staff Committee under Article 47. International peacekeeping was widely understood and used as an informal means of effectively containing warring states and it was supported by states as 'a great power instrument for managing relations and preventing war of a far more catastrophic kind'.[27]

A few operations became controversial within the Council. The United Nations Emergency Force I (UNEF I), undertaken from 1956–67 in pursuance of General Assembly Resolutions,[28] was to secure and supervise the cessation of hostilities, including the withdrawal of the armed forces of France, Israel, and the United Kingdom from Egyptian territory and, after the withdrawal, the creation of a buffer between the Egyptian and Israeli forces and an impartial supervision of the ceasefire. The Security Council was unable to act because of British and French vetoes, and the General Assembly acted under the *Uniting for Peace* Resolution. Opérations des Nations Unies au Congo (ONUC) from 1960–64 were authorized by the Security Council[29] with the mandate to provide military assistance to the

---

[25] Article 12 of the UN Charter.

[26] UNGA Res 377 (V) of 3 November 1950, adopted by 52 votes to 5 (Czechoslovakia, Poland, USSR, Ukrainian SSR, Byelorussian SSR), with 2 abstentions (India and Argentina). See D. Zaum, 'The Security Council, the General Assembly, and War: The Uniting for Peace Resolution', in V. Lowe, A. Roberts, J. Welsh, and D. Zaum (eds), *The United Nations Security Council and War. The Evolution of Thought and Practice since 1945* (Oxford: Oxford University Press, 2008), 154–74.

[27] M. Berdal, 'The Security Council and Peacekeeping', in V. Lowe (n 26), 175–204 at 176.

[28] UNGA Res 997 (ES-1) of 2 November 1956; 998 (ES-1) and 999 (ES-1) of 4 November 1956; 1000 (ES-1) of 5 November 1956; 1001 (ES-1) of 7 November 1956; 1121 (XI) of 24 November 1956, 1125 (XI) of 2 February 1957; and 1263 (XIII) of 14 November 1958.

[29] UNSC Res 143 (14 July 1960), adopted with 8 votes to 0 with 3 abstentions (China, France, United Kingdom); UNSC Res 161 (21 February 1961), adopted with 9 votes to 0 with 2 abstentions (France, USSR);

Government of the Republic of the Congo[30] and to prevent the occurrence of civil war in the country.

When, as a form of protest against the Secretary-General, some states including France and the USSR refused to pay their share of the expenses for UNEF I and ONUC, the ICJ was asked for an Advisory Opinion to solve the dispute.[31] The Court confirmed, despite several dissenting opinions that neither the General Assembly nor the Security Council had acted *ultra vires*, as UNEF I was not an enforcement action under Chapter VII but rather a measure recommended under Article 14 of the Charter, and for ONUC it was in conformity with the Charter that the Council had authorized the Secretary-General to select and invite member states willing to assist, hence the expenditures for both operations constituted 'expenses of the Organization' within the meaning of Article 17(2) of the Charter. But states disagreeing with these operations continued to use non-payment as a means of protest. A compromise was reached two years later in 1965, by not raising the question of voting rights in the General Assembly (Article 19 of the Charter), and by solving the budget difficulties of the Organization through voluntary contributions.[32]

In many crisis situations, however, no international action was taken due to impasse within the Council. When this situation changed with the end of the Cold War in 1989, the number and intensity of UN peace operations increased considerably, but the higher expectations as to their effectiveness were not met. The trauma of mass atrocities in Cambodia (1975–79)[33] with no foreign power intervening was soon matched by the genocide in Rwanda 1994,[34] and the fall of Srebrenica in 1995,[35]

---

and UNSC Res 169 (24 November 1961), adopted with 9 votes to 0 with 2 abstentions (France, United Kingdom). The authorization of ONUC was not cancelled by UNSC Res 157 (17 September 1960), adopted with 8 votes to 2 (Poland, USSR) and 1 abstention (France), by which the Council, considering the lack of unanimity of its permanent members, decided to call an emergency special session of the General Assembly under the Uniting for Peace Resolution. Indeed, UNSC Res 143 (1960) was fully supported by UNGA Res 1474 (ES-IV) of 20 September 1960.

[30] UNSC Res 142 (7 July 1960) had recommended to admit the 'Republic of the Congo' (capital: Leopoldville) to membership in the United Nations. Weeks later a similar recommendation was issued by UNSC Res 152 (23 August 1960) with respect to 'the Republic of the Congo' (capital Brazzaville). On 20 September 1960 both states were admitted by the General Assembly (UNGA Res 1480 and 1486 (XV)).

[31] ICJ, *Certain Expenses of the United Nations* (n 6). See R. Jennings, 'Advisory Opinion of July 20, 1962, Certain Expenses of the United Nations', 11 *ICLQ* (1962) 1169ff.

[32] UNGA (XIX), Official Records, 1331st Plenary Meeting, 1 September 1965, §§ 3, 4; Tomuschat, 'Article 19', margin number 22 in Simma (ed) (n 15).

[33] See C. Etcheson, 'The Politics of Genocide Justice in Cambodia', in C.P.R. Romano, A. Nollkaemper, and J.K. Kleffner (eds), *Internationalized Criminal Courts. Sierra Leone, East Timor, Kosovo, and Cambodia* (Oxford: Oxford University Press, 2004), 181–205.

[34] Report of the Independent Inquiry into the Actions of the United Nations During the 1994 Genocide in Rwanda, UN Doc S/1999/1257 (16 December 1999), <http://www.un.org/News/dh/latest/rwanda.htm>.

[35] Report of the Secretary-General pursuant to General Assembly Resolution 53/35. The fall of Srebrenica. UN Doc A/54/549 (15 November 1999).

both happening in the presence of UN forces lacking resources, adequate man-dates, and a firm political commitment by the Council and the United Nations as a whole. Extensive peace operations in Somalia (1992–95) failed and the tragedy in Sudan (1982–2012) has added a new dimension of atrocities which cannot be contained by the UN alone.

In many cases UN peace operations have reached their limits due to concrete problems in the field. The United Nations Mission in Sudan (UNMIS), a UN peace support operation with a robust mandate under Chapter VII of the UN Charter,[36] was made up of some 9,000 civilian, military, and police components; further military and police personnel were engaged in the United Nations–African Union Hybrid Mission in Darfur (UNAMID), an even larger Chapter VII mission[37] which still carries out confidence-building measures, night patrols, patrols escorting women, and humanitarian assistance. UNAMID has frequently been attacked by militias using heavy weapons. As the African Union's Special Envoy for Darfur, for-mer Prime Minister of Tanzania Salim Ahmed Salim, has concluded: 'the mission could be an effective corner-stone for a long-term development of peace, but its lack of resources including helicopters is a permanent danger for the personnel involved; this must destroy confidence of the civilian population and undermine the reputa-tion of the United Nations'.[38] Sudan as the receiving state frequently failed to provide necessary support for both UNMIS and UNAMID. Delivered goods were held up at customs and minimum infrastructure was provided only hesitatingly. While the current agreements concluded by the Government of Sudan[39] are still considered as the basis for the peace process in the country, and the secession of South Sudan followed in 2011, the country might again be dragged into violence.

The *Agenda for Peace*,[40] commissioned by the Security Council at its first meet-ing at the level of heads of state and government[41] and later endorsed by the Council and the General Assembly,[42] had identified four separate components to

---

[36] See UNSC Res 1590 (2005), § 16, see also UNSC Res 1663 (2006), UNSC Res 1812 (2008), UNSC Res 1870 (2009), and UNSC Res 1919 (2010), <http://www.unmis.org/english/en-main.htm>.

[37] See UNSC Res 1881 (2009). Authorized strength under UNSC Res 1769 (2007): up to 19,555 mili-tary personnel; 6,432 police, including 3,772 police personnel and 19 formed police units compris-ing up to 140 personnel each; and a significant civilian component, <http://www.un.org/Depts/dpko/missions/unamid/>.

[38] Salim Ahmed Salim, 'Kathastrophale Ergebnisse in Darfur', *Frankfurter Allgemeine Zeitung*, 31 July 2008.

[39] *Comprehensive Peace Agreement* with the Sudan People's Liberation Movement/Army (9 January 2005), <http://www.unmis.org/English/documents/cpa-en.pdf, http://www.reliefweb.int/rw/RWB.NSF/db900SID/EVIU-6AZBDB?OpenDocument>, *Cairo Peace Agreement* with the National Democratic Alliance (16 June 2005), <http://www.goss-brussels.com/agreements/gov-south/cairo_agreement_between_gos_nda.pdf>; *Darfur Peace Agreement* with the Sudan Liberation Movement/Army and the Justice and Equality Movement (5 May 2006), <http://www.sd.undp.org/doc/DPA.pdf>; *Eastern Sudan Peace Agreement* with the Eastern Sudan Front (14 October 2006), <http://www.sd.undp.org/doc/Eastern_States_Peace_Agreement.pdf>.

[40] 'An Agenda for Peace—Report of the Secretary-General', UN Doc A/47/277-S/24111, 17 June 1992.

[41] UN Doc S/23500 (31 January 1992).   [42] UNGA Res 47/120 A (18 December 1992).

the maintenance of international peace and security: preventive diplomacy, peace-making, peacekeeping, and post-conflict peace-building. Advocating an early warning system to identify potential conflicts, and a 'reinvigorated and restructured Economic and Social Council' the *Agenda for Peace* tried to establish a system of preventive deployment in situations of national crisis, to discourage hostilities in inter-state disputes, and serve to deter conflict in situations of external threats.[43] Three years later, its *Supplement*[44] reiterated the need for hard decisions in view of a dramatic increase in relevant UN activities, as the end of the Cold War enabled the Council to begin using its authority under the Charter more extensively.

The Brahimi Report,[45] conspicuously avoiding the traditional classification between peacekeeping and peace enforcement, addressed doctrinal issues of peace-making, peacekeeping and peace-building in context. The Report is an important contribution towards adapting the three principles of peacekeeping—ie consent of local parties, impartiality, and the non-use of force except in self-defence—to more complex conditions of internal conflicts in which consent of local parties may be unreliable, Charter principles are often neglected at least by one of the parties, and peacekeepers have to operate in a rather volatile safety and security environment. The Report developed practical recommendations, in particular for 'clear, credible and achievable mandates' to be formulated by the Security Council.[46] Accordingly, rules of engagement (if necessary robust ones) were called for, and should be adopted with relevant specifications for each mission.[47]

The doctrine of *Responsibility to Protect* (R2P),[48] developed on basic principles of state responsibility and intervention in extreme situations,[49] has been described by its authors as 'a new international security and human rights norm to address the

---

[43] See n 40, §§ 26–32.

[44] 'Supplement to An Agenda for Peace', UN Doc A/50/60-S/1995/1, 3 January 1995.

[45] *Brahimi Report* (n 8); see N. White, 'Commentary on the Report of the Panel on United Nations Peace Operations', 6(1) *Journal of Conflict and Security Law* (2001) 127–46; C. Gray 'Peacekeeping After the Brahimi Report', 6(2) *Journal of Conflict and Security Law* (2001) 267–88.

[46] The Security Council has endorsed these proposals in UNSC Res 1327 (2000), adopting detailed decisions and recommendations resulting from the *Brahimi Report*, and decided to review periodically their implementation. For a critical assessment, see W. Durch, V. Holt, C. Earle, and M. Shanahan, *The Brahimi Report and the Future of UN Peace Operations* (Washington DC: The Henry Stimson Center, 2003).

[47] T. Gill, J.A.M. Léveillée, and D. Fleck, 'The Rule of Law in Peace Operations. General Report', XVII *Recueils de la Societé Internationale de Droit Militaire et de Droit de la Guerre* (Brussels, 2006), 109–57.

[48] Report of the International Commission on Intervention and State Sovereignty, *The Responsibility to Protect* (December 2001), <http://www.responsibilitytoprotect.org/>; G.J. Evans and M. Sahnoun, 'The Responsibility to Protect', 81(6) *Foreign Affairs* (2002) 99–110.

[49] Report of the International Commission on Intervention and State Sovereignty (n 48) at xi: 'A. State sovereignty implies responsibility, and the primary responsibility for the protection of its people lies with the state itself. B. Where a population is suffering serious harm, as a result of internal war, insurgency, repression or state failure, and the state in question is unwilling or unable to halt or avert it, the principle of non-intervention yields to the international responsibility to protect.'

international community's failure to prevent and stop genocides, war crimes, ethnic cleansing and crimes against humanity'.[50] Yet certain limitations must be considered in this context. At the 2005 World Summit, the assembled heads of state and government, accommodating concerns that an unqualified reference to R2P might result in 'an obligation to intervene under international law',[51] gave a remarkable response to more progressive approaches by invoking three pillars on which the responsibility rests: first the responsibility of the state to protect its population from genocide, war crimes, ethnic cleansing, and crimes against humanity including their incitement, through appropriate and necessary means; secondly, the commitment of the international community to assist states in meeting these obligations, through the United Nations in accordance with Chapters VI and VIII of the Charter; and thirdly the responsibility of states 'to take collective action, in a timely and decisive manner, through the Security Council, in accordance with the Charter, including Chapter VII, on a case-by-case basis and in cooperation with relevant regional organizations as appropriate, should peaceful means be inadequate and national authorities are manifestly failing to protect their populations from genocide, war crimes, ethnic cleansing and crimes against humanity'.[52]

The three pillars, later referred to as the responsibility to prevent, the responsibility to react, and the responsibility to rebuild[53] are not so much new law, but a different way of presenting some existing legal obligations and sound policy objectives in a new form. They are equally important for doctrine and practice and beyond any doubt they clearly have a bearing on peace operations.[54] Relevant deliberations and decisions are to be made far above command level and it will be up to the Security Council to translate R2P principles into mandates of peace operations. Where the Council fails to take responsible action, the General Assembly may be called to act under the 'Uniting for Peace' Resolution.[55] Regional organizations and states remain fully responsible to cooperate in the restoration of peace and security as well. But in no case could mission mandates be derived from R2P without appropriate authorization.

---

[50] See n 48, Introduction.

[51] See eg US Ambassador John Bolton, letter dated 30 August 2005, <http://www.responsibilityto-protect.org/files/US_Boltonletter_R2P_30Aug05[1].pdf>.

[52] UNGA Res 60/1 (24 October 2005), *2005 World Summit Outcome*, §§ 138–40. See E.C. Luck, 'The United Nations and the Responsibility to Protect', Policy Analysis Brief (Muscatine, IA: The Stanley Foundation, August 2008), <http://www.humansecuritygateway.com/documents/TSF_theUNandR2P.pdf>.

[53] S.C. Breau, 'The Impact of the Responsibility to Protect on Peacekeeping', 11(3) *Journal of Conflict and Security Law* (2006) 429–64 at 431.

[54] See Breau (n 53); V.K. Holt and J.G. Smith, *Halting Widespread or Systematic Attacks on Civilians: Military Strategies and Operations Concepts* (Washington, DC: The Henry L. Stimson Center, 2008); J.H.S. Lie, *Protection of Civilians, the Responsibility to Protect and Peace Operations* (Oslo: NUPI, 2008).

[55] See n 26.

The concept of R2P is not to be misunderstood as a simple coinage replacing the term 'humanitarian intervention' with its highly disputed justification.[56] Developing realistic perspectives for peace enforcement even against objections raised by affected states, R2P does not construe a new 'right to intervene' that was not foreseen under the UN Charter, but does challenge states to meet their existing responsibilities. In the end, if all the recommendations regarding a state's duty to protect human rights and the duty of the UN to take effective measures within the Charter are not forthcoming, the old debate about humanitarian intervention reappears and cannot be wiped away. The legal character of the concept of R2P may be questioned,[57] but there is a responsibility under international law to protect populations from genocide, war crimes, ethnic cleansing, and crimes against humanity, a responsibility the General Assembly and the Secretary-General have expressly evoked.[58]

As confirmed by the Security Council in its resolutions on the protection of civilians in armed conflicts,[59] this is first a 'primary responsibility' of states towards their citizens, and of parties to an armed conflict with respect to civilians affected by the hostilities; but very deliberately all 'relevant provisions of the 2005 World Summit Outcome Document', ie all three pillars of R2P, have been referred to in this context.[60] The responsibility to respond is essentially rooted in Chapter VII of the Charter and thus depends on Security Council action. The commitment to assist rests on the duty of states to cooperate, to bring an end to serious breaches of obligations arising under peremptory norms.[61] State sovereignty is no obstacle for taking responsible action under Chapter VII, as sovereignty and responsibility are to be understood as mutually enforcing principles.

The United Nations Peace-building Commission, established under concurrent Resolutions of the UN General Assembly[62] and the Security Council,[63] is a forum for responding to these considerations. It has accomplished useful work in assisting relevant UN bodies—in particular the Security Council, the General Assembly, the Economic and Social Council, and the Secretary-General—in their efforts to improve the situation in conflict-torn countries. Along with the Peace-building

---

[56] See A. Roberts, 'The So-Called "Right" of Humanitarian Intervention', 3 *Yearbook of International Humanitarian Law* (2000) 3–53; T.D. Gill, in Gill and Fleck (n 11), Ch 13.

[57] See C. Stahn, 'Responsibility to Protect: Political Rhetoric or Emerging Legal Norm?', 101 *American Journal of International Law* (2007) 99–120; D. Chandler, 'The Responsibility to Protect? Imposing the "Liberal Peace"', 11(1) *International Peacekeeping* (2004) 59–81.

[58] See Report of the High Level Panel on Threats, Challenges and Change, *A More Secure World: Our Shared Responsibility* (UNGA Res A/59/565 of 2 December 2004); Report of the Secretary-General *In Larger Freedom* (UN Doc A/59/2005).

[59] See eg UNSC Res 1674 (2006), 1894 (2009).   [60] Cf UNSC Res 1894 (2009), preamble § 7.

[61] See Art 41 of the Articles on Responsibility of States for Internationally Wrongful Acts, ILC, Report on the Work of its 53rd Session (23 April–1 June and 2 July–August 2001), UN GAOR, 55th Session, Supplement No 10, UN Doc A/561/10; J. Crawford, *The International Law Commission's Articles on State Responsibility: Introduction, Text and Commentaries* (Cambridge: Cambridge University Press, 2002), commentary to Art 41, §§ 2 and 3.

[62] UNGA Res 60/180.   [63] UNSC Res 1645 (2005).

Fund and the Peace-building Support Office, the Commission has gained experience in dealing with developments in Burundi, Sierra Leone, the Central African Republic, Guinea-Bissau, Liberia, and more recently in Guinea. This may contribute to resource mobilization, national capacity development, and interaction.[64] While the Commission has not succeeded yet in dealing with many of the other post-conflict situations in the world, and has not been involved in any preventive missions that should play an important role under the concept of R2P, it requires and deserves full support by states and civil society.

The past two decades have seen dramatic changes for international peace operations. The Security Council took firm action for reversal of aggression in Kuwait in 1990.[65] It was not as successful in imposing peace in Bosnia and Herzegovina and in Croatia 1992–95, and it again arrived at an impasse on humanitarian intervention in Kosovo 1999 and regime change in Iraq 2003.[66] The Secretary-General had to face particular problems where the Security Council did not provide specific guidance and failed to exercise political control. Due to disagreements between member states, safe havens were established in Bosnia and Herzegovina without the corresponding resources to implement them. In many situations, including the conflicts in Afghanistan and Darfur, the Council has to rely on groups of states, regional organizations, and arrangements exercising command and control of their operations.[67] Personnel recruitment, equipment, and funding are increasingly posing problems.

The UN works extensively in partnership with other international and regional organizations, such as the African Union (AU),[68] the European Union (EU), and the North Atlantic Treaty Organization (NATO). Again, within a few years UN peace operations have exploded to an eight-fold growth of personnel deployed.[69]

[64] Report of the Peace-building Commission on its 5th session, A/66/675–S/2012/70 (30 January 2012).

[65] See *The United Nations and the Iraq-Kuwait Conflict 1990–1996.*The United Nations Blue Book Series, vol IX (1996).

[66] For a well-informed assessment of events, see R. Zacklin, *The United Nations Secretariat and the Use of Force in a Unipolar World* (Cambridge: Cambridge University Press, 2010).

[67] See eg IFOR/SFOR; KFOR; ISAF, since 1995; the Italian-led 'Operation Alba' in Albania 1997; Mission Inter-africaine de Surveillance des Accords de Bangui (MISAB) in the Central African Republic 1997; African (AU and other) missions: AMIB in Burundi 2003, UNAMID in Darfur; ECOWAS Missions in Liberia 2003, Monitoring Group (ECOMOG) in Sierra Leone 1998–2000; the International Force in East Timor (INTERFET) 1999–2000; Peace-Truce Monitoring Group in Bougainville (BELISI) 1998–2003; the European Missions 'Operation Concordia' in FYROM 2003, 'Operation Artemis' in the Democratic Republic of Congo 2003, 'Operation Turquoise' in Rwanda; EUFOR Democratic Republic of Congo; EUFOR Tchad/RCA; EU NAVFOR ATALANTA Horn of Africa.

[68] Article 4(h) of the Constitutive Act of the African Union (2000) asserts 'the right of the Union to intervene in a Member State pursuant to a decision of the Assembly in respect of grave circumstances, namely: war crimes, genocide, and crimes against humanity'.

[69] Almost 116,000 personnel are serving on 17 peace operations led by the DPKO on four continents. In addition, DFS, established in 2007 to provide support and expertise in the areas of personnel,

The Permanent Members of the Security Council, hitherto reluctant to provide military contingents themselves, have adjusted that policy in order to meet greater demands, to demonstrate the serious intent of the United Nations, and to avoid negative consequences of opposing its peace operations.[70] As the Secretary-General stated in his 2009 annual report, 'United Nations peacekeeping is at a crossroads. The Organization needs a renewed global partnership with Member States and its partners within and outside the United Nations system'.[71]

Aligning military mandates and resources to address a concentration on disarmament, demobilization, and reintegration (DDR), and on military aspects of security sector reform (SSR) is particularly salient.[72] This will require greater awareness of the need to strengthen civilian actors in their efforts to establish the rule of law, ensure good governance, and promote economic and social recovery. Proposals by DPKO/DFS,[73] aimed at a more comprehensive approach to generating resources and creating incentives to deliver results in the field, still need to be implemented.

In this complex environment any plea for legal regulation must be treated with caution.[74] Freedom of action in extreme situations and firm political commitment remain essential for the success of peacekeepers. Yet the task to maintain and restore the rule of law requires adherence to balanced principles and rules. These rules

finance and budget, communications, information technology and logistics, supports another 15 special political and/or peace-building field missions managed by the Department of Political Affairs, as well as a number of other UN peace offices requiring administrative and logistical assistance from UN Headquarters. The budget has risen to nearly US$ 7.8 billion a year. Nearly 87,000 of those serving are troops and military observers and over 12,000 are police personnel. In addition, there are more than 6,000 international civilian personnel, nearly 15,000 local civilian staff and some 2,200 UN Volunteers from over 160 nations. Given constant rotation of personnel and new mission requirements the overall personnel comprises more than 200,000 in real terms. See Fact Sheet United Nations Peacekeeping, <http://www.un.org/en/peacekeeping/documents/factsheet.pdf>.

[70] Cf Matheson, (n 5), 125. British troops participated in UNAVEM III in Angola and UNAMIR in Rwanda; French and US troops in UNOSOM II in Somalia; British, Chinese, French, Russian, and US troops in UNTAC in Cambodia; British, French, Russian, and US troops in the United Nations Protection Force (UNPROFOR) in the former Yugoslavia. With US troops in Haiti and Russian troops in Georgia, Permanent Members of the Security Council even deployed military units in areas they had occupied in the past.

[71] Cf UN Secretary-General, Report on the Work of the Organization (UN Doc A/64/1 of 6 October 2009), § 57.

[72] Norwegian Ministry of Foreign Affairs, *Implementing United Nations Multidimensional and Integrated Peace Operations* (Oslo, May 2008), <http://www.regjeringen.no/upload/UD/Vedlegg/FN/final_operations.pdf>.

[73] DPKO and DFS, *A New Partnership Agenda: Charting a New Horizon for UN Peacekeeping* (New York: DPKO/DFS, July 2009), available at <http://www.un.org/en/peacekeeping/documents/newhorizon.pdf>.

[74] For a cautious approach, see eg D. Kennedy, *The Dark Sides of Virtue: Reassessing International Humanitarianism* (Princeton: Princeton University Press, 2004), 343–4: 'When pragmatists in governance lose their edge they need the wake-up call of principle. When principled advocacy drifts toward impracticality, we can rely on the corrections of policy pragmatism'.

derive from various branches of international law (*jus ad bellum, jus in bello, jus post bellum*, law of peace, law of international organizations) and must be implemented and promulgated in a transparent manner.

3 LEGAL BASIS AND POLITICAL CONTROL

As peace operations are essentially based on cooperation between the host country, contributing states, and the United Nations or a regional organization, there is a constant tendency that practical performance will be shaped according to existing needs, capabilities, and the various interests of the parties rather than sticking to pre-established standing rules. For many operations, questions concerning their exact legal foundations have not been raised at all, and in almost all cases, the pressure of emergencies overshadows legal considerations.

An absence of pre-existing legal rules may negatively affect the success of an operation designed to maintain or restore international peace and security. When operations are undertaken based on doubtful legality, the rule of law as a condition for stable peace is in danger of being jeopardized. Similarly, the conduct of a mission itself may be disturbed by legal uncertainties as to the mandate, the command system, and existing rights and obligations. It is for these reasons that legal principles and rules should be given closer attention. They must be interpreted in a convincing manner and all participating states and international organizations should ensure strict compliance with and full implementation of relevant rules. Many applicable rules are, indeed, subject to interpretation. This may apply even to the basic principles of consent of the parties, impartiality, and non-use of force.[75] Adherence to existing rules and Security Council control, which should be seen as an essential requirement for effective peace operations, are matters of constant challenge.

A. Consent of the parties

The consent of the receiving state is key to the success of any peace operation. In certain situations it may be replaced by the Security Council acting under Chapter VII, but even then consent remains of political importance for both peace enforcement

[75] See n 14.

and post-conflict peace-building. Where peace operations are conducted during or after an internal armed conflict, the question arises whether consent is to be given not only by the host government but also by non-state entities. That issue will depend from the role of the latter in the peace process.

B. Impartiality

For any peace operation the impartiality of peace forces towards conflicting parties is essential for providing convincing assistance in the peace process. The impartiality of peacekeepers is challenged in the case of non-compliance by the host government or factions in the receiving state with existing obligations and commitments. The Brahimi Report has rightly emphasized that impartiality of peacekeepers should not be misconceived as 'neutrality or equal treatment of all parties in all cases for all time'. The Report insisted that impartiality must 'mean adherence to the principles of the Charter and to the objectives of the mandate that is rooted in these Charter principles'.[76]

As elaborated in a comparable situation, ie for the international activities of the Red Cross, impartiality and neutrality must, indeed, be kept distinct from one another. For the Red Cross, impartiality serves to relieve the suffering of victims by concentrating on their needs and giving priority to the most urgent cases of distress. Neutrality, as an additional Red Cross principle, which is not applicable to UN peace operations, excludes taking sides in hostilities or engaging in controversies of a political, racial, religious, or ideological nature.[77] A neutral person refuses to make a judgement whereas the one who is impartial judges a situation in accordance with pre-established rules.[78] For the Security Council neutrality is not a viable option, as the world organization cannot be neutral to a threat to the peace, breach of the peace, or act of aggression. This has been confirmed in UN practice in the case of states being denied membership in the United Nations for adhering to a policy of neutrality without reservation. Article 48 of the UN Charter opens the way for exempting a neutral state from carrying out sanctions.

---

[76] See n 8, § 50.

[77] Fundamental Principles of the International Red Cross and Red Crescent Movement, proclaimed by the 20th International Red Cross Conference (Vienna, 1965) and contained in the Statutes of the International Red Cross and Red Crescent Movement, adopted by the 25th International Red Cross Conference (Geneva, 1986).

[78] J.S. Pictet, *Les Principes Fondamentaux de la Croix-Rouge. Commentaires* (Genève: Institut Henry Dunant, 1979) [*The Fundamental Principles of the Red Cross.Commentary* (Geneva: Henry-Dunant Institute, 1979); *Die Grundsätze des Roten Kreuzes. Kommentar* (Genf und Bonn: Institut Henry-Dunant und Deutsches Rotes Kreuz, 1990)], Ch 4 (Neutrality).

C. Non-use of force and necessary exceptions

The principle of non-use of force is challenged whenever states or non-state actors choose to oppose a peace operation and obstruct or jeopardize its mandate. The right of individual or collective self-defence is not to be questioned here, as it is recognized as an inherent right not only in the Charter, but also in national legal orders. It allows for reactive measures against attacks, including by peacekeepers, irrespective of whether their mandate was given under Chapter VI, VII, or VIII.

At the beginning of UN peacekeeping in Cyprus the UN Secretary-General confirmed that self-defence by peacekeepers may include the use of force against attempts by force to prevent them from carrying out their responsibilities as ordered by their commanders.[79] This position was confirmed in subsequent UN practice.[80] This wider notion of self-defence in UN operations was never contested, although not expressly confirmed under Chapter VII.[81]

The Security Council has taken a very differentiated position in such cases. Far from falling into the trap of giving peace forces *plein pouvoir* for all necessary measures to restore security and safety, it has rather called upon 'the parties, movements and factions concerned' to take all necessary measures to ensure the safety and security of United Nations personnel,[82] and facilitate the latter's efforts to provide urgent humanitarian assistance to the affected population.[83] For UN personnel, often no more than an implicit authorization for the use of force was given by the Council even when the task 'to provide security, as appropriate, to assist in the repatriation of refugees'[84] or 'to ensure security and freedom of movement of United Nations personnel and the safety and security of United Nations property'[85] was referred to as part of their mandate.

In extreme situations, Security Council authorization to use 'all necessary means' included the use of force more explicitly, but this was mostly part of a variety of

---

[79] See Report of the Secretary-General on UNFICYP of 10 September 1964, <http://www.unficyp. org/nqcontent.cfm?a_id=1565&tt=graphic&lang=l1>, 'the expression of self-defense includes the defense of United Nations posts, premises and vehicles under armed attack, as well as the support of other personnel of UNFICYP under armed attack. When acting in self-defense, the principle of minimum force shall always be applied and armed force will be used only when all peaceful means of persuasion have failed. The decision as to when force may be used in these circumstances rests with the Commander on the spot. Examples in which troops may be authorized to use force include attempts by force to compel them to withdraw from a position which they occupy under orders from their commanders, attempts by force to disarm them, and attempts by force to prevent them from carrying out their responsibilities as ordered by their commanders.'

[80] For example, Report of the Secretary-General on UNEF II of 27 October 1973 (UN Doc S/11052/ Rev.1); see also K.E. Cox, 'Beyond Self-Defence: The United Nations Peacekeeping Operations and The Use of Force', 27(2) *Denver Journal of International Law and Policy* (1999) 239–73 at 254.

[81] For the differences between this notion of self-defence and the normal meaning of the term under domestic criminal law, see T.D. Gill (sub-Chapter 5.1) and H. Boddens Hosang (Chs 22 and 23) in Gill and Fleck (n 11).

[82] UNSC Res 745, § 6 (1992) on UNTAC.   [83] UNSC Res 794 (1992), § 2 on UNOSOM I.

[84] UNSC Res 814 (1993), §12 on UNOSOM II.

[85] See eg UNSC Res 1159 (1998), § 10(d) on MINURCA.

political measures focusing on diplomatic pressure and also aiming to secure a balanced outcome.

Thus in the Congo crisis of 1960, the Council called upon the Government of Belgium to implement the withdrawal of its troops and authorized the Secretary-General 'to take all necessary action to this effect',[86] expecting of course that Belgium would cooperate in the withdrawal and not obstruct it by using force. The mandate given to ONUC a few months thereafter, to take 'all appropriate measures to prevent the occurrence of civil war in the Congo, including [...] the use of force, if necessary, in the last resort',[87] was designed to avoid the escalation of events rather than to authorize deadly force right away. Four decades later in the Second Congo War, the Council mandated the Mission de l'Organisation des Nations Unies en République Démocratique du Congo (MONUC) to 'take the necessary action, in the areas of deployment of its infantry battalions and as it deems it within its capabilities, to protect United Nations and co-located [Joint Military Commission] personnel, facilities, installations and equipment, ensure the security and freedom of movement of its personnel, and protect civilians under imminent threat of physical violence',[88] a mandate clearly designed to avoid that peace forces become involved in the conduct of hostilities.

Following Iraq's armed attack against Kuwait in 1990 the Council authorized member states to use 'all necessary means [...] to restore international peace and security in the area',[89] thus leaving open whether more than the exercise of collective self-defence was at stake.

In 1994, when systematic and widespread killings of the civilian population continued in Rwanda, member states cooperating with the Secretary-General in the United Nations Assistance Mission in Rwanda (UNAMIR) were authorized to conduct the operation 'using all necessary means' to contribute to the security and protection of displaced persons, refugees, and civilians at risk in Rwanda, and to provide security and support for the distribution of relief supplies and humanitarian relief operations,[90] again a mandate which was broad enough to include civilian and law enforcement action.

Also in 1994, during the crisis in Haiti, the Council did not focus on the use of armed force alone. It rather authorized a multinational force 'to use all necessary means to facilitate the departure from Haiti of the military leadership, consistent with the Governors Island Agreement [of 3 July 1993, S/26063], the prompt return of the legitimately elected President and the restoration of the legitimate authorities of

---

[86] UNSC Res 145 (1960), § 1.   [87] UNSC Res 160 A (1961), § 1.   [88] UNSC Res 1291 (2000), § 8.
[89] UNSC Res 678 (1990), § 2.
[90] UNSC Res 929 (1994), § 3, referring back to UNSC Res 925 (1994), § 4, where UNAMIR's mandate had been reaffirmed.

the Government of Haiti, and to establish and maintain a secure and stable environment that will permit implementation of the Governors Island Agreement',[91] thus facilitating President Jean-Bertrand Aristide's return to the country. Ten years later in 2004, after Aristide's resignation in a state of insurgency, the Council authorized member states participating in the Multinational Interim Force in Haiti (UNMIH), 'to take all necessary measures to fulfil its mandate'.[92]

The mandate for SFOR in Bosnia and Herzegovina in 1996 expressly confirmed the 'right of the force to take all necessary measures to defend itself from attack or threat of attack', and did so in the broader political context of authorizing member states 'to take all necessary measures, at the request of SFOR, either in defence of SFOR or to assist the force in carrying out its mission',[93] again without going beyond what is written already in Article 51 of the Charter.

Even in Afghanistan after 11 September 2001, the Resolution calling on member states to take 'all necessary measures to fulfil [ISAF's] mandate'[94] clearly observed the relevant political framework established under the Bonn Agreement and cannot be interpreted as a general authorization to use force.

The same attitude was shown in the conflict in Côte d'Ivoire, when the Council, which had asked all Ivorian parties 'to take all the necessary measures to prevent further violations of human rights and international humanitarian law, particularly against civilian populations'[95] authorized the United Nations Operation in Côte d'Ivoire (UNOCI) 'to use all necessary means to carry out its mandate, within its capabilities and its areas of deployment' and renewed the authorization given to the French forces not without qualifications.[96]

In the war in Sudan, after several Security Council Resolutions[97] had remained unheeded, the Council still used very carefully crafted terms to describe the mandate for UNMIS.[98] This mandate was later specified so that UNIMIS was authorized to use all necessary means to protect UNMIS, prevent attacks against civilians, and

[91] UNSC Res 940 (1994), § 4.
[92] UNSC Res 1529 (2004), § 6.   [93] UNSC Res 1088 (1996), § 20.   [94] UNSC Res 1386 (2001), § 3.
[95] UNSC Res 1479 (2003), § 8.
[96] UNSC Res 1527 (2004); UNSC Res 1528 (2004), §§ 8 and 16 ('to use all necessary means in order to support UNOCI in accordance with the agreement to be reached between UNOCI and the French authorities, and in particular to: – Contribute to the general security of the area of activity of the international forces, – Intervene at the request of UNOCI in support of its elements whose security may be threatened, – Intervene against belligerent actions, if the security conditions so require, outside the areas directly controlled by UNOCI, – Help to protect civilians, in the deployment areas of their units').
[97] UNSC Res 1547, 1556, 1564, 1574 (2004).
[98] UNSC Res 1590 (2005), § 4(b): 'To facilitate and coordinate, within its capabilities and in its areas of deployment, the voluntary return of refugees and internally displaced persons, and humanitarian assistance, inter alia, by helping to establish the necessary security conditions'.

support implementation of the Darfur Peace Agreement.[99] A similar mandate was given to UNAMID.[100]

The terms and conditions of these Resolutions clearly show that what may be necessary in the understanding of the Security Council includes political and diplomatic activities, and that the commander's decision on the use of military force must always be subject to the availability and effectiveness of peaceful means. In taking this position the Council may also be influenced by the fact that the contributing forces are bound to act under national command and control and must observe national *caveats*.[101] The Security Council has thus developed practice below the threshold of Article 42 of the Charter by (1) endorsing and supporting the actions of states in individual or collective self-defence; (2) giving limited authority to use force for the protection of international personnel and its mission and for the protection of the civilian population; or (3) delegating Chapter VII authority to use force to states where the use of force to end serious atrocities may be militarily necessary.[102]

While it may be questioned whether in the first two instances the Council was in fact acting under Chapter VII, as it is legally unnecessary (although preferable for political reasons) to seek Security Council approval for recourse to individual and collective self-defence, the third case is foreseen in Article 48 of the Charter, yet as an exception rather than a rule. Agreement within the Council and in particular among its permanent members is difficult to achieve. It will frequently depend on 'political accommodation and political pressure'.[103] It may be unlikely as well in the future that the world organization will be in a position to deploy military forces against serious military opposition.[104] But the general understanding is that '[o]nce deployed, United Nations peacekeepers must be able to carry out their mandate professionally and successfully. This means that United Nations military units must be capable of defending themselves, other mission components and the mission mandate.'[105]

---

[99] UNSC Res 1706 (2006), § 12(a): '*Decides* that UNMIS is authorized to use all necessary means, in the areas of deployment of its forces and as it deems within its capabilities: – to protect United Nations personnel, facilities, installations and equipment, to ensure the security and freedom of movement of United Nations personnel, humanitarian workers, assessment and evaluation commission personnel, to prevent disruption of the implementation of the Darfur Peace Agreement by armed groups, without prejudice to the responsibility of the Government of the Sudan, to protect civilians under threat of physical violence, – in order to support early and effective implementation of the Darfur Peace Agreement, to prevent attacks and threats against civilians, – to seize or collect, as appropriate, arms or related material whose presence in Darfur is in violation of the Agreements and the measures imposed by §§ 7 and 8 of resolution 1556, and to dispose of such arms and related material as appropriate'.

[100] UNSC Res 1769 (2007), §15(a): 'to take the necessary action, in the areas of deployment of its forces and as it deems within its capabilities in order to: (i) protect its personnel, facilities, installations and equipment, and to ensure the security and freedom of movement of its own personnel and humanitarian workers, (ii) support early and effective implementation of the Darfur Peace Agreement, prevent the disruption of its implementation and armed attacks, and protect civilians, without prejudice to the responsibility of the Government of Sudan'.

[101] D. Stephens, 'The Lawful Use of Force by Peacekeeping Forces: The Tactical Imperative', 12(2) *International Peacekeeping* (2005) 157–72.

[102] See Matheson (n 5), 164–5.   [103] See Matheson (n 5), 166.   [104] See Matheson (n 5), 144, 165.

[105] Cf *Brahimi Report*, (n 8), § 49.

Another lesson from this practice may even be more important: the Security Council, even when authorizing 'all necessary means', has never called for unlawful action exempting states and the United Nations themselves from their responsibility under international law. This will be discussed below in the context of human rights (Section 5.D.1)) and operational detentions (Section 5.D.4).

D. Security Council Control

The Security Council's (and, exceptionally, as happened so far in the cases of UNEF I[106] and UNSF/UNTEA:[107] the General Assembly's) substantive, formal, and organizational powers should allow for a comprehensive management of legal issues through the Secretary-General to ensure that a peace operation is based on the rule of law and can be sustained *vis-à-vis* the host country and the contributing states alike. This will include a clear description of the mandate, a definition of pertinent rights and responsibilities, a continuous review of the operation and its development, and both the ability and political will to decide on exit strategies.

In practice, however, enabling resolutions have left important issues unsolved. The size of forces was determined by the degree of political support of states rather than a realistic assessment of actual needs. Many missions had to be started with unclear regulations, an uncertain time schedule, and insufficient support. While consensual arrangements may be preferable to enforcement measures under Chapter VII, if no guidance is provided on contentious issues this can lead to difficult situations.

The Secretary-General is not fully in a position to fill gaps that have been left in an enabling resolution. He may see to it that rules of engagement (ROE) are issued to ensure coordinated action in accordance with existing international law.[108] Yet where the use of force is not authorized under Chapter VII, the ROE may not authorize it, except in self-defence. Law enforcement activities may not be included without consent of the host state, nor may national *caveats* by troop-contributing states be disregarded. The ROE have to reflect the mandate and the scope of the host state's consent. The Secretary-General has also prepared standardized agreements

---

[106] See n 28.

[107] Under the Agreement between the Republic of Indonesia and the Kingdom of the Netherlands concerning West New Guinea (West Irian) of 15 August 1962, Official Records of the General Assembly, Seventeenth Session, Annexes, agenda item 89, UN Doc A/5170, Annex, the Secretary-General was to establish the United Nations Temporary Executive Authority (UNTEA) in the territory and to provide the UNTEA with such security forces (the UNSF) as the United Nations Administrator deemed necessary. UNGA Res 1752 (XVII) of 21 September 1962 (not facing any limitation under Art 12 UN Charter at the time and consequently not acting under *Uniting for Peace* procedures, see n 26) authorized the Secretary-General to carry out the tasks entrusted to him in the Agreement. UNSF was withdrawn in 1963.

[108] See n 47.

to secure the contribution of personnel and equipment by member states,[109] but unless these agreements are formally concluded by states and sufficiently implemented in practice, UN control of peace operations will be limited and may fall short of meeting its objectives.

As demonstrated with respect to the situation in Sudan,[110] regional arrangements may effectively enlarge existing possibilities. They may even enable certain forms of robust peace operations which would not be possible otherwise. But they cannot fill gaps left by a Security Council unwilling to authorize action under Chapter VII.

Finally, Security Council control should be exercised continuously. For the performance of special functions the Council may also establish subsidiary organs under Article 29 of the UN Charter, as recently happened with the Peace-building Commission.[111] The Council is widely supported by the Secretary-General who may also take initiatives himself. In specific situations independent investigations are necessary and appropriate, to establish facts and decide on consequences and remedies for the victims. This may apply to alleged human rights violations and crimes committed by deployed forces in Afghanistan, Iraq, Kosovo, or other missions. Experience shows that appropriate measures are not always taken upon national initiative by contributing states. Even fact-finding may be a problem. The need for international cooperative solutions is obvious, but in the absence of binding decisions under the authority of the UN or a competent regional arrangement under Chapter VIII of the UN Charter, not very much will be achieved.

The Security Council should include in its resolutions, irrespective of whether these are adopted under Chapters VI, VII, or VIII, provisions on effective human rights protection for people affected by peace operations. This aspect has been neglected in UN practice. The inherent role of peace forces in protecting human rights and restoring justice should be explicitly confirmed. The Council should also consider the adoption of a mandate that authorizes the international military force to intervene in cases of illegal use of force against civilians in the area of operations. Appropriate measures should be taken against any wrongful acts committed by members of a peace operation themselves. This includes effective action to ensure monitoring, independent legal control, and remedies for victims of violations.

---

[109] See *Model Agreement between the United Nations and Member States Contributing Personnel and Equipment to United Nations Peace-Keeping Operations* (UN Doc A/46/185 of 23 May 1991), <http://www.amicc.org/docs/UNContributionAgrmnt.pdf>; *Manual on Policies and Procedures Concerning the Reimbursement and Control of Contingent-Owned Equipment of Troop/Police Contributors Participating in Peacekeeping Missions* (COE Manual, UN Doc A/C.5/63/18 of 29 January 2009), <http://daccess-dds-ny.un.org/doc/UNDOC/GEN/N09/223/21/PDF/N0922321.pdf?OpenElement>.

[110] See nn 36–39 and accompanying text.   [111] See n 63.

4 THE STATUS OF PEACEKEEPERS

For effective peace operations it is essential that military and civilian personnel deployed in the receiving state and transiting through third states in their official capacity enjoy certain privileges and immunities. The purpose of such privileges and immunities is not for individuals to benefit in their private affairs but rather to ensure an unimpeded performance of their official functions. Immunity does not imply impunity for any crimes committed by forces of a sending state; neither does it limit the accountability of that state for any wrongful act (see below, Section 6). But it bars the receiving state from taking direct action *vis-à-vis* the members of a foreign force. Any matter of concern remains to be solved in cooperation with the sending state.

While it is often held that immunities are granted and the jurisdiction of the receiving state is waived by consent of the latter to the stationing of forces of a sending state,[112] it is more correct to view functional immunity of foreign military forces as deriving from general principles of international law and confirmed by custom. As the principle of immunity is essentially based on the sovereignty of the sending state, it may be confirmed (but not created) by the receiving state's consent to the stationing. Consequently, status-of-forces agreements (SOFAs) do not constitute that immunity. Yet they can limit it insofar as the sending state agrees to certain standards and procedures of cooperation with the receiving state.[113] Of particular importance in this respect is the exclusive jurisdiction of the sending state with regard to any act committed by a member of their forces,[114] a principle which— unless regulated by SOFA—finds only one exception, ie the general competence

---

[112] See eg W.T. Worster, 'Immunities of United Nations Peacekeepers in the Absence of a Status of Forces Agreement', 47(3)–(4) *Revue de Droit Militaire et de Droit de la Guerre* (2008) 277–375.

[113] See D. Fleck (ed), *The Handbook of the Law of Visiting Forces* (Oxford: Oxford University Press, 2001), 3–6; Fleck, sub-Chs 5.2 and 6.2 in Gill and Fleck (eds) (n 11). The principle of sovereign immunity is generally recognized in national jurisprudence. Recently the US Supreme Court (in *Samantar v Yousuf et al*, decision of 1 June 2010) has created some doubts as to the reach of personal immunity of former state officials. The Court held, that while a foreign state's immunity may extend to an individual for official acts, it does not follow that Congress intended to codify that 'official immunity' in the Foreign Sovereign Immunities Act 1976 (FSIA). In the case under decision the petitioner, a former First Vice President and Minister of Defence of Somalia from 1980 to 1986, who had served from 1987 to 1990 as its Prime Minister was sued by respondents, natives of Somalia who alleged that they, or members of their families, were the victims of torture and extra-judicial killings during those years. Considering that respondents have sued the petitioner in his personal capacity in an effort to seek reparation from his own pocket, the Court concluded that this case is not a claim against a foreign state as defined by the FSIA, yet the Court also emphasized the narrowness of this holding and stated that whether petitioner may be entitled to common-law immunity and whether he may have other valid defences are matters to be addressed in the first instance by the District Court, to which the case was remanded for further proceedings, <http://www.supremecourt.gov/opinions/09pdf/08-1555.pdf>.

[114] See Sections 7, 15, 24–31, and 46–49 of the Model Status-of-Forces Agreement for Peacekeeping Operations, UN Doc A/45/594 (9 October 1990), reprinted in Fleck (ed) (n 113), 603–14.

of the International Criminal Court (ICC) for matters under its jurisdiction (Article 27 of the ICC Statute[115]). The 1994 UN Safety Convention[116] does not affect existing privileges and immunities, as expressly confirmed in its Article 6(1).

Applicable SOFA standards depend on the purpose of stationing, the relationship between the sending and the receiving state, and specific requirements of the military operation in question. There are no unified SOFA conditions that could be applied in each case. In particular, SOFAs applicable for peacetime cooperation within, for example, the North Atlantic Treaty Organization and its Partners,[117] or within the European Union,[118] while being useful to elucidate certain aspects of foreign military presence in a receiving state, cannot be used as blueprints for peace operations. For the latter, specific SOFAs are to be concluded in each single case, as the UN Model SOFA[119] has not been generally adopted in treaty form.[120]

5 SELECTED PROBLEMS OF APPLICABLE LAW AND POLICY FOR THE CONDUCT OF PEACE OPERATIONS

Applicable rules for the conduct of peace operations may derive from the law of peace as well as *jus ad bellum, jus in bello*, or an emerging *jus post bellum*. To identify

---

[115] Rome Statute of the International Criminal Court of 17 July 1998 (ICC Statute).

[116] See n 2.

[117] *Agreement Between the Parties to the North Atlantic Treaty Regarding the Status of Their Forces* (NATO SOFA) of 19 June 1951, <http://www.nato.int/cps/en/natolive/official_texts_17265.htm>, *Agreement Among the States Parties to the North Atlantic Treaty and the Other States Participating in the Partnership for Peace Regarding the Status of Their Forces* (PfP SOFA) of 19 June 1995; with Additional Protocol of 19 June 1995 relating to the prohibition to carry out death sentences and FurtherAdditional Protocol of 19 December 1997 relating to the application of the Paris Protocol on the Status of International Military Headquarters set up pursuant to the North Atlantic Treaty of 28 August 1952, <http://www.aschq.army.mil/gc/sofas/Parternership.rtf>.

[118] *Agreement between the Member States of the European Union concerning the status of military and civilian staff seconded to the institutions of the European Union, of the headquarters and forces which may be made available to the European Union in the context of the preparation and execution of the tasks referred to in Article 17(2) of the Treaty on European Union, including exercises, and of the military and civilian staff of the Member States put at the disposal of the European Union to act in this context* (EU SOFA) of 17 November 2003, <http://www.statewatch.org/news/2009/mar/eu-uk-military-staff-agreement.pdf>.

[119] See n 114.

[120] See D. Fleck, *Drafting Status-of-Forces Agreements (SOFAs): A Guide* (Geneva: Geneva Centre for the Democratic Control of Armed Forces (DCAF), 2012).

and properly implement these rules, case-specific differentiations are required: law enforcement operations are distinct from the conduct of hostilities, each following their specific principles and rules; *jus in bello* rules are no longer legally applicable in a fully pacified situation post conflict; and cooperation with the host country, troop-contributing states, and civilian authorities remains essential. This will be exemplified here by addressing three important problem areas, ie security and safety (A), command and control (B), and logistics (C). Furthermore, some prevailing uncertainties with respect to operational law issues (D) will be discussed.

A. Security and safety

Many peace operations fall short of establishing a secure environment. Often fighters are not completely disarmed, nor mines removed;[121] the maintenance of order is far from achieved in many cases and at times not even recognized as a joint responsibility of the host country and troop contributing states. Training of and cooperation with local security forces remains a demanding task. Training requires close cooperation, respect for the host country's law by sending states and their contingents, and full acceptance of existing responsibilities by both the sending and the receiving state. Unfortunately deficiencies in cooperation have often become the rule rather than an exception.

An increasing number of security incidents have affected United Nations personnel and their premises. It is in such situations that peace forces must apply unit and personal self-defence (see below, Section 5.D.3) against any attack, hostile act and hostile intent, without relying on military means alone and in an effort to maintain or regain consensual approaches in cooperation with the local authorities. The UN Secretary-General has strengthened the unified security management system for the United Nations.[122] The UN Department for Safety and Security (UNDSS) is tasked to enhance the security of all UN civilian personnel including those serving in UN-led peacekeeping operations.[123] Yet severe problems for

---

[121] The Capstone Doctrine (n 14, 26), refers in this context to disarmament, demobilization and reintegration of combatants; mine action; Security Sector Reform (SSR) and other rule-of-law related activities to achieve effective, accountable, and sustainable security institutions operating under civilian control within the framework of the rule of law and respect for human rights; protection and promotion of human rights; electoral assistance; and support to the restoration and extension of state authority.

[122] UN Doc A/64/532.

[123] <http://www.unssc.org/web/programmes/PS/sss/programme.asp>. See also United Nations Security Coordination Office, *United Nations Field Security Handbook: System-wide Arrangements for the Protection of United Nations Personnel and Property in the Field*, New York 1995 (January 2006), <http://pbpu.unlb.org/PBPS/Library/Field%20Security%20Handbook%20-%20FULL.pdf>; *UN Security Operations Manual, Operational instructions and guidelines for use by officials involved in security management* (1995), <http://europeandcis.undp.org/uploads/public1/files/OM%20Workshop%20 2008/Security%20Operations%20Manual%201995.pdf>.

security and safety prevail, a situation that requires cooperative efforts far beyond the use of force.[124]

B. Command and control

The notions of authority, command, and control in peace operations will be subject to uncertainties as long as objectives, mandates, and resources are not clearly specified by the Security Council and implementing activities are left to the discretion of contributing states. The new peacekeeping doctrine,[125] together with standard operating procedures and contingency planning, may help to improve overall coordination and efficacy of operations even under adverse circumstances. Yet military leadership of UN peace operations is still subject to national influence and it should also be considered that the UN Secretariat with its various relevant departments[126] is not fully structured to fulfil the role of an operational headquarters.[127]

Legal definitions of pertinent terms and conditions have been elaborated by DPKO.[128] In an effort to provide clear command and control arrangements and achieve greater cohesiveness amongst all elements of a peacekeeping operation, the DPKO guidance defines the 'United Nations Operational Authority' to be transferred by the troop contributing states. It also includes definitions of 'Command', 'United Nations Operational Control', 'United Nations Tactical Command', 'United Nations Tactical Control', and 'Tasking Authority'. The guidance further aims at

[124] The General Assembly has considered the issue of safety and security of humanitarian personnel and protection of United Nations personnel annually since its 52nd session (UNGA Res 52/167, 53/87, 54/192, 55/175, 56/127, 57/155, 58/122, 59/211, 60/123, 61/133, 62/95, 63/138, and 64/77). An *Independent Panel on Safety and Security of United Nations Personnel and Premises Worldwide* chaired by LakhdarBrahimi has delivered its Report in 2008, <http://www.un.org/News/dh/infocus/terrorism/PanelOnSafetyReport.pdf>.

[125] See Capstone Doctrine (n 14).

[126] DPKO; DFS; Department of Political Affairs (DPA), Department of Humanitarian Affairs (DHA), Department of Administration and Management (DAM), the Office of Legal Affairs; the United Nations Development Programme (UNDP); the United Nations High Commissioner for Refugees (UNHCR); the United Nations High Commissioner for Human Rights (UNHCHR).

[127] See R.H. Palin, 'Multinational Military Forces: Problems and Prospects', *Adelphi Paper* No 294 (Oxford: Oxford University Press/IISS, 1995); Stuart Gordon, 'Icarus Rising and Falling. The Evolution of UN Command and Control Structures', in D.S. Gordon and F.H. Toase (eds), *Aspects of Peacekeeping* (London: Frank Cass, 2001), 19–41; Ronald Hatto, 'UN Command and Control Capabilities: Lessons from UNIFIL's Strategic Military Cell', 16(2) *International Peacekeeping* (2009) 186–98.

[128] DPKO and DFS, *Policy (February 2008): Authority, Command and Control in United Nations Peacekeeping Operations*, on file with author. See J.-M. Guéhenno and J. Sherman, 'Command and Control Arrangements in United Nations Peacekeeping Operations', Background Paper for the International Forum for the Challenges of Peace Operations 2009 (9 November 2009), <http://www.challengesforum.org/cms/images/pdf/Background%20Paper_Command%20and%20Control%20Arrangements%20in%20UN%20Peacekeeping%20Operations_9%20November%202008.pdf>.

improving interaction at the political and strategic level, in the relationship between headquarters and the mission, and within the mission itself. In so doing, it should be possible to avoid what has been characterized within DPKO in the following terms: 'The UN model seems to combine the worse of two worlds: too much military decentralization and too much political control over the conduct of military operations'.[129]

Command and control provisions must serve practical needs at the operational level and strengthen military leadership. They should be adopted in a formal review process and duly published to facilitate cooperation and ensure accountability for wrongful acts. Regional regulations should be coordinated and implementation measures effectively scrutinized. National *caveats* should be continuously reviewed in the course of planning at the international level and the evaluation of practice in lessons-learned processes. To allow for adequate joint action national *caveats* must be limited.

Effective contingency planning and timely deployment in a situation of crisis remains dependent on the availability of personnel and equipment; but states are not ready to commit themselves to provide such personnel and equipment without being involved in the decision process. The United Nations Standby Arrangements System (UNSAS), initiated in 1994 and strongly supported in the Brahimi Report,[130] undertakes to respond to this situation. It serves several objectives. At the first level, it provides the United Nations with an understanding of the forces and other capabilities a member state will have available at an agreed state of readiness. The second level requires detailed technical information to facilitate planning, training, and preparation for both participating member states and the United Nations. At the third level, UNSAS provides the United Nations not only with foreknowledge of a range of national assets and equipment, but also with a conditional commitment to participate on request, following governmental approval in any given case.

Based on a memorandum of understanding, UN planners now have the option of developing contingency and 'fall-back' strategies when they anticipate delays or when one or more members refrain from participating in an operation. No specific binding commitment (level 4 agreement) has been concluded so far. Recommendations have been made to bridge the existing 'commitment-capacity gap' and improve readiness for deployment in military operations other than enforcement operations (ie for advisory services; preventive action and protection of civilians; peacekeeping; policing; peacebuilding; and humanitarian assistance).[131] They include encouragement of all member states to participate in the UNSAS, to which a fifth level (specification of personnel and resources that governments are

---

[129] Guéhenno and Sherman (n 128), 2.   [130] See n 8, Ch III.
[131] See H.P. Langille, *Bridging the Commitment–Capacity Gap. A Review of Existing Arrangements and Options for Enhancing UN Rapid Deployment* (Wayne, NY: Center for UN Reform Education, 2002), <http://www.pugwashgroup.ca/publications/Langille%20Exec%20Sum%20Small.pdf>.

willing to commit to more demanding Chapter VII operations) and also a sixth level (a renewed commitment to Article 43 of the Charter and the use of UNSAS as an important transitional measure facilitating that goal) could be added.

In order to put these procedures into practice there has been discussion of a phased development of a UN Emergency Service as a rapid reaction capability composed of military, police, and civilian volunteers and supplemented by member states.[132] A recent US proposal calls for a UN Rapid Deployment Police and Security Force (PSF) of at least 6,000 volunteers recruited globally and directly employed by the United Nations as a standing force, to address the *time gap*, the *training gap*, and the *political will gap* with well-trained, professional military and police units that can respond to a crisis within 15 days of a Security Council resolution.[133] Once adopted, this project might provide considerable assets to the UN and also be of some influence on the practice of other states. Yet this would require a lasting general solution to the command and control difficulties referred to above.

C. Freedom of movement and communication, logistic support

The general consent of the receiving state does not normally assure peace forces' freedom of movement and communication. Existing restrictions are often not lifted, exemptions from customs and taxes not granted without reservations and impediments, and logistic support not provided by local authorities. Clear arrangements on practical matters should be made beforehand in a SOFA, and implemented in close cooperation with the local authorities. But in practice this is often not the case. Many peace operations have started without such arrangements and continued without concluding an agreement. Time and money have to be spent to solve resulting practical problems and this may negatively affect the successful accomplishment of the mission.

While it is to be admitted that each situation is unique and the capabilities of host countries in need of a peace operation are often very limited, it is worth considering that peace support and post-conflict peacebuilding cannot be successful without strong commitments by the receiving state. In most cases there will be an enormous imbalance between the economic resources of troop contributing states and the state in which a peace operation is to be conducted. To improve the effectiveness and secure the ultimate success of a peace operation it may be necessary to reduce military spending and increase employment opportunities for unskilled

---

[132] See n 131, 12–13.

[133] United Nations Rapid Deployment Act of 2001 (HR 938), <http://www.govtrack.us/congress/bill.xpd?bill=h107-938>, a proposed bill that has not been passed.

young men and women.[134] The economic factor of the presence of peacekeepers in a conflict-shaken country may be seen as a practical contribution to stabilize peace. Yet inappropriate high payments for local services may endanger stable market development; and the absence of appropriate commitments by the host government may undermine local ownership in the peacebuilding process.

If a peace operation is to strengthen good governance in a country, it must not only offer benefits, but also assist local authorities in meeting their obligations. There is an obvious lack of regulation in this field. Customs and tax exemptions as well as logistic support for peace forces in a receiving state are not generally settled. The UN Model SOFA,[135] far from addressing these issues in comprehensive form, provides for the use of roads, bridges, port facilities, and airports without the payment of dues, tolls, or charges, while the United Nations will not claim exemption for charges which are in fact charges for services rendered.[136] The Model SOFA also has provisions on privileges and immunities of peacekeepers including locally recruited members of the operation.[137] For logistic supplies and services it refers to purchases on the local market, expressly mentioning the aim that adverse effects on the local economy must be avoided.[138] It may be worth considering that such adverse effects may not only be created by buying goods which would better be rationed in a situation of general need, but also by accepting prices which the local population cannot afford to pay.

In many cases there is a practical requirement for transit rights and support from neighbouring countries. Yet no general standards exist in this field and pre-arrangements have often not been made. Transit states may be tempted to make economic profit from peace operations rather than participating themselves to ensure security for the region. It appears necessary to devote more efforts to reach a comprehensive assistance system for peace operations and to lend support at the political level, including by the Security Council, to ensure operations enjoy assistance in contentious cases.

D. Operational law issues

Force commanders must comply with the internal regulations of the Organization (eg general doctrine and guidelines, rules of engagement) in the conduct of their operations. Such regulations may include references to relevant principles and provisions of international law, in order to facilitate compliance with existing obligations. Yet in many operations there is insufficient guidance at the operational level,

---

[134] See eg P. Collier, 'Post-Conflict Recovery: How Should Strategies be Distinctive?', *Journal of African Economies* 18 suppl 1, see <http://users.ox.ac.uk/~econpco/research/pdfs/PostConflict-Recovery.pdf>.

[135] See n 114.   [136] See n 114, Section 14.   [137] See n 114, Sections 24–31.
[138] See n 114, Sections 20–2.

a general lack of information, and differences of opinion as to the relevance and exact meaning of pertinent rules. The select issues to be addressed here derive from existing priorities[139] and the specific legal problems involved.

1. *Compliance with human rights obligations*

The obligation to respect and to ensure respect for human rights (including civil and political, economic, social, and cultural rights) plays a significant role in all peace operations. This may be considered under the following three aspects: first, the protection of human rights is an important goal of the operation, and in an ideal situation this would be expressly included in the mandate given by the Security Council and/or a regional organization. Secondly, even where such a commitment has not been expressly stated, peacekeepers are to respect the law of the receiving state including its obligations under international law of which human rights protection is an important part. Thirdly, it is part of binding *lex lata* that the human rights obligations of the sending states apply extraterritorially for acts committed within their jurisdiction. Where applicable, international humanitarian law will be relevant as *lex specialis*.[140] Furthermore, specific codes of conduct must be considered.[141]

While states may take measures derogating from certain human rights obligations in times of emergency, this option is diminishing in practice. National derogations have rarely been declared in armed conflicts or situations of national emergency.[142] Existing cases of derogation remain singularized and are often highly controversial.[143] No derogation may be declared on behalf of international organizations, which are

---

[139] See on setting priorities, n 73: *A New Partnership Agenda*.

[140] ICJ, *Legality of the Threat or Use of Nuclear Weapons*, Advisory Opinion of 8 July 1996, § 25; ICJ, *Legal Consequences of the Construction of a Wall in the Occupied Palestinian Territory*, Advisory Opinion of 9 July 2004, §§ 102–42 at 106; ICJ, *Case Concerning Armed Activities on the Territory of the Congo (Democratic Republic of the Congo v Uganda)*, judgment of 19 December 2005, §§ 216–21. See also B. Klappe in Fleck (ed) (n 1), Section 1307.

[141] See eg *Code of Conduct for Law Enforcement Officials*, adopted by General Assembly resolution 34/169 of 17 December 1979.

[142] Th. Buergenthal, 'To Respect and to Ensure: State Obligations and Permissible Derogations', in L. Henkin (ed), *The International Bill of Human Rights* (New York: Columbia University Press, 1981), 72; R. Higgins, 'Derogations under the Human Rights Treaties', 48 *BYBIL* (1976–77) 281; P. Rowe, *The Impact of Human Rights Law on Armed Forces* (Cambridge: Cambridge University Press, 2006), 118–21.

[143] Rowe (n 142), 159–61. A recent example is the British Anti-terrorism, Crime and Security Act (2001). It remains questionable, however, whether the material conditions for derogation under Art 15 of ECHR and Art 4 of ICCPR are met in this case, see J. Black-Branch, 'Powers of Detention of Suspected International Terrorists under the United Kingdom Anti-Terrorism, Crime and Security Act 2001: Dismantling the Cornerstones of a Civil Society', 27 *European Law Review Human Rights Survey* (2002) 19–32 at 26; V.H. Henning, 'Anti-terrorism, Crime and Security Act 2001: Has the United Kingdom Made a Valid Derogation from the European Convention on Human Rights?', 17 *American University International Law Review* (2002) 1263–98; *A v Secretary of State for the Home Department* [2004] UKHL 56; *A and others v United Kingdom* ECtHR App No 3455/05, judgment of 19 February 2009.

not parties to human rights treaties, but which nevertheless are bound by custom and policy to comply with human rights standards in their operations.

Given the importance of human rights protection in peace operations, the possibility of exemptions declared by the Security Council is unlikely. While such exemptions would be theoretically possible in accordance with Articles 25 and 103 of the UN Charter, unless *jus cogens* norms are concerned, the Council has a long record of support for human rights and humanitarian law compliance.[144] Such compliance may rightly be considered key to the success of future peace operations as well. The Council has never authorized any deviation from human rights or substantial humanitarian law principles, even when adapting certain obligations of Occupying Powers[145] to allow for legal, economic, and political reforms in a specific post-conflict situation.[146]

2. *Protection of civilians*

In many peace operations the protection of civilians against atrocities and armed attack has become a litmus test for the credibility of peace forces. The applicable legal conditions, however, have largely been left in a grey area. While the Brahimi Report referred to 'the actions of the Security Council to give United Nations peacekeepers explicit authority to protect civilians in conflict situations' as a positive development,[147] such authority has not been given in certain critical situations and deploringly small numbers of under-equipped peace forces have found themselves physically unable to effectively protect civilian populations against exploitation and attack. The opinion expressed in the Brahimi Report that peacekeepers witnessing violence against civilians 'should be presumed to be authorized to stop it, within their means'[148] has merely remained a discussion point that is not mirrored in many rules of engagement and—as practice shows—may even create problems for effective conduct of the mission.

It is to be welcomed that an independent study was commissioned by the UN Office for the Coordination of Humanitarian Affairs (OCHA) and the DPKO 'to begin the process of drawing practical lessons from UN peacekeeping missions implementing

---

[144] See eg UNSC Resolutions 1325 (2000) on women, peace and security, to mainstream gender issues into operational activities; 1612 (2005) on children and armed conflict, to ensure a coordinated response to children and armed conflict concerns; and 1674 (2006) on the protection of civilians in armed conflict, to ensure that the mandates of peacekeeping operations, where appropriate and on a case-by-case basis, include provisions regarding: (i) the protection of civilians, particularly those under imminent threat of physical danger within their zones of operation, (ii) the facilitation of the provision of humanitarian assistance, and (iii) the creation of conditions conducive to the voluntary, safe, dignified, and sustainable return of refugees and internally displaced persons. See also G. Nolte, 'The Different Functions of the Security Council With Respect to Humanitarian Law', in V. Lowe, A. Roberts, J. Welsh, and D. Zaum (eds), *The United Nations Security Council and War. The Evolution of Thought and Practice since 1945* (Oxford: Oxford University Press, 2008), 519–34.

[145] Articles 43 of the Hague Regulations (1907) and 64 of the Fourth Geneva Convention (1949).

[146] Cf UNSC Res 1483 and 1511 (2003).   [147] See n 8, § 62.   [148] See n 8, § 62.

civilian protection mandates', with a view to identify required capacities, equipment and training and develop a clear and comprehensive concept and appropriate guidance.[149] That study, submitted in November 2009, stressed the need to fully brief the Security Council about existing threats to civilians and to provide relevant guidance to peace forces in partnership with troop contributing states.[150] Based on four case studies of current peace operations specifically mandated to afford protection to civilians[151] the authors recommended that peace operations, rather than exhausting their resources and abilities by 'protecting everyone from everything' should 'manage expectations', ensure timely and accurate reporting on protection concerns, and definitely do more to protect civilians.[152] The study thus identifies shortcomings that, ten years after the Security Council's first engagement on protection of civilians in armed conflict,[153] still exist.

The Security Council, continuously seized by the matter upon initiatives of the Secretary-General,[154] follows a practice of including provisions regarding the protection of civilians into mandates of UN peace operations and other relevant missions 'where appropriate and on a case-by-case basis'. It has reaffirmed 'the importance of a greater awareness in the Security Council of the resource and field support implications of its decisions', and requested the Secretary-General: 'to develop in close consultation with Member States including troop and police contributing countries and other relevant actors, an operational concept for the protection of civilians' and 'to ensure that all relevant peacekeeping missions with protection mandates incorporate comprehensive protection strategies into the overall mission implementation plans and contingency plans which include assessments of potential threats and options for crisis response and risk mitigation and establish priorities, actions and clear roles and responsibilities'.[155]

While the Security Council has adopted an updated Aide Memoire on the Protection of Civilians in Armed Conflict in November 2010,[156] important open issues in the legal discussion on the nature and extent of the obligation of peacekeepers to protect civilians remained unsolved.[157] Beyond a consideration of notorious

---

[149] See n 73, 20–1.

[150] V. Holt, G. Taylor, and M. Kelly, *Protecting Civilians in the Context of UN Peacekeeping Operations. Successes, Setbacks and Remaining Challenges* (New York: United Nations, November 2009).

[151] Mission de Organisation des Nations Unies en République Démocratique du Congo (MONUC); United Nations Operation in Côte d'Ivoire (UNOCI); United Nations Mission in Sudan (UNMIS); and UNAMID.

[152] Holt, Taylor, and Kelly (n 152), 216.   [153] See UNSC Res 1265 (1999).

[154] See United Nations Security Council, Report of the Secretary-General on the Protection of Civilians in Armed Conflicts, UN Doc S/2009/277 (29 May 2009), and debate in the Security Council on 26 June 2009, UN Doc S/PV.6151.

[155] See UNSC Res 1894 (2009), §§ 19, 20, 22, and 24.

[156] Statement by the President of the Security Council, UN Doc S/PRST/2010/25 (22 November 2010), published by OCHA, Policy and Studies Series, Vol. I No 4, 2011.

[157] See eg S. Wills, *Protecting Civilians. The Obligations of Peacekeepers* (Oxford: Oxford University Press, 2009); N.D. White, 'Empowering Peace Operations to Protect Civilians: Form Over Substance?', 13(3)–(4) *Journal of International Peacekeeping* (2009) 327–55.

factual limitations in terms of personnel and equipment, it is important to extend the discussion also to 'a diagnosis of the motivations of fighting parties to resort to often atrocious violence against civilians'.[158] This latter issue is most relevant for developing effective protection strategies which should include *responsive action* to prevent, stop, or mitigate patterns of abuse; *remedial action* to assist victims, restore their dignity, and support adequate living conditions; and *environment-building action* to foster an environment conducive to respect for the rights of individuals in accordance with relevant bodies of law.[159]

The independent study commissioned by OCHA and DPKO[160] did investigate motives for large-scale crimes against civilians within each of its four case studies, albeit in general terms. Yet it also explained that information and analysis capacity is limited as to the motives and *modus operandi* of the perpetrators.[161] For the Second Congo War the Study noted 'ethnic sectarianism, economic opportunism, political manipulation, strategies of barbarism, and, in some cases, apparent nihilism as a consequence of societal breakdown'.[162] In Côte d'Ivoire (between 2004 and 2007, following the signing of the 2003 Linas-Marcoussis Agreement) the study again found 'barbarism, and, in some cases, apparent nihilism as a consequence of societal breakdown'.[163] In the second civil war in Sudan (1983–92) the study noted 'widespread attacks on civilians by both sides, although the largest scale atrocities were attributed to the Government of Sudan',[164] and still in 2008 the study referred to 'the dynamics of conflicts that, in the context of Sudan, have consistently involved attacks on civilians'.[165] In the conflict in Darfur (since 2003) 'a mixture of systematically targeted violence against civilians and collateral damage' was observed.[166] The latter conclusion is supported by the Report of the International Commission of Inquiry on Darfur to the United Nations Secretary-General,[167] which added that no genocidal policy had been pursued and implemented in Darfur.[168]

This complex list of motivations for deliberate attacks against civilians may be expanded by looking at the root causes for other conflicts. Religious motives, at least in the perception of fighters, and the inability of religious leaders to ensure that civilians are not legitimate targets and that religious belief should not make anyone

---

[158] E. Schmid, 'Re-Focusing on Protecting Civilians' Basic Safety and Why We Need to Know Why People Kill: On the Latest Reports of the Secretary-General on the Protection of Civilians in Armed Conflict', 13(3)–(4) *Journal of International Peacekeeping* (2009) 356–82.

[159] See S. Giossi-Caverzasio, *Strengthening Protection in War: A Search for Professional Standards* (Geneva: ICRC, 2001); ICRC, *Enhancing Protection for Civilians in Armed Conflicts and Other Situations of Violence* (Geneva: ICRC, 2008).

[160] See n 150.   [161] See n 150, 227.   [162] See n 150, Case Study 1, 242.

[163] See n 150, Case Study 2, 242–3.   [164] See n 150, Case Study 3, 316.   [165] See n 150, 331.

[166] See n 150, Case Study 4, 340.

[167] Report pursuant to UNSC Res 1564 (2004), available at <http://www.un.org/News/dh/sudan/com_inq_darfur.pdf>.

[168] For the contrary view, see J. Hagan and W. Rymond-Richmond, *Darfur and the Crime of Genocide* (Cambridge: Cambridge University Press, 2009).

the object of armed attack, sadly play a dominating role in many conflicts, with no effective remedy being pursued until today.

A stricter focus on root causes and the motives of fighters is essential for developing successful protection strategies in peace operations. While military action appears necessary to respond to imminent threats and acknowledging that peace forces must be prepared and properly equipped to fulfil this task, military action cannot replace political, educational, and economic efforts to be taken to restore peace and security.

3. *Force protection*

In all peace operations the overall context of establishing and maintaining security and safety is absolutely essential for the success of the mission. There is no doubt that peace forces and their individual members have a right to defend themselves against attacks as against armed attempts to interfere with the execution of their mandate.[169] Yet the means to be employed must be carefully balanced. Even if the use of force may be legally based on a broad notion of self-defence as including mission defence (see above, Section 5.A) any forceful action may pose problems for the peaceful environment to be achieved.

It is therefore important to issue rules of engagement limiting what is permissible to that which is necessary, while fully respecting the inherent right of self-defence.[170] The Brahimi Report, which recommended employing robust rules of engagement 'against those who renege on their commitments to a peace accord or otherwise seek to undermine it by violence',[171] did not resolve the tension which may exist between the requirement for robust reaction and the need to limit the use of force in the larger interest of re-establishing a peaceful environment.

It is suggested that a key element for any effort to overcome this tension is participation by the host country, its government, local security forces and civil society. While peace operations must be ready to take firm action and uphold their credibility by deterring any attack, it is for the host country to accept and demonstrate its ownership in a convincing solution of the problem by active and appropriate police intervention, visible improvements in living conditions and a readiness to find political solutions to ensure a credible and comprehensive approach to peacebuilding. The use of force by peacekeepers is an expression of failure on the side of the receiving state. It may be necessary in extreme situations, but must be deployed only exceptionally, if that failure is not to be continued or even enlarged.

---

[169] See H. Boddens Hosang in Gill and Fleck, (n 11), Chs 22 and 23.
[170] See P.C. Cammaert and B. Klappe in Gill and Fleck (n 11), sub-Ch 6.4.
[171] The *Brahimi Report* (n 8), § 55; see also Stephens, (n 101), 163.

4. *Operational detention*

It is widely considered unrealistic and even counterproductive in armed conflicts to give captured fighters the benefit of *habeas corpus* as defined by human rights law.[172] Yet it may be questioned whether this opinion makes sense in peace operation, even in situations of protracted armed conflict. As experience in the former Yugoslavia, Iraq, and Afghanistan has shown, the denial of judicial review of detention becomes more problematic, the longer the conflict lasts. The argument drawn from the law of international armed conflict, that prisoners of war shall normally be released after the cessation of active hostilities (Article 118 of GC III), would hardly be fitting in situations in which peace operations are to be conducted.

Judicial control is an essential element of post-conflict peacebuilding. The pertinent ICRC principles underline the requirement of judicial review under Article 78 of GC IV and Article 9(4) of the International Covenant on Civil and Political Rights (ICCPR).[173] An independent judicial review of detention is essential for any legal system, and is all the more important for peace operations.[174]

The opinion, at times also propounded in this context, that the Security Council, based on the text of Articles 25 and 103 of the UN Charter, may authorize a derogation from existing obligations, is not at all convincing.[175] First, that power does not exist *vis-à-vis* rules that have achieved the status of *jus cogens*; secondly, it remains open to question in the light of the meaning and purpose of peace operations; and thirdly, it is not supported by Security Council practice. It is certainly true that Article 103 equally applies to obligations imposed by the Security Council and to action taken under the authorization of the Council; but it would be going too far to assume that the effect of Article 103 is to qualify existing human rights or humanitarian law obligations and that the only possible exception applies to *jus cogens* norms.[176]

When the Council authorizes 'all necessary measures' in the performance of a mandate this may not be interpreted as permitting unlawful action and exempting states and the United Nations themselves from their responsibility under international law. The Security Council, indeed, has never authorized any deviation from the rule of law in peace operations. In the very rare cases where the Council has referred to detention, this was done as a short-term measure to prevent or to end

---

[172] M. Sassòli and L. Olson, 'The Relationship Between International Humanitarian Law and Human Rights Law Where it Matters: Admissible Killing and Internment of Fighters in Non-International Armed Conflicts', 90(871) *IRRC* (2008) 599–627.

[173] J. Pejic, 'Procedural Principles and Safeguards for Internment/Administrative Detention in Armed Conflict and Other Situations of Violence', 87(858) *IRRC* (2005) 375–91 at 386–7.

[174] See J.K. Kleffner, in Gill and Fleck (eds) (n 11), Ch 25.

[175] See Sections 3(C) and 5(D)(1) above.

[176] M. Wood, 'Detention During Military Operations: Article 103 of the United Nations Charter and the *Al-Jedda* Case', 47 (1)–(2) *Revue de Droit Militaire et de Droit de la Guerre* (2008) 139–65 at 157. See now *Al-Jedda v United Kingdom*, ECtHR App No 27021/08, judgment of 7 July 2011.

a warlike situation,[177] or to explicitly mention prosecution, trial, and punishment as the purpose of detention.[178] In no case, not even in the fight against terrorism, did the Security Council authorize operational detention disregarding procedural principles and judicial safeguards.[179]

6 ACCOUNTABILITY AND JUDICIAL CONTROL

As peace operations are to assist in providing security and safety for establishing and maintaining the rule of law, it must be ensured that all actors, including the peacekeepers themselves, are accountable for any wrongful acts. This accountability has legal, political, administrative, and financial aspects to ensure not only that the responsibility of the United Nations and other relevant international organizations will be properly implemented, but also the responsibility of participating states and individual responsibilities of non-state actors as well. Requirements for ensuring international and individual responsibility in peace operations have been discussed against the background of the failures and shortcomings of legal regulation.[180]

A. Responsibility of states and international organizations

A general culture of accountability in peace operations would require a clear division of responsibilities between the United Nations, contributing states and the host country, which should be fully transparent to everyone who may become affected by wrongful acts committed by peacekeepers. A comprehensive set of rules covering the responsibilities for all activities of the United Nations does not exist. Years ago the ICJ had found it necessary to state that 'compensation for any damages incurred as a result of acts performed by the United Nations or by its agents acting in their official capacity' is not excluded by the immunity of the agent.[181]

---

[177] UNSC Res 169 (1961), § 4 (Congo); UNSC Res 1546 (2004), § 10 and annexed letters of the Prime Minister of the Interim Government of Iraq and the US Secretary of State.

[178] UNSC Res 837 (1993), § 5 (Somalia); UNSC Res 1638 (2005), § 1 (Liberia).

[179] See nn 145–6 and accompanying text.

[180] A comprehensive assessment of current issues and proposals for best practice is now available. It provides insight on practical experience and failures, thus revealing *lacunae* and the need for progressive legal development: B. Kondoch in Gill and Fleck (eds) (n 11), Ch 30.

[181] See ICJ, *Difference Relating to Immunity from Legal Process of a Special Rapporteur of the Commission on Human Rights*, Advisory Opinion of 29 April 1999, [1999] ICJ Rep 62, § 66.

For peacekeepers and officials engaged in international territorial administration this issue is all the more important. In Kosovo, the absence of a review mechanism for potential human rights violations by the United Nations Interim Administration Mission in Kosovo (UNMIK), the Kosovo Force (KFOR), and the then provisional institutions of self-government, was convincingly criticized.[182] Yet follow-up appears to be difficult.[183] In 2009, when the European Union Rule of Law Mission in Kosovo (EULEX) had taken over most of the remaining tasks of policing and justice from UNMIK, that situation did not change, although a local Ombudsperson was recruited, and the Kosovo Office of the UN High Commissioner for Human Rights supported the United Nations and other international presences with advice on human rights issues.[184] Forms of UN accountability include local claims offices and review boards established under special arrangements. The same may be true for relevant regional arrangements. But too often a transparent application of legal standards was not ensured.

Particular problems may arise from the cooperation between states and international organizations in peace operations. While state responsibility as a rule of secondary or concurrent liability in international law appears to be limited,[185] the International Law Commission's Articles on Responsibility of International Organizations[186] suggest that a state member of an international organization bears (subsidiary) responsibility for an internationally wrongful act of that organization if '(a) [i]t has accepted responsibility for that act towards the injured party; or (b) [i]t has led the injured part to rely on that responsibility'.[187] Similar arguments might be developed for states assisting an international organization in the commission of an internationally wrongful act, a case not expressly foreseen in the Articles on Responsibility of States for Internationally Wrongful Acts,[188] but not too different from aid or assistance to another state. Responsibility of states and international organizations may be joint, separate, or several. Doctrine and practice should be developed in a way to avoid grey zones and bring clarity to the matter.

---

[182] Opinion on human rights in Kosovo: Possible establishment of review mechanisms, adopted by the Venice Commission at its 60th Plenary Session (Venice, 8–9 October 2004), CDL-AD (2004)033, §§ 63, 113.

[183] F. Sperotto, 'The International Security Presence in Kosovo and the Protection of Human Rights', no 48 *Human Rights and Human Welfare Working Papers*, <http://www.du.edu/korbel/hrhw/workingpapers/2008/48-sperotto-2008.pdf>.

[184] Office of the High Commissioner for Human Rights, *2009 Report: Activities and Results*.

[185] A. Stumer, 'Liability of Member States for Acts of International Organizations: Reconsidering the Policy Objections', 48(2) *Harvard International Law Journal* (2007) 553–80.

[186] As adopted by the International Law Commission at its 63rd session, in 2011, and submitted to the General Assembly as a part of the Commission's report covering the work of that session (UN Doc A/66/10, § 87).

[187] Articles on Responsibility of International Organizations, Art 62.

[188] Articles on Responsibility of States for Internationally Wrongful Acts (UN Doc A/RES/56/83 of 28 January 2002), Art 16.

B. Individual responsibility

While reparation for wrongful acts committed in peace operations, and in particular the settlement of claims, will be mostly an issue for international organizations and participating states, disciplinary and criminal prosecution of peacekeepers remain necessary to ensure individual accountability. In this regard international organizations will be less involved than states, as the latter have retained full command including disciplinary powers and their national criminal courts are competent to prosecute crimes. The UN Secretary-General should, however, be notified of any action taken. Should the International Criminal Court (ICC) have jurisdiction in a case committed by any member of a peace operation, immunity—as noted above[189]—would not be an issue, as the ICC is not barred by the official capacity of the actor from exercising its jurisdiction (Article 27 of the ICC Statute), yet the Court may not proceed with a request for surrender or assistance which would require the requested state to act inconsistently with its obligations with respect to a person or property of a third state (Article 98(1) of the ICC Statute).[190]

It may be noted that attacks against personnel or equipment involved in a peacekeeping mission conducted in accordance with the UN Charter are war crimes in both international and non-international armed conflicts, as confirmed in Article 8(2)(b)(iii) and (e)(iii) of the ICC Statute. There is currently no jurisprudence concerning this matter, but it would be interesting to see whether these two provisions will be applied to acts against personnel involved in more robust action in defence of a mandate originally designed for a peacekeeping mission in the classical sense.[191] This scenario is, indeed, very realistic, as peacekeepers often have to act in a volatile security environment and existing security risks may be aggravated when the host state is 'unwilling or unable genuinely to carry out the investigation or prosecution', as provided in Article 17(1)(a) of the ICC Statute.

[189] See n 115.

[190] See D. Fleck, 'Are Foreign Military Personnel Exempt from International Criminal Jurisdiction under Status of Forces Agreements?', 1 *Journal of International Criminal Justice* (2003) 651–670.

[191] The ICC is currently dealing with a situation for which this issue may be of some relevance. Investigating an attack of 29 September 2007, against personnel, installations, material, units, and vehicles of the African Union Mission in Sudan (AMIS) that were stationed at the Haskanita Military Group Site (MGS Haskanita) in North Darfur during the 'protracted armed conflict not of an international character' that existed in Darfur 'between the Government of Sudan and several organised armed groups, including the Justice and Equality Movement (JEM)', the Pre-Trial Chamber I refused to confirm charges under Art 8(2)(e)(iii) of the Rome Statute against Bahar Idriss Abu Garda on 8 February 2010 due to lack of evidence of his participation. The Prosecutor's application to appeal that decision was rejected on 23 April 2010 (Case no ICC-02/05-02/09, <http://www.icc-cpi.int/menus/icc/situations%20and%20cases/situations/situation%20icc%200205/related%20cases/icc02050209/icc02050209?lan=en-GB>). But in June 2010 two other suspects, Abdallah Banda Abakaer Nourain and Saleh Mohammed Jerbo Jamus, were brought before the ICC (Case no ICC-02/05-03/09, <http://www.icc-cpi.int/Menus/ICC/Situations+and+Cases/Situations/Situation+ICC+0205/Related+Cases/ICC02050309/ICC02050309.htm>). The question whether during that armed conflict AMIS was involved in the conduct of hostilities may be of some relevance for the qualification of the charges.

C. Circumstances precluding wrongfulness of conduct

Circumstances precluding wrongfulness are a matter of extensive legal discussion. They are now defined in the Articles on State Responsibility[192] and the Articles on the Responsibility of International Organizations.[193] To preclude wrongfulness in the conduct of a peace operation, the circumstances of self-defence, necessity, and *force majeure* may be the most important.

There should be no doubt about the fact that the right of self-defence precludes any wrongfulness of conduct. Where this becomes relevant for a peace operation the force commander must provide all necessary support to ensure objective fact-finding. Independent review by an outside authority may become necessary at an early stage of investigation.

The same applies in situations where necessity is invoked for an otherwise wrongful action. The UN Secretary General insisted in 1996 that the Organization's liability for property loss and damage caused by its forces in the ordinary performance of a peace operation was subject to the exception of operational necessity. He defined operational necessity as 'a situation in which damage results from the necessary actions taken by a peace-keeping force in pursuing its mandate' and concluded that '[t]he determination of such a necessity remains the discretion of the force commander'.[194] It may be questioned whether this can be upheld in the light of Article 25 on the Responsibility of International Organizations which widely reproduces Article 25 on State Responsibility and does not cover the doctrine of 'military necessity'.[195] It is also open to doubt whether the force commander could have the last word in making such a decision. A commander is bound in any peace operation to assist in establishing the rule of law, and certainly cannot derogate from existing obligations. A binding decision on the lawfulness of an action which was considered necessary by the actor will often be possible only in retrospect. As confirmed in Article 25 on State Responsibility and Article 25 on the Responsibility of International Organizations, it is under rather limited conditions that necessity may constitute a circumstance precluding wrongfulness.

The loss of control of an area where a peace operation is to be conducted may amount to *force majeure* making it materially impossible in the circumstances to perform a certain obligation. Under such limited conditions, acts of peacekeepers may be precluded from wrongfulness whereas similar action taken by the host state would not be precluded, if the situation of *force majeure* is due to the conduct of that state (Article 23 on State Responsibility, Article 23 on the Responsibility

---

[192] See n 188, Arts 20–7 of the Articles on State Responsibility.

[193] See n 186, Arts 20–7 of the Articles on the Responsibility of International Organizations.

[194] Cf *United Nations Peace Forces in the Former Yugoslavia and on the Administrative and Budgetary Aspects of the Financing of Peace-keeping Missions*, UN Doc A/51/389 (20 September 1996), §§ 13–15.

[195] Cf J. Crawford, *The International Law Commission's Articles on State Responsibility* (Cambridge: Cambridge University Press, 2002), commentary to Art 25 § 20.

of International Organizations). This aspect, which may affect the cooperation between the force commander of a peace operation and the military and civilian authorities of the host state, has to date not become the subject of judicial decisions and hopefully can be avoided in the future. Rather than invoking *force majeure* under high pressure of events, it is suggested that self-defence may provide a better option. This could help avoid putting the mandate into doubt.

D. Monitoring and independent fact-finding

Monitoring and independent fact-finding will face particular problems in peace operations. Access limitations and rapidly changing events may create factual difficulties. In-country support and assistance by sending states, international organizations, and the peace forces themselves may be impeded by lack of regulation, frictions in civil-military cooperation, and even diverging interests. In many situations there are no better facts available than those published by media, official press releases, and non-governmental organizations. Such information, however, is often not sufficient to adjudicate claims, take appropriate measures to ensure non-repetition of wrongful acts, or prosecute wrongdoers.

The victims of violations have an interest in establishing relevant facts objectively, as does anyone who wants to bring about a successful peace operation. It is part of the peacekeeping doctrine, to not only monitor and investigate complaints of violations of a cease-fire, but also help investigate human rights violations and develop the capacity of national actors to do so on their own.[196] This task should be given more prominence in many operations. It is in the interest of effectiveness and success of a peace operation that objective fact-finding should be ensured proactively, even in those cases where peacekeepers themselves may have committed wrongful acts.

E. Judicial control

The competent UN organs are obliged under treaty law to 'make provisions for appropriate modes of settlement of: (a) disputes arising out of contracts or other disputes of a private law character to which the United Nations is a party; (b) disputes involving any official of the United Nations who by reason of his official position enjoys immunity, if immunity has not been waived by the Secretary-General'.[197] To implement

---

[196] Capstone Doctrine (n 14), 27.

[197] Article VIII(29) of the 1946 Convention on the Privileges and Immunities of the United Nations; see also Procedures in Place for Implementation of Article VIII, Section 29, of the Convention on the Privileges and Immunities of the United Nations, Report of the Secretary-General, UN Doc A/C.5/49/65 (24 April 1995).

this provision the Secretary-General has sought ad hoc solutions by negotiation or conciliation, and—as far as necessary—by mediation or arbitration. The UN Model SOFA provides for the settlement of any dispute or claim of a private law character by a standing claims commission with the possibility to permit an appeal to a tribunal of three arbitrators.[198] This procedure has been used only occasionally[199] and there is no consistent practice in this field.

Under current international law, judicial control over UN operations by the ICJ is practically limited to Advisory Opinions requested by UN organs such as the General Assembly or the Security Council in accordance with Article 96 of the UN Charter. As experience has shown,[200] this may be too weak a tool. The ICJ has recognized the legal personality of the United Nations as being 'capable of possessing international rights and duties' in regard to peace operations,[201] but the UN cannot be party to contentious cases before the ICJ. Regional human rights courts will hardly be in a position to bring clarity in this situation of mixed responsibilities. The ECtHR has declared cases concerning human rights violations in the course of peace operations inadmissible.[202] National courts have generally denied their jurisdiction for claims against the United Nations. Their competence for the settlement of claims against their territorial state is often obscured by uncertainties concerning command and control of the latter's troop contingents, uncertainties that cannot be easily clarified by the claimants, and often not even by the judges. There are only a few relevant national court decisions, all more or less dismissing individual claims filed against United Nations organs, and rarely holding states responsible for acts committed in peace operations.[203] The recent decision of the House of Lords in *Al Jeddah*[204] does not offer a counter-example, as it held by majority that the

---

[198] UN Model SOFA (n 114), Sections 51 and 53.

[199] See UNPROFOR, Report of the Secretary-General, UN Doc A/51/389 (1996) §§ 20–33; Administrative and Budgetary Aspects of the Financing of the United Nations Peacekeeping Operations, Report of the Secretary-General, UN Doc A/51/903 (1997) §§ 7–11.

[200] See nn 31 and 32.

[201] ICJ, *Reparation for Injuries Suffered in the Service of the United Nations*, Advisory Opinion of 11 April 1949, [1949] ICJ Rep 174 at 179.

[202] ECtHR, *Behrami v France* (App no 71412/01), *Saramati v France, Germany and Norway* (App no 78166/01), Admissibility Decision of 31 May 2007, 45 *EHRR* SE10; see also *Kasumaj v Greece* (App no 6974/05), judgment of 5 July 2007; *Gajic v Germany* (App no 31446/02) Admissibility Decision of 28 August 2007; *Berić and Others v Bosnia and Herzegovina* (App no 36357/04), Admissibility Decision of 16 October 2007; *Kalinić and Bilbija v Bosnia and Herzegovina* (App nos 45541/04 and 16587/07), Admissibility Decision of 13 May 2008.

[203] See J. Wouters and P. Schmitt, *Challenging Acts of Other United Nations' Organs, Subsidiary Organs and Officials*, Working Paper No 49, Leuven Centre for Global Governance Studies (Katholieke Universiteit Leuven, April 2010), <http://www.ggs.kuleuven.be/nieuw/publications/working%20papers/new_series/wp49.pdf>.

[204] *R (Al Jeddah) v Secretary of State for Defence* (2005) EWHC 1809 (Administrative Court); *R (Al Jeddah) v Secretary of State for Defence* (2006) EWCA Civ 327 (Court of Appeal); *R (Al Jeddah) v Secretary of State for Defence* (2007) UKHL 58; *R (Al Jeddah) v Secretary of State for Defence* (2008) 1 AC 332.

multinational task force which had detained the plaintiff was not mandated to operate under UN auspices and was not a subsidiary organ of the UN.

It may be questioned whether the *lex lata* is really sufficient to convincingly settle disputes and secure the rule of law in peace operations. A solution would be to create effective international jurisdiction for contentious cases in which the United Nations, competent regional organizations, and states would be parties. Such international jurisdiction would not undermine, but strengthen the sovereignty of states, as it could help to ensure that peace operations are conducted with full respect for the rule of law. In the absence of such a wide-reaching solution, all parties should be encouraged to ensure proactive use be made of existing means of negotiation, conciliation, mediation, and arbitration. To ensure judicial control, command and control relationships in peace operations should be regulated clearly and transparently, so that actors and authorities involved cannot hide behind each other.

7 CONCLUSIONS

UN peace operations have a long history. They are characterized by an enormous reach and professional diversification. The sheer size of these activities, in addition to existing uncertainties as to rights and responsibilities, will make increased efforts to improve legal regulation inevitable. Such efforts should not limit improvising action which will remain necessary as long as peace operations must be conducted, but additional legal steps may increase transparency and help to limit implementation gaps.

Legal regulation is required in three areas specifically: *Command and control* arrangements should be improved, formally adopted within the UN and enacted in a way that makes them binding for contributing states and accessible to the public. *Support by host countries* should be further developed to improve the working conditions for peacekeepers and increase ownership by the host country and local actors of the peace process. For that purpose a set of standard rules on the responsibilities of receiving states and transit states would be helpful to deepen cooperation, save resources, and improve security and safety. Finally the *responsibility* of the United Nations and participating states for any wrongful acts committed by peacekeepers in their official capacity should be firmly recognized and made subject to effective judicial control.

In the difficult process from armed conflict through various post-conflict stages to stable peace, many uncertainties will remain as to the applicability of relevant rules of international and national law. This continues to affect the conduct of peacekeepers and requires close cooperation of participating states and the United Nations with a view to develop and accept realistic qualifications of any given situation. As peacekeepers may be involved in both law enforcement activities and the conduct of hostilities, appropriate guidance must be given to ensure compliance with the mandate and avoid any regression in the peace process.

Military operations are no substitute for a political peace process, and they are not enough to secure a process leading to peace and stability. Rather the root causes and the motives of fighters must be explored and overcome in a sustainable manner. The living conditions of the population must be improved and local actors must be encouraged to assume their role in post-conflict peace-building. Hence, while UN peacekeeping, and in some cases peace enforcement under UN mandate, remain important tools and have a specific role to play alongside other essential elements for the peace process and the creation of lasting stability, states and regional arrangements have to support this process with political and economic measures adjusted to the specific situation.

The establishment of and support for the rule of law, as expressed in clear mandates, effective rules of engagement, and an independent legal control is obviously of vital importance for the success of the mission. There is also a need for further interdisciplinary studies to progressively develop strategies of peacekeepers and improve civil–military cooperation. Respect for the law and effective cooperation between the host country and troop contributing states, between states and international organizations, and between governmental authorities and non-state actors may turn out to be the cornerstone for any successful peace effort in an intercultural setting.

CHAPTER 10

THE LAW OF NEUTRALITY

PAUL SEGER[*]

1 Introduction

In today's world, the term 'neutrality' is used and understood as a concept of foreign policy rather than a legal norm. In common language it means not taking sides, being impartial or even indifferent to one party's side or cause. More often than not, it is also associated with political isolationism which gives it a negative connotation. While neutrality, as generally understood, may cover a wide range of behaviour, the *law* of neutrality is not only narrower, but also more precise in its scope. First, the duties and rights of neutrality only apply to sovereign states and not to any other subjects of international law. Secondly, they only apply in a situation of an international armed conflict between two or more states. Thirdly, they impose a limited set of obligations upon the state, these will be explained further in this Chapter. In essence, the core duty of a neutral state is to refrain from supporting, through militarily means, warring parties in an international armed conflict.

2 Definition and Content

The term 'neutrality' stems from the Latin expression *'ne uter'*, meaning neither the one nor the other. According to the *Max Planck Encyclopaedia of Public*

---

[*] This Chapter contains strictly personal opinions and does not reflect the position of the Swiss government.

International Law, 'NEUTRALITY' means the particular status, defined by international law, of a state not party to an armed conflict.[1] The two Hague Conventions of 1907 Respecting the Rights and Duties of Neutral Powers and Persons in Case of War on Land (HC V), and of Neutral Powers in Naval War (HC XIII) respectively, which constitute the main body of the law of neutrality, do not contain any definition of neutrality, but they codify to a large extent the applicable rights and obligations of neutral states. In essence, these obligations are threefold.

The first and foremost obligation of a neutral state is not to involve itself militarily in an armed conflict between states.[2] Secondly, the neutral state is prohibited from providing military assistance to the warring parties, eg through putting its own troops, arms, or its territory at the disposal of either party. Because of this latter obligation, a neutral state must undertake the appropriate measures to protect its land, sea, or air space from intrusion from a belligerent party. Finally, but not less importantly, the neutral power has a duty of equal treatment of belligerents. This principle becomes relevant if it adopts certain restrictions against the parties in conflict.

In return, the neutral state can rightfully require states in conflict to respect its neutrality, including its neutral territory. It is also entitled to continue its political, commercial and other relations with the warring parties. In principle, this even includes the right to export armaments and ammunition from private stocks which is an important exception from the obligation not to support states at war by military means. If, however, the neutral state decides to restrict or to prohibit the private export of military goods then it must apply these measures equally to all parties in conflict.

3 ORIGINS AND HISTORY OF THE LAW OF NEUTRALITY

The concept of neutrality is closely tied to war. It seems natural that peoples, principalities, kingdoms, or states wanted to be able to keep out of a military conflict whenever

---

[1] M. Bothe, 'Neutrality, Concept and General Rules', in R. Wolfrum (ed), *The Max Planck Encyclopedia of Public International Law* (Oxford: Oxford University Press, 2008), <http://www.mpepil.com>), (hereafter *MPEPIL*).

[2] P. Hostettler and O. Danai, 'Neutrality in Land Warfare', in *MPEPIL*, margin number (mn) 7.

wars occurred. The underlying motives for being neutral were usually based on national security interests. By maintaining neutrality the neutral power tried to protect its territory, its population and its economy from the consequences of an armed conflict which normally took place somewhere in the neighbourhood. It is therefore no coincidence that militarily weaker powers embraced the principle of neutrality.

Scholars disagree on the origins of neutrality or neutral behaviour.[3] The first agreements on non-participation in warfare are found in the Middle Ages. Hugo Grotius uses the term neutrality in one of his books on the law in times of peace and war, but he only gives it a very brief description.[4] The concept of neutrality slowly took shape during the eighteenth century when the Dutch lawyer Bynkershoek and his Swiss counterpart Emer de Vattel started to define the rights and duties of neutrals.[5] In essence, neutrality in early times meant impartiality and equal treatment towards both belligerents. However, the concept of *bellum iustum* (the 'just' war) questioned the principle of neutrality since a state could not remain neutral if the cause for war was rightful.

The first major treaty on neutrality was concluded on the initiative of Russia in 1780 and was known as the 'First Armed Neutrality'. The treaty sets rules on the treatment of neutral ships and contraband in sea warfare and it was signed by Denmark, Sweden, the Netherlands, Austria, Portugal, Prussia and others. In 1800, a 'Second Armed Neutrality' was concluded between Russia, Sweden, Denmark, and Prussia as a consequence of the naval blockade of Great Britain against Napoleonic France when the British navy refused to exempt neutral ships from visit and search. It is thus fair to say that the laws of neutrality have been influenced as much through the wars at sea as through the wars on land, if not more so. The Paris Declaration respecting Maritime Law of 1865[6] confirmed certain rights of neutral shipping,[7] but it was more than another forty years before a major codification of the laws of neutrality was achieved. The Hague Conventions of 18 October 1907 on the Rights and Duties of Neutral Powers in War on Land and in Naval War contain the core body of rules on neutrality which are still relevant to this day. The two treaties complement

---

[3] Stefan Oeter offers an excellent overview over the historical development of the laws of neutrality: S. Oeter, 'Ursprünge der Neutralität—Herausbildung der Instituts der Neutralität im Völkerrecht der frühen Neuzeit', 48 *Zeitschrift für ausländisches öffentliches Recht und Völkerrecht* (ZaöRV) (1988) 447–88 at 470ff.

[4] '[…] it is the Duty of those that are not engaged in the War, to sit still and do nothing, that may strengthen him that prosecutes an ill Cause, or to hinder the Motions of him that hath Justice on his Side…'. Hugo Grotius, *The Rights of War and Peace*, vol III (R. Tuck (ed), Indianapolis: Liberty Fund, 2008), Ch XVII: Of Neuters in War, <http://oll.libertyfund.org/title/1427/121250->.

[5] E. de Vattel, *The Law of Nations, Or, Principles of the Law of Nature, Applied to the Conduct and Affairs of Nations and Sovereigns, with Three Early Essays on the Origin and Nature of Natural Law and on Luxury* (B. Kapossy and R. Whitmore (eds) Indianapolis: Liberty Fund, 2008), Ch VII: 'Of Neutrality—and the Passage of Troops through a Neutral Country'.

[6] <http://www.icrc.org/ihl.nsf/FULL/105?OpenDocument>.

[7] M. Torrelli, 'La neutralité en question', XCVI *Revue générale de droit international public* (1992), 5–43 at 8.

the Hague Regulations on Land Warfare of 1899, which already mentioned some obligations and rights of neutral powers, especially in the field of humanitarian law. One should note, however, that the codification of the laws of neutrality is not complete as no rules on neutrality in air warfare have been adopted.

Neutrality reached its high point at the end of the nineteenth century, and, in strict legal terms, we could end the history of the laws of neutrality in 1907 since no major revision of these rules has occurred since.[8] However, the two World Wars and their consequences for international relations have fundamentally changed the ways in which neutrality is perceived. As a consequence of World War I the League of Nations was created and the major powers signed the so-called 'Briand-Kellogg-Pact' of 1928 on the renunciation of war. In the aftermath of World War II the United Nations (UN) with its system of collective security was established. While neither the Treaty on the League of Nations nor the UN Charter specifically mentioned neutrality, it was clear from the outset that the concept of collective security left little or no room for a neutral attitude. Since going to war was banned as a means of national foreign policy, there seemed no need to remain neutral from a conceptual viewpoint. Accordingly, the attitude of major international powers regarding neutrality changed considerably. Another important factor which substantially diminished the political and practical relevance of neutrality was the increase of armed conflicts or violence involving non-state actors for which the Hague Conventions offer no legal answer. While doctrine considers neutrality to be far from becoming obsolete[9] considering relevant state practice, certain authors see the law of neutrality eroding.[10]

4 Sources of Law

As mentioned above, the main sources of the laws of neutrality are the two 1907 Hague Conventions on the Rights and Duties of Neutral Powers in War on Land and in Naval War. Only 32 states are parties to the former Convention and only 28 states have joined the latter. Both treaties have not been amended since their adoption over a hundred years ago, and the last state which acceded to both Conventions was Ethiopia in 1935.

[8] M. Bothe, 'The Law of Neutrality', in D. Fleck (ed), *The Handbook of International Humanitarian Law* (2nd edn, Oxford: Oxford University Press, 2008), 571–604 at 574.

[9] C. Greenwood, 'The Concept of War in Modern International Law', 24 *International and Comparative Law Quarterly* (1987) 283–306 at 299.

[10] Torelli (n 7), 9.

Since the treaty law has now been left unchanged for over a hundred years, one would imagine that customary international law would play a considerable complementary role for developing the law of neutrality. But although this source of law indeed remains important[11] it has only developed to a limited extent. In 1923, a Commission of Jurists tried to codify the rules on air neutrality in the Hague Rules for Aerial Warfare,[12] but these rules never came into effect.[13] More recently, the San Remo Institute for International Humanitarian Law (IIHL) developed a 'Manual on International Law applicable to Armed Conflicts at Sea' (1994)[14] and a 'Handbook on Rules of Engagement' (2009),[15] both of which contain some references to neutrality on sea and in the air. Also, certain national manuals on the law of armed conflict contain references to the law of neutrality applicable to aerial combat.[16] Although not binding under international law, these and other documents constitute useful guidelines which complement both Hague Conventions and allow us to identify the scope of customary neutrality law. The International Court of Justice, in its Advisory Opinion of 1996 on the threat and use of nuclear weapons and in its judgment on the 'Nicaragua case',[17] recognized the validity of the law of neutrality as part of customary international law. Besides, the sovereign right of each state to choose neutrality as a means of foreign policy has been reaffirmed by the UN General Assembly in its Resolution 58/80 of 1995 recognizing Turkmenistan's neutrality. Although the Resolution is not legally binding itself, it can be qualified as an expression of *opinio juris* on the existence and legitimacy of the institution of neutrality. Finally, several field manuals of national armed forces extensively deal with issues of neutrality, which also serve as proof of its continued validity.[18] Despite these reconfirmations in principle, it remains that the law of neutrality contains lacunae which leave considerable room for doubt when applying the rules in modern warfare. To cite just two examples, the extent of the rights and duties of neutrals in missile warfare, especially the definition of aerial space regarding long-distance or ballistic missiles, is largely left open. The same can be said of the whole complex

---

[11] Bothe (n 8), 573; Torelli (n 7), 9.

[12] Rules concerning the Control of Wireless Telegraphy in Time of War and Air Warfare. Drafted by a Commission of Jurists in the Hague, December 1922–February 1923 (Hague Rules), <http://www.icrc.org/ihl.nsf/FULL/275?OpenDocument>.

[13] Some rules became part of customary international law, however see (n 3), 9.

[14] <http://www.icrc.org/ihl.nsf/full/560?opendocument>.

[15] <http://www.iihl.org/iihl/Documents/ROE%20handbook%20ENG%20May%202011%20PRINT%20RUN.pdf>.

[16] See, for instance, UK Ministry of Defence, *Manual of the Law of Armed Conflict* (Oxford: Oxford University Press, 2004) (hereinafter 'UK Manual').

[17] ICJ, *Legality of the Threat or Use of Nuclear Weapons*, Advisory Opinion, 8 July 1996, 226. ICJ, *Case concerning Military and Paramilitary Activities in and against Nicaragua (Nicaragua v United States of America)*, Merits, Judgment, 27 June 1986, 14.

[18] Among others the Field Manual FM 27-10 'The Law of Land Warfare' of the US Department of the Army <http://armypubs.army.mil/doctrine/DR_pubs/dr_a/pdf/fm27_10.pdf>.

of cyber war,[19] which of course the drafters of the Hague Conventions could not even contemplate.

5 THE RIGHTS AND OBLIGATIONS OF NEUTRALS AND BELLIGERENTS

A. Conditions for and duration of the applicability of the law of neutrality

The law of neutrality is only applicable when an armed conflict between two or more states occurs. In contrast, it is not applicable in situations of non-international conflict or even to transnational conflicts between armed forces of state and non-state armed actors.[20] Neither is it applicable in peace operations of the United Nations which includes enforcement through military means according to Article 42 of the UN Charter.

The obligations of the law of neutrality start in principle with the outbreak of an international armed conflict although certain legal obligations may arise in peace-time for permanently neutral states. Since the times are well past when war was officially declared between states, the question arises for the neutral power which kind of conflict qualifies as a war in the sense of the Hague Conventions and from what moment on it is obliged to apply the law of neutrality. The threshold test which is applied in international humanitarian law (IHL) may offer an indication, although for the sake of the protection of victims, this threshold is fairly low and does include surgical strikes or skirmishes which do not qualify as a war in the sense of the laws of neutrality.[21] Thus, there exists no automaticity between the application of IHL and neutrality law. Literature and state practice suggest that the applicability of the law of neutrality is conditioned to a 'generalized state of hostilities'.[22] Switzerland, for instance, considered the Second Gulf War of the Allied Forces against Iraq in 2003

---

[19] J. Kelsey, 'Hacking into International Humanitarian Law: The Principles of Distinction and Neutrality in the Age of Cyber Warfare', 106(7) *Michigan Law Review* (2008) 1427–51. Hostettler and Danai (n 2), mn 24.

[20] There are some scholars, however, who argue the applicability of neutrality to non-international conflicts as well: T. Bridgeman, 'The Law of Neutrality and the Conflict with Al Qaeda', 85 *New York University Law Review* (2010) 1186–1224 at 1213.

[21] Bothe (n 8), 578.

[22] G. Petrochilos, 'The Relevance of the Concepts of War and Armed Conflict to Neutrality', 31 *Vanderbilt Journal of Transnational Law* (1998) 575–616 at 605.

as war according the law of neutrality, and officially declared its applicability as from the beginning of the aerial attacks on Iraq on 20 March 2003.[23] Conversely, the obligations under neutrality law end with the cessation of hostilities. Unless a formal armistice or peace agreement is signed between the warring parties, the determination of the appropriate moment to cease applying the law of neutrality is left to the appreciation of the neutral power. In the case of the Iraq war Switzerland considered this moment to have come on 16 April 2003 when the Iraq army was seen as defeated, and lifted the measures taken in application of the Hague Conventions of 1907. The issue of military occupation is left unanswered by the Hague Conventions. One may find arguments for and against the continued applicability of the law of neutrality: the fact that occupation is a direct consequence of the armed conflict and is still a military act speaks in favour. On the other hand, occupation is also the consequence of military defeat of the occupied power. Since the hostilities between the former belligerents have come to an end (at least provisionally), the law of neutrality which is intended for active war is no longer applicable.[24]

B. Content of the rights and obligations under the law of neutrality

(i) *The protection of the neutral sovereign territory*

The Hague Conventions oblige the belligerents to respect the sovereignty and territory, including the territorial waters, of the neutral power (Article 1 of HC V and HC XIII). The Exclusive Economic Zone (EEZ) of a coastal state does not constitute neutral waters[25] since this zone is not part of the sovereign territory of the state.[26] The neutral airspace is protected solely by customary international law[27] since both Hague Conventions are silent on this issue. In essence, belligerents

[23] Report of the Swiss Federal Council (government) to the Parliament: 'La neutralité à l'épreuve du conflit en Irak, Synthèse de la pratique suisse de la neutralité au cours du conflit en Irak en réponse au postulat Reimann et à la motion du groupe UDC, 2 décembre 2005' Feuille fédérale (FF) 2005, 6535, <http://www.admin.ch/ch/f/ff/2005/6535.pdf>; English abstract available at <http://www.eda.admin.ch/etc/medialib/downloads/edazen/topics/intla/cintla.Par.0029.File.tmp/NeutralitaetspraxisSchweizIrak-Konflikt.en.pdf>.

[24] According to the Swiss Federal Council, the occupation of the Palestinian territories by Israel does not qualify as an international conflict in the sense of the law of neutrality: 'Rapport de politique étrangère, juin 2007, du 15 juin 2007'; Annexe 1 Neutralité, FF 2007, 5286.

[25] Bothe (n 8), 590.

[26] United Nations Convention on the Law of the Sea (1982), Arts 2(1), 55, and 56.

[27] HPCR Manual on International Law Applicable to Air and Missile Warfare of 15 March 2009 (hereinafter HPCR Manual), <http://www.ihlresearch.org/amw/manual/category/section-x-neutrality>, Canadian Forces, Office of the Judge Advocate General, Law of Armed Conflict at the Operational and Tactical Level, Chapter 13 Rights and Duties of Neutral Powers, Rule 1304 <http://www.fichl.org/uploads/media/Canadian_LOAC_manual_2001.English.pdf>, Hague Rules (FN 4), Ch VI.

are prohibited from penetrating neutral territory for military purposes, or from establishing military installations such as recruitment centres, army, navy, or air force bases on neutral ground. Regarding transit trough neutral territory, there seems to exist an interesting difference between the rules applicable on land and on sea. While Article 2 of the Hague Convention on neutrality in case of war on land clearly forbids the movement of troops, or convoys of munitions of war or supplies, across the territory of a neutral power, Article 10 of HC XIII states that '[t]he neutrality of a Power is not affected by the mere passage through its territorial waters of warships or prizes belonging to belligerents'.[28] In contrast, such shortcuts are not allowed in airspace, according to the wording of Rule 40 of the Hague Rules of 1923 on Aerial Warfare which prevents belligerents from penetrating the jurisdiction of the neutral state. Doctrine and state practice suggest that this principle has become part of customary law.[29] Also, the Hague Convention on neutrality in naval warfare is quite specific under which circumstances, and for how long, warships may enter neutral territorial waters or stay in neutral ports. As a general rule, a limited number of warships are allowed to stay in neutral waters or ports for a maximum of 24 hours to accomplish necessary repairs to make a ship seaworthy (Articles 12–20 of HC XIII).

(ii) *The prohibition assisting the belligerents*

As a counterpart to the protection of its territory the neutral power is prohibited to intervene directly in an ongoing conflict or to support the military campaign of either belligerent by providing armed forces, or armament and ammunition coming from its own arsenals. It must further prevent acts which violate its neutrality from occurring on its territory (Article 5 of HC V, Article 25 of HC XIII). In practice this could require the establishment of an adequate defensive capacity commensurate with the potential threats and the likelihood of a war in the neighborhood. While the view seems to prevail among scholars that a neutral state needs to able to defend its neutrality militarily,[30] the Hague Conventions on Neutrality do not formally oblige a neutral state to have armed forces.[31] Indeed, the wording of Article 25 of HC XIII according to which the neutral power is obliged to 'exercise such surveillance as the means at its disposal to prevent any violation of the provisions of the above Articles', does not suggest a legal obligation to intervene by force. However, HC V clearly states that the forcible resistance by the neutral power to combat violations of its neutrality cannot be deemed as a hostile act (Article 10). Here again, HC XIII is somewhat less specific in its wording

---

[28] See also Rule 20 of the *San Remo Manual on International Law Applicable to Armed Conflicts at Sea*, 12 June 1994 (hereinafter San Remo Manual), <http://www.icrc.org/ihl.nsf/full/560?opendocument>.

[29] See namely Rules 14 and 18 of the San Remo Manual. Rule 167(a) of the HPCR Manual (FN 10), see also Commentary to Rule 167(a), <http://ihlresearch.org/amw/Commentary%20on%20the%20HPCR%20Manual.pdf>.

[30] Bothe (n 8), 581, 584. Torrelli (n 7), 33.   [31] Hostettler and Danai (n 2), mn 12.

(Article 25), but essentially means the same. Costa Rica, for instance, considers itself a neutral state and does not possess any military, and this fact has so far not been contested.[32] Ultimately, the question whether or not the neutral state needs to have armed forces to defend its neutrality is not so much a matter of law,[33] but of credibility which is a critical political and strategic asset for the neutral power. In the eyes of potential aggressors a credible defence force strengthens the resolve of the neutral state to defend its neutrality at all costs. It also avoids the risk of countermeasures from one of the belligerents, acting in self-defence, against an opponent who has penetrated neutral territory.[34]

(iii) *Economic and commercial rights and obligations of neutral states*

In general, the law of neutrality allows neutral states to maintain their commercial ties with the belligerents during an armed conflict. This is made clear by Article 7 of HC V which states that '[a] neutral Power is not called upon to prevent the export or transport, on behalf of one or other of the belligerents, of arms, munitions of war, or, in general, of anything which can be of use to an army or a fleet'. Article 7 of HC XIII contains an analogous provision. Also, the neutral power is not obliged 'to forbid or restrict the use on behalf of the belligerents of telegraph or telephone cables or of wireless telegraphy apparatus belonging to it or to companies or private individuals' (Article 9 of HC V). If freedom for the private economy applies to goods or services of strategic nature it is obvious that it must be all the more true for any other product, service, or commodity. Neutral states are entitled, however, to restrict the commercial relations of their subjects with belligerents. But in doing so they must apply such restrictions equally to all parties to the conflict (Article 9 of HC V and XIII). Anyhow, the distinction made in Article 7 of HC V between the delivery of armament, and ammunition from either private or governmental sources seems artificial nowadays as many states have enacted laws which control private arms exports. If the state regulates such commerce the delivery of armament and ammunition to a belligerent is not compatible with the status of neutrality.[35] Yet, neutral states may adopt economic sanctions, either unilaterally or collectively

[32] H. Gros Espiell, 'La neutralidad permanente de Costa Rica y el sistema interamericano', 39 *Revista española de derecho internacional* (1987) 7–22 at 13. A. André Tinoco, 'Völkerrechtliche Grundlagen dauernder Neutralität. Die dauernde aktive und demilitarisierte Neutralität Costa Ricas unter der Satzung der Vereinten Nationen' (Baden-Baden: Nomos Verlagsgesellschaft, 1989), 191, 211.

[33] The Swiss Government argues that the neutral power has an international duty to defend its territory through military means: see 'Neutrality Under Scrutiny in the Iraq Conflict', Summary of Switzerland's neutrality policy during the Iraq conflict in response to the Reimann Postulate (03.3066) and to the Motion by the SVP. In contrast to Switzerland, Austria seems to understand the duty to defend its neutrality rather as a *national* obligation. In its Federal Constitutional Law on Neutrality of Austria of 26 October 1955 it 'declares herewith its permanent neutrality which it is resolved to maintain and defend with all the means at its disposal'.

[34] UK Manual, 20.   [35] Bothe (n 8), 585.

with other nations, against another state without violating the law of neutrality as long as the targeted state is not engaged in an active military conflict. On the other hand, the neutral power would be required to apply the principle of equal treatment if the sanction concerns goods or services 'which can be of use to an army or a fleet' (Article 9 of HC V) and the measure is directed against a belligerent.[36]

(iv) *Obligation of equal treatment*

Apart from the above-mentioned specific obligations, under the rules of neutrality, a core principle is that the neutral state must treat the belligerents equally. Partial behaviour, through which the neutral state offers a military advantage to one or the other warring party, violates the law of neutrality and fundamentally undermines the credibility of the neutral power. As explained above, the principle of equal treatment applies especially if the neutral state decides to restrict the commercial or economic relations of individuals or companies with the belligerents. In naval warfare a neutral power 'must apply impartially to the two belligerents the conditions, restrictions, or prohibitions made by it in regard to the admission into its ports, roadsteads, or territorial waters of belligerent war-ships or of their prizes' (Article 9 of HC XIII). However, the principle of equal treatment only applies to acts of the neutral state which are of military relevance to the belligerents. It does not require the neutral to treat them impartially or equally in other areas, such a politics, human rights, or the media.[37] For instance, a neutral state may criticize one party for resorting to armed force or for not respecting the laws of armed conflict without violating its neutrality.

C. Neutral persons, ships, and aircraft

According to Article 15 of HC V '[t]he nationals of a state which is not taking part in the war are considered as neutrals' as long as they do not actively engage in hostilities against one of the belligerents, namely by voluntarily joining the armed forces of one of the parties to an international armed conflict. While the neutral state must

---

[36] In the Kosovo conflict of 1998/99 Switzerland was struggling between its moral and political duty to show solidarity with the international community to combat ethnic cleansing and other atrocities committed in the region and its obligations under the laws of neutrality when NATO decided to intervene without a mandate of the UN Security Council. While Switzerland participated in EU economical sanctions against former Yugoslavia up to the beginning of the Kosovo conflict, it applied the laws of neutrality with regard to measures of a strategic nature such as oil. See the report of an inter-agency working group of 20 August 2000 following the Kosovo conflict published by the Federal Department of Foreign Affairs: <http://www.eda.admin.ch/etc/medialib/downloads/edazen/topics/intla/cintla. Par.0028.File.tmp/Bericht_zur_Neutralitaetspraxis_Kosovo_2000_e.pdf>.

[37] D. Schindler, 'Neutrality and Morality', 14 *American University International Law Review* (1998) 155–70 at 168.

prohibit the establishment of, or publicity for, 'volunteer corps' on its territory,[38] the fact that individuals of a neutral state offer their services to one of the belligerents does not engage the responsibility of the state (Article 6 of HC V). In that regard, the trend to rely more and more on Private Military Companies (PMCs) poses challenging legal questions from the viewpoint of the law of neutrality. These companies may offer a wide range of services. But to comply with its obligations, the neutral state must prevent them from assisting the belligerents as 'corps of combatants' or 'recruiting agencies' according to Articles 4 and 5 of HC V.[39] While neutral persons may not be treated as enemies as long as they do not engage in hostile acts, individuals joining the armed forces of a belligerent forfeit their neutral status and are regarded as combatants (Article 17 of HC V). Although the Hague Conventions do not spell out the consequences of neutral status, it follows that neutral persons or enterprises are protected from any measures such as internment or confiscation which a belligerent could otherwise take against subjects of the enemy.[40] Save for specific situations (Article 18 of HC V) neutral persons or companies are also allowed to continue supporting a belligerent through private economic or financial activities.

The status of sea and air vessels flying the flag of a neutral state is not governed by the Hague Conventions, but rather by customary international law. Flying the flag of a neutral state is *prima facie* evidence of the neutral character of a vessel,[41] but re-flagging ships has become a contentious issue, namely during the Iran–Iraq war.[42] In general, neutral vessels, both military and civil, enjoy the right of transit and passage through international straits and archipelagos even in times of armed conflict.[43] At least civil vessels may generally also enter the territorial waters or the airspace of belligerent parties. However, there are two important exceptions: first, neutral vessels are obliged to respect naval blockades[44] or its equivalent in the air, so-called 'no-fly-zones'. Secondly, the belligerent may intercept and inspect these

---

[38] Bothe (n 8), 587.

[39] It seems that Switzerland is associating PMCs to such corps or agencies if they recruit combatants to participate directly in hostilities. See the explanatory report of the Swiss Department of Justice of 5 September 2011 (in French) on the draft Federal Law on Private Security Companies, <http://www.ejpd.admin.ch/content/dam/data/sicherheit/gesetzgebung/sicherheitsfirmen/vn-ber-f.pdf>. See also: F. Schreier and M. Caparini, 'Privatising Security: Law, Practice and Governance of Private Military and Security Companies', Geneva Centre for the Democratic Control of Armed Forces (DCAF), Occasional Paper No 6, March 2005, 103, <http://dspace.cigilibrary.org/jspui/bitstream/123456789/27442/1/Privatising%20Security%20-%20Law,%20Practice%20and%20Governance%20of%20Private%20Military%20and%20Security%20Companies.pdf?1>.

[40] Neutral persons are protected by the laws of neutrality first, and only fall under the purview of GC IV relative to the Protection of Civilian Persons in Time of War of 1949 if they are in the territory of a belligerent which has no diplomatic relations with the state of origin of these persons (Art 4 and 11 of GC IV).

[41] UK Manual, 330.   [42] Bothe (n 8), 597.   [43] San Remo Manual, Rule 26.

[44] See esp Art 7, 9, and 11 of the London Declaration of 1909 concerning the Laws of Naval War, <http://www.icrc.org/ihl.nsf/FULL/255?OpenDocument>.

THE LAW OF NEUTRALITY   259

vessels if it has reason to believe that they are engaged in activities contrary to the law of neutrality, especially if they are suspected of carrying contraband.[45] If inspection proves that neutral vessels are engaged in illicit acts they lose their neutral status and may be treated like an enemy merchant vessel.[46] Under certain circumstances a neutral civil vessel may be exempt from inspection, namely if it is accompanied by a military aircraft or warship which warrants that the vessel is not carrying any contraband.[47]

6 Temporary and Permanent Neutrality

As has been shown, neutrality is closely linked to the existence of a state of international armed conflict, and it usually begins with the outbreak of hostilities, and ends with their cessation. In general, neutrality is therefore a temporary condition, and the Hague Conventions on neutrality have been drafted with such situations in mind. The concept of permanent neutrality, as is practised by Switzerland and other states, is neither mentioned in these Conventions nor in any other international treaty. Switzerland's permanent neutrality has, however, been recognized by the major powers in the Conferences of Vienna and Paris of 1815. The same was true when Switzerland joined the League of Nations in 1920. But none of these proclamations define the content of or the obligations under permanent neutrality. Also, the United Nations General Assembly recognized the neutrality of Turkmenistan in its Resolution 58/80 and declared it to be in the interest of international peace and security although this recognition is not legally binding. The main difference between occasional and permanent neutrality is that, in the first case, a state can choose, each time a military conflict occurs, to be neutral or not. A permanently neutral state, on the other hand, stipulates to remain neutral in any possible future war. As a consequence permanent neutrality deploys certain legal effects during peacetime which derive from the principle of good faith or *pacta sunt servanda*. Since no universally agreed definition of permanent neutrality exists the exact scope and extent of legal obligations arising from permanent neutrality in peacetime remain imprecise. In any event, obligations that bear upon a permanently neutral state must be interpreted in a restricted

---

[45] For more details, see HPCR Manual, Section X on Neutrality. UK Manual, 320.
[46] Article 46 of the London Declaration of 1909 concerning the Laws of Naval War.
[47] UK Manual, 331.

way since they constitute limitations to the state's sovereignty. In short, a permanently neutral state should not subscribe to any international legal commitment
in peacetime which would prohibit the fulfilment of its obligations under the
laws of neutrality in a situation of international armed conflict. The main restriction generally associated with the status of permanent neutrality is that a neutral
state cannot join a military or defence alliance[48] such as NATO since an attack
upon one member triggers a right to military assistance by the whole alliance.[49]
One would also argue that the long-term establishment of foreign army bases is
incompatible with the status of permanent neutrality, but this view may be subject
to debate. The example of Ireland which traditionally affords landing and refuelling facilities to the US air force in Shannon seems to indicate that it is possible
to reconcile such arrangements with neutrality.[50] One thing is clear, however: any
legal restrictions that may result from the status of permanent neutrality only
concern the military domain. Apart from the very limited exceptions mentioned
above the neutral state remains entirely free to conduct its foreign, economic, and
security policy in its own best interest. If a permanently neutral state nevertheless
decides to limit its freedom of action beyond the strict limits required by neutrality law this is a consideration of its own neutrality policy only.[51] Besides, permanent neutrality does not mean perpetual neutrality: the state is entitled to change
its policy according to its needs and may also decide unilaterally to terminate its
status.[52] In the latter case, the principle of good faith would require, however, that
the neutral state gives due notice to other interested states and does not abruptly
change its status immediately before or during an international armed conflict
without being attacked itself.

[48] Bothe (n 8), 1 at mn 17. See also: Report of the Swiss government 'Neutrality under Scrutiny in
the Iraq Conflict Summary of Switzerland's neutrality policy during the Iraq conflict in response to
the Reimann Postulate (03.3066) and to the Motion by the SVP Parliamentary Group (03.3050)' of 2
December 2005 (English abstract), 1–17 at 8.

[49] However, agreements with allied states on military training, joint exercises or the sale of armament or ammunition are compatible with permanent neutrality.

[50] During the second Iraq War of 2003 Ireland continued its long-standing practice of granting
the United States overfly and transit facilities through Shannon airport. The then Minister of Foreign
Affairs maintained the viewpoint that this practice was compatible with Ireland's policy of military
neutrality. See Minister Cowen's statement of 20 March 2003 on the situation regarding Iraq, <http://
www.dfa.ie/home/index.aspx?id=26100>.

[51] Report of the Swiss Government (n 48), 9.

[52] Swiss 'White Paper on Neutrality', Annex to the Report on Swiss Foreign Policy for the Nineties
of 29 November 1993, 1–29 at 6, <http://www.eda.admin.ch/eda/en/home/topics/intla/cintla/ref_neutr.
html>.

7 Neutrality, Collective Security, Collective Defence

A. Neutrality and the United Nations

To understand the relationship between neutrality and the system of collective security of the United Nations one needs to recall that the concept of neutrality dates back to times when war was considered legitimate or, as Clausewitz put it, the pursuit of politics with other means.[53] Historically, the main motive for a state to choose neutrality was to shield itself from the effects of a war waged in the proximity in order not to become involved in it. Before the invention of the idea of collective security the law of neutrality offered a sort of security guarantee under which the belligerents promised to respect the territorial integrity and sovereignty of the neutral power in return for complete military abstention and equal treatment without distinguishing between aggressors and aggressed.

As a consequence of World War I war was banned by the Briand-Kellogg-Pact of 1928. The prohibition of armed aggression became part of the fundamental norms of international law. The existence of such a norm entails an obligation *erga omnes* not to support an aggressor and not to recognize the effects of a military aggression. This raises the question how the idea of neutrality can coexist with the prohibition of aggression? First, the prohibition of assisting an aggressor militarily does not apply only to a neutral power but to any state. Secondly, the prohibition of aggression puts into question the principle of equal treatment of belligerents is one of the cornerstones of the law of neutrality. History has shown, however, that the outlawing of war and the prohibition of aggression did not have the desired effect of ending all wars, and the law of neutrality has retained its practical relevance. Institutionally, things started to improve only with the adoption of the United Nations Charter in 1945. Article 2(5) of the Charter stipulates that '[a]ll Members shall give the United Nations every assistance in any action it takes in accordance with the present Charter, and shall refrain from giving assistance to any state against which the United Nations is taking preventive or enforcement action'. In accordance with Articles 24 and 25 of the Charter, the Security Council has been given the primary responsibility for the maintenance of international peace and security and the members of the United Nations are obliged 'to carry out the decisions of the Council' in accordance with the Charter.

The emergence of the principle of collective security has important consequences for the law of neutrality: while there is not a fundamental contradiction between the

---

[53] C. von Clausewitz, 'On War' Book 1, vol I, title 24 (trans Colonel J.J. Graham, new and revised edn), e-book edn 2006, <http://www.gutenberg.org/files/1946/1946-h/1946-h.htm#2HCH0001>.

notion of neutrality and the principles of the UN Charter, the system of collective security, if it worked effectively, simply would leave no room for neutrality. This is already evident from a conceptual point of view: the law of neutrality has been conceived to allow the neutral power to remain outisde an international armed conflict between two or more belligerents, each of them pretending to have a good cause for going to war. Such a situation is fundamentally different from the effective application of collective security where the international community as a whole acts against a threat to international peace and security through the Security Council of the United Nations. Accordingly, there exists general agreement among scholars that the laws of neutrality do not apply to measures of collective security adopted under Chapter VII of the UN Charter.[54] The neutral power is therefore entitled to participate in all necessary measures, including the use of force, which the Security Council may have adopted or authorized to restore the international order, peace, and security. Besides, the neutral power is, as a UN member, not only allowed to disregard its obligations under the law of neutrality, but obliged to comply with resolutions adopted by the Security Council since Article 103 of the UN Charter stipulates that the provisions of the Charter prevail over any other treaty obligation. There is no duty under international law to participate actively in a peace operation mandated under Chapter VII of the UN Charter, but the neutral state must not impede the operation and it is entitled to assist it, for instance by granting transit or overflight rights to participating armed forces, if necessary for the fulfilment of the mandate.[55] State practice confirms this conclusion. When the UN General Assembly reaffirmed Turkmenistan's right to neutrality,[56] it did so with the understanding that it 'does not affect the fulfillment of its obligations under the Charter and will contribute to the achievement of the purposes of the United Nations'. The security policy doctrines of neutral states such as Switzerland,[57] Austria,[58] or Ireland are unanimous in stating that the law of neutrality does not apply to measures taken by the Security Council in accordance with the UN Charter to restore international peace and security. Accordingly, neutral powers have granted overflight and other transit facilities to troops mandated by the United Nations under Chapter VII of the Charter. Besides, neutral states like Austria[59] and Ireland[60] are traditional troop contributors to United Nations' peace operations. Sweden went so far as providing

---

[54] Bothe (n 8), 575. Hostettler and Danai (n 2), mn 21.   [55] Schindler (n 37), 162.

[56] UN General Assembly Resolution 58/80, 12 December 1995.

[57] Swiss 'White Paper on Neutrality' (n 52), 28.

[58] Heinz Gaertner and Otmar Hoell, 'Austria', in E. Reiter and H. Gärtner (eds), *Small States and Alliances* (Heidelberg and New York: Springer Verlag, 2001), 157–68, <http://www.bmlv.gv.at/pdf_pool/publikationen/05_small_states_14.pdf>.

[59] Austria is currently active in Kosovo and Bosnia <http://www.bmlv.gv.at/english/introle/introle.shtml>.

[60] Ireland's defence forces serve in several UN Missions, among others in MINURSO (Western Sahara), MONUC (Democratic Republic of Congo) and UNIFIL (Lebanon), <http://www.military.ie/overseas/current-missions>.

fighter airplanes to support the mission in Libya mandated by Security Council Resolution 1973 (2012). Even Switzerland, which has long maintained a very prudent approach, amended its Federal Military Act in 2000 allowing armed participation in operations under UN mandate provided that its troops do not engage in combat action for peace enforcement.[61]

B. Neutrality in the context of the European Union

In its Maastricht (1993), Amsterdam (1997), and Lisbon (2009) Treaties the European Union (EU) has gradually developed a Common Foreign and Security Policy (CFSP) with the ultimate goal a common European defence. This raises the question for the neutral EU member states of how to reconcile respect for the law of neutrality with their obligations of solidarity under European treaty law. The most problematic clause from a neutrality law point of view seems to be Article 42(7) of the Treaty on European Union which stipulates that member states 'shall have an obligation of aid and assistance by all the means in their power', in accordance with Article 51 of the United Nations Charter, towards a member state which becomes the victim of armed aggression on its territory. This clause basically establishes a system of mutual assistance whereby an attack against one is considered an attack against all. Yet, the laws of neutrality clearly prevent a neutral power from intervening by armed force on behalf of another state or from offering any form of military assistance, regardless of the reasons. While this contradiction may be more theoretical in nature since the solidarity clause will hopefully never have to be put to the test, other elements of the CFSP raise more practical problems from a neutrality viewpoint. This is especially so for the so-called 'Petersberg tasks' which have been codified in Article 42(1) and Article 43 of the TEU. According to these provisions, the Common Defence and Security Policy (CDSP), which forms part of the CFSP, shall provide the Union 'with an operational capacity drawing on civilian and military assets' which the 'Union may use [...] on missions outside the Union for peace-keeping, conflict prevention and strengthening international security in accordance with the principles of the United Nations Charter'. These tasks 'shall include joint disarmament operations, humanitarian and rescue tasks, military advice and assistance tasks, conflict prevention and peace-keeping tasks, tasks of combat forces in crisis management, including peace-making and post-conflict stabilization. All these tasks may contribute to the fight against terrorism, including by supporting third countries in combating terrorism in their territories' (Article 43 of TEU). In analysing these 'out of area' mandates under the aspect of the law of neutrality one should distinguish between civilian and military

[61] Articles 66 and 66a de la Loi fédérale sur l'armée et l'administration militaire, 3 February 1995, <http://www.admin.ch/ch/f/rs/510_10/index.html>.

operations. While civilian missions do not pose any problems for neutrality, mandates which foresee the (potential) use of force need to be examined more carefully. From a neutrality perspective, it does not matter whether the purpose of a military operation of the European Union is humanitarian, rescue, crisis management, or peace-making. The two determining factors are whether (a) the military operation is likely to pass the threshold of an armed conflict in the sense of the law of neutrality[62] and (b) if so, whether or not the operation is mandated or authorized by the UN Security Council. Although Article 42 specifies that out of area operations of the European Union are to be undertaken 'in accordance with the principles of the United Nations Charter', it cannot be excluded that the European Union decides on the use of military force without the approval of the Security Council. Some even argue that such an option should be retained.[63] A participation of a neutral EU member in a military intervention leading or amounting to an international armed conflict, without such Security Council approval or the consent of the state concerned, would constitute an 'unneutral' service. One could even ask the question whether neutrality is not already infringed by subscribing in principle to the obligations under the CFSP/CSDP since Article 24(3) of TEU provides that '[t]he Member States shall support the Union's external and security policy actively and unreservedly in a spirit of loyalty and mutual solidarity.' The strong emphasis on solidarity also resonates in the decision-making process on CFSP matters. Such decisions are to be taken unanimously which would in principle allow the neutral EU member the opportunity to block an EU action incompatible with its neutrality obligations. But in practice, it would be very difficult for a neutral state to block an EU action entirely. Abstention seems to offer an elegant way out, but Article 43 of TEU requires abstaining member states to 'refrain from any action likely to conflict with or impede Union action'. Accordingly, even abstention would not solve the dilemma between solidarity and neutrality since the neutral EU member state could not behave in a completely impartial way. Given the formulation of these provisions and the specific nature of the European Union, the duty of solidarity appears to prevail over the obligations of neutral EU members under the law of neutrality.

However, the European Union made an effort, to the extent possible, to accommodate the interests of neutral EU members when developing the CFSP. Already the Maastricht Treaty, as the first EU instrument to establish a common foreign and security policy, tried to deal with the split between the two conflicting requirements of European solidarity and neutrality by introducing in Article J.4 paragraph 4 the *caveat* that the CFSP 'shall not prejudice the specific character of the security and

---

[62] Petrochilos (n 22), 605.

[63] M. Ortega, 'Military Intervention and the European Union', *Chaillot Paper 45*, Western European Union, Institute for Security Studies (Paris, March 2001), <http://www.iss.europa.eu/uploads/media/cp045e.pdf>.

defence policy of certain Member states'. This clause has subsequently been used and reused in all later amendments of the TEU and it is mentioned twice (Article 42(2) and Article 42(7) of TEU).

The meaning of the CFSP and of the solidarity clause in particular was further specified when Ireland obtained 'legal guarantees' from the European Council in 2009, after its rejection of the Lisbon Treaty in a popular referendum. In fact, the Council declared that the 'Treaty of Lisbon does not affect or prejudice Ireland's traditional policy of military neutrality'.[64] More generally, the Declaration adopted by the European Council repeated that the CSDP 'does not prejudice the security and defence policy of each Member State, including Ireland or the obligations of any Member State'. Section C of the said Declaration further continued that '[i]t will be Member States—including Ireland, acting in a spirit of solidarity and without prejudice to its traditional policy of military neutrality—to determine the nature of aid or assistance to be provided to a member state which is the object of a terrorist attack or the victim of armed aggression on its territory'. Finally, the formulation of Article 42(7) of TEU requiring EU members to assist a fellow member in case of an armed aggression 'by all means in their power' legally leaves open the option of unarmed solidarity.

Neutral EU members interpret these 'special situation' clauses and declarations differently according to their attachment to neutrality. Ireland, which was at the origin of the 2009 Declaration, stated that the European Union had effectively recognized its military neutrality. But the fact that Ireland also considers the permanent granting of transit right for US military aircraft in Shannon as compatible with its notion of 'military neutrality', leads to the conclusion that Ireland has a rather narrow interpretation of neutrality which is not fully in line with the law of neutrality, as laid down in the Hague Convention and international customary law. Austria, on the other hand, came to the conclusion that its foreign policy had commuted from neutrality to European solidarity with the unreserved acceptance and support of the CFSP/CSDP. By an amendment to its constitutional law (Article 23f) Austria ensured that its participation in CFSP/CSDP actions, including full participation in the decision-making process, was not impeded by its neutrality law. With this step, Austria terminated its status as a permanently neutral power[65] and has to be regarded rather as an alliance-free state.[66] Sweden and Finland, too, do not consider themselves as 'neutral' in the sense of the rules of neutrality but rather as states which pursue a policy of non-participation in military alliances.[67]

---

[64] Council of the European Union, Brussels European Council 18/19 June 2009. Presidency Conclusions, Doc 11225/2/09 Rev.2 CONCL 2.

[65] J. Niederberger, 'Österreichische Sicherheitspolitik zwischen Solidarität und Neutralität', Bulletin 2001 zur schweizerischen Sicherheitspolitik.

[66] Österreichische Sicherheits- und Verteidigungsdoktrin, 2001.

[67] H. Himanen 'Finland', in H. Ojanen (ed), *Neutrality and Non-aligment in Europe Today*, Report 6/2003 of the Finnish Institute for International Affairs (Helsinki, 2003), 20–6 at 21; in the same publication: Anders Bjuner 'Sweden', 41–6 at 42.

In its policy brief on security policy, the Swedish Government declares that 'Sweden's security is built on solidarity, together with others. Threats to peace and security are countered in partnership and cooperation with other countries and organisations', and it continues to state that 'Sweden will not take a passive stance if another EU Member State or other Nordic country suffers a disaster or an attack. We expect these countries to act in the same way if Sweden is affected. Sweden should therefore have the capability to provide and receive military support'. The country also played an active role outside of Europe, for example by providing jet fighters to the NATO operation 'Unified Protector' in Libya authorized by Security Council Resolution 1973 (2011).

To sum up, the concept of a unified Europe based on the principle of mutual solidarity and equipped with a common foreign, security and defence policy seems hardly compatible with the obligation of a neutral power as stipulated by international law. As a logical and coherent conclusion Austria, Finland, and Sweden have therefore effectively exchanged their status of neutrality for a more flexible position of non-participation in a military alliance. Time will tell if they will have to abandon even this posture should the European Union ultimately establish a common defence, as stated in Article 42(2) of TEU. Ireland maintains—more for domestic political reasons as it seems—its position that the TEU is compatible with its policy of military neutrality. But since its understanding of neutrality is quite restrictive in itself, it can hardly be used as a case in point for the coexistence of neutrality and European solidarity obligations.

8 Neutrals as Opposed to Non-Belligerent, Non-Aligned or 'Bloc Free' States

There seems to exist some confusion between the terms 'neutral', 'non-belligerent', 'non-aligned', and 'bloc free'. Let us start with the terminological distinction between neutrality and non-belligerence. Is a state not participating in an armed international conflict automatically a neutral power? Doctrine and practice do not seem to sustain such a conclusion. While the status of neutrality implies certain rights and duties, non-belligerence is a (non-legal) factual statement that a state is not participating in an armed conflict between two or more states.[68] But such a state

---

[68] Torrelli (n 7), 14.

cannot claim the rights under the law of neutrality for itself and its subjects if it does not comply with the respective obligations.[69]

What is then the difference between a truly neutral and a non-aligned or bloc free state? At first glance there seem to exist similarities since politically the positions of these states may well overlap.[70] However, if we look closer we are able to separate neutrality from being non-aligned (or bloc free) from a conceptual viewpoint. The main differences could be described as follows: first, neutrality—as we have seen— is based upon a defined legal concept clearly related to the notion of war. It imposes a duty of abstention from military assistance to warring parties. In contrast, the terms 'non-aligned' or 'bloc free' denote political principles.[71] While a neutral state is thus obliged to respect certain rules of international law, the commitments of a non-aligned state are of a purely political character. Historically, the Non-Aligned Movement (NAM) was created in the 1950s by mainly developing countries as a manifestation against imperialism and colonization.[72] In its origins, it was strongly influenced by the Cold War. The NAM takes its *raison d'être* from its opposition to the major military or political blocs which emerged at the time. The group thus clearly defends an anti-hegemonic stance and one may question whether such an attitude could be described as 'neutral' even in political terms. On the other hand, countries such as Sweden have transformed their former status of neutrality into a *sui generis* form of bloc free policy with the understanding that this policy means non-membership in military blocs or alliances.

9 CONCLUSION

The law of neutrality is a law emanating from the nineteenth and early twentieth centuries. It has never been formally adapted since the Hague Conventions of 1907. Although it has to a certain extent been developed by state practice, namely in the field of air and missile warfare, it leaves several legal questions unanswered, for instance the subject of cyber war. More and more armed conflicts are taking place within and not between states, and the protagonists are increasingly non-state

---

[69] Hostettler and Danai (n 2), mn 4. According to Schindler, however, 'all the rights of neutrals can be claimed by all the States not participating in an armed conflict': D. Schindler, 'Transformation in the Law of Neutrality Since 1945', in A. Delissen and G. Tanja (eds), *Humanitarian Law of Armed Conflict, Challenges Ahead: Essays in Honor of Frits Karlshoven* (Dordrecht/Boston/London: Martinus Nijhoff, 1991), 367–86 at 380.

[70] S.K. Singh, 'Non-Alignment and Neutrality', in P.A.N. Murthy and B.K. Shrivastava, *Neutrality and Non-Aligment in the 1990s* (New Delhi: Radiant Publishers, 1991), 1–9 at 2.

[71] Bothe (n 8), 572; Torrelli (n 7), 14.   [72] Singh (n 70), 4.

armed groups. The banning of war and the concept of collective security seem to question the validity and legitimacy of the law of neutrality itself. Does this mean that the law of neutrality has become obsolete? That would probably be too simplistic a conclusion. The fact of the matter is that wars—or international armed conflicts as they are called nowadays—still remain a reality, despite their delegitimization by the UN Charter. The war between Iran and Iraq, for instance, raised numerous questions regarding neutral shipping,[73] and the second Iraq war of 2003 is another case in point. The spectre of future inter-state wars is not simply a theoretical one: the consequences of climate change and competition over the water, arable land, and precious natural resources contain the risk of new armed conflicts between states. For states wanting to keep out of such conflicts, neutrality offers a useful instrument to do so. Whether or not the warring parties respect the neutrality of the third state will to an extent depend on the credibility of that state with regard to upholding its neutrality. The better the neutral state complies with its duties of neutrality, the stronger claim it can make on warring powers to respect its neutrality. In that sense, the law of neutrality still offers an important and very useful legal framework and guideline for the behaviour of both the neutral power and the states at war. This being said, a continued development of the law through state practice would help to maintain its relevance in the future.

But looking beyond its purely normative aspects, how does neutrality stand the test of time from a moral and political perspective? We must recognize that the idea as such has been criticized since its inception. From the concept of 'bellum justum' of the Middle Ages to President George W. Bush's phrase in September 2001 'Every nation [...] now has a decision to make. Either you are with us or you are with the terrorists',[74] those who feel righteous about their cause for war do not accept a neutral attitude. Not taking sides is often perceived as a sign of cowardice, indifference, egoistic isolationism, or all of these taken together. Neutrality will have a better chance of long-term survival if it is perceived as being useful to the international community. As a political idea, it may take a fairly broad variety of meanings. Some forms clearly have an isolationist undertone, but not necessarily all. While, for example, US neutrality before World War II clearly had isolationist motives,[75] countries like Austria, Finland, and Sweden had a fairly active and

[73] M. Bothe, 'Neutrality in Naval Warfare', in A. Delissen and G. Tanja (eds), *Humanitarian Law of Armed Conflict, Challenges Ahead: Essays in Honor of Frits Kalshoven* (Dordrecht/Boston/London: Martinus Nijhoff, 1991), 387–405 at 402–3. A. de Guttry and N. Ronzitti (eds), *The Iran-Iraq War (1980–1988) and the Law of Naval Warfare* (Cambridge: Grotius Publishers, 1993), 253. Greenwood (n 9), 300.

[74] Speech of the US President on 20 September 2001 before the Joint Congress, <http://georgew-bush-whitehouse.archives.gov/news/releases/2001/09/20010920-8.html>.

[75] US Department of State, Office of the Historian, 'American Isolationism in 1930s', <http://history.state.gov/milestones/1937-1945/AmericanIsolationism>.

engaged foreign policy, even when they still considered themselves formally neutral. Besides, neutrality is an evolving concept which needs to adapt itself to the existing geopolitical environment.[76] In this context, it is important to differentiate between the law and the policy of neutrality. While the legal obligations only apply with respect to a war between states, either an ongoing one in the case of occasional neutrality, or any future war for permanently neutral powers, the policy of neutrality describes the measures which the neutral state adopts in peacetime in order to be able to strengthen the credibility of its neutrality. In order to define such a national neutrality policy, the law of neutrality offers the basic yardstick to determine what is required to be a neutral power and what not. In essence, the laws of neutrality prohibit military assistance or interference, but leave other parts of the neutral's foreign policy untouched. Thus, a permanent neutral state fully respects its obligations if it practises a military neutrality and a 'political' neutrality is not required. As an example, a neutral power is entirely free to recognize other states, to establish diplomatic relations or not, and to take positions on violations of human rights or international humanitarian law.[77] The neutral power may even be obliged, under certain peremptory norms of international law, to take non-violent measures against a state which is gravely violating certain fundamental obligations, such as the prohibition of genocide, crimes against humanity, or war crimes.[78]

In sum, neutral powers, especially permanent neutral ones, can be useful to the international community mainly in two ways: first, they contribute to international predictability and stability. Their commitment to neutrality is a commitment not to resort to armed violence. Even nowadays, and regardless of the obligations under the UN Charter, such an undertaking by a state constitutes a positive contribution to international peace and security. Secondly, experience shows that the world still needs neutral powers which can mediate and play a useful role as honest brokers.[79] Switzerland's longstanding tradition of good offices is a telling example.[80] If the neutral power understands neutrality not as a pretext for isolationism, but as an instrument of peace, and accordingly practices a policy of active neutrality, it can play not only an important role as a useful member of the international community,[81] but also promote its own security interests. By using its comparative advantage as being internationally recognized as an 'inoffensive' power, a permanently neutral state can—and should—promote initiatives which reduce international tensions and prevent conflicts. If it engages in creating a framework where peace, security, human rights, humanitarian law, and the rule

---

[76] Swiss 'White Paper on Neutrality' (n 52), 5, 7.
[77] Swiss 'White Paper on Neutrality' (n 52), 27.   [78] Schindler (n 37), 169.
[79] Hostettler and Danai (n 2), mn 24.   [80] Swiss 'White Paper on Neutrality' (n 52), 27.
[81] Torrelli (n 7), 30.

of the law prevail as the foundations of international order, it contributes at the same time to creating an international environment which is conducive to preserving its own national security and well-being. While neutrality has been born out of war, its future lies in its potential as an instrument for peace.

PART IV

KEY CONCEPTS FOR HUMANITARIAN LAW

CHAPTER 11

THE DEVELOPING LAW OF WEAPONS

HUMANITY, DISTINCTION, AND PRECAUTIONS IN ATTACK[1]

STEVEN HAINES

1 INTRODUCTION

IT is often suggested that weapons law has a long history. Ancient bans on the use of poison are, for example, frequently mentioned to support this view. Weapons were also famously a source of mediaeval controversy. The English victories against the much more numerous French forces at both Crécy in 1346 and Azincourt in 1415 were delivered largely by the longbow, regarded as a good example of a paradigm shifting technology ushering in what some have referred to as a 'revolution in military affairs.'[2] That phrase may be an exaggeration, but the longbow certainly

[1] I am most grateful to both Louise Doswald-Beck and Peter Herby for their very constructive comments on an initial draft of this Chapter. This does not mean it should be assumed that both are in full agreement with all of my comments; nor are they responsible for any flaws that remain.
    [2] See M. Boot, *War Made New: Technology, Warfare and the Course of History, 1500 to Today* (New York: Gotham Books, 2006), 21; J. Barker, *Agincourt: The King; The Campaign; The Battle* (London: Little Brown, 2005), esp 86–90 on the attributes and importance of the longbow.

signalled the end of the dominance of mounted knights over infantry. The French at Crécy had, in contrast to the English, deployed Genoese crossbowmen. The winding mechanism of the crossbow resulted in bolts fired with greater force than the arrows fired from longbows. In a comparison of rates of fire, however, the longbow won by a substantial margin, with an expert longbowman able to fire between ten and 20 arrows per minute compared with a mere two shots from a crossbow. Importantly, both could pierce armour. Whether it was the sheer quantity of arrows fired by the longbowmen or the extra armour piercing quality of the crossbow fired bolts, each weapon posed a serious threat to the noble or aristocratic mounted knights and esquires.

The Second Lateran Council in 1139, over two centuries before the Battle of Crécy, is generally assumed to have banned both crossbows and longbows, forbidding their use within the Christian world (though not by Christian armies against the Muslim infidel, it should be noted). In fact, this mediaeval attempt at a weapons ban was generally ignored, even by the Papacy itself, which employed mercenary cross-bowmen in its wars against the Empire.[3] This vain attempt, the best part of a millennium ago, to ban the crossbow and the longbow is notable in retrospect, however, not because it was in any way typical of such measures at that time but because it was, on the contrary, an isolated and totally ineffective mediaeval example of what we now call weapons law.

Despite the paucity of weapons law prior to the seventeenth century, the Dutch jurist Hugo de Groot (Grotius), in his *De Jure Belli ac Pacis* published in 1625, confidently asserted that law imposed limitations on the destructive power of weapons. It is difficult to understand how he drew this conclusion except that his position was arguably arrived at through rational thought reflecting his particular approach to natural law.[4] Important though Grotius was in the early development of international law, not all of his views were prevalent thereafter. During the modern period of European history, as the Westphalian state system developed, and the notion of state sovereignty crystallized, the classic era of balance of power politics gave rise to the almost routine resort to war as an instrument of policy. Indeed, with war viewed as almost a moral imperative in the maintenance of the balance of power, and as natural law gave way to positivism, so the law governing warfare—both resort to and conduct of—went into progressive decline. The natural law doctrine of Just War had become virtually irrelevant by the time of the Revolutionary and Napoleonic

---

[3] See S. Neff, *War and the Law of Nations: A General History* (Cambridge: Cambridge University Press, 2005), 65; R.C. Stacey, 'The Age of Chivalry', in M. Howard, G. Andreopoulos, and M. Shulman, *The Laws of War: Constraints on Warfare in the Western World* (New Haven and London: Yale University Press, 1994), 27–39 at 30; and A. Roberts and R. Guelff, *Documents on the Laws of War* (3rd edn, Oxford: Oxford University Press, 2000), 53.

[4] Grotius's contribution is noted in Commentary AP I and II, 390.

Wars. Even the *jus in bello* element of the doctrine was little more than a vague notion rarely enforced. Clausewitz, a professional military product of those wars, was utterly dismissive of the influence of law on military operations.[5]

It was not until the later decades of the nineteenth century that the *jus in bello* began to re-emerge and the contemporary law of armed conflict (LOAC) began seriously to evolve.[6] It did so through such milestones as the Union Army's Lieber Code, published in 1863 during the American Civil War, the formation of the International Committee of the Red Cross and the subsequent drafting of the first ever Geneva Convention in 1864. Weapons law, being a part of that body of law, also began to evolve at the same time (although separately from the Geneva Convention process), with its first instrument being the 1868 St Petersburg Declaration on explosive projectiles.[7] That is the starting point. References to earlier attempts to restrict weapons are of historical interest only; they contribute virtually nothing to the development of modern weapons law which, for all intents and purposes, has existed for rather less than 150 years.

As technology developed with increasing rapidity from then on, the law also developed in response. Indeed, one can discern a clear tendency initially for the law to follow the technology, with new platforms as well as weapons prompting attempts to regulate. Mines, aircraft, and submarines, for example, were all well developed, deployed and used to significant effect prior to attempts (by no means all successful) to regulate their use through formal treaty making. More recently, however, there has been a clear attempt to render the law more influential and to frame it in such a way that it effectively restricts the development of new weapons technology. Indeed, one of the important requirements laid down in the Additional Protocol I to the Geneva Conventions (AP I) is that states parties are to assess the legality of potential new weapons long before they are put in the hands of those who would use them in conflict.[8] Article 36 of AP I requires that new weapons should be checked for legality, not merely at the point of deployment or use but also in their 'study, development, acquisition or adoption'. Implicit in this requirement is an assumption about the relationship between technology and law by which the existing law should constrain weapon development rather than new weapons technology drive the shaping of new law. This relationship between law and technology is a profoundly important issue, and one to which we shall return.

---

[5] C. von Clausewitz, *On War*, ed and trans by M. Howard and P. Paret (Princeton NJ: Princeton University Press, 1984), 87.

[6] The term 'law of armed conflict' is used throughout this Chapter in preference to 'the laws of war' or 'international humanitarian law', although all three are synonymous in describing the contemporary *jus in bello*.

[7] Full title: 1868 St Petersburg Declaration Renouncing the Use, in Time of War, of Explosive Projectiles Under 400 Grammes Weight.

[8] Full title: Protocol Additional to the Geneva Conventions of 12 August 1949, and relating to the Protection of Victims of International Armed Conflicts, 8 June 1977.

This Chapter will cover seven key issues. First, the term 'weapon' will be discussed and a definition will be provided. Secondly, the weapons law element of LOAC (which is the primary subject of this Chapter) will be explored, including how it relates to other existing bodies of law dealing with weapons which, it should be noted, are not discussed here in detail. Thirdly, an account will be given of the development of the conventional law of weapons, because the bulk of current weapons law is contained in treaties. Those treaties contain important principles underpinning weapons law and define its nature. A fourth aim of the Chapter is to identify these principles and comment on their importance. Fifthly, since conventional law has a vital relationship with customary law, we will offer some comment on the current state of the customary law of weapons. Sixthly, we return to the issue of technology, in particular new technologies that represent significant challenges to existing law. Finally, some attempt will be made to assess where the law might go in the future and what issues are likely to be on the agenda in the immediate term.

2 Defining 'Weapons'

We must start with an understanding of what is meant by the word 'weapon'. In fact, the terminology used today refers not simply to 'weapons' but to 'weapons, means and methods of warfare'.[9] The term 'weapon' is synonymous with the term 'means' of warfare, although it can be useful to use 'weapon' as a generic descriptor and 'means' as indicating something more specific. As illustration, one might define a 'weapon' generically as a capability that can be applied to a military objective or an enemy combatant with the aim of either destroying or reducing the military effectiveness of the objective or incapacitating the combatant to the extent that he (or she) is rendered incapable of further effective combat. 'Means', in contrast, can be used to describe a device, a munition, an implement, a substance, an object, or a piece of equipment.

A mere vehicle or platform on its own, while it might be a military objective in its own right, is not strictly a weapon or means of warfare unless it is weaponized in some way—that is to say, it is fitted with or carries something that can deliver destructive or incapacitating effect. A weaponized vehicle or platform will, however, almost invariably be regarded as a part of a 'weapon system'. The same is true of a sensor, such as a radar. On its own, a radar may be a military objective without being a weapon. If a weapon requires a fire control radar to be effective, however,

---

[9] Article 36 of AP I.

then the radar will, almost certainly, need to be regarded as an integral part of the weapon. In such a case, the radar's own capabilities will probably be an essential consideration when assessing the legality of a weapon in relation to its capacity to discriminate between military objectives and civilian objects.

In contrast to a weapon or means of warfare, 'method' is understood to relate to the manner in which a weapon is actually used during hostilities. Legality is questioned on two levels. First, is the weapon itself inherently lawful or unlawful, for whatever reason? Secondly, is the way in which a particular weapon is used in a particular set of circumstances compliant with the law? It is invariably the case that any weapon, though in and of itself lawful, will have the potential to be used for an unlawful purpose. To give a very basic example, a standard pistol is not itself unlawful. If, however, it were to be used to inflict excessive injury by, for example, deliberately and systematically destroying a victim's kneecaps, its actual use would be unlawful. Another example is white phosphorous, a means of warfare that is designed for either illumination or for applying intense heat to something like an ammunition store in order to cause its contents to ignite or explode. White phosphorous is not a banned weapon or means of warfare but its direct use against combatants, which would inevitably have truly dreadful effects, melting flesh and causing superfluous injury and unnecessary suffering, would be unlawful.[10] The key to determining the inherent lawfulness of a weapon or means of warfare is to assess it in relation to its defined and designed purpose. We shall return to this issue below.

3   Weapons Law in Context

There are effectively four bodies of international law dealing specifically with weapons, only one of which is the concern of this Chapter. The first two categories concern reducing or eliminating the possibilities of war or reducing its consequences. On the one hand there are disarmament agreements; on the other there are arms control agreements. The two are not synonymous. The third category covers LOAC and the fourth relates to the law governing the trade in arms.

Disarmament agreements are predicated on a degree of optimistic idealism. Essentially, it is assumed by disarmament's most enthusiastic advocates that it is

---

[10] This is reflected, for example, in the United Kingdom's position on white phosphorous contained in: UK Ministry of Defence, *The Manual of the Law of Armed Conflict* (Oxford: Oxford University Press, 2004), 112, para 6.12.6.

possible to eliminate warfare by the simple expedient of banning the implements by which wars are fought. Ultimately, if there are no weapons, there are no wars. The whole idea of disarmament is constructed upon the optimistic assumption that states will be willing to trust each other to the extent necessary both to achieve agreement and comply with the terms of the accord.

The theory of arms control, in contrast, is predicated on pessimistic assumptions about human nature allied with a parallel belief in security being potentially a shared value which rival states can seek together. One might regard this as rational pessimism. War is regarded as a natural condition that is only avoided by the effective management of the strategic relationships between potential adversaries. Arms control agreements are an important mechanism for managing strategic relationships, the aim being not the elimination of war through the elimination of weapons but rather the reduction of the risk of war through the maintenance of an effective balance of power. If two sides in a strategic relationship mutually control the level of armaments, neither side is left with the military potential to give it a competitive advantage in war-fighting terms. This is a fundamentally important mechanism for the effective management of what came to be referred to as 'strategic deterrence'— not exclusively about atomic or nuclear weapons but undoubtedly especially associated with them.[11]

For International Relations theorists, disarmament is favoured by those idealists whom Martin Wight referred to as Revolutionists. Arms control as a method of strategic management is a tool favoured by pessimistic Realists. For those of a Rationalist persuasion—neither overly optimistic nor unduly pessimistic—there are, of course, middle positions that recognize the value and shortcomings of each of the two approaches, and try to take advantage of them both while reducing the possession of armaments to reasonable levels.[12]

In contrast to both disarmament and arms control agreements, the law governing the conduct of hostilities—that is to say, LOAC—is also of relevance. This law is a product of the rational centre ground just alluded to, although it is not about preventing war. This body of law is based on the understandable and pragmatic assumption that war is an enduring and probably inevitable feature of the international system. Depending on whether one approaches it with a pessimistic or an optimistic frame of mind, either the most we can achieve or the very least we can do is mitigate the worst effects of war by putting in place pragmatically arrived at regulations enshrined in law. These regulations will include agreements to ban particular weapons on grounds of humanity.

---

[11] See H. Morgenthau, *Politics Among Nations: The Struggle for Power and Peace* (5th edn, New York: Alfred A. Knopf, 1978), in particular the discussion on disarmament and arms control at 391–416.

[12] M. Wight, *International Theory: The Three Traditions*, ed by G. Wight and B. Porter, (Leicester: Leicester University Press, 1991).

The fourth and final body of law is that which places some measure of control on the arms trade and arms proliferation. The Arms Trade Treaty (ATT) is a case in point. Certain weapons and means of warfare are covered by the terms of the treaty. Instruments dealing with the proliferation of weapons and such measures as UN Security Council resolutions dealing with arms embargoes can also conveniently be regarded as part of this body of law. We will not be dealing with this law at all in this Chapter, although there is some overlap with those LOAC weapons law treaties whose ban on specific weapons includes provisions dealing with weapons transfer.[13]

While all four of these bodies of law deal with weapons, it is at times difficult to determine in which of the four a particular agreement principally belongs. They overlap to some degree. Periodic arms control agreements may appear to be leading eventually to full disarmament. Indeed, the official rhetoric of political statements made at the time of agreement may even state this as the ultimate aim. One would be well advised to regard such statements with caution. The 2010 New START agreement between the United States and Russia dealing with numbers of strategic nuclear warheads is an arms control agreement and not a disarmament treaty. This is despite frequent political references to a desire to move towards the complete elimination of nuclear weapons—the so-called 'zero option'. Of course, total bans on specific weapons or means of warfare may well be referred to as a form of disarmament, even though they are, for reasons to do with their humanitarian motive in *jus in bello* terms, more appropriately regarded as a part of LOAC. Recent agreements that aim at banning both anti-personnel land mines and cluster munitions are examples of such agreements. While the various bodies of law are distinct, it is clearly sensible to acknowledge that they are not as precise and exclusive as a definitional purist might like.

4 CONVENTIONAL SOURCES OF LAW

As already stated, the 1868 St Petersburg Declaration is regarded as the founding document of reference. It was followed by the unsuccessful attempt, six years later, to move the law on through the 1874 Brussels Declaration.[14] Undoubtedly, the first

---

[13] See eg the ban on transfer in Art 1, para 1(b) of the 1997 Ottawa Convention on the Prohibition of the Use, Stockpiling, Production and Transfer of Anti-Personnel Mines and on their Destruction.

[14] The 1874 Brussels Declaration was concerned with the laws of land warfare, including acknowledging that belligerents were limited in what they could employ as 'means of injuring the enemy'. It

major attempt to develop the law on weapons took place in the context of the two Hague Peace Conferences of 1899 and 1907. In 1899 there were declarations on asphyxiating gases and on expanding bullets.[15] The most relevant outcomes of the 1907 conference were conventions dealing with land warfare and naval mines.[16] As a result of the work conducted in The Hague, that part of LOAC dealing with weapons came to be referred to as 'Hague Law', distinguished from 'Geneva Law' which owed its label to the development of the series of conventions signed in Geneva that were about the treatment of victims of war. Somewhat confusingly, however, the 1925 Gas Protocol (clearly an example of Hague Law) was actually signed in Geneva and is known generally as the Geneva Protocol.[17]

In 1972 agreement was reached to ban biological weapons and, a little over 20 years later, in 1993, a similar (though not identical) ban was agreed on chemical weapons.[18] As was discussed previously with respect to the different bodies of law dealing with weapons, these two conventions create a clear overlap between disarmament, arms control agreements and the law of weapons forming part of LOAC. Indeed, given their relevance in the context of broader debates about so-called 'weapons of mass destruction' (or WMD), these conventions tend generally to be regarded as disarmament agreements rather than instruments of weapons law falling within LOAC.[19] The fact is, of course, that they can and should be regarded as both. By banning the use of biological and chemical weapons 'in any circumstances', the Conventions have effectively clarified the law in relation to their use in non-international armed conflicts (something not addressed in the 1925 Geneva Protocol).

In the sphere of conventional weapons, by the 1970s the apparent distinction between so-called Hague and Geneva categories of law was viewed as being increasingly inappropriate, not least because weapons were regulated principally for reasons of humanity and to reduce the suffering experienced by those caught up in war (principally combatants, as these are the category of individuals against

mentioned that poison and poisoned weapons were forbidden and restricted the use of means of warfare 'calculated to cause unnecessary suffering'. It did not, however, achieve status as a formal source of law.

[15] The 1899 Hague Declaration 2 Concerning Asphyxiating Gases, and 1899 Hague Declaration 3 Concerning Expanding Bullets.

[16] 1907 Hague Convention IV Respecting the Laws and Customs of War on (hereinafter: Hague Convention IV) and 1907 Hague Convention VIII Relative to the Laying of Automatic Submarine Contact Mines.

[17] 1925 Geneva Protocol for the Prohibition of the Use in War of Asphyxiating, Poisonous or Other Gases, and of Bacteriological Methods of Warfare.

[18] The 1972 Convention on the Prohibition of the Development, Production and Stockpiling of Bacteriological and Toxin Weapons and their Destruction (1015 UN Treaty Series, 163) and the 1993 Convention on the Prohibition of the Development, Production, Stockpiling and Use of Chemical Weapons and their Destruction (1974, UN Treaty Series, 45).

[19] Neither convention is contained in Roberts and Guelff (n 3), very much the standard collection of LOAC conventions.

whom weapons may legitimately be used). Accordingly, the two separate bodies of law were effectively joined as one in the context of AP I and AP II. Although occasional references to the distinction between Hague law and Geneva law are still made, any difference, as applied to weapons, is now effectively moribund.

Following AP I and AP II, the 1980 Conventional Weapons Convention, frequently referred to by the abbreviation 'CCW', was an extremely important development in weapons law.[20] The Convention itself is a relatively brief document. Apart from Article 1, which refers to Article 2 common to the four Geneva Conventions and Article 1(4) of AP I (which was amended with effect from 2004 to cover non-international armed conflicts) the most important provisions arising from the CCW are contained in a series of additional protocols.[21]

Although the CCW was intended to become the main means of regulating or banning specific conventional weapons (and, through the mechanism of nego-tiating subsequent protocols, has become effectively a 'live' convention) there have been two important conventions negotiated separately: the 1997 Ottawa Convention; and the 2008 Oslo Convention.[22] One of the key political issues in relation to conventional weapons law is the extent to which the CCW should remain the principal means of achieving regulation. No such process can ever be perfect and shortcomings will be obvious to both states and civil society bodies concerned about the effects of new and emergent means of warfare. Both the CCW and those conventions negotiated separately have relied on official governmental as well as civil society or non-governmental influence in their development. The process of negotiation in both cases must, of course, principally involve states, as they become parties to the resultant conventions. What both the Ottawa and Oslo processes have demonstrated in particular is the extent to which civil society, in the form of non-governmental interest groups (especially when they are allied with sympathetic states), can significantly influence opinion towards agreement on weapons bans.[23]

[20] 1980 UN Convention on Prohibitions or Restrictions on the Use of Certain Conventional Weapons Which May be Deemed to be Excessively Injurious or to Have Indiscriminate Effects, amended in 2001 with the entry into force of the amendment in 2004.

[21] Protocol I on Non-Detectable Fragments (1980); Protocol II on Mines, Booby Traps and Other Devices (1980); Protocol III on Incendiary Weapons (1980); Protocol IV on Blinding Laser Weapons (1995); and Protocol V on Explosive Remnants of War (2003). An Amended Protocol II on Mines, Booby Traps and Other Devices was also agreed in 1996.

[22] 1997 Ottawa Convention on the Prohibition of the Use, Stockpiling, Production and Transfer of Anti-Personnel Mines and their Destruction, was followed by the 2008 Oslo Convention on Cluster Munitions.

[23] One important difference between the CCW and Ottawa/Oslo processes is that the former is conducted through consensus while the latter both adopted two-thirds majority voting during negotia-tions. The consensus approach in the CCW process leads to a 'lowest common denominator' result that is arguably less demanding than majority voting.

5 Basic Principles of Weapons Law

The basic principles of weapons law are reflected in the range of treaties just summarized. It is generally assumed that there are three basic principles. The first of these is the fundamental basis for weapons law: the principle that the means and methods of warfare are not unlimited. The 1899 Hague Convention II and the 1907 Hague Convention IV of 1907 each addressed the 'Laws and Customs of War on Land'. Article 22 was common to both. It confirmed that the right of belligerents to adopt means of injuring the enemy is not unlimited. Both Conventions also stressed that issues relating to tactical or strategic necessity cannot be used as a justification for an effective departure from weapons law. The plea of necessity by a state, occasioned by the likelihood of an inevitable defeat in conflict, could not be used to justify resort to banned weapons *in extremis*.

The other two principles relate to the need for weapons to be used in a manner that distinguishes between combatants and military objectives on the one hand and non-combatants and civilian objects on the other (the principle of distinction); and rendering as unlawful weapons that are likely to cause superfluous injury and unnecessary suffering (the principle of humanity).

A. The principle of distinction

The principle of distinction has not emerged purely from within weapons law. It is also a fundamental principle of LOAC. Indeed, the International Court of Justice in its Advisory Opinion in *The Nuclear Weapons Case* described it as one of the 'cardinal principles of international humanitarian law'.[24] Essentially, belligerents are forbidden from targeting either civilians or civilian objects and this is, therefore, a rule of targeting law. Nevertheless, it is surely dependent on the existence of weapons that enable such distinctions to be made in attack. Ultimately, therefore, it must be the case that a weapon quite incapable of being used in a manner consistent with that principle—a weapon that was inherently indiscriminate—would be unlawful.

While this would seem to be a perfectly logical and reasonable corollary of the general principle of distinction, it has been argued very recently that no rule existed in either conventional or customary law prohibiting inherently indiscriminate weapons prior to the entry into force of AP I.[25] While it is certainly the case that treaty law prior to 1977 did not address the issue of distinction in a manner directly

[24] ICJ, *Legality of the Threat or Use of Nuclear Weapons*, Advisory Opinion, 8 July 1996, § 78.
[25] See W. Boothby, *Weapons and the Law of Armed Conflict* (Oxford: Oxford University Press, 2009), 75.

related to weapons, at the time the drafts of the Additional Protocol were being agreed, Cassese believed that its ban on indiscriminate weapons was simply a codification of a prior customary ban.[26] One can only agree. It is certainly by no means clear how the fundamental principle of distinction can be squared with the lawful existence of weapons and means of warfare, the use of which would inevitably lead to the breach of that principle. Indeed, this conclusion would seem to rely on the assertion that weapons not the subject of a specific treaty ban cannot be unlawful, a view that would necessitate the dismissal of the importance of customary law. The only inherently indiscriminate weapon that remains lawful is the strategic nuclear weapon (for not uncontroversial reasons related to the strategy of nuclear deterrence and the role of the threat of reprisals in that context).[27]

Today, the principle of distinction is dealt with in Article 51(4) of AP I. However, this Article only addresses indiscriminate attacks, and not weapons that are themselves indiscriminate. It links means of warfare to the particular circumstances in which weapons might be used, stating that weapons incapable of being directed at a specific military objective will probably result in an indiscriminate attack in relation to specific objectives. It certainly does not refer to weapons that would be indiscriminate against any target, implying that a weapon's discriminatory capacity is ordinarily related to particular targets and is not something that is likely to be an inherent feature of any weapon.

In fact, this is going too far. Bacteriological weapons, for example, would not be capable of discriminating between combatants and non-combatants, both being equally vulnerable to disease. Poisons such as those designed for deployment into a water supply, for example, would not discriminate. Actual examples of weapons that were incapable of discrimination in relation to their designed target (London) were the German V1 and V2 rockets that were deployed towards the end of World War II. A contemporary example with similar indiscriminate effect is the Katyusha rocket, used by Hezbollah against Israeli controlled territory (although this is perhaps best explained by reference not to designed purpose but to inappropriate use).

Clearly, most weapons are more capable of discrimination than these examples, although it is also the case that virtually any weapon can be used indiscriminately. Once again we are in the realm of the difference between means and methods, between designed use and inappropriate use. Even a precision guided munition

[26] See A. Cassese, 'The Prohibition of Indiscriminate Means of Warfare', in P. Gaeta and S. Zappalà (eds), *The Human Dimension of International Law: Selected Papers* (Oxford: Oxford University Press, 2008), 172–91 at 173.

[27] Nuclear weapons are not considered in this Chapter, although their actual use would almost certainly breach the principles of distinction and humanity. The nature of strategic deterrence, however, is such that strategic nuclear weapons deserve separate consideration, not least because their only legitimate purpose today is, arguably, to prevent their actual use by an opposing belligerent. Essentially and fundamentally, they are not war-fighting weapons, even though for a nuclear weapon state to admit as much would serve to undermine their deterrent effect. So-called tactical nuclear weapons would not be covered by this consideration and would almost certainly be unlawful, except if used at sea, with minimum or no risk to civilians.

(PGM), designed for very precise targeting of particular military objectives, could be rendered indiscriminate by its use in wholly inappropriate circumstances. An air to surface PGM might accurately pinpoint aircraft hangars and similar buildings on the ground but could prove to be profoundly indiscriminate if it were employed in urban warfare. Cluster munitions might be accurately targetable at the point of use but can leave numerous unexploded and potentially lethal bomblets lying around for long periods following an attack. These 'left over' munitions (or lethal remnants of war) often kill or severely injure civilians, especially curious children who stumble across them. This might be an unintentional indiscriminate consequence of this type of weapon, but it is an unlawful consequence nevertheless. The indiscriminate nature of these weapons is the principal reason why they have been the subject of a highly motivated attempt to eliminate them altogether (through the Oslo Convention, which will hopefully achieve universal support).

B. The principle of humanity

The preamble to the 1868 St Petersburg Declaration states that:

Considering that the progress of civilization should have the effect of alleviating as much as possible the calamities of war;

- The only legitimate object which states should endeavour to accomplish during war is to weaken the military forces of the enemy;
- For this purpose it is sufficient to disable the greatest possible number of men;
- This object would be exceeded by the employment of arms which uselessly aggravate the sufferings of disabled men, or render their death inevitable;
- The employment of such arms would therefore be contrary to the laws of humanity [...]

In the context of the subsequent Hague Peace Conferences, the use of the two different phrases 'superfluous injury' (in 1899) and 'unnecessary suffering' (in 1907) arguably enhanced the obligations in relation to the limiting of a weapon's effects. The two phrases are now as a matter of course employed together, as they are in both Article 35(2) of AP I and the third preambular paragraph of the CCW. That is not to say that they are not problematic, however.

While the words themselves are not in dispute, it is by no means entirely clear what they mean. As Cassese pointed out in the mid-1970s, as both AP I and APII and the CCW were being conceived, neither phrase was defined.[28] What exactly is

---

[28] See A. Cassese, 'Weapons Causing Unnecessary Suffering: Are They Prohibited?', in P. Gaeta and S. Zappalà (eds), *The Human Dimension of International Law: Selected Papers* (Oxford: Oxford University Press, 2008), 192–217.

suffering that is unnecessary? And what sort of injury might be regarded as superfluous? Against what are these being tested? Military necessity is the obvious response,
given that injury must presumably only be necessary if it is inflicted in pursuit of a
military purpose that is itself judged to be necessary under the circumstances. How
exactly does one go about comparing the necessity of suffering or the superfluity of
injury against an equally subjective assessment of military necessity? Clearly, what
might be regarded as necessary in one instance, may not be in another. Any test
would, therefore, only be feasible at the point of decision on weapon use, or even
retrospectively when the extent of injury and suffering is known and the resultant
military advantage revealed. If that is even remotely true, how can such a principle
be used to determine the inherent lawfulness of a weapon that is not yet in service,
let alone not fully developed? That is what states are under an obligation to do—to
review legality during the process of weapons development and procurement in
accordance with Article 36 of AP I.

One notable attempt to objectivize the assessment of the health effects of weapons
was the ICRC's SIrUS project. This established that a number of potential effects
of weapons on humans had not been seen commonly during armed conflict in the
preceding 50 years (including disease, permanent disability specific to the kind
of weapons, and inevitable or virtually inevitable death) and it was proposed that
these should be considered when new weapons were being reviewed for legality, in
particular determining whether the purpose of the weapon 'could reasonably be
achieved by other lawful means that do not have such effect'.[29] The SIrUS project
was controversial and regarded by some key governmental experts as fundamentally
flawed.[30] A significant issue was, as McClelland pointed out, the perception that
SIrUS seemed to ignore the requirement to balance medical factors against the
military necessity to use a particular weapon. Nevertheless, one should not dismiss
SIrUS out of hand. It focused attention on the need legally to review weapons and to
take due account of scientific evidence. Although Boothby suggests that the SIrUS
project was essentially withdrawn from further consideration at an expert meeting
convened in January 2001, Peter Herby of the ICRC's Legal Division has pointed
out that the ICRC's proposals were taken forward, although specific reference to the
SIrUS Project was thereafter avoided.[31]

---

[29] See R. Coupland and P. Herby, 'Review of the Legality of Weapons: A New Approach, the SIrUS
Project', 835 *International Review of the Red Cross* (1999) 583–92.
[30] See eg the comments in Boothby (n 25), 65–6 and J. McClelland, 'The Review of Weapons in
accordance with Article 36 of Additional Protocol 1', 850 *International Review of the Red Cross* (2003)
397–415 at 399–400. Both Boothby and McClelland (together with the author) were British Ministry of
Defence officials responsible for conducting the UK's weapons reviews at the time of the SIrUS Project.
Both were involved with formulating the official British response to the SIrUS Project (although the
current author was not directly involved).
[31] I am extremely grateful to Peter Herby for his clarifying comments on a previous draft of this
section of the Chapter.

We are, however, left with the conclusion that the superfluity of injury and the necessity of suffering can only ever be matters for subjective judgment (albeit informed by relevant objective data), regardless of the time or circumstances in which we are obliged to consider them. This should not be regarded as fundamentally problematic, however. There are some issues about which it is impossible to be other than subjective and attempts to achieve total objectivity in relation to them would be intellectually flawed. Subjective judgment is inevitable, although it must, one assumes, be influenced by a reasonable and responsible understanding of what will be generally acceptable and understood in humanitarian terms. Despite the difficulties associated with assessments of superfluous injury and unnecessary suffering, the principle arising from the desire to eradicate them is vitally important and it is an essential permanent customary backdrop to weapons law.

The existence of the three principles already described as the essential basis of weapons law is not in dispute. It is, however, worth discussing whether or not any other principles deserve consideration as contributors to the essential framework for contemporary weapons law. Possible candidates for inclusion include those arising from both the nature of weapons and the need to allow for compliance with standard precautions in attack, essentially the need for proportionality.

C. The nature of weapons and means of warfare

In both the 1899 Hague Convention II and 1907 Hague Convention IV, Article 23 appears to be common. In fact, while very similar in both, the two Articles 23 are different nevertheless. The 1899 Convention states that '[...] it is especially prohibited [...] to employ arms, projectiles or material *of a nature to cause* superfluous injury....'.[32] In contrast, the 1907 Convention states '[...] it is especially forbidden [...] to employ arms, projectiles or material *calculated to cause* unnecessary suffering [...]'.[33] Ambiguity arose because of the two different phrases 'of a nature to cause' and 'calculated to cause'. This difference in wording (a consequence of a difference in the translation into English from the original and authentic French text, itself identical in 1899 and 1907) was considered in the drafting process for AP I and a decision taken to retain the phrase 'of a nature to cause' in Article 35(2).[34]

This decision has not been without its critics, with both Parks and Boothby regretting it because they regard 'calculated to cause' as a 'clearer expression of the intent of governments to focus on design and intended purpose rather than every remote possibility of injury'.[35] Although Parks' and Boothby's strict linguistic concerns are

---

[32] Emphasis added.   [33] Emphasis added.

[34] See J.-M. Henckaerts and L. Doswald-Beck, *Customary International Humanitarian Law* (Cambridge: Cambridge University Press, 2005) (hereinafter 'Customary Law Study'), at 406–7.

[35] From H. Parks, 'Conventional Weapons and Weapons Reviews', *Yearbook of International Humanitarian Law* (2005) 86–7, quoted in Boothby (n 25), 58.

understandable, there is certainly no evidence to suggest that this textual ambiguity has had the unfortunate effect of causing weapons law to fall into disrepute, as it surely would if it insisted that any weapon needed to be judged on the full extent of its potential to cause superfluous injury and unnecessary suffering (rather than on its intended use). There has been no widespread interpretation of this sort. Among those states known to conduct legal reviews of weapons in accordance with Article 36 of AP I, the practice certainly appears to be to judge them in relation to their designed or intended use.[36] It is, of course, vitally important that, no matter what the words are, their actual meaning in practice relates to the designed or intended use of a weapon rather than virtually any effect it might possibly have if used inappropriately. Surely this ought to be regarded as a principle of weapons law.

D. The need for precautions in attack

In conducting military operations there is a constant obligation to spare the civilian population and civilian objects. Article 57(2) of AP I states that those who plan or decide upon attack shall:

refrain from deciding to launch any attack which may be expected to cause incidental loss of civilian life, injury to civilians, damage to civilian objects, or a combination thereof, which would be excessive in relation to the concrete and direct military advantage anticipated.

This is the rule of proportionality. The need to apply it has traditionally not been regarded as a part of weapons law—and certainly not a principle of it. Technologies that open up the possibility or expand the use of remotely operated weapons platforms or suggest semi-autonomy, or even complete autonomy, raise an important weapon related question, however: is a remotely operated or autonomous weapon system able to facilitate the degree and quality of data collection and analysis necessary to inform decision-making in relation to potential civilian casualties when targeting a military objective? The capability of sensors and data links, for example, will certainly need to be a consideration during a weapon review process for any weapon controlled by remote operators. In many ways this is not a new issue (it has long been a factor with any weapon capable of being fired at targets beyond the visual horizon) but it is certainly assuming an increasing importance as the development

---

[36] Regrettably, very few states seem to have adopted formal weapons review processes to date, the United States being perhaps one of no more than a dozen that have (and the United States is not as yet a party to AP I). In 2006, the ICRC reported only four others that had made available to them the instruments setting up their review processes (Belgium, the Netherlands, Norway, and Sweden), although it also acknowledged a further four that had reported their compliance (Australia, France, Germany, and the United Kingdom). See ICRC, *A Guide to the Legal Review of New Weapons, Means and Methods of Warfare: Measures to Implement Article 36 of Additional Protocol 1 of 1977* (Geneva: ICRC, 2006), 5, note 8.

of unmanned weapon platforms (including unmanned aerial vehicles—or UAVs) proceeds apace. As an extreme example of this, UAVs deployed in Afghanistan are being controlled by military personnel sitting in offices in the continental United States. The quality and quantity of data flow will be crucial in relation to both the principle of distinction and that of proportionality. As it happens, remotely controlled weapons can be more effective at achieving distinction and providing data to the operators who need to be able to make decisions related to proportionality. Certainly, the ability to deploy unmanned drones to obtain close-in data means that they have some advantage over manned aircraft used for the same purpose that would put military personnel at some risk.

Nevertheless, as we move from remote weapons towards semi-autonomy and autonomy, the question becomes one of vital and increasing importance. Onboard data analysis capability will inevitably be a significant consideration as technology moves us in that direction. Although we are some way away from this situation at present, the issue of 'judgement' in relation to essentially subjective matters relating to what degree of injury to civilians or collateral damage to civilian objects is proportionate to concrete and direct military advantage, will become a profound challenge. Although the issue of proportionality is a factor to be taken into account during targeting, it certainly has the additional potential to have significant influence on the legality or otherwise of a weapon system with semi-autonomous or autonomous features. Technology of this sort is developing apace and it is certainly necessary to include some consideration of the proportionality challenge in assessments of the lawfulness of weapons intended to be deployed in that way. Perhaps this need for a weapon to be capable of use in a manner compliant with the need for proportionality should also be regarded as a principle of contemporary weapons law.

E. Summarizing the principles affecting weapons law

There are certainly three longstanding and basic principles of weapons law that are well established and which are today largely accepted without dissent:

- the means and methods of warfare are not unlimited;
- the principle of humanity requires that weapons should not inflict either superfluous injury or unnecessary suffering;
- weapons should not be indiscriminate.

To these it is perhaps worth considering a further three:

- neither tactical nor strategic necessity may be used as a justification for non-compliance with weapons law;
- the inherent lawfulness of a weapon is related to its designed purpose or expected normal use and not its potential to cause either superfluous injury or unnecessary suffering, or indiscriminate effect if used inappropriately;

- weapon systems, in particular those involving remote, semi-autonomous or autonomous targeting, must include adequate technical provision to enable judgments to be made about the potential for disproportionate effect in attack.

Of this second group of possible additional principles of weapons law, the first and second undoubtedly contribute to making weapons law meaningful today. The third is a consequence of technological developments that may become increasingly influential as time moves on. It is certainly the case that all six principles (if one chooses to describe them as such) need to be applied in the process of reviewing the legality of new weapons and means of warfare. Even if one were to regard each of the second group as having a status below that of a fundamental or guiding principle of weapons law, it is certainly the case that they are strong contenders for being regarded as rules of customary law, to which we now turn.[37]

6 CUSTOMARY WEAPONS LAW

Comment on customary law as it relates to weapons will, inevitably, represent a critique of the Customary Law Study's treatment of weapons law.[38] The Study is the obvious starting point and, whether we agree with the relevant rules contained therein or are critical of them, we certainly cannot ignore it.

There is an almost symbiotic relationship between conventional and customary law in this particular body of law. The basic principles apparent from a study of the conventional law and outlined above, have already achieved, or are perhaps close to achieving, the status of customary weapons law. The best established of these are clearly (1) the fundamental principle by which the means of warfare are not unlimited, (2) the principle of distinction, and (3) the humanitarian principle dealing with superfluous injury and unnecessary suffering. The first of these, strangely, is not mentioned in the ICRC's Customary Law Study; this is surprising. Humanity and distinction are reflected in Rules 70 and 71 respectively.[39]

---

[37] Article 35 of AP I lists the Basic Rules of weapons law as being: (1) methods or means of warfare are not unlimited; (2) the principle of humanity; and (3) that it is prohibited to employ means of warfare which are intended, or may be expected, to cause widespread, long-term, and severe damage to the natural environment. This latter rule made its first treaty appearance in AP I but was not included as a rule of customary law in the Customary Law Study.

[38] The full Customary Law Study consisted not only of the volume listed at n 24 above, but also a volume of 'practice' in two parts in which was detailed the evidence supporting the rules contained in vol 1.

[39] Customary Law Study, 237–50.

As suggested, the principles reflected in Rules 70 and 71 are not the only elements making up the full framework for the contemporary development of weapons and means of warfare. Certainly, the inadmissibility of any departure from weapons law predicated on operational or tactical necessity is almost certainly established in custom. Additionally, Rule 70 could easily have been amplified to clarify that it is the intended and designed use of a weapon that should form the basis of a review of its legality, not its potential to produce unlawful results if used inappropriately. This, as we have argued elsewhere, would certainly have been a more accurate reflection of custom.[40] It could, for example, have contained two clauses, one referring to a weapon's actual designed properties related to purpose and the other referring to the inappropriate use of weapons.[41] Finally, as we have acknowledged, although the application of the rule of proportionality has traditionally been regarded as a part of targeting law, there is at least a case that consideration of modern and likely future technological developments relating to remote, semi-autonomous, and autonomous systems should be reflected in weapons law. There is sufficient *prima facie* evidence to support serious consideration of the customary status of the additional principles which have been identified above but which are not included in Rules 70 and 71 of the Customary Law Study.

The way that weapons law has developed in the past and continues to be developed today is the key to the position stated in this Chapter in relation to the overall status of customary weapons law. It seems to make logical sense that there are certain principles underpinning the law of weapons that provide an essential framework for the development of conventional law on the subject. With the possible exception of poison, the accepted customary principles alone have not led directly to any effective acceptance of a ban on a specific weapon or means of warfare. For such to be achieved seems invariably to require a formal international treaty, even in the case of weapons that seem manifestly to breach fundamental principles (blinding laser weapons, for example).[42] This shapes the relationship between custom and convention.

The customary framework of principles is the backdrop and arguably the motive for the additional effort required to ban specific weapons. Without specific weapons bans incorporated in treaty law, however, no effective progress in the banning of weapons seems possible based on recent evidence. In brief, while the customary basic principles provide the framework, the detailed technical details need to

---

[40] S. Haines, 'Weapons, Means and Methods of Warfare', in E. Wilmshurst and S. Breau (eds), *Perspectives on the ICRC Study on Customary International Humanitarian Law* (Cambridge: Cambridge University Press for the Royal Institute of International Affairs and the British Institute of International and Comparative Law, 2007), 258–81.

[41] Customary Law Study, discussion of Rule 70, 237–44.

[42] For a comprehensive account of the negotiation of CCW Protocol IV, see L. Doswald-Beck, 'New Protocol on Blinding Laser Weapons', 312 *International Review of the Red Cross* (1996) 272–99.

be included in treaty law. It is the treaty law, however, that gives real effect to the principles enshrined in custom. It is important that the essential relationship between these two dimensions of the law be recognized; they rely on each other and do not have substantial independent existence.

The Customary Law Study's approach to weapons law may appear to regard treaty law as having evolved into custom, especially in relation to the CCW protocols, unless there was significant actual dissent that effectively denied customary status. The Ottawa Convention is not converted into a customary ban on anti-personnel land-mines, for this reason. It is a notable exception, with significant states withholding support. With the CCW protocols, however, the decision to regard all weapon bans then available as already forming a part of customary law may have been premature. Inevitably, this can only be a matter of opinion and neither the Customary Law Study's view in favour of such nor this author's more cautious approach can be definitive. The latter position has been outlined elsewhere but, in summary, it favours acceptance of the principles described earlier as the rules of customary law while formal bans remain as contained within treaty law.[43]

7. NEW AND EMERGING TECHNOLOGIES

Weapons law has to be able to cope with the development of technologies that might lead to innovative new means of warfare or to the weaponization of otherwise benign platforms. The relationship between law and technology is therefore a key issue. Which should be the most influential in relation to the development of the other? Should the law shift as technology produces new possibilities or should technology only be used to develop new weapons within the parameters laid down in existing law?

The mainstream view would appear to be that weapon technology should only advance within pre-existing guidelines. The weapons review process, in accordance with Article 36 of AP I, effectively prescribes this relationship between law and technology by insisting that at every stage in the process of developing new weapons—at the initial conceptual phase, during development and testing, at the production stage, and prior to entry into service—they should be checked against existing law. If contrary to it, the evolution of a new weapon should be halted. While not advocating at this stage a necessary departure from this approach, it is possible that entirely new technologies could require an alternative way forward as the century proceeds. What are the full consequences, for example, of developments

---

[43] Cf Haines (n 40).

in nano-technology? Will these cause us to reassess precisely what we mean by chemical and biological weapons? If new technologies, currently constrained by the law, were to provide added humanitarian benefit, would it be right effectively to prevent their development simply because the existing law requires that we should? The ban on bacteriological and chemical weapons is clearly a result of humanitarian concern for their effect on people. But what if a technology (perhaps based on nano-technology) emerged that could have a positive (or less negative) influence on the ways that people are affected (through some form of less-lethal weapon)? Would such a technology need to remain banned or would there be a case for allowing it to proceed to development? A less-lethal weapon based on quasi chemical/biological development could in theory have very positive humanitarian effects. While fully appreciating the concerns to which such a comment will give rise, technology is challenging and the directions in which it might develop could surprise us.

One area of emerging or developing technology that is already having an impact on armed conflict involves producing remote effect. That is to say, remote vehicles are being used (controlled at great distance from the conflict zone) to track and analyse potential targets and also to provide platforms for weapons that are then activated from similar distances. UAVs are a common feature of the so-called war against terrorism and modern hybrid conflict. It is still early days for the development of unmanned vehicles/platforms, but UAVs provide a significant capability and they can and do carry weapons. Unmanned ground vehicles, in contrast, are still restricted to doing the so-called 'dull, dirty and dangerous' jobs that do not involve attacks on combatants or military objectives. They are not as yet weaponized to any significant degree.[44] The fact that weaponization is possible, however, means that it is inevitable.

With unmanned weaponized vehicles the questions of concern relate to the role of humans: the so-called 'man in the loop' issue. Remote control implies control from a distance by an operator. Semi-Autonomous implies a degree of automaticity in the processes of data capture, data analysis and target acquisition. Autonomous means just that. The unmanned vehicle is in a position to make targeting 'decisions'. Such technology on the horizon raises a number of concerns related to the ability of a weapon and its operator (if it has one) to comply with the requirements of weapons law. Can the technology distinguish between combatants and non-combatants (including in hybrid forms of warfare where it is difficult to distinguish between civilians and insurgents, for example)? Can it judge the degree of suffering and the nature of likely injury to those targeted? Can it make any sort of judgement in relation to what is a proportionate level of civilian casualties against the necessity of targeting a particular military objective? There are those who believe that this

---

[44] The most obvious weaponized ground vehicles are those used for mine clearance—robots used to investigate and detonate mines.

is either possible already or that the computational technology is on the brink of achieving that ability.

The work being conducted by Professor Ron Arkin, Director of the Mobile Robot Laboratory at the Georgia Institute of Technology in Atlanta is especially relevant in this respect. Arkin believes that the speed of data capture and analysis that computers achieve (far exceeding that of the human brain) combined with complex sophisticated programmes creating something that might well be digital but which achieves a result remarkably similar to human judgement, may well produce humanitarian benefit. Ultimately, the decision output of a machine or robot could be more humane than the decision made by a human. To quote Arkin on research he has conducted for the US Army's Research Office, on the ethical bases for autonomous system deployment, 'This effort has an overarching goal of producing an "artificial conscience", to yield a new class of robots termed *humane-oids*—robots that can perform more ethically in the battlefield than humans are capable of doing'.[45]

Humans are not only slower at data analysis, they are also subject to emotional effect and under stress may well commit a breach of the law when a well programmed machine simply would not. At least that is the argument. A key ethical question concerns the extent that we ought to remove humans from the process of combat. War is a moral activity and those who are conducting it are moral actors. One wonders about the ethical consequences of taking 'humans out of the loop' altogether.

Perhaps even more concerning is current research being undertaken by Dr Kevin Warwick, Professor of Cybernetics at the University of Reading in the United Kingdom. He has created small machines that are capable of making very basic decisions. The decision-making element in them is not simply computer technology. Warwick has taken neurons from the brains of mice, cultured them in the laboratory and created mini-biological components that he has then inserted into the circuitry of his machines. Those components contribute to the decision as to what the machines will do and how they will react. At present the result is small vehicles carrying out the simple task of avoiding obstacles while navigating around a test area.[46] Very basic, of course, but the continued development of such technology could be moving us towards the development of what some refer to as 'androids'— fully autonomous machines endowed with a measure of human judgement.

This may sound like a form of science-fiction but such technology should not be dismissed; we cannot afford to ignore it for the simple reason that the theoretical science of today may well turn into the reality of tomorrow. What impact would

---

[45] R. Arkin, *Governing Lethal Behavior in Autonomous Robots* (Boca Raton, New York and London: Chapman and Hall, 2009), xvi.

[46] The author shared a panel with Dr Warwick (and Professor Arkin) at a conference 'Ground Robotics: Lightening the Load, Enhancing Effectiveness and Delivering the Edge', at the Royal United Services Institute for Defence and Security Studies (RUSI), Whitehall, London, 18 February 2010 at which this technology was demonstrated.

genuinely autonomous robots have on the battle space? Who would be responsible if such a robot 'committed' a war crime due to malfunction? If robots will be capable of sophisticated assessment of such issues as the identity of targets and what constitutes a reasonable proportion in relation to the targeting of military objectives close to civilian population, how will the law deal with this?

It is impossible to provide sound answers to such questions. We are, however, already over three decades on from the agreement of AP I and AP II. Wind forward the same period to the middle of this century and it is impossible to predict what technology will be available for military professionals and specialist LOAC lawyers to grapple with.[47] Nevertheless, with the sophistication of technology advancing in an exponential manner and with increases in computational capability seemingly complying with Moore's Law, the next three or four decades could generate serious challenges for weapons law. While this author, approaching the end of his professional life, may not have to confront such realities, those embarking on their military or legal careers today will almost certainly have to do so.

8   Immediate Issues

Until recently it was generally thought most likely that efforts to ban particular weapons would concentrate on existing weapons that are manifestly problematic rather than on likely future weapons that are only at this stage theoretically so. Three weapons in particular seemed likely candidates: weapons using white phosphorous; those containing flechettes; and those utilising depleted uranium. As this volume goes to press, however, existing weapons that seem to be in focus are all explosive weapons, the intention being either to ban or to at least discourage their use in populated areas. A number of states have raised concerns about such use, in the context of the CCW. This has prompted the UN Secretary General, in his 2013 Report on the Protection of Civilians in Armed Conflict, to task UNOCHA to develop practical measures, including a political commitment by member states to address the problem and to produce operational guidelines. This call was discussed by a group of experts at a meeting hosted by the Royal Institute of International Affairs and UNOCHA in London at the end of September 2013. That meeting confirmed the production of guidelines for the use of such weapons rather than a development in conventional law.

---

[47] For further discussion of the ethical and legal issues arising from such technology, see A. Krishnan, *Killer Robots: Legality and Ethicality of Autonomous Weapons* (Farnham: Ashgate, 2009).

Interestingly, however, a first move has recently been taken to impose a ban on a particular weapons technology not yet fully developed. In November 2012, the highly respected human rights NGO, Human Rights Watch, in cooperation with the Harvard Law School's Human Rights Clinic, published a pamphlet that seems to have set the immediate future agenda for those involved in the development of conventional weapons law.[48] The pamphlet was a critique of so-called 'Killer Robots' and dealt with the likely future emergence of wholly autonomous weapons, with computer technology making decisions on attack. One can, with justification, regard the Human Rights Watch initiative as a direct response to the work of those, like Ron Arkin, who believe that at some point the human can be taken out of the decision-making loop. The immediate contrary response has come principally from the International Law Department at the US Naval War College. Jeffrey Thurner, a member of the War College Faculty, published an article in the influential *Joint Force Quarterly* in December 2012. This was followed by a substantial legal response in the *Harvard National Security Journal* from Michael Schmitt, the Chair of the International Law Department.[49] The next major weapons law debate may, therefore, have commenced. Autonomous weapons are in the sights of civil society activists; government experts are preparing their response. One approach may be to attempt to delay that debate. As Schmitt has noted:

No such weapons have even left the drawing board. To ban autonomous weapons systems altogether based on speculation as to their future form is to forfeit any potential uses of them that might minimize harm to civilians and civilian objects when compared to other systems in military arsenals.[50]

It is far too early to predict the outcome of this debate but a wide-ranging series of legal, moral and ethical arguments are in prospect.

The law must develop but it must also be regarded as responsibly flexible and able to accommodate new technologies that might deliver more humane (or less inhumane) effects than those currently available. And, of course, those who specialize in this area of law need to keep one eye on the most innovative technologies as they develop. Serious ethical and moral questions about the nature of warfare almost certainly need to be grappled with before the law itself is changed to any significant degree. There are several areas of international law in armed conflict today that represent challenging fields of study; weapons law is certainly one.

---

[48] Human Rights Watch, *Losing Humanity: The Case Against Killer Robots* (New York: Human Rights Watch, 2012).

[49] J.S. Thurner, 'Legal Implications of Fully Autonomous Targeting' in *Joint Force Quarterly*, Issue 67, 4th Quarter, 2012, 77–84; and M. N. Schmitt, 'Autonomous Weapons Systems and International Humanitarian Law: A Reply to the Critics', in *Harvard National Security Journal Features*, 2013, 1–37.

[50] 'Autonomous Weapons Systems and International Humanitarian Law: A Reply to the Critics' (n 49) at 3.

CHAPTER 12

THE PRINCIPLE OF DISTINCTION BETWEEN CIVILIANS AND COMBATANTS

NILS MELZER

1 Basic Outline and Contemporary Challenges

THE primary aim of the law of armed conflict, here referred to as international humanitarian law (IHL), is to protect the victims of armed conflict and to regulate the conduct of hostilities based on a balance between military necessity and humanity. The undisputed cornerstone of IHL is the principle of distinction between civilians and combatants, which obliges belligerents to distinguish at all times between persons who may be lawfully attacked, and persons who must be spared and protected from the effects of the hostilities. In order to avoid any ambiguity, these two categories of persons must be mutually exclusive and absolutely complementary. In other words, in a situation of armed conflict, every person is either a legitimate military target (military objective)[1] or a protected person[2]—*tertium non datur*. The principle of distinction reflects the idea that belligerent hostilities constitute limited confrontations between organized armed forces, and not between entire populations, and that their sole legitimate aim is to weaken and defeat the military forces of the enemy.[3] The cardinal importance of this principle was confirmed in the *Nuclear Weapons Opinion* of the International Court of Justice, where the Court held that a number of basic principles of humanitarian law, including the principle of distinction between combatants and non-combatants, are 'intransgressible principles of international customary law' and are so fundamental to the respect of the human person that they can be derived directly from a general principle of law, namely 'elementary considerations of humanity'.[4] In view of the Court's statements, the International Law Commission considered it justified to regard the principle of distinction as part of *jus cogens*.[5] Although the principle of distinction may appear to be simple and straightforward at first sight, the transformation of warfare in the past century has put considerable strain on its practical application. In the nineteenth century, when most of the concepts and principles underlying modern IHL were conceived and formulated, the dividing line between civilians and combatants was still comparatively clear. At that time, war generally involved large-scale military confrontations between uniformed formations of regular state armies on battlefields distant from the civilian population. This pattern has changed fundamentally.

Today, the majority of armed conflicts are of a non-international character, that is to say, they involve at least one belligerent party composed entirely of non-state actors, whose organization, equipment, training, and discipline rarely match those of state armed forces. At the same time, there has been a continuous shift of military operations into civilian population centres. The ensuing intermingling of armed

[1] The term 'military objective' is most commonly used for objects but, as the text of Art 52(2) AP I illustrates ('Attack shall be limited strictly to military objectives. In so far as objects are concerned, military objectives are [...]'), is the accurate technical term (*terminus technicus*) also for persons subject to lawful attack. Nevertheless, for the sake of clarity, the term 'legitimate military target' will here be preferred.

[2] For the sake of simplicity, the term 'protected person' will here be used as referring to persons entitled to protection against direct attack. This terminology should not be confused with the specific meaning given to the concept of 'protected persons' in the context of the Fourth Geneva Convention (Art 4 of GC IV), which has only limited relevance for the conduct of hostilities.

[3] St Petersburg Declaration (1868). See also J.S. Pictet, *Development and Principles of International Humanitarian Law* (Geneva: Martinus Nijhoff Publishers, 1985), 62.

[4] ICJ, *Legality of the Threat or Use of Nuclear Weapons Opinion*, Advisory Opinion (8 July 1996) § 78, where the 'cardinal principles' of IHL are said to include the principle of 'distinction between combatants and non-combatants', the prohibition 'to cause unnecessary suffering to combatants' and the Martens Clause. Affirmative with regard to the customary nature of the principle of distinction in both international and non-international armed conflicts. See also J.-M. Henckaerts and L. Doswald-Beck, *Customary International Humanitarian Law*, vol 1 (Cambridge: Cambridge University Press, 2005), Commentary Rule 1 at 3ff (hereinafter: Customary Law Study).

[5] International Law Commission, Report on State Responsibility, *Yearbook of the International Law Commission, 2001*, vol II, Part Two, Draft Article 40, Commentary, 112.

actors with the civilian population has not only exposed the latter to increased collateral dangers, but has also facilitated the involvement of civilians themselves in activities more closely related to military operations, from providing food, shelter, equipment, and intelligence to combatants, up to direct participation in combat. Even more recently, the increased outsourcing of traditionally military functions has inserted numerous private contractors and civilian intelligence personnel or other civilian government employees into the modern battlefield. Moreover, contemporary military operations often attain an unprecedented level of complexity, involving the coordination of a great variety of interdependent human and technical resources in different locations.

All of these factors have caused confusion and uncertainty as to the distinction between legitimate military targets and persons protected against direct attacks. These difficulties are further aggravated where combatants do not distinguish themselves from the civilian population, for example during undercover military operations or when acting as farmers by day and fighters by night. As a result, civilians are more likely to fall victim to erroneous or arbitrary targeting, while armed forces—unable to properly identify their adversary—bear an increased risk of being attacked by persons they cannot distinguish from the civilian population. This trend, which threatens to undermine some of the most fundamental achievements made in 'humanizing' warfare, calls for a careful analysis of the legal concepts and rationale underlying the principle of distinction with a view to clarifying its meaning in light of the circumstances prevailing in contemporary armed conflicts.

2 INTERNATIONAL ARMED CONFLICT

A. The rule of distinction in international armed conflict

For situations of international armed conflict, the principle of distinction is expressed in the following provision:

In order to ensure respect for and protection of the civilian population and civilian objects, the Parties to the conflict shall at all times distinguish between the *civilian population* and *combatants* and between civilian objects and military objectives and accordingly shall direct their operations only against military objectives.[6]

---

[6] Article 48 AP I.

The most common formulation of the principle in terms of distinction between 'civilians' and 'combatants' does not cover all categories of persons which may be present in a context of hostilities and, therefore, does not constitute a sufficiently precise basis for targeting decisions. In fact, treaty and customary IHL prohibits direct attacks not only against civilians,[7] but also against medical, religious and civil defence personnel of the armed forces[8] and, more generally, all persons *hors de combat*.[9] The underlying rationale is that, since the concerned persons do not directly participate in hostilities, considerations of humanity require their immunity against direct attack regardless of any potential military advantage that could be achieved. The protection of persons against direct attack also includes the protection against belligerent reprisals. Treaty IHL governing international armed conflict generally prohibits reprisals against the wounded, sick and shipwrecked, against medical and religious personnel,[10] against prisoners of war[11] and persons protected under the Fourth Geneva Convention,[12] as well as against civilians and the civilian population in general.[13] The prohibition of reprisals against persons protected by the Geneva Conventions has become part of customary IHL applicable in international armed conflict.[14]

With regard to legitimate military targets, IHL provides an express definition of military objectives only as far as objects are concerned.[15] While Article 48 of Additional Protocol I implies that combatants are military objectives, this basic rule is not completely accurate in view of the fact that not only, and not all, combatants may be lawfully attacked. A more comprehensive overview of persons constituting legitimate military targets results from identifying those categories of persons which IHL does not protect against direct attack. This includes, first of all, combatants provided they are not *hors de combat*. Moreover, persons normally entitled to immunity from direct attack may lose their protection due to their personal conduct. Civilians lose their protection for such time as they 'take a direct part in hostilities'.[16] Similarly, medical, religious, and civil defence personnel lose

---

[7] Article 51 AP I. See also Customary Law Study, vol I, Rule 1.

[8] With regard to medical and religious personnel, see Art 24 of GC I (on land), Art 36 of GC II (on hospital ships), and Customary Law Study, vol I, Rules 25 (medical) and 27 (religious). See further Art 12(1) of AP I for medical units, and Art 8(2)(b)(xxiv) of the Rome Statute, which lists as a war crime in international armed conflict 'intentionally directing attacks against [...] personnel using the distinctive emblems of the Geneva Conventions in conformity with international law'. Both medical and religious personnel are entitled to use the distinctive emblems. For definitions of medical and religious personnel see Art 8 of AP I. With regard to civil defence personnel, see Art 67(1) of AP I.

[9] Article 41(1) and (2) of AP I, and Customary Law Study, vol I, Rule 47. See also the prohibition of killing or wounding an 'enemy who [...] has surrendered at discretion' in Art 23(c) of the 1907 Hague Regulations. Of course, persons *hors de combat* also benefit from extensive protection under the Geneva Conventions. However, the Geneva Conventions focus primarily on the prevention of arbitrary exercise of power and less on protection from direct attack.

[10] Article 46 of GC I; Art 47 of GC II; Art 20 of AP I.   [11] Article 13(3) of GC III.

[12] Article 33(3) of GC IV.   [13] Article 51(6) of AP I.

[14] Customary Law Study, vol I, Rule 146.   [15] Article 52(1) and (2) of AP I.

[16] Article 51(3) of AP I, and Customary Law Study, vol I, Rule 6.

their protection if they carry out, outside of their humanitarian or civil defence function, 'acts harmful' to the adversary,[17] and persons *hors de combat* when they commit 'hostile acts' or try to escape.[18]

In sum, in situations of international armed conflict, the category of persons protected from direct attack includes 'peaceful civilians',[19] medical, religious, and civil defence personnel of the armed forces, and all persons *hors de combat*. Persons constituting legitimate military targets, on the other hand, include combatants, civilians directly participating in hostilities, as well as individuals carrying out hostile or harmful acts despite the special protection afforded to them as medical, religious, and civil defence personnel of the armed forces or as persons *hors de combat*.

B. Armed forces, combatants and civilians

(i) *Treaty law pre-dating the Additional Protocol I of 1977*

(a) *Hague Regulations of 1907*

In Chapter I on 'The Qualifications of Belligerents', the 1907 Hague Regulations declare the laws, rights, and duties of war applicable to 'armies' and to 'militia and volunteer corps' fulfilling the four conditions of: (a) responsible command, (b) fixed and recognizable distinctive emblem, (c) carrying arms openly, and (d) compliance with the laws and customs of war.[20] Included in the notion of 'belligerents' are not only regular and irregular armed forces, but also participants in a *levée en masse*, if they carry arms openly and respect the laws and customs of war.[21]

It is obvious that these regulations were a model for the corresponding provisions in the Geneva Conventions of 1949.[22] The Hague Regulations further clarify that the armed forces of the belligerent parties may consist of both combatants and non-combatants and that both are entitled to the status of prisoner of war (POW) upon capture.[23] While the Hague Regulations determine the basic categories of persons that may legitimately represent a belligerent sovereign on the battlefield, and while they provide a fairly precise description of participants in a *levée en masse*,

---

[17] With regard to medical and religious personnel, see Art 21 of GC I, and Customary Law Study, vol I, Rules 25 (medical) and 27 (religious). Although, strictly speaking, Art 21 of GC I is limited to medical *units*, this rule can be applied by analogy also to medical personnel of the armed forces and, *mutatis mutandis*, to religious personnel. Customary Law Study, vol I, Commentary Rule 25, 85; Commentary AP I and II, para 520. With regard to civil defence personnel of the armed forces, see Art 67(1)(e) of AP I.

[18] Article 41(2) of AP I.

[19] The phrase 'peaceful civilians' is here used to refer to civilians who are not, at the time, directly participating in hostilities.

[20] Article 1 of the 1907 Hague Regulations.   [21] Article 2 of the 1907 Hague Regulations.

[22] See Arts 13 of GC I and GC II and Art 4 of GC III.   [23] Article 3 of the 1907 Hague Regulations.

they do not sufficiently elucidate the criteria upon which a person can be objectively identified as belonging to the combatant or non-combatant armed forces of a belligerent or, respectively, to the civilian population.

(b) *Geneva Conventions of 1949*

The four Geneva Conventions of 1949 contain few rules concerning the conduct of hostilities and, instead, focus on distinguishing and protecting various categories of persons who have fallen into the power of the adversary, namely the wounded, sick and shipwrecked members of the armed forces (GC I and II), prisoners of war (GC III), and essentially all other persons who find themselves in the hands of a party to the conflict of which they are not nationals (GC IV). Although the Geneva Conventions do not define the terms 'armed forces', 'combatant', or 'civilian', there are sometimes attempts to derive such definitions by implication from the description of the Conventions' personal scopes of application. Strictly speaking, however, despite the reference to 'armed forces' (GC I, GC II) and 'civilians' (GC IV) in their titles, none of the four Conventions has a personal scope of protection that would even approximately match the categories of 'armed forces', 'combatant', or 'civilian'.

Accurately understood, the first three Geneva Conventions afford protection and/or POW-status not only to combatants *hors de combat*, but also to medical and religious personnel of the armed forces, to certain categories of civilians accompanying the armed forces without being part thereof, and to participants in a *levee en masse*.[24] Therefore, the remark made in the ICRC's Commentary that the entitlement to POW-status under Article 4 of GC III 'implies' combatant status must be read with appropriate caution and cannot be generalized.[25] Particularly states that have not ratified Additional Protocol I of 1977 often inaccurately refer to Article 4A(1) and (2) of GC III in order to define armed forces or combatants under IHL. Apart from the fact that this provision deals with the entitlement of persons to POW-status after capture and not with the operation of the principle of distinction during the conduct of hostilities, its text does not even mention the notion of combatant and refers to armed forces only as a notion of domestic law.[26] Under domestic law, however, the notion of armed forces is not necessarily defined for the same purposes as under IHL, and membership in the armed forces may have a series of implications unrelated to the conduct of hostilities.[27] Therefore, when defining

---

[24] Articles 13 of GC I and GC II, Art 4A of GC III.

[25] See Commentary AP I and II, para 1677. For example, civilians accompanying the armed forces within the meaning of Art 4A(4) and (5) of GC III may be entitled to POW-status, but do not have combatant privilege and, by definition, are not members of the armed forces.

[26] Article 4A(1) of GC III refers to militias that are 'part of the armed forces' and Art 4A(2) of GC III to 'other' militias, ie that are not part of the armed forces. As both categories of persons are generally recognized as members of the armed forces and combatants within the meaning of IHL, the notion of 'armed forces' used in Art 4 of GC III must refer to the armed forces as defined by national law.

[27] For example, factors likely to influence the definition of 'armed forces' in domestic law are national policies with regard to the subjection of individuals to military jurisdiction, or with regard to coverage of military insurance and pension systems.

armed forces for the purposes of the principle of distinction, the analysis should be conducted based on universally recognized principles of IHL and not based on domestic legislation.

Similarly, GC IV, although entitled 'Geneva Convention relative to the Protection of Civilian Persons in Time of War', does not prove very useful in clarifying the definition of categories of persons for the purpose of the conduct of hostilities. Not only does the Convention fail to provide a definition of 'civilian person', but Article 4 GC IV also leaves no doubt that the Convention does not protect all civilians, and not only civilians, but also members of the armed forces who, for whatever reason, have lost their entitlement to POW-status.[28] In the final analysis, therefore, the Geneva Conventions do not provide definitions of 'armed forces', 'combatants', or 'civilians', which would be sufficiently precise for the purposes of the principle of distinction.

(ii) *Armed forces*

The first treaty definition of armed forces for situations of international armed conflict is provided in Article 43(1) of AP I:

The armed forces of a Party to a conflict consist of all organized armed forces, groups and units which are under a command responsible to that Party for the conduct of its subordinates, even if that Party is represented by a government or an authority not recognized by an adverse Party.[29]

This definition was adopted by consensus at the Diplomatic Conference of 1974 to 1977 and has become part of customary international law.[30] According to its text, the armed forces of a belligerent party are composed of all organized armed personnel fighting on its behalf, including those which previous treaties listed separately and in addition to the regular armed forces. Thus, even members of irregular armed forces, such as organized resistance movements and other militia or volunteer corps are considered part of the armed forces, as long as they operate under a command responsible to that party.[31] The underlying assumption is that all organized armed actors who engage in hostilities on behalf of a belligerent state do so as organs of a subject of

---

[28] For civilians who are not protected by GC IV, see Art 4A(4) and (5) of GC III and, respectively, Art 13(4) and (5) of GC I and GC II, as well as Art 4(2) of GC IV. For the possibility of members of the armed forces coming within the protection of GC IV, see Art 4 of GC IV (generalized personal scope of application), Arts 46(1) of AP I and 5 of GC IV (spies captured in the act), Art 44(4) of AP I (combatants failing to distinguish themselves). See also Commentary of GC IV (Art 4), 50.

[29] Article 43(1) of AP I.   [30] Customary Law Study, vol 1, Commentary Rule 4, 14.

[31] See the reference to militia and volunteer corps in Art 1 of the 1907 Hague Regulations and, additionally, to organized resistance movements in Arts 13 of GC I, 13 of GC II, and 4A of GC III. See also K. Ipsen, 'Combatants and Non-Combatants', in D. Fleck (ed), *The Handbook of Humanitarian Law in Armed Conflicts* (Oxford: Oxford University Press, 1995), § 304.

international law, thus entailing that state's international responsibility for their conduct.[32] Whether the government or authority representing that state has been recognized as legitimate by the adversary is irrelevant.[33]

While the entitlement of irregular forces to combatant privilege and POW-status depends on their collective fulfilment of the four requirements listed in Article 1 of HC IV Regulations and Article 4 of GC III (ie responsible command, fixed and recognizable distinctive emblem, carrying arms openly, and compliance with IHL), Article 43 of AP I makes clear that their qualification as 'armed forces' distinct from the civilian population depends on two pre-requisites only: (1) the existence of an organized armed force, unit or group, which is (2) under a command responsible to a party to the conflict.[34] Thus, although visibility and respect for IHL are legal obligations which may be relevant for individual and collective entitlement to POW-status or combatant privilege, they are not *defining elements* of armed forces within the meaning of IHL.[35] Also, failure of a party to a conflict to notify the other parties when it incorporates a paramilitary or armed law enforcement agency into its armed forces constitutes a violation of its legal duties but does not prevent the incorporated forces from becoming part of the armed forces within the meaning of IHL.[36]

[32] See Ipsen (n 31).

[33] Provisions of the Geneva Conventions dealing with the protection of members of the armed forces in the hands of an adversary (Art 13(3) of GC I, Art 13(3) of GC II, and Art 4A(3) of GC III) are similar in this respect. This principle was relevant, for instance, for the accurate determination of the status of members of the Taliban forces captured by the United States during the international armed conflict with Afghanistan after 7 October 2001.

[34] Customary Law Study, vol 1, Commentary Rule 4, 15.

[35] Articles 43(1) and 44 of AP I. See also Commentary AP I and II, paras 1672–3; Customary Law Study, vol 1, Commentary Rule 4, 15–16. At the Diplomatic Conference of 1974 to 1977, the Israeli delegation held that this solution modified existing law. When the Article was adopted by consensus at a final plenary meeting, the delegation made the following statement: 'With regard to Article 41 (43), paragraph 1, of draft Additional Protocol I, the delegation of Israel wishes to declare that the enforcement of compliance with the rules of international law applicable in armed conflict is a "conditio sine qua non" for qualification as armed forces. Moreover, it is not sufficient that the armed forces be subject to an internal disciplinary system which can enforce compliance with the laws of war, but—as the expression "shall enforce" indicates—there has to be effective compliance with this system in the field' (CDDH 1974–77, Official Records, vol VI, 116, CDDH/SR.39). As violations of IHL invariably occur on all sides participating in an armed conflict, such an absolute requirement would introduce unacceptable uncertainty regarding the status of all armed actors involved in the hostilities, including uniformed governmental soldiers. Therefore, the status of armed forces must depend on factual 'organship' for a belligerent party and not on compliance with IHL while exercising this function. Consequently, while non-compliance with IHL exposes members of armed forces to prosecution under international criminal law, it generally does not terminate the combatant privilege (but see exceptions according to Art 44(2) of AP I).

[36] Article 43(3) of AP I and see Customary Law Study, vol 1, Commentary Rule 4, 14.

Three particular categories of persons deserve separate mention here, namely participants in a *levée en masse*, mercenaries, and other private contractors. Participants in a *levée en masse*, are inhabitants of a non-occupied territory who, on the approach of the enemy, spontaneously take up arms to resist the invading forces without having had time to form themselves into regular armed units, provided they carry arms openly and respect IHL. According to a longstanding rule of customary and treaty IHL, participants in a *levée en masse* are entitled to combatant privilege and POW-status.[37] They are the only armed actors who are not regarded as civilians although, by definition, they operate spontaneously and lack sufficient organization and command to qualify as members of the armed forces. All other persons who directly participate in hostilities on a merely spontaneous, sporadic, or unorganized basis must be regarded as civilians.

Mercenaries, on the other hand, are presumably both organized and under a command responsible to a belligerent party. Admittedly, Article 47(2) of AP I defines a 'mercenary' as a person who, inter alia, 'is not a member of the armed forces of a Party to the conflict'. If this definition were to be based on the definition of 'armed forces' in Article 43(1) of AP I, then only persons who are either (a) not *organized*, or (b) not *armed* or (c) not *under a command responsible to a party to the conflict* may qualify as mercenaries. In operational reality, however, each of these elements must necessarily be given in the case of mercenaries, as their very *raison d'être* is to directly participate in hostilities on behalf of a party to the conflict. The only reasonable conclusion is that Article 47(2)(e) of AP I, similar to Article 4A(1) of GC III, refers to membership in the armed forces as defined in national law only and that mercenaries, despite confusing treaty terminology which may suggest the contrary, do qualify as members of the armed forces within the meaning of Article 43 of AP I, albeit without entitlement to POW-status and combatant privilege.

Finally, private contractors whose function it is to directly participate in hostilities on behalf of a state but who, nevertheless, do not qualify as mercenaries (eg because they are nationals of the contracting state), not only qualify as members of its irregular armed forces but, in principle, are also entitled to POW-status and combatant privilege in case of capture. Private contractors whose function does not involve direct participation in hostilities, on the other hand, remain civilians and lack combatant privilege but, if formally authorized to accompany the armed forces, may still be entitled to POW-status after capture.[38] In sum, in contemporary IHL, the notion of armed forces refers not only to regular state armed forces, but

---

[37] Article 2 of the 1907 Hague Regulations; Art 4(6) of GC III. See also the reference to Art 4(6) of GC III in Art 50(1) of AP I.

[38] Article 4(4) of GC III. See also the discussion of private contractors and civilian employees in: ICRC, *Interpretive Guidance on the Notion of Direct Participation in Hostilities under International Humanitarian Law* (Geneva: ICRC, 2009) (hereafter: DPH Interpretive Guidance), 37–40.

essentially to all organized armed actors whose function it is to conduct hostilities on behalf of a belligerent party.

(iii) *Combatants*

Building on the preceding definition of armed forces, Additional Protocol I then goes on to define the notion of combatant. Article 43(2) of AP I states:

Members of the armed forces of a Party to a conflict (other than medical personnel and chaplains covered by Article 33 of the Third Convention) are combatants, that is to say, they have the right to participate directly in hostilities.[39]

Thus, in international armed conflict, combatants are those members of the armed forces who have a 'right' to directly participate in hostilities on behalf of a party to the conflict. They are 'privileged combatants'. Expressly excluded are religious and medical personnel who, as non-combatant members of the armed forces, and in accordance with the special protection against direct attack afforded to them, do not have a 'right' to directly participate in hostilities.[40] Additionally, Article 2 of the 1907 Hague Regulations and customary law dating back to the Lieber Code and the Brussels Declaration require that combatant status be given to participants in a *levée en masse*, provided they carry their arms openly and respect the laws and customs of war. According to a long-standing treaty definition, participants in a *levée en masse* are inhabitants of unoccupied territory who spontaneously take up arms to resist invading armed forces without having time to organize themselves into an armed force.[41]

It is important not to misconstrue the implications of the 'right' of combatants to participate directly in hostilities. This so-called 'combatant privilege' provides combatants with immunity from prosecution for lawful acts of war, but not for conduct contrary to IHL or international criminal law. This has been expressed with skillful precision in the following words: 'Those who are entitled to the juridical status of "privileged combatants" are immune from criminal prosecution for those warlike acts that do not violate the laws and customs of war but that might otherwise be common crimes under municipal law'.[42] Consequently, lack of combatant privilege

---

[39] As the notion of 'combatant' has not been previously defined in international law, it is difficult (and therefore not meaningful) to determine how far Art 43(2) of AP I actually expands the personal scope of this notion. As far as POW-status is concerned, Art 43(1) and (2) of AP I, in conjunction with Art 44 of AP I, expands the category of 'beneficiaries' compared to Art 4 of GC III by reducing the 'four requirements' listed in Art 4A(2) of GC III to those inherent in the definition of 'armed forces', and by loosening the requirements of distinction in Art 44(3) of AP I.

[40] See Customary Law Study, vol 1, Commentary Rule 3, 13, according to whom this definition of combatants has become part of customary international law.

[41] See the virtually synonymous definition of a *levée en masse* in Art 4A(6) of GC III and Art 2 of the 1907 Hague Regulations.

[42] W.A. Solf, 'The Status of Combatants in Non-International Armed Conflicts Under Domestic Law and Transnational Practice', 33 *American University Law Review* (1983) 58–9 at 57.

does not mean that 'unprivileged' participation in hostilities, as such, constitutes a war crime or otherwise a violation of IHL, but it simply exposes the concerned persons to the full force of domestic criminal law for death, injury, destruction or other harm caused during their direct participation in hostilities.[43]

(iv) *Civilians*

Additional Protocol I also provides the first codified definition of 'civilian'. Article 50(1) of AP I reads:

A civilian is any person who does not belong to one of the categories of persons referred to in Article 4 (A) (1), (2), (3) and (6) of the Third Convention and in Article 43 of this Protocol. In case of doubt whether a person is a civilian, that person shall be considered to be a civilian.[44]

The term 'civilian' is negatively defined and, in essence, includes all persons who are neither members of the armed forces within the meaning of IHL, nor participants in a *levée en masse*.[45] It follows that, in principle, the law of hostilities governing international armed conflict assigns each individual to one of two mutually exclusive categories, namely 'members of the armed forces' or 'civilians'. In case of doubt, a person shall be presumed to be a civilian.[46] The negative definition of civilians as all persons who are not members of the armed forces has become part of customary law.[47] The only exception to this basic dichotomy are participants in a *levée en masse*, which both treaty and customary IHL recognizes as combatants, but which neither qualify as members of the armed forces nor as civilians.[48] Apart from participation in a *levée en masse*, however, civilians cannot become combatants unless they

[43] For the same reasons, the term 'unlawful' combatant—in contrast to 'unprivileged' combatant—belongs to the realm of domestic law and not of IHL.

[44] Article 50(1) of AP I.

[45] The categories of persons referred to in Art 4(A)(1), (2), (3) are already included in the definition of armed forces of Art 43 of AP I. This definition of civilian is affirmed by the ICTY, Trial Chamber, *Prosecutor v Tihomir Blaškić*, Judgment of 3 March 2000, § 180: 'Civilians [...] are persons who are not, or no longer, members of the armed forces', and DPH Interpretive Guidance, 20–6: 'For the purposes of the principle of distinction in *international* armed conflict, all persons who are neither members of the armed forces of a party to the conflict nor participants in a *levée en masse* are civilians and, therefore, entitled to protection against direct attack unless and for such time as they take a direct part in hostilities'.

[46] Article 50(1) of AP I. Upon ratification of Additional Protocol I, the United Kingdom and France expressed their understanding that this presumption does not override the commanders' duty to protect the safety of troops under their command or to preserve their military situation, in conformity with other provisions of Additional Protocol I. See: France, Reservations and declarations made upon ratification of AP I, 11 April 2001, para 9; United Kingdom, Reservations and declarations made upon ratification of AP I, 28 January 1998, para h.

[47] Customary Law Study, vol 1, Commentary Rule 5, 17f.

[48] While a comparison of the definition of 'armed forces' in Art 43 of AP I and the definition of 'civilians' in Art 50(1) of AP I shows that participants in a *levée en masse* belong to neither category, Art 2 of the 1907 Hague Regulations expressly recognizes their 'belligerent' status. The customary nature of this exception to the absolute complementarity between 'civilians' and 'armed forces' is confirmed in Customary Law Study, vol 1, Commentary Rule 5, 18.

become members of the armed forces of a party to the conflict. Therefore, as far as situations of international armed conflict are concerned, civilians taking a direct part in the hostilities without becoming members of armed forces must remain civilians, even though they temporarily lose their protection against direct attack.[49]

3 NON-INTERNATIONAL ARMED CONFLICT

A. The rule of distinction in non-international armed conflict

While treaty IHL governing non-international armed conflict contains a few provisions on the conduct of hostilities, the most important rules and principles applicable in situations of international armed conflict are today recognized as having attained customary status with respect to non-international armed conflict as well. The customary rule of distinction applicable in situations of non-international armed conflict has been formulated as follows:

The parties to the conflict must at all times distinguish between civilians and combatants. Attacks may only be directed against combatants. Attacks must not be directed against civilians.[50]

The term 'combatant' is used in its generic meaning, that is to say, as describing persons who do not enjoy civilian protection against attack but it does not imply a right to combatant privilege or POW-status.[51] Just like the corresponding rule applicable in international armed conflict, this general rule does not cover all categories of persons which may be present in a context of hostilities and, therefore, does not provide sufficiently precise guidance for targeting decisions.

In fact, during the conduct of hostilities in non-international armed conflict, treaty and customary IHL protects the same basic categories of persons as in international armed conflict, namely civilians,[52] medical, and religious personnel[53] and,

---

[49] Article 51(3) of AP I; Customary Law Study, vol 1, Commentary Rule 6, 19f; DPH Interpretive Guidance, 70. See also Israeli High Court of Justice, *The Public Committee Against Torture et al v The Government of Israel et al* (HCJ 769/02), Judgment of 13 December 2006 (hereinafter: Israel HCJ, *PCATI v Israel*), § 39.

[50] Customary Law Study, vol 1, Rule 1.   [51] Customary Law Study, vol 1, Commentary Rule 1, 3.

[52] Article 13 of AP II. See also Customary Law Study, vol 1, Rule 1. See also Art 8(2)(e)(i) of the Rome Statute, according to which 'intentionally directing attacks against the civilian population as such or against individual civilians not taking direct part in hostilities' constitutes a war crime in non-international armed conflicts.

[53] Article 9(1) of AP II; Customary Law Study, vol 1, Rules 25 (medical) and 27 (religious). With regard to the wording of Art 9(1) of AP II it has been held that '[t]he concept of respect implies a duty not to

more generally, all persons *hors de combat*.[54] Treaties governing non-international armed conflict are silent with regard to civil defence personnel but, to the extent that their assignment to civil defence duties is permanent and involves a prohibition of direct participation in hostilities just as in international armed conflict,[55] permitting direct attacks against these individuals would run counter to the fundamental rationale of the principle of distinction. Of course, where civil defence functions are carried out by civilians, they remain entitled, at the very least, to the general protection afforded to civilians. The protection of persons against direct attack also includes the protection against belligerent reprisals by way of direct attack. Although not expressly mentioned in treaty IHL governing non-international armed conflict, the prohibition of belligerent reprisals against persons protected against direct attack has attained customary status in situations of non-international armed conflict as well.[56]

As in the case of international armed conflicts, the category of individuals constituting legitimate military targets in non-international armed conflict includes all persons which IHL does not protect against direct attack. Common Article 3 affords protection to all persons 'taking no active part in the hostilities' against arbitrary exercise of power by the parties to the conflict including violence to life and person, murder and extra-judicial execution. 'Members of armed forces' benefit from such protection only once they have 'laid down their arms' or are 'placed *hors de combat*'.[57]

Common Article 3 therefore implies, *a contrario*, that members of the armed forces are not regarded as 'taking no active part in the hostilities' and, therefore, are not entitled to protection until they have laid down their arms or are placed *hors de combat*. This view is supported by Article 4(1) of AP II, which provides essentially the same scope of protection to '[a]ll persons who do not take a direct part or who have ceased to take part in hostilities, whether or not their liberty has been

attack' and '[t]he scope of the protection granted by Articles 9 and 11 (*Protection of medical units and transports*) is in fact the same. Thus, the reference to attacks in the latter article, and not in the former, is an error of methodology which is regrettable. It would have been better to be consistent' (Commentary AP I and II, para 4674). See also Art 8(2)(e)(ii) of the Rome Statute, which includes into the notion of 'war crime' for non-international armed conflicts 'intentionally directing attacks against [...] personnel using the distinctive emblems of the Geneva Conventions in conformity with international law'. Article 12 of AP II entitles both medical and religious personnel to use the distinctive emblem.

[54] Article 7(1) of AP II; Customary Law Study, vol 1, Rule 47. According to the Commentary AP I and II, para 4635, the obligation 'to respect' means 'to spare, not to attack' or 'to abstain from any hostile act', which is additional to the duty to protect. See also the protection afforded to all persons 'taking no active part in hostilities', including, inter alia, 'those placed *hors de combat* by sickness, wounds, detention, or any other cause' by Common Art 3, as well as by Art 4(1) of AP II, which refers to all persons 'who do not take a direct part or who have ceased to take part in hostilities'.

[55] Article 67(1)(e) of AP I.   [56] Customary Law Study, vol 1, Rule 148.

[57] Article 41 of AP I, '*hors de combat*'; 'A person is *hors de combat* if: (a) He is in the power of the adverse party; (b) He clearly expresses an intention to surrender; or (c) He has been rendered unconscious or otherwise incapable by wounds or sickness, and is therefore incapable of defending himself provided that in any of the cases he abstains from hostilities and does not escape.'

restricted'. The ICRC's Commentary on this matter specifies that: '*Ratione temporis* combatants are protected as soon as they are *hors de combat*'.[58] While treaty IHL applicable in non-international armed conflict does not use the term 'combatant', the principle of distinction operates based on the same criteria which define that category in international armed conflict.[59] Thus, in non-international armed conflict, members of armed forces are not protected against direct attack, unless they serve as medical and religious personnel or have been placed *hors de combat*. This also applies to the armed forces of non-states parties to the conflict, whether they are referred to as 'armed forces' (Common Article 3) or as 'dissident armed forces' and other 'organized armed groups' (Article 1(1) of AP II). As the ICRC's Commentary unambiguously declares: 'Those who belong to armed forces or armed groups may be attacked at any time'.[60] Moreover, just as in international armed conflict, persons normally benefiting from protection against direct attack may lose such immunity due to their individual conduct. Thus, civilians lose their protection for such time as they take a direct part in hostilities,[61] medical and religious personnel if they carry out, outside of their humanitarian function, hostile acts or acts harmful to the adversary,[62] and persons *hors de combat* when they commit hostile acts or try to escape.[63]

In sum, for the purposes of the principle of distinction, the pertinent rules of international humanitarian law distinguish essentially the same categories of persons in international and non-international armed conflict. In both cases, persons protected against direct attack includes peaceful civilians, medical and religious personnel, as well as persons *hors de combat*. Persons not entitled to immunity against direct attack includes members of the armed forces—that is to say: state armed forces, dissident armed forces, and other organized armed groups—of a belligerent party, civilians directly participating in hostilities, as well as medical, religious, and civil defence personnel or persons *hors de combat* who commit hostile or harmful acts despite the special protection afforded to them.

B. Armed forces, organized armed groups, civilians, and combatants

Treaty IHL governing non-international armed conflict uses the terms 'armed forces', 'organized armed groups', and 'civilians' without defining them. The meaning of these terms must therefore be determined based on a comprehensive reading

---

[58] Commentary AP I and II, para 4520 and note 5.
[59] See also *infra*, at 23ff.   [60] Commentary AP I and II, para 4789.
[61] Article 13(3) of AP I. Customary Law Study, vol 1, Rule 6.
[62] Article 11(2) of AP II; Customary Law Study, vol 1, Rules 25 and 27. Although limited to medical *units*, Art 11(2) of AP II can by analogy be applied also to medical personnel of the armed forces and, *mutatis mutandis*, to religious personnel. Affirmative: Customary Law Study, vol 1, Commentary Rule 25, 85; Customary Law Study, vol 1, Commentary Rule 28, 91.
[63] Customary Law Study, vol 1, Rule 47.

of IHL applicable in non-international armed conflict and in light of current state practice. In should also be determined to what extent the notion of 'combatant' has any legal relevance in non-international armed conflict.

(i) *Armed forces*

Treaty IHL governing non-international armed conflict uses the term 'armed forces' with different meanings. A preliminary source of confusion is the question of whether the notion of armed forces in non-international armed conflict covers only state armed forces or also the fighting forces of non-state parties to the conflict.

Common Article 3 to the Geneva Conventions extends protection against arbitrary exercise of power to 'members of armed forces who have laid down their arms and those placed *hors de combat* by sickness, wounds, detention, or any other cause'. Thus, 'members of armed forces' are to be considered as 'persons taking no active part in the hostilities' only once they have definitely disengaged or have been placed *hors de combat*. Mere suspension of combat is insufficient. Since it was considered necessary to make this clarification with regard to the obligations of 'each' party to the conflict, these special provisions could not have been intended to apply exclusively to state armed forces but must also extend to the armed forces of non-states parties to the conflict.[64] This interpretation becomes even more compelling in view of the fact that a non-international armed conflict within the meaning of this provision does not require the involvement of a state but can also take place exclusively between opposing non-states parties. Hence, the notion of 'armed forces' in Common Article 3 must be interpreted as referring to the fighting forces of both state and non-state belligerents.[65]

Article 1(1) of AP II

The clarity and simplicity of Common Article 3 was unnecessarily blurred by Article 1(1) of AP II, which refers to non-international armed conflicts between the 'armed forces' of the High Contracting Party on the one hand, and 'dissident armed forces' or 'other organized armed groups' on the other. Unfortunately, this provision fails to properly distinguish between the 'parties' to the conflict and their respective 'armed forces'. Of course, contrary to the wording of Article 1(1) of AP

---

[64] According to the ICRC's Commentary 'it must be recognized that the conflicts referred to in Article 3 are armed conflicts, with "armed forces" on either side engaged in "hostilities"—conflicts, in short, which are in many respects similar to an international war [...]' Commentary GC III, Art 3, 37). Similarly also Commentary GC II, Art 3, 33; Commentary GC IV, Art 3, 36. See also R.K. Goldman, 'International Humanitarian Law: American Watch's Experience in Monitoring Internal Armed Conflicts, 9(1) *American University Journal of International Law and Policy* (1993) 49–94 at 60; ICRC, *Report Expert Meeting 'Direct Participation in Hostilities'* (2005), 43f.

[65] See also DPH Interpretive Guidance, 28–30.

II, the state party to the conflict cannot be the governmental armed forces, but only the state itself. Thus, the provision leaves unclear whether 'organized armed groups' and 'dissident armed forces' are referred to as 'parties' to the conflict or as 'armed forces' conducting the hostilities for the respective parties.

However conflated the non-governmental party to the conflict and its 'armed forces' may be as a matter of fact, it is imperative to keep these concepts separate as a matter of law. For example, if the notion of 'organized armed group' were to be equated with a 'party' to the conflict as a whole, the functional distinction between that party and its armed forces would have to be made by distinguishing the 'armed' and 'political' wings or, on the level of individual membership, 'combatant' and 'non-combatant' members of the organized armed group in question. Although the result may be the same, equating the notion of 'organized armed groups' in Article 1(1) of AP II with the fighting forces of a non-state party to the conflict better reflects the terminological and conceptual approach of treaty and customary IHL.[66] The described confusion is further compounded by the juxtaposition of armed forces, dissident armed forces, and other organized armed groups, which seems to exclude organized armed groups not qualifying as dissident armed forces from the concept of 'armed forces' altogether. This has led to the suggestion that such organized armed groups in non-international armed conflict should be regarded as 'civilians' who may only be directly attacked when they directly participate in hostilities.[67] As will become apparent, this view is a misconception of major proportions, which necessarily entails a distortion of the fundamental concepts of 'civilian', 'armed forces', and 'direct participation in hostilities' and, ultimately, leads to irreconcilable contradictions in the interpretation of these terms.

(a) Status of organized armed groups in state practice

While the ICRC's study on customary IHL comes to the conclusion that state armed forces are not considered civilians,[68] it finds that 'practice is ambiguous as to whether members of armed opposition groups are considered members of armed forces or civilians' and asserts that 'most manuals define civilians negatively with respect to combatants and armed forces and are silent on the status of armed opposition groups'.[69] It is here submitted that this purported ambiguity is not, in

[66] Where IHL otherwise refers to the concept of an organized armed group, it appears to use it as an equivalent of 'armed forces' rather than of 'party to the conflict'. For example, Art 4(3)(c) of AP II provides that children under 15 years of age shall not be recruited into 'armed forces or groups'. See also the terminology used in Customary Law Study, vol 1, Rule 4 and in IHL applicable to international armed conflict, where 'organized armed groups' or 'organized resistance movements' are referred to as a functional part of the armed forces of a party to the conflict (Art 43(1) of AP I; Art 4A(2) of GC III).

[67] See eg Moodrick-Even Khen, Can We Now Tell What 'Direct Participation in Hostilities' Is?, 12, Report of Expert Meeting on the Right to Life in Armed Conflict and Situations of Occupation, 1–2 September 2005, University Centre for International Humanitarian Law, available at <http://www.adh-geneva.ch/events/expert-meetings.php>, 35.

[68] Customary Law Study, vol 1, Commentary Rule 5, 19.

[69] Customary Law Study, vol 1, Commentary Rule 5, 17, and 19.

fact, reflected in state practice. As it is quite common for states to carefully avoid statements or actions that could be interpreted as giving a direct recognition of any kind to armed opposition groups, it is not surprising that military manuals—just as treaty IHL—generally do not expressly regulate their status. The lack of formal regulation on this sensitive issue does not necessarily indicate ambiguous state practice. Rather, it suggests that qualifying organized armed groups as civilians is a matter where relevant state practice and *opinio juris* are more reliably deduced from operational conduct, conclusive indirect statements and the absence of condemnation than from formal statements prone to political misinterpretation.

Treaty IHL and state practice are very clear as to the rule that, in any armed conflict, civilians may not be directly attacked unless and for such time as they directly participate in hostilities.[70] Consequently, if states viewed organized armed groups as civilians, they would have to express through statements and general conduct that members of such groups cannot be attacked unless and for such time as they directly participate in hostilities. Contrary practice would either have to be denied or, alternatively, would have to be regarded as unlawful by other states. However, even a cursory glance at almost any non-international armed conflict— be it in South East Asia in the 1960s and 1970s, in Central America in the 1980s, or in Colombia, Sri Lanka, Uganda, Chechnya or the Sudan today—is sufficient to conclude that governmental armed forces do not hesitate to attack insurgents even while they are not engaged in a particular military operation. In practice, such attacks generally are neither denied by the operating state nor internationally condemned as long as they do not cause excessive incidental harm to protected persons or objects. Where there has been condemnation of a state's direct attack against individuals supporting an insurgency, it has been in relation to doubts concerning whether the targeted persons belonged to the military wing of the insurgency rather than doubts as to the lawfulness of direct attacks against members of such fighting forces. In sum, state practice suggests that, as far as the principle of distinction is concerned, organized armed groups belonging to a non-state belligerent are not regarded as civilians but, instead, are seen as being functionally equivalent to state armed forces.[71]

(b) *Reconciliation of Common Article 3 and Article 1 of AP II*

In order to restore clarity and reconcile potential conflicts between Common Article 3 and Article 1(1) of AP II, it must be recognized that the two provisions refer to 'armed forces' from different perspectives, but without contradiction in terms of concept. Common Article 3, similar to Article 43 of AP I, adopts a wide and

---

[70] Article 51(3) of AP I; Art 13(3) of AP II; Customary Law Study, vol 1, Rule 6 and Commentary Rule 6, 19ff; Customary Law Study, vol 1, 107ff.

[71] With regard to slight differences in the conception of membership, see below.

functional notion of armed forces which distinguishes the organized fighting forces of all parties to the conflict from the civilian population. Conversely, the notion of 'armed forces' in Article 1(1) of AP II refers exclusively to forces which have at some point and in some form been drafted into service by the governmental side of the conflict, whether they remain loyal or turn against the government as dissident armed forces.[72] Nevertheless, similar to Article 43 of AP I, the notion of 'armed forces' in Article 1(1) of AP II remains functionally broad enough to include police forces, intelligence agents, and border guards assuming combat function for the state without formally qualifying as members of its armed forces under domestic law.[73] Moreover, it has rightly been argued that the description of 'dissident armed forces' and 'other organized armed groups' in Article 1(1) of AP II 'inferentially' recognizes the essential conditions prescribed under Article 43 of AP I, namely 'that the armed force be linked to one of the parties to the conflict; that they be organized; and that they be under responsible command'.[74] Accordingly, in the final analysis, the functional notion of 'armed forces' employed in Common Article 3 includes all three categories juxtaposed in Article 1(1) of AP II, namely 'armed forces' of a High Contracting Party, 'dissident armed forces' and 'organized armed groups'. It is here submitted that the functional interpretation of the notion of 'armed forces' expressed in Common Article 3 best corresponds to the concepts underlying the principle of distinction and, therefore, is tailor-made for the conduct of hostilities.

(c) *Resulting concept*

The ICRC's study on customary IHL comes to the conclusion that, for the purposes of the principle of distinction in situations of non-international armed conflict, the following definition of state armed forces has attained customary nature:

The armed forces of a party to the conflict consist of all organised armed forces, groups and units which are under a command responsible to that party for the conduct of its subordinates.[75]

In the conduct of hostilities, the generic functions of the armed forces of a party to the conflict are essentially the same irrespective of whether they belong to a state or a non-state party and irrespective of whether the conflict is of international or non-international character. It therefore seems reasonable to apply the same functional definition of armed forces also to the organized fighting forces of a non-state party to the conflict. Whether such forces are categorized as 'state armed forces', 'dissident

---

[72] According to Commentary AP I and II, para 4460, the notion of 'dissident armed forces' in Art 1(1) of AP II simply refers to part of the state armed forces, which have become a non-state party to the conflict by turning against the government.

[73] See also also Commentary AP I and II, para 4462.

[74] M. Bothe, K.J Partsch, and W.A. Solf, *New Rules for Victims of Armed Conflicts* (The Netherlands: Martinus Nijhoff Publishers, 1982), 672. See also Goldman (n 64), 49–94 at 66.

[75] Customary Law Study, vol 1, Rule 4.

armed forces', and other 'organized armed groups' (Article 1(1) of AP II), or whether they are simply described as 'armed forces' of a party to the conflict (Common Article 3) is irrelevant, as long as there is clarity as to the functional purpose of the definition as part of the principle of distinction.

(ii) *Organized armed groups*

(a) *Distinction from civilians directly participating in hostilities*

In functional terms, organized armed groups (including dissident armed forces) constitute the armed forces of a non-state party to an armed conflict.[76] As such they are no longer part of the civilian population and must also be distinguished from civilians who may be directly participating in hostilities on a merely unorganized, sporadic, or spontaneous basis. In line with the generic concept of 'armed forces' outlined above, the qualification of armed actors as an organized armed group requires that they be armed, organized, and under a command responsible to one of the parties to the conflict. This does not imply that the structure and organization of such groups must be as sophisticated as that of state armed forces. As pointed out in the ICRC's Commentary:

The existence of a responsible command implies some degree of organization of the insurgent armed group or dissident armed forces, but this does not necessarily mean that there is a hierarchical system of military organization similar to that of regular armed forces. It means an organization capable, on the one hand, of planning and carrying out sustained and concerted military operations, and on the other, of imposing discipline in the name of a *de facto* authority.[77]

Admittedly, the requirement of *de facto* authority is a condition of applicability of Additional Protocol II rather than a generic defining element of an organized armed group engaged in a non-international armed conflict. More accurate with respect to the minimal constitutive elements of any organized armed group are probably the requirements which have been accepted with regard to irregularly constituted resistance movements in international armed conflict, namely that they should form 'a body having a military organization',[78] must be commanded by a 'person responsible for his subordinates'[79] and that they must 'belong to' a party to the conflict.[80] The concept of 'belonging to' denotes a *de facto* relationship between an armed force and a party to the conflict, which may be officially declared, but may also be expressed through tacit agreement or conclusive behaviour.[81]

---

[76] DPH Interpretive Guidance, 32.   [77] Commentary AP I and II, para 4463.

[78] Commentary GC III (Art 4), 58.

[79] Commentary GC III (Art 4), 59. Interestingly, according to the Commentary, 'the leader may be either civilian or military'.

[80] Article 4A(2) of GC III.

[81] In international armed conflict, the notion of 'belonging to' is best expressed in terms of state responsibility, so that an armed group can be said to 'belong to' a state to the extent that its conduct

In conjunction with the functional definition of armed forces, these elements provide margins which are flexible enough to take into account organizational, structural, cultural, political, and other contextual diversities while maintaining the core content of what constitutes the armed forces of a belligerent party in distinction to the civilian population. Where armed actors fulfil these criteria, they are no longer civilians but can be regarded as an 'organized armed group' or as 'armed forces' of a party to the conflict within the meaning of IHL. Where armed non-state actors do not meet these criteria, on the other hand, they remain civilians even for such time as they directly participate in hostilities on an unorganized, sporadic or spontaneous basis.[82]

(b) *Individual membership*

In the case of organized armed groups, it may be particularly difficult to distinguish the 'party' to the conflict as a whole from its 'armed forces', a distinction that is of paramount importance for the protection of civilians supporting a party to the conflict without engaging in organized hostilities on its behalf. For example, such civilians would include political and religious leaders, instigators, or militants making up the 'political wing' of a non-state belligerent. In addition, financial contributors, informants, collaborators, and other service providers without fighting function may support or belong to an opposition movement or an insurgency as a whole. These individuals can hardly be regarded as members of its 'armed forces' in a functional sense.[83] For the purposes of the principle of distinction, such persons remain civilians and, as such, may be attacked only for such time as they directly participate in hostilities.

Membership in state armed forces is normally regulated in domestic law and expressed through uniforms, distinctive signs, emblems and identity cards or disks. Membership in state armed forces is of a formal nature and not necessarily tied to the actual exercise of a fighting function. For example, armed forces can include cooks, secretaries, and administrative personnel unlikely to take a direct part in hostilities. Due to the formal nature of their membership, such non-combatant personnel cannot be regarded as civilians and, with the sole exception of medical and religious personnel, are subject to direct attack regardless of the individual function assumed.

---

is legally attributable to that state. Based on the experience of World War II, the ICRC's Commentary interprets the notion of 'belonging to' as follows: 'It is essential that there should be a "de facto" relationship between the resistance organization and the party to international law which is in a state of war, but the existence of this relationship is sufficient. It may find expression merely by tacit agreement, if the operations are such as to indicate clearly for which side the resistance organization is fighting. But affiliation with a Party to the conflict may also follow an official declaration, for instance by a Government in exile, confirmed by official recognition by the High Command of the forces which are at war with the Occupying Power'. See Commentary GC III (Art 4), 57.

[82] On the meaning of 'direct participation in hostilities', see Section 4 below.

[83] See also DPH Interpretive Guidance, 32.

Similarly, where dissident armed forces remain organized according to structures that are comparable to those of state armed forces, these structures should continue to determine individual membership in these forces. After all, there is no reason to assume that a member of the armed forces becomes a civilian simply by turning against his government.[84]

Much more difficult is the determination of membership in irregularly constituted organized armed groups. Such groups operate in a wide variety of cultural, political, and military contexts, and membership may depend on a range of factors including individual choice, involuntary recruitment, or more traditional notions, such as membership in a clan, tribe, or family. The actual beginning and end of membership in such organized armed groups will largely depend on the particular context and will not necessarily be recognizable to the adversary. Also, in reality, organized armed groups rarely operate in isolated, exclusively military surroundings but are often accompanied by civilians, which provide them with a wide variety of essential services, comparable to private contractors accompanying state armed forces.[85]

In the absence of a formal concept of 'membership' in irregularly constituted armed groups, subjective or overly flexible criteria of distinction are prone to lead to erroneous and arbitrary targeting. This can only be avoided where membership in such groups remains closely tied to the actual function assumed. More specifically, irregularly constituted organized armed groups should be construed as comprising only persons who assume a continuous fighting function on behalf of a party to the conflict, that is to say, a continuous function which involves, at least potentially, direct participation in hostilities.[86] Whether this is the case will in practice have to be deduced from the concrete circumstances. In case of doubt, the concerned individual is presumed to be a civilian.[87] While this interpretation may be criticized, as it results in a narrower (more protective) concept of membership for organized armed groups than for state armed forces, the practical relevance of this perceived imbalance should not be overestimated. In reality, personnel assuming non-combat functions for state armed forces (other than medical and religious personnel) are almost always armed, trained, and expected to directly participate in hostilities should the need arise and, therefore, must be regarded as assuming a combat function.[88]

---

[84] DPH Interpretive Guidance, 31–2.

[85] Article 4A(4) and (5) of GC III.   [86] DPH Interpretive Guidance, 32–5.

[87] See DPH Interpretive Guidance, 74–6; L. Moir, The *Law of Internal Armed Conflict* (Cambridge: Cambridge University Press: 2002), 59.

[88] For a detailed discussion of the functional membership approach proposed by the ICRC, see K. Watkin, 'Opportunity Lost: Organized Armed Groups and the ICRC "Direct Participation in Hostilities" Interpretive Guidance', 42 *NYU Journal of International Law and Politics* (2010) 641–95 (critique), and N. Melzer, 'Keeping the Balance between Military Necessity and Humanity', 42 *NYU Journal of International Law and Politics* (2010) 833–916 (response).

(iii) *Civilians*

Treaty IHL governing non-international armed conflict does not define the concept of civilian. While Common Article 3 makes no express reference to this category, Additional Protocol II seems to use the notion of 'civilian' to describe any person not belonging to one of the categories mentioned in Article 1(1) of AP II. Thus, Article 1(1) of AP II describes armed forces, dissident armed forces and other organized armed groups as able 'to carry out sustained and concerted military operations', whereas Article 13(1) of AP II emphasizes that the civilian population and individual civilians 'shall enjoy general protection against the dangers arising from military operations' conducted by these forces.

Draft Article 25(1) of AP II adopted by consensus in Committee III of the Diplomatic Conference of 1974 to 1977 provided the following definition: 'A civilian is anyone who is not a member of the armed forces or of an organized armed group'. The category of persons qualifying as civilians for the purposes of the principle of distinction in non-international armed conflict has been aptly described in the following terms:

The following persons generally should be considered civilians and, thus, not subjected to individualized attack:

1. The *peaceful population not directly participating in hostilities*, even though their activities may contribute to the war effort.
2. (a) *Persons providing only indirect support* to a party to the conflict by, inter alia, working in defence plants, distributing or storing military supplies outside of combat areas, supplying labour and food, serving as messengers, or disseminating propaganda. These persons may not be subject to direct individualized attack because they pose no immediate threat to the adversary. However, if they are present in or near military targets, they implicitly assume the risk of death or injury incidental to direct attacks against such military targets. (b) Persons providing such indirect support to dissident forces are clearly subject to prosecution by the government for giving aid and comfort to the enemy. Such prosecutions must conform to the obligatory fair trial guarantees set forth in Common Article 3 and, where applicable, Article 6 of Protocol II.
3. Persons, other than members of a party to the conflict's armed forces, who take a direct part in the hostilities. They, however, temporarily lose their immunity from attack while they assume a combatant's role.[89]

In sum, as in the case of international armed conflict, a civilian in non-international armed conflict is anyone not belonging to the 'armed forces' of a party to the conflict (Common Article 3) or, respectively, to state 'armed forces', 'dissident armed forces' or other 'organized armed groups' of a party to the conflict (Article 1(1) of

---

[89] Goldman (n 64), 84.

AP II).[90] Where persons directly participate in hostilities without being integrated into such organized armed forces or groups, even if they intend to support one of the parties to the conflict, they remain civilians and lose protection against direct attack only for such time as their direct participation lasts.[91]

(iv) *Combatants*

(a) *Combatant privilege*

Treaty IHL governing non-international armed conflict does not use the notion of combatant, nor does it provide for combatant privilege (ie immunity from prosecution for lawful acts of war). While domestic legislation in most countries provides members of state armed forces with protection from prosecution for lawful acts of state (ie a status equivalent to combatant privilege), members of organized armed groups remain subject to prosecution for violations of domestic law even if they comply with IHL. Although states can hardly be expected to provide insurgents with immunity from prosecution for death, injury, and destruction caused in rebellion against their government, the lack of any form of combatant privilege for non-state belligerents is not unproblematic.

Most importantly, apart from the general encouragement to afford the 'broadest possible amnesty to persons who have participated in the armed conflict' at the end of hostilities,[92] IHL does not provide members of organized armed groups with any incentive to respect IHL and to distinguish themselves from the civilian population. This may contribute to a destructive downward spiral, with non-state belligerents distancing themselves from their obligations under IHL and, in turn, states stigmatizing non-state belligerents with blanket labels such as 'terrorists' and 'unlawful combatants' and increasingly questioning the appropriateness of the rights and protections afforded to them under IHL.

(b) *Functional combatancy*

The combatant privilege, which separates persons who are entitled to immunity from domestic prosecution for lawful acts of war from persons who are not, must not be confused with our discussion of the principle of distinction between civilians and combatants, which separates persons who may lawfully be attacked from those who may not. Indeed, the concept of combatancy in a strictly functional sense is anything but alien to IHL governing non-international armed conflicts. Already the

---

[90] Affirmative also: *DPH Interpretive Guidance*, 27–36; Bothe et al. (n 74), 672.

[91] Article 13(3) of AP II. See DPH Interpretive Guidance, 70–1. See also IACtHR, *Report Colombia 1999*, Ch IV, § 55 (n 96 and accompanying citation); Customary Law Study, vol 1, Commentary Rule 6, 19f; Goldman (n 64), 67; D. Kretzmer, 'Targeted Killing of Suspected Terrorists: Extra-Judicial Executions or Legitimate Means of Defence?', 16 *EJIL* (2005) 171–212 at 199. On the meaning of 'direct participation in hostilities', see below.

[92] Article 6(5) of AP II.

draft of Additional Protocol II proposed by the ICRC in 1973 and the amended draft Protocol adopted by consensus in Committee III of the Diplomatic Conference of 1974 to 1977 used the term combatant without implying the existence of *privileged* combatancy in non-international armed conflict. Draft Article 24(1) of AP II reads as follows:

In order to ensure respect for the civilian population, the parties to the conflict shall confine their operations to the destruction or weakening of the military resources of the adversary and shall make a distinction between the civilian population and combatants, and between civilian objects and military objectives.[93]

When, in the last moment, this draft Article was discarded along with 23 others, the reason was not that the contracting states wanted to dispense with the principle of distinction between civilians and combatants in non-international armed conflict but, rather, their fear that the use of the term combatant in the treaty text could be misconstrued as indicating the legitimacy of an insurgency or would otherwise encourage insurrection.

(c) *International jurisprudence*

The concept of combatancy has also been used in international jurisprudence dealing with situations of non-international armed conflict. In the *Tadić Case*, for instance, the ICTY referred to 'an individual who cannot be considered a traditional "non-combatant" because he is actively involved in the conduct of hostilities *by membership* in some kind of resistance group',[94] thus permitting no other conclusion than that the individual in question is a combatant. Significantly, in the view of the Tribunal, the decisive element for combatancy appears to be 'membership' in some kind of an organized armed force or group. Further, in its Country Report on Colombia (1999), the Inter-American Commission on Human Rights made clear that combatants must be distinguished from civilians directly participating in hostilities. Thus, according to the Commission, '[i]t is important to understand that while these persons forfeit their immunity from direct attack while participating in hostilities, they, nonetheless, retain their status as civilians. *Unlike ordinary combatants*, once they cease their hostile acts, they can no longer be attacked, although they may be tried and punished for all their belligerent acts'.[95]

(d) *State practice*

As far as state practice is concerned, many military manuals use the term 'combatant', but most were drafted with a view to international armed conflicts and

---

[93] ICRC, Draft Additional Protocols to the Geneva Conventions of 12 August 1949 (Geneva, June 1973), Draft Art 24(1) of AP II, printed in CDDH 1974–77, Official Records, vol I, Part III, 40.

[94] ICTY, *Tadić Case* (Judgment of 7 May 1997), § 639 (emphasis added).

[95] IACtHR, *Report Colombia 1999*, Ch IV, § 55 (emphasis added).

do not necessarily provide for the formal applicability of the same categories in non-international armed conflicts. An instructive example of national practice referring specifically to non-international armed conflicts is the 2009 US Field Manual on 'Tactics in Counterinsurgency' (FM 3-24.2) which 'establishes doctrine [...] for tactical counterinsurgency (COIN) operations' and is based 'on lessons learned from historic counterinsurgencies and current operations'.[96] According to the manual, an insurgent organization normally consists of five elements, namely leaders, guerrillas, underground, auxiliaries, and mass base.[97] The four non-combatant categories are defined as follows:

Leaders provide direction to the insurgency. They are the 'idea people' and the planners. [...] Generally, they convey the ideology of the insurgency into objectives and direct the military efforts of the guerrillas.[98]

The underground is a cellular organization of active supporters of the insurgency [...]. They are more engaged than the auxiliaries are and may at times be guerrillas, if they use weapons or conduct combat operations. [...] Members of the underground often continue in their normal positions in society, but lead second, clandestine lives for the insurgent movement. [...] The underground may: Spread propaganda; Support sabotage, assassination and subversion; Support intelligence and counterintelligence operations; Run safe houses; Provide transportation; Manufacture and maintain arms and explosives.[99]

[...] Auxiliaries are active sympathizers who provide important logistical services but do not directly participate in combat operations. If they participate in guerrilla activities, they become guerrillas. [...] Examples of support that auxiliaries provide include: Store weapons and supplies; perform courier operations; provide passive intelligence collection; give early warning of counterinsurgent movements; acquire funds from lawful and unlawful sources; provide forged or stolen documents; promote and facilitate desertion of security forces; recruit and screen new members; create and spread propaganda; provide medical support; manufacture and maintain equipment.[100]

The mass base consists of the population of the state who are sympathetic to the insurgent movement. [...] This mass base, by default, passively supports the insurgency. As occasions arise, they may provide active support. [...][101]

Most relevant for the present discussion, however, is the description of guerillas (combatants) and of certain activities associated with combatant function:

A guerrilla is any insurgent who uses a weapon of any sort and does the actual fighting for the insurgency. They may conduct acts of terror, guerrilla warfare, criminal activities, or conventional operations. They are often mistaken for the movement or insurgency itself; but they are merely the foot soldiers of the movement or insurgency [...].[102]

[96] US FMI 3-24.2: *Tactics in Counterinsurgency*, Preface.
[97] US FMI 3-24.2: *Tactics in Counterinsurgency*, Chapter 2.II.
[98] US FMI 3-24.2: *Tactics in Counterinsurgency*, Chapters 2–4.
[99] US FMI 3-24.2: *Tactics in Counterinsurgency*, Chapters 2–9.
[100] US FMI 3-24.2: *Tactics in Counterinsurgency*, Chapters 2–10.
[101] US FMI 3-24.2: *Tactics in Counterinsurgency*, Chapters 2–11.
[102] US FMI 3-24.2: *Tactics in Counterinsurgency*, Chapters 2–7.

Guerrillas may continue in their normal positions in society and lead clandestine lives for the insurgent movement. Guerrillas tend to organize themselves based upon the activity they will be conducting. Those focused on using terrorism usually operate individually or in small cells and are often armed with explosives instead of weapons.[103]

In sum, the Field Manual on Tactics in Counterinsurgency makes clear that there are several levels of support for an insurgent party to the conflict, which range from general and political support to movement leadership, and that only persons assuming actual fighting function are regarded as combatants (guerrillas).

(e) Generic use of the term 'combatant' for all persons subject to lawful attack

As has been shown above, the ICRC's study on customary IHL comes to the conclusion that, even in situations of non-international armed conflict, '[t]he parties to the conflict must at all times distinguish between civilians and combatants. Attacks may only be directed against combatants. Attacks must not be directed against civilians'.[104] The study emphasizes that the term combatant in this rule is used in its generic meaning, that is to say, that it does not imply an entitlement to combatant privilege or POW-status but describes persons who do not enjoy civilian protection against attack.[105] According to this interpretation, the notion of combatant would not only include members of state armed forces and organized armed groups (regular and functional combatants), but also civilians directly participating in hostilities. While the terminology chosen by the ICRC is perfectly justified in the generic context in which it is used, it should not be misunderstood as a technical definition of combatancy. The danger of using the term 'combatant' in this expansive sense is that it implies a continuous status or function. Describing civilians directly participating in hostilities as 'combatants', therefore, is likely to lead to their targeting not only while they are actually carrying out an act amounting to direct participation in hostilities, but even in the interval between specific hostile acts. This would be contrary to customary and treaty IHL, according to which civilians lose protection against direct attack only 'for such time as they take a direct part in hostilities'.[106] The description of civilians directly participating in hostilities as combatants also contradicts the very formulation of the principle of distinction, according to which civilians and combatants must be mutually exclusive categories. It

---

[103] US FMI 3-24.2: *Tactics in Counterinsurgency*, Chapters 2–8.
[104] Customary Law Study, vol 1, Rule 1.
[105] Customary Law Study, vol 1, Commentary Rule 1, 3. See also the definitions of 'fighters' and 'civilians' in Section 1.1 of the International Institute of Humanitarian Law, Manual on the Law of Non-International Armed Conflict (San Remo Manual), 2006: 1.1.2. Fighters: 'a. […] fighters are members of armed forces and dissident armed forces or other organized armed groups, or taking an active (direct) part in hostilities. b. Medical and religious personnel of armed forces or groups, however, are not regarded as fighters and are subject to special protection unless they take an active (direct) part in hostilities'. 1.1.3. Civilians: 'Civilians are all those who are not fighters'.
[106] Article 51(3) of AP I; Art 13(3) of AP II; Customary Law Study, vol 1, Rule 6.

is therefore generally preferable to restrict the use of the term 'combatant' to state armed forces and organized armed groups and exclude civilians directly participating in hostilities.

(f) Expansive use of the term 'combatant' as a legal basis for detention

In the wake of the 9/11-attacks (2001) and the second Palestinian uprising (2000), particularly the United States and Israel have used terms such as 'unlawful combatant' or 'enemy combatant' to create categories of persons in their domestic law, which are not entitled to combatant privilege, but are subject to preventive or administrative detention or internment for security reasons (security detention).[107] This category of persons includes not only the fighting personnel of a belligerent party and civilians directly participating in hostilities, but also a wider circle of persons whose function or conduct poses a security threat without necessarily entailing loss of protection against direct attack. The use of the term 'combatant' for all persons liable to security detention is particularly dangerous because, in the conduct of hostilities, the term 'combatant' also suggests lack of protection against direct attack. The category of persons for which IHL permits detention for security reasons, however, is significantly wider than the category of persons for which IHL allows attacks. The risk associated with the misguided use of the term 'combatant' is that, in practice, it may invite the blanket use of 'capture or kill' operations or even the method of 'targeted killing' against any person perceived to pose a security risk, both of which would clearly be unlawful under IHL.

In sum, in non-international armed conflict, the category of combatant is best interpreted to include those persons whose continuous function it is to conduct hostilities on behalf of the belligerent parties, namely members (except for medical and religious personnel) of state armed forces, dissident armed forces, and other organized armed groups. Civilians, including those directly participating in hostilities, are

---

[107] See eg the US Government's position taken in: *Adel Hamlily v George W. Bush et al*, Memorandum in Support of the Government's Definition of Enemy Combatant, filed on 7 January 2009 in the US District Court for the District of Columbia, Case 1:05-cv-00763-JDB: 'At a minimum, the President's power to detain includes the ability to detain as *enemy combatants* those individuals who were part of, or supporting, forces engaged in hostilities against the United States or its coalition partners and allies. This includes individuals who were *part of or directly supporting Taliban, al-Qaida, or associated forces*, that are engaged in hostilities against the United States, its coalition partners or allies. This also includes any persons who have *committed a belligerent act or supported hostilities* in aid of enemy forces' (emphasis added). See also Israel's Law on the Internment of Unlawful Combatants (2002), which defines the term as 'a person who *has taken part in acts of hostilities* against the State of Israel, *directly or indirectly*, or who *belongs to a force* which carries out acts of hostility against the State of Israel in relation to whom the conditions bestowing the status of Prisoner of War according to International Humanitarian Law, and in particular Article 4 of the Third Geneva Convention of 12 August 1949 regarding the treatment of detainees of war are not met' (non-official translation, emphasis added).

not combatants. In terms of legal consequences, in contrast to *privileged* combatancy in international armed conflict, *functional* combatancy in non-international armed conflict does not imply immunity from prosecution for lawful acts of war. Lastly, in contrast to civilians directly participating in hostilities, functional combatants do not regain protection against direct attack between specific military engagements, but instead remain subject to direct attack for as long as they assume combatant function within the organized forces of a belligerent party.

4 DIRECT PARTICIPATION IN HOSTILITIES

A. Basic rule and absence of definition

The principle of distinction is based on the assumption that civilians do not pose a military threat and, therefore, are to be protected against direct attacks. Hostile activities by civilians run counter to this assumption and, depending on the circumstances, may require a military response. Therefore, customary and treaty IHL provide that civilians shall be protected against the effects of military operations 'unless and for such time as they directly participate in hostilities'.[108] In other words, for such time as civilians directly participate in hostilities, they may be directly attacked as if they were combatants. Contrary to combatants, however, civilians regain protection against direct attack as soon as their individual conduct no longer amounts to direct participation in hostilities. Furthermore, just like combatants, civilians directly participating in hostilities must comply with IHL and, if they fail to do so, may be liable to prosecution for war crimes.[109] Direct participation in hostilities by civilians is not, as such, prohibited under international law.[110] However, since

[108] Article 51(3) of AP I; Art 13(3) of AP II; Customary Law Study, vol 1, Rule 6. As the Israeli Supreme Court unambiguaously stated: 'As mentioned, our position is that all of the parts of article 51(3) of The First Protocol express customary international law' (Israel HCJ, *PCATI v Israel*, § 30).

[109] This follows from the case law of the Nuremberg IMT, the ICTY and the ICTR, which established that even individual civilians could commit war crimes by violating provisions of IHL applicable to international armed conflicts. It is not the *status of the perpetrator*, but the *character of the acts* and their *'nexus' to the conflict*, which are decisive in making them relevant under IHL. Nevertheless, in *Rutaganda* (Judgment of 26 May 2003), § 569f, the ICTR pointed out that, in determination whether individual conduct has a nexus to the armed conflict, '(p)articular care is needed when the accused is a non-combatant'. For a discussion of the nexus criterion see eg ICTY, Appeals Chamber, *Prosecutor v. Dragoljub Kunarac et al* Judgment of 12 June 2002, §§ 57ff; ICTY, Trial Chamber, *Prosecutor v Mitar Vasiljević* Judgment 29 November 2002, §§ 24ff.

[110] See DPH Interpretive Guidance, 83–5; R.W Gehring, 'Loss of Civilian Protections under the Forth Geneva Convention and Protocol I', XIX(1)–(2) *Military Law and Law of War Review* (1980) 11–48 at 13; J. Quéguiner, 'Direct Participation in Hostilities under International Humanitarian Law', *International Law Research Initiative Working Paper* (2003), 11; K. Watkin, 'Humans in the Cross-Hairs: Targeting and

civilians lack combatant privilege, they remain subject to prosecution not only for war crimes, but also for acts which, although not prohibited under IHL, amount to crimes under domestic law.[111]

Despite the significant consequences of direct participation in hostilities for the protection of the involved civilians, treaty IHL provides no express definition of the notion, nor can a clear interpretation be derived from state practice, international jurisprudence, or the *travaux préparatoires*.[112] It is therefore important that the meaning of the notion of direct participation in hostilities be clarified in good faith and in accordance with the ordinary meaning to be given to the terms in their context and in the light of the object and purpose of the notion within IHL.[113] This was the aim of an informal clarification process conducted by the ICRC, which involved 50 distinguished international legal experts from academic, military, governmental, and humanitarian circles, as well as from international and non-governmental organizations, and led to five expert meetings from 2003 to 2008. The process concluded in June 2009 with the publication by the ICRC of an 'Interpretive Guidance' which provides the organization's recommendations as to how IHL relating to the notion of direct participation in hostilities should be interpreted in light of the circumstances prevailing in contemporary armed conflict.[114] While the conclusions reached by the ICRC have given rise to a certain amount of academic controversy,[115] no theoretically coherent and practically viable alternative has been proposed, and even the

---

Assassination in Contemporary Armed Conflict', in D. Wippman and M. Evangelista (eds), *New Wars, New Laws? Applying the Laws of War in 21st Century Conflicts* (New York: Transnational Publishers, Inc, 2005), 137–80 at 177. None of the previous or current statutes of international criminal tribunals and courts (ie IMT, IMTFE, ICTY, ICTR, ICC, and SCSL) lists civilian direct participation in hostilities as a war crime. However, as correctly pointed out by Customary Law Study, vol 1, Commentary Rule 6, 23, 'international law does not prohibit States from adopting (i.e. domestic) legislation that makes it a punishable offence for anyone to participate in hostilities, whether directly or indirectly'.

[111] Clearly, this does not mean that such persons fall outside the law. Treaty IHL expressly establishes minimum guarantees for the protection and treatment of all persons, regardless of status, who are captured by the adversary after having directly participated in hostilities. See Art 45 of AP I and, if the nationality requirements of Art 4 GC IV are fulfilled, GC IV. Certain civilians may also be protected by GC I to III (see Arts 13 of GC I, 13 of GC II and 4 of GC III).

[112] See DPH Interpretive Guidance, 41; Customary Law Study, vol 1, Commentary Rule 6, 22; Quéguiner (n 111), 2; Gehring (n 111), 17f; M.N. Schmitt, 'The Interpretive Guidance on the Notion of Direct Participation in Hostilities: A Critical Analysis', 1 *Harvard National Security Journal* (2010) 5–44; Watkin (n 110), 140; W.H. Parks, *Memorandum EO 12333*, 6.

[113] Article 31(1) of the Vienna Convention on the Law of Treaties (1961). See also the unanimous opinion of the experts as to the need for a clarification of the notion of direct participation in hostilities in ICRC, 'Expert Meeting, Summary Report Direct Participation in Hostilities under International Humanitarian Law' (2003), 10f.

[114] DPH Interpretive Guidance, 9–11. The present author, in his function as legal adviser for the ICRC, was directly responsible for this clarification process and authored the 'Interpretive Guidance' on behalf of the ICRC. For further information and documentation concerning the ICRC's clarification process, see <http://www.icrc.org>.

[115] For supportive views see eg D.Fleck, 'Direct Participation in Hostilities by Non-state Actors and the Challenge of Compliance with International Humanitarian Law' (2010) 4 *Public Diplomacy*

sharpest critics admit that the ICRC's defining elements of direct participation in hostilities 'represent a useful step forward in understanding the notion'.[116]

B. The ICRC's interpretation

In essence, the notion of direct participation in hostilities comprises two basic components; that of 'hostilities' and that of 'direct participation' therein. While the concept of 'hostilities' refers to the collective resort by parties to an armed conflict to means and methods of warfare,[117] 'participation' refers to the individual involvement of a person in these hostilities.[118] Depending on the quality and degree of such involvement, individual participation in hostilities may be described as 'direct' or 'indirect'.[119] Direct participation refers to hostile acts carried out as part of the conduct of hostilities between parties to an armed conflict and leads to loss of protection against direct attack. Indirect participation, by contrast, may contribute to the general war effort, but does not directly harm the enemy and, therefore, does not entail loss of protection against direct attacks.

In its Interpretive Guidance, the ICRC interprets the notion of direct participation in hostilities as referring to specific acts designed to support a belligerent party by harming its enemy, either by directly causing military harm or, alternatively, by directly inflicting death, injury or destruction on protected persons or objects. More precisely, according to the ICRC's Interpretive Guidance, in order to qualify as direct participation in hostilities, a specific act must meet three cumulative requirements. First, the harm likely to result from the act must reach a certain threshold

Magazine 40–51; D. Akande, 'Clearing the Fog of War? The ICRC's Interpretive Guidance on Direct Participation in Hostilities', 59 *International and Comparative Law Quarterly* (2010) 180–92; and, depsite certain concerns, UN Special Rapporteur on extrajudicial, summary or arbitrary executions, Philip Alston, Study on Targeted Killings, 28 May 2010 (A/HRC/14/24/Add.6), 62–9. For four detailed critiques of the Interpretive Guidance and the ICRC's response thereto, see Watkin (n 88); M.N. Schmitt, 'Deconstructing Direct Participation in Hostilities: The Constitutive Elements', 42 *NYU Journal of International Law and Politics* (2010) 697–739; B. Boothby, ' "And For Such Time As": The Time Dimension to Direct Participation in Hostilities', 42 *NYU Journal of International Law and Politics* (2010) 741–68; W. Hays Parks, 'Part IX of the ICRC "Direct Participation in Hostilities" Study: No Mandate, No Expertise, and Legally Incorrect', 42 *NYU Journal of International Law and Politics* (2010) 770–830; N. Melzer, 'Keeping the Balance between Military Necessity and Humanity, a Response to Four Critiques of the ICRC's Interpretive Guidance on the Notion of Direct Participation in Hostilities', 42 *NYU Journal of International Law and Politics* (2010) 833–916.

[116] Schmitt (n 112), 43.

[117] See Art 35(1) of AP I and, similarly, Art 22 of the 1907 Hague Regulations.

[118] See Arts 43(2) of AP I; 45(1) and (3) of AP I; 51(3) of AP I; 67(1)(e) of AP I; 13(3) of AP II.

[119] As evidenced by the consistent use of the term *participent directement* in the equally authentic French versions of the relevant treaty texts, the terms 'active' (Art 3 of GC I–IV) and 'direct' (Arts 51(3), 43(2), 67(1)(e) of AP I; 13(3) of AP II) used in the English treaty texts refer to the same quality and degree of individual participation in hostilities. See also ICTR, *Prosecutor v Akayesu*, Judgment of 2 September 1998, 629.

(threshold of harm). Secondly, there must be a direct causal relation between the act and the expected harm (direct causation). Thirdly, there must be close relation between the act and the hostilities occurring between parties to an armed conflict (belligerent nexus).[120]

(i) *Threshold of harm*

For a specific act to qualify as direct participation in hostilities, the harm likely to result must attain a certain threshold. This threshold is reached, most notably, whenever the military operations or capacity of a party to an armed conflict are adversely affected, for example through the use of weapons against the armed forces, or by impeding their operations, deployments, or supplies.[121] Where no military harm is caused, the required threshold of harm can also be reached by inflicting death, injury, or destruction on persons or objects protected against direct attack.[122] For example, the shelling or bombardment of civilian residential areas, sniping against civilians, or armed raids against refugee camps may constitute participation in hostilities even though they would not necessarily cause an immediate military harm to the enemy. It should be noted that direct participation in hostilities does not require the actual materialization of harm but merely the objective likelihood that the conduct in question will result in such harm. Therefore, the relevant threshold determination must be based on 'likely' harm, that is to say, harm which may reasonably be expected to result from an act in the prevailing circumstances.[123]

(ii) *Direct causation*

Not all conduct likely to cause the required threshold of harm necessarily amounts to direct participation in hostilities. Throughout history, civilian populations have contributed to the general war effort, whether through the production and supply of weapons, equipment, food, and shelter, or through financial, administrative, and political support.[124] In order to qualify as 'direct' rather than 'indirect' participation in hostilities, however, there must be a direct causal relation between the act in question and the resulting harm.[125] In this context, direct causation should be interpreted to mean that the harm is brought about in one causal step.[126] Accordingly, acts that merely build or maintain the capacity of a party to harm its adversary in unspecified future operations do not amount to 'direct' participation in hostilities, even if they are connected to the resulting harm through an uninterrupted chain of events, and may even be indispensable to its causation, such as the production

---

[120] DPH Interpretive Guidance, 46.   [121] DPH Interpretive Guidance, 47–9.
[122] DPH Interpretive Guidance, 49–50.   [123] DPH Interpretive Guidance, 47.
[124] See also Commentary AP I and II, paras 1679 and 1945; also ICTY Appeals Chamber, *Prosecutor v Strugar*, Judgment of 17 July 2008, §§ 175–6.
[125] DPH Interpretive Guidance, 51–8. See also Commentary AP I and II, paras 1679, 1944, 4787.
[126] DPH Interpretive Guidance, 53.

of weapons and ammunition or general recruiting and training of personnel.[127] The notion of direct participation in hostilities can also include acts which cause harm only in conjunction with other acts, namely where the act in question is an integral part of a coordinated tactical operation that directly causes the required threshold of harm.[128] In addition, measures preparatory to the execution of a specific act of direct participation in hostilities, as well as the deployment to, and the return from, the location of its execution, constitute an integral part of that act.[129]

(iii) *Belligerent nexus*

In order to amount to direct participation in hostilities, the conduct of a civilian must not only be objectively likely to inflict harm that meets the first two criteria, but it must also be specifically designed to do so in support of a party to an armed conflict and to the detriment of another party (belligerent nexus).[130] Belligerent nexus relates to the objective purpose and design of an act or operation as part of the conduct of hostilities and does not necessarily have to reflect the subjective desires or intent of every participating individual.[131] Quite obviously, armed violence which is not designed to harm a party to an armed conflict, or which is not designed to do so in support of another party, cannot amount to 'participation' in hostilities taking place between these parties.[132] For example, as a general rule, civilian violence remains of a non-belligerent nature if it is used: (a) in exercise of authority over persons or territory having fallen into the power of a party to the conflict (eg the use of force against prisoners),[133] (b) as part of civil unrest against such authority (eg violent demonstrations or riots),[134] (c) in individual self-defence against violence prohibited by IHL (eg civilians defending themselves against marauding soldiers),[135] (d) during inter-civilian violence (eg uncontrolled looting due to breakdown of law and order),[136] or (e) for reasons otherwise unrelated to the conduct of hostilities (eg murder, arson or other violent crimes carried out for private motives).[137] Where armed violence lacks belligerent nexus, it remains an issue of law and order, even if it occurs in the wider context of an armed conflict. Therefore, any resort to force in

---

[127] DPH Interpretive Guidance, 52–4.   [128] DPH Interpretive Guidance, 54–5.
[129] DPH Interpretive Guidance, 65–8.
[130] DPH Interpretive Guidance, 58. The requirement of belligerent nexus refers to the relation between an act and the conduct of hostilities between the parties to an armed conflict and, therefore, is conceived more narrowly than the general nexus requirement developed in the jurisprudence of the ICTY and the ICTR as a precondition for the qualification of an act as a war crime, which refers to the relation between an act and a situation of armed conflict as a whole.
[131] DPH Interpretive Guidance, 59–60.   [132] DPH Interpretive Guidance, 59.
[133] DPH Interpretive Guidance, 61–2.   [134] DPH Interpretive Guidance, 63.
[135] DPH Interpretive Guidance, 61. Direct attacks against persons and objects protected against attack are prohibited under IHL. The use of force by civilians not exceeding what is necessary and proportionate to defend themselves or others against such unlawful attacks lacks belligerent nexus and, therefore, does not amount to direct participation in hostilities.
[136] DPH Interpretive Guidance, 63.   [137] DPH Interpretive Guidance, 60–1.

response to such violence must comply with international standards governing law enforcement operations.[138]

In the ICRC's view, the above-described requirements of threshold of harm, direct causation, and belligerent nexus, when applied in conjunction, permit a reliable distinction between activities amounting to direct participation in hostilities and activities which, although occurring in the context of an armed conflict, are not part of the conduct of hostilities between parties to that conflict and, therefore, do not entail loss of protection against direct attack within the meaning of IHL.[139]

C. Temporal scope of loss of protection

Civilians lose protection against direct attack for the duration of each specific act amounting to direct participation in hostilities.[140] Where preparatory measures and geographical deployments or withdrawals constitute an integral part of a specific hostile act, they extend the beginning and end of such an act beyond the phase of its immediate execution. This temporary loss of protection, which is designed to respond to spontaneous, sporadic, or unorganized hostile acts carried out by civilians, must be distinguished from the continuous loss of protection entailed by membership in state armed forces or organized armed groups belonging to the parties to an armed conflict. Members of such forces or groups lose protection for as long as their membership lasts, regardless of whether membership must be determined based on formal (regular state armed forces) or functional (organized armed groups) criteria.[141]

5 USE OF FORCE IN ATTACK AGAINST LEGITIMATE TARGETS

In regulating the use of force against legitimate military targets, IHL neither provides an express 'right to kill', nor does it impose a general obligation to 'capture rather than kill'. Instead, it simply refrains from providing certain categories of persons with protection against attacks, that is to say, against 'acts of violence against the adversary, whether in offence or in defence'.[142] The fact alone that a person is not protected against acts of violence, however, is not equivalent to a legal entitlement

[138] DPH Interpretive Guidance, 59.   [139] DPH Interpretive Guidance, 64.
[140] DPH Interpretive Guidance, 70–1.   [141] DPH Interpretive Guidance, 71–3.
[142] Article 41(1) of AP I.

of the adversary to kill that person without any further considerations. As will be seen, even in the conduct of hostilities, elementary considerations of humanity require that no more death, injury, or destruction be caused than is actually necessary to accomplish a legitimate purpose.[143]

From a theoretical perspective, the restrictive function of considerations of humanity can be based on three distinct legal arguments. First, in situations where operating forces exercise sufficient territorial control to carry out an arrest, the parallel applicability of human rights law arguably imposes additional restraints on the use of force even against legitimate military targets.[144] Secondly, a similar argument can be made based on a wider proportionality requirement, which constitutes a general principle of international law.[145] In contrast to the specific proportionality test stipulated by IHL for the conduct of hostilities, this general principle of proportionality balances the military advantage expected to result from an attack not only against expected incidental harm, but also against the harm likely to be inflicted on the targeted persons themselves.[146] The third approach is to derive the restrictive function of considerations of humanity directly from the fundamental principles of military necessity and humanity underlying and informing the entire normative framework of IHL.[147]

[143] According to the famous Martens clause, in cases not regulated by the law in force, both civilians and combatants remain under the protection and authority of the principles of international law derived from established custom, from the principles of humanity and from the dictates of public conscience (eg Art 1(2) of AP I; Preamble Additional Protocol II). According to the International Court of Justice, this rule constitutes an 'intransgressible' principle of customary international law, which is so fundamental to the respect of the human person that it can be derived directly from a general principle of law, namely, 'elementary considerations of humanity' (ICJ, *Nuclear Weapons Opinion*, n 4, § 78). See also the Chapter by Y. Sandoz in this volume.

[144] See eg the expert discussions recorded in: ICRC, Report DPH Expert Meeting (2006), 78ff.

[145] This argument has most recently been made by the Israeli High Court of Justice in its judgments on a particular section of the West Bank Barrier (2004) and on the Israeli policy of targeted killing (2006). In *Beit Sourik Village Council v The Government of Israel et al* (HCJ 2056/04), Judgment of 30 June 2004, § 37 the Court held: 'Proportionality is recognized today as a general principle of international law [...] From the foregoing principle springs the Principle of Humanitarian Law (or that of the law of war): Belligerents shall not inflict harm on their adversaries out of proportion with the object of warfare, which is to destroy or weaken the strength of the enemy'. Furthermore, in Israeli High Court of Justice, *The Public Committee Against Torture et al v The Government of Israel et al* (HCJ 769/02), Judgment of 13 December 2006, § 40, the Court held that 'a civilian taking a direct part in hostilities cannot be attacked at such time as he is doing so, if a less harmful means can be employed. In our domestic law, that rule is called for by the principle of proportionality. Indeed, among the military means, one must choose the means whose harm to the human rights of the harmed person is smallest. Thus, if a terrorist taking a direct part in hostilities can be arrested, interrogated, and tried, those are the means which should be employed [...]. Trial is preferable to use of force. A rule-of-law State employs, to the extent possible, procedures of law and not procedures of force'.

[146] For a more detailed discussion of this approach, see N. Melzer, 'Targeted Killing or Less Harmful Means?—Israel's High Court Judgment on Targeted Killing and the Restrictive Function of Military Necessity', 9 *Yearbook of International Humanitarian Law* (2006) 87–113.

[147] This is the view taken in DPH Interpretive Guidance, 77–82.

In the conduct of hostilities, the requirement of 'strict necessity' developed in human rights jurisprudence for the use of force in law enforcement operations is replaced by the requirement of 'military necessity', which no longer refers to the removal of an imminent threat, but to the achievement of a legitimate military purpose. Today, the principle of military necessity is generally recognized to permit 'only that degree and kind of force, not otherwise prohibited by the law of armed conflict, that is required in order to achieve the legitimate purpose of the conflict, namely the complete or partial submission of the enemy at the earliest possible moment with the minimum expenditure of life and resources'.[148] Complementing the principle of military necessity is the principle of humanity, which 'forbids the infliction of suffering, injury or destruction not actually necessary for the accomplishment of legitimate military purposes'.[149] In conjunction, the principles of military necessity and of humanity could be said to reduce the sum total of permissible military action from that which IHL does not expressly prohibit to that which is actually necessary for the accomplishment of a legitimate military purpose in the prevailing circumstances.[150]

The kind and degree of force to be used against legitimate military targets obviously cannot be pre-determined for all conceivable military operations, but must be determined by the operating forces based on the circumstances prevailing at the relevant time and place. As a general rule, circumstances which would allow an attempt at capture, or the issuing of a warning prior to the use of military force, are

---

[148]   United Kingdom: Ministry of Defence, *The Manual of the Law of Armed Conflict* (Oxford: Oxford University Press, 2004), Section 2.2 (Military Necessity). Similar interpretations are provided in numerous other contemporary military manuals and glossaries. See eg NATO: *Glossary of Terms and Definitions (AAP-6V)*, 2-M-5; United States: Department of the Army, *Field Manual 27-10* (1956), § 3; US Department of the Navy, *The Commander's Handbook on the Law of Naval Operations*, NWP 1–14M/MCWP 5-12-1/COMDTPUB P5800.7A (2007), § 5.3.1, 5–2; France: Ministry of Defence, *Manuel de Droit des Conflits Armés* (2001), 86f; Germany: Federal Ministry of Defence, *Triservice Manual ZDv 15/2: Humanitarian Law in Armed Conflicts* (August 1992), § 130; Switzerland: Swiss Army, *Regulations 51.007/IV, Bases légales du comportement à l'engagement* (2005), § 160. Historically, the modern notion of 'military necessity' has been strongly influenced by the definition provided in Art 14 of the Lieber Code (United States: *Adjutant General's Office, General Orders No 100*, 24 April 1863).

[149]   United Kingdom, *Manual of the Law of Armed Conflict* (n 148), Section 2.4 (Humanity). Although no longer in force, see also the formulation provided in: United States: Department of the Air Force, *Air Force Pamphlet, AFP 110–31* (1976), §§ 1–3(2), 1–6. Thus, as far as they aim to limit death, injury, or destruction to what is actually necessary for legitimate military purposes, the principles of military necessity and of humanity do not oppose, but mutually reinforce, each other. Only once military action can reasonably be regarded as necessary for the accomplishment of a legitimate military purpose, do the principles of military necessity and humanity become opposing considerations which must be balanced against each other as expressed in the specific provisions of IHL.

[150]   DPH Interpretive Guidance (n 39), 79. See also the determination of the International Court of Justice that the prohibition on the use of means and methods of warfare of a nature to cause unnecessary suffering to combatants constitutes an intransgressible principle of international customary law and a cardinal principle of IHL, which outlaws the causation of 'harm greater than that unavoidable to achieve legitimate military objectives' (ICJ, *Nuclear Weapons Opinion*, n 4, § 78). Further: Commentary AP I and II, para 1395.

more likely to arise in territory over which the operating forces exercise effective control.[151] This may be the case, for example, where an unarmed adversary or civilian is observed while transmitting targeting information, marking targets on the ground, transporting ammunition to a firing position, or sabotaging military installations, always provided that the circumstances are such that the persons in question could be confronted and arrested without additional risk to the operating forces or the surrounding civilian population.[152] In sum, while military forces certainly cannot be required to take additional risks for themselves or the civilian population in order to capture an armed adversary alive, it would defy basic notions of humanity to shoot to kill an adversary or to refrain from giving him or her an opportunity to surrender where the circumstances are such that there manifestly is no necessity for the application of lethal force.[153]

6 CONCLUDING OBSERVATIONS

Although the principle of distinction between civilians and combatants remains the undisputed cornerstone of IHL, its practical application in contemporary armed conflicts has become increasingly difficult. Factors such as the growing asymmetry of military confrontations, the intermingling of armed actors with the civilian population, the privatization of military and security functions, and the increasing involvement of civilians in the conduct of hostilities put considerable strain on the ability of belligerents to properly distinguish between legitimate military targets and protected persons. Despite the resulting confusion and uncertainty, however, the military rationale and the humanitarian imperative underlying the principle of distinction have not lost their validity. To ensure the principle's continued operability in the face of current challenges, care must be taken not to seek refuge in one-sided simplifications. Instead, what is needed is a sober and disciplined analysis of the circumstances prevailing in contemporary armed conflicts in conjunction with a careful interpretation of longstanding legal concepts in line with the delicate balance between military necessity and humanity underlying and informing IHL as a whole.

---

[151] DPH Interpretive Guidance, 80–1.

[152] See also the expert discussions recorded in: ICRC, Report DPH Expert Meeting (2006), 65.

[153] DPH Interpretive Guidance (n 39), 82. During a series of expert meetings conducted by the ICRC, the proposition that the force permissible against legitimate targets is subject not only to express restrictions imposed on specific means and method of warfare, but also to a general requirement of military necessity, remained highly controversial. For an overview of the relevant discussions, see ICRC, Report DPH Expert Meeting (2004), 17ff; ICRC, Report DPH Expert Meeting (2005), 31f, 44ff, 50, 56f, 67; ICRC, Report DPH Expert Meeting (2006), 74–9; ICRC, Report DPH Expert Meeting (2008), 7–32.

CHAPTER 13

....

PROPORTIONALITY IN THE LAW OF ARMED CONFLICT

....

ENZO CANNIZZARO

1 INTRODUCTION

....

PROPORTIONALITY has long been a mysterious topic in international law. Its critics have tended to highlight its inherent indeterminacy and the subjective character of its assessment. They argue that this indeterminacy undermines the capacity of rules based on proportionality to define a predictable frame of reference for state conduct. Nonetheless, proportionality is over time becoming a constant presence in the international legal landscape. It is frequently referred to in legal scholarship and case law as a useful legal device, capable of explaining the functioning of an ever-increasing number of international rules.

The reasons for this success are manifold. First, proportionality offers an alternative model of law-making. In the classical model, general and abstract rules are based on a predetermined balance of values and interests that are presumed to remain stable over time. These rules consequently determine the conduct to be pursued, or the result to be achieved, and they distribute rights and duties accordingly. The change of the predetermined balance of interests entails the need to change the rule.

A different model is the one based on proportionality. This alternative model applies to situations in which a number of different interests entitled to legal protection can be identified but cannot be *a priori* composed in a predetermined behavioural scheme. Rather, the various interests and values at stake can be combined according to a potentially infinite range of possible combinations, each for the potentially infinite range of concrete situations in which the legal rule can apply. It is from this combination, to be applied on a case-by-case basis, that concrete rules of conduct will ultimately emerge.

This changing balance of interests requires unusual capacities for a legal rule, in particular the capacity to adapt its content to the specific features of every single case: a property at odds with the structured theoretical character of legal rules. Whereas in the classical model the normative content is determined directly by the rule, in the case of proportionality the normative content emerges, rather, from a secondary process of law-making based on the assessment of proportionality.

A further reason that accounts for the extraordinary success of proportionality probably lies in the structural deficiencies of the process of change to international rules. Rules based on proportionality incorporate a mechanism that adapts their content to the evolving legal environment. By referring to a plurality of values and interests to be conveniently composed as each new case arises, rules based on proportionality are therefore not immutable over time. Rather, they change their content in correspondence with the changing content of the values and interests they refer to, and in correspondence with changes in their respective importance in the international community. In other words, proportionality can be seen as a law-making process that continuously adapts the content of the rule to changing social needs, circumventing the complexities of the rules of change in the international legal order.[1]

2 PROPORTIONALITY AS A FORM OF LEGAL CONTROL OF ARMED CONFLICTS

These virtues of proportionality make it a normative device particularly appropriate to the law of armed force.[2] This is a highly politically sensitive field where states are particularly reluctant to accept strict rules imposing objective forms of control.

---

[1] See E. Cannizzaro, *Il principio della proporzionalità nell'ordinamento internazionale* (Milan: Giuffrè, 2000), 429ff; T.M. Franck, 'On Proportionality of Countermeasures in International Law', 102 *American Journal of International Law* (2008) 715–67.

[2] For a specific study on the role and contents of proportionality in the law of armed conflict, see J. Gardam, *Necessity, Proportionality and the Use of Force by States* (Cambridge: Cambridge

Moreover, this field presents itself as a permanent ground of confrontation among competing interests and values: the interests of states to pursue their military objectives free from restraint, on the one hand; and humanitarian and other individual, collective and even universal interests, on the other hand. The precise identification of permitted conduct can therefore hardly be determined in the abstract. It emerges from the combination of a plurality of competing interests whose respective weight must be determined with specific reference to facts and circumstances existing on a given moment.[3] To determine the rules governing the conduct of military hostilities thus becomes an impossible exercise of law-making. It might thus prove to be impossible to encapsulate, in detailed legal rules, all the infinite situations in which states employ armed force. Recourse to rules based on proportionality thus makes it possible to cover an ample spectrum of conduct in a relatively small number of quite simple rules, which, moreover, evolve over time in correspondence to the development of social custom.

The purpose of this Chapter is to reappraise legally the notion of proportionality in humanitarian law (*ius in bello*), by itself and in its relations with the law governing the resort to the use of armed force (*ius ad bellum*). The relationship between the rules that determine the legality of the use of force and those which tend to impose restraints on military action, presents an interesting object of analysis and a litmus test for assessing the future development of the law of armed conflict.

This purpose also dictates the structure of the Chapter and explains the unequal space devoted respectively to *ius in bello* and *ius ad bellum*. The following two sections will separately analyse the structure and content of proportionality in *ius in bello*, and in *ius ad bellum*. The final section will be devoted to the role of proportionality in the relationship between the two regimes.

University Press, 2004). For detailed reference to proportionality in the frame of recent overall analysis on the law governing the use of force, see Y. Dinstein, *War, Aggression and Self-Defence* (5th edn, Cambridge: Cambridge University Press, 2011); C. Gray, *International Law and the Use of Force by States* (3rd edn, Oxford: Oxford University Press, 2008); O. Corten, *The Law Against Force: The Prohibition on the Use of Force in Contemporary International Law* (Oxford: Hart, 2010).

[3] Although sometimes referred to as a unitary normative tool, proportionality seems rather to be a general scheme, which includes a number of different techniques having as a common denominator the power of a state to determine the appropriate balance among a plurality of competing interests. In particular, a distinction must be drawn between two categories of rules: on the one hand, those rules which predetermine a dominant interest, which takes priority over other competing interests upon condition that this does not entail excessive damages to other competing values and interests and, on the other hand, those rules which refer to a plurality of competing interests, none of which taking priority over the other, which must be conveniently composed taking into account the circumstances of each specific situation.

3 PROPORTIONALITY IN *IUS IN BELLO*

A. Proportionality in symmetrical legal relations

The basic reference for proportionality in *ius in bello* is given by Articles 51(5)(b), and 57(2) of Additional Protocol I to the four Geneva Conventions of 1949.[4]

The first provision tends to complete the rules established in the other provisions contained in Article 51, which prohibit indiscriminate attacks against civilians. Article 51(5)(b) regards as 'indiscriminate' not only attacks directed against civilians and attacks that do not distinguish between military and civilian objectives, but also attacks directed against military objectives which cause disproportionate collateral damage. These are attacks 'which may be expected to cause incidental loss of civilian life, injury to civilians, damage to civilian objects, or a combination thereof, which would be excessive in relation to the concrete and direct military advantage anticipated'.[5]

Article 57(2)(a)(iii) and (b) lay down a detailed regime for belligerents in their decision to launch attacks likely to produce disproportionate collateral damage to civilians or civilian objects. The first makes it necessary to consider the proportionality between military advantage expected and prospective collateral damage in making the decision to launch an attack. The second imposes an obligation to consider proportionality also in the successive phase in which the decision has already been taken or the attack has already been launched. Attacks planned or being carried out must be respectively cancelled or suspended if they might be expected to cause excessive loss or damage.

From these two provisions, commonly considered part of customary law,[6] we can gather important information on the structure of the rule and, therefore, on the standard of proportionality.

First, they draw a link between interests equally entitled to legal protection: the need of the combatants to perform military action and the need of non-combatants to remain unaffected by the pursuit of hostilities. Since neither of them takes clear priority over the other, the balance must be struck among interests of equal rank. Belligerents do not enjoy complete freedom to determine the goal of their action and the means to attain it. Nor are humanitarian interests entitled to claim absolute immunity from damages arising from military operations. The degree and forms of

---

[4] There are also other rules of *ius in bello* incorporating reference to a technique of proportionality. See Additional Protocol I, Arts 35 and 51(5).

[5] Additional Protocol I, Art 57(2)(a)(iii).

[6] For a detailed analysis of international practice, see J.-M. Henckaerts and L. Doswald-Beck (eds), *Customary International Humanitarian Law*, vol II, part 1 (Cambridge: Cambridge University Press, 2005), 297ff.

the protection accorded to either interest strictly depend on the prejudice that this protection might inflict upon the other.

This observation is theoretically interesting, as it shows that proportionality in *ius in bello* does not include a previous assessment of necessity.[7] This is easily explained. In the classical *ius in bello* conception, belligerents do have an unfettered discretion to use force to overcome the defence of their respective enemy. In other words, in *ius in bello*, unlike in *ius ad bellum*, the use of force is not functionally linked to the achievement of a pre-determined goal. Belligerents do not possess a functional power to use force, but a fully-fledged right. This right is only curtailed by the competing rights of civilians to remain distinct from military objectives. Proportionality is thus a tool that determines the conditions of exercise of two competing and equally ranking rights.

In practical terms, the right to pursue a military attack depends upon the tolerability of the rights of the civilians to remain unaffected by military operation, namely upon proportionality, to be assessed prospectively, on the basis of the prognostic military advantage to be gained with the attack and the presumed damage it might cause.[8]

A second observation, of a systemic character, is that the duty to balance military gains expected with prospective collateral damage is also subjectively symmetrical since it is equally incumbent upon both sides, regardless of any inquiry upon the legality of their ultimate goal. As explained above, proportionality in *ius in bello* has no regard for the reasons which led a state to use force but only concerns the specific objective of each military action. None of the actors involved can claim to be exempted from this balance of interests on the basis of any alleged moral or legal superiority.

---

[7] For a discussion on the role of necessity in *ius in bello* and for its distinction from necessity as part of the proportionality equation, see Gardam (n 2), 7ff.

[8] The idea that the assessment of proportionality only requires the military commander to minimize the collateral damage deriving from the attack is inconsistent with the balancing philosophy of Arts 57(2)(a)(iii) and (b). The idea that a military commander has unfettered power to achieve a military objective has the effect of radically transforming proportionality into a standard of necessity. Instead of accommodating equally ranking competing interests, proportionality would have the more limited function to prohibit unnecessary collateral damage. See the decision of the ICTY, *Prosecutor v Galić*, IT-98-29-T, Appeal Judgment, 30 November 2006, § 190: 'One of the fundamental principles of international humanitarian law is that civilians and civilian objects shall be spared as much as possible from the effects of hostilities. This principle stems from the principles of distinction and the principle of protection of the civilian population, "the cardinal principles contained in the text constituting the fabric of humanitarian law", constituting "intransgressible principles of international customary law". According to the principle of distinction, warring parties must at all times distinguish between the civilian population and combatants, between civilian and military objectives, and accordingly must direct attacks only against military objectives. These principles establish an absolute prohibition on the targeting of civilians in customary international law, but they do not exclude the possibility of legitimate civilian casualties incidental to the conduct of military operations. However, those casualties must not be disproportionate to the concrete and direct military advantage anticipated before the attack (the principle of proportionality)'. For a different view, see S. Estreicher, 'Privileging Asymmetric Warfare (Part II)?: The "Proportionality" Principle under International Humanitarian Law', *Chicago Journal of International Law* 12.

B. Objective vs. subjective proportionality

By nature, proportionality is an objective standard. There would be no use in requiring a state to consider humanitarian interests in the pursuit of its military objectives if the balance of interests could be struck according to the state's subjective perception.

There are obvious difficulties, however, in determining which standards apply for measuring the relative weight of highly heterogeneous interests such as, on the one hand, the military advantage expected from an attack and, on the other hand, prospective damages to humanitarian values. This is quite a complex logical operation, which entails the need to determine in advance what can be objectively considered a reasonable cost for the achievement of a military goal.

Protocol I provides some methodological guidance. Both Article 51(5) and 57(2) refer to the objectives of each individual attack. The idea that a higher humanitarian toll is more acceptable in the light of the overall strategic goals of military campaign is at odds with the conceptual structure of the proportionality assessment since the degree of protection of humanitarian values would vary—and indeed, considerably— in relation to the long-term objective of a military campaign.

But even confined to an assessment in the context of each military action, proportionality still remains a difficult exercise of combining competing interests. Under which conditions is an attack against a military installation located within an inhabited area to be regarded as proportionate? How can the military importance of the installation and the likely humanitarian damage be weighed against each other?

Neither international practice nor case law provides definite answers. The logic of proportionality seems to entail that relatively minor and indirect expected military advantages cannot justify massive casualties among civilians. However, in its decision of 20 December 2006, the Supreme Court of Israel, while identifying proportionality as the proper standard for measuring on a case-by-case basis the legality of targeted killings in the light of the military importance of the killing and of the likely collateral damage,[9] abstained from identifying appropriate tests.

---

[9] Supreme Court of Israel sitting as the High Court of Justice, *The Public Committee against Torture in Israel and Others v The Government of Israel and Others*, HCJ 769/02, Judgment of 13 December 2006, § 46: 'Take the usual case of a combatant, or of a terrorist sniper shooting at soldiers or civilians from his porch. Shooting at him is proportionate even if as a result, an innocent civilian neighbor or passerby is harmed. That is not the case if the building is bombed from the air and scores of its residents and passersby are harmed'. In the same paragraph, the Court went on to say: 'The state's duty to protect the lives of its soldiers and civilians must be balanced against its duty to protect the lives of innocent civilians harmed during attacks on terrorists'. In spite of the intuitiveness of this statement, it does seem fully correct. The proper test for measuring the proportionality of collateral damages to civilians under Protocol I, indeed, is the 'military advantage' test. Whereas belligerents tend comprehensibly to minimize the risk for their own soldiers, this element does not come into consideration as a balancing factor and it cannot justify a higher level of casualties among 'innocent civilians'. This issue will be further discussed below in the text.

Absent substantive quantitative tests, an important role must be assigned to the procedure to be followed for measuring the relative importance of the diverse values at stake. In this regard, two issues emerge from recent practice.

The first concerns the perspective from which the various interests at stake must be evaluated and balanced against each other. Is that a subjective assessment, to be conducted by the acting agent with the best means at his disposal in the factual conditions in which the assessment is performed, or is it rather an objective assessment, entailing the use of best practices and the gathering of all the pertinent information?

The difference between the two options reveals different conceptions of proportionality. The best example comes from so-called aerial war. On a number of occasions, belligerents tended to justify excessive collateral damages caused by high altitude bombing with the difficulty of the agent, acting from a height adequate to ensure his safety, to assess the situation on the ground. A different assessment could have been made by the agent only at the cost of exposing himself to a higher risk: an impossible condition in the opinion of the supporters of the subjective test.[10]

This example clearly shows the philosophical dilemma between the underlying options: does the safety of the agent enter into account in the balancing of interests, and can it make the attack proportionate? In other words, is the agent entitled to minimize his own risk, and therefore to assess the proportionality of the attack from a perspective which guarantees to his person the highest degree of safety, or is the agent rather compelled to expose himself to a reasonable amount of risk in order to objectively assess the proportionality of the risk incumbent upon civilians and civilian objects?

This theoretical dichotomy has considerable implications in practice. What is the amount of information necessary to decide to launch an attack against a dual use building suspected of hosting a military unit? Is the agent justified to act on the basis of summary information on the presumed absence of civilians, or should he endanger himself, and also the success of the operation, with an effort to gather more accurate information on the ground? Which is to be preferred in such a situation: the safety of civilians, or the life of the agent and the success of the operation?

The scant available evidence of practice does not definitively uphold either of these two options. On the one hand, a certain indulgence emerges for the agents who minimized the risk for their own safety, even at the cost of increasing the imprecision of the calculation of prospective damage for civilians and, therefore, of transferring the higher risk on to them.[11]

---

[10] See the Report of the United Nations Fact-Finding Mission on the Gaza Conflict, *Human Rights in Palestine and Other Occupied Arab Territories* (Goldstone Report), UN Doc A/HRC/12/48, 25 September 2009, § 1888.

[11] This view emerges from certain conclusions adopted by the Final Report to the Prosecutor by the Committee Established to Review the NATO Bombing Campaign Against the Federal Republic of Yugoslavia subsequently endorsed by the ICTY Prosecutor in 1998. The Committee was set up to review the consistency with humanitarian law of the actions carried out in the course of the NATO

The subjective approach seems to have been further stretched, becoming infused with a radical relativism, by the Eritrea–Ethiopia Claims Commission in its Partial Award, Central Front, with regard to Ethiopia's Claim 2, handed down within the context of a wider dispute between Ethiopia and Eritrea on 28 April 2004. The decision is pervaded by the idea that proportionality must be assessed in the light of the personal conditions of the acting agent, even if these conditions relate to inexperience or, perhaps, even ineptitude.[12]

A different course has been taken in other circumstances. There is a certain agreement that proportionality must be assessed from the perspective of the 'reasonable commander', a notion which on the one hand tends to locate the assessment of proportionality with the subjective situation of the agent, but on the other hand seems to require an objective degree of diligence.[13] The standard of the reasonable commander was also adopted by the Israeli Supreme Court in its decision of the lawfulness of targeted killings mentioned earlier. Whereas in some passages the idea seems to emerge that proportionality must be assessed

bombing campaigns in the former Yugoslavia. From the report, the idea seems to emerge that that proportionality of targeting a military objective from a bomber flying from a high altitude must be assessed from the viewpoint of the acting agent. The report also seems to support the idea that casualties caused by high-altitude bombers flying above the range of air-defence systems on the ground were proportionate inasmuch as the resulting damage could not, precisely because of the high altitude, be envisaged by the aircrew. The suggestion seems to rest on the premise that the decision to maximize the security of the military personnel aboard is beyond the reach of proportionality. Consequently, proportionality is not violated even if it were proven that a different strategy of attack would have allowed a better calculation of the ratio between the humanitarian cost and military benefits of the action.

[12] Partial Award, Central Front, Ethiopia's Claim 2, The Hague, 28 April 2004, § 110: 'the Commission believes that the governing legal standard for this claim is best set forth in Article 57 of Protocol I, the essence of which is that all feasible precautions to prevent unintended injury to protected persons must be taken in choosing targets, in the choice of means and methods of attack and in the actual conduct of operations. The Commission does not question either the Eritrean Air Force's choice of Mekele airport as a target, or its choice of weapons. Nor does the Commission question the validity of Eritrea's argument that it had to use some inexperienced pilots and ground crew, as it did not have more than a very few experienced personnel. The law requires all "feasible" precautions, not precautions that are practically impossible'.

[13] See Prosecutor v Galić (n 8), § 58: 'One type of indiscriminate attack violates the principle of proportionality. The practical application of the principle of distinction requires that those who plan or launch an attack take all feasible precautions to verify that the objectives attacked are neither civilians nor civilian objects, so as to spare civilians as much as possible. Once the military character of a target has been ascertained, commanders must consider whether striking this target is "expected to cause incidental loss of life, injury to civilians, damage to civilian objectives or a combination thereof, which would be excessive in relation to the concrete and direct military advantage anticipated." If such casualties are expected to result, the attack should not be pursued. The basic obligation to spare civilians and civilian objects as much as possible must guide the attacking party when considering the proportionality of an attack. In determining whether an attack was proportionate it is necessary to examine whether a reasonably well-informed person in the circumstances of the actual perpetrator, making reasonable use of the information available to him or her, could have expected excessive civilian casualties to result from the attack'.

under the given conditions of time and place, the opinion of the Court and the individual opinions of its members made frequent recourse to the notion of the 'responsible agent'.[14] The same standard was adopted in the Goldstone report, from which the implication seems to be drawn that proportionality prevents shifting the entire risk onto the civilian population, but requires a reasonable share of risk to be assumed by the actors involved.[15]

The subjective approach seems to be logically at odds with the basic premise on which the proportionality assessment rests. Proportionality does not require the agent simply to be prudent and charitable. It requires his or her actions to be based on a careful apprehension of facts and on an objective balance of interests. This character would be illusory if the agent were allowed to conduct the assessment on the basis of his subjective situation. If an agent does not possess sufficient information objectively necessary to proceed to the balance of interests, he or she cannot but abstain from acting. A different conclusion would run overtly against the logic of proportionality, which is based precisely on the objective character of the balancing of interests, which entails that all the interests at stake must be properly appreciated in their factual dimension.[16]

However, the objective standard is not completely free from inconvenience. A standard which requires states to adopt the best available practice is more easily complied with by states which possess the necessary technology. Yet it might seem inappropriate to assume that proportionality imposes conditions that cannot be complied with symmetrically by all belligerents.[17] In order to be realistic, proportionality must impose requirements that can be met by every state engaged in military action, and it should be based on a reasonable balance between the aim

---

[14] In *Prosecutor v Galić* (n 8), § 57, dealing with the scope of judicial review, the Court stated that the scope of judicial review does not extend to the executive decisions of military command provided that this is a decision made by a reasonable commander: 'the question is [...] whether the decision which the military commander made is a decision that a reasonable military commander was permitted to make'. Also the Final Report to the Prosecutor by the Committee Established to Review the NATO Bombing Campaign Against the Federal Republic of Yugoslavia (see n 11) refers to the standard of the 'reasonable commander'. See, in particular, § 50.

[15] See n 10: 'The Mission recognizes fully that the Israeli armed forces, like any army attempting to act within the parameters of international law, must avoid taking undue risks with their soldiers' lives, but neither can they transfer that risk onto the lives of civilian men, women and children. The fundamental principles of distinction and proportionality apply on the battlefield, whether that battlefield is a built up urban area or an open field' (at § 1888).

[16] See, albeit in a different context, *Prosecutor v Galić* (n 8), § 51: 'In case of doubt as to whether an object which is normally dedicated to civilian purposes is being used to make an effective contribution to military action, it shall be presumed not to be so used. The Trial Chamber understands that such an object shall not be attacked when it is not reasonable to believe, in the circumstances of the person contemplating the attack, including the information available to the latter, that the object is being used to make an effective contribution to military action'.

[17] One might wonder whether the objective nature of the assessment of proportionality ends up favouring developed states, who possess sophisticate means of information, to the detriment of states which do not possess the necessary technology and which therefore must necessarily act on the basis

to protect civilians and the need to avoid exposure to excessive risk of military personnel.

The standard of the reasonable agent can appropriately balance the diverse needs respectively underlying the subjective and objective options. It does not impose excessive or impossible conditions. It also avoids the incongruence of making proportionality, and therefore the standard of security of civilians, dependent on the standard of security subjectively chosen by the military commanders or their troops. It certainly avoids the incongruence of making the standard of safety of civilians dependent upon the degree of experience or the degree of training of the military personnel.

C. Proportionality and the treatment of civilians

Asymmetric forms of warfare pose new challenges to the classical paradigm of proportionality in *ius in bello*. As seen above, this paradigm was developed with regard to conventional forms of conflict and presupposes the existence of two distinct entities, the belligerents and the civilians, each of which has a distinctive set of interests.

One may wonder whether this paradigm, and in particular the distinction between belligerents and civilians, still makes sense in new forms of conflict, erupting between military armies and irregular groups and which see an ever more active involvement of civilians.

These difficulties are epitomized by the illegitimate tactic of using civilians as human shields. This is a strategy mostly adopted by irregular militias, which consist of locating military operations in densely inhabited areas, thus making it highly problematic for the military response to comply with the principles of distinction and proportionality. The adoption of this strategy has the effect of deeply altering the symmetry in the legal position of the belligerents. Compliance with the principle of distinction and proportionality by one of the belligerents has the effect of limiting significantly the choice of the military strategies, whilst the other belligerents, namely the irregular militias, take advantage of these rules, careless of the possible harm to their own population (not to mention others).

of summary information or, alternatively, must give up the attack. However, the dichotomy between developed states, who can avail themselves of strategies which are out of the reach of developing states, appears misplaced. Proportionality does not require states to endow themselves with the most sophisticated technological equipment. It simply requires states not to launch an attack without collecting convincing evidence that the collateral damage will be proportionate to the military advantage. Thus, international law does not impose impossible requirements on states, but only requirements which can be complied with by every state which behaves in accordance with normal practice.

Not surprisingly, therefore, the idea has been put forward that, with regard to these forms of conflict, the distinction between belligerents and civilians is an obsolescent one and must be set aside.[18] Instead, the protection of civilians should be graduated according to the degree of their involvement in the conflict.

The assumption that the distinction between belligerents and civilians tends to be fuzzy in asymmetric conflicts appears correct and deserves attention. From this premise, however, the consequence can hardly be drawn that this basic paradigm of humanitarian law has lost its function and must be abandoned. Indeed, humanitarian law has developed a tool that can be employed in order to cope with the involvement of civilians in warfare. Article 51(3) reads: 'Civilians shall enjoy the protection afforded by this section, unless and for such time as they take a direct part in hostilities'.

Admittedly, the protection of civilians under this provision is an all-or-nothing notion lacking the flexibility necessary to follow the nuances of various forms of partial involvement in hostilities. However, the strictness of this approach is offset by the flexibility of the standard measuring the direct involvement in hostilities, which can be conveniently adapted in order to cope with different situations on the ground. It seems to require, as a minimum, active conduct entailing military benefits, performed with a certain degree of wilful participation to the pursuit of military objectives. This standard can be reasonably deemed to meet situations in which civilians, albeit not performing activities typically conducted by military troops, are nonetheless voluntarily contributing to the military operations. It is met, for example, by civilians who voluntarily consent to act as human shields in the awareness that their presence will constitute a deterrent for military attacks. Voluntary consent, however, must be ascertainable by the other belligerent party before they take action on this basis.

To go beyond this assumption, and to conclude that the protection of civilians which do not meet the standard of direct involvement in hostilities can nonetheless be graduated in relation to their conduct appears highly controversial and potentially unsound. From this suggestion one could infer that civilians, who are or must be aware of being utilized as human shields and do not actively avoid it, must bear an additional amount of risk in consequence of their indirect support for the military operations. In order to avoid this additional amount of risk, which would make collateral damage 'more acceptable' as a consequence of their 'indirect part' in hostilities, there would need to be a new rule that civilians must refuse to be used as human shields, abandoning the zone of operations or even actively resisting the presence of the militias in inhabited areas.[19]

---

[18] See eg M. Galchinsky, 'Quaint and Obsolete: The "War on Terror" and the Right to Legal Personality', 14 in *International Studies Perspectives* (2013) 255–68.

[19] The presumption that the civilians which do not follow the warning of belligerents are exposing themselves voluntarily to risk and, consequently, are entitled to a lesser degree of protection is a *caveat*

Although suggestively fashioned, the question cannot be answered but in the negative. The idea that civilians have a positive obligation to act in order to prevent belligerents from using them as human shields has two significant setbacks.

First, it has the effect of inverting the *onus probandi* in regard to the distinction between belligerents and civilians, which is incumbent upon the former. It appears unacceptable that the burden of proof concerning the principle of distinction should rest on the person used as human shield.

Secondly, and perhaps more importantly, it has the further effect of subverting the logic of the system of protection of civilians established by *ius in bello*. To presume that civilians who remain idle are taking 'indirect' part in hostilities and must therefore accept a higher risk of collateral damage has the effect of circumventing the principle of distinction and to make them indistinguishable from military personnel. The principle of proportionality, incorporated into humanitarian law in order to enhance the protection of civilians, would be used in order to attain the inverse objective, that is, to grant belligerents the right to demand from civilians of the other party a positive action and to punish their idleness.

4 PROPORTIONALITY IN *IUS AD BELLUM*

A. The structure of the proportionality assessment in asymmetrical legal relations

A different structure applies to the assessment of proportionality in *ius ad bellum*. The basic premise of this assessment is that the aggression is unlawful conduct, which justifies an armed response. In other words, international law establishes a clear hierarchy between the interests of the two classes of actors: whilst the victim

---

canem argument which, as such, has no place in contemporary humanitarian law. In *Public Committee Against Torture v Israel*, its decision on targeted killings (see n 9), the Supreme Court of Israel reasoned in the following way: 'what is the law regarding civilians serving as a "human shield" for terrorists taking a direct part in the hostilities? Certainly, if they are doing so because they were forced to do so by terrorists, those innocent civilians are not to be seen as taking a direct part in the hostilities. They themselves are victims of terrorism. However, if they do so of their own free will, out of support for the terrorist organization, they should be seen as persons taking a direct part in the hostilities' (§ 36). Yet the problem is precisely to determine the fate of those who neither are forced to serve as human shields nor do so with the specific intent intent to contributing to the military strategies of one of the belligerents.

of aggression is entitled to legal protection, the aggressor is protected only against excessive defensive measures.

It follows that proportionality is not a technique designed to combine conflicting interests and values entitled to the same level of protection. In *ius ad bellum*, proportionality is traditionally conceived as a means to establish a relation of appropriateness between asymmetrically protected interests: the paramount interest of the attacked state to repel the armed attack, on the one hand; and an open set of other interests which might be affected by the defensive action, be they individual, collective, or universal, on the other hand.

The different function of proportionality also explains its different logical structure. In *ius ad bellum*, proportionality traditionally limits the power conferred on a state to use force unilaterally for the achievement of a predetermined end. It therefore presents the classical three-step structure that typically defines the proportionality assessment in the context of functional powers: the military response must be suitable and necessary to achieve its goal, and must not entail an excessive sacrifice of other legally protected interests.

However, there is no unanimous view in legal scholarship or in the case law on the identification of the goal of a forcible response to an armed attack. Quite the contrary: this issue was addressed by a heated scholarly debate whose terms can be broadly grouped in two major streams. A restrictive view tends to regard the need to repel the attack as the only goal of a unilateral forcible response to an armed attack.[20] According to this view, the power to use unilaterally defensive force is an exception to the general prohibition on the use of force designed to give to the attacked state the means to resist the aggression, to avoid defeat and to restore its territorial sovereignty. The definitive removal of the threat, and the permanent restoration of conditions of peace and security, is a function to be discharged through collective action. From the opposite perspective, the objectives and the scope of unilateral resort to force are broader and include aims of prevention and deterrence or, more broadly, the aim to create a safe environment for the attacked state.[21]

Although the former view seems to the current author more in accordance with practice and the logic of the system, there is no need, for the limited purposes of the present contribution, to engage in a thorough analysis of this issue. We will see that the analysis of the structure and functioning of proportionality can also contribute, to an extent, to the identification of the ultimate goal of self-defence.

---

[20]   See also for further reference, Corten (n 2), 480ff.

[21]   A thorough presentation of the theoretical foundations of this thesis is contained in Dinstein (n 2), esp 185ff.

B. Applicable standards: quantitative proportionality and qualitative proportionality

The idea that proportionality is measured by quantitative standards stems from a primitive view of proportionality as a requirement of rough quantitative equivalence between attack and defence. Equivalence, in turn, could be measured in terms of the means employed or the damage inflicted by each.

Although quite simplistic, the tendency to anchor proportionality to quantitative terms of measurement nonetheless has deep roots in the international legal thought.[22] Its success is probably due to the belief that quantitative standards are easily measurable and therefore bestow a certain degree of objectivity on the highly indeterminate standard of proportionality. In other words, objective standards might prove to limit better unilateral use of force and to reduce arbitrariness.[23]

Other reasons, however, plead for the adoption of a different standard. The most obvious is that the primary objective of the rules of *ius ad bellum* is not so much to give to the states the power to punish unlawful conduct, but rather to repel the attack or even, according to some, to prevent or deter it. If the use of lawful force were determined by recourse to a standard of equivalence, that primary goal might remain unattained.

This consideration might prompt the adoption of qualitative standards of measurement of proportionality. A qualitative approach tends to measure proportionality not by reference to equivalence between material goods, but rather by reference to the appropriateness of the means to achieve their ends. In the case of *ius ad bellum*, force is lawfully employed if it proves to be necessary and appropriate and does not unduly interfere with other interests and values.

The adoption of a qualitative standard highlights the exceptional function attributed to the unilateral use of force in contemporary international law. The use of force does not have the function of inflicting retribution on the counterpart, which could in principle be governed by a standard of equivalence. Rather, it is a means necessary to discharge the essential function of self-defence. In international law, self-defence is therefore conceived as a temporary remedy for responding to an aggressive use of force, thus complementing the function of the institutional

---

[22] See Art 51 of the International Law Commission Articles on the Responsibility of States for Internationally Wrongful Acts, UNGA Res 56/83, UN Doc A/RES/56/83, 12 December 2001, Art 51, according to which 'Countermeasures must be commensurate with the injury suffered, taking into account the gravity of the internationally wrongful act and the rights in question.'

[23] A mixed approach was taken by the International Court of Justice in *Oil Platforms (Islamic Republic of Iran v United States of America)* [2003] ICJ Rep 161, 6 November 2003. At §§ 75 and 76 the Court seems to point out that necessity and proportionality must be measured by different standards: a qualitative standard will measure the necessity of the response, whereas its proportionality should be assessed by a quantitative standard. This reasoning appears at § 77, where the Court compared the relatively minor scale of the Iranian attack alleged with the large scale of the response adopted by the United States and concluded that the response was disproportionate.

mechanism of collective security. It follows that a state acting in self-defence must have at its disposal all the means necessary to respond to an armed attack. To impose a quantitative limit of equivalence on the means employed by the attacker or on the damage inflicted would be tantamount to denying the essence of the function that the armed response is designed to serve.

This explains why proportionality in *ius ad bellum* must be measured in purely qualitative terms,[24] thus allowing the use of the means necessary and proportionate to the strategic goal of self-defence. Unlike proportionality in *ius in bello*, which looks only to the short-term goal of each military action, proportionality in *ius ad bellum* is measured against the strategic objective of self-defence.

The adoption of qualitative standards, however, does create additional questions. Beyond the rhetoric of self-defence, determining the long-term goal of military actions is a difficult exercise. States would then have an ample degree of discretion at their disposal. This degree of discretion would further increase if self-defence were considered not to be necessarily limited to create security within one's border, but as extending to the means necessary to create overall conditions of security and to remove permanently the source of threat even beyond borders.

Furthermore, a qualitative standard establishes a direct relationship between the purported objective and the means appropriate to achieve it. The appropriateness of the armed action must be measured by reference to the interest that the acting state is entitled to pursue. It follows that the level of protection of that interest, and not only the interest itself, must be determined objectively. Otherwise a paradoxical situation would arise: by setting unilaterally the level of protection of its own interest, the defending state could circumvent the limits set up by reference to a standard of proportionality. This proposition is valid whatever the ultimate objective of self-defence might be. The higher the level of protection which a state tends to secure for its defensive interest, the more extensive the set of means employed and the damage that constitutes a fair 'price' for its attainment.

This observation also seems to highlight the different functions of necessity and proportionality in *ius ad bellum*. Whereas the former tends to secure the existence of a functional link between military action and the defensive purpose, the latter has a wider scope and includes a comparison of the benefits and the costs entailed by the full achievement of that purpose. In particular, the adoption of a qualitative standard implies that not only the means of the action, but also ultimate strategic goals must be determined through a 'balance of interests' analysis.

We are thus led, through a logical analysis of proportionality, to conclude that the strategies of the state acting in self-defence cannot be determined on the basis

[24] See R. Higgins, *Problems and Process. International Law and How We Use It* (Oxford: Clarendon Press, 1994), 231: 'What marks the transition from the *ius in bello* to the *ius ad bellum* is that, in the former, the hostile act should be proportionate to the specific injury received, while in the latter the use of force should be proportionate to the legitimate objective to be achieved'.

of the state's subjective perception of the level of security needed but must be rather based on a cost-benefit analysis which must take into account, beyond the interest of the attacked state, other interests and values prospectively affected by the action in self-defence.[25] Since these interests and values are primarily, even if not exclusively, expressed by *ius in bello*, we now proceed to an analysis of the relationship between *ius ad bellum* and *ius in bello*. This analysis epitomizes the complex interplay between the security and non-security based interests that underlie the assessment of proportionality.

5 The Relationship between Proportionality in *Ius in Bello* and Proportionality in *Ius ad Bellum*

A. The independence paradigm

As noted at the beginning of this Chapter, *ius in bello* and *ius ad bellum* are traditionally regarded as two set of limits which apply fully independently of each other. Both must be complied with by belligerents, since they pertain to different situations. The victim of aggression must comply with proportionality in choosing the means to respond to the attack; both belligerents must ensure that performance of a single military action does not entail excessive collateral damage.[26]

The idea that *ius ad bellum* and *ius in bello* apply independently of each other is probably due to the historical vicissitudes of the two notions. It is common knowledge that *ius in bello* developed at a time in which, supposedly, no legal restraint was deemed to curtail the discretion of states to use force unilaterally. A further argument militating in favour of the independence of the two legal regimes derives from their antithetical logic. *Ius ad bellum* is pervaded by the idea of the moral and legal superiority of the interest of the attacked state, whereas *ius in bello* is based

[25] On this point, see the critical remarks by D. Kretzmer, 'The Inherent Right to Self-Defence and Proportionality in *Jus Ad Bellum*', in 24 *European Journal of International Law* (2013) 235–82.

[26] See *Prosecutor v Boškoski and Tarculovski*, IT-04-82-A, Appeal Judgment, 19 May 2010, esp at §§ 31, 44 and 51. At § 31, the Court said: 'The fact that a State resorted to force in self-defence in an internal armed conflict against an armed group does not, in and of itself, prevent the qualification of crimes committed therein as serious violations of international humanitarian law'. To make it even more explicit, at § 51 the Court added: 'The fact that a State is acting in lawful self-defence (*jus ad bellum*) is irrelevant for a determination as to whether a representative of this state has committed a serious violation of international humanitarian law during the exercise of the state's right to self-defence which constituted part of an armed conflict (*jus in bello*).' See also ICTY, *Prosecutor v Kordic and Cerkez*, IT-95-14/2-A, Appeal Judgment, 17 December 2004.

on the opposite premise of equal moral and equal legal legitimacy of the various interests at stake.

However, this premise is fallacious. As observed in previous sections, far from being two separate and distinct legal regimes, *ius in bello* and *ius ad bellum* continuously overlap. Proportionate action according to one sub-system might prove to be disproportionate according to the other.[27] The full achievement of the aims of one might even make more difficult, and even impossible, the achievement of the aims of the other. It might prove difficult to determine the standard to measure the proportionality of a military action aimed at destroying a missile base located in densely inhabited area. Yet, according to the standard chosen, the conclusion could drastically change. The action could appear indispensable to respond to an actual or prospective armed attack but disproportionate against the more stringent standard of protection of civilians from the perspective of *ius in bello*.

Not surprisingly, therefore, in international practice it is not uncommon for these two conceptually very different techniques of proportionality to be used interchangeably and even, in the grey area of overlap, for them to be conflated in a sort of global assessment of proportionality.[28] A word of clarification might thus be opportune.

B. Expansive vs restrictive view

According to a first option, proportionality in *ius ad bellum*, and the need to give to the attacked state the power necessary to respond to the aggression, has the effect of enlarging its discretion in determining the expected advantage of the military

---

[27] See the Final Award on Ethiopia's Damages adopted by the Ethiopia-Eritrea Claims Commission (2009). At § 316, the Commission addressed the issue of the compensation to be awarded for violations of *ius ad bellum* which did not amount to violations of *ius in bello* and found that 'if [...] a State initiating a conflict through a breach of the *jus ad bellum* is liable under international law for a wide range of ensuing consequences, the initiating State will bear extensive liability whether or not its actions respect the *jus in bello*. Indeed, much of the damage for which Ethiopia claims *jus ad bellum* compensation involves conduct that the Commission previously found to be consistent with the *jus in bello*. Imposing extensive liability for conduct that does not violate the *jus in bello* risks eroding the weight and authority of that law and the incentive to comply with it, to the injury of those it aims to protect. The Commission believes that, while appropriate compensation to a claiming State is required to reflect the severity of damage caused to that State by the violation of the *jus ad bellum*, it is not the same as that required for violations of the *jus in bello*.'

[28] In the course of the second Lebanon war, many states argued that the violation of proportionality under *ius in bello* also entailed the illegality of the intervention under *ius ad bellum*. For more specific reference, see A. Zimmermann, 'Jus ad bellum, jus in bello and the Issue of proportionality', 11 *MaxPlanck Yearbook of United Nations Law* (2007) 99–141. I refer to my writing 'Contextualizing Proportionality: *Jus ad Bellum* and *Jus in Bello* in the Lebanese War', 88 *International Review of the Red Cross* (2006) 779–92. An interesting case of conceptual overlap might be found in *Public Committee Against Torture v Israel* before the Israeli Supreme Court. At § 40 the Court said: 'Second, a civilian taking a direct part in hostilities cannot be attacked at such time as he is doing so, if a less harmful means

action. The second, and logically antithetical option is rather to use proportionality in *ius in bello* as a limit to the discretion conferred by *ius ad bellum* to the attacked state to determine its strategy of reaction.

The first option tends to highlight the impact of *ius ad bellum*, a deeply asymmetrical legal regime establishing a clear hierarchy among the belligerents, on the egalitarian legal regime of *ius in bello*. This perspective is grounded on the premise that the need to repel the attack represents the essential yardstick against which the lawfulness of every military action must be assessed. If the only means to repel the attack consists in using means or methods entailing a high number of casualties, this should be nonetheless acceptable because the only alternative would be defeat. *Salus rei publicae suprema lex esto!*

The supporters of this perspective would have at their disposal a wide range of arguments. The most insidious is a systematic argument; namely that the two sub-systems, *ius in bello* and *ius ad bellum*, must be construed consistently. Compliance with one cannot entail disregarding the other. Moreover, a logical and practical argument should also be considered. To require a state to forgo its indispensable means of defence and to submit to inexorable defeat in order to avoid excessive civilian damage might seem a morally and legally untenable proposition. No damage is excessive if the ultimate end is self-preservation.

These arguments, very seductive indeed, seem however to highlight the limits of legal analysis in situations of extreme danger. The idea that law imposes upon states confronted with an armed attack the obligation not to use disproportionate force when they have no other means to avoid the defeat is an extreme and somewhat artificial position. Indeed, it presents a situation that even the ICJ was unprepared to prejudge.[29]

---

can be employed. In our domestic law, that rule is called for by the principle of proportionality. Indeed, among the military means, one must choose the means whose harm to the human rights of the harmed person is smallest'. The Court did not unveil the source of this rule, which, interestingly, seems to apply only to civilians taking direct part in the hostilities and not to military personnel. It might be argued that such a rule derives from human rights law, which, unlike humanitarian law, requires that any deprivation of life must be based on necessity. This view was suggested in M. Milanovic, 'Norm Conflicts, International Humanitarian Law and Human Rights Law', in O. Ben-Naftali (ed), *International Humanitarian Law and International Human Rights Law* (Oxford: Oxford University Press, 2011), 95. This view seems to be upheld by a short reference to human rights law contained in the decision a few lines below. However, it is interesting to note that a similar structure also inspires the rule of proportionality in *ius ad bellum*, where a state can use force only insofar as it is necessary to repel the attack. One might plausibly assume that the notion of proportionality in *ius in bello* employed by the Supreme Court was also, if not even pre-eminently, inspired by *ius ad bellum*. This would be a case in which a standard of proportionality in *ius ad bellum* also has the effect of limiting proportionality in *ius in bello*. Indeed, classical humanitarian law seems to accord to the belligerents a full-blown right to kill the enemy, be it a regular soldier or a civilian actively involved in the conduct of hostilities, only limited by an obligation to avoid unnecessary suffering.

[29]   See the famous finding of the International Court of Justice in its Advisory Opinion on the *Legality of the Threat or Use of Nuclear Weapons* [1996] ICJ Rep 226, 8 July 1996: 'In view of the current state of international law, and of the elements of fact at its disposal, the Court cannot conclude definitively whether the threat or use of nuclear weapons would be lawful or unlawful in an extreme circumstance of self-defence, in which the very survival of a State would be at stake' (*Dispositif*, § 2E).

Much more frequent is the situation in which a self-defending state has at its disposal a number of strategies of defence which combine, in different measures, humanitarian and security interests: from those giving paramount or exclusive importance to security objectives to those which accept that the level of security sought by a state acting in self-defence also depends upon humanitarian needs.

The difference is easily understood. In the first option, humanitarian values are protected only incidentally, to the extent that might prove possible without impairing the full attainment of the primary goal of self-defence. Thus, for example, a state can use all the means at its disposal to remove a source of insecurity, such as a group of irregulars performing raids across its borders, even if the attainment of this goal entails a high number of casualties. In the second option, the requirement of self-defence and humanitarian interests must be balanced against each other in order to determine their appropriate combination. In the example referred to above, the primary goal of permanently removing this source of threat becomes legally unattainable, and the state must tolerate a certain degree of instability across its borders if the full attainment of security entails excessive collateral damage to civilians.

The first solution, which corresponds to the expansive option, has the effect of giving the defending state the power to determine unilaterally the degree of protection of its security. By elevating the standard of its own security, that state can correspondingly diminish the standard of security imposed by humanitarian law. The effectiveness of humanitarian law would be sacrificed on the altar of the protection accorded by *ius ad bellum* to the attacked state.

The second perspective is one that tends to include the assessment of proportionality in *ius in bello* as part of the assessment of proportionality in *ius ad bellum*. This would imply that proportionality is not only a technique curtailing the discretion of a state in the choice of the means designed to achieve the objective of military action. Its primary function seems, rather, to limit the appropriate standard of protection of the interest of the attacked state to act in self-defence.[30]

By nature, proportionality can offer a suitable means to reconcile the apparently disparate requirements of *ius in bello* and *ius ad bellum*. More precisely, the proportionality in *ius in bello* can be regarded as part of proportionality in *ius ad bellum* insofar as it helps to determine the appropriate balance of interests underlying the adoption of a defensive strategy by the attacked state. If the achievement of that standard subjectively sought by the defender prospectively entails too many casualties, it must be abandoned and a new standard, guaranteeing a lower level

---

[30] The consideration that lack of proportionality of *ius in bello* can also affect the proportionality of the action under *ius ad bellum* also seems to emerge from the Report of the Secretary-General's Panel of Inquiry on the 31 May 2010 Flotilla Incident (September 2011), concerning the legality of the attack carried out by the Israeli navy on certain neutral vessels which attempted to reach Gaza past the sea blockade. See, in particular, §§ 69ff and 77ff. See also Appendix I to the Report: The Applicable International Legal Principles.

of security at a much lesser humanitarian cost, must be adopted. *Salusreipublicae* must be balanced with humanitarian values and other collective values that have emerged in contemporary international law.

6 Conclusions: Towards a Common Standard of Proportionality in the Law of Armed Conflict?

The analysis undertaken in the previous sections seems to suggest a unitary notion of proportionality in the law of armed conflict. Proportionality rules out measures which are unnecessary or unsuitable to achieve the legitimate aim of forcible action, or which entail excessive or inappropriate sacrifice to other competing values and interests. Measures which do not pursue a legitimate end, such as those involving use of force short of self-defence, or measures which, while pursuing a legitimate end, nonetheless entail excessive collateral damages, are unlawful, albeit for different reasons and to different degrees.

Proportionality not only represents a flexible tool capable of establishing an objective standard of measurement of unilateral use of force. It also serves as a tool that connects *ius in bello* and *ius ad bellum*. Each of these regimes has its own scope and has developed a substantive and procedural test for assessing the proportionality of armed actions. However, experience has proven that neither regime is self-contained. It is common to find that the one refers to the other in order to provide for a comprehensive evaluation of proportionality. Thus, far from constituting fully independent legal regimes, *ius in bello* and *ius ad bellum* may be regarded as constituting sub-systems of a basic but comprehensive system of rules governing the use of force.

This assumption confirms the prevailing opinion that the proportionality of the use of force under one of the two regimes does not condone disproportionality under the other.[31] Thus, compliance with humanitarian law does not condone the illegality of aggressive action and, vice versa, the defensive character of forcible action does not grant immunity under *ius in bello*.

---

[31] See C.J. Tams and J.G. Devaney, 'Applying Necessity and Proportionality to Anti-Terrorist Self-Defence', 45 *Israel Law Review* (2012) 91–106.

Beyond these obvious conclusions, however, there are other implications. This contribution has dealt mainly with the impact of *ius in bello* on the balancing of values underlying the assessment of proportionality in *ius ad bellum*. The conclusion has been drawn that *ius in bello* requires a state acting in self-defence to consider the humanitarian cost of the prospective actions before adopting a defensive strategy. This strategy should balance the various interests at stake: the interest in responding effectively to armed attacks, on the one hand, and other individual, collective, or universal interests presumably to be affected by the defensive action, on the other hand.

A different line of research could be undertaken with a view to examining the potential impact of *ius ad bellum* on the assessment of proportionality in *ius in bello*. In particular, a comprehensive assessment of proportionality might bridge the gap consisting in the absence of a requirement of necessity in *ius in bello*. This makes it possible for belligerents to decide to launch attacks causing unnecessary loss among military personnel of the other party, the sole limit being the need to respect other rules of humanitarian law, including those prohibiting the employment of means and methods of warfare that cause unnecessary suffering.[32] If and to what extent such a development has already taken place, and if it might be likely to further develop in the future, is left to other scholarly inquiries.

---

[32] Compare Ch 11 in this volume.

CHAPTER 14

INTERNAL (NON-INTERNATIONAL) ARMED CONFLICT

ERIC DAVID

1. INTRODUCTION

By definition, the law of armed conflict only applies to armed conflicts. This raises the question; when is there an armed conflict?[1] This is a question of fact that precedes the law as '*l'existence précède l'essence*'.[2]

Originally, the law of armed conflict only applied to international armed conflicts, not because civil wars did not exist, but simply because states felt that such conflicts pertained to the sphere of their domestic affairs and they were not prepared to allow international regulation of this type of situation.[3] As is well known, the first international humanitarian law (IHL) instruments date back to the 1864 Geneva Convention and the 1868 Saint-Petersburg Declaration, while the first codifications of IHL date back to the 1899 and 1907 Hague Conventions. Yet all those rules only applied to conventional international wars. The first text which expressly addressed

---

[1] See *amplius* E. David, *Principes de droit des conflits armés* (5th edn, Bruxelles: Bruylant, 2012) § 1.45ff.

[2] J.-P. Sartre, *L'existentialisme est un humanisme* (Paris: Nagel, 1946), 29.

[3] Cf Burma's position in 1949, in *Actes de la conférence diplomatique de Genève de 1949*, Berne, Département politique fédéral, nd, T. II, B, 320–3.

non-international armed conflicts was Article 3 common to the four 1949 Geneva Conventions (GCs). The resistance of some states at that time to include this provision in the GCs was yet another demonstration of the reluctance of states to regulate internal armed conflicts at the international level.[4]

Things have changed today. Article 3 common to the four 1949 GCs—a single Article, out of about 400 provisions contained in the GCs—has been joined by an increasing number of provisions that regulate internal armed conflicts. Thus, 18 substantive provisions of the second Additional Protocol of 1977 (AP II) to the 1949 GCs have been devoted entirely to non-international armed conflicts. The criminalization as war crimes of serious violations of Common Article 3 and other rules applicable to non-international armed conflicts, however, has come as a later development in customary international law, as recognized by the seminal 1995 decision of the Appeals Chamber of the International Criminal Tribunal for the former Yugoslavia (ICTY) in *Tadić*,[5] and in part codified by Article 4 of the Statute of the International Criminal Tribunal for Rwanda (ICTR), adopted in 1994 by the Security Council.[6]

The quantitative development of norms applicable to internal armed conflicts was confirmed in the recent ICRC Study on Customary International Humanitarian Law (2005), that shows that among the 161 rules contained in the study, at least 137 (and perhaps even 144 rules) are applicable to both non-international and international armed conflicts.[7]

This Chapter will briefly examine the variety and complexity of IHL rules applicable to non-international armed conflicts (NIACs), and then turn to the criteria for identifying the existence of a non-international armed conflict.[8]

2 THE VARIETY AND COMPLEXITY OF IHL RULES ON NIACs

The IHL rules applicable to NIACs are essentially the following:

- Artice 3 common to the 1949 GC;
- Article 19 of the 1954 Hague Convention for the Protection of Cultural Property (1954 Hague Convention);

---

[4] Cf Burma's position in 1949 (n 3), 322–6.
[5] ICTY Appeals Chamber, *Decision on the Defence Motion for Interlocutory Appeal on Jurisdiction*, 2 October 1995, §§ 128–34.
[6] S/RES/955, 8 November 1994.   [7] See David (n 1) § 1.63.
[8] For further reading see eg S. Sivakumaran, *The Law of Non-International Armed Conflict* (Oxford: Oxford University Press, 2012); A. Cullen, *The Concept of Non-International Armed Conflict*

- the 1977 AP II to the 1949 GC;
- Article 2, paragraph 2 (c–f), of the Statute of the International Criminal Court adopted in Rome on 17 July 1998;
- Article 22 of the Hague Protocol of 26 March 1999;
- the 1980 UN Convention on Prohibitions or Restrictions on the Use of Certain Conventional Weapons Which May be Deemed to be Excessively Injurious or to Have Indiscriminate Effects (hereafter: 'the 1980 Convention'), as amended on 21 December 2001 with the result that its five Protocols are now applicable to NIACs for the states parties which have accepted the amendment made in 2001;
- the majority of customary IHL rules defined and published by the ICRC Study.[9]

Among the above, AP II is the only conventional instrument fully dedicated to NIACs.[10]

Not all the rules mentioned above, however, apply to all kinds of NIACs. While Common Article 3 and Article 19 of the 1954 Hague Convention apply to any non-international armed conflict, AP II only applies to a specific category of NIAC, namely one which takes place in the territory of a state between its armed forces and dissident armed forces or other organized armed groups exercising control over a part of its territory. Article 8 paragraph 2(f) of the ICC Statute adds more complexity, since it states that it applies to protracted NIACs which take place in the territory of one state between governmental authorities and organized armed groups or between such groups.

Today, it seems no longer very useful to consider the detail of these provisions and the situations they govern: adopted in 1949, 1954, 1977, and 1998, these rules have changed, and the Statute of the ICC, given its recent adoption, seems largely to express the current state of customary international law. (The ICRC Study on Customary IHL has not dealt with the issue of the definition of non-international armed conflict, and it is not therefore a point of reference in this respect.)

However, it is important to observe that all the rules mentioned above share a common element: since the adoption in 1977 of AP II, they state that they do not govern situations of internal disturbances and tensions such as riots, isolated and sporadic acts of violence and other acts of a similar nature (AP II, Article 1 paragraph 2; the 1999 Protocol to the 1954 Hague Convention, Article 22 paragraph 2; the 1980 Convention amended in 2001, Article 2; and the ICC Statute, Article 8 paragraph 2(d)). It is therefore vital to distinguish between armed conflict and internal disturbances and tensions, as we shall see below.

in International Humanitarian Law (Cambridge: Cambridge University Press, 2010); E. La Haye, *War Crimes in Internal Armed Conflicts* (Cambridge: Cambridge University Press, 2008); L. Moir, *The Law of Internal Armed Conflict* (Cambridge: Cambridge University Press, 2002).

[9] L. Doswald-Beck and J.-M. Henckaerts, *Customary International Humanitarian Law* (Cambridge: Cambridge University Press, 2005), 3 vols.

[10] On the difficulties relating to the adoption of this Protocol, see David (n 1), § 1.64.

3 THE CRITERIA FOR DEFINITION OF INTERNAL ARMED CONFLICTS

In the *Tadić* case, the ICTY Trial Chamber maintained:

The two determinative elements of an armed conflict, intensity of the conflict and level of organisation of the parties, are used 'solely for the purpose, as a minimum, of distinguishing an armed conflict from banditry, unorganized and short-lived insurrections, or terrorist activities, which are not subject to international humanitarian law'.[11]

To distinguish an armed conflict from banditry, terrorism, and short rebellions, the nature of hostilities and the quality of the actors will serve as defining criteria.

A. The nature of hostilities

The *Tadić* judgment just cited requires that hostilities reach a certain level of intensity, ie a certain level of gravity and duration.

(i) *The gravity of hostilities*

NIACs involve open hostilities between the warring parties. Some examples show what the case law considers as open hostilities. Thus, concerning the question of whether the clashes between the *UÇK* (*Ushtria Çlirimtare e Kosovës* or Kosovo Liberation Army) and the Serb forces in Kosovo in the 1990s amounted to an armed conflict, the ICTY noted that,

- from February to July 1998, the *UÇK* had attacked villages and even cities;
- the *UÇK* had closed roads, established checkpoints;
- in June 1998, the UNHCR counted 15,000 refugees in Montenegro who had fled Kosovo.[12]

In another case, the ICTY found that

- the number of attacks by the KLA increased from nine in 1995 to 1486 in 1998;
- these attacks were directed against civilians and Serbian police or security;
- buildings had been bombed;
- the conflict fulfilled the criterion of intensity so that one could speak of armed conflict.[13]

Concerning the violence that took place in the Central African Republic (CAR), the ICC Pre-Trial Chamber noted that the former Chief of Staff of the CAR Armed

---

[11] ICTY, *Tadić*, Trial Judgment, 7 May 1997, § 562.
[12] ICTY, *Limaj*, Trial Judgment, 30 November 2005, §§ 135–73.
[13] ICTY, *Haradinaj et al*, Trial Judgment, 3 April 2008, §§ 90–9.

Forces (FACA), Fr Bozize, 'led mainly dissident *FACA* forces towards Bangui',[14] in October 2002, in order to overthrow President Patassé; JP Bemba sent between 1000 and 1500 soldiers of the Movement for the Liberation of Congo (MLC) to assist Patassé in repelling the FACA;[15] and according to witness accounts:

- the MLC forces engaged 'in combat' and established 'their strategic bases';
- 'the conflict was of a certain intensity'.[16]

Therefore, the ICC Pre-Trial Chamber found there was an armed conflict in the CAR.

In short, hostilities must reach a magnitude that requires confrontation almost similar to those between regular armies.[17]

(ii) *The duration of hostilities*

Article 8 paragraph 2(f), of the ICC Statute refers to 'protracted armed conflict'. In 1995, the ICTY had already limited non-international armed conflict by reference to 'protracted armed violence':

an armed conflict exists whenever there is a resort to armed force between States or protracted armed violence between governmental authorities and organized armed groups or between such groups within a State.[18]

How does one define a protracted armed conflict? The ICTY has held that crimes committed in Bosnia-Herzegovina, in April 1993, were part of a 'protracted conflict', because, in this territory, 'in the time following October 1992 there was serious fighting for an extended period of time'.[19] The Pre-Trial Chamber of the ICC held that clashes during a period of five months (late October 2002 to mid-March 2003) were 'to be regarded as "protracted" in any event';[20] *a fortiori* the hostilities that stretched from July 2002 until end 2003 in Ituri,[21] or the Darfur conflict in 2003–04[22] are obviously protracted hostilities.

However, the protracted nature of the armed conflict does not seem to be a condition for the applicability of Common Article 3. Thus, the Inter-American

---

[14] ICC, Pre-Trial Chamber, *Bemba, Decision Pursuant to Article 61(7)(a) and (b) of the Rome Statute on the Charges of the Prosecutor against Jean-Pierre Bemba Gombo*, 15 June 2009, § 240.

[15] *Bemba, Decision* (n 14), §§ 340–4.

[16] *Bemba, Decision*, (n 14), § 244.

[17] For other examples drawn from practice, see David, (n 1), § 1.84.

[18] ICTY, Appeals Chamber, *Tadić, Decision on the Defence Motion for Interlocutory Appeal on Jurisdiction*, 2 October 1995, §§ 128–34, § 70; ICTY, *Tadić*, Trial Judgment, 7 May 1997, §§ 561ff; ICTY, *Aleksovski*, Trial Judgment, 25 June 1999, § 43; ICTY, *Jelisić*, Trial Judgment, 14 December 1999, § 29.

[19] ICTY, *Kordić et Čerkez*, 17 December 2004, § 341.

[20] ICC, *Bemba, Decision Pursuant to Article 61(7)(a) and (b) of the Rome Statute on the Charges of the Prosecutor against Jean-Pierre Bemba Gombo*, 15 June 2009, §§ 235, 248–55.

[21] ICC, *Katanga*, Pre-Trial Chamber, *Decision on the evidence and information provided by the Prosecution for the issuance of a warrant of arrest for Germain Katanga*, 5 November 2007, § 28.

[22] ICC, *Al Bashir*, Pre-Trial Chamber, *Decision on the Prosecutor's Application for a Warrant of Arrest*, 4 March 2009, § 63.

Commission of Human Rights ruled that a clash of 30 hours between the Argentine army and rebel soldiers was governed by Common Article 3 due to:

the concerted nature of the hostile acts undertaken by the attackers, the direct involvement of governmental armed forces, and the nature and level of the violence attending the events in question.[23]

It added:

More particularly, the attackers involved carefully planned, coordinated and executed an armed attack, *i.e.*, a military operation against a quintessential military objective—a military base. The officer in charge of the Tablada base sought, as was his duty, to repulse the attackers, and President Alfonsin, exercising his constitutional authority as commander-in-chief of the armed forces, ordered that military action be taken to recapture the base and subdue the attackers. [...] Despite its brief duration, the violent clash between the attackers and members of the Argentine armed forces triggered application of the provisions of Common Art. 3, as well as other rules relevant to the conduct of internal hostilities.[24]

This finding suggests that the criterion of protracted conflict affects only the application of AP II and Article 8 paragraph 2(e)–(f), of the ICC Statute, not the application of Common Article 3 of GC.

B. The nature of the actors

As in international armed conflicts, the nature of the actors in an armed conflict is a fundamental criterion for the application of IHL. Once an international armed conflict opposes states or international organizations, the public nature of the actors does not raise many difficulties since states and international organizations are, by definition, statutory bodies that can assume the acts of their forces and be legally accountable for them. IHL being premised on oppositions between armed actors under public international law, this criterion should be reflected in IHL applicable to non-international armed conflicts to the extent that IHL must also determine which entities are responsible for the actions of their forces and can therefore be accountable for them on the international plane. The texts are not this specific, but a logical interpretation leads us to this conclusion. At the Diplomatic Conference of 1949, states had already stressed that the conflicts referred to in the future Common Article 3 only concerned warring parties recognized as such by the legal government and having the characteristics of a state or a governmental authority,[25] but these criteria were then abandoned because of the difficulties of their application.[26]

---

[23] Case No 11.137, *Abella case*, 18 November 1997, § 155.
[24] Case No 11.137, *Abella case*, 18 November 1997, § 155.   [25] *Actes* (n 3), 119.
[26] See intervention of Switzerland, *Actes* (n 3), 330–1.

In the case of an insurgency against a government, the latter is clearly an actor under public international law. In contrast, the insurgent authorities fulfil this criterion only to the extent they meet the definition of an 'organized armed group', an expression found in Article 1(1) of AP II, in Article 8(2)(f) of the Rome Statute of the ICC, and in the cases quoted above.

If the concept of 'state' is fairly simple to define in international law,[27] that of 'organized armed group' requires some elaboration. It is clear from the jurisprudence and practice that an organized armed group is characterized by the fact that, first, it exerts a form of public power (i), secondly, it is responsible and identifiable (ii).

(i) *A form of public power*

Article 1(1) of AP II refers to 'organized armed groups [...] under responsible command'. According to the commentary to this provision, the group in question must be organized, not as a regular army, but in a way to ensure a military strategy and impose discipline on the group's forces:

It means an organization capable, on the one hand, of planning and carrying out sustained and concerted military operations, and on the other, of imposing discipline in the name of a *de facto* authority.[28]

Thus, the ICTY, in cases relating to Kosovo, showed that the crimes imputed to the accused were committed in an armed conflict and that the *UÇK* met the criteria of an organized group; to this end, the Trial Chamber noted that:

- the *UÇK* had established an embryo of administrative organization of the territory of Kosovo;
- Kosovo was divided into seven areas of command;
- the *UÇK* forces were surrounded and subjected to a hierarchic military command;
- the supply of arms was organized.

The Chamber also says:

With respect to the organisation of the parties to the conflict Chambers of the Tribunal have taken into account factors including the existence of headquarters, designated zones of operation, and the ability to procure, transport, and distribute arms. [...] progressively from late May to late August 1998 the territory of Kosovo was divided by the KLA into seven zones [...] the KLA soldiers were provided with military training.[29]

The Chamber further notes that the leadership of the *UÇK*:

- was making public statements, coordinating military actions, regulated the duties of commanders;

---

[27] Cf T.A.M., *Deutsche Continental Gas-Gesellschaft*, 1 August 1929, *Recueil*, IX, 336; Montevideo Convention of 26 December 1933 on the Rights and Duties of States, Art 1; Arb Comm of the EC, 29 November 1991, *RGDIP* (1992), 264.

[28] Commentary AP I and II, § 4463.

[29] ICTY, *Limaj et al*, Trial Judgment, 30 November 2005, §§ 90, 95, 119.

- had established a military police, provided military uniforms to its forces, was negotiating with the EU diplomatic missions in Belgrade, was considered a key player in political negotiations to resolve the Kosovo problem.[30]

The ICC has made a similar analysis, determining the clashes which occurred in Ituri (Eastern Congo) in 2002–03 between 'organized local armed groups' (UPC/FPLC, FNI, FRPI PUSIC) to be an 'armed conflict' because these groups:

(i) had a certain degree of organization, insofar as such groups acted under a responsible command and had an operative internal disciplinary system; and

(ii) had the capacity to plan and carry out sustained and concerted military operations, insofar as they held control of parts of the territory of the Ituri District.[31]

An organized armed group must not necessarily have a legal personality since no text requires or suggests this. In a different context, the European Union (EU) Council's Common Position 2001/931/CFSP provides for measures to fight terrorism committed by 'groups and entities' (Article 1);[32] interestingly, the EU General Court ruled that the expression could refer to 'any other types of social organisations which although they do not have legal personality nonetheless exist in a more or less structured form'.[33] This finding could be applied to organized groups involved in a non-international armed conflict.

(ii) *An accountable and identifiable power*

The concept of 'responsible authority' is linked to that of responsible command that appears in IHL with regard to resistance movements (Hague Regulations, Article 1; GC III, Article 4A(2)(a)). The underlying idea is that the 'person responsible' for acts of his/her forces will ensure 'the discipline which must prevail in volunteer corps'.[34] However, it is reasonable to think that the concept of command responsibility goes further and implies the idea of a responsible authority at the international level. In 1874 at the time of the Brussels Declaration, which became the model for the second Hague Convention of 1899, in 1907 the time of the Hague Conventions, and in 1949 when the Geneva Conventions were adopted, the authority was the state. Today, an organized armed group may also appear as a subject of international law and bear responsibility for the actions of its armed forces, provided it is 'organized' (see above) and identifiable (see below).

---

[30] *Limaj et al* (n 29), §§ 100, 103, 108, 112, 123, 125, 129; also, ICTY, *Haradinaj et al*, Retrial Judgment, 29 November 2012, §§ 402–5, 410.

[31] ICC, *Katanga et Ngudjolo Chui*, Pre-Trial Chamber, *Decision on the Confirmation of Charges*, 30 September 2008, § 239; in the same way, ICC, *Lubanga*, Pre-Trial Chamber, *Decision on the Confirmation of Charges*, 29 January 2007, § 234; ICC, *Bemba*, Pre-Trial Chamber, *Decision Pursuant to Article 61(7)(a) and (b) of the Rome Statute on the Charges of the Prosecutor against Jean-Pierre Bemba Gombo*, 15 June 2009, § 234.

[32] *OJEC* L 344/93 of 28 December 2001.   [33] Case T-348/07, *Al-Aqsa*, 9 September 2010, § 58.

[34] Commentary GC III, 59.

Thus, the ICTR suggests, incidentally, that violations of Common Article 3 of the GCs and AP II committed during the conflict in Rwanda in April–July 1994, could be imputed to the parties to the conflict by reason of the governmental character of one of the parties, the organized nature of the other and its submission to a responsible command:

The ability of the governmental armed forces to comply with the provisions of such instruments is axiomatic. In the instant case, the two armies were well organised and participated in the military operations under responsible military command. Therefore, based on Art. 6 (1) of the ICTR Statute, it could be concluded that the appropriate members of the FAR and RPF shall be responsible individually for violations of Common Article 3 and Protocol II if factually proven.[35]

The ICC links organization of the armed group and responsible command because, as the Pre-Trial Chamber of the Court said with regard to Article 1(1) of AP II:

responsible command impl[ies] some degree of organization of the armed groups, capable of planning and carrying out sustained and concerted military operations and imposing discipline in the name of a *de facto* authority, including the implementation of the Protocol.[36]

The criterion of responsible command, however, has meaning only insofar as it is known and accessible, like a state. It must therefore be identifiable. In 2004, the ICRC best demonstrated the link that must exist between the existence of an identifiable party and the application of IHL:

Armed conflict of any type requires a certain intensity of violence and, among other things, the existence of opposing parties. Party to an armed conflict is usually understood to mean armed force or armed groups with a certain level of organization, command structure and, therefore, the ability to implement international humanitarian law. The very logic underlying IHL requires *identifiable* parties in the above sense because this body of law—while not parties' legal status—establishes equality of rights and obligations among them under IHL [...] In the case at hand, it is difficult to see how a loosely connected, clandestine network of cells...] could qualify as a "party" to the conflict.[37]

Three years later, the ICRC repeats the same idea:

The parties to the conflict have to be *identifiable, i.e.* they must have a minimum of organization and structure, and a chain of command.[38]

One can understand the logic of limiting the application of IHL to hostilities where the parties to the conflict are responsible and identifiable: this allows

---

[35] ICTR, *Kayishema and Ruzindana*, Trial Judgment, 21 May 1999, § 174.

[36] ICC, *Lubanga*, Pre-Trial Chamber, *Decision on the Confirmation of Charges*, 29 January 2007, § 232.

[37] Excerpts of the Report prepared by the ICRC for the 28th International Conference of the Red Cross, *IRRC*, 2004, 234 (emphasis added).

[38] *Increasing Respect for International Humanitarian Law in Non-International Armed Conflicts*, ICRC, 2008, 7 (emphasis added).

authorities to determine who can and should be held responsible for violations of
IHL. To ensure accountability of the parties to the conflict, they must be known or at
least be identifiable, like a state authority. Thus, the Al Qaeda group has no address
in the phone book! On the other hand, the People's Mojahedin Organization of Iran
is acting under the authority of the National Council of Resistance for Iran, whose
members are known; therefore, its armed actions against a regime which, since 1980,
continues to attack parts of the population, amount to episodes of an armed conflict
fully regulated by IHL. *In casu*, the characterization of 'armed conflict' seems even
more justified as today the ICTY jurisprudence equates the mistreatment of a civilian
population to 'armed attacks'.[39]

4 CONCLUDING REMARKS

It is clear that a NIAC falls within the scope of IHL only if the criteria of intensity (open hostilities) and nature of the belligerents (responsible and identifiable
actors) are satisfied. The underlying idea is that the application of IHL requires
a degree of external accountability of the protagonists so that they can appear as
actual 'parties to the conflict': states are willing to accept the applicability of IHL
to armed hostilities on condition that the actors demonstrate their ability to 'play
the game' like 'big boys'. If this condition is not met, the situation is not outside the
law, but it falls more under the domestic law of the state, without prejudice to the
application of international rules other than those found in IHL—namely human
rights law and international criminal law.

In substance, any situation of NIAC meeting the aforementioned conditions of
intensity of hostilities and accountability of the parties is governed by Common
Article 3, Article 19 of the 1954 Hague Convention, its 1999 Protocol, the 1980
Convention as amended in 2001, and Article 8 (2)(c) of the Rome Statute of the
ICC. If, moreover, the conflict is protracted, it also falls under Article 8(2)(e)–(f) of
the Rome Statute of the ICC and AP II interpreted in the light of this provision of
the Statute.

---

[39] ICTY, *Kunarac*, Appeals Judgment, 12 June 2002, § 86; *Stakić*, Trial Judgment, 31 July 2003, § 623.

PART V

KEY RIGHTS IN TIMES OF ARMED CONFLICT

CHAPTER 15

....

THE RIGHT TO LIFE

....

WILLIAM A. SCHABAS

IT is estimated that the two great wars of the twentieth century were responsible for the deaths of somewhere between 65 and 90 million persons. That is an average of between 17,599 and 24,200 deaths on every single day of the two conflicts. It should be borne in mind that the total population of the world at the time was about 2 billion; it is 3.5 times that number today. A conflict of similar scale today would bring deaths of about 60,000 to 75,000 people each day. If nothing else, these staggering numbers show how much more civilized a place the world has become in recent decades, despite appearances and popular impressions. Several factors may explain this progress, including the emergence of international legal standards on human rights and the use of force and international mechanisms for their enforcement and implementation.[1]

In modern times, certainly, armed conflict has posed one of the greatest threats to human life. The purpose of war may not be mass killing, but it is almost inevitably its consequence. Armed conflict is therefore one of our era's greatest challenges to the right to life.

---

[1] For the analysis of a social scientist, see Steven Pinker, *The Better Angels of Our Nature: The Decline of Violence in History and Its Causes* (London: Allen Lane, 2011).

1 Origins and Scope of the Right to Life

The 'right to life' has been described as 'the supreme right',[2] 'one of the most important rights',[3] 'the foundation and cornerstone of all the other rights',[4] the 'prerequisite for all other rights',[5] 'one of the rights which constitute the irreducible core of human rights',[6] and a right which is 'basic to all human rights'.[7] Yet basic as it appears, it is at the same time intangible in scope and vexingly difficult to define with precision. Perhaps more than any other, it is a right whose content is continuously evolving, in step with the hegemony of ever more progressive attitudes to capital punishment, nuclear arms, abortion, and euthanasia, to mention only a few of the many issues that interpreters of the right to life have addressed.

In positive law, probably the earliest recognition of this protection appears in the *Magna Carta*:

No freedman shall be taken or imprisoned, or be disseised of his freehold, or liberties, or free customs, or be outlawed, or exiled, or any other wise destroyed, nor will we pass upon him, nor condemn him, but by the lawful judgment of his peers, or by the law of the land.[8]

Declarations of the right to life are also found in a number of pre-revolutionary American documents, authored by Puritans who had fled religious persecution in England. For example, the Massachusetts Body of Liberties, which is prophetically dated 10 December 1641, proclaims: 'No mans life shall be taken away [...] unlesse it be by bertue or equitie of some expresse law of the country narrating the same, established by a generall Cort and sufficiently published [...]'.[9] The Virginia Bill of Rights, drafted by George Mason at the dawn of the American revolution, referred to 'inherent rights' to 'the enjoyment of life'.[10] The Declaration of Independence

---

[2] *General Comment 6(16)*, UN Doc CCPR/C/21/Add.1, also published as UN Doc A/37/40, Annex V, UN Doc CCPR/3/Add.1, 382–3. See also, *de Guerrero v Columbia* (No 45/1979), UN Doc C/CCPR/OP/1, 112, at 117.

[3] ECtHR, *Stewart v United Kingdom* (App No 10044/82), (1985) 7 *EHRR* 453.

[4] Inter-American Commission of Human Rights, *Diez Años de Actividades, 1971–1981*, Washington, DC: Organization of American States, 1982, 339; *Annual Report of the Inter-American Commission on Human Rights, 1986–1987*, OAS Doc OEA/Ser.L/V/II.71 doc 9 rev 1, 271.

[5] 'Initial Report of Uruguay', UN Doc CCPR/C/1/Add.57.

[6] ICJ, *Legality of the Threat or Use of Nuclear Weapons*, Advisory Opinion, ICJ Rep 1996, 226, Dissenting Opinion of Judge Weeramantry, 506.

[7] *General Comment 14(23)*, UN Doc A/40/40, Annex XX, UN Doc CCPR/C/SR.563, § 1.

[8] 6 Halsbury's Statutes (3rd edn) 401.

[9] R. Perry and J. Cooper, *Sources of Our Liberties* (Washington: American Bar Association, 1952), 148.

[10] Perry and Cooper (n 9), 311. See also: Perry and Cooper (n 9), 'Constitution of Pennsylvania', 329; Perry and Cooper (n 9), 'Constitution of Massachusetts', 374; Perry and Cooper (n 9), 'Constitution of New Hampshire', 382.

followed by a few weeks: 'We hold these truths to be self-evident, that all men are created equal; that they are endowed by their Creator with certain unalienable rights; that among these are life, liberty, and the pursuit of happiness.' Article 5 of the American Bill of Rights states that no person shall 'be deprived of life, liberty, or property, without due process of law'.

The post-World War I period was seminal for the development of international law, including the international law of human rights. It provides what appears to be the first recognition in treaty law of the right to life. Article 2 of the agreement establishing Poland declares: 'Poland undertakes to assure full and complete protection of life and liberty to all inhabitants of Poland without distinction of birth, nationality, language, race or religion.'[11] A similar provision is found in the treaty establishing Yugoslavia.[12] These texts appear to have inspired the Institut de droit international, which adopted an international declaration of human rights at its meeting held at Briarcliff Manor, New York in 1929. Article I of that declaration recognizes the right to life: 'It is the duty of every State to recognize the equal right of every individual to life, liberty and property, and to accord to all within its territory the full and entire protection of this right, without distinction as to nationality, sex, language, or religion.'[13] René Cassin credited the Institut de droit international with playing an important role in the history of the Universal Declaration of Human Rights, noting in particular that the right to life was included as part of the 1929 Declaration.[14]

Inexorably, then, the right to life took a prominent position in the first proposals of the Universal Declaration of Human Rights that were considered by the United Nations Commission on Human Rights in 1947 and 1948. A study of national constitutions conducted by John Humphrey for the Commission found 26 provisions in various national constitutions that recognized a right to life.[15] Based on these materials, Humphrey proposed the following in his 48-article initial draft: 'Everyone has the right to life. This right can be denied only to persons who have been convicted under general law of some crime to which the death penalty is attached.'[16] When the provision was first discussed in the Drafting Committee, Eleanor

[11] Treaty of Peace Between the United States of America, the British Empire, France, Italy and Japan, and Poland [1919] TS 8.

[12] Treaty of Peace between the Principal Allied and Associated Powers and the Serb-Croat-Slovene State [1919] TS 17, Art 2. Also: Treaty between the Principal Allied and Associated Powers and Roumania (1921) 5 *LNTS* 336, Art 1; Treaty between the Principal Allied and Associated Powers and Czechoslovakia [1919] TS 20, Art 1. Article 63 of the Treaty of Saint-Germain-en-Laye [1919] TS 11, protects 'life and liberty, without distinction of birth, nationality, language, race or religion'.

[13] *Annuaire de l'Institut de droit international*, vol II (Brussels: Goemaere, 1929), 118–20; the original is in French, but an English version was published many years later: Institut de droit international, 'Declaration of International Rights of Man' (1941) 35 *American Journal of International Law* 663.

[14] R. Cassin, 'La déclaration universelle et la mise en oeuvre des droits de l'homme', (1951) 79 *Receuil des cours* 241, at 272.

[15] UN Doc E/CN.4/AC.1/3/Add.1, 14–19.

[16] UN Doc E/CN.4/AC.1/3/Add.1, 14; E/CN.4/AC.1/3, 2; UN Doc E/CN.4/21, Annex A.

Roosevelt remarked 'that she understood that there is a movement underway in some States to wipe out the death penalty completely. She suggested that it might be better not to use the phrase death penalty'.[17] Other members joined in the view that the Declaration should not appear to sanction capital punishment.[18] René Cassin reworked the text and, after further discussion in the Drafting Committee, agreement on the following text was reached: 'Every human being has the right to life, to personal liberty and to personal security'.[19] The provision underwent only minor subsequent changes. Article 3 of the Universal Declaration, adopted on 10 December 1948, reads: 'Everyone has the right to life, liberty and security of person'.[20]

The treaty formulations of the right to life are more complex. In the European Convention on Human Rights there is an enumeration of specific exceptions, such as self-defence and quelling a riot or insurrection.[21] The drafters of the European Convention specifically contemplated the issue of the right to life in armed conflict by allowing its derogation 'in respect of deaths resulting from lawful acts of war'.[22] The International Covenant on Civil and Political Rights,[23] the American Convention on Human Rights,[24] and the African Charter on Human and Peoples' Rights[25] eschew attempts to enumerate exceptions to the right to life other than the death penalty. Instead, they declare that no one shall be 'arbitrarily' deprived of the right to life. Even the European Court of Human Rights has in effect interpreted the right to life as ensuring that life is not deprived 'arbitrarily'.

The right to life has many dimensions. Some of them, such as the question of when the right to life begins (abortion) and whether the right can be waived (suicide) seem to have little or no connection with issues of armed conflict. On the other hand, three issues are relevant in this context: (i) the relationship between the right to life as set out in international human rights law and international humanitarian law; (ii) the interplay between the norms on capital punishment as they appear in both the international humanitarian law treaties and the human rights treaties;[26] (iii) the impact on the right to life of the rules of international law on the recourse to armed force. Each of these issues is examined in turn.

---

[17] UN Doc E/CN.4/AC.1/SR.2, 10.   [18] UN Doc E/CN.4/AC.1/SR.2, 10–11.

[19] UN Doc E/CN.4/AC.1/W.2/Rev.2; UN Doc E/CN.4/AC.1/SR.12; Annex F of UN Doc E/CN.4/21.

[20] UNGA Res 217 A (III), UN Doc A/810.

[21] *Convention for the Protection of Human Rights and Fundamental Freedoms* (1955) 213 UNTS 221, Art 2(2).

[22] *Convention for the Protection of Human Rights and Fundamental Freedoms* (1955) 213 UNTS 221, Art 15(2).

[23] *International Covenant on Civil and Political Rights* (1976) 999 UNTS 171, Art 6.

[24] *American Convention on Human Rights* (1979) 1144 UNTS 123.

[25] *African Charter on Human and Peoples' Rights* (1986) 520 UNTS 217, Art 4.

[26] Several protocols to the right to life provisions have been adopted with the aim of abolishing capital punishment. Generally, they acknowledge the special circumstances of armed conflict by contemplating the possibility of capital punishment in time of war. See *Protocol No. 6 to the Convention for the Protection of Human Rights and Fundamental Freedoms Concerning the Abolition of the Death*

2 THE HUMAN RIGHTS
PROVISIONS ON THE RIGHT TO LIFE
AND INTERNATIONAL HUMANITARIAN LAW

In its 1996 Advisory Opinion on Nuclear Weapons, the International Court of Justice confirmed the application of Article 6 of the International Covenant on Civil and Political Rights—and, by implication, other relevant provisions, such as Article 3 of the Universal Declaration of Human Rights and equivalent texts in regional human rights treaties—in wartime. According to the Advisory Opinion, the protection of the International Covenant on Civil and Political Rights (ICCPR) does not cease in times of war, except by operation of Article 4 of the Covenant whereby certain provisions may be derogated from in a time of national emergency.[1] Respect for the right to life is not, however, such a provision. In principle, the right not to be arbitrarily deprived of one's life applies also in hostilities.[27] Logically, then, other instruments that do not contemplate derogation at all, such as the Universal Declaration of Human Rights, must be applicable during armed conflict as well as in peacetime.

If intentional deprivation of life is very much the exception in peacetime, it would seem to be the rule during wartime. Yet the law of armed conflict is also largely concerned with the protection of human life at a time when it is most in peril. For example, the Hague Regulations prohibit the random and arbitrary execution of prisoners of war[28] and, when military authority is exercised over the territory of the hostile state, 'the lives of persons [...] must be respected.'[29] The 1949 Geneva Conventions set out similar norms. Explaining the absence of a reference to protection of life similar to that found in the Hague Regulations, the authoritative *Commentary* to the Geneva Conventions states:

What about the right to life itself? Unlike Article 46 of the Hague Regulations the present Article does not mention it specifically. It is nevertheless obvious that this right is implied, for without it there would be no reason for the other rights mentioned. This is a simple conclusion *a majori ad minus*, and is confirmed by the existence of clauses prohibiting murder, reprisals and the taking of hostages, in Articles 32, 33 and 34 of the Convention.

Penalty, ETS no 114, Art 2; *Second Optional Protocol to the International Covenant on Civil and Political Rights Aimed at Abolition of the Death Penalty* (1991) 1642 UNTS 414, Art 2(1); *Additional Protocol to the American Convention on Human Rights to Abolish the Death Penalty*, OASTS 73, Art 2(1). Only one of these instruments prohibits the death penalty at all times: *Protocol No 13 to the Convention for the Protection of Human Rights and Fundamental Freedoms, concerning the abolition of the death penalty in all circumstances*, ETS no 187, Art 2.

[27] ICJ, *Legality of the Threat or Use of Nuclear Weapons, Advisory Opinion*, [1996] ICJ Rep, 226, § 25.
[28] *Convention Regulating the Laws and Customs of Land Warfare (Hague Convention No IV), Regulations Concerning the Laws and Customs of Land War*, 3 Martens (3rd) 461, 2 AJIL Supp 2 [1910] TS 9, Art 23.
[29] [1910] TS 9, Art 46.

Furthermore, the death penalty may only be applied to protected persons under the circumstances strictly laid down in Article 68.[30]

As the *Commentary* explains, the Geneva Conventions contain explicit guarantees for the lives of protected persons. Article 12 common to the first two Conventions, which concerns wounded, sick, and shipwrecked combatants, states: 'Any attempts upon their lives, or violence to their persons, shall be strictly prohibited; in particular, they shall not be murdered or exterminated, subjected to torture or to biological experiments; they shall not wilfully be left without medical assistance and care, nor shall conditions exposing them to contagion or infection be created.'[31] All of the Conventions treat the wilful killing of protected persons as grave breaches.[32] The application of these principles has been upheld in an important ruling of the European Court of Human Rights.[33] More than half of a recent study on the right to life is devoted to situations of armed conflict. The specific issues addressed include collateral damage, the status of prisoners, so-called unlawful combatants during military occupation, and targeted killings.[34]

In addition to non-combatants and combatants who are *hors de combat*, the law of armed conflict also protects the right to life of those who directly participate in hostilities. The International Committee of the Red Cross has reinforced the view that even combatants benefit from a right to life, to the extent that 'the kind and degree of force which is permissible against persons not entitled to protection against direct attack must not exceed what is actually necessary to accomplish a legitimate military purpose in the prevailing circumstances.'[35] Its position finds support in the work of Jean Pictet, who wrote: 'If we can put a soldier out of action by capturing him, we should not wound him; if we can obtain the same result by wounding him, we must not kill him. If there are two means to achieve the same military advantage, we must choose the one which causes the lesser evil.'[36] Along similar lines, Hersch Lauterpacht wrote that the law on conduct of hostilities 'must be shaped—so far as it can be shaped at all—by reference not to existing law but to more compelling considerations of humanity, of the survival of civilization, and of the sanctity of the individual human being.'[37] Such conclusions flow inexorably

---

[30] Commentary GC IV, 201 (hereinafter: '*Commentary*').

[31] Article 12 of GC I; Art 12 of GC II.

[32] Article 49 of GC I; Art 50 of GC II; Art 129 of GC III; Art 146 of GC IV.

[33] ECtHR, *Kononov v Latvia* [GC], no 36376/04, Judgment, 17 May 2010, §§ 202–204.

[34] C. Tomuschat, E. Lagrange, and S. Oeter (eds), *The Right to Life* (Leiden/Boston: Martinus Nijhoff, 2010).

[35] 'Interpretive Guidance on the Notion of Direct Participation in Hostilities under International Humanitarian Law', 90 *International Review of the Red Cross* (2008) 991 at 1040–4.

[36] Jean Pictet, *Development and Principles of International Humanitarian Law* (Dordrecht: Martinus Nijhoff, 1985), 75 ff.

[37] Hersch Lauterpacht, 'The Problem of the Revision of the Law of War', 29 *British Yearbook of International Law* (1952) 360 at 379.

from the earliest codifications of the law of armed conflict, the 1868 Declaration of St Petersburg and the 1899 Martens Clause.[38]

The broader issue of the rapport between human rights law and the law of armed conflict cannot be avoided here. In its celebrated decision on jurisdiction, the Appeals Chamber of the International Criminal Tribunal for the former Yugoslavia set out 'the more recent and comprehensive notion of "international humanitarian law", which has emerged as a result of the influence of human rights doctrines on the law of armed conflict'.[39] There is in fact a mild degree of reciprocity because the law of armed conflict has contributed to the development of certain human rights norms, notably in the field of capital punishment. Vera Gowlland-Debbas has written of the 'humanisation' of international humanitarian law and the 'humanitarisation' of international human rights law.[40] Some modern legal instruments bridge the divide, incorporating elements from both bodies of law; for example, the Convention on the Rights of the Child[41] and the Rome Statute of the International Criminal Court.[42]

Nevertheless, as Dietrich Schindler has explained, '[h]uman rights and the law of war evolved along entirely different and totally separate lines, but their spiritual roots may be traced in part to the same origin and, from the nineteenth century, a certain degree of similarity may be observed in the development of each'.[43] There was initial reluctance to address issues relating to the legal regulation of armed conflict within the United Nations, a fact that helps to explain why the relationship between the two bodies of law was sometimes not explicitly considered in early human rights instruments. In 1949, the International Law Commission declined to study the laws of war. Several of its members considered the subject to be incompatible with the principles and purposes of the United Nations.[44] For example, James L. Brierly said that the Commission should 'refrain from taking up the question

[38] See Nils Melzer, 'Keeping the Balance Between Military Necessity and Humanity: A Response to Four Critiques of the ICRC's Interpretive Guidance on the Notion of Direct Participation in Hostilities', 42 International Law and Politics (2010) 831; Ryan Goodman, 'The Power to Kill or Capture Enemy Combatants', European Journal of International Law (2013) 863–6.

[39] ICTY, Tadić (IT-94-1-AR72), Decision on the Defence Motion for Interlocutory Appeal on Jurisdiction, 2 October 1995, § 87.

[40] V. Gowlland-Debbas, 'The Right to Life and the Relationship between Human Rights and Humanitarian Law', in C. Tomuschat, E. Lagrange, and S. Oeter (eds), The Right to Life (Leiden/Boston: Martinus Nijhoff, 2010), 123–50 at 126–8.

[41] (1990) 1577 UNTS 3.   [42] (2002) 2187 UNTS 90.

[43] D. Schindler, 'The International Committee of the Red Cross and Human Rights', 203 International Review of the Red Cross (1979) 3. Also L. Doswald-Beck and S. Vité, 'International Humanitarian Law and Human Rights Law', 293 International Review of the Red Cross (1993) 94; Robert Kolb, 'Aspects historiques de la relation entre le droit international humanitaire et les droits de l'homme', 37 Canadian Yearbook of International Law (1999) 57; 'Working paper on the relationship between human rights law and international humanitarian law by F. Hampson and I. Salama', UN Doc E/CN.4/Sub.2/2005/14, §§ 41–4.

[44] UN Doc A/CN.4/SR.6, §§ 45–67.

of the laws of war because if it did so its action might be interpreted as a lack of confidence in the United Nations and the work of peace which the latter was called upon to carry out'.[45]

This began to change with the 1968 Tehran Conference on Human Rights. Anti-colonial and liberation struggles, as well as the Vietnam war and the civil conflict in Nigeria, had placed war at the centre of the agenda for civil society. The Conference adopted a celebrated resolution on human rights in armed conflict. It began by affirming that 'peace is the underlying condition for the full observance of human rights and war is their negation', noting that 'nevertheless armed conflicts continue to plague humanity'. The Resolution called for observance of humanitarian norms during armed conflict, a view that was affirmed in a General Assembly Resolution later the same year.[46]

But as successive generations of scholars, experts, and activists began to peel this onion, layers of complexity and difficulty that had not previously been contemplated began to emerge. There have been attempts to merge the two bodies of law, or at least to ensure that they are viewed as consistent components of a larger whole. This rather holistic view was taken by the International Court of Justice in its Advisory Opinion on Nuclear Weapons. It declared that for the purposes of determining the scope of the right to life in armed conflict, the law of armed conflict was the *lex specialis*. Thus, the right to protection of life from arbitrary deprivation applies also in hostilities. However, according to the Court, the test of what is an arbitrary deprivation of the right to life then falls to be determined by the applicable *lex specialis*, namely, the law applicable in armed conflict which is designed to regulate the conduct of hostilities. Whether a particular loss of life, through the use of a certain weapon in warfare, for example, is to be considered an arbitrary deprivation of life contrary to Article 6 of the Covenant can only be decided by reference to the law applicable in armed conflict and not deduced from the terms of the Covenant itself.[47] From this perspective, the law of armed conflict may appear to constitute a limit to the application of human rights norms.

The *lex specialis* formulation used by the ICJ in the *Nuclear Weapons* case to describe the relationship between the right to life as set out in human rights law and the law of armed conflict was clumsy at best. In the Advisory Opinion in *The Wall* case, the ICJ proposed a more nuanced gloss on its earlier pronouncement. It described the relationship between international human rights law and international humanitarian law as follows:

More generally, the Court considers that the protection offered by human rights conventions does not cease in case of armed conflict, save through the effect of provisions for derogation

[45] UN Doc A/CN.4/SR.6, § 55.
[46] Respect for Human Rights in Armed Conflicts. Resolution 2444 (XXIII) of the United Nations General Assembly, 19 December 1968.
[47] ICJ, *Legality of the Threat or Use of Nuclear Weapons*, Advisory Opinion, ICJ Rep 1996, 226, § 25.

of the kind to be found in Article 4 of the International Covenant on Civil and Political Rights. As regards the relationship between international humanitarian law and human rights law, there are thus three possible situations: some rights may be exclusively matters of international humanitarian law; others may be exclusively matters of human rights law; yet others may be matters of both these branches of international law. In order to answer the question put to it, the Court will have to take into consideration both these branches of international law, namely human rights law and, as *lex specialis*, international humanitarian law.[48]

This statement is not incompatible with the dictum in *Nuclear Weapons*, but it is not identical to it either. In *Nuclear Weapons*, the ICJ stated that international humanitarian law is the window through which arbitrary deprivation of life in armed conflict is to be examined, but it did not develop the discussion with respect to other human rights that may be at issue during armed conflict. In *The Wall* case, the Court seemed to withdraw from what appears to be as a rather too absolute statement. According to Professor Hampson, the above citation from the *The Wall* case makes it 'clear that *lex specialis* is not being used to displace [human rights law]. It is rather an indication that human rights bodies should interpret a human rights norm in the light of [the law of armed conflict/international humanitarian law]'.[49]

In the case of *Democratic Republic of the Congo v Uganda*, the Court again considered the concrete application of these principles. It repeated the paragraph cited above from the Advisory Opinion on *The Wall*.[50] Determining that Uganda was an Occupying Power in Ituri during the relevant period, it said that Article 43 of the Hague Regulations of 1907 imposed an obligation 'to secure respect for the applicable rules of international human rights law and international humanitarian law, to protect the inhabitants of the occupied territory against acts of violence, and not to tolerate such violence by any third party'.[51] It said that Uganda's international responsibility was engaged 'for any lack of vigilance in preventing violations of human rights and international humanitarian law by other actors present in the occupied territory, including rebel groups acting on their own account'.[52] In addition, 'Uganda at all times has responsibility for all actions and omissions of its own military forces in the territory of the DRC in breach of its obligations under the rules of international human rights law and international humanitarian law which are relevant and applicable in the specific situation'.[53] In effect, then, the Court did not address a possible conflict between the two systems, or suggest that violations of

---

[48] ICJ, *Legal Consequences of the Construction of a Wall in the Occupied Palestinian Territory,* Advisory Opinion, 9 July 2004, § 106.

[49] 'Working paper on the relationship between human rights law and international humanitarian law by F. Hampson and I. Salama', UN Doc E/CN.4/Sub.2/2005/14, § 57.

[50] ICJ, *Armed Activities on the Territory of the Congo (Democratic Republic of the Congo v Uganda),* 19 December 2005, § 216.

[51] *Democratic Republic of the Congo v Uganda* (n 50), § 178.

[52] *Democratic Republic of the Congo v Uganda* (n 50), § 179.

[53] *Democratic Republic of the Congo v Uganda* (n 50), § 180.

international human rights law would be examined through the lens of international humanitarian law. Rather, it treated them as two complementary systems, as parts of a whole.

When the right to life is concerned, in many cases the result will be the same whether it is the law of armed conflict or human rights law that governs. In other words, the *lex specialis* issue need not arise at all. For example, to the extent that it is deemed impermissible to kill a combatant when lesser means of rendering that person *hors de combat* may be employed, there is probably no tension whatsoever between the two bodies of law. However, as will be discussed later in this Chapter, to the extent that human rights law may condemn any unlawful resort to armed force, there will be a conflict with international humanitarian law which espouses an indifference as to the responsibility of one or another party for the war itself.

3 CAPITAL PUNISHMENT

The progressive restriction and abolition of capital punishment has been one of the central themes of modern human rights law. Arguably, it is one of the great success stories of the modern human rights movement. When the Universal Declaration of Human Rights was adopted in 1948, only a handful of states had abandoned capital punishment. The international community sentenced several men to death after they were condemned by the first international criminal tribunals, in Nuremberg and Tokyo. Six decades later, more than three-quarters of United Nations member states are considered abolitionist, according to the quinquennial studies produced by the Secretary-General.[54] More than 80 states have confirmed their abolitionist stance by ratifying one of the treaties or protocols, thereby binding themselves on this issue as a matter of international obligation.[55]

The 1929 Prisoner of War Convention was the first multilateral international instrument to deal with the imposition of capital punishment.[56] It set out two principles with respect to the death penalty: notification of the sentence to the prisoner's government (via the protecting power) and a moratorium on execution of the sentence for the three months following sentencing, in order to permit political and

---

[54] 'Capital punishment and implementation of the safeguards guaranteeing protection of the rights of those facing the death penalty', UN Doc E/2010/10, 7.

[55] UN Doc E/2010/10 (n 54), 30–2.

[56] *International Convention Relative to the Treatment of Prisoners of War* (1932–33) 118 *LNTS* 343.

diplomatic efforts at obtaining commutation or reprieve.[57] One of the military tribunals that sat in Nuremberg following World War II held that 'most of the provisions' of the 1929 Geneva Convention were 'an expression of the accepted views of civilized nations' and therefore norms of customary international law.[58]

The treaty was substantially revised and made more stringent in the 1949 Convention with respect to the imposition of the death penalty on prisoners of war.[59] But probably of more consequence were the provisions adopted in the civilian convention, for which there was no predecessor or precedent. According to Claude Pilloud of the International Committee of the Red Cross, '[a]fter the second world war a very strong feeling arose against the numerous death sentences inflicted on inhabitants of occupied territories and there was a general desire that the possibility of inflicting capital punishment should be as restricted as possible'.[60] In this debate, the International Committee of the Red Cross made no secret of its real intention and ultimate objective: abolition of the death penalty.[61]

The fourth Geneva Convention (GC IV) contains important innovations: a severe restriction on the crimes for which the death penalty may be imposed and a total prohibition on the execution of juvenile offenders.[62] The latter measure resulted from a proposal at the Seventeenth International Conference of the Red Cross by the International Union for the Protection of Children and recognizes the principle that children are not fully responsible for their actions, either because of immaturity or because of coercion.[63] According to the authoritative *Commentary*, '[t]he clause corresponds to similar provisions in the penal codes of many countries, and is based on the idea that a person who has not reached the age of eighteen years is not fully capable of sound judgment, does not always realize the significance of his actions and often acts under the influence of others, if not under constraint'.[64]

In addition, Article 75 of GC IV grants a right to petition for pardon or reprieve to all persons condemned to death. The death sentence may not be carried out before expiration of a period of at least six months from the date the Protecting Power

---

[57] *Report on the Work of the Conference of Government Experts for the Study of the Conventions for the Protection of War Victims (Geneva, 14–26 April 1947)*, Series I, no 5b (Geneva: International Committee of the Red Cross, 1947), 231.

[58] *The High Command Case (US v Von Leeb)*, (1950) 11 TWC 462, 535.

[59] Articles 87, 100, 101, 107 of GC III.

[60] C. Pilloud, 'Reservations to the Geneva Conventions of 1949', *International Review of the Red Cross* [1976] 163 at 184–5.

[61] *Report on the Work of the Conference of Government Experts for the Study of the Conventions for the Protection of War Victims (Geneva, 14–26 April 1947)*, Series I, no 5b (Geneva: International Committee of the Red Cross, 1947), 231; *Remarks and Proposals Submitted by the International Committee of the Red Cross, Document for the Consideration of Governments Invited by the Swiss Federal Council to Attend the Diplomatic Conference at Geneva (April 21, 1949)* (Geneva: International Committee of the Red Cross, 1949), 75.

[62] Articles 68 and 75 of GC IV.

[63] Commentary GC IV, 371–2.

[64] Commentary GC IV, 371–2.

receives notification of the final judgment confirming the sentence or an order denying pardon or reprieve. The Diplomatic Conference modified the Stockholm draft somewhat, providing for a reduction of the six-month moratorium in individual cases, under circumstances of grave emergency involving the security of the Occupying Power or its forces.[65] However, even in such cases, the Protecting Power must receive prior notification and be given reasonable time and opportunity to make representations on the subject.[66]

Besides the specific provisions concerning capital punishment in GC III and GC IV, Common Article 3 prohibits 'the passing of sentences and the carrying out of executions without previous judgment pronounced by a regularly constituted court, affording all the judicial guarantees which are recognized as indispensable by civilized peoples'.[67] Although ostensibly applicable to non-international armed conflicts not otherwise governed by the Conventions themselves, these provisions are now held to be applicable to international armed conflicts as well.[68] According to the ICJ, Common Article 3 is a 'minimum yardstick' expressing 'elementary considerations of humanity'.[69] Although the judicial guarantees cited in Common Article 3 are not elaborated upon, such instruments as Article 14 of the International Covenant on Civil and Political Rights,[70] the 'Safeguards Guaranteeing Protection of the Rights of Those Facing the Death Penalty',[71] and Article 75(4) of Additional Protocol I (AP I)[72] provide an indication of what is 'recognized as indispensable by civilized peoples'.

The 1977 Additional Protocols go somewhat further in the limitation of capital punishment than the 1949 Geneva Conventions, reflecting an evolution within the human rights sphere. They extend the prohibition on execution of juvenile offenders to all persons 'in the power of a party to the conflict' and not only to 'protected persons', as is the case with the fourth Convention.[73] According to the Commentary on Article 77(5) of AP I, 'it can be said that the death penalty for persons under

---

[65] *Final Record of the Diplomatic Conference of Geneva of 1949*, vol IIA (Bern: Federal Political Department, 1949) (Summary record of eighteenth meeting of Committee III), 675; Summary record of forty-third meeting of Committee III, 771; Report of Committee III, 835; *Final Record of the Diplomatic Conference of Geneva of 1949*, vol III (Bern: Federal Political Department, 1949), 144–5 (Annex 310); *Final Record of the Diplomatic Conference of Geneva of 1949*, vol IIB (Bern: Federal Political Department, 1949) (Minutes of the twenty-eighth plenary meeting), 439.

[66] Article 75 of GC IV.

[67] Article 3 of GC IV. See R. Sapienza, 'International Legal Standards on Capital Punishment', in Bertrand G. Ramcharan (ed), *The Right to Life in International Law* (Boston: Martinus Nijhoff, 1985), 284–96 at 293.

[68] ICTY, *Delalic et al* (IT-96-21-A), Judgment, 20 February 2001, § 150.

[69] ICJ, *Military and Paramilitary Activities in and Against Nicaragua (Nicaragua v United States)* [1986] ICJ Rep 14, § 218.

[70] (1976) 999 UNTS 171.   [71] ESC Res 1984/50. Subsequently endorsed by UNGA Res 39/118.

[72] Article 75(4) of AP I.

[73] Article 77(5) of AP I. For non-international armed conflict, the same norm applies: see Art 6(5) of AP II.

eighteen years of age is ruled out completely'.[74] Probably inspired by evolving norms in human rights treaties, to which reference is made in the *travaux préparatoires*,[75] the Additional Protocols also prohibit capital punishment for pregnant women. They actually improve upon human rights norms in force at the time, to an extent, by also banning executions of mothers following childbirth. AP I prohibits execution of 'mothers having dependent infants'.[76] Curiously, Additional Protocol II (AP II), which applies to non-international armed conflict, appears to go further than AP I by prohibiting execution of 'mothers of young children'. There is no real explanation for the inconsistency, aside from the occasional incoherence that inevitably occurs from time to time in complex treaty negotiations, where different working groups operate in parallel, with a shortage of time at the end of the process so as to ensure consistency.

It is in the area of juvenile executions where the synergy between human rights law and the law of armed conflict may be most visible. The provision in GC IV prohibiting the death penalty for protected persons who were under 18 at the time of the offence very evidently inspired human rights lawmakers in the United Nations system. They agreed to incorporate the norm in a draft of the ICCPR during the 1957 session of the Third Committee of the General Assembly.[77] It became Article 6(5) in the final version of the Covenant, adopted in 1966: 'Sentence of death shall not be imposed for crimes committed by persons below eighteen years of age [...]'. An essentially identical provision is found in Article 4(5) of the American Convention on Human Rights, which was adopted in 1969.

In 1987, two petitioners before the Inter-American Commission on Human Rights invoked Article 68(4) of GC IV, arguing that it informed the right to life article of the American Declaration of the Rights and Duties of Man. The American Declaration was adopted in 1948, several months prior to the Universal Declaration, and contains a very general formulation of the right to life without reference to the death penalty ('Every human being has the right to life, liberty and the security of his person'). The issue was whether the prohibition of juvenile executions was implied within the text of Article I of the Declaration. In accordance with the law of the Inter-American human

---

[74] Claude Pilloud and Jean Pictet, 'Article 77—Protection of Children', in Commentary AP I and II, 897–905 at 904.

[75] ICRC Doc CDDH/I/SR.64, § 42. Similar views were expressed by Japan: ICRC Doc CDDH/I/SR.64, § 82. See also A. Eide, 'The New Humanitarian Law in Non-International Armed Conflict', in A. Cassese (ed), *The New Humanitarian Law of Armed Conflict, I* (Naples: Editoriale Scientifica, 1979), 276–309, 286. The *Commentary* on *Protocol Additional II* suggests some guidance in construing the term can be obtained from the fourth Convention, Art 14(1), which refers to mothers of children under seven years old, and *Protocol Additional I*, Art 8, which uses the narrower term 'new-born babies': Sylvie-Stoyanka Junod, 'Article 6—Fundamental guarantees', in Commentary AP I and II, 1395–1402 at 1402.

[76] Article 76(3) of AP I.   [77] UN Doc A/C.3/SR.820, § 25.

rights system, petitions based upon compliance with the American Declaration may be lodged against states that have not ratified the American Convention on Human Rights, where the prohibition on such executions is explicit.

The two petitioners made the following submission:

As of January 1, 1986 there are 162 states parties to [the Geneva Conventions], including the United States. This Convention applies to periods of international armed conflict and Article 68 forbids the execution of civilians and military personnel no longer in combat, who committed offenses prior to the age of 18. If nearly all the nations of the world, including the United States, have agreed to such a norm for periods of international armed conflict, the norm protecting juvenile offenders from execution ought to apply with even greater force for periods of peace.[78]

The United States responded that GC IV applies only in international armed conflicts, and therefore cannot be applied for the execution of juveniles in the United States in normal times and in the absence of an international conflict.[79] The Commission did not expressly respond to the Geneva Convention argument, but it said it was 'convinced by the U.S. Government's argument that there does not now exist a norm of customary international law establishing 18 to be the minimum age for imposition of the death penalty'.[80] Apparently, the Commission was influenced by the argument that the norms in GC IV concerning the human rights of protected persons in occupied territories could not automatically be transposed to a more general context. Certainly there is some merit to this position. State practice in 1949, when GC IV was adopted, and at a time when many states still conducted executions for juvenile crimes, must be borne in mind. Surely the drafters of GC IV did not consider that the norms they were adopting would also apply to their own territories in peacetime. If that had been the issue, they would probably never have accepted Article 68 of the Geneva Convention.

By 2002, the views of the Inter-American Commission on Human Rights had evolved. Reconsidering the issue it had contemplated 15 years earlier, the Commission said it could 'identify no appropriate justification for applying a more restrictive standard for the application of the death penalty to juveniles in times of occupation than in times of peace, relating as this protection does to the most basic and non-derogable protections for human life and dignity of adolescents that are common to both regimes of international law'.[81] The Inter-American Commission's finding was premised upon the idea that if a norm is important enough in wartime, it ought also to apply in peacetime. The opposite proposition, namely that standards of humane treatment in wartime will be lower than those in peacetime, seems

---

[78] *Roach and Pinkerton v United States*, Resolution No 3/87, Case No 9647, 22 September 1987, § 36(g).

[79] See *Roach and Pinkerton v United States*, Dissenting Opinion of Dr Marco Garado Monroy Cabra, 22 September 1987.

[80] *Roach and Pinkerton v United States*, Resolution No 3/87, Case No 9647, 22 September 1987, § 60.

[81] *Domingues v United States*, Report No 62/02, Merits, Case 12.285, 22 October 2002, § 67.

almost intuitive. Perhaps for that reason, the Inter-American Commission thought it made sense to take the logic in the other direction.

4 *JUS AD BELLUM* AND THE RIGHT TO LIFE

Unlike torture, where the prohibition by international law has been held to be absolute,[82] the right to life is not envisaged in the same uncompromised manner. In addition to capital punishment, under certain circumstances, other examples of widely-recognized exceptions to or limitations upon the right to life can be found. Examples include killing in self-defence and the lethal use of force by the authorities in order to prevent crime. These are either set out explicitly, as is the case in Article 2 of the European Convention on Human Rights, or are subsumed within the concept of 'arbitrary deprivation', leaving the court to clarify their scope. General principles dictate that these exceptions or limitations follow the same general approach as in the case of other human rights norms, as clarified in the case law of bodies like the European Court of Human Rights and the UN Human Rights Committee. They must be established by law, serve a legitimate purpose and have a reasonable relationship of proportionality between the means employed and the aim sought to be achieved. Where lethal force is employed, it must be 'no more than absolutely necessary in defence of persons from unlawful violence'.[83]

The legal situation may be different in the case of armed conflict, or so it is contended. When the International Court of Justice declared that the determination of arbitrary deprivation of life during wartime should be assessed with reference to the *lex specialis*, namely international humanitarian law, it seemed to be implying that the rules of *jus ad bellum*—that is, the rules of international law regulating the legality of recourse to armed force in international relations—were irrelevant to the assessment. It is beyond real debate that international humanitarian law does not concern itself with *jus ad bellum*. It attempts to confront both sides in a conflict as equals, without regard to whether one or the other party has a just cause or is acting unlawfully. There is considerable wisdom in the approach taken by international humanitarian law, because this neutrality facilitates the effectiveness of bodies that intervene in order to mitigate violations, such as the International Committee of the Red Cross. It is conceivable that an aggressor, acting unlawfully and in breach of *jus*

---

[82] *Gäfgen v Germany* [GC] (no 22978/05), Judgment, 1 June 2010, § 87.
[83] ECtHR, *McCann et al v United Kingdom* [GC], Series A, vol 324, § 213.

ad bellum, may scrupulously respect the *jus in bello*. Likewise, it is also possible that a combatant force fighting a just war may commit atrocities.[84]

The anti-war dimension of international humanitarian law is sometimes forgotten. Yet the preamble of the 1907 Hague Convention begins with these words: 'Seeing that, while seeking means to preserve peace and prevent armed conflicts between nations, it is likewise necessary to bear in mind the case where the appeal to arms has been brought about by events which their care was unable to avert [...]'. It may therefore be overstating things slightly to suggest that international humanitarian law is purely and exclusively focused on *jus in bello*. Article 1 of AP I admits a special regime applicable to 'armed conflicts which peoples are fighting against colonial domination and alien occupation and against racist regimes in the exercise of their right of self-determination'.[85] In addition, it has been held, by the International Court of Justice, that norms of humanitarian law relative to the use of weapons that cause unnecessary suffering or superfluous harm, or are indiscriminate, do not apply strictly in the case of a country placed in an extreme situation of self-defence.[86] But these are really the exceptions that confirm the general rule of the neutrality of international humanitarian law with respect to the responsibility of one or other of the combatant parties for a breach of the law on the use of force.

The view that international human rights should also profess indifference to *jus ad bellum* has been adopted by important non-governmental organizations. During the negotiations proceeding the adoption of amendments to the Rome Statute of the International Criminal Court enabling the exercise of jurisdiction over the crime of aggression, Human Rights Watch said that its

institutional mandate includes a position of strict neutrality on issues of *jus ad bellum*, because we find it the best way to focus on the conduct of war, or *jus in bello*, and thereby to promote our primary goal of encouraging all parties to a conflict to respect international humanitarian law. Consistent with this approach, we take no position on the substance of a definition of the crime of aggression.[87]

In a footnote, Human Rights Watch added:

The only exceptions that Human Rights Watch has made to this policy is to call for military intervention where massive loss of human life, on the order of genocide, can be halted through no other means, as was the case in Bosnia and Rwanda in the 1990s.[88]

Amnesty International came to a similar conclusion, although without explicitly adopting the *jus ad bellum/jus in bello* philosophy derived from the law of armed conflict. According to Amnesty International, the organization

---

[84] ECtHR, *Kononov v Latvia* [GC], no 36376/04, Judgment, 17 May 2010.
[85] Article 1(4) of AP I.
[86] ICJ, *Legality of the Threat or Use of Nuclear Weapons*, Advisory Opinion, ICJ Rep 1996, 226, § 97.
[87] Human Rights Watch, 'Memorandum for the Sixth Session of the Assembly of States Parties of the International Criminal Court'.
[88] Human Rights Watch (n 87).

has not taken a position on the definition of the crime of aggression because its mandate—to campaign for every person to enjoy all of the human rights (civil and political and economic, social and cultural rights) enshrined in the Universal Declaration of Human Rights and other international human rights standards—does not extend to the lawfulness of the use of force.[89]

Despite these pronouncements by influential organizations, it is not apparent that the approach to *jus ad bellum* that features in the law of armed conflict should be transposed into the analysis undertaken pursuant to international human rights law when violations of the right to life are concerned.

The first stumbling block is represented by the Universal Declaration of Human Rights itself, which constitutes the authoritative statement of human rights norms within an organization, the United Nations, premised on the illegality of the resort to force. The Universal Declaration cannot be dissociated from the Charter of the United Nations; rather it must be interpreted in such a manner as to reconcile its provisions with those of the Charter, and the purposes and principles of the United Nations. Surely this explains the first sentence of the preamble to the Universal Declaration with its reference to 'peace in the world' and the allusion, in the second sentence, to Franklin D. Roosevelt's concept of 'freedom from fear' (the reference also appears in the preambles to the two International Covenants). In his January 1941 speech, Roosevelt explained the notion's content: 'The fourth is freedom from fear—which, translated into world terms, means a world-wide reduction of armaments to such a point and in such a thorough fashion that no nation will be in a position to commit an act of physical aggression against any neighbour—anywhere in the world.' Article 28 of the Universal Declaration of Human Rights affirms: 'Everyone is entitled to a social and international order in which the rights and freedoms set forth in this Declaration can be fully realized.' In his commentary on Article 28 of the Universal Declaration, Asbjørn Eide wrote: 'It does not take much reflection to recognize that violence and war negatively affect the enjoyment of human rights. A social and political order in which all the rights in the Universal Declaration could be enjoyed would be possible only if there were peace on both the international and the national levels.'[90]

The relevance of peace to the application of human rights treaties was affirmed by the Human Rights Committee in its first General Comment on the right to life:

The Committee observes that war and other acts of mass violence continue to be a scourge of humanity and take the lives of thousands of innocent human beings every year. Under the Charter of the United Nations the threat or use of force by any State against another State, except in exercise of the inherent right of self-defence, is already prohibited. The Committee considers that States have the supreme duty to prevent wars, acts of genocide and other acts

---

[89] Amnesty International, 'International Criminal Court, Concerns at the Seventh Session of the Assembly of States Parties', October 2008, Index: IOR 40/022/2008, 22.

[90] A. Eide, 'Article 28', in A. Gudmundur and A. Eide (eds), *Universal Declaration of Human Rights* (Dordrecht: Kluwer Academic Publishers, 1999), 620.

of mass violence causing arbitrary loss of life. Every effort they make to avert the danger of war, especially thermonuclear war, and to strengthen international peace and security would constitute the most important condition and guarantee for the safeguarding of the right to life. In this respect, the Committee notes, in particular, a connection between article 6 and article 20, which states that the law shall prohibit any propaganda for war (para. 1) or incitement to violence (para. 2) as therein described.[91]

The 'right to peace' is expressly recognized in the African Charter on Human and Peoples' Rights: 'All peoples shall have the right to national and international peace and security'.[92] The UN Human Rights Council has adopted several resolutions on the promotion of 'the peoples' right to peace'.[93] Most recently, it has spoken of the 'right to peace' without qualifying this as a 'peoples' right'.[94] The Council was divided, with countries of the global south by and large voting in favour, while those of the north were opposed. On both sides, there seems to be no great clarity about what this right entails. Moreover, the entire concept of 'peoples' rights' is contested by some experts.[95]

If human rights law enshrines a right to peace, even implicitly, then it is logical to consider that a threat to peace could result in an 'arbitrary' deprivation of the right to life. If the conflict itself is unlawful, resulting from an act of aggression, then the deaths of those who are attacked that result are arbitrary. The problem is perhaps more acute with civilian victims, for whom there is little solace in suggesting that human rights law takes no position on the legality of the use of force. In the law of armed conflict it is rather common to speak of 'collateral damage' in describing the loss of life (and property) of non-combatants who unfortunately happen to be in the line of fire. Modern treaty law proscribes 'an attack which may be expected to cause incidental loss of civilian life, injury to civilians, damage to civilian objects, or a combination thereof, which would be excessive in relation to the concrete and direct military advantage anticipated'.[96] The collateral death of those who do not participate in the conflict is tolerated by the law of armed conflict, as long as it is actually the military objectives that are targetted, and to the extent that limitations imposed by proportionality are respected. Human rights law may provide a different answer, one that better addresses the rights of victims, precisely because it does not stand indifferent to the arbitrariness that lies behind the use of force. It should be said that while the victimization of non-combatants may be at the centre of concerns

[91] 'General Comment 6', UN Doc CCPR/C/21/Add.1, § 2. See also 'General Comment 14', § 2.
[92] African Charter on Human and Peoples' Rights (1986) 1520 UNTS 217, art 23(1).
[93] 'Promotion of the right of peoples to peace', UN Doc A/HRC/RES/8/9; 'Promotion of the right of peoples to peace', UN Doc A/HRC/RES/11/4; 'Promotion of the right of peoples to peace', UN Doc A/HRC/RES/14/3; 'Promotion of the right of peoples to peace', UN Doc A/HRC/RES/17/16.
[94] 'Promotion of the right to peace', UN Doc A/HRC/20/15.
[95] P. Alston, 'Introduction', in P. Alston (ed), *Peoples' Rights* (Oxford: Oxford University Press, 2001), 1–6 at 1.
[96] Article 51(5)(b) of AP I.

in this respect, members of the armed forces who are victims of an unlawful attack may also suffer breaches of the right to life.

Although the law of armed conflict addresses the proportionality of the measures employed in an attack in assessing whether the levels of collateral damage are tolerable, human rights law has also confronted the issue. The European Court of Human Rights has considered the problem of incidental loss of civilian life in cases dealing with the civil war in the Russian territory of Chechnya. It has steered clear of any attempt to apply international humanitarian law, or to articulate the principles governing the relationship it may have with human rights law. The European Court seems to have found an entirely adequate legal framework within human rights law, without the need to resort to a *lex specialis* theory, in contrast with the approach taken by the International Court of Justice. In one case before the European Court, a bomb dropped by a Russian plane had exploded near the mini-van of the applicant and her relatives as they were fleeing the village of Katyr-Yurt through what they had perceived as a safe exit from heavy fighting.[97] In another, bombs were dropped on a civilian convoy at the border between Chechnya and Ingushetia. Russian authorities had issued a press statement denying civilian damage, claiming that a column of trucks with fighters and ammunition had provoked the encounter by firing upon a government aircraft.[98] According to the Court, Article 2 of the European Convention on Human Rights 'covers not only intentional killing but also the situations in which it is permitted to "use force" which may result, as an unintended outcome, in the deprivation of life'.[99] The test to be applied in considering the exceptions to the right to life in time of conflict, said the Court, was one of 'absolute necessity'; the force used must be strictly proportionate to the achievement of the permitted aims.[100] Nevertheless, in a situation of armed conflict 'the obligation to protect the right to life must be interpreted in a way which does not impose an impossible or disproportionate burden on the authorities'.[101]

In the Katyr-Yurt case, the Court said

the State's responsibility was not confined to circumstances where there was significant evidence that misdirected fire from agents of the state has killed a civilian. It may also be engaged where they fail to take all feasible precautions in the choice of means and methods

---

[97] ECtHR, *Isayeva v Russia*, no 57950/00, Judgment, 24 February 2005.

[98] ECtHR, *Isayeva, Yusopova and Bazayeva v Russia*, nos 57947/00, 57948/00, and 57949/00, Judgment, 24 February 2005, § 32.

[99] ECtHR, *Isayeva v Russia*, no 57950/00, Judgment, 24 February 2005, § 173; ECtHR, *Isayeva, Yusopova and Bazayeva v Russia*, nos 57947/00, 57948/00, and 57949/00, Judgment, 24 February 2005, § 169.

[100] See cases at n 99. Also, ECtHR, *Akhmadov et al v Russia*, no 21586/02, Judgment, 14 November 2008, §§ 92, 94.

[101] ECtHR, *Akhmadov et al v Russia*, no 21586/02, Judgment, 14 November 2008, § 97; *Albekov et al v Russia*, no 68216/01, Judgment, 9 October 2008, § 79; *Arzu Akhmadova et al v Russia*, no 13670/03, Judgment, 8 January 2009, § 163.

of a security operation mounted against an opposing group with a view to avoiding and, in any event, minimising, incidental loss of civilian life.[102]

In the case of the bombing of the convoy on the Chechnya-Ingushetia border, the Court said:

The situation that existed in Chechnya at the relevant time called for exceptional measures on behalf of the State in order to regain control over the Republic and to suppress the illegal armed insurgency. These measures could presumably include employment of military aviation equipped with heavy combat weapons. The Court is also prepared to accept that if the planes were attacked by illegal armed groups, that could have justified use of lethal force, thus falling within paragraph 2 of Article 2.[103]

The Court has also held that Article 2 of the Convention—the right to life—imposes a positive duty on the state to locate and deactivate mines, to mark and seal off mined areas so as to prevent anyone from freely entering them, and to provide comprehensive warnings concerning mines laid in the vicinity of non-combatants.[104]

The European Court of Human Rights pointed out in the Katyr-Yurt case that Russia had not declared martial law or a state of emergency in Chechnya, and that no derogation had been formulated in accordance with Article 15 of the European Convention. As a result, the situation had to be judged 'against a normal legal background'.[105] According to the Court, 'the use of aviation bombs in a populated area, outside wartime and without prior evacuation of the civilians, is impossible to reconcile with the degree of caution expected from a law-enforcement body in a democratic society'.[106] Thus, although the Court accepted that the military operation in Katyr-Yurt was pursuing a 'legitimate aim', it could not accept that it was planned and executed with the requisite care for the lives of the civilian population.[107]

In the border convoy case, the Court did not repeat the same caveat about 'normal legal background' and the absence of a declaration of martial law. It said that 'even assuming that the military were pursuing a legitimate aim in launching 12 S-24 non-guided air-to-ground missiles on 29 October 1999, the Court does not accept that the operation near the village of Shaami-Yurt was planned and executed with the requisite care for the lives of the civilian population'.[108] In another case involving an attack on civilians fleeing Grozny by way of what they had been led to believe was a safe humanitarian corridor, the Court rapidly concluded there had been a violation of the right to life, absent any attempt by Russia to justify the military action.[109]

---

[102] ECtHR, *Isayeva v Russia*, no 57950/00, Judgment, 24 February 2005, § 176.

[103] ECtHR, *Isayeva, Yusupova and Bazayeva v Russia*, nos 57947/00, 57948/00, and 57949/00, Judgment, 24 February 2005, § 178.

[104] ECtHR, *Albekov et al v Russia*, no 68216/01, Judgment, 9 October 2008, § 90.

[105] ECtHR, *Isayeva v Russia*, no 57950/00, Judgment, 24 February 2005, § 191.

[106] ECtHR, *Isayeva v Russia*, no 57950/00, Judgment, 24 February 2005, § 191.

[107] ECtHR, *Isayeva v Russia*, no 57950/00, Judgment, 24 February 2005, § 200.

[108] ECtHR, *Isayeva, Yusupova and Bazayeva v Russia*, nos 57947/00, 57948/00, and 57949/00, Judgment, 24 February 2005, § 199.

[109] ECtHR, *Umayeva v Russia*, no 1200/03, Judgment, 4 December 2008, §§ 82–3.

None of the European Court cases concerning armed conflict have found that the respondent state failed to demonstrate a 'legitimate aim'. In the Chechen jurisprudence, the Court accepted that Russia was entitled to repress a secessionist movement. Thus, its findings were confined to the rules of *jus in bello*. The argument that killing of non-combatants in a conflict conducted in violation of international law, that is, contrary to *jus ad bellum*, would be per se contrary to the European Convention, regardless of issues of necessity and proportionality, remains to be considered by the Court. If it is, the *lex specialis* approach of the International Court of Justice will likely be invoked by the respondent state to suggest the issue is irrelevant. But, as explained above, there is much to support the view that human rights law differs in one fundamental aspect from the law of armed conflict: killing that results from resort to illegal war and acts of aggression is *prima facie* a violation of the human right to life.

5 CONCLUSION

'[P]eace is the underlying condition for the full observance of human rights and war is their negation.'[110] These words begin the Resolution adopted at the 1968 Tehran Conference on human rights that is regularly cited as the point of departure of efforts to reconcile the law of armed conflict with human rights law. The UN Secretary-General, in his first report on human rights and armed conflict, said: 'The Second World War gave conclusive proof of the close relationship which exists between outrageous behaviour of a Government towards its own citizens and aggression against other nations, thus, between respect for human rights and the maintenance of peace.'[111] Somehow, over time, the primacy of peace within the overall philosophy of human rights law has become blurred. Perhaps this is due to a certain infatuation with the use of armed force to prevent human rights violations. This often appears in the guise of fine slogans like 'humanitarian intervention' and the 'responsibility to protect', but in practice seems to degenerate inexorably into the atrocities of Abu Ghraib and Guantánamo. That resort to armed force may be necessary to prevent human rights violations cannot be ruled out, but nor should its benefits be exaggerated. As a general rule, it is a case of killing the patient to cure the illness, as we have seen in Iraq and Afghanistan. Another explanation for the

[110] Resolution XXIII 'Human Rights in Armed Conflicts' adopted by the International Conference on Human Rights, Tehran, 12 May 1968.
[111] Respect for human rights in armed conflicts, UN Doc A/7720, § 16.

marginalization of peace within the overall vision of human rights may be a consequence of the growing insistence upon international justice. Peace is often held up as a counterweight to justice. Some enthusiasts for justice take an absolute view, where there is no room to balance peace with individual accountability.

The conclusion of the June 2010 Kampala Review Conference provides a helpful correction, repositioning the ultimate atrocity, aggressive war, within the realm of international criminality. The Conference adopted, by consensus, a definition of the crime of aggression and modalities for prosecution that allow the Court to proceed even in the absence of a determination or authorization from the UN Security Council.[112] The message of the Nuremberg trial is revived: war is the 'supreme international crime differing only from other war crimes in that it contains within itself the accumulated evil of the whole'.[113] The International Military Tribunal did not use the language of human rights law, which only really emerged in the months and years following its judgment of the Nazi criminals. The judges might well have said that 'war is the supreme violation of the right to life'. Protection of the right to life requires the prohibition of aggressive war, and of the resort to force for the settlement of international disputes. That the law of armed conflict does not speak directly to the prohibition of war is a consequence of its unique mission which involves the regulation of behaviour on the battlefield. Human rights law need observe no such limitation.

[112] 'The Crime of Aggression', RC/Res.6.
[113] *Göring et al,* Judgment and Sentence of 1 October 1946, *in Trial of the Major War Criminals before the International Military Tribunal* (Nuremberg: IMT, 1948) vol 22, at 427.

CHAPTER 16

TORTURE AND OTHER CRUEL, INHUMAN, OR DEGRADING TREATMENT OR PUNISHMENT

MANFRED NOWAK[*]

1 INTRODUCTION

SINCE its beginnings in the nineteenth century, international humanitarian law (IHL) has drawn its major inspiration from respect for the dignity and integrity of the human being.[1] IHL was developed to reduce human suffering during armed conflicts by requiring combatants to act as humanely as possible and to avoid cruelty. The Lieber Code of 1863 clearly stated that military necessity does not admit cruelty, including torture.[2] Similar minimum standards of humane treatment were developed shortly thereafter in the context of international treaties under the auspices of

---

[*] The author expresses his sincere gratitude to Dr Julia Kozma, member of the European Committee for the Prevention of Torture, for her feedback, advice and input to this article.

[1] See eg the preliminary remarks of the International Committee of the Red Cross (ICRC) in its edition of 'The Geneva Conventions of August 12 1949', 1: 'Each of these fundamental international agreements is inspired by respect for human personality and dignity'.

[2] Instructions for the Government of the Armies of the United States in the Field, promulgated as General Order No 100 by President Abraham Lincoln, Washington DC, 24 April 1863, Art 16: 'Military

the International Committee of the Red Cross. In his Commentary on the Fourth Geneva Convention, Jean Pictet called the obligation to grant protected persons humane treatment 'in truth the *leitmotiv* of the four Geneva Conventions'.[3]

International human rights law (IHRL) was developed much later than IHL, in principle only as a reaction to 'barbarous acts which have outraged the conscience of mankind'[4] during World War II and the Nazi Holocaust. At first sight it seems surprising that human rights violations in times of war were taken up by the international community almost a century earlier than human rights violations in times of peace. Would it not have been more logical that the international community first developed minimum standards of civilized behaviour which governments should respect towards their own populations under 'normal' circumstances (in times of peace), and only thereafter consider which of these standards must also be secured in times of war towards the population (combatants and civilians) of 'enemy' states? The reasons why international human rights standards were first developed for times of war and only later for times of peace have to do with the concept of state sovereignty.[5] International armed conflicts are, by definition, a matter of international relations and, therefore, a legitimate concern of international law. How states treat their 'own' people was, however, for a long time regarded as a purely internal matter. The atrocities of the Nazi Holocaust convinced political leaders that genocide and similar crimes against a state's 'own' population were a matter of legitimate international concern. The development and implementation of IHRL as well as of IHL in relation to non-international armed conflicts even today is often confronted with arguments of state sovereignty and regarded as undue interference with domestic affairs. As a justification for taking up human rights as a matter of legitimate international concern, the preambles of both the 1945 Charter of the United Nations and the 1948 Universal Declaration of Human Rights explicitly link the need for human rights to the inherent dignity of the human person.

While all human rights are based on the desire to protect human dignity, not all human rights violations necessarily infringe human dignity.[6] Slavery and torture, however, are the strongest examples of human rights violations which at the same time constitute a direct attack on the core of human dignity. This link between slavery

---

necessity does not admit of cruelty—that is, the infliction of suffering for the sake of suffering or for revenge, nor of any maiming or wounding except in fight, nor of torture to extort confessions.'

[3] Commentary GC IV, 204. See also C. Droege, 'In Truth the *Leitmotiv*'—The Prohibition of Torture and Other Forms of Ill-Treatment in International Humanitarian Law', 89 *International Review of the Red Cross* (2007) 515–541.

[4] Preamble of the Universal Declaration of Human Rights (UDHR) 1948.

[5] M. Nowak, *Introduction to the International Human Rights Regime* (Leiden/Boston: Martinus Nijhoff Publishers, 2003), 33ff.

[6] Cf Progress Report of the Eminent Persons Panel by Manfred Nowak, Protecting Dignity, An Agenda for Human Rights, 12, available at <http://www.udhr60.ch/agenda/ENG-Agenda.pdf>.

and torture on the one hand, and dignity on the other, is best explained by Article 5 of the African Charter of Human and Peoples' Rights (African Charter) of 1981:

Every individual shall have the right to the respect of the dignity inherent in a human being and to the recognition of his legal status. All forms of exploitation and degradation of man, particularly slavery, slave trade, torture, cruel, inhuman or degrading punishment and treatment shall be prohibited.

The prohibition of slavery and torture, therefore, ranks among very few human rights, which are absolute and non-derogable. This means that slavery and torture can never be justified or balanced against other human rights or state interests. Even in time of war or other public emergency threatening the life of the nation, such as terrorism, states are not permitted to derogate from their obligations not to torture or enslave human beings.[7] This absolute character of the right to personal integrity and human dignity is underlined by Article 2(2) of the 1984 UN Convention against Torture and Other Cruel, Inhuman or Degrading Treatment or Punishment (CAT): 'No exceptional circumstances whatsoever, whether a state of war or a threat of war, internal political instability or any other public emergency, may be invoked as a justification of torture.' Today, the prohibition of torture is considered to be part of customary international law and having a *jus cogens* character.[8]

Under IHRL, the right to human dignity and personal integrity[9] is sometimes formulated in purely negative terms, ie as the prohibition of torture, cruel, inhuman, or degrading treatment or punishment.[10] These phenomena of ill-treatment can be divided into three categories: (i) torture; (ii) cruel and inhuman treatment or punishment; (iii) degrading treatment or punishment. The prohibition of these three types of ill-treatment is absolute and applies equally in times of peace and times of war.[11] During international and non-international armed conflicts, IHRL is supplemented by IHL. Both spheres of law apply equally and their

---

[7] Cf eg Art 15(2) of the European Convention on Human Rights (ECHR) 1950; Art 4(2) of the International Covenant on Civil and Political Rights (ICCPR) 1966; Art 27(2) of the American Convention on Human Rights (ACHR) 1969.

[8] See eg the judgment of the International Criminal Tribunal for the Former Yugoslavia (ICTY) of 16 November 1998 in *Prosecutor v Delalić*, Case No IT-96-21-T citing the first report of the Special Rapporteur on Torture, Pieter Kooijmans, of 19 February 1986, UN Doc E/CN.4/1986/15.

[9] Cf Art 5 of ACHR, Art 5 of the African Charter, Arts 1 and 3 of the Charter of Fundamental Rights of the European Union.

[10] Cf Art 3 of ECHR, Art 7 of ICCPR.

[11] That human rights continue to apply in times of armed conflict is clear already from the derogation clauses in Arts 4 of ICCPR, 15 of ECHR, and 27 of ACHR. Since certain states questioned the applicability of human rights during armed conflict, this issue was also clarified by the International Court of Justice in its Advisory Opinion on the *Legal Consequences of the Construction of a Wall in the Occupied Palestinian Territory* of 9 July 2004, [2004] ICJ Rep, 136. See also the joint reports of various special procedures of the United Nations in relation to the situation of detainees at Guantánamo Bay, UN Doc E/CN.4/2006/120 of 27 February 2006; and on secret detention in the fight against terrorism, UN Doc A/HRC/13/42 of 19 February 2010.

relationship needs to be clarified by means of interpretation, including the principle *lex specialis derogat legi generali* (a law governing a specific subject matter (*lex specialis*) overrides a law which governs general matters (*legi generali*)).[12] Since respect for human dignity constitutes a kind of *leitmotiv* for both IHL and IHRL, the absolute prohibition of torture and other forms of ill-treatment plays a central role in both legal frameworks. Although the terminology is slightly different in IHL, interpretation should seek to reconcile these differences as far as possible. If provisions of IHL have a wider scope of application or are simply more detailed than IHRL, they should be given preference. If provisions of IHL grant less protection than IHRL, they should have priority only if so required by the necessity of armed conflict. In the following, the three phenomena of ill-treatment outlined above will be analysed under both IHRL and IHL in light of relevant literature and jurisprudence. Should there be any major differences or contradictions between the relevant norms under the respective legal frameworks, an interpretation aimed at clarifying which norms have precedence will be offered.

2 THREE TYPES OF ILL-TREATMENT UNDER HUMAN RIGHTS LAW

A. Distinguishing criteria

Much has been written about the distinction between torture, cruel and inhuman treatment or punishment, as well as degrading treatment or punishment under IHRL.[13] Since all three types of ill-treatment are absolutely prohibited, even in times of war and emergency, there is no need to consider legal distinctions between them, and the UN Human Rights Committee as well as the two regional human rights courts in Europe and Latin America often only establish a violation of Article 7 of the ICCPR or the respective provisions in regional treaties.[14]

---

[12] On the relationship between international human rights law and international humanitarian law, see the Chapter by D. Jinks in this volume.

[13] Cf M. Nowak and E. McArthur, *The United Nations Convention against Torture—A Commentary* (Oxford/New York: Oxford University Press, 2008), 66ff and 557ff, with further references to the relevant literature and jurisprudence.

[14] Cf eg M. Nowak, *U.N. Covenant on Civil and Political Rights—CCPR Commentary* (2nd edn, Kehl/Strasbourg/Arlington: N.P. Engel Publisher, 2005), 160; P. van Dijk, F. van Hoof, A. van Rijn,

Under the UN Convention against Torture (CAT), the distinction between torture on the one hand, and other forms of ill-treatment on the other, does, however, have major legal consequences. Many provisions of CAT, above all the obligation to criminalize torture and to submit alleged cases of torture to the competent prosecuting authorities, the prohibition of non-refoulement and the prohibition against invoking any confession or information extracted by torture as evidence in any judicial or other proceedings, only apply to torture.[15] There is general agreement that torture constitutes an aggravated form of ill-treatment.[16] But there is disagreement concerning what is meant by aggravation.

In principle, two schools of thought have emerged. One opinion, which was originally developed by the European Court of Human Rights (ECtHR) in the Northern Ireland case and which is followed by most authors commenting on the ECtHR,[17] regards the intensity of pain and suffering as the decisive distinguishing criterion between torture and other forms of ill-treatment. Others see the intensity of pain or suffering as one distinguishing criterion between degrading and other forms of ill-treatment, but not between torture and cruel or inhuman treatment. According to this opinion, severe pain or suffering is required for both torture and cruel/inhuman treatment, and torture does not demand an even higher threshold. The intention and purpose of the infliction of pain or suffering (above all extraction of a confession or information) are, therefore, regarded as the main distinguishing criteria between torture and other forms of ill-treatment.[18]

In my role as UN Special Rapporteur on Torture, I also added the powerlessness of the victim as an additional element for the definition of torture, which means that a person can only be tortured in detention or a similar situation under the absolute control of the torturer.[19] In my opinion, the powerlessness of the victim is

and L. Zwaak (eds), *Theory and Practice of the European Convention on Human Rights* (4th edn, Antwerpen/Oxford: Intersentia, 2006), 405ff; L. Hennebel, *La Convention Américaine des Droits de l'Homme, Mécanismes de Protection et Étendue des Droits et Libertés* (Bruxelles: Bruylant, 2007), 455ff.

[15] Article 16(1) of CAT.

[16] See Art 1(2) of the Declaration on the Protection of All Persons from Being Subjected to Torture and Other Cruel, Inhuman or Degrading Treatment or Punishment, General Assembly Resolution 3452 (XXX) of 9 December 1975.

[17] See eg van Dijk et al, (n 14), 406ff; A. Cassese, 'Prohibition of Torture and Inhuman or Degrading Treatment or Punishment', in R. Macdonald, F. Matscher, and H. Petzold (eds), *The European System for the Protection of Human Rights* (Dordrecht/Boston/London: Martinus Nijhoff Publishers, 1993), 241. Christoph Grabenwarter, *Europäische Menschenrechtskonvention* (4th edn, Munich: Verlag C.H. Beck, 2009), 146.

[18] Cf eg N. Rodley, 'The Definition(s) of Torture in International Law', 55 *Current Legal Problems* (2002) 467–93; M. Evans, 'Getting to Grips with Torture', 51 *International and Comparative Law Quarterly* (2002) 365–83; M. Nowak, 'Challenges to the Absolute Nature of the Prohibition of Torture and Ill-Treatment', 23 *Netherlands Quarterly of Human Rights* (2005) 674–88; M. Nowak, 'What Practices Constitute Torture? US and UN Standards', 28(4) *Human Rights Quarterly* (2006) 809–41.

[19] UN Doc E/CN.4/2006/6 of 23 December 2005, paras 39ff; see also Nowak and McArthur (n 13), 76ff.

the essential criterion which the drafters of the Convention had in mind when they introduced the legal distinction between torture and other forms of ill-treatment. The element of powerlessness also links the torture definition under CAT with the one in the Rome Statute of the International Criminal Court ('Rome Statute').[20] In the following section, I will provide a short definition of the three types of ill-treatment on the basis of the second line of thought outlined above.

B. Degrading treatment or punishment

Degrading treatment or punishment can be defined as the infliction of pain or suffering, whether physical or mental, which aims at humiliating the victim.[21] Even the infliction of pain or suffering which does not reach the threshold of 'severe' must be considered as degrading treatment or punishment if it contains a particularly humiliating element. According to Article 16 of CAT, these acts can only be considered as degrading treatment when they 'are committed by or at the instigation of or with the consent or acquiescence of a public official or other person acting in an official capacity'. A certain degree of *state responsibility*, at least by means of acquiescence, was stressed by the drafters of CAT which means that ill-treatment inflicted by purely private actors, including rebel groups, is not covered by the provisions of CAT. Although there are certain developments in IHRL aimed at holding states accountable for not acting with due diligence to protect individuals against violence by private actors (eg domestic violence, traditional practices such as female genital mutilation),[22] CAT is among those traditional human rights treaties which only relate to state conduct.

Typical examples of *degrading treatment* are excessive use of force by the police outside detention (eg when dealing with public gatherings or riots) aimed at humiliating, or discriminating against, specific individuals (eg slapping or hair pulling), or humiliating prison conditions (eg forced nudity, insulting the religion of a detainee, sexual harassment, bad hygienic conditions). Typical examples of *degrading punishment* are light forms of corporal punishment or certain disciplinary punishments which aim at humiliating the person concerned among his or her peers (eg, hazing in the military, forcing a person to conduct humiliating exercises in front of others).

---

[20] Article 7(2)(e) of the Statute of the International Criminal Court: 'Torture means the intentional infliction of severe pain or suffering, whether physical or mental, upon a person in the custody or under the control of the accused'.

[21] Article 16 of CAT. See Nowak and McArthur (n 13), 558.

[22] Cf A. Clapham, *Human Rights Obligations of Non-State Actors* (Oxford/New York: Oxford University Press, 2006); M. Nowak, *Introduction* (n 14), 54ff and 243ff; Report of the UN Special Rapporteur on Torture to the UN Human Rights Council on 'Strengthening the Protection of Women from Torture', UN Doc A/HRC/7/3 of 15 January 2008, paras 44ff.

C. Cruel or inhuman treatment or punishment

No significant distinction has been drawn between cruel and inhuman treatment either in case law or legal scholarship.[23] While most international and regional treaties refer to cruel and inhuman treatment or punishment, Article 3 of the European Convention on Human Rights only prohibits inhuman treatment or punishment. Cruel/inhuman treatment or punishment can be defined as the infliction of severe pain or suffering,[24] whether physical or mental, on a person by or at least with the acquiescence of a public official without all aggravating conditions required for torture (intention, purpose, powerlessness). Any negligent or reckless infliction of severe pain or suffering (eg particularly harsh prison conditions, incommunicado detention) or the deliberate infliction of severe pain or suffering on a person outside detention or the direct control of a public official without a proper justification amounts to cruel/inhuman treatment.

Typical examples of cruel/inhuman treatment are excessive use of force by the police when arresting a person, during search and seizures, when quelling a riot or insurrection, dispersing an unlawful public gathering etc. Since the use of force by the police is, in principle, lawful for such purposes, the conduct of the police can only be qualified as cruel or inhuman if it is excessive, ie non-proportional in relation to the legitimate objective at stake. The typical example of *cruel/inhuman punishment* is corporal punishment by which severe pain or suffering is inflicted on the victim.[25] Since punishment is also explicitly mentioned as one of the purposes of torture in Article 1 of CAT, severe forms of corporal punishments also amount to torture. In my opinion, capital punishment as an aggravated form of corporal punishment also constitutes cruel/inhuman punishment and torture, but this issue is still highly controversial among states.[26] Other punishments which might be considered as cruel or inhuman are life imprisonment for children, hard labour, or prolonged solitary confinement.

[23] See also Droege (n 3), 519.

[24] This interpretation is based on the legal opinion mentioned above that the intensity of pain or suffering (severe) is no criterion distinguishing torture from cruel/inhuman treatment. This opinion has also been confirmed by the Elements of Crime of the International Criminal Court in relation to the war crime of inhuman treatment (Art 8(2)(a)(ii)-2 of the Rome Statute: '1. The perpetrator inflicted severe physical or mental pain or suffering upon one or more persons.').

[25] See the respective jurisprudence of the UN Human Rights Committee, the Committee against Torture, the European and Inter-American Courts of Human Rights in Nowak and McArthur (n 13), 561ff.

[26] See UNGA Resolution 62/149 of 26 February 2008; Report of the UN Special Rapporteur on Torture to the UN Human Rights Council on 'The Death Penalty in the Light of the Prohibition of Cruel, Inhuman and Degrading Punishment', UN Doc A/HRC/10/44 of 14 January 2009, §§ 29ff; W. Schabas, *The Death Penalty as Cruel Treatment and Torture* (Boston: Northeastern University Press, 1996); and Nowak and McArthur (n 13), 564ff; Juan Méndez, Interim report of the Special Rapporteur on torture and other cruel, inhuman or degrading treatment or punishment, UN Doc A/67/279; see also Juan Méndez, 'The Death Penalty and the Absolute Prohibition of Torture and Cruel, Inhuman, and Degrading Treatment or Punishment', 20(1) *Human Rights Brief* (2012) 2ff.

D. Torture

Torture is the only form of ill-treatment explicitly defined in Article 1 of CAT:

For the purpose of this Convention, the term 'torture' means any act by which severe pain or suffering, whether physical or mental, is intentionally inflicted on a person for such purpose as obtaining from him or a third person information or a confession, punishing him for an act he or a third person has committed or is suspected of having committed, or intimidating or coercing him or a third person, or for any reason based on discrimination of any kind, when such pain or suffering is inflicted by or at the instigation of or with the consent or acquiescence of a public official or other person acting in an official capacity. It does not include pain or suffering arising only from, inherent in or incidental to lawful sanctions.

The 'lawful sanctions' clause in the last sentence of Article 1(1) was inserted by a mistake of the drafters, lacks any meaningful scope of application and must simply be ignored.[27] According to Article 1 of CAT, there are four definition criteria of torture: infliction of severe pain or suffering, intention, purpose, and the involvement of a public official. In my opinion, the element of powerlessness should be added.[28] Since I disagree with the opinion of the ECtHR and others that torture requires a higher threshold of pain or suffering than cruel or inhuman treatment,[29] it follows that any form of cruel/inhuman treatment or punishment amounts to torture if all three additional (aggravating) criteria are fulfilled: (i) intention, (ii) purpose, and (iii) powerlessness of the victim.

(i) *Intention*

Torture can never be inflicted by negligent or even reckless behaviour. Even if a prisoner is forgotten by the prison staff and is slowly starving to death, this does not amount to torture, but 'only' to cruel and inhuman treatment. The intention must be directed at inflicting severe pain or suffering for a specific purpose.

(ii) *Purpose*

Article 1(1) of CAT contains a specific list of purposes of torture: extracting information or a confession, punishment, intimidation, coercion, discrimination. Although this list is non-exhaustive, torture can only be inflicted for a purpose that is similar to those mentioned in Article 1. In my experience as UN Special Rapporteur on Torture, in the vast majority of torture cases I investigated in many countries of the world, torture was inflicted by police interrogators for the purpose

---

[27] Cf Nowak and McArthur (n 13), 79ff. It is difficult to understand why the 'lawful sanctions' clause in Art 1 of CAT was reaffirmed in the definition of torture as a crime against humanity in Art 7(2)(e) of the Rome Statute of the International Criminal Court.

[28] See above, 2.A.

[29] See above, 2.A. Evans (n 18), 49, has rightly observed that it is somewhat absurd to think of treatment more severe than inhuman.

of extracting a confession. Intelligence agencies use torture for the purpose of extracting intelligence information. Punishment figures as the purpose of torture in the case of severe corporal or capital punishment, but in the jurisprudence of most courts or international human rights bodies, corporal or capital punishment is more likely to be qualified as cruel, inhuman, or degrading punishment than torture. This might have to do with the colloquial understanding of the word 'torture' or with the 'lawful sanctions' clause, which was only inserted in relation to torture in Article 1 of CAT but not in relation to cruel, inhuman, or degrading punishment in Article 16. The other purposes listed in Article 1 (intimidation, coercion, discrimination) often constitute only further elements in addition to the main purpose, ie extracting a confession or other information from the victim.

(iii) *Powerlessness*

If a police officer deliberately shoots at a person who attempts to escape or who attacks a third person, he or she intentionally inflicts severe pain on the person concerned. One of the purposes, in addition to preventing the escape of the person or protecting a third person, might be intimidation, punishment, or discrimination. Nevertheless, such conduct can never amount to torture. It might constitute cruel or inhuman treatment if the use of force was excessive, ie not proportional to the legitimate aim of law enforcement. If the use of force was proportional (eg the person was a dangerous criminal who seriously threatened the life of a third person), it was lawful and, therefore, does not constitute a violation of the right to personal integrity and dignity at all. Even if the person was killed, the use of force might still be lawful and, therefore, not qualified as a violation of the right to life.[30]

Torture is such a barbaric act and constitutes a direct attack on the dignity of the victim because severe pain or suffering is deliberately and purposefully inflicted on a powerless and defenceless person. If a police officer uses force to arrest a person who resists such arrest, such conduct might be perfectly lawful. As soon as this person is handcuffed and shackled, ie under the full control of the police officers, no further use of force is permissible. If the person is put under police custody, no use of force is permissible either, whether in the police cell or during interrogation. That is the reason why I felt it necessary in my function as UN Special Rapporteur on Torture to introduce the element of powerlessness as an additional definition criterion although not explicitly mentioned in Article 1(1) of CAT. This element is based on the *travaux préparatoires* of the Convention[31] and has been confirmed by

[30] Cf Art 2(2) of ECHR and the respective case law of the European Court of Human Rights in this respect. See van Dijk et al (n 14).

[31] Cf H. Burgers and H. Danelius, *The United Nations Convention Against Torture: Handbook on the Convention Against Torture and Other Cruel, Inhuman or Degrading Treatment or Punishment* (Dordrecht/Boston/London: Martinus Nijhoff Publishers, 1988), 120; C. Ingelse, *The UN Committee Against Torture: An Assessment* (The Hague/London/Boston: Kluwer Law International, 2001), 211; Nowak and McArthur (n 13), 29ff.

the definition of torture as a crime against humanity in Article 7(2)(e) of the Rome Statute of the International Criminal Court.

Typical examples and methods of torture used in all too many countries around the world are similar to the methods used in the darkest times of the Middle Ages: detainees are stripped naked, hooded or blindfolded, often in a dark cell, kept in stress positions, deprived of sleep, food and water, suspended from the ceiling in very painful positions, subjected to severe beatings, electric shocks, burnings, water boarding, loud noise, rape, extraction of nails, mutilation, mock executions, and similarly horrendous treatment.

E. Obligations of states under Human Rights Law

Under IHRL, states have various obligations to respect, protect, and fulfil the right to personal integrity and human dignity. First of all, they are under an *obligation to respect*, in all circumstances, the absolute prohibition of torture and other forms of ill-treatment by state officials. Secondly, they should take all necessary measures, as required by the principle of due diligence, to *protect* human beings from torture and ill-treatment by private actors, including domestic violence, trafficking in human beings, cruel traditional practices, such as female genital mutilation and honour crimes. If states fail to take the required measures, this constitutes torture or ill-treatment by acquiescence. Finally, states are under an obligation to take comprehensive positive measures to *fulfil* the right to personal integrity and human dignity.

The Convention against Torture contains a comprehensive set of such positive obligations to prevent torture and ill-treatment, to fight impunity for perpetrators of torture, and to provide victims of torture with a right to remedy and reparation. The obligation to prevent torture and ill-treatment includes the right of detainees to prompt access to lawyers, judges, doctors, and family members; the prohibition of incommunicado and secret detention; the right to habeas corpus; the audio- or video-taping of interrogations; the prohibition against the use of evidence extracted by torture in any judicial and administrative proceedings; anti-torture training of law enforcement officials; systematic review of interrogation methods and prison rules; the prohibition of expelling or extraditing a person to a country where he or she faces a serious risk of being subjected to torture (principle of *non-refoulement*); and the prompt and impartial investigation of every suspicion of torture by a competent state authority (a 'police-police'). Under the Optional Protocol to the Convention against Torture of 2002 (OPCAT), states parties are also required to establish so-called 'national preventive mechanisms', ie independent commissions to carry out regular and unannounced visits to all places of detention with the aim of preventing torture and improving conditions of detention.

The obligation to fight impunity of perpetrators of torture includes the criminalization of torture with adequate penalties taking into account the grave nature of the crime of torture; establishing comprehensive jurisdiction for the crime of torture in accordance with the principles of territorial, personal (active and, if the state considers it appropriate, passive nationality) and, if the suspect is present on the territory of the state, universal jurisdiction; arresting suspected perpetrators of torture present in the territory of states with the aim of either extraditing them to another state or submitting them to the competent prosecuting authorities.

The obligation to provide victims of torture with an effective remedy and adequate reparation includes the obligation of the competent authorities to promptly and impartially investigate every allegation of torture and the obligation to provide all victims with adequate reparation for the harm suffered, including compensation, medical, psychological, and social rehabilitation.

The most serious human rights violations, whether committed in times of peace or during armed conflict, also constitute crimes against humanity, ie 'when committed as part of a widespread or systematic attack directed against any civilian population, with knowledge of the attack'.[32] Perpetrators of crimes against humanity shall be prosecuted primarily before domestic courts. If states are, however, not able or willing to investigate and prosecute such perpetrators, the International Criminal Court or ad hoc international criminal tribunals established in relation to certain countries, such as the former Yugoslavia, Rwanda, or Sierra Leone, may exercise jurisdiction. The list of crimes against humanity under Article 7(1)(f) of the Rome Statute of the International Criminal Court includes torture, but not cruel, inhuman and degrading treatment. This is in line with Article 4 of CAT, which establishes an obligation to arrest and prosecute perpetrators only in relation to torture.

The explicit definition of torture as a crime against humanity in Article 7(2)(e) of the Rome Statute is, however, much broader than the definition of torture in Article 1 of CAT (no need of state involvement, no purpose requirement).[33] On the other hand, states have an obligation under the CAT to prosecute every individual act of torture whereas the International Criminal Court has jurisdiction only for acts of torture committed as part of a widespread or systematic attack.

---

[32] Article 7(1) of the Rome Statute. Article 5 of the ICTY Statute (UNSC Res 827 of 25 May 1993) still relates crimes against humanity to an armed conflict in the former Yugoslavia since 1991. Article 3 of the Statute of the International Criminal Tribunal for Rwanda (ICTR) (UNSC Res 955 of 8 November 1994) for the first time accepted crimes against humanity in times of peace 'when committed as part of a widespread and systematic attack against any civilian population on national, political, ethnic, racial or religious grounds'. Torture committed in Rwanda between 1 January and 31 December 1994 is included as a crime against humanity in Art 3(f) of the ICTR Statute. Cruel and degrading treatment are only to be prosecuted as violations of Common Art 3 of the Geneva Conventions, ie as war crimes, according to Art 4(a) and (e) of the ICTR Statute. See Section 3.B below.

[33] See Section 3.C in this Chapter.

Interestingly enough, under IHL and the International Criminal Court Statute, the definition of torture as a war crime is broader than the one enshrined in the CAT and in the Rome Statute (for torture as a crime against humanity). First of all, in contrast to torture as a crime against humanity, there is no requirement in IHL of a widespread or systematic attack as a necessary contextual element, which means that individual acts of torture can constitute grave breaches of the 1949 Geneva Conventions or violations of Common Article 3 to those Conventions and therefore war crimes. Secondly, also other forms of cruel, inhuman, or degrading treatment are listed as war crimes pursuant to Article 8 of the Rome Statute, both in international and non-international armed conflict.[34]

3   THREE TYPES OF ILL-TREATMENT UNDER INTERNATIONAL HUMANITARIAN LAW

Although IHL uses a somewhat different terminology, its safeguards for the right to personal integrity and human dignity can be classified in a similar way as under IHRL.[35] Common Article 3 of the 1949 Geneva Conventions applying to non-international armed conflict requires the parties to such conflict to treat persons humanely. To this end, a number of acts are absolutely prohibited. They include 'violence to life and person, in particular murder of all kinds, mutilation, cruel treatment and torture', as well as 'outrages upon personal dignity, in particular humiliating and degrading treatment'. These different notions of ill-treatment (torture; cruel treatment, including mutilation; degrading and humiliating treatment) are so similar to IHRL that both bodies of law mutually influence each other.[36] In the following, these three different types of ill-treatment are analysed with respect to relevant case law and literature.

---

[34] Article 8(2)(a)(ii): torture and inhuman treatment as grave breaches of the GCs in international armed conflict; Art 8(2)(b)(xxi): degrading treatment as part of other serious violations of the laws and customs applicable in international armed conflict; Art 8(2)(c)(i) and (ii): torture, cruel and degrading treatment as a serious violation of Common Art 3 of the four GCs in non-international armed conflict. See Sections 3.A and 3.B in this Chapter.

[35] For the following, cf also Droege (n 3).

[36] Cf eg the ICTY judgment of 10 December 1998 in *Prosecutor v Furundžija*, Case No IT-95-17/1 (Trial Chamber), § 159; see also Droege (n 3), 517.

A. Outrages upon personal dignity, in particular humiliating and degrading treatment

In addition to Common Article 3, outrages upon personal dignity are also prohibited by Article 75(2)(b) of Additional Protocol I ('outrages upon personal dignity, in particular humiliating and degrading treatment, enforced prostitution and any form of indecent assault') and Article 4(2)(e) of Additional Protocol II ('outrages upon personal dignity, in particular humiliating and degrading treatment, rape, enforced prostitution and any form of indecent assault'). In the ICRC Commentary to Additional Protocol I, outrages upon personal dignity have been defined as 'acts which, without directly causing harm to the integrity and physical and mental well-being of persons, are aimed at humiliating and ridiculing them, or even forcing them to perform degrading acts'.[37] In the jurisprudence of the ICTY, outrages upon personal dignity were considered as a serious attack on human dignity,[38] which requires no purpose as the crime of torture.[39] Examples of degrading treatment found by the ICTY include the use of human shields,[40] inappropriate conditions of confinement, performing subservient acts and being forced to relieve bodily functions in one's clothing.[41]

The notions of humiliating and degrading treatment seem to be synonymous.[42] The grave breaches provisions of the 1949 Geneva Conventions[43] require states to provide effective penal sanctions for persons committing torture and inhuman treatment, but not for degrading treatment or outrages upon personal dignity. This can be interpreted as an indication that the threshold of pain and suffering is lower for degrading treatment than for inhuman treatment. This is confirmed by a comparison of the respective provisions relating to war crimes in the Rome Statute of the International Criminal Court. While torture or inhuman treatment is considered a grave breach under Article 8(2)(a)(ii), outrages upon personal dignity, in particular humiliating and degrading treatment, fall under other serious violations of the laws and customs applicable in international armed conflict pursuant to Article 8(2)(b)(xxi). The Elements of Crimes of the International Criminal Court underline this distinction: while the war crime of inhuman treatment requires that the perpetrator inflicted severe physical or mental pain or suffering upon one or

---

[37] Commentary AP I and II, § 3047.

[38] ICTY, *Prosecutor v Kunarac and Others*, Case Nos IT-96-23 and IT-96-23/1 (Trial Chamber), 22 February 2001, § 161.

[39] ICTY, *Prosecutor v Kvocka and Others*, Case No IT-98-30/1-A (Appeals Chamber), 28 February 2005, § 226.

[40] ICTY, *Prosecutor v Aleksovski*, Case No. IT-95-14/1 (Trial Chamber), 25 June 1999, § 229.

[41] ICTY, *Prosecutor v Kvocka and Others* (n 39).   [42] Cf Droege (n 3), 532.

[43] Articles 50 of GC I, 51 of GC II, 130 of GC III, and 147 of GC IV.

more persons, this threshold is not required for the war crime of outrages upon personal dignity.

This short analysis confirms that outrages upon personal dignity constitute the least serious type of ill-treatment under IHL and can be compared to the notion of degrading treatment under IHRL. It does not require infliction of severe pain or suffering, but rather refers to particularly humiliating and insulting treatment.

B. Cruel or inhuman treatment

While Common Article 3 of the Geneva Conventions prohibits cruel treatment and torture, the grave breaches provisions in Articles 50, 51, 130, and 147 of the four Geneva Conventions respectively refer to 'torture or inhuman treatment, including biological experiments, wilfully causing great suffering or serious injury to body or health'. Under the heading 'humane treatment', Article 4(2)(a) of Additional Protocol II prohibits the following acts: 'violence to the life, health and physical or mental well-being of persons, in particular murder as well as cruel treatment such as torture, mutilation or any form of corporal punishment'. As under IHRL, there seems to be no difference between the notions of cruel and inhuman treatment.[44]

The Rome Statute of the International Criminal Court covers cruel or inhuman treatment in relation to the crime of genocide (Article 6(b): 'Causing serious bodily or mental harm to members of the group'), crimes against humanity (Article 7(1)(k): 'Other inhumane acts of a similar character intentionally causing great suffering, or serious injury to body or mental or physical health'), war crimes in international armed conflicts (Article 8(2)(a)(ii): 'Torture or inhuman treatment, including biological experiments') and war crimes in non-international armed conflicts (Article 8(2)(c)(i): 'Violence to life and person, in particular murder of all kinds, mutilation, cruel treatment and torture'). This again confirms that the notions of cruel and inhuman treatment are used interchangeably.

The Elements of Crimes of the International Criminal Court require for the crime against humanity 'other inhuman acts' which in Article 7(1)(k) specify that 'the perpetrator inflicted great suffering, or serious injury to body or to mental or physical health, by means of an inhumane act'. For the war crime of inhuman treatment, the Elements of Crimes require that the perpetrator inflicted severe physical or mental pain or suffering upon one or more persons.

This short analysis confirms again a broad similarity between the notions of cruel/ inhuman treatment in both IHL and IHRL. The threshold of great suffering or severe physical or mental pain or suffering is the same under both legal frameworks.

---

[44] Cf eg ICTY, *Prosecutor v Delalić and Others*, Case No IT-96-21 (Trial Chamber), 16 November 1998, § 552; *Prosecutor v Blaškić*, Case No IT-95-14 (Trial Chamber), 3 March 2000, § 186. See also Droege (n 3), 520.

While war crimes include both torture and cruel/inhuman treatment, crimes against humanity only include torture and other inhuman acts which are, however, restricted to intentional acts whereas cruel/inhuman treatment can also be inflicted by negligence. Although of no great importance, the fact that the ICTY defines inhuman treatment as 'an intentional act or omission, that is an act which, judged objectively, is deliberate and not accidental, which causes serious mental or physical suffering or injury or constitutes a serious attack on human dignity',[45] must be considered as a more fundamental difference to the understanding of inhuman treatment under IHRL. The introduction by the ICTY of the element of intention into the crime of inhuman treatment seems inconsistent with humanitarian and human rights law standards, given that it is an important criterion distinguishing torture from inhuman treatment.

Typical examples of cruel/inhuman treatment include corporal punishment, which is absolutely prohibited under IHL,[46] mutilation,[47] biological experiments,[48] imprisonment without daylight,[49] or other inhuman conditions of detention.

C. Torture

'Torture to extort confessions' was already prohibited in the Lieber Code, long before torture became outlawed in IHRL.[50] The report of the Commission on Responsibility submitted to the Versailles Conference on the basis of evidence of outrages committed during World War I, listed violations of the laws and customs of war which should be subject to criminal prosecution, including torture of civilians.[51] The Versailles Treaty, however, led only to a handful of prosecutions before German courts, not resulting in any convictions of torture.[52] While the Nuremberg Charter of the International Military Tribunal dealing with Nazi crimes only referred to

[45] Cf eg ICTY, *Prosecutor v Delalić and Others* (n 8), para 543; *Prosecutor v Blaškić* (n 44), §§ 154–5; *Prosecutor v Naletilic and Martinovic*, Case No IT-98-34-T (Trial Chamber), 31 March 2003, § 246. See also Droege (n 3), 520.

[46] Cf Arts 87(3), 89, and 108 of GC III; Arts 32, 118, and 119 of GC IV; Art 75 of AP I; Art 4 of AP II.

[47] Cf Art 13 of GC III; Art 32 of GC IV; Art 75 of AP I; Art 4 of AP II; Art 8(2)(c)(i) of the Rome Statute of the International Criminal Court.

[48] Cf Arts 50, 51, 130, and 147 of the GCs respectively; Art 12 of GC I; Art 12 of GC II; Art 13 of GC III ('medical or scientific experiments'); Art 32 of GC IV ('medical or scientific experiments'); Art 8(2)(a) (ii) of the Rome Statute of the International Criminal Court. See also Art 7 of CCPR 2nd sentence: 'In particular, no one shall be subjected without his free consent to medical or scientific experimentation'.

[49] Cf Art 87(3) of GC III; Art 118(2) of GC IV.

[50] See J.-M. Henckaerts and L. Doswald-Beck, *Customary International Humanitarian Law* (Cambridge: Cambridge University Press, 2005), Rule 90 (Torture and Cruel, Inhuman or Degrading Treatment) and Practice Relating to Rule 90, 1-165; Droege (n 3), 524ff; W. Schabas, 'The Crime of Torture and the International Criminal Tribunals,' 37 *Case W. Res. J. Int'l L.* (2005) 349–64.

[51] Report submitted to the Preliminary Conference of Versailles by the Commission on Responsibility of the Authors of War and on Enforcement of Penalties, Versailles, 29 March 1919.

[52] See Schabas (n 50), 349ff.

ill-treatment as a war crime and inhumane acts as crimes against humanity,[53] the Allied Control Council Law No 10 provided that torture should be prosecuted as a crime against humanity.[54] Nevertheless, torture played no significant role in prosecutions after World War II.[55]

The 1949 Geneva Conventions contain, however, various references to torture. Common Article 3 explicitly prohibits cruel treatment and torture. Articles 12 of Conventions I and II prohibit torture and biological experiments. Article 17(4) of Convention III provides that 'No physical or mental torture, nor any other form of coercion, may be inflicted on prisoners of war to secure from them information of any kind whatever'. In Convention IV, the prohibition of physical or moral coercion to obtain information is prohibited in Article 31, whereas torture figures in Article 32 among other 'measures of brutality', such as corporal punishment, mutilation and medical and scientific experiments. In the context of prohibiting collective punishments, corporal punishment and similar penalties, Article 87(3) of Convention III also reiterates that 'any form of torture or cruelty' is forbidden. The grave breaches provisions in Articles 50, 51, 130, and 147 respectively of the four Geneva Conventions require states to provide effective penal sanctions for persons committing 'wilful killing, torture or inhuman treatment, including biological experiments, wilfully causing great suffering or serious injury to body or health,' etc. Article 75 of AP I prohibits 'torture of all kinds, whether physical or mental'; and Article 4(2)(a) of AP II prohibits 'cruel treatment such as torture, mutilation or any form of corporal punishment'. The Statutes of the Yugoslavia and Rwanda Tribunals and the Special Court for Sierra Leone contain torture as a war crime and refer to the relevant provisions of the 1949 Geneva Conventions, above all Common Article 3.[56]

The combined reading of these provisions illustrates that torture is regarded as a particular form of cruel treatment or brutality aimed at extracting information from a person, usually a detainee. This interpretation is confirmed by the ICRC Commentaries. Jean Pictet, by commenting on the grave breaches provision in the Fourth Geneva Convention, commented as follows:[57]

The word torture has different acceptations. It is used sometimes even in the sense of purely moral suffering, but in view of the other expressions which follow (i.e. inhuman treatment including biological experiments and suffering, etc.) it seems that it must be given here its, so to speak, legal meaning—i.e., the infliction of suffering on a person to obtain from that person, or from another person, confessions or information. Looked at from this angle, torture is a concept which in general is not dealt with as such by national penal codes. It is more

[53] Article 6 of the Charter of the International Military Tribunal for Germany of 8 August 1945.

[54] Article II(1) of the Allied Control Council Law No 10 of 20 December 1945.

[55] See Schabas (n 50), 351.

[56] Article 2(b) of the ICTY Statute; Art 4(a) of the ICTR Statute; Art 3(a) of the Statute of the Special Court for Sierra Leone.

[57] Commentary GC IV, 598.

than a mere assault on the physical or moral integrity of a person. What is important is not so much the pain itself as the purpose behind its infliction. This, therefore, is a point which will require additional clauses in most national legislations; fortunately, judicial torture has disappeared from all civilized penal systems.

This quote shows that Jean Pictet, already in 1958, long before the misleading judgment of the European Court of Human Rights in the Northern Ireland case, rightly noted that the purpose of extorting information and confessions, and not the intensity of pain, is the decisive criterion distinguishing torture from other forms of cruel and inhuman treatment. This finding corresponds to the interpretation of IHRL outlined above.[58]

The Rome Statute of the International Criminal Court contains torture both as a crime against humanity and a war crime.

As a crime against humanity, torture can only be prosecuted 'when committed as part of a widespread or systematic attack directed against any civilian population, with knowledge of the attack'.[59] Other forms of cruel, inhuman, or degrading treatment or punishment are not included in the list of crimes against humanity, but rape, sexual slavery, enforced prostitution, forced pregnancy, enforced sterilization, other forms of sexual violence of comparable gravity, enforced disappearances, and other inhumane acts of a similar character intentionally causing great suffering, or serious injury to body or to mental or physical health are listed as crimes against humanity.

Torture as a crime against humanity, which can be committed both during and outside of any armed conflict, is explicitly defined in the Rome Statute as 'the intentional infliction of severe pain or suffering, whether physical or mental, upon a person in the custody or under the control of the accused; except that torture shall not include pain or suffering arising only from, inherent in or incidental to, lawful sanctions'.[60] The Elements of Crimes add little to this definition but clarify that it is 'understood that no specific purpose need be proved for this crime'.[61] While the definition of torture in the Rome Statute is based on the definition in Article 1 of CAT, there are significant differences. The requirement of infliction of severe pain or suffering, which also applies to cruel and inhuman treatment,[62] corresponds to the correct interpretation of IHRL as outlined above.[63] The requirement that the victim was 'in the custody or under the control' of the perpetrator is not contained

---

[58] See Section 2.A in this Chapter.
[59] Article 7(1)(f) of the Statute of the International Criminal Court.
[60] Article 7(2)(f) of the Statute of the International Criminal Court.
[61] Elements of Crime, footnote 14, adopted by the Assembly of States Parties to the Statute of the International Criminal Court on 9 September 2002 in accordance with Art 9 of the Statute.
[62] Cf Elements of Crime in relation to the war crime of inhuman treatment in Art 8(2)(a)(ii) and in relation to the crime against humanity of other inhumane acts in Art 7(1)(k) of the Statute of the International Criminal Court.
[63] See Section 2.A in this Chapter.   •

in the definition of Article 1 of CAT but corresponds to the element of *powerlessness* characteristic for torture as developed by the Special Rapporteur on Torture.[64]

That the definition of the International Criminal Court does not refer to the involvement of a *public official* is understandable in relation to a non-international armed conflict with non-state actors as combatants, but not necessarily in relation to a crime against humanity. Nevertheless, the state-centred definition of torture in CAT can be considered as somewhat old-fashioned. When the Disappearance Convention was drafted on the model of CAT in the early twenty-first century, a specific provision was inserted which obliges states parties to investigate acts of enforced disappearance 'committed by persons or groups of persons acting without the authorization, support or acquiescence of the state and to bring those responsible to justice'.[65] This shows that IHRL today also recognizes obligations of states in relation to serious human rights violations by non-state actors. It is indeed difficult to understand why torture committed by rebel groups, organized crime gangs, or other non-state actors should not be subjected to criminal investigation by states parties to CAT.

The definition in the Rome Statute can, therefore, be seen as a further development of international law aimed at broader protection against torture. It may also be used by international human rights monitoring bodies for the interpretation of the term 'torture', eg in Article 7 of ICCPR. Why the drafters of the Rome Statute omitted the element of *purpose* from the definition of torture is, however, more difficult to understand. After all, the deliberate infliction of severe pain or suffering for a specific purpose, such as extracting a confession or information from the victim, is the main criterion distinguishing torture from other forms of cruel and inhuman treatment, both in IHRL[66] and in IHL.[67] This is also confirmed by the definition of torture as a war crime in the Elements of Crimes, as outlined below. The waiver of the purpose element in the definition of torture as a crime against humanity, although deliberately chosen as a compromise between different schools of thought,[68] contains the risk of using the term 'torture' in an inflationary manner and of blurring the legal distinction between three different types of ill-treatment. But since the definition in the Elements of Crimes of the International Criminal Court goes beyond the CAT definition and covers all acts of torture prohibited by CAT, this does no harm and raises no difficult questions of interpretation.

As a war crime, torture is both covered as a grave breach of the four Geneva Conventions in international armed conflicts according to Article 8(2)(a)(ii) of the

[64] See Sections 2.A and 2.D in this Chapter.

[65] International Convention for the Protection of All Persons from Enforced Disappearance 2006, Art 3.

[66] See Sections 2.A and 2.D in this Chapter.

[67] See eg the understanding of torture in the GCs and in the ICRC-Commentary to the GCs above.

[68] Cf M. Politi, 'Elements of Crimes', in A. Cassese, P. Gaeta, and J. Jones, *The Rome Statute of the International Criminal Court—A Commentary*, vol I (Oxford/New York: Oxford University Press, 2002), 470ff.   ˙

Rome Statute, and as a serious violation of Common Article 3 of the four Geneva Conventions in non-international armed conflicts pursuant to Article 8(2)(c)(i) of the Rome Statute. Article 8 does not contain any definition of torture as a war crime, but the Elements of Crimes stipulate that the perpetrator inflicted severe physical or mental pain or suffering upon one or more persons protected under the Conventions 'for such purposes as: obtaining information or a concession, punishment, intimidation or coercion or for any reason based on discrimination of any kind'.[69] It is interesting to note that the inclusion of the element of purpose follows the definition in Article 1 of CAT and the general understanding of torture under IHL whereas, as noted above, the element of purpose is missing from the Elements of Crimes of torture as a crime against humanity.

In the *Akayesu* case, the ICTR found Jean-Paul Akayesu, a mayor in the Prefecture of Gitarama in Rwanda guilty of torture as a crime against humanity. It explicitly interpreted the word 'torture' in Article 3(f) of the ICTR Statute in accordance with the definition set forth in Article 1 of CAT.[70] In the *Čelebići prison camp* case of November 1998, the ICTY also based its conviction of torture as a crime against humanity on the definition of torture in Article 1 of CAT, which was considered to reflect customary international law.[71] In the *Furundžija* case which concerned only one single act of torture and, therefore, could not be prosecuted as a crime against humanity, the ICTY convicted the Bosnian Croat army commander Anton Furundžija of the war crime of torture and noted that the prohibition of torture constitutes *jus cogens*.[72] Since the Croat Defence Council (HVO) had to be considered as a non-state actor in Bosnia and Herzegovina, the ICTY broadened the public official element in the definition of torture to also encompass a *de-facto* organ of a state or any other authority-wielding entity.[73] In the *Kvocka* case, the ICTY, by citing Article 7(2)(e) of the Rome Statute of the International Criminal Court, fully departed from the requirement of the involvement of a public official by stating that 'the state actor requirement imposed by international human rights law is inconsistent with the application of individual criminal responsibility for international crimes found in international humanitarian law and international criminal law'.[74] Rape was considered by both the ICTR and the ICTY as a form of torture, since it constitutes a violation of human dignity involving severe pain or suffering.[75]

---

[69] Elements of Crime, above, in relation to the war crime of torture in Art 8(2)(a)(ii) of the Statute of the International Criminal Court.

[70] ICTR, *Prosecutor v Akayesu*, Case No ICTR-96-4-T, 2 September 1998, §§ 121–3.

[71] ICTY, *Prosecutor v Delalić and Others* (n 8), § 459.

[72] ICTY, *Prosecutor v Furundžija* (n 36), §§ 144, 153–6.

[73] ICTY, *Prosecutor v Furundžija* (n 36), § 162.   [74] ICTY, *Prosecutor v Kvocka* (n 41), § 139.

[75] ICTR, *Prosecutor v Akayesu* (n 70), § 597; ICTY, *Prosecutor v Kunarac*, Case No IT-96-23/1-A (Appeals Chamber), 12 June 2002, §§ 149–51.

D. Obligations under IHL

IHL creates obligations for both states and certain non-state actors. The absolute and non-derogable prohibition of torture and other forms of ill-treatment, first of all, requires states and other parties to armed conflicts to refrain from committing any acts of torture, cruel/inhuman treatment and outrages upon personal dignity, including degrading treatment. These acts include rape and other forms of sexual violence, mutilation, biological, medical and scientific experiments, corporal punishment, imprisonment without daylight and other inhuman conditions of detention. CG III contains the general obligation of treating prisoners of war humanely and many specific provisions relating to conditions of detention. These provisions can be regarded as a *lex specialis* for prisoners of war in relation to the general obligation under Article 10 of ICCPR to treat all persons deprived of their liberty with humanity and with respect for the inherent dignity of the human person.

The grave breaches provisions in all four Geneva Conventions create the obligation on states parties to enact special legislation to criminalize grave breaches, to search for persons alleged to have committed grave breaches, and to bring such persons, regardless of their nationality, before their own courts or to hand them over to other states parties for the purpose of prosecution. While torture and inhuman treatment are included in the concept of grave breaches, degrading treatment falls below this threshold. But outrages upon personal dignity, including degrading treatment, also constitute serious violations of the laws and customs applicable in international armed conflict as well as serious violations of Common Article 3 and, therefore, war crimes in all kinds of armed conflicts.

Under IHRL, by comparison, states parties to CAT are required to criminalize torture and to bring perpetrators of every act of torture, regardless of their nationality and where the act of torture was committed, to justice under the principle *aut dedere aut iudicare*.[76] However, there is no obligation to criminalize either cruel/inhuman or degrading treatment. Apart from the obligation to respect the right to personal integrity and dignity and to bring perpetrators of war crimes of torture, inhuman and degrading treatment to justice, IHL does not contain specific obligations to prevent such acts or to provide victims with an effective remedy and adequate reparation for the harm suffered. In this respect, IHRL provides more comprehensive protection.

---

[76] Articles 4–9 of CAT; see Section 2.E in this Chapter.

4 CONCLUSIONS

The comparative analysis of the prohibition of torture and other forms of ill-treatment under IHL, IHRL, and international criminal law shows major similarities and only minor differences between these legal frameworks. All forms of torture, cruel, inhuman, or degrading treatment or punishment are absolutely prohibited under the different spheres of international law, and no derogations from the right to personal integrity and dignity are permitted in times of war or other emergency situations.

Three different types of ill-treatment can be distinguished according to the gravity of the behaviour under both IHL and human rights law: degrading treatment (or outrages upon personal dignity) which does not reach the level of severe pain or suffering but which shows particularly humiliating treatment; cruel or inhuman treatment which requires the infliction of severe pain or suffering but which lacks certain aggravating elements only required for torture, namely intention, a specific purpose (above all extraction of information or confession) and the powerlessness of the victim (meaning a situation of custody or other direct control of the perpetrator).

In certain respects, protection under IHL goes beyond that available under international human rights law. First of all, human rights treaties, at least in principle, only create legal obligations for states to respect, protect, and fulfil human rights, whereas international humanitarian law also applies to *non-state actors*. Notwithstanding certain tendencies under human rights law to go beyond mere state responsibility, the UN Convention against Torture is among those human rights treaties which include the requirements of the involvement of a public official (at least by acquiescence) even in the legal definition of torture and other forms of ill-treatment. Rebel groups or other non-state actors cannot be held accountable for torture and ill-treatment under human rights law, nor can states be held accountable for acts of rebel groups.[77] International humanitarian law, on the contrary, does create direct obligations for non-state actors not to practice torture or other forms of ill-treatment. This is also reflected in international criminal law. In the context of torture and ill-treatment as war crimes, but also in relation to torture as a crime against humanity, state officials, members of rebel groups, and other non-state actors are equally liable to prosecution before the International Criminal Court and other courts and tribunals.

The second reason for the broader protection of IHL, as compared to IHRL, relates to the *use of criminal law*. Under the CAT, states parties have an obligation to criminalize every act of torture, but not acts which constitute other forms of cruel, inhuman, or degrading treatment or punishment. If torture (not, however,

---

[77] Cf the Chapter on the 'Focusing on Armed Non-State Actors' in this volume.

cruel, inhuman or degrading treatment) is practised as part of a widespread or systematic attack against any civilian population, both in times of peace and war, it also constitutes a crime against humanity triggering the jurisdiction of domestic courts as well as of the International Criminal Court and other international criminal tribunals. Under IHL, on the other hand, every individual act of both torture and inhuman treatment could be considered as a grave breach of the Geneva Conventions, which needs to be prosecuted by domestic courts and international tribunals. In addition, even degrading treatment constitutes a serious violation of the laws and customs applicable in international and non-international armed conflict. This means that every single act of torture, cruel, inhuman, or degrading treatment constitutes a war crime and is, therefore, subject to the jurisdiction of the International Criminal Court and other international criminal tribunals.

In the Elements of Crimes treatment of torture as a crime against humanity, the *purpose requirement* is lacking. Although this omission is inconsistent with the relevant rules of international humanitarian law and with human rights law standards and with the definition of torture as a war crime in the same Elements of Crimes, it could mean in effect a broader scope of application for torture as a crime against humanity in peace time as compared to torture as a war crime. Even the deliberate infliction of severe pain or suffering without any purpose might be prosecuted by the International Criminal Court as torture rather than as inhuman treatment.

The definition of torture under the Elements of Crimes of the International Criminal Court also seems to be less comprehensive than in CAT from another perspective: when it requires that the victim of torture must be in the *custody or under the direct control of the perpetrator*. However, this requirement of the powerlessness of the victim has also been included by means of interpretation into the definition of torture under CAT. Consequently, this slight difference can easily be reconciled through interpretation.

In certain respects, international humanitarian standards are more detailed than those found in human rights treaties and provide better protection. While minimum human rights standards for *conditions of detention* have only been developed in the context of soft law,[78] Geneva Convention III contains binding minimum standards for prisoners of war that should be applied in addition to the general obligation under Article 10 of ICCPR to treat all detainees with humanity and respect for the inherent dignity of the human person. Another example is *corporal punishment*. Although international jurisprudence considers every form of corporal punishment as at least degrading punishment in violation of the right to human

---

[78] In my function as UN Special Rapporteur on Torture, I have repeatedly called for the drafting and adoption of a binding UN Convention on the Rights of Detainees: see UN Doc A/HRC/13/39 of 9 February 2010, § 77(e).

dignity, this issue is still highly controversial under human rights law, and many states continue to apply corporal punishment as judicial or disciplinary sanctions under domestic law.[79] However, any form of corporal punishment is explicitly prohibited under various provisions of the Geneva Conventions.[80]

In other respects, human rights treaties contain specific obligations of states that go beyond state obligations under IHL. In particular, CAT provides a broad range of positive obligations to prevent torture and ill-treatment, to refrain from sending persons to countries where they face a serious risk of torture, and to provide victims of torture with an effective remedy and adequate reparation for the harm suffered. Since international human rights law continues to be applicable during armed conflicts, these specific obligations must be considered as *lex specialis*.

In conclusion, I wish to emphasize that there are no contradictions between IHL and IHRL in relation to the prohibition of torture and other forms of ill-treatment which would need to be solved by applying the principle *lex specialis derogat legi generali*, or any similar method of interpretation. In general, the standards under both spheres of international law are very similar. In certain respects, IHL provides a somewhat better protection than IHRL and should, therefore, given preference in the context of armed conflicts. But, in principle, all the obligations under IHRL for the protection of the right to personal integrity and human dignity also remain applicable during armed conflicts, and in certain respects these obligations, above all those enshrined in the CAT, are more detailed and provide better protection than those contained in the relevant rules of IHL.

[79] Cf eg Report of the UN Special Rapporteur on Torture to the UN Human Rights Council, Study on the phenomena of torture, cruel, inhuman or degrading treatment or punishment in the world, including an assessment of conditions of detention, UN Doc A/HRC/13/39/Add.5 of 5 February 2010, §§ 209–28.

[80] See n 47.

CHAPTER 17

....

INTERNATIONAL FAIR TRIAL GUARANTEES

....

DAVID WEISSBRODT[*]

1 INTRODUCTION

....

THE right to a fair trial is a fundamental human right.[1] It ensures that no one is deprived of liberty without due process of law.[2] The use of military commissions by the United States for the trial of 'unprivileged enemy belligerents' has initiated a new debate over the scope and meaning of fair trial guarantees, particularly during periods of armed conflict.[3]

[*] The author thanks Matthew Randol and Mary Rumsey for their assistance in preparing this Chapter.

[1] See eg Universal Declaration of Human Rights (UDHR), Art 10: 'Everyone is entitled in full equality to a fair and public hearing by an independent and impartial tribunal, in the determination of his rights and obligations and of any criminal charge against him'.

[2] UDHR, Art 3: 'Everyone has the right to life, liberty and security of person'; International Covenant on Civil and Political Rights (ICCPR), Art 9(1): 'Everyone has the right to liberty and security of person. No one shall be subjected to arbitrary arrest or detention. No one shall be deprived of his liberty except on such grounds and in accordance with such procedure as are established by law'. See generally Amnesty International, *Fair Trial Manual* (London: Amnesty International Publications, 1998).

[3] Much has been written about the Bush Administration's efforts to establish military commissions to try detainees, and the Obama Administration's handling of the related problems it inherited. See generally J. Bravin, *The Terror Courts: Rough Justice at Guantánamo Bay* (New Haven: Yale University Press, 2013); F. Ni Aoláin and O. Gross (eds), *Guantánamo Bay and Beyond: Exceptional Courts and Military Commissions in Comparative Perspective* (New York: Cambridge University Press, 2013); T. Sparks and G. Sulmasy (eds), *International Law Challenges: Homeland Security and Combating Terrorism* (Newport, RI: Naval

The main purpose of this Chapter is to chart the basic contours of fair trial guarantees as articulated in international humanitarian law (IHL) and international human rights law (IHRL). I will first identify the principal treaty provisions that guarantee the right to a fair trial during armed conflict; then I will explore the concept of a 'regularly constituted court', a vital element in fair trial guarantees, to move to examine the actual content of the fair trial guarantees as expressed in treaties and other instruments of international law. Finally, I will explore how the normative standards of the fair trial guarantees apply in the practice of military commissions.

2 FAIR TRIAL GUARANTEES UNDER INTERNATIONAL LAW: A BRIEF OVERVIEW

The right to a fair trial has been elaborated and guaranteed by no less than 20 global and regional human rights treaties and other instruments. Among the most important are the Universal Declaration of Human Rights (UDHR),[4] the International

War College, 2006); J. Margulies, *Guantánamo and the Abuse of Presidential Power* (New York: Simon & Schuster, 2006); National Institute of Military Justice, *Annotated Guide: Procedures for Trials by Military Commissions of Certain Non-United States Citizens in the War Against Terrorism* (Newark, NJ: Matthew Bender/LexisNexis, 2002); K. Alexander, 'In the Wake of September 11th: The Use of Military Tribunals to Try Terrorists', 78 *Notre Dame Law Review* (2003) 885–916; L. Dickinson, 'Using Legal Process to Fight Terrorism: Detentions, Military Commissions, International Tribunals, and the Rule of Law', 75 *South California Law Review* (2002) 1407–92; J. Fitzpatrick, 'Jurisdiction of Military Commissions and the Ambiguous War on Terrorism', 96 *American Journal of Int'l Law* (2002) 345–54; S. Murphy (ed), 'Instructions for Military Commissions on Trying Aliens Charged with Terrorism', 97 *American Journal of Int'l Law* (2003) 706–9; H. Koh, 'The Case Against Military Commissions', 96 *American Journal of Int'l Law* (2002) 337–44; M. Matheson, 'US Military Commissions: One of Several Options', 96 *American Journal of Int'l Law* (2002) 354–8; D. Mundis, 'The Use of Military Commissions to Prosecute Individuals Accused of Terrorist Acts', 96 *American Journal of Int'l Law* (2002) 320–8; D. Orentlicher and R. Goldman, 'When Justice Goes to War: Prosecuting Terrorists Before Military Commissions', 25 *Harvard Journal of Law and Public Policy* (2002) 653–63; J. Paust, 'Antiterrorism Military Commissions: Courting Illegality', 23 *Michigan Journal of Int'l Law* (2001) 1–29; J. Paust, 'Antiterrorism Military Commissions: The Ad Hoc DOD Rules of Procedure', 23 *Michigan Journal of Int'l Law* (2002) 677–94; A. Rubin, 'Applying the Geneva Conventions: Military Commissions, Armed Conflict, and Al-Qaeda', 26 *Fletcher Forum of World Affairs* (2002) 79; C. Tobias, 'Detentions, Military Commissions, Terrorism, and Domestic Case Precedent', 76 *South California Law Review* (2003) 1371–1407; J. Torruella, 'On the Slippery Slopes of Afghanistan: Military Commissions and the Exercise of Presidential Power', 4 *University of Pennsylvania Journal of Constitutional Law* (2002) 648–734; S. Murphy (ed), 'US Department of Defense Rules on Military Commissions', 96 *American Journal of Int'l Law* (2002) 731–4; R. Wedgwood, 'Al Qaeda, Terrorism, and Military Commissions', 96 *American Journal of Int'l Law* (2002) 328–37; R. Wilson, 'Can US Courts Learn from Failed Terrorist Trials by Military Commission in Turkey and Peru?', 11 *Human Rights Brief* (2003) 11–13; American Bar Association Task Force on Terrorism and the Law, 'Report and Recommendations on Military Commissions' (January 2002) *Army Law* 1–18.

[4] UDHR, Art 10.

Covenant on Civil and Political Rights (ICCPR),[5] the International Convention on the Elimination of All Forms of Racial Discrimination (ICERD),[6] and the Convention on the Rights of the Child (CRC).[7] International humanitarian law, codified in the four Geneva Conventions and two Additional Protocols, ensures that the right to a fair trial and related criminal justice standards are upheld during periods of non-international and international armed conflicts. Regional treaties such as the African Charter on Human and Peoples' Rights,[8] the American Convention on Human Rights (American Convention),[9] and the European Convention for the Protection of Human Rights and Fundamental Freedoms (European Convention),[10] contain fair trial guarantees and other provisions relevant to criminal justice.

The most visible and recent elaboration of the right to a fair trial has been in the context of the activities of the ad hoc international tribunals for the former Yugoslavia,[11] Rwanda,[12] and other mixed national/international tribunals[13] as well as the International Criminal Court.

The remainder of this section offers a brief survey of the treaties and non-treaty instruments that address fair trial guarantees in situations of armed conflict. It surveys treaty sources from humanitarian law and human rights law. It then concludes by distilling from these sources the essential elements of fair trial guarantees as they apply in situations of armed conflict.

A. Fair trial guarantees in IHL

IHL comprises the body of protective norms extended to combatants and civilians in an international or non-international armed conflict irrespective of the legality of the conflict. Contemporary international law imposes criminal liability for certain breaches of humanitarian law in both international[14] and non-international armed conflicts.[15] The prospect of a violation of fair trial guarantees being prosecuted as a war crime means that fair trial takes on a special importance in times of armed conflict.

---

[5] ICCPR, Art 14.   [6] ICERD, Art 5(a).   [7] CRC, Art 40.

[8] African Charter on Human and Peoples' Rights, Art 7.

[9] American Convention, Art 8.   [10] European Convention, Art 6.

[11] Statute of the International Tribunal for the Prosecution of Persons Responsible for Serious Violations of International Humanitarian Law Committed in the Territory of Former Yugoslavia, S/RES/827 (1993).

[12] Statute of the International Tribunal for Rwanda, S/RES/955 (1994).

[13] In addition, the Special Court for Sierra Leone, the Extraordinary Chambers in the Courts of Cambodia, and the Special Tribunal for Lebanon are recent ad hoc tribunals established by agreement between the United Nations and the respective governments.

[14] See the Chapter on 'Grave Breaches' in this volume. See also O. Gross, 'The Grave Breaches System and the Armed Conflict in the Former Yugoslavia', 16 Michigan Journal of Int'l Law (1995) 783–829.

[15] Tadić Case (IT-94-1-AR 72), Appeals Chamber (Jurisdiction), Decision of 2 October 1995, §§ 84–137.

(i) *Fair trial provisions relating to international armed conflict*

The IHL provisions relevant to fair trial guarantees in international armed conflicts are set forth in the Geneva Convention relative to the Treatment of Prisoners of War (1949) (GC III), the Geneva Convention relative to the Protection of Civilian Persons in Time of War (1949) (GC IV), and Article 75 of Additional Protocol I (1977) (AP I).

Articles 96 and 99–108 of GC III prescribe the rights of prisoners of war in judicial proceedings, essentially creating fair trial standards in international armed conflicts. Articles 54, 64–74, and 117–26 of GC IV contain provisions relating to the right to fair trial in occupied territories. Article 75 of AP I extends fair trial guarantees in an international armed conflict to all persons, including those arrested for actions relating to the conflict.

(ii) *Fair trial provisions regulating non-international armed conflict*

In non-international armed conflict, the primary humanitarian law provisions include Article 3 common to all four Geneva Conventions and Article 6 of Additional Protocol II (AP II).

Common Article 3 applies in all situations of non-international armed conflict[16] and applies to all persons not engaged in hostilities, including both civilians and military personnel who have laid down their arms or who are wounded.[17]

AP II supplements Common Article 3 by extending its protections to situations of non-international armed conflict more restrictively defined than Common Article 3 in the Geneva Conventions. Article 1(1) of AP II defines the limited scope of its application to non-international conflicts between the armed forces of a High Contracting Party and 'dissident armed forces or other organized armed groups which [...] exercise such control over a part of its territory as to enable them to carry out sustained and concerted military operations [...]'. Article 6 of AP II extends the fair trial guarantees articulated in Common Article 3 to these forms of non-international armed conflict.

B. The fair trial guarantees in IHRL

Fair trial guarantees are also expressed in IHRL. The most relevant provisions are found in the Universal Declaration of Human Rights and the International Covenant on Civil and Political Rights.

(i) *Universal Declaration of Human Rights*

In 1948 the UN General Assembly adopted the UDHR which provides a worldwide definition of the human rights obligations undertaken by all UN member states

---

[16] Common Art 3, at chapeau.   [17] Common Art 3(1).

pursuant to Articles 55 and 56 of the UN Charter, including several provisions relating to the administration of justice. For example, Article 10 of the UDHR states that 'Everyone is entitled in full equality to a fair and public hearing by an independent and impartial tribunal, in the determination of his rights and obligations and of any criminal charge against him'. Article 11 further provides for the presumption of innocence, public trial, and 'all guarantees necessary for [one's] defence'. It also assures that a 'conviction can only be based on the law applicable at the time of the offence',[18] and forbids retroactive punishment or penalties. Other provisions of the Universal Declaration—for example, those regarding arbitrary arrest, the right to an effective remedy, the right to be free from torture, the right to security of person, and the right to privacy—are relevant to the criminal justice system and the fairness of the trial process.

(ii) *International Covenant on Civil and Political Rights*

Following the adoption of the UDHR, the UN Commission on Human Rights drafted the remainder of the International Bill of Human Rights which includes the ICCPR. The Covenant establishes an international minimum standard of conduct for all participating governments, and further elaborates—primarily in Articles 14 and 15 but also in Articles 2, 6, 7, 9, and 10—on the criminal justice standards identified in the UDHR.

Article 14 is the most extensive provision on the right to a fair trial in the Covenant. It recognizes the right in all proceedings to 'a fair and public hearing by a competent, independent and impartial tribunal established by law'. Every person is 'equal before the courts and tribunals' under Article 14(1). Article 14 also extends the right to a fair hearing to both civil cases and criminal cases and emphasizes that parties to such proceedings are entitled to equality before courts and tribunals. As construed by the UN Human Rights Committee (Committee) in General Comment No 13, Article 14(3) deals with the minimum guarantees required in the determination of any criminal charge, the observance of which is not always sufficient to ensure the fairness of a hearing.[19] The minimum guarantees in criminal proceedings prescribed by Article 14(3) include: the right for the accused to be informed of the charge against him or her in a language which he or she understands; to have adequate time and facilities for the preparation of a defence, and to communicate with counsel of their own choosing; to be tried without undue delay; to examine or have examined the witnesses against them, and to obtain the attendance and examination of witnesses on their behalf under the same conditions as witnesses against them; to the assistance of an interpreter free of any charge, if they cannot understand or speak the language used in court; and not to be compelled to testify against

---

[18] D. Weissbrodt, *The Right to a Fair Trial: Articles 8, 10 and 11 of the Universal Declaration of Human Rights* (The Hague Netherlands: Kluwer Law International, 2001), 33.

[19] HRCttee, General Comment No 13 on equality before the courts and the right to a fair and public hearing by an independent court established by law (Art 14) (General Comment No 13). General

him or herself or to confess guilt. Article 14 also gives the accused the right to have one's conviction and sentence reviewed by a higher tribunal according to law; to compensation if there was a miscarriage of justice; and not to be subjected to trial or punishment for a second time (*non bis in idem*) for the same offence. Under Article 14(4) of the Covenant, juvenile persons have the same right to a fair trial as adults, but are also entitled to certain additional safeguards.

Article 15 codifies the principle of *nullum crimen sine lege* (no crime without law) and also gives the accused the benefit of any decrease in penalty which is promulgated after the person has committed an offence. Other relevant provisions of the Covenant forbid torture or cruel, inhuman, or degrading treatment or punishment; forbid arbitrary arrest; and require equality before the law.

C. Derogation from fair trial guarantees

(i) *Derogation under IHL*

Fair trial guarantees under IHL are not subject to any possibility of derogation during periods of armed conflict. According to the ICRC Commentary on the Geneva Conventions, the obligations set forth in Common Article 3 constitute 'a compulsory minimum'.[20] Courts have followed the Commentary's interpretation at both the domestic and international levels in finding IHL obligations non-derogable during both international and non-international armed conflict. For example, in *Nicaragua v United States*, the International Court of Justice (ICJ) found that Common Article 3 constitutes a 'minimum yardstick' for rules applicable to conflicts of both an international and non-international character.[21] More recently, the United States Supreme Court held that Common Article 3's procedural and judicial guarantees form 'the barest of the trial protections recognized by customary international law'.[22] The Supreme Court went on to note that Article 75 of Protocol I, which addresses judicial guarantees in greater detail than Common Article 3, is also binding on all states as a matter of customary international law.[23]

(ii) *Derogation under IHRL*

Some human rights provisions are not open to derogation at any time. Article 4(2) of the ICCPR prohibits derogation under any circumstances from rights enshrined

Comment No 13 has been superseded by HRCttee General Comment No 32 on the Right to Equality before Courts and Tribunals and to a Fair Trial, UN Doc. CCPR/C/GC/32 (2007) (General Comment No 32).

[20] J. Pictet (ed), *The Geneva Conventions of 12 August 1949: Commentary*, vol IV (Geneva: International Committee of the Red Cross (ICRC), 1958), 37.

[21] *Case Concerning Military and Paramilitary Activities in and Against Nicaragua (Nicaragua v United States of America)*, (1986) ICJ Rep, 14.

[22] *Hamdan v Rumsfeld*, 548 US 557 (2006) at 556.

[23] *Hamdan v Rumsfeld*, 548 US 557 (2006) at 633–4.

in Articles 6,[24] 7,[25] 8(1), 8(2),[26] 11,[27] 15,[28] 16,[29] and 18.[30] Article 15 (*nullem crimen sine lege*) is the only fair trial guarantee explicitly treated as non derogable under Article 4. Conspicuously absent from protection against derogation are the more extensive fair trial guarantees found in Article 14 of the Covenant. The omission of Article 14 raises the question of whether states are free to derogate from the wide range of fair trial guarantees which the Covenant does not explicitly treat as non-derogable under Article 4?

The UN Human Rights Committee has gradually interpreted the Covenant to prohibit derogation from fundamental fair trial norms, regardless of whether such norms are classified explicitly as non-derogable under Article 4. The Committee's jurisprudence is predicated, in part, on the view that non-derogable rights under Article 4 constitute but a small part of a much larger body of rights regarded as generally protected under international law. As the Committee noted in its General Comment on Article 4, '[s]tates parties may in no circumstances invoke Article 4 of the Covenant as justification for acting in violation of humanitarian law or peremptory norms of international law'.[31] On this view, certain portions of Article 14 may be treated as non-derogable so long as they are coterminous with humanitarian law or peremptory norms of international law. Such is the case in regard to Article 14(3)(g), which ensures that no person shall 'be compelled to testify against himself or to confess guilt'. According to the Committee, the wording of Article 14(3)(g) 'must be understood in terms of the absence of any direct or indirect physical or psychological pressure [...] [used] with a view of obtaining a confession of guilt'.[32] Given that coercive uses of physical or psychological pressure can rise to the level of torture or cruel, inhuman or degrading treatment, a court could find violations of Article 14(3)(g) to be coterminous with violations of Common Article 3, customary international law,[33] the Convention Against Torture and Other Cruel, Inhuman

---

[24] Article 6 ensures that every person is entitled to the inherent right to life. The Article addresses the right to life and the acceptable limits in which capital punishment may be imposed and includes a cross-reference to the guarantees under the Genocide Convention.

[25] Article 7 ensures that no one will be subject to 'torture, or to cruel, inhuman or degrading treatment or punishment'.

[26] Article 8(1) and (2), ensure that no person will be held in slavery or servitude.

[27] Article 11 prohibits imprisonment solely on the grounds of failure 'to fulfil a contractual obligation'.

[28] Article 15 articulates the principles of *nullum crimen sine lege* (no crime without law).

[29] Article 16 establishes the equality of all persons before the law.

[30] Article 18 ensures that all persons enjoy 'the right to freedom of thought, conscience and religion', and that '[n]o one shall be subject to coercion' which would impair the enjoyment of these rights.

[31] HRCttee, General Comment No 29 on States of Emergency (Art 4) (General Comment No 29), § 11.

[32] *Johnson v Jamaica*, HRCttee Comm No 588/1994, UN Doc A/51/40 (1994), § 8.7 (quoting ICCPR).

[33] See T. Thienel, 'The Admissibility of Evidence Obtained by Torture under International Law', 17 *European Journal of Int'l Law* (2006) 349–67 at 351 (arguing that the inadmissibility of evidence procured by torture is 'generally understood to be without any exceptions whatsoever' under international law).

or Degrading Treatment or Punishment,[34] or Article 7 of the Covenant.[35] In this circumstance, Article 14(3)(g) should be treated as a non-derogable right, even though it is not explicitly classified as such under Article 4.

Even for certain fair trial guarantees which may be considered to fall within the ambit of derogable rights, the Covenant only permits states to derogate 'to the extent strictly required by the exigencies of the situation'.[36] The Committee has interpreted this limitation very narrowly such that derogation from the fair trial guarantees set forth in Article 14 are permitted only in circumstances constituting 'a threat to the life of the nation', and where the facts of the actual situation demonstrate that derogation is the only reasonably available option.[37] Hence, the mere occurrence of an armed conflict or other national security threat is an insufficient basis for setting aside the fair trial guarantees of Article 14.

An additional limitation on the right to derogate is inherent in the fact that preserving the rights explicitly recognized as non-derogable under Article 4 often requires adherence to the procedural and judicial guarantees of Article 14. Article 6 of the Covenant, which ensures that '[n]o one shall be arbitrarily deprived of his life',[38] offers a good example of the interdependence that exists between the substantive rights considered nonderogable under Article 4 and the procedural and judicial guarantees of Article 14. To give effect to the substantive right of Article 6, states must ensure that 'any trial leading to the imposition of the death penalty [...] conform[s] to the provisions of the Covenant, including all of the requirements of Articles 14 and 15'.[39] By linking the substantive right to life with the procedural guarantees of a fair trial, states are able to ensure that any deprivation of life occurs only after an adequate defence has been made before an independent and impartial tribunal.

Though the Covenant permits derogation from Article 14 in certain cases of public emergency, the limitations on the right to derogate, as discussed above, leave

[34] Convention Against Torture and Other Cruel, Inhuman or Degrading Treatment or Punishment (CAT), (1984). Article 15 of CAT states: 'Each State Party shall ensure that any statement which is established to have been made as a result of torture shall not be invoked as evidence in any proceedings, except against a person accused of torture as evidence that the statement was made'.

[35] See *Higginson v Belarus*, HRCttee Comm No 792/1998, UN Doc CCPR/C/74/D/792/1998 (2002), § 4.6 (stating that 'irrespective of the nature of the crime that is to be punished or the permissibility of corporal punishment under domestic law, it is the consistent opinion of the Committee that corporal punishment constitutes cruel, inhuman and degrading treatment or punishment contrary to Article 7 of the Covenant').

[36] ICCPR, Art 4(1).

[37] General Comment No 29 (n 31), § 3. On the question of what may be considered to threaten the life of the nation, see the House of Lords judgment in *A v Secretary of State for the Home Department* [2004] UKHL 56, esp §§ 16–44, 88–97, 109–33, 153–4, 162–6. This case also addresses the issue of derogations involving discrimination.

[38] ICCPR, Art 6(1).   [39] General Comment No 29 (n 31), § 15.

states little room in which to exercise that right. This practical difficulty in combination with the uniformity of fair trial protections and the breadth of situations in which they apply—even during armed conflicts—strongly suggests that the right to a fair trial is nonderogable.[40]

D. Fair trial rights apply universally

In order to try detainees captured during an armed conflict, it is necessary to understand their status in international law. The specific rights of detainees depend on who they are and which body of international law applies to them. For example, in the recent international armed conflict in Iraq, individuals taken during the initial stages of the war are either covered under the Third Geneva Convention if they are prisoners of war (POWs) or under the Fourth Geneva Convention if they are civilians. Individuals detained following the end of the conflict and the occupation were detained either in the context of a non-international armed conflict and are thus covered under Common Article 3, or were simply detained for reasons unconnected with the conflict and therefore remained under the protection of human rights law. Finally, those who were detained outside of the conflict with Iraq, are now under United States' control and are thus covered under the ICCPR and customary international law. As the Human Rights Committee has emphasized in its General Comment No 32, 'the right of access to courts and tribunals equality before them is not limited to citizens of States parties', rather it 'must be available to all individuals, regardless of nationality or statelessness, or whatever their status ... who may find themselves in the territory or subject to the jurisdiction of the State party.'

The context-bound nature of the humanitarian and human rights treaties, as illustrated above, means that each treaty provision must be carefully examined before it is cited in a particular case, but such differences are of no practical significance in regard to the scope and content of the fair trial guarantees. The same standards for the purposes of fair trial rights apply in all cases: all defendants are entitled to a fair trial by a competent court. Each of the treaty provisions already considered set out two essential requirements for fair trial: (1) a regularly constituted court; that (2) affords judicial guarantees. The two sections that follow examine more fully what these requirements were designed to ensure.

---

[40] See Lawyers Committee for Human Rights, *What is a Fair Trial?: A Basic Guide to Legal Standards and Practice* (New York: Lawyers Committee for Human Rights, 2000), 7 (stating the fundamental importance of the right to a fair trial is illustrated by a proposal to add Art 14 to the non-derogable rights listed in Art 4(2) of the ICCPR); Weissbrodt, (n 18) (explaining that aspects of the right to a fair trial are impliedly included as non-derogable rights under Art 4 of the ICCPR).

3 WHAT IS A REGULARLY
CONSTITUTED COURT?

The regularly constituted court requirement is found in Common Article 3, Article 75 of Protocol I, and Article 14 of the ICCPR. Common Article 3 and Article 75 of Protocol I address the requirement in broad language. Article 3(1)(d) prohibits at any time and in any place '[t]he passing of sentences and the carrying out of executions without previous judgment pronounced by a *regularly constituted court* [...]'. Article 75 of Protocol I, relying on similar language, requires that 'all judicial sentences be passed by an *impartial and regularly constituted court* respecting the generally recognized principles of regular judicial procedure'. As noted by the ICRC Commentary on the Additional Protocols, the slight change in language offered in the Protocol is significant because it underlines the importance of administering impartial justice even in the most difficult of armed conflict situations.[41]

The text of Article 14 of the ICCPR and its subsequent jurisprudence before the Committee offer further explanation of the regularly constituted court requirement. Article 14(1) states that 'everyone shall be entitled to a fair and public hearing by a competent, independent, and impartial tribunal established by law'. According to the Committee's General Comment on Article 14, these requirements form 'an absolute right that is not subject to any exception'.[42]

Independence and impartiality are, at least in theory, two distinct concepts.[43] Independence refers to the structural arrangement ensuring that the judiciary and individual judges can make decisions free from interference.[44] There are numerous components necessary to ensure independence (the UN Basic Principles on the Independence of the Judiciary provides twenty basic principles), but they can be loosely divided into two categories: separation of powers and conditions of service.[45] Concerning separation of powers, the judicial branch must be structurally

---

[41] C. Pilloud et al (eds), *Commentary on the Additional Protocols of 8 June 1977 to the Geneva Conventions of 12 August 1949* (Geneva: ICRC, 1987), 878. The US Supreme Court found that the term 'regularly constituted court' in Common Article 3 excluded specially-constituted military commissions. *Hamdan v. Rumsfeld*, 548 US 557, 631–32 (2006).

[42] General Comment No 32 (n 19), § 19.

[43] See eg *R v Genereux* [1992] 1 SCR 259 (Canada) ('[T]he Court has drawn a firm line between the concepts of independence and impartiality [...] Although the basic concerns of independence and impartiality are the same, the focus of each concept is different').

[44] See *Gonzalez del Río v Peru*, HRCttee Comm No 263/287, UN Doc CCPR/C/46/D/263/1987 (1992), § 5.1.

[45] See eg General Comment No 32 (n 19), § 19 ('The requirement of independence refers, in particular, to the procedure and qualifications for the appointment of judges, and guarantees relating to their security of tenure until a mandatory retirement age or the expiry of their term of office, where such exist, the conditions governing promotion, transfer, suspension and cessation of their functions, and the actual independence of the judiciary from political interference by the executive branch and the legislature').

independent from other governmental branches or institutions,[46] so as to prevent 'inappropriate or unwarranted interference with the judicial process' by external actors (including prosecutors).[47] To secure a separate judicial power, the judiciary must possess functions and competencies that are clearly distinguishable in law from those of the executive and legislative branches of government,[48] as well as exclusive jurisdiction over issues within its competence.[49] Further, judges should have personal immunity from civil suits in the exercise of judicial functions and should only be subject to suspension or removal for reasons of incapacity or unfit behavior.[50] There must also be a protected realm for internal judicial matters, such as court administration and case assignment.[51] Regarding conditions of service, factors such as the selection and appointment of judges, term of office, security of office, adequate remuneration, promotion, tenure, pension, and age of retirement must be secured by law in a manner that protects judges from threats to their personal or professional security.[52]

The impartiality requirement seeks to regulate the individual biases of judges.[53] Individual biases derive from two sources of pressure: external pressure, such as bribes or threats, and internal pressure, such as psychology or morality.[54] Although theoretically no judge acts without some level of partiality,[55] cases and academic commentary have highlighted two basic tests for the impartiality demanded by legal

---

[46] See United Nations, *Basic Principles on the Independence of the Judiciary* (UN Basic Principles), UNGA Res 40/32, UN Doc A/RES/40/32 (29 November 1985), UNGA Res 40/146, UN Doc A/RES/40/146 (13 December 1985), Art 1. See also Amnesty International, (n 2), 76–7.

[47] See Guidelines on the Role of Prosecutors, 8th UN Congress on the Prevention of Crime and the Treatment of Offenders, Havana, 27 August to 7 September 1990, UN Doc A/CONF.144/28/Rev.1 at 189 (1990), Art 10 ('The office of prosecutors shall be strictly separated from judicial functions').

[48] General Comment No 32 (n 19), § 19.   [49] UN Basic Principles (n 46), Arts 3 and 4.

[50] UN Basic Principles (n 46), Arts 16, 18–20.

[51] UN Basic Principles (n 46), Art 14; S. Shetreet, 'The Normative Cycle of Shaping Judicial Independence in Domestic and International Law: The Mutual Impact of National and International Jurisprudence and Contemporary Practical and Conceptual Challenges', 10 *Chicago Journal of Int'l Law* (2009) 275–332 at 286.

[52] See UN Basic Principles, (n 46), Arts 10–13; General Comment No 32 (n 19), § 19; Amnesty International (n 2), 78–9; Shetreet (n 51), 284–5; Office of Democracy and Governance, *US Agency for International Development, Guidance for Promoting Judicial Independence and Impartiality* 5 (rev edn 2002), 13–23 (discussing regional variations of these factors and suggesting general guidelines).

[53] See UN Basic Principles (n 46), Art 2 (requiring judges to decide cases impartially, 'on the basis of facts and in accordance with the law, without any restrictions, improper influences, inducements, pressures, threats or interferences, direct or indirect, from any quarter or for any reason'); B. Barry, *Justice as Impartiality* (New York: Oxford University Press, 1995), 13 ('Judges are supposed to be unmoved by personal interests or the congeniality or otherwise of those who appear before them [...] Partiality [...] is the introduction of private considerations into a judgment that should be made on public grounds').

[54] See T. Franck, *The Structure of Impartiality: Examining the Riddle of One Law in a Fragmented World* (New York: Macmillan, 1968), 243.

[55] Franck (n 54), 243 ('Can any man, or group of men, administer justice impartially in an ideologically and culturally divided world?').

instruments. According to the Committee, impartiality may be violated subjectively where judges rely on 'personal bias or prejudice [...] in ways that improperly promote the interests of one of the parties to the detriment of the other'.[56] Judges may also fail to meet the impartiality standard where an objective observer would find the appearance of bias.[57] In applying the objective test of impartiality, the ICTY found that the appearance of bias may manifest itself in two ways: either if the judge has a financial or proprietary interest in the outcome of the case, or if 'the circumstances would lead a reasonable observer, properly informed, to reasonably apprehend bias'.[58] In the situation of objectively perceived bias, even if the judge concludes that he can act impartially, he nonetheless should recuse himself 'to preserve the integrity of his court and the concept of law'.[59] Trials with 'faceless judges', where the accused cannot know the identity of the judge, will likely fail the objective impartiality test.[60]

The concepts of independence and impartiality seek to address the same concern: guaranteeing a fair trial by providing parties with a tribunal where the outcome is not predetermined. It is perhaps for this reason that the two concepts have been intertwined since the drafting of the UDHR.[61] Nonetheless, depending on the actual facts before a reviewing court, the two concepts identify different issues in ensuring a fair trial. On the one hand, while conceptually distinct, independence and impartiality are functionally related and often overlap.[62] Tribunals without structural independence can hardly be perceived to be objectively impartial.

[56] General Comment No 32 (n 19), § 21 (citing *Karttunen v Finland*, HRCttee Comm No 387/1989, UN Doc CCPR/C/46/D/387/1989 (1992), § 7.2).

[57] General Comment No 32 (n 19), § 21. See also Suzannah Linton, 'Safeguarding the Independence and Impartiality of the Cambodian Extraordinary Chambers', 4 *Journal of Int'l Criminal Justice* (2006) 327–41 at 328.

[58] *Prosecutor v Furundžija* (IT-95-17/1-A), Judgment, 21 July 2000. See Linton (n 57), 328 (describing the objective prong as 'covering appearance or structural linkages, e.g. composition or powers that raise doubt as to impartiality'); see also T. Meron, 'Judicial Independence and Impartiality in International Criminal Tribunals', 99 *American Journal of Int'l Law* (2005) 359–69 at 366-7.

[59] See Meron (n 58), 366.

[60] See UN Working Group on Arbitrary Detention, Decision No 26/1994 (Colombia), UN Doc E/CN.4/1995/31/Add.2 (1994), § 40 (declaring that if a state uses 'faceless judges' in order to protect the judge, then it must take additional action to ensure the judge's independence and impartiality, including in the specific case). But see General Comment No 32 (n 19) (stating that even if an independent authority verifies the status of anonymous judges, such proceedings usually contain other procedural irregularities rendering them inadequate).

[61] See Weissbrodt (n 18), 12–15 (detailing the *travaux préparatoires* of the UDHR and noting the basis for proposing the right to 'independent and impartial' tribunals).

[62] See S. Trechsel, *Human Rights in Criminal Proceedings* (Oxford, New York: Oxford University Press, 2005), 49 (observing that independence and impartiality 'can hardly be distinguished in a clear way'); see eg *Sultanova v Uzbekistan*, HRCttee Comm No 915/2000, UN Doc CCPR/C/86/D/915/2000 (2006), § 7.5 (finding a violation of Art 14(1) of the ICCPR because 'the court did not act impartially and independently').

Therefore, if a reviewing court finds a tribunal not to have been structurally independent, it can fairly conclude that the tribunal did not provide an independent or impartial trial.[63] On the other hand, while some interpretive bodies or courts simply consider whether a previous proceeding violated the right to an independent and impartial tribunal without meaningfully differentiating the two,[64] others, such as the Committee, clearly distinguish the two concepts.[65] Even if the review court does not question the independence of the tribunal system, it may still need to examine whether the specific trial was conducted impartially (both subjectively—personal bias—and objectively, the reasonable appearance of bias).[66]

Human rights courts and other institutions around the world have found numerous violations of these requirements, especially in the context of military commissions, military courts asserting jurisdiction over civilians, or other special courts. To provide a few examples, the Inter-American Commission on Human Rights found 'courts of special jurisdiction' in Guatemala that conducted secret trials and imposed death penalties to have breached provisions of the American Convention related to lack of independence and impartiality, lack of defence of the accused, and a denial of the right to appeal.[67] The African Commission on Human and Peoples' Rights found that when a special tribunal in Nigeria composed of a judge, a member of the armed forces, and a police officer, and with no right to appeal, sentenced two men to death, it violated fair trial provisions of impartiality and the right to appeal.[68] The European Court of Human Rights held that Turkey's State Security Court violated the right to a fair trial both because the presence of a military judge cast doubt on the court's impartiality and because: the accused had no assistance from his lawyers during questioning in police custody; he was unable to communicate with his lawyers in full confidence due to third party monitoring; he was unable to gain direct access to the case file until a very late stage in the proceedings; restrictions were

---

[63] See eg Inter-American Commission, Annual Report 18, OEA/Ser.L/V/II.61 Doc 22 Rev.1 (1983) (finding that the prefix of 'anti' in Nicaragua's Anti-Somoza Courts and the fact that the courts were composed of political enemies of the accused seriously compromised 'their impartiality, fairness and independence'). See also Linton (n 57), 328 ('It is only where there is an independent judiciary that a judge can adjudicate impartially, because the Rule of Law requires that he or she should not be apprehensive of repercussions or retaliation from outside influences').

[64] See Trechsel (n 62), 50 ('It appears that the European Court of Human Rights itself does not attach much importance to the distinction [between independence and impartiality]').

[65] See generally, General Comment No 32 (n 19) (detailing the different aspects of independence and impartiality).

[66] See eg *Castedo v Spain*, HRCttee Comm No 1122/2002, UN Doc CCPR/C/94/D/1122/2002 (2008), §§ 9.7, 9.8 (finding that a judge's personal connections to the defendant university violated the appearance of impartiality without questioning the independence of the judiciary).

[67] Resolution No 15/84, Case 9038, IACHR 81, OAS/Ser.L/V/II.66, Doc 10 Rev.1 (1984).

[68] *Constitutional Rights Project v Nigeria*, Comm No 60/91, 8th Annual Activity Report of the Commission on Human and Peoples' Rights, 1994–95, ACHPR/RPT/8th/Rev.I.

imposed on the number and length of his lawyers' visits; and his lawyers were not given proper access to the case file.[69]

In a cogent analysis of the difficulties of ensuring fair trials in special courts, the Inter-American Court of Human Rights found that convictions by 'faceless' Peruvian military courts of civilians accused of terrorist activities violated the right to a fair trial.[70] Peru defended its military courts, arguing that it had legally established them, that their independence and impartiality were guaranteed under the national constitution, and that given the danger of terrorism, it was necessary to try the civilians in a military court.[71] The Inter-American Court rejected Peru's arguments, stating that 'military tribunals are not the tribunals previously established by law for civilians', and that since the armed forces 'fully engaged in the counter-insurgency struggle [were] also prosecuting persons associated with insurgency groups', the judges were not independent or impartial.[72] The case is also notable because although Peru claimed it had 'scrupulously complied with the procedural guarantees established in Peruvian law',[73] and the Inter-American Court did not question that it had, the court found that the procedures established under national law nonetheless violated the basic right to a fair trial, as provided under the American Convention.[74]

4 FAIR TRIAL GUARANTEES: THE SUBSTANTIVE CONTENT

A regularly constituted court under Common Article 3 must accord 'judicial guarantees that are recognized as indispensable by civilized peoples'[75] and that

---

[69] *Ocalan v Turkey* (2003).

[70] *Castillo Petruzzi et al Case*, IACHR (1999) (Judgment), in Annual Report of the Inter-American Court of Human Rights 1999, OEA/Ser.L./V/III.47, Doc 6, App IX, 211–300 (2000).

[71] *Castillo Petruzzi et al Case*, § 126.   [72] *Castillo Petruzzi et al Case*, §§ 128, 130.

[73] *Castillo Petruzzi et al Case*, § 171.   [74] *Castillo Petruzzi et al Case*, § 226.

[75] See D. Jinks, 'The Declining Significance of POW Status', 45 *Harvard Int'l Law Journal* (2004) 367–442 at 406–10 (suggesting that the use of military tribunals instead of 'regularly constituted court[s]' and the relaxed due process protections of tribunal proceedings violate Common Art 3); D. Jinks and D. Sloss, 'Is the President Bound by the Geneva Conventions?', 90 *Cornell Law Review* (2004) 97–202 at 119–20 ('[Common Art 3 establishes] an evolving standard that, by design, tracks relevant customary international law' (citation omitted)).

reflect an 'evolving standard' of fair trial norms based on customary international law.[76] Internationally recognized fair trial rights[77] include:

- presumption of innocence;[78]
- right to counsel of choice before and after trial;[79]
- right of defendants not to testify against themselves or to confess their guilt;[80]
- right to a speedy trial, including the right to be promptly informed of charges or reasons for detention;[81]
- defendant's right to confront evidence and witnesses,[82] including the defendant's right:

  ○ to be present at proceedings,[83]
  ○ to call witnesses,[84] and
  ○ to examine witnesses against him/herself;[85]

---

[76] Jinks (n 75), 406–10.

[77] Jinks (n 75), 409 ('Article 75 requires, in all circumstances, trials by impartial and regularly consti- tuted courts that, at a minimum, afford the presumption of innocence; the right to counsel before and during trial; the right of defendants to be present at proceedings, call witnesses, and examine witnesses against them; the right to be promptly informed of the charges or reasons for detention; the right to a public judgment; and the right of defendants not to testify against themselves or to confess their guilt, among other rights'). See also William W. Burke-White, 'Regionalization of International Criminal law Enforcement: A Preliminary Exploration', 38 *Texas Int'l Law Journal* (2003) 729–61 at 760 (finding core judicial rights embedded in the Civil and Political Covenant, the American Convention, the Cairo Declaration on Human Rights in Islam, the African Charter on Human and People's Rights, and the European Human Rights Convention).

[78] See Additional Protocol I, Art 75(4)(d); General Comment No 32 (n 19), § 30.

[79] General Comment No 32 (n 19), 55 at § 10 (citing *Kennedy v Trinidad & Tobago*, HRCttee Comm No 845/1998, UN Doc CCPR/C/74/D/845/1998 (2002), § 7.10; *Henry v Trinidad and Tobago*, HRCttee Comm No 752/1997, UN Doc CCPR/C/64/D/752/1997 (1998), § 7.6; *Taylor v Jamaica*, HRCttee Comm No 707/1996, UN Doc CCPR/C/62/D/705/1996 (1998), § 8.2; *Shaw v Jamaica*, HRCttee Comm No 704/1996, UN Doc CCPR/C/62/D/704/1996 (1998), § 7.6; and *Currie v Jamaica*, HRCttee Comm No 377/1989, UN Doc CCPR/C/50/D/377/1989 (1994), § 13.4). These Human Rights Committee cases derive from communications submitted pursuant to the Optional Protocol to the International Covenant on Civil and Political Rights.

[80] General Comment No 32 (n 19), 55, § 38 (citing *Kurbonov v Tajikistan*, HRCttee Comm No 1208/2003,UN Doc CCPR/C/86/D/1208/2003 (2006), §§ 6.2–6.4; *Shukurova v Tajikistan*, HRCttee Comm No 1044/2002, UN Doc CCPR/C/86/D/1044/2002 (2006), §§ 8.2–8.3; *Singarasa v Sri Lanka*, HRCttee Comm No 1033/2001, UN Doc CCPR/C/81/D/1033/2001 (2004), § 7.4; *Deolall v Guyana*, HRCttee Comm No 912/2000,UN Doc CCPR/C/82/D/912/2000 (2004), § 5.1; and *Kelly v Jamaica*, HRCttee Comm No 253/1987, UN Doc CCPR/C/41/D/253/1987 (1991), § 5.5); see also Additional Protocol I, Art 75(4)(f).

[81] General Comment No 32 (n 19), 55, § 27 (citing *Muñoz Hermoza v Peru*, HRCttee Comm No 203/1986, UN Doc Supp No 40 (A/44/40) (1988), § 11.3, and *Fei v Columbia*, HRCttee Comm No 514/1992, UN Doc CCPR/C/53/D/514/1992 (1995), § 8.4); see also Additional Protocol I, Art 75(4)(a).

[82] General Comment No 32 (n 19), 55, §§ 36, 39; see also Additional Protocol I, Art 75(4)(g); D. Weissbrodt, *The Right to a Fair Trial* 136–9 (The Hague: Martinus Nijhoff, 2001).

[83] General Comment No 32 (n 19), § 36.   [84] General Comment No 32 (n 19), § 39.

[85] General Comment No 32 (n 19), § 39.

- right to a public forum,[86] most importantly a public judgment;[87] and
- right to an appeal,[88] in the form of

  ○ a challenge to the legality of detention,[89] and
  ○ the right to review by a higher court.[90]

In order to meet Common Article 3's requirement of a regularly constituted court, any court or tribunal must, at a minimum, provide for the above rights and judicial guarantees,[91] the analogous requirements of the ICCPR, or those of Article 75 of Additional Protocol I to the Geneva Conventions.

The introductory nature and required brevity of this Chapter does not permit a comprehensive examination of all of these rights. The following subsections represent a sample of fair trial rights under humanitarian and human rights law but as can be seen from the law described in the previous subsections, this is not a comprehensive survey.

A. Presumption of innocence

The presumption of innocence is set out in 1977 Additional Protocols to the Geneva Conventions. Article 75(4)(d) requires that '[a]nyone charged with an offence

---

[86] General Comment No 32 (n 19), §§ 28–9 (citing *Kavanagh v Ireland*, HRCttee Comm No 819/1998, UN Doc CCPR/C/76/D/1114/2002 (2002) (pre-trial decisions), § 10.4; *Van Meurs v Netherlands*, HRCttee Comm No 215/1986, P 6.2, UN Doc CCPR/C/39/D/215/1986 (1990) (regarding reasonable limits on public nature of trial proceedings); and *R.M. v Finland*, HRCttee Comm No 301/1988, P 6.4, UN Doc CCPR/C/35/D/301/1988 (1989) (regarding appellate hearings)).

[87] Additional Protocol I, Art 75(4)(i).

[88] General Comment No 32 (n 19), § 45 (citing *Henry v Jamaica*, HRCttee Comm No 230/1987, P 8.4, UN Doc CCPR/C/43/D/230/1987 (1991)).

[89] General Comment No 32 (n 19), § 45.   [90] General Comment No 32 (n 19), § 45.

[91] See Fitzpatrick, (n 3), 345, 352 (noting that judicial guarantees under the Civil and Political Covenant are non-derogable and that Human Rights Committee General Comment No 29 indicates that 'the military commissions under consideration here must comply with international humanitarian law and may not deny fair trial rights where not strictly required'); M. Spetber, J. Lindh, and Y. Hamdi, 'Closing the Loophole in International Humanitarian Law for American Nationals Captured Abroad While Fighting with Enemy Forces', 40 *American Criminal Law Review* (2003) 159–215 at 174–5 (commenting that the requirements established by Common Art 3 are minimum standards that must be met and should be viewed as inviting a greater level of protection); L. Vierucci, 'Prisoners of War or Protected Persons Qua Unlawful Combatants? The Judicial Safeguards to Which Guantánamo Bay Detainees Are Entitled', 1 *Journal of Int'l Criminal Justice* (2003) 284–314 at 307, 314 (noting that Common Art 3 sets out basic judicial guarantees); cf D. Jinks, 'The Applicability of the Geneva Conventions to the "Global War on Terrorism"', 46 *Virginia Journal of Int'l Law* (2005) 165–95 at 185 ('[The dual purposes of Common Art 3 are] the minimization of human suffering and the respect for state sovereignty'). But see C. Bradley, 'Military Commissions and Terrorist Enemy Combatants', 2 *Stanford Journal of Civil Rights and Civil Liberties* (2006) 253–7 at 256 (arguing that indispensable guarantees are presumably less than court-martial procedures and that the then current military commissions guarantee extensive rights).

is presumed innocent until proved guilty according to law'. Article 6(2)(d) of Additional Protocol II uses the same language as Article 75, thereby extending the right to non-international armed conflict situations.

Article 14 of the ICCPR provides further detail on the scope and meaning of the presumption of innocence. In interpreting Article 14, the Committee notes that the presumption requires (1) that the prosecution carry the burden of proving its case; (2) that no penalty of law be imposed without proof beyond a reasonable doubt; and (3) that all persons held on criminal charges be given the benefit of the presumption.[92] According to the Commentaries on the Additional Protocols, the presumption of innocence rule has been incorporated into all human rights documents and is not a matter which the accused must prove.[93]

B. Right to counsel

Article 75(4)(a) devotes only a few lines to the right to counsel by guaranteeing that the accused be given access, before and after trial, to 'all necessary rights and means of defence'.[94] According to the Commentary on the Additional Protocols, certain rights expressed elsewhere in Article 75 are impliedly incorporated within the right to counsel. These include the right to an interpreter and the right to 'understand the assistance given by a qualified defence lawyer'.[95]

The ICCPR devotes more space to the right to counsel. Article 14(3)(b) requires that the accused 'have adequate time and facilities for the preparation of his defence and to communicate with counsel of his own choosing'. According to the Committee, what is adequate time depends on the facts and circumstances of the particular case.[96] The defence first bears the burden of requesting adjournment if the time available to prepare an adequate defence is insufficient.[97] Once a request for adjournment has been made, the court has an obligation to grant all reasonable requests, especially in capital cases.[98]

C. Right to not testify against oneself

The right to not testify against oneself is a right that protects accused persons from becoming subjects of torture for the purposes of obtaining confessions. The right is enshrined in Article 14(3)(g) of the ICCPR, Article 75(4)(f) of Protocol I, Article 6(2)(f) of Protocol II, and Common Article 3. It is also found in Article 17 of the

---

[92] General Comment No 32 (n 19), § 30.
[93] *Commentary on the Additional Protocols* (n 19), 882.   [94] Additional Protocol I, Art 75(4)(a).
[95] *Commentary on the Additional Protocols* (n 19), 880.
[96] General Comment No 32 (n 19), § 32.   [97] General Comment No 32 (n 42), § 32.
[98] General Comment No 32 (n 19), § 32.

Third Geneva Convention and Article 31 of the Fourth Geneva Convention which include the rule for prisoners of war that: 'Every prisoner of war, when questioned on the subject, is bound to give only his surname, first names and rank, date of birth, and army, regimental, personal or serial number, or failing this, equivalent information. [...] No physical or mental torture, nor any other form of coercion, may be inflicted on prisoners of war to secure from them information of any kind whatever. Prisoners of war who refuse to answer may not be threatened, insulted, or exposed to unpleasant or disadvantageous treatment of any kind' and that for protected civilians that 'No physical or moral coercion shall be exercised against protected persons, in particular to obtain information from them or from third parties'.

The Committee defines the protective right in terms of 'the absence of any direct or indirect physical or undue psychological pressure from the investigating authorities on the accused, with a view to obtaining a confession of guilt'.[99] The Committee goes on to note that any domestic authority must erect adequate safeguards 'to ensure that statements or confessions obtained in violation of [the right] are excluded from the evidence'.[100] According to the ICRC Commentary on the Additional Protocols, government safeguards against the use of torture must be strengthened especially during periods of armed conflict 'if [governments] are to be certain that they will not be held responsible for acts of torture committed by their agents, whether civilian or military'.[101]

D. Tried without undue delay: rights of notice and speedy trial

According to the Committee, the right to be tried without undue delay requires prompt action at every stage of the judicial proceeding, from formal charging of the accused (notice), to trial, and to final judgment on appeal.[102] The right to notice protects against excessive delays between the time of initial detention and trial. The Human Rights Committee's interpretation of 'undue delay' has varied depending on the case before it, but generally detention without charges for over three years is found to violate international norms.[103] Further, administrative difficulty has

---

[99] General Comment No 32 (n 19), § 41.   [100] General Comment No 32 (n 19), § 41.
[101] *Commentary on the Additional Protocols* (n 41), 873.   [102] General Comment No 32 (n 19), § 35.
[103] See *Morrison v Jamaica*, HRCttee Comm No 635/1995, UN Doc CCPR/C/63/D/635/1995 (1998) (not finding a violation of prompt trial right when trial occurred approximately 18 months after arrest and delay included a preliminary inquiry); *Leslie v Jamaica*, HRCttee Comm No 564/1993, UN Doc CCPR/C/63/D/564/1993 (1998) (finding no prompt trial when trial occurred 29 months after arrest); *Borroso v Panama*, HRCttee Comm No 473/1991, UN Doc CCPR/C/54/D/473/1991 (1995) (finding an undue delay between indictment and trial when a murder suspect was held without bail for more than three-and-a-half years before his acquittal); *Shalto v Trinidad and Tobago*, HRCttee Comm No 447/1991, UN Doc CCPR/C/53/D/447/1991 (1995) (finding no prompt trial when there was a delay of

not been accepted as an excuse for failure to give prompt notice.[104] The Appeals Chamber for the International Criminal Tribunal for Rwanda decided that holding a suspect longer than 20 days without notice of the charges was a violation of the suspect's rights, as was holding a suspect longer than 90 days without indictment.[105]

Once placed on notice of the charges, the defendant has a right to proceed to trial and final judgment without undue delay. According to the Committee, courts must determine what is a reasonable time based on the facts and circumstances of each case, 'taking into account mainly the complexity of the case, the conduct of the accused, and the manner in which the matter was dealt with by the administrative and judicial authorities'.[106]

5 MILITARY COMMISSIONS
THE UNITED STATES POST-9/11

The right to a fair trial, as set out above, provides an international standard for assessing the procedures of extraordinary adjudicative institutions such as the military commissions established by the United States in the context of the 'War on Terror'.

almost four years between the judgment of the court of appeal and the beginning of the retrial, a period during which the petitioner was kept in detention); *Bozize v Central African Republic*, HRCttee Comm No 428/1990, UN Doc CCPR/C/50/D/428/1990 (1994) (finding that trial did not take place within a 'reasonable time': military leader arrested in a foreign country, repatriated, imprisoned, held incommunicado for a period, and mistreated, as well as denied rights of access to counsel, of notice, and of prompt review of the legality of his detention; he had not yet been formally charged, let alone tried, four years after his arrest).

[104] *Vivanco v Peru*, HRCttee Comm No 678/1996, UN Doc CCPR/C/74/D/678/1996 (2002).

[105] *Barayagwiza v Prosecutor* (ICTR-97-19), Decision, 3 November 1999, § 109. Barayagwiza was held 29 days without being notified of the charges—nine days longer than allowed by Rule 40bis of the ICTR: § 43. He was also held for 233 days without being indicted—143 days longer than allowed by Rule 62 of the ICTR: § 45. Additionally, the ICTR failed to provide the necessary review of his detention by not providing a habeas corpus hearing: § 90. The ICTR initially held that the appropriate remedy for these violations of Barayagwiza's rights, especially the latter two, was his immediate release and the dismissal of charges with prejudice: § 106. Upon review, the prosecutor submitted new evidence which the court found 'diminish[ed] the role played by the failings of the Prosecutor as well as the intensity of the violation of the rights of the Appellant': *Prosecutor v Barayagwiza* (ICTR-97-19-AR72), Decision on Prosecutor's Request for Review or Reconsideration, 31 March 2000, § 71. The remedy was reduced to commuting the sentence from life to 35 years' imprisonment: *Prosecutor v Nahimana* (ICTR-99-52-T), Judgment and Sentence, 3 December 2003, § 1107 (sentencing Barayagwiza at the same time as other defendants).

[106] General Comment No 32 (n 19), § 35. In 2013, the US Court of Appeals for the Second Circuit found that a trial in the Federal Court after five years' detention in Guantánamo did not violate the defendant's right to a speedy trail. *US v Ghailani*, 733 F3d 29 (2d Cir 2013).

US military commissions in the post-9/11 era have evolved under three distinct regimes: unilateral executive control (2001–06); the Military Commissions Act of 2006 (2006–09); and the Military Commissions Act of 2009 (2009–present). The following sections briefly set out the practice of the military commissions during these three periods, and assess the degree to which the commissions have proved capable of meeting international fair trial standards.

A. Military commissions under unilateral executive control: 2001–06

Most cases of terrorist attacks committed prior to 11 September 2001 were prosecuted in federal courts under federal criminal laws. On 13 November 2001, the Administration of George W. Bush deviated from this practice in issuing a Military Order that established military commissions for the purpose of bringing Al Qaeda members and their associates to justice.[107]

The Bush Administration defended the need for military commissions on a number of grounds. It argued that members of Al Qaeda and their associates were not covered by the Third Geneva Convention since Al Qaeda—as a terrorist organization—was not a party to the Convention.[108] It further argued that the Taliban did not qualify for protection under the Third Geneva Convention because, their forces did not 'distinguis[h] themselves from the civilian population of Afghanistan' or 'conduc[t] their operations in accordance with the laws and customs of war'.[109] Further, the Administration concluded that the minimal protections provided by Common Article 3 in cases of 'conflict not of an international character' were not applicable to the 'War on Terror', because the war against the Taliban and Al Qaeda were both international conflicts.[110]

The Bush Administration's initial effort to establish military commissions quickly came under criticism of two kinds. First, many constitutional scholars argued that the President lacked the authority to establish military commissions without prior congressional approval.[111] Secondly, human rights observers pointed out that even with congressional authorization, the military commissions failed to

---

[107] Detention, Treatment, and Trial of Certain Non-Citizens in the War against Terrorism (2001) 66 Federal Regulations 57, § 833.

[108] The White House, Office of the Press Secretary, 'Statement of the Press Secretary on the Geneva Conventions', 7 February 2002, available at <http://www.state.gov/s/l/38727.htm>.

[109] 'Statement of the Press Secretary on the Geneva Conventions' (n 108).

[110] See White House Memorandum, 'Humane Treatment of Al Qaeda and Taliban Detainees', 7 February 2002, available at <http://www.pegc.us/archive/White_House/bush_ memo_ 20020207_ ed. pdf>.

[111] N. Katyal and L. Tribe, 'Waging War, Deciding Guilt: Trying the Military Tribunals', 111 *Yale Law Journal* (2002) 1259–1310 at 1266.

meet the minimal guarantees provided by humanitarian and human rights law.[112] For example, President Bush's Military Order: did not define a reasonable time for pre-trial detention; excluded Article III courts from conducting habeas corpus proceedings; and left the determination of the meaning of 'fair trial guarantees' a matter solely of executive prerogative.[113]

In *Hamdan v Rumsfeld*,[114] the US Supreme Court held that the President's initial attempt at trying detainees before military commissions was not authorized either by congressional legislation or the President's war powers in the US Constitution.[115] Furthermore, the Court held that the military commission procedures constituted an impermissible violation of the Uniform Code of Military Justice (UCMJ)[116] and of the Geneva Conventions.[117] The *Hamdan* decision resulted in the suspension of all proceedings before military commissions. It also forced the Bush Administration to seek legislation from Congress to remedy the constitutional and international law concerns identified by the court in *Hamdan*. On 17 October 2006, Congress specifically responded to the *Hamdan* decision by passing the Military Commissions Act of 2006 (2006 MCA), which expressly authorized new military commissions and announced that the commissions were in full compliance with the Geneva Convention requirements of 'regularly constituted courts' and complied with sufficient 'judicial guarantees' requirements.

B. 'The war on terror' and the Military Commissions Act of 2006

The 2006 MCA renewed the effort 'to try alien unlawful enemy combatants engaged in hostilities against the United States for violations of the law of war and other offenses triable by military commission'.[118] To govern the commissions' proceedings, the Secretary of Defense published the Manual for Military Commissions of 18 January 2007 (The Manual). The Manual set forth guidelines[119] for trials of 'unlawful

---

[112] See eg Human Rights Watch, 'Human Rights Watch Briefing Paper on U.S. Military Commissions', 25 June 2003, available at <http://www.pegc.us/archive/Organizations/HRW_military-commissions. pdf> (arguing that the use of military courts to try civilians constitutes a violation of 'the right to trial by an independent and impartial court').

[113] See Department of Defense, 'Military Commission Order No 1', 21 March 2002, available at <http://www.defense.gov/news/Mar2002/d20020321ord.pdf>.

[114] 126 S Ct 2749 (2006).   [115] 126 S Ct 2749 at 2774–5 (2006).

[116] 126 S Ct 2749 at 2771 (2006).   [117] 126 S Ct 2749 at 2793 (2006).

[118] Military Commissions Act of 2006, Pub L.109-366, 120 Stat 2600, codified at 10 U.S.C. §§ 948a–950w (2007).

[119] See US Department of Defence, *Manual for Military Commissions* (The Manual) (2007), available at <http://www.defenselink.mil/pubs/pdfs/The%20Manual%20for%20Military%20Commissions. pdf>. Part II: Rules for Military Commissions, § 103(a)(24). The Manual contains four parts; in this section, 'Manual Rules', or 'RMC' refer to Part II: Rules for Military Commissions, and 'Evidence Rules'

enemy combatants' at Guantánamo Bay and other US detention sites. Pursuant to these guidelines, prosecutors renewed their effort to charge some detainees and bring them to trial.[120] The prosecutors faced bringing the detainees to justice amidst circumstances of prolonged detention, considerable indications that many of the detainees had been severely ill-treated,[121] criticism of the military commissions by the Supreme Court,[122] and international pressure to comply with human rights and international humanitarian law obligations.[123]

The Manual for Military Commissions guaranteed several of the fair trial rights necessary to comply with internationally accepted standards, but failed to protect other necessary safeguards. With regard to what the Manual *did* protect, Rules for Military Commissions (RMC) 290(e)(5)(A) established the proper standard for findings, noting '[t]he accused must be presumed to be innocent until the accused's guilt is established by legal and competent evidence beyond reasonable doubt [...]'.[124] No definition of competent evidence was given in The Manual, however, which raised concerns—particularly if the evidence was adduced by torture or ill-treatment. RMC 910(c) provided substantial protections regarding counsel for the defendant, including the right to be represented by counsel,[125] though that right only applied after the detainee was accused and was not applicable during pretrial questioning and investigation, which took years in the case of most Guantánamo detainees. The Manual partially guaranteed the defendant's right not to testify against himself through RMC 910(a)(1), which allowed the defendant to plead not guilty.[126] Conversely, the right to counsel was open to restriction under the national security privilege.

or 'RMCE' refer to Part III: The Military Commission Rules of Evidence, available at <http://www.defense.gov/pubs/pdfs/Part%20III%20-%20MCREs%20(Final).pdf>.

[120] See eg W. Glaberson, 'Court Advances Military Tribunals for Detainees', *New York Times*, 25 September 2007 (describing the trial court and appellate decisions in the case of Canadian detainee Omar Ahmed Khadr).

[121] See generally S. Miles, *Oath Betrayed: Torture, Medical Complicity and the War on Terror* (New York: Random House, 2006), 8–9 (summarizing and analysing the information available regarding US interrogation tactics, including ill-treatment, at Guantánamo Bay and elsewhere). See also J. Martinez, 'Process and Substance in the War on Terror', 108 *Columbia Law Review* (2008) 1013–92 at 1073–4 (providing further documentation and support for the perpetration of ill-treatment on the part of the US government).

[122] See *Boumediene v Bush*, 533 US 723 (2008).

[123] See T. Meron, 'The Humanization of Humanitarian Law', 94 *American Journal of Int'l Law* (2000) 239–78 at 266 (stating that human rights law should be a part of the interpretation and application of international humanitarian law specifically in the case of 'regularly constituted courts' under Common Art 3); see also Testimony of Elisa Massimino: Hearing Before the H Comm on Armed Services in the Military Commission Act and the Future of Detention at Guantánamo Bay, 110th Cong (2007) (statement of Elisa Massimino, Washington Director, Human Rights First) (discussing the negative effects of the manner and prolonged nature of the Guantánamo Bay detentions).

[124] See The Manual (n 119), 133 at RMC 920(e)(5)(A).

[125] See The Manual (n 119), 133 at RMC 910(c), RMC Preamble, § 19(f)(2).

[126] See The Manual (n 119), 133 at RMC 910(a)(1).

Particularly problematic portions of The Manual with regard to fair trial rights arose in the context of the right to notice, the right to counsel during interrogations, the right to confront witnesses, the right to be present at trial, the right to a public trial, the right to review by a higher court, and the privilege against self incrimination. RMC 308 addressed a defendant's right to notice, and stated that a detainee must be made aware of the charges against him or her 'as soon as practicable'.[127] This language provided considerable amount of leeway, especially in light of the fact, as noted above, that many of the detainees in US custody had been held for months or years without charges and without access to counsel.[128] Furthermore, Rule 909(b) presumed the defendant mentally capable of standing trial,[129] without taking into account the fact that prolonged detention may in fact diminish that capacity to a great extent.[130]

RMC 701(f), concerning the treatment of classified information for purposes of national security,[131] also raised concerns for fair trial rights. Information became classified for the purposes of Military Commissions Rule of Evidence 505(b)(3) through an *in camera* proceeding, which could have excluded the defendant at the trial counsel's request, or could be made *ex parte*, in writing, 'outside the presence of the accused and defense counsel'.[132] National security could also be invoked under RMC 806(b)(2)(a), which authorized closure of a session to 'protect information the disclosure of which could reasonably be expected to damage national security [...]'.[133] While generally a state possesses the right to exclude the press and

---

[127] See The Manual (n 119), 133 at RMC 308.

[128] See eg A. Grey, 'Guantánamo Trials on Track for Summer: Pentagon', *Reuters*, 28 February 2007, available at <http://www.reuters.com/articlePrint?articleId=USN2816949620070228>; S. Labaton, 'Court Endorses Curbs on Appeal by US Detainees', *New York Times*, 21 February 2007; W. Glaberson, 'A U.S. Trial by Its Looks, But Only So,' *New York Times*, 29 July 2008.

[129] See The Manual (n 119), 133 at RMC 909(b).

[130] See generally J. Dingwall, 'Unlawful Confinement as a War Crime: The Jurisprudence of the Yugoslav Tribunal and the Common Core of International Humanitarian Law Applicable to Contemporary Armed Conflicts', 9 *Journal of Conflict and Security Law* (2004) 133–79 at 177 (stating that 'the recognition that isolation may amount to cruel treatment [is] evidence that inclusion of unlawful confinement as a war crime in internal armed conflict has a basis in customary international law').

[131] See The Manual (n 119), 133 at RMC 701(f) ('Classified information shall be protected and is privileged from disclosure if disclosure would be detrimental to the national security. This rule applies to all stages of proceedings in military commissions, including the discovery phase').

[132] See The Manual (n 119), 133 at RMCE 505(b)(3). While the former chief prosecutor for the military commissions, Morris Davis, defended The Manual rules by arguing that 'the [Military Commissions Act] gives the accused the right to be present for all open sessions of the trial', he neglected to address the denial of an accused's rights at the point where trial procedures are closed. See M. Davis, 'In Defense of Guantánamo Bay', 117 *Yale Law Journal Pocket Part* (2007) 21. Mr Davis later changed his mind about the overall fairness of the proceedings. See W. Glaberson, 'Claim of Pressure for Closed Guantánamo Trials', *New York Times*, 20 October 2007, available at <http://www.nytimes.com/2007/10/20/us/nationalspecial3/20gitmo.html>.

[133] See The Manual (n 119), 133 at RMC 806(b)(2)(A). This closure includes information regarding 'intelligence or law enforcement sources, methods, or activities [...]'. Cf W. Schabas, 'Fair Trials

public from portions of hearings under exceptional circumstances,[134] these provisions, if taken to the extreme, threaten a defendant's rights to confront the witnesses and evidence, to be present at trial, and to have a public trial.

The military commissions under the 2006 MCA also lacked adequate protections for the right to appeal, as well as adequate *habeas corpus* procedures.[135] According to the Manual for the 2006 MCA, military commissions only had jurisdiction over 'alien unlawful enemy combatants'. The Combatant Status Review Tribunal (CSRT) was responsible for determining an individual's status as an 'unlawful enemy combatant' and 'provide[d] detainees with the opportunity to challenge their status'.[136] Accordingly, in theory, a defendant had the opportunity to challenge his or her detention prior to coming before the military commission. In fact, however, the defendant's status was questionable, as the CSRT process inherently violated the rights to a fair trial and habeas corpus.[137] With regard to appellate review, the 2006 MCA seemed to guarantee the right to review by the United States Court of Appeals for the District of Columbia Circuit, and, if necessary, by the Supreme Court.[138] Under RMC 1201, however, the Court of Military Commission Review performed the initial review of decisions by the commissions.[139] Unfortunately, RMC 1201 then

and National Security Evidence', 4 *Int'l Commentary on Evidence* (2006) 1–4, available at <http://www.bepress.com/cgi/viewcontent.cgi?article=1056&context=ice> (pointing to the danger of drawing inferences in international criminal trials from state claims to withhold evidence on grounds of national security). The Obama Administration supports revised legislation 'incorporating classified information procedures that are more similar to those applicable in federal court, but appropriately modified for the military commissions context, and to reflect lessons learned in terrorism prosecutions [...]'. B. Wiegmann and M. Martins, *Memorandum for the Attorney General & the Secretary of Defense*, Detention Policy Task Force, 20 July 20 2009, § 4.

[134] See ICCPR, Art 14 (allowing for the exclusion of the press and public for reasons of 'public order (ordre public) or national security in a democratic society'); see also *United States ex rel Knauff v Shaughnessy*, 338 US 537 (1950), 551 (Jackson, J, dissenting) ('In the name of security the police state justifies its arbitrary oppressions on evidence that is secret [...]'). For more on accommodating national security via in camera inspection and the exclusion of the general public, see GV III, Art 105 ('[E]xceptionally [...] held in camera in the interest of State security'); Rome Statute, Art 68(2) ('[T]o protect victims and witnesses or an accused, [the court may] conduct any part of the proceedings in camera') and Rome Statute, Art 72 (regarding protection of national security information).

[135] See Fitzpatrick (n 3), 245, fn 2 (outlining issues regarding the legality of the appeals process under the 13 November 2002 order negating the possibility of a review of the outcome of military commission proceedings); *Boumediene v Bush*, 127 S Ct 2240 (2007) (finding that the Military Commissions Act operates as an unconstitutional suspension of the writ of habeas corpus).

[136] The Manual (n 119) at RMC 202(b). At least one military commission, however, has questioned a defendant's classification. See *United States v Khadr*, Order on Jurisdiction (US CM Commission, 4 June 2007), available at <http://www.defenselink.mil/news/jun2007/khadrJudgesDismissalOrder(June%204).pdf>.

[137] In determining a detainee's status, the CSRT review asks whether the detainee is an 'alien unlawful enemy combatant' under 10 USC § 948a(1)(ii): see The Manual (n 119) at RMC 202(b). This is not the correct question under the GC III: see GC III, Arts 4, 5. Further, the CSRT process has been found to 'fall well short of the procedures and adversarial mechanisms that would eliminate the need for habeas corpus review': see *Boumediene v Bush*, 127 S Ct 2260 (2007).

[138] The Manual (n 119) at RMC 1205.   [139] The Manual (n 119) at RMC 1201.

provided that 'No relief may be granted unless an error of law prejudiced a substantial trial right of the accused'.[140] This limitation restricted appeals to issues of law and did not permit challenges to convictions for insufficient evidence to support the conviction or review of sentences.

The treatment by military commissions of evidence procured through coercive methods also raised fair trial concerns. The definition of coercion may include methods that rise to the level of cruel, inhuman, or degrading treatment, forbidden by all of the international treaties and instruments discussed earlier.[141] The Manual for Military Commissions, while rightly excluding statements adduced by torture, specifically allowed for 'statements "in which the degree of coercion is disputed" [...] if reliable, probative, and the admission would best serve the interests of justice'.[142] In light of the fact that the Bush Administration authorized 'coercive' interrogation conduct[143] which was later claimed to be 'so brutal that it essentially amounts to torture',[144] this provision arguably allowed for evidence procured by torture to be admitted at trial. This process not only violated international

---

[140] The Manual (n 119) RMC 1201(d)(1). The Obama Administration supported the Military Commissions Act of 2009, which added the opportunity to appeal adverse verdicts to the United States Court of Appeals for the District of Columbia Circuit, but only 'with respect to the findings and sentences as approved by the convening authority and as affirmed or set aside as incorrect in law by the United States Court of Military Commission Review'.

[141] See R. Pattenden, 'Admissibility in Criminal Proceedings of Third Party and Real Evidence Obtained by Methods Prohibited by UNCAT', 10 *Int'l Journal of Evidence and Proof* (2006) 1–41 at 6 (examining international standards of what constitutes torture and noting that 'it is a grave crime to extract information from prisoners or civilians by torture or ill-treatment'); see also Rome Statute, Art 8(2)(a)(ii) (declaring that grave breaches of the Geneva Convention include torture or inhuman treatment); GC III, Arts 3, 17, 130. Human Rights Committee jurisprudence further elucidates the parameters of what constitutes cruel, inhuman, and degrading treatment. In *Conteris v Uruguay*, the Human Rights Committee found that a confession obtained only after ill-treatment violated the accused's right not to be compelled to confess guilt under Art 14(3)(g) of the ICCPR: HRCttee Comm No 139/1983, UN Doc A/40/40 (1985), § 10. Arrested by security police for crimes associated with subverting the constitution, the victim spent three months in incommunicado detention: § 1.4. Subjected to various forms of torture, he eventually signed a confession: § 1.4. The Human Rights Committee held that he did not voluntarily sign the confession: § 9.2. See also *El-Megreisi v Libyan Arab Jamahiriya*, HRCttee Comm No 440/1990, UN Doc CCPR/C/50/D/440/1990 (1994), § 5.4 (holding that the detainee, 'by being subjected to prolonged incommunicado detention in an unknown location is the victim of torture and cruel and inhuman treatment, in violation of Articles 7 and 10').

[142] The Manual (n 119), 'Preamble' (1)(g), citing 10 USC § 948r(b) and (c) (2006).

[143] *Memorandum from William J. Haynes II, General Counsel, Department of Defense, to Donald Rumsfeld, Secretary of Defense, Counter-Resistance Techniques* (27 November 2002), available at <http://www.slate.com/features/whatistorture/LegalMemos.html> (memo signed as approved by Secretary of Defense Donald Rumsfeld).

[144] See Press Release, Senator John McCain, Statement of Senator John McCain on Detainee Amendments on (1) The Army Field Manual and (2) Cruel, Inhumane, Degrading Treatment, 4 November 2005, available at <http://mccain.senate.gov> (follow 'Press Office' hyperlink, then follow 'Press Releases' hyperlink, then enter November 2005 in 'Recent Press Releases' search field) (arguing for the passage of the Detainee Treatment Act because without it the United States 'is the only country in the world that asserts a legal right to engage in cruel and inhumane treatment').

norms regarding torture and ill-treatment[145] but also the fair trial right against self-incrimination, since a witness from whom such statements are obtained will say whatever he or she believes may stop the infliction of pain—rather than the truth.[146] Such techniques may easily lead to coerced confessions.

C. Prospects for reform of the military commissions: 2009 MCA

As one of his first acts as President of the United States, President Barack Obama suspended operation of the 2006 MCA.[147] The stated purpose of the suspension was to 'restore the Commissions as a legitimate forum for prosecution, while bringing them in line with the rule of law'.[148] To accomplish this task, President Obama ordered the Department of Defense to review several specific areas of concern, including: the admissibility of evidence obtained by the use of cruel, inhuman, or degrading interrogation methods; the use of hearsay evidence; equality of arms and the selection of counsel; greater protection for those who refuse to testify; and greater independence of military commission judges.[149]

Congress soon took up the President's initiative to reform the Commissions. In October 2009 Congress passed the Military Commissions Act of 2009.[150] It is worthwhile to compare certain provisions of the two Acts to determine the extent to which the recent reforms were successful at reconciling the practice of military commissions with the normative obligations of international law.

---

[145] See UDHR, Art 5; ICCPR, Art 7; Common Art 3, § 1(a); European Convention, Art 3; Additional Protocol I, Art 75; Rome Statute, Art 55. Each of these instruments, in much the same language, prohibits 'any form of coercion, duress or threat, to torture or to any other form of cruel, inhuman or degrading treatment or punishment'. On 15 May 2009, the Obama Administration notified Congress of five rule changes in the military commissions, including a provision that 'statements that have been obtained from detainees using cruel, inhuman and degrading interrogation methods will no longer be admitted as evidence at trial'. *Statement of President Barack Obama on Military Commissions*, 15 May 2009, available at <http://www.gpoaccess.gov/presdocs/2009/DCPD-200900364.pdf>; Wiegmann and Martins (n 133), 4. The Obama Administration also supports 'adopting a "voluntariness" standard for the admission of statements of the accused, while taking into account the challenges and realities of the battlefield [...]: Wiegmann and Martins (n 133), 4.

[146] See Center for Victims of Torture, Eight Lessons of Torture, available at <http://www.cvt.org/main.php/Advocacy/TheCampaigntoStopTorture/WhatCVTknowsaboutTorture> (explaining why torture does not yield reliable information).

[147] See S. Shane, 'Obama Orders Secret Prisons and Detention Camps Closed', *New York Times*, 22 January 2009, available at <http://www.nytimes.com/2009/01/23/us/politics/23GITMOCND.html>.

[148] The White House, Office of the Press Secretary, 'Statement of President Barack Obama on Military Commissions', 15 March 2009, available at <http://www.whitehouse.gov/the_press_office/Statement-of-President-Barack-Obama-on-Military-Commissions/>.

[149] 'Statement of President Barack Obama on Military Commissions' (n 148).

[150] Military Commissions Act of 2009 (2009 MCA), Title XVIII, Pub L 111-84, 123 Stat 2190, to be codified at 10 USC §§ 948a–950t (2009).

Section 948b(a) of the 2009 MCA establishes the procedures governing the use of military commissions. Following the logic of the 2006 MCA, the new legislation carves out a category of persons over whom military commissions are empowered to exercise jurisdiction. In the language of the 2009 MCA, these persons are referred to as 'unprivileged enemy belligerents,' instead of 'unlawful enemy combatants'. But the substantive effect is the same: military commissions have been given primary jurisdiction over a category of persons not recognized under international law.

The *ex post facto* issue which plagued the 2006 MCA is still very much a problem in the new legislation. Military commissions have traditionally prosecuted war crimes without triggering *ex post facto* concerns, because the offences tried were already known under international law.[151] The 2006 MCA deviated from this tradition by giving military commissions the jurisdiction to prosecute a novel category of individuals for newly defined offences. The new MCA in section 950p(d) perpetuates this error by claiming that prior offences are open to prosecution on the view that they are offences traditionally triable by the laws of war.

One notable change in the new legislation concerns the degree to which the Geneva Conventions apply as a source of law before military commissions. Originally, the 2006 MCA sought to prevent any use of the Geneva Conventions as a source of law, in any setting or for any purpose. Section 948b(g) of the 2006 MCA declared that '[n]o unlawful enemy combatant subject to trial by military commission under this chapter may invoke the Geneva Conventions as a source of rights'. In section 948b(e) of the 2009 MCA, Congress bars reference to the Geneva Conventions only in the context of a 'private right of action'. Accordingly, the new legislation recognizes the application of the Geneva Conventions to habeas corpus proceedings and in defensive penal proceedings.

The 2009 MCA makes further changes in regard to application of the Common Article 3 requirement of a 'regularly constituted court'. Passed in the wake of the *Hamdan* decision, the 2006 MCA had sought to make clear that the military commissions were consistent with the minimal requirements of Common Article 3. In Section 948b(f), the Act had boldly asserted that '[a] military commission under this chapter is a regularly constituted court, afforded all of the necessary "judicial guarantees which are recognized as indispensable by civilized people" for purposes of Common Article 3 of the Geneva Conventions'. In removing this language from the 2009 MCA, Congress has recognized that only the courts can decide whether military commissions comply with international law obligations.

---

[151] C. Rose, 'Criminal Conspiracy and the Military Commissions Act: Two Minds That May Never Meet', 13 *Int'l Law Students Association Journal of Int'l and Comparative Law* (2007) 321–7 at 326–7 (finding an *ex post facto* problem with the MCA's changing of the definition of conspiracy).

D. Minor changes: the 2010 Military Commissions Manual

On 27 April 2010, the Obama administration issued a new Manual of Military Commissions. Many of the troubling rules identified earlier still persist, but some have been adapted or eliminated to provide more rights to the defendant.

Most prominently, the 2010 Manual changed the category of persons over whom military commissions are empowered to exercise jurisdiction. Instead of 'unlawful enemy combatants', defendants are now known as 'unprivileged enemy belligerents'.[152] The military commission itself is designated a 'competent tribunal' to determine whether a person is subject to its jurisdiction.[153] The Combatant Status Review Tribunal (CSRT)[154] no longer plays any role in the military commission process as outlined in the manual.[155] No specific procedure for appealing a determination of status is provided. Presumably, all appeals—including appeals of status—now proceed directly to the Court of Military Commission Review. This modification eliminates the violations inherent in the CSRT process. The substantive effect is the same, however; military commissions have been given primary jurisdiction over a category of persons not recognized under international law.

The process for handling classified information has also been improved slightly. The 2007 Manual stated that examination of classified evidence, as well as decisions about its use, could be done in presentations from 'which the accused may be excluded'.[156] The 2010 Manual still allows trial counsel to present potential classified evidence to the military judge *ex parte*.[157] In deciding whether to permit the evidence to be introduced or alternatively presented, the judge is now instructed to keep the interests of the defence foremost.[158] Nonetheless, once the judge makes a decision, the government retains its right to appeal, but the defence is not permitted to ask for reconsideration.[159]

---

[152] See US Dept of Defense, Manual for Military Comms, Part II: Rules for Military Comm § 103(a) (30) (2010), available at <http://www.defense.gov/news/2010_Manual_for_Military_Commissions. pdf> (hereinafter 'The 2010 Manual'). The Manual contains four parts; in this section, 'Manual Rules', or 'RMC', refer to Part II, Rules for Military Commissions, and 'Evidence Rules' or 'R Mil Comm Evid', refer to US Dept of Defense, Manual for Military Comms, Part III, The Military Commission Rules of Evidence, available at <http://www.defense.gov/news/2010_Manual_for_Military_Commissions.pdf>.

[153] The 2010 Manual, RMC 202(c).   [154] See text at n 151.

[155] The drafters of The Manual apparently forgot to remove a reference to the CSRT in The 2010 Manual, RMC 707(b)(4)(F).

[156] The 2007 Manual (n 119), R Mil Comm Evid 505(b)(3), 505(h)(1), 505(h)(3).

[157] The 2010 Manual (n 152), R Mil Comm Evid 505(f)(2)(B).

[158] Evidence should be admittted if the information is 'noncumulative, relevant, and helpful to a legally cognizable defense, rebuttal or sentencing.' The 2010 Manual (n 152), R Mil Comm Evid 505(f)(1)(B).

[159] The 2010 Manual (n 152), R Mil Comm Evid 505(f)(3).

Perhaps the most notable change is in the appellate process. Formerly, the Court of Military Commission Review and higher appellate courts were limited to finding only errors of law.[160] This process limited the scope of appeal and made evidentiary rulings unreviewable. The 2010 Manual requires appellate courts to support the judgment only if it is correct in both law and fact.[161] Hence, the appellate court may overturn a judgment if it lacks the support of 'competent evidence'. Unfortunately, the lack of definition for 'competent evidence' persists from the 2007 Manual.[162] It is unclear what standard the appellate court would use to find insufficient evidence to support the conviction.

Many other problems in the 2007 Manual remain unaddressed. There is no definite timeline for notifying the defendant of charges against him.[163] The defendant's competence to stand trial is still presumed.[164] Most egregiously, the admissibility of evidence procured through coercive methods was not substantially changed. Instead, the rule permitting the introduction of evidence in which 'the degree of coercion is disputed' was moved from the Preamble to less prominent display in RMC 104(f).[165] It references Rule 304, which was changed so that the Detainee Treatment Act of 2005 is retroactively applicable and no statements obtained via cruel, inhuman or degrading treatment are admissible.[166] Hence, even if the defence alleges that a statement was obtained in violation of the Act, it can still be admitted into evidence.

E. Current proceedings

The United States' post 9/11 experiment with military commissions remains largely untested. In March 2011, the Obama Administration reversed its earlier decision to halt military commission proceedings at Guantánamo Bay, and ordered their resumption.[167] As of December 2013, the military commissions have completed four cases; five are pending/active; sixteen have been withdrawn or dismissed.[168]

Despite the military commissions' new mandate, the Obama Administration attempted to try several Guantánamo detainees in Article III (civil) courts.

---

[160] The 2007 Manual (n 119), RMC 1201(d).   [161] The 2010 Manual (n 152), R.M.C. 1201(d)(1).
[162] See The 2010 Manual (n 152), RMC 920(e)(5)(A).   [163] The 2010 Manual (n 152), RMC 308.
[164] The 2010 Manual (n 152), RMC 909(b).   [165] The 2010 Manual (n 152), RMC 104(f).
[166] The 2010 Manual (n 152), R Mil Comm Evid 304(a)(1).
[167] Military Commission Proceedings Resume; Capital Charges against Abd Al-Rahim Al-Nashiri, 105 *American Journal of Int'l Law* (2011) 596–7 at 596.
[168] US Office of Military Commissions, Cases, http://www.mc.mil/CASES/MilitaryCommissions.aspx.

Congress, however, blocked most such attempts.[169] On 13 November 2009, Attorney General Eric Holder announced that five detainees, including accused 9/11 mastermind Khalid Sheikh Mohammed, would stand trial in the US District Court for the Southern District of New York.[170] But Congressional opposition forced the trial back to the military commissions, where the proceedings have been marked by violations of fair trial rights.[171]

For now, the military commissions remain the Obama Administration's primary tool for trying detainees who are deemed 'unprivileged enemy belligerents'.

Conclusion

Though it is well settled that fair trial protections apply to all courts, whether regular or special, the problem of military commissions in the United States illustrates that there is a serious disconnect between fair trial norms and their application. Unfortunately, too many nations have mounted unfair trials in such exceptional courts. For example, the UN Working Group on Arbitrary Detention has 'found by experience that virtually none of [the special courts, military or otherwise,] respects the guarantees of the right to a fair trial'.[172] Regional human rights bodies and the Human Rights Committee have similarly found special courts to violate fair trial protections.[173]

[169] D. Boehm, 'Guantánamo Bay and the Conflict of Ethical Lawyering', 117 *Penn State Law Review* (2012) 283–327 at 343.

[170] L. Robbins, 'Profiles of Four Terror Suspects', *New York Times*, 14 November 2009, available at <http://www.nytimes.com/2009/11/14/us/14khallad.html>.

[171] R. Bejesky, 'Closing Girmo Due to the Epiphany Approach to Habeas Corpus during the Military Commission Circus', 50 *Willamette Law Review* (2013) 43-113 at 95–6 (footnotes omitted).

[172] Report of the Working Group on Arbitrary Detention, UN Doc E/CN.4/1996/40 (1995), § 107.

[173] See nn 8–10 and 80–90 with related text.

That special courts violate fair trial standards should come as no surprise. In the words of the Human Rights Committee, 'quite often the reason for the establishment of such courts is to enable exceptional procedures to be applied which do not comply with normal standards of justice'.[174] Nonetheless, the problem of extraordinary courts presents an opportunity to reinforce respect for the system of international fair trial guarantees and the rule of law.

[174] HRCttee, General Comment No 13 on equality before the courts and the right to a fair and public hearing by an independent court established by law (Art 14) (General Comment No 13), (replaced by General Comment No 32 (n 19)), § 14.

CHAPTER 18

ECONOMIC, SOCIAL, AND CULTURAL RIGHTS IN ARMED CONFLICT*

EIBE RIEDEL

1 INTRODUCTION

INTERNATIONAL human rights law (IHRL) primarily focuses on rights protection in peace-time, and historically this has been reflected both at national and international levels. International humanitarian law (IHL) by contrast focuses on the Hague and Geneva law of armed conflict. The changing nature of conflict situations in recent times has had important effects on the applicability of IHRL and IHL.[1] Fundamental IHL principles, including distinction, humanity, and proportionality have gained general acceptance, and the position of the civilian population and of individuals has gradually been enhanced. As Articles 72, 75, and 76 of Additional Protocol I to the 1977 Geneva Conventions (AP I) clearly show, the interrelationship

* This Chapter is based on the inaugural lecture in the Academy Lecture Series delivered on 6 May 2010. I wish to thank Giulia Testa and Gilles Giacca for their editorial assistance.

[1] For an overview, see L. Doswald-Beck and S. Vité, 'International Humanitarian Law and Human Rights Law', 293 *International Review of the Red Cross (IRRC)* (1993) 94–119; see also R. Kolb, 'The Relationship Between International Humanitarian Law and Human Rights Law', 324 *IRRC* (1998) 409–19.

between IHL and IHRL by now is well established, but the exact scope of that inter-relationship still needs clarification.[2]

The general practice of the UN human rights treaty bodies over the last decades has been to continue the traditional peace-time focus, leaving war-time situations to other methods of conflict resolution. Gradually, however, conflict situations in all their complex varieties have also gained special attention from a human rights perspective. Previously, states parties in the midst of violent conflict tended to be excused from effective monitoring and implementation of their human rights obligations until peace-time conditions were restored. States were referred to IHL and other international law rules in armed conflict situations. In the last 20 years, however, the practice of human rights treaty bodies has gradually changed.

2 EQUAL TREATMENT OF ECONOMIC, SOCIAL, AND CULTURAL RIGHTS AND OF CIVIL AND POLITICAL RIGHTS

Today the human rights treaty bodies regularly question states parties on the realization of human rights, even in times of armed conflict, and a number of authors have addressed how human rights obligations can apply alongside or instead of IHL rules. The focus of debate has been primarily on the relationship between civil and political rights (cp-rights) and IHL rules, in particular the protection of the right to life during armed conflict situations.[3] Economic, social, and cultural rights (esc-rights), by contrast, have received little or no attention. This has been due in part to the legacy of contentions made during the Cold War that esc-rights, unlike cp-rights, merely had programmatic effect, were cost-intensive, obscure, or vague in formulation, and not justiciable,[4] and allegedly only could apply in state-run

---

[2] See H.J. Heintze, 'On the Relationship Between Human Rights Law Protection and International Humanitarian Law', 86 *IRRC* (2004) 789–814; N. Luball, 'Challenges in Applying Human Rights Law to Armed Conflict', 860 *IRRC* (2005) 737–54. See also the Chapter by D. Jinks in this volume.

[3] C. Droege, 'Elective Affinities? Human Rights and Humanitarian Law', 871 *IRRC* (2008) 501–48.

[4] On the justiciability of economic, social and cultural rights, cf C. Courtis, *Courts and the Legal Enforcement of Economic, Social and Cultural Rights, Comparative Experiences of Justiciability* (Geneva: International Commission of Jurists, 2008), and also by C. Courtis, *Commentary on the Optional Protocol to the Covenant on Economic, Social and Cultural Rights* (Inter-American Institute of Human Rights/International Commission of Jurists, 2008) (English version 2010).

planned economies.[5] While these debates have largely subsided since the end of the Cold War, a number of experts still seem to hold similar views,[6] and thus will only choose examples from the sphere of cp-rights, when discussing the relationship with IHL.[7]

As a basic premise, greater attention should be given to a newer direction in the general debate on human rights in armed conflict situations, which maintains that esc-rights have largely and undeservedly been reduced to a side role in dealing with both IHRL and IHL. However, violations of esc-rights affect the survival and well-being of millions if not billions of people all over the world in a dramatic fashion, at least as much as violations of cp-rights.[8] Although nearly all authorities on IHL and IHRL seem to agree that esc-rights need to be taken into account, usually they do so only in passing, by paying lip-service to the mantra of universality, equality, inter-dependence, and covariance of all human rights, and then apologetically highlighting that the nature of esc-rights allegedly differs fundamentally from cp-rights.

Examples given in the IHL context usually focus on the prohibition of torture and inhuman and degrading treatment, violations of the right to life, the prohibition of slavery, restrictions of freedom of movement, etc, which of course mark grave violations of human rights.[9] Yet the Geneva Conventions of 1949 and the Additional Protocols of 1977 also contain specific obligations in respect of esc-rights.

People who die of hunger or starvation, are denied access to basic health care, face deplorable working conditions, lack housing, water, and adequate sanitation, all suffer as much, if not more than those whose rights are violated under many provisions of the International Covenant on Civil and Political Rights (ICCPR).

---

[5] *Per contra* E. Riedel, 'International Law Shaping Constitutional Law, Realization of Economic, Social and Cultural Rights', in E. Riedel (ed), *Constitutionalism—Old Concepts, New Worlds, German Contributions to the VIth World Congress of the International Association of Constitutional Law* (Berlin: Berliner Wissenschaftsverlag, 2005), 105–21.

[6] C. Tomuschat, 'An Optional Protocol for the International Covenant on Economic, Social and Cultural Rights?', in K. Dicke et al (eds), *Weltinnenrecht: Liber amicorum Jost Delbrück* (Berlin: Duncker & Humblot, 2005), 815–34; M.J. Dennis and D.P. Stewart, 'Justiciability of Economic, Social and Cultural Rights: Should There be an International Complaints Mechanism to Adjudicate the Right to Food, Water, Housing and Health', 98 *AJIL* (2004) 462–515; *per contra* M. Ssenyonjo, *Economic, Social and Cultural Rights in International Law* (Oxford and Portland: Hart Publishing, 2009), 30–9.

[7] See Droege (n 3), and Heintze (n 2), 794ff.

[8] See E. Riedel, 'The Right to Life and the Right to Health, in particular the Obligation to Reduce Child Mortality', in C. Tomuschat, E. Lagrange, and S. Oeter (eds), *The Right to Life, Journées d'études conjointes, Société Francaise pour le Droit International/Deutsche Gesellschaft für Rechtsvergleichung, Hamburg 2008* (Leiden/Boston: Martinus Nijhoff Publishers, 2010), 351–69.

[9] In the seminal study by J. M. Henckaerts and L.Doswald-Beck, *Customary International Humanitarian Law, vol I Rules* (Cambridge: Cambridge University Press, 2005), the examples given on the fundamental guarantees in Ch 32, rules 87–105 only partially cover esc-rights.

In reality, both the ICCPR and the International Covenant of Economic, Social and Cultural Rights (ICESCR or the Covenant) are legally binding treaties, spelling out human rights standards, elaborated conjointly in the Universal Declaration of Human Rights (UDHR),[10] to which nearly all states at the time consented. The 'mantra' of human rights, ie indivisibility, inter-dependence, equality, and universality of all human rights as stated in the Vienna Declaration on Human Rights[11] has been religiously stated in all UN bodies, almost like liturgical incantations, and gains credibility through the fact that both sets of rights deeply relate to the preservation of human dignity.[12]

Without the right to an adequate standard of living, health, education, and equal access to available work, efforts to protect cp-rights would suffer, if not be rendered meaningless. The UN Committee on Economic, Social and Cultural Rights (ESCR Committee) has continuously stressed that basically every Covenant right contains elements that have immediate effect, obliging states parties to take steps to realize rights at once.[13]

In General Comment 3 of 1990, the ESCR Committee addressed the issue, and by way of example stated that there are quite a number of rights in the Covenant that closely resemble those found in the ICCPR and could, therefore, be treated in a similar manner.[14] By way of example, the non-discrimination and equality provisions in Articles 2(2) and 3 of the ICESCR could be mentioned, as well as equal pay for equal work in Article 7(a), trade union rights (Article 8), protection of children from exploitation (Article 10(3)), the right to compulsory primary education free of charge (Article 13(2)(a)), and protections relating to scientific or other research or intellectual productions (Article 15(1)(c) and (3)), to name but some.

Since 1990, the ESCR Committee has elaborated 21 General Comments on specific Covenant rights, and now holds that every Covenant right contains 'a minimum core obligation to ensure the satisfaction of, at the very least, minimum essential levels of each of the rights of the Covenant'.[15] As the ESCR Committee has stressed since its General Comment No 3 of 1990, 'a state in which any significant number of individuals is deprived of essential foodstuffs, of essential healthcare, of basic shelter and housing, or of the most basic forms of education for all, is prima facie failing to discharge its obligations under the Covenant'.[16]

---

[10] UNGA Res 217A(III), UN Doc A/810 (1948); see J. Morsink, *The Universal Declaration of Human Rights: Origins, Drafting and Intent* (Philadelphia: University of Philadelphia Press, 1999); H. Hannum, 'The Status of the Universal Declaration of Human Rights in National and International Law', 25 *Georgia Journal of International and Comparative Law* (1995/96) 287.

[11] Vienna Declaration and Programme of Action, World Conference on Human Rights, Vienna, 14–25 June 1993, UN Doc A/CONF 157/23; see W. Kälin and J. Künzli, *The Law of International Human Rights Protection* (Oxford: Oxford University Press, 2009), 20; see also Ssenyonjo (n 6), 4.

[12] Riedel (n 8).   [13] Courtis (n 4), 26.

[14] Articles 7(a), 8(1), 10(3), 11(2), and 13(2)(a) of the International Covenant on Economic, Social and Cultural Rights.

[15] General Comment No 3, § 10; Maastricht Guidelines 1997, § 9.

[16] General Comment No 3, § 9; Riedel (n 8), 112f.

In recent years, the ESCR Committee has started to distinguish generic structural and specific obligations relating to resource allocation by looking at systemic and individual infringement cases.[17] In so doing it has identified what could be called a *micro-* and a *macro*-dimension of each Covenant right.

The '*micro*'-level addresses the immediate core obligations for rights realization for individuals concerned—as outlined in 'minimum core obligations'. These usually involve discrimination and equal access questions, which usually do not require large budget allocations to ensure implementation, but do imply the need for a willingness on the part of the state to change laws and practices where necessary.[18]

The '*macro*'-level, by contrast, addresses the need for substantial system changes, such as preparing new legislation to bring domestic law in line with the international obligation. Such systemic changes obviously cannot be implemented immediately. Article 2(1) of the ICESCR acknowledges this by referring to the obligation of each state party to 'take steps' to achieve 'progressively the full realization of the rights' set out.

A good example can be taken from the Convention on the Rights of Persons with Disabilities (CRPD),[19] which foresees in Article 24 the provision of inclusive education for disabled persons. At the *micro-level*, states that have ratified the Convention must take immediate steps to enable individual disabled children to be admitted to regular schools, in order to avoid a situation where they would lose required time in regular schools. Bringing national education laws in line in a comprehensive manner usually involves drafting amending laws, which clearly cannot be done from one day to the next. States should be granted up to a full legislative term, presumably not more than four years, during which such *macro-level* changes in the curricula and school admission system must be brought about.[20] In some cases,

[17] See eg CESCR Statement: An evaluation of the obligation to take steps to the 'maximum of available resources' under an Optional Protocol to the Covenant, E/C.12/2007/1, 21 September 2007, § 8, where the CESCR outlined the conditions under which it would evaluate the reasonableness and appropriateness of steps taken by states parties: (a) whether the measures taken were deliberate, concrete and targeted towards the fulfilment of esc-rights; (b) whether the state party exercised its discretion in a non-discriminatory and non-arbitrary manner; (c) whether the state party's decision not to allocate available resources was in accordance with international human rights standards; (d) where several policy options are available, whether the state party adopted the option least restricting Covenant rights; (e) the time frame in which the steps were taken; and (f) whether the steps had taken into account the precarious situation of disadvantaged and marginalized individuals or groups, whether they were non-discriminatory and whether they prioritized grave situations or situations of risk.

[18] This notion has been taken from General Comment No 3, § 10, and been applied consistently in all General Comments since General Comment No 14 on the Right to the Highest Attainable Standard of Health.

[19] UNGA Res 61/106 of 13 December 2006.

[20] E. Riedel, The Impact of the UN Convention of Persons with Disabilities and its Optional Protocol on School Education in a Federal State: the case of Germany, Legal Opinion for Landesarbeitsgemeinschaft, Gemeinsam Leben, Gemeinsam Lernen' Nordrhein-Westfalen, Mannheim/Geneva 15 January 2010, Berlin 2010.

states misunderstand this obligation as only requiring the development of a plan or programme, and fail to provide any indication of how such a policy, plan, or strategy will be implemented. The ESCR Committee has, however, been adamant that states must at least show that immediate and concrete steps in the right direction are being taken, and will question delegations at the dialogue stage about the success and preliminary results achieved by those undertakings and measures.[21]

Other *macro*-questions, such as those relating to poverty reduction or seeking international cooperation and assistance, or concerning environmental or right to development issues which impede the full realization of rights contained in the Covenant fall under this category of esc-rights fulfilment. As *macro*-issues, they are best dealt with in the state reporting procedure, and are regularly addressed in questions from the ESCR Committee on the general provisions of the Covenant.

Now that the Optional Protocol to the ICESCR[22] has entered into force, '*micro*'-level issues will undoubtedly receive more attention, but that cannot be elaborated here.

In sum, when dealing with provisions of the ICESCR, the ESCR Committee has increasingly begun to address the effect of the human rights guarantees in situations of armed conflict, as much as in peace time.

3 THE RELEVANCE OF ESC-RIGHTS TO PEACE AND ARMED CONFLICT

Following World War II and the adoption of the UDHR, the human rights of every individual became the new trump cards against which abuses by states would be challenged. Ensuring universal respect for these rights, however, could not be achieved easily. No individual complaint against home or host states was foreseen at the universal level, and human rights protection was developed only indirectly: individuals were not granted the possibility to claim rights directly, but

---

[21] See generally E. Riedel, 'The International Covenant on Economic, Social and Cultural Rights', *Max Planck Encyclopedia of Public International Law* (EPIL) (Oxford: Oxford University Press, 2007), rev 2010; by the same, The Committee on Economic, Social and Cultural Rights, in *Max Planck Encyclopedia of Public International Law* (Oxford: Oxford University Press, 2008), rev 2010; by the same, 'Economic, Social and Cultural Rights', in C. Krause and M. Scheinin (eds), *International Protection of Human Rights, A Textbook* (Abo, 2009), 129–49.

[22] Entry into force on 5 May 2013 following ratification by 10 states. In addition, some 40 states have signed the Optional Protocol.

obligations were placed on sovereign states to guarantee human rights for everyone under their control.

From a standard-setting point of view, the UDHR drew a comprehensive picture of human rights protection, putting all major civil, cultural, economic, political, and social rights side by side. All rights were seen as exemplifications of the fundamental obligation to protect the human dignity of everyone. The monitoring system set up by treaty law consequently consisted in establishing treaty bodies with mandates to review and monitor state reports, and in the case of the ICCPR also to receive inter-state complaints and even individual communications.[23] Other treaty bodies were given similar powers.[24] Governments did not agree to a draft Optional Protocol to the ICESCR until 2008.

The rights enshrined in the ICESCR are comprehensive and cover many areas of rights protection. As set out in the UDHR, the overriding *raison d'être* of all esc-rights is the protection of human dignity, just as with cp-rights. If we look at the full range of rights in the Covenant, (including the rights to health, food, housing, water and sanitation, work and social security, family rights, education, and culture) we see that all of these rights impose detailed obligations on states parties, and are supplemented by a series of overriding general principles, such as non-discrimination and equal rights of men and women, to name but some.

All these rights have been spelled out as applying primarily in peacetime. Subsequent treaties focusing on more specific issues, all started from this peacetime premise. Only in recent years has the ESCR Committee begun to address the realization of Covenant rights during armed conflict, and requiring states parties to do everything in their power to address the situations of populations concerned in terms of enjoyment of esc-rights. The ESCR Committee now regularly considers how conflict and post-conflict situations affect states parties' ability to address questions of homelessness under the right to housing, protection of women, equal access to health services under the right to health, guarantees of schooling for children under the right to education,[25] and of children enlisted in armed forces. Sexual violence against women and children during conflict situations are also addressed in detail during the ESCR Committee's dialogue with the state party concerned, and strong recommendations follow in concluding observations.

Moreover, the ESCR Committee has—in several instances—noted with alarm the high levels of sexual violence and atrocities, including rapes committed collectively and publicly by armed groups and in some cases by regular armed forces, to intimidate

---

[23] A. Clapham, *Human Rights: A Very Short Introduction* (Oxford: Oxford University Press, 2007), 1–57.

[24] C. Tomuschat, *Human Rights: Between Idealism and Realism* (2nd edn, Oxford: Oxford University Press, 2008).

[25] For an excellent overview, see B. O'Malley, *Education under Attack, A Global Study on Targeted Political and Military Violence Against Education Staff, Students, Teachers, Union and Government Officials, Aid Workers and Institutions* (Paris: UNESCO, 2010), in particular case discussions 65–93.

the population, in clear violation of IHL and IHRL rules. Perpetrators are often granted bail or are released from detention while survivors of sexual violence (women, children, and often also men) frequently end up rejected by their families and communities, and are left without healthcare, support, or compensation being provided by the state party concerned.

In the early years of the ESCR Committee's work, concluding observations relating to armed conflicts did not stand out prominently. In fact, armed conflict situations in a particular state party usually were referred to—if at all—in the opening paragraphs of the Concluding Observations under the heading, 'factors and difficulties impeding the full realization of esc-rights'. This reference had an apologetic ring to it, and showed that the Committee, while insisting on states parties fulfilling their Covenant obligations, also accepted such conflicts as a reality, which made it impossible, at least in the current situation, to meet fully the obligations under each of the rights in question. Consequently, the ESCR Committee would only urge the state party in question to make genuine efforts to move, albeit slowly, towards meeting its obligations under the prevailing adverse conditions.[26]

During the 1990s, many states parties were in arrears of their reporting duties, as happened with all other UN Human Rights Treaty Bodies. The ESCR seldom put pressure on states parties that were engaged in armed conflicts, and did not usually threaten the related non-reporting procedure. As a consequence, states experiencing situations of armed conflict as well as battling with natural catastrophes like earthquakes, floods, tsunamis, and other major emergencies often did not appear before the Committee at all. An implied understanding made clear that it might not be useful for states parties facing such circumstances to go through the required periodic monitoring exercise under the ICESCR as this may distract from their efforts to address the immediate effects and consequences of such man-made or natural catastrophes.

Needless to say, special procedures mechanisms (country mandates and thematic mandates) of the UN Commission on Human Rights and later the UN Human Rights Council filled that gap to a certain extent. As with other treaty bodies, the situation since the end of the 1990s has changed considerably. The ESCR Committee increasingly reviews the performance of states parties even in times of armed conflict. The reasons are manifold, and they cannot be reviewed here in full, but a brief survey with respect to some specific rights will show why monitoring of esc-rights is particularly relevant during armed conflict.

---

[26] In line with Art 2(1) of ICESCR which states: 'Each State Party to the present Covenant undertakes to take steps, individually and through international assistance and co-operation, especially economic and technical, to the maximum of its available resources, with a view to progressively achieving the full realization of the rights recognized in the present Covenant by all appropriate means, including particularly the adoption of legislative measures'.

4 ESC-Rights in Armed Conflict Before the ESCR Committee

Three reports by states to the ESCR Committee illustrate the importance of these rights in armed conflict situations. These few examples show very clearly that esc-rights must apply in peacetime, as well as in times of armed conflict, even if in the latter situation the treaty bodies can only ask the state party to do as much as is feasible under those adverse conditions. The ESCR Committee takes great care to assess the actual effects of armed conflicts on the ability of governments to fulfil their obligations under the Covenant.

A. Afghanistan

When Afghanistan reported to the ESCR Committee in 1990,[27] the concluding observations made scant reference to the prevailing armed conflict situation in that country. The head of the delegation which reported to the Committee stressed at the time that 'his country had been torn by civil strife for 14 years which had taken terrible toll in human lives and economic resources' and concluded that this had 'obviously inhibited the full exercise of economic, social and cultural rights'. Moreover, the delegation pointed out that the government could not guarantee the application of international norms and conventions in areas that were under the control of opposition forces.

The ESCR Committee took the view that despite the armed conflict situation, the government had to do everything in its power to fulfil its obligations under the Covenant to the best of its ability. In particular, the government was asked to address the plight of many refugees across Afghan borders. The Committee also asked the delegation whether the extent of homelessness in the country 'was due to the absence of accommodations rather than the ravages of war'. In the ensuing dialogue between the Committee and the government's delegation, general concerns under the Covenant were discussed, irrespective of the post-war situation. Special emphasis was placed on the situation of women, including their equal access to health services, measures to address the problem of female genital mutilation, education rights of girls and women, and the extent to which steps were being taken to guarantee equal rights of women under Islamic law. The Committee also looked at the position of children in Afghan society. In its concluding observations, the Committee focused particular attention on the plight of children as victims of the war.

---

[27] UN Doc E/C.12/1991/SR.2, 4–6 and 8; Concluding Observations CESCR UN Doc E/1992/23.

Seventeen years later, the ESCR Committee revisited the situation in Afghanistan. In addition to its review of specific aspects of the state's latest report, the Committee also took up the recommendations it made to the government in 1991, and systematically assessed state performance under each Covenant Article.[28] For example, it took up the issue of equal rights of women and men under Article 3 of the Covenant and asked whether Afghanistan had implemented or envisaged implementing a comprehensive strategy to eliminate negative traditional attitudes and practices, and deep-rooted stereotypes, which discriminated against Afghan women. It also raised questions with respect to steps taken by Afghanistan to 'eliminate the stereotypes associated with the traditional roles of men and women in the family and in society at large'.[29]

It should be noted that the ESCR Committee did not differentiate in its comments between armed conflict and peace time situations. Similar and precise questions were posed in relation to all the other Covenant rights, but reference in the report to the armed conflict situations existing between 1991 and 2010 are oblique. Thus, information on quality primary education is sought for all children, but particularly for the most disadvantaged and marginalized individuals and groups.[30] In this context, Afghanistan was asked how it intended to ensure access to education 'in view of the deteriorating security situation for children in, and on the way to and from, school'. In the Committee's Concluding Observations, many of these issues were taken up, in particular, shortcomings in efforts to combat impunity, abuses linked to the recruitment of child soldiers, and health problems associated with war-related traumatic disorders.[31]

B. Colombia

In the case of Colombia, the ESCR Committee's concluding observations on the fourth periodic report in 2001 include few references to armed conflict situations in parts of the country.[32] Again, the Committee's focus at the time was primarily on the state's general record with respect to its obligations under the Covenant, irrespective of the conflict situation. The specific references made to armed conflict in the report were cursory and only discussed *en passant*, such as those concerning the persistence of child labour in Colombia, despite all efforts undertaken by the government to make progress in this area. The Committee remained deeply concerned about the high numbers of street children, and of children affected by the conflict, and

---

[28] Afghanistan, E/C.12/AFG/CO/2-4, of 7 June 2010.

[29] Afghanistan, List of Issues, E/C.12/AFG/Q/2-4, 22/12/2009, question 9.

[30] List of Issues, para 38; see also UNESCO Report Education under Attack, 2010, esp 173–8.

[31] E/C.12/AFG/CO/2-4, 7 June 2010, §§ 15 (corruption and impunity), 30 (child soldiers), 42 (health problems of war-related traumatic disorders).

[32] E/C.12/1/Add.74,30/11/2001.

was particularly concerned that children were being forced to participate in armed violence.[33]

In 2009, the Committee provided a detailed list of issues following from the most recent state report,[34] and asked Colombia, inter alia, whether the current transitional justice process mainstreams esc-rights.[35] It also enquired about the steps taken to give effect to a Constitutional Court order ensuring the protection of internally displaced women against the risk of violence and sexual abuse. In addition, it enquired about what efforts had been made to prevent the forced recruitment of children by armed groups,[36] and address the continuing effects of the armed conflict, 'in particular on women and children who have suffered excessive physical, sexual or psychological violence used as a strategy of war',[37] emphasizing social rehabilitation measures for victims, particularly for those who are displaced or live in remote areas. This theme was taken up in several other questions on Article 11, and on Articles 13 and 14 of the ICESCR, in relation to the right to education, putting particular emphasis on measures Colombia had taken, or was contemplating, to protect school premises from occupation by armed groups and the consequent interruption of classes.[38] These examples demonstrate that the full spectrum of rights in the Covenant were considered, albeit drawing special attention to the effects of the persisting armed conflict in some parts of the country.

C. Democratic Republic of the Congo

One of the most recent examples of a country report submitted while armed conflict in some parts of the state party continued, is the report of the Democratic Republic of the Congo. The Committee made clear[39] that while acknowledging that persisting instability and recurrent armed conflicts in some the provinces made it difficult for the government to fulfil its obligations under the Covenant, this did not absolve it from all human rights obligations. In fact, the Committee insisted that impunity for human rights violations and the illegal exploitation of the country's natural resources, including by foreign companies, constitute major obstacles to the enjoyment of economic, social and cultural rights. The Committee reiterated, however, that the primary responsibility for ensuring security in its territory, and for protecting its civilians regarding the rule of law, human rights and international humanitarian law, rests with the government. The Committee is thus taking an increasingly

---

[33] See E/C.12/1/Add.74,30/11/2001, §§ 19 and 20.

[34] List of Issues, E/C.12/COL/Q/5, 27/07/2009.   [35] List of Issues, question 5.

[36] List of Issues, questions 12, 23, and 24.   [37] List of Issues, question 24.

[38] Cf the detailed analysis of the Colombian situation in B. O'Malley, *Education under Attack*, (Paris: UNESCO, 2010), 180–4.

[39] E/C.12/COD/CO/4, 16/12/2009, § 6.

bolder position in addressing economic, social and cultural rights, even in times of armed conflict in the country under review, and flatly rejects attempts by some governments to excuse themselves from their Covenant obligations by reference to such conflicts.

In its dialogue with the delegation of the government of the Democratic Republic of the Congo, Committee members made quite clear, however, that Western and Southern provinces of the country, not directly affected by the armed conflict situation in Eastern provinces would be subjected to a full review, and addressed many specific issues arising under each of the Covenant rights. For these provinces, the Committee stressed that peacetime human rights standards must be upheld. Yet even in the Eastern provinces experiencing conflict, the Committee stressed that the government must do everything possible under the prevailing adverse circumstances, to realize at least some core aspects of the Covenant's provisions, until a stabilized situation in the entire country enables fuller implementation.

To single out just one recommendation,[40] the Committee noted the high level of sexual violence and atrocities, including ethnically motivated rapes committed collectively and publicly by all armed groups, including by the Congolese Army (FARDC) and the national Congolese Police (PNC), in clear violation of international human rights and humanitarian law.[41] It further expressed alarm that men accused of rape were often granted bail or released while survivors of sexual violence (women, children and often also men) frequently experienced rejection by their families, as well as lack of access to health care, support or compensation being provided to them by the state.[42] The Committee recommended immediate action by the state party, and widened its recommendation to combat all gender-based violence, and to take appropriate measures to combat domestic violence and to support gender empowerment under Article 10 of the Covenant. The plight of 1.7 million Internally Displaced Persons (IDPs) who rely exclusively on assistance provided by international humanitarian organizations was also highlighted. Owing to the continuing outbreaks of armed conflict in the Eastern provinces, IDPs often have no choice but to hide in the forest, deprived of any assistance, and in constant fear of being abused and violated by all factions engaged in the fighting.[43]

---

[40] E/C.12/COD/4,16/12/2009, § 25.

[41] §§ 27 (children recruited in FARDC and detention in military facilities) and 32 (Illegal detentions in prisons and detention centres).

[42] See in particular B. O'Malley, *Education under Attack* (Paris: UNESCO, 2010), 89–91 and 184–6 on the education situation in Eastern Congo.

[43] E/C.12/COD/4,16/12/2009, § 33.

5 THE SLIDING SCALE OF
CONFLICT SITUATIONS

As these few examples of state reporting under the ICESCR have demonstrated, the realization of human rights differs, depending on whether peacetime conditions or armed conflict situations prevail. The concrete application of rights depends on the actual conflict situation at hand, and results in various degrees of applicability. It follows that a range of conflict situations, which essentially cannot be treated alike, need to be distinguished. The conflict escalation ladder, as originally proposed by *Kahn* in his book 'On Escalation', may serve as a structuring guide for the ensuing analysis of conflict situations relating to realization of IHRL standards.[44]

A. Peacetime

In peacetime, the first level set out in Kahn's analysis, the whole tableau of esc-rights obligations must be met, under conditions outlined at the outset. The ESCR Committee has emphasized the issues of domestic application of Covenant obligations in its General Comment No 9, highlighting that the national implementation of internationally agreed esc-rights is the priority. The law to be applied is human rights law and domestic law implementation.

B. Sporadic violence

The second level covers sporadic or larger-scale outbreaks of violence below the level of organized violence, while the government with few exceptions still exercises ultimate control. Here human rights law applies across the board, and domestic law, usually criminal and administrative law, applies as well. The most recent outbreaks of violence in Kyrgyzstan (and Thailand) probably fit this form of internal conflict situation. International Humanitarian Law rules do not apply in such cases.[45]

---

[44] See H. Kahn, *On Escalation: Metaphors and Scenarios* (Praeger, 1965), new edn (New Brunswick N.J: Transaction Publishers, 2010), where he presents a 44-step conflict escalation ladder.

[45] For a further analysis of the threshold of application of International Humanitarian Law in situations of non-international armed conflict, see S. Vité, 'Typology of Armed Conflicts in International Humanitarian Law: Legal Concepts and Actual Situations', 91(873) *IRRC* (2009) 76. See also A.J. Carswell, 'Classifying the Conflict: A Soldier's Dilemma', 91(873) *IRRC* (2009) 150.

C. Insurrections

Next on the scale of increasing conflict are insurrections. Here it is submitted that both international IHL and IHRL as well as domestic law all apply. But IHL only comes into play if the threshold for the applicability of Common Article 3 of the Geneva Conventions is met. But IHRL and domestic law clearly also apply.[46] In such a conflict situation, each of the conflicting parties exercising territorial control must see to it that the esc-rights are not violated, ie that access to health care facilities, schools, and basic subsistence provisions are guaranteed. To cut off water supplies or to generally withhold access to housing in such conflict situations would clearly violate core obligations under the Covenant and would also require domestic law remedies to the extent feasible under the prevailing adverse circumstances.[47]

D. Additional Protocol II non-international armed conflicts

At the next level, the conflict has widened and reached the required threshold of Additional Protocol II of the Geneva Conventions (AP II), which applies alongside domestic law on which the government still having control over certain parts of the country relies. It may be difficult to assess the actual situation, as the developments during the Spanish Civil War from 1936–38 showed.[48] In such situations of civil war, as in Afghanistan, Colombia, or the Democratic Republic of Congo, IHRL also applies throughout, but the Committee has clearly limited the full scope to that degree of rights realization possible under civil war conditions.[49]

Under IHRL, the addressee always is the state party that has ratified the ICESCR. Disputes remain concerning whether such human rights obligations also apply to the non-state armed group opposing the government in a civil war. One view holds that the non-state armed group must declare voluntarily that it regards itself as bound by the treaty.[50] The better view would appear to be that non-state actors

---

[46] See generally R. Prévost, *International Human Rights and Humanitarian Law* (Cambridge: Cambridge University Press, 2002), 54–6.

[47] Again this is mirrored in General Comment No 3 (1990) of the CESCR.

[48] See M.N. Shaw, *International Law* (6th edn, Cambridge: Cambridge University Press, 2008), 462ff.

[49] See eg UN Committee on Economic, Social and Cultural Rights (CESCR), Concluding Observations on Colombia (2010), UN Doc E/C.12/COL/CO/5, § 7; Concluding Observations on Afghanistan (2010), UN Doc E/C.12/AFG/CO/2-4, § 12; Concluding Observations on the Democratic Republic of the Congo (2009), UN Doc E/C.12/COD/CO/4, § 6.

[50] For further information about these unilateral undertakings, see A. Clapham, 'Human Rights Obligations of Non-State Actors in Conflict Situations', 88(863) *IRRC* (2006) 511–12. *Per contra*, according to Christian Tomuschat, non-state actors are bound by international human rights law, whether or not they have consented to the relevant human rights rule: 'The rule that any obligation requires the consent of the party concerned has long been abandoned. The international community has set up a

are also bound by IHRL, whether or not they have consented to relevant human rights instruments.[51] It should, however, be noted that the ESCR Committee has no possibility to deal with non-state actors directly under its terms of reference.[52] From a human rights perspective, we encounter here a possible protection gap. This gap can be filled by international humanitarian law, particularly under AP II.

E. International armed conflicts

Another step on the ladder of armed conflicts is a situation of international armed conflict (in some cases with third states intervening to help one of the belligerents). Here IHL squarely applies, particularly AP I. In cases where the state party to the armed conflict has not ratified this Protocol, the prevailing view of the relevant literature holds that most of the rules laid down in the 1977 Protocols by now have become part of customary international law.[53] Domestic law of both parties to the conflict, however, continues to apply in the respective territories. In such situations, some argue that IHL rules are *lex specialis*, and IHRL would only come into play where protection gaps under IHL would occur.[54] For instance, under Article 12 of the ICESCR health care facilities must be kept accessible for the general population in those areas where the government retains control during armed conflict. The same applies to ensuring the right to education under Covenant Article 13, as the Committee clearly outlined in its Concluding Observations on the Democratic

---

general framework of rights and duties which every actor seeking to legitimize himself as a suitable player at the inter-State level must respect'. C. Tomuschat, 'The Applicability of Human Rights Law to Insurgent Movements', in H. Fischer and U. Froissant et al (eds), *Crisis Management and Humanitarian Protection: Festschrift für Dieter Fleck* (Berlin: Berliner Wissenschafts-Verlag, 2004), 587.

[51] See Tomuschat (n 50), 587.

[52] The CESCR usually tries to overcome this obstacle by emphasizing the obligation of the state to monitor and regulate the conduct of non-state actors, according to their responsibility to protect the rights provided for in the ICESCR. Other human rights bodies have done the same by referring to the principle of due diligence of states. However, it is clear that this is not the ideal way to deal with human rights violations committed by non-state actors.

[53] See J.M. Henckaerts and L. Doswald-Beck, *Customary International Law* (Cambridge: Cambridge University Press, 2005), Vol I: Rules, as regards fundamental guarantees, see Ch 32, 299–383, and *passim*; see also C. Tomuschat, *Human Rights, Between Idealism and Realism* (2nd edn, Oxford: Oxford University Press, 2008), 302–4; W. Kälin, 'The ICRC's Compilation of the Customary Rules of Humanitarian Law', in T. Giegerich (ed), *A Wiser Century? Judicial Dispute Settlement, Disarmament and the Laws of War 100 Years after the Second Hague Peace Conference* (Berlin: Duncker & Humblot, 2009), 417–28.

[54] For an overview on this problem, see D. Richter, 'Humanitarian Law and Human Rights: Intersecting Circles or Separate Spheres?', in T. Giegerich (ed), *A Wiser Century? Judicial Dispute Settlement, Disarmament and the Laws of War 100 Years after the Second Hague Peace Conference* (Berlin: Duncker & Humblot, 2009), 257–322, esp at 311ff.

Republic of the Congo.[55] It is submitted that the more correct view holds that IHRL always applies, but is complemented by IHL rules.

F. *Post-bellum* situations

The review of the scale of armed conflict situations and the inter-relationship between IHL and IHRL does not end here, however: a whole range of post-conflict situations, with '*ius post bellum*' rules, must be looked at separately as well. Such situations reflect the evolution of armed conflict situations during the last few decades.

G. Other scenarios

The question concerns what rules apply in: (a) occupation situations, particularly long-term occupation; (b) transformation situations; (c) failed states; (d) humanitarian interventions/or missions; and (e) mixed conflicts.

(a) During periods of *occupation*, the Occupying Power must ensure that the status quo of the territory is preserved, and that deployment of relief operations is facilitated.[56] Occupation forces must not destroy the civilian population's food stocks, especially by placing mines in agricultural areas, or by immobilizing the transport system.[57] Here humanitarian and human rights regimes overlap. Articles 11 and 12 of the ICESCR confirm duties of the Occupying Power to respect, protect, and fulfil rights set out in the treaty.[58] The obligation to fulfil includes the duty to set

---

[55] Even though the categorization of the conflict as an international armed conflict is debatable. If anything, it applies to the conflict situation in the Eastern Provinces bordering Rwanda and Burundi. In the rest of the country, HRL remains fully applicable.

[56] Article 43 of the Hague Regulations concerning the Laws and Customs of War on Land (1907) provides that 'The authority of the legitimate power having in fact passed into the hands of the occupant, the latter shall take all the measures in his power to restore, and ensure, as far as possible, public order and safety, *while respecting, unless absolutely prevented, the laws in force in the country*'. Furthermore, Art 49 of the Fourth Geneva Convention provides that 'the Occupying Power shall not deport or transfer parts of its own civilian population into the territory it occupies'. As for the facilitation of relief operations, according to Art 55 of the Fourth Geneva Convention relative to the Protection of Civilian Persons in Time of War (1949) the Occupying Power 'has the duty of ensuring the food and medical supplies of the population'. Moreover, Art 59 of the Fourth Geneva Convention provides that 'If the whole or part of the population of an occupied territory is inadequately supplied, the Occupying Power shall agree to relief schemes on behalf of the said population, and shall facilitate them by all the means at its disposal'.

[57] S. Vité, 'The Interrelation of the Law of Occupation and Economic, Social and Cultural Rights: the Examples of Food, Health and Property', 90(871) *IRRC* (2008) 639.

[58] R. Kolb and S. Vité, *Le droit de l'occupation militaire, Perspectives historiques et enjeux juridiques actuels* (Brussels: Bruylant, 2009), Ch IV, 299, esp 440–5; see also Voluntary Guidelines to support the progressive realization of the right to adequate food in the context of national food security, adopted by 127th Session of the FAO Council November 2004, Rome 2005, guidelines 15 and 16.

up an effective relief distribution scheme, as the Committee outlined in detail in its concluding observations on Israel in 2003.[59] In relation to the right to health, access to medical services must be maintained, under IHL[60] and IHRL. The core content of the right to health must at all times be respected, ie access to medical facilities, essential medicines, and an adequate supply of safe drinking water.[61]

In the case of Israel, the ESCR Committee received reports of pregnant women with birth complications being held back at security points, as they wished to cross from A to B territories for medical treatments, resulting in great suffering.[62] The various occupation zones set up under the Oslo process did not change the overall responsibility of Israel under the Covenant with respect to the occupied territories.[63] The government of Israel maintained that it was only responsible for reporting within the Green Line, and that humanitarian law issues were beyond the competency of the Committee.[64] The Committee rejected this line of argument, as did other treaty bodies.[65] The Committee made it clear that peacetime application of human rights standards also applies in conflict situations, including the legal consequences of being an Occupying Power.[66]

A question remains as to how Palestinian authorities might be taken into account under the Covenant in cases where the authorities themselves have contravened obligations of the state party. Paul Hunt, for example, has argued that since the Palestinian authorities, through the Declaration of Principles on Interim Self-Government Arrangements (also known as the Oslo Accords), have assumed important responsibilities with regard to education, health, and social welfare in the

---

[59] CESCR, Concluding Observations on Israel (2003), UN Doc E/C.12/1/Add.90, §§ 31, 35, 4–3.

[60] International Humanitarian Law offers a very detailed system of rules concerning the protection of the right to health during armed conflicts, concerning three different categories: wounded and sick, prisoners of war (POW), and civilians. The access to medical service for the first category is granted by Arts 12(2) and 15 of the First Geneva Convention, as well as by Art 12(2) of the Second Geneva Convention. As of POWs, they are granted access to medical service by Arts 15, 17, 20, 46, 55, and 98 of the Third Geneva Convention. Lastly, the access to medical service of civilians is protected by Arts 14 and 18–22 of the Fourth Geneva Convention.

[61] CESCR, General Comment No 14 on the Right to Health (2000), UN Doc E/C.12/2000/4, §§ 43–4; see also Kolb and Vité (n 58), 410.

[62] According to the Information Health Centre of the Palestinian Ministry of Health, from 2000 to 2006, 69 cases of Palestinian pregnant women giving birth at Israeli checkpoints had been recorded. This information was cited in a Report of the High Commissioner for Human Rights on the issue of Palestinian pregnant women giving birth at Israeli Checkpoints (2007), UN Doc A/HRC/4/57, § 4.

[63] CESCR, Concluding Observations on Israel (2003) (n 59), § 31.

[64] Kolb and Vité (n 58), § 15.

[65] Kolb and Vité (n 58), § 31 (as for the CESCR). For the position of other treaty bodies, see for example Human Rights Committee, Consideration of the First Report submitted by Israel (1998), UN Doc CCPR/C/SR.1675, §§ 55, 70–1, 76, 79–80; Committee on the Elimination of Discrimination Against Women, Concluding Comments on Israel (2005), UN Doc CEDAW/C/ISR/CO/3, §§ 23–4; Committee Against Torture, Concluding Observations on Israel (2009), UN Doc CAT/C/ISR/CO/4, § 11.

[66] CESCR, Concluding Observations on Israel (2003) (n 59), §§ 15 and 31.

Occupied Palestinian Territory, they would as a consequence have at least indirect obligations with respect of the rights enshrined in the Covenant.[67] Palestine is, as yet, not a fully recognized state, and not a party to the International Covenant. But, in fact, both the Palestinian Authority and Hamas have declared their commitment to respect customary international human rights law.[68] Moreover, both the Palestinian Authority and Hamas are bound to respect customary humanitarian law.[69] Thus, under humanitarian customary rules it can be argued that such authorities would be seen as having responsibility under the Covenant.[70]

(b) Difficult problems occur when *transformation processes* are under way. For example, after the demise of the Soviet Union, many Central and Eastern European countries encountered difficult economic and social challenges, often in the wake of government or regime change.[71] If such transformation processes are accompanied by armed conflicts, then humanitarian rules and human rights standards apply simultaneously. Esc-rights, like all other binding human rights obligations, continue to apply, but due regard is paid to the capacity of the state party to fulfil its treaty obligations to the best of its ability under the prevailing economic or political situation.[72]

(c) In situations of *failed states*, such as in Somalia, Rwanda, and Haiti, all state obligations relating to economic, social, and cultural rights still applied,[73] even

---

[67] For a further analysis of this position, see P. Hunt, 'Economic and Social Rights: Issues of Implementation', in S. Bowen (ed), *Human Rights, Self-Determination and Political Change in the Occupied Palestinian Territories* (M. Nijhoff Publishers, 1997), 201.

[68] See the Report of the High Commissioner for Human Rights on the Implementation of Human Rights Council Resolution 7/1 on human rights violations emanating from Israeli military attacks and incursions, in the Occupied Palestinian Territory, particularly the recent ones in the occupied Gaza Strip (2008), UN Doc A/HRC/8/17, §§ 8–9.

[69] See, generally, J.M. Henkaerts and L. Doswald-Beck, *Customary International Law* vol 1 (Cambridge: Cambridge University Press, 2005), Vol I: Rules, esp Ch 32, 299–383.

[70] The Palestinian Authority has given a unilateral undertaking to apply the Fourth Geneva Convention in 1982; that undertaking has been considered valid, see International Court of Justice (ICJ), *Legal Consequences of the Construction of a Wall in the Occupied Palestinian Territory*, Advisory Opinion, 9 July 2004 (hereinafter: ICJ, *Advisory Opinion on the Wall*), § 91.

[71] See eg Concluding Observations, Russian Federation, E/C.12/1/Add.94, 12 December 2003, §§ 10, 30, 38, and 58 on the situation in Chechnya, particularly as regards health care, education, and temporary housing for those fleeing conflict areas; see also Concluding Observations on Georgia, E/C.12/1/Add.83, 19 December 2002, §§ 6 and 31 on internally displaced persons and esc-rights.

[72] See eg Concluding Observations on Sri Lanka, UN Doc E/C.12/LKA/CO/2-4,9.12.2010 or Concluding Observations on Democratic Republic of Congo, UN Doc E/C.12/COD/CO/4,16.12.2009, § 6: 'The Committee acknowledges the persistent instability and recurrent armed conflicts in some of the provinces in the State party, which pose great challenges to the ability of the State to fulfil its obligations under the Covenant. The Committee considers, however, that impunity for human rights violations and the illegal exploitation of the country's natural resources, including by foreign companies, constitute major obstacles to the enjoyment of economic, social and cultural rights in the State party.'

[73] See, generally, K. Schmalenbach, 'Preventing and Rebuilding Failed States', in T. Giegerich (ed), *A Wiser Century? Judicial Dispute Settlement, Disarmament and the Laws of War 100 Years after the Second Hague Peace Conference* (Berlin: Duncker & Humblot, 2009), 231–56.

though it was acknowledged that addressing the responsible government would likely be difficult. IHL provides more detailed and specific rules in such situations, if armed conflicts with rebel forces take place. At this conflict stage, the UN Security Council (under Chapters VI and VII of the UN Charter) is involved, and—to the extent of the mandate given—deals exclusively with such situations. Military personnel provided by member states of the UN must respect humanitarian norms.[74] The ESCR Committee has, however, looked at such situations and emphasized that peacekeeping operations and economic sanctions should not disproportionately impede the realization of economic, social, and cultural rights, even in conflict situations. In its General Comment No 8, the Committee, in response to the Gulf War situation, pointed out that a review of sanctions should take place, to see whether the targeted effects of sanctions are proportional to the suffering incurred by millions of women, children, and older persons not party to the armed conflict.[75] The Covenant guarantees thus also apply in such situations. Similarly, humanitarian rules continue to serve as standards, even when the Security Council regime takes over the execution of UN decisions.[76]

(d) The most recent form of armed conflict concerns so-called *humanitarian interventions*, or *humanitarian missions*, as seen in Iraq, then Somalia, Rwanda, and Kosovo. Here it is submitted that a whole range of international law rules apply: humanitarian standards, under APs I or II as well as esc-rights under the ICESCR all apply. In addition, the special regime of Security Council involvement— and failing that—General Assembly legitimation of individual or collective self-defence also apply. The veto exercised in the Security Council in the case of Kosovo led to extensive debates concerning whether a new category of intervention under the heading of the *responsibility to protect* should be created. The protection of fundamental human rights, amongst them economic, social, and cultural rights, to health, food, housing, and education among others, clearly served as a strong argument in favour of such UN-legitimated missions.

---

[74] See W. Kälin and J. Künzli, *The Law of International Human Rights Protection* (Oxford: Oxford University Press, 2009), 161–4.

[75] CESCR, General Comment No 8 on the Relationship between Economic Sanctions and Respect for Economic, Social and Cultural Rights (1997), UN Doc E/C.12/1997/8.

[76] For an overview, see E. Riedel, 'Quo vadis Europe? The EU Treaty Reforms, Human Rights, Rule of Law and the Fight against Terrorism', 31 *Adelaide Law Review* (2010) 241–70, esp 262; for an overview, see M. Bothe, 'Peacekeeping', in B. Simma (ed), *The Charter of the United Nations. A Commentary* (2nd edn, Oxford: Oxford University Press, 2002), 648–70; A. Orakhelashvili, 'Legal Basis of the United Nations Peacekeeping Operations', *Virginia Journal of International Law* (2003) 484–524; P. Alston, 'The Security Council and Human Rights: Lessons to be Learned from the Iraq-Kuwait Crisis and Its Aftermath', 13 *Australian Year Book of International Law* (1992) 107–76; N. Krisch, 'Unilateral Enforcement of the Collective Will: Kosovo, Iraq, and the Security Council', 3 *Max Planck Yearbook of United Nations Law* (1999) 59–103; see also W. Kälin and J. Künzli, *The Law of International Human Rights Protection* (Oxford: Oxford University Press, 2009), 161–4.

The 'humanitarian interventions' or 'humanitarian missions' as they should be referred to in order to distinguish them from outlawed humanitarian interventions under modern international law, must fulfil several conditions, as suggested by Antonio Cassese,[77] if they are to legitimize state action not endorsed by Security Council decisions. These include: (1) the situation must be one of gross and massive violations of human rights reaching the threshold of crimes against humanity; (2) systematic, wilful disregard of appeals, recommendations, and decisions of UN organs must have taken place by the government concerned; (3) the Security Council must be blocked by veto, after the conditions under Article 39 of the UN Charter have been met; (4) all Chapter VI measures of peaceful settlement of disputes under the UN Charter must have been exhausted;[78] (5) a group of states decides collectively to end atrocities. It would seem that a majority of UN member states would be necessary for this criteria to be met. In the case of NATO action in Kosovo, such a vote in the UN General Assembly for Peace was not attempted, because a majority vote in favour of military action was not expected. Above all, no territorial changes can be included as an objective for such armed conflict, to stress the exclusively humanitarian nature of the operation; (6) lastly, only limited use of force would be permissible, in order to combat crimes against humanity and/or massive, large-scale human rights violations. Moreover, the principle of proportionality must be respected at all times.

These conditions have been taken up in the Report on Responsibility to Protect (R2P) of the International Commission on Intervention and State Sovereignty.[79] The R2P criteria emphasize that state sovereignty implies that the primary responsibility for the protection of people rests with the state itself.[80]

Underlying problems of these missions include potential loss of neutrality, efforts by states to by-pass the prohibition of the use of force, in effect disempowering the Security Council, and the selectivity of application.

---

[77] A. Cassese, 'Ex Iniuria Ius Oritur: Are We Moving Towards International Legitimation of Forcible Humanitarian Countermeasures in the World Community?', 10(1) *European Journal of International Law (EJIL)* (1999) 27; see also B. Simma, 'NATO, the UN and the Use of Force: Legal Aspects', 10 *EJIL* (1999) 1–22.

[78] See Cassese (n 77).

[79] The scope of protection has been limited to the four international crimes, namely of genocide, war crimes, ethnic cleansing, and crimes against humanity. ICISS, *The Responsibility to Protect*, Report of the International Commission on Intervention and State Sovereignty, Ottawa: International Development Research Centre, 2001; UN High Level Panel Report, 'A More Secure World: Our Shared Responsibility', UN Doc A/59/565, 2 December 2004, §§ 201–9; UN Report of the Secretary-General (Kofi Annan), 'In Larger Freedom: Towards Development, Security and Human Rights for All', UN Doc A/59/2005, § 135; UN General Assembly, 2005 World Summit Outcome, UN Doc A/RES/60/1, New York, 24 October 2005, §§ 138–9; see also G. Giacca, 'Responsibility to Protect', in V. Chétail (ed), *Post-conflict Peacebuilding Lexicon* (Oxford: Oxford University Press, 2009), 291–306.

[80] C. Stahn, 'Responsibility to Protect: Political Rhetoric or Emerging Legal Norm?', 101(1) *AJIL* (2007) 99–121.

In humanitarian missions, however, the ESCR Committee has taken the view,[81] like the Human Rights Committee,[82] that human rights standards must not be pushed aside, but continue to apply in such situations, as do humanitarian rules for all parties to armed conflict.

(e) This sliding scale of conflict situations is rendered more complicated by the fact that often *mixed conflicts* of both civil war and international armed conflict are present,[83] where several stages of conflict intensity occur, or where a particular conflict changes in character from a purely internal domestic matter, via a non-international armed conflict to an international conflict, and back, each with different and overlapping responsibilities for the parties to the conflict.

H. Final remarks

The analysis of the sliding scale of conflict situations has demonstrated that in all such cases IHRL standards must be maintained, recognizing however that limits of applicability are triggered when parties to a conflict are objectively unable to fulfil the ICESCR or other human rights obligations. But such inability has to be distinguished from unwillingness to comply; the burden of proof rests squarely on

---

[81] Cf Concluding Observations on Israel, E/C.12/1/Add.90, 26 June 2003, §§ 11, 15, and particularly at 31: 'The Committee recognizes that the State party has serious security concerns, which must be balanced with its efforts to comply with its obligations under international human rights law. However, the Committee reaffirms its view that the state party's obligations under the Covenant apply to all territories, and populations under its effective control. The Committee repeats its position that even in a situation of armed conflict, fundamental human rights must be respected and that basic economic, social, and cultural rights, as part of the minimum standards of human rights, are guaranteed under customary international law and are also prescribed by international humanitarian law. Moreover, the applicability of rules of humanitarian law does not by itself impede the application of the Covenant or the accountability of the state under Art 2(1) for the actions of its authorities [...]'. The recommendation then goes on to request the state party to report more extensively on the rights realization of those living in the Occupied Territories in its next periodic report.

[82] Concluding Observations on Israel CCPR/CO/78/ISR, 21 August 2003, § 11: 'The Committee has noted the State party's position that the Covenant does not apply beyond its own territory, notably in the West Bank and Gaza, especially as long as there is a situation of armed conflict in these areas. The Committee reiterates the view, previously spelled out in para 10 of its concluding observations on Israel's initial report (CCPR/C/79/Add.93 of 18 August 1998), that the applicability of the regime of international humanitarian law during an armed conflict does not preclude the application of the Covenant, including Article 4 which covers situations of public emergency which threaten the life of the nation. Nor does the applicability of the regime of international humanitarian law preclude accountability of States parties under Article 2, para. 1 of the Covenant for the actions of their authorities outside their own territories, including in occupied territories [...]' and that these duties 'fall within the ambit of state responsibility of Israel under the principles of public international law'. The concluding observations then go on in § 12 to discuss the state party's reliance on the state of emergency.

[83] For an analysis of the law applicable to mixed conflicts, see Vité (n 45), 85–7; see also W. Kälin and J. Künzli, *The Law of International Human Rights Protection* (Oxford: Oxford University Press, 2009), 150–80 at 155–9.

the state party under review, as the ESCR Committee clearly outlined in its General Comment No 3 (1990).

6 IHL AND ESC-RIGHTS

Various theories have been developed which seek to explain how IHRL and IHL should interact in armed conflicts.[84] It is often argued, however, that IHRL gives way to IHL standards in times of a declared public emergency. The majority of IHRL treaties do provide for derogation clauses, allowing states to limit the enjoyment of certain rights in public emergency situations.[85] However, the African Charter on Human and Peoples' Rights and the ICESCR, as well as all other major human rights treaties with similar economic and socially related provisions,[86] contain no such derogation clauses. By contrast, the ICCPR, following the example of the European Convention on Human Rights, the Revised European Social Charter, and the Inter-American Convention on Human Rights, makes derogation possible because of express clauses in the treaties.[87] But, of course, there are inherent limits to such limitation clauses, as the European Court of Human Rights and UN Human Rights Committee have clearly outlined.[88]

The absence of a specific clause under the ICESCR essentially could mean one of two things: (i) that no derogations of rights under the Covenant are possible at all, or (ii) that they are permissible, as long as they do not affect the core obligations of each right. The *travaux préparatoires* of the Covenant do not reveal a preference for one of these positions. The omission of an express clause thus leaves room for speculation: it could mean that a combination of factors caused this different

---

[84] See the Chapter by D. Jinks in this volume.

[85] The term 'public emergency' undoubtedly covers times of armed conflict, including military occupation, as well as post-conflict situations and other natural causes, such as earthquakes, Tsunamis, floods, or hurricanes, see M. Ssenyonjo, *Economic, Social and Cultural Rights in International Law* (Oxford: Hart Publishing, 2009), 39–42.

[86] Such as the UN Convention on the Elimination of All Forms of Discrimination against Women (CEDAW), the UN Convention on the Rights of the Child (CRC), the International Convention on the Elimination of All Forms of Racial Discrimination (ICERD), and the International Convention on the Protection of the Rights of All Migrant Workers and Members of their Families (MWC).

[87] European Convention for the Protection of Human Rights and Fundamental Freedoms, Art 15; European Social Charter (revised), 3 May 1996, Part V, Art F—Derogations in time of war or public emergency; Part V, Art G—Restrictions; International Covenant on Civil and Political Rights, Art 4; Inter-American Convention on Human Rights, Art 27.

[88] Ssenyonjo (n 85), 100–2.

treatment as compared to the Civil and Political Rights Covenant. Such factors relate to: (a) the nature of the rights protected in the Covenant, (b) the formulation of a general limitations clause in Article 4 of the ICESCR, and (c) the 'more flexible and accommodating' nature of the generic obligation laid down in Article 2(1) of the ICESCR.[89] Since its General Comment No 3 (1990), the Committee has maintained that states parties have a core obligation to ensure the satisfaction of minimum essential levels of each of the Covenant rights. This position has been confirmed in later General Comments, particularly in General Comment Nos 14 and 15.[90] This does not, however, mean that the Covenant renders limitations impossible.[91] Under Article 4, limitations may be declared, but only 'insofar as this may be compatible with the nature of (the Covenant rights)' and 'solely for the purpose of promoting the general welfare in a democratic society'.[92] Article 5 makes clear that nothing in the Covenant may be interpreted 'as limiting any of the rights or freedoms recognized therein to a greater extent than is provided for'[93] in the Covenant.

In the ESCR Committee's practice this has meant that in principle even in times of armed conflict or general emergency the Covenant rights have to be upheld, as far as their core content is concerned. In fact, in those crisis situations, the population generally, but in particular marginalized and disadvantaged individuals and groups within society, are in even greater need of protection than in peacetime. Thus, while the ICCPR expressly names specific rights which can be limited in times of conflict, albeit with limitations, the ICESCR has broader application, and assumes that in principle each Covenant right maintains its validity, even in times of an emergency. This means, for example, that on no account can the rights to health, to food, housing, access to water, or to education be set aside in respect of their core content, even during times of armed conflict.[94]

While the scope of the ICESCR thus would appear to be wider than that of its ICCPR counterpart, the formulations in Article 2(1) of ICESCR offer some limitation possibilities: states parties only have to ensure what they can realistically

[89] Ssenyonjo (n 85), 40; P. Alston and G. Quinn, 'The Nature and Scope of State Parties' Obligations under the International Covenant on Economic, Social and Cultural Rights', 9 *Human Rights Quarterly* (1987) 156, at 217.

[90] General Comment No 14 (right to health), § 47: 'It should be stressed, however, that a State party cannot, under any circumstances whatsoever, justify its non-compliance with the core obligations set out in para.43 [...] which are non-derogable'; and General Comment No 15 (right to water), § 40: 'A State party cannot justify its non-compliance with the core obligations set out [...] which are non-derogable'.

[91] E. Mottershaw, 'Economic, Social and Cultural Rights in Armed Conflict: International Human Rights Law and International Humanitarian Law', 12(3) *The International Journal of Human Rights* (2008) 451.

[92] International Covenant on Economic, Social and Cultural Rights (ICESCR), 1966, Art 4.

[93] ICESCR, Art 5.

[94] See eg CESCR, General Comment No 15 on the Right to Water, 2002, UN Doc E/C.12/2002/11, § 40.

guarantee 'within the available resources'. This open formulation could easily be misinterpreted as essentially allowing any limitation. However, the ESCR Committee has emphasized repeatedly, in particular since General Comment No 3, that this is not a *carte blanche* for states parties to restrict the application of the Covenant guarantees as they please. The onus is on states to show they have done everything in their power under prevailing circumstances, within their available resources, to maintain, respect, protect, and fulfil the core content of each Covenant right, even in times of armed conflict, public emergency, or natural catastrophes.[95]

It thus becomes clear that the rights in the ICESCR apply at all times, and their core content represents the existential minimum—the survival kit[96] in all situations—including in times of armed conflict. Under the preferred fusion or convergence theory, the task simply is to assess humanitarian and human rights rules in the concrete situation and determine which provides greatest protection to the individuals concerned.

The strongest support for this view can be found in Article 72 of AP I, where reference is made to Geneva Convention IV and to 'other applicable rules of international law relating to the protection of fundamental human rights during international armed conflict'.[97] The fundamental humanitarian guarantees laid down in Articles 75, 76, and 77 in this context can almost be regarded as a miniature charter of human rights during international armed conflict.[98]

The ICJ in its Advisory Opinion on the *Wall* case left open the question of the relationship between IHRL and IHL, but has at least mentioned specifically esc-rights.[99] As Walter Kälin and Jörg Künzli have cogently pointed out, the ICJ, while referring to *lex specialis* in this context, 'has not used the term to mean specific provisions pre-empting the more general rules of human rights law, but rather specific rules that are relevant when it comes to determining the content of the general rule'.[100]

---

[95] See eg CESCR General Comment No 14 on the right to health, 2000, UN Doc E/C.12/2000, §§ 28–9, 40–1; see also CESCR Statement 'An evaluation of the obligation to take steps to the "maximum of available resources" under an Optional Protocol to the Covenant', E/C.12/2007/1, 10 May 2007, § 4.

[96] E. Riedel, 'The Human Right to Health: Conceptual Foundations', in A. Clapham and M. Robinson (eds), *Swiss Human Rights Book: Realizing the Right to Health* vol 3 (Zürich: Rüffer und Rub, 2009), 32.

[97] Additional Protocol I to the Geneva Conventions: Protection of Victims of International Armed Conflicts (1977) (hereinafter: Additional Protocol I), Art 72.

[98] T. Buergenthal and D. Thürer, *Menschenrechte, Ideale, Instrumente, Institutionen* (Zürich/St Gallen: Dike Verlag AG, 2010), 119.

[99] ICJ, *Advisory Opinion on the Wall*, § 112.

[100] Kälin and Künzli (n 83), 180.

7 IMPLEMENTATION AND ENFORCEMENT

Under IHRL the mechanisms for monitoring, implementation, and enforcement of applicable Geneva standards are relatively weak.[101] The key role of the ICRC and of national Red Cross and Red Crescent societies must be acknowledged at the outset. However, the main advantage of IHL is to provide different and detailed rules of application in three types of situations: (a) protected persons in international armed conflicts; (b) persons in the power of a party to an international armed conflict who enjoy minimum guarantees; and (c) persons in the power of a party to a non-international armed conflict who are not—or no longer—taking part in hostilities, who enjoy the minimum guarantees of Common Article 3 and AP II.

Practice shows that the ICRC and national Red Cross and Red Crescent Societies operate effectively at the level of quiet diplomacy, so that, for example, access to prisoners of war will not be jeopardized.[102] All the procedures of peaceful settlement of disputes as outlined in Chapter VI of the UN Charter, such as good offices, fact-finding, inquiries, and mediation are possible. The mode of inquiries and fact-finding under Article 90 of AP I, however, have to date not been used,[103] even though Article 90 contains detailed and useful rules on the composition and working modalities of such an international fact-finding commission. Once violations of IHL rules have been established, it is possible that other international bodies address the issues, such as involvement of the ICJ at the request of states in contentious proceedings or at the request of the UN in Advisory Opinion procedures.[104] This, however, happens rarely, usually takes many years, and thus may come too late. Breaches of IHL

---

[101] C. Droege, 'The Interplay Between International Humanitarian Law and Human Rights Law in Situations of Armed Conflict', 40(2) *Israel Law Review* (2007) 348; Heintze (n 2), 800.

[102] Delegates of the International Committee of the Red Cross are allowed to visit prisoners of war according to Art 126 of the Third Geneva Convention, relative to the Treatment of Prisoners of War. The Article provides that 'Representatives or delegates of the Protecting Powers shall have permission to go to all places where prisoners of war may be, particularly to places of internment, imprisonment and labour, and shall have access to all premises occupied by prisoners of war; they shall also be allowed to go to the places of departure, passage and arrival of prisoners who are being transferred. They shall be able to interview the prisoners, and in particular the prisoners' representatives, without witnesses. [...] The delegates of the International Committee of the Red Cross shall enjoy the same prerogatives'.

[103] Article 90 of Additional Protocol I provides for the creation of an International Fact-Finding Commission, charged with investigating on allegations of grave breaches of the Geneva Conventions and other serious violations of international humanitarian law. The Commission has been officially constituted in 1991 but remains inactive; see F. Kalshoven, 'The International Humanitarian Fact-Finding Commission: a Sleeping Beauty?', 4 *Humanitäres Völkerrecht—Informationsschriften* (2002) 213–16; E. Kussbach, 'The International Humanitarian Fact-Finding Commission', *ICLQ* 174ff.

[104] The ICJ has been dealing with international humanitarian law both in Advisory Opinion procedures and in contentious proceedings. See eg (ICJ), *Legality of the Threat or Use of Nuclear Weapons*, Advisory Opinion, 1996 (8 July); ICJ, *Advisory Opinion on the Wall*; ICJ, *Case Concerning Armed Activities on the Territory of the Congo, Judgment (DRC v Uganda)*, 19 December 2005.

rules can also be addressed by the UN Security Council, as happened in Iraq in the first and second phases of the Second Gulf War.[105] The Security Council can then take enforcement action under Chapter VII of the UN Charter.[106] Failing Security Council action, the UN General Assembly can also legitimate enforcement action through member states under the 'Uniting for Peace' procedure,[107] but again this rarely happens in practice. The same applies to the involvement of the International Criminal Court (ICC) which can only deal with certain breaches of IHL rules.[108] Quite evidently, the ICRC role is primarily one of rendering *assistance humanitaire*, a very important and effective procedure, but of quite limited application in times of armed conflict. In addition, there are other methods of implementation, such as the naming of a protecting power, or diplomatic demarches, and ultimately self-help within narrow confines.[109]

IHRL, by contrast, is slightly stronger on monitoring compliance with treaty guarantees, as applying comprehensively, but does not, as yet, provide truly effective implementation and enforcement at the international level. It leaves this task to the national level. Follow-up to recommendations at the universal level remain quite weak as well. Leaving more effective mechanisms at regional levels aside, IHRL protection does, at least, provide public scrutiny of state behaviour at regular intervals, either via the various UN treaty bodies for member states, or for all UN member states in the Charter-based procedures under the Human Rights Council. And yet, as far as esc-rights are concerned, the regular treaty monitoring practice has had quite considerable effects on states parties' actual behaviour. In some cases laws and administrative practices have been changed as a result of the recommendations made by the treaty bodies, and not infrequently even constitutional provisions are revised, in the light of public criticisms coming from the treaty bodies and from national and international civil society.

As states generally do not wish 'to lose face' at the international level, and do not wish to be regarded as flagrant and systematic violators of human rights, the weak enforcement mechanisms at the international level are no real obstacle to better implementation of human rights.[110] Although some states do not act on the recommendations coming from treaty bodies, they are likely to be reviewed critically in

---

[105] See eg UN Security Council, Resolution 1472 (2003), UN Doc S/RES/1472 (2003); Resolution 1483 (2003), UN Doc S/RES/1483 (2003); Resolution 1637 (2005), UN Doc S/RES/1637 (2005).

[106] UN Charter, Ch VII: Action with Respect to Threats to the Peace, Breaches of the Peace and Acts of Aggression.

[107] Procedure based on UN General Assembly Resolution 377(V), UN Doc A/RES/377(V).

[108] According to the Rome Statute of the International Criminal Court (Art 8), the Court has jurisdiction on grave breaches of the Geneva Conventions of 1949, considered as war crimes, and on other serious violations of International Humanitarian Law.

[109] Buergenthal and Thürer (n 98), 124–7.

[110] See E. Riedel, 'The Examination of State Reports', in E. Klein (ed), *The Monitoring System of Human Rights Treaty Obligations, Colloquium Potsdam, 22/23 November 1996* (Berlin: Berlin Verlag Arno Spitz, 1998), 95–105.

required follow-up procedures. The mechanisms under the Human Rights Council supplement those legal procedures, ie by the Universal Periodic Review as well as reports on state performance prepared by the Council's special procedures mechanisms. Needless to say, much reliance still is placed on national implementation as an obligation of member states, with limited progress with respect to monitoring national implementation and enforcement action. At the same time, there is evidence of growing involvement of national parliamentary committees on humanitarian matters and human rights, with ombudspersons, national human rights commissions, and institutes taking an ever-greater interest in these matters.[111] All of these mechanisms seek to render enforcement of internationally accepted obligations more effective.

The establishment of a World Human Rights Court would certainly enhance such implementation steps. Today that still seems to be a distant vision.[112] Then again, it should be noted that it took more than 50 years before the International Criminal Court became a reality.

8 Conclusion

In comparing IHL and IHRL implementation mechanisms, it is evident that human rights procedures are more varied, comprehensive in scope, and potentially more effective. This Chapter's analysis of the relationship between esc-rights legal protections and IHL rules has shown that both bodies of law, despite differences in the scope of their applicability and focus on individuals concerned, nevertheless are intricately interwoven, and have become more so in recent times.[113]

---

[111] Cf C. Koenig and R.A. Lorz (eds), E. Riedel, 'Die Universalität der Menschenrechte' (Berlin: Duncker & Humblot, 2003), 105–37 at 126–9; on justiciability and enforceability see the dissertation of K. Klee, Die progressive Verwirklichung wirtschaftlicher, sozialer und kultureller Menschenrechte, Richard Boorberg Verlag, Stuttgart, etc, 2000, 88–96; on national implementation and national institutions, see the dissertation of V. Aichele, Nationale Menschenrechtsinstitutionen, Peter Lang Verlag, Frankfurt a M, 2003, 1–68, esp 54ff.

[112] For a further analysis of this vision, cf M. Nowak, 'The Need for a World Court of Human Rights', 7(1) Human Rights Law Review (2007) 251–9; see also J. Kozma, M. Nowak, M. Scheinin, A World Court of Human Rights—Consolidated Statute and Commentary (Vienna: Neuer Wissenschaftlicher Verlag, Recht, 2010); Ssenyonjo (n 85), 401–6; E. Riedel, 'New Bearings in Social Rights? The Communications Procedure under the ICESCR', in From Bilateralism to Community Interest: Essays in Honour of Bruno Simma (Oxford: Oxford University Press, 2011), 574–89 at 580.

[113] See Mottershaw (n 91), and Vité (n 45).

It is submitted that IHRL serves as a chapeau over both areas of international legal protection, and applies in all armed conflict situations, just as in peacetime, but to varying degrees, depending on the specific conflict conditions. At a minimum, the core content of esc-rights provisions, which the ESCR Committee responsible for monitoring state compliance with the Covenant has carefully and meticulously outlined in 21 General Comments to date, must be respected, protected, and fulfilled even in times of armed conflict.[114] When battles rage, authorities frequently are hindered from rendering all assistance needed to fully realize the affected rights, but the Covenant requires that states parties do everything in their power to realize the rights to the extent feasible under the prevailing economic, political, social, and military conditions, in line with Article 2, paragraph 1 and Article 4 of the ICESCR. These rights certainly may not be set aside completely during times of conflict.

The analysis in this Chapter has therefore shown that although implementation procedures associated with human rights have the edge over related provisions in humanitarian law, those procedural advantages should not be over-estimated. What is needed is close interaction, at the theoretical level, but above all at the practical level. The ESCR Committee has long cooperated closely with UN specialized agencies, and cooperation with the ICRC in Geneva has also been close and fruitful, particularly when it comes to drafting General Comments, where the ICRC has made numerous contributions for finding suitable formulations consistent with the humanitarian law dimensions of the rights discussion at hand. During Committee sessions, ICRC representatives frequently provide input on the countries under review. That cooperation can, of course, always be intensified. When surveying the developments of the last two decades, it becomes evident that the nature of conflicts has changed rapidly, reinforcing the need to find uniform or at least harmonious international rules, which combine relevant aspects of humanitarian and human rights law regimes. An important step in this direction would include the development of minimum human rights and humanitarian law standards and principles[115] shaped through a conjoint Charter that includes the establishment of joint procedural mechanisms.

---

[114] See eg CESCR, General Comment No 7 on the Right to Adequate Housing (1997), UN Doc E/C.12/1997/4, §§ 6–7; General Comment No 14 (n 18), para 35; General Comment No 15 on the Right to Water (n 94), §§ 21–2.

[115] An attempt to set these minimum standards has been made at the end of the 1980s, with the elaboration and adoption by a group of experts of the Turku Declaration of Minimum Humanitarian Standards (1990), UN Doc E/CN.4/1995/116. The Declaration has been followed in 1998 by a Report of the High Commissioner for Human Rights concerning fundamental standards of humanity, UN Doc E/CN.4/1998/87.

CHAPTER 19

PROTECTION OF THE NATURAL ENVIRONMENT

JEAN-MARIE HENCKAERTS AND DANA CONSTANTIN[*]

1 INTRODUCTION

ARMED conflicts have always been a threat to the natural environment and thereby also to the survival and well-being of those who depend on it for their livelihood, during the conflict and long thereafter. These threats may take a variety of forms, among them:

- direct attacks on the environment, such as the use of Agent Orange, a herbicide and defoliant, during the war in Vietnam; the consequences of the use of this substance, most notably the prevalence of congenital deformities, are being felt to this day;
- the release of hazardous substances as a result of attacks on industrial sites, such as those which took place in Kosovo in 1999 and in Lebanon in 2006;
- the actual or potential use of certain means or methods of warfare, such as biological, chemical and nuclear weapons; and
- the exploitation of natural resources (diamonds, gold, copper, coltan, timber, etc) to finance armed forces and buy weapons, or for personal enrichment, which has recently become a major source of concern for the international community.

---

* The views expressed in this Chapter are personal and do not necessarily reflect those of the ICRC.

The international effort to better protect the natural environment during armed conflict can be roughly divided into three phases.

The first time the issue became a major concern was during the war in Vietnam. This eventually led to the adoption of the Convention on the Prohibition of Military or any Hostile Use of Environmental Modification Techniques of 1976 (the ENMOD Convention).[1] A year later, the first norms of international humanitarian law explicitly addressing the issue of environmental protection during armed conflict came into being: these were the two provisions—Articles 35(3) and 55—that had been included for that particular purpose in Protocol I of 8 June 1977 additional to the Geneva Conventions (AP I).[2]

A second phase is discernible during the Gulf War of 1990–91, when the adequacy of the existing legal framework was called into question: retreating Iraqi armed forces had caused massive damage to oil wells in Kuwait, but despite its scale, the destruction they had wrought appeared to fall below the threshold established by Articles 35(3) and 55 of AP I ('widespread, long-term and severe damage'). As a result, attention shifted to the *general* principles and rules of international humanitarian law: more precisely, their applicability to the natural environment.

In 1994, a third phase began when these principles and rules were restated in the ICRC's Guidelines for Military Manuals and Instructions on the Protection of the Environment in Times of Armed Conflict.[3] Assessing the legality of incidental damage to the natural environment is beset with difficulties and concern is mounting over the role natural resources and environmental degradation play in armed conflict. For these and other reasons, efforts to increase protection for the natural environment during armed conflict are being made with renewed intensity.

This Chapter seeks to give an overview of the existing legal protection for the natural environment during armed conflict. Part 1 focuses on general rules of international humanitarian law and Part 2 on specific rules. Part 3 identifies some of the gaps and deficiencies in the law and presents possible remedies, including efforts currently under way.

It may be useful to begin with a precise description of the object of our analysis. International law does not contain a uniform definition of the 'natural environment'.

---

[1] Convention on the Prohibition of Military or any Hostile Use of Environmental Modification Techniques, adopted by UN General Assembly Res 31/72, 10 December 1976, 1108 UNTS 151.

[2] Protocol Additional to the Geneva Conventions of 12 August 1949, and relating to the Protection of Victims of International Armed Conflicts (Protocol I) of 8 June 1977, 1125 UNTS 3.

[3] International Committee of the Red Cross (ICRC), 'Guidelines for Military Manuals and Instructions on the Protection of the Environment in Times of Armed Conflict', Geneva, 1994, UN GAOR, 49th Sess, Annex, Agenda Item 139, 49–53, UN Doc A/49/323 (1994), reprinted in H.-P. Gasser, 'For Better Protection of the Natural Environment in Armed Conflict: A Proposal for Action', 89 *American Journal of International Law* (1995) 637–44 at 641–3. Some thought was also given to the possibility of a 'Fifth Geneva Convention' dealing with environmental protection, see, in particular, G. Plant (ed), *Environmental Protection and the Law of War—A 'Fifth Geneva' Convention on the Protection of the Environment in Time of Armed Conflict?* (London: Belhaven Press, 1992).

Having evaluated existing environmental treaties and given the value of everything that surrounds, and in some respects, precedes human activity it seems that the concept should be understood in the widest sense possible. The 'natural environment' should include everything that is not man-made: the atmosphere, the oceans, and other bodies of water, soil, rocks, plants and animals.[4] Quite remarkably, then, while perhaps 95 per cent of what exists on our planet today would fall under this definition, international humanitarian law is for the most part concerned with the protection of the remaining 5 per cent—man-made structures such as roads, bridges, and buildings.

2 General Rules of International Humanitarian Law Applicable to the Natural Environment

The first strand of protection provided by international humanitarian law for the natural environment consists of a number of general rules, ie rules that were not adopted specifically with that end in mind, but which do in fact provide such protection. It is widely agreed that a number of general rules of international humanitarian law are applicable and provide protection for the natural environment. These

---

[4] On the antagonism between the 'anthropocentric' and 'intrinsic' approach to environmental protection and the discussions during the Diplomatic Conference on the Reaffirmation and Development of International Humanitarian Law applicable in Armed Conflicts of 1974–77, see K. Mollard-Bannelier, *La Protection de l'Environnement en Temps de Conflit Armé* vol 53 (Paris: Pedone, 2001), 76ff. While Art 55 of Additional Protocol I reflects at least at the outset the former approach, Art 35(3) of the Protocol clearly protects the environment as such; see with regard to Art 55, Commentary AP I and II, para 2126: 'The concept of the natural environment should be understood in the widest sense to cover the biological environment in which a population is living. It does not consist merely of the objects indispensable to survival mentioned in Article 54 [...]—foodstuffs, agricultural areas, drinking water, livestock—but also includes forests and other vegetation mentioned in the Convention of 10 October 1980 on Prohibitions or Restrictions on the Use of Certain Conventional Weapons, as well as fauna, flora and other biological or climatic elements.' Article 35(3), on the other hand, 'even continues to apply in the absence of any direct threat to the population or to the flora and fauna of the enemy State. It is the natural environment itself that is protected. It is common property, and should be retained for everyone's use and be preserved' (Commentary AP I and II, § 1462). See also Art 2 of the ENMOD Convention which defines 'environmental modification techniques' as 'any technique for changing—through the deliberate manipulation of natural processes—the dynamics, composition or structure of the Earth, including its biota, lithosphere, hydrosphere, and atmosphere, or of outer space'.

include: (a) the rules protecting enemy property from wanton destruction, (b) the prohibition against pillage, (c) the rules protecting civilian objects during hostilities, (d) the rules protecting objects indispensable to the survival of the civilian population, and (e) the rules regulating the use of weapons during armed conflict.[5]

A. Protecting enemy property from wanton destruction

The first general rule protecting the natural environment prohibits the destruction or seizure of enemy property except for reasons of imperative military necessity. This rule goes back to the 1899 and 1907 Hague Regulations.[6] It was restated in the Fourth Geneva Convention of 1949 (GC IV).[7] Under the 1998 Rome Statute of the International Criminal Court (the Rome Statute), '[d]estroying or seizing the enemy's property unless such destruction or seizure be imperatively demanded by the necessities of war' amounts to a war crime in both international and non-international armed conflicts.[8] This rule is now considered to reflect customary international law in both types of conflict.[9]

In addition, GC IV states that 'extensive destruction and appropriation of property, not justified by military necessity and carried out unlawfully and wantonly' amounts to a grave breach of the Convention.[10] Such destruction and appropriation also constitutes a war crime under the Rome Statute.[11]

The general rule prohibiting destruction of enemy property unless imperatively required by military necessity is equally applicable to the natural environment.[12]

---

[5] See eg J.-M. Henckaerts and L. Doswald-Beck (eds), *Customary International Humanitarian Law, Volume I: Rules* (Cambridge: ICRC and Cambridge University Press, 2005) (hereinafter 'Customary International Humanitarian Law Study'). Rule 43 provides: 'The general principles on the conduct of hostilities apply to the natural environment'.

[6] Convention (II), with respect to the Laws and Customs of War on Land, Annex, Regulations respecting the Laws and Customs of War on Land, The Hague, 29 July 1899; Convention (IV) respecting the Laws and Customs of War on Land and its annex: Regulations concerning the Laws and Customs of War on Land, The Hague, 18 October 1907 (hereinafter 'the Hague Regulations'). Article 23(g) of both the 1899 and 1907 Hague Regulations forbids: 'To destroy or seize the enemy's property, unless such destruction or seizure be imperatively demanded by the necessities of war.'

[7] Convention (IV) relative to the Protection of Civilian Persons in Time of War, Geneva, 12 August 1949, 75 UNTS 287. Article 53 prohibits '[a]ny destruction by the Occupying Power of real or personal property belonging individually or collectively to private persons, or to the State, or to other public authorities, or to social or cooperative organizations [...], except where such destruction is rendered absolutely necessary by military operations'.

[8] Statute of the International Criminal Court, 17 July 1998, 2187 UNTS 90, Art 8(2)(b)(xiii) and (e) (xii) (the war crime for non-international armed conflicts refers to 'the necessities of the conflict').

[9] See Customary International Humanitarian Law Study (n 5), Rule 50: 'The destruction or seizure of the property of an adversary is prohibited, unless required by imperative military necessity.'

[10] GC IV (n 7), Art 147.   [11] Rome Statute (n 8), Art 8(2)(a)(iv).

[12] See Customary International Humanitarian Law Study (n 5), Rule 43(B): 'Destruction of any part of the natural environment is prohibited, unless required by imperative military necessity.' See also UN General Assembly, Res 47/37, 9 February 1993, Preamble, fifth paragraph ('*Stressing* that destruction

Unlike Articles 35(3) and 55 of AP I, which prohibit only high-level damage ('widespread, long-term, and severe damage'), this general rule applies regardless of the amount of damage. This also adds to the practical relevance of the rule, particularly during conventional warfare. For example, although it was a subject of controversy whether the destruction of oil wells during the Gulf War reached the high level of damage prohibited under AP I ('widespread, long-term, and severe damage to the natural environment'), it was more plausible to conclude that the destruction amounted to a violation of the prohibition against the wanton destruction of enemy property.[13]

B. The Prohibition against pillage

The prohibition against the destruction or seizure of enemy property except for reasons of imperative military necessity is complemented by the prohibition against pillage in the Hague Regulations,[14] GC IV,[15] and Protocol II of 8 June 1977 additional to the Geneva Conventions (AP II).[16] This prohibition is now considered to reflect customary international law in both international and non-international armed conflict.[17] Under the Rome Statute, '[p]illaging a town or place, even when taken by assault' constitutes a war crime in both international and non-international armed conflict.[18] This prohibition has a particular bearing on the exploitation of natural resources by conflicting parties.[19] A recent study by the United Nations

of the environment, not justified by military necessity and carried out wantonly, is clearly contrary to existing international law'). But see R. Desgagné, 'The Prevention of Environmental Damage in Time of Armed Conflict: Proportionality and Precautionary Measures', 3 *Yearbook of International Humanitarian Law* (2000) 109–29 at 115 (sceptical at least as far as the *treaty* provisions ('enemy property') are concerned).

[13] See eg Y. Dinstein, 'Protection of the Environment in International Armed Conflict', 5 *Max Planck Yearbook of United Nations Law* (2001) 523–49 at 544 (referring to Art 23(g) of the Hague Regulations and Art 53 of the Fourth Geneva Convention); K. Hulme, *War Torn Environment: Interpreting the Legal Threshold* (Leiden: Martinus Nijhoff, 2004), 176ff ('arguably'); US Department of Defense, 'Conduct of the Persian Gulf War: Final Report to Congress', Appendix O, The Role of the Law of War, 10 April 1992, [1992] 31 *ILM* 615 at 633 (finding a violation of Art 23(g) of the Hague Regulations as well as Art 53 of the Fourth Geneva Convention, amounting to a grave breach under Art 147 of that Convention).

[14] See 1899 and 1907 Hague Regulations (n 6), Art 28 (on hostilities) and Art 47 (on occupied territory).

[15] GC IV (n 7), Art 33(2).

[16] Protocol Additional to the Geneva Conventions of 12 August 1949, and relating to the Protection of Victims of Non-International Armed Conflicts (Protocol II) of 8 June 1977, 1125 UNTS 609, Art 4(2)(g).

[17] See Customary International Humanitarian Law Study (n 5), Rule 52: 'Pillage is prohibited.'

[18] Rome Statute (n 8), Art 8(2)(b)(xvi) and (e)(v).

[19] See eg International Court of Justice, *Case Concerning Armed Activities on the Territory of the Congo (Democratic Republic of the Congo v Uganda)*, Judgment of 19 December 2005, [2005] ICJ Reports 168, § 245 ('Thus, whenever members of the UPDF were involved in the looting, plundering and exploitation of natural resources in the territory of the DRC, they acted in violation of the *jus in*

Environment Programme (UNEP) concluded that such exploitation was a major driving force behind many contemporary armed conflicts.[20]

C. Protecting civilian objects during hostilities

The natural environment is also implicitly protected by the general rules protecting civilian objects during the conduct of hostilities, namely the principles of distinction, proportionality, and precaution.[21] In theory, the constituent elements of the natural environment should qualify as civilian objects, unless they make, by their location or use, 'an effective contribution to military action and [unless their] total or partial destruction, capture or neutralization, in the circumstances ruling at the time, offers a definite military advantage'.[22] The general rules involved are, most notably, these: the prohibition of direct attacks against civilian objects,[23] the prohibition of indiscriminate attacks,[24] the principle of proportionality according to which 'an attack which may be expected to cause incidental loss of civilian life, injury to civilians, damage to civilian objects, or a combination thereof, which would be excessive in relation to the concrete and direct military advantage anticipated' is unlawful,[25] and the obligation to take precautions in attack.[26] These rules are now generally considered to be of a customary nature in both international and non-international armed conflicts.[27]

---

bello, [...] The Court notes in this regard that both Article 47 of the Hague Regulations of 1907 and Article 33 of the Fourth Geneva Convention of 1949 prohibit pillage.'). For a more detailed discussion of the law governing pillage and its application to the exploitation of natural resources most notably with regard to violations committed during World War II, see J.G. Stewart, 'Corporate War Crimes: Prosecuting Pillage of Natural Resources' (Open Society Foundations, October 2010), available at <http://www.soros.org>.

[20] UNEP, 'From Conflict to Peacebuilding. The Role of Natural Resources and the Environment' (Nairobi, 2009), available at <http://www.unep.org/pdf/pcdmb_policy_01.pdf>, Table 1, at 11.

[21] See also C. Droege and M-L Tougas, 'The Protection of the Natural Environment in Armed Conflict—Existing Rules and Need for Further Legal Protection', 82 *Nordic Journal of International Law* (2013) 21–52.

[22] See AP I (n 2), Art 52(2). See also M. Bothe, C. Bruch, J. Diamond, and D. Jensen, 'International Law Protecting the Environment During Armed Conflict: Gaps and Opportunities', 92 *International Review of the Red Cross* (2010) 569–92 at 576: 'Elements of the environment are most often civilian objects.'

[23] See AP I (n 2), Arts 48 and 52(1).   [24] See AP I (n 2), Art 51(4).   [25] See AP I (n 2), Art 51(5)(b).
[26] See AP I (n 2), Art 57.

[27] See Customary International Humanitarian Law Study (n 5), Rules 7, 11, 14, and 15. On their applicability to the environment see: Rule 43(A) ('No part of the natural environment may be attacked, unless it is a military objective'), Rule 43(C) ('Launching an attack against a military objective which may be expected to cause incidental damage to the environment which would be excessive in relation to the concrete and direct military advantage anticipated is prohibited'), and Rule 44, second sentence, arguably also applicable to non-international armed conflicts ('In the conduct of military operations, all feasible precautions must be taken to avoid, and in any event to minimize, incidental damage to the

While the applicability of the general rules for protecting civilian objects seems largely uncontested with respect to the natural environment, problems may arise with their *application* in specific cases. This is especially true of cases involving the principle of proportionality: they necessitate difficult assessments in which variables that cannot be compared have to be balanced. These difficulties may be seen in a number of instances of incidental damage to the natural environment, such as the bombardment of the Pancevo industrial complex and of a petroleum refinery in Novi Sad by NATO forces during the war in Kosovo in 1999, which led to the release of some 80,000 and 73,000 tons of crude oil into the soil.[28] More recently, during the war in Lebanon in 2006, the Israeli attack on the Jiyeh power plant south of Beirut led to the release of an estimated 12,000 to 15,000 tons of burning fuel oil into the Mediterranean Sea.[29] Whether the incidental damage caused to the natural environment in these cases was proportionate to the military advantage may not be easy to assess. Defining and quantifying precisely the variables involved in the comparison, ie the extent of the environmental damage caused in relation to the expected military advantage gained, may be difficult.[30] In addition, the decisive elements of comparison are the damage that is *expected* and the advantage that is *anticipated* on the basis of the information reasonably available to the military commander at the time of the attack. Even when these variables can be correctly identified, they are so different in nature as to make a simple quantitative comparison impossible; what emerges is a value judgement.[31]

environment'). See also International Court of Justice, *Legality of the Threat or Use of Nuclear Weapons*, Advisory Opinion of 8 July 1996, [1996] ICJ Rep 226, § 30 ('Respect for the environment is one of the elements that go to assessing whether an action is in conformity with the principles of necessity and proportionality').

[28] See UNEP, 'Protecting the Environment During Armed Conflict. An Inventory and Analysis of International Law' (Nairobi, November 2009), available at <http://www.unep.org/PDF/dmb/ProtectEnvDuringConflict_en.pdf>, 19 and 25.

[29] See UNEP, 'Protecting the Environment During Armed Conflict' (n 28), 23. See also UN General Assembly Res 61/194, 20 December 2006, § 1 (the UN General Assembly expresses its deep concern over the incident).

[30] Equally stressing this aspect Bothe, Bruch, Diamond, and Jensen (n 22), 577f.

[31] See Final Report to the Prosecutor by the Committee Established to Review the NATO Bombing Campaign Against the Federal Republic of Yugoslavia, available at <http://www.icty.org/x/file/About/OTP/otp_report_nato_bombing_en.pdf>, § 19 ('It is difficult to assess the relative values to be assigned to the military advantage gained and harm to the natural environment, and the application of the principle of proportionality is more easily stated than applied in practice'). See also §§ 20ff with the conclusion that, based on information at that time available to the Committee, no investigation into the collateral environmental damage caused by the NATO bombing campaign should be commenced. For further analysis of the attack on the Pancevo industrial complex, see Hulme (n 13), 200ff.

D. Protecting objects indispensable to the survival of the civilian population

Rules protecting objects indispensable to the survival of the civilian population are also of relevance to the protection of the natural environment. These rules were first introduced in the two Additional Protocols of 1977. Article 54(2) of AP I makes it unlawful to 'attack, destroy, remove or render useless objects indispensable to the survival of the civilian population, such as food-stuffs, agricultural areas for the production of food-stuffs, crops, livestock, drinking water installations and supplies and irrigation works, for the specific purpose of denying them for their sustenance value to the civilian population or to the adverse Party, whatever the motive, whether in order to starve out civilians, to cause them to move away, or for any other motive.'[32] Article 14(2) of AP II contains a similar provision that makes it unlawful to 'attack, destroy, remove or render useless [for the purpose of starving out civilians] objects indispensable to the survival of the civilian population'.[33] Article 54(2) of AP I is subject to some exceptions,[34] but Article 14(2) of AP II is not. Both provisions are also considered to reflect customary international law.[35] The relevance of these rules for the natural environment is self-evident, as they protect agricultural areas, drinking water supplies, and livestock, which are constituent elements of the natural environment.

In 2005, the Eritrea–Ethiopia Claims Commission found that Ethiopia had violated the customary law rule expressed in Article 54(2) of AP I by carrying out air strikes on the Harsile water reservoir in February 1999 and June 2000. In the Commission's view, the government of Ethiopia had been well aware that the reservoir was a vital source of water for the city of Assab. From this the Commission drew the following conclusions: that Ethiopia's purpose in targeting the reservoir was to deprive Eritrea of the sustenance value of its water and that it did not do so on the erroneous assumption that the reservoir provided water *solely* to the Eritrean armed forces, as required by Article 54(3)(a). Although this provision was not formally applicable because Eritrea was not party to the Protocol when the air strikes took place, the

---

[32] AP I (n 2), Art 54(2).   [33] AP II (n 16), Art 14(2).

[34] See AP I (n 2), Art 54(3) (attacks against objects indispensable for civilian survival may be lawful if the objects in question 'are used by an adverse Party (a) as sustenance solely for the members of its armed forces; or (b) if not as sustenance, then in direct support of military action, provided, however, that in no event shall actions against these objects be taken which may be expected to leave the civilian population with such inadequate food or water as to cause its starvation or force its movement'). A further exception may be made pursuant to Art 54(5) when, required by imperative military necessity, a state applies a so-called 'scorched earth' tactic in defence of its national territory against invasion.

[35] See Customary International Humanitarian Law Study (n 5), Rule 54: 'Attacking, destroying, removing or rendering useless objects indispensable to the survival of the civilian population is prohibited.'

Commission nevertheless considered the protection of objects indispensable to the survival of the civilian population to be part of customary international law.[36]

E. Weapons law

Lastly, the rules regulating the use of weapons during armed conflict may also benefit the natural environment. Among these rules, the following must be mentioned: the prohibition against 'employ[ing] poison or poisoned weapons' expressed in the Hague Regulations,[37] the prohibition against biological weapons established by the Geneva Gas Protocol of 1925,[38] and the Biological Weapons Convention of 1972 (hereinafter 'Biological Weapons Convention'),[39] and the prohibition against chemical weapons established by the Geneva Gas Protocol and the Chemical Weapons Convention of 1993 (hereinafter 'Chemical Weapons Convention').[40]

The Chemical Weapons Convention specifically protects humans *and* animals as the Convention bans toxic chemicals, which it defines as 'any chemical which through its chemical action on life processes can cause death, temporary incapacitation or permanent harm to humans or animals'.[41] Furthermore, by recognizing the prohibition against using herbicides as a method of warfare, the Chemical Weapons Convention grants protection to plants, at least implicitly.[42] The use of chemical agents to attack plants can have devastating effects on the natural environment; the use of herbicides during the war in Vietnam is a well-known example.[43] In addition, the Chemical Weapons Convention obliges states parties to 'assign the highest

---

[36] Eritrea–Ethiopia Claims Commission, Partial Award, *Western Front, Aerial Bombardment and Related Claims—Eritrea's Claims 1, 3, 5, 9–13, 14, 21, 25, and 26*, Decision of 19 December 2005, [2009] XXVI Reports of International Arbitral Awards 291, §§ 104f.

[37] 1899 and 1907 Hague Regulations (n 6), Art 23(a). See also Customary International Humanitarian Law Study (n 5), Rule 72: 'The use of poison or poisoned weapons is prohibited.'

[38] Protocol for the Prohibition of the Use in War of Asphyxiating, Poisonous or Other Gases, and of Bacteriological Methods of Warfare, Geneva, 17 June 1925.

[39] Convention on the Prohibition of the Development, Production and Stockpiling of Bacteriological (Biological) and Toxin Weapons and on their Destruction, London, Moscow and Washington, DC, 10 April 1972, 1015 UNTS 163. See also Customary International Humanitarian Law Study (n 5), Rule 73: 'The use of biological weapons is prohibited.'

[40] Convention on the Prohibition of the Development, Production, Stockpiling and Use of Chemical Weapons and on their Destruction, 13 January 1993, 1974 UNTS 45. See also Customary International Humanitarian Law Study (n 5), Rule 74: 'The use of chemical weapons is prohibited.'

[41] Chemical Weapons Convention (n 41), Art II(2). See also UN General Assembly Res 2603 (XXIV) (A) of 16 December 1969: '*Declares* as contrary to the generally recognized rules of international law, as embodied in the [Geneva Gas Protocol], the use in international armed conflicts of: (*a*) Any chemical agents of warfare—chemical substances, whether gaseous, liquid or solid—which might be employed because of their direct toxic effects on man, *animals or plants*; [...]' (emphasis added).

[42] Chemical Weapons Convention (n 41), Preamble. See also Customary International Humanitarian Law Study (n 5), Rule 76.

[43] See Hulme (n 13), 4ff.

priority to ensuring the safety of people and to protecting the environment' during the implementation of the Convention.[44] Similarly, the Biological Weapons Convention stresses the need for states parties to observe 'all necessary safety precautions' to 'protect populations and the environment' in implementing their obligations.[45]

As regards the legal review of new means and methods of warfare, Article 36 of AP I provides that '[i]n the study, development, acquisition or adoption of a new weapon, means or method of warfare, a High Contracting Party is under an obligation to determine whether its employment would, in some or all circumstances, be prohibited by this Protocol or by any other rule of international law applicable to the High Contracting Party'.[46] This includes assessing the environmental effects of such means and methods of warfare to the extent that the rules of AP I and other rules of international law protect the natural environment.[47]

3 SPECIFIC PROTECTION PROVIDED BY INTERNATIONAL HUMANITARIAN LAW FOR THE NATURAL ENVIRONMENT

The second strand of protection provided by international humanitarian law for the natural environment during armed conflict consists of those rules that *specifically* provide such protection. As far as treaty law is concerned, the only two provisions in this category are Articles 35 and 55 of AP I, both of which protect the environment only against 'widespread, long-term and severe damage'.

Article 35(3) of AP I makes it unlawful to 'employ methods or means of warfare which are intended, or may be expected, to cause widespread, long-term and severe damage to the natural environment'. Article 55(1) of AP I complements Article 35(3) by providing the following:

Care shall be taken in warfare to protect the natural environment against widespread, long-term and severe damage. This protection includes a prohibition of the use of methods

---

[44] Chemical Weapons Convention (n 41), Art VII(3), see also Arts IV(10) and V(11).

[45] Biological Weapons Convention (n 40), Art II, second sentence.   [46] AP I (n 2), Art 36.

[47] See eg International Committee of the Red Cross, 'A Guide to the Legal Review of New Weapons, Means and Methods of Warfare: Measures to Implement Article 36 of Additional Protocol I of 1977', Geneva, January 2006, available at <http://www.icrc.org/eng/assets/files/other/icrc_002_0902.pdf>, 17 ('In order to be capable of assessing whether the weapon under review [...] contravenes one or more of the general rules of IHL applicable to weapons, means and methods of warfare [...], the reviewing authority will have to take into consideration a wide range of military, technical, health and environmental factors.') See also 19f on environment-related considerations.

or means of warfare which are intended or may be expected to cause such damage to the natural environment and thereby to prejudice the health or survival of the population.

The prohibition to use methods or means of warfare that are intended, or may be expected, to cause widespread, long-term, and severe damage to the natural environment is considered to reflect customary international law in international and, arguably, also in non-international armed conflicts.[48] In this regard, it is noteworthy that the preamble to the Conventional Weapons Convention (hereinafter 'CCW') contains the reminder 'that it is prohibited to employ methods or means of warfare which are intended, or may be expected, to cause widespread, long-term and severe damage to the natural environment'.[49] The related war crime in the Rome Statute is formulated differently, stating that the 'widespread, long-term and severe damage to the natural environment [...] *be clearly excessive in relation to the concrete and direct overall military advantage anticipated*'.[50]

The exact meaning of 'widespread, long-term and severe damage' is not entirely clear. According to the 1975 report of Committee III of the Diplomatic Conference on the Reaffirmation and Development of International Humanitarian Law applicable in Armed Conflicts of 1974–77,

the time or duration required (i.e., long-term) was considered by some to be measured in decades. References to twenty or thirty years were made by some representatives as being a minimum. Others referred to battlefield destruction in France in the First World War as being outside the scope of the prohibition. The Biotope report states that 'Acts of warfare which cause short-term damage to the natural environment, such as artillery bombardment, are not intended to be prohibited by the article,' and continues by stating that the period might be perhaps for ten years or more. However, it is impossible to say with certainty what period of time might be involved.[51]

[48] See Customary International Humanitarian Law Study (n 5), Rule 45: 'The use of methods or means of warfare that are intended, or may be expected, to cause widespread, long-term and severe damage to the natural environment is prohibited. Destruction of the natural environment may not be used as a weapon.' But see K. Hulme, 'Natural Environment', in E. Wilmshurst and S. Breau (eds), *Perspectives on the ICRC Study on Customary International Humanitarian Law* (Cambridge: Cambridge University Press, 2007), 204–37 at 232 (concluding that Rule 45 'may have been more appropriately worded as "arguably" custom even for international armed conflict'); Y. Dinstein, 'The ICRC Customary International Humanitarian Law Study', 36 *Israel Yearbook of Human Rights* (2006) 13–14; J. Bellinger and W. Haynes, 'A US Government Response to the International Committee of the Red Cross Study *Customary International Humanitarian Law*', 89 *International Review of the Red Cross* (2007) 455–60 at 443.

[49] Convention on Prohibitions or Restrictions on the Use of Certain Conventional Weapons which may be Deemed to be Excessively Injurious or to have Indiscriminate Effects, Geneva, 10 October 1980, 1342 UNTS 137, Preamble.

[50] Rome Statute (n 8), Art 8(2)(b)(iv) (emphasis added).

[51] *Official Records of the Diplomatic Conference on the Reaffirmation and Development of International Humanitarian Law Applicable in Armed Conflicts* vol XV (Bern: Federal Political Department, 1978), 268f (CDDH/215/Rev.1, § 27).

But even if the lower threshold of ten years was applicable, this standard would still be highly impracticable as the full extent of the environmental effects of an attack may become apparent only gradually.[52] In fact, even in the case of the burning oil wells in Kuwait there was no agreement on whether the threshold of Article 35(3) of AP I had been met.[53]

Interestingly, the same three conditions—widespread, long-term, and severe— are used in Article I(1) of the ENMOD Convention, which makes it unlawful to 'engage in military or any other hostile use of environmental modification techniques having widespread, longlasting or severe effects as the means of destruction, damage or injury to any other State Party'. Unlike Articles 35(3) and 55 of AP I, the ENMOD Convention affirms that the three criteria are *disjunctive*. According to the 'understandings' annexed to the Convention, for the purposes of the Convention— and *only* for its purposes—'longlasting' means 'lasting for a period of months, or approximately a season'. The threshold stipulated by the ENMOD Convention is thus significantly lower than that of Articles 35(3) and 55 of AP I, which, owing to the vagueness and cumulative nature of their requirements, have remained on the whole of rather marginal importance, certainly with regard to conventional warfare.[54]

A more workable alternative might be the concept of 'ecocide', which emerged in the wake of the war in Vietnam. Ecocide—criminalized by the legislation of several states—is defined as 'the mass destruction of the flora and fauna and poisoning of the atmosphere or water resources, as well as other acts capable of causing an ecological catastrophe'.[55] The damage caused to the environment at the end of the Gulf War in 1991 could very well have fallen within this definition, and thus constituted 'ecocide', even though it might not have amounted to 'widespread, long-term and severe damage'.

Moreover, a *general* duty of due regard for the natural environment—even beyond the threshold of 'widespread, long-term and severe damage'—has now

---

[52] See eg Final Report to the Prosecutor by the Committee Established to Review the NATO Bombing Campaign Against the Federal Republic of Yugoslavia (n 32), § 17 ('Moreover, it is quite possible that, as this campaign occurred only a year ago, the UNEP study may not be a reliable indicator of the long term environmental consequences of the NATO bombing, as accurate assessments regarding the long-term effects of this contamination may not yet be practicable').

[53] See Final Report to the Prosecutor by the Committee Established to Review the NATO Bombing Campaign Against the Federal Republic of Yugoslavia (n 32), § 15 ('In any case, Articles 35(3) and 55 have a very high threshold of application. Their conditions for application are extremely stringent and their scope and contents imprecise. [...] This may partly explain the disagreement as to whether any of the damage caused by the oil spills and fires in the 1990/91 Gulf War technically crossed the threshold of Additional Protocol I'). See also Mollard-Bannelier (n 4), 94; Hulme (n 13), 170ff; Dinstein (n 13), 545ff.

[54] On a possible lowering of the threshold since the adoption of Protocol I in 1977 see Bothe, Bruch, Diamond, and Jensen (n 22), 576; Desgagné (n 12), 112ff; and most favourable to this proposition, É. David, *Principes de Droit des Conflits Armés* (4th edn, Brussels: Bruylant, 2008), § 2.101.

[55] See Customary International Humanitarian Law Study (n 5), 158. The definition used stems from the penal codes of a number of countries of the former Soviet Union, as well as Vietnam.

emerged and must be taken into account in all military operations (attacks, prepa-rations, etc). Arguably, it extends also to non-international armed conflicts.[56] This obligation reflects the international community's ever-growing recognition that the environment is an 'essential interest'.[57] It is also reflected in the general trend to comprehensively review actions from an environmental perspective, which may now be discerned among states and their armed forces, the United Nations and its agencies and specialized organizations, and humanitarian organizations.[58] As far as the principle of precaution is concerned, lack of scientific certainty about the envi-ronmental consequences of certain military operations does not absolve parties to a conflict from taking proper precautionary measures to prevent undue damage to the environment.[59] This appears to be particularly pertinent for legal reviews of new means and methods of warfare, such as the use of depleted uranium, for which no specific treaty regulation yet exists.[60]

[56] See Customary International Humanitarian Law Study (n 5), Rule 44: 'Methods and means of warfare must be employed with due regard to the protection and preservation of the natural environ-ment.' See also Bothe, Bruch, Diamond, and Jensen (n 22), 575 ('The "due regard" principle formulated in Rule 44 seems to be well accepted'); Program on Humanitarian Policy and Conflict Research at Harvard University (HPCR), 'Manual on International Law Applicable to Air and Missile Warfare', Bern, 15 May 2009, available at <http://ihlresearch.org/amw/HPCR%20Manual.pdf>, Rule 89 ('When planning and conducting air or missile operations, due regard ought to be given to the natural environ-ment'); United Kingdom, *The Manual of the Law of Armed Conflict*, Ministry of Defence, 1 July 2004, § 15.20 ('Regard must be had to the natural environment in the conduct of all military operations'), §§ 12.24 (air operations) and 13.30 (maritime warfare). But see K. Hulme, 'Taking Care to Protect the Environment Against Damages: A Meaningless Obligation?', 92(879) *International Review of the Red Cross* (2010) 675 at 686 and 691.

[57] See International Court of Justice, *Case Concerning the Gabčíkovo-Nagymaros Project (Hungary/Slovakia)*, Judgment of 25 September 1997, [1997] ICJ Rep 7, § 53.

[58] See eg the 'Environmental Guidebook for Military Operations' of March 2008 developed by a multinational working group consisting of representatives from the defence organizations of Finland, Sweden and the United States, available at <http://www.denix.osd.mil/international/Publications.cfm>; see also International Court of Justice, *Nuclear Weapons* (Advisory Opinion) (n 27), § 29 ('The existence of the general obligation of States to ensure that activities within their jurisdiction and con-trol respect the environment of other States or of areas beyond national control is now part of the corpus of international law relating to the environment').

[59] See ICRC, Customary International Humanitarian Law Study (n 5), Rule 44, third sentence ('Lack of scientific certainty as to the effects on the environment of certain military operations does not absolve a party to the conflict from taking such precautions'). For a critical assessment, see Hulme (n 49), 227.

[60] See eg UN General Assembly Res 62/30 of 5 December 2007, Preamble and Res 63/54 of 2 December 2008, Preamble (the General Assembly takes into consideration 'the *potential* harmful effects of the use of armaments and ammunitions containing depleted uranium on human health and the environment' (emphasis added)). In the latter resolution, the General Assembly declares itself moreover '[c]onvinced that as humankind is more aware of the need to take immediate measures to protect the environment, any event that could jeopardize such efforts requires urgent attention to implement the required meas-ures' (Preamble, § 5). See also A. McDonald, J. Kleffner, and B. Toebes, *Depleted Uranium Weapons and International Law: A Precautionary Approach* (The Hague: T.M.C. Asser Press, 2008).

Finally, the protection offered by international environmental law might usefully supplement that offered by international humanitarian law. However, of the multilateral environmental treaties in existence, only a few specifically address the issue of their applicability to situations of armed conflict. Some others address the subject implicitly, while the remaining instruments are completely silent on the issue. Even among those treaties that do continue to apply during armed conflict, some allow for exceptions the exact scope of which is not always entirely clear. Questions may also arise about the adequacy of the stipulations contained in these treaties as they are usually not drafted to bear specifically on the conduct of military operations.[61] Overall, there is thus little certainty about the value of these instruments for protecting the natural environment during armed conflict.[62] The situation can be summarized as follows:[63]

(i) Multilateral Environmental Agreements Applicable during Armed Conflict:

- UN Convention on the Law of the Sea (LOSC) (1982)[64]
- International Convention for the Prevention of Pollution of the Sea by Oil (OILPOL) (1954)[65]
- International Convention for the Prevention of Pollution from Ships (MARPOL) (1973)[66]
- Convention for the Protection of the Marine Environment and the Coastal Region of the Mediterranean and its Protocols (Barcelona Convention) (1976/1995)[67]
- Convention for the Protection and Development of the Marine Environment of the Wider Caribbean Region (Cartagena Convention) (1983)[68]

---

[61] In this sense, see also D. Bodansky, *Legal Regulation of the Effects of Miltiary Activity* vol 5/03 (Berlin: Erich Schmidt Verlag, 2003), 63f.

[62] Similarly Bothe, Bruch, Diamond, and Jensen (n 22), 570. See in detail 579 ff. including an overview of the existing theories in legal doctrine.

[63] Information taken from UNEP, 'Protecting the Environment During Armed Conflict' (n 28), 34ff.

[64] 10 December 1982, 1833 UNTS 3. But see the partial exception for warships and other state-operated vessels and aircraft in Art 236.

[65] 12 May 1954, 327 UNTS 3. But see the possibility to suspend the operation of the Convention in case of war or other hostilities provided by Art XIX(1).

[66] 2 November 1973, 1340 UNTS 184, as amended by the Protocol of 1978 Relating to the International Convention for the Prevention of Pollution from Ships, 17 February 1978, 1340 UNTS 61. But see Art 3(3) which contains an exception similar to that of Art 236 of the UN Convention on the Law of the Sea.

[67] Convention for the Protection of the Mediterranean Sea against Pollution, 16 February 1976, 1102 UNTS 27, amended and renamed Convention for the Protection of the Marine Environment and the Coastal Region of the Mediterranean, 10 June 1995. Article 3(5) of the amended Convention contains an exception similar to that of LOSC and MARPOL. The International Maritime Organization invoked the Barcelona Convention as a basis for providing assistance to Lebanon following the bombing of the facility at Jiyeh during the 2006 conflict. See UNEP, 'Protecting the Environment During Armed Conflict' (n 28), 36.

[68] 24 March 1983, 1506 UNTS 157.

- Convention on Wetlands of International Importance especially as Waterfowl Habitat (Ramsar Convention) (1971)[69]
- Convention Concerning the Protection of the World Cultural and Natural Heritage (World Heritage Convention) (1972)[70]
- Convention on Long-Range Transboundary Air Pollution (LRTAP) (1979)[71]
- African Convention on the Conservation of Nature and Natural Resources (Revised) (2003)[72]
- Convention on the Prevention of Marine Pollution by Dumping of Wastes and Other Matter (London Convention) (1972)[73]
- UN Convention on the Law of the Non-Navigational Uses of International Watercourses (International Watercourses Convention) (1997).[74]

(ii) Multilateral Environmental Agreements Not Applicable During Armed Conlict:

- Convention on Civil Liability for Damage Resulting from Activities Dangerous to the Environment (1993)[75]
- Convention on Third Party Liability in the Field of Nuclear Energy (1960)[76]
- Vienna Convention on Civil Liability for Nuclear Damage (1963)[77]
- International Convention on Civil Liability for Oil Pollution Damage (1971).[78]

(iii) Multilateral Environmental Agreements Silent on the Matter:

- Convention on Early Notification of a Nuclear Accident (1986)[79]
- Convention on Biological Diversity (1992)
- Control of Transboundary Movements of Hazardous Wastes and their Disposal (Basel Convention) (1989)[80]

---

[69] 2 February 1971, 996 UNTS 245. But see Art 2(5) that provides for the deletion or restriction of the boundaries of wetlands because of 'urgent national interests' of the Contracting Parties.

[70] 23 November 1972, 1037 UNTS 151. UNESCO has been running a pilot project in the Democratic Republic of Congo since 2000 to try to use the Convention as an instrument to improve the conservation of World Heritage sites in regions affected by armed conflict. See UNEP, 'Protecting the Environment During Armed Conflict' (n 28), 38.

[71] 13 November 1979, 1302 UNTS 217.

[72] 11 July 2003, 1001 UNTS. Article XV(1) establishes specific obligations for times of armed conflict reiterating and expanding upon the basic protection provided under international humanitarian law. See also Art XV(2).

[73] 29 December 1972, 1046 UNTS 120.

[74] Adopted by UN General Assembly Res 51/229 of 21 May 1997. According to Art 29, '[i]nternational watercourses and related installations, facilities and other works shall enjoy the protection accorded by the principles and the rules of international law applicable in international and non-international armed conflict and shall not be used in violation of those principles and rules'.

[75] 21 June 1993, 32 *ILM* 1228. See Art 8(a).

[76] 29 July 1960, amended 28 January 1964, 956 UNTS 264. See Art 9. Austria and Germany, however, made reservations to this provision (Annex I).

[77] 21 May 1963, 1063 UNTS 266. See Art IV(3)(a).

[78] 29 November 1969, 973 UNTS 4. See Arts III and XI.   [79] 26 September 1986, 1439 UNTS 276.

[80] 22 March 1989, 1673 UNTS 126.

- UN Convention to Combat Desertification (1994)[81]
- Convention on International Trade in Endangered Species of Wild Fauna and Flora (CITES) (1973)[82]
- Vienna Convention for the Protection of the Ozone Layer (1985)[83]
- Montreal Protocol on Substances that Deplete the Ozone Layer (1987)[84]
- United Nations Framework Convention on Climate Change (1992)[85]
- Stockholm Convention on Persistent Organic Pollutants (2001)[86]
- Convention on the Conservation of Migratory Species of Wild Animals (CMS) (1979)[87]
- Rotterdam Convention on the Prior Informed Consent Procedure for Certain Hazardous Chemicals and Pesticides in International Trade (1998).[88]

4 STRENGTHENING THE LEGAL PROTECTION PROVIDED BY INTERNATIONAL HUMANITARIAN LAW FOR THE ENVIRONMENT

In view of the foregoing and given the growing concern over environmental protection during armed conflict and in other contexts—as manifested, for instance, in the 1992 UN Conference on Environment and Development in Rio de Janeiro and in follow-up Conferences—there seems to be significant room and also a need for improvement in this regard. Indeed, there has been, for a few years now, a renewed interest in protecting the environment during armed conflict. For example, UNEP has made the issue of 'disasters and conflicts' one of the six priority areas that 'define [its] focus on the environmental challenges of the 21st century'.[89]

In March 2009, the ICRC and UNEP organized a joint expert workshop in Nairobi, which called upon the ICRC to update its 1994 Guidelines to reflect developments in the law and practice.[90] After the workshop, in November 2009, the

---

[81] 17 June 1994, 1954 UNTS 3.   [82] 3 March 1973, 993 UNTS 243.
[83] 22 March 1985, 1513 UNTS 293.   [84] 16 September 1987, 1522 UNTS 3.
[85] 9 May 1992, 1771 UNTS 107.   [86] 22 May 2001, 2256 UNTS 119.
[87] 23 June 1989, *ILM* 19 [1980] 15.   [88] 10 September 1998, 2244 UNTS 337.
[89] See <http://www.unep.org/>.
[90] See also UNEP, 'Protecting the Environment during Armed Conflict' (n 28), 52f. Recommendation 2 provides that '[t]he ICRC *Guidelines on the Protection of the Environment during Armed Conflict* (1994) require updating and subsequent consideration by the UN General Assembly for adoption, as

Secretary-General of the United Nations, Ban Ki-moon, called on member states in an address on the occasion of the International Day for Preventing the Exploitation of the Environment in War and Armed Conflict 'to clarify and expand international law on environmental protection in times of war'.[91] In addition, the ICRC carried out an internal research study on the current state of international humanitarian law in order to identify gaps or weaknesses in the law of armed conflict and devise possible solutions in terms of legal development or clarification. Gaps or weaknesses in the current legal framework were found to exist in four main areas, one of which was protection for the natural environment.[92]

Against this background, eight different areas for further development can be identified:

(i) *Disseminating, implementing, and enforcing the law.* The existing rules must be better disseminated, implemented, and enforced by states and international organizations. This is probably the case for all rules of international humanitarian law. However, it seems especially pertinent for the rules protecting the natural environment. Updating the ICRC's Guidelines for Military Manuals and Instructions on the Protection of the Environment in Times of Armed Conflict will be helpful. The Guidelines were elaborated by the ICRC after consultation with a group of international experts and submitted to the United Nations in 1994. While it did not give the Guidelines its formal approval, the UN General Assembly invited all states to disseminate them widely and 'to give due consideration to the possibility of incorporating them into their military manuals and other instructions addressed to their military personnel'.[93] The Guidelines should be updated to reflect developments since 1994 in international humanitarian law, including the adoption of new treaties and the evolution of customary international law.

(ii) *Clarifying the law.* The existing legal framework—particularly rules relating to the conduct of hostilities and the practical applicability of these rules to the environment—could usefully be clarified on a number of points. Most notably,

---

appropriate' (emphasis removed). The update was on going at the time of completion of this Chapter. As soon as it is released, it will be available at <http://www.icrc.org/eng/war-and-law>.

[91] Message of the UN Secretary-General, Ban Ki-moon, on the occasion of the International Day for Preventing the Exploitation of the Environment in War and Armed Conflict, 6 November 2009, available at <http://www.un.org/en/events/environmentconflictday/2009/sgmessage2009.shtml>.

[92] *Strengthening Legal Protection for Victims of Armed Conflict. The ICRC Study on the Current State of International Humanitarian Law*, Address by Dr Jakob Kellenberger, President of the International Committee of the Red Cross, 21 September 2010, reprinted in 92(879) *International Review of the Red Cross* (2010) 799. The other areas identified in the study are the protection of persons deprived of liberty, especially in situations of non-international armed conflict, the implementation of humanitarian law and reparation for victims of violations, and the protection of internationally displaced persons.

[93] UN General Assembly, Res 49/50, 9 December 1994, § 11.

the principle of proportionality should be clarified in terms of operational impact and precise scope of application with respect to environmental damage.

The notion of 'widespread, long-term and severe damage' should also be further clarified. Clear definitions are needed for each of these terms if they are to have any practical value.[94] In this connection, another issue requiring closer examination concerns the extent to which the high threshold of 'widespread, long-term and severe damage' is still pertinent today. As Bothe, Bruch, Diamond, and Jensen have observed:

Natural resources and the environment are essential to post-conflict peacebuilding, and significant environmental damage can undermine efforts to provide for livelihoods, promote economic recovery, and allow society to return to a 'normal' peacetime way of life. A framework that is too permissive of environmental damage during armed conflict can thus undermine long-term peace. One can ask whether this high threshold is still valid, or whether it has fallen into desuetude in light of the continually increasing recognition of environmental concerns in international relations. This is arguable, but not certain.[95]

It would be useful to establish with more certainty whether the threshold has fallen into disuse and, if not, whether it can be replaced by stricter and more protective, yet realistic standards. This might entail the development of new norms in addition to clarifying existing law.

(iii) *Further developing the law of non-international armed conflict.* As far as the development of new norms is concerned, it should be mentioned that there is a particular dearth of specific norms in the law of non-international armed conflict, which contains no provisions comparable to Articles 35 and 55 of AP I. The ICRC study of 2005 considers the corresponding customary norm to be only 'arguably' part of customary international humanitarian law.[96] Given the fact that most armed conflicts today are of a non-international character, this difference in regulation does not reflect well on the clarity and coherence of international humanitarian law and on the protection it grants to the natural environment.[97]

(iv) *Place-based protection.* In order to better protect areas of great environmental importance existing rules should be supplemented by provisions specifically intended to protect such areas against environmental damage. This would overcome an inherent weakness in the protection granted to the natural environment as a civilian object, namely that such areas can be turned into military objectives by the presence of combatants.[98] This weakness is reflected

---

[94] See UNEP, 'Protecting the Environment during Armed Conflict' (n 28), 52 (recommending that the definitions used for the 1976 ENMOD Convention should serve as the minimum basis for these definitions).

[95] Bothe, Bruch, Diamond, and Jensen (n 22), 576.

[96] See Customary International Humanitarian Law Study (n 5), 156–7.

[97] See ICRC, 'Strengthening legal protection for victims of armed conflict', Report for the 31st International Conference of the Red Cross and Red Crescent, Doc No 31IC/11/5.1.1, Geneva, October 2011, 15.

[98] See Bothe, Bruch, Diamond, and Jensen (n 22), 576–7 ('Elements of the environment are most often civilian objects. As such, they are protected against attacks. [...] This protection is, however,

in Protocol III of 1980 (on Prohibitions or Restrictions on the Use of Incendiary Weapons) to the CCW, which specifically deems it unlawful 'to make forests or other kinds of plant cover the subject of attack by incendiary weapons *except when such natural elements are used to cover, conceal or camouflage combatants or other military objectives, or are themselves military objectives.*'[99]

A proposal to protect publicly recognized nature reserves has already been made, during the Diplomatic Conference of Geneva of 1974–77 that led to the adoption of Additional Protocols I and II. A Working Group of Committee III submitted a draft Article 48*ter* providing that '[p]ublicly recognized nature reserves with adequate markings and boundaries declared as such to the adversary shall be protected and respected except when such reserves are used specifically for military purposes'. This proposal was not, however, received with great enthusiasm in Committee III of the Diplomatic Conference and was ultimately dropped.[100]

In 1995, the International Council of Environmental Law and the Commission on Environmental Law of the International Union for the Conservation of Nature produced the Draft Convention on the Prohibition of Hostile Military Activities in Protected Areas, which provided among other things that:

[e]ach resolution adopted by the Security Council under Chapter VII of the UN Charter, in response to a situation of armed conflict shall include a list of the relevant internally protected areas, thereby designated as non-target areas in which all hostile military activities shall not be permitted during the armed conflict in question.[101]

This draft has remained without effect, but UNEP and the ICRC have recently revived the idea of granting place-based protection to areas of great environmental importance.[102]

---

shaky, as environmental elements can easily become military objectives. Once armed forces are located in a protected area, the area may contribute effectively to military action and its neutralization may offer a definite military advantage. [...] In the case of herbicide use in Vietnam, the trees provided cover for the enemy. Their defoliation constituted a definite military advantage, and the trees—more precisely their leaves—became a military objective').

[99] Protocol on Prohibitions or Restrictions on the Use of Incendiary Weapons, to the Convention on Prohibitions or Restrictions on the Use of Certain Convention Weapons which may be Deemed to be Excessively Injurious or to have Indiscriminate Effects (Protocol III), Geneva, 10 October 1980, 1342 UNTS 171, Art 2(4) (emphasis added).

[100] See Commentary AP I and II, paras 2138ff.

[101] Article 2, cited in A.S. Tolentino, Jr, 'The Law of Armed Conflict *Vis-à-Vis* the Environment', in B. Vukas and T.M. Šošić, *International Law: New Actors, New Concepts—Continuing Dilemmas. Liber Amicorum Božidar Bakotić* (Leiden: Martinus Nijhoff, 2010), 595–606 at 603.

[102] See UNEP, 'Protecting the Environment during Armed Conflict' (n 28), 54 ('A new legal instrument granting place-based protection for critical natural resources and areas of ecological importance during international and non-international armed conflicts should be developed'); Address of Dr Jakob Kellenberger (n 92), 803 and ICRC, 'Strengthening legal protection for victims of armed conflict' (n 97), 17; see also Droege and Tougas (n 21), 43–5.

(v)   *International cooperation.* When environmental damage occurs, there is an urgent need to contain it as much as possible and clean up affected areas.[103] As cleaning up such damages may be a challenging task that might exceed the resources of the country or region concerned, particularly during armed conflict, consideration should be given to the establishment of international cooperation schemes, regardless of legal responsibility. In this regard, the 1997 Convention on the Prohibition of the Use, Stockpiling, Production and Transfer of Anti-Personnel Mines and on their Destruction (hereinafter 'Anti-Personnel Mine Ban Convention') and the 2008 Convention on Cluster Munitions may serve as models. Both instruments specifically provide for international cooperation and assistance in the implementation of their obligations.[104] The 2008 Convention on Cluster Munitions, for example, grants each state party 'the right to seek and receive assistance' in fulfilling its obligations under the Convention and envisages, as far as possible, the provision of 'technical, material and financial assistance to State Parties'.[105] The spirit of these provisions fits well with the needs encountered in areas that have suffered significant environmental damage during armed conflict.

(vi)   *Victim assistance.* Better protection must also be afforded to the victims of environmental damage: they should not be left without assistance, material or non-material. This is particularly important because the natural environment and natural resources are vital for the existence and wellbeing of present and future generations. If the natural environment is damaged and resources depleted, the civilian population may struggle and need assistance to rebuild their livelihoods. Once again, the Anti-Personnel Mine Ban Convention and the Convention on Cluster Munitions provide guidance as both contain innovative provisions on victim assistance. The Convention on Cluster Munitions requires each state party 'with respect to cluster munition victims in areas under its jurisdiction or control' to 'adequately provide age- and gender-sensitive assistance, including medical care, rehabilitation and psychological support, as well as provide for their social and economic inclusion'.[106] The Convention also obliges each state party 'in a position to do so' to 'provide assistance for the implementation of the obligations referred to in Article 5 [victim assistance]' and 'to contribute to the economic and social recovery needed as a result of cluster munition use in affected States Parties'.[107] Again,

---

[103] See Kellenberger (n 92), 803.

[104] Convention on the Prohibition of the Use, Stockpiling, Production and Transfer of Anti-Personnel Mines and on their Destruction, 18 September 1997, 2056 UNTS 211; Convention on Cluster Munitions, 30 May 2008, CCM/77.

[105] Convention on Cluster Munitions (n 104), Art 6(1) and (2). The Anti-Personnel Mine Ban Convention (n 104), Art 6 contains similar provisions.

[106] Convention on Cluster Munitions (n 104), Art 5(1).

[107] Convention on Cluster Munitions (n 104), Art 6(7) and (8). See also Anti-Personnel Mine Ban Convention (n 104), Art 6(3).

the spirit of these provisions fits well with the problems encountered after environmental damage.

(vii) *Compensation*. In order to enforce the law and assist those in need, it is necessary to develop better mechanisms for providing victims with *compensation* for damages. Such compensation schemes could be based either on liability for violations or simply on victims' needs.[108]

(viii) *International monitoring*. Finally, on the institutional level, international mechanisms should be created to monitor and assess the nature and extent of environmental damage caused by armed conflicts. Mechanisms of this kind may also be given the task of conducting legal reviews of responsibility to ensure better enforcement of existing rules.[109] In this regard, UNEP has recommended that '[a] permanent UN body to monitor violations and address compensation for environmental damage [...] be considered'.[110] According to UNEP, this body could then be given a mandate to:

- investigate and decide on alleged violations of international law during international and non-international armed conflicts;
- handle and process compensation claims related to environmental damage and loss of economic opportunities as well as remediation activities; and
- develop norms and mechanisms on victim assistance, international assistance, and cooperation to assess and redress the environmental consequences of armed conflict.[111]

The existence of such a body with comprehensive authority would have far-reaching consequences for the effective implementation of a number of proposals formulated here—not only with regard to monitoring, but also for international cooperation, victim assistance, and compensation. The ICRC has also called for new mechanisms and procedures in this respect.[112]

There are mixed signs as for the prospects of success of these different areas. A recent consultation of states on the ICRC's initiative aimed at strengthening legal protection for victims of armed conflict brought to light 'no clear trend in favour of one or the other possible options' and concluded that, notwithstanding some support, 'States were apparently not yet ready to undertake an exercise aimed at

[108] See eg the United Nations Compensation Commission that was established by Security Council Res 687 of 3 April 1991 to pay compensation for losses and damage resulting from Iraq's invasion and occupation of Kuwait (§§ 16 and 18f) even though the Commission was not concerned with breaches of the *ius in bello*.

[109] On the absence of mechanisms for the implementation of state responsibility for environmental damage, see generally Mollard-Bannelier (n 4), 391ff.

[110] UNEP, 'Protecting the Environment during Armed Conflict' (n 28), 53.

[111] UNEP, 'Protecting the Environment during Armed Conflict' (n 28), 53.

[112] ICRC, 'Strengthening legal protection for victims of armed conflict' (n 97), 16. See also Droege and Tougas (n 21), 45–6.

strengthening the international law protecting the natural environment in time of armed conflict'.[113]

On the other hand, at its sixty-fifth session, in 2013, the International Law Commission decided to include the topic 'Protection of the environment in relation to armed conflicts' in its programme of work, on the basis of the recommendation of the Working Group on the long-term programme of work.[114] The Commission decided to appoint Marie Jacobsson as Special Rapporteur for the topic. The outcome of the ILC work in this area remains to be seen but it may contribute to further clarification and strengthening of the legal protection of the environment in time of armed conflict.

5 CONCLUSION

Over the last few decades, international law has been widened and deepened to protect the natural environment. This may be attributed to increased awareness of the dangerous degradation of the natural environment brought about by man. The development of international environmental law has not, however, been tailored to the specific protection needs of the natural environment and resources during armed conflict. As a result, the applicability of existing environmental treaties during armed conflict is quite often uncertain.

Moreover, international humanitarian law has not developed to the same degree as international environmental law. As the above overview of the existing rules of international humanitarian law has made clear, there are still only two provisions in humanitarian treaty law that deal specifically with environmental protection (Articles 35(3) and 55 of AP I). Because of their high threshold ('widespread, long-term and severe damage'), these provisions have been of limited importance in practice. Meanwhile, the law of non-international armed conflict does not contain any corresponding provisions.

However, a number of general rules of international humanitarian law, both treaty law and customary law, also protect the natural environment or certain aspects of it. Because these general rules protect the natural environment at lower levels of damage, they may be of greater practical importance. In general, these rules must be

---

[113] ICRC, 'Strengthening legal protection for victims of armed conflict' (n 97), 26. As a result, the 31st International Conference of the Red Cross (Geneva, 28 November–1 December 2011) in Resolution 1 'Strengthening legal protection for victims of armed conflict' invited the ICRC to 'pursue further research, consultation and discussion' in two of the four areas the ICRC had identified—detention and compliance—but not the protection of the environment (§ 6).

[114] See <http://www.un.org/law/ilc>.

better disseminated, implemented, and enforced; and in some instances they must be clarified to reveal their scope and the practical implications for the protection of the natural environment and resources.

Gaps in international law and institutions continue to exist. With regard to preventive action, there are no established rules or mechanisms for designating areas of great ecological importance as specially protected areas. Such rules or mechanisms also do not exist for post-conflict recovery of affected areas or for international cooperation to accomplish such undertakings. Agreed mechanisms for victim assistance and compensation are also lacking. Finally, effective and permanent monitoring mechanisms that could have a role in all of the above currently do not exist.

For the sake of the natural environment and the people who depend on it for their livelihood and well-being, it is imperative that the international community address the issues identified in this Chapter.

CHAPTER 20

....

PROTECTION OF CULTURAL PROPERTY

....

ROGER O'KEEFE

1 INTRODUCTION

....

MUCH greater attention has been paid to protecting cultural property in armed conflict by means of international law than might be assumed. Perhaps this is not saying much, given the seemingly popular view that belligerents have always looked to raze or plunder the enemy's cultural heritage. But it is no less true for that, and an account of the international rules and institutions in place for the protection of cultural property in armed conflict ought to serve as a useful corrective to just this sort of corrosive assumption. By 'protection' here is meant protection from damage and destruction and from all forms of misappropriation. What is meant by 'cultural property' depends to an extent on the context, but in essence the term refers to buildings and other monuments of historic, artistic or architectural significance, to archaeological sites, to artworks, antiquities, manuscripts, books, and collections of the same, to archives, and the like. The terminology distinguishes between 'immovable' and 'movable' cultural property, the labels being self-explanatory.

States and other international actors have in fact expended considerable energies on a sophisticated body of international law for the protection of cultural property in armed conflict. Indeed, enthusiasm for the task has led to a degree of over-sophistication. The relevant international rules consist of what at first blush can seem a bewildering matrix of specialized conventions on the protection of cultural property in armed conflict, general conventions on the law of armed conflict, the customary international law of armed conflict, general conventions on the protection of cultural property, conventional and customary international human rights law, and customary international criminal law. To add to the complexity, the precise scope of the cultural property covered by the law can vary depending on the rules in question. On top of this, the law of armed conflict, both conventional and customary, on the treatment during hostilities of 'enemy property', 'civilian objects' and similar broad genera of immovable and movable property apply as much in respect of cultural property as generally. The same goes for the basic conventional and customary rights and obligations of a belligerent occupant. Nor is there anything to indicate that certain treaty provisions on the so-called 'world cultural heritage' cease to apply in armed conflict. Next, to superimpose a further layer of complication, questions as to the implementation and enforcement of the relevant rules fall within the respective purviews of a range of different international and other bodies. And to make matters worse, not everything provided for on paper is how things work in practice, even leaving aside the question of compliance and breach. All this said, however, the applicable international rules boil down to some relatively straightforward propositions, while the mandates or jurisdictions of the interested international bodies are mutually supportive. In short, while the newcomer to the field may feel intimidated and confused, there is no reason why the surprising abundance of international law relevant to the protection of cultural property in armed conflict should be viewed as a cause for concern.

The following account outlines the relevant bodies of international law one by one.[1]

2 INTERNATIONAL HUMANITARIAN LAW

A. The conventional and customary context

Over the course of the last century, states concluded four multilateral treaties specifically dedicated to the protection of cultural property in armed conflict, treaties which trace their immediate origins to a 1919 report of the Netherlands

---

[1] For fuller accounts, see R. O'Keefe, *The Protection of Cultural Property in Armed Conflict* (Cambridge: Cambridge University Press, 2006); R. O'Keefe, 'Protection of Cultural Property', in D. Fleck (ed), *The Handbook of International Humanitarian Law* (3rd edn, Oxford: Oxford University Press, 2013), Ch 9; R. O'Keefe, 'Protection of Cultural Property under International Criminal Law', 11 *Melbourne Journal of International Law* (2010) 339–92; R. O'Keefe, 'Tangible Cultural Heritage and International Human Rights Law', in L. Prott, R. Redmond-Cooper, and S. Urice (eds), *Realising Cultural Heritage Law: Festschrift for Patrick O'Keefe* (Builth Wells: Institute of Art and Law, 2013), 87–95.

Archaeological Society,[2] as reflected subsequently in an optional provision of the 1923 draft Hague Rules on Aerial Warfare[3] and later in a 1938 Preliminary Draft International Convention for the Protection of Historic Buildings and Works of Art in Times of War with annexed Regulations for its execution.[4] In 1935, a number of states of the Pan American Union concluded the Treaty on the Protection of Artistic and Scientific Institutions and Historic Monuments,[5] known as the Roerich Pact, applicable to both war and peace. This rudimentary treaty is still in force among 10 American states, including the United States, although it is outdated and effectively in desuetude. Far more significantly, in 1954 states concluded, under the aegis of the United Nations Educational, Scientific and Cultural Organization (UNESCO), the Hague Convention for the Protection of Cultural Property in the Event of Armed Conflict, along with Regulations for its execution,[6] as well as a separate optional protocol,[7] now known as the First Protocol. The Convention was supplemented in 1999 by the adoption of a Second Protocol.[8] This 'Hague' regime—premised, in the words of the Convention's preamble, on the conviction that 'damage to cultural property belonging to any people whatsoever means damage to the cultural heritage of all mankind, since each people makes its contribution to the culture of the world'—remains the cornerstone of the international legal protection of cultural property in the event of armed conflict.[9]

The 1954 Hague Convention and its two Protocols are the only treaties in the field of international humanitarian law actually to use the term 'cultural property', the formal legal definition of which for the purposes of all three instruments[10] is found in Article 1 of the Convention. In accordance with Article 1(a), 'cultural property' within the meaning of the Convention refers to 'movable or immovable cultural property of great importance to the cultural heritage of every people'[11]—that is, to cultural property of great importance to the national cultural heritage of each respective high contracting party, as determined by that party. In the practice of the high contracting parties, the total immovable cultural property to which the Convention and its First and Second Protocols apply is generally in the order of tens of thousands of items in the territory of each party, while the few figures available for movable cultural property tentatively

---

[2] 26 *Revue Générale de Droit International Public* (1919) 329.

[3] Article 26 of the Rules of Aerial Warfare.   [4] LNOJ, 19th Year, No 11 (November 1938) 937.

[5] Washington, DC, 15 April 1935.   [6] The Hague, 14 May 1954 (1954 HC and Regs).

[7] Protocol to the Convention for the Protection of Cultural Property in the Event of Armed Conflict, The Hague, 14 May 1954 (FP).

[8] Second Protocol to the Hague Convention of 1954 for the Protection of Cultural Property in the Event of Armed Conflict, The Hague, 26 March 1999 (SP).

[9] 1954 HC currently has 126 parties, FP 102, and SP 64.

[10] See para 1 of FP (FP referring to its provisions as 'paragraphs'); Art 1(b) of SP.

[11] Article 1(a) of 1954 HC goes on to give examples of such property. The term 'cultural property' for the purposes of 1954 HC also refers, in accordance with Art 1(b), to buildings whose main and effective

point to the contents of a hundred to a few hundred museums, art galleries, libraries and archives per party.

The Convention applies during international armed conflict between two or more high contracting parties, whether or not a legal state of war exists between them, as well as to all cases of partial or total occupation of the territory of a party.[12] The provisions relating to respect for cultural property, by which is meant the various paragraphs of Article 4 (headed 'Respect for cultural property'), also apply to non-international armed conflict occurring within the territory of one of the parties.[13] The Second Protocol applies to international and non-international armed conflict without distinction,[14] while the First Protocol applies in practice only in respect of belligerent occupation.

Ostensibly the 1954 Hague Convention offers two levels of protection for cultural property. What is commonly referred to as 'general protection'[15] extends to all immovables and movables satisfying the definition of cultural property in Article 1, whereas 'special protection' imposes a supplementary and nominally stricter standard in respect of a narrower range of property.[16] But the second is a dead letter, and for present purposes can be ignored.[17] The Convention also lays down rules on the transport of cultural property during armed conflict,[18] to date never formally applied; on the treatment of personnel engaged in the protection of cultural property;[19] and on the creation and use of a 'distinctive emblem' for cultural property,[20] which again has proved unpopular with high contracting parties.

The Second Protocol to the 1954 Hague Convention, which supplements rather than supplants the Convention,[21] leaves intact the latter's basic architecture and operates by reference back to its provisions, elaborating on, refining, and in places

purpose is to preserve or exhibit the movable cultural property defined in Art 1(a), as well as refuges intended to shelter such movables in the event of armed conflict; and, in accordance with Art 1(c), to centres containing a large amount of cultural property as defined in Art 1(a) and (b), labelled 'centres containing monuments'.

[12] Article 18(1) and (2) of 1954 HC. See also the situation provided for in Art 18(3) of 1954 HC.
[13] Article 19(1) of 1954 HC.
[14] Articles 3(1) and 22(1) of SP. Article 3(2) of SP provides as per Art 18(3) of 1954 HC, *mutatis mutandis*.
[15] See Ch I of 1954 HC.   [16] See Ch II of 1954 HC and Ch II Regs.
[17] Chiefly on account of the difficulty of satisfying the criterion of eligibility laid down in Art 8(1)(a) of 1954 HC, only one centre containing monuments, the Vatican City, and eight refuges for movable cultural property (six of them in the Netherlands) have ever been entered in the International Register of Cultural Property under Special Protection provided for in Ch II of 1954 HC and Ch II Regs, and the Vatican City's entry was possible only thanks to a special undertaking by Italy ostensibly under Art 8(5) of 1954 HC. Four of the refuges have since been removed at the request of the respective parties, leaving the Register to comprise now only four refuges (three in the Netherlands and one in Germany) and the Vatican City: see UNESCO Doc CLT/CIH/MCO/2008/PI/46, December 2000, as manually amended. As between parties to the Second Protocol, special protection has effectively been replaced by the regime of 'enhanced' protection provided for in Ch 3 of SP.
[18] See Ch III of 1954 HC and Ch III Regs.   [19] See Ch IV of 1954 HC.
[20] See Ch V of 1954 HC and Ch IV Regs.   [21] Article 2 of SP.

adding to the various obligations as between parties to the Second Protocol, which as a precondition to participation must be parties to the Convention.[22] The Second Protocol maintains in effect the distinction between general and special protection of cultural property, but it replaces, for all intents and purposes, the second of these with a more promising regime of 'enhanced' protection,[23] available to 'cultural heritage of the greatest importance for humanity' which is protected by 'adequate domestic legal and administrative measures recognising its exceptional cultural [...] value and ensuring the highest level of protection' and which is not used for military purposes or to shield military sites.[24]

For its part, the brief First Protocol deals solely with questions regarding the exportation and importation of cultural property from occupied territory, and with the return of cultural property deposited abroad for the duration of hostilities.

Of the general multilateral treaties on the law of armed conflict, the most significant for contemporary purposes are the 1977 Additional Protocols to the Geneva Conventions,[25] both of which embody provisions specifically relating to respect for what can be referred to as cultural property, even if neither actually uses the term.[26] The scope of the immovables and movables encompassed by Article 53 of AP I, applicable to international armed conflict, and Article 16 of AP II, applicable to non-international armed conflict, is essentially the same as that covered by the 1954 Hague Convention.[27] The motivation behind the two provisions was to affirm in a single, concise article in each instrument the essential obligations of respect for cultural property embodied more exhaustively in the Convention. The subsidiary

---

[22] See Arts 40–2 of SP.   [23] See Art 4 and Ch 3 of SP.

[24] Article 10 of SP. The first entries in the List of Cultural Property under Enhanced Protection were made by the Committee for the Protection of Cultural Property in Armed Conflict in November 2010. All four—namely Choirokoitia, the Painted Churches of the Troodos region and Paphos (both site I, Kato Paphos town, and site II, Kouklia village) in Cyprus and Castel del Monte in Italy—are also inscribed on the World Heritage List provided for in Art 11(2) of the Convention concerning the Protection of the World Cultural and Natural Heritage ('World Heritage Convention'), Paris, 16 November 1972 (WHC). To these were added in December 2011 the Kernavé Archaeological Site (Cultural Reserve of Kernavé) in Lithuania, which is also on the World Heritage List.

[25] See Protocol Additional to the Geneva Conventions of 12 August 1949, and relating to the Protection of Victims of International Armed Conflicts, Geneva, 8 June 1977 (AP I) and Protocol Additional to the Geneva Conventions of 12 August 1949, and relating to the Protection of Victims of Non-International Armed Conflicts, Geneva, 8 June 1977 (AP II). There are currently 173 parties to AP I and 167 to AP II.

[26] Article 53 of AP I and Art 16 of AP II speak of 'the historic monuments, works of art or places of worship which constitute the cultural or spiritual heritage of peoples'.

[27] See eg *Prosecutor v Kordić and Čerkez*, Appeals Chamber, Judgment, IT-95-14/2-A, 17 December 2004, § 91, citing Commentary AP I and II, 646, para 2064. This was followed in *Prosecutor v Strugar*, Trial Chamber, Judgment, IT-01-42-T, 31 January 2005, § 307, which left open '[w]hether there may be precise differences'. But cf *Central Front, Eritrea's Claims 2, 4, 6, 7, 8 & 22 (Eritrea/Ethiopia), Partial Award*, (2004) 135 ILR 295 at 330, § 113.

nature of the pair is highlighted by the 'without prejudice' clause in the chapeau to each,[28] which makes it clear that the provisions are not intended to modify the existing legal obligations of those high contracting parties to AP I and AP II which are also parties to the Convention, a point underscored in Resolution 20 (IV) of the Diplomatic Conference of Geneva.[29] The desire was to avoid the 'parallel application of two divergent systems for the protection of cultural property, which could only be a source of confusion'.[30] Beyond the *lex specialis* represented by Article 53 of AP I and Article 16 of AP II, cultural property is considered a *prima facie* civilian object like any other,[31] with the result that it benefits in international armed conflict from, inter alia, the prohibition on indiscriminate attacks and from the mandatory precautions in attack laid down in AP I.[32] In addition, Article 38(1) of AP I prohibits the improper use of the distinctive emblem of cultural property.

The Additional Protocols were not the first general conventions on the laws of war to include provisions on cultural property, generically speaking. The 1899 and 1907 Hague Regulations on the Laws and Customs of War on Land and the 1907 Hague Convention on naval bombardment contained such articles.[33] Nor were the Additional Protocols the last of the general treaties on international humanitarian law to regulate aspects of the protection of cultural property in armed conflict, with the 1980 and 1996 Protocols to the Conventional Weapons Convention on mines, booby-traps, and other devices both containing provisions to this end.[34]

---

[28] Article 53 of AP I and Art 16 of AP II state in relevant part: 'Without prejudice to the provisions of the Hague Convention for the Protection of Cultural Property in the Event of Armed Conflict of 14 May 1954 […]'. Article 53 of AP I continues 'and of other relevant international instruments'.

[29] *Official Records of the Diplomatic Conference on the Reaffirmation and Development of International Humanitarian Law Applicable in Armed Conflicts, Geneva (1974–1977)* (Bern: Federal Political Department, 1978), vol I, part I, 213 (*Records 1974–77*).

[30] CDDH/SR.53, para 4, *Records 1974–77*, vol VII, 142 (FRG).

[31] Civilian objects are defined negatively in Art 52(1) of AP I as those objects which are not military objectives as defined in Art 52(2) of AP I, namely 'objects which by their nature, location, purpose or use make an effective contribution to military action and whose total or partial destruction, capture or neutralization, in the circumstances ruling at the time, offers a definite military advantage'.

[32] See Art 51(4) and (5)(b) and Art 57 of AP I respectively.

[33] See Arts 27 and 56 of the Regulations concerning the Laws and Customs of War on Land, annexed to Convention concerning the Laws and Customs of War on Land, The Hague, 29 July 1899; Arts 27 ('buildings dedicated to religion, art, science, or charitable purposes, [and] historic monuments') and 56 ('institutions dedicated to religion, charity and education, the arts and sciences', plus 'historic monuments [and] works of art and science') of the Regulations concerning the Laws and Customs of War on Land, annexed to Convention concerning the Laws and Customs of War on Land, The Hague, 18 October 1907 ('1907 HR'); Art 5 ('sacred edifices, buildings used for artistic, scientific, or charitable purposes, [and] historic monuments') of the Convention concerning Bombardment by Naval Forces in Time of War, The Hague, 18 October 1907.

[34] See Art 6(1)(b)(ix) of the Protocol on Prohibitions or Restrictions on the Use of Mines, Booby-Traps and Other Devices to Convention on Prohibitions or Restrictions on the Use of Certain Conventional Weapons Which May be Deemed to be Excessively Injurious or to Have Indiscriminate Effects, Geneva, 10 October 1980; Art 7(1)(i) of the Amended Protocol on Prohibitions or Restrictions on the Use of Mines, Booby-Traps and Other Devices to Convention on Prohibitions or Restrictions

It also pays to note that the 1907 Hague Regulations laid down highly relevant and significant rules on the destruction and seizure of enemy property generally, as well as on pillage and on the rights and duties of an Occupying Power,[35] while the Fourth Geneva Convention does the same in respect of the destruction by an Occupying Power of 'real or personal property belonging individually or collectively to private persons, or to the State, or to other public authorities, or to social or co-operative organizations.'[36]

Alongside these various treaty provisions, a body of customary international humanitarian law, both *lex specialis* and *lex generalis*, serves to protect cultural property in armed conflict. Many of the relevant conventional rules, if not declaratory of custom when agreed, have come to reflect it in the period since, while others must now be interpreted in the light of later custom.

B. The fundamental rules

The foregoing bodies of law can be summed up in the following fundamental rules, which are not intended to be exhaustive and which can be divided into four sets.

(i) *Customary international law and the 1954 Hague Convention*

A first, core set of rules—all of which, unless otherwise stated, apply in international armed conflict, including belligerent occupation, and non-international armed conflict alike—apply, *qua* customary international law, among states not parties to any of the relevant treaties and between the government of such a state and any armed opposition group involved in a non-international armed conflict against it. They also apply, partly *qua* custom and treaty in parallel and partly *qua* custom alone, among the high contracting parties to the 1954 Hague Convention, whether or not they are also parties to the First or Second Protocol and/or to AP I and II, as well as between the government of a party to the Convention and any armed opposition

---

on the Use of Certain Conventional Weapons Which May be Deemed to be Excessively Injurious or to Have Indiscriminate Effects, Geneva, 3 May 1996. The relevant provisions speak of 'historic monuments, works of art or places of worship which constitute the cultural or spiritual heritage of peoples'. In other words, the property protected is identical to the property covered by Art 53 of AP I and Art 16 of AP II, which in turn is essentially the same as cultural property within the meaning of Art 1 of 1954 HC. In the last regard, see eg the Russian Federation's Declaration on Becoming Party to the Protocol on Prohibitions or Restrictions on the Use of Mines, Booby-Traps and Other Devices as Amended on 3 May 1996, 2 March 2005, 2308 UNTS 134, at § 3, which reads: 'For the purposes of interpreting subparagraph 1(i) of article 7, of Protocol II, the Russian Federation understands the cultural or spiritual heritage of peoples as cultural property in the terms of article 1 of the Convention for the Protection of Cultural Property in the Event of Armed Conflict of 1954.'

[35] See Arts 23(g), 28, 43, and 47 of 1907 HR.
[36] See Art 53 of the Convention Relative to the Protection of Civilian Persons in Time of War, Geneva, 12 August 1949 (GC IV).

group involved in a non-international armed conflict against it. All of these rules apply to cultural property as defined in the Convention, at the very least.[37]

As for what these rules are, to begin with it is prohibited to direct attacks[38] against cultural property unless by its nature, location, purpose, or use such property constitutes a military objective (that is, it makes an effective contribution to military action and its total or partial destruction, capture or neutralization, in the circumstances ruling at the time, offers a definite military advantage)[39] and there is no feasible alternative for obtaining a similar military advantage.[40] It is also illegal to attack a military objective, such as a tank, a military headquarters, or a munitions factory, if this cannot be done without inflicting on nearby cultural property damage which would be excessive in relation to the concrete and direct military advantage anticipated.[41] Wilful destruction or damage by a party to the conflict of or to cultural property under its control is forbidden too unless military necessity imperatively requires it.[42] Reprisals against cultural property are absolutely prohibited.[43] It is prohibited as well to make any use of cultural property likely to expose it to destruction or damage in the event of armed conflict unless there is no other feasible way to obtain a similar military advantage.[44] Next, all forms of theft, pillage, misappropriation, confiscation, or vandalism of cultural property are unlawful,[45] and parties to a conflict are required to prohibit, prevent and, if necessary, put a stop to all such

[37] In fact, the first four rules apply more broadly to historic monuments, works of art and the like *tout court.*

[38] The customary definition of the word 'attacks' comports with that in Art 49(1) of AP I, namely 'acts of violence against the adversary, whether in offence or defence'.

[39] The customary definition of a military objective accords with that in Art 52(2) of AP I as reproduced in, inter alia, Art 1(f) of SP: see eg *Prosecutor v Brđanin*, Trial Chamber, Judgment, IT-99-36-T, 1 September 2004, § 596 note 1509; *Western Front, Aerial Bombardment and Related Claims, Eritrea's Claims 1, 3, 5, 9–13, 14, 21, 25 & 26 (Eritrea/Ethiopia), Partial Award* (2005) 135 ILR 565 at 608, § 113; J.-M. Henckaerts and L. Doswald-Beck, *Customary International Humanitarian Law* vol 1 (Cambridge: Cambridge University Press, 2005), 29 (Rule 8).

[40] See Art 4(1) and (2) of 1954 HC (in light of subsequent customary international law), Art 6(a) of SP, the 'without prejudice' clauses of Art 53 of AP I and Art 16 of AP II, and customary international law. Consider also the associated precautions in attack mandated by Art 7(a) and (d)(i) of SP and Art 57(2)(a)(i) and (b) of AP I, which accord with customary international law in at least international armed conflict.

[41] See Art 7(c) and (d)(ii) of SP, Arts 51(4) and (5)(b) and 57(2)(a)(iii) and (b) of AP I, and customary international law. Consider also the associated precaution in attack mandated by Art 7(b) of SP, Art 57(2)(a)(ii) of AP I, and customary international law.

[42] See Art 4(1) and (2) of 1954 HC, Arts 23(g) and 56 of 1907 HR, Art 53 of GC IV, and customary international law.

[43] See Art 4(4) of 1954 HC, Art 53(c) of AP I, and customary international law.

[44] See Art 4(1) and (2) of 1954 HC, Art 6(b) of SP, the 'without prejudice' clauses of Art 53 of AP I and Art 16 of AP II, and customary international law.

[45] See Art 4(3) of 1954 HC, Art 56 of 1907 HR, and customary international law. For the same *a fortiori* reasoning as used to read a prohibition into Art 4(3) of 1954 HC, see *Application of the Convention on the Prevention and Punishment of the Crime of Genocide (Bosnia and Herzegovina v. Serbia and Montenegro), Merits, Judgment,* [2007] ICJ Rep 43 at 112, § 166 (*Application of the Genocide Convention*).

acts.[46] Parties to an international armed conflict are forbidden to seize or requisition cultural property situated in the territory of an opposing party.[47] In the event of the partial or total occupation of the territory of the opposing party in international armed conflict,[48] the Occupying Power must prohibit and prevent any illicit export, other removal or transfer of ownership of cultural property,[49] and must as far as possible support the competent authorities of the territory in safeguarding and preserving cultural property.[50]

When it comes to applying these rules, starting with the first, in the overwhelming majority of cases cultural property will not constitute a military objective, meaning that its intentional attack will generally be unlawful. But there are rare circumstances in which it may. Historic fortresses, barracks, arsenals and the like might be said by their nature to make an effective contribution to military action. That said, when decommissioned or used for purely ceremonial purposes they are better characterized as historic monuments, and when still in service they are better seen as contributing to military action through their use. Next, historic bridges, railway stations, docks, and other forms of civil infrastructure could conceivably make an effective contribution to military action via their purpose, which is defined as 'the future intended use of an object'.[51] Today, however, one might expect more modern transport links to bear most if not all of the military burden. The location of cultural property—that is, its position on the battlefield in relation to the positions of the opposing parties—could make an effective contribution to either's military action, for example by obstructing a line of sight or line of fire. But at least where a party has deliberately positioned itself so as to take advantage of the obstruction, the contribution to military action is better characterized as a function of the passive or *de facto* use of the cultural property. In practice, then, of the four bases on which an object is theoretically capable of constituting a military objective, it is its use to make an effective contribution to military action which will be the principal one by reference to which an attack against cultural property may be held to be lawful.[52]

---

[46] See Art 4(3) of 1954 HC and customary international law.

[47] See Art 4(3) of 1954 HC, Arts 23(g) and 56 of 1907 HR, and customary international law.

[48] Note that the concept of belligerent occupation is limited to international armed conflict.

[49] See para 1 of FP, Art 9(1)(a) of SP, and customary international law. See also Arts 2(2) and 11 of the Convention on the Means of Prohibiting and Preventing the Illicit Import, Export and Transfer of Ownership of Cultural Property, Paris, 14 November 1970. For the same *a fortiori* reasoning as used to read a prohibition into Art 9(1)(a) of SP, see again *Application of the Genocide Convention* (n 45), 112, para 166.

[50] See Art 5(1) of 1954 HC and customary international law.

[51] *Western Front, Aerial Bombardment and Related Claims* (n 39), 611, § 120, endorsing UK Ministry of Defence, *The Manual of the Law of Armed Conflict* (Oxford: Oxford University Press, 2004), 56, § 5.4.4, in turn endorsing Commentary AP I and II, 636, para 2022 ('intended future use').

[52] See eg the finding in *Prosecutor v Prlić, Stojić, Praljak, Petković, Ćorić and Pušić*, Trial Chamber, Judgment, IT-04-74-T, 29 May 2013, vol 3, § 1582 that, on account of its use by the adversary for reinforcement and resupply, the Old Bridge at Mostar constituted a military objective at the time of the attacked which destroyed it.

In terms of the prohibition on attacks against military objects that are likely to cause incidental damage which would be excessive in relation to the concrete and direct military advantage anticipated, the test is one of proportionality,[53] even if the word is not used; and although the assessment called for is not an exact science, it must be made in good faith. In its application to cultural property, proportionality implicates qualitative as much as quantitative factors. The extent of incidental loss likely to be occasioned by damage to or destruction of such property is a question not just of square or cubic metres but also of the cultural value represented thereby.[54] As for the qualified prohibition on wilful destruction of or damage to cultural property other than by way of attacks, imperative military necessity may justify demolitions in order to impede the progress of enemy columns, to clear a line of fire or to deny cover to enemy fighters, although the extent of the destruction will need to be calibrated to the degree of the military necessity. Turning, finally, to the use of cultural property in any manner likely to expose it to destruction or damage in the event of armed conflict, the qualified prohibition goes beyond the use of cultural property for hostile purposes to its *de facto* or passive use in any manner likely to draw fire on it. Examples include the deliberate interposition of cultural property in the line of fire, for example by retreating to a position obscured from the opposing party's view by a monument, and the effective incorporation of such property into a defensive line, as with the German 'Gustav line' around the abbey at Monte Cassino during World War II. Nor is it only use in combat that the rule prohibits. If it is foreseeable that the use of a protected building as a field headquarters or barracks, for example, will expose it to attack, such use is forbidden. Nor, indeed, need such use expose the property to attack for it to fall foul of the rule. The qualified prohibition is on any use likely to expose cultural property to damage during armed conflict, with the result that the likelihood of more than *de minimis* deterioration in the fabric of a monument, and *a fortiori* the risk of vandalism, through its use as a headquarters, barracks or the like is enough to render such use impermissible. It is important to note too that the rule prohibits the use of cultural property in any manner likely to expose it to damage or destruction 'in the event of armed conflict'. In other words, if its use in peacetime is likely to expose such property to attack on the outbreak of hostilities, it is not permitted.

---

[53] *Prosecutor v Galić*, Appeals Chamber, Judgment, IT-98-29-A, 30 November 2006, § 190.

[54] A textbook example of the application of the rule of proportionality came during the Gulf War in 1991, when Iraq positioned two fighter aircraft next to the world-renowned ancient ziggurat at Ur. Coalition commanders decided not to attack the aircraft 'on the basis of respect for cultural property and the belief that positioning of the aircraft adjacent to Ur (without servicing equipment or a runway nearby) effectively had placed each out of action, thereby limiting the value of their destruction by Coalition air forces when weighed against the risk of damage to the temple': US Department of Defense, 'Report to Congress on the Conduct of the Persian Gulf War—Appendix on the Role of the Law of War', 31 *ILM* (1992) 612 at 626.

Some of these rules have been enforced in the past by way of reparations provisions in post-war treaties. In the wake of World War I, Article 245 of the Treaty of Versailles compelled Germany to restore to France 'works of art carried away from France by the German authorities in the course of the war of 1870–1871 and during this last war', in accordance with a list prepared by the French government.[55] Similar terms were imposed on Austria by the Treaty of St Germain, on Hungary by the Treaty of Trianon, and on Bulgaria by the Treaty of Neuilly.[56] Restitution and, in the event that this was materially impossible, compensation were later obliged of the defeated European Axis states in respect of cultural property unlawfully removed from occupied territory during World War II, with the compensation payable by most of them being in kind.[57] In Italy's case, the obligation of restitution extended to cultural treasures taken during its post-World War I occupation of parts of what became Yugoslavia and during its later invasion of Ethiopia.[58] When it comes to the destruction of cultural property, compensation in kind was imposed on Germany by Article 247 of the Treaty of Versailles by way of reparation for its unlawful torching of the university library in Leuven (Louvain) and its devastation of other cultural property in Belgium during World War I.

As for enforcement of the relevant rules by international courts and tribunals, the Eritrea Ethiopia Claims Commission, having found Ethiopia responsible as Occupying Power for deliberate damage to a historic monument (the Stela of Matara) contrary to customary international law,[59] awarded Eritrea compensation equal to the sum spent restoring the stela 'plus an additional amount to reflect, in part, [its]

[55] Treaty of Peace between the Allied and Associated Powers and Germany, Versailles, 28 June 1919.

[56] See Arts 184 and 191 of the Treaty of Peace between the Allied and Associated Powers and Austria, St Germain-en-Laye, 10 September 1919; Arts 168 and 175 of the Treaty of Peace between the Allied and Associated Powers and Hungary, Trianon, 4 June 1920; Art 126 of the Treaty of Peace between the Allied and Associated Powers and Bulgaria, Neuilly-sur-Seine, 27 November 1919.

[57] See Art 22(1) and (3) of the Treaty of Peace with Bulgaria, Paris, 10 February 1947; Art 24(1) and (3) of the Treaty of Peace with Hungary, Paris, 10 February 1947; Art 75(1) and (9) of the Treaty of Peace with Italy, Paris, 10 February 1947. The reference to 'the United Nations Declaration of 5 January 1943' in the relevant provisions is to the Inter-Allied Declaration against Acts of Dispossession committed in Territories under Enemy Occupation or Control, 5 January 1943, Misc No 1 (1943), Cmd 6418, which names 'works of art' as the first example of property systematically spoliated by the Axis powers. See also, in terms of restitution, Art 24 of the Treaty of Peace with Finland, Paris, 10 February 1947 (restitution of historic monuments and museum valuables). For its part, the treaty between Germany and the United States, United Kingdom, and France (concluded two years before 1954 HC) refers in its restitutionary provisions to 'cultural property' *eo nomine*, defining this to comprise 'movable goods of religious, artistic, documentary, scholarly or historic value, or of equivalent importance, including objects customarily found in museums, public or private collections, libraries or historic archives': see Ch 5, Arts 1 and 2 of the Convention on the Settlement of Matters Arising out of the War and the Occupation, Bonn, 26 May 1952 (definition in Art 1(4)), as amended by Sch IV to the Protocol on the Termination of the Occupation Regime in the Federal Republic of Germany, Paris, 23 October 1954.

[58] See respectively Art 12(1) and (3) and Art 37 of the Treaty of Peace with Italy.

[59] See *Central Front, Eritrea's Claims 2, 4, 6, 7, 8 & 22* (n 27), 329–30, §§ 107–14. It went without saying in the Commission's discussion that the damage inflicted on the stela by way of an explosive fastened at its base by one or several soldiers of the Ethiopian army was not justified by military necessity.

unique cultural significance'.[60] At the national level, in response to an interim decision of the Supreme Court of Israel (sitting as the High Court of Justice) questioning its military necessity,[61] the commander of the Israel Defence Forces in the West Bank revised his original order for the demolition, with a view to preventing armed attacks by Palestinian militants, of 22 Ottoman and Mameluke buildings within the historic streetscape of the Old City of Hebron. Although eventually upholding as consonant with military necessity the destruction of a single building, the Court ruled that the demolition was to be supervised by an expert in the preservation of historic structures and an archaeologist, so as to salvage as much heritage value as possible.[62]

(ii) *The 1954 Hague Convention alone*

A second, supplementary set of rules—which go beyond customary international law and which apply only in international armed conflict and, where relevant, peacetime—are applicable, in respect of cultural property within the meaning of the Convention, only to and among the high contracting parties to the 1954 Hague Convention, again whether or not they are also parties to the Second Protocol and/ or to AP I and II. First, Parties to the Convention must prepare in time of peace, by taking such measures as they consider appropriate, for the safeguarding of cultural property situated within their own territory against the foreseeable effects of armed conflict.[63] Measures of this sort may include (and, where the party in question is also party to the Second Protocol, 'shall include, as appropriate'[64]) the preparation of inventories, the planning of emergency measures for protection against fire or structural collapse, the preparation for the removal of movable cultural property, or the provision for it of adequate *in situ* protection, and the designation of authorities responsible for the safeguarding of cultural property. Secondly, parties to the Convention must plan or establish in peacetime services or specialist personnel within their armed forces responsible for securing respect for cultural property and for co-operating with the civilian authorities responsible for safeguarding it,[65] whether the latter be the authorities of their own state or, in the case of occupied territory, of the displaced state.

(iii) *The Second Protocol to the 1954 Hague Convention alone*

Over and above the preceding sets of rules, certain rules apply, in respect of cultural property within the meaning of the Convention, only among parties to the Second Protocol (which, it will be recalled, must also be parties to the Convention) and,

---

[60] *Final Award, Eritrea's Damages Claims (Eritrea/Ethiopia)* (2009) 140 ILR 235 at 319, § 223.
[61] *Hess v Commander of the IDF in the West Bank*, HCJ 10356/02, Interim Decision, 12 February 2003.
[62] *Hess v Commander of the IDF in the West Bank* (2004) 58(3) Piskei Din 443.
[63] Article 3 of 1954 HC.   [64] Article 5 of SP.   [65] Article 7(2) of 1954 HC.

where relevant, between the government of a party to the Second Protocol and any armed opposition group involved in a non-international armed conflict against it. Parties to a conflict to which the Second Protocol applies must, to the maximum extent feasible, remove cultural property from the vicinity of military objectives or provide for adequate protection *in situ*,[66] and they must avoid locating military objectives near cultural property.[67] Next, parties to the Second Protocol must prohibit and prevent any archaeological excavation in territory occupied by them, save where this is strictly required to safeguard, record, or preserve cultural property.[68] The same obligation of prohibition and prevention applies in respect of occupied territory, although obviously without the exception, to any alteration to, or change of use of, cultural property which is intended to conceal or destroy cultural, historical, or scientific evidence.[69] In addition, parties to a conflict to which the Second Protocol applies owe certain special obligations towards cultural property placed under Chapter 2's select regime of 'enhanced' protection. They are prohibited from attacking such property unless by its use, and use alone, it becomes a military objective and the attack is the only feasible means of terminating such use.[70] All acts of hostility against cultural property under enhanced protection other than attacks, such as its demolition even for military ends, are absolutely forbidden.[71] Conversely, parties to a conflict to which the Second Protocol applies are absolutely forbidden from using cultural property under enhanced protection in support of military action.[72]

(iv) *AP I and AP II alone*

Finally, in the rare event that a state is party to AP I, AP II, or both but not to the 1954 Hague Convention, and *a fortiori* not to its Second Protocol, the obligations it owes, in international and non-international armed conflict respectively, as regards the cultural property covered by Article 53 of AP I and Article 16 of AP II will in three main[73] respects be higher, paradoxically, than if it were party to the specialist regime. States parties to AP I and II on their own are prohibited from attacking cultural property unless by its use, and use alone, it becomes a military objective;[74]

---

[66] Article 8(a) of SP. Consider also Art 58(a) and (c) of AP I.   [67] Article 8(b) of SP.
[68] Article 9(1)(b) of SP.   [69] Article 9(1)(c) of SP.
[70] Articles 12 and 13(1)(b) and (2)(a) of SP. Given, however, that its use to military ends is by far the chief reason in practice why specific cultural property might constitute a military objective, the difference between the baseline level of protection from attack afforded to all cultural property and the protection afforded in this respect to cultural property under enhanced protection is not, in substance, great.
[71] Article 12 of SP, read in the light of the wording of Art 4(1) of 1954 HC ('any act of hostility directed against').
[72] Article 12 of SP.
[73] Consider also the precautions in attack mandated in respect of all civilian objects by Art 58(a) and (c) of AP I.
[74] Article 53(a) of AP I in combination with Art 52(2) of AP I and Art 16 of AP II in combination with customary international law.

they are absolutely prohibited from engaging in any other act of hostility against cultural property, including its demolition for military purposes;[75] and they are absolutely prohibited from using cultural property in support of the military effort.[76] In other words, where a state is party to AP I and II alone, the obligations it owes in respect of the cultural property covered by those instruments—which is equivalent to all cultural property within the meaning of the Convention—are in substance the same as those owed by parties to the Convention and Second Protocol only in respect of the select range of cultural property under enhanced protection.

C. The institutional framework

The application of the 1954 Hague Convention brings with it an institutional regime. The Convention and its Regulations provide for an elaborate and cumbersome international system of 'control', meaning implementation and compliance, in the event of an international armed conflict to which the Convention applies,[77] although it has proved a white elephant,[78] and is hardly worth mentioning. Of more practical relevance is the right of initiative granted to UNESCO in both international and non-international armed conflict,[79] which by default has come to serve as a compliance mechanism.[80] Conversely, the high contracting parties may seek technical assistance from UNESCO in organizing the protection of cultural property or in connection with any other problem arising out of the application of the Convention or its Regulations.[81] In addition, the parties must submit to the Organization's Director-General periodic reports on their implementation of the Convention and its Regulations,[82] supposedly every four years but in practice when UNESCO requests them. The Convention further provides for meetings of the parties,[83] which, while taking place only once prior to 1995, have now become a biennial fixture.

---

[75] Article 53(a) of AP I and Art 16 of AP II.   [76] Article 53(b) of AP I and Art 16 of AP II.
[77] See Art 20 of 1954 HC and Ch I Regs.
[78] In no international armed conflict to which 1954 HC has applied has the unwieldy and impracticable control regime laid down in Ch I Regs been implemented in whole. Indeed, in only a single such conflict (the Six Day War of 1967) has any provision of Ch I Regs been invoked, and even then only dysfunctionally.
[79] See respectively Arts 23(2) and 19(3) of 1954 HC.
[80] UNESCO has also acted pursuant to the general mandate conferred on it by Art I(2)(c) of the Constitution of the United Nations Educational, Scientific and Cultural Organisation, London, 16 November 1945, namely to assure 'the conservation and protection of the world's inheritance of books, works of art and monuments of history and science', to urge member states of the Organization to act in accordance with the provisions of 1954 HC, by which it has meant the fundamental obligations of respect for cultural property embodied in Art 4 of 1954 HC, in conflicts to which they have not in fact applied.
[81] See Art 23(1) of 1954 HC.   [82] See Art 26(2) of 1954 HC.
[83] See Art 27 of 1954 HC. As of 15 March 2011, eight such meetings had taken place.

Even if it has not abolished the Convention's effectively defunct control regime, the Second Protocol creates a new institutional framework to facilitate and supervise *inter partes* the protection of cultural property in armed conflict.[84] This framework comprises an intergovernmental Committee for the Protection of Cultural Property in the Event of Armed Conflict, whose tasks include the grant of enhanced protection to eligible cultural property via its inclusion in the List of Cultural Property under Enhanced Protection;[85] a centralized Fund for the Protection of Cultural Property in the Event of Armed Conflict;[86] and a biennial Meeting of the Parties,[87] to which the Committee reports on the implementation of the Protocol. In 2009, in accordance with the Protocol,[88] the third Meeting of the Parties endorsed both the Guidelines for the Implementation of the Second Protocol and the Guidelines concerning the use of the Fund, each prepared by the Committee.[89] The Second Protocol also incorporates obligations relating to international cooperation and assistance.[90] UNESCO is once more granted a right of initiative in both types of armed conflict,[91] and the parties may seek technical assistance from it in organizing the protection of cultural property or in connection with any other problem arising out of the application of the Protocol.[92] Finally, parties to the Second Protocol are required to submit periodic reports on their implementation of the Protocol,[93] although to the Committee, not to the Director-General of UNESCO as under the Convention.

As for the Additional Protocols to the Geneva Conventions, these are the province of the International Committee of the Red Cross and, in relation to international armed conflicts between parties accepting its competence, of the International Fact-Finding Commission provided for in Article 90 of AP I.

---

[84] See Ch 6 of SP.

[85] See Arts 24–27 of SP. Consider also the relations between the Committee and non-governmental organizations—among them the International Committee of the Blue Shield (ICBS), the International Centre for the Study of the Preservation and Restoration of Cultural Property (Rome Centre/ICCROM), and the International Committee of the Red Cross (ICRC)—envisaged in Art 11(3) and especially Art 27(3) of SP. As of 13 August 2013, the Committee had held seven ordinary meetings and one extraordinary meeting.

[86] See Art 29 of SP.

[87] See Art 23 of SP. As of 15 March 2011, there had been three Meetings of the Parties to SP.

[88] See Arts 23(3)(b) and (c), 27(1)(a), and 29(3) of SP.

[89] See Guidelines for the Implementation of the 1999 Second Protocol to the Hague Convention of 1954 for the Protection of Cultural Property in the Event of Armed Conflict, UNESCO Doc CLT-09/CONF/219/3 REV.3, 24 November 2009, and Guidelines concerning the Use of the Fund for the Protection of Cultural Property in the Event of Armed Conflict, UNESCO Doc CLT-09/CONF/219/4 REV, 24 November 2009.

[90] See respectively Arts 31 and 32 of SP.   [91] See Art 33(3) of SP.   [92] See Art 33(1) of SP.

[93] See Art 37(2) of SP.

3 International Human Rights Law

International human rights law does not cease to apply in armed conflict,[94] although, where both international human rights law and international humanitarian law apply to the same conduct, the question whether the state to which the conduct is attributable has acquitted its international human rights obligations is to be determined by reference to the standard laid down in the relevant rule of international humanitarian law.[95] Furthermore, an Occupying Power is obliged—by virtue of the customary rule on the obligations of a belligerent occupant codified in Article 43 of the 1907 Hague Regulations—to ensure, as far as possible, that the competent national authorities respect any international human rights treaties to which the displaced Power may be party.[96] There are a number of international human rights relevant to the protection of cultural property in armed conflict.[97] The most generally applicable of these is Article 15(1)(a) of the International Covenant on Economic, Social and Cultural Rights (ICESCR),[98] guaranteeing the right of everyone to take part in cultural life.[99]

Article 15(1)(a) of the ICESCR imposes on states parties an obligation to '[r]espect and protect cultural heritage in all its forms, in times of war and peace', in the words

[94] There may, however, be separate questions in any given instance as to the scope of application *ratione loci* of the relevant human rights treaty and as to derogation from the right in question. For a fuller account, see the Chapter by D. Jinks in this volume.

[95] See *Legality of the Threat or Use of Nuclear Weapons, Advisory Opinion*, [1996] ICJ Rep 226 at 240, § 25; *Legal Consequences of the Construction of a Wall in the Occupied Palestinian Territory, Advisory Opinion*, [2004] ICJ Rep 136 at 177–8, §§ 104–6 ('*The Wall Case*'); *Armed Activities on the Territory of the Congo (Democratic Republic of the Congo v Uganda), Judgment*, [2005] ICJ Rep 168 at 242–3, § 216 (*Armed Activities*).

[96] *Armed Activities* (n 95), 231, § 178.

[97] In addition to the right discussed in detail below, consider eg the rights of minorities and indigenous peoples.

[98] New York, 16 December 1966, 993 UNTS 3 ('ICESCR'). In *The Wall Case* (n 95), 180, § 112, the ICJ considered it 'not to be excluded' that the ICESCR 'applies both to territories over which a State party has sovereignty and to those over which that State exercises territorial jurisdiction', the latter including territories under that party's belligerent occupation, and it held in the event that the Covenant applied to Israel's conduct in the Occupied Palestinian Territory. See also *Armed Activities* (n 95), 243, § 216 ('The Court further concluded [in *The Wall Case*] that international human rights instruments are applicable "in respect of acts done by a State in the exercise of its jurisdiction outside its own territory", particularly in occupied territories [...]'). The nature of a state party's obligations under the ICESCR is one of progressive realization to the maximum of that party's available resources, as per Art 2(1) of ICESCR. This may have a bearing on the measures required of a party to acquit its positive duty to protect cultural property from vandalism and theft, although it does not affect the negative obligation to refrain from wilfully destroying such property.

[99] Article 15(1)(a) of ICESCR embodies in binding form 'the right freely to participate in the cultural life of the community' recognized in Art 27 of the Universal Declaration of Human Rights, UNGA Res 217A (III), 10 December 1948.

of General Comment No 21 of the Committee on Economic, Social and Cultural Rights,[100] the relevant treaty-monitoring body. This obligation encompasses a duty to protect such property from vandalism and theft,[101] as well as a prohibition on its intentional destruction,[102] the link between the latter and Article 15 of the Covenant being underlined by the United Nations Human Rights Council in its Resolution 6/11 of 28 September 2007, entitled 'Protection of cultural heritage as an important component of the promotion and protection of cultural rights'. The Human Rights Council has further made clear that Article 15 of the ICESCR is applicable during armed conflict. In its Resolution 6/1 of 27 September 2007 ('Protection of cultural rights and property in situations of armed conflict'), the Council, '[a]cknowledging that human rights law and international humanitarian law are complementary and mutually reinforcing' and '[r]eaffirming that the destruction of or any other form of damage to cultural property may impair the enjoyment of cultural rights, in particular of article 15 of the International Covenant on Economic, Social and Cultural Rights', emphasized 'that protection of cultural property during armed conflicts can contribute to the full enjoyment of the right of everyone to take part in cultural life'.[103] Less specifically, in a series of resolutions, the Human Rights Council, reiterating 'that international human rights law and international humanitarian law are complementary and mutually reinforcing', has demanded 'that the occupying Power, Israel, stop [...] the systematic destruction of the cultural heritage of the Palestinian people'; has condemned 'the disrespect of the religious and cultural rights provided for in core human rights instruments and humanitarian law by the occupying Power, Israel, in the Occupied Palestinian Territory, including al-Haram al Ibrahimi in Hebron and Bilal Mosque ("Tomb of Rachel") in Bethlehem and the walls of the old city of Jerusalem, which are on its list of national heritage sites'; has expressed grave concern 'at the excavation of ancient tombs [...] [in] part of the historic Ma'man Allah (Mamila) Cemetery in the holy city of Jerusalem'; and has further demanded 'that Israel, the occupying Power, immediately cease all diggings and excavation works beneath and around Al-Aqsa mosque compound and other religious sites in the old city of Jerusalem, and refrain from any act that may endanger the structure or foundations or change the nature of the holy sites, both Islamic and Christian, in the Occupied Palestinian Territory, particularly in and around Jerusalem'.[104]

---

[100] Committee on Economic, Social and Cultural Rights, *General Comment No 21: Right of everyone to take part in cultural life (art. 15, para. 1(a), of the International Covenant on Economic, Social and Cultural Rights)*, UN Doc E/C.12/GC/21, 21 December 2009, para 50(a).

[101] See eg UN Docs E/1993/22, para 186 and E/CN.4/1994/73, paras 118–22.

[102] See eg UN Doc E/1995/22, para 136.

[103] UNHRC Res 6/1, 27 September 2007, at preamble (fifth and eighth recitals) and para 4 respectively.

[104] UNHRC Res 16/29, 25 March 2011, at preamble (eighth recital) and paras 4, 5, 7, and 8 respectively, echoing UNHRC Res 13/8, 24 March 2010, at preamble (eighth recital) and paras 3, 4, and 7, UNHRC Res S-9/1, 12 January 2009, at preamble (seventh recital) and para 5, UNHRC Res 10/19, 26 March 2009, paras 3 and 4, and UNHRC Res S-12/1A, 16 October 2009, para 4.

4 INTERNATIONAL CULTURAL HERITAGE LAW

In Article 2(2) of the Convention on the Means of Prohibiting and Preventing the Illicit Import, Export and Transfer of Ownership of Cultural Property, concluded in 1970 under the auspices of UNESCO, states parties undertake to oppose the illicit import, export, and transfer of ownership of movable cultural property with the means at their disposal. Article 3 states that the import, export, or transfer of ownership of cultural property 'effected contrary to the provisions adopted under [the] Convention by the States Parties thereto' shall be illicit; and, more specifically, Article 11 provides that the export and transfer of ownership of cultural property 'under compulsion arising directly or indirectly from the occupation of a country by a foreign power' shall be regarded as illicit. For the purposes of the Convention, the term 'cultural property' is defined in Article 1 to mean 'property which, on religious or secular grounds, is specifically designated by each State as being of importance for archaeology, prehistory, history, literature, art or science' and which belongs to one of the categories of movables listed in subparagraphs (a) to (k) of the provision. Articles 6 to 10 of the Convention impose on states parties a range of measures in pursuance of the general obligation laid down in Article 2(2), and, in accordance with Article 17(4), UNESCO may, on its own initiative, make proposals to the parties for the Convention's implementation. The Convention plays a central role in legal attempts to combat the import, export, and transfer of ownership of cultural property misappropriated during armed conflict, including belligerent occupation.[105]

Each state party to the UNESCO-sponsored Convention concerning the Protection of the World Cultural and Natural Heritage 1972 (World Heritage Convention) recognizes in Article 4 its 'duty of ensuring the [...] protection, conservation, presentation, and transmission to future generations' of the cultural heritage situated in its territory, and undertakes to 'do all it can to this end'. Each party further recognizes in Article 6(1) that 'such heritage constitutes a world heritage for whose protection it is the duty of the international community as a whole to co-operate', and undertakes in Article 6(3) 'not to take any deliberate measures which might damage directly or indirectly the cultural and natural heritage [...] situated on the territory of other States Parties to [the] Convention'. The term 'cultural heritage' is defined in Article 1 to mean monuments, groups of buildings and sites—in other words, immovable cultural property—'of outstanding universal value' from a cultural

---

[105] For consideration of the 1970 UNESCO Convention in this context, see *Autocephalous Greek-Orthodox Church of Cyprus and the Republic of Cyprus v Goldberg and Feldman Fine Arts, Inc*, ILR 108 (1990) 488 at 507–9, which concerned four Byzantine mosaics illicitly removed from the Kanakaria church in the Turkish-occupied north of Cyprus. (Note, however, that the assertion of Cudahy, Circuit

point of view; and, in practice, the obligations imposed by Articles 4 and 6(3) of the Convention apply to all cultural heritage inscribed on the World Heritage List in accordance with Article 11(2), included in a so-called 'tentative list' submitted in accordance with Article 11(1) by the state party in the territory of which it is situated, or otherwise identified and delineated by that party in accordance with Article 3.[106] No provision states that the Convention is inapplicable in situations of armed conflict. On the contrary, Article 11(4) includes 'the outbreak [...] of an armed conflict' as one reason justifying the inscription of an item of the world cultural heritage on the List of World Heritage in Danger, and the World Heritage Committee— the treaty body charged with a range of tasks in relation to the Convention—has placed on the List a number of sites threatened by armed conflict.[107] In this light, and especially in view of 'the repeated requests of UNESCO [to the belligerents] to observe the obligations of the Convention'[108] during the war in Croatia in 1991, one can conclude that Articles 4 and 6(3) of the Convention apply not only during peacetime but also during armed conflict, the latter encompassing both hostilities and belligerent occupation.[109] By analogy, however, with the relationship between international humanitarian law and international human rights law, whether a party to the Convention has complied with the instrument's provisions in armed conflict is to be assessed by reference to the standards laid down in the applicable rules of international humanitarian law.

5 International Criminal Law

Alongside rules the breach of which gives rise to state responsibility has evolved a body of international law capable of holding criminally accountable individuals responsible for the unlawful destruction, damage, and misappropriation of cultural

Judge, at 508, that 1954 HC 'applies to international trafficking during peacetime in cultural property unlawfully seized during an armed conflict' is plainly mistaken.)

[106] See Art 12 of WHC. See also eg *Queensland v Commonwealth of Australia*, ILR 90 (1988) 115 at 129–30 (Mason CJ, Brennan, Deane, Toohey, Gaudron, and McHugh JJ) and esp at 134 (Dawson J).

[107] See the respective inscriptions on the List of World Heritage in Danger of World Heritage sites in Croatia (1991), Afghanistan (2002 and 2003), Iraq (2003), Mali (2012), and Syria (2013).

[108] *World Heritage Committee, Fifteenth Session (Carthage, 9–13 December 1991)*, UNESCO Doc SC-91/CONF.002/15, 12 December 1991, para 29. Consider also *Strugar*, Trial Chamber Judgment (n 27), § 279, where the ICTY, referring to Dubrovnik and the attack against it on 6 December 1991, stated: 'The Old Town is also legally distinct from the rest of the wider city because the Old Town, in its entirety including the medieval walls, enjoys a World Heritage listing and the protections and immunities that are consequent on that listing.'

[109] As regards belligerent occupation, the Old City of Jerusalem and its walls were placed on the List of World Heritage in Danger in 1982. In Decision 35 COM 7A.22, para 18, the World Heritage

property in armed conflict. Such accountability is provided for under the respective rubrics of war crimes and crimes against humanity.[110] A general condition of both is that they be committed with intent and knowledge.[111]

A. War crimes

There is a range of both customary and treaty-based offences to which acts of hostility against and misappropriation of cultural property in armed conflict may give rise. Some of these are expressed in terms applicable to all civilian objects,[112] to undefended places and buildings,[113] to 'the enemy's property' or the like,[114] or to all property,[115] while others pertain to cultural property as such, even if the term itself may not be used. The former are as significant as the latter for the protection of cultural property in armed conflict.[116] Take, for example, the war crimes of 'plunder of public or private property' and 'devastation not justified by military necessity' over which Article 6(b) of the Charter of the International Military Tribunal at

---

Committee reaffirmed that no measures were to be taken in relation to the Old City of Jerusalem and its walls that were 'in contravention [of] the relevant provisions of the Hague Convention for the Protection of Cultural Property in the Event of Armed Conflict of 1954 and of the Convention for the Protection of the World Cultural and Natural Heritage of 1972'. See *Decisions adopted by the World Heritage Committee at its 35th Session (UNESCO, 2011)*, UNESCO Doc WHC-11/35.COM/20 (2011), 31–3. This more explicit reaffirmation of a series of previous resolutions was itself reiterated in Decision 36 COM 7A.23.II, para 8: see *Decisions adopted by the World Heritage Committee at its 36th Session (St Petersburg, 2012)*, UNESCO Doc WHC-12/36.COM/19 (2012), 34–6.

[110] Note that the law of war crimes, the latter term referring to those violations of the law of armed conflict which implicate the criminal responsibility of individuals, is as much a part of international humanitarian law as it is of international criminal law, and could, if it were wished, be treated under that heading. Crimes against humanity, on the other hand, form part of international criminal law alone. Note also that, although speculative academic reference is sometimes made to 'cultural genocide', the crime of genocide does not extend under positive international law to acts of hostility against and plunder of cultural property, whether in armed conflict or peacetime: see *Prosecutor v Krstić*, Appeals Chamber, Judgment, IT-98-33-A, 19 April 2004, §§ 25–6, affirming *Prosecutor v Krstić*, Trial Chamber, Judgment, IT-98-33-T, 2 August 2001, § 580; *Application of the Genocide Convention* (n 45), 185–6, § 344. At the same time, '[t]he destruction of culture may serve evidentially to confirm an intent, to be gathered from other circumstances, to destroy the group as such': *Krstić*, Appeals Chamber Judgment, partial diss op Shahabuddeen, § 53, endorsing *Krstić*, Trial Chamber Judgment (n 110), § 580; *Application of the Genocide Convention*, 186, § 344.

[111] See eg Art 30 of the Rome Statute of the International Criminal Court, Rome, 17 July 1998 (Statute of the International Criminal Court).

[112] See eg Art 8(2)(b)(ii) and (iv) of the Statute of the International Criminal Court.

[113] See eg Art 3(c) of the Statute of the International Criminal Tribunal for the former Yugoslavia, UN Doc S/25704, 3 May 1993, Annex (as amended) (ICTY); Art 8(2)(b)(v) of the Statute of the International Criminal Court.

[114] See eg Art 8(2)(b)(xiii) and (e)(xii) of the Statute of the International Criminal Court.

[115] See eg Arts 2(d) and 3(b) and (e) of ICTY; Art 8(2)(a)(iv), (b)(xvi), and (e)(v) and (xii) of the Statute of the International Criminal Court.

[116] In addition to the cases mentioned in the text, see *Prosecutor v MP et al*, Zadar District Court, K 74/96, 24 July 1997, in which 19 persons were convicted *in absentia* of war crimes in violation of, inter

Nuremberg[117] granted the Tribunal jurisdiction. Several of the major German war criminals were convicted of these offences by the Tribunal for their roles in the systematic emptying and razing during World War II of the galleries, museums, libraries, and historic buildings and sites of occupied Poland and the Soviet Union, as well as in the Europe-wide seizure of private Jewish-owned collections, contrary to, among other rules, the customary prohibition reflected in Article 56 of the 1907 Hague Regulations.[118] Almost 60 years later, in *Prlić*, Bosnian Croat forces were held by the ICTY to have committed the war crime of 'devastation not justified by military necessity', triable under Article 3(b) of the Tribunal's Statute, in relation to their destruction of eleven Ottoman mosques in Mostar and Stolac and of the Ottoman Old Bridge ('*Stari Most*') from which the former town takes its name.[119] The destruction of the Sultan Selim mosque in Stolac was additionally held to constitute the grave breach of the Fourth Geneva Convention, triable under Article 2(d) of the ICTY Statute,[120] of 'extensive destruction [...] of property, not justified by military necessity and carried out unlawfully and wantonly'.[121]

When it comes to war crimes specifically relating to cultural property, contemporary customary international law embodies individual criminal responsibility for,[122] and the Rome Statute of the International Criminal Court grants the

alia, Art 25 of 1907 HR—prohibiting the 'attack or bombardment, by whatever means', of undefended places or buildings—for their roles in the bombardment of the historic centre of Zadar in 1991, including the deliberate targeting of the pre-Romanesque church of Saint Donatius and the Romanesque cathedral of Saint Anastasia.

[117] Charter of the International Military Tribunal, annexed to Agreement by the Government of the United Kingdom of Great Britain and Northern Ireland, the Government of the United States of America, the Provisional Government of the French Republic and the Government of the Union of Soviet Socialist Republics for the Prosecution and Punishment of the Major War Criminals of the European Axis, London, 8 August 1945.

[118] See Judgment of the International Military Tribunal for the Trial of German Major War Criminals, Nuremberg, 30 September and 1 October 1946, Misc No 12 (1946), Cmd 6964, reproduced in 41 *American Journal of International Law* (1947) 172–333 (Nuremberg Judgment), esp 237–8, 287, and 330. Chief among the perpetrators was Alfred Rosenberg, head of the Einsatzstab Rosenberg, the special corps created by Hitler and mandated with the plunder of the public artworks and antiquities of Central and Eastern Europe, including the Soviet Union, and of private Jewish-owned collections across the continent.

[119] See *Prlić et al*, Trial Chamber Judgment (n 52), vol 3, §§ 1579–87 and 1590–1. In the event, in accordance with the ICTY's approach to cumulative convictions, the accused were convicted on these accounts solely of the overlapping but more specific war crime, constituted by the same acts, of 'destruction or wilful damage done to institutions dedicated to religion' under Art 3(d) of ICTY. The Trial Chamber's decision in this regard appears to have overlooked the Old Bridge at Mostar, the destruction of which was not pleaded (or at least, in one instance, was not adequately pleaded) under Art 3(d) of ICTY.

[120] See also Art 8(2)(a)(iv) of the Statute of the International Criminal Court.

[121] See *Prlić et al*, Trial Chamber Judgment (n 52), vol 3, §§ 1548–9.

[122] See, inter alia, *Strugar*, Trial Chamber Judgment (n 27), §§ 229–30; *Prosecutor v Hadžihasanović and Kubura*, Appeals Chamber, Decision on Joint Defence Interlocutory Appeal of Trial Chamber Decision on Rule 98*bis* Motions for Acquittal, IT-01-47-AR73.3, 11 March 2005, §§ 44–8; *Prosecutor*

Court jurisdiction over,[123] directing attacks against cultural property in the broad sense of the term,[124] whether in international or non-international armed conflict, unless such property constitutes a military objective. As made clear by the Appeals Chamber of the ICTY in *Strugar*, upholding the accused's conviction for his role in the bombardment of the Old Town of Dubrovnik on 6 December 1991,[125] this responsibility is distinct from that recognized for unlawfully directing attacks against a civilian object,[126] a species of which cultural property *prima facie* constitutes, even if the requisite material and mental elements of the two offences are, *mutatis mutandis*, the same. Acts of hostility against cultural property other than attacks, such as its demolition by the planting of explosives or by bulldozers, jackhammers, or other wrecking equipment, have been prosecuted before the ICTY, alongside attacks, under Article 3(d) of its Statute, which vests the Tribunal with jurisdiction over the war crime of 'destruction or wilful damage done to institutions dedicated to religion, charity and education, the arts and sciences, historic monuments and works of art and science', a provision treated as applicable to international and non-international armed conflict alike.[127] The accused in *Blaškić, Kordić, Naletilić, Brđanin*, and *Prlić* were all convicted on this count of acts of this nature not justified by military necessity, while the accused in *Plavšić* pleaded guilty, and those in *Hadžihasanović* were acquitted, in respect of the same.[128] Article 3(d) of

---

v Brdanin, Appeals Chamber, Judgment, IT-99-36-A, 3 April 2007, § 337; *Prlić et al*, Trial Chamber Judgment (n 52), vol 1, §§ 171–8 and vol 3, §§ 1579–87.

[123] See Art 8(2)(b)(ix) and (e)(iv) of the Statute of the International Criminal Court. When opening her investigation into the situation in Mali, the ICC Prosecutor identified a reasonable basis to believe that the war crime of intentionally directing attacks against, inter alia, buildings dedicated to religion and historic monuments contrary to the laws and customs applicable in non-international armed conflict, as triable under Art 8(2)(e)(iv) of the Statute of the International Criminal Court, had been committed in the course of the armed conflict in Mali by members of the organized armed groups Ansar Dine, AQIM, and possibly also MUJAO. The acts in question comprise the premeditated destruction of nine mausoleums and two mosques on the World Heritage List, along with two other historic monuments, in the city of Timbuktu. See Office of the Prosecutor, *Situation in Mali: Article 53(1) Report*, 16 January 2003, §§ 7, 109–13, 154–60, and 173.

[124] By this is meant not just cultural property as defined in Art 1 1954 of HC but rather all 'institutions dedicated to religion, charity and education, the arts and sciences, historic monuments and works of art and science', in the words of Art 3(d) of ICTY, or, in the words of Art 8(2)(b)(ix) and (e) (iv) of the Statute of the International Criminal Court, all 'buildings dedicated to religion, education, art, science or charitable purposes, [and] historic monuments'.

[125] The accused in *Prosecutor v Jokić*, Trial Chamber, Sentencing Judgment, IT-01-42/1-S, 18 March 2004, pleaded guilty in respect of the same attack.

[126] See *Prosecutor v Strugar*, Appeals Chamber, Judgment, IT-01-42-A, 17 July 2008, § 277.

[127] The Statute of the International Criminal Court, for its part, treats those criminal acts of hostility against cultural property not amounting to attacks under more general rubrics: see Art (2)(a)(iv), (b) (xiii), and (e)(xii) of the Statute of the International Criminal Court.

[128] See *Prosecutor v Blaškić*, Trial Chamber, Judgment, IT-95-14-T, 3 March 2000, one count being vacated in *Prosecutor v Blaškić*, Appeals Chamber, Judgment, IT-95-14-A, 29 July 2004, § 533; *Prosecutor v Kordić and Čerkez*, Trial Chamber, Judgment, IT-95-14/2-T, 26 February 2001, one count being overturned in *Kordić and Čerkez*, Appeals Chamber Judgment (n 27) § 471; *Prosecutor v Naletilić and Martinović*, Trial

the ICTY Statute also grants the Tribunal jurisdiction over the war crime, whether in international or non-international armed conflict, of 'seizure of [...] institutions dedicated to religion, charity and education, the arts and sciences, historic monuments and works of art and science'.[129]

As regards treaty-based war crimes, each of the 1954 Hague Convention, AP I and the Second Protocol contains a provision or provisions on individual criminal responsibility for, variously, acts of hostility against and misappropriation of cultural property in armed conflict, although none of these has yet served as a basis for prosecution in national or international proceedings, and none is likely ever to play a significant role. Article 28 of the 1954 Hague Convention requires the High Contracting Parties 'to take, within the framework of their ordinary criminal jurisdiction, all necessary steps to prosecute and impose penal or disciplinary sanctions upon those persons, of whatever nationality, who commit or order to be committed a breach of the [...] Convention'. It is unclear whether this provision is applicable only to international armed conflict or to non-international armed conflict as well.[130] War crimes within the meaning of Article 28 of the Convention fall within the jurisdiction of the Extraordinary Chambers in the Courts of Cambodia,[131] mandated to try the remnants of the Khmer Rouge leadership, but no charges have been laid on this basis. Next, Article 85(4)(d) of AP I, applicable only to international armed conflict, defines as a grave breach of the Protocol, with the various consequences that this entails:

making the clearly-recognized historic monuments, works of art or places of worship which constitute the cultural or spiritual heritage of peoples and to which special protection has been given by special arrangement, for example, within the framework of a competent international organization, the object of attack, causing as a result extensive destruction thereof,

---

Chamber, Judgment, IT-98-34-T, 31 March 2003; *Brđanin*, Trial Chamber Judgment (n 122); *Prosecutor v Plavšić*, Trial Chamber, Sentencing Judgment, IT-00-39&40/1-S, 27 February 2003; *Prosecutor v. Hadžihasanović and Kubura*, Trial Chamber, Judgment, IT-01-47-T, 15 March 2006; *Prlić et al*, Trial Chamber Judgment (n 52), in relation to the Baba Besir mosque in Mostar and the Sultan Selim mosque in Stolac. See also, not dissimilarly, the post-World War II case of *Trial of Karl Lingenfelder* (1947) 9 Law Reports of Trials of War Criminals 67 (French Permanent Military Tribunal at Metz).

[129] The Statute of the International Criminal Court again treats such war crimes under more general headings: see Art 8(2)(a)(iv), (b)(xiii) and (xvi), and (e)(v) and (xii) of the Statute of the International Criminal Court.

[130] The UN's Group of Experts for Cambodia established pursuant to UNGA Res 52/135, 12 December 1997, suggested not very helpfully that breaches of 1954 HC committed during non-international armed conflict 'perhaps' give rise to individual criminal responsibility: UN Doc A/53/850-S/1999/231, 16 March 1999, Annex, § 76.

[131] See Art 7 of the Law on the Establishment of Extraordinary Chambers in the Courts of Cambodia for the Prosecution of Crimes Committed During the Period of Democratic Kampuchea, as amended 27 October 2004, Doc NS/RKM/1004/006, read in combination with Art 2 of the Agreement between the United Nations and the Royal Government of Cambodia concerning the prosecution under Cambodian law of crimes committed during the period of Democratic Kampuchea, Phnom Penh, 6 June 2003.

where there is no evidence of the violation by the adverse Party of Article 53, sub-paragraph (b), and when such historic monuments, works of art and places of worship are not located in the immediate proximity of military objectives.[132]

As for the Second Protocol, Article 15(1) enumerates five war crimes, capable of commission in international and non-international armed conflict alike and known collectively as 'serious violations' of the Protocol, in respect of which Articles 15(2) to 20 lay down a range of obligations on states parties. These serious violations comprise making cultural property under enhanced protection the object of attack; using cultural property under enhanced protection or its immediate surroundings in support of military action; extensive destruction or appropriation of cultural property protected under the 1954 Hague Convention and the Second Protocol; making cultural property protected under the Convention and Protocol the object of attack; and theft, pillage or misappropriation of, or acts of vandalism directed against, cultural property protected under the Convention.[133] In addition, Article 21(a) and (b) of the Second Protocol would justify, although not require, legislative measures by a state party to establish as criminal offences under its domestic law any use of cultural property in violation of the Convention or Protocol and any illicit export, other removal or transfer of ownership of cultural property from occupied territory in violation of the Convention or Protocol. The obligation in Article 21 is declared to be without prejudice to Article 28 of the Convention.

It is important to emphasize that, while the existence of an armed conflict (be it of an international or non-international character) is a necessary legal criterion for the commission of a war crime, it is not a sufficient one. In order to qualify as a war crime, the destruction or plunder of cultural property, as well as occurring in time of armed conflict, must have some nexus to that conflict.[134] That is, it must be 'closely related' to the armed conflict,[135] by which is meant that the existence of the conflict must, at a minimum, play 'a substantial part in the perpetrator's ability to

---

[132] The requirement in Art 85(4) chapeau of AP I that the act be committed in violation of the Geneva Conventions or of AP I means that, for the purposes of Art 85(4)(d), the attack must constitute a breach of Art 53(a) AP I.

[133] See Art 15(1)(a)–(e) of SP. Article 15(1) chapeau of SP requires that the acts be in violation of 1954 HC or SP.

[134] *Prosecutor v Akayesu*, Appeals Chamber, Judgment, ICTR-96-4, 1 June 2001, § 444; *Prosecutor v Rutaganda*, Appeals Chamber, Judgment, ICTR-96-3-A, 26 May 2003, §§ 569–70; *Prosecutor v Stakić*, Appeals Chamber, Judgment, IT-97-24-A, 22 March 2006, § 342. The ICC Elements of Crimes, ICC-ASP/1/3(part II-B), requires with respect to each species of war crime found in Art 8 of the Statute of the International Criminal Court not only that the impugned conduct take place in the context of an armed conflict but that it be 'associated with' that conflict.

[135] *Prosecutor v Tadić*, Appeals Chamber, Decision on the Defence Motion for Interlocutory Appeal on Jurisdiction, IT-94-1, 2 October 1995, § 70; *Prosecutor v Kunarac, Kovač and Vuković*, Appeals Chamber, Judgment, IT-96-23&23/1-A, 12 June 2002, § 55; *Rutaganda*, Appeals Chamber Judgment (n 134), §§ 569–70; *Stakić*, Appeals Chamber Judgment (n 134), § 342; *Katanga and Ngudjolo*, Pre-Trial Chamber I, Decision on the Confirmation of Charges, ICC-01/04-01/07-717, 30 September 2008, § 380; *Situation in the Republic of Côte d'Ivoire*, Pre-Trial Chamber III, Decision Pursuant to Article 15 of the Rome

commit [the crime], his decision to commit it, the manner in which it was committed or the purpose for which it was committed'.[136] It is for this reason, for example, that the demolition of the Buddhas of Bamiyan in 2001 did not constitute a war crime. While sporadic non-international armed conflict continued in the far north-east of Afghanistan at the time of their destruction, the Buddhas were not destroyed in the course of fighting,[137] the Bamiyan Valley and the rest of the country being free of hostilities and securely under the Taliban government's control, and their demolition, which was essentially an act of fundamentalist religious iconoclasm, was in no way facilitated or motivated by the conflict.

B. Crimes against humanity

The International Military Tribunal at Nuremberg held that the unlawful destruction and plunder of cultural property in the occupied territories of the East amounted not only to war crimes but also to crimes against humanity,[138] and it found several of the major German war criminals guilty of the latter. Over half a century later, a Trial Chamber of the ICTY—quoting from, inter alia, the Nuremberg judgment and the International Law Commission's draft commentary to its draft Code of Crimes against the Peace and Security of Mankind as provisionally adopted at its forty-third session[139]—held in *Blaškić* that the specific crime against humanity of 'persecutions on political, racial and religious grounds' recognized in Article 5(h) of the Tribunal's Statute[140] 'encompasses not only bodily and mental harm and infringements upon individual freedom but also acts [...] such as those targeting property, so long as the victimised persons were specially selected on grounds linked to their belonging to a particular community'.[141] The Chamber accepted the prosecution's contention that

Statute on the Authorisation of an Investigation into the Situation in the Republic of Côte d'Ivoire, ICC-02/11, 3 October 2011, § 150.

[136] *Kunarac et al*, Appeals Chamber Judgment (n 135), § 58. See also *Rutaganda*, Appeals Chamber Judgment (134), 569–70; *Stakić*, Appeals Chamber Judgment (n 134), § 343; *Katanga and Ngudjolo*, Decision on the Confirmation of Charges (n 135), § 380; *Situation in the Republic of Côte d'Ivoire*, Decision on the Authorisation of an Investigation (n 135), § 150.

[137] Nor, as mentioned, can there exist a legal state of belligerent occupation in non-international armed conflict.

[138] Nuremberg Judgment (n 118), 249.

[139] See *Blaškić*, Trial Chamber Judgment (n 128), §§ 228 and 231 respectively.

[140] Although the provision refers conjunctively to persecution on 'political, racial and religious grounds', the ICTY has held that this should be read disjunctively, in accordance with customary international law, so that persecution on any one of these grounds suffices: *Prosecutor v Tadić*, Trial Chamber, Judgment, IT-94-1-T, 7 May 1997, § 713, affirmed in *Kunarac et al*, Appeals Chamber Judgment (n 135), §§ 93 and 97.

[141] *Blaškić*, Trial Chamber Judgment (n 128), § 233. See also *Tadić*, Trial Chamber Judgment (n 140), §§ 703–4.

persecution could take the form of the discriminatory confiscation or destruction of symbolic buildings belonging to the Muslim population of Bosnia-Herzegovina.[142]

Various ICTY Trial Chambers have since affirmed that discriminatory destruction of or extensive damage to cultural property in the broad sense, when committed as part of a widespread or systematic attack against a civilian population,[143] can, as a matter of customary international law, amount to persecution as a crime against humanity,[144] and the Appeals Chamber has in effect endorsed this position.[145] As summarized by the Trial Chamber in *Milutinović*, 'the Tribunal's jurisprudence specifically [recognizes] destruction of [...] cultural monuments as persecution, a crime against humanity'[146] (extensive damage being treated on the same footing[147]), where such destruction results from an act directed against the cultural property[148] and not justified by military necessity,[149] the latter implicating, in cases involving attacks, the question whether the property constituted a military objective.[150]

The conclusion that the destruction of cultural property may amount to the crime against humanity of persecution is in no way contradicted by Article 7(1)(h) of the Statute of the International Criminal Court, which recognizes as a crime against humanity, when carried out as part of a widespread or systematic attack on a civilian population,[151] '[p]ersecution against any identifiable group or collectivity [...] in connection with any [other crime against humanity] or any crime within the jurisdiction

[142] *Blaškić*, Trial Chamber Judgment (n 128), § 227.

[143] Article 5 chapeau of ICTY, as consonant with customary international law.

[144] See *Kordić and Čerkez*, Trial Chamber Judgment (n 128), § 207; *Brdanin*, Trial Chamber Judgment (n 122), § 1023; *Plavšić*, Trial Chamber Sentencing Judgment (n 128), § 15; *Prosecutor v Stakić*, Trial Chamber, Judgment, IT-97-24-T, 31 July 2003, § 768; *Prosecutor v Deronjić*, Trial Chamber, Sentencing Judgment, IT-02-61-S, 30 March 2004, § 122; *Prosecutor v Babić*, Trial Chamber, Sentencing Judgment, IT-03-72-S, 29 June 2004, §§ 30–1; *Prosecutor v Martić*, Trial Chamber, Judgment, IT-95-11-T, 12 June 2007, § 119; *Prosecutor v Krajišnik*, Trial Chamber, Judgment, IT-00-39-T, 27 September 2006, §§ 782–3; *Prosecutor v Milutinović, Šainović, Ojdanić, Pavković, Lazarević, and Lukić*, Trial Chamber, Judgment, IT-05-87-T, 26 February 2009, §§ 205 and 207 (now listed as '*Šainović*'); *Prosecutor v Đorđević*, Trial Chamber, Judgment, IT-05-87/1-T, 23 February 2011, §§ 1770–1; *Prosecutor v Stanišić and Župljanin*, Trial Chamber, Judgment, IT-08-91-T, 27 March 2013, vol 1, §§ 86–9. See also, effectively, *Prlić et al*, Trial Chamber Judgment (n 52), vol 3, §§ 1711–13 and 1725–6.

[145] See *Blaškić*, Appeals Chamber Judgment (n 128), § 149; *Kordić and Čerkez*, Appeals Chamber Judgment (n 128), § 108.

[146] *Milutinović et al*, Trial Chamber Judgment (n 144), § 205.

[147] See *Milutinović et al*, Trial Chamber Judgment (n 144), §§ 206–10. See also, subsequently, *Đorđević*, Trial Chamber Judgment (n 144), §§ 1770–3; *Stanišić and Župljanin*, Trial Chamber Judgment (n 144), vol 1, § 89.

[148] *Milutinović et al*, Trial Chamber Judgment (n 144), §§ 206 and 209; *Đorđević*, Trial Chamber Judgment (n 144), § 1773.

[149] *Milutinović et al*, Trial Chamber Judgment (n 144), § 208; *Đorđević*, Trial Chamber Judgment (n 144), §§ 1772–3; *Stanišić and Župljanin*, Trial Chamber Judgment (n 144), vol 1, § 88.

[150] *Milutinović et al*, Trial Chamber Judgment (n 144), § 208; *Stanišić and Župljanin*, Trial Chamber Judgment (n 144), vol 1, § 90.

[151] Article 7 chapeau of the Statute of the International Criminal Court, as consonant with customary international law.

of the Court'.[152] Since unlawful destruction of cultural property, whether as such or as some other genus of property, constitutes a war crime in both international and non-international armed conflict under Article 8 of the Statute, it can also constitute a crime against humanity under Article 7(1)(h).

Several ICTY Trial Chambers have similarly held that the plunder of public or private property, if carried out as part of a widespread or systematic attack on a civilian population and on a discriminatory basis, can amount to the crime against humanity of persecution,[153] a ruling which would encompass the plunder of cultural property. In *Blaškić*, on the other hand, the Appeals Chamber, while not referring specifically to cultural property, thought that 'there may be some doubt [...] as to whether acts of plunder, in and of themselves, may rise to the level of gravity required for crimes against humanity'.[154] It did acknowledge, however, that Article 7(1)(h) of the Statute of the International Criminal Court was more expansive in this regard.[155] In the subsequent Trial Chamber judgment in *Krajišnik*, the Chamber, referring to the Nuremberg judgment and to the case law of the US Military Tribunal at Nuremberg, concluded that 'an act of appropriation or plunder that has a severe impact on the victim, carried out on discriminatory grounds, and for which the general elements of crimes against humanity are fulfilled, constitutes the crime of persecution',[156] an approach effectively followed by the Trial Chamber in *Stanišić and Župljanin*;[157] and it is relevant that in *Strugar*, in relation to the destruction of cultural property, the Trial Chamber stated not only that 'the victim of the offence at issue is to be understood broadly as a "people", rather than any particular individual', but also that the consequences of the offence for this victim (namely, that people) could be said to be grave.[158] In terms of Article 7(1)(h) of the Statute of the International Criminal Court, since various unlawful forms of appropriation of property constitute war crimes under Article 8 of the Statute, these same acts can represent crimes against humanity if committed as part of a widespread or systematic attack on a civilian population and on a discriminatory basis.

As for the grounds of discrimination deemed impermissible in the context of the crime of persecution, while Article 5(h) of the ICTY Statute restricts itself to political, racial, and religious traits, customary international law probably accords

---

[152] 'Persecution' is defined in Art 7(2)(g) of the Statute of the International Criminal Court to mean 'the intentional and severe deprivation of fundamental rights contrary to international law by reason of the identity of the group or collectivity'.

[153] *Tadić*, Trial Chamber Judgment (n 140), § 704; *Kordić and Čerkez*, Trial Chamber Judgment (n 128), § 205; *Naletilić and Martinović*, Trial Chamber Judgment (n 128), § 698. See also *Plavšić*, Trial Chamber Sentencing Judgment (n 128), § 15.

[154] *Blaškić*, Appeals Chamber Judgment (n 128), § 148.

[155] *Blaškić*, Appeals Chamber Judgment (n 128), § 148 note 300.

[156] *Krajišnik*, Trial Chamber Judgment (n 144), § 711.

[157] See *Stanišić and Župljanin*, Trial Chamber Judgment (n 144), §§ 84–5.

[158] *Strugar*, Trial Chamber Judgment (n 27), § 232.

with the more expansive approach taken by Article 7(1)(h) of the Rome Statute, which refers to persecution 'on political, racial, national, ethnic, cultural, religious, gender [...] or other grounds that are universally recognized as impermissible under international law'.

Since a state of armed conflict is not a legal precondition to the commission of a crime against humanity,[159] it is *a fortiori* immaterial, if crimes against humanity are committed in armed conflict, whether the conflict is international or non-international and whether the crime against humanity has a nexus to it.

6 Conclusion

There are limits to what international law can do to civilize war. No rules will ever stop parties to an armed conflict or individual combatants who, motivated by malice, ideology, or arrogance and convinced of their impunity, bear contempt for law itself. This applies as much in relation to the protection of cultural property as to the protection of any other value in armed conflict. The Nazis' systematic seizure and devastation of the cultural heritage of the occupied Soviet Union was a phenomenon beyond the power of law to prevent. The same is probably true of Saddam Hussein's plunder of the cultural institutions of Kuwait, the destruction of historic and religious sites in the wars in the former Yugoslavia and more recently in Mali, the use by armed militants of the Imam Ali mosque in Najaf as both arsenal and refuge, and former Secretary of Defense Rumsfeld's breathtaking disregard for the security of Baghdad's museums. International law has purchase only where abiding with it holds intrinsic value. History shows that international legal compliance mechanisms can do little on their own to restrain the die-hards.

As it is, perhaps the gravest threat to cultural property in armed conflict today is its organized theft by private, civilian actors not bound to this extent by international law. The breakdown of order that accompanies armed conflict and the corrupting lure of the worldwide illicit market in art and antiquities continue to drive the looting of movable cultural property in war-zones and occupied territory. And while international law obliges belligerents to prevent and put a stop to this,

---

[159] See eg *Tadić*, Trial Chamber Judgment (n 140), § 713. While Art 5 of ICTY makes the existence of an armed conflict (international or non-international) a condition of a crime against humanity for the purposes of the Tribunal's jurisdiction, it was recognized by the drafters that customary international law was not so restrictive: see *Report of the Secretary-General pursuant to paragraph 2 of Security Council resolution 808 (1993)*, UN Doc S/25704, 3 May 1993, § 47.

it is ultimately a question of capacity. Even the best will in the world cannot post guards on all 10,000 archaeological sites in Iraq.

Insofar, however, as international law is capable of mitigating the consequences of war, the rules on the wartime protection of cultural property are as capable as any. The record shows, no doubt again to the surprise of many, that the international rules on the protection of cultural property in armed conflict are by and large observed. Flagrantly unlawful destruction and plunder of cultural property by armed forces and other legally impermissible disregard for its wartime fate have been exceptions over the past 200 years—devastating and not uncommon exceptions, it has to be acknowledged, but exceptions nonetheless, and usually condemned as such by other states, leading on occasion to reparation and/or prosecution under international law. In short, the framework of mutually supportive international rules and institutions outlined here give cultural property a fighting chance of surviving armed conflict unscathed.

Increasingly, moreover, there are synergies between the wartime and peacetime protection of cultural property. Nor is this just on account of the fact that international human rights law, international cultural heritage law, and the international law of crimes against humanity, all of which serve to protect cultural property in armed conflict, apply as much outside it. Rather, the greater emphasis in the Second Protocol to the 1954 Hague Convention on peacetime contingency planning for, inter alia, 'emergency measures for protection against fire or structural collapse' and 'the removal of movable cultural property or the provision for [its] *in situ* protection'[160] stands such property in good stead in the event of natural disaster, while the requirement that cultural property be protected by 'adequate domestic legal and administrative measures recognising its exceptional cultural [...] value and ensuring the highest level of protection'[161] before it can be eligible for the Protocol's regime of enhanced protection provides an added incentive to states to put their day-to-day heritage law and practice in order. In this way, the international law for the protection of cultural property in armed conflict can help to preserve 'the cultural heritage of all mankind'[162] without a shot being fired.

---

[160] Article 5 of SP.   [161] Article 10(b) of SP.   [162] Preamble to 1954 HC.

CHAPTER 21

MEMBERS OF THE ARMED FORCES AND HUMAN RIGHTS LAW

PETER ROWE

1 INTRODUCTION

IT is now too late to argue that human rights law has no applicability during an international armed conflict. Like the invention of gunpowder, human rights law will be a constituent part of the battlefield and its surroundings for the foreseeable future. To soldiers, however, human rights law may appear to be a concept out of place in the inherently dangerous environment of armed conflict.

This Chapter will discuss what is encompassed by the term 'armed forces' and who are entitled to be called members of the armed forces. It will also explore the role of human rights law from the standpoint of members of the armed forces and others who take an active part in hostilities. How a state, or an organized armed group, treats its own members in the light of this law is a variant on this theme and also requires discussion.

2 WHAT ARE THE 'ARMED FORCES'?

International law allows for a considerable margin of appreciation as to how the armed forces of a state are constituted.[1] There are, however, a number of key ingredients that must be possessed by all armed forces belonging to a state. They must be commanded by a person responsible for his or her subordinates[2] and wear a uniform or, at the least, have a fixed and distinctive sign recognizable at a distance so as to distinguish themselves from civilians not taking an active part in hostilities.[3] The individual members (not merely the commander) must also be subject to a disciplinary system.[4] The armed forces of a state should reflect the division between officers and other ranks.[5] They must be able to provide some form of medical

---

[1] See L. Oppenheim, *International Law*, vol II (7th edn, London: Longmans, 1952), 255, § 78.

[2] This is a long-standing requirement. See now Additional Protocol I, Art 43(1) of AP I. It implies that armed forces have 'a hierarchy [...] subordinate to a command which is responsible to one of the Parties to conflict for their operations', Commentary AP I and II, § 1672 and see Protocol I, Art 43(1). As such, they must be 'organized'. In turn, the state (as a party to the conflict) is responsible for 'all acts committed by persons forming part of its armed forces', Hague Convention IV, 1907, Art 3; Art 91 of AP I.

[3] See Art 44(7) of AP I; Art 4(A)(2) of GC III, reflecting the earlier Regulations to the Hague Convention 1907, Art 1. The other requirements of those Articles, such as the requirements to carry arms openly and to conduct their operations in accordance with the laws and customs of war apply to units, which have not become part of the armed forces as such, although they belong to a party to the conflict. There can, for instance, be no requirement that members of the armed forces of a state, while wearing the appropriate uniform, carry their arms openly. These issues refer, strictly, to the status of individuals following capture, 'Interpretive Guidance on the Notion of Direct Participation in Hostilities under International Humanitarian Law', 90 *International Review of the Red Cross* (2008) 991–1047 (DPH Interpretive Guidance), 999; *Osman bin Haji Mohamed Ali and another v The Public Prosecutor* [1969] 1 AC 430.

[4] The Geneva Conventions do not specifically require members of armed forces to be subject to a disciplinary system but assume that they will be. It is also assumed that this disciplinary code will be wider in ambit than merely enforcing compliance with international humanitarian law. See Arts 95, 102, 103, 106, and 108 of GC III. Article 43(1) of AP I requires armed forces to be subject to an internal disciplinary system 'which, inter alia, shall enforce compliance with the rules of international law applicable in armed conflict'. Commanders have an obligation to prevent and suppress breaches of the Conventions and Protocol I, see Art 87(1) of AP I. For an obligation to provide training to members of the armed forces in the Conventions and Protocols see Art 47 of GC I Art 48 of GC II; Art 127 of GC III; Art 144 of GC IV; Arts 82, 87(2) of AP I. Compare Art 19 of AP II, where reference is made only to dissemination and not to instruction of armed forces, dissident armed forces or other organized armed groups. The requirement of an internal disciplinary system is also one of the key features distinguishing a foreign national serving in the armed forces of a state from a mercenary, see Art 47(2)(e) of AP I. Although no reference is made in Art 47 to an internal disciplinary system this is a requirement when Arts 43(1) and 87(1) of AP I are read together.

[5] See Art 96 of GC III (disciplinary punishment of prisoners of war may be ordered only by an officer having disciplinary powers); Art 49 of GC III (work of prisoners of war); Art 97 (para 3) of GC III. There is no comparable reference to officers as such in the Additional Protocols, perhaps because of the lack of such a structure in organized armed groups not belonging to the state.

services, particularly during an international armed conflict,[6] as well as training in international humanitarian law.[7]

The national law of individual states is normally clear as to which entities comprise the armed forces. This may not be the case, however, should the state become involved in an armed conflict and units of a civilian police force, for example, are incorporated into the armed forces.[8] In a coalition of states taking part in an armed conflict, the individuals involved retain their status as part of the armed forces of their own state and will, in consequence, be subject to their own disciplinary system.[9] This may mean that the rules of engagement which they have been issued are different from those of other armed forces. Paramilitary units[10] or organized resistance movements in occupied territory may also become a part of the armed forces of the state with or without the imprimatur of national law.[11]

[6] Although the obligation rests on parties to the conflict under Art 15 of GC I, which imposes a mandatory obligation to 'search for and collect the wounded and sick [whether enemy or not] [...] to ensure their adequate care', it is possible that a state could comply with this obligation solely through civilian medical services. The structure of the whole Convention, however, assumes that medical services will be provided by the armed forces, even though others, such as national Red Cross societies may assist. Indeed, it would, in practical terms, be difficult for civilian personnel acting alone to comply with Art 15. Part II of Protocol I expressly protects civilian medical services and transport without detracting from the obligations on the armed forces medical services. During a non-international armed conflict the obligation on armed forces to collect and care for the wounded and sick would include non-state armed forces. See J-M. Henckaerts and L. Doswald-Beck, *Customary International Humanitarian Law* (Cambridge: Cambridge University Press, 2005), Rule 109.

[7] Commanders must 'ensure that members of the armed forces under their command' are aware of their obligations under international humanitarian law. See Art 87(2) of AP I.

[8] Article 43(3) of AP I. This may occur on a *de jure* or a *de facto* basis. It is more likely to occur where an armed conflict might appear to be an internal one but is, in fact, international, see *Prosecutor v Tadić*, IT-94-1-A, Judgment, 15 July 1999.

[9] This will also be the position where a national contingent forms part of a UN peacekeeping force. The disciplinary system may also apply to certain civilians who accompany the armed forces abroad, *Martin v United Kingdom* (24 October 2006).

[10] For expert evidence on the meaning of a 'paramilitary' unit in Bosnia in 1995 see *Prosecutor v Krstić*, IT-98-33-T, Judgment, 2 August 2001, transcript of evidence, 28 June 2000, 4790–2. Such a unit is described as one 'operating outside the legal framework of the laws which establish the army, the laws which establish the military interior units'. Depending on the facts it may, or may not, belong *de facto* to a state party to the conflict, under Art 4A(2) of GC III. A paramilitary unit may belong to a party to the conflict without any of its participants becoming members, through national law, of the state's armed forces. If a paramilitary unit is not a *de jure* or a *de facto* state organ that state will not be responsible under the European Convention on Human Rights for its acts, *Tasatayevy v Russia*, App No 37541/05, Judgment, 8 April 2010, § 70, unless its activities come within the principle of *Osman v United Kingdom* (28 October 1998).

[11] Members of militias and other volunteer corps may become part of the armed forces of a state within Art 4(1) of GC III. See Commentary GC III, 52. An organized resistance movement may become part of the armed forces of its own state or 'belong to' its own or another state engaged in the armed conflict, see Commentary GC II, 57.

National law will also determine who is entitled to be a member of the armed forces at any one time. So, reservists are likely to be called up for service.[12] Those called up will be members of the armed forces, but those who are not required, or who are not on duty with the armed forces, will remain civilians.[13] The term 'combatant' as applied during an international armed conflict is not wholly synonymous with being a member of the armed forces.[14]

Although the term 'armed forces' is wide enough to cover non-state organized armed groups, the latter groups can be distinguished from the armed forces of a state if they are not fighting on behalf of a state.[15] This may be the case during a non-international armed conflict. The appellation 'armed forces' will not be won by all groups[16] that have taken up arms. An organized armed group must be sufficiently well organized on a military basis and conduct 'military tactics in order to achieve military objectives'[17] so as to compare, *mutatis mutandis*, with the armed forces of a state.[18] These requirements will be easier to display if the armed group controls

---

[12] In some circumstances only reservists with certain skills (such as medical personnel) will be called up for service. National law may provide that certain reserve units will not be called up in any circumstances or that reservists (or members of its regular units) will not be required to take part in armed conflict until they reach a particular age.

[13] Article 50 of AP I.

[14] Article 43(2) of AP I identifies combatants as 'members of the armed forces [other than medical personnel and chaplains]'. It must be taken as referring to those individuals who, according to their national law, are at the time they take part in hostilities members *de jure* or *de facto* of the armed forces. A member of a reserve unit who is neither called up for service nor on duty with the armed forces would not be a member at that time. He could not then be a combatant entitled to take part in hostilities or be the subject of a direct attack against him. See generally, K. Ipsen, 'Combatants and Non-combatants', in D. Fleck (ed), *The Handbook of International Humanitarian Law* (2nd edn, Oxford: Oxford University Press, 2008), 78–118, 79–80.

[15] See H. Grotius, *De Jure Belli Ac Pacis Libri Tres: The Translation* vol 2 (Oxford: Clarendon Press, 1925), 97. For the re-organization of military units to create the armed forces of a new state, see *Prosecutor v Halilović*, IT-01-48-T, Judgment, 16 November 2005, §§ 102–11. As to non-state actors, see Common Art 3(1) of the Geneva Conventions; Arts 1(4) and 43(1) of AP I. Although Common Art 3(1) uses the term 'armed forces' this cannot be limited to the armed forces of the state since the *chapeau* refers to obligations placed on 'each Party to the conflict'. Protocol I only includes those non-state parties which are covered by Art 1(4). Article 1 of Protocol II draws a distinction between 'dissident armed forces' and 'other organized armed *groups* [emphasis supplied]'. The former appears to cover a 'part of the government army' which has rebelled, Commentary AP I and II, § 4460. See also DPH Interpretive Guidance (n 3), 1006. In general, Protocol II avoids imposing obligations directly on parties to the conflict but, instead, does so indirectly through prohibiting certain activities or by declaring how individuals are to be treated.

[16] A distinction is drawn below between an organized armed group being described as armed forces and the members of such groups not being considered to be *members* of armed forces.

[17] *Prosecutor v Haradinaj*, IT-04-84-T, Judgment, 3 April 2008, § 54; J-M. Henckaerts and L. Doswald-Beck (n 6), Rule 8, discussing non-international armed conflicts. The commission of acts by the armed group which were not directed against 'military objectives' as defined, for instance in Art 52 of AP I, would not, merely by that fact, deprive the group of the title 'armed forces'.

[18] The requirement to show that individuals formed an organized armed group stems from *Prosecutor v Tadić*, Appeals Chamber Decision of 2 October 1995 on the defence motion for interlocutory appeal on jurisdiction, § 70. It 'serves to distinguish armed conflict from banditry, riots, isolated acts of terrorism, or similar situations', *Prosecutor v Haradinaj*, IT-04-84-T, Judgment, 3 April 2008, § 38. The UN Security

territory,[19] is able to negotiate agreements applying to the whole of its armed forces, or takes its orders from a state or other governmental authority.[20] It is not clear whether, like a state, an armed group bears responsibility for the acts of its members,[21] although its commanders may do so.[22]

Two distinct views can be discerned as to how these armed groups should be seen when they take part in a non-international armed conflict. The traditionalist view is that their members are not lawful combatants and should be dealt with in line with the criminal law of the state concerned and, at the international level, with international humanitarian law. They have obligations under international humanitarian law[23] but not under human rights law.[24] What might be termed the 'postmodern' view is that members of such groups should be treated as akin to the armed forces of a state. This would mean that the organized armed group should be able to make a deed of commitment to uphold what for states would be treaty obligations,[25] establish courts,[26] and possess human rights obligations.[27]

Council distinguished the Taliban in Afghanistan from 'Al-Qaida, illegally armed groups, criminals and those involved in the narcotics trade', UNSC Res 1917 (2010) § 17. Any form of military organization would include activities such as recruitment, weapons, or other training, the implementation of military discipline and training in the basic principles of international humanitarian law, a hierarchy for the purposes of issuing and receiving military orders and providing some care for the wounded and sick. It must be of a size capable of performing these functions. See eg *Prosecutor v Boškoski*, IT-04-82-A, Judgment, 19 May 2010, § 2; *Prosecutor v Haradinaj*, IT-04-84-T, Judgment, 3 April 2008, § 51-60 (which refer to a number of earlier decisions of the ICTY). The wearing of a uniform may not be a significant factor in determining the existence of an organized armed group, *Prosecutor v Haradinaj*, § 56. See also *Ends and Means: Human Rights Approaches to Armed Groups* (International Council on Human Rights Policy, 2000), 20–1.

[19] Although Common Art 3 to the Geneva Conventions does not formally require the parties to an armed conflict to control territory it will, it is suggested, be easier for a group to show that it comes within the term, 'armed forces' in that Article if it can show that it does control territory. See eg *Prosecutor v Haradinaj*, § 71; *Prosecutor v Halilović*, IT-01-48-T, Judgment, 16 November 2005, § 163.

[20] *Prosecutor v Haradinaj*, § 60. This may also show that the armed group is, in reality, under the overall control of another state, see *Prosecutor v Tadić*, IT-94-1-A, Judgment, 15 July 1999.

[21] See Henckaerts and Doswald-Beck (n 6), 536.

[22] See Henckaerts and Doswald-Beck (n 6), Rule 153; Statute of the International Criminal for Rwanda, Art 6(3); *Prosecutor v Hadžihasanović*, IT-01-47-AR72, Decision of 16 July 2003, § 27; G. Mettraux, *The Law of Command Responsibility* (Oxford: Oxford University Press, 2009), 110.

[23] See eg Common Art 3; Art 48 of AP I; 'to implement this Protocol', Art 1(1) of AP II.

[24] This is an issue discussed below.

[25] See the draft Deed of Commitment for Adherence to a Total Ban on Anti-Personnel Mines and Cooperation in Mine Action initiated by Geneva Call, available at <http://www.genevacall.org/>.

[26] See S. Sivakumaran, 'Courts of Armed Opposition Groups: Fair Trials or Summary Justice?', 7 *Journal of International Criminal Justice* (2009) 489–513 at 505, who draws the conclusion that 'the greater the degree of organisation, the more refined the disciplinary process'; J. Somer, 'Jungle Justice: Passing Sentence on the Equality of Belligerents in Non-International Armed Conflict', 89 *International Review of the Red Cross* (2007) 655–90. For codes of conduct adopted by organized armed groups, see A-M. La Rosa and C. Wuerzner, 'Armed Groups, Sanctions and the Implementation of International Humanitarian Law', 90 *International Review of the Red Cross* (2008) 327–41 at 333; *Ends and Means: Human Rights Approaches to Armed Groups* (n 18), 51–2.

[27] A. Clapham, *Human Rights Obligations of Non-State Actors* (Oxford: Oxford University Press, 2006), 280 and 328–9. Compare C. Greenwood, 'Scope of Application of Humanitarian Law', in

The postmodern view aims to ensure maximum accountability for those who are directly participating in hostilities and maximum protection for those who are not.

Although an organized armed group may be described as 'armed forces' within Common Article 3, it does not follow that its members can be described as being '*members* of armed forces'. Rather, they will be civilians. This is because the identification of members of armed forces is ascribed by international law to the realm of national law, and it is hard to imagine a state granting such status to an armed opposition group[28] or to certain types of members.[29] Indeed, the Interpretive Guidance issued by the ICRC on the Notion of Direct Participation in Hostilities is careful to avoid describing members of organized armed groups as *members of armed forces*.[30] In much the same way, it is difficult to describe members of organized armed groups as 'soldiers'.[31]

Where the nature of the organization may mean it has both a political and a military wing, members of each would need to be clearly defined, as within the organs of a state. Those who do not form part of the 'continuous command' of the organization will be civilians who will not be considered to have taken a direct part in hostilities.[32] Members of the 'military wing' are in a different category since, although civilians, they are more likely to resemble, to some extent, the armed forces of a state as described above.

It has become an increasingly widespread practice for some states to employ civilian security contractors to perform functions traditionally carried out by members of the armed forces, such as guarding duties. These employees cannot be considered

---

D. Fleck (ed), *The Handbook of International Humanitarian Law* (2nd edn, Oxford: Oxford University Press, 2008), 45–78 at § 259. A number of UN Security Council resolutions are directed specifically at non-state actors. See eg Resolutions 1325 (2000), § 10; 1917 (2010), § 22, 35; See also J. Kleffner, 'The Collective Accountability of Organized Armed Groups for Systems Crimes', in H. Van der Wilt and A. Nollkaemper (eds), *System Criminality in International Law* (Cambridge: Cambridge University Press, 2009), 238–69 at 238.

[28] This may be otherwise where the armed opposition group is a resistance movement in occupied territory.

[29] Whilst certain organized armed groups will recruit child soldiers, a state is unlikely to recognize these individuals as members of the armed forces. See generally, N. Quenivet, 'Child Soldiers and Participation in Hostilities', 16 *African Journal of International and Comparative Law* (2008) 219–35.

[30] See DPH Interpretive Guidance (n 3), 999, 1036. Members of such groups, who are labelled by the Interpretive Guidance as possessing a 'continuous combat function', can, in consequence, be attacked at any time and not merely when taking a direct part in hostilities. By taking this approach the ICRC has, in my view, added a new category of civilian, ie a member of an organized armed group but who may be attacked (like a member of the armed forces of a state) at any time. This is despite their conclusion that such individuals 'cease to be civilians for as long as they remain members', 136. They remain civilians under Art 50(1) of AP I.

[31] Although it has become common to refer to children forced to take part in military activities by organized armed groups as 'child soldiers'.

[32] DPH Interpretive Guidance (n 3), 1007. The national law of the territorial state may not, however, draw such a distinction. It could treat all members of a particular organization as 'terrorists' or criminals merely by virtue of their association with it, particularly if the organization has been proscribed.

to be members of the armed forces.[33] They do not become lawful combatants during an international armed conflict and are subject to the law of their own state and, possibly, the law of the state in which they are operating.[34]

3 ARMED FORCES AND HUMAN RIGHTS GENERALLY

The question whether a state is bound by its human rights obligations whilst taking part in an international armed conflict outside its own territory is a complex one. Some states may not be party to a relevant human rights treaty or may not permit individual applications to any particular human rights body. In these situations a state may consider itself free from any specific legal obligation to comply with human rights treaties, particularly if engaged in armed conflict abroad. Alternatively, a state may adopt the view that even if in theory its human rights obligations apply during armed conflict, their limits have not been worked out. Indeed, the demarcation line between international humanitarian law and human rights law is unclear, although there is, without doubt, a considerable degree of overlap.[35] Armed forces may see this uncertainty as unwelcome.

---

[33] Should they take a direct part in hostilities they can be classified as mercenaries if all the conditions of Art 47 of API apply.

[34] They are not usually included in a status of forces agreement so as to make them subject to the exclusive jurisdiction of the visiting force. Montreux Document on Pertinent International Legal Obligations and Good Practices for States related to Operations of Private Military and Security Companies during Armed Conflict, 17 September 2008.

[35] Although there is much in common between international humanitarian law and human rights law there are substantial differences. See generally, Ch 26 in this volume. United Nations resolutions seem to treat international humanitarian law and human rights law as being virtually synonymous and they do not define what the term 'human rights' means. See eg UNGA Res 52/1145 (1997); UNSC Resolutions 1019 (1995); 1034 (1995); 1674 (2006); 1738 (2006); 1868 (2009); 1882 (2009); 1894 (2009); 1917 (2010); 2085 (2012); 2088 (2013); 2093 (2013); 2095 (2013). During armed conflict the basic norms of international humanitarian law are relatively clear, once it is accepted that an armed conflict is taking place, but this cannot be said of the applicability of specific human rights owed to individuals. To link both branches of international law together in this way may lead to a weakening of the impact of human rights law. The cautious use of human rights law by the ICRC is discussed by S. Sayapin, 'The International Committee of the Red Cross and International Human Rights Law', *Human Rights Law Review* (2009) 95–126.

A. Human rights obligations imposed on members of armed forces

To say that the armed forces of a state must comply with human rights may be no more than an attractive proposition.[36] Collectively, the armed forces may have a deeply entrenched image of what their role is within their own state. It is not an uncommon position for the armed forces to see their primary role as being to train for and, if necessary, to fight in an international armed conflict.

The perception by armed forces of their role is an important indicator of how they will perform during other types of military operations, particularly during an armed conflict within the state. If the entire training process for soldiers has been based upon fighting an international armed conflict it is likely that they will act on this basis, to some extent, during armed conflict within their own state.

There will, however, be two significant differences in the minds of soldiers should they be engaged in fighting a non-international conflict. The first is that soldiers will know that if captured by 'rebels' they can expect to be murdered or held in captivity under very harsh conditions.[37] The effect of this may cause them to take every means of avoiding capture. The prospect of being treated as a prisoner of war if captured during an international armed conflict has, at least, the virtue of civilizing to some extent the way in which soldiers behave on the battlefield and how they will treat enemy prisoners of war.

Secondly, in a non-international armed conflict there may be confusion amongst soldiers as to whether their function is to act as combatants, in which case international humanitarian law will provide the principal ground rules for action, or as law enforcers, in which case human rights law will assume greater importance. A combat role might justify the deployment of combat aircraft or artillery, whereas in the context of law enforcement such deployment would hardly ever be justified.[38]

---

[36] See G. Verdirame, 'Human Rights in Wartime: A Framework for Analysis', *European Human Rights Law Review* (2008) 689–705 at 692, who argues that 'we should not persuade ourselves that a human rights-compliant war is ever a possibility'.

[37] A report of a soldier who was released after almost one year spent in captivity by the FARC in Colombia, is available at <http://www.amnesty.org/en/news-and-updates/farc- releases-colombian-soldier-2010-0 3-29>. The ICRC may be able to facilitate the release of detainees on both sides of a non-international armed conflict, *Prosecutor v Boškoski*, IT-04-82-A, Judgment, 19 May 2010, § 22.

[38] See *Isayeva v Russia* (15 November 2007), § 191. Compare *Isayeva, Yusupova, Bazayeva v Russia* (2005) 41 *EHRR* 39, § 178. See the example given by C. Droege, 'Elective Affinities? Human Rights and Humanitarian Law', 90 *International Review of the Red Cross* (2008) 501–48 at 529; C. Von Der Groeben, 'The Conflict in Columbia and the Relationship between Humanitarian Law and Human Rights Law in Practice: Analysis of the New Operational Law of the Columbian Armed Forces', 16 *Journal of Conflict & Security Law* (2011) 141 referring to 'red card operations' at 151.

This perception of role is important in understanding why the armed forces of some states prefer to use the overarching title of 'law of armed conflict' (LOAC)[39] rather than 'international humanitarian law'. There is clearly no dispute as to the contents of this body of law between those who adopt one title and those who use the other. Rather, the inclusion of the word 'humanitarian' in one and its absence from the other illustrates the preferred emphasis. Such a preference may also roughly indicate how the armed forces of states view the applicability of human rights law to their military operations.

That said, it is important to be cautious about drawing any conclusions from this. It is probably safe to assume that many military lawyers (and international lawyers) would not, until fairly recently, have thought that human rights law applied during an armed conflict. Even if they did, they would have assumed that human rights law applied only to acts within the territory of a state[40] and not where the armed forces of that state are engaged in military operations abroad.[41] Even if they had thought that human rights law might apply, the potential different and overlapping obligations under that body of law and the law of armed conflict would need to be resolved.[42]

Since training for an international armed conflict is, of course, much more prevalent than actually taking part in one, some attention should be paid to the type of training soldiers are likely to receive. Given the primary role perceived by the armed forces themselves, as discussed above, it is likely in most states that the overwhelming focus of training will be international humanitarian law. Based as it is upon the lawfulness of individual actions, IHL fits well with the nature of military law itself and the concomitant need to ensure discipline.

Adherence to military discipline is as important to an army as it is to those with whom armed forces come into contact, such as other combatants and, more particularly, civilians not taking an active part in hostilities. Military discipline will only be effective if it is enforced on a routine basis, with the possibility of impunity for infractions being reduced as much as possible. The incidence of actual enforcement of military discipline rules can, normally, be compared very favourably with the enforcement of criminal law in civilian life. Any international war crimes tribunal will only have the capacity to try those most responsible for crimes within its jurisdiction. It is, therefore, the armed forces to which we should look

[39] Or 'the laws of war'. See eg J. Bellinger and W. Haynes, 'A US Government Response to the International Committee of the Red Cross Study *Customary International Humanitarian Law*', 89 *International Review of the Red Cross* (2007) 443–71.

[40] Particularly where the nature of the situation did not amount to an armed conflict.

[41] No state, for instance, has issued a derogation notice under Art 15(2) of the European Convention on Human Rights; *Bankovic v United Kingdom [and other NATO States]* (2007) 44 EHRR SE5, § 62.

[42] See generally, N. Milanovic, 'A Norm Conflict Perspective on the Relationship between International Humanitarian Law and Human Rights Law', 14 *Journal of Conflict & Security Law* (2009) 459–83 at 482.

principally for the enforcement of any norms governing armed conflict, in whatever form they take.[43]

One further feature of the military codes of many states is the requirement on members of the armed forces to secure the maintenance of military discipline among themselves. Soldiers with some form of command responsibility, from corporal to general, will be required to undertake such a role. Failure to prevent misconduct or to report its occurrence can amount to a breach of the military code itself. A corporal who, for instance, witnesses others mistreating a detainee commits an offence against his military code if he fails to report this incident to his superior.[44] Although it may be naïve to assume that all soldiers will report their colleagues, this is not so unlikely where the soldier-witness belongs to a different unit from the observed soldiers.[45]

Human rights obligations do not fit easily within this paradigm. First, they are obligations owed by the state and not directly by individual members of the armed forces. They will, of course, create individual liability where they reflect international humanitarian law, the criminal law of the state or the military code of the armed forces. Thus, the killing of a detainee under interrogation could be seen as a breach of the human rights of that detainee, a breach by the soldier of the criminal law (murder or torture) of the state to which he belongs, a war crime or some other breach of the military code. In terms of preventing soldiers killing detainees it is much more effective to instil in them a prohibition against such acts. If, nevertheless, such an act is committed, soldiers are subject to some form of trial by their own state. This is what the disciplinary code is designed to do. By way of a secondary process, such a trial will show that the state has complied with its obligation to investigate the killing under human rights law.[46] It will also be responsible for providing redress to the individual's family as well as meeting any other claims, including the individual's, that might be successful before a human rights body.

It has been argued here that it is more than likely in well-disciplined armed forces that soldiers will be much more familiar with the basic principles of international

---

[43] See generally, G. Nolte (ed), *European Military Law Systems* (Berlin: de Gruyter Recht, 2003), 129ff.

[44] See eg the US Code of Military Justice, Art 134; National Defence Act, RSC 1985 (Canada), s 129; Armed Forces Act 2006 (UK), s 19; Defence Force Discipline Act 1982, s 60. Other military law offences might include the negligent performance of a duty; *R v Brocklebank* (1996) 134 DLR (4th) 377.

[45] An example would be the fact that after the My Lai massacre it was the US helicopter pilot who reported the incident committed by Lt Calley's platoon and not any of its members who did not take part in the killing of civilians, J. Olson and R. Roberts, *My Lai. A Brief History with Documents* (Boston: Bedford Books, 1998), 205.

[46] If conducted properly, see *Case of the 'Las Dos Erres' Massacre v Guatemala, Preliminary Objection, Merits, Reparations and Costs*, Judgment, 24 November 2009 (Inter-American Court of Human Rights), § 105. One of the functions of an investigation is to bring those responsible to account. By so doing human rights obligations may be enforced indirectly against individuals. Compare the situation where a breach of human rights does not map on to a criminal offence, where the national emergency law gives soldiers considerable latitude of action or where no prosecutions are brought as a result of the involvement of senior commanders in what would otherwise amount to a criminal offence.

humanitarian law than with human rights law, the latter affirming rights including the right to life and the prohibition of detention without the decision of a court. 'How', soldiers might ask, 'can that apply to us since in an international armed conflict our job is likely to involve the killing of enemy combatants and if we are captured we can be detained until the armed conflict comes to an end without any involvement of a court?'[47]

Moreover, soldiers may not know whether their state has issued a derogation notice from particular human rights obligations. Even if this is the case, the derogating state may face a challenge from another state party to that particular treaty. In practice, derogations are not common during an international armed conflict.[48]

International criminal law has a well-developed notion of command responsibility.[49] The importance of this concept lies not so much in the fact that a commander may also be liable, in certain circumstances, where his subordinates have acted in breach of international humanitarian law, but rather in the effect that this potential liability can have on a commander. Commanders have, in consequence, a considerable incentive to ensure their subordinates do not act in ways that could, in turn, impose criminal responsibility on them as commanders. By way of contrast, human rights law is blind as to which individual within a state's organ has caused a breach of the human rights of an individual. It might be argued that, purely in terms of human rights law, a military commander has less incentive to prevent a breach of another's human rights, particularly where that breach does not involve a criminal offence. The commander's actions may, however, cause the state to be in breach of its human rights obligations to another even though neither he nor his subordinates may have committed a breach of their military discipline code.[50]

In terms of preventing violations of human rights during armed conflict, the military discipline code of the armed forces is likely to be a much more effective and practical weapon than any concentration on the human rights of individuals with whom soldiers come in contact. For this human rights protection to be effective, some form of pressure external to the armed forces needs to be in place. This frequently takes the form of international or national press coverage of their activities.

It must be recognized, however, that not all armed forces maintain a high level of discipline or, if they do, not at all times. It is when they are engaged in military operations that the need to maintain a high standard of discipline is at its most acute. It is then that it is most likely to crack or to fail altogether. To avoid this, norms must be made clear and relatively simple to the soldier, particularly during a non-international armed conflict, where animosity against the 'rebels' may be

---

[47] Soldiers are unlikely to be familiar with the concept of the *lex specialis*.

[48] See n 41.

[49] Article 86(2) of AP I; Rome Statute of the International Criminal Court, 1998, Art 28 It applies also in non-international armed conflict, J-M. Henckaerts and L. Doswald-Beck (n 6), Rules 152, 153. See generally, G. Mettraux, *Command Responsibility* (n 22).

[50] *McCann v United Kingdom* (1996) 21 *EHRR* 97 and see § 200.

at a much higher level than against enemy combatants in an international armed conflict.

B. International norms as part of national law

If the paradigm of an effective and enforceable military discipline code is a model for the prevention of breaches of international humanitarian and human rights law, it is essential that relevant international norms find their way into the national law of a state.

Although most states are party to the International Covenant on Civil and Political Rights and possibly to a regional human rights treaty, these treaties may or may not have any impact upon the national law of a state. The impact in the national legal order will depend on how that state sees the relationship between its own international law obligations and its national law.[51]

A number of states require a treaty to be incorporated in whole or in part into national law, while customary international law will usually be received automatically into that law.[52] Whilst this approach respects the constitutional arrangements of individual states, it can mislead individuals about the nature of any protection offered to them by a human rights treaty. This can be seen most clearly when the armed forces of one state occupy another and the inhabitants under occupation seek a legal remedy against that occupying state. It is likely that should any legal remedy be made available it will be in the courts operating within the homeland of the occupying state or by military courts in the occupied territory.[53]

Let us assume that the occupying state is a party to the ICCPR and the 1949 Geneva Conventions but that none of these treaties has been implemented into the national law. A classic example of this would be the occupation of territories by Israel since 1967. An inhabitant, for example, of Gaza may seek a remedy before the Supreme Court of Israel as a result of the intentional demolition of his house by the military authorities in Gaza. Although Israel is a party to the Geneva Conventions, it has not implemented them in its national law, although the Hague Regulations of 1907 are considered to have been automatically received in that law by virtue of their status as customary international law.[54] This will also be the case for the rules

---

[51] See generally, I. Brownlie, *Principles of Public International Law* (7th edn, Oxford: Oxford University Press, 2008), 31; A. Aust, *Modern Treaty Law and Practice* (Cambridge: Cambridge University Press, 2000), Ch 10.

[52] This assumes that a particular norm of customary international law is not inconsistent with national legislation or with binding decisions of the national court. In England it has been held that customary international law cannot create criminal offences within English law, *R v Jones (Margaret)* [2006] UKHL 16.

[53] See eg, Y. Dinstein, *The International Law of Belligerent Occupation* (Cambridge: Cambridge University Press, 2009), 137.

[54] Dinstein (n 53), 28.

in the Geneva Conventions to the extent that they codify or have attained the status of customary law.[55]

A court in Israel faced with such a claim could apply only its national law. By the Defence (Emergency) Regulations 1945[56] the forfeiture and destruction of property is permitted where a specified offence has been committed or in which its inhabitants have committed an offence involving violence. For the claimant to argue that collective penalties are prohibited by Article 33 of Geneva Convention IV will be of no avail since this is not 'law' before the Israeli court, particularly when it appears to be in conflict with national law, in this case the Defence (Emergency) Regulations 1945.[57]

The effect of this dualist approach can have a number of undesirable consequences. First, it can place national courts in a difficult position, requiring them to apply only the law binding upon them and to ignore international treaty obligations to which their state is a party, unless the latter can be interpreted in such a way as to be consistent with the former. This can lead to a substantial problem if the courts are concerned with the rights of individuals in occupied territory, where the inhabitants could assume quite reasonably that their rights will be governed by international law.

Secondly, it can militate against the rule of law within occupied territories, where the state is bound by international law. The interpretation of a treaty provision by an international court can, in consequence, be ignored by national authorities.[58]

The different treatment of treaty law and customary international law can result in a national court having to consider 'old' and not 'modern' law. The national courts in Israel can consider the Hague Regulations 1907 as part of customary international law but not the whole of Geneva Convention IV in interpreting property rights. The Supreme Court of Israel has decided that the sixth paragraph of Article 49 of Geneva Convention IV, which directs that 'the Occupying Power shall not [...] transfer parts of its own population into the territory it occupies' did not reflect customary international law. Neither the treaty provision nor the norms underlying Article 49 were therefore part of Israeli national law. The Court could, however, rely on Articles 46 and 52 of the Hague Regulations 1907 as customary international law to determine the issue.[59] The wording of these Articles was not the same as that contained in Article 49 of Geneva Convention IV.

The consequence of this dualist approach can be to shut out international law when it is most needed by a claimant in occupied territory who wishes to challenge the acts of the military authorities of the Occupying Power. This can have serious

---

[55] See J-M. Henckaerts and L. Doswald-Beck, *Customary International Humanitarian Law* (Cambridge: Cambridge University Press, 2005).

[56] See Dinstein (n 53), 162, note 838.   [57] See Dinstein (n 53), 156.

[58] See Dinstein (n 53), 255, where Dinstein refers to the *Legal Consequences of the Construction of a Wall in the Occupied Palestinian Territory*, Advisory Opinion (2004) International Court of Justice, which he criticizes on a number of grounds.

[59] See Dinstein (n 53), 242.

ramifications for the lives of individuals when the belligerent occupation lasts for a prolonged period. In this situation the Occupying Power is required to place its authority over the hostile territory. To a greater or lesser extent, governmental powers will need to be exercised over the territory. In any democracy the exercise of governmental powers will be subject to some form of legal review in the courts. Where a legal challenge may be most needed against the decisions of military authorities, the dualist system may deny reliance on the law intended by all states party to the Geneva Conventions to govern this unusual exercise of state power.

In exactly the same way, the inhabitants of occupied territory may not be protected by any part of a human rights treaty that has not been implemented in the national law of the occupying state, even if it is assumed they come within the jurisdiction of that state whilst in occupied territory. Should there be no mechanism established to enforce any rights before a human rights body, any human 'rights' owed to them in theory can be ignored in practice.

4 PEACEKEEPING AND HUMAN RIGHTS

When large-scale abuse of human rights occurs, calls for the deployment of a UN peacekeeping force become ever stronger. Following a call by the UN Secretary-General for peacekeeping forces, some states will volunteer national contingents which will have the effect of safeguarding the human rights of individuals in the affected state. In this role, the armed forces can be seen as protectors of human rights.[60]

In their peacekeeping role, national contingents will not wish to become a party to an armed conflict, although they are often deployed to areas where such conflicts are actually taking place.[61] Operating on behalf of the United Nations, they will be expected to uphold the human rights of the individuals with whom they come into contact, even though a particular national contingent is not necessarily a party to any human rights treaty.[62]

Should a breach of the human rights of an individual occur as a result of acts or omissions by a national contingent, there may be some doubt as to whether this should be attributed to the United Nations itself or to the state to which the national

[60] Compare enforcement actions under Ch VII of the UN Charter.
[61] Secretary-General's Bulletin; Observance by United Nations Forces of International Humanitarian Law, ST/SGB/1999/13, (1999) 38 *ILM* 1656.
[62] Pakistan has been one of the largest contributors of peacekeeping forces to the United Nations but became a party to the ICCPR only in June 2010.

contingent belongs.[63] A decision that the responsibility lies with the United Nations and not the contributing states may lead to a belief among soldiers of the national contingent, whose state is a party to a human rights treaty, that breaches of human rights will have no consequences for them. This is, however, to ignore the fact that most serious breaches of human rights will also amount to disciplinary offences for which they can be punished individually. It is likely to be the case that most UN peacekeeping operations will involve contributing states being responsible at least for disciplinary action for members of their armed forces for breaches which may also amount to human rights violations.[64]

5 The Role of the United Nations

In theory, a resolution of the UN Security Council could deprive an individual of a particular right guaranteed under a human rights treaty. Resolution 1546 (2004), which granted powers to the multinational force in Iraq to intern civilians for imperative reasons of security, appeared to conflict with the obligation of the United Kingdom to respect the right to liberty granted by the European Convention of Human Rights. The European Court of Human Rights[65] held, however, that Resolution 1546 neither 'explicitly or implicitly required the United Kingdom to place an individual [...] into indefinite detention without charge' and that there was therefore no conflict between the Resolution and the Convention. It is likely, but not certain, that other human rights bodies would take the same view.

---

[63] *Behrami v France; Seramati v France, Germany and Norway* (2007) 45 *EHRR* SE 85; *Nuhanović v The Netherlands*, BR5388, Gerechtshof's Gravenhage (5 July 2011). See for discussion H. Krieger, 'A Credibility Gap: The Behrami and Saramati Decision of the European Court of Human Rights', 13 *Journal of International Peacekeeping* (2009) 159–80; M. Milanovic and T. Papic, 'As Bad as it Gets: The European Court of Human Right's Behrami and Saramati Decision and General International Law', 58 *International and Comparative Law Quarterly* (2009) 267–96. See T. Dannenbaum, 'Translating the Standard of Effective Control into a System of Effective Accountability', 51 *Harvard International Law Journal* (2010) 113–92; C. Leck, 'International Responsibility in United Nations Peacekeeping Operations: Command and Control Arrangements and the Attribution of Conduct', 10 *Melbourne Journal of International Law* (2009) 346–64; O. Spijkers, 'The Immunity of the United Nations in Relation to the Genocide in Srebrenica in the Eyes of a Dutch District Court', 13 *Journal of International Peacekeeping* (2009) 197–219; *Al-Jedda v United Kingdom*, ECHR, 7 July 2011.

[64] *R (Al-Jedda) v Secretary of State for Defence* [2007] UKHL 58; *Attorney-General v Nissan* [1970] AC 179.

[65] *Al-Jedda v United Kingdom*, 7 July 2011, § 109; *Hassan v United Kingdom*, App No 29750/09 (communicated case, 30 August 2011).

6 WHY DO SOLDIERS
BREACH HUMAN RIGHTS?

If the armed forces are normally the most disciplined body within a state, why does misconduct amounting to breach of human rights occur? We have seen that many breaches of human rights will also contravene international humanitarian law, with the result that wrongdoing can be viewed as such, even if a human rights treaty does not apply in the circumstances involved. The argument that wrongdoing by soldiers is committed by 'bad apples' and, once removed, the problem is solved, appears to be artificial.[66] Military structures, based as they are on a requirement to obey orders and on soldiers acting as a group rather than as individuals, exhibit the conditions necessary for group wrongdoing, particularly where uncertainty of action is created or weak leadership is present.

One of the principal factors where misconduct occurs is the perception by soldiers of members of organized armed groups as unworthy, for a variety of reasons, of decent treatment. In this atmosphere, individuals can become mere numbers for the purposes of body counts or 'terrorists', 'rebels', or 'internal enemies'[67] whose death will pose little concern among the general population. Respect by members of particular units of the armed forces, acting as a group, for the human rights of these individuals can be minimal. It is noticeable that, in virtually all reported incidents of egregious breach of human rights, soldiers do not act as individuals but as a group.[68]

The nature of military training, with its subordination of the individual to the group, should be seen not only for the military effectiveness which it produces, but also for its potential to cause serious human rights breaches in certain circumstances. In armed conflict, compliance with human rights by individual soldiers is, like international humanitarian law, based to some extent upon a desire for reciprocity of treatment. It is, therefore, in the interests of soldiers to generate such reciprocity. Training in human rights standards and effective discipline are the only means to achieve it.

Although a need for better training and discipline of soldiers may appear to be relatively easy solutions to prevent military misconduct in international armed conflicts, in non-international conflicts other factors are likely to be present. These can include: the virtual impossibility of differentiating between a civilian taking an active part in hostilities and innocent civilians, and the characterization of rebels

---

[66] See generally, P. Rowe, 'Military Misconduct During International Armed Operations: "Bad Apples" or Systemic Failure?', 13 *Journal of Conflict & Security Law* (2008) 165–89.

[67] See the Case of the 'Las Dos Erres' Massacre (n 46), § 71.

[68] The abuse of prisoners at Abu Ghraib is one particularly extreme example.

as not being 'honourable soldiers' but those who hide behind innocent civilians. Where either or both of these factors are present, soldiers can justify to themselves that the civilians killed were participating in some form in the conflict or that the rebels did not deserve any 'human rights', or that they (the soldiers) made mistakes of fact. In some cases, however, they may be at a total loss to understand why they committed what could only be described as an atrocity.

The possibility of their misconduct coming to light and some form of judicial process being instigated, which may or may not materialize, is also a factor to be taken into account by soldiers. It explains why soldiers may try to disguise their identities, leave weapons or other equipment in the hands of civilians whom they have killed, or give false evidence before investigating officers.[69]

During a non-international armed conflict, members of organized armed groups are likely to face similar pressures. In addition, the motives of different armed groups will vary depending on their political or other objectives. A group which wishes to replace the existing government may do more to protect at least some human rights than one which merely wishes to control territory to exploit its mineral resources. The former group may well be more highly motivated to respect human rights than the armed forces of the latter group, since the moral support of other states may be an important political goal should they eventually be successful in replacing the government.[70]

7 HUMAN RIGHTS OF MEMBERS OF THE ARMED FORCES

So far we have discussed the obligation on members of the armed forces to respect the human rights of those with whom they come in contact during an armed conflict. The issue now is to what extent a state owes human rights obligations to its own soldiers. In peacetime there can be no doubt that a state owes the obligations accepted under a human rights treaty to all those within its jurisdiction, whether soldiers or

---

[69] Although such allegations are frequently made by applicants to the European Court of Human Rights, the Court is often unable to establish the facts on such issues. See eg *Pad and others v Turkey*, App No 60167/00, Admissibility Decision of 28 June 2007, § 8; *Tasatayevy v Russia*, App No 37541/05, Judgment, 8 April 2010, § 67; *Ozcan v Turkey*, App No 18893/05. In most cases such activities will be under the orders of a superior or with his connivance.

[70] See Ch 30 and generally, J. Kleffner (n 27); S. Ratner, J. Abrams, and J. Bischoff, *Accountability for Human Rights Atrocities in International Law* (3rd edn, Oxford: Oxford University Press, 2009), 281.

civilians.[71] Soldiers may be thought of as 'citizens in uniform' but their position is not identical to a citizen for two reasons. First, the characteristics of military life must be taken into account in determining whether certain conduct would amount to a breach of a human right. Should a civilian employer confine an employee to the workplace for a day as a result of a disciplinary infraction it is likely to amount to a deprivation of liberty, whilst it will not amount to such where a soldier is confined to barracks for the same period of time. Secondly, armies that rely to some extent on conscription must take reasonable steps to guard against suicides where they know that a particular soldier is at risk of taking his or her own life.[72]

Certain human rights will gain a sharp edge during a non-international armed conflict. The right to life, freedom from torture, inhuman or degrading treatment, and the right to liberty are of this nature. Soldiers are entitled to respect for these rights from their own armed forces and, possibly, from the organized armed group with which they are fighting.[73] In relation to, for instance, the right to life, the nature of the obligation will be quite different since the organized armed group will seek to kill soldiers (let it be assumed, in accordance with international humanitarian law as the *lex specialis*)[74] whereas the armed forces of the state will be required under human rights law to take reasonable steps to protect the lives of its soldiers.[75] The same principles will apply during an international armed conflict should the obligation, particularly of the right to life, apply to the state operating outside its own territory. It is likely to do so where an enemy soldier has been captured.

The extent of the obligation imposed upon the state to protect the lives of its own soldiers during an armed conflict, as distinct from peacetime, is not easy to measure. The nature of armed conflict can vary considerably. In some circumstances, the use of air power may be appropriate to provide protection to soldiers on the ground;

---

[71] *Voulanne v Finland* Comm No 265/1987, CCPR C/35/D/265/1987, § 9.5; *Engel et al v Netherlands* (1976) 1 *EHRR* 647, § 59; Council of Europe Committee of Ministers to member states on human rights of members of the armed forces, Recommendation CM/Rec (2010) 4 (24 February 2010). See generally, *Handbook on Human Rights and Fundamental Freedoms of Armed Forces Personnel* (OSCE/ODIHR, 2008).

[72] *Bayram v Turkey*, App No 75535/01, Judgment, 26 May 2009. As to an inadequate investigation following the death of a soldier in barracks, see *Beker v Turkey*, App No 27866/03, Judgment, 24 March 2009; *Mosendz v Ukraine*, App No 52013/08, Judgment, 17 January 2013.

[73] This assumes that the organized armed group owes human rights obligations, as compared with those derived from international humanitarian law. It must follow that if an organized armed group owes human rights obligations this will also operate for the benefit of its own fighters.

[74] Although under international humanitarian law they must not kill those taking no active part in their conflict with the armed forces of the state.

[75] The obligation on the part of state agents to protect life has been well developed by the European Court of Human Rights. See, in particular, *Osman v United Kingdom* (28 October 1998). See also Recommendation CM (2010) (n 71), Recommendation 1, 'members of the armed forces should not be exposed to situations where their lives would be avoidably put at risk without a clear and legitimate military purpose or in circumstances where the threat to life has been disregarded'. It must follow that if an organized armed group owes human rights obligations this will benefit its own fighters.

in others the risk to innocent civilians may be too great. Adequate training and equipment would seem to be the bedrock of this protection, although this may be too general a statement. Should, for instance, a greater number of helicopters be made available to ensure that soldiers do not fall prey to roadside bombs, or better armoured vehicles supplied so as to withstand such attacks? The state may not actually possess this type of equipment in the numbers required to make a meaningful difference or at all. The form of the conflict may change quickly with a need for equipment which had not been previously been foreseen as necessary.

The standard of responsibility of the state is not to protect the lives of its soldiers under all circumstances. War is, after all, a dangerous business. It is, instead, to assess whether there is a real and immediate risk to an identified individual (or group of such individuals) and, if so, to take steps which, in the circumstances and judged reasonably, would have been expected to avoid that risk.[76] It can be distinguished from the duty of care that a state is likely to owe all its employees.[77] The provision of medical services at a base from which soldiers leave to take part in military operations would seem to fall within the type of services reasonably required to protect soldiers engaged in combat. Equipment and training to provide a reasonable chance of withstanding the use of foreseen chemical weapons would be a further example. The provision of a large force of helicopters to transport all soldiers over ground where the risk of unexploded ordnance is high may fall on the other side of the line of what human rights law requires.[78]

Where it is decided that the state has a human rights obligation to protect the lives of its soldiers during military operations, a further requirement involves conducting an independent investigation into the deaths of such individuals. Such an obligation will not flow from the deaths of enemy soldiers[79] but it will exist in respect of a death caused to an alleged member of a rebel group within a state's own

[76] *Osman v United Kingdom* (28 October 1998), § 116. As to the duty of a state in relation to members of its armed forces during 'military activities and operations', see *Mosendz v Ukraine*, App No 52013/08, Judgment, 17 January 2013, § 91.

[77] Under English law a duty of care is not owed by one soldier to another in battle conditions in the course of hostilities, *Mulcahy v Ministry of Defence* [1996] QB 732.

[78] See also the examples given by Collins J in *R (Smith) v Oxfordshire Assistant Deputy Coroner* [2008] EWHC 694 (Admin), § 20. This case involved the application of the Human Rights Act 1998 to a British soldier who died while serving in Iraq. A more narrow view of 'jurisdiction' under Art 1 of the European Convention on Human Rights was taken by the Supreme Court in this case, see [2010] UKSC 29, so as to refer only to acts on a soldier's military base although see now *Smith v Ministry of Defence* [2013] UKSC 41. The European Court of Human Rights may be required to determine whether the 'jurisdiction' of the United Kingdom extended to one of its soldiers killed by enemy action off base, see *Pritchard v United Kingdom*, App No 1573/11 (communicated case). Corporal Pritchard was killed during the period when the United Kingdom was an Occupying Power in Iraq.

[79] This will be either because the enemy soldier does not come within the jurisdiction of the state, whose soldiers killed him or because, in this case, international humanitarian law is the *lex specialis*.

territory.[80] A distinction can be made here between those who are acting on behalf of the state and those, the rebels, who are fighting against it. The steps required to protect the right to life of the former group will likely exceed those of the latter group, simply because the state can do more.[81]

Soldiers can expect the right to a fair trial to be respected during time of armed conflict as well as in peacetime should they be subjected to some form of military trial or summary procedure.[82] Members of organized armed groups can expect the same protection from their leaders, if the proposition is correct that such groups are not merely recipients of human rights obligations but have obligations as well. Could a rebel fighter expect to be tried by the armed group in an independent and impartial tribunal established by law if accused of, for example, conduct that would amount to a war crime committed during a non-international armed conflict?

An obvious difficulty would arise from the fact that a rebel tribunal could not be established 'by law' unless this term is taken to mean 'established by some formal process imposed by the rebel group to provide equivalent standards of justice to those of states'.[83] What is the alternative? By the very nature of the conflict, the state is unable to exercise its authority over the organized armed group. As a result, it cannot ensure the right of fair trial of the member of that group. It cannot, however, merely ignore that member's rights. It will, in consequence, have to accept that an organized armed group can attempt to establish its own independent and impartial tribunals. This will offer some protection[84] to a member of the group, but it will also provide a means by which the armed group, like the armed forces, can exercise discipline over its members to the benefit of innocent civilians and to members of the armed forces, both of which groups are owed the right to life by the state.

---

[80] *McCann v United Kingdom* (1996) 21 EHRR 97; Case of the *'Las Dos Erres' Massacre v Guatamala*, Inter-American Court of Human Rights, Judgment of 24 November 2009, § 105, 140. The purpose of such an investigation is set out in *Rantsev v Cyprus and Russia*, App No 25965/04 (Judgment, 7 January 2010), § 232. It may mean the court will require access to 'military campaign plans and [...] to military files', *'Las Does Erres Massacre'* case, concurring opinion of Judge Ramila.

[81] Compare the three IRA suspects shot and killed by British soldiers in Gibraltar. The European Court of Human Rights decided that these individuals were owed the right to life and held the United Kingdom responsible for their deaths, *McCann v United Kingdom* (1996) 21 EHRR 97. See also *Inter-American Commission on Human Rights Report No 55/97, Case No 11.137, Argentina*, 30 October 1997; L. Zegweld, 'The Inter-American Commission on Human Rights and International Humanitarian Law: A Comment on the Tablada Case', 324 *International Review of the Red Cross* (1998) 505–11; C. McCarthy, 'Human Rights and the Laws of War under the American Convention on Human rights', 6 European Human Rights Law Review (2008) 762–80 at 765.

[82] This may be more likely to arise as a result of the complementary provisions of the Rome Statute 1998 of the International Criminal Court.

[83] See n 26.

[84] The same principle will apply to the nature of any punishment imposed on a member by the armed group tribunal. The state will remain responsible for preventing conduct which would amount to torture, inhuman or degrading treatment and, for parties to the European Convention on Human Rights, the death penalty. In practical terms, the state may be able to do little, *Catan v Moldova and Russia*, App No 43370/04, Judgment (Grand Chamber) 19 October 2012 (the position of Moldova).

8 Conscientious Objection

Although the right to conscientious objection to military service has now become well established, the same cannot be said for objections, based upon conscience, expressed by members of the armed forces required to take part in particular military operations. For example, a small number of individuals serving in the British armed forces have refused, on grounds of conscience, to take part in operations in Iraq or Afghanistan.[85] If the opportunity is not available within the armed forces of a particular state to request deployment elsewhere, a soldier may be faced with having to argue before a military court that the particular operation in which he refuses to participate on grounds of conscience is unlawful.[86]

In some states, it will be difficult to argue successfully in a court that a particular military operation is unlawful under international law. This is likely to be because either the national court takes the view that the issue before it is non-justiciable, or that the court is unable to secure sufficient evidence to make a decision. In any event, it is a difficult course for the soldier to take since his belief that it is unlawful, which forms the basis of his conscientious objection, will be irrelevant. A national court will normally stand on more secure ground in its ability to make a decision where the alleged unlawfulness of the military operation is based upon national law.[87]

See in general, C. Ryngaert and A. Van de Meulebroucke, 'Enhancing and Enforcing Compliance with International Humanitarian Law by Non-State Armed Groups: An Inquiry into Some Mechanisms', 16 *Journal of Conflict & Security Law* (2011) 443.

[85] See *Khan v Royal Air Force Summary Appeal Court* [2004] EWHC 2230 (Admin), § 43 (reservist refused to join his unit because he did not want to be posted to Iraq) where the court stated that 'whether the imposition of sanctions on conscientious objection to compulsory military service, might, notwithstanding Art. 4(3)(b) of the European Convention on Human Rights infringe Art 9(1) was a point left open by the European Court of Human Rights'. See, however, *Bayatyan v Armenia*, App No 23459/03, Judgment, 7 July 2011, where the Grand Chamber broke the link between Arts 4(3)(b) and 9. See also *R v Kendall-Smith*, unreported but discussed in *R (Gentle and another) v Prime Minister and others* [2008] UKHL 20, § 50; *R v Lyons* [2012] 1 WLR 2702 which discusses the effect of *Bayatyan v Armenia*, above.

[86] See the Committee of Ministers, CM/Rec (2010) 4, Recommendations 43–5.

[87] See eg *Distomo Massacre Case (Greek Citizens v Federal Republic of Germany)* (2009) 135 ILR 186 (Federal Constitutional Court, Germany, 2006); *Amnesty International Canada v Chief of the Defence Staff for the Canadian Defence Forces*, 2008 FC 336.

9 CONCLUSION

We need to be clear what we mean by human rights law when we consider it in relation to the armed forces. Are they obligations placed upon the soldier, much like international humanitarian law, or rights possessed by others with whom they come into contact during an armed conflict, or do both apply? Since armed forces have the physical power to prevent the enjoyment of rights and fundamental freedoms by others during the conduct of an armed conflict, it may be better to think of human rights law as imposing obligations on armed forces in order to protect the enjoyment of rights by those with whom they come into contact. This approach is supported by the nature of the internal discipline system to be found in all legitimate armed forces. It seems more satisfying than according *rights* to others which, except in limited cases, cannot be enforced.

It is likely, however, that the future will see more attention being given to the human rights of the soldier during armed conflict. In this context it is, perhaps, correct to speak of the *rights* of the soldier. The limits of the state's obligation to protect the lives of its soldiers in battle will need to be considered carefully to ensure that human rights law provides a realistic balance between military risk and the protection of those who take those risks on behalf of a state.

PART VI

KEY ISSUES IN TIMES
OF ARMED CONFLICT

CHAPTER 22

....

USE OF FORCE

....

GIOVANNI DISTEFANO

1 INTRODUCTION

....

ARTICLE 2(4) of the Charter of the United Nations[1] (UN Charter) introduced for
the first time a comprehensive ban on the use of force in international relations
between states. Indeed, the use of force is prohibited outright, applying not only
to the waging of war (as in the Briand-Kellogg Pact of 1928) but also to forcible
measures short of war such as intervention, blockades, and reprisals. Moreover, the
ban extends not only to the actual use of force but also to its threat. The prohibition is accompanied by a robust system of collective security embodied primarily
in Chapter VII of the UN Charter. As a matter of interpretation under the Vienna
Convention on the Law of Treaties[2] (Vienna Convention), the content and scope of
the prohibition must be construed in context,[3] that is, in the light of other relevant
provisions in the UN Charter and its Preamble; 'any agreement relating to the treaty
which was made between all the parties in connection with the conclusion of the
treaty'; and 'any instrument which was made by one or more parties in connection
with the conclusion of the treaty and accepted by the other parties as an instrument
related to the treaty'.[4]

---

[1] (1945) 1 UNTS XVI. [2] *Vienna Convention on the Law of Treaties* (1969) 1155 UNTS 331.
[3] Vienna Convention, Art 31(1).
[4] Vienna Convention, Art 31(2). See also the *ICJ Advisory Opinion on the Legality of the Threat or Use
of Nuclear Weapons*, [1996] ICJ Rep 244, § 38.

2 THE PROHIBITION OF THE USE
OF FORCE BETWEEN STATES

In order to assess the content and scope of Article 2(4), it ought to be observed from the outset that while the prohibition is incumbent on all member states of the United Nations, its beneficiaries are states in general, whether or not they are UN members. If such specification is today irrelevant, given the customary international law nature of the prohibition enshrined in Article 2(4), this was not the case when the UN Charter was adopted and for a long time since then.

Quite obviously, Article 2(4) outlaws the use of military force, but it is still vociferously debated whether it covers other kinds of force, such as political, economical, and the like, to which states resort in their international life. Far from exhausting this highly sensitive matter, one could briefly list the elements in favour and against the extension of the prohibition to other species of force on the basis of a systemically integrated approach, requiring that relevant rules of international law applicable between the parties be taken into account in interpreting treaties.[5]

On the one hand, an expansive interpretation is supported as a matter of contextual interpretation and application of the textual canon *expressio unius est exclusio alterius*. Some provisions in the UN Charter including Article 2(4) refer only to 'force'[6] while other provisions refer to 'armed force'[7] (although the reference to 'force' in Article 44 is clearly intended only to refer to armed force). Further, General Assembly Resolution 2625 (XXV) on Friendly Relations[8] forbids 'armed intervention and all other forms of interference'[9] and clearly affirms that 'economic, political or any other types of measures'[10] aimed at subordinating sovereign rights breach the principle of non-intervention. While such measures are not expressly mentioned in Article 2(4), the propositions in the Resolution are consistent with a broad reading of the word 'force'. Arguably, therefore, Article 2(4) should not be read as excluding other kinds of force outside military force.

On the other hand, there are strong arguments in favour of a restrictive interpretation of Article 2(4). During the framing of the 1975 Helsinki Final Act on Security and Cooperation in Europe (Helsinki Final Act), a Soviet amendment to insert 'other' types of force was rejected by the Conference. The same had occurred in 1945, during the drafting of the UN Charter itself at the San Francisco Conference,

---

[5] See generally C. McLachlan, 'The Principle of Systemic Integration and Article 31(3)(c) of the Vienna Convention' (2005) 54 *ICLQ* 279.

[6] UN Charter, Arts 2(4), 44.   [7] UN Charter, Preamble, Art 41, 46.

[8] Declaration on Principles of International Law Concerning Friendly Relations and Cooperation Among States in Accordance with the Charter of the United Nations, UNGA Res 2625 (XXV) Annex, 25 UN GAOR, Supp (No 28), UN Doc A/5217 (24 October 1970).

[9] UN Doc A/5217 (24 October 1970), 123.   [10] UN Doc A/5217 (24 October 1970), 123.

where a similar proposition tabled by the Brazilian delegation was eventually dismissed.[11] In these two cases, the recourse to *travaux préparatoires* as a supplementary means of interpretation (one relating to the UN Charter itself and the other to a subsequent international instrument) conveys a restrictive interpretation of Article 2(4). In its 1973 judgment in the *Fisheries Jurisdiction Case*, the International Court of Justice (ICJ) seemed to suggest that only military force is envisaged by Article 2(4).[12] Later, in the seminal 1986 *Nicaragua Case*, the International Court of Justice clearly divided its analysis of allegedly wrongfully US actions into two categories: use of force under Article 2(4) and non-intervention under Article 2(1).[13] Non-military activities of the United States were scrutinized under the latter provision, and not under Article 2(4). Similarly, the Permanent Court of Arbitration in the 1981 *Dubai/Sharjah Border Case*[14] seemed cautiously to support a restrictive interpretation of Article 2(4). Finally, in this connection Article 52 of the Vienna Convention provides for the invalidity of treaties concluded 'by the threat or use of force in violation of the principles of international law embodied in the Charter of the United Nations'. By referring reflexively to the principles embodied in the Charter, this provision purposely abstains from specifying what type of force is eligible to nullify a treaty. A proposal aimed at the insertion of economic coercion within the scope of Article 52 was rejected by the Vienna Conference,[15] though it ultimately adopted a non-binding Declaration condemning 'Military, Political or Economic Coercion in the Conclusion of Treaties'.

At the end of the day, while it can be tentatively suggested that Article 2(4) only encompasses military force, one can nonetheless agree that 'it cannot be concluded that [this] issue has definitively been settled'.[16]

Some words must now be devoted to the second and third clauses of Article 2(4). The second clause ('against the territorial integrity or political independence of any State'), added at the San Francisco Conference,[17] has been hastily and wrongly construed by some authors as being an overt loophole in the general prohibition of the use of force, allowing forcible actions that do not directly compromise territory or political status. Luckily, this is refuted by interpreting the clause 'in the light of its object and purpose' in accordance with Article 31(1) of the Vienna Convention.

---

[11] UN Doc 784, 1/1/27, *UNCIO Documents* 331, 334–5.

[12] *Fisheries Jurisdiction (Federal Republic of Germany v Iceland)*, Jurisdiction of the Court, Judgment, [1973] ICJ Rep 59, § 24.

[13] *Military and Paramilitary Activities in and against Nicaragua*, Judgment, [1986] ICJ Rep 98–102, §§ 187–92 (98–102) and 123–9, §§ 239–53.

[14] Arbitral Award of 19 October 1981 (1993) 91 *ILR* 569.

[15] Amendment sponsored by 19 states purporting to add 'including economic or political pressure' after the term 'force' (Official Documents of the Conference, at 171).

[16] O. Corten, 'Article 52. Convention of 1969', in O. Corten and P. Klein (eds), *The Vienna Conventions on the Law of Treaties* (Oxford: Oxford University Press, 2011), 1207. By contrast, it is undisputed that any kind of political or economic coercion is likely to amount to an unlawful intervention in matters within the domestic jurisdiction of the affected state, thus breaching Art 2(1) of the UN Charter.

[17] UN Doc 784, 1/1/27, *UNCIO Documents* VI, 342–6.

According to its Preamble and reiterated in substance in its first Article,[18] one para-mount purpose of the UN Charter is to restrict the unilateral use of force by states in their international relations. This construction is further supported by the UN Charter's *travaux préparatoires*, which record that the majority of delegations voted for the insertion of the second clause in an attempt to strengthen rather than to dilute the prohibition.[19] It was contended that small-scale or short-lived uses of force on another state's territory did not amount to the infringement of its territo-rial integrity and political independence. This interpretation is not correct. Rather, 'independence' must be read as 'inviolability' (that is, any forcible trespassing of state boundaries),[20] albeit of limited duration and scope. Hence, 'political integ-rity' does not merely cover attempts to modify the legal status of the invaded terri-tory (for instance through annexation), but also any use of force directed within or against another state. In this respect, some scholars[21] have tried to demonstrate that military actions aimed at eradicating military or paramilitary non-state actors on another states territory without clashing, or targeting, the latter military forces, is not inconsistent with Article 2(4). This contention is not well founded for the same reasons as above (see also *infra* 1.B.3).

The third clause ('or in any other manner inconsistent with the Purposes of the United Nations') has likewise given birth to daredevil interpretations aimed at showing that some types of military interventions *on* another state's territory may be compatible with Article 2(4). Such interpretations suggest that, for instance, humanitarian inter-vention, or the germane intervention for the protection of human rights, and interven-tion for the protection of nationals abroad, allegedly being carried out in pursuance of UN goals, would not be at odds with its purposes. Protection of nationals abroad will be dealt with later on; it suffices here to emphasize that this clause aimed, again, at hard-ening the general prohibition as it clearly appears from the UN Conference in 1945.[22]

---

[18] '[T]o ensure [...] that armed force shall not be used, *save in the common interest*' (emphasis added).

[19] See R.B. Russell, *A History of the United Nations Charter* (Washington, The Brookings Institution, 1958), 456–7.

[20] In accordance with General Assembly Res 2625 (XXV) (n 22), 'state boundaries' must be here interpreted according to its widest meaning, thus including (in addition to internationally agreed and recognized state boundaries): 'international lines of demarcation, such as armistice lines, established by or pursuant to an international agreement to which it is a party or which it is otherwise bound to respect'. The ICJ's case law (*Legal Consequences of the Construction of a Wall in the Occupied Palestinian Territory*, Advisory Opinion, [2004] ICJ Rep 171, § 87) and UN Security Council practice (Res 111 (19 January 1956), 228 (25 November 1966) and so forth) concur to this interpretation.

[21] J.E.S. Fawcett, 'Intervention in International Law', 103 *RCADI* (1961-II) 359; B.A. Feinstein, 'The Legality of the Use of Armed Force by Israel in Lebanon—June 1982' (1985) 20 *ILR* 372–3; R.A. Friedlander, 'Retaliations as an Anti-Terrorist Weapon: The Israeli Lebanon Incursions and International Law', 8 *Israel Yearbook on Human Rights* (1978) 72; B. Levenfeld, 'Israel's Counter-Fedayeen Tactics in Lebanon: Self-Defense and Reprisals Under Modern International Law', 21 *Columbia Journal of Transnational Law* (1982) 20, 29, 45–6.

[22] 'The Delegate of the United States made it clear that the intention of the authors of the original text was to state in the broadest terms an absolute all-inclusive prohibition; the phrase "or in any other manner" was designed to insure that there should be no loopholes' (*Documents of the United Nations*

Finally, it is worth recalling that—whatever the actual or overrated deficiencies of the UN system of collective security[23]—Article 2(4) (and the overall régime concerning the use of force embodied therein) reflects customary international law as the ICJ rightfully stressed in *Nicaragua*.[24]

3 THE DEFINITION OF AGGRESSION

The UN Charter refers to 'aggression' and 'act of aggression' several times (Articles 1(1), 39, 53)[25] without defining these terms. In reality, during the San Francisco Conference, several propositions were submitted (by small and medium-sized states)[26] for the insertion in the UN Charter of a definition of aggression binding on the UN Security Council, but all of them were met by the hostility of the future UNSC permanent members. This was unsurprising, as it is likely to be within the interests of larger states and more powerful states to keep definitions as malleable as possible. Since then, the General Assembly approved a definition of aggression drafted by a Special Committee on the Question of Defining Aggression in Resolution 3314 (XXIX).[27]

Although, as stated above, the UN Charter régime pertaining to the use of force is comprised of several provisions and must be considered and construed as a whole, some significant differences exist between, Article 2(4) on the one hand and, on the other, those Articles referring to aggression. In other words, the scope of force prohibited under the former is not coextensive with the notion of aggression, the

Conference on International Organization, San Francisco, 1945, vol VI, 335). '[T]he Committee [Special Committee of the General Assembly mandated to the elaboration of resolution 2625] regarded the concluding phrase of Article 2(4) as a limitation on State action and not an escape clause' (quoted in E. Jiménez de Aréchaga, 'International Law in the Past Third of a Century. General Course in Public International Law', 159 *RCADI* (1978-I) 92).

[23] 'Whatever the fate of Chapters VI and VII of the United Nations Charter, Article 2(4) remains. That norm, I stress, is independent of collective enforcement. The argument that, under the principle *rebus sic stantibus*, or some variation of it, the failure of the intended enforcement system vitiates Article 2(4), has no foundation. Clearly, that was not the intent of the framers of the Charter. No Government has claimed it. Not many scholars have argued it', L. Henkin, 'International Law: Politics, Values and Functions. General Course on Public International Law', 218 *RCADI* (1989-IV) 145–6; *Corfu Channel* case (*UK v Albania*), Judgment, [1949] ICJ Rep, 35; UNGA Res 377 (V) 'Uniting for Peace', adopted 3 November 1950 (7th and 8th Preambles). See likewise *infra* 112.

[24] *Nicaragua* 1986 (n 13), 99–100 (§ 188).

[25] This list omits Art 51, which surprisingly—contrary to the French text—refers to 'armed attack'. See *infra* 1.A.1.

[26] Russell (n 19), 670–2.

[27] UNGA Res 3314 (XXIX) adopted the 14 December 1974 (Definition of Aggression).

existence of which can trigger the right for the victim-state to respond in accordance with Article 51 (which enshrines the right of self-defence).[28]

How do we know that not all acts prohibited as per Article 2(4) constitute aggression? First of all, this provision also bans the *threat* of force, which is clearly outside the scope of *actual* use of force. Secondly, and more importantly, not all *actual* uses of force amount to (an act of) aggression. Aggression is a subset of use of force, as the General Assembly declared in its Resolution 3314 (XXIX) defining aggression as 'the most serious and dangerous form of the illegal use of force'.[29] This discrepancy is corroborated by the majority, if not all, of the elements of the general rule of interpretation, codified by Article 31 of the Vienna Convention. First of all, in terms of literal interpretation, 'use of force' and 'aggression' have different 'ordinary' meanings; contextual[30] and judicial interpretation concur likewise to support this discrepancy;[31] systemic interpretation points to the same conclusion, through the recourse to the aforementioned General Assembly Resolutions 2625 (XXV) and 3314 (XXIX) and to the International Law Commission's Articles on the Responsibility of States for Internationally Wrongful Acts[32] (ILC Articles on State Responsibility). Furthermore, this is confirmed by recourse to the supplementary means of interpretation, *travaux préparatoires* (Article 32 of the Vienna Convention), from which clearly emerges the intention to restrict the grounds for unilateral use of force by states.[33]

Article 3 of the Definition of Aggression annexed to General Assembly Resolution 3314 (XXIX) takes a case-by-case approach to defining aggression, providing an open-ended list of situations that shall qualify as acts of aggression. Its non-exhaustive character can also be inferred explicitly from Article 4, which provides that '[t]he acts enumerated above are not exhaustive' and that 'the Security Council may determine that other acts constitute aggression'. In fact there are two conditions which determine the existence of an act of aggression: first, the temporal element, according to which '[t]he first use of armed force by a State in contravention of the Charter shall constitute *prima facie* evidence of an act of aggression'; secondly, the

---

[28] See *infra* 1.A.1.

[29] UNGA Res 3314 (XXIX) adopted the 14 December 1974 (Definition of Aggression).

[30] It suffices to recall that, as the ICJ said in 1996, 'The prohibition of the use of force is to be considered in the light of other relevant provisions of the Charter. In Article 51, the Charter recognizes the inherent right of individual or collective self-defence': *Threat or Use of Nuclear Weapons* (n 4), 244 (§ 38).

[31] *Nicaragua* 1986 (n 13), 101, 110–11, 119, 126–7 (§§ 191, 210–210, 230, 247); *Threat or Use of Nuclear Weapons* (n 4), 244 (§§ 37–8); Eritrea–Ethiopia Claims Commission, Partial Award *Jus ad bellum* (Ethiopia's Claims 1–8), 19 December 2005, §§ 11, 12 (<http://www.pca-cpa.org/showfile.asp?fil_id=158>); *Oil Platforms (Islamic Republic of Iran v United States)*, Judgment, [2003] ICJ Rep 186–7, § 51; 186–7; *Armed Activities on the Territory of the Congo (Democratic Republic of the Congo v Uganda)*, Judgment, [2005] ICJ Rep 222–3 (§§ 146–7).

[32] 'The wrongfulness of an act of a State is precluded if the act constitutes a lawful measure of self-defence taken in conformity with the Charter of the United Nations', Art 21 (Self-defence as a circumstance precluding wrongfulness), UN Doc A/56/10, 74–5.

[33] Russell (n 19), 560–5.

substantive element, for the acts concerned must attain the severity and magnitude required in order to fall within the definition. Otherwise, the use of force will not amount to an (act of) aggression, even though it may still infringe Article 2(4).

In this regard, it must be noted that this list constitutes the core of the definition of aggression (as the contextual interpretation in light of Article 4 corroborates), to the extent that any (act of) aggression whatsoever should *at least* possess these features. On scanning this list, it is obvious that in all the situations listed there are a number of common themes: (a) inter-state relations;[34] (b) in all but one (3(d)), the territorial dimension is the focal point of the act of aggression.

In this connection it must be observed that it seems that even a series of acts that do not individually reach the threshold of aggression can be considered as a whole, *globally taken* as such. The so-called pin-prick doctrine[35] was discussed by the ICJ in the seminal *Nicaragua* case[36] and reiterated in 2003[37] and 2005, thus conceding that a 'series of deplorable [military] attacks could be regarded as cumulative in character',[38] resulting in an aggression. Therefore a series of 'localized incidents'[39] of low intensity and restricted scope can, if taken *cumulatively*, amount to an aggression. In other words, while each one of them infringes Article 2(4), the whole set *additionally* constitutes an aggression. This point of view is consistent with the logic underlying the concept of aggression and its commission. In this vein, it is pertinent to refer to a well-established concept in international state responsibility, now codified by Article 15 of the ILC Articles on State Responsibility: composite act. As Article 15(1) recites, such an act comprises a 'a series of acts or omissions defined in aggregate as wrongful', for they are bound together by the same intention, plan, policy,[40] or even premeditation[41] and they pursue *as a whole* 'the same internationally wrongfully objective'.[42]

---

[34] Directly or indirectly (as encompassed by Art 3(g)), to which will be devoted a sub-section later on (1.B.1).

[35] In German: 'Nadelstichtaktik'.

[36] The question was whether some military incursions 'may be treated for legal purposes (ie ascertainment of Nicaragua's aggression against some border states) as *amounting, singly or collectively,* to an "armed attack" by Nicaragua [...]', (n 13), 120 (§ 231).

[37] *Oil Platforms* (n 31), 192 (§ 64): 'Even taken *cumulatively* [...]' (emphasis added).

[38] *Armed Activities on the Territory of the Congo* (n 31), 223 (§ 146).

[39] See Eritrea–Ethiopia Claims Commission (n 31), §§ 11, 12.

[40] See ILC Commentary to its Article 15 of the ILC Articles on State Responsibility (n 32), 65.

[41] In fact, it was thanks to Latin-American states at the San Francisco Conference (defending their regional arrangement of collective self-defence) that Art 51 was *moved* from Ch VIII (Regional Arrangements) to its current place (Ch VII). Indeed, as Art 53(1), in UN Charter Ch VIII, provides, no state belonging to any of the regional arrangements can take an 'enforcement action' without Security Council authorization. See in this regard, Russell (n 19), 696–7, 700–2.

[42] Seventh Report on State Responsibility by Mr Roberto Ago, Special Rapporteur—The Internationally wrongful act of the state, Source of international responsibility (continued), UN Doc A/CN.4/307 and Add 1 & 2 and Corr 1 & 2 (*YILC*, 1978, vol I(1), 47 (§ 39)).

4 SELF-DEFENCE

As Article 51 of the UN Charter stipulates, all (member) states have an 'inherent right'[43] of self-defence.[44] As the legislative history of this provision shows, it was undisputed that member states do not need to be authorized by the UNSC in order to avail themselves of the right of self-defence.[45] However, like any subjective right, this too is constitutionally limited by the legal order by which it is envisaged and within which it is implemented. That is why the implementation of the right of self-defence is subject to the fulfilment of several conditions provided for by public international law. These cumulative requirements are enunciated by Article 51 of the UN Charter *and* by customary international law, which complements the former.[46] In sum, three conditions (armed attack, proportionality, and necessity) are required by general international law (that is, by the UN Charter *and* customary international law) while two are posited only by the UN Charter (ie the obligation to report to the UNSC and that of submitting the right of self-defence to the latter).[47]

Besides, self-defence can be individual and collective. In the first scenario the target state, after having reckoned that it has been *attacked* by one (or more) state(s), reacts alone in order to push back the aggressor. In the second case, the target state requests other states to help it to halt the aggression. The same conditions apply in both cases. However, as far as collective self-defence is concerned, there are two additional requirements to be met. First, that only the target state[48] can make the determination that it has been attacked; third states are not empowered to do so on its behalf.[49] Secondly, and more important, third states cannot intervene without being explicitly (and validly) requested or invited to this effect.[50]

---

[43] In the French text, '*droit naturel*'.

[44] '[T]he use of arms in legitimate self-defence remains admitted and unimpaired', in Documents of the United Nations Conference of International Organization (UNCIO) (n 22), 334.

[45] In this connection, it ought to be reminded that for this very reason Art 51 had been moved from Ch VIII (n 41).

[46] 'The Charter, having itself recognized the existence of this right, does not go on to regulate directly all aspects of its content. For example, it does not contain any specific rule whereby self-defence would warrant only measures which are proportional to the armed attack and necessary to respond to it, a rule well established in customary international law', *Nicaragua* 1986 (n 13), 94 (§ 176); *Oil Platforms* (n 31), 183 (§ 43); Resolution ('Present Problems of the Use of Armed Force in International Law') adopted by the Institut de Droit International during its 2007 session in Santiago de Chile: 'Necessity and proportionality are essential components of the normative framework of self-defence' (§ 2).

[47] *Nicaragua* 1986 (n 13), 105 (§ 200).

[48] In addition obviously to the UN Security Council, by virtue of Art 39 of the UN Charter.

[49] Quite naturally, UNSC may at any time determine by virtue of Art 39 of the UN Charter 'the existence [...] of an act of aggression'.

[50] 'The exercise of the right of collective self-defence presupposes that an armed attack has occurred; and it is evident that it is the victim State, being the most directly aware of that fact, which is likely to draw general attention to its plight. It is also evident that if the victim State wishes another State to

A. Conditions

(i) *Previous armed attack*

In accordance with Article 51 of the UN Charter, an 'armed attack' constitutes the *conditio sine qua non* triggering the right to self-defence,[51] be it individual or collective.[52] The armed attack must be underway (already launched) or, at most, imminent; hence, a simple threat (whatever be the meaning and effectiveness of it) does not suffice to trigger the right of self-defence.[53] The formula of 'armed attack' in the English version of the Charter correlates with the expression '*aggression armée*'[54] in the French text, but the meaning of the two is not exactly the same. Notwithstanding this linguistic discrepancy, 'armed attack' must be considered, for the purposes of application of Article 51, as being equivalent to '*agression armée*'. All interpretative methods point to this conclusion: judicial,[55] contextual, systemic interpretation,[56] *travaux préparatoires*.[57] Furthermore, Article 33 of the Vienna Convention (relating to treaties 'authenticated in two or more languages') requires adoption of the 'meaning which best reconciles the texts, having regard to the object and purpose of the treaty'. Once the link is established between 'armed attack' and 'aggression', the reader may recall the discussion of the definition of 'aggression' above.

The existence of this discrepancy between use of force under Article 2(4) and (acts of) aggression may give rise to the question of what a state can lawfully do in reaction to uses of force falling below the threshold of aggression. We will address this issue later in the Chapter.

come to its help in the exercise of the right of collective self-defence, it will normally make an express request to that effect', *Nicaragua* 1986 (n 13), 120 (§ 232). In the same vein: resolution adopted by the Institut de Droit International (n 46), 46: 'Collective self-defence may be exercised only at the request of the target State', § 8 <http://www.idi-iil.org/idiE/navig_chon2003.html>.

[51] *Nicaragua* 1986 (n 13), 103 (§ 195).   [52] *Nicaragua* 1986 (n 13), 110 (§ 211).

[53] See resolution adopted by the Institut de Droit International (n 46), § 7: 'In case *of threat of an armed* attack against a State, only the Security Council is entitled to decide or authorize the use of force' (emphasis added). *Infra* 1.B.2.

[54] 'When it came (in San Francisco) to defining the criteria to be used in determining aggression, it was decided to avoid the words "war" and "aggression". The use of these words in the Covenant of the League had led to prolonged *legalistic debate*, as over the Manchurian affair in 1931, for example', Russell (n 19), 234 (emphasis added).

[55] With regard to Art 51 of the UN Charter, both the ICJ and other international tribunals consider armed attack as being the English equivalent of '*agression armée*'. For the purposes of its interpretation recourse is systematically made to the aforementioned General Assembly Res 3314 (XXIX), which purports to define 'Aggression'.

[56] See the French version of the Institut de Droit International's resolution (n 46), which states clearly this equivalence between 'armed attack' ('*attaque armée*') and 'armed aggression' (§ 3).

[57] Russell (n 19), 697–8.

(ii) *Necessity*

The doctrine of necessity embodies the requirement that force should only be used where there is no other *effective* means at the disposal of the attacked state to repel the aggression. If this is so then the target state is no longer required to exhaust peaceful means of dispute settlement, as mandated under Article 2(3) of the UN Charter. The leading and recurrently cited authority on this point emerged from the *Caroline* affair (1837–42) between the United States and Britain. The *Caroline*, a vessel used by US nationals to supply Canadian rebels across the border, was destroyed on US territory by British soldiers, causing a diplomatic incident. After lengthy correspondence, the dispute was settled through an agreement between the two states. In fact, what counts here is a diplomatic note sent on 24 April 1841 by US Secretary of State (Mr Webster) to the British minister at Washington (Mr Fox), which reads as follows: 'It will be for that Government [that is, Britain] to show a necessity of self-defence, instant, overwhelming, leaving no choice of means, and no moment for deliberation'.[58]

A caveat must nonetheless be imposed in this regard; as Ago showed as Special Rapporteur on State Responsibility,[59] at that time it was nonsense (both logically and historically)[60] to speak of self-defence, for recourse to the use of force to enforce legal rights (so-called self-help or self-protection)[61] was the prerogative of sovereign

---

[58] 'Correspondence between Great Britain and the United States, respecting the Arrest and Imprisonment of Mr. McLeod, for the Destruction of the Steamboat *Caroline.*—March, April, 1841', 29 *British and Foreign State Papers (1840–1841)* (1857) 1126 at 1138; see further 'The *Caroline* Case', 2 *Moore's Digest of International Law* (1906) 409–14.

[59] 'What is the fundamental reason why these publicists argue so strenuously that the scope of self-defence under general international law is much wider than that of resistance to armed attack, and thus conclude that Art 51 of the Charter, in expressly safeguarding only the right of a State to react in self-defence only in the case of armed attack, was not intended to cover the entire field of application of the concept of self-defence and left intact the much wider scope of that concept in general international law? The reason is largely that many of these writers remain wedded to notions and to a terminology—which this writer regards as incorrect—drawn from a relatively antiquated portion of State practice with which they are more familiar. It is no accident that, in their arguments, they often cite practical cases, such as that of the *Caroline* and others, which they place under the heading of self-defence in keeping with the examples set by the diplomats of the time. It has, it is submitted, been clearly shown that these cases are in fact illustrations of different circumstances; admittedly, what they have in common with self-defence is that their effect is to preclude the wrongfulness of certain kinds of State conduct, but in many other essential respects they are quite unlike self-defence. It is indispensable to differentiate, clearly, the concept of self-defence properly so-called from the various notions that are often grouped together under the common label of self-help [...] The confusion between so very different situations hampers the task of arriving at an accurate definition of self-defence', Addendum—Eighth report on State responsibility by Mr Roberto Ago, Special Rapporteur—The internationally wrongful act of the State, Source of international responsibility (Part 1), *YILC*, 1980, vol II (1), 65–6 at 62 (§§ 113, 106).

[60] D. Anzilotti, *Cours de droit international* (transl from Italian, Paris: Sirey, 1929), 506.

[61] *Corfu Channel* case (n 23), 35: 'The United Kingdom Agent, in his speech in reply, has further classified "Operation Retail" among methods of self-protection or self-help. The Court cannot accept this

states. The right of self-defence is a separate concept, which permits the target state to resort to force *only if* it has been attacked by another state and not to enforce its own rights or to react to minor infringements of Article 2(4) (uses of force under the threshold of armed attack or mere threats to use force). That said, the *Caroline* test is useful in order to elucidate the concept of necessity, that is, the requirement that there be no other effective means available to the attacked state to repel the aggressor.

(iii) *Proportionality*

The condition of proportionality, closely intertwined with that of necessity, puts emphasis on the outcome of self-defence, that is, stopping the armed attack and pushing back the aggressor. Military reaction by a target state cannot lawfully either assume a punitive character or cause unnecessary pain and suffering.[62] Proportionality can be assessed from two perspectives: proportionality of means and proportionality of result. In respect of the first meaning, there should be a 'proportionality of that action (by the target state) to the attack to which it was said to be a response'.[63] On the contrary, from the standpoint of the second perspective, 'the action needed to halt and repulse the attack may well have to assume *dimensions disproportionate to those of the attack suffered*. What matters in this respect is the *result to be achieved by the "defensive" action*, and not the forms, substance and strength of the action itself'.[64]

In this connection, one needs to make clear the differences between *jus ad bellum* (in the light of which self-defence must be analysed) and *jus in bello* (that is, international humanitarian law at large). In the same manner, we have to distinguish between the legality of the use of force at a macroscopic level and the legality of each singular military action *during* the conflict, to which of course relevant rules of international humanitarian law shall apply. In this regard, the ICJ's observations in its *Nuclear Weapons* Advisory Opinion are crystal clear: 'at the same time, *a use of force that is proportionate under the law of self-defence, must, in order to be lawful, also meet* the requirements of the law applicable in armed conflict which comprise in particular the principles and rules of humanitarian law'.[65] Hence, under the

---

defence either. Between independent States, respect for territorial sovereignty is an essential foundation of international relations'.

[62] G. Abi-Saab, 'Cours général de droit international public', vol 207, 371.

[63] *Oil Platforms* (n 31), 198 (§ 77). Perhaps in the same vein, yet not fully elaborated: *Nicaragua* 1986 (n 13), 122 (§ 237).

[64] Ago (n 59), 69 (§ 120, emphasis added). In the same vein: 'it does not seem unreasonable as a rule to allow a State to retaliate beyond the immediate area of attack when that State has sufficient reason to expect a continuation of attacks (with substantial military weapons) from the same source' (O. Schachter, 'International Law in Theory and Practice. General Course of Public International Law', 1978 *RCADI* (1982-V) 156.

[65] *Threat or Use of Nuclear Weapons* (n 4), 245 (§ 42, emphasis added).

rules of *jus ad bellum*, a state's use of force can be (qualitatively and quantitatively) different[66] from that of the aggressor, if it is *necessary* in order to repel the latter.[67] In the light of the aforesaid, it can be maintained that proportionality in self-defence, under a *jus ad bellum* perspective, is related to the goal pursued by the military response and not to its means. However, as noted in *Nuclear Weapons*, such a use of force would not necessarily be lawful under *jus in bello*.

(iv) *Two conventional requirements*

First, Article 51 adamantly specifies that the right of self-defence can be exercised by a state 'until the Security Council has taken measures necessary to maintain international peace and security'. Secondly, the measures taken by the target state 'shall be immediately reported to the Security Council'. As the ICJ made clear in 1986 in *Nicaragua*, even though it can hardly be contended that these requirements are exacted by customary international law, 'if self-defence is advanced as a justification for measures which would otherwise be in breach both of the principle of customary international law and of that contained in the Charter, it is to be expected that the conditions of the Charter should be respected. Thus for the purpose of enquiry into the customary law position, the absence of a report may be one of the factors indicating whether the state in question was itself *convinced* that it was acting in self-defence'.[68]

As these two institutional conditions show, self-defence fits into the general scheme for the maintenance (or restoration) of international peace and security, the main responsibility for which is vested in the UN Security Council.[69] Member states need not be authorized by the Security Council to resort to force in self-defence, yet the exercise of this right is no longer unfettered once the Security Council has taken the necessary measures to maintain or restore international peace and security. The following fragment of Article 51 affirms the subordination of the right of self-defence to the system of collective security established in Chapter VII: 'Measures taken by Members [...] shall not in any way affect the *authority and responsibility of the Security Council*' to this effect. In this respect,

---

[66] Each single 'attack' (as per Art 49 of the 1977 Geneva Protocol I) must satisfy IHL requirements in order to be considered as lawful *under this branch of law*.

[67] Even a temporary military occupation of the aggressor state's territory (or parties thereof) can be envisaged, but not its annexation or forceful modification of its legal status. This is explicitly banned by Art 2(4) of the UN Charter as authoritatively interpreted by General Assembly Resolutions 2625 (XXV) (n 20) and 3314 (XXIX) (n 29). Most authorities support this sound principle of public international law: R.R. Baxter 'Treaties and customs', 129 *RCADI* (1970-I) 69. In addition: 'However, the practice of States and the writings of eminent publicists show that self-defence cannot be invoked to settle territorial disputes' (Eritrea–Ethiopia Claims Commission (n 20), § 10).

[68] *Nicaragua* 1986 (n 13), 105 (§ 200, emphasis added).

[69] '[T]he authorization of self-defence is a provisional measure intended to protect the integrity and independence of a member State until the United Nations takes collective action', M. Lachs, 'The Development and General Trends of International Law in Our Time', 169 *RCADI* (1980-IV) 165.

though, no true precedent[70] can be cited to depict the application of this rule, with perhaps the sole exception of a debatable interpretation of Security Council action following Iraq's invasion of Kuwait in 1990.[71]

B. Two selected controversial topics

(i) Self-defence against non-state actors

For more than a couple of decades or so, no textbook or monograph study on the use of force has avoided this seemingly new topic (often in conjunction with another seemingly new topic—that of international terrorism). In fact, the large majority, if not all, of the classics of the Law of Nations, at least until Emer de Vattel, devoted substantial developments to what was then called 'private war', that is, conflict between a public authority (a state or state-like entity) and other generally non-sovereign entities (which did not possess territorial sovereignty).

However, the alleged analogy with Grotius' private war cannot be upheld, especially as a result of massive structural modifications of the international legal order since then (on the side of both substantive and institutional law). It suffices to glance at Vattel's *The Law of Nations* in order to realize that this kind of war had from then on fallen outside the scope of public international law; as it has been affirmed by an authoritative commentator, sovereign states cannot *literally* wage war against non-state actors.[72] Under traditional international law, states can only use force against their equals.[73] Sovereign states have a monopoly on the use of force within their territory; the UN Charter has enshrined this competence in Article 2(4) where it forbids the use of force by states *only* in their international relations, leaving unaffected their rights within their respective territories.

From this perspective, it is not too bold to affirm that, with regard to the régime of the use of force and self-defence, the international legal order is (still) essentially

---

[70] The paucity of practice can explained at the same time by the passivity during the Cold War of the Security Council and by the highly sensitive prerogative which is that of a state right of self-defence. This is not to mention the Security Council's lack of 'armed forces, assistance, and facilities [...] necessary for the purpose of maintaining peace and security', as envisaged by the never-implemented Art 43 of the UN Charter.

[71] Reference is made to Res 678 (29 November 1990), a dispositive paragraph of which ('Member States co-operating with the Government of Kuwait') could allude to a Kuwaiti right of collective self-defence. However, apart from this sole indication, all other elements (textual and contextual) seem to point more convincingly to another ground of use of force, that is, Art 42 providing for collective security under UN Charter, Ch VII.

[72] According to Kelsen, armed attack under Art 51 solely covers cases where 'one State attacks another State with its armed forces', H. Kelsen, *The Law of the United Nations. A Critical Analysis of its Fundamental Problems* (New York: Praeger, 1950), 930.

[73] S. Laghmani, 'Vattel et le *Ius ad Bellum*', in V. Chetail and P. Haggenmacher (eds), *Vattel's International Law in a XXIst Century Perspective* (Leiden: Martinus Nijhoff Publishers, 2011), 308–10.

state-centred and fundamentally territorial. This entails that, technically speaking, a state cannot lawfully avail itself of the principle of self-defence in order to justify military force *on the territory* of another state unless, as stated in Article 3(g) of the Annex to General Assembly Resolution 3314 (XXIX): (a) that other state has sent the 'armed bands, groups, irregulars or mercenaries' on its 'behalf' and they commit acts 'of such gravity as to amount' to aggression, or (b) it can be proved that the other state had 'substantial involvement' in their acts.

Hence, public international law requires a *link* between the state towards which self-defence is directed and the military groups that have carried out acts of aggression against the target state. This is arguably the position taken by the ICJ when faced with acts of aggression carried out by non-state actors from another state and directed at the target state. In addition to its judgment in *Nicaragua*, the ICJ has more recently addressed the link requirement:

[W]hile Uganda claimed to have acted in self-defence, it did not ever claim that it had been subjected to an armed attack by the armed forces of the DRC. The 'armed attacks' to which reference was made came rather from the ADF. The Court has found above (paragraphs 131–135) that there *is no satisfactory proof of the involvement in these attacks, direct or indirect, of the Government of the DRC. The attacks did not emanate from armed bands or irregulars sent by the DRC or on behalf of the DRC, within the sense of Article 3(g) of General Assembly resolution 3314 (XXIX) on the definition of aggression, adopted on 14 December 1974. The Court is of the view that, on the evidence before it, even if this series of deplorable attacks could be regarded as cumulative in character, they still remained non-attributable to the DRC.*[74]

The test of attribution clearly remands to the body of rules codified in the ILC Articles on State Responsibility, notably under Article 4 (the conduct of state organs) and Article 8 (conduct directed or controlled by a state).[75] In its judgment in the *Genocide* case, the ICJ reaffirmed its position with regard to each of these two Articles. As to the first title of attribution, the Court required that in order for some individuals to 'be equated with State organs even if that status does not follow from internal law' it must be proved that 'in fact the persons, groups or entities act in "complete dependence" on the State, of which they are ultimately merely the instrument'.[76] As to the second ground of attribution, and by reference to the very heading of the International Law Commission's Article 8, the Court held that the person or entity must have acted in accordance with the state's instructions or under

---

[74] *Armed Activities* (n 31), 222–3 (§ 146, emphasis added). In the same vein, see Wall in Palestine (n 20), 194 (§ 139): 'Article 51 of the Charter thus recognizes the existence of an inherent right of self-defence in the case of armed attack by one State against another State. However, Israel does not claim that the attack against it are imputable to a foreign State'; *Nicaragua* 1986 (n 13), 138–9 (§ 277)

[75] *Nicaragua* 1986 (n 13), 61–2, 64–5, 103–4, (§§1069, 11516, 195); Application of the Convention on the Prevention and Punishment of the Crime of Genocide (*Bosnia and Herzegovina v Serbia and Montenegro*), Judgment, [2007] ICJ Rep, 202–10 (§§ 385–407).

[76] Crime of Genocide (n 75), 205 (§ 392). The Court makes further references to 'proof of a particularly great degree of State control over them' and 'complete dependence' (§ 393).

its 'effective control'. With regard to the latter, the Court's interpretation requires that, in order for the acts of private individuals to be attributable, it must be proved that the state concerned exercised 'effective control' over them. This criterion can be thus split in two dimensions, the horizontal and the vertical. In other words, 'it must [...] be shown that this "effective control" was exercised, or that the state's instructions were given, in respect of each operation in which the alleged violations occurred, not generally in respect of the overall actions taken by the persons or groups of persons having committed the violations'.[77]

In order to grasp the concrete meaning of 'effective control', it can be said, on the footing of the ICJ's considerations in *Nicaragua*, that a state's participation 'even if preponderant or decisive, in the financing, organizing, training, supplying and equipping of the *contras*, the selection of its military and paramilitary targets, and the planning of the whole of its operation, is still insufficient in itself [...] for the purpose'[78] of attribution. Or, in other words, this participation does not amount to the '*substantial* involvement' required for the purposes of Article 3(g) of General Assembly Resolution 3314 (XXIX). However, as the ICJ made clear, the United States, albeit not committing aggression against Nicaragua through the actions of the Contras, had infringed Article 2(4) of the UN Charter by 'organizing or encouraging the organization of irregular forces or armed bands [...] for incursion into the territory of another State' and 'participating in acts of civil strife [...] in another State', in the terms of General Assembly Resolution 2625 (XXV).[79] Hence, the Court rightly insisted on the aforementioned discrepancy between (mere) use of force and aggression.[80]

If no link can be established in accordance with the legal grounds of attribution or, alternatively, if no 'substantial involvement' can be proved, then the target state cannot, on account of self-defence, react by armed force in or against the state where those groups have their facilities or camps.[81] In the absence of such a link, the only situation in which a state can resort to self-defence is when an 'armed

[77] Crime of Genocide (n 75), 207 (§ 398), 208 (§ 400). In this connection, it must be recalled that, in 1999, ICTY Appeals Chamber, in the *Tadić case* (IT-94-1-A, 15 July 1999, <http://www.icty.org/case/tadic/4>), contested the application of such a stringent test of control in situations where the acts concerned are carried out by 'individuals making up an organised and hierarchically structured group, such as a military unit, in case of war or civil strife, armed bands of irregulars or rebels. [...] Consequently, for the attribution to a State of acts of these groups it is sufficient to require that the group as a whole be under the over control of the State' (§ 120). In sum, it must be proved that most of the time, most of the actions carried put by this organized group of individuals have been under the 'overall control' of the state concerned. For instance, while the ICJ rejected the attribution of Contras' acts to the United States in *Nicaragua*, the application of the ICTY's 'overall control' would have reached the opposite conclusion.

[78] *Nicaragua* 1986 (n 13), 65 (§ 115).   [79] *Nicaragua* 1986 (n 13), 119 (§ 228).

[80] Not unsurprisingly, the Institut de Droit International follows the Court's established case law in this regard.

[81] *Contra* Judge Simma's and Judge Kooijmans' separate opinions appended to the ICJ Judgment in the *Armed Activities on the Territory of the Congo* (n 31), respectively 335-7 and 310-16.

attack by non-State actors is launched from an area beyond the jurisdiction of any State'; then 'the target State may exercise its right of self-defence in that area against those non-State actors'.[82] Once again, the interstate and territorial paradigm of the current international legal order is reaffirmed thus influencing the régime of use of force.

(ii) *Temporal aspects related to self-defence (anticipatory, preventive, pre-emptive)*

More than elsewhere, in the law of self-defence we are faced with a blossoming of labels, tags, neologisms, the result (and no doubt on occasion the aim) of which is to bewilder the critical mind. The stakes of this debate are in fact quite high, for we are dealing with the only ground allowing a state unilaterally to resort to force in international relations. Hitherto, great efforts have been made by states and scholars (sometimes even jointly) to expand self-defence by reference to the time element.

If we assume a large correspondence between Article 51 of the UN Charter and customary international law,[83] it is beyond doubt that a state possesses an 'inherent' right to react to an armed attack *already launched*.[84] What then of an armed attack which is about to be launched? Or what about of the imminent threat of an attack? On the basis of a brief review of doctrinal positions in the current debate, the following adjectives associated with self-defence can be put forward: (a) interceptive; (b) anticipatory; (c) pre-emptive; (d) preventive. We will tentatively sketch their distinctive features in turn.

As for the first ('interceptive'), it means, in a nutshell, the right of a state squarely to obstruct an armed attack already launched, yet not having physically hit its target; in other words, once an armed attack has been irremediably and irreversibly triggered. In this regard, Dinstein speaks of 'nipping an attack in the bud'.[85] Most scholars cite, in this respect, the right of the United States to intercept Japanese bombers airborne outside its territorial waters approaching Pearl Harbour[86] as well as Israel's right to intercept Iraqi Scuds launched during the second Gulf War in 1991.[87] In these examples drawn from state practice, the emphasis is thus put not only on the 'opening of fire' but also, and foremost, on the feature of 'irreversibility'.[88]

---

[82] Resolution adopted by the Institut de Droit International (n 46), § 10(ii).

[83] See *Nicaragua* 1986 (n 13), 93–5 (§§ 175–7).

[84] *Oil Platforms* (n 31), 186 (§ 51): 'in order to establish that it was legally justified in attacking the Iranian platforms in exercise of the right of individual self-defence, the United State *has to show that attacks had been made upon it* for which Iran was responsible'.

[85] Y. Dinstein, *War, Aggression and Self-Defence* (4th edn, Cambridge: Cambridge University Press, 2005), 91.

[86] I. Brownlie, *International Law and the Use of Force by States* (Oxford: Clarendon Press, 1963), 368.

[87] R. Kolb, *Self-Defence and Preventive War at the beginning of the Millennium* (Vienna: Springer Verlag, 2004), 125.

[88] Dinstein (n 85), 191.

A tenuous wall separates the previous scenario from that of 'anticipatory' self-defence. Notwithstanding a strong similarity, the time factor is more remote insofar as in the case of anticipatory self-defence the target state is faced with an armed attack 'on the brink of launch'.[89] This form of self-defence is considered lawful under current international law.

Between inceptive and anticipatory self-defence and the scenarios of pre-emptive and preventive self-defence lies an invisible though significant dividing-line—that of legality. While the former two reflect current customary international law, the last two do not, in spite of recurrent and relentless attempts made by certain states and a minority of scholars. 'Pre-emptive'[90] self-defence is based on the premise that a state apprehends that in the short term it may become a (potential) target of an armed attack by another state. In effect, there lies a perception of a threat of aggression. In order to respond to this perceived threat, the (potential) target state attempts to *pre-empt*[91] its realization by acting 'while these processes [embodying the threat of aggression] still embody only a low level of coercion'.[92] The aim thereby pursued is to put an end to the threat by resorting to less costly means than those which would have been required later on when the threat materialized into actual aggression.

The fourth and last kind of self-defence is the notion of preventive self-defence or preventive war *tout court*; if the notion of 'pre-emptive' self-defence strongly resembles an oxymoron,[93] the latter concept of preventative self-defence is less hypocritical insofar as it unveils the real goal pursued, that is, to wage war when the (potential) target state is of the view that in the long-term another state could do the same. Unlike the 'pre-emptive' self-defence, in this case the perception of a threat is not only more remote in time, but also it rests on vague (and probably subjective) indicators of fear. At the end of World War II, German dignitaries accused before the International Military Tribunal at Nuremberg argued that the Third Reich was 'compelled' to invade Norway (a neutral state) in order to prevent a feared invasion of the latter by Great Britain. The Tribunal, relying on the requirements in the *Caroline* test, categorically rejected this form of 'preventive' self-defence by stating that: 'In the light of all the available evidence it is

---

[89] M.E. O'Connell, 'The Myth of Preemptive Self-Defense', *American Society of International Law Taskforce on Terrorism* (2002) 2. The United States invoked this kind of self-defence with a view to justify the shooting down by *USS Vincennes* of Iran Air Airbus (3 July 1988).

[90] Not to be misled with the same use of 'pre-emptive' in the Report of the Secretary-General's High-level Panel on Threats, Challenges and Change (Doc A/59/565, 2 December 2004, 63, § 189), discussed later in this Chapter.

[91] It is not by accident that the word 'pre-empt' comes from Middle Latin '*prae-emere*': to 'buy beforehand'. In other words, to 'wage' war before others do it.

[92] M.S. McDougal and F.P. Feliciano, *Law and Minimum World Public Order: The Legal Regulation of International Coercion* (New Haven: Yale University Press, 1961), 211.

[93] See, in this respect, Abi-Saab (n 62), 371.

impossible to accept the contention that the invasions of Denmark and Norway were defensive, and in the opinion of the Tribunal they were acts of aggressive war'.[94]

A vivid example of a similar strategy can be found in the 2006 US National Security Strategy.[95] Contrariwise, nearly six decades earlier, the US Truman Administration issued a Strategic Security Document that consecrated the Cold War policy of containment. This text adamantly affirmed that the United States would never have launched an armed attack 'unless it is demonstrably in the nature of a counter-attack to a blow which *is on its way or about to be delivered*'.[96] It must be observed in this regard that what was applicable for a threat of a nuclear aggression is all the more true for armed attack by conventional weapons. In short, this strategy, while implicitly admitting 'anticipatory' self-defence ('about to be delivered'), straightfor-wardly rejected preventive (and even pre-emptive) self-defence.

In conclusion, the first two kinds of self-defence are nowadays admitted as law-ful whilst the last two are not. This is consonant with the Report of the Secretary-General's High-level Panel on Threats, Challenges and Change, which strongly opposed the right for a state to act preventively, that is, in response to a 'non-immi-nent or non-proximate' threat. In this regard, this report reaffirmed the discrepancy of scope between Articles 39, 2(4), and 51 of the UN Charter: the first including even the threat to peace, thus situations not perforce encompassing the use of force in international relations, or being solely restricted within a single state; the second including only threat and use of force between states in international relations; and the third envisaging *exclusively and restrictively* inter-state aggression. In fact, the Panel added that 'if there are good arguments for preventive military action, with good evidence to support them, they should be put to the Security Council, which can authorize such action if it chooses to'. The Panel then concluded that:

[T]he risk to the global order and the norm of non-intervention on which it continues to be based is simply too great for the legality of unilateral preventive action, as distinct from collectively endorsed action, to be accepted [...] We do not favour the rewriting or reinter-pretation of Article 51.[97]

This is on par with a recent stand taken by the Institut de Droit International, which vigorously rejected any form of '"preventive" self-defence (in the absence of an actual or manifestly imminent armed attack)'.[98] Authorities, with the exception of a

---

[94] IMT, Judgment, 1 October 1946 (1947) 41 *AJIL* 207.

[95] Second edition (16 March 2006), <http://georgewbush-whitehouse.archives.gov/nsc/nss/2006/>.

[96] <http://www.mtholyoke.edu/acad/intrel/nsc-68/nsc68-3.htm> (*NSC 68: United States Objectives and Programs for National Security* (14 April 1950). A Report to the President Pursuant to the President's Directive of 31 January 1950), emphasis added.

[97] Report of the Secretary-General's High-level Panel on Threats, Challenges and Change (n 90), 63 (§§ 190–2, bold emphasis in the original).

[98] 'Present Problems of the Use of Armed Force in International Law' (n 46), § 6.

few authors, largely concur in rejecting these forms of self-defence.[99] Lastly, it must be noted that the ICJ has not yet had the chance to elaborate explicitly on the right of a state to resort to self-defence in a situation of an 'imminent threat of armed attack'.[100]

5 What Beyond? Unanswered Questions on Some Alleged Exceptions to the Comprehensive Ban on the Use of Force

Leaving aside the exception represented by the collective security system established by the UN Charter, we ought to address the issue whether there are other ways for states to resort unilaterally to force which may be admitted as legal under current public international law. In fact, as the ICJ affirmed in 1969, '[t]he general rule prohibiting force allows for certain exceptions';[101] the plural can be interpreted as including the aforementioned system of collective security or not, thus leaving room for other exceptions.

A. General prefatory remarks

The primary means by which a new exception can be introduced in the realm of positive international law is through custom, which can either modify the relevant provisions of the UN Charter or sit alongside it. The theoretical underpinnings of the two options are different, but the outcome is the same—that is, the modification of general international law. If international custom is the means, it is pertinent briefly to sketch out the customary process with a view to determining whether either of the alleged exceptions has crystallized into positive law. Without dwelling upon the customary source as such, it is important to highlight the inescapable jurisprudential conditions for the creation of a new customary rule or a new customary exception to the prohibition of the use of force.

---

[99] See eg T. Franck, 'Fairness in the International Legal and International System. General Course on Public International Law', 240 *RCADI* (1993-III) 254. See n 53.

[100] *Nicaragua* 1986 (n 13), 103 (§ 194). To our knowledge, no useful hints can be drawn either from the ICJ's subsequent decisions or from other international judicial bodies' practice.

[101] *Nicaragua* 1986 (n 13), 102 (§ 193).

The first clue is given by the ICJ in its landmark judgment in *Nicaragua*, where, in dealing with the need to verify an alleged new exception to the prohibition of the use of force, it concluded that: '[r]eliance by a State on a novel right or an unprecedented exception to the principle might, if shared in principle by other States, tend towards a modification of customary international law'.[102] The question, then, is how to assess whether the novel exception is truly 'shared by other States'. The relevant requirements have been put forward by the Court, namely, a systematic practice of non-condemnation by a very large number of representative states including those specially affected.[103] Inversely, a lack of condemnation by *other states* of the use of force in a particular incident, even if widespread, does not amount to a change of the law in this respect.[104] Any other conclusion would lead to an unacceptable mechanical conception of the law, that is, that the validity of a norm in a given legal system would depend from either approbation or the condemnation of its violation in each specific case. Such a construction of law is tantamount to its negation. A second clue has likewise been elucidated by the ICJ in the *North Sea Continental Shelf* judgment, which clearly underlined that 'a very widespread and representative participation in the convention might suffice of itself, provided it included [...] States whose interests were specially affected'.[105]

Hence, three conditions must be met: (a) a quantitative requirement of 'very widespread' adherence to the given practice (falling short of a requirement of absolute unanimity); (b) a qualitative requirement of representation, meaning that all sections of the international community (be they geographical, ideological, religious, economic, or political) must take part in the law-making process; (c) effectiveness, that is, those states and groups that have a special interest in the regulation or field concerned shall adhere to the practice, proving their *opinio juris* and ultimately the customary international law rule.

The meaning of 'representative' must be understood as pertaining to the different sections (or even sub-sections) of the international community, according not only to general dividing lines (North-South, East-West, Western/African/Asian, and so on), but also to the more specific field of international regulations in point.[106] As for the meaning of 'specially affected' states, it is worth quoting the International Committee of the Red Cross, affirming that '[w]ith respect to any rule of international humanitarian law, countries that participated in an armed conflict are "specially affected" when their practice examined for a certain rule was relevant to that armed conflict'.[107] In this connection, the US challenged this affirmation by asserting

---

[102] *Nicaragua* 1986 (n 13), 109 (§ 207).   [103] In this vein: *Nicaragua* 1986 (n 13), 98 (§ 186).

[104] Abi-Saab (n 62), 378.

[105] *North Sea Continental Shelf (Germany/Denmark/Netherlands)*, Judgment, [1969] ICJ Rep 42 (§ 73).

[106] See, in this respect, *Texaco Overseas Petroleum Co and California Asiatic Oil Co v Libya*, Arbitral award, ILR, vol 53, § 84 (the original French version in 104 *JDI* (1977) 350–89).

[107] J.-M. Henckaerts and L. Doswald-Beck (eds), *Customary International Humanitarian Law* vol I (Cambridge: Cambridge University Press/ICR, 2005), xxxix.

that 'specially affected States [by a given regulation]' are those states which are *usually* involved in those problems, with regards to which state practice is accordingly analysed.[108]

Still on the same point, a distinguished scholar has remarked that *among* 'specially affected States', *special relevancy* must be given to those acts which go against states' interests:

> Particularly significant are manifestations of practice that go against the interest of the State from which they come, or that entail for them significant costs in political, military, economic or other terms, as it is less likely that they reflect reasons of political opportunity, courtesy etc.[109]

Treves has thus proposed a 'unit of evaluation' for evidence of state practice within the international process, put forward from time to time by the ICJ itself. Hence, the behaviour of the state more deeply involved in a given situation is deemed to be more *representative* than that of other states that are but rarely 'affected'.[110] In addition, it can be contended that because Article 2(4) is a *jus cogens* rule, any state is by definition entitled to the same weighting coefficient in the assessment of its 'specially affected' status in a manner similar to the integral treaties under Article 60(2)(c) of the Vienna Convention. Therefore, since all the states are 'specially affected', none of them is ultimately, so that all states' practice is characterized (weighted) by the same coefficient of importance.

Finally it needs also to be stressed that, according to a general principle of law in the matter of interpretation, any exception to a rule must be construed restrictively; moreover, in the case in point, this is all the more true since the rule concerned is a peremptory norm of public international law.[111]

Another argument, often invoked in order to soften the prohibition of the use of force, relies on the asserted dysfunction or inefficacy of the UN collective security system. Without having to dwell upon this allegation, one ought to recall what the ICJ in 1949 affirmed in this respect: 'The Court can only regard the alleged right

---

[108] The letter, sent to the ICRC, read as follows: 'Not every State that has participated in an armed conflict is "specially affected"; such States do generate salient practice, but it is those States that have a distinctive history of participation that merit being regarded as "specially affected". Moreover, those States are not simply "specially affected" when their practice has, in fact, been examined and found relevant by the ICRC. Instead, specially affected States generate practice that must be examined in order to reach an informed conclusion regarding the status of a potential rule' (US Gov, 445). In this same letter also quoted is the opinion of one of the Committee's members (T. Meron) who drafted the customary IHL study: 'The practice of "specially affected states"—such as nuclear powers, other major military powers, and occupying and occupied states—which have a track record of statements, practice and policy, remains particularly telling': 'The continuing role of custom in the formation of international humanitarian law', 90 *AJIL* (1996) 249.

[109] T. Treves, 'Customary International Law', in R. Wolfrum (ed), *The Max Planck Encyclopedia of Public International Law* (Oxford: Oxford University Press, 2008), para 30.

[110] Treves (n 109), para 30.

[111] In this connection, one shall remind that in accordance with Art 53 of VCLT, a *jus cogens* rule cannot but be modified by another norm 'having the same character'.

of intervention as the manifestation of a policy of force, such as has, in the past, given rise to most serious abuses and such as cannot, *whatever be the present defects in international organization*, find a place in international law'.[112] In the same vein, one year later, the General Assembly adopted the famous Resolution 377 (V) on 'Uniting for Peace', the Preamble of which declares, at paragraph 7, that 'failure of the Security Council to discharge its responsibilities on behalf of all the Member States [...] does not relieve Member States of their obligations or the United Nations of its responsibility under the Charter to maintain international peace and security'. Moreover, pursuant to the law of treaties, the oft-cited argument relying on a 'fundamental change of circumstances' as a cause for at least softening, if not squarely terminating, UN Charter provisions pertaining to the use of force must be straightforwardly and irrevocably rebutted.[113] In fact, even assuming that all Article 62 of VCLT's stringent (five) conditions—enunciated in paragraph 2—are met in the case in point, paragraph 2 would apply for the fundamental change invoked—ie the dysfunction (lack of unanimity and/or the failed implementation of Article 43 of the UN Charter) of the collective security system is due to member states which, in turn attempt to avail themselves of this ground of termination/suspension.

B. Sampling of alleged exceptions

(i) *Armed counter-measures or 'self-defence lite'*

In *Nicaragua*, the Court suggested that if a state is affected by a 'use of force of a lesser gravity' it could then resort to 'proportionate counter-measures'.[114] Therefore, the Court, after adamantly rejecting collective armed counter-measures—invoked in this case by the United States—opened this possibility for a state that has been

---

[112] *Corfu Channel* case (n 23) (italics added).

[113] By the way, as it has been observed: 'But no responsible voice, surely no government, has suggested that the failures of the organization vitiated the agreement and nullified or modified the Charter's norms', L. Henkin, 'Use of Force: Law and U.S. Policy', in *Right v. Might. International Law and the Use of Force* (New York: Council on Foreign Relations Book, 1989), 37–70 at 38.

[114] *Nicaragua* 1986 (n 13), 127 (§ 249). In this connection, it must be observed that in a puzzling previous paragraph, the Court had affirmed that: 'Since the Court is here dealing with a dispute in which a wrongful use of force is alleged, it has primarily to consider whether a State has a right to respond to intervention with intervention going so far as to justify a use of force in reaction to measures which do not constitute an armed attack but may nevertheless involve a use of force. The question is itself undeniably relevant from the theoretical viewpoint. However, since the Court is bound to confine its decision to those points of law which are essential to the settlement of the dispute before it, it is not for the Court here to determine what direct reactions are lawfully open to a state which considers itself the victim of another state's acts of intervention, possibly involving the use of force. Hence it has not to determine whether, in the event of Nicaragua's having committed any such acts against El Salvador, the latter was lawfully entitled to take any particular counter-measure': *Nicaragua* 1986 (n 13), 110 (§ 211).

victim of uses of force which fell below the threshold of armed attack.[115] Hence, as the Institut de Droit International declared:

[A]cts involving the use of force of lesser intensity may give rise to countermeasures in conformity with international law. In case of an attack of lesser intensity the target State may also take strictly necessary police measures to repel the attack. It is understood that the Security Council may take measures referred to in paragraph 3.[116]

Therefore, despite the Court's ambiguities in 1986 and its subsequent silence, Judge Simma has concluded that:

[A]gainst smaller-scale use of force, defensive action—by force also 'short of Article 51'—is to be regarded as lawful. In other words, I would suggest a distinction between (full-scale) self-defence within the meaning of Article 51 against an 'armed attack' within the meaning of the same Charter provision on the one hand and, on the other, the case of hostile action, for instance against individual ships, below the level of Article 51, justifying proportionate defensive measures on the part of the victim, equally short of the quality and quantity of action in self-defence expressly reserved in the United Nations Charter.[117]

    This is fair enough; yet, while insisting on the 'defensive' character of these armed counter-measures (which could be crudely labelled 'self-defence lite'), it could be awkward in some circumstances to distinguish them from their companions, that is, armed reprisals in times of peace. For the latter are undoubtedly banned in public international law, as the ICJ itself affirmed in *Nuclear Weapons*,[118] relying on General Assembly Resolution 2625 (XXV).[119] Other international instruments uphold this prohibition, such as the ILC Articles on State Responsibility[120] and the Helsinki Final Act,[121] to name only two. Hence, a thin red line must be drawn between defensive counter-measures (short of self-defence) and (punitive) armed reprisals. To this end, timing ('leaving no moment for deliberation') and purposes—on the one hand to repel the hostile use of force, while on the other to punish its author and at the same time deter the latter from doing it again[122]—must be taken into account

---

[115] Quite obviously, the state concerned can make likewise recourse to peaceful counter-measures, the lawfulness of which is clearly attested by Arts 22 and 49–53 of the ILC Articles on State Responsibility; see in this regard: the ILC's Commentary to the aforementioned provisions (n 32), 75–6, 129–38.

[116] Resolution IDI, § 5.

[117] Individual opinion of Judge Simma appended to the Court's Judgment in the *Oil Platforms* case (n 31), 331–32 (§ 12).

[118] *Threat or Use of Nuclear Weapons* (n 4), 246 (§ 46).

[119] Declaration on Principles of International Law Concerning Friendly Relations and Cooperation Among States in Accordance With the Charter of the United Nations, UNGA Res 2625 (XXV) Annex, 25 UN GAOR, Supp (No 28), UN Doc A/5217 (24 October 1970), 122.

[120] Article 50(1)(c).   [121] Principle II.3.

[122] 'A reprisal is an act of self-help (*Selbsthilfehandlung*) by the injured state, responding—after an unsatisfied demand—to an act contrary to international law committed by the offending state [...] Its object is to obtain reparation from the offending state for the offense or a return to legality by the avoidance of further offenses': *Naulilaa* case (Portugal/Germany), arbitral award of 31 July 1928, *RIAA*, vol II, 1026 (our translation). Hence, the Tribunal clearly ranks (armed) reprisals among the states' means of

with a view to determining whether the facts present a defensive counter-measure or an armed reprisal. While the former is lawful, the latter remains unlawful since it is a means of forcible self-help, and as such 'cannot find a place in international law'.[123]

(ii) *Protection of nationals abroad*

In the past, states have regularly invoked this title in order to justify their interventions by forcible means in another state's territory. Franco-British intervention in Egypt during the Suez Canal crisis,[124] Belgian intervention in Congo,[125] US intervention in the Dominican Republic (1965), Grenada (1983),[126] and Panama (1989)[127] well illustrate the case in point; not to mention the notorious Entebbe case.[128]

self-help. As already underlined, the latter banned by Art 2(4) of the UN Charter does not coincide at all with self-defence; see also nn 23 and 112.

[123] *Corfu Channel* case (n 23), 35.

[124] The UK representative at the Security Council argued in these terms: 'In Egypt there are many thousands of British and French nationals. The chain of events which began with the Israel moves into Egypt has developed into hostilities and hostilities have created a disturbed situation. In those circumstances, French and British lives must be safeguarded. I again emphasize [...] that we should certainly not want to keep any forces in the area for one moment longer than it is necessary to protect our nationals' (quoted in N. Ronzitti, *Rescuing Nationals Abroad through Military Coercion and Intervention on Grounds of Humanity* (Dordrecht: Martinus Nijhoff Publishers, 1985), 28).

[125] France backed Belgian intervention on grounds of its humanitarian purposes: 'their mission of protecting lives [...] is the direct result of the failure of the Congolese authorities is in accord with a recognized principle of international law, namely, intervention on humanitarian grounds' (UNSC Doc S/PV. 873 (1960), § 144).

[126] Operation 'Urgent Fury'. US President Reagan justified the intervention in the following terms: 'When I received reports that a large number of our citizens were seeking to escape the island thereby exposing themselves to great danger, and after receiving a formal request for help [...] I concluded the United States had no choice but to act strongly and decisively' (interview, President Reagan with reporters, White House, 25 October 1983, weekly Compilation of Presidential Documents, 3l October 1983, l487) (cited in: R.H. Cole, *Operation Urgent Fury. Grenada* (Joint History Office, Office of the Chairman of the Joints Chiefs of Staff, Washington DC, 1997), 46. UNSC was unable to adopt a draft resolution submitted by Nicaragua and purporting to condemn US invasion, due to the latter's veto (11 affirmative votes and 3 abstentions). On the contrary, both the General Assembly (Res 38/7 of 2 November 1983) and CARICOM (see W. Gilmore, *The Grenada Intervention. Analysis and Documentation* (London: Mansell Publishers, 1984), 38) condemned the US raid on the Caribbean island.

[127] Operation 'Just Cause', see US President George Bush statement (*NYT*, 21 December 1989).

[128] On 27 June 1976, a French carrier airliner, flying from Tel-Aviv to Paris, was hijacked by a commando of four Palestinians who compelled the pilot to land at the Ugandan airport of Entebbe. All non-Israeli passengers were quickly freed while the hijackers ransomed the Israeli Government to liberate Palestinians jailed in different countries in exchange for the remaining 86 Israeli hostages. On 3 July, a special Israeli force landed at the airport, without prior Ugandan authorization, and managed to free the hostages. During the raid some Ugandan military forces were wounded and the Israeli forces destroyed ten or so Ugandan airplanes. Upon Uganda's request, the Security Council was convened five days later. While Israel asserted its right 'to take military action to protect its nationals in mortal danger', several other states categorically rejected this argument, with Uganda tagging the intervention as a 'barbaric aggression'. The United States stood up for Israel's right which 'flow[s] from the right

Neither the ICJ (nor its predecessor) has heretofore been called upon to examine the lawfulness of forcible actions aimed at rescuing nationals abroad. However, some hints can be drawn from its Judgment in *Hostages in Tehran*,[129] initiated by a US application asking the Court to assess the responsibility of Iran arising out of the invasion and occupation of the US embassy and general consulate in Tehran as well as from the detention of US nationals and diplomatic and consular staff. While the case was before the Court, the US Government decided to set up a rescue expedition, but the mission ended in a crushing fiasco. The Court ultimately determined that Iran's responsibility was engaged, yet it also noted that:

[I]t cannot let pass without comment the incursion into the territory of Iran made by United States military units on 24–25 April 1980 [...] No doubt the United States Government may have had understandable preoccupations with respect to the well-being of its nationals held hostage in its Embassy for over five months. No doubt also the United States Government may have had understandable feelings of frustration at Iran's long-continued detention of the hostages, notwithstanding two resolutions of the Security Council as well as the Court's own Order of 15 December 1979 calling expressly for their immediate release. Nevertheless, in the circumstances of the present proceedings, the Court cannot fail to express its *concern* in regard to the United States' incursion into Iran.[130]

The Court could not go further to assess the wrongfulness of US action (a hint of which can be inferred by the use of the word 'concern') for the substantive scope of its jurisdiction was limited to the two Vienna Conventions of 1961 and 1963 in a matter of diplomatic and consular relations. Therefore, as it took care to emphasize, 'neither the question of the legality of the operation of 24 April 1980, under the Charter of the United Nations and under general international law, nor any possible question of responsibility flowing from it, is before the Court'.[131] The Court

of self-defence', while France argued that the Israeli intervention infringed Uganda's sovereignty yet not its 'territorial integrity'. India's and Sweden's stances must be briefly recalled in this connection. The former underlined that the UN Charter recognizes a state right to self-defence only if it has been the victim of an armed attack; in the case in point, it is not Israel which is the target State, but rather Uganda. India thus rebutted the legality of Israeli intervention. Sweden, in an articulate speech, recalled that the UN Charter makes room for two exceptions only (self-defence and forcible measures under Ch VII), adding that 'Any formal exceptions permitting the use of force or of military intervention in order to achieve certain aims; however laudable, would be bound to be abused, especially by the big and strong, and to pose a threat, especially to the small and weak. In our view, the Israeli action which we are now considering involved an infringement of the national sovereignty and territorial integrity of Uganda'. Yet, in spite of that, the Swedish Government did 'not find it possible to join in a condemnation in this case' (S/PV.1940, §§ 121–2 at 14). The UN Security Council could not ultimately adopt any resolution condemning Israel's raid, on the account of lack of unanimity between its permanent members.

    [129] *United States Diplomatic and Consular Staff in Tehran*, Judgment, [1980] ICJ Rep.
    [130] *United States Diplomatic and Consular Staff in Tehran*, Judgment, n 129, 44, § 93 (italics added).
    [131] *United States Diplomatic and Consular Staff in Tehran*, n 129, 44, § 94.

was thus impeded by its jurisdictional limits in the case in point to go further than the—already eloquent—expression of its 'concern'.

In the same vein, reference can be made to the works of the ILC pertaining to diplomatic protection. The second Special Rapporteur on Diplomatic Protection, John Dugard, recommended in his First Report to the ILC a provision that envisaged the right for a state to rescue its nationals abroad by resorting to forcible means.[132] The exercise of this right to intervention was subject to five stringent and cumulative conditions.[133] Moreover, the first paragraph of the proviso was framed in conditional and negative terms, for it stated the principle of non-intervention applied 'except in the case [...] where' all the requirements were fulfilled. Yet, notwithstanding all these strictures, this draft provision was rejected by the ILC in 2000, on the ground 'that diplomatic protection did not include the use of force. It was thus quite clear that [Dugard's proposed article] was not acceptable to the Commission'.[134]

In the light of the foregoing it can hardly be contested that, at least *de lege lata*, public international law does not admit any right of a state to rescue its nationals abroad by forcible means. In this regard, the mechanism of diplomatic protection, that ancient institution of the law of nations, well reconciles each state's conflicting interests arising out of the infringement of public international law against aliens.

(iii) *(Hot) pursuit*

A right of (hot) pursuit has been asserted by some scholars and governments; so that it would be lawful for a state to send its troops into another state's territory for the purposes of catching military or paramilitary bands that have found a safe haven there. Quite obviously, in the case in point neither an organic link nor a 'substantial implication' can be established between the host-state and the private individuals, otherwise this action would constitute indirect aggression on the terms of Article 3(g) of the General Assembly Resolution 3314 (XXIX).[135]

Indeed, while some authors have sought to fit this hypothesis into a stretched definition of aggression,[136] so as to trigger a right of self-defence,[137] others, no

---

[132] First Report to the ILC, UN Doc A/CN.4/506, 16.

[133] They were: (a) 'The protecting State has failed to secure the safety of its nationals by peaceful means'; (b) 'The injuring State is unwilling or unable to secure the safety of the nationals of the protecting State'; (c) 'The nationals of the protecting State are exposed to immediate danger to their persons'; (d) 'The use of force is proportionate in the circumstances of the situation'; (e) 'The use of force is terminated, and the protecting State withdraws its forces, as soon as the nationals are rescued' (First Report to the ILC, UN Doc A/CN.4/506, 17).

[134] ILC's Report to the General Assembly, UN Doc A/55/10, 76.

[135] This scenario has been already analysed (*supra* 1.B.1).

[136] For example, A.D. Sofaer, 'Terrorism and the Law', 64 *Foreign Affairs* (1986) 920–2; O. Schachter, 'The Extraterritorial Use of Force Against Terrorist Bases', 11 *Houston Journal of International Law* (1989) 312–15.

[137] Fewer authors have relied, even less convincingly, on state of necessity (D. Bowett, *Self-Defense in International Law* (Oxford: Oxford University Press, 1956), 38–41). Without dwelling upon this

more plausibly, have endeavoured to establish a separate title of intervention, notably by analogy with the law of the sea. In fact, according to Article 111 of the LOSC:

The hot pursuit of a foreign ship may be undertaken when the competent authorities of the coastal State have good reason to believe that the ship has violated the laws and regulations of that State. Such pursuit must be commenced when the foreign ship or one of its boats is within the internal waters, the archipelagic waters, the territorial sea or the contiguous zone of the pursuing State, and may only be continued outside the territorial sea or the contiguous zone if the pursuit has not been interrupted.[138]

Therefore, the right of pursuit is subject to the condition that the chase has commenced in one of the maritime areas where the coastal state has sovereign rights or functional competencies and it can accordingly continue—with no discontinuation—into the High Seas (hence the label 'hot'). It must of course stop at the outer limit of another state's territorial waters.[139]

However, the propounded analogy cannot be sustained, not only in the light of state (and UN) practice but also from a juridical standpoint. Under the first heading, several elements bolster the refutation of a right of pursuit on foreign territory. UN Security Council practice in condemning or simply determining the unlawfulness of this behaviour abounds; for instance, in 1985, it 'denounc[ed] and reject[ed] racist South Africa's practice of "hot pursuit" to terrorize and destabilize Botswana and other countries in southern Africa'.[140] Other Security Council resolutions can be

---

argument, it suffices to recall that state of necessity as a circumstance precluding wrongfulness—codified in Art 25 of the ILC Articles on State Responsibility (n 32)—is barred from being invoked when the breached obligation flows from a peremptory rule of public international law (see Art 26 of the Draft Articles). As already made clear, the prohibition of the use of force belongs to this body of international norms.

[138] The customary international law rule reflected in this proviso seemingly ripened during the US prohibition era (aimed at preventing and punishing the smuggling of alcohol in the Federal territory).

[139] In this connection it is relevant to note that in Res 1846 (2008) the Security Council authorized 'States and regional organizations cooperating (with the transitional Somali Government) to enter into the latter's territorial waters in order to "fight against piracy and armed robbery at sea off the coast of Somalia"': at [10], albeit with the consent of the State concerned. It is important to underline in this respect the following paragraph, by which Security Council stressed that its 'resolution applies only with respect to the situation in Somalia and shall not affect the rights or obligations or responsibilities of Member States under international law, including any rights or obligations under the Convention, with respect to any other situation, and underscores in particular that this resolution shall not be considered as establishing customary international law; and *affirms further* that such authorizations have been provided only following the receipt of the 20 November letter conveying the consent of the TFG'. Hence, it ought to be observed not only that this resolution cannot be taken into account as state practice likely to substantiate their *opinio juris*, but also that this was made possible only thanks to the prior consent given by the state concerned (even though it can be argued that it was not required for the Security Council to act under Ch VII, the resolution adopted under this heading being binding upon member states pursuant to Art 25 of the UN Charter).

[140] UNSC Res 568 (21 June 1985), § 4.

cited, the content of which clearly attests the consistent condemnation of the right of pursuit.[141]

Moreover, the alleged analogy with the Law of the Sea must be challenged from a purely juridical point of view. Of course, while exercising the right of (hot) pursuit in the High Seas, state action occurs in a space which is *res omnium*, that is, beyond the jurisdiction of any state. In the case of pursuit on foreign territory, the state action is under the exclusive jurisdiction of a sovereign state. According to the *Island of Palmas* case, 'territorial sovereignty [...] involves the exclusive right to display the activities of a State', 'to the exclusion of any other State'.[142] In conclusion, since the legal status of spaces concerned are far from being identical, the analogy cannot be upheld. Consequently, there can be no right of pursuit—be it hot or not—on a territory under the jurisdiction of another state, unless of course the latter gives beforehand its consent to this effect.[143]

6 Conclusions

In the light of the aforesaid, a few observations ought to be put forward in addition to the intermediate conclusions drawn in each individual section of this study.

It can hardly be contested that the UN Charter not only provided for a comprehensive ban on the use and threat of force between states in their international relations, but it also established—for the first time ever—a substantive and institutional framework making this prohibition a truly attainable goal. To this effect, UNSC (and secondarily the General Assembly) have been entrusted by the UN Charter with the duty—and corresponding powers—to maintain (and restore) international peace and security.[144] By this oft-cited formula, the UN Charter means a collective enforcement of law, a function which beforehand was of one of the states' main prerogatives and was labelled under the tag 'self-help'. As already pointed out, the UN

---

[141] A far from exhaustive list would comprise, in addition to South Africa: South Rhodesia (against Botswana, 1977: Resolutions 403 and 406; Mozambique, 1976: Resolution 386; Zambia, 1978: Resolution 424); Israel (on Lebanon, 1982: Resolutions 517 and 520; Tunisia, 1985: Resolution 573; on Jordan's occupied West Bank, 1953: Resolution 101; on Jordan, 1966: Resolution 228; on Syria, 1956 (Resolution 111), 1962 (Resolution 171)); Great Britain (on Yemen, 1964: Resolution 188).

[142] *Island of Palmas* case (Netherlands/United States), arbitral award (1982) *RIAA*, vol II, 8–9.

[143] See, for instance, Art 41 of the Schengen Agreement between some European countries (19 June 1990); Mauritania, Algeria, Mali and Niger have presumably entered into an agreement (Tamanrasset agreement, 2010), or have at least reached and understanding, granting a reciprocal right of hot pursuit in their respective territories (parts of the Sahel) with a view to fight Al-Qaeda Organization in the Islamic Maghreb's terrorists (see *Le Temps*, 27 July 2010; *FT*, 22 April 2010).

[144] Article 24(1) of the UN Charter.

Charter has stripped states of their forcible self-help rights, so that use of force with a view of 'self-preservation' is thenceforth lawful only 'if an armed attack occurs' (Article 51 of the UN Charter).

Furthermore, as shown above, the obligation not to resort to threat or use of force is not subordinated to the actual functioning of the UN collective security system.[145] Kelsen was then right to stress, shortly after the entry into force of the UN Charter, its fundamental difference *vis-à-vis* the League of Nations system:

The delinquent [State] which is in actual possession of the illegal advantage is *protected by the Charter against any enforcement action other than that taken by the Security Council.*[146]

Indeed, the UN Charter Preamble, the interpretative value of which is undisputed in accordance with Article 31(2) of VCLT, adamantly declares that 'armed forces shall not be used, *save in the common interest*'.[147] Now, the ascertainment of the 'common interest' can hardly be carried without and outside the endowed organs of the UN and certainly cannot be left to the self-interpretation of a few states.

Lastly, one cannot but share Georges Abi-Saab's illuminating thought according to which:

To each level of normative density must correspond a certain level of institutional density allowing the norms to be enforced in a satisfactory way.[148]

It can thus be easily argued that either the international legal order has not yet found a *satisfactory* machinery, or that the latter is seldom resorted to by those in the interest of which it has been established. In the light of historical records, we tentatively lean towards the second hypothesis.

---

[145] See nn 23 and 112.   [146] Kelsen (n 72), 269 (emphasis added).   [147] Emphasis added.
[148] Abi-Saab (n 62), 95 (our translation).

CHAPTER 23

....

TERRORISM[*]

....

ANDREA BIANCHI AND
YASMIN NAQVI

1 INTRODUCTION
....

THE belief that international humanitarian law (IHL) may provide a suitable legal framework for the regulation of international terrorism and responses thereto is fairly widespread. After all, IHL clearly prohibits acts of terrorism, it revolves around the principles that civilians and their property must be protected, that a distinction must be made between civilian and military objectives and that unnecessary suffering must be prevented. Most, if not all, acts of terrorism would violate these fundamental principles. Moreover, IHL lays down specific rules allowing for the targeting of individuals taking direct part in hostilities, for the detention of persons posing a threat to state security and for effectively enforcing all these principles and rules. Upon closer scrutiny, however, terrorism and war should be seen as clearly distinct phenomena. Terrorism comes under the regulation of IHL only in limited circumstances, when the existence of an armed conflict, characterized by a certain threshold of intensity and organization of the parties, can be established.

  * The topics discussed in this Chapter are developed by the authors at length in their book Andrea Bianchi and Yasmin Naqvi, *International Humanitarian Law and Terrorism* (Oxford: Hart Publishing, 2011). The views expressed herein are those of the authors alone and do not necessarily reflect the views of the International Criminal Tribunal for the former Yugoslavia or the United Nations in general.

This Chapter first examines in which circumstances IHL applies to acts of terror or terrorism.[1] It then looks at how acts of terror and terrorism are prohibited forms of warfare in situations of armed conflict, as well as the rules applicable to operations of so-called 'counter-terrorism'. Subsequently, the issue of how individual criminal responsibility has come to be attached to acts of terrorism and acts of terror under international humanitarian law will be examined. Issues connected to the status, detention, and treatment of terrorist suspects in international humanitarian law will be briefly discussed as well. Overall, the Chapter focuses on the so-called 'grey areas' of international humanitarian law, where the existing framework and rules of IHL seem to struggle to accommodate contemporary manifestations of armed conflict, particularly when actors, qualified by one of the parties as 'terrorists', are involved. The concluding section offers some thoughts on how these areas of uncertainty might be eventually resolved and on how the international community can meet the main challenges in the interpretation and implementation of IHL.

2 When Does IHL Regulate Terrorism or Acts of Terror?

A. The phenomenology of war: a preliminary look at *jus ad bellum* and *jus in bello*

The linkage between IHL and acts of terrorism is premised upon an understanding of what constitutes armed conflict and war. Both war and terrorism are ancient phenomena related to the use of violent measures to gain and/or maintain power or to influence public opinion.[2] Terrorism has almost always been a factor in

---

[1] These terms are found in the Geneva Conventions and their Additional Protocols (see section 3 below).

[2] The English word 'terrorism' comes from the *régime de la terreur* that prevailed in France from 1793–94 (see J.R. Thackrah, *Dictionary of Terrorism* (2nd edn, London: Routledge, 2004); H.W. Kushner, *Encyclopedia of Terrorism* (Thousand Oaks: Sage Publications, 2002), 360). Originally an instrument of the state, the regime was designed to consolidate the power of the newly installed revolutionary government, protecting it from elements considered 'subversive'. Always value-laden, terrorism was, initially, a positive term. The French revolutionary leader, Maximilien Robespierre, viewed it as vital if the new French Republic was to survive its infancy, proclaiming in 1794 that: 'Terror is nothing other than justice, prompt, severe, inflexible; it is therefore an emanation of virtue; it is not so much a special principle as it is a consequence of the general principle of democracy applied to our country's most urgent needs'. 'On the Moral and Political Principles of Domestic Policy', Speech (5 February 1794) 'Rapport sur les principes de morale politique qui doivent guider la Convention national dans l'administration

war,[3] and has sometimes been a trigger for it.[4] In fact, 'acts of terrorism are usually part of or indirectly linked in some ways to an armed conflict'.[5] During armed conflict, irregular means of warfare[6] have been used by state armed forces, militias employed by states, and by non-state armed groups.[7] However, acts of terror also frequently occur in situations falling short of war such as periods of internal disturbances or may be perpetrated as isolated attacks during periods of peace.[8] Acts of a terrorist nature differ little from the 'elemental violence' of war;[9] what differs is the irregularity of the method and means of warfare and the often-sporadic nature of the act. Both acts of war and terrorism are violent measures with political ambition. Nonetheless, terrorism has historically straddled the uncertain divide between war and other forms of violence. For this and other reasons, its regulation by international law has turned out to be difficult and controversial.

Although the use of terrorist tactics has always been part of the experience of war, the evolution of both the *jus ad bellum* and the *jus in bello* has remarkably restrained the scope as well as the modalities of the use of violence. As regards the legality of resorting to force, the UN Charter set strict limits, which have been increasingly called into question especially with regard to the use of force against terrorist groups. Under current international law on the use of force, as laid down in the relevant provisions of the UN Charter of 1945, offensive war, described as 'the threat or use of force against the territorial integrity or political independence of any state', is prohibited.[10] States are only allowed to use military force in self-defence in response to an armed attack[11] or if authorized to do so by the Security Council acting under Chapter VII (once it has identified a threat to the peace, breach of the

---

intérieure de la République' (5 février 1794) in 10 *Oeuvres de Maximilien Robespierre: 27 juillet 1793–27 juillet 1794* (Paris, 1967), 356–7. For an historical perspective on terrorism, see recently, M. Williamson, *Terrorism, War and International Law: The Legality of the Use of Force against Afghanistan in 2001* (Farnham: Ashgate, 2009), 40ff.

[3] See H. Smith, *On Clausewitz: A Study of Military and Political Ideas* (New York: Palgrave Macmillan, 2005).

[4] For instance, the assassination of the Archduke Franz Ferdinand on 28 June 1914 in Sarajevo carried out by an activist from the 'terrorist' group, the 'Young Bosnians' has been commonly cited as being the catalyst for the chain of events leading to World War I. By the same token, the attacks by Al Qaeda on 11 September 2001 in the United States led to the invasion of Afghanistan.

[5] H.-P. Gasser, 'Acts of Terror, "Terrorism" and International Humanitarian Law', 847 *IRRC* (2002) 547–70.

[6] While irregular warfare has been defined in political terms, 'more strictly viewed, irregular warfare simply encompasses military organization, tactics and style in combat'. C.S. Gray, *War, Peace and International Relations: An Introduction to Strategic History* (London: Routledge, 2007), 246.

[7] M. Tse-tung, *On Guerrilla Warfare* (Illinois: University of Illinois Press, 2000), Apps 1–4.

[8] Many well-known terrorist attacks fall into this category, such as the Oklahoma City bombing on 19 April 1995 by Timothy McVeigh and Terry Nichols.

[9] Clausewitz theorized that there were three elements of warfare: the intrinsic violence of its components, the creativity of the strategists, and the rationality of the political decision-makers.

[10] Article 2(4) of the UN Charter.

[11] Article 51 of the UN Charter. See further the Chapter in this volume by G. Di Stefano.

peace, or act of aggression). The Security Council, in its Resolution 1368 passed on 12 September 2001, referred to the terrorist attacks perpetrated in the United States the previous day as a 'threat to the peace'.[12] What was controversial about Resolution 1368 was whether the Security Council had meant indirectly to authorize the use of force by the victim state, the United States, by qualifying the terrorist attacks as a 'threat to the peace' and making reference in the last paragraph of the Resolution's preamble to states' 'inherent right to self-defence'.[13] If the Resolution were to be so construed, the Security Council would recognize that a terrorist group could carry out an 'armed attack', an unprecedented characterization until then.

In fact, an almost instant consensus materialized in the international community about the 9/11 attacks being tantamount to an armed attack.[14] Unfortunately, such a consensus has rapidly dissolved over subsequent developments and the fight against terrorism has acted as a catalyst for profound divergences among states on the international regulation of the use of force. The tendency to stretch the contours of the notion of self-defence to its outer limits, the discussion about the possibility of applying the traditionally inter-state regulation of the use of force to non-state actors, the tolerance shown by states towards uses of force against terrorist groups located in the territory of other states, in particular, in so-called 'failed states',[15] as

[12] See, generally, C. Stahn, 'Security Council Resolutions 1368 (2001) and 1373 (2001): What They Say and What They Do Not Say', *EJIL Forum* (2001). Notably, the Security Council had already qualified 'acts of international terrorism' as 'threats to peace' in the past, in particular with regard to the attacks attributed to Libya regarding Lockerbie and Flight UTA 772; yet this did not provoke any articulation that the hijackings and the resulting death and devastation in Lockerbie were acts of war, or could trigger war-like responses. Rather, there were calls for criminal prosecution of the alleged culprits. It is perhaps of some significance that the Security Council has never referred to terrorist acts as a 'breach' of the peace or as an act of aggression. Jinks makes the interesting observation that while the UN Charter on self-defence rules seek to minimize international aggression and hence push the threshold for what constitutes an 'armed attack' higher, the Geneva Conventions seek to minimize suffering in war, and thereby the inclination is to interpret the threshold for 'armed conflict' lower. D. Jinks, 'The Applicability of the Geneva Conventions to the "Global War on Terrorism"', 46 *Virginia Journal of International Law* (2005–06) 165–96 at 172.

[13] In UNSC Res 1368 (12 September 2001) UN Doc S/RES/1368, the Security Council did not characterize the attacks as an 'armed attack'—language which would have clearly legitimized self-defence under Art 51 of the UN Charter. Nonetheless, operative para 5 expresses the Security Council's 'readiness to take all necessary steps to respond to the terrorist attacks [...] in accordance with its responsibilities under the Charter of the United Nations'—a clear reference to its readiness to use military and other action, if need be. A similar preambular paragraph was also included in Res 1373.

[14] As aptly noted by Cassese 'in a matter of a few days, practically all states [...] have come to assimilate a terrorist attack by a terrorist organization to an armed aggression by a State, entitling the victim state to resort to individual self-defence and third states to act in collective self-defence'. A. Cassese, 'Terrorism is Also Disrupting Some Crucial Legal Categories', 12 *EJIL* (2001) 993–1001.

[15] See further, G. Cavallar and A. Reinisch, 'Kant, Intervention and the "Failed State"', in B.S. Byrd and J. Hruschka (eds), *Kant and Law* (Aldershot: Ashgate, 2006), 431–46; M. Ignatieff, 'Intervention and State Failure', in 3 *Globalization and Violence* (London: Sage, 2006) 287–98; IDI Resolution on Self-Defence, § 10(i); Chatham House, *Principles of International Law on the Use of Force by States in Self-Defence* ILP WP 05/01 by E. Wilmshurst (London: Chatham House, 2005), 12; *Leiden Policy Recommendations on Countermeasures and International Law* (Leiden: Grotious Centre, 2010), 25–6.

well as the 'controversial doctrine' of pre-emptive/anticipatory self-defence against imminent terrorist attacks,[16] are good illustrations of the current challenges posed by international terrorism to the international regulation of the use of force. Many of these issues are still characterized as 'grey areas'. In fact, there does not seem to be a sufficiently wide interpretive consensus on the content and scope of application of the rule of self-defence, which, besides the system of collective security enforced by the Security Council, is the only admissible exception to the unilateral use of force.[17]

From the perspective of *jus in bello*, international humanitarian law applies only in situations of armed conflict. The existence of an armed conflict needs to be ascertained on a case-by-case basis. This has the consequence that terrorist violence, whether committed by state or non-state actors, may or may not be regulated under IHL depending on the context in which it occurs. In fact, different factual situations exist in which terrorist violence is distinctively regulated. In times of peace, applicable international law includes sectoral treaties covering certain types of terrorist acts[18] as well as human rights treaties. Furthermore, where a government considers that a situation created by terrorism is such as to represent a threat to the life of the nation, a state of emergency might be invoked, leading to the derogation of certain human rights norms such as the right to be free from arbitrary detention and the right to fair trial.[19] As soon as the threshold of armed conflict is crossed, however, the pertinent regime becomes IHL, either that applicable to international armed conflicts where more than one state is involved, or that applicable to non-international armed conflicts (Common Article 3 and, also, possibly AP II).

A brief overview of the factual/material distinctions between armed conflict and other forms of violence underlines the difficulty of maintaining a bright-line

---

[16] Although we are mindful of the differences in the use of the expressions 'anticipatory self-defence' and 'pre-emptive self-defence', we find such differences to matter little in this context. Both the United States and the United Kingdom relied on an ambiguous notion of self defence, presumably of an anticipatory character, to justify their military intervention in Afghanistan. See the letters addressed to the UNSC by the Permanent Representatives of the United States and the United Kingdom, UN Doc S/2001/946 (US), reproduced in 40 *ILM* (2001) 1280: 'to prevent and deter further attacks against the United States'; and UN Doc S/2001/947 (UK), reproduced in 72 *BYIL* (2001) 682: 'to avert the continuing threat of attacks from the same source'. For two conflicting views on the legality of the intervention, see M. Bothe, 'Terrorism and the Legality of Pre-emptive Force', 14 *EJIL* (2003) 227–40, and A. Sofaer, 'On the Need of Pre-emption', 14 *EJIL* (2003) 209–26.

[17] See A. Bianchi, 'The International Regulation of the Use of Force: The Politics of Interpretive Methods', 22 *LJIL* (2009) 651–76, and C. Tams, 'The Use of Force against Terrorists', 20 *EJIL* (2009) 359–97.

[18] The so-called 'anti-terror treaties' can be found at <http://www.un.org/terrorism/instruments.shtml>.

[19] For an examination of whether such human rights are also non-derogable in situations of emergency in view of the role they play in upholding other peremptory rights (such as the right to be free from torture), see T. Meron, *Human Rights in Internal Strife: Their International Protection* (Cambridge: Cambridge University Press, 1987); and UN Human Rights Committee General Comment 29, 31 August 2001.

rule between 'terrorism' and genuine 'war'. The distinctions that have traditionally helped to legally characterize the threshold of applicability of IHL have become blurred with the intense use of force by and against groups considered to be terrorist organizations. Given this blurring, the question of the applicable law in situations falling below the threshold or on the borderline of armed conflict has become increasingly significant for the debate on the use of force against terrorist groups. For this reason, the criteria traditionally used in IHL to identify the applicable law to specific types of armed conflict are discussed below.

B. International armed conflict

IHL is clear and precise on the definition of international armed conflict. Common Article 2 of the Geneva Conventions of 1949 defines an international armed conflict as 'all cases of declared war or of any other armed conflict which may arise between two or more of the High Contracting Parties, even if the state of war is not recognized by one of them'.[20] The essential characteristic of armed conflict for the purposes of Article 2 is thus the resort to armed force between states. The military intervention by the United States and other states against Afghanistan in 2001, in response to the 9/11 attacks, can be characterized as a recent example of an international armed conflict regulated by the Geneva Conventions.

Arguably the only noticeable exception to the traditional inter-state conflict paradigm, to which the IHL of international armed conflict applies, is in situations in which 'peoples are fighting against colonial domination and alien occupation and against racist regimes in the exercise of their right of self-determination'.[21] An armed conflict between a terrorist organization such as Al Qaeda and a state cannot amount to an international armed conflict within the meaning of AP I: irrespective of their level of organization, terrorist groups of that kind are not peoples fighting for self-determination. The question arises, however, as to whether peoples fighting for self-determination can, in their method of combat, legitimately resort to terrorism. Such was the concern, for example, of the US Government in its explanation of its arguments against adopting Protocol I.[22]

[20] The same article also states with regard to the applicability of the Conventions, that they 'shall also apply to all cases of partial or total occupation of the territory of a High Contracting Party, even if the said occupation meets with no armed resistance'.

[21] Article 1(4) of AP I. However, its customary nature is often contested (and a lot of important states have not ratified the Protocol).

[22] Abraham D. Sofaer, then Legal Adviser to the United States Department of State cautioned against the intent of Protocol I, 'which aims to encourage and give legal sanction not only to "national liberation" movements in general, but in particular to the inhumane tactics of many of them'. See 2 *American Journal of International Law* (1987) 415, 463.

Although the prohibition of terrorism in armed conflict enjoys widespread accept-ance, there is disagreement concerning the exception to the prohibition, namely to exclude from the definition of terrorism the acts of national liberation movements (so-called 'freedom fighters'). Despite the refusal by developing countries to include in the definition of terrorism acts of violence committed by those struggling for their right to self-determination, a consensus emerged in the 1990s regarding the prohibition of acts of terrorism, irrespective of their motivation.[23] It should be noted, however, that the Arab Convention for the Suppression of Terrorism excludes from its definition of terrorism acts 'by whatever means' committed in struggles for the self-determination of peoples.[24] Similarly, the Convention on Combating Terrorism adopted by the Organization of the Islamic Conference (1999) exempts from the definition of terrorism, armed struggle aimed at self-determination.[25] The methods adopted in exercising the right to self-determination are not unlimited, however, for they must be carried out 'in accordance with the principles of international law'.[26] The discussions on the Draft Comprehensive Convention on International Terrorism[27] reveal that the debate concerning this exclusion remains ongoing. The

---

[23] See eg UNGA Res 49/60 (9 December 1994) UN Doc A/RES/49/60, §2: 'Criminal acts intended or calculated to provoke a state of terror in the general public, a group of persons or particular persons for political purposes are in any circumstances unjustifiable, whatever the considerations of a political, philosophical, ideological, racial, ethnic, religious or other nature that may be invoked to justify them'; Security Council 'unequivocally condemn(ed) all acts, methods and practices of terrorism as criminal and unjustifiable, regardless of their motivation, in all their forms and manifestations, wherever and by whomever committed' UNSC Res 1269 (1999) §1. In Res 1566 (2004) the Security Council '*Recalls* that criminal acts, including against civilians, committed with the intent to cause death or serious bodily injury, or taking of hostages, with the purpose to provoke a state of terror in the general public or in a group of persons or particular persons, intimidate a population or compel a government or an international organization to do or to abstain from doing any act, which constitute offences within the scope of and as defined in the international conventions and protocols related to terrorism, are under no circumstances justifiable by considerations of a political, philosophical, ideological, racial, ethnic, religious or other similar nature and *calls upon* all States to prevent such acts, and if not prevented, to ensure that such acts are punished by penalties consistent with their grave nature'.

[24] Article 2(a) states that: 'All cases of struggle by whatever means, including armed struggle, against foreign occupation and aggression for liberation and self-determination, in accordance with the prin-ciples of international law, shall not be regarded as an offence'.

[25] Article 2(1).

[26] This clause appears in both the Arab Convention for the Suppression of Terrorism (adopted 22 April 1998), Art 2(a); and the OIC Convention on Combating International Terrorism (adopted 1 July 1999), Art 2(1). The exclusion of any reference to the 'struggle for self-determination' from the scope of the Draft Comprehensive Convention was the object of a long debate. A compromise solu-tion was found in the wording of current Art 18(1) with added reference to *peoples*. This provision, which is no longer contentious, reads: 'Nothing in this Convention shall affect other rights, obligations and responsibilities of States, peoples and individuals under international law, in particular the pur-poses and principles of the Charter of the United Nations, and international humanitarian law', 'Draft Comprehensive Convention' (14 October 2005) UN Doc A/C.6/60/L.6, paras 9–10; UN Doc A/C.6/62/SR.16 (19 November 2007), para 117.

[27] Last consolidated version: 'Draft Comprehensive Convention' (12 August 2005) UN Doc A/59/894, Annex II 7.

member states of the Organization of the Islamic Conference have been against the application of the Convention during armed conflicts, including occupation.[28] If we turn back to the law of international armed conflict, the prohibition in Article 51(2) of AP I of '[a]cts or threats of violence the primary purpose of which is to spread terror among the civilian population' clearly suggests that Article 1(4) of the same Protocol would not permit peoples in their struggle for self-determination to legitimately resort to such acts of terrorism.

Coming back to the definition of international armed conflict under Common Article 2, difficulties remain in determining the required elements of 'armed conflict' and 'state involvement'. As regards the first requirement, one may note that some degree of intensity, to be appreciated on a case-by-case basis, appears to be required even when the armed forces of two or more states are involved. This criterion is instrumental to distinguish 'border clashes', 'skirmishes', and 'minor incidents' that states do not tend to regard as giving rise to an international armed conflict

Given that two or more states must be directly or indirectly involved for an armed conflict to be characterized as international, the issue of determining state involvement is crucial, particularly in those cases in which such involvement may be controversial. The most difficult issue has turned out to be the determination of the criteria whereby state involvement is to be ascertained for the purposes of characterizing a conflict as an international one.

In the *Genocide* case,[29] the ICJ decoupled the issue of state involvement for the purpose of attributing responsibility from that of determining the extent to which state involvement is necessary for characterizing an international conflict. After *Tadić*,[30] the issue seemed to be one and the same. In particular, the ICJ suggested that the 'overall control' test, elaborated by the ICTY in *Tadić*, might well be a suitable one to be applied for the determination of the international nature of a conflict.[31]

---

[28] Current Art 18(2) as presented by the Chairperson of the Ad-Hoc Working Group in 2007, reads: 'The activities of armed forces during an armed conflict, as those terms are understood under international humanitarian law, which are governed by that law, are not governed by this Convention'. The decision not to include in the scope of the Draft Comprehensive Convention situations covered by IHL would not have the consequence of excluding criminal responsibility. It would simply be a choice of applicable law. The proposal by the Organisation of the Islamic Conference, which added the explicit reference 'including in situations of foreign occupation' to the text, met with the resistance of other delegations. According to some, the exclusion of activities regulated by IHL necessarily covers situations of occupation, thus making an explicit reference to the latter redundant. 'Report of the Ad Hoc Committee established by General Assembly Resolution 51/210 of 17 December 1996', 11th session (5, 6, and 15 February 2007) UN Doc A/62/37, 8, para 14.

[29] *Application of the Convention on the Prevention and Punishment of the Crime of Genocide (Bosnia and Herzegovina v Serbia and Montenegro)* (Merits) 2007.

[30] *Prosecutor v Dusko Tadić a/k/a 'Dule'* (Appeal Judgment) ICTY-94-1-A (15 July 1999).

[31] *Application of the Convention on the Prevention and Punishment of the Crime of Genocide*, §§ 404–5. The ICJ added that the determination of state involvement for the purpose of characterizing a conflict as international may well differ 'without logical inconsistency' to the test used to attribute conduct to a state under the law of state responsibility (§ 405), which should be based on the 'effective control' test (§ 401).

The criteria for 'armed conflict' and 'state involvement' can be evaluated in relation to the scope and object of the Geneva Conventions; in this way an expansive reading would include situations of sustained and protracted violence where two or more states are involved with a view to ensuring the protections laid down in the Conventions. If one considers the involvement of armed bands and militias controlled by another state, the degree of the required control can be satisfied by the laxer 'overall control' test elaborated by the ICTY or by even more tenuous links. Ultimately, the weight to be given to relevant elements appears likely to be influenced by political considerations, which are hardly apt to fit strict legal categories. A sound policy argument can be advanced that the application of the enhanced guarantees of the law applicable to international armed conflicts should not be hampered by such restrictive criteria as those applicable to attribution of an act to a state under the law of state responsibility.

The criteria with respect to Article 2 notwithstanding, grey areas remain. In particular, recent practice attests to the interpretive difficulties inherent in the characterization of international armed conflict and the identification of rules applicable to it, particularly in relation to extraterritorial enforcement operations and uses of force short of armed force or to the use of force in a foreign state's territory not controlled by that state, against terrorist groups.[32] Extraterritorial operations may occasionally be carried out with the authorization of the territorial state. This seems to have been the case in the 2002 targeted killing of six Al Qaeda operatives in Yemen by a missile fired by a CIA-operated drone. Similar air strikes were undertaken by the United States in January and June 2007 in Somalia against suspected terrorists linked with Al Qaeda. The strikes seem to have been part of an operation in which the US military would be supporting Somali security forces, having faced no opposition or protests by the local authorities.

Most of the time, however, armed strikes against terrorist objectives in foreign territory are conducted against the will of the territorial state. The strikes by US forces against Taliban strongholds in Pakistan, although protested against by the Government of Pakistan,[33] are not perceived as acts directed against the country and are unlikely to trigger an international armed conflict with that state.[34] Nor is the legality of such acts evaluated through the looking glass of international

---

[32] See C. Tams, 'The Use of Force against Terrorists', 20 *EJIL* (2009) 359–97, and A. Bianchi, 'The International Legal Regulation of the Use of Force: The Politics of Interpretive Method', 22 *LJIL* (2009) 651–76. See also G.L. Neuman, 'Humanitarian Law and Counterterrorist Force', 14 *EJIL* (2003) 283–98.

[33] For an interesting discussion on the legal parameters to assess the lawfulness of such conduct, see the 'Report of the Special Rapporteur on extrajudicial, summary or arbitrary executions: Addendum. Study on Targeted Killing', Philip Alston, UN Doc A/HRC/14/24/Add.6 (28 May 2010).

[34] See eg Ministry of Foreign Affairs of Pakistan, 'Drone Attacks' (24 January 2009) Press Release No 40/2009 (protesting against a drone attack, in infringement of Pakistan's sovereignty); and 'Response to US Defence Secretary's Statement' (28 January 2009) Press Release No 42/2009 (denying the existence of any understanding between the two states on predator attacks).

humanitarian law rules. Along similar lines, the March 2008 incident in which the Colombian army penetrated into Ecuador to pursue and kill 25 FARC fighters is of relevance.[35]

If a certain threshold of violence is required to trigger the applicability of international humanitarian law, one can question whether the above-mentioned instances easily meet the requirement of sustained and protracted violence, which could justify finding that an armed conflict exists. The illegality of these operations may, however, be self-evident, either because they represent unauthorized acts of enforcement in the territory of another state, the territorial sovereignty of which is thereby violated, or because they amount to a violation of the prohibition of the use of force. But could one reasonably claim that any transnational use of force by a state's military force triggers the applicability of the Geneva Conventions? At the very least, such a claim could be legitimately questioned.

Distinguishing between extraterritorial acts of enforcement and uses of force against terrorist groups in foreign territory is not easy and must be done on a case-by-case basis, taking into account the characteristics of the operation, its magnitude, as well as its effects.[36] But the fact that the armed forces of a state are involved in another state does not automatically trigger the full applicability of international humanitarian law rules if the existence of a conflict cannot be established.

C. Non-international armed conflict

The definition of non-international armed conflicts (NIACs) has historically been an area of controversy in IHL.[37] States have tended to be reluctant to admit the existence of a level of hostilities between governmental and non-governmental forces or between such forces that would trigger the obligations of warfare.[38] This is largely

---

[35] For a detailed account of the factual background, which concerned an operation of the Colombian military carried out by air bombings and troops on the ground, prompting a protest by Ecuador for violation of its territorial sovereignty, see the OAS, 'Report of the OAS Commission that visited Ecuador and Colombia' (16 March 2008) OAS Doc RC.25/doc7/08. While Ecuador had sponsored a draft resolution of the OAS condemning Colombia, the incident was eventually closed by the apologies offered by Colombia, together with the guarantee that such extraterritorial operations will not be repeated in the future (taken note also in OAS Res RC.25/RES.1/08, para 6).

[36] See D. Kretzmer, 'Targeted Killing of Suspected Terrorists: Extra-Judicial Executions or Legitimate Means of Defence?', 16 *EJIL* (2005) 171–212. On targeted killings, see the Chapter by N. Mezler in this volume as well as his study, *Targeted Killings in International Law* (Oxford: Oxford University Press, 2008).

[37] See, generally, D. Schindler, 'International Humanitarian Law and Internationalized Internal Armed Conflicts', 22 *IRRC* (1982) 255–64; H. Salinas Burgos, 'The Application of International Humanitarian Law as Compared to Human Rights Law in Situations Qualified as Disturbances and Tensions, or Public Emergency, with Special Reference to War Crimes and Political Crimes', in F. Kalshoven and Y. Sandoz (eds), *Implementation of International Humanitarian Law* (Boston: Martinus Nijhoff, 1989); L. Moir, *The Law of Internal Armed Conflict* (Cambridge: Cambridge University Press, 2002).

[38] F. Bugnion, 'Jus Ad Bellum, Jus in Bello and Non-International Armed Conflicts', 6 *YIHL* (2003) 167–98.

due to the fear that recognizing an insurgent group as a party to a conflict would result in the non-state group being accorded legal status and legitimacy.[39] For this reason, the notion of terrorism has been linked with the unlawful use of force by non-state groups and states have often referred to rebels or insurgents as 'terrorists' as a way to distinguish them from a party to a legally cognizable state of armed conflict.[40]

With respect to non-international armed conflicts, the scope of Common Article 3 of the Geneva Conventions has become a bone of contention *vis-à-vis* its application to conflicts that take place within the territory of more than one High Contracting Party. The rules set out in Common Article 3 to the Geneva Conventions of 1949 apply in case of 'armed conflict not of an international character occurring in the territory of one of the High Contracting Parties'.

Two particular aspects have troubled those interpreting the provision. The first is that without a definition of armed conflict, it is unclear exactly which factual situations Common Article 3 is supposed to regulate. A cursory consideration of recent practice highlights a number of relevant factors that are instrumental to ascertain the existence of a conflict. The ICTY Appeals Chamber's 1995 decision in *Tadić* stressed the importance of 'protracted armed violence' between a government and armed groups or between such groups.[41] In fact, the Trial Chamber in *Tadić* interpreted the test laid down by the Appeals Chamber as requiring evidence of (1) intensity; and (2) organization of the parties.[42] Many Trial Chambers have subsequently adopted this two-pronged test, which serves to distinguish 'an armed conflict from banditry, unorganized and short-lived insurrections, or terrorist activities, which are not subject to international humanitarian law'.[43]

Inconsistencies remain, however. While the ICTY Trial Chamber determined that the criterion of protracted armed violence refers more to the intensity of

---

[39] Y. Sandoz, 'International Humanitarian Law in the Twenty-First Century', 6 *YIHL* (2003) 3–40 at 14.

[40] See eg the attitude of the Russian Federation towards the situation in Chechnya and the Government of Colombia's view of FARC. It was argued (unsuccessfully) in the *Boškoski* case before a Trial Chamber of the ICTY that the commonly held view that the ethnic Albanian armed group the National Liberation Army (NLA) was a terrorist group meant that the situation in 2001 did not amount to an armed conflict. See *Prosecutor v Boškoski, Ljube and Tarčulovski, Johan* (Judgment) ICTY-04-82-T (10 July 2008), § 191.

[41] *Tadić* (Decision on the defence motion for Interlocutory Appeal on Jurisdiction), ICTY, Appeals Chamber, Decision of 2 October 1995, Case No IT-94-1-AR72, 35 *ILM* 32 (1996) § 70.

[42] *Tadić*, ICTY, Trial Chamber, Opinion and Judgment of 7 May 1997, Case No IT-94-1-A, § 562.

[43] See eg *Delalić and others* (*Čelebići case*), ICTY, Trial Chamber II, Judgment of 16 November 1998, Case No IT-96-21-T, § 184; *Kordić and Čerkez*, ICTY, Appeals Chamber, Judgment of 17 December 2004, Case No IT-95-14/2-A, § 341; *Limaj, Fatmir et al*, ICTY, Trial Chamber II, Judgment of 30 November 2005, Case No IT-03-66-T, §§ 84 and 89; *Haradinaj, Ramush et al*, ICTY, Trial Chamber I, Judgment of 3 April 2008, Case No IT-04-84-T, § 38.

the armed violence than to its duration,[44] the ICC Pre-Trial Chamber opted for a slightly different interpretation, finding that the criterion of 'protracted armed conflict between [...] [organized armed groups]' focused on the need for the armed groups 'to have the ability to plan and carry out military operations for a prolonged period of time'.[45]

Be that as it may, the definitional guidance for 'armed conflict' provided by the ICTY Appeals Chamber in *Tadić* has not only been influential at the level of international tribunals. It was accepted by the 2005 Commission of Inquiry on Darfur, it is reflected in the ICC Statute, and it appears to have affected the case law of domestic courts as well.[46]

Secondly, difficulties have arisen in interpreting the condition that the armed conflict must take place in the territory of one of the High Contracting Parties. This could either mean that at least one state party to the Geneva Conventions must be the locus for fighting for the provision to be triggered, or, more literally, it could mean that the fighting must be contained within the borders of one state.

In recent years, the phenomenon of trans-national terrorist groups not linked to any particular territory perpetrating massively violent attacks primarily directed against the civilian population and the military response to these by certain states has raised the question of whether this is a new type of armed conflict 'not of an international character' to which IHL does or should apply. In June 2006, the US Supreme Court in the *Hamdan* case came to a positive conclusion to this question, finding that Common Article 3 applied to the 'armed conflict not of an international character' occurring between the United States (a signatory to the Geneva Conventions) and Al Qaeda (obviously, as a non-state group, a non-signatory) on the territory of a signatory state (Afghanistan).[47]

The US Supreme Court interpreted the scope of application of Common Article 3 extremely broadly—as applying to all armed conflicts, which do not fall into the category of inter-state armed conflicts. For the time being, it is difficult to contend that international consensus on expanding the scope of application of Common Article 3 has been reached; a few decisions of domestic or international courts are unlikely

---

[44] *Haradinaj, Ramush et al*, ICTY, Trial Chamber I, Judgment of 3 April 2008, Case No IT-04-84-T, § 49.

[45] *Lubanga Dyilo, Thomas*, ICC, Pre-Trial Chamber I, Decision on the Confirmation of Charges of 29 January 2007, Case No ICC-01/04-01/06-803, § 234.

[46] *Report of the International Commission of Inquiry on Darfur to the United Nations Secretary-General pursuant to Security Council Resolution 1564 of 18 September 2004*, Geneva, 25 January 2005, § 4. Compare ICC Statute, Art 8(2)(c) and (d) with Art 8(2)(e) and (f). For examples of the adoption of the test by domestic courts, see (*HH et al (Mogadishu: Armed Conflict: Risk) Somalia v Secretary of State for the Home Department* CG [2008] UKAIT 00022 (28 January 2008), §§ 72–3 and *KH (Article 15(c) Qualification Directive) Iraq v Secretary of State for the Home Department*, [2008] UKAIT 00023, §§ 81–3).

[47] *Hamdan, Salim Ahmed v Rumsfeld, Donald H, Secretary of Defense, et al* (Judgment) 126 SCt 2749 (2006) (US Supreme Court) 67.

to meet the threshold. Certainly, if some key participant in the IHL interpretive community, such as the ICRC, decided to promote such a reading of Common Article 3, this could act as a catalyst for coalescing consensus by states parties to the Geneva Conventions on such an interpretation.

The problems of fitting different factual scenarios into the existing categories of IHL, with the ensuing difficulty of determining which rules are applicable, suggests the importance that the recognition of the proposed 'minimum standards of humanity' applicable in all circumstances would have faced, had such standards been adequately developed and endorsed at the UN level. It is somewhat unfortunate that the process of the elaboration of such standards has lost momentum, given that factual mischaracterizations and the blurring of legal categories have often contributed to circumvention of fundamental humanitarian standards.[48]

The adoption of the arguably clearer threshold of applicability of AP II in 1977[49] has unfortunately not been accompanied by an increased likelihood of states recognizing the existence of this type of armed conflict. The banner of terrorism has often been used by states to denounce the legitimacy of non-state groups fighting in internal armed conflicts and thereby to deny the applicability of the Protocol or Common Article 3 to such situations. This can be seen in conflicts lasting decades such as in Colombia or Sri Lanka. Such a tendency has been even more pronounced since 2001, when governments have tended to use the political power of the terrorist label to delegitimize non-state opponents and shy away from peace talks with armed groups on the basis that they cannot negotiate with 'terrorists'. The recognition that non-state groups still remain parties to armed conflicts, regardless of their unlawful use of acts of terror or terrorism to further their causes, would help correct the current misalignment of the principles of the applicability of IHL *vis-à-vis* the acts of non-state armed groups.

---

[48] See 'Fundamental standards of humanity: Report of the Secretary-General submitted pursuant to Commission Resolution 2000/69' (12 January 2001) UN Doc E/CN.4/2001/91. See also the '1990 Declaration on Minimum Humanitarian Standards' (the Turku Declaration) (31 January 1995) UN Doc E/CN.4/1995/116.

[49] The scope of application of AP II as set out in Art 1(1) covers: 'all armed conflicts which are not covered by Article 1 of [Protocol I] [...] and which take place in the territory of a High Contracting Party between its armed forces and dissident armed forces or other organized armed groups which, under responsible command, exercise such control over a part of its territory as to enable them to carry out sustained and concerted military operations and to implement this protocol'.

3 The Conduct of Hostilities
Vis-à-Vis Terrorism and
'Counter-Terrorist' Operations

A. The prohibition on terrorism and terrorist acts in armed conflict

The use of terrorism has almost always been present in the history of warfare, and remains a commonly used means of combat. The structure and basic tenets of IHL form a solid body of principles and specific regulations that unequivocally prohibit and condemn terrorism in armed conflict. The principles of humanity[50] and distinction[51] and the protection of the civilian population form the basis of the specific rules found in the Fourth Geneva Convention and the two additional Protocols prohibiting acts of terrorism and acts of terror. This entails that the civilian population or individual civilians may not be the object of attack. The prohibition of acts of terror(ism) in IHL forms part and parcel of this protection.[52] Apart from some need for interpretative distinctions to be made between 'acts of terrorism' as prohibited in GC IV and AP II and 'acts of terror' in AP I, these rules are comprehensive and there seems to be no need for further development or revision.

B. The law on counter-terrorism

While the law prohibiting terrorism and acts of terror by state and non-state actors in both international and non-international armed conflicts is clear, the law on the conduct of hostilities related to counter-terrorism is subject to numerous practical difficulties. Questions relating to whether a terrorist may be considered a civilian

---

[50] This principle is considered as one of the 'intransgressible principles' of IHL. *Legality of the Threat or Use of Nuclear Weapons* (Advisory Opinion) [1996] ICJ Rep 226, § 79. See also *Legal Consequences of the Construction of a Wall in Occupied Palestinian Territory* (Advisory Opinion) [2004] ICJ Rep 136, § 89.

[51] The law related to the conduct of hostilities seeks to minimize the suffering of the civilian population from the effects of war, and therefore sets down the fundamental principle of distinction between civilians and combatants. Article 48 of AP I sets out the basic rule: 'In order to ensure respect for and protection of the civilian population and civilian objects, the Parties to the conflict shall at all times distinguish between the civilian population and combatants and between civilian objects and military objectives and accordingly shall direct their operations only against military objectives'.

[52] Article 51(2) of AP I provides: 'The civilian population as such, as well as individual civilians, shall not be the object of attack. Acts or threats of violence the primary purpose of which is to spread terror among the civilian population are prohibited'. See also Art 33 of GC IV and Art 13(2) of AP II.

within the categories of Article 4A of GC III (defining a prisoner of war and thereby, indirectly, a combatant), have led to differing interpretations as to the adequacy of the two categories of legal status (combatant and civilian) under IHL. While the US Government between 2001 and 2009 took the legally dubious view that such persons are neither combatants, nor civilians, but unlawful combatants—a term unknown to IHL[53]—the Israel Supreme Court held, by contrast, that members of Palestinian terrorist organizations who are captured during hostilities would retain their civilian status.[54]

Whether the conditions of Article 4A(2) of GC III should also formally apply to members of the armed forces in order for them to receive POW status has been a troubling issue of lingering uncertainty, not only for members of the Taliban captured by US forces during hostilities in Afghanistan in 2001–02, but also for counter-terrorist forces such as members of special forces who wear non-standard uniforms and therefore risk being denied POW status if captured.

While a strict reading of the conditions has been applied to deny POW entitlement to the group as a whole where members of armed forces (such as the Taliban) are suspected of terrorism or where dealing with those who support terrorist groups, commentators have often argued for a broader interpretation of the requirement to wear a fixed distinctive sign in the case of members of special forces.[55] This in turn raises the question of whether in contemporary armed conflict such a binary approach to the interpretation of Article 4A of GC III is sound as a matter of both law and policy.

Arguably, the simpler definition of armed forces, as contained in Article 43 of AP I, is the preferable solution to identifying persons entitled to POW status.[56] Under Article 43 of AP I, the four conditions have been reduced to two: (1) the existence of an organized armed force, unit, or group, which is (2) under a command responsible to a party to a conflict. This simplified definition has two consequences. First, it means that visibility is no longer a *collective defining element* of armed forces, but an *individual obligation*, the respect of which may be relevant for a member's entitlement to POW status or combatant privilege, but not for his or her unit's legal qualification as part of the 'armed forces of a Party to the conflict'.[57] Secondly, the collective requirement of compliance with IHL is no longer a defining element of

---

[53] Although this was changed by the Obama Administration and by Congress with the Military Commission Act of 2009, the legal definition of 'unprivileged enemy belligerent' is equally alien to IHL categories. See further the Chapter by K. Dörmann in this volume.

[54] *Public Committee against Torture v Israel* HCJ 769/02 (14 December 2006) (Israel, Supreme Court), § 28.

[55] See eg W. Hays Parks, '"Special Forces" Wear Non-standard Uniforms', 4 *Chicago Journal of International Law* (2003) 493–547 at 493 and 510, fn 30.

[56] See Art 44 of AP I.

[57] Article 43(1) of AP I. See also, N. Melzer, *Targeted Killing in International Law* (Oxford: Oxford University Press, 2008), 307.

what constitutes armed forces, but has been reduced to a legal obligation of the parties to the conflict to enforce the compliance of their armed forces with IHL through an internal disciplinary system.[58] Universal ratification of AP I would be the logical solution to this particular conundrum. Even if ratification does not occur, however, it can be reasonably argued that the definition of armed forces in Article 43 of AP I, which was adopted by consensus at the Diplomatic Conference of 1974 to 1977, has become part of customary law.[59]

When military operations are launched against armed groups qualified as terrorist groups, the application of the principles of the means and methods of warfare—distinction, proportionality and protection of the civilian population—acquires a heightened level of complexity in view of the fact that non-state actors engaged in terrorism are civilians; they are mostly located in civilian population centres, and themselves often target civilians in their means of warfare. This has meant that in order to comply with IHL rules of engagement, the targeting of such individuals by governmental forces has needed to be precise and contained. However, factual examples abound of the targeting of 'terrorists' in urban settings in which, rather than relying on precision targeting, a looser proportionality metric has been applied, so that 'collateral damage' is considered as justified in view of the importance of the terror figure targeted.[60]

Another difficult instance of assessing the lawfulness of targeting has arisen in connection with drone attacks against terrorist targets in Afghanistan and elsewhere. The use of drones in such contexts as Afghanistan and Pakistan has turned out to be highly controversial due to the number of civilian casualties involved, the lack of publicly available information about the selection of targets, and the lack of transparency generally associated with this type of operation. Furthermore, the law applicable to such attacks is relatively uncertain when these operations take place in contexts the factual and legal qualification of which is unclear. For instance, while drone attacks in Afghanistan are carried out under the supervision of the military in a situation of armed conflict, the attacks against alleged terrorist targets in Pakistan, in the regions close to the Afghan border, are conducted by the CIA

---

[58] Melzer (n 57), 307–8.

[59] J.-M. Henckearts and L. Doswald-Beck, *Customary International Humanitarian Law*, vol I (Cambridge: Cambridge University Press, 2005), Rule 4, 14. See also the discussion by N. Melzer in his Chapter in this volume at section 2 B(ii) 'Armed Forces' in particular with regard to the position of Israel.

[60] Well-publicized instances of 'urban combat' were the Israeli incursion into the Palestinian settlement of Jenin in 2002 and the US-led incursion into Fallujah in 2004. Excessive civilian casualties have been claimed as a result of both operations. See R. Wedgwood, 'Propositions on the Law of War after the Kosovo Campaign: *Jus Ad Bellum* and the Personal Factor in History', 78 *US Naval War College International Law Series* (2003) 435 (arguing that '[w]hether one's framework is utilitarian or pure principle, it is possible to admit that the merits of a war make a difference in our tolerance for methods of war fighting. This teleological view can be incorporated, albeit awkwardly, in the metric for "military advantage" in judging proportionality, for surely we do not value military objectives for their own sake').

and are allegedly not subject to the same degree of supervision under IHL rules. The United States has not officially taken a stance on the legality of the programme, but the legal adviser to the State Department has stated that the United States 'has carefully reviewed the rules governing targeting operations' to ensure that they conform with the laws of war, including the principles of distinction and proportionality, which 'are implemented rigorously throughout the planning and execution of lethal operations to ensure that such operations are conducted in accordance with all applicable law'.[61] Given that the applicable law may differ depending on the factual characterization of any given situation, this statement does not solve all the doubts raised by drone attacks and the rules applicable to them. It would appear, however, that the Administration sees itself still engaged in 'the armed conflict with al-Qaeda, the Taliban and associated forces'.[62] From a strictly legal point of view, however, this justification is presented jointly with arguments based on legitimate self-defence. Either justification would, in the State Department legal adviser's view, make the use of drone attacks lawful.[63] The blurring of categories regulating the use of force and the conduct of hostilities, and justifications under different legal regimes propounded by the US Administration, has not gone unnoticed. In his recent Study on Targeted Killings,[64] the UN Special Rapporteur on extrajudicial, summary or arbitrary executions, criticizes this approach, maintaining that the justification for a targeted killing cannot be provided under the rules on the use of force, and that the issue of whether a specific killing is lawful depends on 'whether it meets the requirements of IHL and human rights (in the context of armed conflict) or human rights alone (in all other contexts)'.[65] According to the Special Rapporteur, '[o]utside the context of armed conflict, the use of drones for targeted killings is almost never likely to be legal', as it would hardly meet the human rights limitations on the use of lethal force.[66] Under the laws of armed conflict recourse to such targeted killings must be appreciated against the background of strict conditions (like any other targeted killings), ranging from the requirement for state armed forces and agents to use all reasonably available sources (including technological ones such as intelligence and surveillance) to obtain reliable information to verify that the target is lawful, to ensuring that compliance with the IHL proportionality principle is assessed for each attack individually, and not for an overall military operation.[67]

---

[61] H. Koh, 'The Obama Administration and International Law', Keynote Address at the Annual Meeting of the American Society of International Law (25 March 2010), <www.state.gov/s/l/releases/remarks/139119.htm>.

[62] Koh (n 61).   [63] Koh (n 61).

[64] 'Report of the Special Rapporteur on extrajudicial, summary or arbitrary executions, Philip Alston, Study on Targeted Killings, Addendum', UN Doc A/HRC/14/24/Add.6 (28 May 2010).

[65] UN Doc A/HRC/14/24/Add.6 (28 May 2010), para 44.

[66] UN Doc A/HRC/14/24/Add.6 (28 May 2010), para 85.

[67] UN Doc A/HRC/14/24/Add.6 (28 May 2010), IV Conclusions and Recommendations, para 93. Other conditions include the need to ensure: 'that even after a targeting operation is under way, if it

The problem, however, does not seem to lie in the rules on proportionality or distinction as such, but rather in the way they are being applied or, as in the case of the drone attacks, in the issue of whether IHL rules or international human rights standards should apply to certain factual situations.

In addition, debate continues in military and academic circles as to the precise meaning of 'direct participation in hostilities' for the purpose, inter alia, of deciding whether and in which circumstances a terrorist suspect could be killed. Arguably, the tendency has been not to regard a person belonging to a terrorist organization as merely a civilian if he or she is actively involved in perpetrating attacks or is in a 'continuous fighting function', and could therefore be targeted at any time, even when not directly participating in hostilities.[68] The serious ramifications of such an approach could be somewhat ameliorated by the adoption of human rights standards in the decision as to whether to arrest—if possible—or kill, if necessary and proportionate to the threat posed. This approach was applied by the Israeli Supreme Court in the *Targeted Killings* case.[69] In addition, 'in case of reasonable doubt, the concerned individual would have to be presumed to be a civilian'.[70] Despite its *lex specialis* status, IHL is able to draw on human rights standards in order to protect the right to life and liberty in these complex security situations taking place outside the theatre of battlefield operations. While the notion of 'direct participation in hostilities' would appear to be sufficiently descriptive to restrict the legal targeting of individuals to some degree, there is little doubt that the identification of its exact contours remains controversial. It is to be hoped that the ICRC 'Interpretative

appears that the target is not lawful, or that the collateral loss of life or property damage is in excess of the original determination, targeting forces have the ability and discretion to cancel or postpone the attack'; that 'procedures are in place to verify that no targeted killing is taken in revenge, or primarily to cause terror or to intimidate, or to gain political advantage [...] especially in heavily populated urban areas, if it appears that a targeted killing will risk harm to civilians, State forces must provide effective advance warning, as specifically as possible to the population'.

[68] See eg Melzer (n 57), 321.

[69] *Public Committee against Torture v Israel* HCJ 769/02 (14 December 2006) (Israel, Supreme Court), § 46. Quite usefully, the Israeli Supreme Court identified a number of cases which should be included in the definition of 'direct part in hostilities': using arms; carrying arms, openly or not, to or from the location of a battle; collecting intelligence on the army, whether on issues regarding the hostilities, or beyond those issues; transmission of information concerning targets directly intended for facilitating an attack on them; transporting combatants to or from the place where the hostilities are taking place; driving ammunition to the place from which it will be used for the purposes of hostilities; operating weapons to be used in battle, or supervising their operation, or providing service to them, be the distance from the battlefield as it may; preparation for a military operation and intention to take part therein; sending combatants to perform an attack, deciding upon the act, or planning it; or serving, out of one's own free will, as a 'human shield' for terrorists taking a direct part in hostilities. On the other hand, according to the Court, the following activities would not be included in the definition of 'taking a direct part in hostilities': providing combatants with general strategic analysis or logistical support, including monetary aid; distributing propaganda supporting the hostilities; employment in the armaments industry; or serving as a 'human shield' due to coercion (§§ 34–7).

[70] Melzer (n 57), 321.

Guidance on the Notion of Direct Participation in Hostilities under IHL' will contribute to establishing some degree of consensus among IHL actors.[71] According
to the Interpretive Guidance, in order to qualify as direct participation in hostilities, a specific act must *either* be likely to adversely affect the military operations or
military capacity of a party to an armed conflict 'or, alternatively, to inflict death,
injury, or destruction on persons or objects protected against direct attack' (emphasis added).[72]

4 Terrorism and Acts of
Terror as War Crimes

In the field of international criminal law, there have been significant developments towards the criminalization of terrorism and/or acts of terror. The ICTY,
ICTR, and the Special Court for Sierra Leone have all recognized that acts of terror may amount to war crimes. As noted, the Geneva Conventions of 1949 and
their Additional Protocols prohibit 'acts of terrorism' and 'acts or threats of violence the primary purpose of which is to spread terror among the civilian population' committed during international or non-international armed conflict when
directed against civilians or civilian objects.[73] However, these offences were not
listed among the grave breaches in the Geneva Conventions nor in AP I. The recognition that such offences may amount to war crimes outside the context of World
War II jurisprudence[74] only transpired in the mid-1990s. The ICTR Statute (1994)

---

[71] *Interpretive Guidance on the Notion of Direct Participation in Hostilities under International
Humanitarian Law* (Geneva: ICRC, 2009) (hereinafter 'DPH Interpretive Guidance'). However, there
are further constitutive elements that must be fulfilled for an act to qualify as direct participation in
hostilities. First, there must be a direct causal link between the act and the harm likely to result; secondly, 'the act must be specifically designed to directly cause the required threshold of harm in support
of a party to the conflict and to the detriment of another'. The latter is termed the 'belligerent nexus'.
The third requirement seems to impose a type of mental element or, at least, intentionality condition
tied to the belligerent nature of the act. It is plausible that certain terrorist attacks committed against
civilians during armed conflict would qualify as direct participation in hostilities under these elements.

[72] DPH Interpretive Guidance, 46; see also 49–50.

[73] Article 33(1) of GC IV; Art 4(2)(d) of AP II; Art 51(2) of AP I; Art 13(2) of AP II; Rules concern-
ing the Control of Wireless Telegraphy in Time of War and Air Warfare. Drafted by a Commission of
Jurists at the Hague (December 1922–February 1923), Art 22. The customary status of Art 51(2) of AP
I and Art 13(2) of AP II has been recognized. See *Galić, Stanislav* (Appeal Judgment) ICTY-98-29-A (30
November 2006), § 87; J.-M. Henckaerts and L. Doswald-Beck, *Customary International Humanitarian
Law*, vol I (Cambridge: Cambridge University Press, 2005), Rule 2.

[74] For an overview, see R. Arnold, *The ICC as a New Instrument for Repressing Terrorism*
(New York: Transnational, 2004), 96ff.

included 'acts of terrorism' within its list of war crimes in non-international armed conflicts.[75] Although the ICTY was not given the same specific competence, a Trial Chamber and the Appeals Chamber held in 2003 and 2006 respectively that 'the crime of terror' is covered by Article 3 of its Statute (violations of the laws and customs of war).[76] The International Law Commission included 'acts of terrorism' in the list of war crimes in non-international armed conflicts in its 1996 Draft Code of Crimes against the Peace and Security of Mankind.[77] However, 'acts of terrorism' did not make it onto the list of war crimes (or for that matter, any other type of international crimes) under the ICC, an exclusion that was criticized by some states that did not sign the Statute. In terms of the so-called 'hybrid' tribunals, neither the Special Panels for Serious Crimes in East Timor nor the Extraordinary Chambers in Cambodia have jurisdiction over 'acts of terrorism', whereas the Special Court for Sierra Leone (SCSL) lists terrorism as a prosecutable war crime.[78] The reason for its absence in the East Timor and Cambodia jurisdictions is possibly explained by the fact that the Special Panels for Serious Crimes in East Timor used essentially the same text as that of the ICC Statute, which excludes acts of terrorism from its list of war crimes. Those negotiating the constitutive instrument of the Extraordinary Chambers in Cambodia decided to include only well-accepted international crimes, and did not wish to enter into the thorny question of state-led terrorism.

The first international criminal court to rule on 'acts of terror' as a war crime was the ICTY. In a 2003 judgment, the majority of a Trial Chamber in *Galić* held that a violation of Article 51(2) of AP I entailed individual criminal responsibility under the treaty law applicable at the time the offences were committed (the 22 May 1992 Agreement), which incorporated Article 51(2) of AP I.[79] The majority did not take a position on the customary character of Article 51(2) of AP I.[80] In its 2006 judgment, the Appeals Chamber held by majority that the 'crime of acts or threats of violence the primary purpose of which is to spread terror among the civilian population' may be prosecuted under Article 3 of the Statute, but it came to this conclusion on the basis of customary law, not treaty law.[81] Although it observed that conventional law can form the basis of the Tribunal's jurisdiction provided that the treaty is unquestionably binding on the parties at the time of the offence and does not conflict with or derogate from peremptory norms of international law,[82] in practice 'Judges have consistently endeavoured to satisfy themselves that the crimes charged

---

[75] Article 4(d), dealing with violations of Art 3 Common to the Geneva Conventions and of AP II.
[76] *Galić* (Judgment) ICTY-98-29-A (5 December 2003); *Galić* (Appeal Judgment) ICTY-98-29-A (30 November 2006).
[77] Article 20(f) in UN Doc A/51/10, (1996 ILC Draft Code) Ch II(2), §§ 46–8.
[78] Article 3(d) of the Statute of the SCSL.
[79] *Galić* (Judgment) ICTY-98-29-A (5 December 2003), §§ 21, 25, 38, 125.
[80] *Galić* (Judgment) ICTY-98-29-A (5 December 2003), § 69.
[81] *Galić* (Appeal Judgment) ICTY-98-29-A (30 November 2006), § 79.
[82] *Delalić* et al (*Čelebići case*) (Appeal Judgment) ICTY-96-21-A (20 February 2001), § 44.

in the indictments before them were crimes under customary international law at the time of their commission and were sufficiently defined under that body of law'.[83] This was the case because although treaty law often identified the violation, it did not always provide for its criminalization or sufficiently define the criminal elements of the offence.[84] A majority was also satisfied that a breach of such a rule gave rise to individual criminal responsibility under customary international law at the time of the commission of the offences for which Galić was convicted.[85] The *Galić* precedent is troubling in certain respects with regard to the Appeals Chamber's manner of ascertaining customary international law. Much of this criticism was voiced by Judge Schomburg who dissented on the finding of the Appeals Chamber in *Galić* that the 'crime of acts and threats of violence the primary purpose of which is to spread terror among the civilian population' was founded on customary law, on the basis that this result was reached 'without sufficient reasoning'.[86]

Be that as it may, the holding of the Appeals Chamber in *Galić* was followed by a Trial Chamber, which assessed the same set of facts in (*Dragomir*) *Milošević*.[87] In this case, the Trial Chamber concluded that the crime of terror constituted an 'aggravated', or more serious form of unlawful attack on civilians, and was thus constituted by the same legal elements as that offence as well as the specific intent of spreading terror among the civilian population.[88]

The *Galić* precedent has also been applied in the subsequent jurisprudence of other international courts. As noted earlier, the Special Court for Sierra Leone is the second international or hybrid court (after the ICTR) to have been given specific jurisdiction over 'acts of terrorism' as a war crime under Article 3(d) of the Statute,[89] which incorporates Article 4(2)(d) of AP II. 'Terrorizing the civilian population' has been charged in every indictment before the court.[90] The types of acts that have

---

[83] *Galić* (Appeal Judgment) ICTY-98-29-A (30 November 2006), § 83. See also § 85.

[84] *Galić* (Appeal Judgment) ICTY-98-29-A (30 November 2006), §§ 83–4.

[85] *Galić* (Appeal Judgment) ICTY-98-29-A (30 November 2006), § 86. Judge Schomburg dissented on this finding.

[86] *Galić* (Appeal Judgment) ICTY-98-29-A (30 November 2006) Judge Schomburg's Partly Diss Op, § 4. Although he agreed that the *prohibition* contained in Art 51(2) of AP I and Art 13 of AP II was part of customary law at the relevant time, Judge Schomburg questioned the Majority's claims that numerous states had criminalized and incorporated this offence in the relevant timeframe, §§ 7–17.

[87] *Milošević, Dragomir* (Judgment) ICTY-98-29/1-T (12 December 2007), §§ 873–82.

[88] *Milošević, Dragomir* (Judgment) ICTY-98-29/1-T (12 December 2007), §§ 882.

[89] Article 3(d) of the Statute grants the SCSL jurisdiction over serious violations of Common Art 3 to the Geneva Conventions and of AP II.

[90] *Foday Saybana Sankoh* (Indictment) SCSL-03-I (7 March 2003), Counts 1–2; *Sam Bockarie* (Indictment) SCSL-2003-04-I (7 March 2003), Counts 1–2; *Johnny Paul Koroma* (Indictment) SCSL-I (7 March 2003), Counts 1–2; *Samuel Hinga Norman, Moinina Fofana and Allieu Kondewa* (Indictment) SCSL-03-14-I (4 February 2004), Counts 6 and 7; *Alex Tamba Brima, Brima Bazzy Kamara and Santigie Borbor Kanu* (Further Amended Consolidated Indictment) SCSL-04-16-PT (18 February 2005), Counts 1–2; *Issa Hassan Sesay, Morris Kallon, and Augustine Gbao* (Corrected Amended Consolidated Indictment) SCSL-2004-15-PT (2 August 2006), Counts 1–2; *Charles Taylor* (Indictment) SCSL-03-01-PT (29 May 2007), Count 1. Charles Taylor was convicted on Count 1. as well as 10 other

been alleged to fall within this charge include unlawful killings, physical violence (including mutilation and maiming), sexual violence and slavery, the use of child soldiers, abductions and forced labour, and looting and burning, including threats to kill, destroy and loot, committed as part of a campaign to terrorize the civilian population of Sierra Leone.

One problem is that the SCSL has seemingly amalgamated the two notions of 'acts of terrorism' and 'acts or threats of violence the primary purpose of which is to spread terror among the civilian population'.[91] The result of this blurring of the rules is that the elements of the latter offence have been transposed on the former prohibition, which is broader in character. While Article 13(2) of AP II and Article 51(2) of AP I are situated within the parts of the treaties dealing with the protection of the civilian population as a whole against the effects of hostilities, Article 33 of GC IV and Article 4(2)(d) come within the parts on the status and treatment of protected persons and humane treatment, respectively. The protections granted therein are broad in nature but may relate to the terrorizing of just one person protected by the provisions.

The questionable results of amalgamating the elements of Article 4(2)(d) of AP II and Article 51(2) of AP I have been borne out in some of the Trial Chambers' findings. For instance, in *Brima et al*, the Trial Chamber found that the primary purpose of acts such as the recruitment of child soldiers and abduction and forced labour by the AFRC during the conflict was military in nature; the primary purpose was not to spread terror among the civilian population. The Chamber made a similar finding with regard to sexual slavery, finding that its primary purpose for AFRC troops was to take advantage of the spoils of war through personal gain.[92] As a result, none of these acts were considered as constituting the crime of 'acts of terrorism'. Similarly, in *Sesay et al*, the Trial Chamber, while not discounting that the abduction and detention of persons from their homes and their subjection to forced labour, including forced mining and living in RUF camps under conditions of violence, did spread terror in the civilian population, it nevertheless found that this 'side effect' of terror was not sufficient to establish the specific intent element of the crime of terror.[93] In the view of the Chamber, the primary purpose behind the commission of abductions and forced labour was utilitarian or military in nature.[94]

---

separate counts of crimes against humanity and war crimes, *Charles Taylor* (Judgment) SCSL-03-01-T (18 May 2012).

[91] See *Brima, Alex Tamba et al* (Judgment) SCSL-04-16-T (20 June 2007), § 666; *Fofana, Moinina and Kondewa, Allieu* (Judgment) SCSL-04-14-T (2 August 2007), § 170; see also §§ 729–31, 743, 779, 879; *Fofana, Moinina and Kondewa, Allieu* (Appeal Judgment) SCSL-04-14-A (28 May 2008), §§ 344–9; *Sesay, Kallon and Gbao* (Judgment) SCSL-04-15-T (2 March 2009), §§ 110–11.

[92] *Brima, Alex Tamba et al* (Judgment) SCSL-04-16-T (20 June 2007), §§ 1450, 1454, 1459.

[93] *Sesay, Kallon and Gbao* (Judgment) SCSL-04-15-T (2 March 2009), § 1359.

[94] *Sesay, Kallon and Gbao* (Judgment) SCSL-04-15-T (2 March 2009), § 1360.

The difficulties of applying the narrower constitutive elements of Article 13(2) of AP II to Article 3(d) of the SCSL Statute, and in particular, the primary purpose test, have therefore arguably resulted in a number of acquittals for crimes that would otherwise have been covered under the category of 'acts of terrorism'.

Finally, doubts remain as to whether a separate crime of international terrorism is already part of customary law, and whether efforts to include the crime in the Rome Statute or codify it in a UN comprehensive convention are justified in view of the seemingly intractable problems of reaching a consensus on the definition. We should recall that various manifestations of terrorism are already criminalized, either on the international level through one of the sectoral treaties, or as a war crime, crime against humanity or genocide, or on the national level, in domestic legislation. There seems to remain a residual feeling in the international community that the general definition of the crime of terrorism must be clearer before it can be said to exist in customary international law or be codified in a treaty. For the regime of IHL, the issue remains a live one given that the relationship between IHL and any comprehensive convention will determine the fate of those taking part in hostilities whose actions may or may not fall under the scope of application of the comprehensive convention. Again in this case the overlap between applicable legal regimes is likely to cause confusion, and non-state actors perpetrating attacks with the intent to compel Government 'to do or not to do any act' during armed conflicts are at risk of finding themselves caught in the blurred lines of the divide between the rules of IHL and the new comprehensive convention on terrorism.[95] However, a revision of IHL texts to account for an eventual crime of international terrorism seems neither necessary nor realistic. It would be hoped, however, for reasons of systemic coherence, that the draft comprehensive terrorism convention clearly delineates its scope of application and does not make acts that are lawful in armed conflict under IHL rules unlawful under the convention. In terms of the prospect of reaching international consensus as to the existence of the international crime of terrorism in customary international law, the elucidation by the Special Tribunal for Lebanon (STL) of the definition of terrorism – and states' reactions to this – may prove a significant source of practice.[96] In this regard, the trial, set to begin in

[95] The Draft elaborated by the Committee (UN Doc A/57/37, Annex II, 6, Art 2) provides: '[a]ny person commits an offence within the meaning of this Convention if that person, by any means, unlawfully and intentionally, causes: Death or serious injury to any person; or Serious damage to public or private property, including a place of public use, a state or government facility, a public transportation system, an infrastructure facility or the environment; or Damage to property, places, facilities, or systems referred to in paragraph 1(b) of this article, resulting or likely to result in major economic loss, when the purpose of the conduct, by its nature or context, is to intimidate a population, or to compel a Government or an international organization to do or abstain from doing any act'.

[96] In a decision of 2011, the STL Appeals Chamber held that terrorism consists of '(i) the volitional commission of an act; (ii) through means that are liable to create a public danger; and (iii) the intent of the perpetrator to cause a state of terror'. *Interlocutory Decision on the Applicable Law: Terrorism, Conspiracy, Homicide, Perpetration, Cumulative Charging,* Case No STL-11-01/I, 16 February 2011, §§ 4, 87–89.

January 2014, and the resulting judgment, and appellate proceedings, may either play a catalyzing role in the formation of such a consensus, or conversely further add to the division of opinion.[97]

5 STATUS, DETENTION AND TREATMENT OF TERRORIST SUSPECTS

For persons captured as terrorist suspects during armed conflict, the determination of their status is the overriding issue, given that under IHL an individual's status determines which body of rules with regard to detention and treatment will apply, in both international and non-international armed conflict. While detailed discussion of questions relating to status, treatment, and detention cannot be provided in this Chapter's limited context,[98] some of the most problematic issues that have emerged recently are addressed briefly below.

As is well known, IHL provides for two types of legal status: combatants and civilians. While a 'third' category of 'unlawful combatant' has been rejected by the ICRC,[99] the ICTY,[100] the Israeli Supreme Court,[101] and authoritative commentators,[102] a certain amount of confusion remains with respect to the minimal protections accorded to those who do not easily fit within the 'civilian' category on account of their participation in terrorist organizations. The Israeli Supreme Court has suggested a 'dynamic interpretation' of IHL rules that would apply to such persons to account for the security risk they present.[103] Others have proposed that such persons might be given 'protected person' status if caught within the context of occupation.

---

[97] Both the Defence Office and the Prosecutor had argued that there is currently no settled definition of terrorism under customary international law. See *ibid.*, § 83.

[98] For extensive treatment of these issues, see A. Bianchi and Y. Naqvi, *International Humanitarian Law and Terrorism* (Oxford: Hart Publishing, 2011), Ch 6. See also, P. Spoerri, 'Law of Occupation' and K. Dormann, 'Unlawful Combatants' in this volume.

[99] See K. Dormann, 'Unlawful Combatants' in this volume. ICRC, Commentary GC IV, 51: 'Every person in enemy hands must have some status under international law: he is either a prisoner of war and, as such, covered by the Third Convention, a civilian covered by the Fourth Convention, [or] a member of the medical personnel of the armed forces who is covered by the First Convention. *There is no* intermediate status; nobody in enemy hands can fall outside the law'.

[100] *Delalić et al (Čelebići case)* (Judgment) ICTY-96-21.T (16 November 1998), § 271.

[101] *Public Committee against Torture v Israel* HCJ 769/02 (14 December 2006) (Israel, Supreme Court), § 28.

[102] See eg J. Steyn, 'Guantánamo: The Legal Black Hole' (2004) 53 *ICLQ* 1–15; K. Dörmann, 'The Legal Situation of "Unlawful/Unprivileged Combatants"', 849 *IRRC* (2003) 45–74.

[103] *Public Committee against Torture v Israel* HCJ 769/02 (14 December 2006) (Israel, Supreme Court), § 28.

This, it is contended, would be the case even where the exclusionary clauses apply in Article 4 of the GC IV where the person is loyal to an enemy force, such as an organization considered by the occupier as engaged in terrorism.[104]

The right not to be subjected to arbitrary detention entails that a person's liberty may be restricted only on a legal basis. Under IHL, the legal basis for detention is significantly wider than under human rights law in the sense that a person may be detained without charge or trial, though there must still be lawful grounds for detention and such a measure remains one of extreme exception.[105] An occupying (and detaining) state may be simultaneously bound by the laws of IHL and its human rights obligations. Those terrorist suspects detained in situations where the threshold of armed conflict is unclear or outside the theatre of war, and therefore not appearing to benefit from protections under IHL, should retain their rights under human rights law, including the right to *habeas corpus* and the right to fair trial.[106] Importantly, the US Supreme Court has repeatedly upheld the rights of persons detained in relation to the so-called 'war on terror' to have the legality of their detention determined by a court of law.[107] Concerted and repeated legislative efforts to deny these rights to foreign terrorist suspects have been consistently found to be unconstitutional.

Recently, some states have subjected certain IHL rules in this area to unilateral reinterpretation.[108] Perhaps the most disturbing aspect of the 'reinterpretation' by the United States of the rules of detention and interrogation of terrorist suspects between 2002 and 2005 was the relaxation of the rules governing torture and

[104] L. Vierucci, 'Prisoners of War or Protected Persons *Qua* Unlawful Combatants? The Judicial Safeguards to Which the Guantánamo Bays Detaineed are Entitled', 1 *JICJ* (2003) 284–314.

[105] J. Pejic, 'Procedural Principles and Safeguards for Internment/Administrative Detention in Armed Conflict and Other Situations of Violence', 858 *IRRC* (2005) 375–91 at 380: 'The exceptional nature of internment lies in the fact that it allows the detaining authority to deprive persons of liberty who are not subject to criminal process, but are nevertheless considered to represent a real threat to its security in the present or in the future'.

[106] See J. Pejic, 'Procedural Principles and Safeguards for Internment/Administrative Detention in Armed Conflict and Other Situations of Violence', 858 *IRRC* (2005) 375–91 at 380; F.J. Hampson, 'Detention, the "War on Terror" and International Law', in H.M. Hensel (ed), *The Law of Armed Conflict: Constraints on the Contemporary Use of Military Force* (Aldershot: Ashgate, 2005), 143.

[107] *Hamdi v Rumsfeld*, 542 US 507 (2004); *Hamdan, Salim Ahmed v Rumsfeld, Donald H, Secretary of Defense et al*, 126 S Ct 2749 (2006); *Boumediene et al, v Bush et al*, 553 US, 128 S Ct 2229 (2008); see also J.K. Elsea and M.J. Garcia, *Enemy Combatant Detainees: Habeas Corpus Challenges in Federal Courts* (Washington: Congressional Research Service, 2010).

[108] For instance, the restrictions on the non-transfer of interned civilians in occupied territory led the US Government to attempt to re-interpret Art 49 of GC IV in such a way as to allow 'temporary' transfers outside of occupied territory for the purpose of intelligence gathering. Draft memorandum from J. Goldsmith (Assistant Attorney-General, Office of Legal Counsel) to W.H. Taft, IV (General Counsel, Dept of State) W.J. Haynes, II (General Counsel, Dept of Defense) J. Bellinger (Legal Adviser for National Security), and S. Muller (General Counsel, Central Intelligence Agency) '*Re Permissibility of Relocating Certain "Protected Persons" from Occupied Iraq*' (19 March 2004) reprinted in Greenberg and Dratel (eds), *The Torture Papers: The Road to Abu Ghraib* (Cambridge: Cambridge University Press, 2005), 367–8.

inhuman treatment, ostensibly justified by the need to extract information about terrorist entities and possible future attacks, as recorded in the so-called 'torture memos'.[109] The wide condemnation in the international community of this seemingly retrograde interpretation of the law relating to torture, together with the Obama Administration's clear disassociation from such interpretations,[110] signal clearly the international consensus on the unconditional illegality of torture, including in relation to the interrogation of terrorist suspects. For its part, IHL is clear and unequivocal on the point.[111] Nonetheless, the willingness of certain states to extradite terrorist suspects to countries where systematic torture is practised on such persons based on diplomatic assurances has proved to be a worrisome chink in the international legal regime preventing the occurrence of torture.[112] The use of 'extraordinary rendition' of terrorist suspects to countries where torture is routinely committed in order to extract information from them is an even more extreme example of the view maintained by some states' authorities that, in certain situations, torture may be justified.[113] While the Obama Administration has taken steps

[109] See J.S. Bybee (Assistant Attorney-General) Memorandum for A.R. Gonzales (Counsel to the President), 'Standards of Conduct for Interrogation under 18 USC. §§2340–2340A', reproduced in Greenberg and Dratel (eds) (n 108), 172, 176, 213–14 (advising that physical torture 'must be of an intensity akin to that which accompanies serious physical injury such as death or organ failure', while mental torture 'requires suffering not just at the moment of infliction but it also requires lasting psychological harm, such as seen in mental disorders like post-traumatic stress disorder'). See also A.R. Gonzales, Memorandum for the President, 'Decision re Application of the Geneva Convention on Prisoners of War to the Conflict with Al Qaeda and the Taliban' (25 January 2002) reproduced in Greenberg and Dratel (eds) (n 108), 119, advising that 'the nature of the new war [on terrorism] places a high premium on [...] the ability to quickly obtain information from captured terrorists and their sponsors in order to avoid further atrocities'.

[110] On 22 January 2009, US President Obama issued Executive Order (EO) 13491, which revoked all executive directives, orders, and regulations inconsistent with the order, including those issued to or by the CIA from 11 September 2001 to 20 January 2009. Executive Order 13491–'Ensuring Lawful Interrogations' (22 January 2009), s 1 74 FR 4893 (27 January 2009).

[111] In international armed conflicts, torture is a grave breach of international humanitarian law: Art 50 of GC I, Art 51 of GC II, Art 130 of GC III, Art 147 of GC III, Art 75(2)(a)(ii) of AP I. See also Art 12(2) of GC I, Art 12(2) of GC II, Arts 17(4) and 87(3) of GC III, Arts 27(1), 37, and 118(2) of GC IV. Torture is also prohibited in conflicts of a non-international character: Art 3(1) common to the Geneva Conventions; Art 4(2)(a) of AP II. Under customary law, torture committed in a non-international armed conflict is a war crime.

[112] On the legality of extraordinary renditions and secret detention policies, see 'Joint Study on Global Practices in Relation to Secret Detention in the Context of Countering Terrorism of the Special Rapporteur on the Promotion and Protection of Human Rights and Fundamental Freedoms', Martin Scheinin; the Special Rapporteur on Torture and Other Cruel, Inhuman or Degrading Treatment or Punishment, Manfred Nowak; the Working Group on Arbitrary Detention Represented by its Co-Chair, Shaeen Sardar Ali; and the Working Group on Enforced or Involuntary Disappearances Represented by its Chair, Jeremy Sarkin (19 February 2010) UN Doc A/HRC/13/42.

[113] Recent domestic judicial decisions on 'extraordinary renditions' include *Arar v Ashcroft* 585 F 3d 559 (2009) (US 2nd Cir); *Adler Monica Courtney et al* n 12428/09 (4 November 2009) (Tribunale Ordinario di Milano in composizione monocratica, Sezione IV Penale, 4th crim section of the Milan Tribunal sitting in 'monocratic' (ie one-judge) composition) judgment delivered by Dr Oscar Magi, filed on 1 February 2010 (officially unreported at the time of writing).

to desist from such practices, past and recent history indicates the need for con-
tinual efforts at building and maintaining international consensus on even the most
basic protections in the case of terrorist suspects.

The legal framework seems, at least at first sight, not to allow for cracks into
which people can fall. IHL is replete with safety nets applicable to persons not
subject to higher, more specific protections under the texts. Yet there have been
repeated examples of people whose conduct is linked to terrorist activity somehow
finding themselves languishing in places of detention with no definite status, no
idea on what basis they are detained and for how long a period, no idea what rights
they are entitled to while detained, and no way to contest these conditions or their
right to have the legal basis of their detention determined by a court of law. This
situation is at odds with the legal provisions of both IHL and human rights law, and
with most domestic law.

It is interesting from this perspective to pay due heed to the important role the
judiciary can play in underlining the illegality of a government's measures to restrict
the rights of such detainees. The important judgments of the US Supreme Court in
the *Hamdi*, *Hamdan* and *Boumediene* cases were crucial to enforcing the legal protection that applied to all those persons arrested and detained in Guantánamo Bay and
elsewhere in the so-called 'war on terror' and no doubt contributed to the change of
approach of the Obama Administration to these issues. The importance of access to a
court and the independence and impartiality of judicial review can hardly be underestimated.[114] However, even for courts it is not always easy to discern the relevant legal
standards, which often result from domestic and international legal sources.

The importance of human rights law as a means to safeguard essential rights of
terrorist suspects who do not easily fall within the purview of IHL has also been
highlighted, indicating the significance of the interrelation between this regime
of international law with IHL. The modalities of such interplay, however, are not
always clear-cut and straightforward and their practical application has proved to
be much more difficult than envisaged by the academic concordance of views about
the complementary character of these two branches of the law.

Finally, the role of customary international law with respect to the treatment of
persons deprived of their liberty has taken on crucial significance, particularly as it
is now recognized that many rules of customary law apply to all persons deprived
of liberty, including POWs, interned civilians, and security detainees. It is notable
that the Chapter of the ICRC *Customary International Law Study* on detention
deals with 'persons deprived of liberty' generally, rather than being divided into
segments dealing with civilians and POWs. Many of these rules also apply in both
international and non-international armed conflict.[115] Given the reticence of some

---

[114] See in this regard the 'Report of the Special Rapporteur on the promotion and protection of
human rights and fundamental freedoms while countering terrorism', Martin Scheinin, UN Doc
A/63/223, §§ 13–30, 7–14.

[115] See J.-M. Henckaerts and L. Doswald-Beck, *Customary International Humanitarian Law*, vol I
(Cambridge: Cambridge University Press, 2005), Ch 37, 428–55.

states to apply basic protections to detainees arrested on grounds related to terrorism, the customary law character of many of these rules represent an important
layer of protection to such persons where they do no easily fit within the categories
of persons protected under the Geneva Conventions or their Additional Protocols.

Interestingly, there seems to be a very ambiguous perception of the relevant rules
of IHL on determination of status and treatment, including detention. On the one
hand, many maintain that the rules are perfectly adequate and that the problem lies
rather in the lack of proper implementation. At the same time, however, several initiatives attest to the need to review, at least partly, the interpretation or the application of relevant legal standards applicable in different factual situations.[116] Against
this background, it is of note that several institutional initiatives as well as political
processes have been put in place in order to provide guidance and seek consensus on
grey areas or principles and rules on which different interpretive stances are possible
or have been taken. For instance, the Danish Government launched in 2005 a diplomatic initiative, the so-called 'Copenhagen Process', geared at establishing an international common understanding of the rules applicable to the handling of detainees
in international military operations as well as devising a code of best practices to give
practical solutions to the challenges faced by armed forces engaged in such operations. Although the output of the process remains uncertain, the Danish Government
underlined the importance of engaging all the actors in the process itself as one of
the fundamental objectives of the diplomatic initiative.[117] Along similar lines, expert
meetings convened by or with the involvement of the ICRC have taken place with a
view to shedding light on or promoting a certain interpretation of IHL rules and principles applicable to particular situations. Overall, all these initiatives seem to indicate
that the international community is seeking a common interpretation of rules, the
understanding and administration of which has become increasingly complex.

6 Conclusion

The contention that the rules of IHL are obsolete or in need of revision *vis-à-vis*
acts of terrorism is in all likelihood unfounded.[118] Indeed, it could be reasonably
argued, first, that IHL categories of legal status have proved fairly resilient in the

---

[116] See for instance, J. Pejic, 'Procedural Principles and Safeguards for Internment/Administrative
Detention in Armed Conflict and Other Situations of Violence', 858 *IRRC* (2005) 375–91.

[117] See T. Winkler, 'The Copenhagen Progress on Detainees: A Necessity', 78 *Nordic Journal of
International Law* (2010) 489–98 at 498.

[118] See also International Commission of Jurists, *Assessing Damage, Urging Action: Report of the
Eminent Jurists Panel on Terrorism, Counter-terrorism and Human Rights* (Geneva: International
Commission of Jurists, 2009), 53.

face of strains caused by developments involving terrorist elements; and secondly, that principles of IHL have helped limit the extent of civilian suffering in actions involving counter-terrorism operations and have denounced those terrorist acts which deliberately seek to spread terror among innocent civilians; and third that thresholds of application of IHL have stymied attempts to draw the world into an armed conflict against transnational terrorist groups, unlimited by time or space. At the same time, there are a number of important lessons to be learned from the recent past, in which IHL has found itself at the core of the international legal and political debate.

Even if its underlying principles are broad and easy to grasp, with the principle of humanity permeating its entire fabric, IHL is a fairly homogeneous body of precise and detailed rules with a long history. Furthermore, the legal categories that shape the regime tend to be rigid, as they are designed to fit the regulation of phenomena that at the time of their establishment were largely experienced in a certain way (mainly state versus state with the use of professional armies). The definition of international armed conflict is a good illustration of this point. The changing phenomenology of war and the appearance on the international scene of transnational terrorists, operating on a large scale and carrying out attacks of war-like magnitude, have unexpectedly impacted the rules that were fundamentally designed to tackle a different factual situation. The attempt to deal with the threat of international terrorism by using a blend of domestic law enforcement and international law rules has blurred many of the traditional IHL categories and has put the whole regime under strain. A similar dynamic characterizes the increasing interplay between IHL and international human rights law. Although both branches of the law are commonly grounded on the protection of the individual, their logic and scope of application, also due to their asynchronous historical development, remain different.

Against the background of recent practice, it is stunning to realize how often reference is made to the gaps and the 'grey areas' of IHL as well as to the uncertainty surrounding the interpretation of some of its rules and to the alleged unsuitability of some provisions to effectively countering the phenomenon of terrorism. Whereas most experts of IHL fiercely maintain the coherence and overall suitability of the system, occasionally acknowledging, at most, a problem of implementation by concerned actors, sweeping proposals for reform have been put forward that would fundamentally alter the logic and well-crafted balance struck by the drafters of the Geneva Conventions. Such postures seem to be oblivious to the real underlying stakes of the debate.

The first element to take into account is that the four 1949 Geneva Conventions are universally ratified, which means that each and every state has expressly consented to them. In an international community of nearly 200 states this is a patrimony of consensus that cannot be underestimated. To re-open a political and diplomatic process geared at formally revising the Geneva Conventions seems inconceivable at present. Similarly, to set aside the consensus existing over IHL principles risks opening a Pandora's box and, most likely, the breaking up of the extant consensus on the overall regulatory structure. Yet, the somewhat outdated and unclear character of some of the provisions laid down in the Geneva Conventions is widely perceived as a source for concern, particularly as regards the issues of asymmetric warfare, international terrorism, status of combatants, and detention.[119]

How to bring about changes that all actors will find desirable or indispensable—within the framework of a treaty structure that cannot be easily altered—is not an insoluble problem. In international law, states are traditionally reluctant to proceed to formally revising multilateral treaties, which have been adopted with lengthy and cumbersome processes, often on the basis of 'package deals' and compromises of different sorts.[120] This is not to say, however, that treaties are immutable and can never be adjusted to changing societal needs, unless they are formally amended.

Interpretation can be a powerful tool to adjust the content of IHL to a changing phenomenology of armed conflict. Interpretation, however, needs to be looked at as a more socially embedded intellectual undertaking than international law rules on treaty interpretation or particular techniques favoured in specific contexts usually allow. For instance, IHL experts usually tend to rely heavily on the Geneva Convention Commentaries, which may not always be appropriate or useful given the factual situations that the drafters might have had in mind at the time. Similarly, the primacy of literal interpretation, as codified in Article 31(1) of the Vienna Convention,[121] does not always help to resolve a particular 'grey' area when the problem lies in the lack of consensus about what these expressions mean or should mean in contemporary armed conflict.

If societal consensus on the interpretation of certain legal categories has broken down, it needs be restored, not through a focus on rules of interpretation but by consensus-building processes. In this respect, it is indeed significant that some recent initiatives of this type have been undertaken, such as the *ICRC Interpretive Guidance on Direct Participation in Hostilities*, which have the merit of spurring the debate and forcing actors to express their views. Over time, such processes

---

[119] See eg the UK House of Commons, Foreign Committee, *Visit to Guantánamo Bay, Second Report of Session 2006–2007* (London: The Stationery Office Ltd, 2007), § 85: 'We conclude that, by its own test, the Government should recognise that the Geneva Conventions are failing to provide necessary protection because they lack clarity and are out of date. We recommend that the Government work with other signatories to the Geneva Conventions and with the International Committee of the Red Cross to update the Conventions in a way that deals more satisfactorily with asymmetric warfare, with international terrorism, with the status of irregular combatants, and with the treatment of detainees'.

[120] A. Boyle and C. Chinkin, *The Making of International Law* (Oxford: Oxford University Press, 2007), 21–2.

[121] On the limits of the plain meaning doctrine and, more generally, of textual determinacy, see A. Bianchi, 'Textual Interpretation and (International) Law Reading: the Myth of (In)Determinacy and the Genealogy of Meaning', in P. Bekker et al (eds), *Making Transnational Law Work in the Global Economy. Essays in Honour of Detlev Vagts* (Cambridge: Cambridge University Press, 2010), 34.

might well produce new interpretive consensus on legal categories, that too often are viewed as rigid and almost immutable, and on legal rules whose understanding and implementation are far too complex to allow for effective regulation.[122] Notably, Article 31(3)(b) of the Vienna Convention allows for taking into account 'any subsequent practice of the parties in the application of the agreement which establishes the agreement of the parties regarding its interpretation'. Furthermore, Article 31(4) establishes that a special meaning can be attributed to a term 'if it is established that the parties so intended'.

As the historical contingencies of the 'war on terror' are yielding, and a new collaborative spirit seems to have emerged, there is a window of opportunity for all actors concerned to engage in interpretive processes of varying nature and scope in order to adjust to the changing circumstances of contemporary armed conflict, and to establish consensus on the various areas requiring further elaboration.

---

[122] For a critical view of such rigidity, see A. Bianchi, 'Terrorism and Armed Conflict: Insights from a Law and Literature Perspective', 23 *LJIL* (2010) 1–21.

CHAPTER 24

UNLAWFUL COMBATANTS

KNUT DÖRMANN[*]

1 INTRODUCTION

ONE of the most debated subjects in international humanitarian law (IHL) over the years has been the legal situation of 'unlawful combatants'. In legal writing it has been addressed in some detail after the adoption of the Geneva Conventions of 1949 and then prior to the adoption of the 1977 Additional Protocols to the Geneva Conventions. The debate emerged again with some intensity following the US-led military campaign in Afghanistan, which started in 2001. The notion was very present in internal US debate when it was discussed how to deal with Taliban and Al Qaeda fighters.

Different understandings have been expressed and thus different approaches suggested with regard to the legal framework applicable to the possible detainability and targetability of 'unlawful combatants'. Consequently, the issue was also taken up intensively in more recent publications, statements, and reports, looking specifically at what the Bush Administration has called the 'Global War on Terror', but also more generically. It was asserted in certain circles that 'unlawful combatants' do not

[*] This Chapter is largely based on an entry in the *Encyclopedia of Public International Law* and the article 'The Legal Situation of "Unlawful/Unprivileged Combatants", 849 *International Review of the Red Cross (IRRC)* (2003) 45–74. It reflects the views of the author alone and not necessarily those of the ICRC. The author would like to thank Tobias Köhler, Legal Attaché to the ICRC Legal Division, for his help on this article.

have any protection whatsoever under IHL, or that they are a category of persons outside the scope of either the Third Geneva Convention[1] or the Fourth Geneva Convention of 1949.[2] Many others opposed these assertions vehemently.

While the term has been used earlier, this contribution will look at the time after the adoption of the Geneva Conventions as these treaties and subsequent treaties— in particular the 1977 Additional Protocols to the Geneva Conventions—as well as customary international law set the legal framework for contemporary armed conflicts. Prior to the Geneva Conventions of 1949 the treatment of unlawful combatants was governed through the Martens' clause. At the time of the two World Wars, in international practice, unlawful combatants were dealt with harshly, even allowing them to be shot after capture.[3]

2 Terminology

The term 'combatant', as well as other related terms designating a specific category of persons ('prisoner of war' and 'civilian'), are used and defined in the treaties of IHL. In contrast, the terms 'unlawful combatant' or 'unprivileged combatant/belligerent' (often used interchangeably) do not appear in them. They have, however, been frequently referred to, at least since the beginning of the last century, in legal literature, military manuals and case law. The connotations given to these terms and their consequences for the applicable protection regime are not always very clear.

In international armed conflicts, the term 'combatants' denotes the right to participate directly in hostilities.[4] The 'combatant's privilege' is in essence a permission to kill or wound enemy combatants and destroy enemy military objectives.[5] Consequently (lawful) combatants cannot be prosecuted for lawful acts of war in the course of military operations even if their behaviour would constitute a serious crime in peacetime. They can be prosecuted only for violations of IHL, in particular for war crimes. Once captured, combatants are entitled to prisoner of war status

---

[1] Convention (III) relative to the Treatment of Prisoners of War, Geneva, 12 August 1949 (GC III).

[2] Convention (IV) relative to the Protection of Civilian Persons in Time of War, Geneva, 12 August 1949 (GC IV).

[3] Jason Callen, 'Unlawful Combatants and the Geneva Conventions', 44 *Virginia Journal of International Law* (2004) 1025–72 at 1026, with references; K. Watkin, 'Warriors Without Rights? Combatants, Unprivileged Belligerents, and the Struggle Over Legitimacy', *Occasional Paper Series, Program on Humanitarian Policy and Conflict Research, Harvard University (Winter 2005)*, 46–7.

[4] See Art 43(2) of AP I.

[5] Inter-American Commission on Human Rights, Report on Terrorism and Human Rights, 22 October 2002, OAS Doc OEA/Ser.L/V/II.116 Doc 5 re. 1 corr, § 68 (IACHR Report).

and benefit from the protection of GC III.[6] Combatants are lawful military targets. Generally speaking, members of the armed forces (other than medical personnel and chaplains) are combatants. The conditions for combatant/prisoner of war status can be derived from Article 4 of GC III and from Articles 43 and 44 of AP I, which developed Article 4 of GC III.

According to the most commonly shared understanding, the term 'unlawful combatant' describes all persons taking a direct part in hostilities without being entitled to do so (ie without having a combatant's privilege) and who therefore cannot be classified as prisoners of war when falling into the power of the enemy.[7] It would include, for example, civilians taking a direct part in hostilities, as well as members of militias and of other volunteer corps—including those of organized resistance movements—belonging to a party to the conflict, if they do not comply with the conditions of Article 4A(2) of GC III.

If a person who has participated directly in hostilities is captured on the battlefield, it may not be obvious to which category that person belongs. In such types of situations, Article 5 of GC III (Article 45 of AP I) foresees a special procedure (competent tribunal) to determine the captive's status.

3 'UNLAWFUL COMBATANTS' IN THE HANDS OF THE ENEMY

A. International armed conflicts

There are essentially two different approaches with different subsets regarding the legal situation of 'unlawful combatants' when they are in enemy hands in international armed conflicts.

The first approach concludes that 'unlawful combatants' are a category of persons that is neither covered by GC III nor GC IV.[8] One subset of this approach limits

---

[6] M. Sassòli, A. Bouvier, and A. Quintin, *How Does Law Protect in War?*, vol I, (3rd edn, Geneva: ICRC, 2011), 177.

[7] See eg, G. Aldrich, 'The Taliban, Al Qaeda, and the Determination of Illegal Combatants', 96 *American Journal of International Law* (2002) 891–8; IACHR Report (n 5), § 69; Sassòli, Bouvier, and Quintin (n 6), 177.

[8] For example I. Detter, *The Law of War* (Cambridge: Cambridge University Press, 2000), 136; R.K. Goldmann and B.D. Tittemore, 'Unprivileged Combatants and the Hostilities in Afghanistan: Their Status and Rights Under International Humanitarian and Human Rights Law', available at <http://asil. org/taskforce/goldman.pdf>, 38; C. Greenwood, 'International Law and the "War Against Terrorism"', 78 *International Affairs* (2002) 301–17 at 316; IACHR Report (n 5), § 74.

the protection to the Martens Clause. Another subset specifically concludes that 'unlawful combatants' are protected by the customary international law standards contained in Common Article 3 of GC, and other fundamental guarantees that have developed into customary international law, in particular Article 75 of AP I. Most authors defending this approach, and thereby disputing the applicability of GC IV, do not give any detailed legal reasoning for their position. It is merely asserted that GC IV does not cover 'unlawful combatants'; an analysis of its Article 4 is not provided. When these authorities refer to case law (in particular *Ex Parte Quirin*[9]), it is case law that predates GC IV.

The second approach—supported by the present author—concludes that 'unlawful combatants' are protected by GC IV provided they satisfy the nationality criteria of Article 4 of GC IV.[10] The protection is subject to possible derogations based on Article 5 of GC IV. The protection is supplemented by Article 45(3) of AP I

---

[9] 317 US 1, 63 S Ct 2 (1942). See, however, more recent international case law: ICTY, Judgment, *The Prosecutor v Delalić et al*, IT-96-21-T, 16 November 1998, § 271: '[...] If an individual is not entitled to the protections of the Third Convention as a prisoner of war (or of the First or Second Conventions) he or she necessarily falls within the ambit of Convention IV, provided that its article 4 requirements are satisfied.'; and national case law: Supreme Court of Israel, *Iyad v State of Israel*, 1 CrimA 6659/06, 11 June 2008, available at <http://elyon1.court.gov.il/files_eng/06/590/066/n04/06066590.n04.pdf>, § 12. See also Supreme Court of Israel, *Public Committee against Torture in Israel v Government of Israel*, Case No HCJ 769/02, 13 December 2006, available at <http://elyon1.court.gov.il/files_eng/02/690/007/A34/02007690.a34.pdf>.

[10] Supreme Court of Israel, *Iyad v State of Israel*, 1 CrimA 6659/06, 11 June 2008, available at <http://elyon1.court.gov.il/files_eng/06/590/066/n04/06066590.n04.pdf>, § 12. K. Ipsen, 'Combatants and Non-combatants', in D. Fleck (ed), *The Handbook of Humanitarian Law in Armed Conflicts* (2nd edn, Oxford: Oxford University Press, 2010), 79–118, § 301; H. McCoubrey, *International Humanitarian Law: Modern Developments in the Limitation of Warfare* (2nd edn, Dartmouth: Aldershot, 1998), 137; E. David, *Principes de droit des conflits armés* (4th edn, Brussels: Bruylant, 2008), 460ff; M. Bothe, K. Partsch, and W. Solf, *New Rules for Victims of Armed Conflicts: Commentary on the Two 1977 Protocols Additional to the Geneva Conventions of 1949* (The Hague: Martinus Nijhoff, 1982), 261ff; Aldrich (n 7), 893, fn 12; G.I.A.D. Draper, 'The Status of Combatants and the Question of Guerrilla Warfare', *British Yearbook of International Law* (1971) 173–218 at 197 (recognizes the applicability of GC IV to persons who do not fulfil the conditions of Art 4 of GC III, but participate in hostilities in enemy territory or in occupied territory, within the limits of Art 5 of GC IV); E. Rosenblad, 'Guerrilla Warfare and International Law', 12 *Revue de droit pénal militaire et de droit de la guerre* (1973) 91–134 at 98 (recognizes the applicability of GC IV to members of organized resistance movements who do not fulfil the conditions of Art 4 of GC III, within the limits of Art 5 of GC IV); F. Kalshoven, 'The Position of Guerrilla Fighters under the Law of War' (1972) 11 *Revue de droit pénal militaire et de droit de la guerre*, 55–91 at 71 (recognizes the applicability of GC IV to persons who do not fulfil the conditions of Art 4 of GC III, but participate in hostilities in enemy territory or in occupied territory). In situations other than fighting in enemy territory or occupied territory, 'the guerrilla fighter who falls into enemy hands will not enjoy the full protection extended to protected persons in occupied territory. It is submitted, however, that he will not be entirely without protection. The principle expounded in Article 3 for non-international armed conflict provides at the same time a minimum below which belligerents may not go in other situations either [...] To my mind, the strongest argument in favour of this thesis lies precisely in the element of their foreign nationality and, hence, allegiance to the opposite Party from the one which holds them in its power'; Watkin (n 3), 50–1, 58, 68, 74; M. Sassòli, '"Unlawful Combatants": The Law and whether it Needs to Be Revised', *Proceedings of the 97th Annual Meeting of the American Society of International Law* (2003) 196–203 at 197.

and customary international law, in particular Article 75 of AP I. The concrete extent of protections based on GC IV depends on the specific field of application of the relevant sections of GC IV, ie whether the unlawful combatant is in occupied territory, or is an alien in enemy territory or is otherwise in the territory of a belligerent state.

Some authors have concluded that GC IV only covers 'unlawful combatants' in occupied territory,[11] and, if they are aliens, in enemy territory. So-called 'battlefield unlawful combatants', ie persons that take part in the fighting against an advancing enemy while the enemy has not (yet) established a situation of occupation would not be covered.[12] In so far as Article 5 of GC IV refers to 'in the territory of a Party to the conflict' and Part III, section I of GC IV refers to 'the territories of the parties to conflict', these authors essentially claim that only the home territory of an enemy country is covered by these terms, thus only deal with aliens in enemy territory.[13]

If GC IV does not apply, either because the nationality criteria are not met (or because some would exclude 'battlefield unlawful combatants' from GC IV) then under this second approach, protection derives from Common Article 3 of GC and other fundamental guarantees that have developed into customary international law, in particular Article 75 of AP I (see also Article 45(3) of AP I).

(i) The legal protection of 'unlawful combatants' under GC IV

In light of the quite explicit wording used in Article 4, which defines the personal scope of application of GC IV, it is submitted that 'unlawful combatants' are protected by GC IV under specific conditions as detailed below.[14]

(ii) Personal field of application of GC IV

The personal field of application of GC IV is defined in Article 4 paragraph 1. According to this provision '[p]ersons protected by the Convention are those who, at a given moment and in any manner whatsoever, find themselves, in case of a conflict or occupation, in the hands of a Party to the conflict or Occupying Power of which they are not nationals'.

This definition is all-embracing. It only excludes nationals of the detaining Power. The scope of application is further limited by specific exceptions contained in the

---

[11] R.R. Baxter, 'So-called "Unprivileged Belligerency": Spies, Guerrillas, and Saboteurs', British Yearbook of International Law (1951) 323–45 at 328ff, 343ff; R.R. Baxter, 'The Duties of Combatants and the Conduct of Hostilities (Law of The Hague)', in Henry Dunant Institute and UNESCO (ed), International Dimensions of Humanitarian Law (The Hague: Martinus Nijhoff, 1988), 105ff.

[12] Callen (n 3), 1062ff; Y. Dinstein, The Conduct of Hostilities under the Law of International Armed Conflict (2nd edn, Cambridge: Cambridge University Press, 2010), 33ff, 36. See, however, Watkin (n 3), 56, arguing against such a terminology.

[13] Callen (n 3), 1040.

[14] For a discussion of the travaux préparatoires, see K. Dörmann, 'The Legal Situation of "Unlawful/Unprivileged Combatants"', 849 International Review of the Red Cross (2003) 45–74 at 52–8.

Article's subsequent paragraphs. According to Article 4 paragraph 2, 'nationals of a State which is not bound by the Convention' are not protected (a theoretical restriction, since the 1949 Conventions now have universal participation). Equally, when the state of which they are nationals has normal diplomatic representation in the state in whose hands they are, nationals of co-belligerent states as well as of neutral states are excluded. The latter are still protected if they are in occupied territory.[15] Lastly, according to Article 4 paragraph 4, GC IV does not protect persons protected by GC I–III.

Based on the plain wording of the text, all persons who are not protected by GC I–III, including those persons who do not respect the conditions which would entitle them to POW status/treatment, are covered by GC IV provided that they fulfil the nationality criteria. The fact that a person has unlawfully participated in hostilities is not a criterion for excluding the application of GC IV. On the contrary, Article 5 of GC IV, which allows for some derogations from the protections of GC IV, uses the term 'protected persons' with regard to persons detained as spies or saboteurs as well as persons definitely suspected of or engaged in activities hostile to the security of the state/Occupying Power. Both the concepts of 'activity hostile to the security of the State/Occupying Power' and of 'sabotage' certainly encompass direct participation (without entitlement) in hostilities. Thus, this article would apply to persons who do not fulfil the criteria of GC I–III and take a direct part in hostilities, ie persons labelled 'unlawful combatants'.[16]

A further argument for the application of GC IV to 'unlawful combatants' may be drawn from Article 45(3) of AP I. This provision stipulates that any person who has taken part in hostilities, who is not entitled to prisoner of war status and who does not benefit from more favourable treatment in accordance with GC IV is entitled to the protection of Article 75 of AP I. In occupied territory, such person—unless he is held as a spy—is also entitled, notwithstanding Article 5 of GC IV, to his rights of communication under GC IV.

Article 45(3) of AP I thus contains an implicit confirmation of the interpretation that 'unlawful combatants' are protected persons under GC IV if they fulfil the nationality criteria. By stating that 'any person who has taken part in hostilities, who is not entitled to prisoner of war status and who does not benefit from more favourable treatment in accordance with the Fourth Convention shall have the right at all times to the protection of Article 75 of this Protocol', it recognizes that GC IV is in fact applicable to some categories of 'unlawful combatants'—otherwise the formulation 'who does not benefit from more favourable treatment in accordance

---

[15] Commentary GC IV, 46. Commentaries concerning the draft Convention, Final Record, vol II A, 814. See also the explanation by the Swiss Rapporteur at the Diplomatic Conference, who confirmed that interpretation, Final Record, vol II A, 793. See also the statement by the US, Final Record, vol II A, 794.

[16] See Kalshoven (n 10), 72, for guerrilla fighters whom he defines as persons (taking a direct part in hostilities) who cannot be regarded as prisoners of war, see 65, 69.

with the Fourth Convention' would be meaningless. The second sentence of that paragraph ('In occupied territory, any such person, unless he is held as a spy, shall also be entitled, notwithstanding Article 5 of the Fourth Convention, to his rights of communication under that Convention') implicitly recognizes that 'unlawful combatants' in occupied territory are protected by GC IV.[17]

The interpretation that GC IV applies to 'unlawful combatants' also finds support in Military Manuals drafted shortly after the adoption of the GCs. Contrary to more recent approaches in the United States, particularly in the context of what it initially labelled the 'Global War on Terror', the US 1956 *Military Manual FM 27-10, The Law of Land Warfare*, developed the law as follows:

> 72. Certain Persons in Occupied Areas
>   Persons in occupied areas not falling within the categories set forth in Article 4 [GC III], who commit acts hostile to the occupant or prejudicial to his security are subject to a special regime [reference is made to the provisions of GC IV, Part III, Section III]
>   [...]
> 73. Persons Committing Hostile Acts Not Entitled To Be Treated as Prisoners of War
>   If a person is determined by a competent tribunal, acting in conformity with Article 5 [GC III] not to fall within any of the categories listed in Article 4 [GC III], he is not entitled to be treated as a prisoner of war. He is, however, a 'protected person' within the meaning of Article 4 [GC IV].
>   [...]
> 247. Definition of Protected Persons
>   [quotation of GC IV, Article 4]
>   Interpretation. Subject to qualifications set forth in paragraph 248, those protected by [GC IV] also include all persons who have engaged in hostile or belligerent conduct but who are not entitled to treatment as prisoners of war.
> 248. Derogations
>   a. Domestic and Occupied Territory
>   [reference is made to GC IV, Article 5]
>   b. Other Areas. Where, in territories other than those mentioned in a. above, a Party to the conflict is satisfied that an individual protected person is definitely suspected of or engaged in activities hostile to the security of the State, such individual person is similarly not entitled to claim such rights and privileges under [GC IV] as would, if exercised in favour of such individual person, be prejudicial to the security of such a State.[18]

---

[17] See in this regard, Bothe, Partsch, and Solf (n 10), 261ff.

[18] See also the British Manual Part III—*The Law of War on Land*, 1957, no 96:

> Should regular combatants fail to comply with these four conditions [of Art 4 of GC III], they may in certain cases become unprivileged belligerents.
> This would mean that they would not be entitled to the status of prisoners of war upon their capture. Thus regular members of the armed forces who are caught as spies are not entitled to be treated as prisoners of war. But they would appear to be entitled, as a minimum, to the limited privileges conferred upon civilian spies or saboteurs by the Civilian Convention, Art. 5. [...] Members of the armed forces caught in civilian clothing while acting as saboteurs in enemy territory are in a position analogous to that of spies.

(iii) *Substantive protections for 'unlawful combatants' under GC IV*

GC IV provides for various standards of protection for protected persons depending on the situation in which they find themselves in the hands of another party to
the armed conflict. Part III, section I contains provisions common to the territories
of the parties to conflict and to occupied territories. These include: rules on humane
treatment; special protection for women; non-discrimination; prohibition of the
use of protected persons as human shields; prohibition of coercion and of corporal
punishment, torture, etc; prohibition of collective punishment, pillage, reprisals,
and hostage taking.

This section is followed by specific provisions on the treatment of aliens in the
territory of a party to conflict (Section II), which deal, inter alia, with: the right to
leave the territory; the treatment of persons in confinement; the right to individual/
collective relief, to medical attention, and to practice their religion; employment;
measures of control, ie assigned residence and internment, and the procedure to be
followed; and transfer to another Power.

Section III, on protected persons in occupied territory, includes rules on: deportation and transfers; children; labour; food and medical supplies for the population;
hygiene and public health; relief operations; penal legislation; penal procedure;
treatment of detainees; and security measures.

Section IV contains regulations for the treatment of internees, inter alia, on: places
of internment; food and clothing; hygiene and medical attention; religious, intellectual, and physical activities; personal property and financial resources; administration and discipline; relations with the outside; penal and disciplinary sanctions;
transfers of internees; deaths; and release, repatriation, and accommodation in neutral countries. Article 79 of that section stipulates that protected persons may not
be interned, except in accordance with the provisions of Articles 41–43 (aliens in
the territory of a party to conflict) and Articles 68 and 78 (protected persons in
occupied territory).

Since, as submitted before, 'unlawful combatants' are protected by GC IV if they
fulfil the nationality criteria set out in Article 4 thereof, the abovementioned forms
of protection also apply to them. These protections may, however, be subject to
derogations under Article 5 of GC IV (see below).

The fact that GC IV only provides for specific protections to aliens in enemy
territory and to persons in occupied territory, who are in the hands of the adverse
party, led some experts to conclude that the situation of 'unlawful combatants' in
the zone of military operations in the 'unlawful combatants' own country, which
is not occupied, was not taken into account in the drafting of GC IV, and in particular in the drafting of Articles 4 and 5.[19] The interpretation of Article 6 of GC

---

[19] See A. Rosas, *The Legal Status of Prisoners of War* (Helsinki: Suomalainen Tiedeakatemia, 1976),
411; Baxter, 'Unprivileged belligerency' (n 11), 329ff; Callen (n 3), 1038–47, 1062–5.

IV proposed in the Commentary by Pictet would lead to a broader protection of 'unlawful combatants' in the zone of military operations:

It follows from this that the word 'occupation' as used in the Article, has a wider meaning than it has in Article 42 of the Regulations annexed to the Fourth Hague Convention of 1907. So far as individuals are concerned, the application of the Fourth Geneva Convention does not depend upon the existence of a state of occupation within the meaning of the Article 42 referred to above. The relations between the civilian population of a territory and troops advancing into that territory, whether fighting or not, are governed by the present Convention. There is no intermediate period between what might be termed the invasion phase and the inauguration of a stable regime of occupation. Even a patrol which penetrates into enemy territory without any intention of staying there must respect the Conventions in its dealings with the civilians it meets. [...] The Convention is quite definite on this point: all persons who find themselves in the hands of a Party to the conflict or an Occupying Power of which they are not nationals are protected persons. No loophole is left.[20]

Based on this interpretation, every person who fulfils the nationality criteria and is captured while enemy armed forces are present (from the moment of invasion until the withdrawal) would be protected by the provisions of GC IV (Part III, Sections I, III, and IV). This interpretation of the concept of occupation, however, is not universally shared.[21] Whether or not one agrees with Pictet's interpretation, the rules of Part III, Section I, containing provisions common to the territories of the parties to conflict would apply to 'unlawful combatants' in the zone of military operations.[22]

(iv) Derogations

The rights and privileges defined in particular in Part III of GC IV are not absolute. Article 5 of GC IV provides for derogations in specific circumstances and contains the following distinction:

- in the territory of a Party to conflict, individual protected persons who are definitely suspected of or engaged in activities hostile to the security of the state are not entitled to claim such rights and privileges under GC IV as would, if exercised in the favour of such individual person, be prejudicial to the security of such state;[23]

---

[20] Commentary GC IV, 64.   [21] See Callen (n 3), 1041–6.

[22] For a more in-depth analysis, see Dörmann (n 14), 62–4.

[23] As for possible derogations under para 1, Commentary GC IV (n 15), 55, indicates the following:

The rights referred to are not very extensive in the case of protected persons under detention; they consist essentially of the right to correspond, the right to receive individual or collective relief, the right to spiritual assistance from ministers of their faith and the right to receive visits from representatives of the Protecting Power and the International Committee of the Red Cross. The security of the State could not conceivably be put forward as a reason for depriving such persons of the benefit of other provisions—for example, the provision in Article 37 that they are to be humanely treated when they are confined pending proceedings or subject to a sentence involving

- in occupied territory, individual protected person detained as a spy or saboteur, or as a person under definite suspicion of activity hostile to the security of the Occupying Power are regarded as having forfeited rights of communication under GC IV in those cases where absolute military security so requires.

The wording of the Article in referring to 'activity hostile to the security of the State/Occupying Power' and of 'sabotage' encompasses direct participation in hostilities (without being entitled thereto).[24] Thus, the Article is particularly relevant to 'unlawful combatants'.[25]

As the bottom line Article 5(3) provides that, in each case, such persons must be treated with humanity and, in case of trial, must not be deprived of the rights of fair and regular trial prescribed by GC IV. They must also be granted the full rights and privileges of a protected person under GC IV at the earliest date consistent with the security of the state or Occupying Power, as the case may be.

(v) *Minimum guarantees under customary international law*

Minimum guarantees as codified in AP I and developed under customary international law protect 'unlawful combatants' excluded from the scope of application of GC IV. These minimum guarantees also complement existing protections under GC IV when applicable to 'unlawful combatants'.

Article 75 of AP I defines the minimum guarantees applicable to all persons in the power of a party to the conflict. It is the widely shared view that these protections now constitute customary international law.[26] The personal scope of application

loss of liberty, or the stipulation in Article 38 that they shall receive medical attention, if their state of health so requires. Furthermore, it would be really inhuman to refuse to let a chaplain visit a detained person who was seriously ill. Torture and recourse to reprisals are of course prohibited. It should, moreover, be noted that this provision cannot release the Detaining Power from its obligations towards the adverse Party. It remains fully bound by the obligation, imposed on it by Article 136, to transmit to the official Information Bureau particulars of any protected person who is kept in custody for more than two weeks. This is not, in fact, a right or privilege of the protected person, but an obligation of the Detaining Power.

[24] See Rosenblad (n 10), 110ff. Rosenblad further states: 'A saboteur, who is [sic] unlawful combatant, is on the one hand punished in accordance with the Civilians Convention. Granted that he is a "protected person" (Article 4) and that in this capacity he shall be unconditionally "treated with humanity" (third paragraph of Article 5). A protected person can, however, if "imperative reasons of security" make this necessary, be subjected to assigned residence or to internment (Article 78). Furthermore, the occupying power can under certain circumstances retain a saboteur without judgement (second paragraph of Article 5) and, in the case of prosecution, sentence him to death (second paragraph of Article 68).'

[25] See Kalshoven (n 10), 72, for guerrilla fighters whom he defines as persons (taking a direct part in hostilities) not regarded as prisoners of war, at 65, 69; Sassòli (n 10), 197.

[26] J.M. Henckaerts and L. Doswald-Beck, *Customary International Humanitarian Law*, vol I (Cambridge: Cambridge University Press, 2005), Rules; see most recently also the statement by US Secretary of State Clinton, who declared that '[…] as of today, the United States, out of a sense of legal obligation, will adhere to the set of norms in Article 75 of Protocol I in international armed conflicts'. Press Statement, Hillary Rodham Clinton, Secretary of State, Washington, DC, 7 March 2011, <http://

extends to all 'persons who are in the power of a Party to the conflict and who do not benefit from more favourable treatment under the Conventions or under this Protocol'.

This Article clearly ensures that no person in the power of a Party to an international armed conflict is outside the protection of IHL.[27] It defines the minimum standards that apply to any such person. Article 45(3) of AP I explicitly recognizes the application of Article 75 to 'unlawful combatants' (see above).

Article 45(3) in conjunction with Article 75 provides for a minimum of protection for those 'unlawful combatants' who are not covered by GC IV because they do not fulfil the nationality criteria of Article 4 of GC IV and—if the interpretation defended by certain authors (eg Baxter, Draper, and Kalshoven) is followed—for those who fall into enemy hands in the battle area.[28] Previously, solely Common Article 3 as customary international law or the Martens Clause provided protection to these types of 'unlawful combatants'.

For 'unlawful combatants' who are protected by GC IV, Article 75 of AP I complements that protection by defining additional minimum guarantees. More specifically, for 'unlawful combatants' in enemy hands on enemy territory, Article 75 of AP I specifically ensures that various judicial guarantees are respected (para 4). In addition, Article 75 of AP I lays down other protections in relation to treatment (paras 1 and 2) and to arrest, detention, and internment (para 3), which in certain cases increase the protections contained in Part III, Sections I, II, and IV of GC IV. For 'unlawful combatants' in enemy hands in occupied territory, Article 75 of AP I adds a few more judicial guarantees, such as the presumption of innocence. The protections in relation to treatment, arrest, detention, and internment are supplemented. In addition, Article 45(3) of AP I restricts the possibility for derogations under GC IV's Article 5.[29]

Most of the authors who question the applicability of GC IV to 'unlawful combatants' share the view that Article 75 of AP I is applicable.[30] Those authors who

www.state.gov/secretary/rm/2011/03/157827.htm>; see also Greenwood (n 8), 316; IACHR Report (n 5), § 76; Aldrich (n 7), 893.

[27] See statement by the ICRC at the Diplomatic Conference of 1974–77, CDDH/III/SR.43, or vol XV, 25ff; Finland, 27, Belgium, 31, Holy See, 34.

[28] See also the ICRC's commentary on the Draft Additional Protocols to the Geneva Conventions of 12 August 1949 (October 1973), on draft Art 65 (Art 75 of API): 'The purpose of this draft is to rectify an omission in the existing treaty law; on the one hand, persons who are not protected by the First, Second and Third Conventions are not necessarily always protected by the Fourth Convention, as is shown by its Article 4; on the other hand, Article 5 of the Fourth Convention relating to derogations is fairly difficult to interpret and appears to restrict unduly the rights of the persons protected', 81ff.

[29] This interpretation is largely shared by Bothe, Partsch, and Solf in their commentary on AP I; see Bothe, Partsch, and Solf (n 10), 261ff. See also Commentary on Art 45, Commentary AP I and II, para 1761. See also Commentary on Art 51, para 1942.

[30] IACHR Report (n 5), § 74; Y. Dinstein, 'The Distinction Between Unlawful Combatants and War Criminals', in Y. Dinstein (ed), International Law in a Time of Perplexity (London: Martinus Nijhoff,

wrote before the adoption of AP I recognized that some minimum humanitarian guarantees apply to all 'unlawful combatants'. They derived those guarantees either from Common Article 3, Article 5(3) of GC IV, or the Martens Clause, depending on whether they accepted the applicability of GC IV to 'unlawful combatants' or not.[31]

(vi) *Penal prosecution of 'unlawful combatants'*

It is generally accepted that 'unlawful combatants' may be prosecuted for their mere participation in hostilities, even if they respect all the rules of IHL.[32] National legislation must, however, provide for such a possibility.[33] If 'unlawful combatants' commit serious violations of IHL, they may be prosecuted for war crimes.[34] Contrary to certain claims, participation in hostilities without combatant privilege is not a war crime in the sense of a crime under international law.[35] In any proceedings, be it for violation of domestic law or for commission of war crimes, 'unlawful combatants' are entitled to the fair trial guarantees of GC IV if applicable (ie if they comply with the nationality requirements), or at least to those contained in Article 75 of AP I. They may not be executed/punished without proper trial.[36]

1989), 112. The authors who limit the applicability of GC IV to some types of unlawful combatants equally recognize the applicability of the said Art 75 to all unlawful combatants, Ipsen, in Fleck (ed) (n 10), 82–3; McCoubrey (n 10), 137; David (n 10), 489 ff; Bothe, Partsch, and Solf (n 10), 261ff; Aldrich (n 7), 893, fn 12.

[31] G. Schwarzenberger, *International Law as applied by International Courts and Tribunals*, vol II (London: Stevens, 1968), 115ff; Draper (n 10), 197; Rosenblad (n 10), 98; Kalshoven (n 10), 71.
[32] C. Rousseau, *Le droit des conflits armés* (Paris: A. Pedone, 1983), 68; Dinstein (n 30), 105; Commentary GC IV (n 15), 50; Kalshoven (n 10), 73ff.
[33] Dinstein (n 30), 114; Kalshoven (n 10), 73.   [34] Baxter, 'Unprivileged Belligerency' (n 11), 344.
[35] Interpretive Guidance on the Notion of Direct Participation in Hostilities under International Humanitarian Law (DPH Interpretive Guidance), ICRC, section X, 83–4.
[36] Draper (n 10), 197–8; Baxter, 'Unprivileged Belligerency' (n 11), 336, 337, 340; Baxter, 'Duties of Combatants' (n 11), 105ff; Schwarzenberger (n 31), 115ff; M.H.F. Clarke, T. Glynn, and A.P.V. Rogers, 'Combatant and Prisoner of War Status', in M.A. Meyer (ed), *Armed Conflict and the New Law: Aspects of the 1977 Geneva Protocols and the 1981 Weapons Convention* (London: British Institute of International and Comparative Law, 1989), 125; Rousseau (n 32), 68; Dinstein (n 30), 112; Kalshoven (n 10), 73ff. It is interesting to note that Dinstein considerably limits the competence of a capturing state to punish unlawful combatants for mere participation in hostilities when he claims '[a]n unlawful combatant may be put on trial only for an act committed in the course of the same mission that ended up in his capture by the adversary. [...] Hence, should the enemy capture [him] at a later stage, it may not prosecute him for the misdeeds of the past', Dinstein (n 30), 112. Thus, Dinstein applies to unlawful combatants the rules of the Hague Regulations relating to spies. This restriction has also been included in Art 44(5) of AP I (which stipulates that '[a]ny combatant who falls into the power of an adverse Party while not engaged in an attack or in a military operation preparatory to an attack shall not forfeit his rights to be a combatant and a prisoner of war by virtue of his prior activities') for members of the armed forces who have not distinguished themselves from the civilian population as required by that Article's paragraph 3.

B. Non-international armed conflicts

While the notion 'unlawful combatant' has been used by some also in the context of non-international armed conflicts, it has a place only within the context of the law applicable to international armed conflicts as defined in the GCs and AP I. The law applicable in non-international armed conflicts does not foresee a combatant's privilege (ie the right to participate in hostilities and impunity for lawful acts of hostility).[37] Once captured or detained, all persons taking no active/direct part in hostilities or who have ceased to take such a part come under the relevant provisions of IHL (ie Common Article 3 of GC, and AP II, in particular Articles 4–6), as well as relevant customary international law. The personal scope of application of these provisions refers to 'persons taking no active part in the hostilities, including members of armed forces who have laid down their arms and those placed *hors de combat* by sickness, wounds, detention, or any other cause',[38] 'all persons who do not take a direct part or who have ceased to take part in hostilities',[39] and 'persons deprived of their liberty for reasons related to the armed conflict, whether they are interned or detained',[40] whereas Article 6 'applies to the prosecution and punishment of criminal offences related to the armed conflict'.[41]

The protective rules apply regardless of the way in which such persons have participated in hostilities (eg in accordance with IHL or not; in accordance with national law or not; etc). Nor does it matter whether the person was a member of an armed rebel group, a member of the armed forces of a state, or a civilian who (temporarily) took a direct/active part in hostilities.

In recent years an important part of the international debate has focused on which rules or standards would apply to internment/detention for security reasons. The issue arose most prominently for people captured in non-international armed conflicts rhetorically subsumed under the designation of the fight against terrorism. While it may be said that IHL allows internment in non-international armed conflicts, it does not expressly provide the grounds or procedures applicable (contrary to GC IV dealing with internment in international armed conflicts). In the absence of a more detailed regulation in existing treaty law, the ICRC has submitted standards of reference based on law and policy.[42] The document reflects the ICRC's official position and now guides its operations. The document sets out a series of broad principles and specific rules that the ICRC believes should, as a minimum, govern any form of detention without criminal charge. As a general rule in the more traditional non-international armed conflicts, taking place within the territory of a state between government armed forces and organized armed groups, grounds and procedure would need to be provided for under domestic law. The situation

---

[37] See also IACHR Report (n 5), § 70.   [38] Common Art 3.
[39] Article 4 of AP II.   [40] Article 5 of AP II.   [41] Article 6 of AP II.
[42] J. Pejic, 'Procedural Principles and Safeguards for Internment/Administrative Detention in Armed Conflict and Other Situations of Violence', 87 *IRRC* (2005) 375–91.

is more complex if third states, often as a part of a coalition, operate in a country with the consent of the government and intern people of the armed opposition. It is submitted that an international agreement between the multinational forces(s) and the 'host' state should be concluded, or specific domestic law provided by the 'host' state for that purpose.

4 'UNLAWFUL COMBATANTS' UNDER THE RULES OF THE CONDUCT OF HOSTILITIES

The general rules on the conduct of hostilities apply to 'unlawful combatants'. Under these rules only the civilian population and individual civilians enjoy general protection against dangers arising from military operations. They are protected against direct attacks, unless and for such time as they take a direct part in hostilities. In accordance with Article 50 of AP I applicable in international armed conflicts, a civilian is any person who does not belong to 'one of the categories of persons referred to in Article 4 A paragraphs 1,[43] 2,[44] 3[45] and 6[46] of the Third Convention and in Article 43 of this Protocol' (ie members of the armed forces). Thus for the purposes of the law on the conduct of hostilities, there is no gap:[47] either a person is a combatant or a civilian. In so far as 'unlawful combatants' do not fulfil the criteria of either Article 4A paragraphs 1, 2, 3, and 6 of GC III or Article 43 of AP I, they are civilians. In such case, for such time as they directly participate in hostilities, they are lawful targets of an attack. When they do not directly participate in hostilities, they are protected as civilians and may not be directly targeted. It must be stressed

---

[43] Members of regular armed forces.

[44] Members of militias and volunteer corps, including organized resistance movements, not included in the regular armed forces.

[45] Members of regular armed forces of a non-recognized government/authority.

[46] *Levée en masse.*

[47] For example, see also Supreme Court of Israel, *Public Committee against Torture in Israel v Government of Israel*, Case No HCJ 769/02, 13 December 2006, available at <http://elyon1.court.gov.il/files_eng/02/690/007/A34/02007690.a34.pdf>. For the different approaches in GC IV and AP I, see Commentary on Art 50, Commentary AP I and II, para 1908: 'Article 4 of the fourth Geneva Convention of 1949 relative to the Protection of Civilian Persons in Time of War contains a definition of the persons protected by that Convention against arbitrary and wanton enemy action when they are in the power of the enemy; this is the main object of the Convention. However, Part II, entitled "General protection of populations against certain consequences of war" has a wider field of application; according to Article 13, that Part covers "the whole of the populations of the countries in conflict". That definition is close to the definition of the civilian population given in Article 50 of the Protocol under consideration here.'

that the fact that civilians have at some time taken direct part in the hostilities does not make them lose their immunity from direct attacks once and for all.[48] While the law is rather straightforward in this regard, the concrete interpretation is not fully clarified. The ICRC has submitted its recommendations how the notion of direct participation should be interpreted.[49]

If 'unlawful combatants' who have laid down their arms or no longer have means of defence, have surrendered at discretion, they must not be killed or wounded.[50] It is likewise prohibited to declare that no quarter will be given.[51]

In non-international armed conflicts, all persons who are not members of state armed forces or organized armed groups of a party to the conflict are civilians and, therefore, entitled to protection against direct attack unless and for such time as they take a direct part in hostilities. Organized armed groups constitute the armed forces of a non-state party to the conflict and consist only of individuals whose continuous function is to directly participate in hostilities.[52]

5 Some National Practice

A. The Israeli incarceration of unlawful combatants law (as amended 30 July 2008)[53]

Israel is probably the only country in the world that has enacted a specific law on detention of 'unlawful combatants'. In very broad strokes, the law contains the following elements: An 'unlawful combatant' is defined as 'a person who has participated either directly or indirectly in hostile acts against the State of Israel or is a member of a force perpetrating hostile acts against the State of Israel, where the

[48] See Art 51(3) of AP I: 'Civilians shall enjoy the protection afforded by this Section, unless and *for such time as* they take a direct part in hostilities' (own emphasis); Commentary on Art 51, Commentary AP I and II, para 1944; Bothe, Partsch, and Solf (n 10), 301.

[49] DPH Interpretive Guidance (n 35), 35.

[50] Article 23(c) of the 1907 Hague Regulations; Art 41 of AP I. See also ICRC, *Rules Applicable in Guerrilla Warfare,* Conference of Government Experts on the Reaffirmation and Development of International Humanitarian Law Applicable in Armed Conflicts, Geneva, 24 May–12 June 1971, Paper submitted by the International Committee of the Red Cross, Geneva, January 1971, 19.

[51] Article 23(d) of the 1907 Hague Regulations; Art 40 of AP I. See also ICRC, *Rules Applicable in Guerrilla Warfare* (n 50), 19; Kalshoven (n 10), 67ff.

[52] DPH Interpretive Guidance on DPH (n 35), section VII.

[53] Incarceration of Unlawful Combatants Law, 5762-2002 (as amended 30 July 2008), <http://www.justice.gov.il/MOJHeb/HeskeminVeKishreiHutz/KishreiChutz/HukimEnglish/>.

conditions prescribed in Article 4 of the Third Geneva Convention [...] do not apply to him'. According to that law an 'unlawful combatant' may be incarcerated if his/her release will harm state security. The incarceration order must generally include the grounds for incarceration. The order must be brought to the attention of the person at the earliest possible date and he/she must be given the opportunity to make a submission, which will be reviewed to determine whether the conditions for incarceration are met. The law also foresees a judicial review no later than 14 days after the incarceration order has been granted. Subsequently once every six months further judicial review takes place to assess whether the release will not harm state security or there are special grounds justifying his/her release. The decisions are subject to appeal. The person has a right to a lawyer. The law contains a far-reaching presumption that the release of the person would harm state security. Lastly, the law prescribes that the person must be held under proper conditions of detention which shall not impair his health or dignity. While the law has been criticized in several aspects, it is interesting to note that it is largely inspired by the indications contained in GC IV.

B. US practice in the fight against terrorism

The initial position of the Bush Administration was that neither GC III nor GC IV would apply to or protect Al Qaida or Taliban fighters.[54] In the White House memorandum of 7 February 2002, President Bush stated that 'our values as a nation [...] call for us to treat detainees humanely, including those who are not legally entitled to such treatment. [...] As a matter of policy, the United States Armed Forces shall continue to treat detainees humanely and, to the extent appropriate and consistent with military necessity, in a manner consistent with the principles of Geneva'.[55] On the face of this statement, a position was endorsed that 'unlawful combatants' have no protections based on IHL and humane treatment is only accorded as a matter of policy. The US understanding of the notion of 'unlawful combatants' in the so-called 'Global War on Terror' and the protection they are entitled to has evolved since. Congressional action and litigation (often at the crossroads between domestic, including constitutional exigencies, and law of war principles) as well as different political landscapes have played a role in this respect. A major development was clearly the US Supreme Court *Hamdan* decision that confirmed the *de iure* applicability of Common Article 3. Four judges of the majority also asserted the applicability of Article 75 of AP I as customary international law. The fifth judge of the majority felt that this question did not need to be addressed. Common Article 3 has since

---

[54] With a view to upholding incentives to comply with the law, Watkin remarks that '[t]he decision to exclude a group from attaining combatant status should not be taken lightly' (n 3), 36.

[55] <http://www.pegc.us/archive/White_House/bush_memo_20020207_ed.pdf>.

become a benchmark of protection and recognized as binding on the United States as treaty law. The US Supreme Court determination and subsequent US practice is significant as it rejects concepts that would have placed a category of persons outside the protections of law and IHL more specifically. Still it is debated what this concretely means for essential questions like detainability and targetability.

The question of detention of persons detained in the context of the fight against terrorism has been discussed and litigated over many years in the United States. Different approaches have evolved during the first and second Bush Administration as well as during the current Obama Administration. The differences in their substantive elements and the different legal nature of the texts involved ranging from statutes such as the 2006 Military Commission Act,[56] amended in 2009,[57] to Department of Defense policy directives binding only on the US Armed Forces have impeded a consolidated understanding of the US position. Since the US Supreme Court in *Hamdan*[58] rejected the idea that the United States was involved in an international armed conflict with Al Qaeda and its affiliates and concluded that the law of non-international armed conflicts (Common Article 3) applied, reference to terms like 'unlawful combatants' became less prevalent. In March 2009 the Department of Justice submitted to the federal District Court for the District of Columbia a new standard for the Government's authority to detain at the Guantánamo Bay Detention Facility, which does not employ anymore the term 'enemy combatant'. The new standard is based on the Authorization for the Use of Military Force, which Congress passed in September 2001. According to Attorney General Holder, 'the government's new standard relies on the international laws of war to inform the scope of the president's authority under this statute'. In the memorandum submitted to the District Court it is stated:

The President has the authority to detain persons that the President determines planned, authorized, committed, or aided the terrorist attacks that occurred on September 11, 2001, and persons who harbored those responsible for those attacks. The President also has the

---

[56] The Act effectively provides two definitions in § 948a: one substantive and one process-based. 'The term "unlawful enemy combatant" means—(i) a person who has engaged in hostilities or who has purposefully and materially supported hostilities against the United States or its co-belligerents who is not a lawful enemy combatant (including a person who is part of the Taliban, al Qaeda, or associated forces); or (ii) a person who, before, on, or after the date of the enactment of the Military Commissions Act of 2006, has been determined to be an unlawful enemy combatant by a Combatant Status Review Tribunal or another competent tribunal established under the authority of the President or the Secretary of Defense'. The term 'lawful enemy combatant' is defined based in Art 4A(1), (2), and (3) of GC III.

[57] 'An "alien unprivileged belligerent" includes an individual (other than a privileged belligerent) who (A) has engaged in hostilities against the United States or its coalition partners; (B) has purposefully and materially supported hostilities against the United States or its coalition partners; or (C) was a part of Al Qaeda at the time of the alleged offense [...]'. The term 'privileged belligerent' is defined in Art 4 of GC III.

[58] <http://www.supremecourtus.gov/opinions/05pdf/05-184.pdf>.

authority to detain persons who were part of, or substantially supported, Taliban or al-Qaida forces or associated forces that are engaged in hostilities against the United States or its coalition partners, including any person who has committed a belligerent act, or has directly supported hostilities, in aid of such enemy armed forces.

Questions as to what procedural principles and safeguards apply remain under discussion as different standards have been applied in Guantánamo, Afghanistan, and Iraq, and US Courts continue to refine their potential.

While much of the preceding developed in the context of the fight against terrorism, the 2007 US *Commander's Handbook on the Law of Naval Operations* poses some more general standards. It defines 'unlawful enemy combatants' as 'persons not entitled to combatant immunity, who engage in acts against the United States or its coalition partners in violation of the laws and customs of war during armed conflict.' With regard to detention it repeats that they do not receive combatant immunity for their hostile acts and are not entitled to prisoner of war status. However, they are entitled to humane treatment as a matter of law and US policy, which includes the protections of Common Article 3 of GC.

All detainees shall
- receive appropriate medical attention and treatment
- receive sufficient food, drinking water, shelter, and clothing
- be allowed the free exercise of religion, consistent with the requirements for safety and security
- be removed as soon as practicable from the point of capture and transported to detainee collection points, holding facilities, or other internment facilities operated by DOD Components
- have their person and their property accounted for and records maintained
- be respected as human beings. They will not be subjected to medical or scientific experiments. They will not be subjected to sensory deprivation.[59]

In the absence of combatant immunity 'they may be prosecuted for their unlawful actions. However, prosecution is not required and unlawful combatants may be detained until the cessation of hostilities without being prosecuted for their acts. [...] a detaining nation may release an unlawful combatant at any time. For example, a detaining nation may decide to end detention before the cessation of hostilities if it determines the detained combatant no longer poses a threat'.[60]

---

[59] NWP 1-14M/MCWP 5-12.1/COMDTPUB P5800.7A, *The Commander's Handbook on the Law of Naval Operations* (July 2007), 11.1 and 11.2.

[60] *The Commander's Handbook* (n 59), 11.3.2.

6 Conclusion

Any interpretation that 'unlawful combatants' are outside the protection of IHL is unfounded. For international armed conflicts, it is submitted that if they fulfil the nationality criteria of Article 4 of GC IV, they are protected by that Convention. The fact that a person has unlawfully participated in hostilities is not a criterion for excluding the application of GC IV, though it may be a reason for derogating from certain rights in accordance with Article 5 thereof. The specific protections of GC IV depend on the situation in which such persons find themselves in enemy hands. They are most extensive if unlawful combatants are in enemy hands in occupied territory. For those in enemy hands in enemy territory the protections are also quite well developed, whereas on the battlefield, where no actual control is established—depending on the interpretation of when the law of occupation starts to apply—protections may be the least developed. The guarantees contained in Article 75 of AP I constitute the minimum protections that apply to all persons, including unlawful combatants, in the hands of a party to an international armed conflict, irrespective of whether they are covered by GC IV or not. The protection in non-international armed conflicts is essentially based on Common Article 3 of GC, Articles 4–6 of AP II, and customary international law.

CHAPTER 25

PRIVATE MILITARY AND SECURITY COMPANIES

JAMES COCKAYNE

1 Introduction: The Challenge of Regulating Commercial Actors on the Battlefield

In the last two decades, private commercial actors offering military and security services have moved from being considered a curious and exotic anomaly—an exception unworthy of forming the basis of systematic regulation—to being regarded as a central contemporary concern for the international law of armed conflict.

That shift in perception is in part due to a shift in reality. The dominance of national military power over the last century has left little space on the battlefield for independent entrepreneurs, except as adjuncts to state forces or in theatres where state military power has remained weak and unsupported by external state patrons—a rarity during the Cold War. As a result, in recent decades organized, commercial military groups largely took the form of small bands of closely-knit mercenaries, operating in the guerrilla wars of Africa. These groups were essentially peripheral players in the geostrategic major military confrontations of the day. They were not seen as destabilizing the central conceptual foundations of the international law of armed conflict, but instead were viewed as anomalies.

In the last two decades, however, these mercenary companies, working with demobilized and retired military and security personnel from all parts of the globe, have capitalized on the entrepreneurial opportunities afforded by globalization. There is now a network of military entrepreneurs operating around the world, recruiting in one country, headquartered in a second, contracted to a third, perhaps operating weapons in a fourth to carry out attacks in a fifth.[1] Private military and security companies (PMSCs) have become significant players in the global force projection strategies of some of the world's most powerful military actors, supplementing authorized troop deployments by providing personal security details, static guarding units, logistics support, training, theatre analysis, covert intelligence assets, psychological operations, weapons maintenance, and language and communications support. The United States, in particular, is seen in the light of its expeditions in Iraq and Afghanistan as increasingly dependent on PMSCs for both its overt and covert military operations.[2]

The arrival of large numbers of PMSC personnel on geostrategic key battlefields has quite literally placed them at the centre of contemporary discussions about the regulation of armed conflict. Their form, statutory duties to contractual clients and shareholders, and often their conduct raise difficult questions for international lawyers. Are PMSC personnel civilians, or combatants, or sometimes one and sometimes the other? Can they be targeted for attack? If they cannot effectively be distinguished from either civilians or combatants, how can opposing forces know whether it is lawful to attack them? And, perhaps centrally, who is ultimately responsible for their conduct before international law—especially if they are merely private actors, working for private clients?

---

[1] See generally P.W. Singer, *Corporate Warriors: The Rise of the Privatized Military Industry* (New York: Cornell University Press, 2004); D.D. Avant, *The Market for Force: The Consequences of Privatizing Security* (Washington DC: George Washington University, 2005); S. Maninger, 'Soldiers of Misfortune—Is the Demise of National Armies a Core Contributing Factor in the Rise of Private Security Companies?', in G. Kümmel and T. Jäger (eds), *Private Security and Military Companies: Chances, Problems, Pitfalls and Prospects* (Wiesbaden: VS Verlag für Sozialwissenschaften, 2007), 69–86; T. Geraghty, *Guns For Hire: The Inside Story of Freelance Soldiering* (London: Portrait, 2007).

[2] See especially the multi-year investigation run by *The Washington Post*, documented at <http://projects.washingtonpost.com/top-secret-america/>.

The persistence of these questions has led to numerous attempts in the last decade at both the national[3] and international[4] levels to clarify laws and policies around the regulation of PMSCs. But continuing allegations of involvement of PMSC personnel in major violations of international law, especially in Iraq,[5] have fuelled a perception that PMSCs must exist in some kind of 'legal vacuum'[6] or 'regulatory gap'.[7] PMSCs combine military functions and civilian and military forms of organization in new ways,[8] capitalizing on the limited control that states can exert—and the reduced responsibility they consequently bear—beyond their borders.

These complexities coalesce around a number of recurring points of disputation, including the legitimacy of PMSCs' presence on the battlefield, the protections PMSC personnel enjoy, and the privileges they benefit from. In this Chapter, I first explore

[3] See eg Afghanistan, Draft Regulations on Private Security Companies, 2008; Australia, Crimes (Overseas) Amendment Act 2003; Coalition Provisional Authority: Order No 17 (Revised), Status of the Coalition Provisional Authority, MNF-Iraq, Certain Missions and Personnel in Iraq (27 June 2004); Coalition Provisional Authority, Memorandum, No 17, Registration Requirements for Private Security Companies; Sierra Leone, National Security and Central Intelligence Act (2005); South Africa, Prohibition of Mercenary Activities and Regulation of Certain Activities in Country of Armed Conflict Act, 2006 (Act No 27 of 2006); Swiss Federal Council, *Rapport du Conseil federal sur les enterprises de sécurité et les enterprises militaries privées*, 2006; Swiss Ordinance on the Use of Private Security Companies, 31 October 2007, and accompanying Model Contract; UK Foreign Affairs Committee, Private Military Companies: Ninth Report of Session 2001–02 ('Green Paper'); United Kingdom, Green Paper, *Private Military Companies: Options for Regulation*, London: The Stationery Office, 2002; UK Foreign and Commonwealth Office, *Private Military and Security Companies (PMSCs): Summary of Public Consultation Working Group*, April 2010; United States, Arms Export Control Act 2002; US Federal Acquisition Regulation 52.225-19, Contractor Personnel in a Designated Operational Area or Supporting a Diplomatic or Consular Mission Outside the United States (March 2008); US Department of Defense Instruction 3020.41, 3 October 2005, in Federal Register, vol 73, no 40, 28 February 2008, Rules and Regulations, 10943; US Department of Defense, 'Private Security Contractors (PSCs) Operating in Contingency Operations', 32 CFR Part 159, *Federal Register*, vol 74, no 136, 17 July 2009, 34690–4.

[4] See eg UNMIK Regulation No 2000/33 on licensing of security services providers in Kosovo and the regulation of their employees; UN, 'Report of the Working Group on the use of mercenaries as a means of violating human rights and impeding the exercise of the right of peoples to self-determination', UN Doc A/HRC/15/25, 2 July 2010; *Montreux Document on Pertinent International Legal Obligations and Good Practices for States related to Operations of Private Military and Security Companies during Armed Conflict*, UN Doc A/63/467–S/2008/636, 6 October 2008.

[5] See eg Major General G.R. Fay, AR 15-6 Investigation of the Abu Ghraib Detention Facility and 205th Military Intelligence Brigade 130–4, 23 August 2004, esp 131–4; Major General A.M. Taguba, Article 15-6 Investigation of the 800th Military Police Brigade, May 2004; Human Rights First, *Private Security Contractors at War: Ending the Culture of Impunity*, New York/Washington DC, 2008.

[6] See eg P. Singer, 'War, Profits and the Vacuum of Law: Privatized Military Firms and International Law', 42 *Columbia Journal of Transnational Law* (2004) 521–50.

[7] See C. Hoppe, 'Passing the Buck: State Responsibility for Private Military Companies', 19 *European Journal of International Law* (2008) 989–1014. See also University Centre for International Humanitarian Law, Geneva, Expert Meeting on Private Military Contractors: Status and State Responsibility for Their Actions, 2005, 20–1 (hereinafter 'UCIHL').

[8] See further, J. Cockayne, 'The Global Reorganization of Legitimate Violence: Military Entrepreneurs and the Private Face of International Humanitarian Law', 88 *International Review of the Red Cross* (2007) 1–32.

these recurring themes, then examine whether 'states are the answer' to these regulatory questions. Highlighting the limits of state power—and desire—to regulate commercial actors on the battlefield, I move on to explain why some commentators in fact see states as 'the problem'. In a final section, I explore whether and how international law might be coming to provide the primary rules of conduct which might serve as the basis for the development of non-traditional mechanisms for enforcing international law: through domestic and civil litigation, and through industry action.

2 Presence, Protections, and Privileges

Much of the commentary on PMSCs—both lay and expert—is polarized around different attitudes to the legitimacy of PMSCs' presence on the battlefield. These poles involve different views of the protections and privileges that PMSC personnel ought enjoy under international law.

Some commentators, pointing to incidents such as the brutal slaying of four American contractors in Fallujah in 2004,[9] or the long-term detention of American contractors in Colombia,[10] suggest that PMSC personnel are particularly vulnerable on the battlefield. Some suggest, therefore, that PMSC personnel should enjoy protections and privileges additional to those afforded civilians—for example it is suggested they should enjoy the right to participate directly in hostilities without losing the protections that civilians enjoy from attack. Others, however, suggest that if PMSCs are particularly vulnerable on the battlefield, that is in part because many PMSCs operate outside the traditional system of integrated responsible command, which facilitates not only distinction between combatants and civilians on the battlefield, but also the reciprocity that underpins effective implementation and enforcement of international law, especially international humanitarian law. Some commentators in this camp suggest that PMSCs' access to the combatant's privilege of lawful direct participation in hostilities should depend on their integration into such a structure.[11] As Lindsey Cameron notes,

the plethora of companies [on the battlefield] means that it will be extremely difficult for an enemy to comply with IHL in terms of knowing who may be directly targeted, considering

[9] J. Gettleman, 'Enraged Mob in Falluja Kills 4 American Contractors', *New York Times*, 31 March 2004.

[10] M. Gonsalves, T. Howes, K. Stansell, and G. Brozek, *Out of Captivity: Surviving 1,967 Days in the Colombian Jungle* (New York: HarperCollins, 2009).

[11] Compare K. Watkin, *Warriors Without Rights? Combatants, Unprivileged Belligerents, and the Struggle over Legitimacy*, HPCR Occasional Paper Series, 2005.

that likely only very few PMCs will have combatant status but they may closely resemble the many other PMCs operating in the conflict zone. It would be a crime for an enemy to target civilian PMC employees directly, but the inability to distinguish the civilian PMCs from combatant PMCs may discourage any attempt to comply with IHL and contribute to an erosion of the principle of distinction.[12]

Behind these contending normative positions, however, there is in fact a clear consensus amongst qualified jurists: while an individual's legal status must be determined on a factual, case-by-case basis, most PMSC personnel will likely qualify only as civilians, even as a minority of PMSC personnel may enjoy PoW protections (but not status) under certain strict conditions (those applying to civilians accompanying the armed forces, and of course only in international armed conflict).[13] In non-international armed conflicts, too, most PMSCs will simply be civilians, protected from attack unless and for such time as they directly participate in hostilities, unless they form part of the state's armed forces.[14]

Some experts, however, also point out that, in addition, in limited cases (explored further below) certain PMSC units active in international armed conflict may themselves constitute organized armed groups under a command responsible to a party to the armed conflict, and thus form a part of the armed forces of the party to the conflict (under Article 43 of API and customary international humanitarian law).[15] This classification probably applies primarily to PMSC combat units, interrogation units, covert operations, and psychological operations personnel co-located with state personnel.[16] Personnel in these units may be privileged belligerents, rather than civilians. They are thus lawfully entitled to participate directly in hostilities (whereas civilian PMSC personnel may take part in hostilities only at the risk of later prosecution). Even if this narrow sub-class of PMSC personnel do not wear a fixed distinctive sign or bear arms openly (contra Article 4(A)(2) of GC III and Article 1 of the Hague Regulations), they may be entitled to participate

---

[12] L. Cameron, 'International Humanitarian Law and the Regulation of Private Military Companies', Paper presented at the Conference on Non-State Actors as Standard Setters: The Erosion of the Public-Private Divide, 8–9 February 2007, Basel, Switzerland, 5. See also L. Cameron, 'Private Military Companies: Their Status under International Humanitarian Law and its Impact on Their Regulation', 88 *International Review of the Red Cross* (2006) 572–98.

[13] See eg Cameron (n 12); M. Schmitt, 'Humanitarian Law and Direct Participation in Hostilities by Private Contractors or Civilian Employees', 5 *Chicago Journal of International Law* (2005) 511–46; E.-C. Gillard, 'Business Goes to War: Private Military/Security Companies and International Humanitarian Law', 88 *International Review of the Red Cross* (2006) 525–72; Hoppe (n 7), 1006–7.

[14] Article 13(3) of AP II. See also J.-M. Henckaerts and L. Doswald-Beck, *Customary International Humanitarian Law* (Cambridge: Cambridge University Press) ('Customary Law Study'), vol I, *Rules*, Rule 4, 14.

[15] See Hoppe (n 7), 1009. For further support for this functional interpretation of Art 43 see M. Bothe, K.J. Partsch, and W.A. Solf, *New Rules for Victims of Armed Conflict: Commentary on the Two 1977 Protocols Additional to the Geneva Conventions of 1949* (The Hague: Martinus Nijhoff, 1982), 234.

[16] Compare Hoppe (n 7), 1009.

in hostilities[17]—though they may also risk losing the entitlement to PoW status they might otherwise enjoy during international armed conflict, had they so distinguished themselves.[18] And these personnel will also be, as a result of their direct participation in hostilities and their classification as combatants—and regardless of their uniforms or open bearing of arms—legitimate military targets. The party to whom they are responsible will bear all the obligations of control, due diligence, oversight—and legal liability—that it bears in relation to its regular armed forces (also explored further below).

Few states, however, seem to have the requisite legal frameworks, bureaucratic incentives, supervision arrangements, or vetting and training mechanisms in place to discharge effectively such obligations of oversight and control.[19] The application of international law to PMSCs is rendered complex not only by the location of PMSCs outside the traditional chain of military command. It is also complicated by the fact that many PMSC personnel operate far from what was traditionally thought of as 'the battlefield', instead operating automated weapons systems from civilian centres or buildings, perhaps a continent away from the on-the-ground kinetic operations, answering not to uniformed personnel but to contractor managers and private boards, accountable not through the chain of command but through contract.[20] Even the US Government, which has spent more time and effort than perhaps any other seeking to address these issues over the last decade, continues to struggle at times to exert effective control over the actions of the PMSCs it has hired—so much so that the US Congress established a special Commission on Wartime Contracting to wrestle with these concerns.[21]

The broader regulatory problem this points to, however, is the limited capacity that states have to control highly decentralized, transnational, commercial networks, operating partly in their territory and partly outside it, partly on the battlefield, and partly outside it. PMSCs do not fit neatly into the conceptual boxes that structure the international law of armed conflict, with its emphasis on territorial control as the basis of legal responsibility, and its preference for hierarchical command structures as avenues for the reciprocal implementation and enforcement of norms.[22]

Generally speaking, two different schools of thought have emerged on how to remedy this mismatch. One suggests that commercial actors should be dis-incentivized from being present on the battlefield, by having access to reduced protections

---

[17] Compare Customary Law Study (n 14), Rule 4, 16.

[18] Customary Law Study (n 14), Rule 106, 15, 16, 386–9.

[19] J. Cockayne et al, *Beyond Market Forces: Regulating the Global Security Industry* (New York: International Peace Institute, 2009), 38–43.

[20] See R. Heaton, 'Civilians at War: Reexamining the Status of Civilians Accompanying the Armed Forces', 57 *Air Force Law Review* (2005) 155–208.

[21] See <http://www.wartimecontracting.gov>.

[22] See Cockayne (n 8). See also A. Leander, *Eroding State Authority? Private Military Companies and the Legitimate Use of Force* (Rome: Centro Militari di Studi Strategici, 2006).

and enjoying reduced privileges. This is the impulse that has underpinned efforts in the OAU and UN to criminalize mercenarism[23] and, more recently, an effort within the UN Human Rights Council to draft a Convention to greatly curtail PMSCs' market access through a complex system of licensing and international oversight.[24] These efforts have had little regulatory impact because states have ensured that the resulting norms do not so much legally constrain their own access to PMSC services as socially stigmatize the operation of PMSCs outside state control.[25]

Existing legal definitions of mercenarism are largely seen as 'unworkable',[26] in the sense that they have little impact on the activities of most PMSCs, and are extremely difficult to apply in the circumstances of limited information, which prevail on the battlefield. By way of example, many PMSC personnel in Iraq and Afghanistan would not be caught by the existing legal provisions specifically pertaining to mercenarism, either because (1) they were nationals of parties to the conflict, or residents of Iraq; or (2) they worked for PMSCs contracted by private clients, rather than a party to the conflict; or (3) they did not take direct part in hostilities. The remainder—primarily 'third-country nationals' (TCNs)—were in fact recruited largely after the conflicts in Iraq and Afghanistan transitioned from being international armed conflicts or situations of occupation to non-international armed conflicts, over which the established provisions relating to mercenarism have even weaker reach. These provisions thus have limited legal 'added-value': instead, their real purpose, as the *travaux préparatoires* of the Diplomatic Conference that drafted the mercenary provision in Additional Protocol I make clear, is political.[27] Unfortunately, the major impact of the stigma of 'mercenarism' has not been to control or regulate PMSC or mercenary conduct, but rather to drive it towards the shadow economy, and to mobilize domestic political support for summary criminal proceedings levelled against mercenaries—such as the trial of mercenaries in Angola in 1976,[28] or the more recent trial of Simon Mann in Equatorial Guinea—sometimes entailing violations of the fundamental guarantees in fact afforded such individuals by Common Article 3 and Article 75 of Additional Protocol I.

---

[23] See *International Convention against the Recruitment, Use, Financing and Training of Mercenaries*, 4 December 1989, UNGA Res A/RES/44/34, entered into force 20 October 2001; and *Convention for the Elimination of Mercenarism in Africa*, Organisation of African Unity, Libreville, 3 July 1997, CM/817 (XXXIX), Annex II, Rev 3, entered into force 22 April 1985. For further discussion of the compatibility between these Conventions and Art 47 of AP I, see Gillard (n 13), 567–8.

[24] UN, 'Report of the Working Group' (n 4).

[25] See Cockayne (n 8). See also S. Percy, *Mercenaries: The History of a Norm in International Relations* (Oxford: Oxford University Press, 2007).

[26] F. Hampson, 'Mercenaries: Diagnosis before Prescription', 3 *Netherlands Yearbook of International Law* (1991) 3–38 at 14–16.

[27] See *Official Records of the Diplomatic Conference on the Reaffirmation and Development of International Humanitarian Law Applicable in Armed Conflicts*, Geneva (1974–77), vol VI, Plenary Meetings, Summary Records of the Thirty-Fourth to Forty-Sixth Meetings, CDDH/SR.41, 156–204.

[28] See M. Hoover, 'The Laws of War and the Angolan Trial of Mercenaries: Death to the Dogs of War', 9 *Case Western Journal of International Law* (1977) 323–406.

The second impulse seeks not to exclude commercial military actors from the battlefield through these mechanisms of international and criminal law, but rather to remedy the mismatch between the transnational commercial activities of PMSCs and the regulation afforded by states, by extending the actual control of states over PMSCs through strengthened state oversight arrangements.

3 ARE STATES THE ANSWER?

Many people see states as the key to effective regulation of PMSC conduct in armed conflict, since states are the subjects of international law and the only entities— many argue—with the wherewithal to effectively regulate this conduct.[29] Yet states seem reluctant, absent some external incentive, to assert such increased control over private, commercial actors, often operating outside their territory. It is often difficult, given the territorial basis of the international legal order, to effectively assert and exercise such control. And to do so would reduce the room to manoeuvre that states enjoy as a result of their arm's length relations with PMSCs.[30]

Many of these issues became clear in the negotiation of the Montreux Document, which sought to identify good practices for territorial, contracting and home states in dealing with PMSCs operating in armed conflict, as well as affirm existing international law as it applied to those relations. The 18 states involved in negotiating the document—which included some of the 'most-affected states' such as the United States, United Kingdom, Iraq, Afghanistan, the Russian Federation, France, Australia, South Africa, and Sierra Leone—focused greater attention on the affirmation of existing legal obligations under IHL and international human rights law than they did on the 'Good Practices' section.[31] Perhaps the most significant aspects of the negotiation, from a legal perspective, turned on the questions of (1) attribution and (2) positive obligations. The first concerns when PMSC conduct would be attributed to a state under international law. The second addresses when non-attributable conduct might nonetheless entail regulatory obligations

---

[29] See eg H.-Y. Liu, 'Leashing the Corporate Dogs of War: The Legal Implications of the Modern Private Military Company', 15(1) *Journal of Conflict and Security Law* (2010) 141–68.

[30] See J. Cockayne, 'Make or Buy? Principal-Agent Theory and the Regulation of Private Military Companies', in S. Chesterman and C. Lehnardt (eds), *From Mercenaries to Markets: The Rise and Regulation of Private Military Companies* (Oxford: Oxford University Press, 2007), 196–217.

[31] See J. Cockayne, 'Regulating Private Military and Security Companies: The Content, Negotiation, Weaknesses and Promise of the Montreux Document', 13(3) *Journal of Conflict and Security Law* (2008) 401–28.

on the part of different states.[32] I address these two questions in the two sections that follow.

4 ATTRIBUTING PMSC CONDUCT
TO STATES

States are responsible for any unlawful conduct under international law which is attributable to them. Yet it will not always be immediately obvious when the conduct of a PMSC is attributable to a state, especially when we consider that PMSCs frequently operate through corporate pyramids that stretch across multiple jurisdictions.[33] Under public international law, there are essentially three avenues by which PMSC conduct may be attributable to a state.[34]

A. When PMSC personnel serve as state organs

The ILC Articles on Responsibility of States for Internationally Wrongful Acts make clear that the conduct of an individual will be attributable to a state if that individual is serving as an 'organ' of the state, as determined by the state's law.[35] For a PMSC to be considered an 'organ' of a state, therefore, there must be more than a mere contractual relationship;[36] they must form a part of the state's official organs; or, as the

[32] Cockayne (n 31). See generally A. Kontos, 'Private Security Guards: Privatized Force and State Responsibility Under International Human Rights Law', 4 *Non-State Actors and International Law* (2004) 199–238; and K. Creutz, *Transnational Privatised Security and the International Protection of Human Rights*, Erik Castrén Institute Research Report 19/2006, University of Helsinki, 2006.

[33] See eg J. Risen and M. Mazetti, '30 False Fronts Won Contracts for Blackwater', *New York Times*, 3 September 2010.

[34] See generally Hoppe (n 7); C. Lehnardt, 'Private Military Companies and State Responsibility', in S. Chesterman and C. Lehnardt (eds), *From Mercenaries to Market: The Rise and Regulation of Private Military Companies* (2007) 139–57; M. Spinedi, 'Private Contractors: Responsabilité Internationale des Enterprises ou Attribution à l'Etat de la Conduit des Personnes Privées?', 7 *FORUM du droit international* (2005) 281–9.

[35] See UN, *ILC Articles on Responsibility of States for Internationally Wrongful Acts, adopted by the International Law Commission at its fifty-third session, and Commentaries thereto*, in 'Report of the International Law Commission on the work of its Fifty-third session (2001)', *Official Records of the General Assembly, Fifty-Sixth Session, Supplement No 10*, UN Doc A/56/10, Ch IV.E.1 (hereinafter 'ILC Articles'), Art 4.

[36] Cameron (n 12), 4; Gillard (n 13), 533; see also K. Ipsen, 'Combatants and Non-Combatants', in D. Fleck, *Handbook of Humanitarian Law in Armed Conflicts* (Oxford: Oxford University Press, 1995), 65–104 at 67.

International Court of Justice recently clarified in the *Bosnian Genocide* case, they must be 'completely dependent' upon the state in question.[37]

There are a limited number of clear-cut cases where the incorporation of a PMSC or its personnel as official (ie *de jure*) organs of the state was, in fact, exactly the manifest intention of both the PMSC and the contracting state. In the late 1990s, Sandline contracted with the governments of both Sierra Leone and Papua New Guinea for its personnel to be incorporated into—and to enjoy formal command powers over parts of—their armed forces. In Colombia, some US contractors have for some time been sworn in as members of the internal security and police services of the state. In the case of international armed conflict, Additional Protocol I seems to suggest that any such incorporation should be communicated to the opposing party.[38] But cases of such communication are rare.

Absent such communication, or some form of statutory basis beyond a contract which suggests PMSC personnel have taken on the role of a state organ, the question becomes whether a PMSC is 'completely dependent' upon a particular state, and thus becomes its *de facto* organ. Mere financial support does not create a situation of complete dependence.[39] Evidence of 'autonomy' on the part of the PMSC will suggest it is not the 'mere instrument' of the state, and thus not its *de facto* organ. The political, military, and logistical relations between the state and the PMSC will be significant in determining the PMSC's autonomy. Any real 'margin of independence', even if qualified, will mean that the PMSC is not a *de facto* organ of the state, for the purpose of attribution of responsibility.[40] As a result, few PMSCs are likely to constitute *de facto* state organs, since they likely have some—even marginal—degree of legal and financial autonomy from any given state. The exception may be where it can be demonstrated that a PMSC in fact serves as a front for covert state activity—as, arguably, some US corporations involved in the US government's aerial renditions programme may.

B. State instruction, direction, or control of PMSCs

PMSC conduct may, however, be attributable to a state even where PMSC personnel are not organs of the state if the PMSC personnel are acting under the instructions, direction, or control of a state.[41]

Exactly how specific such 'instructions' must be in order for the resulting conduct to be attributed to the state remains unclear. Experts disagree on whether a head contract will suffice as 'instructions' or whether there must be specific task

---

[37] ICJ, *Case Concerning Application of the Convention on the Prevention and Punishment of the Crime of Genocide (Bosnia and Herzegovina v Serbia and Montenegro)*, Judgment, 26 February 2007 ('*Bosnian Genocide* case'), §§ 389–93.

[38] See Art 43(3) of AP I.   [39] *Bosnian Genocide* case (n 37), § 388.

[40] *Bosnian Genocide* case (n 37), § 394.   [41] ILC Articles, Art 8.

634 KEY ISSUES IN TIMES OF ARMED CONFLICT

orders, rules of engagement, standard operating procedures, or even commands issued or acquiesced in by state officials.[42] Likewise, there is continuing dispute at the international level over the nature of control that a state must exert over an armed group in order for the group's conduct to be attributable to the state—especially whether it needs to be 'effective control' at an operational level, or whether mere 'overall control' of the group's operations as a whole will suffice.[43] The bottom line seems to be that the likelihood that PMSC conduct will be attributable to a state rises with the level of actual or potential control that a state agent exerts over PMSC personnel.

State agents exercising territorial control or commensurate authority therefore have a higher potential to create state attribution. But with the penetration of the battlefield by remote information technologies, such territorial control may no longer be determinative, given the ability of states remotely to communicate with PMSC personnel while on the battlefield, and their ability to influence PMSC conduct through contractual and other administrative arrangements such as financial or contractual penalties.

The level of control that a state must exert over an armed group in order for that group's conduct to be attributable to the state should also be considered against the background not only of general public international law, but also the *lex specialis* of international humanitarian law. Here, Article 43(1) of Additional Protocol I is particularly relevant. It suggests that organized armed groups under a command responsible to a party to a conflict should be treated, for the purpose of IHL, as part of the armed forces of that party.[44] This does not seem to require that the armed group be commanded by an organ of the state, but rather that it is commanded by some person who is himself or herself 'responsible' to the state. Hoppe argues that 'command responsible' should be construed broadly, simply requiring a factual link between the PMSC and a state to which it must 'respond'.[45] The original (and equally

---

[42] See eg UCIHL (n 7), 18–20.

[43] See ICJ, *Case Concerning Military and Paramilitary Activities in and against Nicaragua (Nicaragua v United States of America)*, Judgment (Merits), 27 June 1986 ('*Nicaragua* case'); ICTY, Appeals Chamber, *Prosecutor v Tadić*, Judgment, 15 July 1999, IT-94-1-A; ICJ, *Legal Consequences of the Construction of a Wall in the Occupied Palestinian Territory*, Advisory Opinion, 9 July 2004 ('*Wall* case'), §§ 108–11; and ICJ, *Case Concerning Armed Activities on the Territory of the Congo (Democratic Republic of the Congo v Uganda)*, Judgment of 19 December 2005 ('*DRC v Uganda*'), § 160 (confirming the *Nicaragua* approach). See also *Bosnian Genocide* case (n 37), §§ 397–400.

[44] Most commentators see the language in Art 4(A)(2) of GC III (discussing carrying arms openly, wearing a fixed and distinctive sign, conducting operations according to international law) not as imposing additional *preconditions* to an armed group being considered to form part of the armed forces of a state for the purpose of *attribution*, but as a stipulation of the conduct expected of such groups if they wish to continue to enjoy the privileges of belligerency: see Hoppe (n 7), 1011. See also UCIHL (n 7); and compare M. Schmitt, 'Humanitarian Law and Direct Participation in Hostilities by Private Contractors or Civilian Employees', 5 *Chicago Journal of International Law* (2005) 511–46 at 527 and following; see also K. Watkin, *Warriors Without Rights? Combatants, Unprivileged Belligerents, and the Struggle over Legitimacy*, HPCR Occasional Paper Series, 2005, 67.

[45] Hoppe (n 7), 1009. See generally M. Bothe, et al (n 15), 234.

authentic) French version uses the phrase 'un commandement responsable de la conduite de ses subordonnés devant cette Partie'. This phrasing 'responsable [...] devant'—rather than 'responsable [...] de'—carries a broader sense of 'accountability to' the party to the conflict, rather than strict control by that party.[46]

Even this clarification does not, however, make entirely clear what level of PMSC 'accountability' to a state will make its conduct attributable to the state. Does attribution kick in if the CEO of the PMSC reports irregularly to a foreign ministry official? Or must the accountability mechanisms stretch down to lower levels of the PMSC, involve more frequent and extensive interaction, and involve state review of the PMSC's conduct? Which part of a PMSC organization is the appropriate level of analysis—should responsibility be sought at the level of the division that oversees the head contract under which a PMSC unit is operating, or must there be interaction between the state and the field manager of the particular unit that carries out the conduct in question? And given how fluid many PMSCs' payrolls are, how 'organized' must a group of PMSC personnel be to fall within this concept of a 'responsible command'?

What we can say is that the likelihood of attribution to the state will rise as the state imposes more extensive administrative or oversight mechanisms over extraterritorial conduct, and as it enjoys greater territorial control. The mere possibility of the exercise of extraterritorial jurisdiction will not, in and of itself, give rise to attribution.[47] That might seem to suggest that attribution of PMSC conduct, especially human rights violations, is primarily a concern for the states who control territory on which PMSCs operate,[48] whether 'home' or 'host' states—rather than 'hiring' states. Human rights norms may, therefore, be particularly relevant to effective regulation of those PMSC units that operate co-located with state agents who control territory, or even specific places of detention—such as interrogators, interpreters, or combat units.

In many cases, however, PMSC personnel will not be collocated with the hiring state's personnel, but instead operating on territory that is effectively controlled by another state. And their client may not be a state at all, but a private company, such as an extractive corporation. In those cases, there is even more uncertainty as to the form of 'control' that a state must exert, even if temporarily, over a non-state agent or the place in which it is operating, in order for the state *either* to exercise jurisdiction (for the purpose of determining the state's human rights obligations)

[46] See also Customary Law Study (n 14), 15.

[47] See the *Wall* case (n 43), §§ 108–11; and *DRC v Uganda* (n 43), §§ 216–20.

[48] See Hoppe (n 7), 996–7. Compare ECtHR, App No 153187/89, *Loizidou v Turkey* (preliminary objections) (1995), ECtHR series A No 310, 62, suggesting that a small group of soldiers temporarily controlling a small area within another state may carry their human rights obligations with them; and ECtHR, App No 46221/99, *Öcalan v Turkey*, Judgment of 12 May 2005, ECHR 2005-IV 131 (GG), suggesting a similar result for the rendering of an individual by state forces in a third country, without consent or collusion by officials of that country (which in that case was present).

or for the non-state agent's actions to be attributable to the state. Yet such cases are increasingly important in regulating the conduct of PMSCs, as revelations of their role in providing targeting intelligence for extra-judicial executions in Pakistan,[49] and participating in enforced disappearances and extraordinary renditions make clear.[50] At a minimum, where PMSC personnel are co-deployed with state agents in such operations the chances of the resulting conduct being found to be attributable to the state seem likely to rise.[51]

Finally, even if state attribution is established via this route, the resulting state responsibility will be *narrower* than it would be if the PMSC had been formally incorporated into the state's armed forces. This is an important distinction: where the PMSC is an organ of the state or (as discussed below) is exercising governmental authority, state responsibility will arise even for actions undertaken *ultra vires*.[52] Where the PMSC is simply operating under the state's instructions, direction, and control, state responsibility will not extend so far unless those actions are sufficiently closely linked to the instructions the PMSC received.[53]

C. PMSC personnel are empowered by law to exercise governmental authority

The central regulatory problem presented by the legal analysis above is that it may actually give states a positive incentive *not* to exert close control or oversight of PMSCs' conduct, especially outside their territory. States that *do* exercise such oversight are more likely to be saddled with responsibility for PMSCs' misconduct. The danger is that this undermines the effective implementation of international law, by encouraging states not simply to avoid responsibility but actually to act irresponsibly. Accordingly, many analysts ask whether there is any other basis for holding states to account for the conduct of PMSCs, regardless of the level of oversight states in fact exert—or in a manner that encourages them to exert effective oversight. The first possibility lies in the concept of 'governmental authority'.

Article 5 of the *ILC Articles* on State Responsibility indicates that the conduct of a person 'empowered by the law' of a state 'to exercise elements of the governmental authority' of that state is attributable to the state, providing the conduct is performed while the person is acting in that capacity—regardless of the instructions, direction, and control provided by the state. This begs two questions: what

---

[49] D. Filkins and M. Mazzetti, 'Contractors Tied to Efforts to Track and Kill Militants', *New York Times*, 14 March 2010.

[50] See *Mohamed v Jeppesen Dataplan, Inc*, 579 F.3d 942 (9th Cir 2009).

[51] In some of these cases there may also be a question whether state responsibility might arise via Art 11, involving state acknowledgment and adoption of conduct. See also the '*Tehran Hostages*' case, ICJ, *United States Diplomatic and Consular Staff in Iran (USA v Iran)*, Judgment, 24 May 1980, 3.

[52] See ILC Articles, Art 7.   [53] ILC Articles, Commentaries, 108.

is 'the law' of a state, and what are 'elements of the governmental authority' of that state?

On the first point, the Commentaries on the *ILC Articles* suggest that a state attracts responsibility for the conduct of entities empowered 'by domestic legislation' to exercise governmental powers.[54] Presumably legislation can include secondary or delegated legislation, such as the Federal Acquisition Regulations and Defence Federal Acquisition Regulation Supplement, which provide the legal basis for much US government contracting with PMSCs. During the preparation of the Montreux Document, some states even suggested that a contract, per se, even absent any underpinning 'legislation' could qualify as 'the law' of a state empowering a contractor to exercise elements of the governmental authority—though this clearly does not qualify as a consensus view.

The second point—what constitutes 'governmental authority'—is even less settled as a matter of law. The Commentaries to the *ILC Articles* suggest that private security firms acting as prison guards, exercising public powers of detention and discipline pursuant to a judicial sentence or prison regulations, are exercising 'governmental authority'. Likewise, they suggest that a private airline exercising delegated immigration or quarantine control powers will be engaged in conduct attributable to the delegating state.[55] During the preparation of the Montreux Document, some experts suggested that since IHL requires the administration of PoW and certain detainee camps to be placed under the authority of a state official, the administration of those camps—and everything that occurred within them— necessarily implicates the exercise of governmental authority. Others argued by analogy that since IHL likewise limits the right to directly participate in hostilities to the members of state armed forces, authorized direct participation in hostilities necessarily involves an exercise of governmental authority[56]—suggesting that all PMSC personnel authorized by a state to directly participate in hostilities on any basis other than self-defence will engage the state's responsibility for their conduct while so doing.

---

[54] See Commentaries to the ILC Articles, para 7 of Commentary on Art 5. See also M. Spinedi (n 34), 277.

[55] ILC Articles, Commentaries, 92.

[56] A view reinforced by the position under US law, which prohibits contracted PMSCs directly participating in hostilities except in certain self-defence related cases: see US Federal Acquisition Regulation 52.225-19, Contractor Personnel in a Designated Operational Area or Supporting a Diplomatic or Consular Mission Outside the United States (March 2008); and US Department of Defense Instruction 3020.41, 3 October 2005, in Federal Register, vol 73, no 40, 28 February 2008, Rules and Regulations, 10943. For the position in the United Kingdom see Ninth Report of the Foreign Affairs Committee, Session 2001–02, Private Military Companies, para 108 and recommendation (k). A 31 January 1997 contract between the PMSC Sandline and the Government of Papua New Guinea reflects a similar analysis: it recognized Sandline's contractual right to 'engage and fight hostile forces', but also formally incorporated Sandline personnel into the PNG command structure, in command positions.

That point has been the subject of close scrutiny in the United States.[57] The Obama Administration indicated that it would revise US procurement rules[58] so that any function that requires a person to 'determine, protect, and advance United States [...] interests by military or diplomatic action [...] [or] to significantly affect the life, liberty, or property of private persons' will be considered 'inherently governmental'—though this will 'not normally include [...] building security'.[59] Such 'inherently governmental' functions should usually be performed by US personnel, rather than contractors. While the proposed policy guidance suggests that 'command of military forces, especially the leadership of military personnel who are members of the combat, combat support or combat service support role' would be 'inherently governmental',[60] 'contingency contracting' would not be so considered, unless the functions contractors are asked to perform involve the exercise of discretion which would 'have the effect of committing the government to a course of action'.[61]

These rules provide significant guidance to those seeking to understand how Article 5 of the *ILC Articles* might be applied in cases involving contracting by the US Government, since any functions that fall in the above categories will be considered by US law to be 'inherently governmental'. More difficult, however, are those functions—including many that PMSCs will perform—that entail a 'risk that their performance, if not appropriately managed, may materially limit Federal officials' performance of inherently governmental functions'. Such functions, under the new guidance, come in for increased scrutiny as functions 'closely associated with inherently governmental' functions.[62]

An Appendix to the policy guidance specifically proposes that this category include 'provision of special non-law-enforcement security activities that do not directly involve criminal investigations, such as prisoner detention or transport and non-military national security details'.[63] What remains unclear is whether such functions, 'closely associated with *inherently* governmental functions' (emphasis added) may nevertheless qualify, for the purposes of international law, as 'exercise of the governmental authority'. Unlike Article 4 (on organs of the state), Article 5 of the *ILC Articles* does not clarify whether the term 'governmental authority' is to be

---

[57] For background on the position under US law at the time of writing, see J. Luckey, V.B. Grasso, and K.M. Manuel, 'Inherently Governmental Functions and Department of Defense Operations: Background, Issues, and Options for Congress', Congressional Research Service, CRS R40641, 22 July 2009.

[58] See Office of Management and Budget, 'Work Reserved for Performance by Federal Government Employees', in *Federal Register*, vol 75, no 61, 31 March 2010, 16188–97.

[59] Federal Activities Inventory Reform Act, Public Law 105-270, section 5.

[60] OMB, 'Work Reserved' (n 58), App A, 16196. See also the GAO Decisions B-298370 and B-298490, relating to 'attacks'.

[61] On the latter, see OMB, 'Work Reserved' (n 58), 16190.

[62] OMB, 'Work Reserved' (n 58), 16191.   [63] OMB, 'Work Reserved' (n 58), App B, 16197.

interpreted with reference to domestic law or whether a uniform interpretation may be applicable across different states.[64]

Even in the US Government, there are different views, too, of how 'inherently' governmental PMSCs' functions actually are. Bills presented in US Congress seek to restrict the US Government's ability to outsource some such functions, including security advice and planning (for the government); military and police training; repair and maintenance for weapons systems; prison administration; interrogation; and intelligence.[65] A 2009 Act of Congress has already expressed the sense of Congress that 'security operations for the protection of resources [...] in uncontrolled or unpredictable high-threat environments should ordinarily be performed by members of the Armed Forces'.[66] And the matter was closely debated in the Commission on Wartime Contracting, a special commission established by both Houses of US Congress to investigate US use of PMSCs and recommend policy changes.[67]

Finally, it is worth considering whether peacekeeping functions involve an exercise of 'governmental authority'. Some experts argue that functions carried out within an inter-governmentally-mandated peace support operation are inherently governmental:[68] any PMSC hired by a state to serve as its national military contingent would, following this analysis, be exercising governmental authority, even for acts that would not otherwise involve the exercise of such governmental authority, but which the state contracts the PMSC to perform. Such an analysis draws support from the legal situation of national contingents in a Peace Support Operation (PSO), which are traditionally expected to carry their own law—and disciplinary arrangements—with them.[69] The problem with such an analysis is that, in reality, the few states that do hire PMSC personnel for PSO roles (to date, primarily for policing, Security Sector Reform (SSR) and demining activities) have not necessarily ensured that such *corporate* accountability systems are put in place, but have rather focused on recruiting individual PMSC personnel as civilians.[70] And as recent litigation in

---

[64] The recent draft Convention presented by the UN Working Group on mercenaries moves in the direction of codifying a uniform standard. See UN, 'Report of the Working Group' (n 4).

[65] The *Stop Outsourcing Security Act*, introduce by Rep Jan Schakowsky (D-IL) and Sen Bernie Sanders (I-VT).

[66] Duncan Hunter National Defense Authorization Act for FY2009, Public Law 110-417, sec 831, 18 October 2008.

[67] See the records of the hearings held on 18 June 2010 in Washington DC, available at <http://www.wartimecontracting.gov/index.php/hearings/commission/hearing2010-06-18>.

[68] UCIHL (n 7), 30–2.

[69] See Model Contribution Agreement between the United Nations and Participating State Contributing Resources to the United Nations Peacekeeping Operation, in 'Administrative and Budgetary Aspects of the Financing of United Nations Peacekeeping Operations', UN Doc A/50/995 (1996), Annex, section X; and see 'Observance by United Nations forces of international humanitarian law', UN Doc ST/SGB/1999/13 (1999), section 2.

[70] For example the United States has long contracted a PMSC to identify and recruit qualified police to deploy into UN CIVPOL missions.

Europe and the United Kingdom makes clear, even in the nominally-clearer case of state agents, it remains unclear whether the sending state, the international organization, or the state commanding the force to which an individual is sent will be responsible under international law for any resulting misconduct.[71]

5 States' Positive Obligations to Regulate and Remedy PMSC Conduct

In certain cases, states retain their legal obligations even if they contract PMSCs: irrespective of the individuals or military units in charge of PoWs or civilian internees, for example, the party to an international conflict that holds these detainees remains responsible for them under international law.[72] If detainees are held in conditions that violate standards recognized under IHL—for example because they receive inadequate healthcare or nutrition—the state is responsible for that violation, even if it had delegated oversight of the place of detention to a PMSC.

This points us to another avenue for demanding effective state regulation of PMSC conduct, by states, under international law: states' positive obligations to regulate and remedy PMSC conduct. Some of these obligations are made explicit by international humanitarian law, and relate to the expectation that parties to a conflict that control territory or populations will provide for their well-being. Occupying Powers, for example, have the obligation to 'take all measures in [their] power to restore, and ensure, as far as possible, public order and safety [...]',[73] which seems to entail an obligation effectively to regulate private actors. In certain cases, international law takes this principle even further, explicitly prohibiting states from contracting out certain activities—such as the overall supervision of a Prisoner of War camp.[74]

At a more general level, states are obliged by international humanitarian law to: (1) take measures to prevent and put an end to violations of IHL committed by the personnel of PMSCs through appropriate means, such as military regulations,

---

[71] *Behrami and Behrami v France and Saramati v France, Germany and Norway*, European Court of Human Rights Grand Chamber, Decision on Admissibility (31 May 2007); *R (Al-Jedda) v Secretary of State for Defence (JUSTICE and another intervening)* [2007] UKHL 58; *Al-Jedda v United Kingdom*, European Court of Human Rights, 7 July 2011.

[72] See Art 12 of GC III, Art 29 of GC IV.

[73] Article 43 of the Hague Regulations.

[74] Article 39 of GC III. See also Arts 51, 52 of the Hague Regulations; Arts 120(2), 121 of GC III, Arts 99, 129(2), 131 of GC IV.

administrative orders, disciplinary and judicial sanctions; (2) not encourage or assist any violations of IHL committed by PMSC personnel; and (3) disseminate IHL and ensure awareness of it amongst PMSC personnel.[75] These obligations flow from Article 1 common to the Geneva Conventions and Protocol I, which stipulates that '[t]he High Contracting Parties undertake to respect and to ensure respect [for these instruments] in all circumstances', as well as from Article 43 of the Hague Regulations (reflecting customary international law)[76] and Article 91 of AP I.[77] The view of the delegate of the United States to the Diplomatic Conference in Geneva in 1949 that crafted Common Article 1 is instructive. He described the 'object of [Common Article 1 as being] to ensure respect of the Conventions by the population as a whole'.[78] This will extend to controlling commercial actors—even if they are working for private clients.[79]

Specific obligations of IHL dissemination and training also flow from other specific provisions of IHL: for example where PMSC personnel are integrated into a state's armed forces, a commander is obliged to ensure they are aware of their obligations under the Geneva Conventions and Additional Protocol I (if the latter is applicable).[80] Significantly, given recent abuses in Iraq and Afghanistan, authorities controlling places of detention have similar obligations.[81] Such training can be provided by a client state, or by the PMSC itself.[82]

State obligations of due diligence and prevention also arise from a variety of human rights norms.[83] Exactly how those obligations relate to states' regulation of commercial actors has been a subject addressed by the Special Representative of the Secretary-General of the United Nations on human rights and transnational corporations and other business enterprises, Professor John Ruggie. Ruggie's conceptual framework, differentiating between the state 'Duty to Protect', the corporate 'Responsibility to Respect' and a shared obligation of providing effective 'Access to Remedy' was unanimously endorsed by the UN Human Rights Council in 2008.[84] In his work to

[75] See especially the Montreux Document (n 4), 4. See further Gillard (n 13), 551–3; and Hoppe (n 7), 993–1005. Compare UCIHL (n 7).

[76] See eg *DRC v Uganda* (n 43), § 84, in which the ICJ found Uganda responsible for its 'lack of vigilance in preventing the violation of human rights and international humanitarian law' by third parties in DRC territory it was occupying.

[77] '[...] responsibility is incurred if the Party to the conflict has not acted with due diligence to prevent such acts from taking place, or to ensure their repression once they have taken place.' Commentary AP I and II, para 3660.

[78] Final Record of the Diplomatic Conference of Geneva, vol III, Ninth Meeting, 25 May 1949, 39.

[79] Compare Hoppe (n 7), 993.   [80] Article 87(2) of AP I.

[81] Articles 39, 127 of GC III; Art 144(2) of GC IV.   [82] Gillard (n 13), 552.

[83] Hoppe (n 7), 998–1005.

[84] See United Nations Human Rights Council, *Business and Human Rights: Mapping International Standards of Responsibility and Accountability for Corporate Acts*, Report of the Special Representative of the Secretary-General on the Issue of Human Rights and Transnational Corporations and other Business Enterprises, John Ruggie, UN Doc A/HRC/4/35 (2007); and Human Rights Council, *Protect, Respect and Remedy: A Framework for Business and Human Rights*, UN Doc A/HRC/8/5, 7 April 2008.

'operationalize' what has now become known as the UN Framework on Business and Human Rights, Ruggie has highlighted the importance of states making greater efforts to prevent and redress human rights abuses occurring in conflict affected areas, as well as the need for corporate actors to respect the principles of IHL (in addition to international human rights law) when they operate in such situations.[85] The resulting UN Guiding Principles on Business and Human Rights were unanimously endorsed by the UN Human Rights Council in 2011.[86]

The UN Guiding Principles provide guidance on global standards for state efforts to prevent corporate abuses of human rights from even occurring. They set out a variety of steps that states ought to take to prevent such violations, such as working with companies operating in conflict-affected zones to identify human rights risks and help them mitigate them.[87] Both the Montreux Document, and the related International Code of Conduct for Private Security Service Providers, can be understood as an effort by states to work with the PMSC industry (and in the latter case, civil society actors), to build frameworks for effectively discharging these obligations. Still, as I explain further below, there may be weaknesses in such a claim.

The development of the UN Framework has also helped to remind states of their earlier commitments to provide access to effective remedies for violations of IHL and human rights by third parties, including commercial actors. Under customary international law, a state has an independent obligation to provide compensation for 'all acts committed by persons forming part of its armed forces' during armed conflict.[88] Accordingly, if as discussed above, a certain PMSC unit forms part of the armed forces of a state because it is an organized armed group under a command responsible to a state—even if it has not formally been incorporated into those armed forces—a state will be obliged to provide compensation for its wrongful acts.

Where this is not the case, states nonetheless have an independent duty to protect people *on their territory or within their jurisdiction* by providing access to effective remedies.[89] This can include providing victims access to judicial or administrative

---

[85] Human Rights Council, *Business and Human Rights: Further Steps Towards the Operationalization of the 'Protect, Respect and Remedy Framework'*, UN Doc A/HRC/14/27, 9 April 2010, paras 44–7, 61.

[86] Human Rights Council, UN Doc A/HRC/RES/17/4, 16 June 2011. The Guiding Principles themselves are contained in an Annex to UN Doc A/HRC/17/31, 21 March 2011.

[87] UN Guiding Principles, Guiding Principle 7.

[88] See Art 3 of the Hague Convention IV of 1907; Art 131 of GC III; Art 148 of GC IV; Art 91 of AP I. See also Customary Law Study (n 14), Rule 150, 537–50; UN Basic Principles and Guidelines on the Right to a Remedy and Reparation for Victims of Gross Violations of International Human Rights Law and Serious Violations of International Humanitarian Law, UN General Assembly Resolution A/RES/60/147, 16 December 2005; *DRC v Uganda* (n 43), §§ 214–50. But see also the *Dissenting Opinion of Judge ad hoc Kateka*, §§ 50–3, in which he argued that Ugandan responsibility for UPDF soldiers should not follow, because the acts in question were committed by those soldiers 'in their private capacity'.

[89] UN Guiding Principles (n 86); Art 2(3) of ICCPR; Art 13 of ECHR; Art 25 of ACHR; Art 6 of CERD; Art 13 of CAT; Art 39 of CRC; UN Basic Principles and Guidelines on the Right to a Remedy and Reparation for Victims of Gross Violations of International Human Rights Law and Serious

mechanisms that are expeditious, fair, inexpensive, and accessible;[90] ensuring those responsible make adequate restitution or otherwise support victims of the worst abuse with compensation themselves;[91] and providing victims access to material, medical, psychological, and social assistance.[92] Where the violation in question involved is a grave breach of the Geneva Convention, there is, additionally, a state obligation to provide a *penal* sanction.[93]

6 ARE STATES THE PROBLEM?

Many commentators in recent years have suggested that the key to effective enforcement of international law on and by PMSCs on the battlefield lies with state regulation at the national level.[94] The great challenge, though, lies not in articulating these standards, but in identifying which states must discharge them in which cases—and ensuring they have the capacity and will so to do. Territorial states and Occupying Powers will, by the nature of armed conflict, have limited (though meaningful) capacity to provide such remedies, and to take the preventive measures of dissemination, due diligence, and public order control discussed earlier. Contracting states

Violations of International Humanitarian Law, UN General Assembly Resolution A/RES/60/147, 16 December 2005; Principles on Remedy and Fair Trial of the African Commission on Human and People's Rights. See also UN Human Rights Committee, General Comment 29 on Derogations during a State of Emergency, UN Doc CCPR/C/21/Rev.1/Add.11, 31 August 2001, para 14.

[90] UN Declaration of Basic Principles of Justice for Victims of Crimes and Abuse of Power, UN General Assembly resolution 40/39, 29 November 1985, Principle 5. See also UN Guiding Principles (n 86), Guiding Principle 31; and Montreux Document (n 4), 8, para 9.

[91] UN Declaration of Basic Principles (n 90), Principles 8 and 12. The obligation to make reparations is most clear cut where the conduct of PMSC personnel gives rise to direct state responsibility.

[92] UN Declaration of Basic Principles (n 90), Principle 14. The right of individuals to reparation for breaches of IHL may also be implied by the decision of the ICJ in the *Wall* case (n 43), which suggested that Israel was obliged to restore confiscated lands to those from whom they had been confiscated: at paras 153, 163. But see Commentary GC III, 603 and 630, suggesting that under Art 131 of GC III individual claims are superseded by peace agreements and war reparations arrangements; though see Commentary AP I and II (n 77), paras 3656-7, pointing in a contrary direction under Art 91 of AP I. Consider also *Burger-Fischer v Degussa AG*, United States District Court for the District of New Jersey, 65 F.Supp.2d 248, 278 (September 1999), in which the court dismissed a World War II reparations claim on the basis that it had been subsumed by the treaty ending World War II.

[93] The rule is best established in relation to a state's nationals or those on its territory: see Customary Law Study (n 14), Rule 158.

[94] See C. Holmqvist, *Private Security Companies: The Case for Regulation*, SIPRI Policy Paper No 9, January 2005, Stockholm; F. Schreier and M. Caparini, *Privatising Security: Law, Practice and Governance of Private Military and Security Companies*, DCAF, Geneva, 2005; Cockayne et al (n 19).

also have leverage, yet often fail to use it. States' obligation to ensure respect for international law is one of *due diligence*, not *result*: the state must only take all reasonable measures that can be expected from it in the given circumstances to prevent and repress violations. It turns out that what *is* at present expected of states (distinct from what *might be* expected in future) is arguably quite low, given the legal and political obstacles to effective regulation of transnational commercial actors—and especially those facing effective regulation of PMSCs.

There are a number of obstacles to effective regulation of PMSCs by states. The first of these is in determining exactly what body of law applies to any given situation in which a PMSC operates, especially as a result of the interaction between international humanitarian and human rights law. Recent jurisprudence strongly suggests that both IHL and human rights norms apply 'on the battlefield'.[95] But the nature of contemporary conflicts and the way that PMSCs are employed means that it will not always be easy to determine whether they are, in fact, operating 'on the battlefield'—in the sense that it may not be clear whether international humanitarian law applies.

The ICTY has long held that '[a]n armed conflict exists whenever there is a resort to armed force between States or protracted armed violence between governmental authorities and organized armed groups or between such groups within a State'.[96] IHL does not apply to situations of internal disturbances and tensions, such as riots, isolated and sporadic acts of violence, or other acts of a similar nature.[97] Yet this leaves unaffected by IHL many situations of protracted violence between non-state elements, especially within one state's borders, which are not necessarily recognized as constituting 'armed conflict', but in which private and state clients have engaged PMSCs to provide security such as in Nigeria, Mexico, parts of the Balkans and parts of South-East Asia.[98] And it also leaves unclear situations where an armed group (such as Al Qaida) engages in protracted violence, but not clearly on behalf of (or attributable to) any state.

Should the use of a PMSC in cross-border operations to tackle these groups be governed by IHL standards (such as the right to target legitimate military targets for execution) or by human rights standards (which might prohibit such killings as

---

[95] See the *Wall* case (n 43), §§ 106–13; and *DRC v Uganda* (n 43), § 216. See also Principle 1 of the UN General Principles on the Effective Prevention and Investigation of Extra-Legal, Arbitrary and Summary Executions, recommended by Economic and Social Council Resolution 1989/65 of 24 May 1989.

[96] *Prosecutor v Tadić*, Case No IT-94-1, Decision on the Defence Motion for Interlocutory Appeal on Jurisdiction, ICTY (2 October 1995), §§ 67–70.

[97] See also ICC Statute Art 8(2)(d). For a review of jurisprudence on these points, see *Prosecutor v Limaj*, Case No IT-04-84-T, Judgment (Trial Chamber), ICTY (30 November 2005), §§ 83–92.

[98] See generally R. Geiss, 'Armed Violence in Fragile States: Low-Intensity Conflicts, Spillover Conflicts, and Sporadic Law Enforcement Operations by Third Parties', 91 *International Review of the Red Cross* (2009) 127–42; S. Vité, 'Typology of Armed Conflicts in International Humanitarian Law: Legal Concepts and Actual Situations', 91 *International Review of the Red Cross* (2009) 69–94.

extra-territorial executions)?[99] The answer to these questions will affect the status of contractors, conduct of hostilities, and state regulatory duties. And the absence of legal clarity undermines effective forward planning and even the pricing of services and insurance, given the inability to quantify accurately corporate and state liability and risk exposure.

Similarly, as Cameron points out, a security guard in a conflict zone confronted by a hostile attack will likely be unaware, at the time, whether the attack they are repelling is a military operation (in which case the guard most likely engages in direct participation in hostilities by repelling the attack), or merely a criminal offensive (in which case their response will likely not constitute direct participation in hostilities).[100]

The larger regulatory challenge, therefore, is in moving from the *ex post* case-by-case characterization required by international law to a more certain basis for *ex ante* planning, control, and regulation by states. This is made particularly difficult by the fluid nature of military operations, which can rapidly alter the context in which PMSC personnel are working, exposing them to attack,[101] and especially by the rapid geographic expansion of the battlefield as a result of networked information and communication technologies. Private contractors now undertake aspects of war-fighting that were traditionally considered central to direct participation in hostilities—such as the selection of targets, the direction and movement of military assets, loading and operating weapons systems, or their maintenance—far from the battlefield.[102] Given such actions may be carried out remotely, perhaps even in a location not under the territorial control of one of the parties to the armed conflict, the application of IHL to such contractors is frequently unclear.

In the absence of bright-line parameters setting out, *ex ante*, where and when IHL begins and ends and where and when direct participation in hostilities begins and ends, activists and decision-makers are increasingly looking not to IHL, but to human rights law as a universally applicable source of substantive standards by which to guide PMSC conduct. This is, for example, the approach taken by the recent International Code of Conduct, organized by the Swiss Government and signed by over 700 PMSCs.[103]

Some of the key human rights questions around contractor conduct relate to protections of the right to life and rights in detention (especially torture), on which

[99] On this point, see United Nations Human Rights Council, Report of the Special Rapporteur on extrajudicial, summary or arbitrary executions, Philip Alston, UN Doc A/HRC/14/24/Add.6, 28 May 2010. See also M.E. O'Connell, 'Defining Armed Conflict', 13 *Journal of Conflict and Security Law* (2008) 393–400; A. Paulus and M. Vashakmadze, 'Asymmetrical War and the Notion of Armed Conflict—An Attempt at a Conceptualization', 91 *International Review of the Red Cross* (2009) 95–120.

[100] Cameron, 'Private Military Companies' (n 12), 589–90.

[101] Cameron, 'International Humanitarian Law' (n 12), 8–9.

[102] Heaton, 'Civilians at War' (n 20).

[103] International Code of Conduct for Private Security Service Providers, 9 November 2010, available at <http://www.icoc-psp.org>.

there is significant coherence between the norms provided by IHL and human rights. For example, the state's duty to ensure respect for IHL is mirrored by a separate duty under human rights law, to take appropriate measures to prevent, investigate, and provide effective remedies for the harmed caused by certain conduct of PMSCs and their personnel—at least where it violates certain human rights, such as the right to life.[104] Yet this does not entirely clarify the basis for any state regulation of PMSCs, because the extra-territoriality of states' human rights obligations remains uncertain. And on key issues—such as targeting—IHL and human rights law in fact operate from fundamentally diverging premises.

The transnational organization and operation of much PMSC activity challenges the territorial basis of jurisdiction in the international legal order. International law has always operated from the presumption of effective sovereignty: a preference for the regulatory primacy of territorial states. But it is precisely because territorial states lack effective regulatory capacity that PMSCs are often employed. And even strong sending states' regulatory capacity is relatively weakened by the transnational nature of these PMSCs.

Increasingly, there is a push to recognize that effective regulation will depend on a coordinated push by all three types of states—home, hiring, and host states— each of which will have different duties to discharge in ensuring respect for IHL and discharging its duty to protect human rights.[105] The UN Guiding Principles on Business and Human Rights also recognize a role for all involved states within the bounds of what is permitted, if not required, by international human rights law.[106] And the Montreux Document seeks to clarify the administrative practices that each of these states might employ to discharge these common but differentiated responsibilities.

Yet the coordinated regulatory approach envisaged by the Montreux Document remains aspirational. The practices it identifies are, in their own terms, 'Good Practices'—they are by no means standard state practice. In reality the implementation of international obligations by states with regard to PMSCs runs up against a series of political and institutional obstacles.[107] The first of these is that many states have strong incentives to keep their oversight of PMSCs weak, not only to reduce the likelihood of attribution of PMSC conduct to the state (as discussed above), but also to reduce the applicability of positive obligations under human rights law, and

---

[104] See for instance UN Human Rights Committee, General Comment No 31 on the Nature of the General Legal Obligation Imposed on States Parties to the Covenant, 26 May 2004, CCPR/C/21/Rev.1/Add.13, para 8; European Court of Human Rights, *X and Y v The Netherlands*, Judgment of 26 March 1985, § 27; Inter-American Court of Human Rights, *Velázquez Rodríguez v Honduras*, Judgment of 29 July 1988, § 74. Specifically on the right to life, see UN Human Rights Committee, General Comment No 6 on the Right to Life (Art 6), 20 April 1982, § 3; European Court of Human Rights, *Osman v UK*, Judgment of 28 October 1998, §§ 115ff.

[105] See further the discussion in Gillard (n 13).   [106] See UN Guiding Principles (n 86).

[107] See Cockayne (n 19). See also Human Rights First (n 5), 23–31 for an examination of the weaknesses in US regulation in 2008.

to maximize states' room to manoeuvre. By engaging PMSCs, states gain plausible deniability and can even circumvent some internal political and policy restrictions they may face, such as, in the United States, congressional limits on the deployment of national troops to specific combat zones.[108] For that reason it seems unlikely that states will, as some authors advocate, simply incorporate privatized 'battlegroups' into national military structures,[109] returning to the system of private commissions by which states raised armed forces in an earlier period.

States have only recently begun to invest seriously in the development of the extra-territorial oversight capacity needed to manage effectively the conduct of PMSCs they hire for off-shore tasks—though the primary motivation has been less to discharge their international obligations than to protect themselves against fraudulent billing and the unintended political, diplomatic, and military consequences of ineffective off-shore oversight. States including the United States, Australia, and South Africa have all adopted laws in the last decade that assert criminal jurisdiction in certain cases over PMSC conduct outside their territory.[110]

Yet criminal investigations and prosecutions, such as the prosecution of two Blackwater guards in January 2010 for homicides in Afghanistan,[111] or the settlement of a case against Mark Thatcher for violating the South African law prohibiting involvement in mercenarism,[112] are the exception, not the rule. Absent any specific political incentive to mount an extra-territorial investigation—usually present only where there has been a major, well-documented atrocity such as the killing of 16 civilians in Nisoor Square in Baghdad in September 2007—home and hiring state investigators and prosecutors have little incentive to take on the challenge of a long, complex case that will pay few dividends at home, and in fact may be seen as a distraction from more immediate local concerns. And as the collapse of most of the US prosecutions in the *Nisoor Square* case makes clear, even where they do choose to take such a case on, investigators face major obstacles to obtaining relevant evidence from abroad, often in insecure locations, and subject to serious national security and commercial confidentiality restrictions.[113]

[108] Cameron, 'International Humanitarian Law' (n 12), 5. See further D. Avant. *The Market for Force* (Cambridge: Cambridge University Press, 2005).

[109] See eg J.K. Wither, 'European Security and Private Military Companies: The Prospects for Privatized "Battlegroups"', 4 *The Quarterly Journal* (2005) 107–26.

[110] See especially the 2000 Military Extraterritorial Jurisdiction Act and provisions in the 2007 Department of Defense Budget Authorization Act—National Defense Authorization Act for Fiscal Year 2007, section 552.

[111] See Indictment, *US v Cannon*, No 2:10cr 1, 2010 WL 28529 (ED Va 6 January 2010). See also US DOJ, 'Two Individuals Charged with Murder and Other Offenses Related to Shooting Death of Two Afghan Nationals in Kabul, Afghanistan', 7 January 2010, available at <http://washingtondc.fbi.gov/dojpressrel/pressrel10/wf0010710.htm>.

[112] BBC, 'Thatcher fined over "coup plot"', *BBC News*, 13 January 2005, <http://news.bbc.co.uk/2/hi/africa/4169557.stm>.

[113] See in particular the dismissal of the charges against six former Blackwater guards charged in relation to the homicides in Nisoor Square in Baghdad in 2007, in *US v Paul A. Slough et al*, US District

Given these realities, it seems unlikely that states will provide 'the answer' to the problems of ensuring respect by PMSCs for international law in armed conflict—and on occasion they may even exacerbate some of the underlying problems. Reaching these conclusions, numerous commentators—and even some within the industry—have called for a system of effective international oversight and monitoring. It remains unclear, though, how any such system could be developed and its access to the information required for effective oversight ensured, absent state consent and support.[114] The UN Working Group on mercenaries has drafted a convention that proposes a complex system of international licensing, reporting, and oversight,[115] but the lack of enthusiasm for this text amongst the PMSC industry and most of the states in which PMSCs are based suggests that the conclusion of such a Convention is unlikely any time soon. Instead, others are increasingly looking to alternative mechanisms for enforcing international law—including through its indirect application to and by PMSCs themselves.

7 THE APPLICATION OF INTERNATIONAL LAW TO AND BY PMSCS AND THEIR PERSONNEL

States might be expected to enforce IHL in their dealings with PMSCs over the long term, in part because it is in their interest to maintain IHL as an effective body of law with clear and workable arrangements, for example protecting the principle of distinction and the reciprocity it is motivated by. But the analysis above suggests that states are unlikely soon to radically alter their *laissez faire* approach to PMSCs' implementation of international law in armed conflict. The proliferation of non-state clients for PMSCs, including local actors, humanitarian organizations, and international agencies[116] also suggests that additional mechanisms may be needed that can ensure respect for international law outside a state-managed command and

Court for the District of Columbia, Criminal Action No 08-0630 (RMU), Memorandum Opinion, 31 December 2009.

[114] Though see the discussion of initiatives in similar industries in Cockayne et al (n 19). Both the UN Working Group and other UN Special Rapporteurs continue to play a key watchdog role highlighting industry misconduct: see eg Alston (n 99), and see Report of the Special Rapporteur on the question of torture, Theo van Boven, 15 December 2004, UN Doc E/CN.4/2005/62, para 37(h).

[115] See 'Report of the Working Group' (n 4). For background on the earlier treatment of these issues by the UN Human Rights Commission, see International Alert, 'The Mercenary Issue at the UN Commission on Human Rights: The Need for a New Approach', January 2001.

[116] See generally J. Cockayne, *Commercial Security in Humanitarian and Post-Conflict Settings: An Exploratory Study* (New York: International Peace Academy, 2006).

control structure. For this reason, some commentators suggest applying international law directly to PMSCs and their personnel—and having PMSCs implement international law norms and standards themselves.

A. Indirect enforcement of international law against PMSCs and their personnel

International law is generally understood as applying to states, not to individuals or companies. But the international law of armed conflict has always taken a somewhat different route, treating some non-state belligerents as both subjects and objects of the law. While some debate continues as to whether customary international humanitarian law has direct applicability to all individuals finding themselves in situations of armed conflict,[117] there is in fact substantial precedent suggesting that private individuals with a factual connection to parties to a conflict far *weaker* than a contractual connection will have direct obligations under international law.[118] The more difficult question remains whether private contractors working for private clients in situations of armed conflict attract liability.[119]

Some precedents suggest they may, so long as the conduct itself reflects the requisite 'nexus' to the armed conflict—which is to say that it was not merely a domestic criminal act, but motivated or facilitated by the armed conflict.[120] But a more satisfactory answer may be that the question is too narrowly cast: the question, increasingly, for PMSC personnel is not simply whether they are exposed to criminal liability for violations of IHL during situations of armed conflict, but whether they are exposed to criminal *or civil* liability for violations of international humanitarian *or human rights* law *in any situation*. Indeed, it falls to state judicial actors—rather than to general international law or international criminal law—to determine the modalities of liability and procedure that attach to violation of international norms. It is up to states to determine the elements of liability, for example relating to the level of knowledge and notice a corporation must enjoy of a violation of international law before it can be held liable for the harms resulting from that violation.[121]

---

[117] See especially C. Lehnardt, 'Individual Liability of Private Military Personnel under International Criminal Law', 19 *European Journal of International Law* (2008) 1015–34 at 1018–19. See also E. David, *Principes de droit des conflits armés* (3rd edn, Brussels: Bruylant, 2002), §§ 1.195, 4.65.

[118] See eg International Military Tribunal, *US v Krauch and 22 others (I G Farben* case), 10 L Reps of Trials of War Criminals (1947) 1; ICTR, *Prosecutor v Musema*, ICTR-96-13, Judgment, 27 January 2000. In the *Musema* case, the ICTR convicted a tea factory director on the basis of both actual perpetration and superior responsibility for the acts of his subordinates.

[119] See Lehnardt (n 117), 1019.   [120] See Lehnardt (n 117), 1020–1.

[121] For discussion of the extensive US litigation on this point, drawing on the jurisprudence of the international criminal tribunals, see K. Gallagher, 'Civil Litigation and Transnational Business: An Alien Tort Statute Primer', 8 *Journal of International Criminal Justice* (2010) 745–67 at 761–6. On

There is no doubt that standards of both conduct and liability are the most clearly established in the area of individual criminal liability for violations of IHL, thanks in no small part to the work of numerous international criminal tribunals in the last two decades. But increasingly, those standards are migrating into domestic and international civil litigation, giving rise to a thickening jurisprudence dealing with private actors' conduct in the kinds of insecure situations in which PMSCs operate, even if it falls short of open armed conflict. This involves figuring out a range of modes of liability (national and international, civil and criminal, individual and collective) for violation of a variety of primary rules of international law (humanitarian law, human rights law, international crimes). PMSC personnel's conduct may, for example, constitute a crime against humanity attracting individual criminal liability—even if it is not a 'war crime' per se—which might entail individual *and* state responsibility.[122] Such distinctions are indeed now becoming the basis for private litigation.[123]

Access to remedies varies enormously across different jurisdictions. This variance has given rise to a patchwork of different approaches for determining the ancillary or collective responsibility of non-state armed groups, their managers, their state handlers, and their financiers. Some conduct violating international norms may result less from the actions of specific individuals than from the conduct of a group or collectivity, or even a common enterprise amongst a network of enablers; it may, in those circumstances, be appropriate to attach liability to the group or enterprise, rather than any specific individual. And victims may prefer to attach such liability to the group, where it controls assets from which they may be compensated. Moreover, civil litigation may hold out a greater prospect of success than criminal prosecution, given it usually entails a lower standard of proof.[124] As a general rule, however, corporate actors are not directly responsible under international law—unless national-level rules make them so responsible.[125]

Much will depend on the exact circumstances of the relationship between PMSC personnel and their clients. Not only state personnel, but also civilian managers and corporate directors may in certain cases face superior responsibility for the acts of their contractors.[126] *De facto* controls, such as the ability to issue instructions that are routinely implemented, or report violations to responsible authorities, will be

corporate complicity, see generally International Commission of Jurists, *Corporate Complicity and Legal Accountability*, vols I, II, and III (Geneva, 2008).

[122] Gallagher (n 121), 1021–2.

[123] See *Genocide Victims of Krajina v L-3 Communications Corpn and MPRI, Inc*, Civil Case filed 17 August 2010 in the United States District Court Northern District of Illinois, Eastern Division.

[124] See further Gillard (n 13), 546–7.

[125] See generally A. Clapham, *Human Rights Obligations of Non-State Actors* (Oxford: Oxford University Press, 2006). For an overview of litigation under the US Alien Tort Statute, see Gallagher (n 121).

[126] For further discussion, see Lehnardt (n 117), 1025–7.

central to determining whether a specific individual enjoyed the form of authority and control necessary to underpin such a finding of individual superior responsibility.[127] Such civilian superior responsibility is well established for conduct that violates IHL, and has also been held to arise in some cases of conduct that violates other peremptory norms.[128]

Another key factor in such situations will frequently be access to information—whether specific individuals or corporate officers had knowledge, awareness, or notice of information that suggested the existence or risk of a violation of the standard in question. Here, corporate culture, information-sharing arrangements, and internal disciplinary arrangements may become crucial in a determination of liability. As Chia Lehnardt has pointed out, it may in fact be easier to establish knowledge and control in PMSCs than in other kinds of corporate entities, given the military nature of many PMSCs' operations, structures, and cultures.[129] And as Hans Vest has pointed out, those businesses that are typically surrounded by greater risks— such as PMSCs—may expect more often to be held by courts to bear responsibility for positive obligations of prevention and due diligence.[130]

Indeed, recent US litigation suggests that while 'conspiracy' will only rarely be recognized as an internationally wrongful act,[131] it may be treated as a distinct mode of liability that attaches to other internationally wrongful acts.[132] PMSCs might expect enlarged exposure to liability as a result—even where they were acting in close concert with state actors and might, previously, have expected *de facto* if not *de jure* immunity from liability for violation of international law. In *Arias v Dyncorp*, a US District Court held that a PMSC could be found responsible for harms caused by aerial fumigation when acting 'under color of law', by wilfully participating in joint activity with state actors.[133] Similarly, in the Netherlands, two businessmen have been convicted for complicity in international crimes.[134] And at the international level, PMSC personnel's knowledge of and contribution to their

[127] See Lehnardt (n 117), 1027. See also Customary Law Study (n 14), vol I, *Rules*, Rule 153, and vol II, *Practice*, Part 2, 3733ff.

[128] See eg Committee against Torture, *General Comment 2 on Implementation of article 2 by States Parties*, UN Doc CAT/C/GC/CRP.1/Rev.4, 23 November 2007, para 26; and see *Hilao v Estate of Marcos*, 103 F.3d 767, 776 to 778 (9th Cir 1996). See also Art 6 of the International Convention for the Protection of All Persons from Enforced Disappearance, UNGA Res 61/177, UN Doc A/RES/61/177 (2006), adopted 20 December 2006, which may be particularly relevant in cases of so-called 'extraordinary rendition'.

[129] Lehnardt (n 117), 1026.

[130] See H. Vest, 'Business Leaders and the Modes of Individual Criminal Responsibility under International Law', 8 *Journal of International Criminal Justice* (2010) 851–72 at 871–2.

[131] See *Hamdan v Rumsfeld*, 548 US 557, 610 (2006), in which the US Supreme Court limited 'conspiracy' as a crime under international law to conspiracy to commit genocide or wage aggressive war.

[132] See *Hamdan v Rumsfeld*, 548 US 611, note 40. See further Gallagher (n 121), 761, note 68.

[133] 517 F.Supp.2d 221, 227–8 (DDC, 2007).

[134] The cases relate to the activities of Frans van Anraat and Guus Kouwenhoven. For an overview, see W. Huisman and E. van Sliedregt, 'Rogue Traders: Dutch Businessmen, International Crimes and Corporate Complicity', 8 *Journal of International Criminal Justice* (2010) 803–28.

partners' criminal activities may also expose them to liability under the doctrines of 'joint criminal enterprise' (as developed in the ad hoc tribunals and picked up in US case law), or 'co-perpetration' (as being developed by the International Criminal Court).[135]

Still, such indirect enforcement of international law faces numerous obstacles. Beyond the very serious practical considerations (victims' lack of access to funds, their lack of access to lawyers and courts in the PMSC's home jurisdiction, the difficulties private litigants face in gathering evidence in a conflict-affected zone, the asymmetry of plaintiff and defendant resources), there are also serious legal obstacles to success. In certain cases, PMSCs and their personnel may be shielded from liability for unlawful conduct because of statutory or conventional provisions adopted to protect them from suit.[136] And traditional doctrines of state secrecy and domestic and foreign sovereign immunity may also create obstacles.

State secrecy will be a particular obstacle in cases involving litigation in the courts of a country whose executive was the contracting party. For example in September 2010 a US Federal Appeals Court held that the 'state secrets' doctrine barred civil litigation against a Boeing subsidiary for alleged participation in 'extraordinary renditions'.[137]

Sovereign immunity will likewise be a potential obstacle to indirect judicial enforcement of international law at the national level. In the United States, two duelling lines of authority on sovereign immunity are currently making their way through the courts towards the Supreme Court. These may have major implications for the exposure of the PMSC industry to private litigation in the United States for violations of international law conducted overseas.

In *Saleh v Titan Corpn*, the US Court of Appeals for the District of Columbia Circuit held that a company that supplied interpreters and translators who participated in abusive interrogations at the Abu Ghraib prison in Iraq was immune from suit as a matter of US tort law, because as a contractor 'integrated into combatant activities over which the [US] military retains its command authority' it was entitled to immunity from suit in tort before a US court due to a pre-emption for suits arising out of combatant activities.[138] It held that '[d]uring wartime, where a private service contractor is integrated into combatant activities over which the military retains its command authority, a tort claim arising out of the contractor's

---

[135] But see the discussion in Vest (n 130), 868–9, suggesting that it may prove difficult to discharge the evidentiary burden associated with the ICC's 'co-perpetration' doctrine in business-related cases. See also N. Farrell, 'Attributing Criminal Liability to Corporate Actors: Some Lessons from the International Tribunals', 8 *Journal of International Criminal Justice* (2010) 873–94, at 878–81.

[136] See eg Coalition Provisional Authority Order No 17 (Revised): Status of the Coalition Provisional Authority, MNF-Iraq, Certain Missions and Personnel in Iraq, 27 June 2004.

[137] See *Binyam Mohamed et al v Jeppesen Dataplan, Inc and USA*, Case No 08-15693, DC No 5:07-CV-02798-JW, US Court of Appeals, Ninth Circuit, Opinion, 8 September 2010.

[138] 580 F.3d 1 (DC Cir 2009), 9. For other Abu Ghraib litigation, see *In Re: Xe Services Alien Tort Litigation*, 665 F.Supp.2d 569 (E.D. Va 2009).

engagement in such activities shall be pre-empted'.[139] But this 'rule' was contested by the United States District Court for the District of Maryland, Greenbelt Division in a July 2010 decision in *Wissam Abdullateff Sa'eed al-Quraishi et al v Adel Nakhla et al*,[140] which held that where a private contractor has acted outside the scope of their contract and not on behalf of the sovereign when they commit an allegedly tortious act, they will 'not be entitled to derivative sovereign immunity'.[141]

Assessing whether the conduct in question was committed 'on behalf of the sovereign' would require 'consideration of [the contractor's] course of dealing with the government' to 'reveal whether deviations from the contract occurred and, if so, whether they were tolerable or ratified'.[142] And, in any case, the judge in this case ruled, 'the Court would still need to consider whether the authority to commit the alleged acts [in this case of torture] was "validly conferred"' since 'if, by its own laws, the sovereign could not lawfully take these actions on its own, it could not delegate the task to a private contractor'.[143]

Hearing an appeal from that decision, the full court of the 4th Circuit of the US Court of Appeals held that the key questions are, ultimately, ones of fact: the 'level of public/private integration' in the contract in question, 'the conduct of activities that may be classified as combat, and the military's retained prerogative concerning the decisionmaking process' in executing the contract.[144] US law thus appears at present to indicate that PMSCs will not be able to claim derivative sovereign immunity in US courts for conduct contrary to international law, if that conduct would be illegal even if committed by a state actor. This may quickly open up a key pathway for 'private attorneys general' to enforce the international law of armed conflict against PMSCs. One example is a case brought by the 'Genocide Victims of Krajina' in a US District Court in Illinois against MPRI Inc, the PMSC that trained the Croatian government prior to Operation Storm, then the largest land-based European military offensive since World War II, alleging complicity in genocide.[145]

B. Application by PMSCs: the responsibility to respect

Such litigation might provide the spur for PMSCs to take preventive measures to ensure their personnel abide by the standards imposed by international law, reducing their exposure to liability. But even absent the shadow of litigation, it might be

---

[139] 580 F.3d 1 (DC Cir 2009), 9.   [140] *Al-Quraishi v Nakhla*, 728 F.Supp.2d 702, 735 (D.Md. 2010).
[141] *Al-Quraishi v Nakhla*, 728 F.Supp.2d 702, 735 (D.Md.2010).
[142] *Al-Quraishi v Nakhla*, 728 F.Supp.2d 702, 735 (D.Md.2010), 37–8, quoting *Al Shimari v CACI Premier Technology Inc*, 657 F.Supp.2d 700, 717 (E.D. Va 2009).
[143] *Al-Quraishi v Nakhla*, 728 F.Supp.2d 702, 735 (D.Md.2010), 38, following *Yearsley v W.A. Ross Construction Corpn*, 309 US 18 (1940), 21.
[144] *Al-Shimari v CACI International, Inc*, 679 F.3d 205 (2012), 222.
[145] *Genocide Victims of Krajina v L-3 Communications Corpn and MPRI, Inc*, 10-cv-5197 (N.D. Ill).

possible to encourage PMSCs to apply international law themselves, to drive industry standards up and secure the industry's reputation, future, and the investments of its financiers.[146]

The importance of direct application of international law *by* PMSCs will only rise as PMSCs proliferate and become more powerful. In theory, a PMSC might itself become responsible for violations of international law by becoming a non-state party to a non-international armed conflict. There are, to date, no clear such cases, since by their nature PMSCs are usually contracted by a party to the armed conflict to fight on their behalf, rather than adopting an independent combat role. Yet given the stated ambitions of some contemporary PMSCs, such a situation is increasingly conceivable. (Witness, for example, the high degree of command and control allegedly exercised by Saracen International SAL (Lebanon) and Sterling Corporate Services over the Puntland Maritime Police Force in Somalia, between 2010 and 2012.[147]) In that event, a PMSC would enjoy all the same rights and responsibilities of any other non-state armed group party to a non-international armed conflict— including the obligation to implement IHL.

Even absent such clear-cut cases, there is an increasing effort by some—including within the PMSC industry itself, and within state apparatus—to encourage PMSCs to behave *as if* they were formally bound by the controlling standards of international humanitarian and human rights law.[148] The UN Guiding Principles on Business and Human Rights detail the corporate 'responsibility' to respect human rights (though this responsibility is based on 'social expectations', and is not a binding duty under international law).[149] How PMSCs might show such respect is becoming increasingly clear, with the adoption of the Montreux Document (which sets out Good Practices for states in dealing with PMSCs, and therefore implicitly reveals what PMSCs should expect to have to do in dealing with states), the Swiss-led International Code of Conduct for Private Security Service Providers, and other ad hoc industry-led codes of conduct.[150] Though less-frequently named, there are also a wide range of other relevant international codes from which PMSCs might draw guidance, such as the UN Basic Principles on the Use of Force and Firearms by Law Enforcement Officials, the UN Code of Conduct for Law Enforcement Officials,[151] and the UN Body of Principles for the Protection of All Persons under Any Form of Detention or Imprisonment.[152] These all point to certain conduct by

---

[146] See Cockayne et al (n 19), 43–8.

[147] See UN Security Council, 'Report of the Monitoring Group on Somalia and Eritrea pursuant to Security Council resolution 2002 (2011)', UN Doc S/2012/544, Annex, 13 July 2012.

[148] Clapham (n 125), 299–310.   [149] See UN Guiding Principles (n 86).

[150] See eg the *Sarajevo Code of Conduct for Private Security Companies*, SEESAC, 2006, and the Code of Conduct of the International Peace Operations Association. For discussion of these Codes, see Cockayne et al (n 19), 43–8, 134–44, 226–33.

[151] UN Doc A/RES/34/169, 17 December 1979.

[152] UN Doc A/RES/43/173, Annex, 43 UN GAOR Supp (No 49), 298, UN Doc A/43/49 (1988).

PMSCs themselves as means to mitigate their exposure to liability and help ensure respect for international law in armed conflict, such as vetting staff for past violations; promoting awareness of IHL and human rights, including through training; issuing standard operating procedures and guidance on IHL and human rights compliance; and creating incident reporting, internal investigations, and effective third-party grievance mechanisms.

8 CONCLUSION: UNANSWERED QUESTIONS

Ultimately, the central criticism of voluntary codes is neatly summarized by Lindsey Cameron: 'people handling weapons in situations of armed conflict clearly need to be bound by more than a voluntary code of conduct'.[153] And as recent UK and Swiss-led consultations have made clear, both states and industry are more than happy to adopt such voluntary codes—but neither are willing to pay for their enforcement, absent, as the UK Foreign and Commonwealth Office put it, 'a clear commercial incentive'.[154] Some states are now signalling they may yet create such incentives, by choosing only to contract with PMSCs that comply with such voluntary codes, implemented through effective external monitoring. Thus both the United Kingdom and Switzerland have indicated they will only contract with PMSCs that comply with the International Code of Conduct. But because international law is made by states for states, purely state regulation—whether through legislation, command and control, contractual oversight officers, partnership with PMSCs in multistakeholder initiatives, or through the courts—will remain crucial to the effective implementation of international law to and by PMSCs.

PMSCs sit in a conceptual and physical position *vis-à-vis* the battlefield precisely where lines of accountability are weakened by jurisdictional barriers and contractual and informal—rather than command and control—relations. Figuring out exactly how international law can be efficiently and effectively applied by and to these highly de-territorialized, networked commercial actors will remain a crucial task in the years ahead. Making substantive progress in this area is vital if the ongoing legitimacy, relevance, and effectiveness of the international law of armed conflict is to be ensured.

---

[153] Cameron (n 12), 10.   [154] UK Foreign and Commonwealth Office (n 3), 9.

CHAPTER 26

INTERNATIONAL HUMAN RIGHTS LAW IN TIME OF ARMED CONFLICT

DEREK JINKS

1 INTRODUCTION

THE Geneva Conventions formalized two important developments concerning when international humanitarian law (IHL) applies: (1) IHL now governs *de facto* as well as *de jure* warfare; and (2) IHL now governs non-international as well as international armed conflict. Both developments were revolutionary. First, the Conventions apply to any 'armed conflict' between states irrespective of whether either state has formally declared war.[1] Prior to the drafting of the Geneva Conventions, the applicability of the 'law of war' was delimited by formal acts of state such as a declaration of war or a formal 'recognition of belligerency'. Why this is so is important, and is not obvious. Traditionally, a 'state of war' meant the complete rupture of legal relations between the belligerent states. In these circumstances, the 'laws of war'

---

[1] See eg Geneva Convention Relative to the Treatment of Prisoners of War, 12 August 1949, Art 2, (hereinafter GC III).

completely displaced the 'laws of peace' (normal law). Most treaties were suspended, as were normal diplomatic relations. Therefore, rules regarding the treatment of war victims—precursors to the Geneva Conventions—were only one, comparatively insignificant, legal consequence of war. Remarkably detailed rules governed the relations between warring states, as well as the relations between belligerents and neutral states. 'War' was, in this sense, a special case of inter-state belligerency, and many varieties of organized hostilities would not trigger the application of the 'laws of war'. In this context, formal declarations of war were considered a condition precedent to the displacement of the 'laws of peace'.

The Geneva Conventions substantially revised this formalistic approach. The treaties are instead applicable during all 'armed conflicts' *irrespective of whether the states involved formally recognize a state of war*. The Conventions are triggered by certain objective conditions. This shift was thought necessary in view of other changes in international law and politics that made formal recognition of a state of war increasingly rare. The problem was that, by the mid-twentieth century, the existence of a 'state of war' no longer played an important role in international law— so states had no incentive to declare war—and international law prohibited 'war' except in narrow circumstances—providing states with an disincentive to declare war. In the wake of World War II, it was clear that the applicability of humanitarian rules, such as those embodied in the Geneva Conventions, should not turn on whether the belligerents formally recognized a state of war.

Secondly, the Geneva Conventions, in Common Article 3, explicitly regulate non-international armed conflicts—that is, conflict between states and non-state armed groups.[2] Prior to the Conventions, no international agreements purported to regulate such conflicts.[3] These conflicts—even when involving sustained, organized, and intense violence—were exclusively governed by domestic law. Indeed, any interference by another state in such matters would have been deemed an unlawful intrusion into the internal affairs of the state and might have been considered an act of war.[4] This regulatory gap nevertheless persisted until the end of World War II. The atrocities perpetrated by the Nazi regime in Germany before and during World War II clearly demonstrated that even wholly internal matters presented grave threats to humanitarian principles. The Spanish Civil War, with highly organized, sustained fighting erupting in 1936, also made clear that the 'recognition of belligerency' doctrine inadequately regulated non-international armed

---

[2] See eg GC III, Art 3, making clear that the provision applies to conflicts involving only one state. The provision also governs conflict between two or more nonstate armed groups.

[3] See L. Moir, *The Law of Internal Armed Conflict* (Cambridge: Cambridge University Press, 2002), 4.

[4] See eg E. Castrén, *Civil War* (Veikko Väänänen ed, Helsinki: Suomalainen Tedeakatemia, 1966), 175–81. There was, in fact, only one circumstance in which the laws of war might govern such a conflict. Under customary international law, the laws of war governed non-international conflicts only if an established state recognized the 'belligerency' of the non-state armed group. This doctrine of 'recognition of belligerency', however, applied to a narrow range of conflicts and was very rarely invoked. J.W. Garner, 'Recognition of Belligerency', 32 *AJIL* (1938) 106–12.

conflicts.[5] Against the backdrop of these events and the general humanitarian trajectory of the laws of war, the Geneva Conventions enacted a limited scheme that
made some elementary humanitarian principles applicable in non-international
armed conflicts.

In all cases of armed conflict, several categories of persons will be placed in an
unusually vulnerable position—arising out of their classification as the 'enemy' by
opposing forces. In such circumstances, there is a unique role for international
legal regimes—and, more fundamentally, a unique role for protection schemes with
exceptionally broad material and personal fields of application. The real difficulty is
defining 'armed conflict', particularly in the context of hostilities between states and
non-state actors. The upshot is that 'armed conflict' should be defined very broadly
to include all cases of sufficiently organized, sufficiently intense fighting.

Broad application of IHL, particularly in the context of international terrorism,[6]
immediately suggests several potentially important collateral consequences for
international law and policy. And many of the most intractable debates about the
role of law in counter-terrorism policy directly or indirectly rest on one or more
assumptions about the collateral legal consequences of the 'armed conflict' characterization. For example, debates about the proper geographic scope of the 'battlefield' often centre on where the IHL framework applies—as opposed to a more
robust legal framework, such as international human rights law—and where it
does not.[7] The focal point in these debates is the contention that the 'battlefield' is
coincident with those *places* in which an 'armed conflict' exits. Debates about US
targeted killing policy—particularly the use of drone strikes in Pakistan, Somalia,
Yemen, and other locales—often centres on the appropriate or optimal legal framework for shooting to kill suspected terrorists. The focal point in these debates is the
contention that IHL provides the relevant legal framework only where the target
is a combatant in an armed conflict—in other words, that IHL is the framework,
perhaps to the exclusion of other frameworks, only where the *persons* in question
are connected to an armed conflict in the right way. Debates about the appropriate legal framework for detaining terrorists under a 'law of war model' exhibit the
same pattern.[8] More generally, debates about whether international human rights

---

[5] See N.J. Padelford, *International Law and Diplomacy in the Spanish Civil Strife* (New York: The
Macmillan Co, 1939), 18–20.

[6] See *amplius* the Chapter by Bianchi and Naqvi in this volume. The point here is not IHL applies to
all, or even most, aspects of international counter-terrorism. Rather, the point is that debates about the
scope of IHL's applicability in this context often centre on concerns about collateral legal consequences
rather than concerns interior to IHL. In other words, these debates often explicitly rely upon, or tacitly
assume, the notion that IHL deactivates (or otherwise sharply delimits) some other more appropriate
legal framework.

[7] See eg M.E. O'Connell, 'Combatants and the Combat Zone', 43 *University of Richmond Law Review*
(2009) 845–64. See also the Chapter by Bianchi and Naqvi in this volume.

[8] See eg M. Hakimi, 'A Functional Approach to Targeting and Detention', 110 *Michigan Law
Review* (2012) 1365–1420; R. Chesney, 'Who May Be Held? Military Detention Through the Habeas

law applies at all in time of armed conflict centre on the contention that mutually exclusive legal frameworks protect individuals from governmental abuses on the international plane. And less visibly, but just as importantly, debates about whether international supervisory and enforcement machinery—including the UN Human Rights Council (including the Special Procedures and individual complaint procedure of the Council), international human rights treaty bodies (including the Human Rights Committee established by the International Covenant on Civil and Political Rights), the European Court of Human Rights, and the Inter-American Commission on Human Rights—have jurisdiction or competence to address matters governed by IHL centre on the institutional implications of certain legal frameworks.[9]

Each of these deeply related debates turns, in part, on whether the characterization of a particular situation as an armed conflict—one that is occurring in a delimited, definable space, at a delimited, definable time, and involving specific, identifiable categories of persons—simultaneously triggers the application of IHL and terminates the application of international human rights law (and other international legal regimes designed to protect individuals). The ostensible implications of this displacement are straightforward. IHL, it is thought, is less restrictive than international human rights law. It also authorizes states to engage in otherwise unlawful actions—such as extra-judicial executions of individuals without an individualized assessment of necessity and the long-term preventive detention of persons without any sort of fulsome procedural guarantees and without any ongoing, robust judicial supervision.

In this Chapter, I maintain that the very notion of competing legal frameworks is incompatible with the text, structure, and history of the Geneva Conventions. And, more fundamentally, it is incompatible with the institutional and behavioural foundations of contemporary IHL.

IHL is best understood as a floor of humanitarian protection—but the application of this law does not require reducing the level of legal protection down to this floor. If this is the case there are sensible reasons to define the material field of application of IHL as broadly as possible. If we conclude otherwise, ie if we see the applicability of IHL as reducing protection to the minimal floor, then we introduce concern about over-application in turn raising the threshold for the application of IHL.

The retail level resolution of concrete legal questions—such as the procedures that must attend detention in a particular context or what amounts to arbitrary, hence unlawful, killing—will ultimately turn on the application of the concepts

Lens', 52 *Boston College Law Review* (2011) 769–870; R. Chesney and J. Goldsmith, 'Terrorism and the Convergence of Criminal and Military Detention Models', 60 *Stanford Law Review* (2008) 1079–133.

[9] See eg P. Alston, 'The CIA and Targeted Killings Beyond Borders', 2 *Harvard National Security Journal* (2011) 283–446; P. Alston, J. Morgan-Foster, and W. Abresch, 'The Competence of the UN Human Rights Council and its Special Procedures in Relation to Armed Conflicts', 18 *EJIL* (2008) 183–209.

of necessity, proportionality, and humanity to specific facts. What is needed in international society is frank, sustained, and principled reflection on what these concepts should mean in specific contexts. The notion of competing international legal frameworks ultimately makes such reflection much less likely by complicating threshold questions of applicability and sharply narrowing the range of relevant legal principles and competent international institutions in any particular context.

2 IHL and Collateral Legal Consequences Generally

Before analysing the relationship between IHL and international human rights law, some conceptual precision about the nature of the 'armed conflict' inquiry is necessary. The most important, seemingly most fundamental, objection to a broad applicability for IHL is that undesirable legal and policy consequences follow from the characterization of any situation as a 'war' or 'armed conflict'. Consider the example of the Global War on Terror (GWOT). Of course, the US Government has adopted several controversial policies based on the premise that the GWOT is a war. For example, the United States characterized the September 11 attacks as 'acts of war' triggering the right of self-defence under the UN Charter. The President also characterized the attacks as 'war crimes', rendering the perpetrators amenable to prosecution before ad hoc military commissions. In addition, the rights of several hundred detainees are sharply delimited, according to the United States, because they are 'enemy combatants'—that is, they took up arms against the United States in time of war. The government nevertheless insists that the relevant law of war does not protect these 'combatants' because they do not qualify as 'prisoners of war'; and because the application of the laws of war, in any case, is sharply limited by the requirements of reciprocity. Critics, of course, have taken issue with each of these claims.

The divergences are the result of divergent policy objectives. The UN Charter self-defence rules seek to minimize international aggression and they are part of a wider regime committed to the elimination of war as an instrument of national policy. As such, the primary concern is the over-application of the self-defence exception—which tends to push the threshold of application higher. The Geneva Conventions, on the other hand, seek to minimize unnecessary suffering resulting from organized hostilities. Therefore, the primary worry in Geneva law is the under-application of humanitarian rules, which tends to push the threshold for application lower. Because there is no necessary relationship between the optimal level of war and the 'optimal' level of suffering in war, there is no necessary relation between the triggering conditions of these regimes. Indeed, any structural linkage of the two regimes risks frustrating the policy objectives of one (or both) of the regimes. Any structural relationship between the two regimes would tend to exert pressure in the opposite direction suggested by regime objectives.

More importantly, the resolution of the 'armed attack' issue turns on considerations unrelated to the applicability of the Geneva Conventions. Because the Charter issue arises only in the context of contemplated force against another state—as was the case after 9/11 when the United States sought to justify the use of force against Afghanistan—the central issue typically will be whether the attacks are attributable to a state.[10] The dispute over the validity of the US self-defence claim is then, at bottom, a disagreement about the circumstances in which states should be deemed responsible for the acts of private persons (or groups). Irrespective of the merits of these criticisms, the important point is that the debate on the type of regime applicable to the use of force (law enforcement or the law of armed conflict) does not turn on whether states have the right to defend themselves against the kind of attacks witnessed on 9/11.[11]

The most important examples, though, are those that implicate the very values the Conventions purport to protect individual rights. Consider the example of emergency powers. The central point here is that the Convention rules do not define, directly or indirectly, when the President may invoke constitutional war powers. If, when, and to what extent the US Constitution empowers the President to suspend civil liberties present questions that have little, if anything, to do with the applicability of the Conventions. The Conventions define the treatment due to vulnerable individuals in the context of organized hostilities. The problem addressed by the Conventions is the radical inhumanity that all too often characterizes warfare. To address this problem, the Conventions prescribe a few simple rules that require humane treatment of captured enemy soldiers and civilians. The limiting principle for these rules is military necessity. Because it is unreasonable to expect warring parties to observe rules that increase the prospect of their defeat, the Conventions require only a modest level of protection—a level that is consistent with the legitimate strategic imperatives of waging war. The Conventions, in this sense, establish minimum rules that apply even when arguably no other law does. Given these limited ambitions, the Conventions should apply *whenever* sufficiently intense fighting erupts between organized enemies.

---

[10] Indeed, this is the formal rationale forwarded by the United States to the UN Security Council. See Letter from Ambassador Negroponte to the UN Secretary General and the President of the UN Security Council (7 October 2001), available at <http://www.un.int/usa/s-2001-946.htm>.

[11] Any suggestion that the attacks are not the kind of injury against which states have the inherent right to defend is normatively suspect given the scale, sophistication, and purpose of the attacks.

More generally, the Conventions, if applicable, do not displace or trigger the application of any other body of rules. Many of the variations of this criticism tacitly trade on the idea that application of the Conventions somehow precludes application of some more robust individual rights scheme such as ordinary constitutional law, criminal law, or, most importantly, international human rights law. This assumption, however, is plainly inconsistent with the Conventions themselves and difficult to square with the purposes of humanitarian law generally. No rule in the Conventions requires the warring parties to abrogate any rights-protecting scheme otherwise recognized in its law. In other words, the United States could accord, consistent with the Geneva Conventions, all captured al Qaeda fighters the full protections of international human rights law and the US Code and Constitution. The applicability of the Conventions does not displace these other potentially applicable regimes. Moreover, the inverse is clearly false; states cannot render the Conventions inapplicable simply by deciding to apply some other body of rules.

One important purpose of the Conventions, and humanitarian law generally, is to define the minimum standard of acceptable treatment. The Conventions establish a floor below which the treatment of individuals may not fall—even in time of war, even with respect to one's enemy.[12] The problem addressed by humanitarian law is that organized hostilities are often characterized by lawlessness and barbarity. The Conventions, then, prescribe the rules that must be observed *even if* no other rules apply. This is, of course, importantly different from the view that the Conventions prescribe rules that apply *because* no other rules apply. And it is manifestly inconsistent with the view that the Conventions prescribe rules that *have the effect of displacing* other rights-regarding rules.

3 IHL AS *LEX SPECIALIS* DISPLACING OR QUALIFYING THE APPLICATION OF INTERNATIONAL HUMAN RIGHTS LAW

This kind of claim about undesirable collateral legal consequences is typically associated with the idea that IHL, as *lex specialis* in time of armed conflict, supersedes any conflicting aspects of the *lex generalis* designed to protect individuals, including international human rights law. The idea is that IHL—as the body of law specifically

---

[12] The Conventions encourage warring parties in multiple contexts to negotiate a higher standard of treatment. See eg GC III, Arts 109, 111; GC IV, Arts 7, 14, 15.

tailored to govern the treatment of individuals in certain circumstances—ought to trump the generally applicable human rights law in the specific circumstances for which IHL was designed. The upshot is that characterization of any situation as an 'armed conflict' would result in the application of IHL *and* the displacement of international human rights law. Though obviously correct on one level—clearly, the Geneva Conventions are applicable only in delimited circumstances and human rights law applies much more broadly—however the inference that the Conventions displace much, if not all, of international human rights law is unwarranted. Before evaluating the claim in a more direct way, some further clarification is needed of the *lex specialis* position—and its various forms as well as some of its ambiguities.

The principle *lex specialis derogat lege generali*—that special law derogates from general law—is a common technique for the resolution of normative conflicts in public international law and national judicial systems. The principle maintains that, in cases of conflict, specific rules should take precedence over general standards. The primary justification for this principle is that it assigns priority to the rule most narrowly tailored to the specific context, suggesting that it would be more effective and that it better reflects the will of the parties.[13]

IHL and international human rights law both govern the treatment of individuals subject to the authority and/or lethality of the obligated power. International human rights law prescribes the treatment states must accord all persons subject to their jurisdiction in all circumstances.[14] Human rights law is, in this important sense, a regime of general application. Of course, human rights law also expressly

---

[13] See eg J. Pauwelyn, *Conflict of Norms in Public International Law: How WTO Law Relates to Other Rules of International Law* (Cambridge: Cambridge University Press, 2003); Report of the Study Group of the International Law Commission, Finalized by Martii Koskenniemi, Fragmentation of International Law: Difficulties Arising From the Diversification and Expansion of International Law, A/CN.4/L.682, 13 April 2006. The idea that special enjoys priority over general has a long pedigree in international jurisprudence as well. Its rationale is well expressed already by Grotius:

> *What rules ought to be observed in such cases* [ie where parts of a document are in conflict]. Among agreements which are equal [...] that should be given preference which is most specific and approaches most nearly to the subject in hand, for special provisions are ordinarily more effective than those that are general.

This passage refers to two reasons why the *lex specialis* rule is so widely accepted. ('A special rule is more to the point ("approaches most nearly to the subject in hand") than a general one and it regulates the matter more effectively ("are ordinarily more effective") than general rules. This could also be expressed by saying that special rules are better able to take account of particular circumstances. The need to comply with them is felt more acutely than is the case with general rules.'). At paras 59 and 60 footnote omitted.

[14] This is not to say that international human rights law applies in all circumstances. The rules arguably do not apply extra-territorially—though it bears mentioning that the near consensus view is that human rights obligations apply extraterritorially whenever a state exercises effective control of a person or territory abroad. See generally L. Doswald-Beck, *International Human Rights in Times of Armed Conflict and Terrorism* (New York: Oxford University Press, 2012); M. Milanovic, *The Extra-Territorial Application of Human Rights Treaties: Law, Principles, and Policy* (New York: Oxford University Press, 2011).

contemplates its application in times of national security crisis, including times of war.[15] IHL, on the other hand, applies only in special circumstances: declared war, armed conflict, and military occupation.

Against this backdrop, the *lex specialis* principle has been applied in this context in two importantly different ways. The first approach maintains that the *lex specialis* rule should apply at the regime level—suggesting that the applicability of IHL should wholly displace the application of international human rights law. On this approach, there are pervasive normative conflicts across the two regimes and that the more fully articulated, more narrowly tailored approach of IHL should govern the treatment of persons associated with the enemy in time of armed conflict. This approach would not only deprive human rights law of any independent normative force in armed conflicts, it would also deprive international human rights machinery of any role in supervising the conduct of hostilities. The second approach maintains that IHL, as *lex specialis*, determines the meaning of important, abstract standards in human rights law. This view is famously associated with the International Court of Justice (ICJ). In its *Advisory Opinion on the Legality of the Threat or Use of Nuclear Weapons*, the ICJ reasoned that both human rights law—in this case, the International Covenant on Civil and Political Rights—and IHL apply 'in times of war'. Whether any killing in this context amounts to an 'arbitrary deprivation of life' under Article 6(1) of the Covenant, however, is 'to be determined by the applicable *lex specialis*, namely the law applicable to armed conflict'.[16] On this approach, the content of human rights law is determined solely by reference

---

[15] Human rights law purports to regulate a broad range of domestic practices that impact security concerns. As a consequence, international law explicitly recognizes that national security concerns will shape domestic application of international standards. International human rights treaties allow the suspension of some rights in public emergencies, such as times of war. Article 4 of the ICCPR, for example, provides that in situations threatening the life of the nation, a government may issue a formal declaration suspending certain human rights guarantees provided that: (1) a state of emergency that threatens the life of the nation exists; (2) the exigencies of the situation 'strictly require' such a suspension; (3) the suspension does not conflict with the nation's other international obligations; (4) the emergency measures are applied in a non-discriminatory fashion; and (5) the government notifies the UN Secretary-General immediately. Some rights, however, are not subject to derogation even in times of public emergency. The ICCPR specifically identifies several non-derogable obligations including the rights to be free from arbitrary killing; torture or other cruel, inhuman, or degrading treatment or punishment; and slavery. Although the rights to fair trial and personal liberty are, as a formal matter, derogable provisions, the UN Human Rights Committee has repeatedly found that many restrictions of these rights are inappropriate even in times of emergency. The UN Human Rights Committee has also emphasized that procedural rights, such as fair trial rights, must be respected even in times of emergency in order to protect other non-derogable rights. Finally, the Committee, following the lead of the Inter-American Court of Human Rights, strongly suggested that, at a minimum, the right to *habeas corpus* (or *amparo*) is non-derogable. See generally Doswald-Beck (n 14).

[16] ICJ, *Advisory Opinion on the Legality of the Threat or Use of Nuclear Weapons*, 8 July 1996. See also ICJ, *Advisory Opinion on the Legal Consequences of the Construction of a Wall in the Occupied Palestinian Territories*, 9 July 2004; *Extrajudicial, Summary or Arbitrary Executions: Report of the Special Rapporteur*, UN ESCOR Commission of Human Rights, 61st Sess, UN Doc E/CN.4/2005/7 (2005).

to IHL, depriving human rights law of independent normative force. The important difference between this approach and the first, however, is that the second approach acknowledges the competence of international human rights supervisory and enforcement machinery in armed conflict, even if the norms to be interpreted and applied in such situations are exclusively drawn from IHL.

Three reasons, to varying degrees, favour these two approaches. First, IHL authorizes states to engage in some acts that would be flatly inconsistent with international human rights law. For example, IHL allows warring parties to target and kill, in the absence of any individualized determination about necessity, enemy combatants and even civilians directly participating in hostilities. IHL also arguably authorizes warring parties to capture and detain persons who are members of the enemy armed forces and enemy national civilians posing a security threat for the duration of the hostilities. On this view, IHL reflects a careful balance of authority and constraint—thus, only IHL constraints should condition the exercise of authority recognized as legitimate in time of armed conflict.[17]

Secondly, human rights law should not fill the gaps in protection afforded by IHL because those gaps promote larger regime objectives in IHL. The point is that IHL calibrates the treatment accorded to enemy individuals to incentivize fighters and civilians to conduct themselves in a manner that is consistent with IHL and that facilitates compliance with IHL by their enemy. This is crucially important, proponents of this view maintain, in hostilities against irregular forces including terrorist organizations. The worry is that the application of international human rights law would systematically over-protect so-called unlawful combatants and that doing so would pose a grave threat to humanitarian values.

Thirdly, IHL is better suited to govern armed conflict because its enforcement is based in substantial part on mutual reciprocity between the warring parties. International human rights law, as is often noted in numerous contexts, cannot be understood as a properly reciprocal regime.

These three claims suggest that the *lex specialis* of IHL is more narrowly tailored to the exigencies of armed conflict and that it is more likely than human rights law to reflect the will of treaty makers and more likely than human rights law to be effective in promoting humane and fair treatment of enemy individuals. The balance of this Chapter assesses, and rejects, each of these claims.

---

[17] See eg G.D. Solis, *The Law of Armed Conflict: International Humanitarian Law in War* (Cambridge: Cambridge University Press, 2010); G. Corn, et al (eds), *The Laws of War and the War on Terrorism: A Military Perspective* (New York: Oxford University Press, 2009).

4 AGAINST THE NOTION OF COMPETING LEGAL FRAMEWORKS: EVALUATING THE *LEX SPECIALIS* CLAIMS

In the remainder of this Chapter, I argue that the application of IHL—meaning the existence of an armed conflict—should not be understood to displace the application of international human rights law. I outline three fundamental respects in which the *lex specialis* claim misconstrues or distorts international humanitarian law.

A. IHL and affirmative authorization

IHL is broadly compatible with human rights law in that it does not require, or authorize, states to engage in conduct prohibited by human rights law. The nature of IHL, the unique work that it is designed to do, and its resulting relationship with other aspects of public international law suggest that IHL should not be understood as conferring authority on states in the strong sense. IHL rules, in the main, are prohibitory. As discussed at the outset of this Chapter, they establish a floor of humanitarian protection—crafted in light of the vulnerable circumstances common to organized hostilities.

Critics of my view might sensibly point out that the Geneva Conventions seemingly authorize states to restrict the rights of 'protected persons'—most notably, they permit the confinement of PoWs and, in a more narrow range of circumstances, civilians.[18] Although accurate at one level, this point involves a categorical mistake. The Conventions do not authorize states to engage in practices otherwise forbidden in law in the way that a domestic statute authorizes actors to exercise some power.[19] The Conventions simply are not an instrument that purports to confer authority where none exists.[20] The provision—as a rule of international law and, more specifically, international humanitarian law—cannot be read in the way that an analogous provision of domestic law might be read. Rather, the Conventions are designed to condition or prohibit the exercise of powers routinely associated with the conduct of war. Consider the relevant provision of the PoW treaty. Remember

---

[18] See eg GC III, Art 21; GC IV, Arts 41–2, 79.

[19] The Conventions provide that PoWs and civilians retain their 'full civil capacity' and they are allowed to exercise all 'rights compatible with their status', GC III, Art 14; GC IV, Art 80.

[20] On another level, the 'authorization to confine' objection involves a more fundamental category mistake. These would-be authorizations apply only in the context of an international armed conflict. There are no parallel provisions in the rules governing non-international armed conflicts. Compare GC III, Art 3. As a consequence, these provisions are relevant to the GWOT only insofar as this conflict assumes an inter-state character.

that the Conventions protect only those persons who have 'fallen into the hands of the enemy'. That is, the Conventions apply from the moment of capture (or surrender) to the time of release and repatriation.[21] It is, after all, a treaty governing the treatment of *prisoners* of war.

The persons protected by the Convention, and the period during which it applies, underscore that the treaty governs the treatment of persons made prisoner by the enemy. The 'authorization' to intern is better understood as a limit on the kinds of force states do and will use to confine PoWs. 'Internment' is explicitly distinguished from 'detention' (which involves the close confinement of individuals) and implicitly distinguished from killing.[22] States cannot 'detain' or kill PoWs as a means to prevent their return to the fight, but they may, though they need not, 'intern' them. The sharp edge of the rule is what it prohibits, or how it qualifies the exercise of some power that states will predictably seek to exercise in war.[23] Another example helps illustrate the same point. The Fourth Geneva Convention allows the detention of peaceful civilians only when necessary to protect the security of the detaining state.[24] This provision is best understood as a *prohibition on the detention of civilians*. In circumstances not satisfying the standard, relating to the need to protect security or perhaps as recognizing a *right to release for all civilians* not satisfying that standard, this provision cannot be understood as conferring on the detaining authority the *legal power to detain*.[25]

---

[21] This is, as a formal matter, an oversimplification. Some aspects of GC IV, for example, govern the targeting of certain civilian institutions and, of course, many provisions of that Convention govern the administration of 'occupied territory'. The oversimplification presented in the text nevertheless helps illustrate the more general point that the Conventions do not augment state power to restrict the rights of persons subject to its authority.

[22] Commentary GC III, 178 (hereinafter 'ICRC Commentary').

[23] The ICRC Commentary makes plain the background assumptions informing the rule.

[24] Articles 42 and 79 of GC IV.

[25] There is one important (potential) exception to this point—though, properly understood, it is orthogonal to my argument here. The Geneva Civilian Convention prescribes rules for the government of occupied territory. One cluster of these rules requires the Occupying Power to preserve, to the extent practicable, the pre-existing criminal laws of the occupied state, GC IV, Art 64. This rule, in some circumstances, might require the Occupying Power to administer and to enforce laws inconsistent with its own commitments to individual rights. The US occupation of Iraq is an obvious example. The 'legal continuity' rules of the Conventions arguably required the United States to enforce Iraqi criminal laws irrespective of whether these laws were inconsistent with US conceptions of individual liberty. For a fuller consideration of this interesting problem, see Y. Dinstein, *The Dilemmas Relating to Legislation Under Article 43 of the Hague Regulations, and Peace-Building* (2004) (IHLRI Background Paper), available at <http://www.hpcrresearch.org/sites/default/files/publications/dinstein.pdf> (discussing the Geneva Convention scheme in light of its predecessor in the Hague Regulations). This rule, however, is a limit on the authority of Occupying Powers, limiting the degree to which the conquering state may impose its sovereign will on the civilians of the occupied power. As such, it is importantly different from the concern that motivates our discussion here.

An important feature of the IHL regime makes clear that it does not provide affirmative authorization to kill, capture, or detain. IHL is, in one important respect, a second-order legal regime—governing only the conduct of hostilities. That is, the legality and, indeed, the justifiability of the organized violence itself is not regulated by IHL. In fact, one central tenet of IHL is that a strict separation between *jus ad bellum* (the law regulating the resort to armed force) and *jus in bello* (the law regulating the conduct of hostilities) considerations is necessary. In other words, the scope and content of IHL does not turn on which side in an armed conflict is in the wrong regarding the initiation of hostilities. This strict separation between *ad bellum* and *in bello* issues is necessary because the conflation of these regimes would systematically weaken IHL. If this were not the case, all, or nearly all, warring parties would claim for themselves the prerogatives associated with the lawful initiation of hostilities and assign to their adversaries the disabilities associated with unlawful initiation of hostilities. IHL, as a matter of sociological imperative, remains indifferent to how or for what reasons the fighting started.

As such, compliance with IHL never ensures that any particular use of force or coercive measure taken against the enemy is lawful as such. In this sense, the ICJ's holding that the meaning of abstract standards in human rights law, such as the meaning of arbitrariness in the prohibition on arbitrary deprivation of life in the ICCPR is simply determined by IHL, is normatively suspect. Although IHL is certainly relevant, and perhaps centrally so, in making arbitrariness determinations under the ICCPR, these determinations surely must also address whether the initiation of the armed conflict on behalf of the entity for which the killer is fighting was and is consistent with the *jus ad bellum*.[26] It seems perverse to characterize as non-arbitrary these killings that are committed in furtherance of an aggressive war in contravention of the UN Charter—irrespective of whether the killing is otherwise consistent with IHL. Arbitrariness inquiries, even in times of armed conflict, would also presumably ask whether the killing was committed pursuant to domestic law. Once again, it would be perverse to suggest that killings committed in violation of national rules of engagement or in a manner that is otherwise *ultra vires* under domestic law would be non-arbitrary simply in view of the fact that the killing was consistent with IHL. This line of argument is related to my claim, developed below, that compliance with IHL does not and cannot determine the legality of any wartime action because of the heavily qualified role that IHL plays in public international law. The notion of 'arbitrary deprivation of liberty' in Article 9 of the ICCPR is amenable to a similar analysis. The upshot is that human rights law must apply alongside IHL and it must retain some independent normative content.

---

[26] See also the Chapter by Schabas in this volume.

B. 'Armed conflict' as determinant of regime boundaries

In addition, the 'armed conflict' concept is manifestly ill-suited to arbitrate between potentially applicable protection schemes. Contemporary IHL is designed to address the problem of under-application of humanitarian norms. It lacks the conceptual or normative resources to resolve over-application problems of the sort that motivate the *lex specialis* claim.

Two features of IHL make this clear. First, the armed conflict threshold is too low to determine the optimal regime boundaries between IHL and human rights law. The abandonment of formal triggers in favour of the *de facto* concept of 'armed conflict'—and the extension of IHL into situations of non-international armed conflict—were driven by concerns about the systematic under-application of humanitarian principles. The only countervailing consideration was state sovereignty—and the inherent prerogative of states to maintain law and order on their territory without unwarranted interference from the international community. In other words, the effort to drive down the threshold for the application for IHL—especially in non-international armed conflict—was resisted solely on the grounds that unorganized, low levels of violence should not be understood as a matter of international concern. States wholly denied the relevance of international law in such circumstances. There is no indication—in state practice from 1949–2001 or in the drafting history of the Geneva Conventions, the Additional Protocols, or the principal global human rights treaties—that states contemplated a rights-regarding, over-application issue in IHL.

Secondly, the 'armed conflict' concept cannot determine the outer limit of human rights law because it would allow, by its nature, ill-motivated states to bootstrap into a more favourable international legal framework. The point here is that the inquiry into the existence of an armed conflict places great weight on the actions of individual states. States enjoy substantial ability to trigger the application of IHL unilaterally. The point here is not that the existence or non-existence of an 'armed conflict' is subjective in nature. This inquiry is, to be sure, an objective assessment. The point, instead, is that the relevant objective considerations obviously centre on the actions and attitudes of the parties to the hostilities. In other words, states declaring war on another state or resorting to sustained military operations against another state or a non-state group have engaged in a course of action that would typically warrant application of IHL. In an international armed conflict, this is obvious. When Iraq invaded Kuwait in 1990, the Iraqi military operations were governed by IHL. Similarly, when the United States and its coalition partners invaded Iraq in 2003, those military operations triggered the application of IHL.

The situation is more complex in non-international armed conflicts, but the inquiry is fundamentally the same. Recall that the *travaux préparatoires* of Common Article 3 reveal several criteria that states thought relevant to the classification of hostilities. The ICRC Commentary identifies a number of 'convenient criteria'[27] drawn from proposed definitions of armed conflict that were favourably received at the Diplomatic Conference.[28]

1. That the Party in revolt against the *de jure* Government possesses an organized military force, an authority responsible for its acts, acting within a determinate territory and having the means of respecting and ensuring respect for the Convention.
2. That the legal Government is obliged to have recourse to the regular military forces against insurgents organized as military and in possession of a part of the national territory.
3. (a) That the *de jure* Government has recognized the insurgents as belligerents; or
    (b) That it has claimed for itself the rights of a belligerent; or
    (c) That it has accorded the insurgents recognition as belligerents for the purposes only of the present Convention; or
    (d) That the dispute has been admitted to the agenda of the Security Council or the General Assembly of the United Nations as being a threat to international peace, a breach of the peace, or an act of aggression.
4. (a) That the insurgents have an organization purporting to have the characteristics of a State.
    (b) That the insurgent civil authority exercises *de facto* authority over persons within a determinate portion of the national territory.
    (c) That the armed forces act under the direction of an organized authority and are prepared to observe the ordinary laws of war.
    (d) That the insurgent civil authority agrees to be bound by the provisions of the Convention.[29]

These criteria identify four kinds of circumstances that constitute 'armed conflicts' within the meaning of Common Article 3. The criteria clearly reflect the dual purposes of Common Article 3: the minimization of human suffering and the respect for state sovereignty. They also recognize that some circumstances pose such substantial risks to humanitarian values that international regulation is justified irrespective of the resultant constraints on state autonomy. As a consequence, two important sets of considerations pertain to (1) the intensity of the violence; and (2) the capacity and willingness of the parties to carry out sustained, coordinated hostilities. In addition, concerns about state sovereignty are not significant in circumstances where the state itself accepts or invokes application of the laws of war. Therefore, another important set of criteria concerns the reaction of the state to the hostilities. In addition, the reaction of the international community straddles these categories, and, as a consequence, may provide evidence relevant to both sets of criteria.

---

[27] ICRC Commentary, 35.
[28] See II.B *Final Record of the Diplomatic Conference of Geneva of 1949*, 121.
[29] ICRC Commentary, 35–6.

The point is that, were the *lex specialis* claims correct, states could often bootstrap into the less protective framework of IHL through resort to sustained, intense military action.[30]

C. The institutional and behavioural foundations of IHL: reciprocity and humanitarian protection as inducement for compliance

Finally, the normative bite of the *lex specialis* claim rests on flawed assumptions about the institutional and behavioural foundations of IHL. The most common assertions are that IHL is better suited to govern armed conflicts, and to promote the sort of second-best humanitarianism appropriate to this context, because unlike international human rights law it is amenable to inter-belligerent, reciprocal enforcement and because it calibrates the treatment due to specific categories of persons in a manner that maximizes humanitarianism in conflict settings. Neither assertion withstands scrutiny. Contemporary IHL substantially abandons any form of reciprocal enforcement that would be inconsistent with international human rights law. And contemporary IHL does not calibrate humanitarian protection to incentivize fighters to comply with, or to facilitate the enemy's compliance with, its rules.

Although the classical law of war included rigid reciprocity constraints on the material field of application and broadly authorized warring parties to utilize reprisals aimed at inducing compliance with the law by the enemy, this formal reliance on bilateral reciprocity is in sharp decline. Contemporary IHL has substantially abandoned any compliance-based reciprocity mechanisms. The applicability of the Geneva Conventions is not subject to reciprocity constraints—other than the modest, now irrelevant, mutuality of obligation requirement. The Geneva Conventions and the Protocols thereto also sharply limit resort to belligerent reprisals. The 1949 Conventions prohibit reprisals against each of the categories of 'protected persons'. The Conventions also expressly forbid the taking of reprisal measures against vessels, equipment, or property protected by the Conventions. And although GC IV prohibited only reprisals directed against civilian internees and civilians in occupied territory, Additional Protocol I now prohibits all reprisals directed against the civilian population or civilian objects. The only remaining reciprocity mechanism is war crimes trials—and the Conventions make clear that such trials must comport with robust procedural rights guarantees that closely track the requirements of international human rights law.

---

[30] Of course, states could not *always* trigger the application unilaterally—at least not in theory. Classification as an 'armed conflict' would be warranted only where there is a sufficiently organized opposing party.

Moreover, the Conventions do not allow incentivization through the manipulation of status categories—or levels of protection. In early law of war treaties, specific status categories are defined in terms that encourage protection-seeking states (and at times individuals) to orient their behaviour in ways that promote the objectives of humanitarian law. Protection, in these treaties, is a carrot for rule-regarding behaviour; harsh, summary treatment at the hands of the enemy, is the stick. Such an approach, by design, includes coverage gaps. Beginning with the 1949 Geneva Conventions, this understanding of status has been in decline. The 1949 Geneva Conventions—though they draw on many structural features of traditional law of war treaties—lay the foundations for the 'human rights' perspective that so clearly predominates in the 1977 Protocols. The Geneva Civilian Convention (GC IV) accords substantial protection, which tracks closely the protection accorded under the PoW Convention (GC III), to all enemy nationals who have 'fallen into the hands of the enemy'. Moreover, the Civilian Convention expressly applies to 'unlawful combatants'—authorizing states in such cases to derogate, where necessary for security reasons, from certain rights recognized in the treaty. Common Article 3 of the Geneva Conventions, Article 75 of Protocol I, and the procedural rights regime embedded in the Conventions' grave breach regime provide important humanitarian protections to persons subject to the authority of the enemy—without regard to the 'status' or pre-capture behaviour of the individual in question.

Inter-belligerent reciprocity and the use of humanitarian protection as a carrot were abandoned by contemporary IHL precisely because they proved to be poor ways to promote respect for humanitarian values—all too often initiating or sustaining spirals into barbarity. Because the classical law of war broadly authorized retaliation in the form of abject disregard of humanitarian principles—recognizing drastic reciprocity constraints on the material field of application, the personal field of application, and the scope and content of specific substantive provisions—this scheme blurred the line between proper reciprocal response and violation. If violations are met with law-disregarding retaliation which is in most relevant respects identical to the initial violations, there is a high risk that the retaliation will be interpreted as a violation by the relevant audiences—which, in turn, risks a spiral into unmitigated barbarity. Of course, reciprocity is an effective enforcement strategy only if the enemy understands when a particular action is a reward and when it is a punishment. A decision to apply the Conventions to a conflict, or the decision to accord humane treatment, is unlikely to be understood by the enemy as a 'reward'. The protections required by the treaties are much more likely to be understood as entitlements. Moreover, a decision not to apply the Conventions, or (worse still) not to accord humane treatment, may not be understood as a punishment. The difficulty is that this type of retaliation can itself be understood as a *violation* of the treaty—which, in turn, risks prompting retaliation from the enemy as a response to this 'violation', ad infinitum, thereby risking a retaliatory spiral. A growing body of sociological and psychological evidence documents multiple mechanisms that might trigger or sustain such a spiral of atrocities. The problem is that both the offender and offending parties are more likely to perpetrate further violations when proper retaliation mirrors violations. The moral disengagement that facilitates radical inhumanities is often triggered by perceived victimization in time of war.[31] Moral disengagement is also encouraged by systematic group-level recourse to (1) justifications for violations and (2) dehumanizing characterizations of the enemy as morally or psychologically defective.[32]

The claim that international human rights is structurally incompatible with, and inferior to, IHL is difficult to square with the text, structure, history of the Geneva Conventions, and the institutional and behavioural foundations they imply. To improve its effectiveness, and to neutralize several ways in which the classical laws of war threatened humanitarian values, contemporary IHL has become increasingly similar to international human rights law. It applies very broadly, protects all persons subject to the authority or lethality of the enemy, and accords an increasingly convergent bundle of humanitarian protections irrespective of the behaviour or affiliation of the individual in question.

5 Concluding Remarks

The vision of IHL embodied in the Geneva Conventions and the Additional Protocols thereto expressly or impliedly relies on a certain understanding of: the most pressing threats to humanitarianism in international society, the role played by that subset of international law designed to protect individual persons in meeting those threats, and the role of international law more generally in minimizing those threats. This understanding of the problem and its (partial) solution builds on several important assumptions about the institutional and behavioural realities of war—and the kind of work we can reasonably expect the rule of law to do in this context. In several important respects, the *lex specialis* claim is inconsistent with this vision. As such, this Chapter provides a sustained critique of the *lex specialis* claim from the theoretical perspective of an IHL regime architect. This critique suggests that IHL and human rights law are broadly and fundamentally compatible and complementary. Reliance on human rights law in the interpretation of IHL is, as a general matter, appropriate. Human rights law should be understood, as the widely

---

[31] See eg D. Munoz-Rojas and J.-J. Fresard, 'The Roots of Behavior in War: Understanding and Preventing IHL Violations', 86 *IRRC* (2004) 189–205.

[32] See eg Munoz-Rojas and Fresard (n 31), 189–205; A. Bandura, 'Moral Disengagement in the Perpetration of Inhumanities', 3 *Personality and Social Psychology Review* (1999) 193–209.

understood gaps and ambiguities in IHL should be addressed, in part, through reliance on international human rights law. And although the meaning of abstract human rights standards in time of armed conflict should be interpreted in light of IHL, the content of IHL should not be understood to determine the meaning of human rights law. The international legal project of humanizing warfare requires no less.

CHAPTER 27

GENDER AND ARMED CONFLICT

CHRISTINE CHINKIN

1 INTRODUCTION

THE construction of social sex and gender roles means that armed conflict is sexed and gendered.[1] Men still make up the majority of the fighting forces, while women's generally unequal and subordinate social and economic position makes them vulnerable in particular ways during conflict. Women and men, girls and boys all suffer gender-based violence. Such violence is directed at a person because of his or her gender.[2] For instance men sustain specific harms such as disappearances and deliberate killings in greater numbers than women, while women disproportionately experience sexual violence. The detention of Bosnian Muslims at Potocari on 12 July 1995 and subsequent separation of women and men is illustrative of gender-based crimes. The International Tribunal for the former Yugoslavia (ICTY) found that after separation, the Bosnian Muslim men had suffered 'severe beatings and other cruel treatments'. In the compound 'rapes and killings were reported by credible

[1] J. Goldstein, *War and Gender: How Gender Shapes the War System and Vice Versa* (Cambridge: Cambridge University Press, 2001).
[2] The UN Committee on the Elimination of Discrimination against Women, defines gender-based violence against women as: 'violence that is directed against a woman because she is a woman or that affects women disproportionately'. The UN Committee on the Elimination of Discrimination against Women, General Recommendation No 19, 1992, Violence against Women.

witnesses and some committed suicide out of terror. The entire situation in Potocari has been depicted as a campaign of terror. As an ultimate suffering, some women about to board the buses had their young sons dragged away from them, never to be seen again.'[3]

While it is not spelled out by the ICTY Judges, witness evidence was that the rapes were of women and girls.[4] The forcible separation of young boys from their mothers had different consequences for both: subsequent execution for the sons, along with thousands of 'military aged' men[5] and the loss of their family members for the mothers. The same phenomenon was reported in Kosovo where 'young men were at risk, more than any other group of Kosovo society, of grave human rights violations. Many were executed on the spot, on occasion after horrendous torture'.[6] Children are forcibly abducted into military units where their subsequent experience is likely to be gendered: boys may be required to become child soldiers and girls are likely to have to perform domestic tasks and become subject to sexual violence. Conflict is also gendered in that acts of violence, including sexual violence, are most frequently, but not exclusively,[7] committed by men. Little attention is given to the role of women as combatants or as the perpetrators of international crimes.[8]

While recognizing the reality of gendered violence for all, this Chapter focuses on the gender-specific harms suffered by women in armed conflict. It outlines these harms and considers the international legal framework for responding to them. Despite the long history of rape and other forms of sexual assault against women during armed conflicts, and explicit evidence offered to tribunals of such offences, such acts of violence had not figured prominently in either the legal restraints on warfare, nor directly in judgments of war crimes trials until those of the 1990s. Although the Hague Regulations and the Geneva Conventions included crimes against women, these crimes remained for many years 'forgotten' and shrouded in silence. This Chapter outlines how the silence has been broken, as these crimes have come to the forefront through the legislative and jurisprudential developments of the ad hoc international criminal Tribunals, the ICTY and the International Criminal Tribunal for Rwanda (ICTR), the hybrid Special Court for Sierra Leone (SCSL), and

---

[3] *Prosecutor v Krstić*, IT-98-33-T, 2 August 2001 (TC), § 517.

[4] *Krstić* (n 3), §§ 45, 46.

[5] The ICTY Trial Chamber noted that 'military aged' 'should be understood in its broadest, non-technical sense as including the men and boys who were broadly defined by the Bosnian Serb authorities as being within the vicinity of military age.' *Prosecutor v Krstić*, IT-98-33-T, 2 August 2001 (TC), § 1, note 3. The victims were all defined by their gender.

[6] OSCE, *Kosovo/Kosova As Seen, As Told* (Kosovo Verification Mission, 1999), Ch 15.

[7] For example, *Prosecutor v Pauline Nyiramasuhuko*, ICTR-97-21.

[8] For example, *Prosecutor v Biljana Plavšić*, IT-00-39&40/1-S. The accused was a member of the Bosnian-Serb leadership. In sentencing, a number of factors were taken into account as both aggravating and mitigating factors, including her age and her behaviour after the conflict, but her sex was apparently irrelevant.

the International Criminal Court (ICC). In addition relevant UN Security Council Resolutions on 'women, peace and security' will be examined. Finally, the Chapter considers some of the tensions generated by the evolving international response to gender-based violence in armed conflict.

2 Gender-based Violence in Conflict

Conflict related gender-based violence is violence that occurs during or in the immediate aftermath of armed conflict and which has a link with the conflict.[9] The concept of gender crimes 'emphasises that sexual crimes such as rape are crimes of gender inequality, enacted violently'.[10] Such crimes occur widely in armed conflict and as the jurisprudence of the ad hoc international criminal Tribunals demonstrates, they are experienced by men as well as women.[11]

The incidence and gendered consequences of such forms of violence for men are becoming better understood, although particular forms of trauma and shame lead to under-reporting and silence. Men may feel that being a victim of sexual violence is 'incompatible with their masculinity [...] both at the level of the attack itself—a man should have been able to prevent himself from being attacked—and in dealing with the consequences of the attack—to be able to cope "like a man"'.[12] While sexual violence against men in armed conflict, in the forms of rape, forced sterilization, and mutilations, still needs a great deal of research, it does not reach the levels of such violence committed against women and it is on this that the next section focuses.

Women's experiences of armed conflict and its aftermath vary greatly depending upon such factors as whether they are civilians or combatants, their national

[9] For examples of how such a link may be established, see Report of the Secretary-General on the implementation of Security Council Resolutions 1820 (2008) and 1888 (2009), A/65/592–S/2010/604, 24 November 2010, § 5.

[10] L. Moreno-Ocampo, 'Sexual Violence as International Crime: Interdisciplinary Approaches to Evidence', 35 *Law and Social Inquiry* (2010) 839–46 at 841.

[11] For example, *Prosecutor v Brdanin*, IT-99-36 (male detainees forced to commit oral sex on each other); *Prosecutor v Mucic*, IT-96-21 (brothers forced to commit oral sex on each other and sexual abuse).

[12] S. Sivakumaran, 'Sexual Violence against Men in Armed Conflict', 18 *European Journal of International Law* (2007) 253–76 at 255. Sivakumaran notes its occurrence in El Salvador, Chile, Guatemala, Argentina, Greece, Northern Ireland, Chechnya, Turkey, former Yugoslavia, Sri Lanka, Iraq-Kuwait, Coalition-Iraq, Sino-Japanese war, Liberia, Sierra Leone, Kenya, Sudan, the Central African Republic, Burundi, Uganda, Rwanda, the Democratic Republic of the Congo, Zimbabwe, and South Africa.

identity, race, class, economic circumstances, urban or rural location, family situation, age, employment, and health. Nevertheless, some frequent experiences can be described,[13] resting on the reality that: '[c]onflict creates a free-fire zone, a sort of free for all in which pre-existing ideas about women as inferior, and other discriminatory [...] ideas may be given free expression by frequently all male groups of soldiers and other combatants'.[14]

Conflict-related sexual violence remains largely unreported for a range of reasons, including social stigma, fear, and a feeling of hopelessness because of both the lack of appropriate services and of any official response.[15] Nevertheless it has been reliably recorded in many areas, including Afghanistan, Burundi, Chad, Colombia, Côte D'Ivoire, Democratic Republic of the Congo, Liberia, Peru, Rwanda, Sierra Leone, Chechnya/Russian Federation, Darfur, Sudan, Northern Uganda, and the former Yugoslavia.[16] Rape and sexual violence are not only widespread, they occur in devastating numbers, with estimates of between 250,000 and 500,000 women raped during the 1994 Rwandan genocide; between 20,000 and 50,000 in Bosnia-Herzegovina in the conflict in the early 1990s; and around 200,000 in Bangladesh in 1971.[17] Sexual violence continues in the conflicts and situations of political unrest of the twenty-first century: the 2012 report of the Special Representative of the Secretary-General on sexual violence in armed conflict records widespread sexual violence, and in some instances mass rapes, in many of the same places as those listed above, as well as in conflicts in Libya (during the violence against the Qadhafi regime), Myanmar (especially in militarized ethnic border areas) and Somalia; in post-conflict in such places as the Central African Republic, Chad, and Sri Lanka; and in election violence and political strife in Egypt, Guinea, and Kenya.[18] In Syria there have been reports of rapes in detention, of abductions, and of rapes at checkpoints and during house searches committed by both Government forces and *Shabbiha* members.[19]

Witness testimony in proceedings before international criminal tribunals provides graphic accounts. For example, in the Central African Republic women have been raped by several perpetrators in turn: 'their clothes were ripped off by force [...] they

[13] M. Urban Walker, 'Gender and Violence in Focus: A Background for Gender Justice in Reparations', in R. Rubio-Marin (ed), *The Gender of Reparations* (Cambridge: Cambridge University Press, 2009), 18.

[14] K. Bennoune, 'Do We Need New International Law to Protect Women in Armed Conflict?', 38 *Case Western Reserve Journal of International Law* (2006) 363–92 at 370.

[15] UN Secretary-General, *Conflict-related Sexual Violence*, UN Doc A/66/657–S/2012/33, 23 February 2012, § 16.

[16] UN Secretary-General, *In-depth Study on All Forms of Violence against Women*, UN Doc A/61/122/Add.1, § 145.

[17] UN Doc A/61/122/Add.1, § 146.

[18] UN Secretary-General, *Conflict-related Sexual Violence*, UN Doc A/66/657–S/2012/33, 23 February 2012.

[19] Report of the independent international commission of inquiry on the Syrian Arab Republic, A/HRC/21/50, 16 August 2012, §§ 96–102.

were pushed to the ground, immobilized by MLC soldiers standing on or holding them, raped at gunpoint, in public or in front of or near their family members'.[20] In the Democratic Republic of the Congo, there is sufficient 'evidence to establish substantial grounds to believe that rape was a common practice following an attack and that combatants who forced women to engage in sexual intercourse intended to commit such acts by force or threat of force'.[21] Girl soldiers, irrespective of their age, were subject to rape, sexual violence, sexual slavery, and forced impregnation.[22] In Sierra Leone too 'women and girls were systematically [...] abducted in circumstances of extreme violence, compelled to move along with the fighting forces from place to place, and coerced to perform a variety of conjugal duties including regular sexual intercourse, forced domestic labour such as cleaning and cooking for the "husband", endure forced pregnancy and to care for and bring up children of the "marriage".'[23]

Rape and sexual violence against women occur in varying circumstances: sometimes the perpetrators move on after the attacks, but may be followed by others; sometimes women and girls are abducted into situations of captivity where they are raped repeatedly;[24] sometimes they are raped prior to being murdered. Women cannot easily flee combat areas when they are pregnant, encumbered with children, or by social mores, which inhibit their presence in public spaces. Among the ten countries with the highest lifetime risk of maternal death, most are at war today or are in a post-conflict situation, such as Afghanistan, Sierra Leone, Chad, Angola, Liberia, Somalia, and the Democratic Republic of the Congo.[25] Women and girls are not safe even after they have fled the conflict zone, experiencing further sexual violence in camps for refugees and IDPs.[26] There are reports of men, in particular from Saudi Arabia and other Gulf states seeking young girls in the Syrian refugee camps to buy, offering them 'marriage'. Some are subsequently sent back, but since they feel shamed many do not return to their families and enter prostitution. Families agree to marriages for young girls as a form of protection against further sexual abuse and for the money they receive.[27]

[20] *Prosecutor v Jean-Pierre Bemba Gombo*, Decision Pursuant to Article 61(7) (a) and (b) of the Rome Statute, ICC-01/05-01/08, 15 June 2009, § 165.

[21] *Prosecutor v Germain Katanga and Mathieu Ngudjolo Chui*, Decision on the confirmation of charges, ICC-01/04-01/07, 30 September 2008, § 443.

[22] *Lubanga Dyilo* (n 22), §§ 70–3.

[23] *Prosecutor v Brima, Kamara, Borbor*, SCSL-2004-16-A, (AC) 22 February 2008, 190 (footnotes omitted).

[24] *Prosecutor v Kunarac, Kovač and Vuković*, IT-96-23-T and IT-96-23/1-T (TC) 22 February 2001 (also known as 'the *Foča* case').

[25] N. Puechguirbal, 'Greater Need, Fewer Resources: Ensuring Adequate Health Care For Women During Armed Conflict' (International Committee of the Red Cross, 3 March 2009) available at <http://www.icrc.org/web/eng/siteengo.nsf/html/women-health-interview-010309>.

[26] 'Sexual and gender-based violence is endemic, occurring too often and in every aspect of the lives of displaced women and girls and their families.' UN High Commissioner for Refugees, *Survivors, Protectors, Providers: Refugee Women Speak Out Summary Report* (2011), 16.

[27] International Civil Society Action Network, *What the Women Say Voices from the Ground: Syria's Humanitarian Crisis* (Winter 2013).

What is only too apparent is the extreme violence of sexual attacks and the humiliation and degradation that accompany them for both women and men victims. As well as the immediate pain and terror, rape survivors frequently experience long-term physical injury and psychological trauma. Sexual violence against women in armed conflict is structural, part of the instrumentality of conflict and often inherent to its very aims. The UN Security Council has affirmed that 'sexual violence, when used or commissioned as a tactic of war in order to deliberately target civilians or as a part of a widespread or systematic attack against civilian populations, can significantly exacerbate situations of armed conflict and may impede the restoration of international peace and security'.[28]

Rape and sexual violence are not the only gender-based ways women experience armed conflict,[29] although these have become the focus of the international legal system. Alongside the fear of physical violence civilians face economic and social hardships, increased by the danger of attacks involved in leaving the home for routine activities such as finding food, water, and fuel. Women's traditional domestic responsibilities mean that these tasks fall most heavily on them, as does caring for physically and psychologically injured fighters, the elderly, and children. Women whose male relatives have been killed or are otherwise absent may be left financially unassisted and without the requisite legal documentation to substantiate claims to property. Collapse of governmental agencies, including those for maintaining law and order, and the physical concentration of armed fighters all undermine community restraints on human rights abuses. Women also suffer from a higher incidence of violence at home during armed conflict, whether or not they are living within the combat zone.

The report of the UN Fact Finding Mission to Gaza illustrates a number of such gender-based consequences of conflict for women. The Mission heard that:

the blockade and the military operations had aggravated poverty, which particularly affected women, who must find food and other essentials for their families. Women were often the sole breadwinners [...] but jobs were hard to come by. [...] women bore a greater social burden, having to deal with daily life made harsher by the crisis and, at the same time, provide security and care for injured family members and children, their own and others who have lost their parents.[30]

Living in tents without any privacy was hard for women who, for example, lacked adequate sanitary protection. 'Psychological pressures on men and women, together with financial difficulties, led to family disputes, family violence and divorce.'[31]

---

[28] UNSC Res 1820, 19 June 2008; UNSC Res 1960, 16 December 2010; UNSC Res 2106, 24 June 2013.

[29] C. Lindsey, 'Women and War—An Overview', 839 *International Review of the Red Cross* (2000) 561, lists issues relating to women combatants, missing persons and widowhood, displaced women, and women in detention as well as sexual violence in armed conflict.

[30] Report of the United Nations Fact-Finding Mission on the Gaza Conflict, A/HRC/12/48, 25 September 2009, §§ 1275–9.

[31] Report of the United Nations Fact-Finding Mission on the Gaza Conflict (n 30).

3 Legal Regimes for Addressing Gender and Armed Conflict

A. International humanitarian law prior to 1990

Legal excavation has shown that 'the laws and customs of war had undoubtedly long prohibited rape and other crimes of sexual violence, where they are core crimes within humanitarian law, and, as such, inductively shape the very interpretation of the procedural doctrines and the breadth of substantive crimes within humanitarian law'.[32] Rape was included in the first recorded war crimes trial in 1474. Hugo Grotius asserted that 'as Part of the Law of Nations *viz.* that whoever ravishes a Woman tho' in time of War, deserves to be punished in every Country'.[33] Modern international humanitarian law with respect to the prohibition of sexual violence has developed since the nineteenth century. The Lieber Code, which gave directions to Union forces during the American civil war, prohibited under penalty of death 'All wanton violence committed against persons in the invaded country, [...] all rape, wounding, maiming, or killing of such inhabitants'.[34] The Hague Regulations 1899, Article 46 required 'Family honour and rights' to be respected.[35] 'Family honour' is a coded way of referring to crimes of sexual violence. The 1929 Geneva Convention on Prisoners of War recognized that women may be combatants and thus detained as prisoners of war. Article 3 required women to be treated 'with all the regard due to their sex'.[36] This provision was repeated in the Third Geneva Convention of 1949 with the addition that women prisoners of war 'shall in all cases benefit by treatment' as favourable as that granted to men'[37] and be provided with separate dormitories,[38] conveniences,[39] and quarters for disciplinary treatment.[40]

The jurisdiction of the Nuremburg and Tokyo International Tribunals included war crimes (violations of the laws and customs of war) and crimes against

---

[32] P. Viseur Sellers, 'The Context of Sexual Violence: Sexual Violence as Violations of International Humanitarian Law', in G.K. McDonald and O. Swaak-Goldman (eds), *Substantive and Procedural Aspects of International Criminal Law*, vol 1 (The Hague: Kluwer Law International, 2000), 263.

[33] H. Grotius, *The Rights of War and Peace* Book III (ed Richard Tuck) (Indianapolis: Liberty Fund, 2005), 1301.

[34] General Orders No 100, 24 April 1863, Art 44.

[35] Regulations concerning the Laws and Customs of War on Land, 1899.

[36] Convention between the United States of America and Other Powers, relating to Prisoners of War, Geneva, 27 July, 1929.

[37] Convention Relative to the Treatment of Prisoners of War, Geneva, 12 August 1949, Art 14.

[38] Convention Relative to the Treatment of Prisoners of War (n 37), Art 25.

[39] Convention Relative to the Treatment of Prisoners of War (n 37), Art 29.

[40] Convention Relative to the Treatment of Prisoners of War (n 37), Arts 97 and 108.

humanity.[41] In neither case was rape and sexual violence spelled out.[42] In the case of war crimes the list of specified crimes was stated not to be exhaustive and crimes against humanity included 'other inhumane acts'. Persecution as a crime against humanity included political, racial, or religious grounds, but not those of sex or gender. The war crimes trials in both instances received a good deal of testimony about such crimes but they barely figured in the judgments.

Article 27 of the Fourth Geneva Convention,[43] provides that states parties are under an obligation to protect women in international armed conflict 'against any attack on their honour, in particular against rape, enforced prostitution, or any form of indecent assault'. This is framed in terms of protection rather than as an express prohibition of the listed offences and designates rape as a crime against 'honour' rather than as one of violence.[44] Nor are rape, enforced prostitution, and sexual assault explicitly designated as grave breaches of the Convention,[45] although the definition of grave breaches to include acts 'wilfully causing great suffering or serious injury to body or health' allows sexual violence to come within it. Common Article 3 to the 1949 Geneva Conventions applicable to non-international armed conflicts prohibits 'at any time and in any place whatsoever [...] outrages upon personal dignity, in particular humiliating and degrading treatment'. This again is a formula that allows for the inclusion of rape and other forms of sexual violence, but without express wording to that effect.

The 1977 Additional Protocols make some further advances. Article 76 of AP I, does not refer to the notion of women's honour, but portrays women as the objects of special respect and protection. The fundamental guarantees stipulated in Article 75 include prohibition of any distinction based, inter alia, on 'sex', and the commission of any 'outrages upon personal dignity, in particular humiliating and degrading treatment, enforced prostitution and any form of indecent assault' by any person, whether civilian or military. AP II, applicable in non-international armed conflicts, omits the language of protection and in Article 4(2)(e) prohibits 'outrages upon personal dignity, in particular humiliating and degrading treatment, rape, enforced prostitution and any form of indecent assault'. However the formula identifies rape as a crime against dignity, not as an act of violence.

Other references to women in the Geneva Conventions emphasize their reproductive, mothering, and caring roles. Analysis of the Geneva Conventions provisions on safeguards for women in armed conflict indicates that the primary target

---

[41] Agreement for the Prosecution and Punishment of the Major War Criminals of the European Axis, and Charter of the International Military Tribunal. London, 8 August 1945, Charter, Art 6; International Military Tribunal for the Far East (IMTFE) Tokyo, 19 January 1946 Charter, Art 5.

[42] Control Council Law, No 10, 1945, Punishment of Persons Guilty of War Crimes, Crimes against Peace and against Humanity, Art II(1)(c) includes rape.

[43] Convention Relative to the Protection of Civilian Persons in Time of War, 12 August 1949 (GC IV).

[44] Lindsey points out that honour is more complex than simply a 'value' term but that it is women that must be protected; Lindsey (n 29), 567.

[45] GC IV, Arts 146, 147.

for protection is children. This reduces the status of women without children and obscures the reality that girls are especially vulnerable to forms of sexual attack. For these reasons Judith Gardam has concluded that international humanitarian law has constructed a gender hierarchy parallel to that found in human rights law that has discounted the interests of women in favour of those of combatants and in the name of the notion of 'military necessity'. Gardam asserts:

Far from being a neutral yardstick, military necessity in fact incorporates a hierarchy of values. It assumes [makes natural] that the military victory of the State is pre-eminent. From this flows the seemingly logical value judgment, that the life of the combatant is more important than that of the civilian, even more so if that civilian belongs to the enemy 'State'. [...] The military resists strongly the notion that combatants should assume risks to protect the civilian population. But their position is not immune to challenge. It assumes that war is inevitable.[46]

B. Legal developments after 1991

International humanitarian law no longer provides the sole legal framework for the protection of women in armed conflict. Indeed, since 1977 there has been no further international humanitarian law convention relating to women in armed conflict. However, there has been considerable advancement through the application of international humanitarian law in international criminal courts, through human rights law, through regional treaties, and through UN Security Council Resolutions under the rubric of 'women, peace and security'. Together these legal regimes provide guidance with respect to the obligations of states and non-state actors for the prevention, protection, prosecution, and punishment of gender-based crimes against women in armed conflict.

4 INTERNATIONAL CRIMINAL LAW

A. Legislative provisions

From late 1991 and throughout 1992 global media coverage created widespread pressure for an international legal response encompassing accountability for the atrocities committed against women and men in the conflicts accompanying the disintegration of the former Yugoslavia. In particular, sufficient outrage was expressed

---

[46] J. Gardam, 'Women and the Law of Armed Conflict: Why the Silence?', 46 *ICLQ* (1997) 72.

about the 'massive, organized and systematic'[47] rapes and other violent assaults against women to ensure that they could not be ignored, or discounted as a normal phenomenon of armed conflict. Crimes of sexual violence against women became the focus of international campaigns by women's groups arguing for their acceptance as constituting violations of international criminal law and for their inclusion in the jurisdiction of the ICTY and subsequently the ICTR. Feminist advocates were active at the negotiations for the Rome Statute for a permanent International Criminal Court in 1998.

The ICTY Statute does not spell out crimes of sexual violence as a grave breach or violation of the laws and customs of war but does list rape as a crime against humanity.[48] The ICTR Statute includes rape as a crime against humanity[49] and Article 4 includes 'Outrages upon personal dignity, in particular humiliating and degrading treatment, rape, enforced prostitution and any form of indecent assault' as a violation of Article 3 common to the Geneva Conventions and of Additional Protocol II. The Rome Statute specifies 'rape, sexual slavery, enforced prostitution, forced pregnancy, enforced sterilization, or any other form of sexual violence of comparable gravity' as crimes against humanity, as 'serious violations of the laws and customs applicable in international armed conflict' and as serious violations of Common Article 3. This list emphasizes that rape and sexual violence are not synonymous and that the latter takes many forms. The disaggregation of sexual violence into diverse categories permits a more focused approach to prevention.[50] In addition, 'Committing outrages upon personal dignity, in particular humiliating and degrading treatment' is a violation of the laws and customs of war in international armed conflict and of Common Article 3. The crime of persecution against a collectivity as a crime against humanity for the first time includes 'gender'.

Article 7(3) provides the first international legal definition of 'gender' as referring to 'the two sexes, male and female, within the context of society'.[51] The Statute of the Special Court for Sierra Leone[52] was agreed after the negotiation of the Rome Statute but before its entry into force. Article 2 includes the same crimes as crimes against humanity and Article 3 includes 'outrages upon personal dignity, in particular humiliating and degrading treatment, rape, enforced prostitution and any form of indecent assault' as violations of Common Article 3 and AP II. An additional crime is that of sexual abuse against girls under Sierra Leone law.

---

[47] UNSC Res 820, 17 April 1993.   [48] ICTY Statute, UNSC Res 827, 25 May 1993, Art 5(g).
[49] ICTR Statute, UNSC Res 955, 8 November 1994, Art 3(g).
[50] Report of the Secretary-General on the implementation of Security Council Resolutions 1820 (2008) and 1888 (2009), UN Doc A/65/592–S/2010/604, 24 November 2010, § 4.
[51] A much fuller definition is given by the Committee on the Elimination of Discrimination against Women, General Recommendation No 28, CEDAW/C/2010/47/GC.2, 19 October 2010, § 5.
[52] Established by Agreement between the United Nations and Sierra Leone under UNSC Res 1315, 14 August 2000.

The package of agreements under the umbrella of the Pact on Peace, Security, Good Governance, Economic Development and Regional Integration Stability in the Great Lakes Region, (Stability Pact) 2006, which seek to bring an end to conflict in the Great Lakes region of Africa, includes the groundbreaking Protocol on the Prevention and Suppression of Sexual Violence against Women and Children. The Protocol is a substantive agreement that seeks to fill the legal void that prevails in most of the legal systems in the region as a response to the systemic and massive rape of women and children that have occurred throughout the conflicts there, notably in the DRC. States parties seek 'to combat sexual violence against women and children through preventing, criminalizing, and punishing acts of sexual violence, both in times of peace and in times of war, in accordance with national laws and international criminal law'.[53] The Protocol also provides model language for other legal systems and peace negotiations. By drawing upon and bringing together language from other international instruments, notably the Convention on the Elimination of All Forms of Discrimination against Women, the Rome Statute, the Palermo Trafficking Protocol,[54] and the Protocol to the African Charter on Peoples' and Human Rights on the Rights of Women in Africa,[55] it enhances its own legitimacy and reinforces those instruments.

The Protocol asserts international standards to address crimes of sexual violence as war crimes and crimes against humanity in the region, defining them in accordance with the Statutes of the ICTY and ICTR and the ICC. It establishes links between sexual violence and the offences of trafficking, slavery, and genocide. The Protocol is not concerned solely with individual criminal responsibility as it incorporates preventive aspects, counselling for the rehabilitation of victims of sexual violence, and it advocates for maximum sentencing. Parties have committed themselves to set up regional mechanisms to protect women and children, and provide legal and material assistance for victims and survivors of sexual violence. The Protocol has not, however, been effective at putting an end to the extreme sexual violence in the Great Lakes region, notably the DRC. It has been followed by the Goma Declaration on Eradicating Sexual Violence and Ending Impunity in the Great Lakes Region, 18 June 2008, which seeks in part to address the Protocol's shortcomings by offering a Plan of Action for implementation and language for future peace negotiations.

Another innovative treaty is the 2011 Council of Europe Convention on Preventing and Combating Violence against Women and Domestic Violence.[56] The Convention requires states parties to criminalize and prosecute forms of gender-based violence

---

[53] Stability Pact, 2006, Art 11.

[54] Protocol to Prevent, Suppress and Punish Trafficking in Persons, especially Women and Children, supplementing the United Nations Convention against Transnational Organized Crime, adopted UNGA Res 55/25, 15 November 2000.

[55] Adopted by the 2nd Ordinary Session of the Assembly of the Union, Maputo, 11 July 2003.

[56] CETS No 210, 11 May 2011 (Istanbul Convention).

(including domestic violence) in their national courts. Article 2(3) makes the Convention applicable in 'times of peace and armed conflict', thereby recognizing the continuation of forms of violence during conflict that do not come within the ambit of war crimes.[57] Further, although the Convention identifies domestic violence as a gender-based crime that 'affects women disproportionately', it encourages states parties to apply it to all victims of domestic violence.[58]

There is thus now a considerable body of treaty law addressing crimes of sexual violence against women. To date, the practical implementation of this body of law has been carried out through the ad hoc criminal Tribunals, which have developed some understandings of gender-based crimes and sexual violence. However, these have not progressed uniformly and there remain inconsistencies and uncertainties. The ICC Statute, Article 54(1)(b) explicitly requires the Prosecutor to 'take into account the nature of the crime, in particular where it involves sexual violence, gender violence or violence against children'. José Luis Moreno-Ocampo, former Prosecutor at the ICC, saw as his challenge 'to capture this "gendered" reality in our different cases and present them in connection with the contextual elements of the crimes as defined by the Rome Statute',[59] but, as discussed below, the first completed trials have been disappointing in this respect.

B. Application of law by international criminal tribunals

This section examines some of the ways in which various institutions have applied the somewhat skeletal legal provisions relating to violence against women in conflict situations. A first step in breaking the silence previously surrounding crimes against women in armed conflict is including relevant crimes within international instruments. A second is prosecuting perpetrators as a step towards ending impunity, ensuring accountability and giving practical application to the legal provisions. A third is ensuring that definitions and implementation take into account women's experiences of the crimes committed against them. A fourth is ensuring adequate and appropriate reparation for survivors.

When the ad hoc Tribunals commenced work they had little to rely upon other than the somewhat stark wording of their Statutes and the jurisprudence of the Nuremburg Tribunal and Tokyo Tribunals. There were, for example, no definitions of the various sexual offences under international law (rape, sexual violence, enforced prostitution) and no accepted applicable general principles. The ad hoc Tribunals have had to determine the understandings of sexual crimes as war crimes,

---

[57] See also the Protocol to the African Charter on Human and Peoples' Rights on the Rights of Women in Africa, Maputo, 11 July 2003, Art 11.

[58] Council of Europe Convention on Preventing and Combating Violence against Women and Domestic Violence, Art 1(2).

[59] Moreno-Ocampo (n 10), 843.

crimes against humanity, and genocide. Although the ICC must work with the definitions in the Elements of Crimes agreed by the Assembly of States Parties, the
Tribunals' jurisprudence is nevertheless likely to be influential, both for the work of
the ICC, and in building understandings of these crimes in national courts.

The Tribunals have addressed issues of gender-based and sexual violence in a
number of their judgments.[60] The Tribunals have determined that where the other
elements are present:[61]

- rape can constitute a freestanding crime against humanity and a war crime;
- rape can constitute torture as a crime against humanity and a war crime when it
  comes within the definition of torture;[62]
- rape and other forms of sexual violence can constitute genocide when committed
  with intent to destroy in whole or in part a national, ethnical, racial, or religious
  group;[63]
- rape and other forms of sexual violence can constitute persecution and enslavement as crimes against humanity;
- sexual violence can constitute part of outrages on personal dignity and inhumane
  treatment.

Some judgments have made especially important contributions to the understanding of these crimes. For example in the *Foča* case the ICTY considered the situation
of Bosnian Muslim women who were detained in a range of local buildings including schools, houses, and apartments.[64] They were forced to carry out tasks such as
cooking and cleaning and were repeatedly raped and degraded in other ways. The
ICTY held that the factors of enslavement include control of a person's movement
and physical environment, psychological control, and control of sex.[65] Enslavement
requires the exercise of any or all of the powers attaching to the right of ownership
over a person,[66] which are present in the refusal of sexual autonomy and denial
of choice to the detained women who had to provide sexual services on demand.
When a woman cannot refuse sexual contact, where such matters as abortion, con-
traception, and personal hygiene are totally under the control of her abusers, and
she has '[n]owhere to go and no place to hide',[67] then her captors exercise ownership
over her and she is enslaved.

[60] UN Department of Peacekeeping Operations, *Review of the Sexual Violence Elements of the
Judgments of the International Criminal Tribunal for the Former Yugoslavia, the International Criminal
Tribunal for Rwanda, and the Special Court for Sierra Leone in the Light of Security Council Resolution
1820* (New York, 2010), 29, 46, 59.

[61] UN Department of Peacekeeping Operations (n 60), 25.

[62] Convention against Torture and Other Cruel, Inhuman or Degrading Treatment or Punishment,
(1984), Art 1; Elements of Crime, ICC-ASP/1/3 (part II-B), 9 September 2002, Art 7(1)(f).

[63] Convention on the Prevention and Punishment of the Crime of Genocide (1948).

[64] *Kunarac*, (n 24).

[65] *Kunarac* (n 24), §§ 542–3.

[66] *Kunarac* (n 25), § 539.   [67] *Kunarac* (n 24), § 740.

The ICTY did not, however, make a finding of sexual slavery, as no such crime is determined as a crime against humanity in its Statute. In contrast, the Statute of the SCSL, Article 2(g) includes sexual slavery as a crime against humanity. The camps at Foča (and elsewhere in the former Yugoslavia) were a modern manifestation of the forced detention of the so-called comfort women detained across Asia by the Japanese military in World War II. Those women, too, had no control over their own destinies, even where they were not physically locked up.[68] Designation as enslavement removes issues of consent to individual acts of intercourse.

It is noteworthy that typical 'women's roles' (cooking, cleaning) were recognized as forced labour and gendered aspects of enslavement. Assignment of domestic tasks to women can be seen as everyday, natural, and as too mundane to be conceived of as constituting crimes against humanity. Forced labour is more readily associated with such atrocities as building the Burmese railway or factory labour, but at Nuremberg it was held that sending 500,000 women domestic labourers to Germany to relieve German housewives and the wives of German farmers also constituted slave labour.[69]

A particular form of sexual slavery in armed conflict is forced marriage. The SCSL Trial Chamber found such occurrences to constitute sexual slavery as a crime against humanity.[70] Justice Doherty, partially dissenting, discussed various elements of 'bush marriages' that had been identified by the prosecution expert: the women's families were not involved in the marriage; there was no official marriage ceremony; it was a means of survival for a woman who by 'belonging' to a single person would be spared gang rapes, at least while the 'marriage' lasted; the woman was required to do as her 'husband' commanded and 'to gratify his sexual wishes whenever he so desired without question'. A bush marriage frequently involved long-term stigmatization and rejection by families and communities.[71] The Appeal Chamber accepted Justice Doherty's characterization of forced marriage and found that a separate crime of forced marriage existed as a crime against humanity in the context of Sierra Leone. The separate element was that of forced conjugal association and sexual exclusivity.[72]

The ICTR has been at the forefront of identifying rape as genocidal when committed with the intention to destroy in whole or in a part a group identified in national, ethnic, racial, or religious terms. Indeed, rape and other forms of extreme sexual violence have been at the very core of group destruction. These include preventing births within a group,[73] for example through sexual mutilation, forced

---

[68] G. Hicks, *The Comfort Women: Japan's Brutal Regime of Enforced Prostitution in the Second World War* (New York: W.W. Norton & Co, 1995); C. Chinkin 'Peoples' Tribunals: Legitimate or Rough Justice?', 24 *Windsor Yearbook of Access to Justice* (2006) 201–20.

[69] *Kunarac* (n 65), § 523.

[70] *Prosecutor v Brima, Kamara and Kanu*, SCSL-04-16-T, 20 June 2007.

[71] *Brima, Kamara and Kanu* (n 70), §§ 27–36 (sep op J Doherty).

[72] *Brima, Kamara and Kanu* (n 70), §§ 190–5.

[73] Genocide Convention, Art II(d).

sterilization, forced birth control, separation of the sexes, prohibiting marriage, and mental trauma.[74] Forced pregnancy may also be directed towards destruction of the group. As the Trial Chamber in *Akayesu* stated:

In patriarchal societies [...] an example of a measure intended to prevent births within a group is the case where, during rape, a woman [...] is deliberately impregnated by a man of another group, with the intent to have her give birth to a child who will consequently not belong to its mother's group.[75]

The Statute of the ICC, Article 7(2)(f), defines forced pregnancy as a crime against humanity. Forced pregnancy is one of the few sexual crimes that can only be committed against women. It comprises two separate acts: forcible impregnation and the forced denial of access to abortion. The ICC definition of forced pregnancy is limited to where there is the 'intent of affecting the ethnic composition of any population'. That religious objections to abortion determined this restrictive understanding of forced pregnancy is made apparent by the rider that the definition 'shall not in any way be interpreted as affecting national laws relating to pregnancy'. In no other instance is there a requirement for an additional intent or motive for an offence to constitute a crime against humanity. Forced pregnancy constitutes a very particular denial of a woman's autonomy and bodily integrity by forcing her to bear a child. Yet in this one instance the continuing insistence for control over women's reproductive capacity has subjugated gender identity (that the crime was committed against her because she is a woman) to ethnic identity.

Rape is central to facts that have led to findings of torture, enslavement, and genocide. A crucial question is how rape is defined under international law. How the law constructs rape determines who has in fact been raped. Where there is dissonance between survivors' perceptions of what has occurred to them, and the law's verdict on this point, the impunity granted means that the law ceases to be relevant to survivors as either an instrument of protection or of punishment. Such impunity is often based upon the myths and stereotypes about male and female sexuality that inform decisions about rape,[76] but which ignore such factors as the trauma of rape, the practical and security reasons against reporting rape, especially in armed conflict, and the fear and shame experienced by the survivors. If impunity for sexual violence in armed conflict is to cease it is essential that such myths are confronted and dispelled. It is therefore important that the definitions, understandings, and procedures for the prosecution of such crimes before international tribunals reflect the perspectives of rape victims.

The Tribunals had to evolve their own definitions of rape and other sexual offences, and there have been divergent views between different Trial Chambers.

---

[74] *Prosecutor v Jean-Paul Akayesu*, ICTR-96-4, 2 September 1998, §§ 507–8.

[75] *Prosecutor v Jean-Paul Akayesu*, (n 74), § 507.

[76] For a discussion of 'rape myths' see *Vertido v the Philippines*, Communication No 18/2008, 1 September 2010, CEDAW/C/46/18/2008.

One view has been to define rape not through specific prohibited acts but to capture the essence of rape as 'a physical invasion of a sexual nature, committed on a person under circumstances which are coercive'.[77] The emphasis on coercive circumstances addresses the situation where an individual may, through fear and desperation, not have actually protested or fought against sexual activity. Coercion is inherent in conflict and in the very presence of armed militia and genocidaires. This definition of rape is consonant with the context of the particular crimes within the Tribunals' jurisdiction—war crimes, crimes against humanity, and genocide—with all the elements of force, terror, and helplessness that are integral to situations where such offences are committed.

An alternative approach is to define rape through a mechanical description of body parts. The ICTY in *Furundžija* held the objective elements of rape to be:

(i)   the sexual penetration, however slight:
    (a) of the vagina or anus of the victim by the penis of the perpetrator or any other object used by the perpetrator; or
    (b) of the mouth of the victim by the penis of the perpetrator
(ii) by coercion or force or threat of force against the victim or a third person.[78]

This definition incorporates rape of men and non-penile rape. Brutal rapes with wood, guns, and other weapons are also prevalent in armed conflict. The Trial Chamber held oral rape to be 'a most humiliating and degrading attack upon human dignity' and stated that 'such an extremely serious sexual outrage as forced oral penetration should be classified as rape'.[79] However, the second part of this definition of rape requires coercion or force of the actual victim or third person. Further, the mechanical description of objects and body parts fails to capture the aggression of rape. In *Kunarac* the Trial Chamber emphasized issues of coercion, consent, and implied consent. It concluded that what appears to be common to legal systems around the world is 'the basic underlying principle [...] that sexual penetration will constitute rape if it is not truly voluntary or consensual on the part of the victim'.[80] It adopted the *Furundžija* definition, but addressed the issue of consent by adding a final sentence derived from *Akayesu*: 'Consent for this purpose must be consent given voluntarily, as a result of the victim's free will, assessed in the context of the surrounding circumstances'.[81] The Trial Chamber accepted the evidence of the witness, who, Kunarac alleged, had consented to, and even initiated, sex with him, that she had been threatened by another soldier, that he would kill her unless she satisfied his commander, Kunarac. The Chamber was unmoved by Kunarac's claim that he did not know she was acting out of fear. In the general context of war and the

[77] *Prosecutor v Jean-Paul Akayesu*, ICTR-96-4, 2 September 1998, § 598.
[78] *Prosecutor v Furundžija*, IT-95-17/1-T, 10 December 1998, § 185.
[79] *Prosecutor v Furundžija*, IT-95-17/1-T, 10 December 1998, § 183.
[80] *Kunarac and others* (n 24), § 440.
[81] *Kunarac and others* (n 24), § 460.

position of Muslim women and girls detained, at that time it was not credible that he was 'confused by her motives'.

The verdict reveals its understanding of the situation, but its analysis brought the issue of consent back into the definition. The Appeal Chamber approved the definition of the Trial Chamber[82] adding that there is no basis in customary international law for requiring resistance on the part of the victim, a requirement that would be 'absurd on the facts'. In 2006 in *Gacumbitsi* the Appeal Chamber was asked by the prosecution to revisit the question of the elements of rape as a crime against humanity or as an act of genocide. The Appeal Chamber adopted the *Kunarac* definition and thus retained the elements of non-consent and knowledge thereof, thereby requiring the prosecution to prove these beyond reasonable doubt. Reference to consent in the Rules of Procedure refers only to the circumstances when evidence of consent is admissible.[83]

5 Women, Peace, and Security

In addition to the development of international humanitarian law through international criminal law, the political organs of the United Nations have addressed gendered crimes and crimes of sexual violence. On 31 October 2000 the UN Security Council adopted Resolution 1325 on Women, Peace, and Security, addressing the important role of women in the prevention and resolution of conflicts and in peace building. In June 2008 the Security Council built upon Resolution 1325 with Resolution 1820. This resolution linked sexual violence to the primary purpose of the Security Council in the maintenance of international peace and security. It noted the jurisprudential developments confirming that rape and other forms of sexual violence can constitute a war crime, a crime against humanity, or a constitutive act with respect to genocide, and stressed the need to end impunity with respect to these crimes. It demanded that parties to armed conflict take appropriate measures 'to protect civilians, including women and girls, from all forms of sexual violence' and spelled out certain measures such as enforcing appropriate military disciplinary measures, upholding the principle of command responsibility, training troops on the categorical prohibition of all forms of sexual violence against civilians, debunking myths that fuel sexual violence, vetting armed and security forces to take into account past actions of rape and other forms of sexual violence, and evacuation to safety of women and children under imminent threat of sexual violence.

---

[82] *Prosecutor v Kunarac and others*, IT-96-23/1-A, 12 June 2002, §§ 128–33.

[83] *Gacumbitsi v Prosecutor*, ICTR-01-64 –A, 7 July 2006, §§ 147–57.

Two Security Council Resolutions in 2009 continued the two-pronged approach of seeking enhancement of women's participation in relevant decision-making, and ensuring accountability for the commission of crimes of sexual violence. Security Council Resolution 1888, of 30 September 2009, reiterates much of Resolution 1820 and calls upon the UN Secretary-General to appoint a Special Representative 'to provide coherent and strategic leadership, [...] to address, at both headquarters and country level, sexual violence in armed conflict, while promoting cooperation and coordination of efforts among all relevant stakeholders'.[84] The Special Representative chairs UN Action against Sexual Violence in Armed Conflict, a network of 12 United Nations agencies established in order to enhance coordinated action and strengthen responses. The Secretary-General was also asked 'to deploy rapidly a team of experts to situations of particular concern with respect to sexual violence in armed conflict, working through the United Nations presence on the ground and with the consent of the host government, to assist national authorities to strengthen the rule of law'.

Resolution 1889, 5 October 2009, returned to women's participation in 'all stages of peace processes, particularly in conflict resolution, post-conflict planning and peacebuilding'. It encourages states to 'increase access to health care, psychosocial support, legal assistance and socio-economic reintegration services for victims of sexual violence, in particular in rural areas'. Security Council Resolution 1960, 16 December 2010, reaffirms the earlier Resolutions and the Council's commitment to the cessation of all acts of sexual violence. It adopts a 'naming and shaming' approach by requesting the Secretary-General to compile lists of those who are 'credibly suspected of committing or being responsible for patterns of rape and other forms of sexual violence in situations of armed conflict' and goes further by indicating the use of such lists for 'more focused United Nations engagement with those parties', including potentially through sanctions.[85] The Security Council reiterates the importance of command responsibility and calls for the 'issuance of clear orders through chains of command prohibiting sexual violence'. In seeking implementation of Resolution 1960, the President of the Council has stressed the need for timely, verified, and reliable data which would assist in determining appropriate action, including possible targeted

[84] In February 2010 Margot Wallström from Sweden was appointed to this post; in 2012 Zainab Bangura from Sierra Leone took up the position.

[85] The 2012 report of the Special Representative on sexual violence in armed conflict lists a number of armed groups as parties to armed conflicts in the Central African Republic, Côte d'Ivoire, the DRC and names a leader (n 18); Annex, List of parties that are credibly suspected of committing or being responsible for patterns of rape and other forms of sexual violence in situations of armed conflict on the Security Council agenda. See also UNSC Res 2078, 28 November 2012 (financial and travel measures applicable to individuals in the DRC committing serious violations involving children or women in armed conflict, including killing and maiming, sexual violence, abduction, and forced displacement). UNSC Res 2106, 24 June 2013, § 13 urges sanctions committees to apply targeted sanctions against perpetrators.

and graduated measures.[86] The Security Council has recalled its Resolutions on women, peace, and security in country-specific resolutions.[87]

The Security Council has thus recognized the systemic use of sexual violence 'for political motivations and as a tactic of war'[88] and its adverse impact on the maintenance of international peace and security. It has called upon parties to conflict, states and institutions, to take concrete measures to prevent such violence, to protect civilians, especially women and children,[89] to strengthen legal provisions and mechanisms to combat impunity, and to address the medical and social-economic consequences of sexual violence. In a range of resolutions it has also instituted a zero-tolerance policy of sexual exploitation and abuse in UN peacekeeping operations[90] and has reiterated the importance of including gender advisers, women protection advisers, and child protection advisers in UN missions.[91]

These Resolutions and Statements go a long way in recognizing the extent and pervasiveness of sexual violence in conflict and the importance of empowering women, for example through enhanced participation.[92] Despite references, inter alia, to gender-based violence, gender advisers, and experts, the Resolutions focus 'in particular' on sexual violence against women and children, thereby conflating 'gender' and 'women' to the detriment of making more visible sexual violence against men. Unlike the Beijing Platform for Action, the resolutions do not make recommendations with respect to the reduction of military expenditures and the availability of armaments.[93]

6 Conclusions: Tensions and Debates

Feminist activism and interventions have ensured that gender and sex-based crimes in armed conflict have become visible and acquired higher priority within the international legal order since the early 1990s. Such crimes are now explicitly recognized

[86] UN Doc S/PRST/2012/3, 23 February 2012.

[87] For example, UNSC Res 2085, 20 December 2012 (Mali); UNSC Res 2062, 26 July 2012 (Côte D'Ivoire); UNSC Res 2121, 10 October 2013 (Central African Republic).

[88] UN Doc S/PRST/2013/2, 12 February 2013.

[89] The Security Council has repeated its condemnation of 'sexual and other forms of violence committed against civilians in armed conflict, in particular women and children' in other resolutions; eg UNSC Res 1674, 28 April 2006, on Protection of civilians in armed conflict.

[90] For example, UNSC Res 2086, 21 January 2013, United Nations Peacekeeping Operations.

[91] UN Doc S/PRST/2013/2, 12 February 2013.

[92] On the limited impact of UNSC Res 1325, see C. Bell and C. O'Rourke, 'Peace Agreements or Pieces of Paper? The Impact of UNSC Resolution 1325 on Peace Processes and their Agreements', 59 *ICLQ* (2010) 941–80. UNSC Res 2122, 18 October 2013 emphasizes the importance of implementation of Resolution 1325.

[93] Beijing Platform for Action, § 143.

by the Security Council as constituting a threat to the maintenance of international peace and security and have been effectively included within the jurisdiction of the ad hoc international criminal Tribunals and the Statute of the ICC. Convictions have been achieved within the former and relevant charges laid before the latter. They have been moved up in the hierarchy of crimes.[94] However, there remain conflicting concerns: on the one hand are considerations which show that much more work is still needed to make international humanitarian law truly responsive to women's experiences of armed conflict; while on the other hand are arguments that these developments themselves undermine women's exercise of autonomy.

The implementation of international humanitarian law through international criminal tribunals is still limited. First, only limited numbers of perpetrators of sexual violence are ever brought to justice.[95] International criminal trials deal only with the most serious incidents of war crimes and crimes against humanity (explicitly so in the case of the ICC[96]). Prosecutorial discretion means that not all such cases are subject to criminal charges and considerations such as the availability, willingness, and credibility of witnesses, the perceived relative importance of diverse charges as well as selected locations for investigation all impact upon decision-making with respect to laying charges. Decisions not to include, or to limit, such charges may be controversial,[97] as illustrated by the *Lubanga* case, the first completed trial before the ICC. Although the Trial Chamber heard witness evidence of the rape and sexual violence committed against girl soldiers,[98] no charges relating to sexual violence were brought. In a separate and dissenting (on particular issues) opinion, Judge Odio Benito expressed her disquiet that by excluding sexual violence from its understanding of 'direct participation in hostilities' the majority had rendered it invisible. She continued that such invisibility leads to discrimination 'against the victims of enlistment, conscription and use who systematically suffer from this crime as an intrinsic part of the involvement with the armed group'. She noted the gender-specific aspect of sexual violence in the potential consequence of pregnancy for girls 'that often lead[s] to maternal or infant's deaths, disease, HIV, psychological traumatisation and social isolation'.[99] These crimes should have been charged and

---

[94] J. Halley, 'Rape in Berlin: Reconsidering the Criminalisation of Rape in the International Law of Armed Conflict', 9 *Melbourne Journal of International Law* (2008) 78, 83.

[95] UNSC Res 1960, 16 December 2010.   [96] Statute of the ICC, Art 1.

[97] For example, while celebrating the indictment in *Kunarac* as 'unparalleled in international, regional or national courts', Kelly Askin considered omission of 'appropriate charges of genocide' as a shortcoming; K. Askin, 'Sexual Violence in Decisions and Indictments of the Yugoslav and Rwandan Tribunals: Current Status', 93 *AJIL* (1999) 97–123 at 118; Askin also regretted that the decision did not use the term 'sexual slavery' referring only to enslavement; K. Askin, 'Prosecuting Wartime Rape and other Gender-related Crimes under International Law: Extraordinary Advances, Enduring Obstacles', 21 *Berkeley Journal of International Law* (2003) 288–349 at 340.

[98] *Prosecutor v Thomas Lubanga Dyilo*, ICC-01/04-01/06, Judgment of 14 March 2012.

[99] *Thomas Lubanga Dyilo* (n 98), separate and dissenting opinion, Judge Odio-Benito, §§ 15–20.

evaluated separately. In setting out principles for determining appropriate reparations the Trial Chamber asserted that the Court 'should formulate and implement
reparations awards that are appropriate for the victims of sexual and gender-based
violence', ensuring a 'specialist, integrated and multidisciplinary approach'.[100]
Nevertheless, in sentencing Lubanga, Judge Odio Benito found herself again in disagreement with the majority in Trial Chamber I, in particular with respect to what
she considered their disregard of the damage caused by sexual violence to victims
and their families.[101] An expert witness had testified as to the post-traumatic stress
disorder suffered by child soldiers following such events as experiencing or witnessing 'killing or mutilation, severe physical or sexual assault, sexual abuse and rape'
and which could be long lasting. Again Judge Odio Benito emphasized the need to
'keep in mind the differential gender effects and damages that these crimes have
upon their victims'.

Acquittals where the evidence cannot sustain conviction of particular accused
persons can also cause distress to victims. Unlike in the *Lubanga* case, charges
of rape and sexual slavery were brought in the case against Mathieu Ngudjolo
Chui.[102] Witnesses had testified to 'horrific attacks, rapes, gang rapes and enslavement' that took place during the attack on Bogoro village in February 2003. The
accused was acquitted on the grounds that it was not proved beyond a reasonable
doubt that he was the commander of the relevant forces at the time of the attack.
Although the ICC stressed that this did not mean that crimes had not been committed, or that the population had not suffered, the decision was nevertheless
described as a devastating outcome to victims and survivors.[103] The trials that take
place represent a selective and limited picture of the reality and therefore cannot truly convey the extent or circumstances of gendered crimes in armed conflict. At the same time, the mediation of witnesses' narratives through the rules
of evidence and procedure may inhibit their ability to provide the story they wish
to tell.

The paucity of international criminal trials and the principle of complementarity
in Article 1 of the Statute of the ICC make clear that the internalization of international criminal law into national legal systems and prosecution in national courts
of international crimes, including those of gender-based and sexual violence, is a
way forward. In this regard the announcement by the UK Foreign Secretary that the
United Kingdom is seeking a Declaration from the G8 Foreign Ministers that rape
and serious sexual violence amount to grave breaches of the Geneva Conventions,

---

[100] *Prosecutor v Thomas Lubanga Dyilo*, ICC-01/04-01/06, 7 August 2012, Decision establishing the principles and procedures to be applied to reparations, §§ 207–8.

[101] *Lubanga Dyilo* (n 22), 40ff.

[102] *Prosecutor v Mathieu Ngudjolo Chui*, ICC-01/04-02/12-4, Judgment of 18 December 2012.

[103] Press statement by Brigid Inder, Women's Initiatives for Gender Justice, 18 December 2012.

and that they are prepared to pursue domestic prosecution of such crimes on the basis of universal jurisdiction is welcome.[104]

Secondly, and linked, while international humanitarian law is regulatory and protective, international criminal law is reactive and its remedies are only punitive. It fails to take account of the multiple harms generated by acts of sexual violence: 'there is no discursive space to document the likelihood that victims of rape will face other secondary harms such as rejection, depression, destitution, and continuing prostitution'.[105] There is a practical need for international criminal law to recognize that many such witnesses are also victims of crime who are entitled to long-term financial and other remedies, such as medical care, support, shelters and refuges, resettlement, and retraining,[106] taking into account the gendered nature of the offences. Thirdly, inclusion of crimes against women within the canon of international criminal law does not address fundamental issues of power or question the 'objectivity' of the international legal system and its hierarchy based on gender. Focusing on specific crimes may exclude broader enquiry into the motives for such offences and result in a failure to ask important questions: Why is it that crimes of sexual violence against women are consistently committed both in armed conflict and non-conflict situations? What is the proper response of international criminal law to the gross inequalities of power that makes their commission so regular? Why does violence against women not stop when a cease-fire or negotiated settlement is achieved but continues in ways directly connected with conflict?[107] In sum, '[r]eparation must go above and beyond the immediate reasons and consequences of the crimes and violations; they must aim to address the political and structural inequalities that negatively shape women's and girls' lives'.[108]

These critiques go to the nature of the legal response. Other critiques consider what Janet Halley has termed 'governance feminism'—successful feminist insistence on the inclusion of crimes of sexual violence against women within the international legal system—as having become excessive with unconsidered consequences. Karen Engle noted that there were disagreements between feminists at the outset of the 1990s, with some arguing that 'genocidal rape' should be distinguished from 'normal, everyday rape' while others disagreed arguing that rape of women in conflict

[104] Parliamentary Debates, House of Commons, 14 February 2013, col 1141, available at <http://www.publications.parliament.uk/pa/cm201213/cmhansrd/cm130214/debtext/130214-0003.htm#13021465000003> The Declaration was adopted by the G8, 11 April 2013.

[105] R. Dixon, 'Rape as a Crime in International Humanitarian Law: Where to From Here?', 13 European Journal of International Law (2002) 697–720 at 705.

[106] UNGA Res 40/34, 29 November 1985, Declaration of Basic Principles of Justice for Victims of Crime and Abuse of Power; UNGA Res 60/147, 16 December 2005, Basic Principles and Guidelines on the Right to a Remedy and Reparation for Victims of Gross Violations of International Human Rights Law and Serious Violations of International Humanitarian Law.

[107] Cf S. Marks, 'Human Rights and Root Causes', 74 Modern Law Review (2011) 57–78.

[108] Nairobi Declaration on Women's and Girls' Right to a Remedy and Reparation, 2007, § 3H, available at <http://www.womensrightscoalition.org/site/reparation/signature_en.php>.

is nothing new, is committed by all sides, and that focus on genocide distorts this reality. She suggests that even though this disagreement was diluted with the founding of the ad hoc criminal Tribunals, nevertheless the focus on criminal prosecution undermines women's political and sexual agency.[109] Halley argues that armed conflict has become routinely represented as rape and forms of sexual violence against women, rendering invisible other atrocities and defining women solely through their sexuality and reproductive capacity rather than as holistic beings.

This indeed could promote sexual violence through the 'weaponization' of rape. Halley finds especially problematic the issue of consent: can a woman consent to intercourse with a person from the opposing side in the coercive circumstances of armed conflict? When a woman consents to intercourse with one man hoping for some security from being raped by other men, and also for some food and other unavailable items, conceptual differences between survival, prostitution, enforced prostitution, collaboration, forced marriage, and rape become blurred. The anonymous 'Woman in Berlin' asks: 'What does it mean—rape? When I said the word for the first time aloud [...] it sent shivers down my spine. Now I can think it and write it with an untrembling hand [...] It sounds like the absolute worst, the end of everything—but it's not.'[110]

Similarities between the coercive circumstances of armed conflict and those that force women into prostitution outside of armed conflict are apparent, and, coupled with the continued myths about rape and implied consent, undermine the applicability of different legal regimes to armed conflict and so-called peacetime. As is apparent from the account of *the Woman in Berlin*, concentration on crimes of sexual violence conceals the many other gender-specific ways in which women experience armed conflict, such as disappearances of male family members, and destruction of property and food sources for women who are the primary carers within family and community. Halley's position has been challenged, for example by Hilary Charlesworth who argues that the inclusion of feminist ideas into international law is not in fact that great, and that it is important not to become 'dazzled by the inclusive language' and the concept of gender integration that has spread through the UN system.[111]

Dianne Otto argues that 'governance feminism' is a misnomer: that the 'the institutional reception and management of feminist ideas' has divested them 'of their emancipatory content', making it more a matter of co-option than governance.[112] Otto, however, is concerned about the continued protective stance towards women

---

[109] K. Engle, 'Feminism and its (Dis)contents: Criminalizing Wartime Rape', 99 *American Journal of International Law* (2005) 778–816 at 780.

[110] Anonymous, *A Woman in Berlin* (Virago, 2005), 83.

[111] H. Charlesworth, 'Talking to Ourselves: Should International Lawyers Take a Break from Feminism?', in S. Kouvo and Z. Pearson (eds), *Between Resistance and Compliance? Feminist Perspectives on International Law* (Oxford: Hart Publishing, 2011), 17–33.

[112] D. Otto, 'The Exile of Inclusion: Reflections on Gender issues in International Law over the Last Decade', 10 *Melbourne Journal of International Law* (2009) 11–26.

that assumes their vulnerability, for example by the conjunction of 'women and children' and the zero tolerance response to sexual abuse committed by UN peace-keepers. This policy gives insufficient attention to 'the grinding poverty or the poorly resourced charity-based models of aid that produce economies of survival sex', diverting attention from the politics of social justice in order to 'save the UN's humanitarianism from scandal. It makes the survival of the "victims" it claims to protect even more precarious'.[113] Otto's intention is not to 'understate the harm that can be inflicted by sexual violence, but rather to demystify it and suggest dealing with the problem in a way that is empowering for women'.[114]

Another concern is that focus on gender-based crimes against women minimizes those offences committed against men. As Adam Jones points out, 'non-combat-ant men have been and continue to be the most frequent targets of mass killing and genocidal slaughter, as well as a host of lesser atrocities and abuses'.[115] He notes that a leading work on 'gendercide' refers only to such behaviours when directed at women.[116] Nevertheless, lessening the unnecessary suffering of mostly male com-batants has been the objective of international humanitarian law and asserting accountability for crimes committed against them has formed the bulk of the work of war crimes tribunals. However, other forms of violence against men in armed conflict have remained less visible and accurate numbers of these offences will most probably never be known.

While acknowledging that the figures are nevertheless unlikely ever to equate to those relating to sexual violence against women, Sandesh Sivakumaran argues con-vincingly that this does not justify exclusive attention being given to female sexual violence.[117] All sexual violence, whoever it is committed against, warrants attention from the international community. Indeed, breaking the silence about crimes com-mitted against women has opened the door to the same with respect to men. As Sivakumaran notes '[i]n some respects, the situation facing male rape victims today is not so different from that which faced female victims, say, two centuries ago'.[118] Further, sexual violence against males is part of the same context—gender dimen-sions of conflict—as that committed against females; understanding more about the causes, circumstances, and outcomes of one facilitates our greater understand-ing of, and therefore appropriate responses to, all kinds of sexual violence. In both manifestations of violence 'the constructions of masculinity and femininity and the

---

[113] D. Otto, 'Making Sense of Zero Tolerance Policies in Peacekeeping Sexual Economies', in V. Munro and C.F. Stychin (eds), *Sexuality and the Law: Feminist Engagements* (Oxon: Glass House Press, 2007).

[114] D. Otto, 'The Exile of Inclusion: Reflections on Gender Issues in International Law over the Last Decade', 10 *Melbourne Journal of International Law* (2009) 11–26 at 24.

[115] A. Jones, 'Gendercide and Genocide', 2 *Journal of Genocide Research* (2000) 185–211 at 186.

[116] Jones (n 115), discussing M. Warren, *Gendercide: The Implications of Sex Selection* (Totowa, NJ. Rowman & Allanheld, 1985).

[117] S. Sivakumaran, 'Sexual Violence against Men in Armed Conflict', 18 *European Journal of International Law* (2007) 253–77 at 260.

[118] Sivakumaran (n 117), 253.

stereotypes involved are similar'.[119] Finally, this may assist in dispelling the stereo-types of women as victims and in need of protection and men only as perpetrators. Thus a more nuanced understanding of the role of gender in conflict can play a part in a transformation of gender relations.

These tensions demonstrate the complexity of gender-based crimes and crimes of sexual violence whether committed by or against women or men. It is evident that the somewhat blunt instruments of international humanitarian law and inter-national criminal law are inadequate to address the multiple issues that are raised by their continuing commission. Nevertheless they are an important step and gov-ernments may find they cannot easily discount the formal legal commitments they have accepted. Without feminist critique and initiative, international criminal law would have continued to exonerate the most blatant gender-based crimes of sexual violence against women, thereby enhancing the expectation of impunity and allow-ing the unchallenged continuation of gender constructs.

[119] Sivakumaran (n 117), 260.

CHAPTER 28

....

ARMED CONFLICT AND FORCED MIGRATION

....

....

A SYSTEMIC APPROACH TO INTERNATIONAL HUMANITARIAN LAW, REFUGEE LAW, AND HUMAN RIGHTS LAW

....

VINCENT CHETAIL

1 INTRODUCTION

....

ALTHOUGH armed conflicts constitute the main cause of forced migrations, the applicable normative framework is plagued by recurrent ambiguities and controversies. Three decades ago, Dinstein asserted that 'in its present form international law does not deal in a systematic fashion with the whole spectrum of the problem of refugees in armed conflict. [...] Still there are several provisions relevant to the issue which are dispersed in various legal instruments'.[1] These instruments are scattered throughout three main branches of international law: international humanitarian

[1] Y. Dinstein, 'Refugees and the Law of Armed Conflict', 12 *Israel Yearbook on Human Rights* (1982) 94.

law, refugee law, and human rights law. Their concurrent applicability in times of armed conflict is arguably both the solution and the problem. On the one hand, the great variety of applicable instruments reflects the multifaceted dimensions of forced migration and its cross-cutting character. On the other hand, such a fragmentation undermines the understanding and cogent application of the existing legal norms.

While sharing the same purpose of protecting individuals against abuses, international humanitarian law, refugee law, and human rights law have largely evolved around their own specific sources, institutions, and ethos. Meanwhile, the academic literature has mainly focused on the interfaces between refugee law and humanitarian law to the detriment of a more holistic approach,[2] thereby excluding human rights law as a source of refugee protection in armed conflict.[3]

Scholars' discussions about the applicable legal regime have been further biased by the natural temptation of specialists to celebrate the virtues of their own discipline. Humanitarian and refugee lawyers have thus been keen to highlight the centrality of their respective fields by relying ironically on the same argument: *lex specialis*

---

[2] See most notably: M. Jacques, *Armed Conflict and Displacement. The Protection of Refugees and Displaced Persons under International Humanitarian Law* (Cambridge: Cambridge University Press, 2012); P.A. Fernández-Sánchez, 'The Interplay Between International Humanitarian Law and Refugee Law', 1(2) *Journal of International Humanitarian Legal Studies* (2010) 329–81; K. Hulme, 'Armed Conflict and the Displaced', 17(1) *International Journal of Refugee Law* (2005) 91–116; F. Bugnion, 'Humanitarian Law and the Protection of Refugees', 24(4) *Refugee Survey Quarterly* (2005) 36–42; F. Bugnion, 'Refugees, Internally Displaced Persons, and International Humanitarian Law', 28(5) *Fordham International Law Journal* (2005) 1397–1420; O. Casanovas, 'La protection internationale des réfugiés et des personnes déplacées dans les conflits armés', 306 *Recueil des cours de l'Académie de droit international* (2003) 9–176; R. Brett and E. Lester, 'Refugee Law and International Humanitarian Law: Parallels, Lessons and Looking Ahead. A Non-Governmental Organization's View', 83(843) *International Review of the Red Cross* (2001) 713–26; W. Kälin, 'Flight in Times of War', 83(843) *International Review of the Red Cross* (2001) 629–50; S. Jaquemet, 'The Cross-Fertilization of International Humanitarian Law and International Refugee Law', 83(843) *International Review of the Red Cross* (2001) 651–74; J. Patrnogic, 'Thoughts on the Relationship Between International Humanitarian Law and Refugee Law, their Promotion and Dissemination', 28(265) *International Review of the Red Cross* (1988) 367–78; K.J. Partsch, 'The Protection of Refugees in Armed Conflicts and Internal Disturbances by Red Cross Organs', 2234 *Revue de droit pénal militaire et de droit de la guerre* (1983) 419–38. By contrast, inclusive approaches tackling with the three applicable branches of international law are conspicuously rare. See essentially: A. Edwards, 'Crossing Legal Borders: The Interface Between Refugee Law, Human Rights Law and Humanitarian Law in the "International Protection" of Refugees', in R. Arnold and N. Quenivet (eds), *International Humanitarian Law and International Human Rights Law: Towards a New Merger in International Law* (Leiden and Boston: Martinus Nijhoff, 2008). For more specific case-studies focusing on the refugee definition or a particular country, see also: M.R. Von Sternberg, *The Grounds of Refugee Protection in the Context of International Human Rights and Humanitarian Law: Canadian and United States Case Law Compared* (The Hague: Martinus Nijhoff, 2002); and A.C. Helton, 'The Role of Refugee, Humanitarian and Human Rights Law in Planning for Repatriation of Kampuchean Asylum Seekers in Thailand', 3 *International Journal of Refugee Law* (1991) 547–63.

[3] For a general overview of the role and potential of human rights law, see V. Chetail, 'Are Refugee Rights Human Rights? An Unorthodox Questioning on the Relations between International Refugee Law and International Human Rights Law', in R. Rubio Marin (ed), *Migrations and Human Rights* (Oxford: Oxford University Press, 2014) and the bibliographical references quoted therein.

derogat lex generalis, though they are not always clear about the exact meaning and impact of this maxim.[4] From a systemic perspective, this superficially attractive maxim is, however, too simplistic to provide a cogent and predictable frame of analysis. It raises more questions than it actually solves for two main reasons. First, resort to *lex specialis* presupposes a conflict of norms which proves to be extremely rare between international humanitarian law, human rights law, and refugee law. As will be shown later, when this arises, such a conflict is resolved in favour of the most protective treatment essentially provided by human rights law, without regard to the alleged speciality of the prevailing norm. Secondly, the *lex specialis* maxim says nothing about what should be 'general' or 'special', and how to interpret these vague terms.[5] The subjectivity inherent to such assessment is exemplified by the contradictory interpretations raised by the position of the International Court of Justice on this issue.[6] There are now as many possible criteria for determining the special or general nature of a particular norm as the number of authors undertaking such an exercise. Some attempt to combine the precision of a norm with the 'systemic goals of the international legal order',[7] whereas others encapsulate 'the operation of *lex specialis* as an aspect making pragmatic judgements about relative "generality" and "speciality", about what is "normal" and what "exceptional"'.[8]

Given the weakness of this approach, the normative interaction between international humanitarian law, refugee law, and human rights law is more convincingly understood through the complementarity approach as notably endorsed by the United Nations (UN) Human Rights Committee.[9] This last approach differs from

---

[4] See for instance: Jacques (n 2), 13–14; H. Storey, 'Armed Conflict in Asylum Law: The "War-Flaw"', 31(2) *Refugee Survey Quarterly* (2012) 1–32 at 14–18; Edwards (n 2), 429. See *contra* Fernández-Sánchez (n 2), 329–81.

[5] For a similar account see: N. Prud'homme, '*Lex Specialis*: Oversimplifying a More Complex and Multifaceted Relationship?', 40 *Israel Law Review* (2007) 355–95 at 369–70; A. Lindroos, 'Addressing Norm Conflicts in a Fragmented Legal System: The Doctrine of Lex Specialis', 74 *Nordic Journal of International Law* (2005) 27–66 at 65.

[6] *Legality of the Threat or Use of Nuclear Weapons*, Advisory Opinion of 8 July 1996, *ICJ Reports* 1996, 226; *Legal Consequence of the Construction of a Wall in the Occupied Palestinian Territory*, Advisory Opinion of 9 July 2004, *ICJ Reports* 2004, 178.

[7] M. Sassòli, 'Le droit international humanitaire, une *lex specialis* par rapport aux droits humains?', in A. Auer, A. Flückiger, and M. Hottelier (eds), *Les droits de l'homme et la constitution: études en l'honneur du Professeur Gorgio Malinverni* (Geneva: Schulthess, 2007), 375–95 at 383.

[8] M. Koskenniemi, *Fragmentation of International Law: Difficulties Arising from the Diversification and Expansion of International Law*, UN Doc A/CN.4/L.682 (2006), 57, § 105. Among many other instances, see also H. Krieger, 'A Conflict of Norms: The Relationship between Humanitarian Law and Human Rights Law in the ICRC Customary Law Study', 11 *Journal of Conflict and Security Law* (2006) 265–91 at 273 ('the relation between two norms depends on an interpretation of the purposes of each norm and of the normative context').

[9] *General Comment No 31: Nature of the General Legal Obligation Imposed on States Parties to the Covenant*, UN Doc CCPR/C/21/Rev.1/Add.13 (2004), § 11. For further discussions, see W. Schabas, '*Lex Specialis*? Belt and Suspenders? The Parallel Operation of Human Rights Law and the Law of Armed Conflict, and the Conundrum of *Jus ad Bellum*', 40(2) *Israel Law Review* (2007) 592–613.

the *lex specialis* approach in two essential respects. It first posits the cumulative application of overlapping norms on a same-subject matter, instead of the exclusive application of one specific norm overriding another. This approach favouring the simultaneous application of humanitarian law, refugee law, and human rights law is more in line with the prevailing interstate practice. Alongside the General Assembly,[10] and the Human Rights Council,[11] the Security Council has steadily reaffirmed that 'parties to armed conflict comply strictly with the obligations applicable to them under international humanitarian, human rights and refugee law'.[12]

The second key difference with the *lex specialis* approach relies on the criteria to be used in resorting to the complementarity approach. Reflecting the ultimate objective of these three branches of international law, the cumulative application of humanitarian law, refugee law, and human rights law requires the most protective norm to be implemented. The most favourable treatment further constitutes a well-established feature of both human rights law and refugee law.[13] While this last principle is also occasionally endorsed by some provisions of humanitarian law,[14] the Martens Clause is apt to play a similar function.

From this angle, a strict compartmentalization of the three branches of international law is artificial and even counterproductive for the purpose of ensuring effective protection. Contrary to the common belief of many humanitarian and refugee law specialists, the most specific norm is not always the most protective one. In fact, rather the contrary is true. The present Chapter will show that the complementarity approach not only constitutes the most cogent frame of analysis for capturing the multifaceted interactions between humanitarian law, refugee law, and human rights law. It also paves the way for a human rights-based approach to armed conflicts.

Three scenarios are identified in this Chapter: (i) refugees in war, (ii) refugees fleeing war, and (iii) refugees in post-war contexts. For each scenario a comparative assessment of the three branches of international law comes to the same conclusion: while humanitarian and refugee law still play a non-negligible role, they are not the panacea in terms of protection. By contrast, human rights law fulfils the central function of filling the gaps in protection left by humanitarian and refugee law.

---

[10] See notably UN Doc A/RES/64/77 (2010), § 2; UN Doc A/RES/57/230 (2002), § 3(b).

[11] See eg HRC Res S-8/1 (2008), § 1.

[12] UNSC Res 1894 (2009), § 1. Among many other similar restatements, see UNSC Res 2085 (2012), §§ 10, 16, and 18; UNSC Res 2062 (2012), § 17; UNSC Res 1973 (2011), § 3; UNSC Res 1856 (2008), § 23; UNSC Res 1843 (2008), preambular § 8; UNSC Res 1790 (2007), preambular § 19.

[13] See for instance Art 5 of the Geneva Convention relating to the Status of Refugees and Art 5(2) of the ICCPR.

[14] See most notably Art 75(8) of AP I ('No provision of this Article may be construed as limiting or infringing any other more favourable provision granting greater protection, under any applicable rules of international law, to persons covered by paragraph 1'). See also Art 72 of AP I ('The provisions of this Section are additional to [...] other applicable rules of international law relating to the protection of fundamental human rights during international armed conflict').

2 REFUGEES IN WAR

Refugees caught in armed conflicts represent an archetypal case for testing the potential of the complementarity approach. The overlapping between international humanitarian law, refugee law, and human rights law is not disputable in this particular situation and their cumulative application reveals some unexpected conclusions. Although international humanitarian law is supposed to be the main branch of international law applicable in times of armed conflict, closer scrutiny of its specific norms proves rather frustrating (Section A). Indeed, international humanitarian law has little to provide for protecting the specific needs of refugees caught up in armed conflicts. The simultaneous application of refugee law and human rights law accordingly proves to be a crucial source of protection (Section B).

A. International humanitarian law and the limits of protection

The impact of international humanitarian law on the refugee protection regime is particularly complex and ambiguous. On the one hand, its primary function in the field of forced migration is a preventive one. The explicit prohibition of forced displacement aims to prevent civilians from becoming refugees.[15] On the other hand, international humanitarian law is relatively indifferent to the specific needs of refugees who are in the territory of a party to an armed conflict.

Among the 576 articles of the Geneva Conventions and their Protocols, only three provisions explicitly refer to refugees.[16] Furthermore, all of them are exclusively applicable in times of international armed conflict and occupation. By contrast, international humanitarian law does not contain any specific provision on refugees in non-international armed conflicts despite these representing the majority of armed conflicts around the world. Neither Common Article 3 of the Geneva Conventions and AP II, nor the International Committee of the Red Cross (ICRC) Customary Study specifically addresses refugees.[17] This curious omission does not mean that refugees are left without protection by international humanitarian law.

---

[15] See Art 49 of GC IV and Art 17 of AP II.

[16] Article 44 of GC IV deals with the relations between the state of asylum and refugees who are nationals of a belligerent state; Art 70 of the same Convention addresses the relations with their state of origin when the latter is occupying the asylum state; and, finally, Art 73 of AP I concerns refugees who have been recognized as such before the armed conflict. See also implicitly at least, Art 45(4) of GC IV.

[17] For a critical account of the ICRC study with regard to forced displacement, see R. Piotrowicz, 'Displacement and Displaced Persons', in E. Wilmshurst and S.C. Breau (eds), *Perspectives on the ICRC Study on Customary International Humanitarian Law* (Cambridge and New York: Cambridge University Press, 2007), 337–53.

They are still protected as civilians provided they are not directly participating in hostilities. Nevertheless, besides the general protection of the civilian population as a whole, refugees are not conceived by international humanitarian law as persons in need of specific protection in non-international armed conflicts.

Even in international armed conflicts, international humanitarian law still apprehends refugees through the particular prism of its own concepts and categorization schemes. From this angle, the distinction between combatants and non-combatants is one of 'the cardinal principles [...] constituting the fabric of humanitarian law'.[18] Though it is frequently assumed that 'one cannot be a refugee and a fighter at the same time',[19] this question remains open both in law and practice. It even constitutes the prerequisite for identifying the relevant applicable norms under international humanitarian law.

Refugees may fall within the definition of 'combatant' under Article 4 of GC III as supplemented by Article 43(1) of AP I, when they belong to a party to the conflict—other than their country of origin—fighting against the latter or any other states.[20] If not, refugees are civilians and accordingly benefit from the protection against the effect of hostilities. The crux of the matter is then whether refugees are 'protected persons' under international humanitarian law. There is, however, no unequivocal answer to this question. International humanitarian law instead provides a piecemeal frame of protection which depends on a complex set of various factors, including the ratification of AP I, the nationality of refugees, and the time of their arrival on the territory of states parties. While some are protected persons under AP I, the great majority of refugees caught in international armed conflicts are not covered by this last instrument. In such a case, they must accordingly fulfil the ordinary conditions required by international humanitarian law to be considered as protected persons.

---

[18]   ICJ, *Legality of the Threat or Use of Nuclear Weapons* (n 6), § 79.

[19]   S. Jaquemet, *Under What Circumstances Can a Person Who Has Taken an Active Part in the Hostilities of an International or a Non-International Armed Conflict Become an Asylum Seeker?* (Geneva: UNHCR Legal and Protection Policy Research Series, Department of International Protection, PPLA/2004/01, 2004), 21.

[20]   If captured by the enemy state, refugee combatants benefit from the status of prisoners of war. If they are instead within the territory of a neutral state, the latter must disarm and intern them as far as possible at a distance from the theatre of hostilities: Art 11 of the Hague Convention V and Art 4B(2) of GC III. For further discussions about the principle of distinction and its relevance for refugees, see notably Jacques (n 2), 217–44; R. Da Costa, *Maintaining the Civilian and Humanitarian Character of Asylum* (Geneva: UNHCR Legal and Policy Research Series, Department of Protection, PPLA/2004/02, 2004); C. Beyani, 'International Legal Criteria for the Separation of Members of Armed Forces, Armed Bands and Militia from Refugees in the Territories of Host States', 12 *International Journal of Refugee Law* (2000) 251–71; M. Othman-Chande, 'International Law and Armed Attacks in Refugee Camps', 59(2)–(3) *Nordic Journal of International Law* (1990) 153–77.

(i) *Refugees as protected persons under AP I*

The question whether refugees are as such 'protected persons' remained surprisingly unclear until 1977 with the adoption of AP I. Its Article 73 explicitly acknowledges that refugees are protected persons 'within the meaning of Parts I and III of the Fourth Convention, in all circumstances and without any adverse distinction'.[21] As protected persons, they benefit from a substantial range of fundamental guarantees, including most notably the right to leave,[22] the grounds and procedures governing their internment or assigned residence,[23] as well as protection against deportation and forcible transfer.[24]

However, Article 73 subordinates their status of protected persons to the fulfilment of two cumulative conditions. First, they must have been recognized as refugees 'under the relevant international instruments accepted by the Parties concerned or under the national legislation of the State of refuge or State of residence'. The relevant international instruments obviously include the Geneva Convention relating to the Status of Refugees as amended by its Protocol, the Organization of African Unity (OAU) Convention governing the Specific Aspects of Refugee Problems in Africa, and the European Union Qualification Directive. According to the ICRC Commentary, they also cover non-binding resolutions,[25] including notably the 1984 Cartagena Declaration on Refugees.[26]

The second condition required by Article 73 to be recognized as a protected person is much more significant and restrictive: they must have been considered as refugees 'before the beginning of hostilities'. Those who have become refugees after the outbreak of hostilities, and most probably because of them, are thus excluded. From a refugee protection perspective, this represents the major shortcoming of international humanitarian law which has been criticized as introducing 'an arbitrary and unnecessary distinction, in direct contradiction to the humanitarian principles of protection of the Geneva Conventions'.[27]

---

[21] Part II of the Fourth Convention already applies to refugees as member of the civilian population.

[22] Articles 35–37 and 48 of GC IV.   [23] Articles 41–43 and 78–133 of GC IV.

[24] Articles 45 and 49 of GC IV.

[25] Commentary AP I and II, § 2951.

[26] Whether binding or not, all these international instruments must have been 'accepted by the Parties concerned' in order to make sure that states would not be indirectly bound by instruments they are not parties to by virtue of AP I (see Commentary AP I and II, § 2952). Despite its broad understanding of the term 'international instruments', the ICRC commentary construes this last requirement as referring to 'States which are Parties to them if they are treaties, or States which have given them binding force, or which recognize their binding force, if they are resolutions' (Commentary AP I and II, § 2952). In any event, however, the decision taken by the asylum state to grant the refugee status or any other forms of complementary protection is binding upon all parties to the conflict whether such decision has been taken under its own domestic law and/or under international instruments it has accepted (Commentary AP I and II, § 2952).

[27] Jacques (n 2), 162. See also among others K. Obradovic, 'La protection des réfugiés dans les conflits armés internationaux', in *The Refugee Problem on Universal, Regional and National Level, Thesaurus*

Such a difference in treatment between those recognized as refugees before the beginning of hostilities and those recognized after is apparently based on the fear of many states that a more protective role would encourage desertion and treason.[28] The rationale behind such far-reaching exclusion is, however, not convincing for two main reasons. First, the alleged risk of desertion is hardly relevant since refugees must be civilians to be considered as protected persons under GC IV as supplemented by Article 73. Secondly, it is precisely when civilians are fleeing their own country because of hostilities that the need for protection is at its greatest.

(ii) *Refugees as non-nationals of a party to the conflict*

If refugees do not fulfil the conditions imposed by Article 73, or if they are in the hands of a state not party to AP I, they may fall under the general definition of protected persons contained in Article 4 of GC IV. This last provision covers most—but not all—refugees once they are 'in the hands of a Party to the conflict or Occupying Power of which they are not nationals'. In such cases, they will benefit from the full range of guarantees contained in GC IV as well as the specific protection granted by Article 44. This last provision acknowledges that refugees who are by definition not protected by their state of origin cannot be treated as an 'enemy alien' because they simply have the nationality of the other party to the conflict.[29] Article 44 thus mitigates the traditional criterion of nationality, which determines the applicability of GC IV, in order to take into account the particular situation of refugees.

Though limited to nationals of the other state party to an international armed conflict, the *rationae personae* scope of Article 44 is more inclusive than Article 73 of AP I. Contrary to the latter, the former is not confined to those who were recognized as refugees before the beginning of hostilities, but also covers those who fled their own country during the conflict. Furthermore, Article 44 retains a broad and factual definition of the term 'refugee' as referring to all nationals of an enemy state 'who do not, in fact, enjoy the protection of any government'. It is thus not limited to the refugees under the UN Convention relating to the Status of Refugees which was adopted two years after GC IV and then amended in 1967 by the New York Protocol. Article 44 also includes beneficiaries of other complementary forms of protection in the state of asylum, whether such protection is based on its domestic law or other international instruments.[30]

Acroasium, vol 13 (Thessaloniki: Institute of International Public Law and International Relations of Thessaloniki, 1987), 147–61 at 150.

[28] Obradovic (n 27), 147.

[29] 'In applying the measures of control mentioned in the present Convention, the Power shall not treat as enemy aliens exclusively on the basis of their nationality de jure of an enemy State, refugees who do not, in fact, enjoy the protection of any government.'

[30] With such a factual focus on the absence of protection, Art 44 might also well cover the significant number of persons in need of protection who fall under the protection mandate of the UNHCR regardless of their official recognition as refugees by the asylum state.

However, the potentially significant number of persons covered by Article 44 is undermined by the vague and permissive obligation contained therein. As confirmed by the drafting history,[31] the ICRC Commentary,[32] and the legal doctrine,[33] the provision's loose wording recommends that belligerents do not consider refugees as enemies exclusively because of their nationality. The Detaining Power thus retains a particularly broad discretion in considering whether or not refugees should be treated as enemy nationals. Hence, Article 44 does not prevent the Detaining Power from taking security measures, such as internment, against refugees who are considered as a danger to its own security.

(iii) *Refugees as nationals of neutral, co-belligerent, or occupying state*

The general definition of 'protected persons' under GC IV does not include all refugees who are non-nationals of a party to an international armed conflict. Article 4(2) explicitly excludes nationals of a neutral or co-belligerent state which has 'normal diplomatic representation' in the belligerent state on whose territory they are located or nationals of a co-belligerent state with diplomatic relations with the occupying state in whose hands they are.[34] In such cases, refugees who have fled from neutral or co-belligerent states will only benefit from the general protection afforded to the civilian population, unless the concerned state has ratified AP I and the refugees have been recognized as such before the outbreak of the hostilities.

Furthermore, nationals of an Occupying Power who are in the territory of the occupied state are not covered by the definition of protected person because Article 4 is circumscribed to non-nationals. Though not considered as protected persons, refugees who are nationals of the Occupying Power are specifically addressed by Article 70(2) of GC IV. The wording of this last provision is again not a model of clarity and needs to be quoted *in extenso*:

Nationals of the Occupying Power who, before the outbreak of hostilities, have sought refuge in the territory of the occupied State, shall not be arrested, prosecuted, convicted or deported from the occupied territory, except for offences committed after the outbreak of hostilities, or for offences under common law committed before the outbreak of hostilities which, according to the law of the occupied State, would have justified extradition in time of peace.

---

[31] Report of the Committee III to the Plenary Assembly of the Diplomatic Conference of Geneva, vol 2A, 826.

[32] Commentary GC IV, 264–5.

[33] See among others: Jacques (n 2), 168–9; Obradovic (n 27); and Dinstein (n 1), 96–7.

[34] The same applies to refugees who are nationals of a state which has not ratified GC IV but such a case is particularly rare given its almost universal ratification.

Article 70(2) is the only provision in the whole Fourth Geneva Convention which explicitly applies to nationals of a state party to an international armed conflict. Such a departure from the traditional stance of international humanitarian law remains nevertheless in line with the general duty of the Occupying Power to respect the laws in force in the occupied country. As stressed by the ICRC Commentary, the rationale of Article 70(2) 'is derived from the idea that the right to asylum enjoyed by them [ie refugees] before the occupation began must continue to be respected by their home country, when it takes over control as Occupying Power in the territory of the country of asylum'.[35]

However, the protection granted by international humanitarian law should not be overestimated. Article 70(2) suffers from three main drawbacks. First, the prohibition expressed in this provision is limited to some specific measures only: arrest, prosecution, conviction, and deportation. As observed by Dinstein, it says nothing about the other measures which may be taken against refugees (such as confiscation of property or denial of religious freedom).[36] This represents a considerable lacuna where Article 73 of AP I does not apply.

Secondly, similarly to Article 73 of AP I, Article 70(2) of GC IV is confined to refugees who reached the occupied territory 'before the outbreak of the hostilities'.[37] This *rationae temporis* qualification creates a dangerous protection gap. Indeed, nationals who fled from their own country during a conflict are the most vulnerable to acts of revenge by their state of origin when the latter occupies the territory of the asylum state.[38] States' obsession not to encourage desertion and treason is further confirmed by this last limitation.

Thirdly, the prohibition contained in Article 70(2) is not absolute. It may be exposed to two significant exceptions which reflect the conflicting interests at stake. First, refugees can be arrested, prosecuted, convicted, and deported for non-political offences committed before the hostilities, provided that these offences would have justified extradition in time of peace under the law of the occupied territory. This subtly qualified exception endorses the traditional distinction made in refugee law between ordinary criminals and refugees.[39] It is aimed at ensuring that refugees are not sanctioned for the reasons they have fled their own state when it becomes

---

[35] Commentary GC IV, 351.   [36] Dinstein (n 1), 104.

[37] One should add that, though circumscribed to nationals of the Occupying Power, the personal scope of Art 70 is slightly broader than Art 73, since it does not require that refugees have been recognized as such by the state of asylum. Although this specificity is rarely underlined, Art 70 refers instead to persons who 'have sought refuge in the territory of the occupied State', including thus not only refugees but also asylum-seekers (who asked for protection but have not been formally recognized as refugees).

[38] For a similar account, see notably: Jacques (n 2), 176.

[39] For further discussions about the origins and rationale of this well-known distinction of international refugee law, see V. Chetail, 'Théorie et pratique de l'asile en droit international classique: étude sur les origines conceptuelles et normatives du droit international des réfugiés', 115 *Revue générale de droit international public* (2011) 625–52.

the Occupying Power. However, the risk of abuse is still apparent since Article 70(2) says nothing about the procedure to be followed, and in particular whether this is up to the Occupying Power or the occupied authorities to interpret and apply the conditions laid down therein.

The other exception is even more straightforward, as it refers to any 'offences committed after the outbreak of hostilities' without any other qualifications. From the angle of international humanitarian law, the refugee is still considered as a national of the Occupying Power. He retains, as such, some duties of allegiance towards his own country in times of armed conflict and must abstain from activities which may be construed as treason.[40] In an echo of the concern of states, the ICRC Commentary assumes that 'once war has broken out, [...] the higher interest of the State take precedence over the protection of individual'.[41]

As exemplified by Article 70(2), the reach of international humanitarian law is equivocal to say the least. Overall, while providing a vital protection to civilians, it has little to offer to refugees as a specific group of concern. Refugee protection under international humanitarian law thus remains incomplete and fragmented. Under both treaty and customary law, international humanitarian law offers no specific protection to refugees caught in non-international armed conflicts. Even in international armed conflict, it does not provide a tailored, specific, and comprehensive regime of refugee protection. International humanitarian law attempts instead to encapsulate refugees within its own notion of protected persons. By doing so, it gives the impression of trying to resolve a problem it has itself created.

More fundamentally, enclosing refugees under the generic label of protected person fails to address their specific needs. On the one hand, the definition of protected persons under international humanitarian law does not include all refugees and other persons in need of protection. Beside the cases mentioned before, it excludes all nationals of a belligerent state who flee to a state that is not a party to the conflict during and/or because of the hostilities. On the other hand, even if refugees correspond to the definition of protected persons, they benefit as such from the same guarantees as ordinary aliens within the territory of a party to the conflict. As demonstrated above, the only two provisions specifically devoted to refugees in GC IV are conspicuously weak and ambiguous.

B. International refugee law and human rights law as a vital source of protection in armed conflicts

Because of the limited protection offered by humanitarian law, refugee law and human rights law are bound to play essential roles. This is not only the case in

---

[40] Commentary GC IV, 351; Dinstein (n 1), 104.   [41] *Commentary GC IV*, 351.

non-international armed conflicts but also in international armed conflicts, where refugees are not protected persons under international humanitarian law or, even when they are, because of the relative lack of a tailored and specific protection granted by this last branch of international law. The concurrent application of refugee law and human rights law highlights the crucial importance of the complementarity approach for ensuring effective protection in armed conflicts. The reach and degree of protection offered by the two branches of law are nevertheless quite different from one another. Thus as we saw with humanitarian law, the most specific norms enshrined in refugee law are not necessarily the most protective ones when compared to human rights law.

(i)   International refugee law in times of armed conflict: between legal mimicry and emancipation from international humanitarian law

International refugee law is as indifferent to armed conflict as international humanitarian law is to refugees. This comes as no surprise as it reflects the segmented approach which prevailed at the end of World War II when the first universal treaties for the protection of individuals were adopted. As a result of such compartmentalization, refugees are approached by humanitarian law within the interstices of its particular norms, whereas refugee law refers to armed conflicts in a transversal and occasional manner.

Nevertheless, the few references to armed conflict in the 1951 Convention relating to the Status of Refugees (Refugee Convention) epitomize the cross linkages and the mutually supportive interactions between refugee law and humanitarian law. The provisions specifically addressing armed conflict in the Refugee Convention are clearly informed by international humanitarian law. The first and most obvious reference appears in the refugee definition.[42] Article 1(F)(a) excludes from the benefit of the Refugee Convention a refugee who 'has committed a crime against peace, a war crime, or a crime against humanity, as defined in the international instruments drawn up to make provision in respect of such crimes'. The grave breaches of GC IV and AP I are instrumental for defining war crimes under the exclusion clause of the refugee definition.[43] Though less ratified than the former international instruments, the Rome Statute of the ICC is also bound to play a substantial role in defining the crimes covered by Article 1(F)(a).

---

[42]   For further discussion on the inclusion clauses of the refugee definition with regards to victims of armed conflict see Section 2.B.

[43]   For an overview, see C. Bauloz, 'L'apport du droit international pénal au droit international des réfugiés: l'article 1F(a) de la Convention de 1951', in V. Chetail and C. Laly-Chevalier (eds), *Asile et extradition: théorie et pratique des clauses d'exclusion au statut de réfugié* (Brussels: Bruylant, 2014) and the bibliographical references contained therein.

Another implicit reference to international humanitarian law may be found in Article 8 of the Refugee Convention[44] which reproduces in substance Article 44 of GC IV.[45] Their respective scope nevertheless differs slightly. On the one hand, exemption from exceptional measures under international refugee law is broader than its humanitarian law counterpart, since Article 8 applies both in time of armed conflict and peace.[46] On the other hand, as mentioned above, the *rationae personae* scope of Article 44 is not circumscribed by the refugee definition under the Refugee Convention.[47]

In any event, under both branches of international law, the relevant provisions suffer from the same weakness: exceptional measures may be taken against refugees provided that they are not applied on the sole ground of their nationality. As underlined during the drafting of the Refugee Convention, 'States would be at liberty to advance a variety of reasons, other than that of nationality, why refugees should be subjected to the measures in question'.[48] According to commentators, this would be notably the case when 'a refugee, in spite of his genuine fear of persecution by the regime in power in his country of origin, contributes or has contributed to the war effort of that country, or otherwise carries on or has been participating in activities which the measure in question aims at suppressing'.[49] The main concern of the drafters was clearly the fear of fifth columnists, namely 'enemy aliens professing to be refugees',[50] carrying out sabotage, espionage and other related activities against the asylum state.

---

[44] 'With regard to exceptional measures which may be taken against the person, property or interests of nationals of a foreign State, the Contracting States shall not apply such measures to a refugee who is formally a national of the said State solely on account of such nationality. Contracting States which, under their legislation, are prevented from applying the general principle expressed in this article, shall, in appropriate cases, grant exemptions in favour of such refugees.'

[45] The influence of international humanitarian law is further confirmed by the fact that no similar provision was contained in the previous arrangements and conventions relating to the status of refugees adopted during the inter-war period. Article 44 of GC IV was adopted as a result of the experiences of World War II in order to take into account the observations made by the International Refugee Organization and the Israel Delegation during the 1949 Diplomatic Conference: Commentary GC IV, 263.

[46] Ad Hoc Committee on Statelessness and Related Problems, Status of Refugees and Stateless Persons—Memorandum by the Secretary-General, 1950, 48 ('if this rule is to be applied in time of war, a similar rule must a fortiori be applied in time of peace').

[47] The added value of Art 8 is further mitigated by its second sentence which enlarges the—already substantial—margin of discretion in implementing this provision.

[48] UN Doc A/CONF.2/SR.27 (1961), 31–2 (Sweden). For similar acknowledgements, see notably the declarations of the United States, Turkey, and Canada: UN Doc E/AC.32/SR.21 (1950), 7–8.

[49] A. Grahl-Madsen, *Commentary on the Refugee Convention 1951* (Geneva: UNHCR, 1963), 25–6. See also U. Davy, 'Article 8', in A. Zimmerman (ed), *The 1951 Convention Relating to the Status of Refugees and its 1967 Protocol. A Commentary* (Oxford: Oxford University Press, 2011), 774; J.C. Hathaway, *The Rights of Refugees under International Law* (Cambridge: Cambridge University Press, 2005), 273; N. Robinson, *Convention Relating to the Status of Refugees: Its History, Contents and Interpretation* (New York: Institute of Jewish Affairs, 1953), 76.

[50] UN Doc E/AC.32/SR.34 (1950). See also UN Doc E/AC.31/SR.21 (1950), § 33.

States' reduced concern towards refugees in times of armed conflict is further displayed by the particularly broad derogation clause contained in Article 9 of the Refugee Convention:

Nothing in this Convention shall prevent a Contracting State, in time of war or other grave and exceptional circumstances, from taking provisionally measures which it considers to be essential to the national security in the case of a particular person, pending a determination by the Contracting State that that person is in fact a refugee and that the continuance of such measures is necessary in his case in the interests of national security.

Article 9 is clearer on what it does not say than on what it does. It does not provide any particular procedure to be followed for invoking such a derogation clause. It does not identify nonderogable rights, nor specify the types and the limits of the measures which can be taken under Article 9. Though virtually applicable to all provisions of the Refugee Convention, this derogation clause has raised considerable debates about its exact scope and content. Authors are divided as to whether it applies in individual cases or in massive influx, and whether it concerns only asylum-seekers during the examination of their request, or all refugees formally recognized as such.[51]

In any event, the vague and permissive wording of this provision offers a considerable margin of appreciation. Davy even argues that 'Article 9 provides a *carte blanche*: contracting States may introduce measures of control as they see fit in order to contain the threat to national security'.[52] In practice, however, although several proposals have been made for using the derogation clause in a refugee context,[53] Article 9 has hardly ever been invoked by states parties.

If the derogation clause is not applied the whole Refugee Convention remains plainly applicable even in times of armed conflict. This does not mean, however, that national security concerns are totally ignored in such exceptional circumstances. They are in fact incorporated into three major provisions which echo the main concerns of asylum states in times of armed conflict.[54] First, under Article 28, states parties are no longer bound to deliver travel documents to refugees wishing to leave their asylum state when 'compelling reasons of national security or public order otherwise require'. Secondly, Article 32(1) of the Refugee Convention restates

[51] Compare for instance: Jacques (n 2), 167 and Hathaway (n 49), 266–7 with U. Davy, 'Article 9', in A. Zimmerman (ed), *The 1951 Convention Relating to the Status of Refugees and its 1967 Protocol. A Commentary* (Oxford: Oxford University Press, 2011), 799–801; A. Edwards, 'Temporary Protection, Derogation and the 1951 Refugee Convention', 13 *Melbourne Journal of International Law* (2012) 623–4.

[52] Davy (n 51), 784.

[53] It is noteworthy that such proposals have been made by refugee lawyers for reasserting the centrality of the Refugee Convention through the use of derogation clause in case of mass influx. J.-F. Durieux and J. McAdam, 'Non-Refoulement Through Time: The Case for a Derogation Clause to the Refugee Convention in Mass Influx Emergencies', 16(4) *International Journal of Refugee Law* (2004) 5–24; Edwards (n 51), 595–635.

[54] This probably explains why Art 9 has been so rarely invoked by states parties as their concerns are already taken into account in the key provisions of the Refugee Convention.

that '[t]he Contracting States shall not expel a refugee lawfully in their territory save on grounds of national security or public order'. When expulsion is resorted to on these two grounds, the procedural guarantees specified in Article 32(2) can also be suspended for 'compelling reasons of national security'.[55] Thirdly, the cornerstone of international refugee law—the principle of *non-refoulement*—may be derogated from on the ground of the two exceptions contained in Article 33(2). The first exception specifically refers to 'a refugee whom there are reasonable grounds for regarding as a danger to the security of the country in which he is'.

However, the tribute paid by the Refugee Convention to national security does not give free rein to asylum states caught in an armed conflict. On the one hand, concerns of national security are incorporated within the Refugee Convention as an exception to the basic guarantees contained therein. As a result, they call for a restrictive interpretation with due regard to the circumstances of each particular case. On the other hand, even when exceptions are clearly justified on the ground of national security, this does not suspend the basic guarantees granted by international humanitarian law and human rights law. Indeed, the three branches of international law must be applied cumulatively so that possible restrictions and exceptions permitted by one of them—can be overridden or conditioned by the rules and guarantees under the other branches.

(ii) *International human rights law as the residual source of refugee protection in armed conflicts*

The continuing applicability of human rights law in times of armed conflict is beyond any doubt. In fact, 'the question is no longer *whether* international human rights law applies in armed conflict but *how* it applies'.[56] Similarly to the Refugee Convention, the answer mainly depends on whether the derogation clause applies or not.

Compared to its refugee law counterpart, derogation clauses under human rights law contain five substantive conditions. First, there must be an emergency threatening the life of the nation.[57] Secondly, the derogation must be limited to, and go no further than that 'strictly required by the exigencies of the situation' in due respect

---

[55] This does not concern, however, the additional guarantees granted by Art 32(3). Thus, even in times of armed conflicts and provided that Art 9 is not invoked by the states parties, they 'shall allow such a refugee a reasonable period within which to seek legal admission into another country. The Contracting States reserve the right to apply during that period such internal measures as they may deem necessary'.

[56] S. Sivakumaran, 'International Humanitarian Law', in D. Moeckli, S. Shah, and S. Sivakumaran (eds), *International Human Rights Law* (Oxford: Oxford University Press, 2010), 538.

[57] Article 4(1) of ICCPR; Art 15(1) of ECHR; Art 27(1) of ACHR; Art 4(1) of the Arab Charter on Human Rights; Art 35(1) of the Commonwealth of Independent States Convention on Human Rights and Fundamental Freedoms (CIS Convention); Art 30(1) of the European Social Charter. Note that the American Convention uses slightly different terminology: 'in a time of war, public danger or other emergency that threatens the independence or security of a State Party'.

with the principle of proportionality. Third that the derogating measures must not be inconsistent with the state's other obligations under international law, thus including international humanitarian law and refugee law. Lastly, derogating measures must not involve discrimination on the ground of race, colour, sex, language, religion, or social origin.[58]

Further to the substantive conditions, some rights cannot be subject to derogation notwithstanding the existence of a public emergency threatening the life of the nation. While the list of these nonderogable rights varies from one instrument to another,[59] some are common to all, namely: the right to life; the prohibition of torture, inhuman, cruel or degrading treatment; prohibition of slavery and servitude; and the prohibition of criminal conviction or punishment not based on a pre-existing law.[60] As basic as they are, these rights are not mentioned at all in the Refugee Convention. Refugee status is indeed relatively weak with regard to civil and political rights; here human rights law provides a vital source of protection.

Finally, a state seeking to invoke the derogation clause, must fulfil the procedural requirement of immediately informing other states parties and the Secretary General of the relevant organization of the provision from which it wishes to derogate from. Such notice should, at the very least, explain the reasons for the derogation,[61] although General Comment 29 of the Human Rights Committee, and the *Siracusa Principles*, call for more detailed information to be provided.[62]

Overall, the conditions required by human rights treaties for a derogation to be valid substantially circumscribe the vast margin of appreciation granted by Article 9 of the Refugee Convention, when the relevant exceptional measures interfere with human rights. From this angle, one could even assert with Davy that 'provisional measures under art. 9 of the 1951 Convention have, over time, become outdated by human rights law'.[63]

The centrality of human rights law in times of armed conflict is even more obvious when the derogation clause under this branch of law does not apply. This may

---

[58] Article 15(1) of ECHR; Art 4(1) of ICCPR; Art 27(1) of ACHR; Art 35(1) of the CIS Convention; Art 4(1) of the Arab Charter on Human Rights; Art 30(1) of the European Social Charter.

[59] The European Convention and the CIS Convention contain the most restrictive list of underogable rights, while the Arab Charter enumerates the most extensive one. It is noteworthy that the Arab Charter consecrates as underogable rights the following key guarantees: freedom to leave any country, prohibition to be compelled to reside in any part of the country, and prohibition of exile and return in his own country (Art 27); the right to seek asylum (Art 28); and the right to nationality (Art 29).

[60] Article 15(2) of ECHR; Art 4(2) of ICCPR; Art 27(2) of ACHR; Art 35(2) of the CIS Convention; Art 4(2) of the Arab Charter.

[61] *Lawless v Ireland (No 3)* [1961] ECHR 2 (ECtHR), § 47.

[62] Human Rights Committee, *General Comment 29: States of Emergency (Article 4)*, UN Doc CCPR/C/21/Rev.1/Add.11 (2001), §§ 5, 16, and 17; UN Economic and Social Council Sub-Commission on Prevention of Discrimination and Protection of Minorities, *Siracusa Principles on the Limitation and Derogation of Provisions in the International Covenant on Civil and Political Rights*, UN Doc E/CN.4/1985/4 (1985), § 45.

[63] Davy (n 51), 803.

happen for a variety of political and legal reasons, mainly when states abstain from using the derogation clause or when such a possibility is not permitted by the relevant instrument. As far as the first is concerned, states frequently abstain from using the derogation clause in order to avoid any sort of recognition that a rebel group is involved in an internal armed conflict. As notably confirmed by the European Court of Human Rights in the leading case *Issayeva v Russia*, when 'no derogation has been made under Article 15 of the Convention [...], the operation in question therefore has to be judged against a normal legal background'.[64]

The same conclusion must be drawn for the great majority of treaties which do not contain any derogation clause. Such a clause remains a purely conventional mechanism established for the exclusive purpose of the relevant treaty. In fact, it is enclosed in a very limited number of six instruments, whereas the vast majority of human rights treaties contain no derogation clause. As confirmed by international courts and treaty-bodies,[65] these conventions remain applicable in armed conflicts. This notably concerns the ten core UN instruments (with the only exception of the ICCPR) as well as a substantial number of regional treaties (including for example the ACHPR, or the European Convention on Action against Trafficking in Human Beings).

In short, even if a state uses its right to derogate from the Refugee Convention and/or the relevant human rights treaties, a broad range of human rights obligations still applies concurrently with humanitarian law. Nevertheless, most human rights are not absolute, and can be restricted with due regard to the conditions spelled out in the relevant treaties. Against such a normative framework, a contextualized approach to human rights law is required in order to take into account the particular situation of armed conflict. While a comprehensive comparison of all applicable norms under humanitarian law, refugee law, and human rights law is beyond the scope of this Chapter, a typical example may be found in the right to leave which constitutes a common guarantee enshrined in the three branches of international law.

Following our frame of analysis, the legal regime governing the right to leave depends on whether the concerned state derogates from the Refugee Convention and all the relevant human rights treaties. If yes, humanitarian law constitutes an important safeguard. Yet, even in such a case, the parallel obligation under human rights law remains utterly applicable as the right to leave is reinforced in a wide range of universal and regional conventions without any possibility of derogation.[66] The

---

[64] ECtHR, *Issayeva v Russia*, Judgment of 24 February 2005, App No 57950/00, § 191.

[65] See eg ICJ, *Legal Consequence of the Construction of a Wall in the Occupied Palestinian Territory* (n 6), § 112; African Commission on Human and Peoples' Rights, *Commission Nationale des Droits de l'Homme et des Libertés v Chad*, Com No 74/92 (1995), § 21.

[66] 1965 International Convention on the Elimination of all Forms of Racial Discrimination (Art 5(d)(i)); 1973 Convention on the Suppression and Punishment of the Crime of Apartheid (Art 2(c)); 1989 International Convention on the Rights of the Child (Art 10(2)); 1990 Convention on

normative prevalence of human rights law is more apparent when the state refrains from using the derogation clause under the few relevant instruments. The personal scope of this basic freedom and the permissible restrictions to it clearly underline the crucial protection provided by this last branch of international law. Under humanitarian law, freedom to leave is limited to non-nationals in the hands of a party to an international armed conflict,[67] whereas refugee law confines its benefit to 'refugees lawfully staying in [the] territory' of asylum states.[68] In stark contrast to humanitarian law, human rights law does apply to everyone including nationals of belligerent states. Furthermore, contrary to refugee law, the human right to leave any country also applies to all non-nationals without regard to their legal status and documentation in the concerned state.[69]

Besides its broad personal scope, human rights law substantially delineates and conditions the permissible restrictions on the right to leave. Both international humanitarian law and refugee law offer a large discretion for prohibiting departure: under the former, leaving the country can be 'contrary to the national interests of the State',[70] whereas, under the latter, 'compelling reasons of national security or public order [may] otherwise require'.[71] By contrast, under human rights law, restrictions are only permissible when the three following conditions are duly fulfilled: (1) permissible restrictions must have a legal basis; (2) they must be necessary to protect national security, public order, public health, morals, or the rights and freedoms of others; and (3) such restrictions must be consistent with the other rights recognized in the relevant instruments.[72]

the Protection of the Rights of All Migrant Workers and Members of Their Families (Art 8(1)); 2006 International Convention on the Rights of Persons with Disabilities (Art 18(1)(c)); ACHPR (Art 12(2)); and Arab Charter (Arts 4(2) and 27).

[67] Article 35 and 48 of GC IV.   [68] Article 28 of the Refugee Convention.

[69] *General Comment No 27: Freedom of movement (Art 12)*, UN Doc CCPR/C/21/Rev.1/Add.9 (1999), § 8.

[70] Article 35(1) of GC IV. According to the ICRC Commentary, '"national interests" is broader than "security considerations." [...] With this wording the belligerents may object to someone's departure not only when it would endanger their security but also when the national economy would suffer as a result. [...] A great deal is thus left to the discretion of the belligerents, who may be inclined to interpret "national interests" as applying to many different spheres': Commentary GC IV, 236.

[71] Article 28(1) of the Refuge Convention. For further discussions about the margin of appreciation granted to states parties when applying this exception, see J. Vedsted-Hansen, 'Article 28', in A. Zimmerman (ed), *The 1951 Convention Relating to the Status of Refugees and its 1967 Protocol. A Commentary* (Oxford: Oxford University Press, 2011), 1206–7.

[72] The Human Rights Committee has recalled that 'Article 12, paragraph 3, clearly indicates that it is not sufficient that the restrictions serve the permissible purposes; they must also be necessary to protect them. Restrictive measures must conform to the principle of proportionality; they must be appropriate to achieve their protective function; they must be the least intrusive instrument amongst those which might achieve the desired result; and they must be proportionate to the interest to be protected. [Moreover] the application of the restrictions permissible under article 12, paragraph 3, needs to be consistent with the other rights guaranteed in the Covenant and with the fundamental principles of equality and non-discrimination': *General Comment No 27* (n 69), §§ 14 and 18.

One should further add that, contrary to refugee law, both humanitarian law and human rights law provide procedural guarantees governing restrictions to the right to leave. According to Article 35(1) of GC IV, any refusal to leave the country must be reviewed by 'an appropriate court or administrative board designated by the Detaining Power for that purpose'. Human rights law achieves the same result through the right to an effective remedy as applied in connection with the right to leave.

3 REFUGEES FROM WAR

When refugees and other victims of armed conflicts have left the belligerent state, the crucial issue is then to find protection in another state. This is primarily governed by the principle of *non-refoulement* which is a common feature of international humanitarian law, refugee law, and human rights law. Its application to refugees from war nonetheless raises two major questions: first, the access to protection and more specifically entry to the territory of an asylum state in a situation of massive influx (Section A); and secondly, the type of protection granted to these persons (Section B).

A. Access to protection: the principle of *non-refoulement* and the spectre of massive influx

Although the principle of *non-refoulement* clearly encompasses rejection at the frontier, its applicability in case of massive influx represents the most vexed controversy of international refugee law.[73] While states' anxiety towards mass influx is

---

[73] For an overview of the issues at stake and the conflicting interpretations raised in the refugee law doctrine, see W. Kälin, M. Caroni, and L. Heim, 'Article 33, para. 1', in A. Zimmerman (ed), *The 1951 Convention Relating to the Status of Refugees and its 1967 Protocol. A Commentary* (Oxford: Oxford University Press, 2011), 1327–96 at 1377–80; J.-Y. Carlier, 'Droit d'asile et des réfugiés: de la protection aux droits', 332 *Recueil des cours de l'Académie de droit international* (2008) 93–101; G.S. Goodwin-Gill and J. McAdam, *The Refugee in International Law* (3rd edn, Oxford: Oxford University Press, 2007), 242–3; Hathaway (n 49), 355–63; J.-F. Durieux and A. Hurwitz, 'How Many is Too Many? African and European Legal Responses to Mass Influxes of Refugees', 47 *German Yearbook of International Law* (2004) 105–59; E. Lauterpacht and D. Bethlehem, 'The Scope and Content of the Principle of Non-Refoulement: Opinion', in E. Feller, V. Türk, and F. Nicholson (eds), *Refugee Protection in International Law, UNHCR's Global Consultations on International Protection* (Cambridge: Cambridge University Press, 2003), 119–21; M. Barutciski, 'Le militantisme juridique et le néo-naturalisme face au droit international positif: les flux massifs de réfugiés et la sécurité nationale', 14(1) *Revue québécoise de droit*

palpable, international refugee law does not provide a clear-cut answer in favour of one or another interpretation. In fact, the two opposite views can be equally justified by sensible arguments.

On the one hand, state delegates made clear during the drafting of the Refugee Convention that 'the possibility of mass migrations across frontiers or of attempted mass migrations was not covered by article 33'.[74] This interpretation has then been endorsed as an exception to the principle of *non-refoulement* in the Declaration on Territorial Asylum adopted by the General Assembly in 1967. According to its Article 3(2), 'exception may be made to the foregoing principle only for overriding reasons of national security or in order to safeguard the population, as in the case of a mass influx of persons'. This resurfaced ten years later, in 1977, at the abortive Conference on Territorial Asylum. Turkey proposed an amendment whereby *non-refoulement* could not be claimed 'in exceptional cases, by a great number of persons whose massive influx may constitute a serious problem to the security of a Contracting State'.[75]

On the other hand, nothing in the text of Article 33 arguably precludes its application to mass influx. Its wording is particularly inclusive as it prohibits 'in any manner whatsoever' any act of forcible removal or rejection towards a country of persecution.[76] The plain applicability of the principle in situations of mass influx has been further acknowledged by the Executive Committee of the United Nations High Commissioner for Refugees (UNHCR).[77] By contrast, the two exceptions endorsed in Article 33(2) do not envisage massive influx: they are instead limited to an individual refugee who is a danger to the security or to the community of the state. Even assuming that the notion of national security has in fact been enlarged to cover similarly exceptional threats arising from massive influxes, effective refusals of entry based on such a ground are relatively rare,[78] when compared

---

international (2002) 37–54; A. Vibeke Eggli, *Mass Refugee Influx and the Limits of Public International Law* (The Hague: Martinus Nijhoff, 2002), 168–72; V. Chetail, 'Le principe de non refoulement et le statut de réfugié en droit international', in V. Chetail and J.-F. Flauss (eds), *La Convention de Genève du 28 juillet 1951 relative au statut des réfugiés—50 ans après: bilan et perspectives* (Brussels: Bruylant, 2001), 55–61.

[74] UN Doc A/CONF.2/SR.35 (1951), 21. See also A/CONF.2/SR.16 (1951), 6.

[75] UN Doc A/Conf.78/C.1/L.28/Rev.1, adopted in the Committee of the Whole by 24 votes to 20 with 40 abstentions.

[76] One should further add that Art 33 applies whether asylum-seekers enter the territory legally or illegally. This basic protection is further reinforced by Art 31(1) of the Geneva Convention. This provision prohibits the imposition of penalties on account of their illegal entry provided that: they come directly from a country of persecution; they present themselves without delay to the national authorities; and they show good cause for their illegal entry.

[77] Among a plethoric number of similar conclusions, see Executive Committee (ExCom) Conclusions Nos 15 XXX (1979), [f]; 22 XXXII (1981), [A.1, 2]; 79 (XLVII) (1996), (i); 100 LV (2004), [i]; 103 LVI (2005), [l].

[78] For a survey of the main closure borders, see K. Long, *No Entry! A Review of UNHCR's Response to Border Closures in Situations of Mass Refugee Influx* (Geneva: UNHCR Policy Development and Evaluation Service, 2010).

to the longstanding state practice of granting temporary protection in a situation of massive influx.[79]

Whatever the respective merits of the two possible interpretations, human rights law compensates for the uncertainty surrounding Article 33 of the Refugee Convention. Two main arguments may be invoked to justify such a stance. First, the principle of *non-refoulement* under human rights law is absolute; it does not permit any exceptions or derogations when there is a real risk of torture, inhuman, or degrading treatment.[80] As a result, a danger to national security arising from a massive influx does not exempt states from their human rights duty of *non-refoulement*. Secondly, the prevalence of human rights law in situations of mass influx finds additional support in its prohibition of collective expulsion. This absolute prohibition is endorsed in all regional human rights treaties.[81] Though not explicitly mentioned in the ICCPR, the Human Rights Committee has also construed Article 13 as implicitly prohibiting collective expulsion.[82] Likewise, the Committee on the Elimination of Racial Discrimination comes to the conclusion that collective expulsions violate the prohibition of racial discrimination.[83]

A parallel prohibition of mass transfers and deportations can be found in international humanitarian law within Article 49(1) of GC IV.[84] Its applicability is nevertheless confined to protected persons in the hands of an Occupying Power. Its content is further qualified by the possibility of undertaking evacuation of a given area 'if the security of the population or imperative military reasons so demand'.[85]

---

[79] For an overview of the state practice in the field of temporary protection, see notably: I.C. Jackson, *The Refugee Concept in Group Situations* (The Hague: Martinus Nijhoff, 1999); J. Fitzpatrick, 'The Principle and Practice of Temporary Refuge: A Customary Norm Protecting Civilians Fleeing Internal Armed Conflict', in D.A. Martin (ed), *The New Asylum Seekers: Refugee Law in the 1980s* (Dordrecht: Martinus Nijhoff, 1988), 87–101; D. Perluss and J.F. Hartman, 'Temporary Refuge: Emergence of Customary Norm', 26 *Virginia Journal of International Law* (1986) 558–75; G.J.L. Coles, 'Temporary Refuge and the Large Scale Influx of Refugees', 8 *Australian Yearbook of International Law* (1978–80) 190–212. At the regional level, temporary protection has been in the EU with the Temporary Protection Directive 2001/55/EC, OJ L 212/12 (2001).

[80] Among many other restatements see *Chahal v United Kingdom*, ECHR (1996) Reports 1996-V, § 80; CAT, *Tapia Paez v Sweden*, UN Doc CAT/C/18/D/39/1996 (1996), § 14.5.

[81] Article 22(9) of ACHR; Art 12(5) of ACHPR; Art 4 of Protocol No 4 of ECHR; Art 26(b) of the Arab Charter; Art 25(4) of the CIS Convention; and Art 19(1) of the Charter of Fundamental Rights of the European Union.

[82] *General Comment No 15: The Position of Aliens under the Covenant*, UN Doc HRI/GEN/1/Rev.1 at 18 (1986), § 10. Though much less ratified, see also for an explicit restatement of this well-established prohibition, Art 22(1) of the International Convention on the Protection of the Rights of All Migrant Workers and Members of Their Families.

[83] *Concluding Observations on Dominican Republic*, UN Doc CERD/C/DOM/CO/12 (2008), § 13; *General Recommendation 30: Discrimination Against Non-Citizens*, UN Doc HRI/GEN/1/Rev.7/Add.1 at 2 (2005), § 26.

[84] 'Individual or mass forcible transfers, as well as deportations of protected persons from occupied territory to the territory of the Occupying Power or to that of any other country, occupied or not, are prohibited, regardless of their motive.'

[85] Article 49(2).

Besides such a margin of appreciation, the exact scope and content of Article 49(1) has also raised some longstanding controversies.[86]

In any event, the continuing applicability of human rights law in times of armed conflict obviates the limits and ambiguities of both refugee law and humanitarian law. The human rights prohibition of collective expulsion suffers from no exception or derogation. It further applies to any non-citizens—whether documented or not—who are within the jurisdiction of the state and without regard to the risk of ill-treatment in the country of destination. One could still contend that the prohibition of collective expulsion does not apply to massive influx, because the term 'expulsion' does not cover 'refusal of entry' or 'rejection at the border'. Such a line of reasoning is, however, not convincing. Although expulsion may have a particular understanding in domestic law, under international law this notion has an autonomous meaning determined by the object and purpose of the relevant treaty and in due accordance with the principle of effectiveness. This has been restated by the European Court of Human Rights in the leading case *Hirsi v Italy*. The Court dismissed the argument of the Italian Government according to which the contested measure (maritime interception) was a 'refusal to authorize entry into national territory rather than "expulsion"'.[87] By doing so, the Grand Chamber unambiguously confirmed that the prohibition of collective expulsion generally applies to any measure 'the effect of which is to prevent migrants from reaching the borders of the State or even to push them back to another State'.[88]

As a result of this general prohibition, expulsion and other related measures of *refoulement* can only take place after an individual examination of each particular case.[89] In sum, under international human rights law, the general prohibition of collective expulsion combined with the principle of *non-refoulement* converges in ensuring that, even in situations of mass influx, asylum-seekers shall have temporary asylum during the examination of their request. The next issue is then to identify on which grounds victims of armed conflict may be protected in asylum states.

---

[86] For an overview of these controversies, see: Y. Arai-Takahashi, *The Law of Occupation. Continuity and Change of International Humanitarian Law and its Interaction with International Human Rights Law* (Leiden: Martinus Nijhoff, 2009), 332–45; J.-M. Henckaerts, *Mass Expulsion in Modern International Law and Practice* (The Hague/Boston/London: Martinus Nijhoff Publishers, 1995), 143–78; Y. Dinstein, 'The Israel Supreme Court and the Law of Belligerent Occupation: Deportations', 23 *Israel Yearbook on Human Rights* (1993) 1–26; R. Lapidoth, 'The Expulsion of Civilians from Areas which Came under Israeli Control in 1967: Some Legal Issues', 2 *European Journal of International Law* (1990) 97–109.

[87] ECtHR, *Hirsi Jamaa and Others v Italy*, Judgment of 23 February 2012, App No 27765/09, § 160.

[88] *Hirsi Jamaa and Others v Italy* (n 87), § 180.

[89] See notably in this sense: ECtHR, *Andric v Sweden*, ECHR (1999), App No 45917/99, § 1; *General Comment No 15* (n 82), § 10; CERD, *General Recommendation 30* (n 83), § 26; IACHR, *Report on Terrorism and Human Rights*, OEA/Ser.L/V/II.116, Doc 5 rev 1 corr (2002), § 404.

B. The grounds of protection: between a rock and a hard place?

The grounds of protection for victims of armed conflicts provide for another paradigmatic illustration of the complementarity approach. Indeed, each of the three branches of international law virtually covers war refugees, though their respective scope significantly varies from one to another.

Under international refugee law, the definition spelled out in Article 1A(2) of the Refugee Convention (as amended by its 1967 Protocol) is normally apt to cover most victims of armed conflicts.[90] Eligibility for refugee status depends on three cumulative conditions: (1) a well-founded fear of (2) being persecuted (3) for reasons of race, religion, nationality, membership to particular social group and political opinion. In fact, each of these requirements is plainly relevant when applied to the particular context of armed conflicts. With regard to the first condition, the very notion of 'well-founded fear' requires a prospective assessment grounded on two prognostic factors: the personal circumstances of the applicant as well as the general situation prevailing in the destination country. Clearly, the existence of an armed conflict is a key consideration for assessing the general situation in the state of origin and thus the risk of ill-treatment in case of return.

Furthermore, even if the fear is individual by nature, such a fear might find its origin in a collective phenomenon affecting a whole group of persons indistinctively. Indeed a distinction must be drawn between the individual nature of the fear and the collective character of the persecution: the former does not exclude the latter. On the contrary, in some circumstances, the collective character of the persecution may even presume the individual nature of the fear. The very notion of collective persecution is further confirmed by the wording of the Refugee Convention. The five grounds of persecution are primarily identified by reference to membership to a group of persons (whether racial, religious, national, social, or political). They further coincide with the typical causes of most contemporary armed conflicts.

---

[90] This view corresponds to the mainstream doctrine on refugee law. See especially V. Holzer, *Protection of People Fleeing Situations of Armed Conflict and Other Situations of Violence and the 1951 Refugee Convention* (Geneva: UNHCR Legal and Protection Policy Research Series, 2012); J.-F. Durieux, 'Of War, Flows, Laws and Flaws: A Reply to Hugo Storey', 31(3) *Refugee Survey Quarterly* (2012) 161–76 at 163–4; C.M. Bailliet, 'Assessing Jus Ad Bellum and Jus in Bello within the Refugee Status Determination Process: Contemplations on Conscientious Objectors Seeking Asylum', 20(1) *Georgetown Immigration Law Journal* (2005) 337–84; Von Sternberg (n 2), 5; M. Kagan and W.P. Johnson, 'Persecution in the Fog of War: The House of Lords' Decision in Adan', 23 *Michigan Journal of International Law* (2002) 247–64; H. Storey and R. Wallace, 'War and Peace in Refugee Law Jurisprudence', 95 *American Journal of International Law* (2001) 349–66 at 353; W. Kälin, 'Refugees and Civil Wars: Only a Matter of Interpretation?', 3 *International Journal of Refugee Law* (1991) 435–51; S. Bodart, 'Les réfugiés apolitiques: guerre civile et persécution de groupe au regard de la Convention de Genève', 7(1) *International Journal of Refugee Law* (1995) 39–59; P. Butcher, 'Assessing Fear of Persecution in a War Zone', 5(1) *Georgetown Immigration Law Journal* (1991) 435–74.

Against such a framework, acts of war perpetrated against civilians on account of their race, religion, nationality, political opinion, or membership to a particular social group arguably constitute the archetype of persecution. In this regard, several commentators have further suggested that international humanitarian law should provide guidance for construing the refugee definition under Article 1A(2) of the Geneva Convention.[91] Such a possibility may nevertheless be counterproductive. On the one hand, defining persecution as a violation of humanitarian law may distract the attention of decision-makers in placing too much emphasis on peripheral issues which are not crucial for assessing an asylum request (eg whether the situation in the state of origin corresponds to the legal definition of an armed conflict, whether the applicant is a protected person, or whether the balance between humanitarian considerations and military necessity has been adequately applied by the belligerents ...). On the other hand, the notion of persecution under the Refugee Convention already benefits from a well-established definition as a serious violation of human rights.[92] With the continuing applicability of human rights law in armed conflicts, there is no need to further complicate the assessment of asylum requests by resorting to another branch of law. In any event, any grave violation of humanitarian law already corresponds in substance to a serious violation of human rights for the purpose of the refugee definition.[93]

In practice, however, the potential of the refugee definition for victims of armed conflicts starkly contrasts with the reticence of states parties to the Geneva Convention. Though nothing precludes the application of the refugee definition to persons fleeing armed conflicts, states' interpretations remain highly divergent and frequently restrictive.[94] This is exemplified by the wide disparity in refugee

[91] See notably Holzer (n 90), 19–22; Storey (n 4), 19–21; Edwards (n 2), 433–4; Von Sternberg (n 2), 320; Jaquemet (n 2), 665–9; Storey and Wallace (n 90), 359; B. Rutinwa, 'Refugee Claims Based on Violation of International Humanitarian Law: The "Victims" Perspective', 15 *Georgetown Immigration Law Journal* (2000) 497–517.

[92] See most notably: *Canada v Ward* (1993) 103 DLR 4th 1; *Horvath v Secretary of State for the Home Department* (2000) 3 All ER 577; *K v Refugee Status Appeals Authority* (2005) NZAR 441 (2004); Art 9 of the Council Directive 2004/83/EC of 29 April 2004 on minimum standards for the qualification and status of third country nationals or stateless persons as refugees or as persons who otherwise need international protection and the content of the protection granted, OJ L 304/12 (2004).

[93] One should further add that the definition of persecution under international criminal law also converges with its refugee law counterpart as referring to a serious violation of human rights. According to Art 7(2)(g) of the Rome Statute, '"Persecution" means the intentional and severe deprivation of fundamental rights contrary to international law by reason of the identity of the group or collectivity'. This definition nevertheless contrasts with the one under refugee law with regard to its collective nature. This last characteristic is required by international criminal law simply because, according to the definition of the crime against humanity, persecution is 'part of a widespread or systematic attack directed against any civilian population'. By contrast, in international refugee law, persecution may be either collective or individual depending on the specific context of the case.

[94] The position of UNHCR has also not always been clear. In its Handbook first published in 1979, it considered: 'Persons compelled to leave their country of origin as a result of international or national armed conflicts are not normally considered refugees under the 1951 Convention or Protocol. However,

recognition rates concerning persons coming from the same countries plagued by conflicts.[95] The most common ground for refusing protection is to require a so-called 'differentiated risk' over and above that of other civilians caught up in the armed conflict.[96]

The uncertainty surrounding the applicability of the refugee definition and the correlative gap of protection have been partially mitigated by some regional instruments following two different approaches. In the Global North, the European Union has consecrated a specific regime of subsidiary protection based, inter alia, on 'indiscriminate violence in situations of international or internal armed conflict'.[97] Subsidiary protection appears as an additional—and arguably concurrent—device to the Refugee Convention. It indirectly gives a pretext for justifying the restrictive interpretation of the refugee definition in the context of armed conflicts. Resort to subsidiary protection for victims of armed conflict has proved to be disappointing and its application has raised many controversies regarding its exact scope and content.[98]

foreign invasion or occupation of all or part of a country can result—and occasionally has resulted—in persecution for one or more of the reasons enumerated in the 1951 Convention': UNHCR, *Handbook and Guidelines on Procedures and Criteria for Determining Refugee Status under the 1951 Convention and the 1967 Protocol relating to the Status of Refugees* (Geneva: UNHCR, 1979), §§ 164-5. UNHCR has since clarified that, in many situations, persons fleeing conflicts may have a well-founded fear of persecution for a 1951 Convention ground: UNHCR, *Note on International Protection*, UN Doc A/ AC.96/850 (1995), § 11.

[95] Such a disparity has been highlighted by the UNHCR in the case of asylum-seekers from Afghanistan, Iraq, and Somalia in EU host countries. According to the Refugee Agency, 'The variation extends to as much as 33 percent with regard to first instance decisions relating to Afghanistan in 2010, 50 percent with regard to Iraq and 72 percent with regard to Somalia'. UNHCR, *Safe at Last? Law and Practice in Selected EU Member States with Respect to Asylum-Seekers Fleeing Indiscriminate Violence* (Geneva: UNHCR, 2011), 17, see also tables at 17–18.

[96] See eg *Mohamed v Ashcroft* (2005) 396 F.3d 999, 1006 (8th Cir); *Adan v Secretary of State for the Home Department* (1998) 2 WLR 702, per Lord Slynn of Hadley; *Isa v Canada* (Secretary of State) (1995) FCJ No 354, 72. For further discussions about the state practice, see the doctrinal references mentioned above.

[97] Article 15(c) of the Qualification Directive 2004/83/EC.

[98] In particular, the determination of the very existence of an 'armed conflict' has led to diverging interpretations among member states. For instance, the situation in Iraq has been recognized as a non-international armed conflict in France and the United Kingdom, while other member states (such as Romania and Sweden) have refused to come to this obvious conclusion: UNHCR, *Asylum in the European Union, A Study of the Implementation of the Qualification Directive* (Geneva: UNHCR, 2007), 76–8. For a critical account of the irrelevance of humanitarian law in construing subsidiary protection, see also C. Bauloz, 'The (Mis)Use of International Humanitarian Law under Article 15(c) of the EU Qualification Directive', in J.-F. Durieux and D. Cantor (eds), *Refuge from Inhumanity: Enriching Refugee Protection Standards Through Recourse to International Humanitarian Law* (The Hague: Martinus Nijhoff, 2014). For further discussions about the controversies raised by subsidiary protection, see also: H. Battjes, 'Subsidiary Protection and Other Alternative Forms of Protection', in V. Chetail and C. Bauloz (eds), *Research Handbook on Migration and International Law* (Cheltenham: Edward Elgar Publishing, 2014); S.S. Juss, 'Problematizing the Protection of "War Refugees": A Rejoinder to Hugo Storey and Jean-François Durieux', 32(1) *Refugee Survey Quarterly* (2013) 122–47; P. Tiedemann, 'Subsidiary Protection and the Function of Article 15(c) of the Qualification Directive', 31(1) *Refugee*

Regional endeavours carried out in the Global South have followed a different approach, ultimately less convoluted and more protective: the refugee definition under the Geneva Convention has been explicitly extended to any person fleeing armed conflicts. The pioneer regional instrument in this area was adopted in 1969 by the Organization of African Unity. Article 1(2) of the Convention Governing the Specific Aspects of Refugee Problems in Africa states:

The term refugee shall also apply to every person who, owing to external aggression, occupation, foreign domination, or events seriously disturbing public order in either part or the whole of his country of nationality, is compelled to leave his place of habitual residence in order to seek refuge in another place outside of his country of origin or nationality.

The African model of refugee protection has been further endorsed in Latin America with the 1984 Declaration of Cartagena.[99]

At the universal level, however, human rights law still remains the most clear-cut avenue for compensating the restrictive interpretation of the refugee definition. Under this branch of law, the principle of *non-refoulement* unequivocally prohibits states from sending back persons who are exposed to a real risk of torture or inhuman and degrading treatment in the midst of an armed conflict.[100] Compared to the Refugee Convention, its large and objective scope highlights two main characteristics: its absolute character impedes any possible derogation and the notion of inhuman or degrading treatment is not qualified by one of the five limitative grounds of persecution.

Furthermore, the human rights principle of *non-refoulement* has been construed as establishing a presumption of inhuman or degrading treatment in some cases of generalized violence. As underlined by the European Court of Human Rights,

Survey Quarterly (2012) 123–38; R. Errera, 'The CJEU and Subsidiary Protection: Reflections on Elgafaji and After', 23(1) *International Journal of Refugee Law* (2011) 93–110; V. Chetail and C. Bauloz, *The European Union and the Challenges of Forced Migration: From Economic Crisis to Protection Crisis?* (San Dimenico di Fiesole: European University Institute, Robert Schuman Centre for Advanced Studies, EU-US Immigration Systems 2011/07, 2011), 17; H. Lambert and T. Farrell, 'The Changing Character of Armed Conflict and the Implications for Refugee Protection Jurisprudence', 22(2) *International Journal of Refugee Law* (2010) 237–73; J. McAdam, 'The European Union Qualification Directive: The Creation of a Subsidiary Protection Regime', 17 *International Journal of Refugee Law* (2005) 461–516; R. Piotrowicz and C. Van Eck, 'Subsidiary Protection and Primary Rights', 53 *International and Comparative Law Quarterly* (2004) 107–38.

   [99] Though a non-binding resolution, the Cartagena Declaration has been endorsed in the domestic law of several states and is considered as a primary instrument of protection in the region. For further discussions about the OAU Convention and the Cartagena Declaration, see G. Okoth-Obbo, 'Thirty Years On: A legal Review of the 1969 OAU Convention Governing the Specific Aspects of Refugee Problems in Africa', 20(1) *Refugee Survey Quarterly* (2001) 79–138; E. Arboleda, 'Refugee Definition in Africa and Latin America: The Lessons of Pragmatism', 3 *International Journal of Refugee Law* (1991) 185–207; P. Nobel, 'Refugee, Law, and Development in Africa', 3 *Michigan Yearbook of International Legal Studies* (1982) 255–88.

   [100] See eg UN Human Rights Committee, *Warsame v Canada*, UN Doc CCPR/C/102/D/1959/2010 (2011); Committee against Torture (CAT), *K.H. v Denmark*, UN Doc CAT/C/49/D/464/2011 (2012); CAT, *Sadiq Shek Elmi v Australia*, UN Doc CAT/C/22/D/120/1998 (1999).

'a general situation of violence in a country of destination [can] be of a sufficient level of intensity as to entail that any removal to it would necessarily breach Article 3 of the Convention'.[101] Though such a level of intensity remains exceptional by nature,[102] the Court has also made clear that membership of a group systematically exposed to ill-treatment is sufficient on its own to trigger the duty of *non-refoulement* without any further distinguishing features.[103]

Protection against forced return in times of armed conflict finds an additional support in international humanitarian law. According to Article 45(4) of GC IV, '[i]n no circumstances shall a protected person be transferred to a country where he or she may have reason to fear persecution for his or her political opinions or religious beliefs'. Although this provision has been partially reproduced in the refugee definition endorsed two years later in the 1951 Convention,[104] it has subsequently been overtaken by human rights law for three main reasons.

First, the notion of torture, degrading and inhuman treatment is broader than the one of persecution on account of political opinions or religious beliefs, even if they may overlap in practice.[105] Secondly, though worded in categorical terms, the prohibition of transfer does not prejudice extradition provided that this is done 'in pursuance of extradition treaties concluded before the outbreak of hostilities' and for 'offences against ordinary criminal law'.[106] By contrast, the human rights principle of *non-refoulement* applies to all measures of removal (including extradition) and without regard to the criminal record of the person at risk of torture, degrading, or inhuman treatment.[107] Thirdly, the scope of the prohibition contained in international humanitarian law is confined to protected persons on the territory of a state party to an international armed conflict.

[101] *N.A. v United Kingdom*, 17 July 2008, App No 25904/07, § 115.

[102] *N.A. v United Kingdom* (n 101), § 115. Such a situation has been nevertheless acknowledged by the Court as regards Mogadishu, Somalia: *Sufi and Elmi v United Kingdom*, 28 June 2011, App Nos 8319/07 and 11449/07, § 248.

[103] *Salah Sheekh v The Netherlands*, 11 January 2007, App No 1948/04, § 149; *N.A. v United Kingdom* (n 101), § 116.

[104] As mentioned before, besides religion and political opinion, three other grounds of persecution have been added in the Refugee Convention (race, nationality, and membership of a particular social group).

[105] One could argue, however, that Art 45(3) further prohibits any transfer when the destination state is unable or unwilling to apply the Fourth Geneva Convention, thereby triggering the risk of violation of any rights and guarantees granted by this Convention. This extensive scope of application is nevertheless mitigated by the fact that it only applies to civilian detainees. See also for prisoners of war, Art 12(2) of GC III.

[106] Article 45(6) of GC IV.

[107] See most notably: *Soering v United Kingdom*, 7 July 1989, App No 1/189/161/217, § 88.

4 REFUGEES IN POST-WAR CONTEXTS

Refugees in post-war contexts constitute another case for highlighting the centrality of human rights law. The termination of hostilities inevitably begs the question
of the end of refugee protection and the correlative return to the state of origin.
This highlights in turn a dilemma inherent to any process of post-conflict peace-
building: can one consider that the end of a conflict constitutes, in and of itself, a
fundamental change of circumstances justifying the withdrawal of refugee protection, when a sustained peace has not yet been established, and the massive return
of refugees may serve as an additional source of destabilization? On the other hand,
return and reintegration of refugees can be a decisive factor in the reconstruction
of a country.

An empirical solution to this normative and political dilemma has been found
through the notion of voluntary repatriation. While voluntary repatriation is commonly referred to as 'the ideal solution to refugee problems',[108] international refugee
law is rather silent on this (Section A). Instead, it is human rights law which gives
voluntary repatriation its full normative scope and content, even when international humanitarian law provides for more specific norms in relation to prisoners
of war and civilian internees (Section B).

A. Voluntary repatriation: the human right to return filling the silence of international refugee law

With the promotion of voluntary repatriation entrusted to UNHCR,[109] one could
legitimately expect its normative framework to be settled by international refugee law. Voluntary repatriation has, however, evolved quite outside the refugee
law framework to become both a practice of states and an institutional policy of
UNHCR.[110]

---

[108] UN Doc A/RES/39/169 (1994). Since then, the General Assembly has constantly referred to
voluntary repatriation as 'the preferred solution' by contrast to the other possible solutions provided
by local integration or resettlement in a third country. See also among the numerous and somewhat
repetitive Excom Conclusions Nos: 109 (LXI) (2009), preambular § 16; 108 (LIX) (2008), (l); 104 (LVI)
(2005), preambular § 1; 101 (LV) (2004), preambular § 5; 95 (LIV) (2003), (i); 90 (LII) (2001), (j); 87
(L) (1999), (r); 85 (XLIX) (1998), (g); 81 (XLVIII) (1997), (q); 79 (XLVII) (1996), (q); 74 (XLV), 1994 (v).
[109] Articles 8(c) and 9 of UNHCR Statute.
[110] For an overview see notably: Hathaway (n 49), 917–63; V. Chetail, 'Voluntary Repatriation in
Public International Law: Concepts and Contents', 23 *Refugee Survey Quarterly* (2004) 1–32; M. Zieck,
UNHCR and Voluntary Repatriation of Refugees: A Legal Analysis (The Hague/Boston/London: Martinus
Nijhoff, 1997); S. Takahashi, 'The UNHCR Handbook on Voluntary Repatriation: The Emphasis of
Return over Protection', 9(4) *International Journal of Refugee Law* (1997) 593–612; B.S. Chimni, 'The
Meaning of Words and the Role of UNHCR in Voluntary Repatriation', 5(3) *International Journal of*

The Refugee Convention is indeed silent on voluntary repatriation. The reason for this can be found in its primary rationale: it exclusively focuses on the obligations of asylum states without envisaging refugee protection from a more holistic perspective encapsulating both states of origin and asylum. Following its specific stance, the Refugee Convention implicitly favours integration in the country of asylum. It associates refugee status with a substantial range of basic guarantees and social benefits,[111] and calls for facilitating naturalization of refugees in asylum countries.[112] The only references to return to country of origin are made in prohibitive terms: Article 32 bars expulsion of refugees, except for exceptional circumstances, and Article 33 lays down the fundamental principle of *non-refoulement*. This focus on prohibiting return comes as no surprise for 'refugees are by definition "unrepatriable" '[113] because of their well-founded fear of being persecuted in their country of origin.

Voluntary repatriation is understood in a similarly oblique way through the cessation clause of Article 1.C(4). According to this provision, the Refugee Convention is no longer applicable when the refugee 'has voluntarily re-established himself in the country which he left or outside which he remained owing to fear of persecution'. But even in such an instance, voluntary repatriation does not justify, on its own, withdrawal of refugee status.[114] This is possible only when the refugee is re-established in his/her country of origin.

While voluntary repatriation is not addressed as such by the Refugee Convention, some regional instruments (including most notably the OAU Convention)[115] have endorsed it as a key principle of refugee protection. By contrast, human rights law provides a solid and universal legal basis with the right to enter one's own country.[116] In this regard, the Human Rights Committee underlines that 'the right of a person to enter his or her own country [...] includes [...] the right to return after having left one's own country' which 'is of the utmost importance for refugees seeking voluntary repatriation'.[117] The human right to return is thus crucial for ensuring both

---

Refugee Law (1993) 442–60; G.S. Goodwin-Gill, 'Voluntary Repatriation: Legal and Policy Issues', in G. Loescher and L. Monahan (eds), *Refugees and International Relations* (Oxford: Oxford University Press, 1989), 255–85; R. Hofmann, 'Voluntary Repatriation and UNHCR', *Zeitschrift für ausländisches und öffentliches Recht* (1984) 327–35.

[111] Refugees lawfully established in the territories of states parties are notably thus entitled to access to courts (Art 16), the right to work (Art 17), access to public education (Art 22), and the right to social security (Art 24).

[112] Article 34.   [113] Zieck (n 110), 101–2.   [114] Hathaway (n 49), 918–19.

[115] Article 5. See also Cartagena Declaration, § 12 and Council Directive 2001/55/EC on Temporary Protection, Art 22.

[116] Article 12(4) of ICCPR; Art 5 of CERD; Art 2 of the 1973 Convention on the Suppression and Punishment of the Crime of Apartheid; Art 10(2) of the 1989 Convention on the Rights of the Child; Art 3(2) of the 1963 Protocol No 4 to the ECHR; Art 22(5) of ACHR; Art 12(2) of ACHPR; and Art 27(a) of the Arab Charter.

[117] *General Comment No 27* (n 69), § 19.

the voluntary nature of repatriation and the correlative obligation of states of origin to admit their nationals.[118]

This contextual understanding of the human right to return has been further developed by the Committee on the Elimination of Racial Discrimination in its *General Recommendation No 22: Article 5 and Refugees and Displaced Persons*:

(a) All such refugees and displaced persons have the right freely to return to their homes of origin under conditions of safety;

(b) States parties are obliged to ensure that the return of such refugees and displaced persons is voluntary and to observe the principle of non-refoulement and non-expulsion of refugees;

(c) All such refugees and displaced persons have, after their return to their homes of origin, the right to have restored to them property of which they were deprived in the course of the conflict and to be compensated appropriately for any such property that cannot be restored to them. Any commitments or statements relating to such property made under duress are null and void;

(d) All such refugees and displaced persons have, after their return to their homes of origin, the right to participate fully and equally in public affairs at all levels and to have equal access to public services and to receive rehabilitation assistance.[119]

This human rights-based approach has also been refined through *The Principles on Housing and Property Restitution for Refugees and Displaced Persons*, endorsed by the UN Sub-Commission on the Promotion and Protection of Human Rights in 2005.[120] Known as the Pinheiro Principles, they elaborate key human rights relating to the equitable restitution of housing and property and provide guidelines to states and international actors for ensuring access to these rights.

In short, human rights law provides an indispensable yardstick for framing the legal content of both return and reintegration of displaced persons in their own countries. Although much remains to be done for ensuring their basic rights in peacebuilding processes,[121] it contributes to fill the silence in the Refugee Convention, highlighting the vital interplay between these two branches of international law for the purpose of promoting a holistic approach to refugee protection.

---

[118] See UNHCR, *Handbook on Voluntary Repatriation* (Geneva: UNHCR, 1996), § 2.1 considering the right to return as 'the basic principle underlying voluntary repatriation'. For further discussions, see: Chetail (n 110), and the bibliographical references mentioned therein.

[119] UN Doc A/51/18 (1996).   [120] UN Doc E/CN.4/Sub.2/2005/17 (2005).

[121] See generally, V. Tennant, 'Return and Reintegration', in V. Chetail (ed), *Post-Conflict Peacebuilding: A Lexicon* (Oxford: Oxford University Press, 2009), 307–19 and the special issue on 'Displacement, Peace Processes and Post-Conflict Peacebuilding' in 28 *Refugee Survey Quarterly* (2009).

B. How voluntary is repatriation? International humanitarian law versus international human rights law

In post-conflict situations, repatriation is nonetheless not solely governed by human rights law but also by international humanitarian law. This last branch provides states with the obligation to repatriate prisoners of war and civilian internees at the end of hostilities. Such a reliance on humanitarian law understanding of repatriation is, however, unable to promote the voluntary nature of reparation, thereby demanding recourse to human rights law.

Under humanitarian law, the obligation to repatriate is framed in categorical terms without reference to the willingness of the concerned person to be so returned. Article 118 of GC III requires that '[p]risoners of war shall be released and repatriated without delay after the cessation of active hostilities'.[122] In fact, during the 1949 Diplomatic Conference, an Austrian amendment was introduced to grant prisoners of war a right 'to apply for their transfer to any other country [than their country of origin] which is ready to accept them'.[123] The proposal was, however, rejected by a large majority of delegations for fear that prisoners might not have the free will to so decide.[124] Moreover, the absolute obligation of repatriation is further reinforced by the inalienability of a prisoner of war's rights, which cannot be renounced under any circumstances.[125]

While the obligation to repatriate civilian internees under Article 134 of GC IV may sound less categorical,[126] the ICRC study reaffirms its unconditional nature under customary international law for both types of protected persons.[127] It even reminds that '[a]n "unjustifiable delay in the repatriation of prisoners of war or civilians" constitutes a grave breach of Additional Protocol I'.[128] Ultimately, such categorical obligations not only require states to enforce repatriation at any price— even on an involuntary basis—but may also conflict in practice with the principle of *non-refoulement*.

This is probably the only case of a true conflict of norms between international humanitarian law, refugee law, and human rights law. The absolute duty to repatriate prisoners of war without delay is in contradiction with, and superseded by,

---

[122] This provision curiously contrasts with the legal regime applicable during armed conflicts for, according to Art 109(3) of GC III, 'no sick or injured prisoner of war [...] may be repatriated against his will during hostilities'.

[123] Commentary GC IV, 542.

[124] Commentary CG III, 542.   [125] Article 7 of GC III.

[126] 'The High Contracting Parties shall endeavour, upon the close of hostilities or occupation, to ensure the return of all internees to their last place of residence, or to facilitate their repatriation.'

[127] Customary International Humanitarian Law, Rule 128.

[128] Customary International Humanitarian Law, Rule 128; see Art 85(4)(b) of AP I.

international refugee law when these prisoners have a well-founded fear of being persecuted in the destination state. This refugee law prohibition of forcible repatria-tion does not apply when prisoners of war have committed war crimes or any other acts falling under the exclusion clause of Article 1F or under the exceptions of the *non-refoulement* duty of Article 33(2). Yet, even in such a case, human rights law still prevails over the humanitarian law obligation of repatriation as it bans any forcible return where there is a real risk of torture, degrading or inhumane treatment.

Instead of a conflict of norms, such a divergence could be simply understood as the successive application of humanitarian law, refugee law, and human rights law.[129] In any event, the result is the same: contrary to Article 118 of GC III, prisoners of war shall not be repatriated without delay after the cessation of active hostilities, when they fall under the refugee definition, or are otherwise exposed to a real risk of degrading treatment.

It is true that, in subsequent practice, Article 118 of GC III has rarely been applied in the automatic way suggested by its categorical wording. Since the Korean War,[130] and especially since the two Gulf wars,[131] the common stand is that of not repatri-ating prisoners unwilling to return home for fear of mistreatments therein. Such practice has been endorsed by the ICRC[132] and it is even advanced as a norm of customary international law for both prisoners of war and civilian internees.[133]

For the ICRC, the customary law obligation of repatriation should thus be inter-preted as including an additional duty of taking into account the wish of the con-cerned person. While this unapparent conclusion could be grounded on Article 45 of GC IV with regard to civilian detainees, the argument advocated in favour of a similar guarantee for prisoners of war is particularly weak. Though the ICRC

[129] Jaquemet (n 2), 663–4.

[130] For further details, see: A.J. Esgain and Colonel W.A. Solf, 'The 1949 Geneva Convention Relative to the Treatment of Prisoners of War: Its Principles, Innovations and Deficiencies', 41 *North Carolina Law Review* (1963) 537–96 at 590–3; S.A. Pasha, 'The Repatriation Problem of the Korean Prisoners of War and India's Contribution in its Solution', 2 *The Indian Journal of International Law* (1962) 1–47; G. Attia, *Le rapatriement des prisonniers de guerre* (Beirut: Dar el Fath, 1960); R.R. Baxter, 'Asylum to Prisoners of War', 30 *British Yearbook of International Law* (1953) 489–98.

[131] For instance, about 15,000 Iraqi prisoners of war refused their repatriation to Iraq after the second Gulf War. H. Fischer, 'Protection of Prisoners of War', in D. Fleck (ed), *The Handbook of Humanitarian Law in Armed Conflicts* (Oxford: Oxford University Press, 1995), 321–67 at 366. See also J. Quigley, 'Iran and Iraq and the Obligations to Release and Repatriate Prisoners of War after the Close of Hostilities', *American University Journal of International Law and Policy* (1989) 82.

[132] Commentary GC III, 546–7: '1. Prisoners of war have an inalienable right to be repatriated once active hostilities have ceased. [...] 2. No exception may be made to this rule unless there are serious reasons for fearing that a prisoner of war who is himself opposed to being repatriated may, after his repatriation, be subject of unjust measures afflicting his life or liberty, especially on grounds of race, social class, religion or political views, and that consequently repatriation would be contrary to the general principles of international law for the protection of the human being. Each case must be exam-ined individually.' The ICRC has taken action according to these principles in a number of conflicts, including the Iran-Iraq eight years conflict (20 ICRC Annual Report 1989, 87), the Gulf War (ICRC Annual Report 1991, 100), and the Ethiopia–Eritrea armed conflict (ICRC Annual Report 2007, 102).

[133] See Rule 128.

recognizes that such provision is absent from GC III, it underlines that every repa-triation in which it has been involved as a neutral intermediary has been conducted after a prior interview ascertaining the person's wish to be so repatriated. One would expect more than ICRC practice for grounding such a customary law interpretation clearly contradicting the unconditional wording of Article 118 of GC III. By con-trast, the lack of any reference to the human rights principle of *non-refoulement* is odd to say the least.

State practice may indeed have evolved into a customary norm but, if so, this development has itself been framed by, and grounded in human rights law, rather than humanitarian law. First, international humanitarian law was originally con-ceived as a set of inter-state obligations (eg the obligation of repatriation); it is thanks to human rights law that the focus has been further placed on individuals as bearers of rights and obligations under international law (eg the right to repatriation).[134] Secondly, this customary norm of international law is nothing else but the acknowl-edgment of the human rights principle of *non-refoulement*.[135] Prisoners of war and civilian internees cannot be repatriated where they would be at risk of torture or inhumane or degrading treatment upon return.

5 Conclusion

Though this has not always been the case, the simultaneous application of interna-tional humanitarian law, human rights law, and refugee law is no longer contested. This common assumption nevertheless belies the complexity of the relationship between the three legal regimes and the difficulties arising from the identifica-tion, interpretation, and application of the relevant norms. Undoubtedly, no single branch offers a definitive answer to the contemporary challenges of armed con-flicts: the reach of international protection can only be apprehended through a complementary, and thereby cumulative, approach of the branches of international law applicable in times of armed conflicts.

---

[134] See Major V.A. Ary, 'Concluding Hostilities: Humanitarian Provisions in Cease-Fire Agreements', 148 *Military Law Review* (1995) 186–273 at 222; and J.E. Rockwell, 'The Right of Nonrepatriation of Prisoners of War Captured by the United States', 83(2) *The Yale Law Journal* (1973) 358–84 at 377–8.

[135] See J.P. Charmatz and H.M. Wit, 'Repatriation of Prisoners of War and the 1949 Geneva Convention', 62 *The Yale Law Journal* (1952–53) 391–415 at 406–8 who already contemplated the poten-tial of international human rights law for repatriation to be conducted on a voluntary basis. See also C. Shields Dellessert, *Release and Repatriation of Prisoners of War at the End of Active Hostilities*, vol 5 (Zürich: Société Suisse de droit international, Schulthess, 1977), 194–9; Rockwell (n 134), 378–82.

Furthermore, while international humanitarian law, refugee law, and human rights law are clearly the three pillars of the refugee protection regime, their multi-faceted interactions constitute a fertile ground for apprehending forced migration through a holistic and systemic approach. From a comparative perspective, international refugee law has more in common with international humanitarian law than it has with international human rights law. The reasons for this are both historical and structural.

The four Geneva Conventions of 1949 and their refugee sister adopted two years later are children of their times. Though both refugee law and humanitarian law have been amended (and partially updated) in the 1960s and 1970s, they have still retained some common distinctive features which arguably reflect their stage of development. The normative structure of international humanitarian law and refugee law converges on three major components. First, the two legal regimes are primarily framed as obligations of states, instead of individual rights. Secondly, under each branch of international law, the traditional distinction between nationals and non-nationals remains a foundation stone for identifying and framing the applicable norms. Thirdly, both international humanitarian law and refugee law rely on a decentralized scheme of implementation without a proper supervisory mechanism. Though the ICRC and the UNCHR are the key humanitarian actors in their respective field, they are not monitoring bodies in charge of supervising states' conduct. Overall, the basic principle underlying the three common attributes of international humanitarian law and refugee law is the tribute paid to the sacrosanct sovereignty of states.

While international human rights law does not fundamentally depart from the state-centric approach to international law, it diverges on each of the three above characteristics of international humanitarian law and refugee law. The human rights-based approach to the law of armed conflict proves to be essential in compensating for the limits inherent to the other applicable legal regimes.

Though international humanitarian law is supposed to be the tailor-made regime applicable in times of armed conflict, it does not endorse the most protective norms. It provides instead a minimum standard within the strict limits of its particular scope (namely the treatment of non-nationals in the hands of a party to the conflict). The minimum, if not minimalist, protection granted by international humanitarian law is upgraded by the cumulative application of the other applicable branches of international law. Nevertheless, even through this approach, international refugee law does not provide the most specific frame of protection for those fleeing armed conflicts.

Even worse, both international humanitarian law and refugee law appear to be relatively indifferent to the specific needs of refugees in war, from war and in post-war contexts. As observed by Kälin,

[A] traditional understanding of the relationship between international humanitarian law and refugee law maintains that refugee law was not really made to address the plight of those who had to flee the dangers of war and seek refuge abroad. At the same time, international humanitarian law does not provide any protection for this large category of persons in need of international protection.[136]

Against such a background, international human rights law is bound to play a vital role for compensating and arguably updating international humanitarian law and refugee law. Human rights law must thus be taken seriously by humanitarian and refugee lawyers. Though every specialist is naturally inclined to comprehend the world through the myopic lens of his/her own discipline, some substantial progress has been made during the last decade for facilitating cross-disciplinary dialogue. It is true that the professional culture and the particular ethos of each discipline are still very present in governmental, non-governmental, and academic circles. However, there is, after all, nothing insurmountable in ensuring that international humanitarian law, refugee law, and human rights law are no longer competitors but brothers in arms.

Besides all their differences, the three branches of international law share the same fundamental objective, notably restated by the International Tribunal for the former Yugoslavia:

The general principle of respect for human dignity is the basic underpinning and indeed the very *raison d'être* of international humanitarian law and human rights law; indeed in modern times it has become of such paramount importance as to permeate the whole body of international law.[137]

Similarly, the very function of international refugee law is to ensure the effective respect for human dignity when victims of abuses have no other option than to leave their own country. From this stance, international refugee law cogently constitutes 'a right to have rights'[138] following Arendt's terminology:

The new refugees were persecuted not because of what they had done or thought, but because of what they unchangeably were—born into the wrong kind of race or the wrong kind of class or drafted by the wrong kind of government [...] but [...] they were and appeared to be nothing but human beings whose very innocence—from every point of view, and especially that of the persecuting government—was their greatest misfortune.[139]

---

[136] Kälin (n 2), 637.
[137] *Prosecutor v Furundžija*, Trial Judgment, Case No IT-95-17/1, 10 December 1998, § 183.
[138] H. Arendt, *The Origins of Totalitarianism* (San Diego: Harcourt, 1958), 296.
[139] Arendt (n 138), 294–5.

PART VII

ACCOUNTABILITY/ LIABILITY FOR VIOLATIONS OF THE LAW IN ARMED CONFLICT

CHAPTER 29

....

WAR CRIMES AND OTHER INTERNATIONAL 'CORE' CRIMES

....

PAOLA GAETA

1 INTRODUCTION

....

IN a book published in 1945, Manfred Lachs, writing 'under the strain of active military service' during World War II, noticed that '[w]ar crimes may appear a minor issue in this deadly conflict'. He pointed out, however, that 'the manner in which the problem is resolved might become a great precedent' for, he explained, raising international law 'to the height it deserves', '[t]he principle that crime does not pay must become law, not only in the everyday life of an individual, but also in inter-State relations'.[1]

This he wrote before the adoption of the London Charter which established the Nuremberg Tribunal[2] and the trials of war criminals from World War II started,

---

[1] M. Lachs, *War Crimes. An Attempt to Define the Issues* (London: Stevens & Sons, 1945), 102.

[2] The Charter of the International Military Tribunal at Nuremberg was signed on 8 August 1945 by France, the United Kingdom, the United States, and the USSR after very difficult negotiations relating to the list and definition of the crimes to be subject to the jurisdiction of the Tribunal, as well as with regard to the rules of procedure and evidence it had to follow. The London Charter conferred on the Nuremberg Tribunal jurisdiction over three classes of crimes: crimes against peace, war crimes, and crimes against humanity.

both at the international and the national level. It was a time when the 'principle that individuals are not subjects of the law of nations' was still an orthodoxy in international law, and even perceived by some commentators as 'axiomatic' in the law of war.[3] Its natural corollary was that penal offences could have only a *municipal* character, including those offences committed in violation of the laws of war. An orthodox approach therefore required war crimes not to be considered as crimes under international law, but simply a means to enforce international rules of warfare at the national level.

The trials against World War II German 'major war criminals' before the Nuremberg Tribunal, and against the 'major war criminals in the Far East' before the Tokyo Tribunal,[4] shook this basic principle of international law. The trials were grounded on the assumption that the individuals in the dock were to be tried for crimes *against international law*, and that the rules proscribing these crimes were *international rules*. The fact that some defendants had committed such crimes in obedience of superior orders lawfully issued under their domestic law was therefore no defence before those Tribunals.[5] Nor could the defendants plead that they had acted on behalf of the state, a plea based on the traditional notion that only states, and not individuals, are responsible for conduct contrary to international law.[6] Manfred Lachs' wish, to see the problem of war crimes committed during World War II solved in a way which would raise international law to 'the height it deserved', was thus fulfilled.

It was, however, not until after the end of the Cold War, and following the establishment of the ICTY and the ICTR by the UN Security Council,[7] that the

---

[3] See for instance G. Manner, 'The Legal Nature and Punishment of Criminal Acts of Violence Contrary to the Laws of War', 37 *AJIL* (1943) 407.

[4] The Tokyo Tribunal was established in January 1946, by virtue of a Decree issued by the US General D. MacArthur to implement amongst others Art 10 of the Potsdam Declaration, which provided that 'stern justice' was to be 'meted out' to all war criminals. Its Statute was very similar to that of the Nuremberg Tribunal and conferred on the Tokyo Tribunal jurisdiction over crimes against peace, war crimes, and crimes against humanity.

[5] Article 8 of the Charter of the Nuremberg Tribunal provided: 'The fact that the defendant acted pursuant to order of his Government or of a superior shall not free him from responsibility, but may be considered in mitigation of punishment if the Tribunal determines that justice so requires'. In the same vein, see Art 6 of the Charter of the Tokyo Tribunal.

[6] Article 7 of the Charter of the Nuremberg Tribunal provided: 'The official position of the defendants, whether as Heads of States or responsible officials in Government Departments, shall not be considered as freeing them from responsibility or mitigating punishment'. The same provision, slightly changed, can also be found in Art 6 of the Charter of the Tokyo Tribunal: '[N]either the official position, at any time, of an accused, [...] shall, of itself, be sufficient to free such accused from responsibility for any crime with which he is charged, but such circumstance may be considered in mitigation of punishment if the Tribunal determines that justice so requires'.

[7] The Security Council established the ICTY with Resolution 827 of 25 May 1993, following consideration of the Secretary-General's Report (S/25704, 3 May 1993). In this Resolution the Security Council determined that the situation in the former Yugoslavia, and in particular in Bosnia and Herzegovina—'where there were reports of mass killings, massive, organized and systematic detention and rape of women and [...] the practice of ethnic cleansing'—constituted a threat to international

revolutionary precedent set by the international criminal trials in Nuremberg and Tokyo could grow into a fully-fledged body of international criminal rules, now known as 'international criminal law'. At the legal level, resistance came mainly from those who supported the 'orthodox' approach to international law. Firmly believing that crimes were a matter exclusively confined to national jurisdictions, they went on to influence the drafting of treaties dealing with individual criminal responsibility for violations of international law. The preeminent example is found in the 1949 GCs. The attempt to declare that certain violations of the GCs amounted to war crimes, thus entailing criminal responsibility for the individual perpetrators under the Conventions, was strenuously resisted by many delegations. Some insisted that the use of the word 'crime' had to be avoided, since violations of the Conventions 'will not be crimes until they are so made by domestic penal legislation'.[8] This approach prevailed. The GCs, far from directly establishing the criminal responsibility of the individuals who violate the Conventions, merely oblige the High Contracting Parties to 'enact any legislation necessary to provide effective penal sanctions' against them and to bring them before their national courts.[9] The term 'war crimes' to describe those violations was carefully avoided, and that of 'grave breaches' was finally chosen.[10]

The 'orthodox' approach to international law in the matter of individual criminal responsibility for war crimes, however, is no longer tenable today. The principle that individuals may be held directly responsible under the law of nations is firmly embedded in customary international law. In addition, the list of acts directly criminalized under international law also includes at least two other classes of crimes: crimes against humanity and genocide.[11]

This Chapter aims to trace the development of the criminalization of war crimes under international law and to compare it with the parallel criminalization of crimes

peace and security under Ch VII of the UN Charter. The ICTR was established in a similar fashion to the ICTY in response to the civil war and genocide in Rwanda. The Security Council adopted the Statute of the ICTR by Resolution 955 of 8 November 1994, after having determined that 'this situation continues to constitute a threat to international peace and security'.

[8] This was the statement of the US Delegation. For the debate, see *Diplomatic Conference of Geneva, Verbatim Report of the Twenty-first Meeting*, 30 July 1949 (CDG/PLEN/CR.21), 10–11.

[9] This is an essential feature of the grave breaches: under the GCs, any contracting state is obliged to search for and bring to trial (or alternatively to surrender to a requesting state showing a *prima facie* case) any person suspected or accused of a grave breach (see Arts 49/50/129/146, para 2, of the GCs). This is what is usually known as the 'mandatory system of universal criminal jurisdiction' over grave breaches.

[10] Article 49/50/129/146, para 1, of the GCs, according to which: 'The High Contracting Parties undertake to enact any legislation necessary to provide effective penal sanctions for persons committing or ordering to be committed, any of the grave breaches of the present Convention defined in the following Article'.

[11] The list of international crimes directly criminalized under customary international law is uncertain, but there is general agreement that it includes at least war crimes, crimes against humanity, and genocide.

against humanity and genocide. It will also examine the legal ingredients of these three classes of international crimes. It will be shown that, while war crimes are intimately connected to international humanitarian law, the same does not hold true for crimes against humanity and genocide. Although they are usually committed in times of armed conflict, crimes against humanity and genocide are internationally criminalized because they constitute a serious and gross infringement of the human rights accruing to all human beings, regardless of their nationality or allegiance.

2 THE CRIMINALIZATION OF WAR CRIMES VERSUS THE CRIMINALIZATION OF CRIMES AGAINST HUMANITY AND GENOCIDE

A. The paths followed

The rationale behind the assertion of individual criminal responsibility under international law for war crimes can be traced back to the eighteenth century, when national criminal codes and military manuals started providing for the right of a belligerent to prosecute and punish its own soldiers for violations of the laws of war.[12] As for war crimes committed by enemy personnel or civilians, it would seem that the power of a belligerent to exercise its criminal jurisdiction was initially limited to the time of the armed conflict and, in any case, only within occupied territories. However, armistice or peace treaties could contain a clause whereby the victorious belligerent imposed upon the defeated states the obligation to surrender alleged war criminals for trial.[13]

World War I abruptly launched the discourse on war crimes in the international arena. Articles 228–9 of the Peace Treaty of Versailles constitute the first clear international recognition of the right of a belligerent party to bring to justice persons belonging to the other belligerents for violations of the laws and customs of war *after* the end of hostilities.[14] Article 227 of the Treaty went so far as to provide for

---

[12] M. Bothe, 'War Crimes', in A. Cassese, P. Gaeta, and J.R.W.D. Jones (eds), *The Rome of Statute of the International Criminal Court. A Commentary*, vol I (Oxford: Oxford University Press, 2002), 382.

[13] See UN War Crimes Commission, *History of the UN War Crimes Commission and the Development of the Laws of War* (1948), 29–30.

[14] Article 228 of the Treaty of Versailles provided as follows: 'The German Government recognizes the right of the allied and associated powers to bring before military tribunals persons accused of having committed acts in violation of the laws and customs of war [...]'. Under Art 229, persons charged with war crimes against the nationals of one of the Allied and Associated Powers, should have been

the accountability of the former German Emperor for 'a supreme offence against international morality and the sanctity of treaties'. It is well known that this was an abortive attempt: Wilhelm II was never brought to trial on account of the refusal of the Netherlands to extradite him (on grounds of national law: Dutch legislation allowed extradition only on the basis of a treaty, and the Netherlands was not party to the Versailles treaty; in addition, the offences provided for in Article 227 did not constitute crimes under Dutch law).[15] Furthermore, the high ranking German military officers indicted under Article 228 were never tried by the Allies.[16]

The path towards criminalization of war crimes however continued through the establishment of the Nuremberg and Tokyo Tribunals,[17] and the adoption of specific provisions on grave breaches in the 1949 GCs,[18] subsequently supplemented by the relevant provisions in Additional Protocol I.[19] This process culminated, as mentioned above, with the establishment of the ICTY and the ICTR[20] and the subsequent creation of the ICC[21] and other international or mixed criminal tribunals.[22]

The rationale behind the international criminalization of war crimes is clear. It lies in the need to guarantee—also by way of a threat of criminal sanction—that some elementary principles and considerations of humanity are respected in warlike situations, so as to reduce as much as possible the suffering and misery caused by war.

The case of crimes against humanity is slightly different. The path towards their international criminalization is not rooted in national criminal legal systems, as it is

brought before the military tribunals of the relevant Power, while persons accused of war crimes against nationals of more than one of these Powers should have been brought before military tribunals composed of members of the military tribunals of the Powers concerned. It should be noted that these articles only deal with violations of law and customs of war; the American view prevailed and no reference was made to the 'laws of humanity'.

[15] See E. Decaux, 'Le statut du Chef d'État déchu', XXVI *AFDI* (1980), 109.

[16] Germany refused to surrender the 896 persons requested by the Allies (among those persons there were many senior military and naval officers). As a compromise, it was decided that instead of handing the accused persons over to the Allies, the German Government would have to bring to trial those persons before the Supreme Court of Leipzig. Only 12 out of the 45 persons, against whom the most serious charges had been brought, were tried by the Leipzig Court (see UN War Crimes Commission (n 13), 46–52).

[17] See Art 6(b) of the Charter of the Nuremberg Tribunal and Art 5 (b) of the Charter of the Tokyo Tribunal, conferring on both Tribunals jurisdiction over war crimes.

[18] See Art 50/51/130/147 of GCs.   [19] See Art 11 and Art 85 of AP I.

[20] Both Tribunals have jurisdiction over war crimes: see Arts 2 and 3 of the ICTY Statute and Art 4 of the ICTR Statute.

[21] The ICC was established by virtue of the Rome Statute, adopted in Rome on 17 July 1998. Its jurisdiction includes war crimes, as defined in Art 8 of the Statute.

[22] For instance, the Special Court for Sierra Leone, whose Statute was drafted by the UN Secretary-General at the request of Sierra Leone and became part of the Agreement of 16 January 2002 between the UN and Sierra Leone (UN Doc S/2000/915). The jurisdiction of the Court comprises serious violations of Common Art 3 and of AP II, as well as other serious violations of IHL.

the case with war crimes. It started at the international level with the adoption of the Statute of the Nuremberg Tribunal and the ensuing criminal trials. The story is well known: the Allies had to find a way to come to grips with odious crimes committed by the Nazis against Germans, or against the civilian population of the Allies of the Third Reich. These crimes did not fall under the notion of war crimes as understood at that time (war crimes could only be committed against an enemy population, or enemy combatants). Moreover, under traditional international law the treatment by a state of its own citizens or those of Allied countries was a matter pertaining to the 'internal and external affairs' of states, and no interference from other states was envisaged or allowed. Crimes against humanity were therefore conceived of as a sort of 'umbrella' notion, to be applied if necessary to fill the lacunae left by the notion of war crimes, subject however to an important limitation: these crimes had to be linked to the perpetration of war crimes or crimes against peace, ie they had to be connected with war.[23] However, after these truly international first steps, the notion of crimes against humanity remained 'dormant' for a long time, and the process of its international criminalization was never subject to the establishment of traditional mechanisms for criminal repression, as was the case for war crimes through the institution of the notion of grave breaches of the Geneva Conventions. In other words, states never felt it necessary to conclude an international treaty by which they obliged themselves, both to criminalize within their legal systems these crimes, and to coordinate their efforts in the field of criminal repression. On the contrary: some national courts conceived the notion of crimes against humanity as strictly connected to World War II and the punishment of German and Japanese criminals, as if there were no international rule prohibiting crimes against humanity except for the one that had evolved from the Nuremberg Charter.[24]

Unlike crimes against humanity, genocide was not included in the list of crimes falling within the jurisdiction of the Nuremberg Tribunal (the Holocaust was punished at Nuremberg as part of the wider notion of crimes against humanity in the form of persecution or 'extermination'). However, the process towards its international criminalization was faster than the process accompanying crimes against humanity, and the adoption in 1948 of the Genocide Convention accelerated this trajectory. True, this Convention, while solemnly proclaiming the international prohibition of genocide, did not directly criminalize genocide. It applied the traditional scheme of repression, by requesting contracting states to criminalize genocide and obliging the territorial state to punish genocide within its legal order. However, Article VI of the Convention went so far as to envisage the future establishment of an international criminal court endowed with jurisdiction over acts of genocide. In addition, the Genocide Convention was rapidly ratified by a large number of states,

---

[23] See Section 4.B.

[24] See the *Boudarel* case (*Sobanski Wladyslav*), decided on 1 April 1993 by the French Court of Cassation, in *RGDIP* (1994) 471.

and the general revulsion against this crime quickly gave rise to a customary rule contemplating genocide, not only as a crime committed by individuals, but also as a very serious international wrongful act of state. This explains why, when the Security Council established the ICTY and ICTR, the definition of genocide was taken verbatim from the Genocide Convention without much discussion, and again inserted in all subsequent instruments instituting international or mixed tribunals for the repression of international crimes. By contrast, at the time of the adoption of the ICTY and ICTR Statutes the notion of crimes against humanity was still highly controversial, as the subsequent Rome negotiations for the ICC made abundantly clear.[25]

B. The reasons for the different paths to international criminalization

One can speculate on the reasons why the process of international criminalization of crimes against humanity and genocide was different from that relating to war crimes.

Arguably, for war crimes the 'national' origin of their international criminalization can be explained by taking into account that states had a sort of 'selfish' interest in their criminal repression within their national legal systems. Whatever the humanitarian reasons behind the birth and development of the laws of war, it is a fact that these laws for a long time applied solely within the context of an interstate relationship (ie they were conceived to regulate international armed conflicts between states). For a long time, no humanitarian reason appeared strong enough to force or convince states to regulate civil strife as well. The notion of war crimes served various purposes: when it applied to national military servicemen, repression of violations of the laws of war served to impose military discipline and to protect the honour of armed forces; with regard to enemy combatants, such repression constituted an effective tool to discourage breaches of the rules of warfare by the enemy belligerent.

The notions of crimes against humanity and genocide emerged from a totally different seed: the concept that states are not the absolute owners of the life, limbs and dignity of their citizens, rather individuals and groups *as such* must be respected in their fundamental rights. At Nuremberg, for the first time in history, they proclaimed the right of the international community to lift the veil of state sovereignty when a state systematically tramples on basic human rights. This was an unexpected revolution. True, the drafters of the Nuremberg Charter carefully tried to confine the

---

[25] See, in this regard, D. Robinson, 'Defining "*Crimes against Humanity*" at the Rome Conference', 93 *AJIL* (1999) 43. See also Section 4.B.

notion of crimes against humanity to the historical events of World War II, in order to avoid future interference in their internal affairs by the international community with regard to the treatment of their citizens.[26] Two US Military Tribunals sitting at Nuremberg even asserted that the notion of crimes against humanity could apply to extermination through euthanasia only if the victims were *foreigners*![27] A similar cautious development can be seen in the UN Charter. For example, the powers of the new United Nations Organization in matters of human rights were originally limited to the adoption of resolutions of a general nature, while the passing of resolutions condemning a given state for violating human rights was argued to fall within the remit of domestic jurisdiction under Article 2(7) of the UN Charter. Notwithstanding these and other sophisticated attempts to avoid perceived undesirable developments, the seeds of the human rights doctrine had been sown. In the 1990s, this doctrine was embedded enough in the 'conscience' of the international community to allow the notion of individual criminal responsibility for large-scale violations of human rights to flourish. The Rome negotiations on the ICC Statute and the adoption of Articles 6 and 7 of this Statute (on genocide and crimes against humanity) are the latest stage of a process that originated and developed almost entirely at the international level.

3 War Crimes and the Rules of IHL

War crimes are traditionally defined as *serious violations* of rules of international humanitarian law (IHL), involving the individual criminal responsibility of the perpetrator under international law. This definition might appear tautological, since it explains what a crime is by referring to its consequence for the perpetrator, ie the fact that he or she may be criminally accountable. However, the key element in the definition is the reference to the criminal responsibility of *an individual under international law*. This is to underline the 'revolutionary' element of war crimes as violations of IHL as a body of rules belonging to international law. Rules of international law traditionally only address states, and their violations traditionally involve only the international responsibility of the state on behalf of which an individual has acted, and not the responsibility of the individual himself or herself. In the case of

---

[26] See Section 4.

[27] See, in this regard, the cases reported in A. Cassese and P. Gaeta, *Cassese's International Criminal Law* (3rd edn, Oxford: Oxford University Press, 2013), 105.

war crimes, the illegal conduct will instead also make the individual who carried it out accountable at the international level.

There is no authoritative list of what violations of IHL constitute war crimes. Rules of IHL usually fail to provide whether their violation is or must be criminalized. Exceptions are the relevant provisions enshrined in the four 1949 Geneva Conventions (GCs) and Additional Protocol (AP) I concerning so-called 'grave breaches'. These provisions expressly indicate the violations of the rules that, in addition to the international responsibility of the party to the conflict, shall entail the criminal responsibility of the individual. In addition, Article 85(5) of AP I expressly clarifies that graves breaches of the GCs and of AP I 'shall be regarded as war crimes'.

Setting aside grave breaches, in order to identify which conduct amounts to a war crime one has therefore to peruse international practice and *opinio juris* to determine whether a customary international law rule provides for the criminalization of a given violation of IHL. The point of departure is whether a violation has been consistently considered a war crime in national legislation and by national courts. There needs to be widespread evidence that states customarily prosecute the violation as a war crime and that they do so because they believe themselves to be acting under a rule of international law. The violation can also be termed a war crime by the Statute of an international criminal court or tribunal. In this case, there exists a strong presumption that the violation of IHL is a war crime under customary international law (in any case, such violation will fall under the jurisdiction of that international criminal court or tribunal). Article 8 of the Rome Statute of the ICC contains a fairly long list of the war crimes which fall within the jurisdiction of the Court. This provision, however, does not codify or crystallize customary international law.[28]

It is undisputed that not every violation of a rule of IHL constitutes a war crime, but only those that are 'serious'. Violations that do not reach the threshold of seriousness may give rise to international responsibility of the party to the conflict to which the violation can be attributed, but do not constitute war crimes under international law.

A. Classes of war crimes

Since a war crime is a serious violation of a rule of IHL, there cannot be a war crime if there is no armed conflict, since IHL rules applies only in this context.

---

[28] See Art 10 of the Rome Statute, expressly declaring that the provisions contained in Part 2 (including the one on war crimes) do not purport to limit or prejudice 'in any way existing or developing rules of international law'.

Traditionally, war crimes proper were held to embrace only violations of international rules regulating international armed conflicts (IACs), ie between states, and not civil wars. After the landmark ICTY Appeals Chamber decision in *Tadić* (*Interlocutory Appeal*), it is now widely accepted that serious infringements of the international humanitarian law of non-international armed conflicts (NIACs) may also be regarded as amounting to war crimes proper, if the relevant conduct is criminalized by international law.[29]

Given the continuing discrepancy between the rules of IHL applicable in IAC and those applicable in NIAC, a particular conduct may be a war crime if committed during an IAC but not if it takes place in the context of a NIAC. For instance, conduct contrary to the IHL rules applicable in occupied territories, or the rules protecting prisoners of war and other 'protected persons' as expressly defined by the GCs, can constitute war crimes only in an IAC (since the relevant rules are not applicable in NIAC). Setting aside these clear-cut examples, however, one can safely assume that in the matter of war crimes the traditional distinction between IAC and NIAC has become obsolete, since illegal conduct that can amount to war crimes is almost the same in both kind of armed conflict.[30]

In this respect, therefore, Article 8 of the Rome Statute of the International Criminal Court (ICC) must be considered as more restrictive than the applicable rules of customary international law. In listing war crimes submitted to the jurisdiction of the ICC, it maintains the distinction between IAC and NIAC and, within it, it further distinguishes between conduct contrary to the Geneva Conventions and 'other serious violations of the laws and customs' applicable either in IAC or in NIAC. In other words, Article 8 refers to four classes of war crimes, on the basis the character of the armed conflict, and the origin of the norm of IHL which was violated. The list of war crimes in IAC comprises: (i) grave breaches of the GCs; and (ii) 'other serious violations of the laws and customs applicable in international armed conflict' (mainly the rules on the means and methods of warfare, principally codified in the Hague Conventions and AP I). The list of war crimes in NIACs consists of: (i) serious violations of Common Article 3 of the Geneva Conventions; (ii) 'other serious violations of the laws and customs applicable in armed conflicts not of an international character'.

The Rome Statute's list of war crimes in IAC is considerably longer than the one applicable to NIAC. For instance, with regard to the IHL rules on prohibited methods of warfare, Article 8 fails to include in the list of war crimes committed in NIAC

---

[29] ICTY, Appeals Chamber, *Tadić*, Decision on the Defence Motion for Interlocutory Appeal on Jurisdiction, 2 October 1995, §§ 94–137.

[30] See the Chapter by E. David in this volume. See also V. Nerlich, 'War Crimes (Non-International Armed Conflict)', in A. Cassese (ed), *The Oxford Companion to International Criminal Justice* (Oxford: Oxford University Press, 2009), 568.

illegal practices such as attacks directed against illegal objects, attacks causing excessive incidental death or injury of civilians, attacks against undefended localities, and so on, that are practices commonly considered as war crimes under customary international law in a NIAC. In addition, since the wording used to describe the illegal acts constituting certain war crimes is taken verbatim from the relevant provisions of the Geneva Conventions, there is a clear discrepancy between the crimes committed as grave breaches in an IAC against protected persons and the crimes committed as serious violations of Common Article 3 in a NIAC against persons not taking part in the hostilities. For instance, while Article 8(2)(a)(iii) refers to the war crime of '[w]ilfully causing great suffering, or serious injury to body or health' to a protected person in IAC, the corresponding war crime in NIAC is that of '[v]iolence to life and person, in particular [...] cruel treatment'. These discrepancies therefore oblige the ICC to classify the nature of the armed conflict, before formulating a specific charge against a suspect. This task can prove extremely difficult in some circumstances, as evidenced by the debate on the classification of armed conflicts involving a non-state armed group operating autonomously from both within a state and a third state.

B. The seriousness of the violation and the distinction between war crimes of conduct and war crimes of result

As noticed above, not every violation of a rule of IHL necessarily constitutes a war crime, but only those involving a degree of 'seriousness'. In the words of the ICTY Appeals Chamber in *Tadić*, a war crime 'must constitute a breach of a rule protecting important values, and *the breach must involve grave consequences for the victim*'.[31] Under this definition, war crimes are therefore *crimes of result*. War crimes consisting in *crimes of conduct*, ie those punishable simply on account of the illegality of the behaviour, irrespective of any prejudicial consequence, seem therefore to be excluded from the notion of war crimes propounded by the ICTY.

In modern criminal law, a crime does not consist only of an illegal act (*actus reus*). The law also requires that the individual carries out the illegal conduct with a 'criminal mind', which constitutes the so-called mental element or *mens rea* of a crime. The ICTY Appeals Chamber decision mentioned above does not clarify the

---

[31] ICTY, Appeals Chamber, *Tadić* (n 29), § 94 (emphasis added). See, however, the notion of seriousness propounded by the ICRC in *Explanatory Note*, 'What Are "Serious Violations of International Humanitarian Law"', available on the ICRC website. For the ICRC, 'violations are serious, and are war crimes, if they endanger protected persons[...] or objects [...] or if they breach important values'.

mental element necessary for a serious violation of a rule of IHL to be a war crime. The mental element, however, is sometimes specified by the international rule prohibiting a certain conduct: for instance, Article 130 of GC III on prisoners of war enumerates, among the 'grave breaches' of the Convention, the 'wilful' killing of prisoners of war. When this is not the case, ie when the relevant international rules of IHL do not provide, not even implicitly, for a subjective element, it would seem appropriate to hold that what is required is intent or, depending upon the circumstances, recklessness, as prescribed in most legal systems of the world, for the illegal conduct to be a crime under municipal law (murder, rape, torture, destruction of private property, pillage, etc).

It would therefore be incorrect to believe that the individual who breaches a rule of IHL commits *ipso facto* a war crime. Further elements must be added, namely: (i) the conduct must be contrary to a rule protecting fundamental values; (ii) the breach must have caused grave consequences to the victims; (iii) the illegal conduct must have been carried out with the requisite criminal mind, that can be expressly or implicitly provided by the rule of IHL that was breached, or be identified through other means.

In the light of the above, it is worth emphasizing, contrary to what may appear at first sight, that some of the war crimes listed in the Rome Statute are not mere reformulations of 'grave breaches' as included in AP I. An obvious example is the war crime of attacking civilians in IACs. Under Article 85(3) of AP I this crime must be committed 'wilfully' and must cause 'death or serious injury to body or health'.[32] In other words under AP I the war crime of attacking civilians is a crime of result (because it requires that a harmful event is caused by the illegal conduct), that must be committed with a given degree of intent (wilfulness). According to the ICTY case law, that adheres to the relevant ICRC Commentary on Article 85(3) of AP I,[33] wilfulness describes a mental element that comprises not only of knowledge and intention (the so called *dolus directus*), but also recklessness or the conscious awareness that one's behaviour will probably result in a violation of a criminal rule.[34] However, this

[32] The *chapeau* of Art 85(3) of Additional Protocol I, preceding the list of grave breaches which includes 'making the civilian population or individual civilians the object of attack', provides as follows: '[...] the following acts shall be regarded as grave breaches of this Protocol, *when committed willfully*, in violation of the relevant provisions of this Protocol, and *causing death or serious injury to body or health*' (emphasis added).

[33] The ICRC Commentary explains the term 'wilfully' used in Art 85(3) of AP I as follows: 'the accused must have acted consciously and with intent, i.e., with his mind on the act and its consequences, and willing them ("criminal intent" or "malice aforethought"); this encompasses the concept of "wrongful intent" or "recklessness", viz., the attitude of an agent who, without being certain of a particular result, accepts the possibility of it happening; on the other hand, ordinary negligence or lack of foresight is not covered, i.e., when a man acts without having his mind on the act or its consequences': see Commentary AP I and II, 994, § 3473.

[34] See ICTY, Trial Chamber, *Galić*, Judgment 5 December 2003, § 54, where the Chamber agreed with the explanation of the term 'willfully' provided by the ICRC Commentary (n 33) and stated as follows: 'The

relatively low *mens rea* required by Article 85(3) of API is counter-balanced by a more stringent *actus reus*, in that an attack against civilians amounts to a war crime only if it causes death or serious injury to body and health.

Article 8(2)(b)(i) (relating to IAC) of the Rome Statute takes a different approach. It provides that there is a war crime under the jurisdiction of the ICC of 'intentionally launching attacks against civilians', without providing for the need of any harmful result.[35] Clearly, under the Rome Statute, the crime of attacking civilians is a crime of conduct (ie a crime that is completed by the mere launching of an attack against a civilian population or individual civilians): no resulting death, injury, or damage is required. Additionally, this differing objective element is accompanied by the adoption of a required *mens rea*, namely 'intentionality', which excludes recklessness.[36] Indeed, whether or not the *mens rea* required for the war crime of attacking civilians under the Rome Statute corresponds to the general subjective element set out by Article 30 of the Rome Statute,[37] it could certainly not be maintained that attacks directed at specific military targets that nonetheless hit civilians due to a conscious disregard of the necessary measures of precaution can be considered an attack intentionally directed against civilians. Once a military attack is directed against military objectives, any subsequent casualty caused to civilians must be assessed according to the proportionality rule,[38] and the separate crime of attacking civilians is no longer at issue.[39]

The differing *actus reus* and *mens rea* elements within the Rome Statute that correspond to grave breaches in AP I (at least as interpreted by the ICTY for the

Trial Chamber accepts this explanation [ie the one provided by the ICRC Commentary], according to which the notion of "wilfully" incorporates the concept of recklessness, whilst excluding mere negligence. The perpetrator who recklessly attacks civilians acts "wilfully". The Appeals Chamber in the same case confirmed this stand' (see ICTY, Appeals Chamber, *Galić*, 30 November 2006, § 140).

[35] See Art 8 (2)(b)(i), providing that for the purpose of the Rome Statute, war crimes means: 'Other serious violations of the laws and customs applicable in international armed conflict, within the established framework of international law, namely any of the following acts: (i) Intentionally directing attacks against the civilian population as such or against individuals not taking part in the hostilities; [...]'. See also, in the context of non-international armed conflicts, Art 8 (2)(e)(i) of the Rome Statute.

[36] See in this regard H. Olásolo, *Unlawful Attacks in Combat Situations. From the ICTY's Case Law to the Rome Statute* (Leiden/Boston: Matinus Nijhoff, 2008), 220.

[37] According to the ICTY Trial Chamber in *Lubanga*, Art 30 of the Rome Statute excludes both *dolus eventualis* and recklessness (where the difference between the two forms of *mens rea* can be identified in the fact that the perpetrator in the former case acts with a degree of intent, ie awareness that the forbidden results will likely occur in the ordinary course of events): see ICC, Trial Chamber I, *Lubanga*, Judgment, 14 March 2012, §§ 1011–12. Recklessness would still not be sufficient even if one accepts the view that in the Rome Statute the *mens rea* of the crime of attacking civilians is set forth by the pertinent provisions of Art 8 and does not correspond to the mental element generally set forth in Art 30. See in this respect Olásolo (n 36), 219–23.

[38] The principle is codified in Art 51(5)(b) of Additional Protocol I, providing that it is considered as indiscriminate, hence prohibited: 'an attack which may be expected to cause incidental loss of civilian life, injury to civilians, damage to civilian objects, or a combination thereof, which would be excessive in relation to the concrete and direct military advantage anticipated'. Compare Art 8(2)(b)(iv).

[39] See Olásolo (n 36), 218.

requisite *mens rea*) are therefore not without consequences. In practice they might allow for a greater application of the potential defence of mistake of fact.[40] Attacks carried out against military targets that instead, due to a reasonable error, hit civilians will not be considered criminal. Similarly, attacks where the mistake concerns whether or not the target is a military objective will not be punishable under the Rome Statute.[41] Considering that many instances of attacks against civilians are justified by the responsible party invoking a fatal error on the facts, one cannot fail to observe that the relevant provisions of the Rome Statute appear to be too restrictive from the point of view of the enhanced protection of victims of armed conflict.

C. The nexus with the armed conflict

Not all crimes committed during an armed conflict constitute war crimes. It is widely held in the case law and legal literature,[42] that in order to qualify as a war crime, the criminal conduct must be closely related to the hostilities, ie it must have a 'nexus' with the armed conflict. The nexus between the criminal conduct and the armed conflict is also demanded by the Elements of Crimes of the ICC, for each war crime listed in Article 8 of the Rome Statute.

The requirement of such a nexus clearly serves to distinguish between war crimes and 'ordinary' criminal conduct that falls under the law applicable in the relevant territory. It applies in particular to offences committed by civilians against other civilians or against combatants, although courts have also required the link, or nexus, with an armed conflict in the case of crimes perpetrated by members of the armed forces. In addition, it should be noted that identifying a nexus between a criminal offence and an armed conflict is relatively easy in the case of an *international* armed conflict: there, normally two or more states face each other, and offences committed by combatants or civilians from one party to the conflict against combatants and civilians from the opposing party will usually be considered as 'linked' to the armed conflict. In contrast, things are less clear in a *non-international* armed conflict, in particular with respect to crimes committed by civilians not taking part in hostilities against other civilians not taking part in hostilities. Here the question of identifying whether the criminal conduct was related to the armed conflict might prove to be particularly challenging, as the case law of the ICTR evinced in a string of cases.[43]

---

[40] See Art 32(1) of the Rome Statute.

[41] See for instance W. Fenrick, 'War Crimes', in O. Triffterer (ed), *Commentary on the Rome Statute of the International Criminal Court* (1st edn, Baden-Baden: Nomos Verlagsgesellschaft, 1999), 187. See also Olásolo (n 36), 223.

[42] For example, G. Mettraux, 'Nexus with Armed Conflict', in Cassese (n 30), 435.

[43] See for instance ICTR, Appeals Chamber, *Akayesu*, Judgment, 1 June 2001, § 444; ICTR, Appeals Chamber, *Rutaganda*, Judgment, 26 May 2003, § 570; ICTR, Trial Chamber, *Semanza*, Judgment and Sentence, 15 May 2003, §§ 518–21. On the nexus requirement, see *amplius* H. van der Wilt, 'War Crimes and the Requirement of a Nexus with an Armed Conflict', 10 *JICJ* (2012) 1113.

The ICTY and ICTR considered the following criteria to be of assistance when assessing whether an offence qualifies as a war crime: the fact that the perpetrator is a combatant; the fact that the victim is a non-combatant; the fact that the victim is a member of the opposing party; the fact that the act may be said to serve the ultimate goal of a military campaign; and the fact that the crime is committed as part of, or in the context of, the perpetrator's 'official duties'.[44]

The 'nexus' standard is objective in linking the armed conflict *with the crime*, not the criminal. The fact that the offender is a soldier and the victim a civilian not taking part in the hostilities does not, in and of itself, provide the necessary link. Rather, it is the inference regarding the conduct of the soldier that might assist in establishing the link. In other words, the conduct is objectively a war crime—even if in the nexus can only be inferred by looking at the personal (subjective) qualification of the perpetrator and the victim. The application of this standard avoids two unwanted outcomes. First, opportunistic crimes that are unrelated to the conflict will not be characterized as war crimes merely because of the existence of an armed conflict (eg where a civilian who holds a personal vendetta against his neighbour takes advantage of lawlessness created by the conflict to murder his neighbour). Secondly, it is not necessary to inquire into the state of mind of the offender in order to establish a nexus.

4 Crimes Against Humanity

Crimes against humanity were defined for the first time by the Charter of the Nuremberg Tribunal as follows:

murder, extermination, enslavement, deportation, and other inhuman acts committed against any civilian population, before or during the war, or persecution on political, racial or religious grounds in execution of or in connection with any crime within the jurisdiction of the [Tribunal], whether or not in violation of the domestic law of the country where perpetrated.[45]

---

[44] In the wording of the ICTY Appeals Chamber in *Kunarac*, Judgment, 12 June 2002, § 58: 'What ultimately distinguishes a war crime from a purely domestic offence is that a war crime is shaped by or dependent upon the environment—the armed conflict—in which it is committed. It need not have been planned or supported by some form of policy. The armed conflict need not have been causal to the commission of the crime, but the existence of an armed conflict must, at a minimum, have played a substantial part in the perpetrator's ability to commit it, his decision to commit it, the manner in which it was committed or the purpose for which it was committed. Hence, if it can be established, as in the present case, that the perpetrator acted in furtherance of or under the guise of the armed conflict, it would be sufficient that his acts were closely related to the armed conflict.'

[45] Article 6(c) of the Charter of the Nuremberg Tribunal.

The inclusion of this category of crimes within the jurisdiction of the Tribunal had the main purpose of allowing prosecution of acts of barbarity committed by the Nazis against their own population (Jews, trade union members, social democrats, communists, members of the church) or those of their allies or of the annexed countries. As such, those crimes could not come under the notion of war crimes, for the latter, in the context of a war such as World War II, only embraced crimes committed against the enemy civilian population or enemy combatants. In addition, some of those acts of barbarity had been committed even before the war started, under the dictatorship established by Hitler since he came to power.

The inclusion of crimes against humanity in the Charter of the Nuremberg Tribunal marked a great advance. After the failed attempt in the first decades of the nineteenth century to assert the international criminal nature of mass crimes committed by governments against their own population,[46] the international community widened the category of acts considered of 'meta-national' concern. This category came to include all action running contrary to the inherent dignity and value that ought to attach to any human being. The Nuremberg Charter showed that in some special circumstances there were limits to the omnipotence of the state in the way it treated its own citizens. The seeds of the international protection of human rights were thus planted.

The definition of crimes against humanity provided in the Charter of the Nuremberg Tribunal was repeated almost verbatim in the Charter of the Tokyo Tribunal[47] and, with some important modifications, in the law passed by the four Occupying Powers in Germany for the prosecution of German war criminals in the respective occupying zones (ie Control Council Law No 10).[48] In addition, on 11 December 1946 the UN General Assembly unanimously adopted a Resolution 'affirming' the principles of the Charter of the Nuremberg International Tribunal and its judgment. On 13 February 1946 it further passed Resolution 3(1) recommending the extradition and punishment of persons accused of the crimes provided for in the Nuremberg Charter. These Resolutions illustrate that the category of crimes against humanity was in the process of becoming part of customary international law.

Despite this momentum, no international treaty was adopted to provide for the express criminalization under international law of this class of crimes. Arguably, this was because the international community preferred to focus on what was perceived at that time as the paradigmatic example of crimes of against humanity, ie genocide. As aptly noted, the 'early international focus on genocide' through the

---

[46] See Cassese and Gaeta (n 27), 84–5.   [47] Article 5(c) of the Charter of the Tokyo Tribunal.

[48] Article II(1)(c) defined crimes against humanity as: 'Atrocities and offences, including but not limited to murder, extermination, enslavement, deportation, imprisonment, torture, rape, or other inhumane acts committed against any civilian population, or persecutions on political, racial or religious grounds whether or not in violation of the domestic laws of the country where perpetrated.'

adoption of the 1948 Genocide Convention, 'resulted in the fragmentation of the law of atrocity crimes and delayed the process of shaping the norm of crimes against humanity'.[49]

As a result of the absence of a convention that could have crystallized the definition of crimes against humanity under customary international law, or at least influenced its development, the clarification of the legal ingredients of this class of crimes was achieved through the establishment of the ICTY, the ICTR, and especially the ICC. The definition now enshrined in Article 7 of the Rome Statute was the object of intense negotiations, in particular as regards the so-called *chapeau* of the provision setting forth the contextual element of the crime. Being included in a treaty to which a large number of states are now parties, it constitutes an indispensable point of reference for any discussion on crimes against humanity.

A. The prohibited conduct and the mental element

Crimes against humanity consist of two distinct categories of conduct, also described as 'underlying offences', that are usually referred to as 'murder-type' offences and 'persecution-type' offences. This distinction serves to underline the fact that the acts that can amount to crimes against humanity are either criminal offences in national legal systems, such as murder; or they can be acts that may not be criminal or may not even be prohibited in national legal systems, but are committed on discriminatory grounds to persecute a specific group of people.

The list of the 'murder-type' offences that can amount to a crime against humanity contained in the Rome Statute is longer than the ones contained in the Statutes of other international criminal courts and tribunals. In the Charter of the Nuremberg and Tokyo Tribunals the list comprised murder, extermination, enslavement, deportation, and other inhumane acts committed against any civilian population. Control Council Law No 10 added imprisonment, torture, and rape, while the ICTY and ICTR Statutes simply cumulatively list all the preceding acts. The Rome Statute, by contrast, adds crimes such as 'forcible transfer of population', 'forced pregnancy', 'severe deprivation of physical liberty in violation of fundamental rules of international law', 'sexual slavery, enforced prostitution, forced pregnancy, enforced sterilization, or any other form of sexual violence of comparable gravity'; 'enforced disappearance of persons'; and 'the crime of apartheid'. In addition, the notion of 'any other inhumane act', which harks back to Article 6(c) of the Statute of the Nuremberg Tribunal, is given looser contours in the Rome Statute. By following the interpretation already given by the ICTY,[50] Article 7(1)(k) provides that

---

[49] M.M. DeGuzman, '*Crimes Against Humanity*', in W. Schabas and N. Bernaz (eds), *Routledge Handbook of International Criminal Law* (London/New York: Routledge, 2011), 121, 123.

[50] ICTY, Trial Chamber, *Kupreškic and others*, Judgment, 14 January 2000, §§ 563–6.

crimes against humanity include 'other inhumane acts [of a character similar to the offences mentioned in Article 7] and causing great suffering or serious injury to body or to mental or physical health'. In spite of its relatively loose character, the offence is important for it may function as a 'residual clause' covering and criminalizing instances of inhuman behaviour that do not neatly fall under any of the other existing categories of crimes against humanity.

There is no comprehensive enumeration of the persecution-type offences constituting a crime against humanity. The ICTY Appeals Chamber clarified that persecution consists of 'an act or omission which discriminates in fact and which denies or infringes upon a fundamental right laid down in international customary or treaty law'.[51] A similar definition is contained in Article 7(2)(g) the Rome Statute, according to which persecution means 'the deprivation of fundamental rights contrary to international law'. The persecutory conduct must be carried out on discriminatory grounds. Here again the Rome Statute is more expansive compared to the constitutive instruments of preceding international courts and tribunals: to the political, racial, and religious grounds already mentioned in the latter, it adds national, ethnic, cultural, and gender grounds, or 'other grounds that are universally recognized as impermissible under international law'.[52] The Rome Statute, however, requires that persecutory conduct is committed in connection with a murder-type offence of crimes against humanity listed in Article 7 or any crime within the jurisdiction of the Court (ie war crimes, genocide, and aggression). It thus narrows considerably the reach of the ICC jurisdiction over discriminatory conduct with respect to the ICTY and ICTR. The two ad hoc Tribunals did not consider the connection with murder-type offences or with other international crimes to be a legal ingredient of the crime of persecution under customary international law.

The conduct constituting crimes against humanity must be carried out with the awareness by the perpetrator of the broader context into which his or her crime fits.[53] In addition, the perpetrator shall possess the criminal mental element appropriate for the underlying offence under domestic or international law (usually intent, but sometimes recklessness). When crimes against humanity take the form of persecution, another mental element is also required: a persecutory or discriminatory animus, ie the intent to subject a person to discrimination, so as to bring about great suffering or injury to that person.

---

[51] ICTY, Appeals Chamber, *Kronjelac*, Judgment, 17 September 2003, § 185. For the contribution of the ICTY to the clarification of the crime of persecution, see J. Nilsson, 'The Crime of Persecution in the ICTY Case-Law', in B. Swart, A. Zahar, and G. Sluiter (eds), *The Legacy of the International Criminal Tribunal for the Former Yugoslavia* (Oxford: Oxford University Press, 2011), 219.

[52] Article 7(1)(h) of the Rome Statute.

[53] See Art 7(1) of the Rome Statute. On the contextual element of crimes against humanity, see below.

B. The severance of the link with armed conflict and the contextual element

Article 6(c) of the Charter of the Nuremberg Tribunal provided that the Tribunal had jurisdiction over crimes against humanity committed before or during the War, but at the same time it linked the definition of crimes against humanity to the other two categories of offences under the jurisdiction of the Tribunal. Article 6(c) actually required crimes against humanity to be perpetrated 'in execution of or in connection with' war crimes or crimes against peace. Since it was only within the context of a war, or of the unleashing of aggression, that these crimes could be prosecuted and punished, the Tribunal decided that such a link certainly existed after 1 September 1939, which was when the War had started. It therefore decided not to take into consideration crimes committed before that date.[54]

After 1945 the link between crimes against humanity and war was gradually dropped. For instance, the definition of crimes against humanity contained in Article II(1)(c) of Control Council Law no 10 did not require crimes against humanity to be committed in connection with war crimes or crimes against peace. Similarly, when passing criminal legislation on crimes against humanity, some countries did not link crimes against humanity to war.[55] By contrast, the definition of crimes against humanity contained in the Statute of the ICTY refers to crimes against humanity committed in armed conflict. This limitation prompted the ICTY Appeals Chamber to clarify in its early case law that this requirement was not needed under customary international law.[56] The question of whether crimes against humanity had to be connected to an armed conflict was discussed at the Rome Conference. Some delegations considered it necessary to include such a link in the definition of crimes against humanity in the Rome Statute, but the majority of the delegations were of a different opinion in light of the post-Nuremberg developments.[57] Article 7 of the Rome Statute therefore drops any reference to armed conflict in the definition of crimes against humanity, and codifies the customary international rule that these crimes against humanity can be committed in time of peace.

[54] The Tribunal stated that: 'To constitute crimes against humanity, the acts relied on before the outbreak of war must have been in execution of, or in connection with, any crime within the jurisdiction of the Tribunal. The Tribunal is of the opinion that revolting and horrible as many of these crimes were, it has not been satisfactorily proved that they were done in execution of, or in connection with, any such crime. The Tribunal therefore cannot make a general declaration that the acts before 1939 were crimes against humanity within the meaning of the Charter' (see Nuremberg Tribunal, Judgment and Sentence, 1 October 1946, in *Trial of the Major War Criminals before the International Military Tribunal*, Nuremberg, 14 November 1945 to 1 October 1946 (Nuremberg, IMT, 1947), vol I, 254).

[55] See § 7 (3.76) of the Canadian Criminal Code and Art 212-1, § 1 of the French Criminal Code (enacted by Law no 92-1336 of 16 December 1992, modified by Law no 93-913 of 19 July 1993).

[56] ICTY, Appeals Chamber, *Tadić* (n 29), § 141.

[57] See *amplius* Robinson (n 25), 43.

It is a fact, however, that the underlying offences comprising crimes against humanity are a frequent occurrence in war. Since they consist of offences that can also amount to war crimes, the need to distinguish crimes against humanity from war crimes and to clarify their mutual relationship therefore arises. To identify whether an offence perpetrated during an armed conflict is a crime against humanity, the key element is whether it belongs to a pattern of widespread or systematic violence against a civilian population. Crimes against humanity were included in the Charter of the Nuremberg Tribunal because the offences perpetrated during the Nazi era were not isolated or sporadic events, but they were part of a widespread or systematic practice carried out in furtherance of the Nazi policy. The offences punishable under the Charter as crimes against humanity were therefore clearly of a *large-scale* or *massive nature*. Subsequent case law, both at the national and international level, has consistently borne out that this is a major feature of the crimes.[58] Article 7(1) of the Rome Statute confirms this feature, and demands that for acts to amount to crimes against humanity they must be 'committed as part of a widespread or systematic attack directed against any civilian population, with knowledge of the attack'.[59]

The need for this contextual element clarifies when an offence committed in the course of an armed conflict that amounts to a war crime also constitutes a crime against humanity, and *vice versa*. Therefore, when a soldier kills a group of innocent civilians in the course of a NIAC, this crime can constitute a war crime if it is committed wilfully and is linked to the armed conflict. It can, however, also amount to a crime against humanity if the killing forms part of a widespread or systematic practice carried out against the civilian population in the course of the armed conflict, and the perpetrator acts in the knowledge of such practice. In such a case, he will be accountable for *both* the war crime of attacking civilians and the crime against humanity of murder. This on the basis of the doctrine of *concours ideal d'infractions* (cumulative convictions), according to which: should an act breach two different criminal rules protecting two different set of values and interests, the perpetrator is

---

[58]   See Cassese and Gaeta (n 27), 92–3, notes 26 and 27.

[59]   The provision must be read in conjunction with Art 7(2)(a), defining 'attack directed against any civilian population' as: 'a course of conduct involving the multiple commission of acts referred to in paragraph 1 against any civilian population, pursuant to or in furtherance of a State or organizational policy to commit such attack'. The ICC Elements of Crime further adds that 'the policy to commit such attack' 'requires that the state or organization *actively promote or encourage* such an attack against a civilian population' (emphasis added). It would thus seem that any practice involving the commission of crimes against the civilian population which is simply tolerated or condoned by a state or an organization would not constitute an attack under the Rome Statute. These crimes would therefore not qualify as crimes against humanity under the Statute. It is doubtful, however, whether the definition of customary international law on crimes against humanity requires the offences to be committed 'pursuant to or in furtherance of a State or organizational policy'. The ICTY and ICTR case law point to a different direction. Both ad hoc Tribunals held that crimes against humanity do not necessarily require a policy. See, however, the critical remarks in this respect by W. Schabas, 'State Policy as an Element of International Crimes', 98 *Journal of Criminal Law and Criminology* (2008) 953 at 959.

accountable for both breaches.[60] By contrast, the isolated and intentional killing of a civilian in an occupied territory by a soldier of the Occupying Power can amount to a war crime, but the same act will not amount to a crime against humanity absent the contextual element described above. Similarly, when a given offence cannot constitute a war crime as the conduct is not a breach of a rule of IHL, the commission of a crime against humanity cannot be excluded. What matters is that the act is an underlying offence within crimes against humanity, and that the act forms part of a widespread or systematic pattern of violence against a civilian population, with knowledge of such practice. One example could be that of the killings of civilians during an armed attack against a military objective that does not contravene the precautionary and proportionality rules under IHL. The killings cannot amount to war crimes, for they do not violate a rule of IHL, but they might still constitute a crime against humanity if they belong to a pattern or practice of violence against a civilian population. For instance, if the 'proportionate collateral damage' inflicted on the civilians are part of a pattern of violence against the civilian population living in a given geographical area.

Finally, in time of peace, the contextual element of crimes against humanity serves to establish whether an offence is a crime against humanity or eventually 'only' amounts to a municipal offence. This legal criterion is indeed crucial to confine the 'intrusion' of international law into criminal matters to serious situations of gross violations of human rights, so as 'to reserve' the criminalization of other violations to domestic criminal legislation.

5 GENOCIDE

The destruction of, or the attempt to destroy, entire groups, whether national, racial, religious, cultural, and so on, is by all evidence an ancient phenomenon in the history of mankind. The word 'genocide', which etymologically describes it, however, was only coined in 1944, by the Polish lawyer R. Lemkin.[61] In just a few short years the term 'genocide' has spread and asserted itself at the authoritative description of an age-old behaviour.[62] The relatively modern construct of the term explains

---

[60] The matter has been discussed intensively at the ICTY and the ICTR: see A. Bogdan, 'Cumulative Charges, Convictions and Sentencing at the Ad Hoc International Tribunals for the former Yugoslavia and Rwanda', 3 *Melbourne Journal of Int'l Law* (2002) 1.

[61] R. Lemkin, *Axis Rule in Occupied Europe: Laws of Occupation, Analysis of Governments, Proposals for Redress* (Washington DC: Carnegie Endowment for International Peace, 1944), 79.

[62] See in this regard, Y. Shany, 'The Road to the Genocide Convention and Beyond', in P. Gaeta (ed), *The UN Genocide Convention. A Commentary* (Oxford: Oxford University Press, 2009), 7.

why the word 'genocide' itself, which is now commonly used as well to describe the Holocaust of the Jews before and during World War II, cannot be located within the Statute of the International Military Tribunal in Nuremberg (IMT), nor in its final judgment.[63] As we have seen, in fact the Holocaust perpetrators were punished by the IMT using charges of extermination and persecution, which constituted two of the underlying offences of crimes against humanity.

On 9 December 1948, in the wake of the Nuremberg trial, the UN General Assembly adopted the Genocide Convention,[64] whose substantive rules may largely be considered as declaratory of customary international law.[65] Among these rules, one can certainly mention Article II, which provides the legal definition for what was until that time a crime without a name.[66] Nonetheless, the existence of a conventional definition of the crime of genocide has rendered the evolution of a parallel, and potentially wider, definition through customary international law more

[63] The word genocide was neither used in the Charter establishing the International Military Tribunal for the Far East (the so-called Tokyo Tribunal), nor in the final judgment issued by this Tribunal. It was, however, used in the indictment before the IMT, in some of the speeches of the Prosecutors before such a Tribunal, and in the *Justice* case before a US military court sitting at Nuremberg and operating under Control Council Law no 10. See also for the necessary reference, Shany (n 62).

[64] The process which led to the adoption of the Convention is concisely described by N. Robinson, *The Genocide Convention. A Commentary* (New York: Institute of Jewish Affairs–World Jewish Congress, 1960), 17–28. See also W.A. Schabas, *Genocide in International Law* (2nd edn, Cambridge: Cambridge University Press), 59–90.

[65] See ICJ, *Reservation to the Convention on Genocide*, 1951 ICJ Report, 23, where the Court stated: 'the principles underlying the Convention are principles that are recognized by civilized nations as binding on states, even without any conventional obligation'.

[66] 'In the present Convention, genocide means any of the following acts committed with intent to destroy, in whole or in part, a national, ethnical, racial or religious group as such:

(a) killing members of the group;
(b) causing serious bodily or mental harm to members of the group;
(c) deliberately inflicting on the group conditions of life calculated to bring about its physical destruction, in whole or in part;
(d) imposing measures intended to prevent births within the group;
(e) forcibly transferring children of the group to another group.

This definition has been reproduced verbatim in the Statutes of the International Criminal Tribunal for the former Yugoslavia (ICTY) (Art 4), the International Criminal Tribunal for Rwanda (ICTR) (Art 2), and the International Criminal Court (ICC) (Art 6). In addition, it has been adopted, usually unchanged, in most national criminal legislation. See, in the last respect, B. Saul, 'The Implementation of the Genocide Convention at the National Level', in Gaeta (ed) (n 62), 62–6.

For the expression 'crime without a name', see 'Prime Minister Winston Churchill's Broadcast to the World About the Meeting with President Roosevelt', 24 August 1941, available at <http://www.ibiblio.org/pha/timeline/410824awp.html>, speaking of the mass killings committed by the Nazis in occupied Russia: 'The aggressor [...] retaliates by the most frightful cruelties. As his Armies advance, whole districts are being exterminated. Scores of thousands—literally scores of thousands—of executions in cold blood are being perpetrated by the German Police-troops upon the Russian patriots who defend their native soil. Since the Mongol invasions of Europe in the Sixteenth Century, there has never been methodical, merciless butchery on such a scale, or approaching such a scale. And this is but the beginning. Famine and pestilence have yet to follow in the bloody ruts of Hitler's tanks. We are in the presence of a crime without a name.'

difficult. The 'rigidity' of the definition of genocide, however, has been softened by way of judicial interpretation. In particular, the International Criminal Tribunal for Rwanda (ICTR) has adopted specific criteria to widen the categories of groups protected by the definition, and has considered that some acts, such as rape, can fall within the purview of the enumerated genocidal acts.

A. The genocidal acts

The conduct that may amount to genocide, as pointed out above, is contained in Article II of the Convention which exhaustively lists the following acts: (a) killing members of the group; (b) causing seriously bodily or mental harm to members of the group; (c) deliberately inflicting on the group conditions of life calculated to bring about its physical destruction in whole or in part; (d) imposing measures intended to prevent births within the group; (e) forcibly transferring children of the group to another group.

The ICTR and the ICTY have both contributed to clarifying the scope of each of these notions. The case law of the two Ad Hoc Tribunals clarifies that the killing under paragraph (a) is equivalent to 'murder', which requires *intentional* killing.[67] Various arguments have been put forward to ground this interpretation, including the fact that the French text refers to *meurtre* and therefore clearly excludes unintentional homicide.

As for the act of causing harm under (b), it does not require that the harm caused be permanent and irremediable,[68] but '[i]t must be harm that results in a grave and long-term disadvantage to a person's ability to lead a normal and constructive life'.[69] The harm caused can be bodily *or* mental, and must be 'serious'. The seriousness of the harm 'must be assessed on a case-by-case basis and with due regard for the particular circumstances'.[70] In the ICTR case law, serious bodily harm has been interpreted as 'harm that seriously injures the health, causes disfigurement or causes any serious injury to the external, internal organs or senses'.[71] With respect to serious mental harm, it has considered that 'minor or temporary impairment of mental faculties' would not meet the seriousness threshold.[72] Serious bodily or mental harm can also be caused by rape and other acts of sexual violence.[73]

---

[67] See, in particular, ICTR, Trial Chamber, *Akayesu*, Judgment, 2 September 1998, §§ 500–1; ICTR, Appeals Chamber, *Kayishema and Ruzindana*, Judgment, 1 June 2001, § 151; ICTR, Trial Chamber, *Semanza* (n 44), § 319.

[68] *Akayesu* (n 67), § 502.   [69] ICTY, Trial Chamber, *Krstić*, Judgment, 2 August 2001, § 513.

[70] *Krstić* (n 69).   [71] *Kayishema and Ruzindana* (n 67), § 109.

[72] *Semanza* (n 44), §§ 321–2; ICTR, Trial Chamber, *Ntagerura, Bagambiki and Imanishimwe*, Judgment, 25 February 2004, § 664.

[73] *Akayesu* (n 67), §§ 706 and 731.

'Deliberately inflicting on the group conditions of life calculated to bring about its physical destruction in whole or in part', provided under (c), includes 'slow death measures', such as 'lack of proper housing, clothing, hygiene and medical care or excessive work or physical exertion'.[74] It is not required that those conditions of life actually result in the physical destruction of the group, in whole or in part; it is only requested that they are 'calculated to bring about its physical destruction', namely that they intended to achieve this result.[75]

The fourth prohibited act that can amount to genocide, namely 'imposing measures intended to prevent births within the group', is intended to cover conduct whose aim is to prevent the biological reproduction of the group. This result can usually be achieved through the sterilization of women (when the transmission of the distinguishing features of the group is matriarchal, as it was in the case of the sterilization of Jewish women). It can also be accomplished through the rape of women of the group by members of another group, when rape aims at changing the ethnic composition of the group whose characteristics are transmitted following the patriarchal line. Other measures intended to achieve the same objective can include segregation of sexes, prohibition of marriage, or forced birth control.[76] As in the preceding hypothesis, it is not required that the measures achieve the desired goal, it is only necessary that they are carried out for that particular purpose.[77]

B. The mental element

As in the case of crimes against humanity, there is a need to distinguish between first, the mental element required for each of the acts that may amount to genocide, and then, secondly, the specific mental element which is necessary to consider that the conduct amounts to genocide.

---

[74] See the Draft of the Convention prepared by the Secretary-General of the UN: Secretariat Draft E/447, reproduced in H. Abtahi and P. Webb, *The Genocide Convention. The Travaux Préparatoires*, vol I (Leiden/Boston: Martinus Nijhoff, 2008), 233.

[75] The relevant comment in the Secretariat Draft explains that '[i]n such cases, the intention of the author of genocide may be less clear. Obviously, if members of a group of human beings are placed in concentration camps where the annual death rate is thirty per cent to forty per cent, the intention to commit genocide is unquestionable. There may be borderline cases where a relatively high death rate might be ascribed to lack of attention, negligence or inhumanity, which, though highly reprehensible, would not constitute evidence of intention to commit genocide. At all events, there are such borderline cases which have to be dealt with on their own merits' (Abtahi and Webb (n 74)).

[76] *Akayesu* (n 67), § 507.

[77] The forcible transfer of children skirts along the borderline of 'cultural genocide'. This conduct may not result in the biological or physical destruction, but cause the disappearance of the group through the severance of the links of the youngest generation with the group of origin. In this way, the children will lose their original cultural identity and their original group will be destroyed.

All the prohibited acts must be carried out *intentionally*, ie they require *intent* on the part of the perpetrator. In addition to requiring intent with regard to the prohibited act, an additional specific mental element is required, namely 'the intent to destroy, in whole or in part' one of the enumerated group 'as such'. In other words, although the victims of the prohibited conducts are individuals, it is against the group as such to which the victims belong that the perpetrator must ultimately direct his or her genocidal activity.[78] This is the specific intent of genocide, also known as genocidal intent. It is an aggravated form of intent that does not demand realization through the material conduct, but that the realization is nonetheless pursued by the perpetrator. In other words, it is not required that the perpetrator actually manages to destroy a member of a protected group by carrying out one of the five acts prohibited under the Convention. It is only necessary that the perpetrator harbours the specific intent to destroy the group while carrying out one of the prohibited acts, regardless of whether by accomplishing the act the intended ultimate objective is achieved. The requirement of this specific intent, therefore, has a preventative function, since it allows the criminalization of genocide before the perpetrator achieves the actual destruction of the group.

The question, however, arises whether the specific intent harboured by the perpetrator has to be 'realistic'; must the perpetrator believe that the intended goal can really be achieved through the commission of one of the prohibited acts? The case law of the ICTR and ICTY has not expressly tackled this issue. In *Mpambara*, however, an ICTR Trial Chamber has stressed that 'even a single instance of one of the prohibited acts' can amount to genocide, 'provided that the accused genuinely intends by that act to destroy at least a substantial part of the group'.[79] The reference to the *genuine* intent to destroy the group is explained by the Trial Chamber in a note to the judgment: 'The perpetrator of a single, isolated act of violence could not possess the requisite intent based on a delusion that, by his action, the destruction of the group, in whole or in part, could be effected'.[80] It seems therefore that for the Trial Chamber the genocidal intent can be 'genuine' only to the extent that the perpetrator realistically considers it possible that the destruction of the group can eventually be achieved.

---

[78] As the Trial Chamber of the ICTR has put it in *Akayesu*, 'the victim is chosen not because of his individual identity, but rather on account of his membership of a national, ethnical, racial or religious group' (*Akayesu* (n 67), § 521). It is, however, not requested that the individual victim actually belongs to the group, for what counts is the perception or belief of the perpetrator that the victim is a member of the targeted group. It has therefore been affirmed by a Trial Chamber of the ICTR that 'if a victim was perceived by the perpetrator as belonging to a protected group, the victim could be considered [...] as a member of the protected group, for the purposes of genocide'. See ICTR, Trial Chamber, *Musema*, Judgment, 27 January 2000, § 161. On this issue, see Schabas (n 64), 125–6, also for further reference to case law.

[79] *Mpambara*, Judgment, 11 September 2006, § 8.

[80] *Mpambara*, Judgment, 11 September 2006, § 8, note 7.

The genocidal intent of the perpetrator must be directed towards a group. Under Article II of the Genocide Convention, the list of the protected groups is exhaustive and it comprises national, ethnical, racial, or religious groups. During the preparatory work on the Genocide Convention, an attempt was made also to include in the list cultural and political groups, but to no avail. The exclusion was justified by the volatile membership of these two categories of groups and the desire to afford protection to groups characterized by a certain degree of stability.[81] The ICTR has tried to identify the distinguishing features of each protected group, and has affirmed that: (i) a national group is a group of people 'who are perceived to share a legal bond based on common citizenship, coupled with reciprocity of rights and duties';[82] (ii) a racial group is made up by members who possess 'hereditary physical traits often identified with a geographical region, irrespective of linguistic, cultural, national or religious factors';[83] (iii) an ethnic group is 'a group whose members share a common language or culture',[84] and (iv) a religious group is made by members who share 'the same religion, denomination or mode of worship'.[85] It is important to stress, however, that the reference to the four enumerated groups is made to the groups as social entities. It would therefore be useless to try to describe the protected groups by applying rigorous scientific or objective notions, also because by so doing one could find that some groups do not scientifically and objectively exist.[86]

It is perhaps because a particular group can be deemed to exist as a national, racial, ethnic, or religious group on account of the perception by the community, that the question of the identification of a given group, as a group protected by the prohibition of genocide, has eventually been solved by applying a subjective test, accompanied by the existence of objective elements. Thus, in the case of the attacks against the Tutsis in Rwanda, the ICTR considered they constituted an *ethnic group*, since the official classifications referred to them as an ethnic group and the Rwandans themselves, without hesitation, answered questions regarding their ethnicity.[87] Similarly, the International Commission of Inquiry on Darfur, found that the members of the tribes attacked in Darfur constituted an ethnic group distinct from that of the attackers on account of the self-perception of the victims as well

---

[81] This is the interpretation put forward by the ICTR Trial Chamber in *Akayesu* (n 67), § 511.

[82] *Akayesu* (n 67), § 512. This definition of 'national goup' has been criticized, among others, by Schabas, who rightly observes that the ICTR Trial Chamber has mixed up the notion of 'nationality' with that of membership in a national group by referring, as it did, to the decision of the International Court of Justice in *Nottembohm* to ground the definition of 'national group'. Schabas correctly underlines that in the *Nottembohm* case the Court focused on the effectiveness of the nationality, in the sense of citizenship, of an individual, and did not examine at all the question of individuals who, while sharing cultural, linguistic and other bonds of a particular 'nation', have in fact the citizenship of another state or have even stateless: see Schabas (n 64), 134–5.

[83] *Akayesu* (n 67), § 514.   [84] *Akayesu* (n 67), § 513.   [85] *Akayesu* (n 67), § 515.

[86] The paradigmatic example is that of 'racial group', since the notion of race or racial group does not find room from a scientific point of view.

[87] *Akayesu* (n 67), § 702.

as the attackers that they were two different ethnic groups, namely the 'Africans' as opposed to the 'Arabs'.[88]

The genocidal intent must be directed at one of the listed groups 'in whole or in part'. This means that it is not required that the perpetrator seeks to destroy the group in its entirety, since an intent to attain only a 'partial' destruction would suffice. It is, however, not clear what 'in part' means exactly. If one applies a quantitative approach 'in part' can describe the numeric size of the group with respect to its totality. By contrast, if one uses a qualitative approach, the intrinsic characteristic of the selected part of the group would count, ie the leadership of the targeted group. In any case, it has been contended that 'in part' seems to mean 'a substantial part'[89] of the group, and that both a quantitative and a qualitative approach can be used to establish whether or not part of the targeted group constitutes a substantial part.[90]

Finally, the genocidal intent must aim at the destruction of the group 'as such'. This requirement makes it clear that the ultimate intended victim of genocide is the group, whose destruction is sought by the perpetrator through carrying out the prohibited acts against its individual members or the group itself.[91]

C. Is the existence of a genocidal policy a legal ingredient of the crime of genocide?

The word genocide reminds us of the extermination of thousands, if not millions of people, on account of their membership in a particular group and in the pursuance of a state policy. The definition of genocide enshrined in the Genocide Convention, however, does not expressly require the existence of such a policy, and as a matter of fact does not even consider the number of the victims of the prohibited acts as relevant. The fact that historically genocide coincides with the actual destruction of a protected group, carried out in furtherance of a genocidal policy, has not been mirrored in the legal definition of genocide, which is aimed at punishing some enumerated acts as genocide on account of the specific intent harboured by the perpetrator. The ICTR and the ICTY have clearly confirmed this view,[92] although

[88] Report of the International Commission of Inquiry on Darfur to the United Nations Secretary General, 25 January 2005 (UN Doc S/2005/60), §§ 509–12.

[89] See the Commentary on Art 17 (on genocide) of the Draft Code of Crimes against the Peace and Security of Mankind, adopted in 1996 by the UN International Law Commission (ILC), 45, § 8, where the ILC observes: 'the intention must be to destroy a group "in whole or in part". It is not necessary to intend to achieve the complete annihilation of a group from every corner of the globe. None the less the crime of genocide by its very nature requires the intention to destroy at least a substantial part of a particular group'.

[90] *Kayishema and Ruzindana* (n 67), §§ 96–7.   [91] *Akayesu* (n 67), § 521.

[92] *Kayishema and Ruzindana* (n 67), § 94; ICTY, Appeals Chamber, *Jelisić*, Judgment, 5 July 2001, § 48.

they have admitted that the existence of a genocidal plan may be useful to estab-lish whether the perpetrator of one of the prohibited acts of genocide possesses the required genocidal intent.[93]

Some distinguished commentators consider this stand to be incorrect and argue that a contextual element, in the form of genocidal campaign, or at least of a pattern of collective violence against the group, is necessary.[94] To bolster this proposition, it is maintained that it would be unrealistic for a single individual to aim at the destruction of a group; therefore the genocidal intent must perforce be directed to the result of a collective endeavour to which the single individual contributes.[95] This view has also been echoed in the case law.[96] It also finds some support in the Elements of Crimes of the International Criminal Court (ICC), according to which the conduct must take place 'in the context of a manifest pattern of similar conduct directed against the group or was conduct that could itself effect [the] destruction [of the group]'.

As is clear, the question of the need for the existence of a genocidal policy is in fact closely intertwined with whether the specific intent to destroy one of the protected group, in whole or in part, must be 'genuine' (to use the expression of the ICTR Trial Chamber in *Mpambara*). The existence of a genocidal policy or campaign against the targeted group will make it possible for the perpetrator to form a 'realistic' intent to attain the destruction of the group; the conduct of the perpetrator will in fact aim at the same result pursued by others, thus creating a genuine threat to the existence of the group.

Nonetheless, it would be incorrect to conclude that a genocidal policy or campaign is one of the legal ingredients of genocide. Even admitting that historically genocide has been perpetrated within a genocidal context, still it is theoretically possible that

---

[93] *Kayishema and Ruzindana* (n 67), § 276; *Jelisić* (n 92), § 48.

[94] See, for instance, Schabas (n 65), 243–56. See also, among others, A.K.A. Greenawalt, 'Rethinking Genocidal Intent: The Case for a Knowledge-Based Interpretation', 99 *Columbia Law Review* (1999) 2259; C. Kress, 'The Darfur Report and Genocidal Intent', 3 *Journal of International Criminal Justice* (2005) 562. Another distinguished commentator argues instead that three out of the five acts that may amount to genocide 'not only presuppose, but rather take the shape of, some sort of collective or even organized action', namely: '(i) deliberately inflicting on a protected group or members thereof con-ditions of life calculated to bring about its physical destruction, in whole or in part; (ii) imposing measures intended to prevent births within a protected group; (iii) forcibly transferring children of a protected group to another group'. It is maintained that these acts 'are necessarily carried out on a large scale and by a multitude of individuals in pursuance of a common plan, possibly with the support of at least the acquiescence of the authorities'. See A. Cassese, 'Is Genocidal Policy a Requirement for the Crime of Genocide?', in Gaeta (ed) (n 62), 134–6.

[95] As Kress put it: 'An individual perpetrator cannot realistically *desire* the destruction of a protected group to occur *as a result* of his or her *individual genocidal conduct*. The perpetrator's desire must rather be related to the *results* to be brought about by the *collective activity* to which he or she contrib-utes' (Kress (n 94), 566).

[96] ICTY, Trial Chamber, *Krstić*, Judgment, 2 August 2001, § 682. The Trial Chamber has stated that the genocidal acts must be committed 'in the context of a manifest pattern of similar conduct, or them-selves [must] constitute a conduct that could in itself effect the destruction of the group, in whole or in part, as such'. What is requested here, as it is clear, is the systematic or widespread attack against a pro-tected group, to use two expressions that describe the contextual element of crimes against humanity.

a lone perpetrator may realistically aim at the destruction of a targeted group in the absence of such a context. An example is that of the individual who possesses a weapon of mass destruction. Another example is the attack, by a single individual, against the leadership of the group that may realistically endanger its existence at least in part.

It is on account of these considerations that one may perhaps understand why the ICC Elements of Crimes provides, with respect to genocide, that the conduct either must take place in the context of a manifest pattern of similar conduct directed against the group, *or* must be of a kind that *could itself effect* the destruction of the targeted group. If a *single* act may pose a concrete risk to the existence of the group, regardless of the existence of a genocidal policy, then the act carried out by the perpetrator could amount to genocide.

6 Concluding Remarks

Writing 'under the strain of military service' during World War II, Manfred Lachs could not perhaps have foreseen the tremendous development of international law in the matter of criminal responsibility of individuals for war crimes and other serious offences against international law. This development, which started with the trials at the Nuremberg and Tokyo Tribunals, culminated with the establishment of the ICTY and the ICTR by the UN Security Council and the adoption of the Rome Statute of the ICC, and is still under way. The international community has now begun to enforce its criminal prohibitions through international or mixed international courts and tribunals, that directly apply international criminal rules. The *jus puniendi* has now ceased to be an exclusive state prerogative; furthermore, it is exercised at the international level on behalf of the international community as a whole. Plainly, states can still prosecute and punish individuals who engage in these criminal acts. However, the current exercise of national criminal jurisdiction in the field of war crimes, crimes against humanity, and genocide can better be described as a judicial activity performed for the international community as such, rather than as a way of exercising sovereign power.[97]

The principle that 'crime does not pay' is now firmly embedded in international law. And, as Manfred Lachs envisaged, '[i]t is, therefore, our task, the task of those who are the guardian of law, to make it work'.[98]

---

[97] One could go so far to say that, national judges, if and when they step in and exercise their criminal jurisdiction over those crimes, also act as judicial organs of the international community thereby accomplishing a sort of *dédoublement fonctionnel*, a phenomenon well known to international lawyers and of which some national courts seemed to have been fully aware. It is as though the international community, still a *communitas imperfecta*, availed itself of national criminal courts to enforce its criminal prohibitions.

[98] Lachs (n 1), 103.

....

CHAPTER 30

FOCUSING ON ARMED
NON-STATE ACTORS

....

ANDREW CLAPHAM

THIS Chapter considers the obligations of armed non-state actors. It covers their obligations both in times of armed conflict, and at all other times as well. We address issues of international humanitarian law, human rights law, and international criminal law; and we make a number of suggestions to ensure respect for the law by armed non-state actors so as to improve the protection of the victims of armed conflict. The topic is a controversial one because some people tend to assume that engaging in this discussion bestows inappropriate recognition on armed groups; these people would prefer that such groups be simply outlawed as criminals or labelled as terrorists.

It is obvious that a state-centric approach to holding armed groups accountable has reigned for many years, but in recent times the need to address the international obligations of these groups has become self-evident, especially for those involved in humanitarian protection work. The legal landscape is being reshaped by the recent practices of some parts of the United Nations and certain non-governmental organizations, who are determined to ensure better protection for civilians in armed conflict.

It would be facile to suggest that today most violations in armed conflict are committed by lawless non-state actors and that these entities should be our primary focus. In fact the record is mixed, some non-state actors are worse than others, some non-state actors commit fewer violations that the states they are fighting against, some commit many more.[1] The point of this Chapter is to show what can be done to address these armed non-state actors directly. While the state has an on-going role to protect people from all sorts of violence—the international law applicable in armed conflicts need not be focused only on states.[2]

1 INTRODUCTION

Although much has been written on the need to engage with non-state armed groups in order to encourage respect for humanitarian norms,[3] less attention has been given to examining the actual obligations of these groups. This is understandable at one level. The exclusion of armed groups from the normal treaty-making process,[4] and their subsequent inability to become parties to the relevant treaties, mean that alternative non-legal regimes have had to be adopted. These regimes, whether established by the UN Security Council, the UN Human Rights Council, NGOs, or by national truth commissions, operate in a grey zone between law and politics: relying on international legal principles for the normative framework, and remaining dependent on political pressure, rather than courts, for the enforcement of these norms. Only rarely do we see court cases brought against armed groups as such (as opposed to the prosecution of their individual members).[5]

---

[1] O. Bangerter, 'Reasons Why Armed Groups Choose to Respect International Humanitarian Law or Not', 93 *IRRC* (2011) 353–84.

[2] This Chapter looks at rebel groups. One could also consider private military companies and international organizations as armed non-state actors. These issues are, however, dealt with in this *Handbook* in the Chapters by J. Cockayne and D. Fleck respectively.

[3] 'Engaging Armed Groups', 93 *IRRC* (2011) 581–808; A. Bellal and S. Casey-Maslen, *Rules of Engagement: Promoting the Protection of Civilians Through Dialogue with Armed Non-State Actors* (Geneva: Geneva Academy of International Humanitarian Law and Human Rights, 2011); T. Whitfield, *Engaging With Armed Groups: Dilemma and Options for Mediators* (Geneva: Centre for Humanitarian Dialogue, 2010); O. Bangartner, 'Disseminating and Implementing International Humanitarian Law Within Organized Armed Groups. Measures Armed Groups Can Take to Improve Respect for International Humanitarian Law', in International Institute of Humanitarian Law, *Non-State Actors and International Humanitarian Law. Organized Armed Groups: A Challenge for the 21st Century* (Milano: FrancoAngeli, 2010), 187–212.

[4] For proposals on how to include such groups in the formation of their international legal obligations, see M. Sassòli, 'Involving Organized Armed Groups in the Development of the Law?', in *Non-State Actors and International Humanitarian Law* (n 3), 213–21; S. Rondeau, 'Participation of Armed Groups in the Development of the Law Applicable to Armed Conflicts', 93(883) *IRRC* (2011) 649–72.

[5] One example would be the case which reached the US Supreme Court: *Mohamed et al v Palestinian Authority and PLO* 3, 566 US ____ (2012).

Again this is not surprising. Why sue a group in court when it is unlikely that the group will have easily traceable assets in the relevant jurisdiction? Governments fighting an armed group will usually proscribe membership in the group, making membership or association a crime; no need then for the government to show that the group is violating international law—when the group as such is already outlawed in national law.

For several observers, armed non-state actors, inevitably labelled as 'criminals' or 'terrorists', have little or no incentive to apply international norms related to humanitarian law and human rights. The challenge is therefore said to be to create a new norm to protect certain 'captured combatants' who have respected the rules of armed conflict. This new law would protect such fighters from being prosecuted for 'the mere fact of having taken up arms against the central authorities'.[6] This in turn would provide an incentive to abide by the laws of war, and would reflect the rule that states that combatants in an international armed conflict have the right to participate in hostilities, and that they cannot be prosecuted for fighting, unless their acts amount to war crimes.

Several authors have therefore suggested that one builds on the encouragement, contained in Additional Protocol II of 1977, which states that those in power at the end of the internal armed conflict 'endeavour to grant the broadest possible amnesty to persons who have participated in the armed conflict, or those deprived of their liberty for reasons related to the armed conflict, whether they are interned or detained'.[7] The idea would be that the law would develop so that such an amnesty would become compulsory.

In effect this train of thought would make it illegal or difficult for a state to punish those non-state actors who took up arms against it. For the present author such a development seems unlikely. While laudable from a humanitarian point of view, it seems implausible that states today would vote to empower those who would do them harm. Not to put too fine a point on it, this seems as likely as turkeys voting for Christmas.

Evidence of how far we are from any right to rebellion can be found in a recent Court of Appeal judgment in the United Kingdom. The Court rejected the argument that any combatant immunity would apply to insurgents involved in attacks on the UK military in Afghanistan and Iraq, such acts were considered terrorism even though they are not outlawed in international humanitarian law.[8]

At a more abstract level, the doctrinal notion that the international legal system has a limited number of 'subjects', and that these subjects are primarily states (or

---

[6] A. Cassese, 'Should Rebels be Treated as Criminals? Some Modest Proposals for Rendering Internal Armed Conflicts Less Inhumane', in A. Cassese, (ed), *Realizing Utopia: The Future of International Law* (Oxford: Oxford University Press, 2012), 519–24 at 523; see also in the same volume N. Melzer, 'Bolstering the Protection of Civilians in Armed Conflict', 508–18; and S. Sivakumaran, 'How to Improve Upon the Faulty Legal Regime of Internal Armed Conflicts', 525–37.

[7] Article 6(5).   [8] *R v Gul* [2012] EWCA Crim 280 at §§ 28–31.

the entities that states create), has meant that many international lawyers see inter-national law (beyond certain traditional rules of armed conflict) as inapplicable to armed groups. And from the point of view of the armed groups, international law is seen as inimical or even hostile to the aims of the armed groups at issue. As long as the armed group is considered to be a non-state actor rather than the government of a state, its rights and responsibilities mostly remain apparently suspended until the day it achieves control of the state or separate statehood.[9] Klabbers concludes: 'A legal system which treats actors as second-rank citizens should not be surprised that those second-class citizens aim to upgrade their status, and the shortest route to being heard and being taken seriously is through violence'.[10]

This Chapter considers that the traditional approach, which sees international law as based solely on inter-state consent, excluding armed non-state actors from its list of suitable subjects, is not only unhelpful, but also dangerous as it creates the impression that armed groups inhabit a lawless world. Moreover, it will be argued that the time has come for a radical rethinking of these issues due to the fact the international legal system itself has undergone major upheavals since the tradi-tional approach first took hold.

One major development has been that international law is now concerned with individuals, and that these individuals have international rights and obligations. Let us consider for a moment the individual insurgent in this context. The indi-viduals that compose these armed groups have rights and responsibilities under international law.[11] It is now uncontroversial that every individual is entitled to a catalogue of international rights under customary international law;[12] these rights are complemented by the rights enjoyed under certain treaties where the state party to the treaty is responsible for its acts or omissions towards that individual. It is also uncontroversial that every individual in the world has certain international

[9] The International Law Commission has suggested that successful insurgents carry over their internationally wrongful acts so that they are then seen as the responsibility of the new state or govern-ment, see A. Clapham, 'Human Rights Obligations of Non-State Actors in Conflict Situations', 88(863) *IRRC* (2006) 491–523 at 508–9; this approach has been challenged on the grounds that there is no legal evidence for such a rule, and that in policy terms it makes sense to limit such attribution to the state where 'a national reconciliation or power sharing agreement leads to democratic elections which even-tually bring the rebels to power'. J. D'Aspremont, 'Rebellion and State Responsibility: Wrongdoing by Democratically Elected Insurgents', 58 *ICLQ* (2009) 427–42 at 437.

[10] J. Klabbers, '(I Can't Get No) Recognition: Subjects Doctrine and the Emergence of Non-State Actors', in J. Petman and J. Klabbers (eds), *Nordic Cosmopolitanism. Essays in International Law for Martii Koskenniemi* (Leiden: Martinus Nijhoff, 2003), 351–69 (reproduced in A. Bianchi, (ed), *Non-State Actors and International Law* (Dartmouth: Ashgate, 2009), 54–5).

[11] See eg Y. Dinstein, 'The Interaction Between Customary International Law and Treaties', 322 *RCADI* (Brill, The Hague, 2006), 228: 'Since the dawn of international law, obligations have been imposed directly on individual human beings through customary prohibitions of certain modes of conduct [...] Only in more recent times has customary international law conferred rights straightly on human beings.'

[12] According to Dinstein: 'But it is impossible to deny today that the core of the Universal Declaration of Human Rights has come to reflect customary international law' (Dinstein (n 11), 338).

obligations not to commit international crimes, such as genocide, crimes against humanity, or war crimes. These international obligations are not dependent on whether or not the individual acts through a state or non-state actor. In both situations, the individual has violated international law, and in some cases there will be a court with jurisdiction ready and willing to prosecute such acts as violations of international law. The question of consent is seen as irrelevant. Individuals are bound by this customary international law, whether or not they or their state or their non-state armed group consented to be bound by the rule.

When we turn to the organizations themselves, the scope of international obligations which attach to armed non-state groups is underdeveloped in law and practice. All relevant existing international courts only allow for cases to be brought against states or individuals. One should not, however, draw the conclusion that the absence of an international jurisdiction means that non-state armed groups have no obligations under international law. First, the historic practice of recognizing such groups as belligerents or insurgents was nothing less than an explicit acceptance by the relevant states that the armed non-state actor had international rights and obligations that were to be respected.[13] Secondly, Common Article 3 to the 1949 Geneva Conventions sets out provisions which 'each Party to the conflict' is bound to apply; and this has been interpreted to confirm that armed non-state groups have a set of international obligations when they become a party to an armed conflict. Thirdly, the Security Council has increasingly called on armed non-state groups to respect international law. Fourthly, the UN Human Rights Council, and its special procedures, have condemned violations of human rights by armed groups and detailed some of the responsibilities of these groups in different contexts. Fifthly, national courts have had occasion to consider the international obligations of armed groups. This can happen, for example, when a court has to determine whether a government supplying arms to an armed non-state actor was facilitating crimes against humanity.[14] Lastly, as we shall see, there are multiple initiatives which focus on the unilateral or negotiated commitments made by armed non-state actors.

A further development has been the growing acceptance that international law imposes various positive obligations on states to ensure that private individuals and non-state actors respect the rights of others. These state obligations are beyond the scope of this Chapter, but we will quickly mention three sources of obligation. First, we might recall the general obligation found in Common Article 1 to the Geneva Convention whereby the states parties undertake to 'ensure respect for the present Convention in all circumstances'. Secondly, in human rights law, the case law of the regional Human Rights Courts and UN treaty bodies is replete with examples of states being held accountable for failing to prevent, investigate, prosecute or punish

---

[13] See further H. Lauterpacht (ed), *Oppenheim's International Law: A Treatise (Disputes, War and Neutrality)*, vol II (7th edn, London: Longmans, 1952), 248 ff.

[14] Dealt with in Section 6 below.

the acts of non-state actors that violated the rights of those falling within the state's jurisdiction.[15] Thirdly, in some circumstances these international obligations on states may flow from UN Security Council resolutions. Obviously an arms embargo adopted by the Security Council may entail binding obligations for states, with the aim of cutting off arms supplies or other support to certain armed non-state actors. With regard to weapons of mass destruction, the Security Council has issued a blanket injunction (acting under Chapter VII) in Resolution 1540 (2004), which created binding obligations for states. It decided that 'all States shall refrain from providing any form of support to non-state actors that attempt to develop, acquire, manufacture, possess, transport, transfer or use nuclear, chemical or biological weapons and their means of delivery'. It also decided that:

all States, in accordance with their national procedures, shall adopt and enforce appropriate effective laws which prohibit any non-state actor to manufacture, acquire, possess, develop, transport, transfer or use nuclear, chemical or biological weapons and their means of delivery, in particular for terrorist purposes, as well as attempts to engage in any of the foregoing activities, participate in them as an accomplice, assist or finance them.

The Council included 'for the purpose of this resolution only', a definition of a non-state actor: 'individual or entity, not acting under the lawful authority of any state in conducting activities which come within the scope of this resolution'.

Our focus, however, for the rest of this Chapter is on the obligations of the groups and their members rather than the obligations of states.

2 INTERNATIONAL HUMANITARIAN LAW

In 2004, the Appeals Chamber of the Sierra Leone Special Court simply held that: 'it is well settled that all parties to an armed conflict, whether states or non-state actors, are bound by international humanitarian law, even though only states may become parties to international treaties'.[16] It has now become quite common to refer to non-state parties to an armed conflict being bound by international humanitarian

---

[15] C. Focarelli, 'Common Article 1 of the 1949 Geneva Conventions: A Soap Bubble?', 21 *EJIL* (2010) 125–71; on the human rights obligations, see A. Clapham, *Human Rights Obligations of Non-State Actors* (Oxford: Oxford University Press, 2006), Chs 8 and 9; W. Kälin and J. Künzli, *The Law of International Human Rights Protection* (Oxford: Oxford University Press, 2009), 96–113 and on the right to life in armed conflict see esp 284–303.

[16] *Prosecutor v Sam Hinga Norman* (Case No SCSL-2004-14-AR72(E)) Decision on Preliminary Motion Based on Lack of Jurisdiction (Child Recruitment), Decision of 31 May 2004, § 22.

law.[17] This is said to happen under a number of competing theories: because the treaties take effect in national law and therefore bind the armed group and its members
(so- called 'legislative jurisdiction'), because the groups aspire to be governments
in charge of states, because the treaties are directly addressed to them, or because
they are bound under customary international law.[18] By searching for the theoretical underpinnings of the binding obligation in international humanitarian law,[19] we
may be able first, to develop these arguments so as to clarify the responsibilities of
armed groups under other branches of international law, and secondly, determine
legal routes for holding armed groups accountable.

A. The law of treaties

The principle that third states cannot be bound by a treaty to which they are not a
party, is so familiar, and so obviously derived from principles of contract law, that
it is often associated with the Latin maxim: *pacta tertiis nec nocent nec prosunt*.
The Vienna Conventions on the Law of Treaties reinforce this message by allowing
an exception to the rule, where the parties intend the provision to be binding on
third states, or international organizations, and those entities agree in writing to be
bound.[20] In the face of these concrete provisions, and a principle apparently dating
back to Roman Law, should we simply conclude that there is nothing an inter-state
treaty can do to bind an armed group? Perhaps not, perhaps we should look a little

---

[17] Consider the Updated European Union Guidelines on promoting compliance with international
humanitarian law (IHL) (2009/C 303/06) 15 December 2009, '§ 5: States are obliged to comply with the
rules of IHL to which they are bound by treaty or which form part of customary international law. They
may also apply to non-State actors. Such compliance is a matter of international concern.' Note that the
source of obligation for non-state actors is not specified. Compare the Swiss Federal Department of
Foreign Affairs: 'Non-state actors—including armed groups—are playing an ever greater role today in
armed conflicts. Although they are not parties to international law treaties, non-state actors are obliged
to respect the rules of customary international law. It follows that international humanitarian law is
also legally binding on non-state actors.' *ABC of International Humanitarian Law* (2009), 32.

[18] For a good discussion, see J.K. Kleffner, 'The Applicability of International Humanitarian Law to
Organized Armed Groups', 93 *IRRC* (2011) 443–61.

[19] For analyses of this question, see S. Sivakumaran, *The Law of Non-International Armed Conflict*
(Oxford: Oxford University Press, 2012), esp 236ff; S. Sivakumaran 'Binding Armed Opposition Groups',
55 *ICLQ* (2006) 369–94; M. Sassòli, *Transnational Armed Groups and International Humanitarian
Law* (Harvard University: Program on Humanitarian Policy and Conflict Research, 2006), esp 14;
K. Nowrot, 'International Legal Personality of Influential Non-State Actors: Towards A Rebuttable
Presumption of Normative Responsibilities', 80 *Philippines Law Journal* (2006) 563–86 at 580–6;
L. Zegveld, *Accountability of Armed Opposition Groups in International Law* (Cambridge: Cambridge
University Press, 2002); A. Cassese, 'The Status of Rebels under the 1977 Geneva Protocol on Non-
International Armed Conflicts', 30 *ICLQ* (1981) 416–39.

[20] Article 34 of the Vienna Convention on the Law of Treaties (1969); Article Vienna Convention
on the Law of Treaties between States and International Organizations or between International
Organizations (1986), 'An obligation arises for a third State or a third organization from a provision of
a treaty if the parties to the treaty intend the provision to be the means of establishing the obligation

more closely at the rules in the law of treaties and consider the changing structure of the international legal system.

The law of treaties states that a third *state* cannot be bound by a treaty it is not a party to. Any other result would violate the rule of sovereign equality. How can two states bind a third state without its consent? The origins in contract law make sense—no two individuals should be able to contract to bind a third party. But it seems reasonable to suggest that two states could contract through treaty to bind certain non-state actors such as individuals or other entities within their jurisdiction. For some time it has been accepted that treaties between states have effects on third parties.[21]

First, as we have already mentioned, a treaty can create not only rights for individuals but also obligations. Dinstein puts it bluntly: 'It is a commonplace today that treaties can directly impose obligations on—and accord rights to—individual human beings'.[22] We can ask why these individual third parties can be bound—and yet conventional doctrine would suggest that a group composed of such individuals is not so bound?[23]

Secondly, the UN Charter is a treaty, and, as such, one might assume that it is merely binding on the member states. And yet from early on in the United Nations' history there has been a sense that the purposes of the United Nations were so essential that non-member states could be bound by decisions of the member states. In the words of one authoritative treatise discussing the effect of the UN Charter on non-member states: 'as international society becomes a more integrated community, a departure from the accepted principle becomes unavoidable, in particular in the sphere of international peace and security'.[24] It seems that, with regard to certain principles in the UN Charter, this treaty can be seen as creating binding obligations on non-parties, but we can admit that this manoeuvre is probably dependent on the fact that those same Charter principles are now seen as binding customary international law.[25]

Thirdly, under the 1949 Geneva Conventions, Common Article 3 is addressed to 'each Party to the conflict', and this Article applies to conflicts 'not of an international character'. The treaties then would seem to have a provision which directly

and the third State or the third organization expressly accepts that obligation in writing'. See further, Sivakumaran, *The Law of Non-International Armed Conflict* (n 19), 277–9.

[21] M. Fitzmaurice, 'Third Parties and the Law of Treaties', in J.A. Fowein and R. Wolfrum (eds), 6 *Max Planck Yearbook of United Nations Law* (2002) 37–137; C. Chinkin, *Third Parties in International Law* (Oxford: Clarendon Press, 1983).

[22] *The Interaction Between Customary International Law and Treaties* (n 11), 339.

[23] Dinstein: 'At the present juncture, there is no decisive authority for holding a constitutive provision of a treaty applicable to insurgents who refuse to abide by it and deny the rights of the State to exercise its treaty-making power on their behalf' (Dinstein (n 11), 344).

[24] R. Jennings and A. Watts (eds), *Oppenheim's International Law*, vol I (9th edn, London: Longman, 1996), 1265.

[25] See M. Shaw, *International Law* (6th edn, Cambridge: Cambridge University Press, 2008), 929.

binds the non-state armed group. This seems to add a further exception to the rule that treaties are considered as only binding on the parties to the treaty. In the case of the Geneva Conventions, only states may become parties.[26]

Applying this reasoning to Common Article 3 of the Geneva Conventions, we might assume that universal adherence to the Geneva Conventions, together with the legal consensus that the Article applies as customary international law,[27] allow us to conclude that this provision is indeed binding on armed groups.[28] It is worth noting that the UK Ministry of Defence relies on the treaty as such, and with reference to Common Article 3 states: 'This purports to bind *all* parties, both states and insurgents, whether or not the latter have made any declaration of intent to apply the principles'.[29] Similarly, the language of the International Court of Justice suggests that the *Contras* in Nicaragua were bound by the terms of Common Article 3 rather than merely by the principles which it embodied: 'The United States is thus under an obligation not to encourage persons or groups engaged in the conflict in Nicaragua to act in violation of the provisions of Article 3 common to the four 1949 Geneva Conventions'.[30]

Before we simply apply this logic to all humanitarian law provisions applicable in internal armed conflict, we need to admit that Common Article 3 was singled out by the International Court of Justice 'as a minimum yardstick [...] rules which, in the Court's opinion, reflect [...] "elementary considerations of humanity"'.[31] While we can conclude that international law accepts that Common Article 3 is binding on non-state parties to a conflict, due perhaps to a combination of the special nature of the norms and the universal acceptance of the treaties, the case may be less certain

---

[26] The Geneva Conventions and related humanitarian law treaties are not normally open for signature by armed non-state groups. There is a sort of exception to this in Art 96(3) of the 1977 Additional Protocol I to the Geneva Convention of 1949 allowing for a declaration by certain armed non-state actors (known as national liberation movements) that such an actor undertakes to apply the Protocol and the Geneva Conventions to that particular conflict. No such Declaration has ever entered into force. Note for the purposes of this provision the non-state actor would have to be an 'authority' representing a people 'fighting against colonial domination and alien occupation and against racist régimes in the exercise of their right of self-determination, as enshrined in the Charter of the United Nations and the Declaration on Principles of International Law concerning Friendly Relations and Co-operation among States in accordance with the Charter of the United Nations'. See Arts 96(3) and 1(4). This issue is dealt with again in more detail in the section on weapons.

[27] See ICJ, *Nicaragua v United States of America*, International Court of Justice, 27 June 1986, §§ 218–20.

[28] Compare the Sierra Leone Special Court: 'It suffices to say, for the purpose of the present case, that no one has suggested that insurgents are bound because they have been vested with personality in international law of such a nature as to make it possible for them to be a party to the Geneva Conventions. Rather, a convincing theory is that they are bound as a matter of international customary law to observe the obligations declared by Common Article 3 which is aimed at the protection of humanity.' Appeals Chamber Decision on Challenge to Jurisdiction: Lomé Accord Amnesty, Case Nos SCSL-2004-15-AR72(E) and SCSL-2004-16-AR72(E), § 47, 13 March 2004.

[29] *The Manual of the Law of Armed Conflict* (Oxford: Oxford University Press, 2004), 385, fn 19.

[30] *Nicaragua v United States* (n 27), § 220.   [31] *Nicaragua v United States* (n 27), § 218.

for other norms found in treaties applicable in non-international armed conflicts. These treaties may enjoy less than universal adherence, and the norms they detail may not always be considered as representing customary international law. In practice, armed groups have at various times rejected norms found in treaties that they did not negotiate or sign.[32] While arguments can be made that Protocol II is an elaboration of the norms contained in Common Article 3,[33] and that many of the norms are now reflected in customary international law,[34] the search for a theory to explain how armed groups become bound by the Geneva Conventions and Protocol II continues.[35]

Another set of treaties we need to consider are those relating to weapons. As with Additional Protocol I (1977),[36] national liberation movements can make a declaration under the Convention on Prohibitions or Restrictions on the Use of Certain Conventional Weapons Which May be Deemed to be Excessively Injurious or to Have Indiscriminate Effects (CCW) (1980).[37] Such a declaration can bring into force, not only the Weapons Convention and its Protocols, but also the Geneva Conventions, even where the state against which the liberation movement is fighting is not a party to 1977 Protocol I.[38] No such Declaration has been successfully made either under this Convention or under 1977 Protocol I.[39]

Since 2001 the CCW has been amended so that it now reads: 'In case of armed conflicts not of an international character occurring in the territory of one of the High Contracting Parties, each party to the conflict shall be bound to apply the prohibitions and restrictions of this Convention and its annexed Protocols.'[40] This applies only in situations where the relevant state has ratified the amendment, in other cases the relevant provisions will only apply to inter-state conflicts, with the exception of the provisions in Amended Protocol II (Prohibitions or Restrictions on the Use of Mines, Booby-Traps and Other Devices) and Protocol V (Explosive Remnant of War).[41]

---

[32] A. Roberts and S. Sivakumaran, 'Lawmaking by Nonstate Actors: Engaging Armed Groups in the Creation of International Humanitarian Law', 37 *Yale Journal of International Law* 1 107–52, esp 127; O. Bangerter, 'Reasons Why Armed Groups Choose to Respect International Humanitarian Law Or Not', 93 *IRRC* (2011) 353–84, esp 380–2.

[33] See R. Geiss, 'Humanitarian Law Obligations of Organized Armed Groups', in International Institute of Humanitarian Law, *Non-State Actors and International Humanitarian Law. Organized Armed Groups: A Challenge for the 21st Century* (Milano: FrancoAngeli, 2010), 93–101.

[34] J.-M. Henckaerts and L. Doswald-Beck, *Customary International Humanitarian Law—Volume 1: Rules* (Cambridge: Cambridge University Press, 2005).

[35] S. Sivakumaran, 'The Addressees of Common Article 3', in A. Clapham, P. Gaeta, and M. Sassòli, (eds), *The 1949 Geneva Conventions: A Commentary* (Oxford: Oxford University Press, forthcoming).

[36] See n 27.   [37] 10 October 1980, see Art 7(4).   [38] Article 7(4)(b).

[39] Although certain declarations have been sent to the ICRC, the procedure demands a communication with the Swiss Federal authorities.

[40] Article 1(3).

[41] Amended Protocol II states: '1(3) In case of armed conflicts not of an international character occurring in the territory of one of the High Contracting Parties, each party to the conflict shall be bound to apply the prohibitions and restrictions of this Protocol.' Protocol V Art 1(3) 'This Protocol

Other weapons treaties may or may not extend to situations of internal armed conflict but there are apparently no explicit provisions aimed at the non-state parties to the conflict.[42] Despite the fact that the Cluster Munitions Convention recognizes the need to prevent the use of cluster munitions by all persons,[43] this recent Convention confines itself to a preambular commitment that the states parties are: '*Resolved* also that armed groups distinct from the armed forces of a State shall not, under any circumstances, be permitted to engage in any activity prohibited to a State Party to this Convention'. Commentators have not seen this as creating any international obligations on the armed groups as such; nevertheless it has been argued that, as the treaty refers to a ban on assistance to 'anyone' engaged in prohibited activities, this must be read to include assistance to such armed groups.[44] So under this reading states parties are prohibited under the treaty from assisting non-state actors to use cluster munitions, while the non-state actors themselves are not considered as subject to obligations under the same treaty.

This duality (obligations for states, nothing internationally binding on armed groups) is apparently not confined to weapons treaties applicable to internal armed conflict. Even where a humanitarian treaty on the methods of war applies to the state party in an internal armed conflict, there may be doubts as to whether international obligations are generated for the armed non-state actor. Like Common Article 3, the 1954 Hague Convention for the Protection of Cultural Property in the Event of Armed Conflict seeks to single out a set of obligations for the non-state armed group. Article 19(1) states that 'each Party to the conflict shall be bound to apply, as a minimum, the provisions of the present Convention which relate to respect for cultural property'. But the 1999 Protocol II to the Hague Convention of 1954, while it extends to internal armed conflicts, seems specifically to address its key obligations to a *state* 'Party' (with a capital P) to the Protocol rather than the 'parties' to the conflict (with a small p). This exclusive capitalization for state 'Parties' is not present in the Geneva Conventions of 1949 nor in the Hague Convention of 1954. Article 1(a) to Protocol II, however, draws this distinction in unambiguous terms: 'For the purposes of this Protocol: a. "Party" means a State Party to this Protocol'.

shall apply to situations resulting from conflicts referred to in Article 1, paragraphs 1 to 6, of the Convention, as amended on 21 December 2001'.

    [42] See W.H. Boothby, *Weapons and the Law of Armed Conflict* (Oxford: Oxford University Press, 2009), Ch 18.

    [43] See Art 9. See further T. Boutruche, S. Casey-Maslen, A. Clapham, T. Nash, M. Reiterer, and M. Smyth, 'The Title and Preamble of the Convention', in G. Nystuen and S. Casey-Maslen (eds), *The Convention on Cluster Munitions: A Commentary* (Oxford: Oxford University Press, 2010), 37–94 at 64–9. National legislation should therefore outlaw the use or possession of cluster munitions without requiring that the individual be a member of the state's armed forces, see eg the UK Cluster Munitions (Prohibition) Act 2010; New Zealand Cluster Munitions Prohibition Act 2009. Similarly see the UK Landmines Act 1998.

    [44] B. Docherty, 'Breaking New Ground: The Convention on Cluster Munitions and the Evolution of International Humanitarian Law', 34 *Human Rights Quarterly* (2009) 934–63 at 959–62, esp 960.

Moreover the Protocol, while it is extended to non-international armed conflicts on the territory of a 'State Party' to the Protocol,[45] nowhere demands substantive obligations from the non-state party, as the obligations are addressed to Parties or a Party. The Protocol seems on its face to refer to non-state actor 'parties' to the conflict (with a small p) simply to remind that the application of the Protocol to an internal armed conflict 'shall not affect the legal status of the parties to the conflict'.[46] This state-centric reading is, however, contradicted by Henckaerts, who participated in the drafting, and who writes that such 'a literal interpretation would lead to a manifestly absurd result of declaring a treaty applicable to non-international armed conflicts and at the same time eliminating most of its practical relevance in such conflicts'.[47] According to Henckaerts' appreciation at the time:[48]

Although Article 22 of the Second Protocol does not spell it out as clearly as it could have, the Protocol applies to all parties to a non-international armed conflict, whether governmental or insurgent forces. This was clearly acknowledged at the final plenary session. A certain confusion arose because Article 1 of the Protocol defines the word 'Party' as a State Party to the Second Protocol. However, the understanding was that throughout the text the word 'Party' in the phrase 'Party to the conflict' includes rebel groups of States party to the Second Protocol but not third States which have not ratified the Second Protocol.[49] The reasoning was that non-governmental forces involved in a non-international armed conflict within a State party to the Protocol are bound by the Protocol through the ratification of the State concerned.[50]

---

[45] Article 22.

[46] See Protocol II of 1999 to the Hague Convention of 1954 for the Protection of Cultural Property in the Event of Armed Conflict, Arts 1 and 22(6), see also Arts 22(7), 32(4), and 35(2). Note the provision for a party to a conflict to accept the protocol only applies to a 'state party', Art 3(2).

[47] 'The Protection of Cultural Property in Non-International Armed Conflicts', in N. van Woudenberg and L. Lijnzaad (eds), *Protecting Cultural Property in Armed Conflict: The First Ten Years of the Second Protocol to the Hague Convention of 1954 for the Protection of Cultural Property in the Event of an Armed Conflict* (Leiden: Martinus Nijhoff, 2010), 81–94 at 84; see also Henckaerts in the same volume, 'New Rules for the Protection of Cultural Property in Armed Conflict: The Significance of the Second Protocol to the 1954 Hague Convention for the Protection of Cultural Property in the Event of an Armed Conflict', 21–42 esp 39–40. See also R. O'Keefe, 'Protection of Cultural Property', in D. Fleck (ed), *The Handbook of Humanitarian Law in Armed Conflict* (2nd edn, Oxford: Oxford University Press, 2007), 433–74 who separates the rules applicable in international and non-international armed conflict in a detailed examination.

[48] 'New Rules for the Protection of Cultural Property in Armed Conflict', 835 *IRRC* (1999) 593–620 at 618–19.

[49] [Third States which have not ratified the Second Protocol are generally referred to as 'party' (in lower case).] Footnote in the original.

[50] [It is unfortunate that recognition of the potential confusion of the definition of 'Party' and the use of the term 'Party to the conflict' came only in the last hours of the Diplomatic Conference. As a result, there was no discussion on whether the general understanding that the Second Protocol applies to governmental forces and rebel groups in a non-international armed conflict is also valid for Article 11(9). It is difficult to say whether this was indeed the intention of States, as the Working Group on Chapter 3 (Enhanced Protection) did not discuss the issue.] Footnote in the original.

We find here an echo of the so called 'legislative jurisdiction' doctrine. Kleffner explains the doctrine as follows: 'According to this construction, the capacity of a state to legislate for all its nationals entails the right of the state to impose upon them obligations that originate from international law, even if those individuals take up arms to fight that state or (an)other organized armed group(s) within it'.[51] It is suggested that this approach is 'fully compatible with other areas of international law, through which states grant rights to, or impose obligations on, individuals and other legal persons'.[52]

But confusion remains: this doctrine seems to rely in part on the idea that states transform their international obligations into binding legal obligations for their nationals. While some states do this some of the time for some obligations, we cannot really reliably infer that the outlawed group as such is considered to be bound simply by the act of a state's ratification of a treaty. Furthermore, the doctrine seems to rely on a nationality link. This is problematic for two reasons. First, the rebels are often rebelling against the state of nationality and rejecting their laws as illegitimate. Engaging a group on the grounds that it should respect national law imposed by the enemy is unlikely to be fruitful. Secondly, this could be taken to suggest that foreign fighters or foreign rebels groups are not so bound. Today's conflicts often involve multinational rebel groups and include cross-border armed conflicts involving multiple armed non-state actors.

Perhaps one way out is to see the obligation as taking effect, not through domestic law, but rather through the will of the states parties to create an obligation for a third party (which is not a state). As we have seen, this has been accomplished without major doctrinal objections in the field of international criminal law. The proof being that individuals have been prosecuted for international crimes even in the absence of identical national law. There is no reason to limit this prosecutorial power of states to obligations for their nationals. States may also agree to international obligations for anyone operating on their territory.[53] In short, the doctrine that treaties only bind those who are parties to them is misleading, as treaties are today considered as capable of creating obligations for other entities (that are not sovereign states). There may be limits as to the scope of the obligations that states can create in this way according to the traditional rules limiting a state's jurisdiction, but a combination of the active personality and territorial jurisdictions should resolve that issue.

While treaty law remains important, as we have seen, it can be ambiguous as to whether the states intended it to bind non-state actors. Even where we can discern at least a developing consensus over its binding nature, the treaty may not have

---

[51] J.K. Kleffner, 'The Applicability of International Humanitarian Law to Organized Armed Groups', 93 *IRRC* (2011) 443–61 at 445.

[52] Kleffner (n 51), 443–61 at 445.

[53] This would seem to be the logic of the Statute for the International Criminal Court (1998) Art 12.

universal application. It is suggested that the tendency today is to focus on those obligations which are considered to be binding due to their customary international status.[54] Let us now see how custom is applied to armed non-state actors.

B. Contemporary customary international law

Inquiries into customary international humanitarian law have taken off in recent years.[55] In part this is due to the perceived need to prove that certain obligations are customary, so that they can form the basis for the prosecution of an individual for an international crime before an international criminal tribunal. International Criminal Tribunals have had to examine whether the events are covered by applicable customary international law,[56] before going on to determine whether customary international law entails individual criminal responsibility.[57]

But the turn to custom is also essential beyond the question of individual prosecution. It has been central in the context of fact-finding missions and commissions of inquiry charged with determining violations of international law by armed non-state actors. In contrast to many provisions of treaty law, customary international law is often seen as binding on the non-state actor as such.[58] In this context the work of the Darfur Commission is instructive. The Commission set a threshold for the capacity of any rebel group to bear international obligations under customary international law.

The SLM/A and JEM, like all insurgents that have reached a certain threshold of organization, stability and effective control of territory, possess international legal personality and

---

[54] See eg Geiss (n 34), 96: 'In any case, given that the vast corpus of rules applicable to non-international armed conflict has acquired the status of customary international law, and given that this particular source of law binds any entity even with a limited personality under international law, the debate has arguably lost much of its verve. Non-state parties to an armed conflict are bound to IHL by virtue of customary international law.' At the time he wrote this, Geiss was a legal adviser in the ICRC. For an example of an international criminal tribunal applying a treaty to ground the war crime of 'acts or threats of violence the primary purpose of which is to spread terror among the civilian population', see *Prosecutor v Galić*, ICTY (Case No IT-98-29-T), 5 December 2003, see also the Appeals Chamber (IT-98-29-A, 30 November 2006): 'However, while binding conventional law that prohibits conduct and provides for individual criminal responsibility could provide the basis for the International Tribunal's jurisdiction, in practice the International Tribunal always ascertains that the treaty provision in question is also declaratory of custom' (§ 85).

[55] See in this regard Henckaerts and Doswald-Beck (n 35).

[56] See *Tadić* (Appeal) (Decision on the defence motion for Interlocutory Appeal on Jurisdiction) ICTY, Appeals Chamber, Decision, 2 October 1995 (Case No IT-94-1-AR72), esp §§ 94–127.

[57] *Tadić* (Appeal) (n 56), §§ 128–36.

[58] '[C]ustom may be opposable beyond States, not only to armed opposition groups but also to other non-State actors and individuals.' D. Bethlehem, 'The Methodological Framework of the Study', in E. Wilmshurst and S. Breua (eds), *Perspectives on the ICRC Study on Customary International Humanitarian Law* (Cambridge: Cambridge University Press, 2007), 3–14 at 8.

are therefore bound by the relevant rules of customary international law on internal armed conflicts referred to above. The same is probably true also for the NMRD.[59]

The next step then is to determine what are the relevant rules. Of course one set of rules can be found in the study on customary international humanitarian law,[60] another much shorter list was attempted in the Darfur Commission's report. The list is reproduced here without the relevant footnotes:

(i)   the distinction between combatants and civilians, and the protection of civilians, notably against violence to life and person, in particular murder (this rule was reaffirmed in some agreements concluded by the Government of the Sudan with the rebels);

(ii)   the prohibition on deliberate attacks on civilians;

(iii)   the prohibition on indiscriminate attacks on civilians, even if there may be a few armed elements among civilians;

(iv)   the prohibition on attacks aimed at terrorizing civilians;

(v)   the prohibition on intentionally directing attacks against personnel, installations, material, units, or vehicles involved in a humanitarian assistance or peacekeeping mission in accordance with the Charter of the United Nations, as long as they are entitled to the protection given to civilians or civilian objects under the international law of armed conflict;

(vi)   the prohibition of attacks against civilian objects;

(vii)   the obligation to take precautions in order to minimize incidental loss and damage as a result of attacks, such that each party must do everything feasible to ensure that targets are military objectives and to choose means or methods of combat that will minimise loss of civilians;

(viii)   the obligation to ensure that when attacking military objectives, incidental loss to civilians is not disproportionate to the military gain anticipated;

[59] Report of the International Commission of Inquiry on Darfur to the United Nations Secretary-General, 25 January 2005, § 172.

[60] J.-M. Henckaerts and L. Doswald-Beck, *Customary International Humanitarian Law—Volume 1: Rules* (Cambridge: Cambridge University Press, 2005) and helpfully available online in summary form at J.-M. Henckaerts, 'Study on Customary International Humanitarian Law: A Contribution to the Understanding and Respect for the Rule of Law in Armed Conflict', 857 *IRRC* (2005) 175–212. The methodology for finding customary obligations for non-state actors is not obvious, in fact where the existing human rights obligations of states have been used to divine customary humanitarian law for non-state actors this methodology has been criticized, for states may have only have intended to create obligations for themselves in this context: R. Piotrowicz, 'Displacement and Displaced Persons', in Wilmshurst and Breua (n 58), 337–53 at 340–1. Some of the transposition of obligations from states to armed non-state actors has been similarly criticized as 'aspirations rather than practical' in the context of the obligation to instruct armed forces in international humanitarian law; D. Turns, 'Implementation and Compliance', in the same volume, 354–76 at 362. A more general caution is expressed by M. Schmitt, 'The Law of Targeting', in the same volume, 131–68 at 135, Schmitt invites a comparison with the rules in the *Manual on the Law of Non-International Armed Conflict*, International Institute of Humanitarian Law, San Remo, 2006 (drafting committee: M.N. Schmitt, C.H.B. Garraway, and Y. Dinstein).

(ix)   the prohibition on destruction and devastation not justified by military necessity;

(x)   the prohibition on the destruction of objects indispensable to the survival of the civilian population;

(xi)   the prohibition on attacks on works and installations containing dangerous forces;

(xii)   the protection of cultural objects and places of worship;

(xiii)   the prohibition on the forcible transfer of civilians;

(xiv)   the prohibition on torture and any inhuman or cruel treatment or punishment;

(xv)   the prohibition on outrages upon personal dignity, in particular humiliating and degrading treatment, including rape and sexual violence;

(xvi)   the prohibition on declaring that no quarter will be given;

(xvii)   the prohibition on ill-treatment of enemy combatants *hors de combat* and the obligation to treat captured enemy combatants humanely;

(xviii)   the prohibition on the passing of sentences and the carrying out of executions without previous judgment pronounced by a regularly constituted court, affording all the judicial guarantees recognized as indispensable by the world community;

(xix)   the prohibition on collective punishments;

(xx)   the prohibition on the taking of hostages;

(xxi)   the prohibition on acts of terrorism;

(xxii)   the prohibition on pillage;

(xxiii)   the obligation to protect the wounded and the sick;

(xxiv)   the prohibition on the use in armed hostilities of children under the age of 15.

Although these prohibitions would normally be seen as binding on both sides, and easily transposable to armed non-state armed groups, the idea of armed non-state actors creating a 'regularly constituted court', or having the right to intern detainees, continues to confound scholars.[61] Clearly, a rebel group has no legal authority to constitute a court in the regular way that a government can. Nevertheless, the practice shows that armed non-state actors do fashion a form of judicial process, and will be judged against international standards in this field.[62] Because these standards

---

[61] Commenting on Rule 100 in the ICRC Study, Hampson writes: 'It is difficult to envisage many circumstances in which a non-State armed group would be able to afford detainees the due process guarantees contained in the Study.' For her 'it is difficult to see how any non-State armed group could ensure that a tribunal was established by law without implying some degree of recognition of legitimacy. To require that a group respect a rule that the State makes it impossible to comply with makes a nonsense of the law.' F. Hampson, 'Fundamental Guarantees', in Wilmshurst and Breua (n 58), 282–301 at 287 and fn 20. See also M. Sassòli, 'The Role of Human Rights and International Humanitarian Law in New Types of Armed Conflicts', in O. Ben-Naftali (ed), *International Humanitarian Law and International Human Rights Law* (Oxford: Oxford University Press, 2011), 34–94, esp 92–3.

[62] See further, S. Sivakumaran, 'Courts of Armed Opposition: Fair Trials or Summary Justice?', 7 *JICJ* (2009) 489–513; J. Somer, 'Jungle Justice: Passing Sentence on the Equality of Belligerents in Non-International Armed Conflict', 89(867) *IRRC* (2007) 655–90.

have to be gleaned from human rights law, this is dealt with in more detail in this section below. For the moment, suffice to say that the question of whether one can adjust the scope of the obligations to meet the capacity of the armed non-state group remains divisive. Some would argue that a 'sliding scale' would be appropriate depending on the situation;[63] others would counter that this would undermine the fundamental premise that the laws of war are equally binding on both sides (often evoking the level playing field metaphor).[64]

C. Special agreements, unilateral declarations, and codes of conduct

A further source of international obligations may be found in the special agreements entered into by armed non-state actors. Such agreements will not be applied in international courts where they conflict with peremptory norms of international law, which according to the International Tribunal for the former Yugoslavia (ICTY) include: 'most customary rules of international humanitarian law'.[65] These agreements are not always easy to find or monitor,[66] but it has been suggested by the ICTY that violations of such agreements can be the basis for international prosecutions where these agreements go beyond customary international law.[67]

Such agreements are encouraged by the Geneva Conventions, which state in their Common Article 3 that '[t]he Parties to the conflict should further endeavour to bring into force, by means of special agreements, all or part of the other provisions of the present Convention'. The Hague Convention of 1954 arguably strengthens this obligation, converting the 'should' into a 'shall'.[68] And the CCW reminds parties to a conflict involving an authority representing a people engaged in a national liberation struggle, that '[t]he High Contracting Party and the authority may also agree to accept and apply the obligations of Additional Protocol I to the Geneva Conventions on a reciprocal basis'.[69]

---

[63] See especially the carefully argued contribution by M. Sassòli, 'Taking Armed Groups Seriously: Ways to Improve their Compliance with International Humanitarian Law', 1 *International Humanitarian Legal Studies* (2010) 5–51.

[64] See the engaging debate between Marco Sassòli, Yval Shany, and René Provost in 93 *IRRC* (2011) 425–42.

[65] *Tadić* (Appeal) (Decision on the defence motion for Interlocutory Appeal on Jurisdiction) ICTY, Appeals Chamber, Decision of 2 October 1995 (Case No IT-94-1-AR72), § 143.

[66] For a useful set of references, see C. Ewumbue-Monono, 'Respect for International Humanitarian Law by Armed Non-State Actors in Africa', 88 *IRRC* (2006) 905–24.

[67] *Tadić* (n 65), §§ 143–4.

[68] 'The Parties to the Conflict shall endeavour to bring into force, by means of special agreements, all or part of the other provisions of the present Convention', Art 19(2) of the Hague Convention of 1958.

[69] Article 7(4).

Such special agreements have been considered international agreements by the Darfur Commission, and can be seen as giving rise to international rights and obligations.[70] The Commission seems to limit international obligations to those rebel groups that have a sufficient degree of control to bear the obligations.[71]

Unilateral declarations by armed non-state actors are of considerable relevance, not only for the obvious sense of ownership they engender, but also for those seeking to ensure compliance with these promises. One can make the case that such a declaration, whether or not it is written or formally witnessed, could be considered binding under international law and therefore a further source of obligation; this would be the case even in a situation where the relevant treaty made no provision for declarations with the depositary. In the words of Klabbers:[72] 'Of course, non-state entities may make unilateral declarations even in the absence of a specific provision to that effect, and following general international law, it may very well be that by making unilateral declarations those entities bind themselves on the international level.'[73]

These unilateral declarations are often at a level of generality, for example agreeing to respect humanitarian law. The ICRC has recently proposed that where an armed group has made such a unilateral declaration, 'the development of a code of conduct that includes IHL can be suggested as a logical "next step"'.[74] Key here is the need to reduce the obligations down to a workable list. According to Sassòli: 'a declaration by an armed group that it will comply with "the Geneva Conventions and Additional Protocols" deserves scepticism. There are some 500 articles in those treaties! Often, a two page code of conduct is preferable, which really addresses the genuine humanitarian issues that arise for a given armed group in the field.'[75]

One study of 11 such codes with regard to Afghanistan, Angola, Burundi, Democratic Republic of the Congo, Democratic People's Republic of Korea, Liberia, Sierra Leone, Somalia, Sudan, the Russian Federation, and East and West Timor

---

[70] 'All the parties to the conflict (the Government of the Sudan, the SLA and the JEM) have recognised that this is an internal armed conflict. Among other things, in 2004 the two rebel groups and the Government of the Sudan entered into a number of international agreements, *inter se*, in which they invoke or rely upon the Geneva Conventions', § 76; and see §§ 168–71 and 173 of the Report on Darfur (n 59) for an application of the principles of international humanitarian law through the special agreements.

[71] Report on Darfur (n 59), § 174.   [72] Klabbers (n 10).

[73] Footnote in the original reads: 'As much follows from in particular the *Nuclear Tests* cases (Australia v France, and New Zealand v France), ICJ Reports (1986) at 253 and 457. But see the *Case concerning the Frontier Dispute (Burkina Faso/Republic of Mali)*, ICJ Reports (1986) 554, in which the Court held that unilateral declarations may not automatically be presumed to create binding commitments if there was a more obvious way to create such commitments, for instance through a negotiating process.'

[74] ICRC, *Increasing Respect for International Humanitarian Law in Non-International Armed Conflicts* (Geneva: ICRC, 2008), 22.

[75] M. Sassòli, 'The Implementation of International Humanitarian Law: Current and Inherent Challenges', 10 *Yearbook of International Humanitarian Law* (2007) 45–73 at 64.

revealed that 'for non-State actors, the agreements refer to international human rights customary law',[76] and that all the agreements state that the beneficiaries of humanitarian aid are to enjoy the following rights:

the right to live in security and dignity,
the right to basic needs,
the right to receive humanitarian assistance without discrimination and according to basic needs,
the right to be involved in humanitarian activities of concern to them,
the right to legal and effective human rights protection, and
the right to protection against forced population transfer.[77]

The ICRC has published a number of codes of conduct (some older and some more recent) covering groups from China, Philippines, Colombia, Uganda, Sierra Leone, and Libya. It introduces the collection in the following way: 'Codes of conduct rarely specify whether a particular rule is derived from a certain branch of law—such as IHL or human rights law—or whether they stem from other ethical or social norms. The content of these documents demonstrates the acceptance of the included norms, rather than their concrete foundations in law.'[78] Reflecting on the utility of such codes the following points are made:

First, codes of conduct have the advantage of being short and simple texts. If integrated properly, IHL rules can be stated in a way that is easy to understand and to be followed by members of the armed group. Complex legal texts are unlikely to capture the attention of fighters.

Second, discussions on, and the drafting of, codes of conduct may cause groups to reflect on IHL and on their behaviour in comparison to it. In some cases, the inclusion of norms of IHL in codes of conduct may mean that the leadership of an armed group expresses its willingness to recognize IHL as the applicable law. Even when an armed group chooses to do so purely for reasons of propaganda, the passing of a code of conduct can represent a first step towards the group's improved 'ownership' of rules originally created by states, and towards ensuring respect for the mentioned provisions of IHL. Acceptance of a code of conduct containing IHL norms may lead to further preventative steps within the group, such as the dissemination of the code itself or the instruction and training of the members in its rules. It is to be hoped that a better overall knowledge of the rules of IHL will induce better compliance with IHL.

Finally, the potential of these instruments lies in the reality that armed actors who commit violations in NIACs are not acting completely autonomously. They are usually part of a hierarchical structure, and their actions depend, at least in part, on orders and rules passed on by the hierarchy. As an expression of such rules, codes of conduct can be a powerful tool for compliance. In many instances, the perceived deterrent value of punishment for violations

---

[76] J.-D. Vigny and C. Thompson, 'Fundamental Standards of Humanity: What future?', 20 *Netherlands Quarterly of Human Right* (2002) 185–99 at 193. See also International Council on Human Rights Policy (ICHRP), *Ends and Means: Human Rights Approaches to Armed Groups* (Versoix: ICHPR, 2000), 52.

[77] Vigny and Thompson (n 76), 194.

[78] 'A Collection of Codes of Conduct Issued by Armed Groups', 93(882) *IRRC* (2011) 483–501 at 484.

of rules stipulated by the group itself may be greater than the threat of international prosecution for violations of IHL.[79]

D. When will an armed non-state actor be the bearer of these international obligations?

Having established that armed non-state actors have international obligations that can stem from treaty law, customary international law, special agreements, and unilateral declarations, we still have to consider when exactly these obligations will attach to the group in question. A first question concerns the issue of attribution. There will be complex questions to answer with regard to which acts of which individuals can be attributed to the group, so that the armed group *as such* is in violation of international law. While considerable case-law exists explaining when states are responsible for the acts of their agents, or those under their control and direction, very little thinking has been done with regard to non-state actors and when they might be responsible for the acts of their 'officials'.[80]

A second question concerns the preconditions for the application of humanitarian law. Common Article 3 and 1977 Protocol II apply to various types of non-international armed conflict where the violence has reached a certain threshold. The test in customary international law is similar. This is not the place to go into detail (the reader can find fuller discussions in the Chapters on Terrorism and Internal Armed Conflict) but a citation from the case law of the ICTY may be helpful to understanding the violence threshold.

The criterion of protracted armed violence has therefore been interpreted in practice, including by the *Tadić* Trial Chamber itself, as referring more to the intensity of the armed violence than to its duration. Trial Chambers have relied on indicative factors relevant for assessing the 'intensity' criterion, none of which are, in themselves, essential to establish that the criterion is satisfied. These indicative factors include the number, duration and intensity of individual confrontations; the type of weapons and other military equipment used; the number and calibre of munitions fired; the number of persons and type of forces partaking in the fighting; the number of casualties; the extent of material destruction; and the number of civilians fleeing combat zones. The involvement of the UN Security Council may also be a reflection of the intensity of a conflict.[81]

---

[79] 'A Collection of Codes of Conduct Issued by Armed Groups' (n 78), 485–6.

[80] For an exception, see J.K. Kleffner, 'The Collective Accountability of Organized Armed Groups for System Crimes', in A. Nollkaemper and H. van der Wilt (eds), *System Criminality in International Law* (Cambridge: Cambridge University Press, 2009), 238–69.

[81] *Prosecutor v Haradinaj*, Case No. IT-04-84-84-T, 3 April 2008, § 49; see also S. Vité, 'Typology of Armed Conflicts in International Humanitarian Law: Legal Concepts and Actual Situations', 91(873) *IRRC* (2009) 69–94.

A second criterion is, however, required for the application of humanitarian law to a non-state armed group in a non-international armed conflict. The armed non-state actor has to fulfil certain organizational requirements.[82] While these might be more demanding in the text of Protocol II, the requirements under custom have most recently been spelt out in some detail by the ICTY.

These cases highlight the principle that an armed conflict can exist only between parties that are sufficiently organized to confront each other with military means. State governmental authorities have been presumed to dispose of armed forces that satisfy this criterion. As for armed groups, Trial Chambers have relied on several indicative factors, none of which are, in themselves, essential to establish whether the 'organization' criterion is fulfilled. Such indicative factors include the existence of a command structure and disciplinary rules and mechanisms within the group; the existence of a headquarters; the fact that the group controls a certain territory; the ability of the group to gain access to weapons, other military equipment, recruits and military training; its ability to plan, coordinate and carry out military operations, including troop movements and logistics; its ability to define a unified military strategy and use military tactics; and its ability to speak with one voice and negotiate and conclude agreements such as cease-fire or peace accords.[83]

In order for international humanitarian law to apply to the armed non-state actor, these two criteria (protracted armed violence and organization) need to be satisfied. Having determined the preconditions for the application of international humanitarian law to armed groups, we now turn to another branch of international law: human rights.

3 Human Rights Law

While it may be seen as 'well settled' that international humanitarian law is applicable to the armed non-state actor party to an internal armed conflict, there is an apparent problem with the application of human rights law to such armed groups. This is for three main reasons. First, because, in contrast to international humanitarian law, human rights law is seen in the doctrine as applicable only to states, and is moreover seen as ill-suited to regulating the non-state actors. Secondly, human rights treaties only rarely address armed non-state armed groups. Thirdly, there is a perception that engaging with rebel groups on human rights issues lends such

---

[82] We saw above how the Darfur Commission introduced such a threshold to distinguish the groups fighting in Darfur.

[83] *Prosecutor v Haradinaj* (n 81), § 60. And see further ICTY *Prosecutor v Boškoski*, Case No IT-04-82, 10 July 2009, § 175.

groups a certain legitimacy. This is in part related to the first issue: by claiming that a group has violated human rights one is implying that they are a state-like entity because it is presumed that only states have human rights obligations. Let us look at these obstacles in turn.

Several commentators insist that only states have human rights obligations in this context, and that the non-state actors are exclusively bound by international humanitarian law. Moir, for example, accepts the full application of international humanitarian law obligations for insurgents, but is adamant that such non-state actors have no human rights obligations: 'Human rights obligations are binding on governments only, and the law has not yet reached the stage whereby, during internal armed conflict, insurgents are bound to observe the human rights of government forces, let alone of opposing insurgents. Non-governmental parties are particularly unlikely to have the capacity to uphold certain rights (e.g. the duty to ensure a "regularly constituted" court, the right to due process, being unlikely to have their own legal system, courts, etc.).'[84] Hampson has suggested that there is little legal (as opposed to political) evidence that human rights law applies to armed non-state actors, and, that if we assume that human rights law is based on the relationship between the individual and the authorities, then 'there may be an assumption that the individual owes some measure of loyalty to those authorities, to the extent of accepting the legal character of the rules they promulgate. Such authorities could legitimately punish attempts to overthrow them. Does Colombia, for example, really accept that the FARC can legitimately criminalize opposition to itself on the part of individuals living in areas under their control?'[85] Zegveld considers the issue, but seems to exclude the application of human rights law on the grounds that: 'The main feature of human rights is that these are rights that people hold against the state only'.[86] Pejic sees little reason to take the inquiry further as: 'Given that in most cases the human rights obligations allegedly binding non-state armed groups would be identical to those that clearly bind them under international humanitarian law, the value added of invoking human rights law remains unclear'.[87]

My insistence on the relevance of human rights law can be explained as follows. First, there will be situations where armed groups abuse people outside an armed conflict. In such situations international humanitarian law does not apply. Recent

[84] L. Moir, *The Law of Internal Armed Conflict* (Cambridge: Cambridge University Press, 2002), 194.

[85] F. Hampson, 'Other Areas of Customary Law in Relation to the Study', in E. Wilmshurst and S. Breau (eds), *Perspectives on the ICRC Study on Customary International Humanitarian Law* (Cambridge: Cambridge University Press, 2007), 55–6 at note 17.

[86] L. Zegveld, *Accountability of Armed Opposition Groups in International Law* (Cambridge: Cambridge University Press, 2002), 53.

[87] J. Pejic, 'Conflict Classification and the Law Applicable to Detention and the Use of Force', in E. Wilmshurst (ed), *International Law and the Classification of Conflicts* (Oxford: Oxford University Press, 2012), 80–116 at 84 fn 22.

examples of where this was an issue include the post conflict period in Nepal, where the in-country field mission of the Office of the High Commissioner for Human Rights had to deal with multiple allegations against the Maoists, and the early stages of the uprising in Syria where allegations against the opposition forces had to be addressed by the UN Human Rights Council's Commission of Inquiry. Secondly, there will be bodies whose mandate is limited to questions of human rights. This includes not only intergovernmental bodies and their secretariats, but also national human rights institutions and non-governmental organizations. International humanitarian law currently has far fewer fora and experts bodies for scrutinizing its implementation. Thirdly, human rights protection may supplement and not just complement international humanitarian law in times of armed conflict. Apart from freedoms which are not reflected in the law of armed conflict, for example freedom of expression or the right to privacy, there will be categories of people who fall out-side the scope of international humanitarian law: deserters, those being detained by their own side for breach of discipline, those subject to sexual violence by their own side, and so on. Moreover, as we shall see below, human rights law has taken an expansive approach to what constitutes an armed group and may reach entities that international humanitarian law cannot reach.

It is suggested, therefore, that armed groups should be subject to a wide range of human rights obligations which go beyond their obligations under the laws of war. If armed groups possess enough international legal personality to be subject to a sliding scale of obligations under international humanitarian law, it seems logical that they should also be subject to international obligations under human rights law.[88]

While political scientists have studied the reasons why some groups are more likely to commit atrocities than other groups,[89] and humanitarians see the case for negotiating with such groups in order to reduce such abuses, international lawyers have done hardly any work in developing a theory as to why such groups might have human rights obligations at all. And while some human rights obligations might be admitted, such obligations are simultaneously seen as problematic, as the actors will either not have the facilities to ensure respect for rights such as those associated with fair trial, or the human rights obligations with regard to liberty of the person will make 'efficient fighting impossible'.

Whereas the assumption that international humanitarian law binds armed non-state actors dates back some time (and arguably to the older practice of recognizing insurgency and civil war), the argument that armed non-state actors are bound by

---

[88] For discussion of the ways in which international law is changing to admit participation by actors other than states, see W.M. Reisman 'The Actors Theory Has Ignored' in his General Course, *The Quest for World Order and Human Dignity in the Twenty-First Century: Constitutive Process and Individual Commitment* (Leiden: Martinus Nijhoff, 2012), vol 351 Collected Courses.

[89] J.M. Weinstein, *Inside Rebellion: The Politics of Insurgent Violence* (Cambridge: Cambridge University Press, 2007).

international human rights law has only recently been made with conviction. Fleck puts it as follows:

Whereas the binding effect of international humanitarian law on non-state actors was never seriously disputed, the extent to which this would also apply to underlying human rights norms was shadowed by a widely believed myth according to which human rights could be claimed against the state, but not against individuals. That myth may have been supported by a limited textual understanding of human rights conventions, but was never keeping with custom, neither with practice, and cannot be upheld.[90]

Similarly, the application 'in principle' of human rights *treaties* has been recently recognized by Greenwood who writes:

The obligations created by international humanitarian law apply not just to states but to individuals and to non-state actors such as a rebel faction or secessionist movement in a civil war. The application to non-state actors of human rights treaties is more problematic and even if they may be regarded as applicable in principle, the enforcement machinery created by human rights treaties can normally be invoked only in proceedings against a state.[91]

Leaving aside the question of the enforcement machinery, we can suggest, along with several other commentators,[92] that international human rights principles are increasingly considered applicable to armed non-state actors. The doctrinal debate continues, but the assumptions may be changing. This is due in part to recent UN practice with regard to human rights reports on non-state actors by Commissions of Inquiry and Special Rapporteurs of the Human Rights Council, as well as demands by the Security Council for armed groups to respect human rights (discussed in more detail below).[93] Furthermore, we should recall the reports of the various truth commissions (such as those in Guatemala and Sierra Leone) which

---

[90] D. Fleck, 'The Law of Non-international Armed Conflicts', in D. Fleck (ed), *The Handbook of Humanitarian Law in Armed Conflict* (2nd edn, Oxford: Oxford University Press, 2007), 605–33.

[91] C. Greenwood, 'Scope of Application of Humanitarian Law', in D. Fleck (ed), *The Handbook of Humanitarian Law in Armed Conflict* (2nd edn, Oxford: Oxford University Press, 2007), 45–118 at 76.

[92] See also E. Crawford, *The Treatment of Combatants and Insurgents under the Law of Armed Conflict* (Oxford: Oxford University Press, 2010), 126–9; C. Tomuschat, 'The Applicability of Human Rights Law to Insurgent Movements', in H. Fischer, U. Froissart, W. Heintschel von Heinegg, and C. Raap (eds), *Krisensicherung und Humanitärer Schutz—Crisis Management and Humanitarian Protection: Festschrift für Dieter Fleck* (Berlin: Berliner Wissenschafts-Verlag, 2004), 573–91; D. Fleck, 'Humanitarian Protection Against Non-State Actors', in J.A. Frowein, K. Scharioth, I. Winkelmann, and R. Wolfrum (eds), *Verhandeln für den Frieden—Negotiating for Peace: Liber Amicorum Tono Eitel* (Berlin: Springer, 2003), 69–94; Institute of International Law, *L'application du droit international humanitaire et des droits fondamentaux de l'homme dans les conflits armés auxquels prennent part des entités non étatiques: résolution de Berlin du 25 août 1999—The application of international humanitarian law and fundamental human rights in armed conflicts in which non-state entities are parties: Berlin resolution of 25 August 1999 (commentaire de Robert Kolb) Collection 'résolutions' no 1* (Paris: Pedone, 2003).

[93] See eg Resolutions 1193, 1213, 1214, 1216, 1471, 1479, 1509, and 1528 discussed in A. Clapham, 'Human Rights Obligations of Non-State Actors in Conflict Situations', 88(863) *IRRC* (2006) 491–523 at 499–504.

detail the human rights violations committed by the relevant armed non-state actors.[94]

A. Human rights treaties addressing the behaviour of armed non-state actors

Let us first, however, look at some recent human rights treaties and dispel the myth that human rights law is exclusively addressed to states. Article 4 of the Optional Protocol to the Convention on the Rights of the Child (2000) reads:

1. Armed groups that are distinct from the armed forces of a State, should not, under any circumstances, recruit or use in hostilities persons under the age of 18 years.
2. States Parties shall take all feasible measures to prevent such recruitment and use, including the adoption of legal measures necessary to prohibit and criminalize such practices.
3. The application of the present article under this Protocol shall not affect the legal status of any party to an armed conflict.

The ICRC Manual on the Domestic Implementation of IHL suggests that this treaty provision gives rise to binding obligations on the armed non-state actor. The authors enumerate a number of guiding principles with regard to the protection of children, and then state that the 'Guiding Principles emphasize the *obligations of the States party to international treaties*, but that in no way alters the fact that these obligations also apply to armed groups involved in armed conflicts'.[95] The footnote reference is then to Article 4(1) of the Optional Protocol. Not everyone will share this interpretation. It has been suggested that the use of the word 'should', with regard to the injunction on the armed groups, means that they have something less than a full immediate international obligation. States are said by some to be expressing a desire rather than a command.[96] Nevertheless, it is suggested that one could interpret the assertion that children should not be recruited or used '*under any circumstances*' as a clear indication that the text creates (or crystallizes) a meaningful obligation that allows for no doubt, delay, or derogation.

Turning to the International Convention for the Protection of All Persons from Enforced Disappearance (2006) we find an Article which states that '[e]ach State Party shall take appropriate measures to investigate acts defined in article 2 [enforced

---

[94] Clapham (n 93), 503–4.

[95] 'Guiding Principles for the Domestic Implementation of a Comprehensive System of Protection for Children Associated with Armed Forces or Armed Groups', in the *Domestic Implementation of International Humanitarian Law: A Manual* (Geneva: ICRC, 2011), 371.

[96] For references to different opinions over the effect of this provision of the Optional Protocol, see A. Clapham, *Human Rights Obligations of Non-State Actors* (Oxford: Oxford University Press, 2006), 75; see also UNICEF and Coalition to Stop the Use of Child Soldiers, *Guide to the Optional Protocol on the Involvement of Children in Armed Conflict* (New York: UNICEF, 2003), 17.

disappearances by state agents] committed by persons or groups of persons acting without the authorization, support or acquiescence of the State and to bring those responsible to justice.' Although there were moments in the negotiations where it seemed as though enforced disappearances would be defined to include acts committed by non-state armed groups, this did not happen.[97] While the definition of enforced disappearance is confined by Article 2 to acts committed 'with the authorization, support or acquiescence of the State', the treaty foresees an obligation on states parties to investigate and prosecute the same acts when committed by armed non-state groups (whether or not there is an armed conflict). Interestingly, the provisions which provide for accountability are not necessarily linked to enforced disappearances carried out by state agents. Articles 30 and 31 allow for communications to be sent to the UN Committee responsible for the supervision of compliance with this treaty. The Committee could therefore find itself dealing with complaints concerning 'a disappeared person' where the principal perpetrators were members of an armed group.

Of course the international crime against humanity (rather than the treaty crime defined in this Convention) can still be committed by an individual operating within an armed non-state armed group where the enforced disappearance is 'part of a widespread or systematic attack directed against any civilian population, with knowledge of the attack', and that group is considered a 'political organization' in the words of the Statute of the International Criminal Court.[98]

The African Union Convention for the Protection and Assistance of Internally Displaced Persons in Africa (Kampala Convention) (2009) is perhaps the most explicit treaty to date with regard to what is expected of armed non-state actors. The first point to note is that two different types of actors are included in the scope of the treaty. According to Article 1(d) of the treaty ' "Armed Groups" means dissident armed forces or other organized armed groups that are distinct from the armed forces of the state'; and under Article 1(n) ' "Non-state actors" means private actors who are not public officials of the State, including other armed groups not referred to in article 1(d) above, and whose acts cannot be officially attributed to the State'. The obligations for the members of the *armed groups* and the *non-state actors* are distinguished. The treaty states that:

Members of armed groups shall be prohibited from:

a. Carrying out arbitrary displacement;
b. Hampering the provision of protection and assistance to internally displaced persons under any circumstances;

---

[97] For detail and the statement made by the Philippines that disappearances by non-state actors should be criminalized at the national level, see T. Scovazzi and G. Citroni, *The Struggle against Enforced Disappearance and the 2007 United Nations Convention* (Leiden: Martinus Nijhoff, 2007), 278–82.

[98] See Statute of the International Criminal Court 1998, Arts 7(1)(d) and 7(2)(i), discussed further in Section 5 below.

c. Denying internally displaced persons the right to live in satisfactory conditions of dignity, security, sanitation, food, water, health and shelter; and separating members of the same family;

d. Restricting the freedom of movement of internally displaced persons within and outside their areas of residence;

e. Recruiting children or requiring or permitting them to take part in hostilities under any circumstances;

f. Forcibly recruiting persons, kidnapping, abduction or hostage taking, engaging in sexual slavery and trafficking in persons especially women and children;

g. Impeding humanitarian assistance and passage of all relief consignments, equipment and personnel to internally displaced persons;

h. Attacking or otherwise harming humanitarian personnel and resources or other materials deployed for the assistance or benefit of internally displaced persons and shall not destroy, confiscate or divert such materials; and

i. Violating the civilian and humanitarian character of the places where internally displaced persons are sheltered and shall not infiltrate such places.[99]

On the other hand Article 3(1) (h) and (i) provides that state parties shall:

> Ensure the accountability of non-State actors concerned, including multinational companies and private military or security companies, for acts of arbitrary displacement or complicity in such acts;
> Ensure the accountability of non-State actors involved in the exploration and exploitation of economic and natural resources leading to displacement.

The bigger point here is that these three human rights treaties have started developing their own terminology for armed non-state actors, and the terms are not dependent on the relatively demanding criteria set out in international humanitarian law. There is no suggestion that the group needs to be organized or be engaged in the level of violence required for it to be considered a 'Party to the conflict' under international humanitarian law.

Turning to the legitimacy question, this still dogs the discussion. The African Union Convention is careful to include references to avoid the treaty ever being used as proof of legitimacy for the groups addressed. 'The provisions of this Article shall not, in any way whatsoever, be construed as affording legal status or legitimizing or recognizing armed groups and are without prejudice to the individual criminal responsibility of the members of such groups under domestic or international criminal law'.[100] The emphasis reflects, not only the importance attached to the issue, but also how apparently simple it is to dispel the spectre of legitimacy with simple treaty language. Now that human rights treaties have started to address the behaviour (and obligations) of armed non-state actors, one might hope that such a savings clause will be considered enough to eliminate any legitimacy

---

[99] Article 7(5).   [100] Article 7(1).

fears in the future.[101] Human rights treaties could address armed groups in the same language that humanitarian law treaties address parties to the conflict.[102] In both situations a simple provision precluding any legitimacy implications ought to be enough to see off any legitimacy implications that might be drawn from the existence of the treaty.

B. Human rights field missions, commissions of inquiry, and the UN human rights council

A recent UN report on the protection of civilians in Afghanistan explicitly addresses the human rights obligations on non-state actors:[103] 'While non-State actors in Afghanistan, including non-State armed groups, cannot formally become parties to international human rights treaties, international human rights law increasingly recognizes that where non-State actors, such as the Taliban, exercise *de facto* control over territory, they are bound by international human rights obligations'.[104] It is suggested that reports such as this which address the various armed groups undermining the enjoyment of human rights will become ever more common. Increasingly, UN field operations have had to address the behaviour of armed non-state actors through the lens of human rights law, this may be due to the absence of an armed conflict, due to the need to avoid the language of civil war (non-international armed conflict), in order to respect the sensibilities of the government, or simply due to the mandate and expertise of the personnel involved.[105] In many cases field operations will simply use the language of human rights obligations to ensure a more productive dialogue.

The UN Commission of Inquiry on Libya, in contrast to the Commission on Darfur, has seemingly eased the restrictions relating to the degree of organization

[101] Note the Convention suggests that the states intended to set out obligations for the non-state actors: 'The objectives of this Convention are to: [...] (e) Provide for the respective obligations, responsibilities and roles of armed groups, non-state actors and other relevant actors, including civil society organizations, with respect to the prevention of internal displacement and protection of, and assistance to, internally displaced persons'.

[102] See for a recent example: Art 1(6) of the Amended Protocol II of 1996 to the CCW: 'The application of the provisions of this Protocol to parties to a conflict, which are not High Contracting Parties that have accepted this Protocol, shall not change their legal status or the legal status of a disputed territory, either explicitly or implicitly.'

[103] *Afghanistan Annual Report on Protection of Civilians in Armed Conflict 2011* (2012), iv.

[104] 'See UN Secretary-General, Report of the Secretary-General's Panel of Experts on Accountability in Sri Lanka, 31 March 2011, § 188. Also see Report of the International Commission of Inquiry to investigate all Alleged Violations of International Human Rights Law in the Libyan Arab Jamahiriya A/HRC/17/44, 1 June 2011.' Footnote in the original.

[105] See also F. Rawski, 'Engaging with Armed Groups: A Human Rights Field Perspective from Nepal', 6(2) *International Organizations Law Review* (2009) 601–26.

and stability required to be the bearer of international obligations, and referred only to *de facto* control of territory when addressing the human rights obligations of armed groups.[106] Although the Libya Commission of Inquiry went on in that report to apply the rules on international humanitarian law, a later report was forced to deal with armed groups operating in the post conflict situation. The Commission took 24 October 2011 as the cut off point for the application of international humanitarian law, and so it applied international human rights law to the continuing activities of armed groups after that date. The Commission separates the same sort of violations by the *thuwar* during the conflict from those committed after the cessation of hostilities, referring in the summary to the former as the war crime or murder and the latter as arbitrary deprivations of life.[107] The full report is more detailed:

The Commission established that *thuwar* from various brigades across the country, as well as other opponents of the Qadhafi government, have executed, otherwise unlawfully killed and tortured to death Qadhafi soldiers, security officials as well as those they perceive to be loyalists or mercenaries. During the armed conflict, killing fighters or others who have surrendered, captured or otherwise rendered *hors de combat* amounts to a war crime. Once the conflict ended, such acts have constituted violations of international human rights law.[108]

Similarly with regard to torture and ill-treatment, the Commission reiterated the same formula: 'These acts are violations of international human rights law, and when committed during armed conflict constitute war crimes'.[109] By contrast, with regard to arbitrary detention and enforced disappearances the Commission uses human rights language to describe the acts of the *thuwar*, but fails to draw any legal conclusions, focusing instead on the obligations of the state of Libya under the International Covenant on Civil and Political Rights.

Thuwar forces have been involved in the arbitrary arrest and enforced disappearance of perceived Qadhafi loyalists, security officers, alleged mercenaries and members of the former government. Detainees have been arrested without a warrant, without being told the reasons for their arrest, and without a reasonable suspicion that they have been individually involved in criminal activity. Such arrests have often been accompanied by extortion and pillaging. Detainees are neither informed of their rights, nor provided them in practice.

---

[106] See esp § 72: 'Non-state actors in Libya, in particular the authorities and forces of the National Transitional Council cannot formally become parties to the international human rights treaties and are thus not formally given obligations under the treaties. Although the extent to which international human rights law binds non-state actors remains contested as a matter of international law, it is increasingly accepted that where non-state groups exercise de facto control over territory, they must respect fundamental human rights of persons in that territory. The Commission has taken the approach that since the NTC has been exercising de facto control over territory akin to that of a Governmental authority, it will examine also allegations of human rights violations committed by its forces.' UN Doc A/HRC/17/44, 1 June 2011 (footnotes omitted).

[107] UN Doc A/HRC/19/68, 2 March 2012, § 36.

[108] UN Doc A/HRC/19/68, 2 March 2012, § 252. The full details of the violations committed by the armed non-state actors can be found at §§ 204–50.

[109] UN Doc A/HRC/19/68, 2 March 2012, § 53.

The Commission has information that a number of detainees are being held outside any legal framework in unacknowledged centres, although it was unable to independently confirm this information. The Commission received accounts of enforced disappearance that it deems to be credible.[110]

The early reports of the Commission of Inquiry on Syria remained within the ambit of international human rights law. Interestingly, in the case of Syria in the early stages of the violence there may have been difficulty in showing that the relevant groups were in *de facto* control of territory. The Commission makes no reference to control as a condition for the application of human rights law, and goes on to apply a limited set of human rights obligations to the armed non-state groups. The Commission stated with regard to the Free Syrian Army (FSA):

> The commission carefully reviewed the information gathered on the operations and activities to date of FSA groups. In this regard, the commission notes that, at a minimum, human rights obligations constituting peremptory international law (*ius cogens*) bind States, individuals and non-State collective entities, including armed groups. Acts violating *ius cogens*—for instance, torture or enforced disappearances—can never be justified.
>
> FSA leaders abroad also assured the commission that the FSA was committed to conducting its operations in accordance with human rights and international law. They requested guidance in shaping rules of engagement consistent with this undertaking. The FSA leadership indicated to the commission that commanders in the field currently made their own rules of engagement in accordance with the training received in the Syrian Armed Forces.[111]

The Syria inquiry relied neither on treaty law, nor on the traditional formation of customary international law, but chose to invoke peremptory norms of international law (or *jus cogens*). Considering the scope of *jus cogens* we might add to the prohibition on torture and enforced disappearances by reproducing some of the lists of *jus cogens*.

Chapter III of the International Law Commission's articles on state responsibility is entitled 'Serious breaches of obligations under peremptory norms of general international law'. The Commentary states: 'Those peremptory norms that are clearly accepted and recognized include the prohibitions of aggression, genocide, slavery, racial discrimination, crimes against humanity and torture, and the right to self-determination.'[112] Other examples included in the Commentary are 'the slave trade [...] and apartheid[,] [...] the prohibition against torture as defined in article 1 of the Convention against Torture and Other Cruel, Inhuman or Degrading Treatment or Punishment[,] [...] the basic rules of international humanitarian law

---

[110] UN Doc A/HRC/19/68, 2 March 2012, § 316, although the details of the report seem directed at the *thuwar*, the Commission seems to be applying the ICCPR to the state of Libya (see §§ 259–61) rather than the non-state entity the *thuwar*, and the conclusions do not refer to human rights violations (at § 41), although reference is made to the crimes against humanity of enforced disappearance and how that can involve not only the support of a state but also of a 'political organization' (at § 267).

[111] UN Doc A/HRC/19/69, 22 February 2012, §§ 106–7.

[112] Commentary to Art 26(5), Report of the ILC, GAOR, Supp No 10 (A/56/10), 208.

applicable in armed conflict'.[113] This list is carefully described as exemplary rather than definitive. For completeness one should note that the UN Human Rights Committee has referred to the following as acts which would violate *jus cogens* norms: arbitrary deprivations of life, torture and inhuman and degrading treatment, taking hostages, imposing collective punishments, arbitrary deprivations of liberty or deviating from fundamental principles of fair trial, including the presumption of innocence.[114]

In related developments the UN High Commissioner for Human Rights and the UN Human Rights Council have had to confront the violence in Mali. In a consensus resolution the Council *condemned* 'the human rights violations and acts of violence committed in northern Mali, in particular by the rebels, terrorist groups and other organized transnational crime networks, including the violence perpetrated against women and children, the killings, hostage-takings, pillaging, theft and destruction of religious and cultural sites, as well as the recruitment of child soldiers, and calls for the perpetrators of these acts to be brought to justice'.[115]

The High Commissioner's January 2013 report goes further than the lists of *jus cogens* norms just mentioned. It catalogues a series of human rights violations committed by the armed groups including: the right to life; extrajudicial and summary executions; torture and other cruel, inhuman, or degrading treatment; arbitrary arrests and detentions; recruitment of child soldiers; sexual abuse; attacks on property; violations of freedom of expression and of the right to information; violations of the right to education; violations of the right to health; violations of cultural rights, and violation of the right to freedom of religion.[116]

The Mali resolutions in 2012 and the 2013 report did not need to address the thorny of issue of the mandate of the Human Rights Council in situations of armed conflict or the relationship between these two branches of law. Unlike the situations in Iraq and Afghanistan the focus was solely on the armed groups and no state sought to question the role of the Human Rights Council. Some governments have suggested in other contexts that the United Nations' human rights bodies and

---

[113] Commentary to Art 40(3)–(5), Report of the ILC, GAOR, Supp No 10 (A/56/10), 283–4.

[114] See General Comment No 29, 'Article 4: Derogations during a state of emergency', adopted on 24 July 2001, § 11, UN Doc HRI/GEN/1/Rev.6, 12 May 2003.

[115] A/HRC/RES/20/17, 6 July 2012, § 2; the subsequent Resolution in October speaks of 'abuses' rather than violations, this probably reflects the ongoing reticence over recognizing that armed groups have legal obligations rather than some sort of moral responsibility (cf Pejic (n 88), who admits that armed groups that control territory so that they have developed and can perform government like functions 'could be said to have de facto human rights *responsibilities*'.) At the level of the UN Human Rights Council it seems to make no difference whether we talk about abuses or violations, about legal obligations or de facto responsibilities, the accountability through public reporting of the facts and condemnation of the groups will be to the same effect.

[116] Report of the United Nations High Commissioner for Human Rights on the situation of human rights in Mali, UN Doc A/HRC/22/33, 7 January 2013.

mechanisms have no mandate in times of armed conflict.[117] This suggestion has been convincingly refuted and need not detain us here.[118] It is quite clear that the United Nations and its mechanisms are now reporting on human rights and humanitarian law violations in times of armed conflict. What is changing is the underlying legal basis for holding armed groups accountable for violating human rights.

The United Nations' Special Rapporteur on Extrajudicial, Summary or Arbitrary Executions, Philip Alston, grappled with the question in the context of his report on Sri Lanka. He concluded in the following terms:

Human rights law affirms that both the Government and the LTTE must respect the rights of every person in Sri Lanka. Human rights norms operate on three levels—as the rights of individuals, as obligations assumed by States, and as legitimate expectations of the international community. The Government has assumed the binding legal obligation to respect and ensure the rights recognized in the International Covenant on Civil and Political Rights (ICCPR). As a non-State actor, the LTTE does not have legal obligations under ICCPR, but it remains subject to the demand of the international community, first expressed in the Universal Declaration of Human Rights, that every organ of society respect and promote human rights [...]. [119]

It is increasingly understood, however, that the human rights expectations of the international community operate to protect people, while not thereby affecting the legitimacy of the actors to whom they are addressed. The Security Council has long called upon various groups that Member States do not recognize as having the capacity to formally assume international obligations to respect human rights.[120] The LTTE and other armed groups must accept that insofar as they aspire to represent a people before the world, the international community will evaluate their conduct according to the Universal Declaration's 'common standard of achievement'.[121]

Alston went on to include specific human rights recommendations addressed to the non-state actor: 'The LTTE should refrain from violating human rights, including those of non-LTTE-affiliated Tamil civilians. This includes in particular respect for the rights to freedom of expression, peaceful assembly, freedom of association with others, family life, and democratic participation, including the right to vote. The LTTE should specifically affirm that it will abide by the North-East Secretariat on

[117] See the discussion by F. Hampson, 'Is Human Rights Law of Any Relevance to Military Operations in Afghanistan?', in M. Schmitt (ed), *The War in Afghanistan: A Legal Analysis* (Rhode Island: Naval War College, 2009), 485–524.

[118] P. Alston, J. Morgan-Foster, and A. William, 'The Competence of the UN Human Rights Council and its Special Procedures in relation to Armed Conflicts: Extrajudicial Executions in the "War on Terror"', 19(1) *EJIL* (2008) 183–209.

[119] Footnote in the original reads: '14 Consistent with this analysis, the LTTE-created North East Secretariat on Human Rights released the final version of the NESOHR Charter of human rights in Oct. 2005. Its stated objectives include promoting respect for human rights "according to the Universal Declaration of Human Rights and the International Covenants on human rights [...]".'

[120] Footnote in the original reads: 'UNSC Res 1265 (1999), preamble; UNSC Res 1193 (1998), §§ 12, 14; UNSC Res 814 (1993), § 13.'

[121] UN Doc E/CN.4/2006/53/Add.5, 27 March 2006 (footnote omitted), §§ 25–7.

Human Rights charter'.[122] This approach was reprised in the joint report on Lebanon and Israel by a group of four UN Special Mechanisms.[123]

It is suggested that the situations in Syria, Libya, and Mali have taken the debate forward into new realms. The groups addressed were not necessarily organized or in control of territory in a government like function, and the human rights issues raised in Mali were not simply similar to the obligations expected from groups under international humanitarian law, but rather related to a broad range of issues. These included, for example, 'degrading treatment by armed groups which, because of their extreme interpretation of sharia, harass, flog and beat women who are not wearing the veil or are not properly veiled, as well as men involved in the sale or consumption of cigarettes and alcohol or any other practices or conduct that they consider as not in conformity with sharia'.[124]

Calling for a group to respect human rights is one thing, engaging with the group over why it has not respected such human rights, or even assisting the group to come into compliance, raises a whole new set of legitimacy problems. The issue is less whether the standards apply, but rather that there is a perceived sense of legitimization through the act of engagement. To the extent that the group is most probably proscribed under national law, or even targeted under international law, then association with or assistance to the group carries with it the risk of being considered to have aided or abetted terrorism. While governments have usually understood that the International Committee of the Red Cross have to engage such groups in a dialogue about the laws of war, human rights monitors have been wary of engagement, and humanitarian workers are becoming cautious regarding their dealings with such armed groups due to the risks of guilt by association in the 'war on terror'.[125]

Alston's report on Afghanistan illuminates the dilemma for human rights monitors. Having recalled the demand from some quarters for more pressure to be brought on the Government of Pakistan, he continues:

Others argued that there was a need for international actors to engage directly with the Taliban to understand the rationales for its abusive tactics and to apply targeted pressure

---

[122] UN Doc E/CN.4/2006/53/Add.5, 27 March 2006, § 85. See also the letter addressed directly to the LTTE concerning prevention of killings, investigation, and the application of the death penalty, 'Allegation letter sent 21 November 2005', UN Doc E/CN.4/53/Add.1, 27 March 2006, 320. Note the 'Urgent appeal' sent to the Palestinian Authority regarding death sentences, on 28 February 2005, 321.

[123] Report of the Special Rapporteur on extrajudicial, summary or arbitrary executions, Philip Alston; the Special Rapporteur on the right of everyone to the enjoyment of the highest attainable standard of physical and mental health, Paul Hunt; the Representative of the Secretary-General on human rights of internally displaced persons, Walter Kälin; and the Special Rapporteur on adequate housing as a component of the right to an adequate standard of living, Miloon Kothari; UN Doc A/HRC/2/7, 2 October 2006, § 19.

[124] UN Doc A/HRC/22/33, § 26.

[125] K. Thorne, 'Terrorist Lists and Humanitarian Assistance', 37 *Humanitarian Exchange* (2007) 13–16; G.J. Andreopoulos, 'The Impact of the War on Terror on the Accountability of Armed Groups', in H.M. Hensel (ed), *The Law of Armed Conflict: Constraints on the Contemporary Use of Military Force* (Aldershot: Ashgate, 2005), 171–91.

for change. Prominent elders in the South told me directly that the problem with visits by international envoys was that they only spoke to one side. An international military commander expressed surprise that I was not speaking with Taliban representatives. In general, when I conduct country visits and fact-finding missions, I speak with armed opposition groups, but I did not speak with any formal representatives of the Taliban or other armed groups during my visit.[126] In retrospect, this was a mistake. Taking account of information provided by such sources would permit a more nuanced understanding of Taliban and other AGE [anti-government-element] strategies. While some of the explanations and justifications provided for engaging in abusive tactics would be self-serving and deceitful, there is no reason to assume that the Taliban could never be persuaded to modify its conduct in ways that would improve its respect for human rights. And purely humanitarian contacts have had a positive impact in the past.[127]

The distinction between the 'purely humanitarian' and the human rights approach is narrowing. Why should 'humanitarian' engagement over the treatment of detainees, or access to food parcels, be seen as radically different from human rights engagement over the treatment of women or extrajudicial execution? The assumption may be that such human rights topics suggest that the addressee is a state-like entity while humanitarian engagement suggests a rebel group that has achieved a degree of control and organization. Moreover some may argue that the human rights norms are less universally accepted than the humanitarian law norms. Neither of these suggestions seems convincing. It seems most likely that the Human Rights Council, through its special procedures and ad hoc fact finding missions will inevitably have to monitor both the behaviour of governments and those armed non-state actors that are operating in their territory. In many cases, and Mali is perhaps just the most recent example, the issues may not relate to an armed conflict, and engagement over issues of punishment, discrimination, health care, education, and discrimination will turn solely on an application of human rights law and principles. Furthermore, the UN Human Rights Council's Special Mechanisms will be more and more likely to engage with these armed groups in order, not only to gather information about the situation, but also in order to attempt to get these actors to change their behaviour.

---

[126] 'Initially, I assumed that security concerns, largely of the armed groups' own making, would make doing so impossible. I was also aware that various actors had reservations about the political implications of doing so. Ultimately, I felt I had no option but to abide by these reservations despite the fact that realistic opportunities were presented to me.' Footnote in the original.

[127] Report of the Special Rapporteur on extrajudicial, summary or arbitrary executions, Mission to Afghanistan, UN Doc A/HRC/11/2/Add.4, 6 May 2009, § 42.

C. The work of the Security Council and the Special Representative on Children in Armed Conflict

The Security Council has over the last decade addressed armed non-state actors directly (using the expressions 'all parties', 'factions', or referring directly to the groups by name) and called on them to respect international humanitarian law and human rights. In 2011 it condemned 'human rights violations perpetrated by the FPR' (*Front Populaire pour le Redressement*) in the Central African Republic,[128] and called on the United Nations Integrated Peacebuilding Office in the Central African Republic 'to report on human rights violations perpetrated by armed groups particularly against children and women'.[129] In 2012 the Council strongly condemned 'all abuses of human rights in the north of Mali by armed rebels, terrorist and other extremist groups, including those involving violence against civilians, notably women and children, killings, hostage-taking, pillaging, theft, destruction of cultural and religious sites and recruitment of child soldiers, *reiterating* that some of such acts may amount to crimes under the Rome Statute and that their perpetrators must be held accountable'.[130]

The reference to the Rome Statue in this context suggests a political will to ensure prosecutions of the individuals from the relevant armed groups, but because Mali was already a state party, and had already referred the situation to the International Criminal Court, it would not seem to change much on the legal plane. This can be contrasted with the referrals to the International Criminal Court by the Security Council with regard to Darfur and Libya. In those situations the Security Council's action led directly to jurisdiction over the international crimes committed by members of the relevant armed groups. But we should not overly focus on these jurisdictional questions, the role of the Security Council in this context is also to send a message about the international community's commitment to prosecution and accountability.

The UN's work on children in armed conflict has led to an innovative approach which details violations by non-state actors. Reports by the UN Secretary-General to the Security Council on certain country situations now list the non-state actors concerned and whether or not they are involved in any of six categories of 'grave violations':

(a) killing or maiming of children;
(b) recruiting or using child soldiers;
(c) attacks against schools or hospitals;
(d) rape or other grave sexual violence against children;

---

[128] S/RES/2031 (2011) § 13; see also S/RES/2088 (2013) § 13.   [129] S/RES/2031 § 14.
[130] S/RES/2085 (2012) preambular § 6. There have also been multiple resolutions on Afghanistan, Liberia, Sierra Leone, the Democratic Republic of Congo, Sudan, Somalia, and Côte d'Ivoire.

(e) abduction of children;

(f) denial of humanitarian access for children.

The UN Secretary-General's initial report explains that these violations are based on international norms, and commitments that have been made by the parties to the conflict, as well as national laws and peace agreements.[131] Subsequent reports on various country situations have detailed the 'grave violations of children's rights' committed by the non-state actors concerned.[132] These reports dedicate as much, if not more, space to the violations committed by the non-state actors, as they do to addressing the states concerned. Although the focus started with recruitment, the Security Council has now requested the Secretary-General to include in his reports 'those parties to armed conflict that engage, in contravention of applicable international law, in patterns of killing and maiming of children and/or rape and other sexual violence against children, in situations of armed conflict'.[133]

The mechanism *vis-à-vis* the non-state actor works not only through naming and shaming, but by encouraging the non-state actor to submit an 'action plan' to the Security Council, in this way the group can be removed from the list of violators. One non-state armed group that has supplied such an action plan and claimed to no longer be a violator is the Forces Nouvelles (FAFN) in Côte d'Ivoire, and they were eventually delisted by the Security Council in 2008.[134] The Security Council also has in mind that it could adopt 'country-specific resolutions, targeted and graduated measures, such as, inter alia, a ban on the export and supply of small arms and light weapons and of other military equipment and on military assistance, against parties to situations of armed conflict which are on the Security Council's agenda and are in violation of applicable international law relating to the rights and protection of children in armed conflict'.[135]

While the focus seems to be on violations of applicable law in situations of armed conflict, the work is not restricted to the applications of international humanitarian law. The question of the criteria for a group to be considered a party to an armed conflict is not carefully examined. The universal standard seems to apply outside

---

[131] UN Doc S/2005/72; for a recent look at the legal aspects of these categories, see *The Six Grave Violations Against Children During Armed Conflict: The Legal Foundation*, Woking Paper No 1, Office of the Special Representative of the Secretary-General for Children and Armed Conflict (2009).

[132] The most recent SG report is S/2009/158. Relevant country reports are: Democratic Republic of the Congo, S/2006/389; Sudan, S/2006/662; Côte d'Ivoire, S/2006/835; Burundi, S/2006/851; Sri Lanka, S/2007/758; Burundi, S/2007/68; Myanmar, S/2007/666; Côte d'Ivoire S/2007/515; Sudan, S/2007/520; Chad, S/2007/400; Democratic Republic of the Congo, S/2007/391; Uganda, S/2007/260; Somalia, S/2007/259; Nepal, S/2006/1007; Sri Lanka, S/2006/1006; Nepal, S/2008/259; Philippines, S/2008/272; Somalia, S/2008/352; Chad, S/2008/532; Democratic Republic of the Congo, S/2008/693; Afghanistan, S/2008/695; Central African Republic, S/2009/66; Sudan, S/2009/84; Sri Lanka, S/2009/325; Myanmar, S/2009/278; Sudan, S/2009/84; Central African Republic, S/2009/66.

[133] UNSC Res 1882 of 4 August 2009.

[134] See UN Doc S/AC.51/2008/5, 1 February 2008 for more detail.

[135] Security Council Resolution 1612, § 9.

the strict framework of international humanitarian law. These reports are complemented by the work of the Special Representative of the Secretary-General, whose
work not only feeds into the reports to the Security Council, but also relies on country visits, engaging with non-state actors and facilitating commitments by those
armed groups.[136] The Special Representative's reports and activities have covered
groups which were not recognized as parties to a conflict by the states concerned.[137]
Furthermore, the Special Representative has developed a methodology based on
commitments by the armed non-state actor rather than a strict application of
humanitarian law to a party to a conflict.[138] For these reasons it seems more appropriate to consider this question as a matter of international human rights standards rather than international humanitarian law, and the obligations can be said to
exist whether or not there is an armed conflict. This technique of applying universal
standards to armed non-state actors, and then engaging with them to monitor and
encourage consent has been developed by various non-governmental organizations
including, in particular, Geneva Call.

4 NON-GOVERNMENTAL APPROACHES
AND THE EXAMPLE OF GENEVA CALL

Engagement with armed groups is not limited to UN human rights mechanisms.
Non-governmental organizations such as Human Rights Watch increasingly report
on human rights abuses committed by armed non-state actors.[139] So far its reports
on Hamas and Fatah emphasize the commitment of the Palestinian Authority to
human rights, and the fact that these groups are seen to be in control of territory.[140]
In other situations human rights law is transposed from the state-based treaty

---

[136] See eg the report A/63/227 of 6 August 2008; see further A. Clapham, *Human Rights Obligations
of Non-State Actors* (Oxford: Oxford University Press, 2006), 289–90.

[137] Discussed in Clapham (n 93), 512–13.   [138] See the discussion in Clapham (n 136), 289–91.

[139] Human Rights Watch: 'You'll Learn not to Cry: Child Combatants in Colombia' (2003); 'No
Exit: Human Rights Abuses Inside the MKO Camps' (2005); 'A Face and a Name: Civilian Victims
of Insurgent Groups in Iraq' (2005); 'A Question of Security: Violence against Palestinian Women
and Girls' (2006); 'Renewed Crisis in North Kivu' (2007); 'All the Men Have Gone: War Crimes in
Kenya's Mt. Elgon Conflict' (2008); 'Internal Fight: Palestinian Abuses in Gaza and the West Bank'
(2008); 'Trapped and Mistreated: LTTE Abuses against Civilians in the Vanni' (2008); 'War on the
Displaced: Sri Lankan Army and LTTE Abuses against Civilians in the Vanni' (2009); 'Pursuit of
Power: Political Violence and Repression in Burundi' (2009); 'Under Cover of War: Hamas Political
Violence in Gaza' (2009); 'The Christmas Massacres: LRA attacks on Civilians in Northern Congo'
(2009); 'Paramilitaries' Heirs: The New Face of Violence in Colombia' (2010).

[140] See n 139.

provisions in ways that allude to customary international law or, in one case, where a non-state actor's justice system was found wanting the report stated: 'The fairness of any justice system should be tested against international human rights law criteria that include independence, impartiality, and competency of judges, presumption of innocence, right to legal counsel and adequate time for preparation of defense, and the right to appeal.'[141] We see here that the apparent doctrinal problem of applying human rights law to armed non-state actors has been overcome through simply invoking universally accepted values: fairness, independence, impartiality, competence, the presumption of innocence, and the right to defend oneself. Amnesty International's reports similarly address their concerns to the armed non-state actors in terms which go beyond the strict obligations found under the laws of war.[142]

Let us now consider the approach of a third organization, Geneva Call. The International Campaign to Ban Landmines, having recognized the limits of the Ottawa Treaty to address the possession and use of landmines by non-state actors, set up their own working group which led eventually to the establishment of the NGO Geneva Call.[143] The organization Geneva Call has engaged armed groups in 'Deeds of Commitment' regarding a 'total ban on anti-personnel mines and for cooperation in mine action'. Having negotiated the signature of the Deed, Geneva Call receives the armed non-state actors' regular reports, monitors compliance with the Deed, and helps arrange mine action including demining and destruction of stocks. It is worth inquiring at this point what might be the incentives for such a non-state actor to bind themselves to such a Deed.

First, rebel groups realize the advantages of being seen to abide by international norms in the context of moves towards peace negotiations; secondly, it is much easier to criticize governments and their armed forces for violating humanitarian norms if the group has policies in place to avoid and punish similar violations;

[141] 'Being Neutral is Our Biggest Crime': Government, Vigilante, and Naxalite Abuses in India's Chhattisgarh State (US: Human Rights Watch, 2008), 98. See further, S. Sivakumaran, 'Courts of Armed Opposition: Fair Trials or Summary Justice?', 7 JICJ (2009) 489–513.

[142] See Israel and the Occupied Territories and the Palestinian Authority: Without distinction— attacks on civilians by Palestinian armed groups, AI Index MDE 02/003/2002; Algeria: Steps towards change or empty promises?, MDE 28/005/2003; DRC: On the precipice: the deepening human rights and humanitarian crisis in Ituri, AFR 62/006/2003; DRC: Addressing the present and building a future, AFR 62/050/2003; Haiti: Abuse of human rights: political violence as the 200th anniversary of independence approaches, AMR 36/007/2003; Iraq: In cold blood: abuses by armed groups, AI Index MDE 14/009/2005; Democratic Republic of Congo North Kivu: No End to War on Women and Children, AI Index AFR 62/005/2008; Carnage and Despair: Iraq five years on AI Index: MDE 14/001/2008; Russian Federation; Rule without law: Human rights violations in the North Caucasus, AI Index EUR 46/012/2009.

[143] See M. Busé, 'Non-State Actors and their Significance', 5(3) Journal of Mine Action (2001), online <http://jmu.edu/cisr/journal/5.3/features/maggie_buse_nsa/maggie_buse.htm>. See also S. Shackle, 'Landmine ban failing', New Statesman, 11 December 2008; P. Bongard and J. Somer, 'Monitoring Armed Non-State Actor Compliance With Humanitarian Norms: A Look at International Mechanisms and the Geneva Call Deed of Commitment', 93(883) IRRC (2011) 673–706.

thirdly, factions may be able to distinguish themselves from other armed groups and thus 'get ahead' in terms of dialogue with the government or other actors; finally, in some circumstances entering into such commitments will facilitate access to assistance from the international community in the form of mine clearance.[144]

Such explicit recognition of specific obligations by the groups themselves helps to transform the debate about the human rights obligations of non-state actors. If armed groups are prepared to take on such obligations, arguments about their non-applicability under international law lose much of their force. States may fear the legitimacy that such commitments seem to imply, and international lawyers may choose to accord them no value, but from a victim's perspective such commitments may indeed be worth more than the paper they are written on. In some cases commitments may even go beyond the obligations that would be applicable to them under international law, or indeed go beyond even the obligations on the states they are fighting. In other cases the commitment may fall below what is considered binding under international law. In both cases we should move beyond doctrinal debate over the legal significance of these commitments, and focus instead on their effectiveness and potential to help the victims of armed conflict and violence.[145]

Two further Deeds of Commitment have now been developed by Geneva Call to address first, the issue of the participation of children (defined as those under 18) in armed conflict, and second gender violence. The first states, inter alia, that the group solemnly commits:

1. TO ADHERE to a total ban on the use of children in hostilities.
2. TO ENSURE that children are not recruited into our armed forces, whether voluntarily or non-voluntarily. Children will not be allowed to join or remain in our armed forces.
3. TO NEVER COMPEL children to associate with, or remain associated with, our armed forces.

The second, states, inter alia, that the group solemnly commits:

1. TO ADHERE to an absolute prohibition of sexual violence against any person, whether civilian, member of state armed forces, or member of an armed non-state actor.

---

[144] For further reflections, see E. Decrey Warner, 'Characteristics and Motivation of Organized Armed Groups', in International Institute of Humanitarian Law, *Non-State Actors and International Humanitarian Law. Organized Armed Groups: A Challenge for the 21st Century* (Milano: Franco Angeli, 2010), 59–66; and more generally on the incentives which drive armed groups to comply with humanitarian norms, see P. Hayner, 'Creating Incentives for Compliance: Between Amnesty and Criminalization', in the same volume, 181–6.

[145] S. Sivakumaran, 'Lessons from the Law of Armed Conflict from Commitments of Armed Groups: Identification of Legitimate Targets and Prisoners Of War', 93 *IRRC* (2011) 463–82.

2. TO TAKE all feasible measures towards effectively preventing and responding to acts of sexual violence committed by any person, in areas where we exercise authority.
3. TO ENSURE that persons deprived of their liberty are protected from sexual violence.

By the beginning of 2014 there were 43 signatories to the deed banning anti-personnel mines, nine with regard to the deed on children in armed conflict, and seven for the deed on gender and armed conflict. Geneva Call investigates complaints concerning non-compliance and examines the periodic reports sent in by the groups concerned. While there is said to be overall compliance with regard to the non-use of land-mines, the crucial point is that signature acts as a catalyst for 'undertaking humanitarian mine action activities, such as demining, stockpile destruction, mine risk education and victim assistance'.[146]

5 INTERNATIONAL CRIMINAL LAW

The development of international criminal law so as to apply to individuals fighting with non-state armed groups has been rapid and sophisticated. The International Criminal Tribunals for the former Yugoslavia and Rwanda have developed, not only a complex catalogue of crimes, but also rules concerning command responsibility and joint criminal enterprise.[147] Furthermore, individual criminal responsibility clearly applies outside the context of armed conflicts to situations which constitute crimes against humanity or genocide. And, in some cases, international criminal law has been used to prosecute the members of armed non-state groups for treaty crimes such as torture and hostage-taking.[148] The list is not closed and one should mention the crimes of piracy, forced labour, and enforced disappearance as clearly relevant in this regard.

A cursory glance at the work of the International Criminal Court reveals that it will be individuals from armed non-state actors who are likely to make up the bulk of the defendants there. Four states have all referred their own situations to the Court (Central African Republic, the Democratic Republic of the Congo, Uganda, and Mali); in all four cases the Government is cooperating in order to see non-state

---

[146] Decrey Warner (n 144), 60.

[147] See S. Sivakumaran, 'Command Responsibility in Irregular Groups', 10(5) *JICJ* (2012) 1129–50.

[148] See eg the *Zardad* trial in 2004; R. Cryer, 'Zardad', in A. Cassese (ed), *Oxford Companion to International Criminal Justice* (Oxford: Oxford University Press, 2009), 979–80.

actors tried before the Court. Nearly all the detainees in custody at the time of writing were non-state actors. Governments will not lightly hand over their own forces for international prosecution.

With regard to crimes against humanity, recent developments suggest that non-state actors can be prosecuted for these crimes even where the group is not 'state-like' or a *de facto* authority. This issue remains divisive in the International Criminal Court. The issue turns on an interpretation of Article 7 of the ICC Statute which defines crimes against humanity for the purpose of the Statute as any of a number of listed acts 'when committed as part of a widespread or systematic attack directed against any civilian population, with knowledge of the attack'. And then states that for these purposes, '"Attack directed against any civilian population" means a course of conduct involving the multiple commission of acts referred to in paragraph 1 against any civilian population, pursuant to or in furtherance of a State or organizational policy to commit such attack'. In the context of the Kenyan case the majority in the Pre-Trial Chamber ruled as follows:

> With regard to the term 'organizational', the Chamber notes that the Statute is unclear as to the criteria pursuant to which a group may qualify as 'organization' for the purposes of article 7(2) (a) of the Statute. Whereas some have argued that only State-like organizations may qualify, the Chamber opines that the formal nature of a group and the level of its organization should not be the defining criterion. Instead, as others have convincingly put forward, a distinction should be drawn on whether a group has the capability to perform acts which infringe on basic human values.[149]

Judge Kaul, in his dissent, sets out a threshold for separating organizations that can commit crimes against humanity from other non-state actors that simply commit serious crimes.

> I read the provision such that the juxtaposition of the notions 'State' and 'organization' in article 7(2)(a) of the Statute are an indication that even though the constitutive elements of statehood need not be established those 'organizations' should partake of some characteristics of a State. Those characteristics eventually turn the private 'organization' into an entity which may act like a State or has quasi-State abilities. These characteristics could involve the following: (a) a collectivity of persons; (b) which was established and acts for a common purpose; (c) over a prolonged period of time; (d) which is under responsible command or adopted a certain degree of hierarchical structure, including, as a minimum, some kind of policy level; (e) with the capacity to impose the policy on its members and to sanction them; and (f) which has the capacity and means available to attack any civilian population on a large scale.
>
> In contrast, I believe that non-state actors which do not reach the level described above are not able to carry out a policy of this nature, such as groups of organized crime, a mob, groups of (armed) civilians or criminal gangs. They would generally fall outside the scope of

---

[149] Decision Pursuant to Art 15 of the Rome Statute on the Authorization of an Investigation into the Situation in the Republic of Kenya, ICC-01/09-19-Corr, dated 31 March 2010 and registered on 1 April 2010, § 90 (footnotes omitted).

article 7(2)(a) of the Statute. To give a concrete example, violence-prone groups of persons formed on an *ad hoc* basis, randomly, spontaneously, for a passing occasion, with fluctuating membership and without a structure and level to set up a policy are not within the ambit of the Statute, even if they engage in numerous serious and organized crimes. Further elements are needed for a private entity to reach the level of an 'organization' within the meaning of article 7 of the Statute. For it is not the cruelty or mass victimization that turns a crime into a *delictum iuris gentium* but the constitutive contextual elements in which the act is embedded.[150]

In some ways, this sharp difference of opinion mirrors the doctrinal differences that surround the issue of whether armed non-state actors can commit violations of human rights law.[151] The final judgment and sentencing in the ICC's Kenyan cases will have implications beyond the actual situation in Kenya. The Court's approach will certainly influence how we see the international responsibilities and accountability of non-state actors and the individuals that comprise them.

6 THE ALIEN TORT STATUTE

We have seen that international tribunals can prosecute individuals. But what of the obligations of the armed non-state actor itself? Is it bound by international criminal law? And, if so, how? It is worth looking at these questions in a little more detail as it is suggested there are some quite unusual practical applications. Although the group as such cannot be tried before the International Criminal Court, national jurisdictions may have to consider the responsibility of the group under these international criminal norms. In this regard it is worth looking in particular at developments surrounding the US Alien Tort Statute.

Let us consider a complaint brought against Chiquita for complicity in crimes against humanity, war crimes, and torture allegedly committed with a paramilitary organization (the United Self-Defence Committees of Colombia, AUC). This civil suit under the Alien Tort Statute depends on proving that the protection money offered by Chiquita facilitated international crimes committed by the group (rather than showing that the crimes were committed by any one or more individuals).[152] Other suits have been brought against Chiquita for contributing to the deaths of

---

[150] Decision Pursuant to Art 15 of the Rome Statute (n 149), §§ 51–2 (footnotes omitted).

[151] See further, G. Werle and B. Burghardt, 'Do Crimes Against Humanity Require the Participation of a State or "State-like" Organization', 10 *JICJ* (2012) 1151–70.

[152] *John Doe et al v Chiquita Brands International*, US District Court, District of New Jersey, filed 18 July 2007.

individuals at the hands of the rebel group the Revolutionary Armed Forces of Colombia (FARC).[153] Whether or not these suits are successful, the point remains that there will be situations where the victims of international crimes committed by armed groups may need to rely on the notion that an armed group can commit violations of international criminal law as a group (even if this is only as a way to recover reparation from a corporate accomplice).

A further example of a third party being accused of complicity in an international crime being committed by an armed opposition group is the suit brought against Libya for complicity in the international crimes committed by the Provisional IRA (PIRA). The suit alleges, inter alia, in Count IX that the:

PIRA bombings utilized Semtex as the primary explosive ingredient against the Alien Plaintiffs and the unarmed British population constitute crimes against humanity in violation of the law of nations [...]

Throughout the 1980s and 1990s, this campaign by the PIRA was widespread and systematic against the civilian population.

Libya, through its officials, employees, and agents including but not limited to defendants Qadhafi, Senoussi, Kusa, Ashour, and Bazelya, knowingly, intentionally and directly aided and abetted, intentionally facilitated, and/or recklessly disregarded crimes against humanity in violation of the law of nations.[154]

The complaint goes on to allege the supply of arms and ammunition, training, training facilities, and a base of operations within Libya. And the complaint also alleges that Libya knew that its provisions of arms, etc, would 'be used to carry out crimes against humanity against the civilian populations in Great Britain and Northern Ireland by the PIRA.'[155] An essential link in the legal argumentation is that the PIRA as such committed international crimes. Knowingly assisting such a group with the provision of arms then becomes a violation of international law.

The most recent decisions of the US courts in this area have set down some parameters for what sort of violations by non-state armed groups might fall under this Statute, and what sort of knowledge or purpose will be necessary to find an organization liable for complicity in a violation of the law of nations. It is now becoming clear that the US Courts will not demand a link to state action for the following violations of international law: war crimes, genocide, and crimes against humanity. A Court of Appeals decision reviewed the case law and recalled the jurisprudence which sees violations of Common Article 3 to the Geneva Conventions as war crimes and mentions that: 'This standard applies to all "parties" to a conflict [...] which includes insurgent military groups." '[156]

[153] 'Families Sue Chiquita in Deaths of 5 Men', New York Times, 17 March 2008.
[154] Class Action, McDonald et al v The Socialist People's Libyan Arab Jamahiriya, US District Court for the District of Columbia, filed 21 April 2006, §§ 313, 319, 320.
[155] McDonald et al v The Socialist People's Libyan Arab Jamahiriya (n 154), § 322.
[156] The Presbyterian Church of Sudan et al v Talisman Energy et al, US Ct of Appeals 2nd Cir, Docket No 07-0016-cv, Decision of 2 October 2009, 35 of the unpublished Decision.

7 Options for Prevention, Prosecution, and Punishment

By way of a summary we list here some of the options that could be considered when addressing violations of international law committed by armed non-state actors. It should be stressed at the outset that the response should vary according to the type of conflict and the sort of group one is dealing with. As the research by Weinstein illustrates, rebel groups may have different incentives to respect international law depending for example on their dependency on certain natural resources, the relationship with the local population, and the situation of their leaders.[157]

1. *Criminal accountability* can be emphasized, and, as the prospect of prosecution becomes better understood and more realistic, there is a chance that this can be dissuasive. The scope of the jurisdiction of the International Criminal Court is potentially universal (as the Security Council or a future territorial government can trigger jurisdiction retroactively). But for the moment there is only sparse evidence that fighters or their leaders are dissuaded by this prospect.[158] Nevertheless, as the sentences against former rebel leaders start to trickle out from the International Criminal Court, the dissuasive effect can only grow. Similarly, a few well-chosen prosecutions at the national level in states that have legislation that allows for universal jurisdiction over international crimes committed abroad, could have a dissuasive effect, especially as this implies restrictions on future freedom to travel abroad or to become a respected partner in any future peace deal.

2. *Sanctions* have been adopted by governments, regional organizations and the UN Security Council with a view to changing rebel behaviour. These can take the form of an embargo on a particular commodity from a particular area (say timber), on a travel ban naming certain individuals or members of their family, the freezing of assets, or the exclusion of certain groups from peace talks or other international initiatives. Of course care should be taken not to engage in sanctions which have unintended consequences such as forcing armed groups or factions within groups to take an even more destructive course.[159]

3. *Monitoring and reporting*, as we have seen, are already undertaken by NGOs, the United Nations, and regional organizations. Detailing the atrocities and describing the acts as violations of international humanitarian law, war crimes, crimes against humanity, and so on can focus the debate and the information

---

[157] Weinstein (n 89).

[158] For examples of the dissuasive effect of possible international criminal prosecution, see Hayner (n 144).

[159] Weinstein (n 89), 346–8.

may build the case for triggering an international jurisdiction or eventual trials at the national level. Reporting acts as violations of human rights has in the past been seen as questionable, however, the examples from Mali, Syria, and Libya demonstrate that there will be situations outside armed conflict where a body will be obliged to report on armed groups as human rights violators under international law. This may be because the mandate is focused on human rights violations, because there is no armed conflict, or because no other international normative framework fits the facts.

4. *Encouraging codes of conduct and deeds of commitment* may be appropriate where an armed group is serious about committing to international standards or adapted humanitarian norms. Such codes or commitments may be tailor-made or based on existing texts such as the Geneva Conventions (and their Protocols), they may involve templates such as those used by Geneva Call in the context of landmines, children associated with armed conflict, or violence against women. Such initiatives may prove worthwhile where the group has realized the incentives to comply are significant.[160] Such incentives may include: enhancing reputation with the local and international community, creating better internal military discipline leading to greater efficiency, and a sense of bringing behaviour into line with professed values and goals.

5. *Initiatives aimed at the underlying causes of the conflict* may sap the support which the group enjoys as the group loses any justification that it might enjoy. Of course, these issues are complex and multiple conflicts may now exist primarily to satisfy the greed of the protagonists rather than for some political or group interest. Grievances are often expressed in terms of human rights complaints thereby giving extra traction to appeals to the armed groups themselves to respect human rights. Thinking about the causes of the conflict is obviously the best way to find a longer-term solution, and prevent the next round of conflict.

---

[160] See for more discussion, A. Bellal and S. Casey-Maslen, *Rules of Engagement: Promoting the Protection of Civilians Through Dialogue with Armed Non-State Actors* (Geneva: Geneva Academy of International Humanitarian Law and Human Rights, 2011), esp 22–4.

CHAPTER 31

STATE RESPONSIBILITY AND THE INDIVIDUAL RIGHT TO COMPENSATION BEFORE NATIONAL COURTS

CHRISTIAN TOMUSCHAT

1 INTRODUCTION

OUTSIDE the system created in Europe on the basis of the European Convention on Human Rights (hereinafter ECHR), one mostly finds a huge gap with regard to civil responsibility for human rights violations. It is trivial to note that in our time primary rights are generously conferred on individuals by many international instruments, the most prominent of which are the two International Covenants of 1966 and the corresponding regional treaties, but that the mechanisms available for sanctioning breaches of those rights through individual reparation claims remain generally weak. In the field of international humanitarian law (IHL), the deficit is even larger. Normally, states parties to an armed conflict settle the financial consequences of that conflict in the traditional way, if ever they reach agreement, by concluding comprehensive treaties that embrace also all the claims that their nationals may have acquired on account of the conflict. The most common form of reparation consists of lump sum payments that do not differentiate between the different groups of victims, leaving it to the recipient to distribute the monies received to the injured persons.[1] Many times, such distribution schemes are defective, payments not reaching those most in need. Remedies for individuals are not available within the framework of IHL at the international level.

Would it not be the best solution to follow the logic inherent in establishing human rights as true legal entitlements by complementing the relevant sets of rules by corresponding sets of secondary rights to reparation in case of a breach of the primary obligations, granting the individuals concerned at the same time the right to access a judge in order to assert and enforce their entitlements? And should not the same apply to IHL inasmuch as humanitarian rules are also designed to protect human rights in time of armed conflict? In terms of pure legal logic, this might be deemed an important step forward on the path of effectuating human rights and IHL. However, would such a new scheme fit into the traditional world of international law—which may have good *raisons d'être*? And would the opening up of judicial channels really help the individual—or would he/she only gain a pyrrhic victory by obtaining a favourable judgment? This is the fundamental question one has to ponder when trying to assess the current legal position. It is an undeniable fact that there is much room for improving the situation of victims of human rights violations and violations of IHL. However, one should not be blind to the systemic difficulties inherent in such attempts to individualize international law by pushing back the traditional processes of collective arrangement on a state-to-state basis.

Right from the very outset, any close look at the topic immediately splits up its unity. The phrase 'compensation claims before national courts' seems to easily identify the subject-matter of the following reflections. But the analysis that follows will have to draw many distinctions. The famous 'Basic Principles and Guidelines on the Right to a Remedy and Reparation for Victims of Gross Violations of International Human Rights Law and Serious Violations of International Humanitarian Law' (hereinafter Basic Principles and Guidelines), adopted by the UN General Assembly in 2005,[2] do not really care to assess different factual patterns according to their respective specificities. However, both in terms of substantive and procedural law, the legal framework changes in accordance with those variegated patterns. One

[1] See R. Bank and F. Foltz, 'Lump Sum Agreements', VI *MPEPIL* (2012) 950.

[2] UNGA Res 60/147, 16 December 2005. For a commentary, see T. van Boven, 'Victims' Rights to a Remedy and Reparation: The New United Nations Principles and Guidelines', in C. Ferstman et al (eds), *Reparations for Victims of Genocide, War Crimes and Crimes against Humanity* (Leiden: Martinus Nijhoff, 2009), 19–40; C. Tomuschat, 'Reparation in Favour of Individual Victims of Gross Violations of Human Rights and International Humanitarian Law', in *Promoting Justice, Human Rights and Conflict Resolution Through International Law. Liber Amicorum Lucius Caflisch* (Leiden: Martinus Nijhoff, 2007), 569–90.

particularity, above all, springs to mind: bringing a case before the domestic courts of the respondent country normally does not raise any specific difficulties, whereas suing a foreign government before the national courts of the claimant goes right to the heart of the sovereign equality of states. The venerable maxim: the King can do no wrong, is dead. In our time, no government should enjoy immunity from legal suits at home. To be sure, in the United States, the doctrine is still upheld that, in principle, except for specific regulations to the contrary, the United States itself is not suable;[3] instead, however, the agent(s) responsible for an act or activity allegedly unlawful may to some extent be sued.[4] Likewise, in Japan the doctrine of Kokka-Mutoseki—irresponsibility of the state—has not yet been completely abandoned.[5] But these are remnants of a past which can hardly be reconciled with the rule of law as understood in our time. Moreover, no government should be able to rely on a dusty theory of the act of state, thereby challenging the admissibility of a claim.[6] According to the International Covenant on Civil and Political Rights (Article 14(1)) and also the European Convention on Human Rights (Article 6 (1)), everyone has a right to go to court in the pursuit of his/her civil rights. The guarantee of a judicial procedure applies also to reparation claims based on a tort allegedly committed by public authorities.[7]

In accordance with the general topic of this book, the main emphasis of the following considerations will be on violations of IHL. Obviously, however, human rights law and IHL can never be seen in total isolation from one another. Human rights law constitutes the background of IHL and will never be totally displaced by

[3] See *United States v Lee*, 106 US 196 (1882); *United States v Mitchell*, 463 US 206, 212 (1983) ('It is axiomatic that the United States may not be sued without its consent and that the existence of consent is a prerequisite for jurisdiction'); *Federal Deposit Ins Corpn v Meyer*, 510 US 471, 474 (1994) (absent an express waiver of sovereign immunity, a plaintiff may not sue the United States in a federal court).

[4] 42 USC § 1983; *Bivens v Six Unknown Federal Narcotics Agents*, 403 US 388 (1970). However, by virtue of the Westfall Act (1988), codified as 28 USC § 2679, the United States may be substituted as the defendant in any action where one of its employees is sued for damages as a result of an alleged common law tort. Thus, in such disputes, the specific immunities enjoyed by the United States with their potential to bar the suit become applicable.

[5] See S. Hae Bong, 'Compensation for Victims of Wartime Atrocities', 3 *JICJ* (2005) 186 at 191–7.

[6] Curiously enough, in the *Markovic* case, the Italian Corte di Cassazione, 5 June 2002, 85 *Rivista di diritto internazionale* (2002) 800, 128 *ILR* 652, dismissed an action brought by Serbian victims of air attacks on Belgrade during the Kosovo war on the ground that operations of the Italian armed forces were unchallengeable as 'atti di Governo' (802). In *El-Shifa Pharmaceutical Industries v US*, the US Court of Appeals for the District of Columbia, 27 March 2009, 48 *ILM* 831 at 835, dismissed an action for compensation of the damage sustained by a factory of the claimant in Sudan through an air strike as raising a 'nonjusticiable political question'.

[7] Human Rights Committee, views in *Karatsis v Cyprus*, Comm No 1182/2003, 25 July 2005, [2005] Report of the Human Rights Committee, UN Doc A/60/40, vol II, 377: 'The Committee recalls that the concept of "suit at law" under Article 14, paragraph 1, is based on the nature of the rights in question rather than on the status of one of the parties'; General Comment No 32 on Art 14 of ICCPR: Right to equality before courts and tribunals and to a fair trial, UN Doc CCPR/C/GC/32, 32 August 2007, § 16; European Court of Human Rights (ECtHR), judgments of 21 November 2001 in *McElhinney*, App No 31253/96, §§ 24, 25; *Al-Adsani*, App No 35763/97, §§ 47, 48.

it, even where it takes the role of *lex specialis*. Accordingly, the fence between the two disciplines has many holes and interconnecting channels that must be taken into account as appropriate.[8]

2 COMPENSATION CLAIMS BEFORE THE COURTS OF THE ALLEGED WRONGDOING STATE

A. National reparation programmes

It is a constant practice of countries that went through the traumatic experience of armed conflict to enact legislation for the equalization of war burdens. Generally, war hits the citizens of the country concerned in the most disparate manner. Some persons lose life and limb, others see their homes and factories destroyed while mostly some other groups of the population remain unaffected or even benefit from the events that brought havoc to their neighbours. In such circumstances, the principle of national solidarity requires that some equalization take place. It would be an affront to social justice to leave alone those who suffered most.

Germany has a rich experience in this field. After World War II, almost every German family needed public assistance to recover from the injuries suffered. A particular challenge was the necessity to resettle in the remaining German territory seven million Germans who had fled from the eastern parts of the German territory or had been expelled from those regions, and additionally the majority of the German population in Eastern Europe who were also driven out from their home countries. At the same time, all the victims of racial persecution, irrespective of their nationality, had to be indemnified. Amidst its huge economic difficulties, West Germany launched a comprehensive programme of compensation not only for the refugees and expellees and other war victims, but also for all those who had suffered persecution on racial grounds. These measures had to be financed from public funds, either on the basis of taxes in general or through special levies that had to be borne by those who had survived the war period relatively unharmed ('*Lastenausgleich*'). In general, such systems of equalization of social burdens lack a background of international law.[9] The General Assembly's 'Basic Principles and

---

[8] In this regard, we agree with R.P. Mazzeschi, 'Reparation Claims by Individuals for State Breaches of Humanitarian Law and Human Rights: An Overview', 1 *JICJ* (2003) 339 at 340.

[9] Obviously, a totally different perspective obtains with regard to racial persecution.

Guidelines' presuppose the commission of grave violations. By contrast, national reconstruction programmes are related to basic human needs, trying to overcome an extensive calamity. Payments are awarded to everyone who has sustained significant damage, without much regard for the legal framework of the armed conflict concerned. As already hinted, it is the principle of national solidarity which acts as the driving force. Only against the background of the provisions of the International Covenant on Economic, Social and Cultural Rights could a responsible government be called upon today to employ their best efforts in order to secure the rights guaranteed by that instrument, the right to food, the right to adequate housing, and the right to work, just to name the most prominent ones of the relevant rights. Entitlements established by national legislation can of course be pursued before the courts of the country concerned without any hindrance—provided they have the nature of true individual rights.

B. Tort claims arising from military operations during non-international armed conflict

Tort claims resulting from military operations inside the national territory have a more complex structure *ratione materiae*. Although hostilities resulting from an international armed conflict may take place on national territory, as this happened, eg during the last months of World War II in Germany, this section shall only deal with non-international armed conflict between governmental armed forces and groups of insurgents. Procedurally, such disputes should not cause any difficulties to the extent that claims are asserted by citizens of the country concerned. For them, the way to a judge, ie their national judge, should be open.

(a) With regard to this type of conflict, reliance on domestic law of responsibility seems to be an almost natural option. However, as already pointed out, nations normally regulate the consequences of civil war and other disturbances of public order by statutes that focus on the actual damage a person has suffered, disregarding the criterion of lawfulness or unlawfulness of the act or activity that caused the damage. In this regard, it is a matter of the utmost importance to clarify whether international law may provide a basis for asserting reparation claims on account of damage sustained as a consequence of non-international conflict.

(b) It is common knowledge that still in the first half of the twentieth century states were fundamentally opposed to accepting any interference of international law with internal power struggles. Thus, the 1907 Hague Rules do not address non-international armed conflict. Only when after World War II the entire edifice of humanitarian law was re-considered, did it become possible to introduce a mini-code for that type of armed conflict through Common Article 3 of the four Geneva Conventions of 1949. In 1977 a further step was taken with the adoption of Additional Protocol II (AP II). But none of these legal texts touches upon the issue of civil responsibility in case that the applicable rules are breached by one of the parties. The aim of the effort undertaken in 1949 was to introduce a minimum of civilized conduct in conflicts hitherto characterized by an extreme degree of brutality. None of the participating states wished to cross that threshold by establishing, in addition, rules on civil responsibility which, in the case of non-international conflict, obviously could not have been of easy application. Humanitarian law relies on reciprocity as one of its central pillars.[10] However, with regard to civil responsibility or liability, reciprocity dwindles down to a hollow chimera during non-international conflict. Insurgent groups are unlikely respondents to claims asserting their collective responsibility. Of course, one finds many examples of violations of the applicable rules of IHL by insurgent groups. But there does not seem to exist any consistent practice of reparation claims made against such groups.[11] Thus, the conclusion seems inescapable that a violation of the rules governing non-international armed conflict does not entail reparation claims in the relationship between the parties to hostilities.[12] Given this state of affairs, it is even less likely that such entitlements may accrue to individual victims.

At first glance, this gap seems to be wholly unsatisfactory. Should one not depart from the reciprocal nature of IHL with regard to non-international armed conflict by sanctioning in any event misconduct on the part of governmental forces by postulating the state's civil accountability? This approach would correspond to the line taken by the 'Basic Principles and Guidelines'. On closer reflection, however, it appears that there is no real need for such a constructive effort. On the one hand, human rights law can serve as a defence bulwark of last resort. On the other hand, to constructively face up to the economic and financial consequences of civil war is the natural task of domestic legislation, which cannot be helped a great deal by some vague principles of international law. It must be acknowledged, though, that on this issue there is wide room for research and reflection.

(c) It remains to examine whether international human rights law may be of any help to claimants who wish to bring a suit before the courts of the alleged tortfeasor.

Within the Inter-American system, the issue arose in the *La Tablada* case where an attack by an armed group on some army barracks in Argentina (1989) had to

[10] For a recent study, see S. Watts, 'Reciprocity and the Law of War', 50 *Harvard International Law Journal* (2009) 365–434.

[11] Just one example is cited by E.-C. Gillard, 'Reparation for Violations of International Humanitarian Law' 85(851) *Review of the International Red Cross* (2003) 529 at 535. Some additional fragmentary evidence is reported in the ICRC Commentary by J.-M. Henckaerts and L. Doswald Beck, *Customary International Humanitarian Law*, vol I: Rules (Cambridge: Cambridge University Press, 2005), 549.

[12] Indeed, Henckaerts and Doswald-Beck note that 'the consequences of such responsibility are not clear', Henckaerts and Doswald Beck (n 11), 536, 550. W. Heintschel von Heinegg, 'Entschädigung für Verletzungen des humanitären Völkerrechts', 40 *Berichte der Deutschen Gesellschaft für Völkerrecht* (2003) 1 at 54, denies the existence of any rule providing for compensation in non-international armed conflict.

be assessed. In this proceeding, the Inter-American Commission affirmed its competence to apply IHL as the most adequate body of law for the assessment of armed hostilities.[13] However, three years later, in *Las Palmeras v Colombia* the Inter-American Court of Human Rights (IACtHR) denied such competence, holding that its was only entrusted with authority to enforce the American Convention on Human Rights (IACHR) and other treaties explicitly committed to its jurisdiction.[14] In a *volte-face*, only a few months later, in *Bámaca Velásquez v Guatemala* it held that it was not debarred from interpreting the Convention in the light of IHL.[15] It specified, however, that responsibility could only be incurred under the provisions of the ACHR.

The ECHR, on the other hand, generally does not apply during armed conflict. Article 15(1) provides that in time of war 'any High Contracting Party may take measures derogating from its obligations under this Convention'. Yet, some core guarantees, in particular the right to life (Article 2), remain unaffected even during a state of emergency. Where such a derogation has not been made, human rights law and IHL exist side by side, IHL constituting *lex specialis*, but not totally displacing the former, as clarified by the International Court of Justice (ICJ) in the *Wall* case[16] and later judgments.[17] This parallelism holds true also for the International Covenant on Civil and Political Rights, where the Human Rights Committee explained in General Comment No 31 (para 11):

As implied in General Comment No. 29 on States of Emergencies, the Covenant applies also in situations of armed conflict to which the rules of international humanitarian law are applicable. While, in respect of certain Covenant rights, more specific rules of international humanitarian law may be specially relevant for the purposes of the interpretation of Covenant rights, both spheres of law are complementary, not mutually exclusive.[18]

In fact, in a number of instances the European Court of Human Rights (ECtHR) has investigated and adjudicated disputes that arose from armed activities that sometimes reached the level of armed conflict. Most of the struggle in the Kurdish provinces of Turkey seems to have remained below that threshold. A case where Turkish troops had invaded Iraq failed because it could not be established that the victims had been under the jurisdiction of Turkey as required by Article 1 of ECHR.[19]

---

[13] Inter-American Commission on Human Rights, Case No 11.137, Report 55/97, Doc OEA/Ser.L/V/II.97, <http://www.cidh.oas.org/annualrep/97eng/Argentina11137.htm>, §§ 157–71.

[14] Judgment of 4 February 2000, C 67, § 33.

[15] Judgment of 25 November 2000, C 70, §§ 206–9.

[16] *Legal Consequences of the Construction of a Wall in the Occupied Palestinian Territory*, ICJ Reports 2004, 136, 178, § 106.

[17] *Armed Activities on the Territory of the Congo (Democratic Republic of the Congo v Uganda)*, ICJ Reports 2005, 168, 242–4, §§ 216–19.

[18] The Nature of the General Legal Obligation Imposed on States Parties to the Covenant, UN Doc CCPR/C/21/Rev.1/Add.13, 26 May 2004.

[19] ECtHR, *Issa and Others v Turkey*, App No 31821/96, 16 November 2004.

It is clear, however, that some of the cases that came to the Court from Chechnya emerged from organized fighting that went well beyond 'internal disturbances and tensions, such as riots, isolated and sporadic acts of violence' (AP II, Article 1). In those cases, the ECtHR referred in particular to the right to life, assessing whether the Russian army had taken all the precautionary measures that were necessary for the protection of the civilian population. By applying the parameters of necessity and proportionality, it used the same yardstick as it would have to be resorted to in a case to be appraised under the auspices of IHL.[20] It may be doubtful whether full military combat between enemy armies could be assessed in the same manner.[21]

Since the ECtHR awarded considerable sums of reparation to the claimants in those cases where it found that the Russian armed forces had operated without due regard for the civilian population, one may well ask whether the Convention provides for reparation claims independently of the procedural situation or whether the compensation amounts awarded to the applicants depend on a specific finding by the ECtHR. If the latter alternative is true, it must be concluded that the ECHR lacks an international reparation regime which travels, together with the other substantive provisions, to the domestic legal orders of the 47 states members.[22] Textual arguments, in particular, militate in fact for this construction. Article 41 of ECHR leaves it primarily to the domestic law of states to make reparation. It specifies that the Court may make a finding on reparation only 'if the internal law of the [...] Party [concerned] allows only partial reparation to be made'. In other words, allocation of compensation under Article 41 of ECHR is a subsidiary remedy that becomes applicable '*à titre subsidiaire*'. Although the ECHR requires states to put an end to any violation found by the ECtHR and to make reparation for the loss suffered by the applicant, this obligation of the wrongdoing state does not seem to be conceptualized by the ECtHR as a true individual right of the individual, in particular because a wide margin of discretion is left to the responsible state as to how the reparation due should be effected.[23]

As far as the International Covenant on Civil and Political Rights is concerned, no relevant practice can be found as yet. It also remains controversial whether the

---

[20] See the two judgments of 24 February 2004: *Isayeva, Yusupova and Bazayeva v Russia*, App Nos 57947/00, 57948/00 and 57949/00, §§ 168–200; *Isayeva v Russia*, App No 57950/00, §§ 172–201. Commenting on these decisions, W. Abresch, 'A Human Rights Law of Internal Armed Conflict: The European Court of Human Rights in Chechnya' 16 *EJIL* (2005) 741. See now *Al-Skeini and Others v United Kingdom*, App No 55721/07, 7 July 2011, § 164.

[21] A lucid analysis of the legal position is provided by C. Droege, 'Effective Affinities? Human Rights and Humanitarian Law', 90(871) *International Review of the Red Cross* (2008) 501–48.

[22] The different modalities of implementation of the ECHR will not be discussed here.

[23] See eg *Brumarescu v Romania*, App No 28342/95, 23 January 2001, §§ 19, 20; *Iatridis v Greece*, App No 31107/96, 19 October 2000, §§ 32, 33; *Verein gegen Tierfabriken v Switzerland*, App No 32772/02, 30 June 2009, §§ 85, 86. However, more recently the ECtHR has not shied away from ordering, under specific circumstances, specific performance, see, in particular, *Fatullayev v Azerbaijan*, App No 40984/07, 22 April 2010.

Covenant confers true individual rights on aggrieved individuals; weighty arguments speak against this reductionist interpretation, though. Lastly, it is well known that the Human Rights Committee can do no more than issue recommendations ('views') to states.

C. Tort claims arising from international armed conflict

Claims can also be brought before the courts of the alleged wrongdoing state on account of torts committed or allegedly committed abroad, in particular by aliens, victims of military activities carried out in the course of international armed conflict. It is particularly tempting to choose this option since the legal hurdles seem to be relatively low. In general, states cannot invoke immunity if they are impleaded before their own tribunals.[24] And the domestic law of responsibility of the alleged wrongdoer may provide a reliable legal foundation.

(a) Logically, a state would become liable under the generally applicable domestic regime of responsibility if its agents infringe any of the obligations incumbent upon them. All states have created such sets of rules that specify what criteria must be met if damage has been caused by governmental authorities. Normally, it pertains to the duties of governmental agents to abide by the rules domestically in force. In respect of international treaties, including IHL, the situation varies from country to country. Some states—like the United Kingdom—do not integrate international treaties into their domestic legal system. It is highly significant that in the Iraqi case of *Al-Skeini v Secretary of State for Defence* the applicability and relevance of IHL was hardly discussed.[25] Therefore, it would appear that no legal claim can be based on the allegation that conventional rules of IHL have been infringed. Other States, like the United States, take the view that humanitarian law is generally non-self-executing and can therefore not be invoked by individuals.[26] In the debate on the Guantánamo prison camp the alleged non-self-executing character of the Geneva Conventions played a key role; only recently has the applicability of the Geneva Conventions been affirmed as so being directed by a US statute.[27]

If, in principle, the legal system of a given country permits invocation of IHL, the next question is whether the ordinary rules on responsibility of the state can be resorted to in case of armed hostilities, as the instrument to make IHL enforceable through compensation claims. Many legal systems exclude from their scope any

---

[24] But see n 3 concerning the legal position in, for example, the United States.

[25] House of Lords, *Al-Skeini v Secretary of State for Defence* [2007] UKHL 26. In § 26 of this judgment, it is solely mentioned that IHL does not provide a right to demand an investigation. See now the judgment of the ECtHR in *Al-Skeini and Others v United Kingdom* (n 20).

[26] *Johnson v Eisentrager*, 339 US 763 (1950).

[27] *Hamdan v Rumsfeld*, 548 US 557 (2006), section VI.D.i. But see the political question doctrine recently raised in *El-Shifa Pharmaceutical Industries v US* (n 3).

damage that has been caused by their security forces in armed conflict. This is the traditional rule in Germany: war damages are not covered by the ordinary regime of state responsibility. In recent years, the Federal Supreme Court had to address this issue at great length in the *Distomo* case, where the relatives of the victims of a massacre perpetrated by German SS units during their withdrawal from Greece (as a revenge act after the killing of several German soldiers by partisans) sought damages against the German state. Their action was dismissed as unfounded by a judgment of 26 June 2003.[28] The Court held that

[a]ccording to the understanding and the overall system of the German law in force at the time the act was committed (1944) the military acts during war in a foreign State, which are attributable under international law to the German Reich, did not fall within the scope of state liability for official act as enshrined [in the legislation at that time in force].[29]

This holding was slightly modified in the later case of the *Bridge of Varvarin* where the Court observed that it could be left open whether a doctrine that was applicable in 1944 could be maintained after the entry into force of the Basic Law since the action brought by the claimants was to be rejected on other grounds.[30] The *Varvarin* dispute had its origin in the Kosovo war where a bridge spanning the river Morava was bombed by NATO airplanes on 30 May 1999. Ten people died, 17 were wounded. They were all civilians. The question arose whether the bridge could legitimately be considered a military target. It was never contended by anyone of the NATO countries that it had been actually used for military purposes during the time of the attack. German planes were not involved in the operation, but Germany had taken part in the strategic planning of the hostilities.

The same ground rule can also be found in other countries. In the United Kingdom, the principle of 'combat immunity' removes the jurisdiction of the courts to adjudicate on the merits of disputes on occurrences during actual fighting. It is true, however, that this exception is narrowly construed to cover only situations where objective military necessity motivated the use of arms.[31] In the United States, the Federal Tort Claims Act (1948), which derogates from the general principle of state immunity, establishes that no claim may be brought that arises 'out of the combatant activities of the military or naval forces'.[32] Additionally, the Act denies access

---

[28] BGHZ 155, 279, English translation: 42 *ILM* (2003) 1030.

[29] BGHZ 155, 279, English translation: 42 *ILM* (2003) 1039.

[30] Federal Supreme Court, 2 November 2006, 62 *Juristenzeitung* (2007) 532, <http://juris.bundesger-ichtshof.de/cgi-bin/rechtsprechung/document.py?Gericht=bgh&Art=en&Datum=2006-11&Sor t=1&nr=38105&pos=2&anz=288>, with critical note by S. Baufeld, 'Die schadensersatzrechtliche Stellung ziviler Opfer von militärischen Operationen', Federal Supreme Court, 2 November 2006, 62 *Juristenzeitung* (2007) 502–9. The Court of Appeals in Cologne, 28 July 2005, 2005 *NJW* 2861, at 2862 s, had previously argued that the denial of an individual reparation claim in instances of war operations could not be maintained under the auspices of the Basic Law, which had introduced a new philosophy based on human dignity.

[31] See *Bici v Ministry of Defence* [2004] EWHC 786 (QB), §§ 84–93.

[32] 28 USC § 2680 (j).

to US courts to 'any claim arising in a foreign country'.[33] If instead under the *Bivens* rule[34] the responsible officials are sued individually, a further defence stands in the way of claims based on the violation of constitutional rights in that the alleged misconduct must have violated 'clearly established rights [...] of which a reasonable person would have known'.[35] Thus, litigation regarding war damages has almost no room in the United States.

It is true that harm resulting from armed conflict pertains to a specific class of damage originating from state conduct that by necessity causes mass injuries. Accordingly, the financial consequences of armed conflict cannot be dealt with as everyday problems that fit into the ordinary legal framework. There are good grounds to argue that the general regime of state responsibility is unsuitable for instances of violations of IHL occurring in armed conflict of either type. It should be noted, in this connection, that, as far as information is available, the United States has never agreed to pay, as a matter of legal obligation, any financial compensation to victims of the wars in Vietnam, Iraq, and Afghanistan, and there have been no attempts by victims to enforce claims by judicial means they believe to have. In fact, this finding corresponds to the objective and spirit of the Federal Tort Claims Act regarding combat activities. Generally, domestic law in this field protects national interests only. There seems to be an international consensus that the settlement of war damages can, if at all, only be effected through collective means, in particular by way of international treaties. Or else, *ex gratia* payments are made.

(b) Given the reluctance of national legislation to provide for war damages caused by their armed forces, the question obviously arises whether individuals may derive rights to reparation, in particular financial compensation, from the relevant rules of IHL. It is not a novelty in international law that states are obligated to make good the harm they or their agents have caused through a breach of their commitments under international law; in fact, this has become the general standard. One can even say that IHL is one of the disciplines where that idea took firm roots at a relatively early stage already. Hague Convention IV of 1907 provides explicitly (Article 3):

A belligerent party which violates the provisions of the said Regulations shall, if the case demands, be liable to pay compensation. It shall be responsible for all acts committed by persons forming part of its armed forces.

At first glance, this is a clear statement. But it does not reveal to whom the right to compensation shall accrue, to the direct victim of the injurious act or to the state whose national has sustained harm. According to the general conception of international law prevailing before World War I, the conclusion seems inescapable that

---

[33] 28 USC § 2680 (k).

[34] *Bivens v Six Unknown Federal Narcotics Agents*, 403 US 388, 397 (1971).

[35] *Harlow v Fitzgerald*, 457 US 800, 818 (1982); *Saucier v Katz*, 533 US 194, 201 (2001).

only the latter answer can be true. Individuals as holders of rights were alien to that conception. International law was regarded as inter-state law; it was conceptualized as a cobweb of relations between sovereign states.[36] Whenever an individual suffered an injury at the hands of a foreign state, no personal claim arose to his/ her benefit: it was the state of nationality that was regarded as the injured actor, and accordingly it was left to that state to assert the right to reparation through the mechanism of diplomatic protection. In the *Mavrommatis* case,[37] the Permanent Court of International Justice held:

By taking up the case of one of its subjects and by resorting to diplomatic action or international judicial proceedings on his behalf, a State is in reality asserting its own rights—its right to ensure in the person of its subjects, respect for the rules of international law.[38]

Accordingly, good grounds militate for interpreting Article 3 of Hague Convention IV in that same sense: if liability occurs, the beneficiary of a right to financial compensation will be the state injured in the person of one of its subjects.

Frits Kalshoven has contended that this understanding of Article 3 of Hague Convention IV is erroneous. In order to challenge the majority view, he relies essentially on the drafting history.[39] It can indeed be shown that the German Government, which had introduced some amendments in one of the Commissions of the Peace Conference, spoke in one of these amendments of compensation for 'persons'. This proposed rule, however, was confined to 'neutral persons', ie citizens of neutral countries, an exception in the course of warfare. The other proposed rule said in a very unspecific manner that in case of prejudice to the adverse party 'the *question* of indemnity will be settled at the conclusion of peace'.[40] In other words, no suggestion was made that generally individual war victims should be compensated, just the contrary: the German proposal proceeded from the assumption that the traditional pattern of making reparation for war damages to the 'adverse party' by way of inter-state treaties should be maintained. In the ensuing debate, a controversy arose concerning the possibility of distinguishing between neutral persons and nationals of the opponent party. It is true that at the same time the speakers referred mostly to *persons* having sustained injury.

---

[36] See eg F. von Liszt, *Das Völkerrecht* (Berlin: Springer, 1898), 21: 'Nur die Staaten [...] sind Subjekte des Völkerrechts: Träger von völkerrechtlichen Rechten und Pflichten'.

[37] Series A No 2, 30 August 1924.

[38] Series A No 2, 30 August 1924, 12.

[39] 'State Responsibility for Warlike Acts of the Armed Forces', 40 *ICLQ* (1991) 827 at 830–2); reconfirmed: 'Some Comments on the International Responsibility of States', in W. Heintschel von Heinegg and V. Epping (eds), *International Humanitarian Law Facing New Challenges* (Berlin et al: Springer, 2007), 207 at 212.

[40] The relevant texts are reproduced in the original French version by M. Frulli, 'When Are States Liable Towards Individuals for Serious Violations of Humanitarian Law? The Markovic Case', 1 *IJCJ* (2003) 406 at 417. For the English version, see *The Proceedings of the Hague Peace Conferences. The Conference of 1907. Acts and Dcouments* (vol III, New York: Oxford University Press, 1921), 139.

But the British delegate, Lord Reay, also said that indemnification of members of the hostile party:

depends upon the conditions which will be inserted in the treaty of peace and which will be the result of negotiations between the belligerents.[41]

Eventually, the texts were merged and got their final shape—where the beneficiary of the proposed reparation claim is not mentioned. A sober assessment of the materials referred to yields no real clue that eventually, at the end of their deliberations, the drafters intended to set forth individual entitlements. Instead, the conclusion seems to be warranted that they renounced setting forth a special rule in favour of nationals of neutral countries.[42] Indeed, the persons convening in The Hague were no inexperienced lawyers. In particular, the German side was certainly well aware of the modalities of the Frankfurt Peace Treaty[43] that had brought to its final conclusion the Franco-German War of 1870/71. There were simply no precedents that could have been relied upon to open up an avenue for individual claims in case of violation of the Hague Rules.

The gap between the alleged agreement on the scope and meaning of Article 3 and the actual practice is also present when a glance is cast at the diplomatic practice following the 1907 Peace Conference. The Versailles Peace Treaty[44] does not care to identify specific violations of the laws of war. It is well known that in a grand gesture it imposed all the guilt concerning the outbreak of World War I on Germany. Article 231 provided:

The Allied and Associated Governments affirm and Germany accepts the responsibility of Germany and her allies for causing all the loss and damage to which the Allied and Associated Governments and their nationals have been subjected as a consequence of the war imposed upon them by the aggression of Germany and her allies.

An approach basing responsibility on specific infringements was irreconcilable with this one-sided assessment of the historical circumstances. It would also have required investigating whether on the part of the Allied Powers, too, violations of the applicable rules had been committed. Similar observations can be made regarding World War II. When the victorious Allied Powers convened at Potsdam in July/ August 1945 in order to establish a programme of reparations which Germany would have to shoulder, none of the statesmen present at the conference table reasoned in terms of individual entitlements in favour of each and every victim of the atrocious crimes that had been committed by Nazi Germany. The document that

---

[41] *The Proceedings of the Hague Peace Conferences* (n 40), 142.

[42] Heintschel von Heinegg (n 12), 31. See also the careful assessment of the drafting history by the Tokyo district court in the judgment of 7 December 1963 (n 63).

[43] Reprinted in: W.G. Grewe (ed), *Fontes Historiae Iuris Gentium*, vol 3/1 (Berlin and New York: Walter de Gruyter, 1992), 89.

[44] Of 28 June 1919, reprinted in W.G. Grewe (ed), *Fontes Historiae Iuris Gentium*, vol 3/2 (Berlin and New York: Walter de Gruyter, 1992), 683.

emerged from the Conference,[45] whatever its correct name and legal character,[46] stated quite unequivocally that 'Germany' had to compensate for the 'loss and suffering' caused by it, and that reparation had to be made to the USSR, on the one hand, and to the United States, the United Kingdom 'and other countries entitled to reparation'. The assumption that the members of the victorious Alliance—and not their citizens—were to be the beneficiaries of the reparation measures underlay also the dispositions over German territory. More than 100,000 sq km (exactly 114,267 sq km) were provisionally separated from the German territory and placed under foreign administration. It stands to reason that in particular such territorial changes do not square within a reparation scheme that would recognize individuals as rights holders.

Thus, taking as the most trustworthy yardstick for the interpretation of Article 3 of the Hague Rules, the Vienna Convention on the Law of Treaties, which acknowledges practice as a factor to be taken into account (Article 31(3)(b)), one arrives unavoidably at the conclusion that inferences that seek to derive individual entitlements from that provision, lack any firm basis.[47]

The clause in the 1949 Geneva Conventions on 'Responsibilities of the Contracting Governments'[48] does not deal directly with the liability deriving from breaches of the new regime of humanitarian law as it was conceived after the tragic experiences of World War II. Nevertheless, the commentary of the International Committee of the Red Cross is quite remarkable. It states categorically:

> As regards material compensation for breaches of the Convention, it is inconceivable, at least as the law stands today, that claimants should be able to bring a direct action for damages against the State in whose service the person committing the breach was working. Only a State can make such claims on another State, and they form part, in general, of what is called 'war reparations'.[49]

Additionally, it is uncontested that Article 91 of AP I, the text of which is almost identical with Article 3 of Hague Convention IV, was drafted with the intention of setting forth a rule of the traditional type, ie a rule giving rise to claims to the benefit of any state injured by a violation of the rules of IHL.[50] The Commentary of

[45] Reproduced by I. von Münch, *Dokumente des geteilten Deutschland* (Stuttgart: Kröner, 1968), 32, section IV.

[46] See J. Abr. Frowein, entry 'Potsdam Agreements on Germany (1945)', in *Encyclopedia of Public International Law*, vol 3 (Amsterdam et al: Elsevier, 1997), 1087–92.

[47] See the careful assessment by A. Alam, 'Is there any Right to Remedy for Victims of Violations of International Humanitarian Law?', 19 *HuV* (2006) 178 at 182, and D. Fleck, 'Individual and State Responsibility for Violations of the Ius in Bello: An Imperfect Balance', in Heintschel von Heinegg and Epping (n 39), 171 at 193.

[48] GC III, Art 131; GC IV, Art 148.

[49] J.S. Pictet (ed), IV *Geneva Convention Relative to the Protection of Civilian Persons in Time of War* (Geneva: International Committee of the Red Cross, 1958), 603.

[50] *Official Records of the Diplomatic Conference on the Reaffirmation and Development of International Humanitarian Law applicable in Armed Conflicts* (Geneva: 1974–77), vol III, 347; vol IX, 355 s, 397.

the International Committee of the Red Cross expresses itself with extreme caution on this issue, obviously wishing to open up new avenues but at the same time
refraining from giving a clear answer. It says that 'those entitled to compensation
will normally be the Parties to the conflict or their nationals'[51]—thus enlarging the
circle of beneficiaries beyond the traditional subjects of international law by noting a 'tendency' to recognize the exercise of rights by individuals.[52] This tendency
has taken some further steps in recent years, as noted by Jean-Marie Henckaerts
and Louise Doswald-Beck in their magnificent work on Customary International
Humanitarian Law.[53] Mostly, however, the mechanisms authorizing private victims of breaches of IHL were established by treaty, like the Eritrea-Ethiopia Claims
Commission,[54] or, exceptionally, by a Resolution of the UN Security Council.[55]

The Advisory Opinion of the ICJ in the *Wall* case[56] does not require modifying the
picture thus far obtained. In paragraph 152 of this opinion it is stated that 'Israel has
the obligation to make reparation for the damage caused to all the natural or legal
persons concerned'. Thus, the ICJ has indeed suggested an individualized reparation scheme. However, the Palestinian situation has peculiar features. There is no
government that could assert claims against Israel according to the model of diplomatic protection; the Palestinian National Authority does not have the full status of
a national government. Furthermore, the Opinion refrains from saying that the victims are holders of individual entitlements against Israel. In fact, the operative part
(C) confines itself to specifying that 'Israel is under an obligation to make reparation
for all damage caused by the construction of the wall in the Occupied Palestinian
Territory', without elaborating on the modalities of discharge of this obligation. In
any event, the Court has refrained from continuing on a path which some authors
had hailed as a welcome departure from a legal regime based on outmoded positiv-
ist thinking. In the recent judgment in the case of *Germany v Italy*, it stated bluntly
that no international practice can be perceived that would support the existence
of a rule 'requiring the payment of full compensation to each and every individual

---

[51] Y. Sandoz et al, *Commentary on the Additional Protocols of 8 June 1977 to the Geneva Conventions of 12 August 1949* (Geneva: International Committee of the Red Cross, 1987), 1067, MN 3656.

[52] Sandoz et al, 1067, MN 3657.

[53] Henckaerts and Doswald-Beck (n 11) 541–5.

[54] Established by virtue of the Peace Agreement between the two countries of 12 December 2000, 40 *ILM* (2001) 260, Art 5. For a first comment on the practice of awarding reparations under this Agreement, see N. Klein, 'State Responsibility for International Humanitarian Law Violations and the Work of the Eritrea Ethiopia Claims Commission So Far', 47 *GYIL* (2004) 214 at 261–4. On 17 August 2009, the Claims Commission handed down its two awards in the case, see <http://www.pca-cpa.org/upload/files/ET%20Final%20Damages%20Award%20complete.pdf>, and <http://www.pca-cpa.org/upload/files/ER%20Final%20Damages%20Award%20complete.pdf>. Only in the award on Eritrea's damages claims were the injuries suffered by a few individual victims dealt with separately, see opera-tive part, 95, para 20. For all the other damages, global amounts were allocated.

[55] Thus, in particular, the UN Compensation Commission for Iraq was created by UN Security Council Resolution 692 (1991).

[56] See n 16.

victim' of grave violations of IHL.[57] Rightly, the judgment emphasizes the importance of the requisite factual underpinnings of customary law. It has put an end to
a debate that arose out of the noble motive to improve the fate of victims of armed
conflict but failed to fully grasp the complexity of financial settlements after armed
conflict.

It cannot be denied that granting direct remedies may provide a fully satisfactory
solution in instances that are suitable for that type of settlement, in particular when
restitution of confiscated property is in issue. As far as cultural property taken away
or looted ('exported') during armed conflict is concerned, this is indeed the solution
generally preferred by the international community.[58] In Bosnia-Herzegovina[59] and
Kosovo,[60] special mechanisms were established to secure the restoration of property
of which the victims of displacement were deprived. However, regarding financial
compensation for war damages in general the traditional modalities of settlement
offer many advantages over individualized settlement schemes. Almost inevitably,
a state having gone through the bitter experience of war finds itself at the brink of
financial and economic collapse. It simply cannot shoulder the burden of making
good all the harm caused by violations of the *jus contra bellum* and the *jus in bello*. It
is well known that Germany went down in financial and political turmoil after it had
been compelled, through the Treaty of Versailles, to compensate the Allied Powers
comprehensively for any loss and injury they had suffered. Some formula has to be
found which, on the one hand, permits the injured nations to obtain reparation, but
which, on the other hand, permits the debtor nation to survive and thereby also to
generate the financial means needed for the reconstruction programmes of the victim nations.[61] A peace treaty can be equated, to some extent, with an insolvency proceeding where the claims of the creditors and the financial capacities of the debtor
have to be assessed and balanced. If every injured individual were entitled to bring
an individual claim before a competent judicial body, such an overall assessment
would be simply impossible.

---

[57] *Jurisdictional Immunities of the State (Germany v Italy: Greece Intervening)*, 3 February 2012,
<http://www.icj-cij.org/docket/files/143/16883.pdf>, § 94.

[58] Article I(3) of the Protocol to the Convention for the Protection of Cultural Property in the Event
of Armed Conflict, 14 May 1954, 249 *UNTS* 358.

[59] General Framework Agreement for Peace in Bosnia and Herzegovina, 14 December 1995,
Annex 7: Agreement on Refugees and Displaced Persons 35 *ILM* (1996) 136, Art 1.

[60] UNMIK, Reg No 1999/23, 15 November 1999, on the Establishment of the Housing and Property
Directorate and the Housing and Property Claims Commission, <http://www.unmikonline.org/regu-
lations/1999/reg23-99.htm>; a comprehensive assessment is made by M. Cordial and K. Rosandhaug,
*Post-Conflict Property Restitution. The Approach in Kosovo and Lessons Learned for Future International
Practice* (Leiden: Martinus Nijhoff, 2009).

[61] The draft on State responsibility adopted by the ILC on first reading, *YILC* 1996, vol II, Part Two,
58, contained a clause in Art 42(3) on reparation in the following terms: 'In no case shall reparation
result in depriving the population of a State of its own means of subsistence'. Unfortunately, this clause
did not find its way into the final version.

Realizing these factual constraints, state practice has generally refrained from allowing war victims to bring civil suits against the wrongdoers. The fight of the so-called 'comfort women' against the Japanese Government before Japanese courts is well-documented.[62] Most Japanese courts have stubbornly refused to grant reparation payments,[63] although the moral case in favour of the claimants was enormous and should have prompted a generous gesture on the part of the Government.[64] In the *Princz* case, a US citizen of Czechoslovak origin sued Germany before US courts on account of forced labour he had to perform in Nazi Germany during World War II. For some bureaucratic reason, he had not benefited from any of the reparation programmes enacted by the new democratic Government in favour of people persecuted on racial grounds. In that proceeding, Germany denied the existence of a cause of action, but was eventually compelled to conclude a special compensation agreement with the United States, given plans in the US Congress to permit suits against Germany like against other states suspected of being engaged in terrorist activities.[65] It is most significant, in this regard, that the ECtHR has found that no right to reparation under international law accrued to victims of infringements of IHL during World War II.[66] As far as the wars in Iraq and Afghanistan are concerned, nothing is known about any claims brought by Iraqi or Afghan victims of violations of IHL before the competent national courts or before US courts. Recently, representatives of the civilian victims of an air strike carried out in Afghanistan on the order of a German colonel against a fuel truck (Kunduz, 4 September 2009) negotiated directly with the German Government with a view to obtaining adequate reparation.[67]

[62] See, for instance, Alam (n 47), 182 s; H.H.L. Roque and D. Desierto, 'Redress for Violations of War Crimes: The Filipino Comfort Women's Continuing Search for Legal Remedies', 19 *HuV* (2006) 241–9; Shin Hae Bong (n 5), 200 s, 205 note 67.

[63] The Japanese courts have consistently taken the position that no individual rights may be derived from Art 3 of 1907 Hague Convention No IV: Tokyo High Court, Judgments of 7 August 1996, 40 *Japanese Annual of International Law* (*JAIL*) 116; 6 December 2000, 44 *JAIL* 173; 11 October 2001, *JAIL* 144; 23 June 2005, 50 *JAIL* 194. Correspondingly, they held inadmissible claims brought against the United States on account of the bombing of Hiroshima and Nagasaki by nuclear devices: Tokyo District Court, 7 December 1963, 32 *ILR* 627, 8 *JAIL* 212 at 246 (although the finding was that the bombing contravened international law). Attempts of the 'comfort women' to bring a claim against Japan in the United States failed as well on grounds of state immunity: *Hwang Geum Joo v Japan*, 172 F.Supp.2d 52 (DDC, 2001). After the Supreme Court had granted a *writ of certiorari*, the case was again dismissed on the basis of the political question doctrine: 413 F.3d 45 (2005).

[64] The cases reported by S. Hae Bong (n 5), 195–7 are inconclusive as yet.

[65] 35 *ILM* (1996) 195.

[66] *Associazione Nazionale Reduci dalla Prigionia, dall'Internamento e dalla Guerra di Liberazione*, App No 45563/04, 4 September 2007: 'there was no legal provision, whether of an international or of a domestic character, supporting the applicants' claims against the Federal Republic of Germany. [...] neither international public law nor domestic law recognised claims for compensation for forced labour at the time [...]'.

[67] However, German jurisprudence is unanimous in holding that international law does not provide victims with individual reparation claims: Federal Constitutional Court, 18 August 2013, 40 *Europäische Grundrechte-Zeitschrift* (*EuGRZ*) (2013) 563, margin numbers 41–7; see also Federal Constitutional Court, 13 May 1996, *Entscheidungen des Bundesverfassungsgerichts* (*BVerfGE*), 94, 315, 329; Supreme Federal Court, 2 November 2006, 62 *Juristenzeitung* 532 at 533.

In sum, however, both in terms of quantity and quality, the prevailing practice speaks plainly against an individual right to reparation arsing from either codified IHL or parallel customary law.[68] Rightly, Lisbeth Zegveld has observed that 'primary rights in IHL do not necessarily translate into secondary rights as a consequence of their breach'.[69] This being the legal position, our analysis should be understood as a call to parties to an armed conflict to set up conventional schemes granting war victims individual remedies to the extent possible, in particular with regard to the restitution of patrimonial items.

In this connection, one must realize that the issue has a temporal dimension. The economic capacity of a wrongdoing state is generally weak immediately after the end of an armed conflict. Many decades later, it will normally have recovered. While at the earlier point in time everyone would agree that an individualized system of financial settlement would drive the debtor state into insolvency, 50 or 60 years later the victims could argue that the law of the first hour should not be the determinative criterion. Germany has undergone that experience. The *Distomo* case, which has its territorial roots in Greece, originated as a judicial proceeding in 1995, almost 50 years after the end of World War II.[70] And the *Ferrini* case, in which the Italian Corte di Cassazione rendered its judgment in 2004,[71] commenced in 1998, more than half a century after that date. Now that Germany had again become one of the wealthiest nations in Europe, the victims took the view that their suffering had not been adequately compensated for. This change of perspective should be taken as an incidental circumstance that cannot re-define the basic legal parameters. Neither can a cause of action arise through a general change of circumstances where it had not existed beforehand, nor would an actual legal entitlement become extinct because of such a change, except under the conditions set out in Article 62 of the Vienna Convention on the Law of Treaties.

---

[68] The International Law Association adopted a Resolution on 'Reparation for Victims of Armed Conflicts' at its Hague Conference in August 2010 (Resolution No 2/2010). According to Art 6 of that Resolution, 'Victims of armed conflicts have a right to reparation from the responsible parties'. It is specifically explained that injured persons enjoy an individual entitlement to reparation. However, the Resolution is not sufficiently supported by actual State practice. During the preceding Conference in Rio de Janeiro in 2008 it was hotly disputed whether the proposed rules were conceived as a codification of *lex lata* or were understood as *lex ferenda*, see ILA, *Report of the 73rd Conference Rio de Janeiro 2008*, Report on the Working Session, 519–33. For the background, see the Rapporteur's study: 'Victims of Violations of International Humanitarian Law: Do They Have an Individual Right to Reparation against States under International Law?', in *Common Values in International Law. Essays in Honour of Christian Tomuschat* (Kehl: N.P. Engel, 2006), 341–59.

[69] 'Remedies for Victims of Violations of International Humanitarian Law', 85(851) *Review of the International Red Cross* (2003) 497 at 507. That there is a qualitative leap from primary to secondary rights is overlooked by C. Greenwood, 'Expert Opinion', in H. Fujita et al (eds), *War and the Rights of Individuals* (Tokyo: Nippon Hyoron-sha Publishers, 1999), 59 at 69. See also the cogent observations by Heintschel von Heinegg (n 12), 26, 52.

[70] The judgment of the Areios Pagos, 129 *ILR* 513, was handed down on 4 May 2000.

[71] 87 *Rivista di Diritto internazionale* (2004) 539; English translation: 128 *ILR* 659.

3 COMPENSATION CLAIMS BEFORE COURTS OUTSIDE THE ALLEGED WRONGDOING STATE

A. The basic rule

Obviously, the crucial issue is whether a victim can bring a suit against a wrong doing foreign state before his/her own courts. The traditional rule excluding such suits is clear. On the basis of sovereign equality (UN Charter, Article 2 (1)), states enjoy jurisdictional immunity *vis-à-vis* the exercise of jurisdiction by judicial bodies of other countries. In shorthand, Latin dicta are currently relied upon to characterize the legal position: *par in parem non habet imperium*. What originally was a comprehensive rule, has shrunk under the influence of international practice to a rule shielding only acts *jure imperii* from review by foreign courts. Military activities are acts *jure imperii* par excellence. Thus, the conclusion seems warranted—or in French: *incontournable*—that suits arising from armed activities are inadmissible if they are introduced before courts other than those of the alleged wrongdoer itself.

It is easily understandable that many legal strategies have been relied upon to avert this outcome, in particular in instances where the aggrieved person feels that his/her rights have not been duly secured by his/her home state. Claimants normally find the courts of their own country more trustworthy than the courts of the alleged wrongdoing state. Lastly, they also place their trust in the political power of their home state. If, for example, a forum can be found in the United States, claimants may have good grounds to hope that a judgment in their favour will be honoured just because of the economic might of the United States. Not all courts everywhere in the world enjoy the same kind of respect.

B. Inapplicability of the commercial activity exception

First of all, it can hardly be maintained that military operations allegedly contrary to rules of IHL constitute a commercial activity which is not immune from scrutiny by foreign tribunals. When conducting hostilities, a state puts into operation its power as a sovereign entity. This characterization is in no way different if a person is deported to perform forced labour in the territory of the occupying state. Only if a person agrees voluntarily to be sent to the foreign country, having signed a genuine work contract, can one seriously speak of an activity *jure gestionis*. However, during World War II, even if sometimes a signature was offered to the members of a foreign workforce, their condition was essentially a status of forced labourers who had no freedom either to accept or to refuse the work offered to them.[72] On the other hand, prisoners of war who were assigned to forced labour remained prisoners of war. Germany was not able to change their status unilaterally, and the prisoners could not take a truly free decision. Accordingly, only in exceptional circumstances could it be correct to hold that all the elements of a private law relationship were met so that state immunity did not constitute an obstacle to legal proceedings.

C. Commission of grave violations as waiver?

A second avenue was embarked upon in the *Princz* case, where the court of first instance argued, following suggestions proffered by the claimants, that the Third Reich impliedly waived Germany's sovereign immunity under the FSIA by violating *jus cogens* norms of the law of nations: 'A foreign state that violates these fundamental requirements of a civilized world thereby waives its right to be treated as a sovereign'.[73] Rightly, however, on appeal the court found that this interpretation was simply fictitious.[74] Waiver is an act whereby a party in a proceeding voluntarily renounces a procedural defence at its disposal. Never does a wrongdoing state have the slightest notion that by perpetrating grave crimes it foregoes at the same time rights that may become relevant in a later proceeding. Moreover, jurisdictional immunity is not a matter of merit or honour. States do not have to 'deserve' immunity and thus cannot forfeit it by engaging in violations of IHL. State immunity serves to ensure a proper functioning of the international legal order where certain mechanisms have been evolved for the settlement of international disputes. It is mainly founded on the realization that the courts of a given country are not the best judges for the assessment of the conduct of the state organs of another country—also because structurally in such situations of international tensions a certain amount of bias in favour of one's own nationals can never be excluded.[75] Today, it is generally recognized that the hurdle of sovereign immunity cannot be overcome by the artificial construct of waiver.

D. The territorial clause

More argumentative power is provided by the territorial clause set out in many instruments regulating sovereign immunity. Pursuant to this clause, immunity is denied in instances where money damages are sought against a foreign state for

---

[72] For a differentiated view, see B. Hess, 'Kriegsentschädigungen aus kollisionsrechtlicher und rechtsvergleichender Sicht', 40 *Berichte der Deutschen Gesellschaft für Völkerrecht* (2003) 107 at 116.

[73] 813 F.Supp.22 at 26 (DDC, 1992).   [74] 26 F.3d 1166 (DCC, 1994).

[75] Rightly underlined by S. Kadelbach, 'Staatenverantwortlichkeit für Angriffskriege', 40 *Berichte der Deutschen Gesellschaft für Völkerrecht* (2003) 63 at 93.

personal injury or death, or damage to or loss of property, occurring in the territory of the forum state and caused by a tortuous act or omission of that foreign state if the author of the injury was present in the foreign territory at the relevant time. The first one of these clauses was to be found in the European Convention on State Immunity[76] (Article 11). Four years later, the US Foreign Sovereign Immunities Act (FSIA) adopted essentially the same rule.[77] The recent UN Convention on Jurisdictional Immunities of States and Their Property[78] has also opted for a territorial clause with the same criteria (Article 12). It must be tempting to base suits filed against a foreign state on that departure from the general principle of immunity. The text of the relevant clauses seems to correspond fully to the factual situation of armed hostilities taking place on the territory of the forum state. However, the Council of Europe made clear in its Explanatory Report that Article 11 was only meant to cover limited risks, in particular those resulting from traffic accidents,[79] and the immunity of armed forces when on the territory of another state is explicitly maintained (Article 31). A similar explanation was forwarded to the US Congress for the deliberations on the FSIA[80] and can also be found in the commentary of the ILC on Article 12 of the UN Convention.[81] The intention behind Article 12 is to grant the inhabitants of the forum state protection against insurable risks that derive from the presence, in particular, of foreign consular and diplomatic agents in the national territory. With regard to the routine activities of such agents, in particular their participation in road traffic offences, foreign states should not enjoy special protection.

It is true that one finds isolated cases where the territorial clause has been used in a wider sense. Here the case of *Letelier v Chile* stands out as the most prominent example.[82] Letelier, a former minister under President Allende, was murdered while living in exile in Washington through a bomb attached by the Chilean Secret Service to his car. The US District Court for the District of Columbia noted that the text of section 1605(a)(5) of the Foreign Sovereign Immunities Act was sufficiently broad to cover also an assassination act committed in the territory of a foreign state, notwithstanding the fact that the legislature had not taken such an eventuality into consideration. However, nowhere does one find the slightest hint that acts of warfare should also be understood as falling within the ambit of the territorial clause. Many countries have included in their national acts provisions which specify explicitly that damage claims arising from acts of foreign armed forces cannot be pursued

---

[76] CETS No 74, 16 May 1972. To date (April 2012), it has no more than eight states parties.

[77] Original version: 15 *ILM* (1976) 1388, section 1605(a)(5).

[78] Of 2 December 2004, adopted by UNGA Res 59/38, not yet in force (in April 2012, it had 13 parties).

[79] 'For example, when a vehicle belonging to a State is involved in a traffic accident, then, provided the driver of the vehicle was present, the State as owner or possessor of the vehicle may be sued, even though the plaintiff does not seek to establish the personal liability of the driver', see <http://conventions.coe.int/treaty/en/Reports/Html/074.htm>.

[80] See observations by the US Supreme Court in *Amerada Hess v Argentina*, 488 US 428 at 439 (1989).

[81] *YILC* 1991, vol II, Part Two, 45, § 4.   [82] 488 F.Supp.665 (1980).

against the responsible state. Concerning the UN Convention, the commentary on the ILC draft articles from which the Convention arose states explicitly that the provision did not apply to 'situations involving armed conflicts'.[83] Accordingly, the Chairman of a working group of the General Assembly entrusted with reviewing the ILC draft took care to specify when introducing the report of that group that military activities are not encompassed by Article 12.[84] This statement is explicitly referred to in the last paragraph of the Preamble of General Assembly Resolution 59/38. Accordingly, it is part of the drafting history. As such, it can of course not be deemed to be the last and final word on the issue, notwithstanding the weight it is given by Article 31(2) of the Vienna Convention on the Law of Treaties. Obviously, much depends on the *raison d'être* of jurisdictional immunity of states. The question is whether it must be considered an illegitimate privilege of states or else an undesirable, but nonetheless useful and perhaps even indispensable, element of the international regime of state responsibility.

The practice of many states that have enacted legal statutes for the regulation of state immunity confirms that military activities are not considered as coming within the purview of the relevant territorial clause. The UK State Immunity Act 1978[85] provides explicitly that the Act does not apply to occurrences related to the presence of foreign armed forces on British territory (section 16(2)), and this clause was widely copied by other Commonwealth countries. Reference can be made in particular to Singapore[86] and Pakistan.[87] In *Germany v Italy*, the ICJ convincingly demonstrated that the territorial clause contained in some of the codifications of the law on state immunity does not cover military activities and has not crystallized as customary law.[88]

E. Precedence of *jus cogens* over jurisdictional immunity?

Seemingly the most powerful of the legal arguments advanced by those denying immunity in instances where suits are brought on account of grave breaches of human rights and IHL relies on *jus cogens*. The contention is that since any rule of *jus cogens* takes precedence over 'ordinary' rules of international law, state immunity is pushed aside: no state can invoke that defence if it is charged with having committed such a breach, which will generally be characterized as an international crime. The

---

[83] *YILC* 1991, vol II, Part Two, 46, para 10.

[84] Reproduced by D.P. Stewart, 'The UN Convention on Jurisdictional Immunities of States and Their Property', 99 *AJIL* (2005) 194 at 197 fn 19.

[85] 17 *ILM* (1978) 1123.

[86] Singapore State Immunity Act 1979, reprinted in United Nations (ed), *Materials on Jurisdictional Immunities of States and Their Property* (New York, 1982), 28, section 19(2).

[87] State Immunity Ordinance, 1981; UN Materials (n 86), 20, section 17(2)(a).

[88] See (n 57), §§ 62–79.

Greek Areios Pagos took the lead in the *Distomo* case by holding that state immunity must fall where a state is made accountable for serious violations of human rights and international humanitarian law.[89] In a parallel case, the Special Supreme Court under Article 100 of the Greek Constitution censured two years later the Areios Pagos, holding that a new rule departing from the principle of state immunity had not yet emerged. Nonetheless, in the *Ferrini* judgment of 11 March 2004 the Italian Court of Cassation observed that 'the recognition of immunity from jurisdiction for States responsible for such misdeeds stands in stark contrast' to the normative con-demnation of such offences. It pointed out that 'a contradiction between two equally binding legal norms ought to be resolved by giving precedence to the norm with the highest status'.[90] Unable to find precedents for its assessment of the legal position, it relied heavily on the minority opinion of the judges of the ECtHR in *Al-Adsani v UK*,[91] where an application arguing that the United Kingdom's refusal to allow repara-tion claims against a foreign state amounted to a violation of the guarantee of access to a judge had been dismissed.[92] In later pronouncements, the Corte di Cassazione has consistently confirmed its holding in *Ferrini* by pursuing an original line of legal reasoning. In a number of decisions of 29 May 2008,[93] it acknowledged that a rule of customary international law derogating from the principle of jurisdictional immu-nity had not yet come into existence but that it was in the process of formation. By denying Germany the right to rely on immunity, it was contributing to shaping a new rule that was required by considerations of equity and justice. It even went so far as to order Germany to pay compensation as 'civilly responsible party' ('*responsabile civile*') in a criminal proceeding against one of the German officers who had partici-pated in a massacre in the Italian village of Civitella.[94]

The ILA Commission on Compensation for Victims of War was seized by a pro-posal of its rapporteur on procedural issues, Japanese lawyer Shuichi Furuya, to fol-low the trend that had emerged in the *Distomo* and *Ferrini* judgments. A draft text submitted by him to the whole Committee was to provide:

A State cannot invoke immunity from the jurisdiction of a court of another State, when a victim files a suit to claim compensation for his or her serious harm as the result of an act or omission attributable to the former State, if

   (a)   that act or omission constitutes a violation of the core norms of international humanitarian law and/or international human rights law which have the character

---

  [89] 129 *ILR* (4 May 2000) 513.

  [90] See (n 71). For a critical comment, see A. Gattini, 'War Crimes and State Immunity in the *Ferrini* Decision', 3 *JICJ* (2005) 224–42.

  [91] Written by judges Rozakis and Caflisch, who were joined by judges Wildhaber, Costa, Cabral Barreto, and Vajić.

  [92] Application No 35763/97, 21 November 2001.

  [93] 91 *Rivista di diritto internazionale* 896 (2008).

  [94] Corte di cassazione, 13 January 2009, 92 *Rivista di diritto internazionale* 618 (2009), commented by A. Ciampi, 'The Italian Court of Cassation Asserts Civil Jurisdiction over Germany in a Criminal Case Relating to the Second World War', 7 *JICJ* (2009) 597–615.

of *jus cogens* or of which violation is supposed to generate criminal responsibility under international law of its individual violator; and

(b) that act or omission occurred in whole or in part in the latter State, or had a direct effect in the latter State.[95]

No substantial grounds were put forward why this new rule should supplant the traditional rule of immunity with regard to acts *iure imperii*. At the 2010 ILA Hague Conference it was decided not to pursue further the project for the time being, given the case of *Germany v Italy* on *Jurisdictional Immunities of the State* which at that time was pending before the ICJ.

The line of reasoning underlying the two judgments just mentioned misses the true sense and meaning of *jus cogens. Jus cogens* seeks to avert and also to prevent actions that infringe fundamental values of the international community. The rules prohibiting genocide and torture are the most prominent rules in that regard. No action that carries out, assists, or encourages such abominable acts can be lawful under international law. Thus, in particular, no treaty may be validly concluded that provides for concerted action pursuing the aim of committing genocide and torture. The international legal order cannot, if it wishes to remain faithful to its essential premises, accept such grave crimes as lawful. However, it is quite another matter to define the consequences of a breach that has been actually committed. There is no pre-determined programme for *jus cogens* breaches. Accordingly, there can be no 'clash' of norms of different hierarchical rank.[96] The most diverse legal inferences may be envisaged.[97] In the case of genocide, just a few options should be mentioned:

– Does a state whose government engages in genocide lose the protection of the principle of non-use of force? Many authors think so. But the world summit outcome of 2005 did not give a green light for humanitarian intervention, confining itself to clarifying that in such instances the Security Council is empowered to take action under Chapter VII of the UN Charter.[98]

– Does a state have to prosecute persons who have engaged in genocide? Only the judiciary of the state on whose territory genocide was committed bears such a

---

[95] Draft Declaration of International Law Principles on Reparation for Victims of Armed Conflict, ILA, *Report on the Rio de Janeiro Conference (2008)*, 494.

[96] See C. Tomuschat, 'L'immunité des Etats en cas de violations graves des droits de l'homme', 109 *Revue générale de droit international public* 51–74 (2005); C. Tomuschat, 'The International Law of State Immunity and Its Development by National Institutions', 44 *Vanderbilt Journal of Transnational Law* (2011) 1105–40 at 1130. The different nature of the relevant substantive rules and the procedural consequences of any breach was also underlined by the ICJ in *Germany v Italy* (n 57), § 93.

[97] This is generally overlooked by Alexander Orakhelashvili, *Peremptory Norms in International Law* (Oxford: Oxford University Press, 2006).

[98] General Assembly Res 60/1, 16 September 2005, § 139.

duty (Genocide Convention, Article VI). The judicial machinery of third states is free to act as it sees fit.[99]

- Can a state whose government is alleged to have committed genocide be automatically sued before the International Court of Justice? Is there a departure from the principle of consent as the foundation of international judicial settlement? This is not the case, the ICJ applies the general regime of jurisdiction to any state, irrespective of the charges brought against it.[100]
- Do third states have a right to take countermeasures against a state that carries out genocide? The ILC hesitates even in that regard, just mentioning that third states may take 'lawful measures' against a state that has breached obligations owed to the international community as a whole (Article 54 of its Articles on State Responsibility for Internationally Wrongful Acts, (ARS)[101]).

The four examples just given illustrate a general principle, namely that according to the current legal order the combat against breaches of *jus cogens* by way of prevention is one thing whereas sanctioning breaches committed is quite another thing. When drafting the ARS the ILC proceeded with the utmost caution. Article 41 of ARS calls on states to cooperate to bring to an end through lawful means any serious breach, and additionally it enjoins them not to recognize as lawful a situation created by such a breach. No further sanctions are provided for. Clearly, it is a grave intellectual error to believe that a state committing breaches of *jus cogens* rules forfeits its general statutory rights under international law. This is not the thrust of *jus cogens*. Regarding any possible consequence under secondary rules, a careful examination is invariably necessary as to its pros and cons.[102] In one of the latest judicial decisions available on the issue, the District Court of The Hague came to the conclusion that Article 105 of the UN Charter, which establishes the immunity of the world organization, will not be affected if the subject matter of a claim is constituted by charges that genocide was not prevented.[103]

In any event, the legal landscape is quite uniform. After the judgment of the Greek Areios Pagos in the *Distomo* case[104] had been censured by the Special Supreme Court according to Article 100 of the Greek Constitution,[105] the Italian Corte di Cassazione

[99] ICJ, *Case concerning the application of the Convention on the Prevention and Punishment of the Crime of Genocide (Bosnia and Herzegovina v Serbia and Montenegro)*, ICJ Reports 2007, § 442; see also V. Thalmann, 'National Criminal Jurisdiction over Genocide', in Paola Gaeta (ed), *The UN Genocide Convention—A Commentary* (Oxford: Oxford University Press, 2009), 231 at 256 s.

[100] ICJ, *East Timor (Portugal v Australia)*, ICJ Reports 1995, 90 at 102, § 29; *Armed Activities on the Territory of the Congo (New Application: 2002) (Democratic Republic of the Congo v Rwanda)*, ICJ Reports 2006, § 64.

[101] Taken note of by General Assembly Res 56/83, 12 December 2001.

[102] See C. Tomuschat, 'Reconceptualizing the Debate on *Jus Cogens* and Obligations *Erga Omnes*', in C. Tomuschat and J. M. Thouvenin (eds), *The Fundamental Rules of the International Legal Order* (Leiden and Boston: Martinus Nijhoff, 2006), 425–36.

[103] Decision of 10 July 2008, case 295247/HA ZA 07-2973, 55 *NILR* 428 at 438.   [104] See (n 70).

[105] *Margellos and Others v Germany*, 17 September 2002, 129 *ILR* 525.

stood quite alone in maintaining that sovereign immunity may be dismissed by advancing arguments of *jus cogens*. Only the United States has introduced legislation according to which sponsoring of terrorism by a foreign state would remove the defence of immunity.[106] This practice has not met with approval by other nations. In fact, the traditional rule of immunity is founded on a broad international consensus. Mention should be made, in the first place, to the highest courts of France[107] and the United Kingdom.[108] The Canadian judiciary has joined this view in *Bouzari v Iran*.[109] Attention should also be paid to a concordant decision of the Constitutional Court of Slovenia.[110] A particularly well-reasoned judgment was delivered by the Polish Supreme Court, which persuasively explained the precedence of conventional settlements at inter-state level over any regime that would fragment the settlement regime by privatizing it in the interest of individual victims.[111] Most of the other decisions where judges correctly follow the established law do not come to the cognizance of a broader public. Yet they exist in great numbers. In its judgment of 3 February 2012 in *Jurisdictional Immunities of the State*,[112] the ICJ has definitively clarified the legal position in the sense exposed above. Contrary to criticism voiced especially in the media, this is not a formalistic judgment but is founded on well-pondered considerations.

F. Public policy considerations

Essentially, the question has to be answered whether the objective of *jus cogens* rules, namely to prevent any breaches and to exert a deterrent effect, requires departing from jurisdictional immunity or makes it advisable to do so. Is this to the advantage of victims? Is reparation of the injury suffered by them better ensured if they can sue the responsible state before the courts of their own countries? Would such an action carry with it real advantages or only theoretical benefits?[113]

---

[106] Torture Victim Protection Act of 1991, 28 USC § 1350; Antiterrorism and Effective Death Penalty Act of 1996, codified as 28 USC § 1605(a)(7).

[107] *Bucheron*, 16 December 2003, 108 *RGDIP* (2004) 259.

[108] *Jones v Ministry of Interior Al-Mamlaka Al-Arabiya AS Saudiya (the Kingdom of Saudi Arabia) and Others*, 14 June 2006, [2006] UKHL 26.

[109] Court of Appeal of Ontario, 30 June 2004, 128 *ILR* 586.

[110] Judgment of 8 March 2001; for a summary see <http://www.coe.int/t/e/legal_affairs/legal_co-operation/public_international_law/state_immunities/documents/Cahdi%20_2005_%206%20bil%20 PartII%20SLOVENIA.pdf>.

[111] Judgment of 29 October 2010, IV CSK 465/09 (Polish), available at <http://www.sn.pl>, commented upon by Tomasz Milej, 'The Position of General Rules of Public International Law in the Polish Legal Order', in Société française pour le droit international (ed), *Comparative International Law Practice in France and Germany* (Paris: Pedone, 2011), 289–305 at 303–5.

[112] See (n 57).

[113] For a sober assessment, see Thilo Rensmann, 'Impact on the Immunity of States and their Officials', in M.T. Kamminga and M. Scheinin (eds), *The Impact of Human Rights Law on General International Law* (Oxford: Oxford University Press, 2009), 151–70.

A realistic assessment must come to the conclusion that, in particular, with regard to damages caused by armed conflict a respondent state would not be prepared to comply with judgments rendered against it by the courts of a foreign country. Foreign civil courts making determinations on the lawfulness of specific military actions of the (former) enemy is an awkward notion. It is inevitable that in dealing with hostilities in a far-away zone a great amount of experience would be necessary; mostly, the evidence would be fragmentary and unreliable. It is significant, in this regard, that the International Fact-Finding Commission under Article 90 of AP I has not yet been seized with a single request. Moreover, almost naturally judges side with the claimants of their own nationality. But the main stumbling block is the structural issue: how should a respondent state deal with thousands or even millions of individual claims? Its capacity to pay is limited. Judges who would wish to apply the standards and parameters they are used to from other proceedings would overburden any respondent state with debt. Examples from the United States are well known. In a number of proceedings against alleged terrorist states, American judges awarded sums of more than $200 million in individual cases.[114] Such irrational judgments are essentially meant as symbolic reparation, but one cannot shove them aside as fanciful and irrelevant hoaxes. They are part of the reality which constructive thinking has to take into account. In any event, equality in the actual enjoyment of a right to reparation could not be guaranteed. Those rushing ahead with the best lawyers could perhaps grab some of the available assets, but the great majority of the victims would not reap any actual benefit.[115] It is a fact of life and law that enforcement against a recalcitrant state is hardly possible. To date, it has not been argued that immunity from enforcement should also be sidestepped. Very few of the assets of a state are located abroad, and in case of need a government concerned would devise ways and means to secure its bank accounts in such a way that no garnishee order can be enforced. In other words, the barrier against civil claims guarantees at the same time that some orderly procedure can take place if the responsible state is prepared to face up to the commitments that have arisen for it as a consequence of its tortuous conduct. Failing such preparedness of the responsible state, the judgments obtained by the claimants are just pieces of paper, beneficial only for the lawyers involved in the proceedings.

Accordingly, preference should always be given to establishing conventional regimes that may reserve a role for the individual victims. Obviously, international judicial bodies are much more appropriate for that purpose than national judges whose decisions come inevitably close to self-help.

---

[114] Thus, in the *Flatow* case, the US District Court for the District of Columbia ordered Iran to pay compensatory and punitive damages in an amount of US$247 million, 93 *AJIL* (1999) 182. This was not an isolated case.

[115] See Gillard (n 11), 549: 'National courts are likely to award very large sums of money to a very small number of victims—usually the most educated and well informed.'

4 Universal Jurisdiction for Reparation Claims?

Could it become a viable solution to entrust jurisdiction for serious violations of international humanitarian law to national courts in accordance with the principle of universal jurisdiction? The only actual model in that regard is provided by the US Alien Tort Claims Act,[116] according to which federal judges enjoy jurisdiction for actions brought by an alien for torts 'committed in violation of the law of nations or a treaty of the United States'. Reading this text, one might assume that the United States has assumed the role of guardian of general international law, to the extent that it protects the interests of individuals. However, experiences with this provision are disillusioning at best. Many actions have been filed on that basis against foreign governments and—given that the bar of immunity cannot be easily overcome—in particular against foreign corporations.[117] On the other hand, according to available information, there is not a single case where a foreigner would have succeeded in obtaining a judgment against the US Government on account of mistreatment. In *Sosa v Alvarez Machain*, the Supreme Court was not prepared to accept the proposition that kidnapping a person in a foreign country in violation of the principle of territorial integrity was covered by the Statute,[118] and in the case of *El Masri*, a German national who had allegedly been kidnapped and thereafter tortured in US prisons, the courts stopped the action by declaring that the case affected governmental secrets.[119] Thus, one can hardly avoid the impression that the Alien Tort Claims Act serves mainly as an instrument to protect American national interests. In the pending case of *Al-Zahrani v Rumsfeld*[120] it will again be tested whether victims of detention in Guantánamo are entitled to compensation for the harm suffered.[121] Other applications were already dismissed, in one case on the basis of the remarkable observation that torture committed by the military official responsible for detaining and interrogating suspected enemy combatants was 'foreseeable'.[122] The thicket of immunities seems impenetrable, which raises serious doubts as to whether the United States is in compliance with the obligations it has undertaken under the International Covenant on Civil and Political Rights and the

---

[116] 28 USC 1350.   [117] Details are given by Hess (n 72), 180–2.   [118] 542 US 692 (2004).

[119] *El-Masri v United States*, US Court of Appeals for the Fourth Circuit, 2 March 2007, 46 *ILM* (2007) 630.

[120] <http://ccrjustice.org/ourcases/current-cases/al-zahrani-v.-rumsfeld>. The case is currently (April 2012) pending on appeal before the US Court of Appeals for the DC Circuit.

[121] See also *Celikgogus v Rumsfeld*, <http://ccrjustice.org/ourcases/current-cases/celikgogus-v.-rumsfeld>.

[122] Federal Appeals Court Washington, *Rasul v Myers*, 512 F.3d 644, 661, available at <http://ccrjustice.org/files/2008-1-11%20Rasul%20DC%20Circuit%20opinion.pdf>; for a cogent comment, see J.A. Menon, 'Guantánamo Torture Litigation', 6 *JICJ* (2008) 323–45.

Convention against Torture and Other Cruel, Inhuman or Degrading Treatment or Punishment.[123]

5 Concluding Observations

The end result of our reflections may sound exceedingly pessimistic to many ears. But the fact is that allowing private claims to proceed does not promote the interests of victims in a true sense. Our recommendation would be to strive for the establishment of procedures under international supervision. One of the most successful mechanisms was the UN Compensation Commission established by the Security Council. Its big advantage was that Iraqi assets were available for distribution to the victims. In any event, to settle war damages by opening up the gates for thousands and maybe millions of individual claims is not the appropriate recipe. To date, the problem of harmonizing global forms of settlement pursuant to the traditional pattern through peace treaties with individualized forms of settlement has neither been addressed nor resolved. Only specific instances like the *Letelier* case may seem to deserve a different assessment.

---

[123] See B. Fassbender, 'Can Victims Sue State Officials for Torture?', 6 *JICJ* (2008) 347–69.

CHAPTER 32

TRANSITIONAL JUSTICE

NICOLAS MICHEL AND KATHERINE DEL MAR*

1 INTRODUCTION

'TRANSITIONAL justice' has been defined as 'a response to systematic or widespread violations of human rights [...] [it] is not a special form of justice but justice adapted to societies transforming themselves after a period of pervasive human rights abuse.'[1] The term encompasses a number of different judicial and non-judicial mechanisms designed to assist the affected population in addressing large-scale violations of human rights and international humanitarian law (IHL), and in 'transitioning' towards national reconciliation, and in some cases, in the establishment of democracy.[2] Central

---

* The reader is advised that this chapter was completed in 2011.

[1] International Center for Transitional Justice, 'What is Transitional Justice?', available at <http://www.ictj.org/static/TJApproaches/WhatisTJ/ICTJ_WhatisTJ_pa2008_.pdf>. See also the definition provided by UN Secretary-General Kofi Annan in his report on 'The rule of law and transitional justice in conflict and post-conflict societies', 23 August 2004, UN Doc S/2004/616, § 8.

[2] UN Secretary-General Kofi Annan stated in his report on 'The rule of law and transitional justice in conflict and post-conflict societies', that '[j]ustice, peace and democracy are not mutually exclusive objectives, but rather mutually reinforcing imperatives', 23 August 2004, UN Doc S/2004/616, 1. On the adoption of democratic forms of governance in post-conflict transitional societies, see S. Ratner, 'New Democracies, Old Atrocities: An Inquiry in International Law', 87 *Georgetown Law Journal* (1999) 707–48.

to the notion of transitional justice is the idea that a comprehensive approach encompassing a number of complementary mechanisms and tailored to the needs of the particular state in question, is required to bring about a stable and ultimately successful transition.[3] These mechanisms may include the establishment of truth commissions, reparation for victims, criminal prosecutions, and penal and other sanctions for the perpetrators of violations.[4]

At first blush, transitional justice appears to be primarily reactive insofar as it directly responds to past violations of IHL and human rights. However, it is important to note the preventive rationale underlying the mechanisms that it encompasses. For example, the criminal prosecution of individuals suspected of having committed a crime that falls under the jurisdiction of the International Criminal Court, is grounded on the logic that such a judicial process will eventually 'contribute to the prevention of such crimes',[5] by acting as a deterrent to future offenders.[6] Similarly, in addition to examining past events, truth commissions also look to the future by providing a government with recommendations on institutional and policy reforms needed to prevent further violations.[7] Ultimately, transitional justice is about adequately and appropriately addressing past events in order to strengthen the prospect for national reconciliation and sustainable peace.

Transitional justice is entwined with broader post-conflict peace-building issues. Indeed, transitional justice mechanisms are often premised on, or they are intended to help bring about, fundamental institutional and policy changes and the establishment of the rule of law within a society, which may involve the participation of international organizations such as the United Nations and other international actors. This Chapter does not address transitional justice in this broader context, including the lustration and vetting of persons from official positions, the vast array of issues that fall under the heading of the 'responsibility to rebuild',[8] the role played

---

[3] Nuremberg Declaration on Peace and Justice, annexed to the letter dated 13 June 2008 from the Permanent Representatives of Finland, Germany, and Jordan to the United Nations addressed to the Secretary-General, 19 June 2008, UN Doc A/62/885, recommendation 3.3, at 7.

[4] A. La Rosa and X. Philippe, 'Transitional Justice', in V. Chetail (ed), *Post-Conflict Peacebuilding: A Lexicon* (New York: Oxford University Press, 2009), 368–79.

[5] Preamble of the Rome Statute of the International Criminal Court, 17 July 1998, entered into force on 1 July 2002, A/CONF.183/9, 2187 UNTS 3.

[6] J. Méndez, Special Advisor to the Prosecutor of the International Criminal Court on Crime Prevention, 'Quantative analysis of the deterrence impact', annexed to 'The Importance of Justice in Securing Peace', Review Conference of the Rome Statute, 30 May 2010, RC/ST/PJ/INF.3, at 8–11.

[7] P. Hayner, *Unspeakable Truths. Transitional Justice and the Challenge of Truth Commissions* (2nd edn, Oxon: Routledge, 2011), 23; Office of the United Nations High Commissioner for Human Rights, 'Rule-of-Law Tools for Post-Conflict States. Truth Commissions', UN Doc HR/PUB/06/1, 2006, 2.

[8] The development of this notion can be traced in a chronological reading of the following documents: Report of the International Commission on Intervention and State Sovereignty, *The Responsibility to Protect*, Ottawa, International Development Research Centre, December 2001, §§ 39–45; Report of the UN Secretary-General, *In Larger Freedom: Towards Development, Security and Human Rights for All*, September 2005, UN Doc A/59/2005; UN Secretary-General, *Implementing the responsibility to protect. Report of the Secretary-General*, 12 January 2009, UN Doc. A/63/677; UN

by UN peace operations in post conflict situations,[9] and the UN Peacebuilding Commission.[10]

This Chapter focuses on transitional justice mechanisms that are established to respond to serious international crimes that have occurred in the context of armed conflict. For the purposes of this Chapter, a 'serious international crime' is a crime that falls under the jurisdiction of the International Criminal Court. Transitional justice mechanisms that are established in order to address human rights violations committed in the context of a repressive predecessor regime of governance, outside the context of armed conflict, are not addressed. Before examining a number of different transitional justice mechanisms, Part 2 of this Chapter addresses an issue that underpins the implementation of transitional justice in general, namely the relationship between peace and justice. Whereas peace and justice were once thought divisive, they are now usually considered to be complementary. Concretely this means that there is no need for transitional justice mechanisms to be put on hold in order for peace processes to go ahead; justice processes should accompany peace processes. Part 3 looks at the transitional justice mechanism of truth-seeking, and it focuses on three different truth-seeking processes: truth commissions, commissions of inquiry,

Secretary-General, *Report of the Secretary-General on the protection of civilians in armed conflict*, 29 May 2009, UN Doc S/2009/277.

[9] See 'Report of the Panel on United Nations Peace Operations', annexed to identical letters dated 21 August 2000 from the Secretary-General to the President of the General Assembly and the President of the Security Council, 21 August 2000, UN Doc A/55/305; Report of the High-level Panel on Threats, Challenges and Change, *A more secure world: our shared responsibility*, UN Doc A/59/565, 2 December 2004; Report of the UN Secretary-General, *In Larger Freedom: Towards Development, Security and Human Rights for All*, September 2005, UN Doc A/59/2005; UNGA Resolution 60/1, 'World Summit Outcome', 24 October 2005; UN Secretary-General, 'Uniting our strengths: Enhancing United Nations support for the rule of law', Report of the Secretary-General, 14 December 2006, UN Docs A/61/636-S/2006/980; UN Secretary-General, 'Strengthening and coordinating United Nations rule of law activities', Report of the Secretary-General, 6 August 2008, UN Doc A/63/226; UN Secretary-General, 'Annual report on strengthening and coordinating United Nations rule of law activities', Report of the Secretary-General, 17 August 2009, UN Doc A/64/298; Statement by the President of the Security Council, 12 February 2010, UN Doc S/PRST/2010/2.

[10] See UN Secretary-General, *An Agenda for Peace. Preventative diplomacy, peacemaking and peace-keeping*, Report of the Secretary-General pursuant to the statement adopted by the Summit Meeting of the Security Council on 21 January 1992, 17 June 1992, UN Docs A/47/277–S/24111; Report of the High-level Panel on Threats, Challenges and Change, *A more secure world: our shared responsibility*, UN Doc A/59/565, 2 December 2004, §§ 224–30; UNGA Resolution 60/1, 'World Summit Outcome', 24 October 2005; UNSC Resolution 1645 (2005), 'Post-conflict peacebuilding', 20 December 2005; UNGA Resolution 60/180, 'The Peacebuilding Commission', 20 December 2005; UN Secretary-General, 'Uniting our strengths: Enhancing United Nations support for the rule of law', Report of the Secretary-General, 14 December 2006, UN Docs A/61/636–S/2006/980; UNSC Resolution 1820 (2008), 19 June 2008; UN Secretary-General, *Report of the Secretary-General on peacebuilding in the immediate aftermath of conflict*, 11 June 2009, UN Docs A/63/881–S/2009/304; UN Secretary-General, 'Women's participation in peacebuilding', Report of the Secretary-General, 7 September 2010, UN Docs A/65/354–S/2010/466. See also V. Chetail, 'Introduction: Post-conflict Peacebuilding—Ambiguity and Identity', in V. Chetail (ed), *Post-Conflict Peacebuilding: A Lexicon* (New York: Oxford University Press, 2009), 1–33.

and truth-seeking as part of the judicial process. Part 4 analyses the emerging culture of the end of impunity for perpetrators of serious international crimes with respect to treaty obligations that require states to prosecute and punish the perpetrators of such crimes including the legality of amnesties, exercises of the International Criminal Court's jurisdiction, and exercises of universal jurisdiction. Finally, Part 5 analyses the issue of reparation for past atrocities.

2 Peace and Justice: Once Thought Divisive, Now Considered Complementary

Peace and justice were once generally considered divisive; that in order to broker a peace agreement between warring parties, sometimes justice had to be sacrificed. Concretely, this meant that in order to bring an armed conflict to an end and achieve short-term peace, forms of impunity—such as amnesties—had to be placed squarely on the negotiating table for individuals suspected of having committed serious international crimes in the course of an armed conflict. In addition to the unlikelihood of criminal investigations and prosecutions being pursued for the alleged commission of such crimes, an application of a 'peace versus justice' approach also meant that other transitional justice mechanisms were equally unlikely to see the light of day. Although Prince Zeid Ra'ad Zeid Al Hussein does not agree with the 'peace versus justice' approach, he aptly captured the frame of mind of those who may feel they are faced with a 'peace versus justice' dilemma, in the following terms:

Whatever the origins of [an] initial contact [among warring parties], which subsequently clears the way for a ceasefire or a condition we define as 'post-conflict', the challenge then confronting the parties, the international community, or a third party mediator, is how do they preserve it, hold on to that contact, how do they strengthen and enliven it, lest it be lost and the sides revert to another round of hostilities, and possibly the commission of further crimes. The means by which the parties can most easily lock a peace process into place, is if the party exercising sovereignty offers to its adversaries an amnesty for crimes thought to have been committed during the course of the conflict [...] Moreover, with the end of bloody conflict, a wounded nation must, it is often said, find rest [...] And this can be accomplished through a simple and official burial of facts, under layers of silence. So all and every effort on the part of a transitional government focuses instead on binding the citizenry in the fulfilment of a common aim: that of building peace and concentrating on what lies ahead.[11]

[11] Remarks by Prince Zeid Ra'ad Zeid Al Hussein, 'Peace v. Justice: Contradictory or Complementary', 100 *American Society of International Law Proceedings* (2006) 361–73 at 364.

The 'peace versus justice' approach is outdated. The establishment of the International Criminal Court can be said to have brought about a 'paradigm shift', according to which there is now 'a positive relation between peace and justice'.[12] Indeed, it is now common to speak of justice reinforcing peace; that 'we cannot have peace without justice'.[13] In 2004 UN Secretary-General Kofi Annan affirmed that '[j]ustice and peace are not contradictory forces. Rather, properly pursued, they promote justice and sustain one another'.[14] The compatibility of peace with justice has been acknowledged by the Security Council which has recognized '[…] that ending impunity is important in peace agreements, and can contribute to efforts to come to terms with past abuses and to achieve national reconciliation to prevent future conflict',[15] and it 'attaches vital importance to promoting justice and the rule of law, including respect for human rights, as an indispensable element for lasting peace'.[16] It has also been recognized in the 2005 Nuremberg Declaration on Peace and Justice, circulated among members of the UN General Assembly.[17] At the opening session of the Review Conference of the International Criminal Court in Kampala in 2010, UN Secretary-General Ban Ki-Moon called the perceived 'balance between peace and justice' a 'false choice'.[18]

Moreover, a 'peace with justice' approach is reflected in the practice of the Security Council, which has responded to situations of armed conflict amounting to threats to international peace and security by taking concrete measures in the pursuit of justice. For example, the Security Council established the International Criminal Tribunal for the former Yugoslavia (ICTY) during the armed conflict in the former Yugoslavia;[19] it referred the situation in Darfur to the International Criminal Court pursuant to Article 13(b) of the Rome Statute,[20] which has been described as a case

[12] Remarks by K. Roth, Executive Director of Human Rights Watch and Moderator of the stock-taking exercise on the issue of peace and justice at the Review Conference of the Rome Statute of the International Criminal Court, in *Official Records of the Review Conference*, RC/11, Annex V(b), 'Stocktaking on international criminal justice. Peace and justice. Moderator's Summary', 106, § 29. See also remarks by D. Tolbert, President of the International Center for Transitional Justice, in *Official Records of the Review Conference*, RC/11, Annex V(b), 'Stocktaking on international criminal justice. Peace and justice. Moderator's Summary', 103, § 4.

[13] Remarks by C. Bassiouni, 'Effectuating International Criminal Law through International and Domestic Fora: Realities, Needs and Prospects', 91 *American Society of International Law Proceedings* (1997), 259–62 at 262.

[14] Report of the UN Secretary-General, 'The rule of law and transitional justice in conflict and post-conflict societies', 23 August 2004, UN Doc S/2004/616, 8, § 21.

[15] Statement by the President of the UN Security Council, 12 July 2005, UN Doc S/PRST/2005/30, 1.

[16] Statement by the President of the UN Security Council, 22 June 2006, UN Doc S/PRST/2006/28.

[17] Nuremberg Declaration on Peace and Justice, annexed to the letter dated 13 June 2008 from the Permanent Representatives of Finland, Germany, and Jordan to the United Nations addressed to the Secretary-General, 19 June 2008, UN Doc A/62/885.

[18] Statement by Mr Ban Ki-Moon, Secretary-General of the United Nations, 'An Age of Accountability', Address at the Review Conference on the International Criminal Court, 31 May 2010, available at <http://www.un.org/sg/selected-speeches/statement_full.asp?statID=829>.

[19] UN Security Council Resolution 827 (1993), 25 May 1993.

[20] UN Security Council Resolution 1593 (2005), 31 March 2005.

in which 'justice is only viewed as instrumental for peace';[21] it referred the situation in Libya of ongoing political violence to the International Criminal Court;[22] and it adopted a Resolution in relation to the transfer of Charles Taylor to The Hague to be tried by the Special Court for Sierra Leone.[23] It is also reflected in the issuance of indictments against key political figures in the former Yugoslavia by successive Chief Prosecutors of the ICTY,[24] and the issuance of arrest warrants against the President of Sudan by the Pre-Trial Chamber of the International Criminal Court,[25] which illustrate that justice should not be sacrificed at the expense of the possibility of brokering peace agreements with key political figures.

The paradigm shift from 'peace versus justice' to 'peace with justice' is grounded on a definition of long-term, sustainable peace and an expansive understanding of justice. The following definitions of these terms were agreed upon by representatives of States and scholars who participated in the drafting of the 2005 Nuremberg Declaration on Peace and Justice:

'Peace' is understood as meaning sustainable peace. Sustainable peace goes beyond the signing of an agreement. While the cessation of hostilities, restoration of public security and meeting basic needs are urgent and legitimate expectations of people who have been traumatized by armed conflict, sustainable peace requires a long-term approach that addresses the structural causes of conflict, and promotes a sustainable development, rule of law and governance, and respect for human rights, making the recurrence of violent conflict less likely.

'Justice' is understood as meaning accountability and fairness in the protection and vindication of rights, and the prevention and redress of wrongs. Justice must be administered by institutions and mechanisms that enjoy legitimacy, comply with the rule of law and are consistent with international human rights standards. Justice combines elements of criminal justice, truth-seeking, reparations and institutional reform as well as the fair distribution of, and access to, public goods, and equity within society at large. Justice may be delivered by local, national and international actors.[26]

In addition to the pursuit of justice benefiting long-term peace, short-term peace—in the form of a peace agreement—could even be achieved more quickly in some cases by pursuing justice. The former Chief Prosecutor of the ICTY, Richard

---

[21] V. Gowlland-Debbas, 'Security Council Change. The Pressure of Emerging International Public Policy', 65 *International Journal* (2009–10), 119–139 at 130.

[22] UN Security Council Resolution 1970 (2011), 26 February 2011.

[23] UN Security Council Resolution 1688 (2006), 16 June 2006.

[24] Indictments were brought against the key political and military figures Radovan Karadžić (Case No IT-95-5/18), Ratko Mladić (Case No IT-09-92), and Slobodan Milošević (Case No IT-02-54). Mr Karadžić and Mr Mladić are currently being tried before the ICTY, while Mr Milošević died in detention on 11 March 2006.

[25] *Prosecutor v Omar Hassan Ahmad Al Bashir ('Omar Al Bashir')*, Warrant of Arrest for Omar Hassan Ahmad Al Bashir, 4 March 2009, Pre-Trial Chamber I, Case No ICC-02/05-01/09; *Prosecutor v Omar Hassan Ahmad Al Bashir ('Omar Al Bashir')*, Second Warrant of Arrest for Omar Hassan Ahmad Al Bashir, 12 July 2010, Pre-Trial Chamber I, Case No ICC-02/05-01/09.

[26] Nuremberg Declaration on Peace and Justice (n 17), 4.

Goldstone, recounted how an indictment he issued against Radovan Karadžić did not hamper, but rather assisted, in brokering the Dayton peace agreement:

In my experience the threat of prosecutions and the issue of indictments against senior political players have aided rather than retarded peace negotiations. In July of 1995, as Chief Prosecutor of the Yugoslav Tribunal, I issued indictments charging Radovan Karadžić [...] with crimes against humanity [...] [He] was the self-appointed President of the Bosnian Serb enclave called Republika Srbska [...] Two months later the Bosnia Serb Army massacred over 8 000 Muslim men and boys near Srebrenica. In November 1995, the United States called a meeting in Dayton, Ohio, of leaders of the former Yugoslavia to discuss an end to the Balkan war that began in 1991. There can be no doubt that had Karadžić been a participant at Dayton, the Bosniak leaders, a mere two months after the massacre, would not have been prepared to attend the meeting. That was indeed confirmed in my presence some months later by the then Bosnian Foreign Minister, Mohamed Sacirbey. The indictment issued against Karadžić effectively prevented his attendance at Dayton [...] The Dayton meeting put an end to the war [...] I might add that I issued a second indictment against Karadžić [...] while the Dayton meeting was actually in progress. That indictment included a count of genocide arising from the Srebrenica massacre. The first indictment enabled the meeting to proceed and the second in no way inhibited the peace negotiations.[27]

However, it is not always clear-cut whether criminal indictments against key political figures have directly assisted the settlement of peace agreements in the short-term. For example, the issuance of an indictment against the former President of Liberia, Charles Taylor, by the Chief Prosecutor of the Special Court for Special Leone disrupted the peace negotiations that were ongoing at that time under the auspices of the United Nations in Accra, Ghana.[28] Although both the criminal trial of Mr Taylor before the Special Court for Sierra Leone and peace negotiations later successfully went ahead, this example raises the delicate question of timing in the joint pursuit of peace and justice processes. As the UN Secretary-General Kofi Annan noted in 2004, '[t]he question [...] can never be whether to pursue justice and accountability, *but rather when and how*.'[29]

There is debate about the timing of efforts to achieve both peace and justice: should these efforts be carried out concurrently? Should one be postponed in order to pursue the other? It could be argued that in cases in which the interests of peace and justice appear to come into conflict with one another, steps towards justice should be carefully calibrated in order not to negatively adversely impact on steps towards peace. However, great care should be taken not to allow the outdated

---

[27] R. Goldstone, 'Peace versus Justice', address delivered at the Law School of the University of Las Vegas on 15 October 2005, reprinted in 6 *Nevada Law Journal* (2005) 421–4 at 421 and 422.

[28] Remarks by M. Wierda, 'Peace v. Justice: Contradictory or Complementary', 100 *American Society of International Law Proceedings* (2006) 361–73 at 369. See also D. Crane, '"Back to the Future"— Reflections on the Beginning of the Beginning: International Criminal Law in the Twentieth Century', 32 *Fordham International Law Journal* (2009) 1761–9 at 1767.

[29] Report of the UN Secretary-General, 'The rule of law and transitional justice in conflict and post-conflict societies', 23 August 2004, UN Doc S/2004/616, at 8, para 21 (emphasis added).

'peace versus justice' approach to re-enter current debates through the backdoor of a question of timing, and for this old doctrine to effectively be re-instated through an indefinite postponement of justice processes. Kenneth Roth noted during the Review Conference of the International Criminal Court in Kampala in 2010 that the sequencing of peace and justice mechanisms 'had been successful in some cases, but had resulted, in others, in *de facto* amnesties'.[30] In principle, there is nothing to prevent both peace and justice processes being carried out simultaneously in many contexts. Practice evinces that long-term peace can only be achieved with justice. It is clear that sensitivity and tact are required to ensure that both peace and justice processes move ahead smoothly,[31] but '[t]he problem is not one of choosing between peace and justice, but of the best way to interlink the one with the other, in light of specific circumstances, without ever sacrificing the duty of justice'.[32]

Regrettably, justice processes continue to be dogged by calls to give way to peace processes in almost all circumstances. The Chief Prosecutor of the International Criminal Court, Luis Moreno Ocampo, noted that:

[...] for each situation in which the ICC is exercising jurisdiction, we can hear voices challenging judicial decisions, their timing, their timeliness, asking the Prosecution to use its discretionary powers to adjust to the situation on the ground, to indict or withdraw indictments according to short term political goals. We also hear officials of States Parties calling for amnesties, granting of immunities and other ways to avoid prosecutions, supposedly in the name of peace; we can hear voices portraying the ICC as an impediment to progressing further with Peace processes.[33]

In this respect, it is worth noting that the power of the Prosecutor under Articles 53(1)(c) and 53(2)(c) of the Rome Statute to conclude that there is no reasonable basis to proceed with an investigation or prosecution because it is not in, or would not serve, the interests of justice, is not viewed by the Office of the Prosecutor (OTP) as a discretionary power that should be used in order to further peace negotiations

---

[30] Remarks by K. Roth, Executive Director of Human Rights Watch and Moderator of the stockingtaking exercise on the issue of peace and justice at the Review Conference of the Rome Statute of the International Criminal Court, in *Official Records of the Review Conference*, RC/11, Annex V(b), 'Stocktaking on international criminal justice. Peace and justice. Moderator's Summary', 106, § 30.

[31] On some of the issues to be taken into account, see P. Hayner, 'Managing the Challenges of Integrating Justice Efforts and Peace Processes', Review Conference of the Rome Statute, 30 May 2010, RC/ST/PJ/INF.4.

[32] Remarks by Mr N. Michel, Under-Secretary-General for Legal Affairs and Legal Counsel of the United Nations, UN Security Council, 5474th meeting, 22 June 2006, UN Doc S/PV.5474, 4. See also the address by Mr K. Annan, Review Conference of the Assembly of State Parties to the Rome Statute of the International Criminal Court, Kampala, Uganda, 31 May 2010, available at <http://www.kofiannanfoundation.org/newsroom/speeches/2010/05/review-conference-assembly-states-parties-to-rome-statute-international>, § 54.

[33] L. Moreno Ocampo, 'Building a Future on Peace and Justice: The International Criminal Court', in K. Ambos, J. Large, and M. Wierda (eds), *Building a Future on Peace and Justice. Studies in Transitional Justice, Peace and Development. The Nuremberg Declaration on Peace and Justice* (Berlin/Heidelberg: Springer-Verlag, 2009), 9–13 at 11.

with persons suspected of having committed crimes that fall under the jurisdiction of the Court.[34] In a policy paper issued in 2007 the OTP stated that 'there is a difference between the concepts of the interests of justice and the interests of peace and that the latter falls within the mandate of institutions other than the [OTP]'.[35] Attempts like those made by members of the Lord's Resistance Army in Uganda to bargain their way to the negotiating table in exchange for assurances that they will not be investigated or prosecuted by the International Criminal Court in the future are not likely to be heeded by the OTP. As the Deputy Prosecutor stated on 17 August 2010, '[w]e can see from some of the situations before the Court that ignoring justice will not help peace efforts. In Northern Uganda, the international community was for a long time keen to appease Joseph Kony both before and after the warrant of the International Criminal Court. Kony, however, was only interested in impunity and repeatedly took advantage of peace talks to re-group and re-arm his forces'.[36]

A potential mechanism for temporarily stalling justice processes before the International Criminal Court (ICC) in order to favour peace processes is Article 16 of its Statute, which allows the Security Council to defer an investigation or prosecution for a period of twelve months, renewable, by adopting a resolution under Chapter VII of the Charter to that effect.[37] According to some commentators, the drafting history of Article 16 confirms the Security Council's 'decisive role in dealing with situations where the requirements of peace and justice seem to be in conflict'.[38] However, the Security Council's primary responsibility for the maintenance of international peace and security, consecrated under the UN Charter, is not a role that *prima facie* conflicts with justice processes undertaken in the framework of the International Criminal Court. As explained above, peace can only be achieved

---

[34] An overview of the different doctrinal positions taken to interpreting the meaning of 'interests of justice' is provide by K. Ambos, 'The Legal Framework of Transitional Justice: A Systematic Study with a Special Focus on the Role of the ICC', in K. Ambos, J. Large, and M. Wierda (eds), *Building a Future on Peace and Justice. Studies in Transitional Justice, Peace and Development. The Nuremberg Declaration on Peace and Justice* (Berlin/Heidelberg: Springer-Verlag, 2009), 19–103 at 82–6.

[35] Office of the Prosecutor of the ICC, 'Policy Paper on the Interests of Justice', September 2007, available at <http://www.icc-cpi.int/NR/rdonlyres/772C95C9-F54D-4321-BF09-73422BB23528/143640/ICCOTPInterestsOfJustice.pdf>, 1.

[36] Ms F. Bensouda, Deputy Prosecutor of the International Criminal Court, 'Peace and Justice, Friends or Foes?', Keynote address at the 74th Conference of the International Law Association, *De iure humanitatis; Peace, justice and international law*, The Hague, 17 August 2010, available at <http://www.icc-cpi.int/nr/exeres/2386f5cb-b2a5-45dc-b66f-17e762f77b1f.htm>.

[37] Article 16 of the Statute of the International Criminal Court reads: 'No investigation or prosecution may be commenced or proceeded with under this Statute for a period of 12 months after the Security Council, in a resolution adopted under Chapter VII of the Charter of the United Nations, has requested the Court to that effect; that request may be renewed by the Council under the same conditions.'

[38] M. Bergsmo and J. Pejić, 'Article 16. Deferral of investigation or prosecution', in O. Triffterer (ed), *Commentary on the Rome Statute of the International Criminal Court. Observer's Notes, Article by Article* (2nd edn, München: C.H. Beck, 2008), 595–604 at 598.

with justice. To this end, a decision to defer an investigation or prosecution by the Security Council should take into account 'the current activity of the Court, and particularly the cases pending before it [...] [T]he evaluation of the existence of a threat to the peace, and of the appropriateness of a deferral as a measure under Chapter VII [...] [must be] determined by [giving due consideration to] the effect of the continuation of specific proceedings before the Court'.[39] The Security Council may consider not making use of its powers under Article 16 of the Rome Statute where a state claims that it is willing and able to prosecute an individual suspected of committing crimes that fall under the jurisdiction of the Court, and the Security Council attaches certain conditions to the temporary suspension of proceedings before the International Criminal Court.

3 TRUTH-SEEKING AS A FORM OF JUSTICE

At the end of hostilities, and after a peace settlement, a society torn apart by serious international crimes committed during the course of an armed conflict may be tempted to simply turn the page; to forget, to forgive, and to move on. Nobel peace prize laureate Elie Weisel, reflecting upon our ability to both forget and remember, stated in his Nobel Lecture that '[o]f course we could try to forget the past. Why not? Is it not natural for a human being to repress what causes him pain, what causes him shame? Like the body, memory protects its wounds [...] [However] [r]emembering is a noble and necessary act'.[40] Placing systematic or widespread violations on record in order to address them is necessary because although memory can be repressed, it cannot be stifled indefinitely. It has been noted in this vein with respect to the establishment of the Extraordinary Chambers in the Courts of Cambodia (ECCC), many years after the atrocities committed by the Khmer Rouge took place, that the establishment of the ECCC 'constituted a long-awaited response to the demands for justice from the victims, who had never forgotten what they had endured, even if their voices had not been heard for a long time'.[41] Truth-seeking processes may also

---

[39] L. Condorelli and S. Villalpando, 'Referral and Deferral by the Security Council', in A. Cassese, P. Gaeta, and J. Jones (eds), *The Rome Statute of the International Criminal Court: A Commentary* (Oxford: Oxford University Press, 2002), 627–55 at 647.

[40] E. Wiesel, 'Hope, Despair and Memory', Nobel Lecture, 11 December 1986, available at <http://nobelprize.org/nobel_prizes/peace/laureates/1986/wiesel-lecture.html>.

[41] Remarks by Y. Chhang, Director of the NGO Documentation Center of Cambodia, Review Conference of the Rome Statute of the International Criminal Court, in *Official Records of the Review Conference*, RC/11, Annex V(b), 'Stocktaking on international criminal justice. Peace and justice. Moderator's Summary', 105, § 18.

constitute prophylactic antidotes to future societal unrest and violence '[...] where mass crimes are not addressed, where the truth is not told, in short where there is no transitional justice, the embers of those conflicts remain, and it is often only a matter of time before they are rekindled'.[42]

The process of truth-seeking is thus a useful transitional justice tool for establishing an accurate and impartial account of past atrocities for a transitional society. In some cases transitional governments may have positive obligations to investigate what happened to victims, and to inform their relatives of their fate.[43] States may be under a general obligation 'to investigate allegations of violations promptly, thoroughly and effectively through independent and impartial bodies'.[44] Philip Alston has noted that '[a]rmed conflict and occupation do not discharge the State's duty to investigate'.[45]

Truth-seeking may constitute a stand-alone transitional justice mechanism in the form of truth commissions (Part A). In other cases, truth-seeking may constitute a preliminary step for other transitional justice mechanisms. For example, truth-seeking undertaken by an independent commission of inquiry may lead to the recommendation that criminal investigations be opened with a view to prosecuting individuals (Part B). Finally, there is an element of truth-seeking integral to other transitional justice mechanisms, such as criminal trials conducted both at the domestic and international levels, where a judicial account of past events is recorded (Part C). All forms of truth-seeking processes during and following an armed conflict face enormous challenges in the gathering of evidence for the purpose of documenting past atrocities,

[42] D. Tolbert and M. Wierda, 'Stocktaking: Peace and Justice', International Center for Transitional Justice briefing paper, May 2010, available at <http://ictj.org/publication/stocktaking-peace-and-justice-rome-statute-review-conference>, 2.

[43] See the treaty-based human rights obligations addressed by R. Pisillo Mazzeschi, 'Responsabilité de l'état pour violation des obligations positives relatives aux droits de l'homme', 333 RCADI (2008) 175–506 at 345–51 ('obligation d'avoir un appareil adéquat d'enquête sur les violations des droits de l'homme'); D. Orentlicher, 'Independent Study on Best Practices, Including Recommendations, to Assist States in Strengthening their Domestic Capacity to Combat All Aspects of Impunity', 27 February 2004, UN Doc E/CN.4/2004/88, paras 14–23 ('the right to know'); D. Orentlicher, 'Report of the independent expert to update the Set of Principles to combat impunity', 18 February 2005, UN Doc E/CN.4/2005/102, §§ 17–35 ('the right to know').

[44] Human Rights Committee, General Comment No 31, 'Nature of the legal obligation on States Parties to the Covenant', 29 March 2004, UN Doc CCPR/C/21/Rev.1/Add.13, § 15. See also UN General Assembly Resolution 55/111 (2001), 'Extrajudicial, summary or arbitrary executions', 4 December 2000, § 6; Inter-American Court of Human Rights, Velasquez Rodriguez Case, Judgment of 29 July 1988 (Ser. C) No 4, § 176 '[t]he State is obligated to investigate every situation involving a violation of the rights protected by the Convention'; European Court of Human Rights, Aksoy v Turkey, Judgment of 18 December 1996, App No 00021987/93, § 98 '[article 13 of the European Convention on Human Rights imposes] an obligation on States to carry out a thorough and effective investigation of incidents of torture'; Human Rights Committee, Bautista de Arellana v Colombia, Comm No 563/1993, UN Doc CCPR/C/55/D/563/1993 (1995), § 8.6 '[t]he Committee nevertheless considers that the State party is under a duty to investigate thoroughly alleged violations of human rights, and in particular forced disappearances of persons and violations of the right to life'.

[45] UN Special Rapporteur on Extra-judicial, Summary or Arbitrary Executions, Report of the Special Rapporteur, P. Alston, 8 March 2006, UN Doc E/CN.4/2006/53, § 36.

both in terms of logistics, and concerning serious ethical dilemmas that may arise. It is not within the scope of this Chapter to address these difficulties.[46]

A. Truth commissions

Truth commissions have been defined as 'official, temporary, non-judicial fact-finding bodies that investigate a pattern of abuses of human rights or humanitarian law, usually committed over a number of years'.[47] They usually examine a broad spectrum of past events, and various issues that may arise in connection with these events. Since the mid-1970s to the present day, some 40 truth commissions have been established.[48] It is to be expected that there is great divergence among truth commissions because each truth commission should be 'unique [and] country-specific'.[49] The core activities of many truth commissions include the collecting of statements from victims, witnesses, and perpetrators; researching and investigating the root causes of an armed conflict; holding public hearings; engaging in outreach programs; and issuing a final report that summarizes the truth commission's findings and recommendations.[50]

The most celebrated example of a truth commission is the South African Truth and Reconciliation Commission.[51] Controversially, the Amnesty Committee of the South African truth commission had the power to grant amnesties to individuals suspected of having committed serious crimes.[52] The legal basis for the granting of amnesties by the truth commission in post-apartheid South Africa was the Promotion of National Unity and Reconciliation Act No 34 of 1995, which in turn was based on the amnesty agreement contained in a 'postamble' to the interim Constitution of 1993.[53] The 'postamble' to the 1993 Constitution provided that

---

[46] A publication by the International Center for Transitional Justice provides useful guidelines for addressing some of the logistical and ethical problems that may be encountered in the process of truth-seeking in general: L. Bickford, P. Karam, H. Mneimneh, and P. Pierce, 'Documenting Truth', International Center for Transitional Justice, 2009, available at <http://ictj.org/publication/documenting-truth>.

[47] D. Orentlicher, 'Report of the Independent Expert to update the Set of Principles to combat Impunity: Addendum', 8 February 2005, UN Doc E/CN.4/2005/102/Add.1, 6.

[48] These are analysed in detail by P. Hayner, *Unspeakable Truths. Transitional Justice and the Challenge of Truth Commissions* (2nd edn, Oxon: Routledge, 2011).

[49] Office of the United Nations High Commissioner for Human Rights, 'Rule-of-Law Tools for Post-Conflict States. Truth Commissions', UN Doc HR/PUB/06/1, 2006, 5.

[50] UN Doc HR/PUB/06/1, 2006, 17–20.

[51] The full report of the South African Truth and Reconciliation Commission is available at <http://www.info.gov.za/otherdocs/2003/trc/>.

[52] See the detailed study on the work of the South African truth commission by A. du Bois-Pedain, *Transitional Amnesty in South Africa* (Cambridge: Cambridge University Press, 2007).

[53] Constitution of the Republic of South Africa, Act 200 of 1993. The amnesty provisions in the 1993 interim Constitution were preserved in Sch 6, s 22, of the Constitution of the Republic of South Africa Act No 108 of 1996.

'[...] gross violations of human rights, the transgression of humanitarian principles in violent conflicts and the legacy of hatred, fear, guilt and revenge [...] can now be addressed on the basis that there is a need for understanding but not of vengeance, a need for reparation but not for retaliation [...] In order to advance such reconciliation and reconstruction, amnesty shall be granted [...].'[54]

The South African truth commission is arguably one of the most successful truth commissions to date, thus warranting considerable scholarly attention. However, because it is exceptional in many respects, too much emphasis on this truth commission can lead to a distorted view of the activities of other truth commissions. Indeed, there is a common misperception that a key function of truth commissions is to grant amnesties to persons suspected of having committed serious international crimes. Whilst some truth commissions have operated in contexts where amnesties were already in place, such as in Sierra Leone and in Ghana, and regrettably a blanket amnesty was put in place in El Salvador after the truth commission issued its report, '[m]ost truth commissions have no formal or informal relationship to amnesties. Those that have the power to recommend amnesty usually are proscribed from doing so for serious international crimes'.[55] For example, in exchange for testifying at a public hearing, the Kenyan Truth, Justice and Reconciliation Commission may grant an individual amnesty, except 'if the act, omission or offence to which the application relates is an act, omission or offence that constitutes crimes against humanity or genocide within the meaning of international human rights law'.[56] The legality of amnesties is addressed in greater detail in Part 4(A)(2) below.

The truth-seeking function of truth commissions means that they may become privy to evidence indicating that serious international crimes may have been committed during the armed conflict under examination. An important issue that arises in this respect is the relationship between truth commissions and other transitional justice mechanisms. Among the recommendations provided in the final reports of truth commissions is sometimes the proposal that the transitional government pursue criminal investigations and prosecutions against individuals suspected of having committed serious crimes. For example, the National Commission for Truth and Reconciliation in Chile concluded its report by stating that:

[...] as an indispensable element for achieving national reconciliation and avoiding the repetition of the deeds that have occurred, the State must exercise fully its powers of prosecution. Human rights can only be effectively protected under the true rule of law. And the rule of law presupposes that all citizens are subject to the law and to the courts of justice, which

---

[54] Constitution of the Republic of South Africa, Act 200 of 1993, Postamble. See P. van Zyl, 'Dilemmas of Transitional Justice: The Case of South Africa's Truth and Reconciliation Commission', 52 *Journal of International Affairs* (1999) 647–67.

[55] P. Hayner, *Unspeakable Truths. Transitional Justice and the Challenge of Truth Commissions* (2nd edn, Oxon: Routledge, 2011), 104.

[56] The Truth, Justice and Reconciliation Commission Bill, 2008, Part III, § 34.

involves the application of the penalties provided in criminal legislation, on an equal basis, to all those who violate the standards that govern respect for human rights.[57]

The relationship between truth commissions and the criminal prosecution of individuals raises delicate questions in relation to the presumption of innocence, the rights of the accused, and evidentiary matters. For example, it is uncertain how the rights of an accused are to be adequately protected if such an individual participates in a truth commission—which may offer incentives for testifying and for confessing to having committed crimes—and this same individual is later indicted before a criminal court with respect to the same matters. Conversely, truth commissions may be in the possession of potentially exculpatory evidence relevant to the criminal trial of an individual. Where witnesses have furnished the truth commission with such evidence under the assurance of confidentiality, it is unclear what recourse a prosecutor, a defence counsel, or a criminal court could have to such evidence.

Some of these concerns may be raised with respect to the dual functioning of the Sierra Leonean Truth and Reconciliation Commission and the Special Court for Sierra Leone. To date there has never been a request made by the Special Court for Sierra Leone for evidence obtained by the Commission on a confidential basis. However, the Commission outlined its concerns that 'at some time in the future, the Special Court for Sierra Leone [...] will seek to obtain information from its archives held under condition of confidentiality', and that for this reason the Commission recommended that 'Parliament should never authorise access by criminal justice mechanisms, either directly or indirectly, to information in the archives of the Commission that was provided on a confidential basis'.[58] Regrettably, and despite calls from the UN Secretary-General for the two mechanisms to 'operate in a complementary and mutually supportive manner, fully respectful of their distinct but related functions',[59] the relationship between the Sierra Leonean Truth and Reconciliation Commission and the Special Court for Sierra Leone was never formalized, leading to a lack of cooperation and no detailed discussion on how to address some of the concerns outlined above.

[57] Report of the Comisión Nacional de Verdad y Reconciliación ('Rettig Report'), February 1991, vol 2, 868. The original Spanish version of the Rettig Report is available at <http://www.ddhh.gov.cl/ddhh_rettig.html>. An English translation of the above cited paragraph is found in Inter-American Commission on Human Rights, Report No 36/96, Case No 10.843, Chile, 15 October 1996, available at <http://www.cidh.org/annualrep/96eng/Chile10843.htm>, para 76. A full English version of the Rettig Report is available on the website of the United States Institute of Peace at <http://www.usip.org/publications/truth-commission-chile-90>, however the wording in this translation of the above cited paragraph differs from the translation provided by the Inter-American Commission on Human Rights, with the latter being preferred.

[58] Report of the Sierra Leone's Truth and Reconciliation Commission, available at <http://www.sierra-leone.org/TRCDocuments.html>, vol 3B, 381, § 68.

[59] Letter dated 12 January 2001 from the Secretary-General addressed to the President of the Security Council, 12 January 2001, UN Doc S/2001/40, 3, § 9.

A future case of interaction between a truth commission and a criminal court is potentially the relationship between the ICC and the Kenyan Truth, Justice and Reconciliation Commission. For his part, the Chief Prosecutor of the ICC has indicated that he 'aims to liaise with the different organizations set up by the Kenyan Government, including the Truth, Justice and Reconciliation Commission'.[60] It remains to be seen how these two transitional justice mechanisms will cooperate with one another in order to bring perpetrators of serious international crimes to justice, whilst ensuring that the rights of the accused, and the interests of witnesses, are protected.[61]

B. Commissions of inquiry

Like truth commissions, commissions of inquiry are temporary mechanisms the primary purpose of which is truth-seeking, and the outcome of their work is also a report which includes conclusions and recommendations. Unlike truth commissions, commissions of inquiry are often viewed as a preliminary step to the establishment of transitional justice mechanisms, rather than as a transitional justice mechanism in their own right. Compared with truth commissions, commissions of inquiry often operate in tighter time constraints, and consequently they place less emphasis on the participation of victims, and more emphasis on providing a general overview of the events that took place. A commission of inquiry may be established at the international level, typically under the auspices of the United Nations or another international organization, or at the domestic level.

Commissions of inquiry may have very narrow scopes of inquiry. In some cases they may only inquire into one particular event that occurred within the broader context of an armed conflict that took place over the course of many months, or even years. For example, The Bloody Sunday Inquiry was established by the House of Commons to inquire into the events of one day—30 January 1972—when 13 people were killed by military forces in Londonderry, Northern Ireland.[62] In other cases, commissions of inquiry may have mandates with wider temporal and spatial scopes. For example, the Independent International Fact-Finding Mission on the Conflict in Georgia established by the Council of the European Union, had to investigate 'the origins and the course of the conflict in Georgia'.[63]

---

[60] 'Press Conference by the Prosecutor of the International Criminal Court, Luis Moreno-Ocampo', Nairobi, Kenya, 7 November 2009, 3.

[61] For a consideration of some of the issues that may arise, see A. Bisset, 'Rethinking the Powers of Truth Commissions in Light of the ICC Statute', 7(5) *Journal of International Criminal Justice* (2009) 963–82.

[62] The Report of The Bloody Sunday Inquiry is available at <http://www.bloody-sunday-inquiry.org/index.html>.

[63] The full report of the Independent International Fact-Finding Mission on the Conflict in Georgia is available at <http://www.ceiig.ch/Report.html>.

It is essential that commissions of inquiry are perceived to be impartial and independent in their examination of past atrocities, and that they have not been set up in order 'to give legal cover to governments and justify or minimise their actions, while constructing an official version or "memory" that denies the original abuse'.[64] To this end, commissions of inquiry are often comprised of persons who are reputed to be independent and impartial, in many cases current or former judges. Some domestic commissions of inquiry may even be comprised of a majority of members who are nationals of other states. The Bloody Sunday Inquiry included two international members: Judge Hoyt of the Court of Appeal, New Brunswick, Canada, and Judge Toohey of the High Court of Australia.

The facts established in reports issued by commissions of inquiry may play an important role in criminal prosecutions and other judicial processes. The terms of reference of the Independent International Fact-Finding Mission on the Conflict in Georgia included the investigation of both inter-state violations, and violations committed by individuals during the course of the armed conflict that could be characterized as serious international crimes.[65] With respect to serious international crimes committed by individuals during the armed conflict, these were contained in Volume II of the Report, which contains 'findings and opinions [...] [that] do not necessarily reflect the views of the Mission'.[66] It is interesting to note that after reaching the conclusion that there was no evidence to support allegations of genocide, a recommendation contained in Volume II of the Report was the dissemination of this information 'to ensure that unfounded allegations of genocide do not further fuel tensions or revengeful acts'.[67] The potential evidentiary weight of the Report in judicial contexts was recognized by the Mission, which recommended that the Report 'be made public in order to provide information in the context of judicial proceedings' before the International Court of Justice, the European Court of Human Rights, and possibly even potential proceedings before the International Criminal Court.[68]

The factual findings of some commissions of inquiry have served to directly assist criminal investigations before the International Criminal Court. Both a domestic commission of inquiry, and an international commission of inquiry, may be cited in this respect. The former is the Commission of Inquiry into Post-Election Violence ('Waki Commission'), established in Kenya in order to examine the violence precipitated by the 2007 Presidential elections. The latter is the International Commission

---

[64] A. Hegarty, 'The Government of Memory: Public Inquiries and the Limits of Justice in Northern Ireland', 26 *Fordham International Law Journal* (2003) 1148–92 at 1151. See also C. Bell, 'Dealing with the Past in Northern Ireland', 26 *Fordham International Law Journal* (2003) 1095–1147 at 1105.

[65] Council of the European Union, Council Decision 2008/901/CFSP, 'Concerning an independent international fact-finding mission on the conflict in Georgia', 2 December 2008.

[66] Report of Independent International Fact-Finding Mission on the Conflict in Georgia, vol II, 1.

[67] Report of Independent International Fact-Finding Mission on the Conflict in Georgia, vol II, 429.

[68] Report of Independent International Fact-Finding Mission on the Conflict in Georgia, vol II, 437.

of Inquiry on violations of international humanitarian law and human rights in Darfur, chaired by Judge Antonio Cassese. Another example of a commission of inquiry that served to directly assist criminal investigations is the United Nations International Independent Investigative Commission (UNIIIC), established to assist the Lebanese authorities in their investigation of the bombing on 14 February 2005 that killed former Lebanese Prime Minister Rafik Hariri and 22 others.[69] The series of reports published by the UNIIIC have proved useful to the work of the Special Tribunal for Lebanon.

An issue that arose in the context of the Waki Commission was whether it should 'name names', and include in its final report a list of individuals alleged to have committed serious international crimes in the context of the violence it investigated. The Waki Commission placed the names of individuals in a sealed envelope together with supporting evidence, and it gave this envelope to the Panel of African Eminent Personalities, chaired by the former UN Secretary-General Kofi Annan. It recommended that this information be passed onto either a yet to be established special tribunal, or '[i]n default of setting up the Tribunal, consideration will be given by the Panel to forwarding the names of alleged perpetrators to the special prosecutor of the International Criminal Court in the Hague to conduct further investigations'.[70] The list of names of alleged perpetrators, together with the supporting evidence, was transferred to the Prosecutor of the International Criminal Court. It is possible that these names and the supporting evidence could have assisted the Court in deciding to respond favourably to the Prosecutor's request to open an investigation in Kenya.[71] On 18 February 2010, the Chief Prosecutor of the International Criminal Court stated that '[t]here is more information from the Waki Commission including names that we can share with the Judges'.[72]

The Darfur Commission was established by the UN Secretary-General at the request of the Security Council to 'investigate reports of violations of international humanitarian law and human rights law in Darfur'.[73] It acted as a fact-finding body by both soliciting information, and by collecting information during visits to Sudan, including the Darfur region; it characterized violations of human rights law and humanitarian law to determine if these violations amounted to genocide under international criminal law; it identified individual perpetrators;

[69] UN Security Council Resolution 1595 (2005), 7 April 2005.

[70] Report of the Commission of Inquiry into Post-Election Violence ('Waki Commission'), 15 October 2008, available at <http://www.usip.org/publications/truth-commission-kenya>, 18.

[71] International Criminal Court, Pre-Trial Chamber II, Decision Pursuant to Article 15 of the Rome Statute on the Authorization of an Investigation into the Situation in the Republic of Kenya, 31 March 2010, ICC-01/09-19.

[72] Statement by Prosecutor Moreno-Ocampo in relation to the 18 February 2010 Pre-Trial Chamber II decision regarding the situation in Kenya, 18 February 2010, available at <http://www.icc-cpi.int/nr/exeres/2386f5cb-b2a5-45dc-b66f-17e762f77b1f.htm>.

[73] UN Security Council Resolution 1564, 18 September 2004.

and it provided recommendations on how to hold these individuals accountable.[74] Among the recommendations set out in its final report, the Darfur Commission 'strongly recommend[ed] that the Security Council refer the situation in Darfur to the International Criminal Court pursuant to article 13(b) of its Statute' because '[m]any of the alleged crimes documented in Darfur have been widespread and systematic. They meet all the thresholds set in the Statute. The Sudanese justice system has demonstrated its inability and unwillingness to investigate and prosecute the perpetrators of these crimes'.[75] In line with this recommendation, the Security Council referred the situation in Darfur to the International Criminal Court in a Resolution adopted under Chapter VII of the Charter, in which it took note of the Commission's report in the preamble.[76] On 5 April 2005, the Office of the Prosecutor of the International Criminal Court received 2,500 items of evidence collected by the Commission, and the names of persons contained in a sealed envelope that the UN Secretary-General passed on to the OTP from the Commission.[77]

C. Truth-seeking in the criminal justice process

Unlike truth commissions and commissions of inquiry, truth-seeking by a court of law, at the domestic or international level, is of course a judicial process. Even if the temporal scope of judicial inquiries into past events may be broader in some instances than the temporal scope of inquiry by a commission of inquiry or even certain truth commissions, judicial truth-seeking in the context of criminal law is limited in many other respects. This form of truth-seeking is undertaken with the specific purpose of prosecuting individuals for certain crimes, and past events will be viewed within the legal parameters required to prove and disprove such crimes. Due to logistical and financial constraints, fewer crimes can be prosecuted at the international level than at the domestic level. Depending on the international or internationalized criminal court or tribunal in question, these may include serious international crimes such as genocide, crimes against humanity, war crimes, and in some cases also specific domestic crimes.[78] Furthermore, the international criminal

[74] Report of the International Commission of Inquiry on Darfur to the Secretary-General, annexed to Letter dated 31 January 2005 from the Secretary-General addressed to the President of the Security Council, UN Doc S/2005/60.
[75] UN Doc S/2005/60, 174, § 647.
[76] UN Security Council Resolution 1593 (2005), 31 March 2005.
[77] Office of the Prosecutor of the International Criminal Court, 'First Report of the Prosecutor of the International Criminal Court, Mr. Luis Moreno Ocampo, to the Security Council Pursuant to UNSCR 1593 (2005)', 29 June 2005, 2.
[78] See Arts 2–5 of the Statute of the ICTY; Arts 2–4 of the Statute of the International Criminal Tribunal for Rwanda; Arts 2–5 of the Statute of the Special Court for Sierra Leone; Arts 3–7 of Cambodian Law NS/RKM/1004/006 with respect to the Extraordinary Chambers in the Courts of Cambodia; Arts 5–8 of the Statute of the International Criminal Court; Art 2 of the Statute of the Special Tribunal for Lebanon.

prosecutor exercises greater prosecutorial discretion than her or his national counterpart, thereby further narrowing the scope of past events that will be examined in
the course of the judicial process from the outset.

Despite the partial account of past events offered by a process of truth-seeking in
the criminal justice context, this mechanism has certain characteristics that arguably ensure that a particularly reliable account of what has occurred will be obtained.
These characteristics include the fact that the accused is provided with legal representation and legal assistance in the preparation of her or his defence, thereby
ensuring that her or his account of events is presented in a rigorous manner; there
are detailed rules in place pertaining to matters of proof and evidence, including
the admissibility of certain forms of evidence, standards of proof, and burdens of
proof; and there is a large body of procedural rules in place to ensure the fairness
of judicial proceedings. It has been commented in the context of transitional justice
that '[…] a society would be better served were the truth to find its origins in, and
emerge from, a judicial process',[79] because a judicial account of past events may offer
'unassailable "pockets of truth" '.[80]

Courts of law cannot examine past atrocities with the breadth that truth commissions and some commissions of inquiry are able to do. It has been noted in the context of the International Criminal Court, that the Court 'will not be in a position to
take down and analyse thousands of statements of victims as, for example, a Truth
Commission might do'.[81] However, judicial accounts of past atrocities may go into
greater depth of detail and allow otherwise reluctant victims to participate in the
truth-seeking process due to the ability of courts and tribunals to address the needs
of vulnerable witnesses through well-developed frameworks of witness protection.
Indeed, some truth commissions and commissions of inquiry have acknowledged
that certain witnesses may have declined to provide them with information due to
personal safety concerns. For example, the Waki Commission of Inquiry (Kenya)
noted in its Final Report that 'we did not have a reliable witness protection program
which might have given greater solace to [some individuals] who avoided speaking
to us'.[82] The challenge in the judicial context is in ensuring that demanding measures
taken to protect witnesses, such as the suppression of names and voice and image
distortion in recorded testimonies, do not unduly place the accused at a disadvantage in defending her or his rights, and ultimately in ensuring the accurate judicial
recording of past events.

[79] Remarks by Prince Zeid Ra'ad Zeid Al Hussein (n 11), 366.
[80] Remarks by Prince Zeid Ra'ad Zeid Al Hussein (n 11), 363.
[81] J. Lindenmann, 'Transitional Justice and the International Criminal Court: Some Reflections on
the Role of the ICC in Conflict Transformation', in M. Kohen (ed), *Promoting Justice, Human Rights
and Conflict Resolution through International Law/La promotion de la justice, des droits de l'homme et
du règlement des conflits par le droit international. Liber Amicorum Lucius Caflisch* (Leiden: Koninklijke
Brill, 2007), 315–38 at 325.
[82] Report of the Commission of Inquiry into Post-Election Violence ('Waki Commission'), 15
October 2008, available at <http://www.dialoguekenya.org/docs/PEV%20Report.pdf>, 9.

There are many challenges faced by criminal courts and tribunals in obtaining and securing evidence during or following an armed conflict, particularly at the international level where international and internationalized criminal courts and tribunals rely on the cooperation and assistance of states and organizations. The assistance provided to the ICTY by the Kosovo Force (KFOR), the military component of the international administration established by the Security Council in Kosovo, and the NATO-led Stabilisation Force in Bosnia and Herzegovina (SFOR, replaced by European Forces in Bosnia and Herzegovina (EUFOR) in 2005), on the basis of a broad obligation to cooperate with the ICTY, has been highly valuable to the work of the ICTY in fulfilling its truth-seeking role. The type of assistance provided to the ICTY has included—in relation to KFOR—finding and securing the sites of mass graves,[83] providing aerial surveillance of reported mass grave sites,[84] assisting in mass grave exhumations,[85] and other investigative activities.[86] In relation to SFOR, it amounted to providing security for the ICTY Prosecutor's investigation missions,[87] assisting in investigation missions,[88] and assisting in mass grave exhumations.[89]

The International Criminal Court may be assisted by evidence supplied to it by commissions of inquiry, as discussed above with respect to the situations in Kenya and in Darfur, Sudan. It is important to stress that although commissions of inquiry may provide significant amounts of material evidence to the OTP, and they may even suggest the names of persons they consider could have committed serious international crimes that fall within the jurisdiction of the International Criminal Court, the Prosecutor will operate independently. The OTP will thus 'conduct its own independent investigations, in accordance with the Rome Statute and the policies of the Office, in order to determine those persons bearing greatest responsibility for the crimes to be prosecuted by the Court', and the names of persons suspected of having committed serious international crimes, submitted to the Prosecutor by a commission of inquiry, are considered by the OTP merely to

---

[83] 'Report of the International Tribunal for the Prosecution of Persons Responsible for Serious Violations of International Humanitarian Law Committed in the Territory of the Former Yugoslavia since 1991', 7 August 2000, UN Docs A/55/273–S/2000/777, 29, § 184.

[84] UN Docs A/55/273–S/2000/777, 29, § 184.

[85] 'Report of the International Tribunal for the Prosecution of Persons Responsible for Serious Violations of International Humanitarian Law Committed in the Territory of the Former Yugoslavia since 1991', 4 September 2002, UN Docs A/57/379–S/2002/985, 40, § 230.

[86] UN Docs A/57/379–S/2002/985, 40, § 230.

[87] UN Docs A/57/379–S/2002/985, 40, § 230.

[88] 'Report of the International Tribunal for the Prosecution of Persons Responsible for Serious Violations of International Humanitarian Law Committed in the Territory of the Former Yugoslavia since 1991', 20 August 2003, UN Docs A/58/297–S/2003/829, 55, § 248.

[89] 'Report of the International Tribunal for the Prosecution of Persons Responsible for Serious Violations of International Humanitarian Law Committed in the Territory of the Former Yugoslavia since 1991', 4 September 2002, UN Docs A/57/379–S/2002/985, 40, § 230.

'represent the conclusions of the Commission'.[90] Similarly, although the OTP of the Special Tribunal for Lebanon continues the investigative function carried out by the UNIIIC, the factual findings made by the UNIIIC are not binding on the OTP, although they serve to assist the work carried out by the OTP.

4 THE EMERGING CULTURE OF THE END OF IMPUNITY FOR PERPETRATORS OF THE MOST SERIOUS INTERNATIONAL CRIMES

For a society in transition, it is crucial that there is no impunity for individuals suspected of having committed the most serious international crimes. Impunity has been defined as 'the exemption from accountability, penalty, or punishment for perpetrators of illegal acts'.[91] The UN Security Council has affirmed that '[…] ending impunity is essential if a society in conflict or recovering from conflict is to come to terms with past abuses committed against civilians affected by armed conflict and to prevent future such abuses'.[92] With respect to perpetrators of the most serious international crimes, the last 20 years have witnessed the emergence of a culture of the end of impunity that builds on the pioneering work of the Nuremberg and Tokyo tribunals at the beginning of the twentieth century.[93] This is evidenced by concerted efforts taken by the international community of states, and a great many dedicated individuals, in the establishment and functioning of different international and internationalized criminal courts and tribunals,[94] culminating in a permanent

[90] Office of the Prosecutor of the International Criminal Court, 'First Report of the Prosecutor of the International Criminal Court, Mr. Luis Moreno Ocampo, to the Security Council Pursuant to UNSCR 1593 (2005)', 29 June 2005, 2.

[91] S. Opotow, 'Psychology of Impunity and Injustice: Implications for Social Reconciliation', in M. Cherif Bassiouni (ed), *Post-Conflict Justice* (Ardsley: Transnational Publishers, 2002), 201–16 at 202.

[92] UN Security Council Resolution 1674 (2006), 'Protecting civilians in armed conflict', 28 April 2006, § 7.

[93] It has even been argued that there is an emerging norm to end impunity for perpetrators of genocide, crimes against humanity, and war crimes: see *Nuremberg Declaration on Peace and Justice* (n 34), 4.

[94] ICTY, established by UN Security Council Resolution 827 (1993) of 25 May 1993; ICTR, established by UN Security Council Resolution 955 (1994) of 8 November 1994; Special Court for Sierra Leone, established by an agreement between the United Nations Organization and the government of Sierra Leone of 16 January 2002; Extraordinary Chambers in the Courts of Cambodia, established by Cambodian law NS/RKM/1004/006, promulgated on 27 October 2004 by Cambodian law NS/RKM/0801/12 KRAM; Special Tribunal for Lebanon, established by an agreement between the United

international criminal court of potential universal reach, the International Criminal Court.[95] It is also evidenced in more recent years—in line with the principle of 'complementarity' within the framework of the International Criminal Court—by a shift in focus from the prosecution of perpetrators of serious international crimes at the international level, to the primary responsibility of states to end impunity for these individuals within the framework of their domestic legal systems. The treaty-based obligations that require states to prosecute and punish perpetrators of the most serious international crimes are addressed in Section A, below.

For states parties to the Rome Statute, this primary responsibility to exercise criminal jurisdiction is complemented by the jurisdiction of the International Criminal Court where a state party is unable or unwilling to exercise its primary responsibility. However, there is also a positive aspect to states parties' conduct concerning the principle of complementarity. This 'positive complementarity' arises where a state is willing, but unable, to exercise its primary territorial criminal jurisdiction. In such cases, it was remarked that '[i]t would appear that States, in particular States parties to the Statute, should make every effort, either individually or collectively, to give appropriate *assistance* to such a State in building its capacities, with a view to the establishment of a functioning criminal justice system in that State. Such assistance represents—politically, not legally speaking—an "extension" of the complementarity principle: states enable other states to better fulfil their primary responsibility under the Rome Statute to investigate and prosecute the most serious crimes.'[96] This 'positive complementarity' was consecrated on 8 June 2010 when the Review Conference of the Rome Statute adopted a Resolution that recognized 'the desirability of States to assist each other in strengthening domestic capacity to ensure that investigations and prosecutions of serious crimes of international concern can take place at the national level'.[97] The role of the International Criminal Court in the culture of the end of impunity for persons suspected of having committed serious international crimes is addressed in Section B, below.

Nations Organization and Lebanon, the provisions of which entered into force by virtue of UN Security Council Resolution 1757 (2007).

[95] Rome Statute of the International Criminal Court, 17 July 1998, entered into force on 1 July 2002.

[96] J. Lindenmann, 'Transitional Justice and the International Criminal Court: Some Reflections on the Role of the ICC in Conflict Transformation', in M. Kohen (ed), *Promoting Justice, Human Rights and Conflict Resolution through International Law/La promotion de la justice, des droits de l'homme et du règlement des conflits par le droit international. Liber Amicorum Lucius Caflisch* (Leiden: Koninklijke Brill, 2007), 315–38 at 334 (original emphasis). See also remarks by Mr N. Michel, Under-Secretary-General for Legal Affairs and Legal Counsel of the United Nations, UN Security Council, 5474th meeting, 22 June 2006, UN Doc S/PV.5474, 4.

[97] Review Conference of the Rome Statute of the International Criminal Court, Resolution RC/Res 1, 'Complementarity', 8 June 2010, § 5 (adopted by consensus). See also International Center for Transitional Justice, 'Complementarity after Kampala: The Way Forward', Meeting Summary of the Retreat, 19 November 2010, available at <http://ictj.org/publication/complementarity-after-kampala-meeting-summary>.

Exercises of 'positive complementarity' can assist a willing albeit unable state party to the Rome Statute ultimately to carry out criminal investigations and prosecutions in line with its primary responsibility to exercise criminal jurisdiction with respect to serious international crimes. For transitional societies, where institutional structures may be in disarray or in need of reform, it will be particularly important to ensure that the state in question is assisted in establishing a robust and effective legal system. However, in cases where a non-state party to the Rome Statute is unwilling to investigate and prosecute suspected perpetrators of serious international crimes, and where such persons are beyond the reach of the jurisdiction of the Court, including in cases where no recourse to Article 13 of the Rome Statute is envisaged by the Security Council, there arise gaps of impunity in the fabric of the emerging culture to bringing alleged perpetrators to trial. It is arguable that in such instances other states could exercise universal criminal jurisdiction in order to bring suspected perpetrators of serious international crimes to justice. This argument is addressed in section C, below.

A. Individual criminal responsibility at the domestic level

The emerging culture of the end of impunity for perpetrators of serious international crimes is manifested in two respects at the domestic level. On the one hand, states must take 'effective action to combat impunity',[98] in line with their existing responsibilities. There exist different treaty obligations to prosecute and punish individuals suspected of having committed serious international crimes that may be binding on states. These obligations are addressed in section (i). On the other hand, a corollary to the obligation to take effective action to combat impunity for serious international crimes is the prohibition on granting amnesties to the suspected perpetrators of such crimes. The granting of amnesties may also conflict with human rights obligations binding on states. The issue of amnesties for the commission of serious international crimes is addressed in section (ii).

(i) *Obligations to prosecute and to punish*

It remains controversial whether—and to what extent—there exists a general obligation binding on states, either under customary international law or as a general principle of law, to prosecute and punish those persons suspected of having committed the most serious international crimes.[99] According to the Basic

---

[98] D. Orentlicher, 'Report of the Independent Expert to update the Set of Principles to Combat Impunity: Addendum', 8 February 2005, UN Doc E/CN.4/2005/102/Add.1, 7.

[99] K. Ambos, 'The Legal Framework of Transitional Justice: A Systematic Study with a Special Focus on the Role of the ICC', in K. Ambos, J. Large, and M. Wierda (eds), *Building a Future on Peace and Justice. Studies in Transitional Justice, Peace and Development. The Nuremberg Declaration on Peace and Justice* (Berlin/Heidelberg: Springer-Verlag, 2009), 19–103 at 30.

Principles and Guidelines on the Right to a Remedy and Reparation for Victims of Gross Violations of International Human Rights Law and Serious Violations of International Humanitarian Law, submitted to the UN General Assembly, '[i]n cases of gross violations of international human rights law and serious violations of international humanitarian law constituting crimes under international law, States have the duty to investigate and, if there is sufficient evidence, the duty to submit to prosecution the person allegedly responsible for the violation and, if found guilty, the duty to punish her or him'.[100] The Security Council has limited itself to emphasizing '[...] the responsibility of States *to comply with their relevant obligations* to end impunity to prosecute those responsible for war crimes, genocide, crimes against humanity and serious violations of international humanitarian law, while recognizing, for States in or recovering from armed conflict, the need to restore or build independent national judicial systems and institutions'.[101]

Although the existence of a general obligation is debatable, it is clear that some states are bound by treaty obligations to prosecute and punish suspected perpetrators of serious crimes that have been committed on their territory. There is no obligation contained in the operative parts of the Rome Statute, according to which states parties must prosecute individuals suspected of having committed serious international crimes that fall under the jurisdiction of the International Criminal Court. However, it is arguable that on the basis of Article 17 of the Statute (principle of complementarity), read together with paragraphs 4 to 6 of the preamble, states parties to the Rome Statute have a primary obligation to prosecute and punish individuals suspected of having committed crimes contained in the Statute, namely war crimes, crimes against humanity, genocide, and possibly aggression, on their territory.[102] Pursuant to the very *raison d'être* of the International Criminal Court set out in paragraphs 4 to 6 of the preamble to its Statute, states parties affirm 'that the most serious crimes of concern to the international community as a whole must not go unpunished and that their effective prosecution must be ensured by taking measures at the national level', they express their determination 'to put an end to impunity for the perpetrators of these crimes [...]', and they recall 'that it is the duty of every State to exercise its criminal jurisdiction over those responsible for international crimes'.[103]

[100] 'Basic Principles and Guidelines on the Right to a Remedy and Reparation for Victims of Gross Violations of International Human Rights Law and Serious Violations of International Humanitarian Law' annexed to UN General Assembly Resolution 60/147, 'Basic Principles and Guidelines on the Right to a Remedy', 21 March 2006, § 4.

[101] UN Security Council Resolution 1674 (2006), 'Protecting civilians in armed conflict', 28 April 2006, § 8 (emphasis added). See also Statement by the President of the Security Council, 12 July 2005, UN Doc S/PRST/2005/30, 1; Statement by the President of the Security Council, 22 June 2006, UN Doc S/PRST/2006/28, 2.

[102] Articles 5–8 of the Rome Statute of the International Criminal Court. For the definition of the crime of aggression, see Annex 1 'Amendments to the Rome Statute of the International Criminal Court on the Crime of Aggression' to Review Conference of the Rome Statue of the International Criminal Court, Resolution RC/Res 6, 11 June 2010 (adopted by consensus).

[103] §§ 4 to 6 of the preamble to the Rome Statute of the International Criminal Court.

States parties to the Convention on the Prevention and Punishment of the Crime of Genocide have undertaken—in addition to their obligation to prevent genocide—to punish genocide.[104] Concretely, this means that states parties to this Convention must exercise their criminal jurisdiction, to ensure that '[p]ersons charged with genocide or any of the other acts enumerated in article III [of the Genocide Convention] shall be tried by a competent tribunal of the State in the territory of which the act was committed [...]'.[105] This obligation to prosecute under the Genocide Convention is limited to exercises of territorial jurisdiction. However, this does not prevent states parties to the Genocide Convention from conferring other forms of jurisdiction on their domestic criminal courts, even though they are not obliged to do so. The International Court of Justice has noted in this respect that '[a]rticle VI [of the Genocide Convention] only obliges the Contracting Parties to institute and exercise territorial criminal jurisdiction; while it certainly does not prohibit States, with respect to genocide, from conferring jurisdiction on their criminal courts based on criteria other than where the crime was committed which are compatible with international law, in particular the nationality of the accused, it does not oblige them to do so'.[106]

States parties to the 1949 Geneva Conventions, and Additional Protocol I to the Geneva Conventions, arguably have a broader obligation to prosecute or extradite those persons suspected of having committed grave breaches of the Geneva Conventions that extends beyond conferring territorial criminal jurisdiction on their domestic courts.[107] Once a state party to the Geneva Conventions 'is aware that a person on its territory has committed such an offence, it is its duty to see that such person is arrested and prosecuted without delay'.[108] Similarly, in accordance with the *aut dedere aut judicare* obligation contained in the Convention against Torture and Other Cruel, Inhuman or Degrading Treatment or Punishment (CAT),[109] states parties have an obligation to either submit a case concerning torture to their relevant

[104] Article I of the Convention on the Prevention and Punishment of the Crime of Genocide, 9 December 1948, entered into force on 12 January 1951, 78 UNTS 277.

[105] Article VI of the Convention on the Prevention and Punishment of the Crime of Genocide, 9 December 1948, entered into force on 12 January 1951, 78 UNTS 277.

[106] *Application of the Convention on the Prevention and Punishment of the Crime of Genocide (Bosnia and Herzegovina v Serbia and Montenegro)*, [2007] ICJ Rep 158–9, § 442. For a critique of the Court's narrow reading of the obligation to prosecute and punish under the Genocide Convention, see O. Ben-Naftali, 'The Obligations to Prevent and to Punish Genocide', in P. Gaeta (ed), *The UN Genocide Convention. A Commentary* (Oxford: Oxford University Press, 2009), 27–57, at 46–52.

[107] Article 49 of GC I; Art 50 of GC II; Art 129 of GC III; Art 146 of GC IV; Art 85 of AP I. See also J.-M. Henckaerts and L. Doswald-Beck, *Customary International Humanitarian Law*, vol I (Cambridge: International Committee of the Red Cross/Cambridge University Press, 2005), 607 (Rule 158).

[108] Commentary GC I, 365–6.

[109] Convention against Torture and Other Cruel, Inhuman or Degrading Treatment or Punishment, 10 December 1984, entered into force on 26 June 1987, 1465 UNTS 85.

prosecutorial authorities, or to extradite the person, in line with the provisions of the Convention Against Torture.[110] Furthermore, Article I of the Convention on the Non-Applicability of Statutory Limitations to War Crimes and Crimes Against Humanity provides that no statutory limitation applies to war crimes, crimes against humanity and genocide, irrespective of the date of the commission of such crimes, and 'even if such acts do not constitute a violation of the domestic law of the country in which they were committed'.[111] It has been argued that this treaty 'by necessary implication places an obligation on States to prosecute' these crimes.[112]

Two remarks are warranted with respect to obligations to prosecute and punish persons suspected of having committed serious international crimes in the context of a transitional society. First, it could be argued that the prosecution and punishment of individuals suspected of committing past abuses could destabilize a fragile, newly established democracy. However, rather than undermining progress towards national reconciliation, such criminal trials conducted in the public sphere may serve as a vehicle for reconciliation. Luis Moreno Ocampo noted in the context of Argentina that '[c]ivil society was strengthened as a result of the investigations and public trials, which increased the public's commitment to, and respect for, democracy and permitted—through the newly-created free press—a constructive public debate'.[113] Secondly, it is important to stress the need for an equal application of the law. The prosecution of individuals suspected of serious international crimes, regardless of their current or past membership or allegiance to an armed group or a regime of governance is desirable. The Security Council noted with regard to Haiti in 2004 that 'an end to impunity is key to national reconciliation in Haiti. The Council stresses that justice should apply equally to all citizens in that country and be carried out by an independent judicial system with the support of a reformed correctional system. The Council expresses its strong concern at reports of double standards in the administration of justice'.[114]

(ii) Amnesties

Amnesties are domestic laws the purpose of which is to provide persons suspected of having committed unlawful conduct in the past with prospective criminal

---

[110] See generally M. Nowak and E. McArthur, *The United Nations Convention Against Torture. A Commentary* (Oxford: Oxford University Press, 2008), 344–67 (Article 7).

[111] Convention on the Non-Applicability of Statutory Limitations to War Crimes and Crimes Against Humanity, 26 November 1968, entered into force on 11 November 1970, 754 UNTS 73.

[112] J. Dugard, 'Possible Conflicts of Jurisdiction with Truth Commissions', in A. Cassese, P. Gaeta, and J. Jones (eds), *The Rome Statute of the International Criminal Court: A Commentary* (Oxford: Oxford University Press, 2002), 693–704 at 696.

[113] L. Moreno Ocampo, 'Beyond Punishment: Justice in the Wake of Massive Crimes in Argentina', 52 *Journal of International Affairs* (1999) 669–89 at 670.

[114] Statement by the President of the Security Council, 10 September 2004, UN Doc S/PRST/2004/32, 2.

impunity and civil indemnity. The attitude of the international community towards amnesties has drastically changed over the years. In the 1960s and 1970s, human rights advocates and legal scholars actively supported amnesties for political prisoners, particularly in the context of dictatorial regimes of governance. The nongovernmental organization Amnesty International even went so far as to adopt the notion as part of its name.[115] In the context of crimes committed during armed conflict, Article 6(5) of Additional Protocol II to the Geneva Conventions famously provides that '[a]t the end of hostilities, the authorities in power shall endeavour to grant the broadest possible amnesty to persons who have participated in the armed conflict, or those deprived of their liberty for reasons related to the armed conflict, whether they are interned or detained'.[116]

Nowadays there is general consensus that 'unconditional amnesties' or 'blanket amnesties', ie amnesties that cover any crime committed in the past, are unacceptable. The reason for this is that a prohibition of amnesties for persons suspected of having committed serious international crimes is a logical corollary of the emerging culture of the end of impunity for perpetrators of such crimes. Amnesties may also be incompatible with other obligations binding on states, such as human rights obligations.[117] The Nuremberg Declaration on Peace and Justice asserts that 'amnesties must not be granted to those bearing the greatest responsibility for genocide, crimes against humanity and serious violations of international humanitarian law'.[118]

Although there is general consensus that amnesties for serious international crimes are unacceptable under international law, it is acknowledged from the outset that there are instances where amnesties for other crimes may not only be acceptable, but desirable. In the context of transitional societies, where large parts of the population may have participated in a non-international armed conflict without having committed serious international crimes, amnesties may be an appropriate mechanism to assist the reintegration of such persons into society by granting them impunity for the domestic crime of participation in the conflict, in line with Article 6(5) of AP II.[119] In this vein, the Nuremberg Declaration on Peace and Justice

[115] A history of Amnesty International is available at <http://www.amnesty.org/en/who-we-are/history>.

[116] Protocol Additional to the Geneva Conventions of 12 August 1949, and Relating to the Protection of Victims of Non-International Armed Conflicts, entered into force on 7 December 1978, 1125 UNTS 609.

[117] See D. Momtaz, 'De l'incompatibilité des amnisties inconditionnelles avec le droit international', in M. Kohen (ed), *Promoting Justice, Human Rights and Conflict Resolution through International Law/La promotion de la justice, des droits de l'homme et du règlement des conflits par le droit international. Liber Amicorum Lucius Caflisch* (Leiden: Koninklijke Brill, 2007), 353–68.

[118] Nuremberg Declaration on Peace and Justice, annexed to the letter dated 13 June 2008 from the Permanent Representatives of Finland, Germany, and Jordan to the United Nations addressed to the Secretary-General, 19 June 2008, UN Doc A/62/885, 4.

[119] F. Bugnion, 'L'amnistie entre l'exigence de justice et l'indispensable réconciliation: lorsque les armes se taisent, que faire des crimes qui ont été commis à l'occasion d'un conflit armé?', in W. Kälin,

noted that '[a]mnesties, other than for those bearing the greatest responsibility for genocide crimes against humanity and war crimes, may be permissible in a specific context and may even be required for the release, demobilization and reintegration of conflict-related prisoners and detainees'.[120] Similarly, the UN has recognized that '[i]t may be necessary and proper for immunity from prosecution to be granted to members of the armed opposition seeking reintegration into society as part of a national reconciliation process'.[121]

The practice of the United Nations provides a guide to the changing attitude towards amnesties for perpetrators of serious international crimes. Although the United Nations may have harboured concerns about amnesties being granted to persons suspected of having committed serious international crimes in the early to mid-1990s, it stopped short of outright condemning them. For example, in response to a general amnesty that was adopted by El Salvador one week after the release of the El Salvador Commission on the Truth's report, the UN Secretary-General did not expressly condemn this measure. Rather, he noted in his Report in 1993 that 'I expressed my concern at the haste with which this step had been taken and my view that it would have been preferable if the amnesty had been promulgated after creating a broad degree of national consensus in its favour'.[122] Similarly, when the Abidjan Agreement between the Government of the Republic of Sierra Leone and the Revolutionary United Front of Sierra Leone was signed on 30 November 1996, it contained an Article granting amnesty to 'any member of the RUF/SL in respect of anything done by them in pursuit of their objectives as members of that organization up to the time of the signing of this Agreement'.[123] The UN Special Envoy who witnessed the signing of the Abidjan Agreement did not raise the issue of the blanket amnesty contained therein. The UN Secretary-General simply noted in his Report that the 'political provisions of the Accord [...] also include the provision of amnesty for members of the RUF [...]'.[124]

R. Kolb, C. Spenlé, and M.D. Voyaume (eds), *International Law, Conflict and Development. The Emergence of a Holistic Approach in International Affairs* (Leiden: Martinus Nijhoff, 2010), 385–409 at 403.

[120] Nuremberg Declaration on Peace and Justice (n 34), recommendation 2.6 at 6. See also The Princeton Principles on Universal Jurisdiction (Princeton: Office of University Printing and Mailing, 2001), available at <http://lapa.princeton.edu/hosteddocs/unive_jur.pdf>, Principle 7(1), 31: 'Amnesties are generally inconsistent with the obligation of states to provide accountability for serious crimes under international law'.

[121] Guidelines for United Nations Representatives on Certain Aspects of Negotiations for Conflict Resolution (1999), reproduced in *United Nations Juridical Yearbook* (2006), 495–7 at 497.

[122] Report of the Secretary-General on the United Nations Observer Mission in El Salvador, 21 May 1993, UN Doc S/25812, 2, § 6.

[123] Article 14 of the Peace Agreement between the Government of the Republic of Sierra Leone and the Revolutionary United Front of Sierra Leone ('Abidjan Peace Agreement'), 30 November 1996, annexed to Letter dated 11 December 1996 from the Permanent Representative of Sierra Leone to the United Nations addressed to the Secretary-General, 11 December 1996, UN Doc S/1996/1034.

[124] UN Doc S/1996/1034, § 6.

Although the United Nations did not openly condemn amnesties during the early and mid-1990s, this period marked a shift in attitude of the international community towards amnesties as a result of the developing culture of the end of impunity for perpetrators of serious international crimes, which in turn impacted upon UN practice. In 1992, the UN General Assembly adopted a 'Declaration on the Protection of All Persons from Enforced Disappearance', containing the principle that '[p]ersons who have or are alleged to have committed [acts of enforced disappearance] shall not benefit from any special amnesty law or similar measures that might have the effect of exempting them from any criminal proceedings or sanction'.[125] Furthermore, it was during this same decade that the UN Security Council established two ad hoc international criminal tribunals: the ICTY on 25 May 1993 and the International Criminal Tribunal for Rwanda (ICTR) on 8 November 1994.

Although the Statutes of these tribunals make no reference to amnesties, it is clear that they were established '[...] for the sole purpose of prosecuting persons responsible for serious violations of international humanitarian law',[126] and '[...] for the sole purpose of prosecuting persons responsible for genocide and other serious violations of international humanitarian law',[127] respectively. The Trial Chamber of the ICTY in the case of *Prosecutor v Anto Furundžjia* stated that the granting of amnesty laws with respect to the commission of torture would have the legal effect of 'international legal [non-]recognition'.[128] The 1990s also marked growing calls for unconditional amnesties to be prohibited by a number of human rights bodies because of the bar that amnesties pose to the protection of certain human rights.[129] In 1994, the UN Human Rights Committee stated in its General Comment No 20 concerning Article 7 of the International Covenant on Civil and Political Rights,[130] that '[a]mnesties are generally incompatible with the duty of States to investigate [...] acts [of torture]'.[131]

One of the most significant developments in the 1990s in the emerging culture of the end of impunity for perpetrators of serious international crimes occurred in

---

[125] UN General Assembly Resolution 47/133, 'Declaration on the Protection of All Persons from Enforced Disappearance', 18 December 1992, Art 18.

[126] UN Security Council Resolution 827 (1993), 25 May 1993, § 2.

[127] UN Security Council Resolution 955 (1994), 8 November 1994, § 1.

[128] ICTY, *Prosecutor v Anto Furundžjia*, Trial Chamber, Judgment of 10 December 1998, Case No IT-95-17/1-T, 60, § 155.

[129] See UN Commission on Human Rights, Revised final report prepared by Mr Louis Joinet pursuant to Sub-Commission decision 1996/119, 'Question of the impunity of perpetrators of human rights violations (civil and political)', 2 October 1997, UN Doc E/CN.4/Sub.2/19997/20/Rev.1, § 32.

[130] International Covenant on Civil and Political Rights, 19 December 1966, entered into force on 23 March 1976, 999 UNTS 171.

[131] UN Human Rights Committee, General Comment No 20, Art 7 (Forty-fourth session, 1992), Compilation of General Comments and General Recommendations Adopted by Human Rights Treaty Bodies, UN Doc HRI/GEN/1/Rev.1 (1994), § 15.

1998 with the adoption of the Rome Statute, a criminal court of potential universal jurisdiction. This occurred with the support of the UN Secretariat, which acted as the Secretariat of the Preparatory Committee until 31 December 2003. The adoption of the Rome Statute put all perpetrators of serious international crimes on notice that once the Rome Statute entered into force, the International Criminal Court could potentially exercise its jurisdiction in large parts of the world by virtue of its various forms of jurisdiction from the date of entry into force of its Statute.[132] It thus tolled the bell for amnesties being granted in relation to serious international crimes that fall under its jurisdiction.

By 1999, it had become apparent that the position of the United Nations was to henceforth take positive steps in expressing its non-acceptance of amnesty provisions contained in peace treaties that would cover serious international crimes. According to paragraph 12 of the 1999 Guidelines for United Nations Representatives on Certain Aspects of Negotiations for Conflict Resolution, UN representatives were put on notice that 'the United Nations cannot condone amnesties regarding war crimes, crimes against humanity and genocide or foster those that violate treaty obligations of the parties in this field'.[133] This practice was first manifested when the Lomé Peace Agreement between the Government of Sierra Leone and the Revolutionary United Front of Sierra Leone was signed on 3 June 1999. The Representative of the UN Secretary-General, when signing the Lomé Peace Agreement, penned the following statement next to his signature: 'The United Nations holds the understanding that the amnesty provisions of the Agreement shall not apply to international crimes of genocide, crimes against humanity, war crimes and other serious violations of international humanitarian law'.[134] Although no legal obligations from peace agreements are opposable to the United Nations, the implication of a UN representative witnessing such a peace agreement is 'an indication of a moral or political support for the principles contained therein', and '[a]s far as the United Nations is concerned, a signature as a witness is a "stamp of legitimacy" of a kind'.[135]

---

[132] Article 11 of the Rome Statute of the International Criminal Court.

[133] Guidelines for United Nations Representatives on Certain Aspects of Negotiations for Conflict Resolution (1999), reproduced in *United Nations Juridical Yearbook* (2006), 495–7 at 497.

[134] This statement does not appear in Peace Agreement between the Government of Sierra Leone and the Revolutionary Front of Sierra Leone, 3 June 1999 (Lomé Peace Agreement), annexed to Letter dated 12 July 1999 from the Chargé d'affaires ad interim of the Permanent Mission of Togo to the United Nations addressed to the President of the Security Council, 12 July 1999, UN Doc S/1999/777. It is reproduced in the fifth preambular paragraph to UN Security Council Resolution 1315 (2000), 14 August 2000.

[135] 'Electronic message to the United Nations Mission in the Sudan, regarding the implications for the United Nations to sign a peace agreement as a witness', Selected Legal Opinions of the Secretariat of the United Nations and Related Intergovernmental Organizations, 4 June 2007, *United Nations Juridical Yearbook* (2007), 457–8 at 458, § (d).

The following year, in 2000, the UN Secretary-General stated in a report on the establishment of the Special Court for Sierra Leone that '[w]hile recognizing that amnesty is an accepted legal concept and a gesture of peace and reconciliation at the end of a civil war or an internal armed conflict, the United Nations has consistently maintained the position that amnesty cannot be granted in respect of international crimes, such as genocide, crimes against humanity or other serious violations of international humanitarian law [...]'.[136] Article 10 of the Statute of the Special Court for Sierra Leone makes clear that there is no amnesty for crimes falling under the jurisdiction of the Special Court.[137] The mounting international condemnation of amnesties for perpetrators of serious international crimes led a respected legal scholar to conclude in 2002 that '[a]lthough international law does not—yet—prohibit the granting of amnesty for international crimes, it is clearly moving in that direction'.[138]

In 2006, the Legal Counsel of the UN stated during a meeting of the Security Council that '[...] amnesty for international crimes has been regarded as unacceptable in international practice. Today, its rejection must be enshrined as a standard to be enforced'.[139] Legal advice issued by the UN Secretariat in 2006 for UN envoys to regions where an amnesty law for persons indicted by the International Criminal Court was in place, stipulated that '[...] in the event that the Special Envoy is called upon to conduct, facilitate or otherwise participate in negotiations of a permanent cease-fire or a peace agreement, especially if the Agreement includes an amnesty clause, the following should be borne in mind. It has been a long-standing position of the United Nations not to recognize, let alone condone any amnesties for the crime of genocide, crimes against humanity, war crimes and other serious

---

[136] Report of the Secretary-General on the establishment of a Special Court for Sierra Leone, 4 October 2000, UN Doc S/2000/915, 5, § 22. The same year, the UN Security Council called on states to exclude amnesties and to prosecute those persons responsible for genocide, crimes against humanity, and war crimes in the context of the Democratic Republic of the Congo: UN Security Council Resolution 1325 (2000), 'Women, Peace and Security', 31 October 2000, § 11.

[137] Statute of the Special Court for Sierra Leone, annexed to the Agreement between the United Nations and the Government of Sierra Leone on the Establishment of the Special Court for Sierra Leone, 16 January 2002. See *Prosecutor v Morris Kallon and Brima Bazzy Kamara*, 'Decision on Challenge to Jurisdiction: Lomé Accord Amnesty', Special Court for Sierra Leone, Appeals Chamber, 13 March 2004, SCSL-2004-15-AR72(E) and SCSL-2004-16-AR72(E); *Prosecutor v Moinina Fofana*, 'Decision on Preliminary Motion on Lack of Jurisdiction: Illegal Delegation of Jurisdiction by Sierra Leone', Special Court for Sierra Leone, 25 May 2004, SCSL-2004-14-AR72(E); *Prosecutor v Augustine Gbao*, 'Agreement between the United Nations and the Government of Sierra Leone on the Establishment of the Special Court', Special Court for Sierra Leone, 25 May 2004, SCSL-2004-15-AR72 (E); *Prosecutor v Allieu Kondewa*, 'Decision on lack of jurisdiction/abuse of process: Amnesty provided by the Lomé Accord', Special Court for Sierra Leone, 25 May 2004, SCSL-2004-14-AR72(E).

[138] J. Dugard, 'Possible Conflicts of Jurisdiction with Truth Commissions', in A. Cassese, P. Gaeta, and J. Jones (eds), *The Rome Statute of the International Criminal Court: A Commentary* (Oxford: Oxford University Press, 2002), 693–704 at 698.

[139] Remarks by N. Michel, Under-Secretary-General for Legal Affairs and Legal Counsel of the United Nations, UN Security Council, 5474th meeting, 22 June 2006, UN Doc S/PV.5474, 4.

violations of international humanitarian law'.[140] Similarly, an interoffice memorandum provided:

The United Nations does not recognize any amnesty for genocide, crimes against humanity, war crimes and other serious violations of international humanitarian law. This principle, which reflects a long-standing position and practice, applies to peace agreements negotiated or facilitated by the United Nations, or otherwise conducted under its auspices. In the event that such a peace agreement nevertheless grants amnesty for such crimes, the United Nations representative, when witnessing the agreement on behalf of the United Nations, shall affix a declaration next to his or her signature, stating that 'the United Nations does not recognize amnesty for genocide, crimes against humanity, war crimes and other serious violations of international humanitarian law'.[141]

There is now general consensus that amnesties for serious international crimes are unacceptable under international law, and that persons suspected of having committed such crimes should be prosecuted. It remains debatable whether the act of granting amnesties for serious international crimes per se is unlawful under international law. It is clear, however, that the granting of amnesties conflicts with obligations binding on states to prosecute perpetrators of serious international crimes, as well as other human rights obligations including a duty to investigate human rights violations. The unacceptable nature of unconditional amnesties has developed in direct proportion to the emergence of the culture of the end of impunity for serious international crimes. Furthermore, with respect to transitional societies, the Security Council has called on amnesties not to be granted for sexual crimes. In 2008, it

stress[ed] the need for the exclusion of sexual violence crimes from amnesty provisions in the context of conflict resolution processes, and call[ed] upon Member States to comply with their obligations for prosecuting persons responsible for such acts, to ensure that all victims of sexual violence, particularly women and girls, have equal protection under the law and equal access to justice, and stress[ed] the importance of ending impunity for such acts as part of a comprehensive approach to seeking sustainable peace, justice, truth, and national reconciliation.[142]

---

[140] 'Note to the Under-Secretary-General for Political Affairs regarding guidance on activities of the Special Envoy in [Rebel Group]-affected areas', Selected Legal Opinions of the Secretariat of the United Nations and Related Intergovernmental Organizations, 31 August 2006, United Nations Juridical Yearbook (2006), 493–7 at 494, § 7.

[141] 'Interoffice memorandum relating to the United Nations position on peace and justice in post-conflict societies', Selected Legal Opinions of the Secretariat of the United Nations and Related Intergovernmental Organizations, 25 September 2006, United Nations Juridical Yearbook (2006), 498–500 at 499.

[142] UN Security Council Resolution 1820 (2008), 19 June 2008, § 4.

B. Individual criminal responsibility at the international level

International and internationalized criminal courts and tribunals play a pivotal role in the emerging culture of the end of impunity for perpetrators of serious international crimes.[143] There are some advantages to prosecuting those persons most responsible for serious international crimes before international and internationalized criminal courts and tribunals, rather than before national courts. Institutional reforms may need to take place before criminal trials can be held within the framework of a domestic court system. The highly charged political environment in a post-conflict transitional society may mean that a criminal trial at the domestic level would raise serious safety concerns for the accused, members of the court, witnesses, and the general public. Indeed, the political environment in the region may be of such intensity that even a criminal trial of a former political leader before an international or internationalized criminal court or tribunal may need to take place on the territory of a state far removed from the region. For example, instead of taking place in Freetown, Sierra Leone, the criminal trial of the former President of Liberia, Charles Taylor, is being conducted by the Special Court for Sierra Leone in The Hague, the Netherlands, initially at the premises of the International Criminal Court, and subsequently at the premises of the Special Tribunal for Lebanon.

The future of international criminal prosecutions is the system created by the Rome Statute, to which an impressive and steadily increasing number of states are parties. It should be emphasized from the outset that unlike other international and internationalized criminal courts and tribunals, which exercise primary jurisdiction over domestic courts in relation to the crimes that fall under their respective jurisdictions, the International Criminal Court functions on the basis of the principle of 'complementarity', meaning that it can only exercise its jurisdiction in situations in which a state is unable or unwilling to exercise its primary, domestic criminal jurisdiction. As explained above, the notion of complementarity extends beyond the primary responsibility of states to exercise their domestic criminal jurisdictions, and it includes 'positive complementarity', namely assistance that states and international organizations can provide to other states in building the capacity of domestic legal systems to ensure the criminal prosecution of suspected perpetrators of serious international crimes.

'Positive complementarity' may also be viewed within the broader context of the notion of the 'responsibility to protect', and in particular, the 'responsibility to prevent'. In 2005, the UN General Assembly adopted a Resolution in which states agreed that '[t]he international community should, as appropriate, encourage and

---

[143] See Remarks by Ambassador de La Sablière (France), UN Security Council, 5474th meeting, 22 June 2006, UN Doc S/PV.5474, 18.

help States to exercise this responsibility [to protect their populations from geno-cide, war crimes, ethnic cleansing and crimes against humanity] and support the United Nations in establishing an early warning capability.[144] According to Sheri Rosenberg, this 'collective responsibility to take coordinated action' also 'implies individual state responsibility to take reasonable steps to prevent the acts it seeks to prohibit'.[145] There is thus a need both for individual states, and the international community of states as a whole, to provide assistance in the form of capacity-build-ing to those states struggling to fulfil their primary obligations to prevent and pun-ish the commission of serious international crimes. The kinds of assistance that may be provided to individual states include:

[...] (a) ensuring that donors place on their agenda the need for legal reform, such as domes-tication of the Rome Statute and implementing legislation; (b) adopting a whole govern-ment approach to complementarity, i.e. aligning development cooperation projects with other forms of bilateral technical cooperation such as among police forces; [...] (c) creating a support community that consists of international justice and humanitarian actors on the one hand, and development and peace-building efforts on the other [...] [and (d)] develop-ing a comprehensive tool kit on complementarity as well as developing a roster of expertise comprising ex-tribunal personnel to be administered by some mechanism.[146]

It is debatable whether the notion of 'positive complementarity' also extends to assistance that the International Criminal Court itself may provide to state parties. The Office of the Prosecutor has adopted a strategy that is 'a *positive approach* to complementarity, meaning that it encourages genuine national proceedings where possible, relies on national and international networks and participates in a system, of international cooperation'.[147] This 'positive' prosecutorial strategy does not equate with assistance in the form of capacity-building. Rather, it is more aptly defined as 'a managerial concept that organizes the relationship between the court and domes-tic jurisdictions on the basis of three cardinal principles: the idea of shared burden of responsibility, the management of effective investigations and prosecutions, and the two-pronged nature of the cooperation regime'.[148] To avoid confusion with the notion of 'positive complementarity' as consecrated in a Resolution adopted by the Review Conference of the Rome Statute in 2010,[149] a prosecutorial strategy of the International Criminal Court that serves to positively encourage states parties

[144] UN General Assembly Resolution 60/1, '2005 World Summit Outcome', 24 October 2005, 30, § 138.

[145] S. Rosenberg, 'Responsibility to Protect: A Framework for Prevention', 1 *Global Responsibility to Protect* (2009) 442–77 at 450.

[146] International Center for Transitional Justice, 'Complementarity after Kampala: The Way Forward' (n 97), § 13.

[147] Office of the Prosecutor of the International Criminal Court, 'Report on Prosecutorial Strategy', 14 September 2006, 5 (emphasis added).

[148] C. Stahn, 'Complementarity: A Tale of Two Notions', 19 *Criminal Law Forum* (2008) 87–113 at 113.

[149] Review Conference of the Rome Statute of the International Criminal Court, Resolution RC/Res 1, 'Complementarity', 8 June 2010, § 5 (adopted by consensus).

to fulfil their primary responsibility to prosecute suspected perpetrators of serious international crimes at the domestic level is perhaps more appropriately referred to as 'proactive complementarity'.[150]

The success of the International Criminal Court is dependent upon the cooperation of states parties with the Court. The Rome Statute obliges states parties to cooperate with the Court in various respects. There exists both a general obligation to cooperate under Article 86 of the Statute, and a number of specific obligations contained under Part IX thereof. Additionally, states parties to the Genocide Convention have a distinct treaty obligation to cooperate with the International Criminal Court contained under Article VI of the Genocide Convention, which requires states parties to cooperate with 'all international criminal courts created after the adoption of the Convention [...] of potentially universal scope, and competent to try the perpetrators of genocide',[151] thus including the International Criminal Court. The Security Council may also require non-states parties to the Rome Statute to cooperate with the Court in a binding resolution adopted under Chapter VII of the UN Charter, as occurred in relation to the Government of Sudan,[152] and in relation to the Libyan authorities.[153]

Although the UN Organization is not, and cannot become, a party to the Rome Statute, it does have an obligation to cooperate and assist the International Criminal Court as stipulated in the Relationship Agreement between the United Nations and the International Criminal Court.[154] From its terms it is clear that '[...] the Relationship Agreement does not oblige the United Nations to support any policy or strategy decision of the ICC'.[155] However, the UN Secretariat has insisted that '[t]he United Nations should, if possible, avoid any action that would undermine or counteract key ICC policies and strategies'.[156] In practice this means that considerable tact should be exercised by representatives of the United Nations who may come into contact with persons indicted by the International Criminal Court in the context of their work. According to a legal opinion issued by the UN Secretariat in 2006, if a UN Special Envoy cannot avoid direct contact with persons indicted by

---

[150] W. Burke-White, 'Proactive Complementarity: The International Criminal Court and National Courts in the Rome System of International Justice', 49(1) *Harvard International Law Journal* (2008) 53–108 at 56.

[151] International Court of Justice, *Application of the Convention on the Prevention and Punishment of the Crime of Genocide (Bosnia and Herzegovina v Serbia and Montenegro)*, Judgment of 26 February 2007, 159, § 445.

[152] UN Security Council Resolution 1593 (2005), 31 March 2005.

[153] UN Security Council Resolution 1970 (2011), 26 February 2011, § 5.

[154] Relationship Agreement between the United Nations and the International Criminal Court, 22 July 2004, entered into force on 4 October 2004.

[155] 'Interoffice memorandum relating to the United Nations position on peace and justice in post-conflict societies', Selected Legal Opinions of the Secretariat of the United Nations and Related Intergovernmental Organizations, 25 September 2006, *United Nations Juridical Yearbook* (2006), 498–500 at 500.

[156] *United Nations Juridical Yearbook* (2006), 498–500 at 500.

the International Criminal Court in carrying out his or her mandate, then such contact should 'be limited to what is strictly required for carrying out [the] mandate. The presence of the Special Envoy in any ceremonial or similar occasions should be avoided. We should also add that when contacts with the [Rebel Group] are necessary, an attempt should be made to interact with *non-indicted [Rebel Group] leaders*, if at all possible'.[157]

C. Filling the 'impunity gap' through exercises of universal criminal jurisdiction

The steady increase in the number of states parties to the Rome Statute is leading to a greater jurisdictional reach of this international judicial body. Pending this future development, there arise 'gaps of impunity' in the fabric of the culture of the end of impunity in cases in which a non-state party to the Statute is unable or unwilling to investigate and prosecute suspected perpetrators of serious international crimes, and when the International Criminal Court does not have jurisdiction. It has been argued that in such cases the domestic criminal courts of other states should exercise universal criminal jurisdiction with regard to the suspected perpetrators.[158] It is important to recall in this respect that the establishment of international and internalized criminal courts and tribunals has not replaced the role of the domestic courts of other states in the fight against impunity. Judges Higgins, Kooijmans, and Buergenthal noted in relation to exercises of universal criminal jurisdiction that the fight against impunity for perpetrators of serious international crimes has not been '[…] "made over" to international treaties and tribunals, with national courts having no competence in such matters'.[159]

'Universal criminal jurisdiction' refers to exercises of domestic jurisdiction 'based solely on the nature of the crime, without regard to where the crime was committed, the nationality of the alleged or convicted perpetrator, the nationality of the victim,

---

[157] 'Note to the Under-Secretary-General for Political Affairs regarding guidance on activities of the Special Envoy in [Rebel Group]-affected areas', Selected Legal Opinions of the Secretariat of the United Nations and Related Intergovernmental Organizations, 31 August 2006, *United Nations Juridical Yearbook* (2006), 493–7 at 494, § 4 (original emphasis). See also 'Interoffice memorandum relating to the United Nations position on peace and justice in post-conflict societies', Selected Legal Opinions of the Secretariat of the United Nations and Related Intergovernmental Organizations, 25 September 2006, *United Nations Juridical Yearbook* (2006), 498–500 at 500.

[158] J. Lindenmann, 'Transitional Justice and the International Criminal Court: Some Reflections on the Role of the ICC in Conflict Transformation', in M. Kohen (ed), *Promoting Justice, Human Rights and Conflict Resolution through International Law/La promotion de la justice, des droits de l'homme et du règlement des conflits par le droit international. Liber Amicorum Lucius Caflisch* (Leiden: Koninklijke Brill, 2007), 315–38 at 334.

[159] *Arrest Warrant of 11 April 2000 (Democratic Republic of the Congo v Belgium)*, Judgment, [2002] ICJ Rep, Joint Separate Opinion of Judges Higgins, Kooijmans and Buergenthal, 78–9, § 51.

or any other connection to the state exercising such jurisdiction.[160] Exercises of this form of jurisdiction—where there is no connecting factor to the forum—are highly controversial.[161] Some scholars advocate exercises of universal jurisdiction only in those cases in which the accused is found on the territory of the state wishing to prosecute, because '[o]therwise, we may be faced with the Belgian situation, where judges are flooded with complaints against dictators and generals from everywhere in the world'.[162] Courts exercising universal jurisdiction must surmount challenges during the judicial process that could be exacerbated by the distance of the court from the scene of the crime, and the court's lack of powers of enforcement in the territory where the serious international crimes occurred, such as the securing of evidence and the protection of witnesses.

Conversely—and to some extent, counter-intuitively—it may be the case that certain aspects of the judicial process are enhanced by virtue of the fact that a court outside the forum is conducting the criminal proceedings. Witnesses reluctant or unable to testify in the forum state may be willing to travel to another state in order to testify. For example, in relation to the exercise of universal criminal jurisdiction by Spanish courts concerning events that took place in Argentina under the dictatorship regime, Judge Garzón was able to hear 'the testimonies of a large number of witnesses, including family members of the disappeared, and victims of torture and other acts of state repression'[163] who had travelled to Spain in order to take part in the proceedings.

There is no general obligation binding on states to confer universal criminal jurisdiction on their domestic courts. However, some states may have treaty-based obligations to extend their criminal jurisdiction in different ways, such as on the basis of the principles of active or passive nationality. For example, under Article 5 of CAT, states parties must establish criminal jurisdiction for acts of torture committed in the jurisdiction of the forum state,[164] when the alleged offender is a national of the forum state,[165] when the victim is a national of the forum state 'if that State

[160] The Princeton Principles on Universal Jurisdiction (n 120), Principle 1(1), at 28.

[161] Universal criminal jurisdiction was an issue that arose in separate cases between the Republic of the Congo and Belgium, and between the Republic of the Congo and France, initiated by the former against the two latter states before the International Court of Justice. The case concerning *Certain Criminal Proceedings in France (Republic of the Congo v France)* was discontinued by the Republic of the Congo and removed from the List of cases by the Court on 16 November 2010 before hearings on the merits could be held. Some aspects of the case concerning the *Arrest Warrant of 11 April 2000 (Democratic Republic of the Congo v Belgium)* are discussed below.

[162] A. Cassese, 'The Role of Internationalized Courts and Tribunals in the Fight Against International Criminality', in C. Romano, A. Nollkaemper, and J. Kleffner (eds), *Internationalized Criminal Courts. Sierra Leone, East Timor, Kosovo, and Cambodia* (Oxford: Oxford University Press, 2004), 3–13 at 12.

[163] D. Rothenberg, '"Let Justice Judge": An Interview with Judge Baltasar Garzón and Analysis of His Ideas', 24 *Human Rights Quarterly* (2002) 924–73 at 931.

[164] Article 5(1)(a) of CAT. See generally M. Nowak and E. McArthur, *The United Nations Convention Against Torture. A Commentary* (Oxford: Oxford University Press, 2008), 253–327.

[165] Article 5(1)(b) of CAT.

considers it appropriate',[166] and when the alleged offender is on the territory of the forum and is not extradited pursuant to other provisions of the Convention Against Torture.[167] In line with the *Case of the S.S. 'Lotus'* before the Permanent Court of International Justice, states are arguably free to extend their criminal jurisdiction in any way that does not violate international law.[168]

Unlike international and internationalized criminal courts and tribunals, a domestic court may be barred from exercising criminal jurisdiction with respect to foreign state representatives who enjoy immunity. Thus, even though a state may have conferred universal criminal jurisdiction on its domestic courts pursuant to a treaty obligation to prosecute and punish serious international crimes, this jurisdiction cannot be exercised by the domestic courts of that state with respect to incumbent Heads of State, Ministers for Foreign Affairs, and other state representatives who enjoy immunity from criminal jurisdiction. The International Court of Justice stated in the *Arrest Warrant* case that:

> [...] although international conventions on the prevention and punishment of certain serious crimes impose on States obligations of prosecution or extradition, thereby requiring them to extend their criminal jurisdiction, such extension of jurisdiction in no way affects immunities under customary international law [...] These remain opposable before the courts of a foreign State, even where those courts exercise such a jurisdiction under these conventions.[169]

Immunity from jurisdiction provides legal protection from prosecution for foreign state representatives, thereby ensuring the day-to-day functioning of states and stability in international relations. This is understandable, but nevertheless frustrating in those situations in which a Head of State suspected of having committed serious international crimes is able to travel freely to other countries without risk of being held accountable for these crimes. The International Court of Justice has taken care to distinguish immunity from impunity, noting that '[j]urisdictional immunity may well bar prosecution for a certain period or for certain offences; it cannot exonerate the person to whom it applies from all criminal responsibility'.[170] It may come to pass that although the domestic criminal courts of a state are barred from exercising jurisdiction *vis-à-vis* an incumbent foreign state representative for serious international crimes committed over a certain period of time, once this person ceases to hold office, the state may be free to prosecute this person based on universal criminal jurisdiction in relation to 'acts committed prior or subsequent to his or her period of office, as well as in respect of acts committed during that period of office in a private capacity'.[171]

---

[166]   Article 5(1)(c) of CAT.   [167]   Article 5(2) of CAT.

[168]   *The Case of the S.S. 'Lotus'*, PCIJ Series A, No 10, Judgment, 7 September 1927.

[169]   *Arrest Warrant* (n 159), 25, § 59.

[170]   *Arrest Warrant of 11 April 2000* (n 159), 25, § 60.

[171]   *Arrest Warrant of 11 April 2000* (n 159), 25, § 61. On whether 'acts committed during the period of office in a private capacity' encompass serious international crimes, see eg *R v Bow Street Metropolitan Stipendiary Magistrate: Ex Parte Pinochet Ugarte*, *(No 3)* [1999] 2 All ER 97, 119 ILR 135.

5 JUSTICE FOR VICTIMS IN THE FORM OF REPARATION

Reparation is premised on 'a principle of international law, that a breach of an engagement involves an obligation to make reparation in an adequate form'.[172] Reparation has been identified as a key component of a holistic approach to transitional justice. According to the Basic Principles and Guidelines, '[a]dequate, effective and prompt reparation is intended to promote justice by redressing gross violations of international human rights law or serious violations of international humanitarian law'.[173] Reparation to victims of serious international crimes may take the form of either individual or collective reparation.[174] Emphasis is placed here on individual reparation.

It is debatable whether there is a right to reparation for victims of serious international crimes,[175] and if so, the scope of this right. In relation to an obligation binding on states to provide reparation to victims, states parties to the 1907 Hague Convention (IV) and the 1977 Additional Protocol I have an obligation to provide reparation to other states parties to these treaties for IHL violations.[176] According to a traditional understanding of these treaty provisions, this means that only states— and not individual victims—can invoke these treaty obligations in a claim for

---

[172] Permanent Court of International Justice, *Case concerning the Factory at Chorzów*, Series A, No 9, Judgment, 26 July 1927, 21.

[173] 'Basic Principles and Guidelines on the Right to a Remedy and Reparation for Victims of Gross Violations of International Human Rights Law and Serious Violations of International Humanitarian Law' annexed to UN General Assembly Resolution 60/147, 'Basic Principles and Guidelines on the Right to a Remedy', 21 March 2006, § 15.

[174] On collective reparation, see F. Rosenfeld, 'Collective Reparation for Victims of Armed Conflict', 92 *International Review of the Red Cross* (2010) 731–46.

[175] In relation to the existence of a customary international law obligation to provide reparation to victims, Riccardo Pisillo Mazzeschi is cautious in noting that '[…] one could perhaps maintain that a customary rule is *slowly developing* in the field of human rights. In contrast, in the field of humanitarian law the conclusion should be more pessimistic because, at least for the time being, both international and domestic case law on reparation is still lacking' (R. Pisillo Mazzeschi, 'Reparation Claims by Individuals for State Breaches of Humanitarian Law and Human Rights: An Overview', 1 *Journal of International Criminal Justice* (2003) 339–47 at 347 (original emphasis)).

[176] Convention (IV) respecting the Laws and Customs of War on Land, 18 October 1907, entered into force on 26 January 1910 (Art 3 provides: 'A belligerent party which violates the provisions of the said Regulations shall, if the case demands, be liable to pay compensation. It shall be responsible for all acts committed by persons forming part of its armed forces'); Protocol Additional to the Geneva Conventions of 12 August 1949, and relating to the Protection of Victims of International Armed Conflicts (Protocol I), 8 June 1977, entered into force on 7 December 1979, 1125 UNTS 3 (Art 91 provides: 'A Party to the conflict which violates the provisions of the Convention or of this Protocol shall, if the case demands, be liable to pay compensation. It shall be responsible for all acts committed by persons forming part of its armed forces'). See eg International Court of Justice, *Armed Activities on the Territory of the Congo (Democratic Republic of the Congo v Uganda)*, Judgment, [2005] ICJ Rep, 168.

reparation.[177] Thus, through diplomatic protection, a state may bring a claim against another state in a judicial forum, or via another mechanism for the peaceful settlement of disputes, and claim reparation for the injury suffered by its nationals.[178] However, a state is not obligated under international law to bring such a claim; it may do so at its discretion. Furthermore, any reparation obtained will pass directly to the claimant state, which may—if it wishes—subsequently transfer some portion of it to the individual victim(s) concerned.

Some scholars have argued that individual victims should be able to directly claim reparation from a state party on the basis of the aforementioned treaties. In this vein, Riccardo Pisillo Mazzeschi argues that '[i]n our opinion, Article 3 [of the] Hague Convention No. IV and Article 91 of Protocol I should [...] be jointly interpreted as rules providing for an obligation of reparation in favour both of states and of injured individuals'.[179] This argument is consonant with the progressive development of international law. However, there remain concrete impediments to its full realization. One of the difficulties that this argument must overcome is determining the forum in which an individual victim could bring such a claim for reparation directly against a foreign state. National courts are barred from examining the merits of a claim for reparation brought by an individual victim against a foreign state for serious international crimes on the basis of the jurisdictional bar of state immunity.[180] There is limited practice in the national courts in Greece and Italy of allowing such claims to reach the merits stage on the basis of the *jus cogens* nature of the norm(s) allegedly violated.[181] Further clarification on the international law

---

[177] R. Pisillo Mazzeschi, 'Reparation Claims by Individuals for State Breaches of Humanitarian Law and Human Rights: An Overview', 1 *Journal of International Criminal Justice* (2003) 339–47 at 341.

[178] For example, Eritrea and Ethiopia brought claims against one another before the Eritrea–Ethiopia Claims Commission for violations of international humanitarian law committed against their respective nationals.

[179] Riccardo Pisillo Mazzeschi (n 177), 342.

[180] See eg *Al-Adsani v United Kingdom*, 35763/97, European Court of Human Rights, 21 November 2001.

[181] *Prefecture of Voiotia v Federal Republic of Germany*, Case No 137/1997, Court of First Instance of Leivadia, Greece, 30 October 1997, excerpts reprinted in M. Gavouneli, 'War Reparation Claims and State Immunity', 50 *Revue Hellénique de Droit International* (1997) 595–608; see also I. Bantekas, 'Case Report: Prefecture of Voiotia v. Federal Republic of Germany', 92 *American Journal of International Law* (1998) 765–8; *Prefecture of Voiotia v Federal Republic of Germany*, Case No 11/2000, Areios Pagos, 4 May 2000, 476. See M. Gavouneli and I. Bantekas, 'Case Report: Prefecture of Voiotia v. Federal Republic of Germany', 95 *American Journal of International Law* (2001) 198–204. However, following this judgment, the Greek Special Highest Court held that Germany enjoyed immunity: *Federal Republic of Germany v Miltiadia Margellos*, Special Highest Court of Greece, Case No 6/17-9-2002, 17 September 2002, discussed in K. Bartsch and B. Elberling, 'Jus Cogens vs. State Immunity, Round Two: The Decision of the European Court of Human Rights in the *Kalogeropoulou et al. v. Greece and Germany* Decision', 4(5) *German Law Journal* (2003) 477–91 at 481. *Ferrini v Federal Republic of Germany*, Cass. Sez. Un. 5044/04, reproduced in 87 *Rivista di diritto internazionale* (2004) 539. See A. Gattini, 'War Crimes and State Immunity in the *Ferrini* Decision', 3 *Journal of International Criminal Justice* (2005) 224–42.

governing state immunity may be provided by the International Court of Justice in due course.[182]

Although state immunity may pose an insurmountable hurdle to claims brought by individuals against foreign states, there is no such jurisdictional bar under international law for claims brought against a state concerning serious international crimes committed by this state in the forum, before this same state's national courts. According to the Basic Principles and Guidelines, '[i]n accordance with its domestic laws and international legal obligations, a State shall provide reparation to victims for acts or omissions which can be attributed to the State and constitute gross violations of international human rights law or serious violations of international humanitarian law'.[183] Some international legal obligations stipulate that there is a requirement for states to provide reparation within the framework of their domestic legal systems. These include the right of reparation for those who have suffered discrimination under Article 6 of the Convention on the Elimination of All Forms of Racial Discrimination,[184] and the right for victims of torture to obtain compensation under Article 14 of the Convention Against Torture.[185]

Aside from national courts, victims of serious international crimes may also be able to bring claims for reparation against a state before human rights courts,[186] once domestic remedies have first been exhausted. Pursuant to Article 41 of the European Convention on Human Rights,[187] '[i]f the Court finds that there has been a violation of the Convention or the protocols thereto, and if the internal law of the High Contracting Party concerned allows only partial reparation to be made, the Court shall, if necessary, afford just satisfaction to the injured party'. Similarly, Article 63(1) of the American Convention on Human Rights provides that '[i]f the Court finds that there has been a violation of a right or freedom protected by this Convention, the Court shall rule that the injured party be ensured the enjoyment of his right or freedom that was violated. It shall also rule, if appropriate, that the consequences of the measure or situation that constituted the

---

[182] International Court of Justice, *Case concerning Jurisdictional Immunities (Federal Republic of Germany v Italian Republic)*. See in this volume, C. Tomuschat, 'State Responsibility and the Individual Right to Compensation before National Courts'.

[183] 'Basic Principles and Guidelines on the Right to a Remedy and Reparation for Victims of Gross Violations of International Human Rights Law and Serious Violations of International Humanitarian Law', annexed to United Nations General Assembly Resolution 60/147, 15 December 2005, § 15.

[184] International Convention on the Elimination of All Forms of Racial Discrimination, 21 December 1965, entered into force on 4 January 1969, 660 UNTS 195.

[185] Convention Against Torture and Other Cruel. Inhuman or Degrading Treatment or Punishment, 10 December 1984, entered into force on 26 June 1987, 1465 UNTS 85.

[186] See C. Tomuschat, 'La protection internationale des droit des victimes', in J.-F. Flauss (ed), *La Protection internationale des droits de l'homme et les droits des victimes. International protection of human rights and victims' rights* (Brussels: Bruylant, 2009), 1–29 at 12–20.

[187] Convention for the Protection of Human Rights and Fundamental Freedoms, 4 November 1950, entered into force on 3 August 1953, 213 UNTS 221.

breach of such right or freedom be remedied and that fair compensation be paid to the injured party'.[188]

Reparation may also be obtained from a state for victims of serious international crimes via mechanisms established at the international level with the assistance of the United Nations. For example, the UN Compensation Commission was created in 1991 as a subsidiary organ of the UN Security Council in Resolution 692 of 20 May 1991, and pursuant to Resolution 687 of 3 April 1991, in which the Security Council established that 'Iraq [was] liable for any [...] injury to foreign Governments, nationals and corporations, as a result of Iraq's unlawful invasion and occupation of Kuwait'. Reparation could also be obtained from a state after the state establishes, of its own volition, mechanisms for providing reparation to victims of serious international crimes with reparation, as Germany provided to some victims of the Holocaust.

Rather than bring a claim against a state, individual victims of serious international crimes may choose to bring claims directly against the individual suspected of having committed the serious international crime.[189] Claims may be brought before the national courts of a state, either as part of the criminal proceedings against the suspected perpetrator where the victim may participate as a 'partie civile' in the proceedings—as is the case in many civil law countries—or as a separate judicial process, as is the case in common law countries. Reparation may also be obtained from the individual perpetrator in the institutional context of an international or internationalized criminal court or tribunal. For example, under Article 75(2), of the Rome Statute of the International Criminal Court, the Court may make an order against a convicted person for reparation to victims that may include restitution, compensation, and rehabilitation.[190] Claims could also be brought against individuals before national courts of a foreign state, depending on the enabling domestic legislation of that state. For example, the US Aliens Tort Claims Act[191] allows US courts to hear civil suits brought by any foreigner who alleges a violation of the 'law of nations'.

---

[188] American Convention on Human Rights, 22 November 1969, entered into force on 18 July 1978, 1144 UNTS 123.

[189] This Chapter does not address the possibility for victims to bring claims against collectives of natural persons, such as non-state armed groups, or other legal persons, such as corporations. See A. Clapham, 'Extending International Criminal Law Beyond the Individual to Corporations and Armed Opposition Groups', 6(5) Journal of International Criminal Justice (2008) 899–926; and articles in the Special Issue on transnational business and international criminal law in 8(3) Journal of International Criminal Justice (2010).

[190] For an overview of the reparation framework of the International Criminal Court, see M. Henzelin, V. Heiskanen, and G. Mettraux, 'Reparations to Victims before the International Criminal Court: Lessons from International Mass Claims Processes', 17 Criminal Law Forum (2006) 317–44. See also C. Ferstman, 'The Reparation Regime of the International Criminal Court: Practical Considerations', 15 Leiden Journal of International Law (2002) 667–86.

[191] 28 USC § 1350 (1994).

Reparation may also be envisaged in the context of non-judicial transitional justice mechanisms, such as truth commissions (discussed above), and traditional justice mechanisms. In relation to traditional justice mechanisms, Rwanda established *Gacaca* courts in order to address the significant number of individuals allegedly involved in the commission of serious international crimes. It was simply not feasible to prosecute every suspect within the framework of the domestic criminal justice system nor before the ICTR, which—in line with the exercise of prosecutorial discretion and the institutional capacity of the Tribunal, including financial constraints—can only prosecute a small number of individuals deemed to be those most responsible. Only very limited forms of reparation are available for genocide survivors before *Gacaca* courts in the form of restitution of property, or symbolic reparation in the form of the provision of information leading to locating the remains of genocide victims.[192]

In cases in which individual perpetrators are unable to provide reparation to their victims, it may be appropriate for the transitional government in the state in question to step in and provide such reparation. However, there is no legal obligation binding on the state to do so. To this end, the Final Report submitted to the UN Commission on Human Rights by Special Rapporteur Bassiouni on the right to restitution, compensation, and rehabilitation for victims of gross violations of human rights and fundamental freedoms, states that '[i]n the event that the party responsible for the violation is unable or unwilling to meet these obligations, the State *should* endeavour to provide reparation to victims [...] To that end, States *should* endeavour to establish funds for reparation to victims and seek other sources of funds wherever necessary to supplement these'.[193] Similarly, the Basic Principles and Guidelines provide that 'States *should endeavour* to establish national programmes for reparation and other assistance to victims in the event that the parties liable for the harm suffered are unable or unwilling to meet their obligations'.[194]

---

[192] P. Clark, *The Gacaca Courts, Post-Genocide Justice and Reconciliation in Rwanda* (New York: Cambridge University Press, 2010), 254. See also L. Waldorf, 'Goats & Graves: Reparations in Rwanda's Community Courts', in C. Ferstman, M. Goetz, and A. Stephens (eds), *Reparations for Victims of Genocide, War Crimes and Crimes Against Humanity. Systems in Place and Systems in the Making* (Leiden: Martinus Nijhoff, 2009), 515–39.

[193] UN Commission on Human Rights, Final Report of the Special Rapporteur Mr M. Cherif Bassiouni, 'The right to restitution, compensation and rehabilitation for victims of gross violations of human rights and fundamental freedoms', 18 January 2000, UN Doc E/CN.4/2000/62, 10, § 18 (emphasis added).

[194] 'Basic Principles and Guidelines on the Right to a Remedy and Reparation for Victims of Gross Violations of International Human Rights Law and Serious Violations of International Humanitarian Law', annexed to United Nations General Assembly Resolution 60/147, 15 December 2005, § 16 (emphasis added).

6 CONCLUSION

Transitional justice demands a coordinated approach among a plurality of mechanisms to assist a society in transitioning from a state of armed conflict in which serious international crimes were committed, to a peaceful and reconciled future. This Chapter has provided on overview of a non-exhaustive number of transitional mechanisms, including the truth-seeking mechanisms of truth commissions, commissions of inquiry, and judicial fact-finding; the criminal prosecution of individuals at the international and national levels within the context of the emerging culture of the end of impunity for suspected perpetrators of serious international crimes; and forms of reparation for victims of serious international crimes. On a theoretical level it is not difficult to demand a coordinated approach among different transitional justice mechanisms. However, it is challenging to achieve such coordination in practice. This Chapter has addressed some of the difficulties that may arise in the interaction among different transitional justice mechanisms, such as protection of the rights of the accused, and of witnesses that may arise in the relationship between a truth commission and a criminal court or tribunal.

INDEX

Lightning Source UK Ltd.
Milton Keynes UK
UKOW03f0758110615

253242UK00003B/4/P